Why Do You Need this New Edition?

If you're wondering why you should buy this new edition of *American Social Welfare Policy*, here are a few good reasons!

1. Coverage of the 2008 election, the significance of the first African American president, and the Democratic majority in Congress.

2. Hot topics, such as the passage of Proposition 8 in California and the global economic crisis, and their far-reaching effects are examined.

3. Cutting edge issues and their impact on social welfare policy include: technology, the fringe economy, religion, tax policy, and more.

4. Coverage of Obama's election win and how his presidency might come to change the welfare state (Ch. 1).

5. Coverage of the ideas of Jacob Hacker's *Great Risk Shift* and the new ownership society (Ch. 1).

6. Latest poverty data and the 2007 minimum wage bill passage (Ch. 5).

7. Content on social entrepreneurship (Ch. 6).

8. Exploitation of the Medicare Modernization Act (Ch. 7).

9. Income and wealth distribution and economic mobility (Ch. 9).

10. *The Pension Protection Act of 2006* (Ch. 10).

11. The Deficit Reduction Act of 2005 (final rules were promulgated in 2006) that reauthorized the Temporary Assistance for Needy Families (TANF) program and modified work participation rules (Ch. 11).

12. Coalitions forming around health care reform in Massachusetts and California (Ch. 12).

13. Veterans' mental health (Ch. 13).

14. The "burst bubble" of the housing market and its impact upon families (Ch. 16).

15. The globalization of capitalism (Ch. 18).

16. **NEW supplement for students!** *MyHelpingKit* is an electronic supplement that offers book-specific Learning Objectives, Chapter Summaries, Flashcards and Practice Quizzes, as well as Research Navigator, Video Clips, Cases, *Social Work in the News* blog as well as Interactive Activities to aid student learning and comprehension. www.myhelpingkit.com

PEARSON

SIXTH EDITION

American
Social Welfare Policy

A PLURALIST APPROACH

Howard Jacob Karger
University of Queensland, Australia

David Stoesz
Virginia Commonwealth University

Allyn & Bacon

Boston • New York • San Francisco
Mexico City • Montreal • Toronto • London • Madrid • Munich • Paris
Hong Kong • Singapore • Tokyo • Cape Town • Sydney

Senior Series Editor: *Pat Quinlin*
Series Editorial Assistant: *Carly Czech*
Marketing Manager: *Wendy Albert*
Production Supervisor: *Patrick Cash-Peterson*
Editorial Production Service: *Progressive Publishing Alternatives*
Manufacturing Buyer: *Debbie Rossi*
Electronic Composition: *Progressive Publishing Alternatives*
Photo Researcher: *Martha Shethar*
Cover Administrator: *Joel Gendron*

Library of Congress Cataloging-in-Publication Data

Karger, Howard Jacob, 1948–
    American social welfare policy : a pluralist approach/Howard Jacob Karger,
David Stoesz. — 6th ed.
        p. cm.
    ISBN-13: 978-0-205-62708-0
    ISBN-10: 0-205-62708-0
    1. Public welfare—United States. 2. United States—Social policy. 3. Welfare State—United States. I. Stoesz, David. II. Title.

    HV95.K354 2010
    361.973—dc22   2008052665

Printed in the United States of America

4 CKV 15 14 13 12 11

Allyn & Bacon
is an imprint of

www.pearsonhighered.com

ISBN 10: 0-205-62708-0
ISBN 13: 978-0-205-62708-0

Contents

Preface xvii

PART ONE
AMERICAN SOCIAL WELFARE POLICY

CHAPTER 1
Social Policy and the American Welfare State 1

CHAPTER 2

Social Welfare Policy Research: A Framework for Policy Analysis   27

CHAPTER 3

Religion and Social Welfare Policy   40

C H A P T E R 4

Discrimination in American Society 61

CHAPTER 5
Poverty in America   109

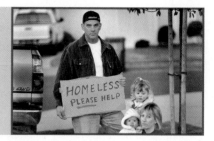

PART TWO
THE VOLUNTARY AND FOR-PROFIT SOCIAL SECTORS

CHAPTER 6
The Voluntary Sector Today   144

CHAPTER 7
Privatization and Human Service Corporations   167

PART THREE
THE GOVERNMENT SECTOR

CHAPTER 8
The Making of Governmental Policy 210

CHAPTER 9
Tax Policy and Income Distribution 238

CHAPTER 10

Social Insurance Programs 257

CHAPTER 11

Public Assistance Programs 275

CHAPTER 12

The American Health Care System 302

CHAPTER 13

Mental Health and Substance Abuse Policy 338

CHAPTER 14
Criminal Justice   361

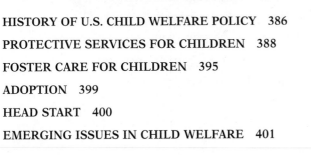

CHAPTER 15
Child Welfare Policy   383

CHAPTER 16
Housing Policies   413

CHAPTER 17
The Politics of Food Policy and Rural Life   444

PART FOUR

THE AMERICAN WELFARE STATE IN PERSPECTIVE

CHAPTER 18

The American Welfare State in International Perspective   472

Preface

*T*he four years since the publication of the last edition have been marked by dramatic events on the domestic and international fronts. By early 2009 the Iraq war had dragged on for six years and cost the lives of more than 4,200 American soldiers (30,000 wounded) and an estimated 1.25 million Iraqis. In 2003, former president GW Bush estimated that it would cost $50 billion to oust Saddam Hussein and install a new government. By 2009 the costs were close to $700 billion with no end in sight. Since the U.S. invasion in 2003, about 20 percent of Iraqis had fled the violence and left the country.[i] According to Linda Bilmes (former chief financial officer at the Commerce Department) and Joseph Stiglitz (former chairman of the Council of Economic Advisers), the Iraq war will end up costing the United States about $3 trillion. In direct appropriations alone, the war cost the United States about $144 billion in 2008.[ii] The war in Iraq has been aggravated by the events in Afghanistan. While the Taliban was routed after the U.S. invasion in 2001, they shortly began to regroup and threaten the fragile Afghan government. By 2009 more than 500 U.S. soldiers had died in Afghanistan.[iii]

By the end of the Bush presidency, American respect and influence abroad had reached a low point not seen for decades. This nadir was exacerbated by the global economic crisis that began in mid-2008, a crisis that much of the world blamed on American-initiated subprime mortgages and dodgy financial ventures like derivatives and hedge funds. It seemed like the United States was responsible not only for an unpopular war in Iraq but also for a global economic crisis.

If the international front looked bleak in 2008, the domestic front did not lag far behind. Housing prices dropped 18 percent.[iv] According to the Standard & Poors/Case-Shiller index, 2008 housing prices in Phoenix, Las Vegas and San Francisco sunk the most, dropping 32.7%, 31.7% and 31.0% of their value in a year's span. Miami, Los Angeles and San Diego followed suit with declines of 29.0%, 27.9% and 26.7%. By late 2008 the United States was officially in a recession.[v] In the midst of these daunting problems, the United States was being led by a president with the highest disapproval rating (more than 70 percent) in modern history.[vi] Long before the end of his presidency, George W. Bush was in contention for being one of the worst presidents on record.[vii] That the United States survived eight years of the Bush administration with its institutions relatively intact is testimony to the nation's resilience.

Many governmental agencies were run by political appointments whose sole credential was their loyalty to the Bush administration. Not surprisingly, these agencies were unable to fulfill their basic mandates. For instance, responding to the outbreak of salmonella-tainted tomatoes, CNN's Lou Dobbs exclaimed:

> You know, I have heard a lot of reasons over the years as to why George W. Bush should be impeached. For them to leave the Food and Drug Administration (FDA) in this state, its leadership in this sorry condition and to have no capacity apparently or will to pro-

[i]Margaret Griffis, "Casualties in Iraq: The Human Cost of Occupation," Antiwar. com (Ralph Bourne Institute), June 20, 2008. Retrieved June 21, 2008, from www.antiwar.com/casualties

[ii]Linda J. Bilmes and Joseph E. Stiglitz, "The Iraq War Will Cost Us $3 Trillion, and Much More," *Washington Post*, March 9, 2008, p. B01.

[iii]Ibid.

[iv]Mike Caggeso, "U.S. Home Prices Post Record 18% Annual Drop in October," *Money Morning*, December 30, 2008. Retrieved January 3, 2009 from http://www.moneymorning.com/2008/12/30/home-prices-2

[v]*Wall Street Journal*, June 13, 2008. Retrieved June 21, 2008 from, http://online.wsj.com/public/resources/documents/info-flash08.html?project=EFORECAST07

[vi]Paul Steinhauser, "Poll: More Disapprove of Bush than Any Other President," CNN, May 1, 2008. Retrieved June 21, 2008, from www.cnn.com/2008/POLITICS/05/01/bush.poll/index.html

[vii]Sean Wilentz, "The Worst President in History?: One of America's Leading Historians Assesses George W. Bush," *Rolling Stone*, April 21, 2006.

tect the American consumer—that is alone to me sufficient reason to impeach a president who has made
this agency impossible and has ripped its guts out in
its ability to protect the American consumer. It's
insane what is going on here.[viii]

The two terms of George W. Bush will likely be
remembered as a nonstarter for social welfare policy.
For one, Bush only mildly tinkered with income
maintenance policy since he inherited a public assistance program already largely disemboweled by the
1996 TANF legislation. Second, Bush's attempt to privatize Social Security met with an ignominious
death, bereft of support even from his own party. The
only concrete social welfare program to come out of
the Bush administration, Medicare Part D (drug benefits), has proven to be little understood, underutilized, and expensive for both senior citizens and the
government. It was also a program that was largely a
federal government subsidy of the pharmaceutical
industry.

There were also bright spots. For the first time
in American history, a woman, Hillary Clinton, ran
against an African American for the Democratic
Party presidential nomination. It seemed like
America might finally outgrow its preoccupation
with race and gender. Both Barack Obama and
Hillary Clinton offered hope to a country mired
down in the politics of division.

By late 2008 America seemed almost bereft of
hope as the country faced a recession, a war with no
end in sight, a $10 trillion federal debt, a 2008 budg-
et deficit of $420 billion, and a $1 trillion federal
bailout of the financial industry. But on November
4, 2008 history was made as America elected its first
African American president in a landslide election.
This was not merely a U.S. election—the eyes of the
world were focused on whether Americans would
elect a candidate representing hope or one associated with maintaining the status quo. In many ways,
the election of Barack Obama not only represented
hope for America but hope for the world.

Since the "revolution" that installed Ronald
Reagan in the White House, the ideological right
has defined the social policy discussion, even during
a democratic presidency (the Clinton period was
essentially an accommodation to welfare conservatism). Aside from his peccadilloes, Bill Clinton
will be remembered as a centrist president, one who

behaved more like a moderate Republican than a
liberal Democrat.

The current policy environment could offer
social welfare advocates multiple opportunities for
change. Consider several of the conservative themes
driving public philosophy: "Privatization," long a
part of human services in the United States, is evident in nonprofit organizations and private practitioners. "Devolution" is familiar to providers of
child welfare, mental health, and corrections—
traditionally state-controlled programs—to say
nothing of professionals who have served as elected
officials in state and local governments. "Faith-
based social services" has been a cornerstone of the
nonprofit sector, evident in such agencies as
Catholic Charities, the Salvation Army, and Jewish
community services, among others. As these examples illustrate, advocates of social justice already
have substantial expertise in domains that conservatives have appropriated. In turn, this expertise
could be mobilized to enhance the public interest
while benefitting social work.

Several changes will be required if human service professionals are to reclaim a prominent role in
social policy. Markets have been a primary means of
distributing goods and services to the nonpoor, and
the application of market dynamics to low-income
families should be evaluated on merit, not discarded
solely on ideological grounds. State and local politics
have been important arenas for introducing innovations in social welfare and for providing social workers a first step on the ladder of public service; such
opportunities should be celebrated, not dismissed.

If social work is to reassert its role in public policy, acceptance of privatization and devolution will
be insufficient for the profession to become an
influential player. Public policy involves the kind of
power that occurs in three basic forms: money,
votes, and networks. Although these resources have
been the staple of politics, the information age
requires players to possess a higher level of sophistication. To be competitive, one must have command of information systems, large data sets, and
complex decision menus.

If social work can educate students about these
methods and begin to insert itself into the policy
environment, the profession will have to again
become an influential force in social policy. On the
other hand, if the profession rests on its historic laurels, it will remain a bit player. Such an eventuality
would essentially waste the substantial assets that
social work brings to social affairs: a distinguished

[viii]*Huffington Post*, "Dobbs: Impeach Bush Over Tomatoes," June
20, 2008. Retrieved June 22, 2008, from www.huffingtonpost.com/
2008/06/20/dobbs-impeach-bush-over-t_n_108350.html

legacy, the altruism of the young, and a unique moral imperative.

This sixth edition of *American Social Welfare Policy* attempts to provide the information necessary for the reemergence of social work in social policy, nationally and internationally. In addition to discussing the basic concepts, policies, and programs that have typified the U.S. welfare state, the text includes chapters on the voluntary nonprofit sector (Chapter 6) and the for-profit corporate sector (Chapter 7). Chapter 9 directs attention to a new strategy in social policy: tax expenditures. Chapter 3 discusses the often neglected role of religion in the formation of social welfare policy. The final chapter, Chapter 18, examines the influence of global capitalism, a development that not only weds the developed nations to the undeveloped nations, but in the process shifts capital and jobs in unprecedented volumes.

We owe many debts in completing the sixth edition. The reviewers of this and previous editions have provided an invaluable service in identifying deficiencies. We would like to thank the reviewers of the sixth edition for their insightful comments and suggestions. In addition, a special thank you to Dr. Stephen Thornton who tirelessly helped to update the data. Thanks for the long hours and weekends. Thanks also to Deanna Machin for helping with the editing. Peter Kindle also deserves a major "thank you" for granting permission to include material from the Policy Update (5th edition) in Chapters 1, 2, 4, 5, 10, 12, 16, and 17, as well as updating his chapter on religion and social policy. Finally, thanks to our families for being there. In anticipation of a seventh edition, comments by students and faculty are welcome. The authors can be contacted via email: Howard Karger at H.karger@uq.edu.au and David Stoesz at Davestoesz@aol.com.

About the Authors

Howard Karger (right) is professor and Head of the School of Social Work and Human Services, The University of Queensland, Brisbane, Australia. David Stoesz (left) is professor, Virginia Commonwealth University. Howard and David have been friends and colleagues for more than 25 years. In 2001 they collaborated on the creation of policyAmerica, a nonprofit organization dedicated to disseminating innovations in social policy. In addition to six editions of *American Social Welfare Policy*, they have coauthored two other books: *The Politics of Child Abuse in America* (with Lela Costin) (Oxford University Press, 1996) and *Reconstructing the American Welfare State* (Rowman and Littlefield, 1992). Howard's book, *Shortchanged: Life and Debt in the Fringe Economy* (Berret-Koehler, 2005) examines the financial practices and products that exploit millions of American families. In 2006 the book won the Independent Publishers Award in Finance/Investment/Economics. David's book, *Quixote's Ghost: The Right, the Liberati, and the Future of Social Policy* (Oxford University Press, 2005), explains how conservatives have assumed control of domestic policy and proposes a new framework for social policy. *Quixote's Ghost* won the 2006 Pro Humanitate Literary Award. Howard lives in Brisbane, Australia; David and his son Julio live in Alexandria, Virginia.

CHAPTER 1

Social Policy and the American Welfare State

Social welfare policy is best viewed through the lens of political economy (i.e., the interaction of economic, political, and ideological forces). This chapter provides an overview of the American welfare state through that lens. In particular, it examines various definitions of social welfare policy, the relationship between social policy and social problems, and the values and ideologies that drive social welfare in the United States. In addition, the chapter examines the effects of ideology on the U.S. welfare state, including the important roles played by conservatism and liberalism (and their variations) in shaping welfare policy. An understanding of social welfare policy requires the ability to grasp the economic justifications and consequences that underlie policy decisions. As such, this chapter contains a brief introduction to Keynesianism, free market economics, socialism, and communitarianism, among others.

American social welfare is in transition. Starting with the Social Security Act of 1935, liberals argued that federal social programs were the best way to help the disadvantaged. Now, after 70 years of experimenting with the **welfare state,** a discernible shift has occurred. The conservatism of U.S. culture—so evident in the Reagan, Bush (both Bushes), and even Clinton presidencies—has left private institutions to shoulder more of the welfare burden. For proponents of social justice, the suggestion that the private sector should assume more responsibility for welfare represents a retreat from the hard-won governmental social legislation that provided essential benefits to millions of Americans. Justifiably, these groups fear the loss of basic goods and services during the transition in social welfare.

The political trajectory shifted with the 2008 election. The election of Barack Obama as the 44th President of the United States not only broke a racial barrier but also swept away the strident conservatism that had defined the presidency of George W. Bush. Winning 52 percent of the vote and increasing Democratic majorities in both chambers of Congress, the Obama victory heartened liberals who anticipated an expansion of government social programs. Obama's platform was crafted to appeal to middle-class voters who had lost ground economically during the second Bush presidency and included the following objectives:

- Increase capital gains taxes on individuals making more than $250,000 per year while providing tax credits for couples earning less than $200,000 annually.
- Jump-start the economy through a $700 billion stimulus package that included $25 billion for infrastructure projects as well as $25 billion for state and local governments.
- Introduce progressivity in the withholding tax by adding a tax of 2 to 4 percent for individuals whose incomes exceed $250,000 a year.
- Require that all children have health insurance, prohibit insurance companies from refusing to insure people with pre-existing conditions, and mandate that employers provide health insurance to workers or pay into a health insurance fund.
- Spend $10 billion to expand and improve pre-school education and $12 billion for higher education in the form of a $4,000 refundable tax credit in exchange for 100 hours of community service.[1]

While liberal pundits hailed the resurgence of "a vast new progressive movement,"[2] structural limits would certain restrain Obama's ambitions. Massive deficits left by the second Bush administration compounded by a looming recession mean that economic issues will not only trump other priorities, but that reduced tax revenues will impede the ability of the government to meet existing obligations let alone expand social programs. Moreover, the Republicans can filibuster Democratic initiatives in the Senate that are perceived as being particularly generous. Obama's centrist inclinations will help build bipartisan support for his legislative agenda. This was evident in his understanding of welfare reform. Acknowledging that "conservatives—and Bill Clinton—were right" to scrap the Aid to Families with Dependent Children program, Obama also recognized that welfare reform had "swelled the ranks of the working poor." Consequently, he argued that a post-welfare reform anti-poverty policy must entail increasing the Earned Income Tax Credit for low-income working families, but also expanding community-based health and education as well as law enforcement.[3] Clearly, economic and political circumstances will test the new president's leadership in managing domestic affairs and therein social welfare.

Despite the Democratic victory in 2008, structural features of the American welfare state militate against a major expansion of government, per se. A pluralistic mix of private and public services is an overriding feature of U.S. social welfare. As in other realms, such as education, in social welfare private institutions coexist alongside those of the public sector. U.S. social welfare has a noble tradition of voluntary citizen groups taking the initiative to solve local problems. Today, private voluntary groups provide important services to AIDS patients, the homeless, immigrants, victims of domestic violence, and refugees.

Social welfare has become big business. During the last 30 years, the number of human service corporations—for-profit firms providing social welfare through the marketplace—has increased dramatically. Human service corporations are prominent in long-term nursing care, health maintenance, child day care, psychiatric and substance abuse services, and even corrections. For many welfare professionals, the privatizing of social services is troubling, occurring as it does at a time when government has reduced its commitment to social programs. Yet human service corporations will likely continue to be prominent players in shaping the nation's social welfare policies. As long as U.S. culture is democratic and capitalistic, entrepreneurs will be free to establish social welfare services in the private sector, both as nonprofit agencies and as for-profit corporations.

The **mixed welfare economy** of the United States, in which the voluntary, governmental, and corporate sectors coexist, poses important questions for social welfare policy. To what extent can voluntary groups be held responsible for public welfare, given their limited fiscal resources? For which groups of people, if any, should government divest itself of responsibility? Can human service corporations care for poor and multiproblem clients while continuing to generate profits? Equally important, how can welfare professionals shape coherent social welfare policies, given the fragmentation inherent in such pluralism? Clearly, the answers to these questions have much to say about how social welfare programs are perceived by human service professionals, their clients, and the taxpayers who continue to subsidize social programs.

The multitude of questions posed by the transition of social welfare in this country is daunting. Temporarily satisfied by the draconian 1996 welfare reform bill (and the dramatic cuts in the nation's public assistance rolls), conservatives later shifted their attention to "reforming" social insurance programs such as Social Security and Medicare

through privatization. Yet past advocates of social justice such as Jane Addams, Whitney Young Jr., and Wilbur Cohen, to name a few, interpreted the inadequacy of social welfare provision and the confusion of their times as an opportunity to further social justice. It remains for another generation of welfare professionals to demonstrate the same imagination, perseverance, and courage to advance social welfare in the years ahead. Those accepting this challenge will need to be familiar with the various meanings of social welfare policy, differing political and economic explanations of social welfare, and the multiple interest groups that have emerged within the U.S. social welfare system.

Definitions of Social Welfare Policy

The English social scientist Richard Titmuss defined **social services** as "a series of collective interventions that contribute to the general welfare by assigning claims from one set of people who are said to produce or earn the national income to another set of people who may merit compassion and charity."[4] Welfare policy, whether it is the product of governmental, voluntary, or corporate institutions, is concerned with allocating goods, services, and opportunities to enhance social functioning.

William Epstein defined social policy as "social action sanctioned by society."[5] Social policy can also be defined as the formal and consistent ordering of human affairs. **Social welfare policy,** a subset of social policy, regulates the provision of benefits to people to meet basic life needs, such as employment, income, food, housing, health care, and relationships.[6]

Social welfare policy is influenced by the context in which benefits are provided. For example, social welfare is often associated with legislatively mandated programs of the **governmental sector,** such as **Temporary Assistance for Needy Families (TANF).** In the TANF program, social welfare policy consists of the rules by which the federal and state governments apportion cash benefits to an economically disadvantaged population. TANF benefits are derived from general revenue taxes (often paid by citizens who are better off). But this is a simplification of benefits provided to those deemed needy.

Benefits provided through governmental social welfare policy include cash, along with noncash or in-kind benefits, including personal social services.[7] Cash benefits can be further divided into social insurance and public assistance grants (discussed in depth in Chapter 11).

In-kind benefits (provided as proxies for cash) include such benefits as food stamps; Medicaid; housing vouchers; Women, Infants, and Children (WIC) coupons; and low-income energy assistance. Personal social services are designed to enhance relationships between people as well as institutions, such as individual, family, and mental health treatment; child welfare services; rehabilitation counseling; and so forth. Although complicated, this classification reflects a common theme—the redistribution of resources from the better-off to the more disadvantaged. This redistributional aspect of social welfare policy is generally accepted by those who view social welfare as a legitimate function of the state. Governmental social welfare policy is often referred to as "public" policy because it is the result of decisions reached through a legislative process intended to represent the entire population.

But social welfare is also provided by non-governmental entities, in which case social welfare policy is a manifestation of "private" policy. For example, a nonprofit agency with a high demand for its services and limited resources may establish a waiting list as agency policy. As other agencies adopt the same strategy for rationing services, clients begin to pile up on waiting lists and some are eventually denied services. Or consider the practice of "dumping," a policy that has been used by some private health care providers to abruptly transfer uninsured patients to public hospitals while they are suffering from traumatic injuries. Patients can—and sometimes do—die as a result of private social welfare policy.

Because U.S. social welfare has been shaped by policies of governmental and nonprofit agencies, confusion exists about the role of for-profit social service firms. The distinction between the public and private sectors was traditionally marked by the boundary between governmental and nonprofit agencies. Profit-making firms are "private" nongovernmental entities that differ from the traditional private voluntary agencies because they operate on a for-profit basis. Within private social welfare, it is therefore important to distinguish between policies of for-profit and of nonprofit organizations. A logical way to redraw the social welfare map is to adopt the following definitions: *Governmental social welfare policy* refers to decisions made by the state; *voluntary social welfare policy* refers to decisions reached by nonprofit agencies; and *corporate social welfare policy* refers to decisions made by for-profit firms.

Social Problems and Social Welfare Policy

Social welfare policy often develops in response to social problems. The relationship between social problems and social welfare policy is not linear, and not all social problems result in social welfare policies. In many instances, existing social welfare policies are funded at ineffectual levels. For example, the Child Abuse Prevention and Treatment Act of 1974 was designed to ameliorate the problem of child abuse, yet underbudgeting left Child Protective Service (CPS) workers in a catch-22 situation. The act required CPS workers to promptly investigate child abuse reports, but agencies had inadequate staff resources to deal with the skyrocketing number of complaints. Caught in a resources crunch, many CPS workers were unable to properly investigate allegations of abuse, resulting in many children dying or undergoing serious injury.

Social welfare is not merely an expression of social altruism; it contributes to the maintenance and survival of society. In this respect, social welfare policy helps hold together a society that may fracture along social, political, and economic stress lines. Social welfare policy is also useful in enforcing social control, especially as a proxy for more coercive measures such as law enforcement and the courts.[8] When the basic minimum needs of the disadvantaged are met, they are less inclined to revolt against the unequal distribution of resources. Social welfare policies also subsidize employers, because welfare benefits supplement low and nonlivable wages, thereby maintaining a work incentive. If wages are insufficient to meet basic food, clothing, and shelter needs, little incentive exists for workplace participation. Without social welfare, like earned income tax credit (EITC), employers would have to raise wages and prices for consumers. Social welfare also supports important industries, such as agriculture (food stamps), housing (Section 8 and various other housing programs), and health care (Medicaid and Medicare). If social welfare benefits were suddenly eliminated, a segment of U.S. business would collapse and prices for commodities and services would rise dramatically. Social welfare benefits help maintain stable price structures and economic growth.

Social welfare policies also relieve the social and economic dislocations caused by the uneven nature of economic development. For example, one of the main features of capitalism and economic globalism is a constantly changing economy where jobs are created in one sector and lost (or exported) in another. The result is large islands of unemployment as workers transition from one employment sector to the other or are lost in the shuffle. Myriad social welfare programs, such as unemployment insurance and food stamps, help soften the transition. Without such social benefits, fundamental questions would also arise about the moral nature of U.S. society. Finally, social welfare policies are a means for rectifying past and current injustices. For example, affirmative action was designed to remedy the historical discrimination that denied large numbers of Americans access to economic opportunities and positions of power. School breakfast and lunch programs, teacher incentive pay, and other policies are designed to help ameliorate the unequal distribution of resources between underfunded inner-city and better-funded suburban school systems.

Social Work and Social Policy

Social work practice is driven by social policies that dictate how the work is done, with whom, for how much, and toward what ends. For example, a social worker employed in a public mental health center may have a caseload of well over 200 clients. Given that caseload size, it is unlikely that the worker can engage in any kind of sustained therapeutic intervention with clients because the size of the caseload permits little more than case tracking. Or consider the worker who must find employment for mothers on public assistance about to lose benefits because of the imposition of time limits, but who are unlikely to locate adequate work because of high area unemployment. In these instances, economic (i.e., underfunding) and political factors contribute to policies that determine the ability of the worker and agency to accomplish their jobs.

An ideological preference among policymakers for private sector social services has resulted in less

funding for public agencies. The conservative focus on cutting taxes—evident in the dramatic tax cuts of the last Bush administration—led to reductions in public revenues and hence reductions for social programs. In response to diminishing revenues, public agencies adjust in predictable ways, such as cutting qualified staff and expecting existing staff to do more with less, utilizing less-qualified and lower-paid staff, promoting short-term or group interventions designed to cheaply process more clients, and freezing or reducing the salaries and benefits for professional staff. Combined, these strategies help shape an agency geared to processing more clients rather than helping individual ones. Hence, what a trained social worker can accomplish depends, in part, on the available resources within the agency.

Although not obvious at first glance, many social workers in private practice who depend on managed care for reimbursement experience similar constraints. Specifically, managed care plans dictate how much a social worker will be paid and how often they will see a client; accordingly, care management dictates the kinds of interventions that will be practical in the allotted time. In fact, these policies have as much impact on what social workers do in their day-to-day work as the microlevel theories taught in much of social work education. Accepted agency policy also helps to dictate what is taught in direct social work practice.

Values, Ideology, and Social Welfare Policy

Social welfare policies are shaped by a set of social and personal values that reflect the preferences of those in decision-making capacities. According to David Gil, "Choices in social welfare policy are heavily influenced by the dominant beliefs, values, ideologies, customs, and traditions of the cultural and political elites recruited mainly from among the more powerful and privileged strata."[9] Charles Prigmore and Charles Atherton list no fewer than 15 values that influence social welfare policy: achievement and success, activity and work, public morality, humanitarian concerns, efficiency and practicality, material comfort, equality, freedom, external conformity, science and secular rationality, nationalism and patriotism, democracy and self-determination, individualism, racism and group superiority, and belief in progress.[10] How these values are played out in the realm of social welfare is the domain of the policy analyst. Despite the best of intentions, social welfare policy is rarely based on a rational set of assumptions and reliable research.

One view of a worthwhile social policy is that it should leave no one worse off and at least one person better off, at least as that person judges his or her needs. In the real world of policy that rarely occurs. More often than not, policy is a zero-sum game, in which some people are advantaged at the expense of others. In fact, it can be argued that major social policies are based on values, not on the careful consideration of alternative policies.

Of course, there are serious consequences when social welfare policy is determined to a high degree by values. Since the late 1970s, social welfare policy has been largely shaped by values that emphasize self-sufficiency, work, and the omniscience of the marketplace. Because policymakers expected disadvantaged people to be more independent, supports from government social programs were significantly cut. Although these reductions saved money in the short run, most of the beneficiaries whose supports fell to the budget ax were children. Eventually, cuts in social programs may well lead to greater expenditures, as the generation of children who have gone without essential services begin to require programs to remedy problems associated with poor maternal and infant health care, poverty, illiteracy, and family disorganization. Although in 2006 the U.S. ranked fourth internationally in purchasing power parity (what a family income can actually buy in a given country), it ranked 22nd in public spending on family benefits.[11]

Social values are organized through the lens of ideology. Simply put, an **ideology** is the framework of commonly held beliefs through which we view the world. It is a set of assumptions about how the world works: what has value, what is worth living and dying for, what is good and true, and what is right. For the most part, these beliefs are rarely examined and are simply assumed to be true. Hence, the ideological tenets around which society is organized exist as a collective social consciousness that defines the world for its members. All societies reproduce themselves partly by reproducing their ideology; in this way, each generation accepts the basic ideological suppositions of the preceding one. When widely held ideological beliefs are questioned, society often reacts with strong sanctions. Ideological trends influence social welfare when adherents of one orientation hold sway in decision-making bodies.

Ideology even more strongly influences social welfare policy during periods of threat, such as the current "War on Terror." In this instance, social welfare policy fades into the background as the perceived need for personal and national security takes center stage. U.S. social history has been intermittently shattered when oppressed groups assert their rights in the face of mainstream norms. Such periods of social unrest strain the capacity of conventional ideologies to explain social problems and offer solutions. Sometimes social unrest is met with force, as during the period of the great labor strikes of 1877. In other instances, such as the Great Depression, social unrest is met with expanding social welfare programs.

The Political Economy of American Social Welfare

The term **political economy** refers to the interaction of political and economic theories in understanding society. The political economy of the United States has been labeled **democratic capitalism**—an open and representative form of government that coexists with a market economy. In that context, social welfare policy plays an important role in stabilizing society by modifying the play of market forces and softening the social and economic inequities that the market generates.[12] To that end, two sets of activities are necessary: state provision of social services (benefits of cash, in-kind benefits, and personal social services) and state regulation of private activities to alter (and sometimes improve) the lives of citizens. Social welfare bolsters ideology by helping to remedy the problems associated with economic dislocation, thereby allowing society to remain in a state of more or less controlled balance.

As noted earlier, the U.S. welfare state is driven by political economy. Ideally, the political economy of the welfare state should be viewed as an integrated fabric of politics and economics, but in reality, some schools of thought or movements contain more political than economic content, and vice versa. For example, most economic schools of thought contain sufficient political implications to qualify them as both economic and political dogmas. Conversely, most political schools of thought contain significant economic content. It is therefore often difficult to separate political from economic schools of thought. For the purposes of this chapter, though, we will organize the political economy of U.S. welfare into two separate categories: (1) predominantly economic schools of thought and (2) predominantly political schools of thought. The careful reader will find a significant overlap among and between these categories.

The U.S. Economic Continuum

In large measure, economics forms the backbone of the political system. For example, we would not have the modern welfare state without the contributions of economist John Maynard Keynes. Conversely, we would not have the conservative movement without the contributions of classical or free market economists such as Adam Smith or Milton Friedman. Virtually every political movement is somehow grounded in economic thought. The three major schools of economics that have traditionally dominated American economic thought are Keynesian economics; classical or free market economics (and its variants); and, to a lesser degree, democratic socialism.

Keynesian Economics

Keynesian economics drives liberalism and most welfare state ideologies. John Maynard Keynes' economic theories formed the substructure and foundation of the modern welfare state, and virtually all welfare societies are built along his principles. Sometimes called demand or consumer-side economics, this model emerged from Keynes's 1936 book, *The General Theory of Employment, Interest and Money*.

An Englishman, Keynes took the classical model of economic analysis (self-regulating markets, perfect competition, the laws of supply and demand, etc.) and added the insight that macroeconomic stabilization by government is necessary to keep the economic clock ticking smoothly.[13] He rejected the idea that a perfectly competitive economy tended automatically toward full employment and that the government should not interfere in the process. Keynes argued that instead of being self-correcting and readily able to pull themselves out of

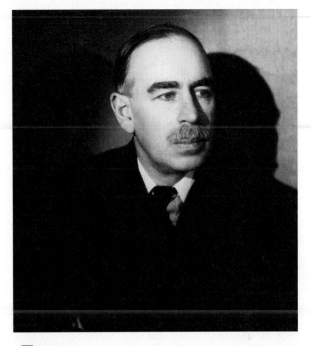

John Maynard Keynes is best known as the economic architect of the modern welfare state.

recessions, modern economies were recession prone and had difficulty providing full employment.

According to Keynes, periodic and volatile economic situations that cause high unemployment are primarily caused by instability in investment expenditures. The government can stabilize and correct recessionary or inflationary trends by increasing or decreasing total spending on output. Governments can accomplish this by increasing or decreasing taxes (thereby increasing or decreasing consumption) and by the transfer of public goods or services. For Keynes, a "good" government is an activist government in economic matters, especially when the economy gets out of full employment mode. Keynesians believe that social welfare expenditures are investments in human capital that eventually increase the national wealth (e.g., by increasing productivity) and thereby boost everyone's net income.

Keynes's doctrine emerged from his attempt to understand the nature of recessions and depressions. Specifically, he saw recessions and depressions as emerging from businesses' loss of confidence in investments (e.g., focusing on risk rather than gain), which in turn causes the hoarding of cash. This loss of confidence eventually leads to a shortage of money as everyone tries to hoard cash simultaneously. Keynes's answer to this problem is that government should make it possible for people to satisfy their economic needs without cutting their spending, which prevents the spiral of shrinking incomes and shrinking spending. Simply put, in a depression the government should print more money and get it into circulation.[14]

Keynes also understood that this monetary policy alone would not suffice if a recession got out of control, as in the depression of the 1930s. In a depression, businesses and households will not increase spending regardless of how much cash they have. To help an economy exit this trap, government must do what the private sector will not—namely, spend. This spending can take the form of public works projects (financed by borrowing) or of direct governmental subsidization of demand (welfare entitlements). To be fair, Keynes saw public spending only as a last resort to be employed if monetary expansion failed. Moreover, he sought an economic balance: Print money and spend in a recession; stop printing and stop spending once it is over. Keynes understood that too much money in circulation, especially in times of high production and full employment, leads to inflation. Although relatively simple, Keynes's theories represent one of the great insights of twentieth-century economic thought.[15] These ideas also formed the economic basis for the modern welfare state.

Conservative or Free Market Economics

Whereas liberalism is guided by Keynesian economics, the conservative view of social welfare is guided by free market economics. It is predicated on a belief in the existence of many small buyers and sellers who exchange homogeneous products with perfect information in a setting in which each can freely enter and exit the marketplace at will.[16] None of these assumptions hold in the real world of economics. For instance, the free market model does not address the dominance of distribution networks by a single retailer like Wal-Mart. There is nothing in the free market model that addresses the lack of equitable distribution of knowledge, experience, opportunity, and access to resources enjoyed by buyers and sellers. The free market model ignores theft, fraud, and deception in cases like Enron, and it ignores the competitive advantages that accrue through lobbying and special interest negotiations like Halliburton's no competition bids for Iraq reconstruction projects. It also ignores the power of large retailers in controlling the market by

instituting late shopping hours or even 24/7 businesses that make it impossible for small family-owned businesses to compete.

The ascendance of the conservative economic (and social) argument accelerated after 1973, when the rise in living standards began to slow for most Americans. Conservatives blamed this economic slowdown on governmental policies—specifically, deficit spending, high taxes, and excessive regulations.[17] In a clever sleight of hand, government went from having the responsibility to address economic problems (à la Keynes) to being the cause of them.

Milton Friedman, considered by some to be the father of modern conservative economics, was one of Keynes's more ardent critics. In opposition to Keynes, Friedman argued that using fiscal and monetary policy to smooth out the business cycle is harmful to the economy and worsens economic instability.[18] He contended that the Depression did not occur because people were hoarding money; rather, there was a fall in the quantity of money in circulation. Friedman argues that Keynesian economic policies must be replaced by simple monetary rules (hence the term *monetarism*). In effect, he believes that the role of government is to keep the money supply growing steadily at a rate consistent with stable prices and long-term economic growth.[19]

Friedman counseled against active efforts to stabilize the economy. Instead of pumping money into the economy, government should simply make sure enough cash is in circulation. He called for a relatively inactive government in economic affairs that did not try to manage or intervene in the business cycle. For Friedman, welfare spending existed only for altruistic rather than economic reasons.[20] To the right of Milton Friedman is Robert Lucas, 1994 Nobel Prize winner and developer of the "theory of rational expectations." Lucas argued that Friedman's monetary policy was still too interventionist and would invariably do more harm than good.[21]

Developing outside of conventional economics, **supply-side economics** enjoyed considerable popularity during the early 1980s. Led by Robert Barth, editorial page head of the *Wall Street Journal*, supply-siders were journalists, policymakers, and maverick economists who argued that demand-side policies and monetary policies were ineffective.[22] They maintained that the incentive effects of reduced taxation would be so large that tax cuts would dramatically increase economic activity to the point where tax revenues would rise rather than fall. (Former president George H. W. Bush referred to this as *voodoo economics* in 1980.[23]) Specifically, supply-siders argued that tax cuts would lead to a large increase in labor supply and investment and therefore to a large expansion in economic output. The budget deficit would not be problematic because taxes, increased savings, and higher economic output would offset the deficit. In the early 1980s, supply-siders seized power from the Keynesians and mainstream conservative economists, many of whom believed in the same things but wanted to move more slowly.[24]

Although some supporters preferred to think of supply-side economics as pure economics, the theory contained enough political implications to qualify as a political as well as an economic approach. Supply-side economics provided the rationale for the punishing cuts in social programs executed under the Reagan administration.

Despite their popularity in the early years of the Reagan administration, supply-side ideas fell out of favor when it became evident that massive tax cuts for the wealthy and corporations did not result in increased capital formation and economic activity. Instead, the wealthy spent their tax savings on luxury items, and corporations used tax savings to purchase other companies in a merger mania that took Wall Street by surprise. Other corporations took advantage of temporary tax savings to transfer their operations abroad, further reducing the supply of high-paying industrial jobs in the United States. For these and other reasons, the budget deficit grew from about $50 billion a year in the Carter term to $352 billion a year in 1992.[25] Although the term "supply-side economics" fell out of favor by the late 1980s, many of its basic tenets, such as massive tax cuts and cuts in social welfare spending, were adopted by the G. W. Bush administration. The result mirrored the earlier effects of supply-side policies: huge federal and state budget shortfalls, corporate hoarding, greater economic inequality, and stagnant wages.[26]

Conservative economists argue that large social welfare programs—including unemployment benefits and public service jobs—are detrimental to the society in two ways. First, government social programs erode the work ethic by supporting those not in the labor force. Second, because they are funded by taxes, public sector social welfare programs divert money that could otherwise be invested in the private sector. These conservative economists believe that economic growth helps everyone because overall prosperity creates more jobs, income, and goods, and these eventually filter down to the poor. For conservative economists, investment is the key to prosperity and the engine that drives the economic machine. Accordingly, many conservative economists favor tax breaks for the wealthy based on the premise that such breaks will result in more disposable after-tax income freed up for investment. High taxes are an impediment to economic progress because they channel money into "public" investments and away from "private" investments.

In the neoconservative paradigm, opportunity is based on one's relationship to the marketplace. Thus, legitimate rewards can occur only through marketplace participation. In contrast to liberals who emphasize mutual self-interest, interdependence, and social equity, conservative economists argue that the highest form of social good is realized by the maximization of self-interest. In the conservative view (as epitomized by author Ayn Rand[27]), the best society is one in which everyone actively pursues their own good. Through a leap of faith, the maximization of self-interest can somehow be transformed into a mutual good. This premise was proved false by the 2008 global economic crisis. This premise was proved false by the 2008 global economic crisis.

Conservative economists maintain not only that high taxation and government regulation of business serve as disincentives to investment, but that individual claims on social insurance and public welfare grants discourage work. Together these factors lead to a decline in economic growth and an increase in the expectations of beneficiaries of welfare programs. For conservatives, the only way to correct the irrationality of governmental social programs is to eliminate them. Charles Murray has suggested that the entire federal assistance and income support structure for working-aged persons (Medicaid, the former Aid to Families with Dependent Children [AFDC], food stamps, etc.) should be scrapped. This would leave working-aged persons no recourse except to actively engage in the job market or turn to family, friends, or privately funded services.[28]

Many conservative economists argue that economic insecurity is an important part of the entrepreneurial spirit. Unless people are *compelled* to work, they will choose leisure over work. Conversely, providing economic security for large numbers of people through welfare programs leads to diminished ambition and fosters an unhealthy dependence on the state. Conservatives further argue that self-realization can occur only through marketplace participation. Hence, social programs harm rather than help the most vulnerable members of society. This belief in the need for economic insecurity forms the basis for the 1996 welfare reform bill that includes a maximum time limit on welfare benefits.

Some conservative economists are influenced by "public choice" theory. The **public choice school** gained adherents among conservative analysts as faith ebbed in supply-side theories. Not widely known outside academic circles until its major proponent, James Buchanan, was awarded the Nobel Prize for economics in 1986, the public choice model states that public sector bureaucrats are self-interested utility-maximizers, and that strong incentives exist for interest groups to make demands on government. The resulting concessions from this arrangement flow directly to the interest group and their costs are spread among all taxpayers. Initial concessions lead to demands for further concessions, which are likely to be forthcoming so long as interest groups are vociferous in their demands. Under such an incentive system, different interests are also encouraged to band together to make demands, because there is no reason for one interest group to oppose the demands of others. But while demands for goods and services increase, revenues tend to decrease. This happens because interest groups resist paying taxes directed specifically toward them and because no interest group has much incentive to support general taxes. The result of this scenario is predictable: Strong demands for government benefits accompanied by declining revenues lead to government borrowing, which in turn results in large budget deficits.[29] Adherents of public choice theory view social welfare as a series of endless concessions to disadvantaged groups that will eventually bankrupt the government.

The Global Economic Crisis and the Flaws in the Free Market Argument

In a rare occurrence in 2008, Alan Greenspan, the former 18-year Federal Reserve chairman, admitted he "made a mistake" in trusting free markets to regulate themselves without government oversight. He also conceded a serious philosophical flaw in his thinking. Namely, that an unfettered free market is an essential part of a superior economy. Greenspan further admitted that "I made a mistake in presuming that the self-interests of organizations, specifically banks and others, were . . . capable of protecting their own shareholders and their equity in the firms."[30] This was an amazing series of admissions from the man known as the "oracle"—or the one thought of as being almost infallible in his economic acumen. More importantly, Greenspan's admissions repudiated the belief that largely unregulated free markets inevitably yield superior economic gain.

The initial event triggering the 2008 global economic crisis was the collapse of the U.S. housing market and the realization that domestic and foreign banks and investment houses and institutions were holding hundreds of billions of dollars of subprime mortgages (i.e., mortgages given to less creditworthy borrowers) that were essentially toxic debt with little hope of repayment. Moreover, investors realized that many subprime mortgages were underpriced in terms of risk. Specifically, the higher interest rate charged to credit-challenged borrowers was below the real interest rate that would have been required to justify the higher risk. Underpricing risk has been a major factor in the subprime mortgage crisis.

It is overly simplistic to blame the economic crisis solely on subprime loans or on families who took out mortgages they could not repay. Multiple factors converged to create the economic crisis, including the largely unregulated derivatives market and various other forms of dodgy financial instruments. Derivatives are used by major banks and businesses to hedge risk or engage in speculation. They are financial instruments whose value depends on that of an underlying commodity, bond, equity, or currency. Investors purchase derivatives to bet on the future (or as a hedge against the potential adverse impacts of an investment), to mitigate a risk associated with an underlying security, to protect against interest rate or stock market changes, and so forth. Derivatives are sold by hedge funds, investment houses, insurance companies, and banks. Derivatives are used in a variety of areas. For example, credit derivatives can involve a contract between two parties that allows one of them to transfer their credit risk to the other. The party transferring the risk pays a fee to the party that assumes it.

All forms of derivatives are risky investments since they are basically big bets made in amounts (often in the billions) that are astounding even to financially sophisticated investors. Like all forms of gambling, derivatives only work if the casino has the money to meet their obligation to bettors. In turn, the system collapses if the house lacks the cash (i.e., it has a liquidity problem) to pay winners. The 2008 economic crisis was partly precipitated by the derivatives market (which hedged bets on portfolios that included subprime mortgages) and the resulting liquidity problem.

Trying to Save the Economy The precursor to the massive federal bailout of Wall Street and the banking industry began in February 2008 when former president G. W. Bush signed the $168 billion stimulus package giving tax rebates to more than 130 million households.[31] Bush administration officials hoped the tax package would be sufficient to kick-start the economy and steer it away from a full-blown recession. He was obviously wrong.

Shortly thereafter, federal loans and bailout proposals came at an almost dizzying pace. In March 2008, the Federal Reserve enticed JP Morgan with a $29 billion credit line to take over the failing Bear Stearns investment house.[32] One financial institution after another failed or was taken over. Later in 2008, Bank of America bought Countrywide Mortgage (the largest U.S. mortgage lender with assets of $209 billion) for a paltry $4.1 billion in stock. Fearing that Merrill Lynch was next, CEO John Thain quickly sold out to Bank of America. In another stunning move, JP Morgan Chase (the third largest U.S. bank) bought Washington Mutual (WaMu), the nation's largest thrift bank, after it was seized by federal regulators. Meanwhile, Wells Fargo was busy acquiring Wachovia Bank for $15.1 billion in stock.[33]

When Freddie Mac and Fannie Mae were facing a bankruptcy that threatened to further destabilize an already devastated housing market, the Feds came to the rescue by buying up to $200 billion of stock (including bad mortgage debt). Since Freddie Mac and Fannie Mae guarantee $5.4 trillion in outstanding mortgage debt, the costs of the bailout could eventually run even higher, especially given the 1.3 million homes in foreclosure in 2008.[34]

While the Feds let the investment banking house Lehman Brothers die (the largest bankruptcy in U.S. history), they relented with American International Group (AIG)—the world's largest insurer—by providing a two-year $85 billion line of credit. In return, the federal government took control of some of AIG's equity and assets. In September 2008, the Central Bank lent AIG an additional $37.8 billion. In total, by late 2008 the U.S. government had put about $123 billion at AIG's disposal.[35] Not wanting to be left out of the party, U.S. automakers also pressed for taxpayer subsidized loans.[36]

After much jockeying, Congress finally approved a $700 billion (a number that swelled to $825 billion) bailout for Wall Street in September 2008. Despite this bailout, world markets continued to convulse with uncertainty. Frightened by increased market instability, the Federal Reserve further cut the U.S. prime rate, a strategy that seemed to have little effect. Taken together, these bailout obligations added up to more than $1 trillion, barring a few billion here and there.

With the exception of Bush's tax stimulus package, the bailouts and financial help were largely directed at the supply side of the economy.[37]

Can the U.S. Government Pay the Bill? To put things into perspective, the proposed $825 billion bailout (inflated by pork) was more than the U.S. government spent on defense ($549 billion), Social Security ($581 billion), or Medicare and Medicaid ($561 billion) in 2007.

Much of the money to pay for the bailouts will come from foreign investors who purchase U.S. Treasury bills. As long as foreign investors are confident in the ability of the United States to solve its problems, the country can borrow. All bets are off if their faith in the United States is shaken, or if foreign investors begin to prefer hard assets like cheap buildings, land, or factories over paper.

Foreign investors are closely watching U.S. economic data. In 2008, the U.S. gross domestic product (GDP) was $14 trillion—the highest in the world. However, the International Monetary Fund (IMF) predicted U.S. economic growth to be 0.6% in 2008 or half that of other industrialized nations like Germany, the UK, France, Spain, Japan, and Canada.[38] Moreover, the 2008 U.S. budget deficit was $410 billion, an amount that significantly added to the existing national debt of $10 trillion.[39]

By 2009, government spending on bailouts and loans could exceed $1.4 trillion or about 10 percent of the GDP, adding 13 percent to the national debt. The national debt could total a whopping 81 percent of the GDP. If Wall Street is not properly regulated, or if the structural problems are deeper than anticipated, current bailout attempts will likely fail.

The 2008 economic crisis led to profound consequences for the nation and its social welfare system. The semi-nationalization of large chunks of the U.S. banking system calls into question the long-term belief in the sanctity of the marketplace and the viability of laissez-faire capitalism. Even more amazing is that the semi-nationalization of the banking system occurred under the former Bush administration. Regardless, the financial crisis will also prove a punishing experience for nonprofit human service organizations that depend on individual and foundation philanthropy as well as government agencies that rely on tax revenues. Not surprisingly, the collapse of Wall Street will chill any subsequent debate around privatizing Social Security (see Chapter 10).

Democratic Socialism

After a long dormant period, the cobwebs of socialism were dusted off in the 2008 presidential election when John McCain falsely accused Barack Obama of being a socialist. Democratic socialism (as opposed to old Soviet-style socialism) is based on the belief that radical economic change can occur within a democratic context. While eschewing capitalism, democratic socialists, such as the late Michael Harrington, have a fundamental belief in the democratic process.

Democratic socialism sharply veers from Keynesianism and conservative economics. Specifically, Keynesians basically believe in the market economy but want to make it more responsive to human needs by smoothing out the rough edges. Conservatives believe that the economy should be left alone except for a few minor tweaks, such as regulating the money flow. Other conservative economists argue that the market should be left totally alone. On balance, both Keynesians and economic conservatives have a basic faith that capitalism can advance the public good and be made compatible with human needs. In that sense, Keynesians and economic conservatives have more in common with each other than Keynesians have with socialists.

Proponents of **socialism** argue that the fundamental nature of capitalism is anathema to advancing the public good. Socialists contend that a system predicated on pursuing profit and individual self-interest can lead only to greater inequality. The creation of a just society requires a fundamental transformation of the economic system, and the pursuit of profit and self-interest must be replaced by the collective pursuit of the common good. Not surprisingly, socialists rebuff Keynesians because of their inherent belief that economic problems can be fixed by simple technicalities instead of major institutional change. Socialists differ from conser-

vatives for obvious reasons, such as the primary importance they place on markets, their belief in subordinating individual interests to market forces, and their overall social conservatism.

Left-wing theorists maintain that the failure of capitalism has led to political movements that have pressured institutions to respond with increased social welfare services. They believe that real social welfare must be structural and can be accomplished only by redistributing resources. In a just society where goods, resources, and opportunities are made available to everyone, all but the most specific forms of welfare (health care, rehabilitation, counseling, etc.) would be unnecessary. In this radical worldview, poverty is directly linked to structural inequality: People need welfare because they are exploited and denied access to resources. In an unjust society, welfare functions as a substitute, albeit a puny one, for social justice.[40]

Some socialists argue that social welfare is an ingenious arrangement on the part of business to have the public assume the costs caused by the social and economic dislocations inherent in capitalism. According to these theorists, social welfare expenditures "socialize" the costs of capitalist production by making public the costs of private enterprise. Thus, social welfare serves both the needs of people and the needs of capitalism. For other socialists, social welfare programs support an unjust economic system that, in turn, continues to generate problems requiring social programs. For these radicals, social welfare programs function like junk food for the impoverished: They provide just enough sustenance to discourage revolution but not enough to make a real difference in the lives of the poor. Within this radical framework, social welfare is seen as a form of social control. Frances Fox Piven and Richard Cloward summarize the socialist argument:

> Relief arrangements are ancillary to economic arrangements. Their chief function is to regulate labor, and they do that in two general ways. First, when mass unemployment leads to outbreaks of turmoil, relief programs are ordinarily initiated or expanded to absorb or control enough of the unemployed to restore order; then, as turbulence subsides, the relief system contracts, expelling those who are needed to populate the labor markets.[41]

In place of liberal welfare reforms, the radical vision proposes that the entire social, political, and economic system undergo a major overhaul. In the radical context, real welfare reform (i.e., a complete redistribution of goods, income, and services) can occur only within a socialist economic system.

The U.S. Political Continuum

Various understandings of the political economy produce differing conceptions of the ultimate public good. Competition among ideas about the public good and the welfare state has long been a knotty issue in the political economy of the United States. Because shifts in government policy are driven largely by an ideologically determined view of the public good, any policy analysis must be based on whose definition is being examined. In a democratic capitalist society, beliefs about the public good often vary depending on the proponent's position in the social order.

The major American ideologies, (neo)liberalism and (neo)conservatism, hold vastly different views of social welfare and the public good. Conservatives believe that the public good is best served when individuals and families meet their needs through marketplace participation. Accordingly, conservatives prefer private sector approaches over governmental welfare and advocate for smaller government social welfare programs. Conservatives are not antiwelfare per se; they simply believe that government should have a minimal role (i.e., serve as a "safety net") in ensuring the social welfare of citizens. Traditional liberals, on the other hand, view government as the only institution capable of bringing a measure of **social justice** to millions of Americans who cannot fully participate in the U.S. mainstream because of obstacles such as racism, poverty, and sexism. Traditional liberals therefore view governmental social welfare programs as a key component in promoting the public good. One of the major differences between conservatives and liberals lies in their differing perceptions of how the public good is enhanced or hurt by welfare state programs.

The understanding of "the public good" is lodged in the political and ideological continuum that makes up the U.S. political economy. An appreciation of this requires an understanding of the interaction of schools of political thought and how they evolved. These ideological tenets also shape the platforms of the major political parties and can be divided into two categories: (1) liberalism and left-of-center movements, and (2) traditional conservatives and the far right.

Liberalism and Left-of-Center Movements

Liberalism   Since Franklin Delano Roosevelt's **New Deal,** advocates of liberalism have argued for advancing the public good by promoting an expanding economy coupled with the growth of universal, non-means–tested social welfare and health programs. Traditional liberals used Keynesian concepts as the economic justification for building the welfare state. As such, the general direction of policy from the 1930s to the early 1970s was for the federal government to assume greater amounts of responsibility for the public good.

American liberals established the welfare state with the passage of the Social Security Act of 1935. Harry Hopkins—a social worker, the head of the Federal Emergency Relief Administration, a confidant of President Roosevelt, a co-architect of the New Deal, and a consummate political operative—developed the calculus for American liberalism: "tax, tax; spend, spend; elect, elect."[42] This liberal approach was elegant in its simplicity: The government taxes the wealthy, thereby securing the necessary revenues to fund social programs for workers and the poor. This approach dominated social policy for almost 50 years. In fact, it was so successful that by 1980 social welfare accounted for 57 percent of all federal expenditures.[43]

By the mid-1960s, the welfare state had become an important fixture in America's social landscape, and politicians sought to expand its benefits to more constituents. Focusing on the expansion of middle-class programs such as Federal Housing Administration (FHA) home mortgages, federally insured student loans, Medicare, and veterans' pensions, liberal policymakers secured the political loyalty of the middle class. Even conservative politicians respected voter support for the middle-class welfare state, and not surprisingly, the largest expansion of social welfare spending occurred under Richard Nixon, a Republican president.

Yet the promise of the U.S. welfare state to provide social protection similar to that in industrialized European nations never materialized. By the mid-1970s, the hope of traditional liberals to build a welfare state mirroring those of northern Europe had been replaced by an incremental approach that narrowly focused on consolidating and fine-tuning the programs of the Social Security Act. One reason for this failure was the ambivalence of many Americans toward centralized government. "The emphasis

Barack Obama was elected president of the United States in 2008.

consistently has been on the local, the pluralistic, the voluntary, and the business-like over the national, the universal, the legally entitled, and the governmental," observed policy analyst Marc Bendick.[44]

Liberalism lost ground for another reason. The Social Security Act of 1935—the hallmark of American liberalism—was primarily a self-financing social insurance program that rewarded working people. Public assistance programs that contained less political capital and were therefore a better measure of public compassion, were rigorously means tested, sparse in their benefits, and operated by the less than generous states. For example, although Social Security benefits were indexed to the cost of living in the mid-1970s, AFDC benefits deteriorated so badly that about half its value was lost between 1975 and 1992. At the same time that Social Security reforms reduced the elderly poverty rate by 50 percent, the plight of poor families worsened.

Neoliberalism By the late 1970s, the liberal belief that the welfare state was the best mechanism to advance the public good was in retreat. What remained of traditional liberalism was replaced by a **neoliberalism** that was more cautious of government, less antagonistic toward big business, and more skeptical about the value of universal entitlements.

The defeat of Jimmy Carter and the election of a Republican Senate in 1980 forced many liberal Democrats to reevaluate their party's traditional position on domestic policy. This reexamination, which Charles Peters christened "neoliberalism" to differentiate it from old-style liberalism, attracted only a small following in the early 1980s.[45] However, by the mid-1990s, most leading Democrats could be classified as neoliberal. Randall Rothenberg charted signs of the influence of neoliberalism on the Democratic domestic policy platform as early as 1982, when he observed that the party's midterm convention did not endorse a large-scale federal jobs program, did not endorse a plan for national health insurance, and did not submit a plan for a guaranteed annual income.[46]

In the late 1980s, a cadre of prominent mainstream Democrats established the Democratic Leadership Council (DLC). In part, their goal was to wrest control of the Democratic Party from traditional liberals and to create a new Democratic Party that was more attuned to the beliefs of the traditional core voters. In 1989 the DLC released *The New Orleans Declaration: A Democratic Agenda for the 1990s*, which promised that Democratic Party politics would shift toward a middle ground combining a corporatist economic analysis with Democratic compassion. Two of the founders of the DLC were Al Gore and Bill Clinton, who chaired the DLC just before announcing his presidential candidacy.[47] President Obama's campaign platform and cabinet-level appointments point to him also being largely in the neoliberal camp.

Compared to traditional liberals, neoliberals were more forgiving of the behavior of large corporations and were opposed to economic protectionism. Grounded in *realpolitik*, neoliberals viewed the New Deal approach (with the exception of Social Security) as too expensive and antiquated to address the mood of voters and the new global realities. Consequently, neoliberals distanced themselves from the large-scale governmental welfare programs associated with Democrats since the New Deal. Like their neoconservative counterparts, they called for reliance on personal responsibility, work, and thrift as an alternative to governmental programs. Accordingly, their welfare proposals emphasized labor market participation (workfare), personal responsibility (time-limited welfare benefits), family obligations (child support enforcement), and frugality in governmental spending. They argued for reduced governmental spending while encouraging businesses to assume more responsibility for the welfare of the population.

Former Secretary of Labor Robert Reich advocated a postliberal formulation that replaced social welfare entitlements with investments in **human capital.** Public spending was divided into "good" and "bad" categories: "Bad" was unproductive expenditures on welfare and price supports; "good" was investments in human capital, such as education, research, and job training.[48]

Neoliberalism altered the traditional liberal concept of the public good. Instead of viewing the interests of large corporations as antithetical to the best interests of society, neoliberals argued for free trade, less regulation, and a more laissez-faire approach to social problems. They also viewed long-time Democratic Party supporters, such as labor unions, with caution. For example, when labor unions fought to stop NAFTA (the North American Free Trade Agreement), former President Clinton continued to endorse it, despite labor's threats to oppose his reelection bid in 1996. The same was true for the GATT (General Agreement on Tariffs and Trade) agreement. In both instances, Clinton was firmly aligned with conservative Democrats and Republicans. Traditional liberal Democrats found themselves alone, bereft of support from the first Democratic White House in 14 years. In effect, the new shapers of the public good had systematically excluded key actors of the old liberal coalition.

The neoliberal view of the public good reflects a kind of postmodern perspective. For neoliberals, the public good is elusive, and its form is fluid. Definitions of the public good change as a social order evolves and new power relationships emerge. Thus, neoliberals do not define the public good as tethered to industrial era allegiances but look to a postindustrial society composed of new opportunities and new institutional forms.

Neoliberalism, then, is more a political strategy and pragmatic mode of operation than a political philosophy embodying a firm view of the public good. This is both its strength and its weakness. Specifically, the strength of neoliberalism lies in its ability to compromise and therefore to accomplish things. Its weakness is that when faced with an ideological critique, neoliberals are incapable of formulating a cogent ideological response. When G. W. Bush argued for staying the course in 2004, voters knew exactly what he meant even if they disagreed with him. When Clinton argued for staying the course in 1994, the public were unsure of the course.

In the American and British contexts, neoliberalism represents a "third way." Anthony Giddens offers a philosophical rationale for neoliberalism: "We should speak of a *positive welfare,* to which individuals and other agencies besides government contribute—and which is functional for wealth creation. The guideline for investment is *human capital* wherever possible, rather than the direct provision of economic maintenance. In place of the welfare state, we should put the *social investment state*, operating in the context of a positive welfare society."[49]

The Self-Reliance School   A perspective gaining influence in economically distressed areas and in developing countries is the **self-reliance school.**[50] This school maintains that industrial economic models are irrelevant to the economic needs of poor communities and are often damaging to the spiritual life of people.[51] Adherents of self-reliance repudiate the emphasis of Western economic philosophies on economic growth and the belief that the quality of life can be measured by material acquisitions. These political economists stress a balanced economy based on the real needs of people, production designed for internal consumption rather than export, productive technologies that are congruent with the culture and background of the population, the use of appropriate and manageable technologies, and a small-scale and decentralized form of economic organization.[52] Simply put, proponents of self-reliance postulate that more is less and less is more. The objective of self-reliance is the creation of a no-poverty society in which economic life is organized around issues of subsistence rather than trade and economic expansion. Accepting a world of finite resources and inherent limitations to economic growth, proponents argue that the true question of social and economic development is not what people think they want or need but what they require for survival. The self-reliance school accepts the need for social welfare programs that ameliorate the dislocations caused by industrialization, but it prefers low-technology and local solutions to social problems. This contrasts with the conventional wisdom of the welfare state, which is predicated on a prescribed set of programs on a national scale, administered by large bureaucracies using sophisticated management systems.

Classical Conservatives and the Far Right

Classic Conservatism   Former conservative political leaders such as Nelson Rockefeller, Richard

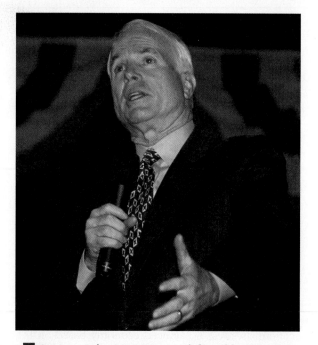

Senator John McCain was defeated by Barack Obama in the 2008 presidential election.

Nixon, and Barry Goldwater represented traditional conservatism. Few traditional conservatives occupy important leadership positions in the Republican party, as most have been replaced by cultural conservatives. Other conservatives like John McCain have had to spin their message to try to gain the approval of cultural conservatives.

On one level, all conservatives agree on important values relating to social policy. Beneath this agreement, however, important differences exist among various conservative factions.

Older, traditional conservatives diverge with the newer cultural conservatives on a range of social issues. First, as strict constitutionalists, traditional or classical conservatives believe strongly in the separation of church and state. They see prayer and religion as personal choices in which government has no constitutional right to intervene. Second, although both classical conservatives and cultural conservatives supposedly advocate for a weaker federal government, cultural conservatives also demand that the federal government use its power to implement their domestic agenda in areas they consider immoral, such as abortion and homosexuality.

Third, classical conservatives are more socially liberal than their cultural counterparts. For example, the late Barry Goldwater, a conservative icon and former U.S. senator and 1964 presidential candidate,

stated that "I have been, and am still, a traditional conservative, focusing on three general freedoms— economic, social, and political. . . . The conservative movement is founded on the simple tenet that people have the right to live life as they please, as long as they don't hurt anyone else in the process."[53] Following that line of reason, Goldwater's outspoken support of homosexuals in the military was directly opposed to the principles of neoconservatives. Regarding reproductive freedom, classical conservatives might challenge cultural conservatives on various measures that limit or ban abortions.

From the late 1970s onward, factions within the conservative movement became more pronounced. Old-style conservatives such as Nelson Rockefeller, Barry Goldwater, and William Cohen, who were more concerned with foreign policy than with domestic issues, were replaced by a new breed of cultural conservatives, such as Dick Armey, Newt Gingrich, Phil Gramm, and Sam Brownback. These cultural conservatives were committed to reversing 50 years of liberal influence in social policy. How the cultural conservatives came to shape social policy warrants elaboration, although it is first important to examine neoconservatives, the forerunners of cultural conservatism.

Neoconservatism Before the 1970s, conservatives were content to merely snipe at welfare programs, reserving their attention for areas more consistent with their traditional concerns such as the economy, defense spending, and foreign affairs. However, by the mid-1970s, younger conservative intellectuals recognized that the conservative stance toward social welfare was myopic because welfare was too important to be lightly dismissed. Consequently, **neoconservatives** sought to arrest the growth in governmental welfare programs while simultaneously transferring as much welfare responsibility as possible from government to the private sector.[54] They faulted government programs for a breakdown in the mutual obligation between groups; the lack of attention to how programs were operated and benefits awarded; the dependency of recipients; and the growth of the welfare industry and its special interest groups, particularly professional associations.[55] To counter the liberal goals of full employment, national health care, and a guaranteed annual income, neoconservatives maintained that high unemployment was good for the economy, that health care should remain in the private marketplace, and that competitive income structures were critical to productivity. They argued that income inequality was socially desirable because social policies that promote equality encourage coercion, limit individual freedom, and damage the economy.[56]

The neoconservative attack on the welfare state was so well crafted because many neoconservatives, among them Irving Kristol and Norman Podhoretz, were former liberals who had developed misgivings about the welfare state and joined the conservative movement in protest. Neoconservatives were effective in critiquing the welfare state, in large measure because they were so familiar with its philosophical origins. (One commentator classified them as liberals who had been mugged.) Despite their opposition to the welfare state, former liberals found their new conservative home anything but tidy. Born out of an urban environment, neoconservatives fashioned themselves as cosmopolitan intellectuals and free thinkers. Social issues such as abortion, school prayer, and the like were not a hot button item for this movement.

By the late 1970s, the position occupied by neoconservatives in the conservative movement began to be usurped by the emerging cultural conservatives. Although the neoconservatives provided the intellectual wedge that fractured the liberal consensus around the welfare state, cultural conservatives, such as Trent Lott and Tom DeLay, attained the leadership positions necessary to take down what was left of the institutional structure of liberal public philosophy. Properly understood, neoconservatism is at odds with the culturally conservative Republican agenda. The rift between the more urbane neoconservatives and the cultural conservatives was illustrated by John McCain's choice of Sarah Palin as his vice presidential running mate in 2008. Neoconservatives such as David Brooks, David Frum, Christopher Buckley, and others abhorred the choice of Palin whom they saw as unqualified but also as representing the culturally conservative faction of the party that believed in creationism, and were opposed to abortion regardless of the circumstances.

Cultural Conservatism   The neoconservative assault on liberal social policy was soon taken over by cultural conservatives, who raged against governmental intrusion in the marketplace while simultaneously attempting to use the authority of government to advance their social objectives in the areas of antiwelfare planks, sexual abstinence, school prayer, abortion, and antigay rights proposals. Cultural conservatives cleverly promoted a dual attitude toward the role of government. Mimicking their classical conservative predecessors in demanding a laissez-faire approach to economics, they steadfastly refused to translate that orientation to social affairs. Instead, cultural conservatives argued for social conformity and a level of governmental intrusion into private affairs that made most classical conservatives gag. In contrast to the classical conservative skepticism about blending religion and politics, cultural conservatives opportunistically embraced the rising tide of fundamentalist religion. As a measure of their success, this cobbled-together coalition of economic conservatives, right-wing Christians, and opportunistic politicians had by the late 1980s virtually decimated what remained of Republican liberalism, whose adherents had become an endangered species like liberal Democrats.

Cultural conservatives view the state as the cause of rather than the solution to social problems. With the exception of protecting people (police and defense) and property, cultural conservatives argue that the very existence of the state is antithetical to the public good because government interferes with the maximization of individual self-interest. Hence, their posture toward government is adversarial, except when the state is used to further their social agenda. Even though cultural conservatives argue for a minimalist state, they have been willing to compromise these libertarian leanings by adopting the agenda of traditionalists in myriad social issues such as school prayer, abortion, sexual orientation, and drug testing.

The conservative agenda of the 1980s was fourfold: (1) end the liberal hegemony in social policy, (2) reroute public policy through the private sector, (3) curtail costly social programs that lessen profits and restrict the global competitiveness of corporations, and (4) preclude the possibility of a resurgence in social programs. In tandem with this agenda, conservative presidents such as Reagan and the two Bushes prohibited the future growth of the welfare state by employing multiple strategies such as tax policy and federal budget deficits that precluded any form of significant public spending. As such, few responsible politicians would argue for increased social welfare spending given the 2008 federal debt of around $10 trillion.

In 1994, frustrated voters seemed ready to give cultural conservatives control of the Senate and the House. Cultural conservatives had learned from past mistakes. Instead of toying with incremental policies, they proposed bold new social initiatives that were incorporated into the Contract with America

Spotlight 1.1

Two groups that exemplify the differences between liberal and conservative political movements are the Green Party and the Moral Majority.

The Green Party

Ten key values serve as guiding principles for the Green Party—grassroots democracy, social justice and equal opportunity, ecological wisdom, nonviolence, decentralization, community-based economics and economic justice, feminism and gender equity, respect for diversity, personal and global responsibility, and future focus and sustainability. To learn more about these key values, go to the Green Party's website at **www.gp.org/tenkey.html.**

The Moral Majority

Traditionalists are characterized by conservative evangelical groups such as the Moral Majority. The Moral Majority and other traditional groups believe that God's laws must be translated into politics, and "higher laws" must become the laws of the state. Traditionalists are highly critical of governmental social programs, which they associate with a liberal social philosophy that is eroding traditional social institutions, particularly the family and the church. To learn more about the Moral Majority platform, visit the group's website at **www.faithandvalues.us.**

(designed to alter most of the safety net programs within a two-year period), a document signed by more than 300 House Republicans in 1994.[57] The crowning victory of the conservative movement occurred with the passage of the Personal Responsibility and Work Opportunity Reconciliation Act (PRWORA) in 1996.

Libertarianism Libertarians reflect another perspective. Specifically, this school of thought believes in virtually no government regulation.

> We, the members of the Libertarian Party, challenge the cult of the omnipotent state and defend the rights of the individual. We hold that all individuals . . . have the right to live in whatever manner they choose, so long as they do not forcibly interfere with the equal right of others to live in whatever manner they choose. We . . . hold that governments . . . must not violate the rights of any individual: namely, (1) the right to life—accordingly we support the prohibition of the initiation of physical force against others; (2) the right to liberty of speech and action—accordingly we oppose all attempts . . . [at] . . . government censorship in any form; and (3) . . . we oppose all government interference with private property. . . .[58]

Libertarians argue that governmental growth occurs at the expense of individual freedom. They also believe that the proper role for government is to provide a police force and a military that possesses only defensive weapons. Libertarians are highly critical of taxation because it fuels governmental growth. Apart from advocating minimal taxation earmarked for defense and police activities, they oppose the income tax. Because libertarians emphasize individual freedom and personal responsibility, they advocate the decriminalization of narcotics and believe that government should intercede in social affairs only when an individual's behavior threatens the safety of another.

The Welfare Philosophers and the Neoconservative Think Tanks

Many welfare professionals envisioned a U.S. welfare state based on a European model.[59] This vision was shared by virtually every social welfare scholar writing in the late 1960s and early 1970s.[60] In turn, most social workers supported a liberal welfare philosophy grounded in a system of national social programs that would be deployed as more citizens demanded greater services and benefits. This framework was informed by European welfare states, especially the Scandinavian variant that spread health care, housing, income benefits, and employment opportunities equitably across the population.[61] It also led Richard Titmuss to hope that the welfare state, as an instrument of government, would eventually lead to a "welfare world."[62]

For U.S. welfare philosophers, government programs that restricted the caprices of capitalism were both desirable and inevitable. In their classic *Industrial Society and Social Welfare,* Harold Wilensky and Charles Lebeaux suggested that "under continuing industrialization all institutions will be oriented toward and evaluated in terms of social welfare aims. The 'welfare state' will become the 'welfare society,' and both will be more reality than epithet."[63]

Despite the widespread acceptance of this liberal vision, an alternative vision arose that questioned the fundamental nature of welfare and social services. Throughout the 1970s and 1980s, conservatives (especially right-wing **think tanks,** or conservative policy institutes) busily made proposals for welfare reform. In fact, no conservative policy institute could prove its mettle until it produced a plan to clean up "the welfare mess." The Hoover Institution at Stanford University helped shape the early conservative position on welfare. "There is no inherent reason that Americans should look to government for those goods and services that can be individually acquired," argued Hoover's Alvin Rabushka, who listed four strategies for reforming welfare: (1) let users pay, (2) contract for services, (3) fund mandated services through the states, and (4) emphasize private substitution.[64] Martin Anderson, a Hoover senior fellow and later a domestic policy adviser to the Reagan administration, elaborated the conservative position on welfare in terms of the need to (1) reaffirm the need-only philosophical approach to welfare and state it as explicit national policy; (2) increase efforts to eliminate fraud; (3) establish and enforce a fair, clear work requirement; (4) remove inappropriate beneficiaries from the welfare rolls; (5) enforce support of dependents by those who have the responsibility and are shirking it; (6) improve the efficiency and effectiveness of welfare administration; and (7) shift more responsibility from the federal government to state and local governments and private institutions.[65] These recommendations formed the backbone of the 1996 PRWORA.

Another conservative think tank, the American Enterprise Institute (AEI), commissioned sociologist Peter Berger and theologian Richard John Neuhaus to prepare a theoretical analysis of U.S. society. Berger and Neuhaus's *To Empower People: The Role of Mediating Structures in Public Policy* identified the fundamental problem confronting the culture, such as the growth of megastructures (big government, big business, big labor, and professional bureaucracies), and the corresponding diminution in the value of the individual. The route to empowerment was to revitalize "mediating structures," among them the neighborhood, family, church, and voluntary associations.[66] In a subsequent analysis, an AEI scholar recategorized the corporation from a megastructure to a mediating structure, thus leaving the basic institutions of liberal social reform—government, the professions, and labor—as the sources of mass alienation.[67]

Not to be outdone, the Heritage Foundation featured *Out of the Poverty Trap: A Conservative Strategy for Welfare Reform* by Stuart Butler and Anna Kondratas.[68] Following along the same lines, the Free Congress Research and Education Foundation proposed reforming welfare through "cultural conservatism;" that is, by reinforcing "traditional values such as delayed gratification, work and saving, commitment to family and to the next generation, education and training, self-improvement, and rejection of crime, drugs, and casual sex."[69]

A handful of other works also served as beachheads for the conservative assault on the liberal welfare state. George Gilder's *Wealth and Poverty* argued that beneficent welfare programs represented a "moral hazard" that insulated people against risks essential to capitalism and thus contributed to dependency.[70] Martin Anderson concluded that income calculations should include the cash equivalent of in-kind benefits, such as food stamps, Medicaid, and housing vouchers, thus effectively lowering the poverty rate by 40 percent.[71] Taken together, these ideas and recommendations provided a potent critique of liberal governmental welfare programs. Unlike classical conservatives of an earlier generation, neoconservatives not only did their homework on social welfare policy but they also prepared proposals for welfare reform.

As Peter Kindle earlier pointed out in a supplement to this book, perhaps the most enduring change engineered by the conservative movement is what Jacob Hacker calls the "Great Risk Shift."[72] The private ownership of property and the acceptance of personal responsibility have long been core American values, which partly explains why opposition to former President Bush's "ownership society" has not materialized until recently. In *The Great Risk Shift*, Hacker exposes Bush's ownership society and the Republican Party's emphasis on personal responsibility as the code for shifting economic risk away from government and corporations and onto the back of the American family.

Simply put, private and public support mechanisms have fallen behind the pace of change in contemporary society. Almost half of marriages end in divorce. Over a third of employed Americans say that they are frequently worried about losing their jobs. Structural changes in the nature of employment, primarily seen in a shift away from manufacturing to the lower-paying service sector, have left many without the skills needed for new jobs or the resources to retrain. The likelihood of family income dropping 50% has almost tripled since the 1970s; personal bankruptcies and home foreclosures have increased by a factor of five; and over any two-year period more than 80 million Americans go without health insurance coverage.[73] During a 30-year period in which middle-class incomes have been stagnant, the need for increased economic security has been met by neglect from private and public institutions.[74]

The risk shift is happening in almost all sectors. Corporate retirement programs are shifting away from defined benefit plans in which retirees are guaranteed a set retirement income to defined contribution plans in which retirement depends on the investment savvy of the employees' investments. Whether these changes will help or hurt the individual depends on many factors, but it is clear that it is a shift in risk from corporation to the individual worker.

The absence of universal health care has underscored the importance of employer-provided health insurance; however, the increasing instability of employment often means that job transitions are accompanied by the inability to acquire health coverage. Conservatives have proposed Health Savings Accounts as a means of activating market forces to control health costs, but they reflect another risk shift from the corporation to the individual worker. The former Bush administration suggested the elimination of employer-provided health insurance in favor of tax deductions for health insurance premiums, yet another shifting of risk from corporations to the individual or family.[75] An important implication of Hacker's argument is that good social welfare policy analysis can no longer be restricted to a focus on income; it also must attend to the shifting dynamics of risk. As such, progressive social welfare policies must help to mitigate the degree of risk the individual family must bear.

Conclusion

John Judis and Michael Lind argue that "Ultimately American economic policy must meet a single test: Does it, in the long run, tend to raise or depress the incomes of most Americans? A policy that tends to impoverish the ordinary American is a failure, no matter what its alleged benefits are for U.S. corporations or for humanity as a whole."[76] To this we would add: "What are the effects of an economic policy on the social health of the nation?" Researchers at Fordham University's Institute for Innovation in Social Policy contend that the nation's quality of life has become unhinged from its economic growth. "We really have to begin to reassess this notion that the gross domestic product—the overall growth of the society—necessarily is going to produce improvements in the quality of life."[77] Constructing an Index for Social Health that encompassed governmental data from 1970 to 1993, researchers found that in six categories—children in poverty, child abuse, health insurance coverage, average weekly earnings adjusted for inflation, out-of-pocket health costs for senior citizens, and the gap between rich and poor—"social health" hit its lowest point in 1993. These indicators have worsened in the years since 1993, and we presume that the downward trend continues.

A corollary question is "What's the economy for, anyway?" In other words, do we exist to serve the economy or should the economy serve us? Economists often talk about the gross national product (GNP) or gross domestic product (GDP), productivity, and overall economic growth as if they were religious truths. Discussions typically revolve around how to best grow the economy, not whether the economy should grow. Meanwhile, too little of the economic discussion involves environmental sustainability or quality of life issues. John de Graaf has addressed these issues in *Affluenza* (the film and the book) as have other authors in various forms. (See Spotlight 1.2.)

As this chapter has demonstrated, social welfare in the United States is characterized by a high degree of diversity and is not a monolithic, highly

spotlight 1.2

What's The Economy For, Anyway?

by *John de Graaf*

In the global economy, it seems *everyone* is dissatisfied and looking for different models. One by one, Latin American countries are moving from Right to Left. On the other hand, in Europe, the parties of social democracy have been losing ground to the Center (Europe's "right-wing" parties would be Centrist or Left in the United States), one after another.

All of this frenetic searching begs the fundamental question: What's the Economy for, Anyway? How much stock can we take in the Dow Jones? Is the Gross Domestic Product the measure (the grosser the better), and stuff the *stuff*, of happiness? Is the good life the *goods* life?

If so, then there's little doubt that the freer-market regimes win big. U.S. per capita GDP is still 30 percent higher than the average in Western Europe, just as it was a generation ago. We've got bigger homes, bigger cars, and more high-definition televisions. On the other hand if we measure success by the happiness, health, fairness and sustainability of economies, the picture looks very different.

I've been doing a little number-crunching lately, comparing data from such sources as the 2007 OECD (Organization for Economic Cooperation and Development) Fact Book, the World Health Organization, and the UN (United Nations) Human Development Index, trying to see how countries are doing in real, empirical terms when it comes to health, quality of life, justice, and sustainability. The results, I'm afraid, would come as a shock to those who look to the United States as the model of economic success.

Let me do a few of the numbers: compared, for example, to western European nations, the United States ranks *worst* or next-to-worst when it comes to child welfare, health care, poverty, income equality, pollution, CO_2 emissions, ecological footprint, personal savings, income and pension security, balance of payments, municipal waste, development assistance, longevity, infant mortality, child abuse, depression, anxiety, obesity, murder, incarceration, motor vehicle fatalities, and leisure time. We do slightly better in education. Our unemployment rate looks pretty low, unless you count those 2.3 million people we've got behind bars, an incarceration rate 7 to 10 times as high as Europe's.

Since 1970, Europeans have traded a portion of their productivity gains for free time instead of stuff, a trade that pays off in many ways. New studies show that long working hours, the norm in the United States, contribute to poor health, weakened family and community bonds, *and* environmental damage. Americans, far less healthy than Europeans, spend twice as much for health care per person. In fact, we spend nearly half the world's *total* health care budget, an amount that will reach 20 percent of our GDP by 2010—with the worst outcomes. Yet, all of that spending counts as a *plus* when it comes to GDP. The leisure that Europeans enjoy, the long meals and café conversations, the long walks and bike rides, count only as wasted time, adding not a single point to GDP. *La dolce vita*, by that measure, is for losers.

But which countries come out on *top* in measures of quality of life? It's the northern European nations, those that combine a strong social safety net with shorter working hours, high but progressive tax rates and strong environmental regulations. *The pattern is as clear as can be.*

I have found no one who refutes these figures. They simply explain them away by saying that the United States can't be like Europe. Why not?

One argument for why the United States can't even have such things as paid maternity leave—a reality in every country on the globe except the United States, Swaziland, Lesotho, Liberia, and Papua New Guinea—is that we're so affected by *globalization*. But with its massive domestic market, the United States is just about the *least* affected by globalization of all industrial countries.

American conservatives argue that Europeans can't continue to compete in the global economy. But according to the World Economic Forum, over the past few years, four of the six most globally competitive countries have been in Europe. Even American businesses invest five times as much each year in Germany as they do in China and more in Belgium than in India. And they make money doing it.

When all else fails, there's the final appeal: the United States may not be very healthy, fair or sustainable, but it's "the land of opportunity," where *anyone* can make it big if they're willing to work hard enough. Yet a recent study finds that Americans actually have only about one-half to one-third as much chance as Europeans of escaping low-income lives and rising to the top.

The steady drone from some European business leaders about the American economic miracle masks what should be obvious—they'd like to join our CEOs in making 400 times as much as their average workers, instead of the miserable 30 to 40 times as much they now make. Their voices speak louder than those of the average European citizen, who enjoys his or her six weeks of vacation, restful meals, family leave, health care, sick pay, free college education, and secure pension plan.

Since Ronald Reagan declared that "government cannot be the solution because government is the problem," indices of American quality of life, fairness, economic security, and environmental sustainability have all fallen sharply in comparison with those in Europe. The conservative economic revolution has produced a *gush-up* instead of a "trickle-down." For most of us, the "ownership society," emphasizing privatization, deregulation and massive tax cuts for the wealthy, is really a *"you're on your own*ership" society.

To make America better, our President tells us, we must do even *more* of these things, making tax cuts for the wealthy permanent, for example. But the working definition of insanity is to keep doing the same things hoping for a different result.

If we want to build societies that really work for people, we need to ask, "What's the Economy for, Anyway?" And then we need to separate the real results from the myths, shed a little of our American hubris and start looking at how other countries are actually edging us out by providing policies that succeed. That way lies a happier, healthier, more just and sustainable world.

John De Graaf is a documentary filmmaker and coauthor (with David Wann, Thomas Naylor, and Vicki Robin) of *Affluenza: The All-Consuming Epidemic* (San Francisco Berrett-Koehler, 2005)

centralized, well-coordinated system of programs. Rather, a great variety of organizations provide a wide range of benefits and services to different client populations. The vast array of social welfare organizations contributes to what is commonly called "the welfare mess." Consequently, different programs serving different groups through different procedures have engendered an impenetrable tangle of institutional red tape that is problematic for administrators, human service professionals, and clients.

The complexity of U.S. social welfare policy can be attributed to several cultural influences, some of which are peculiar to the American experience. For instance, the U.S. Constitution outlines a federal system whereby states vest certain functions in the national government. Although the states have assumed primary responsibility for social welfare through much of U.S. history, this changed with Franklin Delano Roosevelt's New Deal which ushered in a raft of federal programs. Over subsequent decades, federal social welfare initiatives played a dominant role in the nation's welfare effort. Still, states continued to manage important social welfare programs, such as mental health, corrections, and social services. Over time, the relationship between the federal government and the states has changed. From the New Deal of the 1930s through the Great Society of the 1960s, federal welfare programs expanded, forming the American version of the "welfare state." Beginning in the 1980s, the Reagan administration sought to return more of the responsibility for welfare to the states, a process called devolution.[78] This devolution was furthered by the Clinton administration with the signing of the PRWORA.

A second confounding element can be attributed to the relatively open character of U.S. society. Often referred to as a melting pot, the national culture is a protean brew of immigrant groups that competed with one another to become an established part of national life.[79] A staggering influx of

Europeans in the late nineteenth century gave way to waves of Hispanics and Asians entering the United States a century later.[80] Historically, social welfare programs have played an important role in the acculturation of these groups. At the same time, many ethnic groups brought with them their own fraternal and community associations, which not only provide welfare benefits to members of the community but also serve to maintain its norms. Other groups that have exerted important influences on U.S. social welfare are African Americans, the aged, women, and Native Americans. The very pluralism of U.S. society—a diverse collection of peoples, each with somewhat different needs—contributes to the complexity of social welfare.

Third, the economic system exacerbates the complexity of social welfare. The U.S. economy is predominantly capitalist, with most goods and services being owned, produced, and distributed through the marketplace. In a capitalist economy, people are expected to meet their basic needs in the marketplace through labor force participation. When people are unable to participate fully in the labor market, social programs are deployed to support these groups. These programs take various forms. Many are governmental programs. Private sector programs often complement those of the public sector. Within the private sector, two organizational forms are common—nonprofit organizations and for-profit corporations. Often these private sector organizations coexist, proximate to one another.[81]

Finally, various religious or faith-based organizations strongly influence social welfare in the United States. This is seen most clearly in the range of faith-based agencies that offer social services, such as Jewish Family Services, Lutheran Social Services, Catholic Charities, and the Salvation Army. In many cases, religious-based agencies provide services to groups that would not otherwise receive them. Today many faith-based agencies receive federal funds for various services they provide to the public. It is likely that this trend will grow.

The complexity of social welfare in the United States helps account for changes in welfare policies and programs. For example, since 1980 a convergence of social, political, and economic forces has led to a reappraisal of welfare. Liberal and conservative scholars have questioned the dominance of government programs in welfare provision. At the same time, a

firestorm of fundamentalism has swept across the nation, attracting the allegiance of groups associated with evangelicalism. The traditionalist movement flexed its muscles through the elections of Ronald Reagan, the two Bush administrations, the installation of a Republican Senate in the early 1980s and a conservative House of Representatives in 1994, and an effective grassroots mobilization that challenged government policies on issues ranging from the family to affirmative action. By the early 1990s, social conservatism had begun to influence Democratic party leaders, traditional supporters of government welfare programs. To reestablish credibility in an increasingly conservative political milieu, liberals distanced themselves from the large-scale government welfare programs they had been associated with since the New Deal. In place of these programs, many liberals called for a reliance on personal responsibility, work, and thrift.

Conservative public sentiment has served as a backdrop for the debate on the future of welfare policy.[82] An ascendant conservatism has not only checked further expansion of federal social programs, but the unprecedented tax cuts engineered by the former Bush administration threatened to dry up the revenues upon which social programs are dependent. The magnitude of this cannot be overstated: The tax cuts of the George W. Bush presidency eliminated the federal surplus; after September 11, 2001, Social Security and Medicare funds that had been set aside for retiring baby boomers were diverted to national security. As a result, the unfunded obligations of Social Security and Medicare and those of the federal retirement programs totaled $16.7 trillion in 2007.[83] The impact of this on social programs is profound, and the future solvency of social insurances for retirees would require a 91 percent increase in the withholding tax or an 81 percent increase in the income tax paid by individuals. If future workers reject such tax increases, pressure will build to convert Social Security and Medicare to means-tested, welfare programs. "This is the death trap of the welfare state," concluded Paul Samuelson, "here and in Europe and Asia."[84] Given these developments, welfare professionals face a formidable challenge: How can basic goods and services be brought to vulnerable populations within a context of such complexity and uncertainty?

Discussion Questions

1. According to the authors, American welfare is undergoing a transition. Which ideologies, schools of political economy, and interest groups within social welfare stand to gain most from this transition?
2. Ideology tends to parallel schools of political economy. How would classical conservatives and liberals address current social welfare issues such as health care, long-term care for the aged, and substance abuse? How would neoconservatives and neoliberals diverge from traditional conservatives and liberals on these issues?
3. Which schools of political, social, and economic thought discussed in this chapter would come closest to being classified as moderate? Why?
4. The chapter argues that in large measure social policy dictates social work practice. Do you agree with that premise? Explain your position. Can you think of any instances (historic or otherwise) in which social work practice has led to changes in social welfare policy?
5. In your opinion, which schools of economic and political thought are the most compatible with social work practice? Why? What are the incompatibilities in the various schools of thought with macro- and micro-level social work and practice?

Notes

1. Glenn Kessler and Amy Goldstein, "A Guide to the Candidates' Positions," *Washington Post* (November 3, 2008), pp. A10–A11.
2. E. J. Dionne Jr., "The Opening Obama Saw," *Washington Post* (November 3, 2008), p. A21.
3. Barack Obama, *The Audacity of Hope* (New York: Three Rivers, 2006), pp. 256–257.
4. Richard Titmuss, *Essays on the Welfare State* (Boston: Beacon Press, 1963), p. 16.
5. Contained in personal correspondence between David Stoesz and William Epstein, April 2000.
6. Education would logically be included here, except that in the American experience it has been treated separately.
7. See Alfred Kahn, *Social Policy and Social Services* (New York: Random House, 1979).
8. Frances Fox Piven and Richard Cloward, *Regulating the Poor* (New York: Vintage, 1971).
9. David Gil, *Unraveling Social Policy* (Boston: Shenkman, 1981), p. 32.
10. Charles Prigmore and Charles Atherton, *Social Welfare Policy* (Lexington, MA: D.C. Heath, 1979), pp. 25–31.
11. World Development Indicators Database, World Bank, September 2007. Retrieved 2008, from http://siteresources.worldbank.org/DATASTATISTICS/Resources/GNIPC.pdf; and OECD Family Database, Social Policy Division, Directorate of Employment, Labour and Social Affairs, Public Spending on Family Benefits, January 1, 2007. Retrieved March 29, 2008, from www.oecd.org/dataoecd/45/46/37864391.pdf
12. Claus Offe, *Contradictions of the Welfare State* (Cambridge, MA: MIT Press, 1984).
13. John Maynard Keynes, *The General Theory of Employment, Interest and Money* (London: Macmillan, 1936).
14. Paul R. Krugman, *Peddling Prosperity: Economic Sense and Nonsense in the Age of Diminished Expectations* (New York: W.W. Norton, 1994).
15. Ibid.
16. In their book *Economics for Social Workers: The Application of Economic Theory to Social Policy and the Human Services* (New York: Columbia University Press, 2001), Michael Anthony Lewis and Karl Widerquist identify four conditions that must hold for a free market to exist.
17. Ibid.
18. Milton Friedman, *Money Mischief: Episodes in Monetary History* (New York: Harcourt Brace, 1992).
19. Milton Friedman, *Capitalism and Freedom* (Chicago: University of Chicago Press, 1962).
20. Ibid.
21. Robert E. Lucas, *Studies in Business Cycle Theory* (Cambridge, MA: MIT Press, 1981).
22. Krugman, *Peddling Prosperity.*
23. Ibid.
24. Ibid.
25. Congressional Budget Office, *The Economic and Budget Outlook: Fiscal Years 1993–1997* (Washington, DC: Congressional Budget Office, 1992), p. 28.
26. See Beth Shulman, *The Betrayal of Work: How Low Wage Jobs Fail 35 Million Americans* (New York: The

New Press, 2003); Lawrence Mishel, Jared Bernstein, and John Schmitt, *The State of Working America 2000/2001* (Ithaca, NY: Cornell University Press, 2001); and Jared Bernstein, "Economic Growth Not Reaching Middle- and Lower Wage Earners," January 28, 2004, retrieved 2004, from www.epinet .org/content.cfm/webfeatures_snapshots

27. See Ayn Rand, *The Fountainhead* (New York: New American Library, 50th Anniversary Edition, 1996); *Atlas Shrugged* (New York: Signet Book; 35th Anniversary Edition, 1996).

28. Charles Murray, *Losing Ground* (New York: Basic Books, 1984), pp. 227–228.

29. *Privatization: Toward More Effective Government* (Washington, DC: U.S. Government Printing Office, 1988), pp. 233–234.

30. Michael Grynbaum, "Greenspan Concedes Error on Regulation," *New York Times,* October 23, 2008, p. 1.

31. CNN News, "Taxpayers Would Get Checks under Economic Stimulus Plan," January 24, 2008. Retrieved October 25, 2008, from http://edition.cnn. com/2008/POLITICS/01/24/economic.stimulus/

32. Edmund L. Andrews, "Fed Acts to Rescue Financial Markets," *New York Times,* March 17, 2008, p. 4.

33. Mark Landler, "U.S. Is Said to Be Urging New Mergers in Banking," *New York Times,* October 20, 2008, p. 18.

34. Greg Morcroft, "Treasury Set to Bail Out Fannie Mae, Freddie Mac," *MarketWatch,* September 6, 2008. Retrieved October 25, 2008, from www.marketwatch.

35. Matthew Karnitschnig, Deborah Solomon, Liam Pleven, and Jon E. Hilsenrath, "U.S. to Take Over AIG in $85 Billion Bailout," *Wall Street Journal,* September 16, 2008, p. 10; The Associated Press, "AIG Borrows $90.3 Billion from Federal Reserve," *BusinessWeek,* October 24, 2008, p. 2.

36. Paul Wallis, "$25 Billion Fed Loan to Car Industry; It's Not a Bailout, Says Detroit," *Digital Business Journal,* September 29, 2008. Retrieved October 25, 2008, from www.digitaljournal.com/article/260441

37. Uwe E. Reinhardt, "Does the Democrats' Stimulus Package Make Economic Sense?" *New York Times,* October 24, 2008, p. 16.

38. Subir Lall, "World Economic Outlook: IMF Predicts Slower World Growth Amid Serious Market Crisis," *IMFSurvey,* April 9, 2008. Retrieved October 23, 2008, from www.imf.org/external/pubs/ft/survey/so/ 2008/RES040908A.htm

39. Associated Press, "2008 U.S. Budget Deficit Bleeding Red Ink First 4 Months of Budget Year at Nearly $88B, Double Amount Recorded For Same 2007 Period," CBS News, February 12, 2008. Retrieved October 24, 2008, from www.cbsnews.com/stories/ 2008/02/12/national/main3822385.shtml

40. Jeffry Galper, "Introduction of Radical Theory and Practice in Social Work Education: Social Policy." Mimeographed paper, Michigan State University School of Social Work, ca. 1978.

41. Piven and Cloward, *Regulating the Poor,* pp. 3–4.

42. Harry Hopkins, *Spending to Save: The Complete Story of Relief* (Seattle: University of Washington Press, 1936).

43. Neil Gilbert, Harry Specht, and Paul Terrell, *Dimensions of Social Welfare Policy* (Englewood Cliffs, NJ: Prentice Hall, 1993).

44. Marc Bendick, *Privatizing the Delivery of Social Welfare Service* (Washington, DC: National Conference on Social Welfare, 1985), p. 1.

45. Charles Peters, "A New Politics," *Public Welfare* 41, no. 2 (Spring 1983), pp. 34, 36.

46. Randall Rothenberg, *The Neoliberals* (New York: Simon & Schuster, 1984), pp. 244–245.

47. David Stoesz, *Small Change* (New York: Longman, 1995).

48. Robert Reich, *The Next American Frontier* (New York: Times Books, 1983).

49. Anthony Giddens, *The Third Way* (Cambridge, MA: Polity Press, 1999), p. 117.

50. Bruce Stokes, *Helping Ourselves: Local Solutions to Global Problems* (New York: W.W. Norton, 1981).

51. Sugata Dasgupta, "Towards a No-Poverty Society," *Social Development Issues* 12 (Winter 1983), pp. 85–93.

52. Some of these economic principles were addressed by E. F. Schumacher in *Small Is Beautiful* (New York: Harper & Row, 1973).

53. Barry M. Goldwater, *The Conscience of a Conservative* (New York: Putnam, 1960), pp. 109–110.

54. See Peter Steinfels, *The Neoconservatives* (New York: Simon & Schuster, 1979).

55. Interview with Stuart Butler, Director of Domestic Policy at the Heritage Foundation, October 4, 1984.

56. Alan Walker, "The Strategy of Inequality: Poverty and Income Distribution in Britain 1979–89," in I. Taylor (ed.), *The Social Effects of Free Market Policies* (Sussex, England: Harvester-Wheatsheaf, 1990), pp. 43–66.

57. Kristen Geiss-Curran, Sha'ari Garfinkle, Fred Knocke, Terri Lively, and Sue McCullough, "The Contract with America and the Budget Battle," unpublished manuscript, University of Houston, Spring 1996.

58. The Libertarian Party, "Statement of Principles," Washington, DC, 1996.

59. Daniel Patrick Moynihan, *Came the Revolution* (New York: Harcourt Brace Jovanovich, 1988), p. 291.

60. See Harold Wilensky and Charles Lebeaux, *Industrial Society and Social Welfare* (New York: Free Press, 1965); and Mimi Abramovitz, "The Privatization of the Welfare State," *Social Work* 31 (July–August 1986), pp. 257–264.

61. R. Erikson, E. Hansen, S. Ringen, and H. Uusitalo, *The Scandinavian Model* (Armonk, NY: M.E. Sharpe, 1987).

62. Richard Titmuss, *Commitment to Welfare* (New York: Pantheon, 1968), p. 127.

63. Wilensky and Lebeaux, *Industrial Society and Social Welfare*, p. 147.

64. Alvin Rabushka, "Tax and Spending Limits," in Peter Duignan and Alvin Rabushka (eds.), *The United States in the 1980s* (Stanford, CA: Hoover Institution, 1980), pp. 104–106.

65. Martin Anderson, "Welfare Reform," in Peter Duignan and Alvin Rabushka (eds.), *The United States in the 1980s*, pp. 171–176.

66. Peter Berger and John Neuhaus, *To Empower People: The Role of Mediating Structures in Public Policy* (Washington, DC: American Enterprise Institute, 1977).

67. Michael Novak, *Toward a Theology of the Corporation* (Washington, DC: American Enterprise Institute, 1981), p. 5.

68. Stuart Butler and Anna Kondratas, *Out of the Poverty Trap: A Conservative Strategy for Welfare Reform* (New York: Free Press, 1987).

69. William Lind and William Marshner, *Cultural Conservatism: Toward a New National Agenda* (Washington, DC: Free Congress Research and Education Foundation, 1987), p. 83.

70. George Gilder, *Wealth and Poverty* (New York: Basic Books, 1981), p. 118.

71. Anderson, "Welfare Reform," p. 145.

72. Jacob. S. Hacker, *The Great Risk Shift: The Assault on American Jobs, Families, Health Care, and Retirement* (New York: Oxford University Press, 2006).

73. Ibid.

74. Lawrence Mischel, Jared Bernstein, and Sylkvia Allegretto, *The State of Working America 2004/2005* (Ithaca, NY: IRL Press, 2005).

75. Julie Appleby, "Bush Unveils Health Plan Tied to Tax Deduction," *USA Today*, January 24, 2007. Retrieved March 17, 2007, from www.usatoday.com

76. John Judis and Michael Lind, "For a New Nationalism," *The New Republic* (March 27, 1995), p. 26.

77. Mitchell Landsberg, "Nation's Social Health Declined in '93," *Houston Chronicle* (October 16, 1995), p. 1C.

78. Domestic Policy Council, Up from Dependency (Washington, DC: White House Domestic Policy Council, December 1986).

79. For a classic description of the assimilation phenomenon, see Nathan Glazer and Daniel Patrick Moynihan, *Beyond the Melting Pot* (Cambridge, MA: MIT Press, 1970).

80. Thomas Muller et al., *The Fourth Wave* (Washington, DC: Urban Institute, 1985).

81. The three auspices of social welfare in the United States have been termed the "mixed economy of welfare." See Sheila Kamerman, "The New Mixed Economy of Welfare," *Social Work* 28 (January–February 1983), pp. 43–50.

82. For further details, see David Stoesz, "The Functional Conception of Social Welfare," *Social Work* 34 (March 1989), pp. 86–91.

83. U.S. Treasury Office of Economic Policy, "The 2008 Annual Report of the Board of Trustees of the Federal Hospital Insurance and Federal Supplementary Medical Insurance Trust Funds," March 25, 2008. Retrieved March 26, 2008, from www.treas.gov/offices/economic-policy/social_security.shtml

84. Paul Samuelson, "The Deficit Chicken Hawks," *Washington Post* (October 10, 2003), p. A27.

CHAPTER 2

Social Welfare Policy Research: A Framework for Policy Analysis

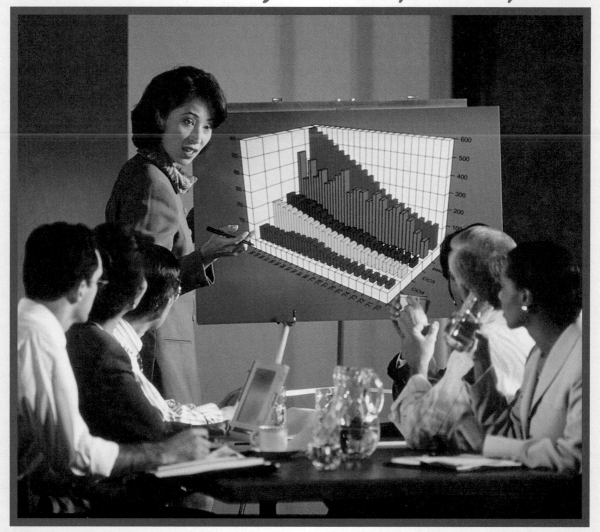

*P*olicy analysts engage in the systematic investigation of a social policy or a set of policies. They are employed in a variety of settings, including federal, state, and local governments; think tanks; universities; social justice or public interest groups or community organizations; and larger social agencies. The goals of policy analysis can range from pure research to providing information to legislators (i.e., congressional researchers) and to advocacy research. In this chapter, examined is one of the major tools used by the policy researcher, a systematic and structured framework for policy analysis. The authors also propose a model for policy analysis.

A **policy framework**—a systematic model for examining a specific social welfare policy or a series of policies—is one means analysts use to evaluate the congruence of a policy with the mission and goals of the social welfare state. Analysts can also employ policy frameworks to assess whether key social welfare values—that is, social justice, redistribution, or equity—are incorporated within a given policy. Moreover, policy frameworks help us determine if policy is consistent with established social welfare values or the historical precedents that have guided social welfare initiatives. For example, let us consider the proposal that foster care should be abolished and that all children suspected of being abused or neglected should be placed in orphanages. The use of a policy framework would illustrate that this proposal reflects a clear break with the general drift of child welfare policy since the end of the twentieth century and that it repudiates established values such as family reunification. In addition, a systematic analysis would reveal that this policy is not economically, politically, or socially feasible.

Apart from examining a given policy, an analytic framework can also be used for comparing existing policies. For example, comparing the mental health policies of Missouri with those of Massachusetts and Minnesota would yield valuable information for all three states. A comparative analysis of the health systems of the United States, Canada, and Sweden would also provide useful information for decision makers. Finally, analytic frameworks are useful in evaluating competing policies and helping analysts make a recommendation as to which policy most effectively addresses a problem or remedies a need.

Policy analysis frameworks are useful for social work practitioners on several levels and can address agency policies and those at the statewide or national level. Agency policies dictate what a social worker will do, with whom, and for how long. They also define who is (or is not) a client and what services will be offered to them. Social work practitioners can examine agency policies around issues like flextime, merit pay, agency-based day care, job shifting, and so forth. Child welfare workers can use policy analysis to evaluate impending state or federal legislation and the concomitant fiscal allocations. Social workers in health care can analyze managed care policies in terms of equity, effectiveness, and a wide range of other issues. Social work practice is clearly influenced—if not driven—by social policy.

Policy analysis is also useful in environmental scanning activities of non- and for-profit agencies. As the delivery of social services becomes more heavily located in the competitive marketplace, social agencies will be forced to replicate private sector corporate behavior. This includes being aware of changing demographics and market trends, and monitoring new legislation. In some social welfare sectors, events change so rapidly that agencies must quickly modify their operations if they are to remain viable. Data-based environmental scanning allows agencies to make long- and short-term plans based on changing demographics, new competing organizations, or the effects of impending legislation. Environmental scanning also allows agencies to discover new markets and to protect their existing ones.[1]

Social welfare policies and programs are complex phenomena. For example, it is easy to propose a social policy such as mandatory drug testing for all governmental employees. On the surface, the policy may appear simple: Drug users are discovered through testing and then forced to seek treatment. On closer scrutiny, however, the hidden issues become problematic. Is it constitutional to require drug treatment if a positive result is found? Is occasional use of marijuana sufficient grounds for requiring drug treatment? Because alcohol is a legal substance, drug tests do not detect it. Is alcohol less debilitating than marijuana? Can mandatory drug testing be misused by supervisors to harass employees? Will drug testing produce the desired results? Without a systematic means to analyze the effects of a policy, decisions become arbitrary and may produce consequences that are worse than the original problem.

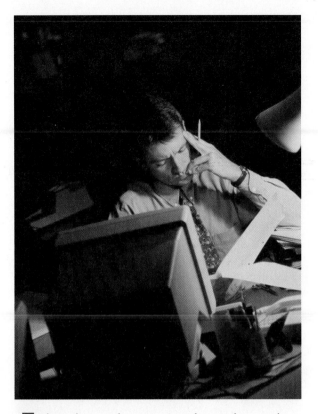

The policy analyst is expected to evaluate policies and make recommendations. To succeed,
the analyst must accept his or her own values
while basing the analysis on objective criteria.

All well-designed policy frameworks are characterized by eight key elements:

- Policy frameworks attempt to systematically
  analyze a social policy or program.
- Policy frameworks reflect the understanding that
  social policy is context sensitive, and that there
  are competing priorities in all policy options.
- Policy frameworks employ rational methods of
  inquiry and analysis. The data used in policy
  analysis must be derived from objective scientific inquiry and must come from legitimate
  sources. Data should be interpreted and analyzed as objectively as possible.
- In theory, the analytic method is explicit and all
  succeeding policy analyses should approximate
  the same conclusion.
- Policy analysis is based on the commitment to
  derive the largest possible social benefit at the
  least possible social cost. A good social policy is

one that benefits at least one person (as he or
she perceives his or her own self-interest) while
at the same time hurting no one (a variation
of the Pareto Optimality). Although rarely
achieved in the real world of finite resources—
and of proliferating claims on them—policy
analysts should nevertheless strive to realize
that goal.
- Policy frameworks should attempt to take into
  account the unintended consequences of a particular policy or program.
- Policy analysts should consider alternative
  social policies or alternative uses of present or
  future resources allocated to a given policy.
- Policy frameworks should examine the potential impact of a policy (or a series of policies) on
  other social policies, social problems, and the
  overall public good.

A policy framework can provide decision makers and the general public with information, an
understanding of the ramifications of a policy on
the target problem as well as on other problems and
policies, and alternative policies that might more
effectively address the problem. Untoward consequences are more likely when the decision-making
process is not based on a systematic framework for
policy analysis.

History is replete with examples of well-
intentioned policies that proved catastrophic. For
example, in 1919 the U.S. Congress enacted a law
prohibiting the manufacture, sale, or transport of
alcohol in an effort to cut down on crime, familial
instability, unemployment, and other social problems. Advocates of Prohibition, including many
social workers, touted the end of alcohol as a major
step forward in the social evolution of the United
States. By the time Prohibition was repealed in 1932,
most of the original supporters were silent. Despite
their best hopes, Prohibition did not decrease crime
or lead to more family stability and greater social
order; instead, it encouraged the growth of an organized crime industry that fed the ongoing taste of
Americans for alcohol. Instead of curbing alcohol-
related nightlife, Prohibition led to the creation of
illegal and well-attended speakeasies. Even many
supporters conceded that alcohol was almost as
abundant as before Prohibition. A systematic analysis of prohibition done before the passage of the bill
might have demonstrated the futility of this policy
initiative.

A similar argument can be made for the current policy of drug interdiction and enforcement. After almost a half-century of vigorous drug enforcement, marijuana, heroin, cocaine, and other drugs continue to be readily available. Vigilant drug enforcement has not resulted in less drug use but in a more than doubling of the prison population from 1980 to 2008. A study by the Pew Center reported that the United States has more adults in jails and prisons than any other nation—2.3 million at the start of 2008 or 1 of every 99.1 adults.[2] More than one in three incarcerated women are there for a drug-related offense.[3] The "war on drugs" has also resulted in the added public expense of new prison construction (about 1,000 new prisons were built from 1990 to 2004[4]), the creation of international drug cartels whose wealth and power rival that of many national governments and multinational corporations, a dramatic increase in the drug-related homicide rate, and the deterioration of inner-city neighborhoods racked by gang warfare fed by the lucrative drug trade. Drug enforcement policies have not stopped the flow of illegal drugs, but they have created a vibrant industry that includes government officials, contractors, private correctional corporations, police departments, and segments of the legal and judicial system. All of these groups have a vested interest in maintaining a status quo drug policy, regardless of its effectiveness. In short, a social problem led to a social policy, which, in turn, led to a powerful industry that depends for its very existence on the continuation of an ineffective policy. As this example suggests, social policy is often driven by politics and rarely, if ever, systematically analyzed. Policy analysis often occurs only after a bill or policy is enacted. As a result, analysts are asked to perform an autopsy to determine why a specific bill or policy failed.

The purpose of a policy framework is to provide the analyst with a model or a set of questions for systematically analyzing a policy. Consequently, the choice of a policy framework must fit the requirements of the project as well as the resources available to the analyst. Every policy framework can be either fine-tuned or modified. In fact, the best policy framework may result from a synthesis of existing models.[5]

A Proposed Model for Policy Analysis

Policy analysts are expected to evaluate a policy and make recommendations. To succeed, the analyst must acknowledge his or her own values while, at the same time, basing the analysis on objective criteria. The policy framework proposed in this text is divided into four sections: (1) the historical background of the policy, (2) a description of the problem(s) that necessitated the policy, (3) a description of the policy, and (4) the policy analysis (see Figure 2.1).

Historical Background of the Policy

The policy analyst should examine similar policies that were adopted in the past and assess how they fared. Understanding the historical antecedents of a policy is important for two reasons. First, continuity requires that the analyst identify the historical problems that led to the original policy. Questions might include the following: What historical problems led to the creation of the policy? How important were

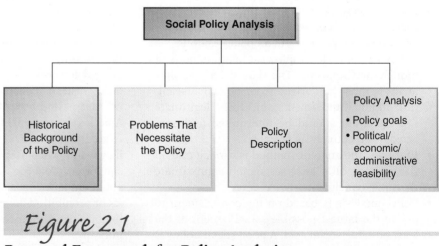

Figure 2.1
Proposed Framework for Policy Analysis

they? How were these problems previously handled? When did the policy originate and how has it changed over time? What is the legislative history of the policy?

Second, a historical analysis helps to curb the tendency of decision makers to reinvent the wheel. Policies that were previously unsuccessful may continue to be so; or the analyst may find that circumstances have changed, thus creating a climate in which a previously failed policy might now be viable. A historical analysis also helps the analyst to understand the forces that were mobilized to support or oppose a given policy. In short, this part of the analysis locates a particular policy within a historical framework, thus helping to explain the evolutionary nature of a social policy or series of policies.

spotlight 2.1

A Model for Policy Analysis

The model for policy analysis can be divided into four sections—the historical background of the policy, a description of the problem that necessitated the policy, a description of the policy, and the policy analysis. Each of these sections requires the policy analyst to ask specific questions.

Historical Background of the Policy

- What historical problems led to the creation of the policy?
- How important have these problems been historically?
- How was the problem previously handled?
- What is the historical background of the policy?
- When did the policy originate?
- How has the original policy changed over time?
- What is the legislative history of the policy?

Description of the Problem That Necessitated the Policy

- What is the nature of the problem?
- How widespread is it?
- How many people are affected by it?
- Who is affected and how?
- What are the causes of the problem?

Policy Description

- How is the policy expected to work?
- What resources or opportunities is the policy expected to provide?
- Who will be covered by the policy and how?

- How will the policy be implemented?
- What are the short- and long-term goals and outcomes of the policy?
- What are the administrative auspices under which the policy will be lodged?
- What is the funding mechanism for the policy?
- What agencies or organizations will be charged with overseeing, evaluating, and coordinating the policy?
- What are the formal or informal criteria that will be used to determine the effectiveness of the policy?
- For what length of time is the policy expected to be in existence?
- What is the knowledge base or scientific grounding on which the policy rests?

Policy Analysis

- Are the goals of the policy legal?
- Are the goals of the policy just and democratic?
- Do the goals of the policy contribute to greater social equality?
- Do the goals of the policy positively affect the redistribution of income, resources, rights, entitlements, rewards, opportunities, and status?
- Do the goals of the policy contribute to a better quality of life for the target population?
- Will the goals adversely affect the quality of life of the target population?
- Does the policy contribute to positive social relations between the target population and the overall society?
- Are the goals of the policy consistent with the values of professional social work?

Problems That Necessitate the Policy

The second step in policy analysis is an examination of the problems that led to the creation of the policy. To fully assess whether a proposed policy will successfully remedy a social problem, the analyst must understand the parameters of the problem. Furthermore, the analyst must be familiar with the nature, scope, and magnitude of the problem and with the affected populations. In this way, the analyst can discern early whether the policy is appropriate. Specific questions might include the following: What is the nature and causes of the problem? How widespread is it? Who and how many people are affected by it?

Policy Description

The next step is the description of the policy. This section requires a detailed explanation of the policy, including a description of (1) how the policy is expected to work; (2) the resources or opportunities the policy is expected to provide (power, cash, economic opportunity, in-kind benefits, status redistribution, goods and services, and so forth); (3) who will be covered by the policy and how (e.g., universal versus selective entitlement, means testing, and so forth); (4) how the policy will be implemented; (5) the expected short- and long-term goals and outcomes of the policy; (6) the administrative auspices under which the policy will be lodged; (7) the funding mechanism, including short- and long-term funding commitments; (8) the agencies or organizations that have overall responsibility for overseeing, evaluating, and coordinating the policy; (9) the criteria used to determine the effectiveness of the policy; (10) the length of time the policy is expected to be in existence (i.e., is it a "sunset law" designed to end at a certain date?); and (11) the knowledge base or scientific undergirding for the policy.

Policy Analysis

This section is the heart of any policy analysis. In this section, the analyst engages in a *systematic* analysis of the policy.

Policy Goals   The policy goals are the criteria by which all else is measured. Often the analyst must conjecture on the overall goals of the policy because they may not be explicitly stated. The following questions may help to explicate the goals of a particular policy:

- Are the goals legal, just, and democratic?
- Do they contribute to greater social equality?
- Do the goals positively affect the redistribution of income, resources, rights, entitlements, rewards, opportunities, and status?
- Do the goals contribute to a better quality of life for the target population? Will they adversely affect the quality of life of the target group?
- Does the policy contribute to positive social relations between the target population and the overall society?
- Are the policy goals consistent with the values of professional social work (i.e., self-determination, client rights, self-realization, and so forth)?

Analysts must understand the value premises of the policy as well as the ideological assumptions underlying it. To this end, several questions should be asked: What are the hidden ideological assumptions in the policy? How is the target population viewed in the context of the policy? What social vision, if any, does the policy contain? Does the policy encourage the status quo or does it represent a radical departure from it? Who are the major beneficiaries of the policy? Is the policy designed to foster real social change or to placate a potentially insurgent group? Uncovering the hidden ideological dimensions of a policy is frequently the most difficult task for the policy analyst.

Despite good intentions, a prospective policy must be viable if it is to be successful. American history is littered with worthy policies that were simply not viable at the time they were proposed. For example, at the height of the Great Depression, a California physician named Francis Townsend proposed that all citizens over the age of 65 be given a flat governmental pension of $200 a month. Although in more prosperous times this proposal might have been granted at least a cursory hearing, in the midst of one of the greatest depressions in U.S. history, policymakers dismissed the proposal as not viable. The overall viability of a policy is based on three factors: political feasibility, economic feasibility, and administrative feasibility.

Political Feasibility   The political feasibility of a policy is a subjective assessment. In order to evaluate a policy, the analyst must assess which groups will oppose or support a particular policy, and they must estimate the constituency and power base of each group. However, in U.S. politics, the size of the constituency base and its relative power are sometimes unrelated. For example, despite its relatively small numbers, the American Medical Association (AMA) is a powerful lobby. Conversely, although more than 30 million Americans are poor, they have negligible political clout.

The political viability of a policy is subject to the public's perception of its feasibility. In other words, for a policy to be feasible, it must be perceived as being feasible. For example, although a sizable portion of the public would welcome some form of national health care, none exists. The United States lacks a national health care partly because of the power of the health care industry, but in part it has not been enacted because the public believes it cannot happen. Thus is born a public myth around what is and what is not possible.

In assessing the political feasibility of a policy, the analyst must examine the public's sentiment toward it. Is a large segment of the public concerned about the policy? Do people feel they will be directly affected by the policy? Does the policy threaten fundamental social values? Is the policy compatible with the present social and political climate? Can either side marshal substantial public support for or against the policy? The answers to these questions will help the policy analyst determine the political feasibility of the policy.

The political feasibility of a policy also encompasses a smaller, but no less important, dimension. In their assessment, the analyst must understand the relationship between the policy and external factors in agencies and institutions. For example, which social welfare agencies, institutions, or organizations support or oppose the policy? What is the relative strength of each group? How strong is their support or opposition to the policy? Which federal, state, or local agencies would be affected by the policy? The world of social policy is highly political and some governmental and private social welfare agencies have political power on par with elected officials and other decision makers. Groups of institutions often coalesce around issues or policies that directly affect them, and, through lobbying efforts, they can defeat legislation. In cases where they cannot defeat a policy outright, these administrative units can implement a policy in ways that ensure its failure. The analyst must therefore take into account whether key administrative units support or oppose a new or existing policy.

Economic Feasibility   Most social policies require some form of direct or indirect funding. In assessing the economic feasibility of a policy, the analyst must ask several questions: What is the minimum level of funding necessary for successfully implementing the policy? Does adequate funding for the policy currently exist? If not, what is the public sentiment toward increased funding for the policy? What are the future funding needs of the policy likely to be?

Given the current political and economic climate, it appears unlikely that new social policy initiatives requiring large revenues will be successful. Perhaps new, revenue-based policy legislation will be based on the reallocation of existing resources (budget-neutral policies) rather than on new revenue sources. This approach—taking money from one program to fund another—is called **pay-go** financing. The danger in this approach is that thinning out fiscal resources among many programs may mean that none will be adequately funded. The analyst must therefore decide whether a new policy initiative should be recommended regardless of the funding prospects. The parameters of this decision are complex. If a new policy is recommended despite insufficient resources, the chances of its failure are greater. If a policy is not recommended, however, the possibility that fiscal resources may be allocated in the future is precluded. As a result, many policy analysts lean toward incremental approaches, tending to recommend policies in the hope that future funding will become available.

Administrative Feasibility   The analyst must also be concerned with the administrative viability of a policy. Regardless of the potential value of a policy, responsible administrative and supervisory agencies must possess the personnel, resources, skills, and expertise needed to effectively implement the policy. In addition, directors and supervisors must be sympathetic to the goals of the policy, have the expertise and skills necessary to implement or oversee the policy, and possess an understanding of the fundamental objectives of the policy. Policy analysts focus on two key aspects of administrative feasibility: effectiveness and efficiency.

Effectiveness is based on the likelihood that the policy will accomplish what its designers intended. This encompasses several questions: Is the policy broad enough to accomplish its stated goals? Will the benefits of the policy reach the target group? Is the implementation of the policy likely to cause new or other social problems? What are the ramifications of the policy on the nontarget sector (i.e., higher taxes, reduced opportunities, diminished freedom, etc.)?

Another challenge facing policy analysts is the nature and extent of the unintended consequences of a policy. Virtually all policies have unforeseen consequences. One example of this is methadone, a drug legally administered to addicts as a substitute for heroin. When introduced in the 1960s, methadone was thought to be a safe way to wean addicts away from heroin. However, by the mid-1970s health experts realized that methadone was almost as addictive as heroin and that some addicts were selling their methadone as a street drug. Despite this unintended outcome, some addicts were able to withdraw from heroin, and on balance, the methadone program was a positive development. Because policy analysts cannot see into the future, recommendations are made on the basis of available data. Nevertheless, analysts must try to investigate the possibility of adverse future consequences.

Policy analysts look closely at *efficiency,* or the cost-effectiveness of the proposed policy compared to alternative policies, no policy, or the present policy. Social policy always involves trade-offs. Even in the best of economic times, fiscal resources are always inadequate to meet the breadth of human need. For example, virtually everyone could benefit from some form of social welfare, whether it is counseling, food stamps, or free health care. But because resources are finite, society must choose the primary beneficiaries for its social allocations. Publicly financed services are often provided on the basis of two criteria: (1) the severity of the problem (services go to those who most need them) and (2) means (services go to those who can least afford them). As a result, adequately funding one policy often means denying or curbing the allocations to another. This is the essential trade-off in social welfare policy. When analysts evaluate a policy, they are cognizant that promoting one policy often means that needs in other areas may go unmet. Hence, important questions remain: Is the policy important enough to justify the allocation of scarce resources? Are there other areas where scarce resources could be better used?

The policy analyst often compares the cost-effectiveness of a proposed policy with an alternative policy. Will the proposed policy have better results than the present policy or no policy at all?

Is it advantageous to enlarge or modify the present policy rather than create a new one? Can an alternative policy provide better results at a lower cost? Can an alternative policy achieve the same results? These questions are often addressed in a thorough policy analysis.

Researching and Analyzing Social Policies

There are two major hurdles in policy analysis. The first is finding and focusing on a manageable social policy, and the second is finding or generating information relevant to it.

One of the most difficult tasks the analyst faces is choosing the actual policy. To do a careful policy analysis, the analyst must select a policy that is specific and discrete. For example, it would be virtually impossible to do an exhaustive analysis of child welfare policy in the United States. For one thing, the United States lacks an integrated child welfare policy; instead, child welfare is characterized by a patchwork quilt of myriad programs. Second, differing child welfare policies on the national, state, and community levels make such a policy analysis even more daunting.

A second task involves locating policy-relevant information. There are seven major avenues for finding information. First, policy analysts may choose to generate their own data through primary research, including surveys, opinion polls, experimental research, longitudinal studies, and so forth. Although this method can yield a rich body of information, time and cost constraints may prove an impossible obstacle. Moreover, the same research may already exist in other places, in which case the replication of the effort would be unwarranted.

Second, governmental or agency records are often useful sources for relevant data. These can include archival material; memos; minutes of boards of directors, governmental officials, and staff meetings; policy manuals; and departmental records. A surprising amount of information can be found online in government or agency websites.

A third avenue for policy research is the records and published minutes of legislative bodies and committees. On the federal level these sources include the *Congressional Record* and the minutes of the various House and Senate committees and subcommittees. All state legislatures have similar record-keeping procedures, and most of these records can be found in regional or university libraries or online.

A fourth source of information is governmental publications. For example, the U.S. Government Printing Office maintains catalogues of all government documents published. Other documents include the Census Bureau's population studies (often updated annually); publications of the Departments of Labor, Commerce, Housing, and Health and Human Services; and the *Green Book* of the House Committee on Ways and Means, a yearly publication containing comprehensive information on social programs and participants.

A fifth source of policy-relevant information includes think tanks, advocacy organizations, and professional associations. All think tanks (many of which are also advocacy organizations) employ research staff who evaluate and analyze social policies. Examples of these include the Brookings Institute, the American Enterprise Institute, the Heritage Foundation, the Hoover Institute, the Urban Institute, the Center on Budget and Policy Priorities, the Reason Foundation, the Hudson Institute, the Progressive Policy Institute, the Economic Policy Institute, and the Independent Sector. Again, much of this information can be accessed through the Internet. Because most think tanks are affiliated with particular political or economic ideologies or political parties, their data and policy recommendations should be viewed critically.

Many national advocacy organizations retain research staff and publish reports that are helpful to the policy analyst. Some of these organizations include the Urban League, the National Association for the Advancement of Colored People (NAACP), the Children's Defense Fund, the National Farm Organization, and the National Organization for Women. Many professional associations, such as the American Medical Association, the American Public Welfare Association, the National Association of Social Workers, and the American Psychological Association, also publish policy-relevant information.

A sixth data source is professional journals, books, and monographs. Articles or books on specific policy topics can be found in various places, including the Social Science Index and the subject headings in library catalogues. Commercial electronic databases such as Lexis/Nexis and Westlaw are also useful. Last, policy-relevant information can be derived from interviews with principals in the policy process, advocates, recipients of services, and government officials. Personal interviews may also help gauge public opinion and assess the opposition or support for a particular policy. Taken together, these sources can be a gold mine for the policy analyst.

Social Policy Research and the Internet

The Internet, e-mail, Listservs, and FTP (File Transfer Protocol) sites have made the job of the policy analyst immeasurably easier, more efficient, and even more fun. Policy analysts no longer have to wait months before their library receives the report or data they are seeking; no longer must they contend with lost, misplaced, or checked-out documents; or wade through library stacks filled with endless feet of government reports. Instead, analysts can now download the newest government data, legislative reports, and governmental bills from the comfort of home. Policy analysts engage in different types of research activities. Although the Internet can provide access to vast stores of information, the degree to which it will facilitate your research will vary. It is helpful at the outset to know your research needs and how the Internet can help.

Journals and Online Research

Although titles, tables of contents, and article abstracts of many professional journals can be found online, the full text is often not available electronically. Full library searches remain the most fruitful way to conduct research when the full texts of print journals are required. Even though many professional journals are beginning to convert to an electronic format, this remains a costly and time-consuming process. Because journals provide income for their publishers, there is little incentive to provide free what journal subscribers must pay for. Still, when research requirements involve locating the most current information available, the Internet is a good starting place. This is especially true as virtually all major newspapers and news services are now online.

Although the full texts of many journal articles are often not available online, there are web-based databases that provide those services. These vary in cost. Some are free, but the majority of them charge an initial sign-up fee; an annual maintenance fee;

fees for time spent searching the database; and a fee for each full article or abstract that is viewed or downloaded.

Online Data Collection

Recruiting subjects and collecting data online for research that requires more formalized qualitative and quantitative data collection has several advantages:

- Posting messages on e-mail lists or newsgroups to recruit and interview subjects is more efficient and less costly than traditional forms of data collection such as mailing questionnaires or using field researchers.
- Data obtained online do not require transcription, which lowers research costs.
- Subjects living anywhere in the world can respond to questionnaires at their convenience.
- Principal investigators living in various parts of the country can quickly and conveniently communicate with each other to clarify aspects of the research, provide feedback, and share reactions to the findings.[6]

There are also disadvantages to relying on the Internet for data collection. First, the danger exists that convenience and cost will dictate sampling methods, resulting in a biased sample. Second, the pool of people available to the researcher is limited to those who possess the following:

- Sufficient education to enable them to express themselves in written form
- The ability to operate a computer and Internet software
- Adequate financial resources to maintain an Internet account, or have access through their place of employment
- The inclination to use the Internet and to participate in research[7]

Ethical Concerns Related to Online Research Involving Human Subjects

Just as copyright and fair use laws dictate the use of online information, ethical principles also apply to research activities. Two major areas that demand vigilance are informed consent and confidentiality.

The rights of research subjects have been codified into laws and codes of professional ethics. Violating these codes puts the researcher at risk of incurring not only professional sanctions but also legal ones. At the heart of this protection is informed consent. The fundamental ethical principle underlying informed consent is respect for subjects' autonomy—their right to make an informed decision about whether to participate in a research activity based on their understanding of the process, risks, and benefits.

Confidentiality involving the subjects and their responses is another hallmark of ethical research. Challenges to confidentiality arise in online research when identifying information on subjects and their responses are published on an online forum, especially because there are no guarantees that all forum users will honor professional ethics. E-mail presents similar concerns as there is no way to ensure that the person accessing the e-mail is the research subject. Opportunities for Internet-related research are abundant as many individuals openly discuss personal information in public forums, such as chat rooms or newsgroups. Unfortunately, there are reports of some researchers who have opportunistically exploited this situation, conducting naturalistic studies by observing a support Listserv or newsgroup.[8] This kind of research is in clear violation of the informed consent rule that guides professionals engaging in responsible human subject research.

Finding and Accessing Online Information

Searching for information on the Internet may initially appear daunting, especially because Internet traffic is growing rapidly with more than 100 million Americans now online.[9] Fortunately, tools for searching the Internet allow users to quickly locate and access the data they need. These include (1) search engines, (2) subject directory guides, and (3) meta-search engines.

Search engines collect and index online data. They are easy to use, and the information is returned ranked by relevancy to the search topic. Some well-known search engines include Google (www.google.com); Yahoo (www.yahoo.com); Excite (www.excite.com), HotBot (www.hotbot.com), and Lycos (www.lycos.com). One drawback of search engines is that all online data are included, thereby forcing the user to sort through many irrelevant hits. To be efficient, search engines require specificity in the choice of words or phrases.[10]

Subject directory guides are helpful when the user knows the broad topic but has not yet decided on a narrower subtopic. The information obtained will be an index of the World Wide Web's contents by subject category, with the results provided in a subject directory. Information in this type of search reflects efforts by editors who have searched for information and reviewed its contents. As with most search engines, retrieved information will be ranked by relevancy. Because of the editorial review of material in these databases, users generally obtain more relevant responses than using search engines. Examples of subject guides include the Library of Congress Web page (http://lcweb.loc.gov), the Argus Clearinghouse (www.clearinghouse.net), Mental Health Net (www.cmhc.com), and Medical Matrix (www.medmatrix.org).

Meta-search engines search across all the other online search engines. Although this search yields a vast amount of information, it collates the results, removes duplications and links that are no longer valid, and then rank orders the results. Examples of meta-search engines include Meta-Crawler (www.metacrawler.com), SavvySearch (www.cs.colostate.edu/~dreiling/smartform.html), and Inference Find (http://m5.inference.com/ifind).

Citing and Documenting Information Obtained Online

Correctly citing online sources is as important as citing print references. Moreover, intellectual property rights apply to online material in much the same way as printed material. Electronic information technologies have transformed the flow of information, but they have not changed our concept of intellectual property ownership. Copyright laws cover online public messages, collections of messages (i.e., message threads), e-mail, computer program files, text files, image files, sound and MIDI files, and electronic databases and trademarks. Shareware, freeware, and public domain software are the only types of software that can move through online networks without potentially violating copyrights.[11] In short, it is important to carefully cite online sources in research papers to avoid plagiarism.

Evaluating Reliable and Legitimate Internet Sources

We all are familiar with the saying "Don't believe everything you read." This warning also applies to information obtained online.

- The Internet is home to many bogus "professional" and hate-based websites containing questionable "facts." Obviously, information obtained from these sources should be avoided.
- Certain types of legal or technical information obtained online may be inappropriate because the website providing the information may be in a different country and subject to different jurisdictions.[12]
- The quality of online information varies from up-to-date research from leading policy institutes to out-of-date or inaccurate research. Information from websites that do not contain a date or a "modified on" notation should be avoided.

The Internet poses a challenge to policy analysts because of the mismatch between the speed with which new data can be disseminated and the length of time required for careful peer review.[13] One strategy for mitigating this problem is to develop innovative peer-reviewed approaches to Internet publishing.

Electronic Journals: An Increasingly Popular Venue

Electronic journals often take two forms: print journals with a website that contains an online copy of articles, and electronic journals with no print counterpart.[14] Online journals are increasingly seen as a way to address the problems libraries have with print journal collections, such as storage, preservation, accessibility, and cost. One project that has facilitated the availability of online information is Journal Storage (JSTOR), a not-for-profit organization of approximately 200 libraries, including Columbia, Harvard, Princeton, and Yale. JSTOR (www.jstor.org/about) has digitalized all or some of more than 52 core journal titles in 12 disciplines, including economics, political science, sociology, and anthropology.

Online Publishing

Electronically distributed information should be subject to the same standards of validity and reliability as printed materials. This is important to keep in mind when considering whether to publish online. For example, publishing an article on an Internet mailing list typically does not carry formal academic recognition. Peer-reviewed journals that appear in print are still considered the normative venue by which to achieve academic distinction. Moreover, if an article is published electronically, many print journals will reject it because prior publication has already occurred. Online publishing may therefore be a problem for policy analysts who must formally document their publications.

Fortunately, there are a growing number of legitimate online publications. One way to discern whether an online journal is legitimate is to determine whether it is peer-reviewed. Specifically, the journal should have a masthead listing an editor, an editorial board, and guidelines for submission and review. In addition, legitimate online journals are sometimes issued an International Standard Serial Number (ISSN) through the Library of Congress or another official agency.[15] The Internet facilitates a wide range of research activities that range from conducting literature searches to publishing in online journals. Just as we adopt a critical stance when evaluating the credibility and quality of print sources, it is important to maintain a critical perspective when evaluating information obtained online.

Conclusion

The choice of a policy analysis framework depends on several factors, including (1) the kind of problem or policy that is being analyzed; (2) the resources available to the analyst, such as time, money, staff, facilities, and the availability of data; (3) the needs of the decision maker requesting the analysis; and (4) the time frame within which the analysis must be completed.

Because it is impossible to evaluate all of the data (data are essentially infinite) and to ask all of the possible questions, no policy analysis is ever complete. Policy analysis is always an approximation of the ideal, and therefore decisions are inevitably made on the basis of incomplete information. How incomplete the information is and how close an approximation to a rational decision is offered to decision makers will depend on the skills of the analyst, the available resources, and the time allotted for the project.

Despite its reliance on an analytic framework, social policy analysis is largely subjective. Because a policy is analyzed by human beings, it is always done through the lens of the analyst's value system, ideological beliefs, and their particular understanding of the goals and purposes of social welfare. Subjectivity may be evident in the omission of facts or questions or in the relative weight given to one variable over another. Other forms of subjectivity include asking the wrong questions about the policy, evaluating it on the basis of expectations that it cannot meet, or expecting it to tackle a problem the policy was not designed to remedy. Finally, political pressure can be put on the policy analyst to come up with recommendations that are acceptable to a certain interest group. Regardless of the causes of subjectivity, policy analysis always approximates the ideal and always involves an informed hunch as to the effects of a policy or a set of policies.

Discussion Questions

1. What are the main advantages of using an analytic framework for social policy analysis? Describe the benefits of using such a framework. What, if any, are the potential drawbacks?

2. Although the *unintended* consequences of a social policy are obviously unpredictable, what can a policy analyst do to minimize the risk? Describe a social policy that has produced unintended consequences that were either positive or harmful.

3. Can a policy researcher neutralize his or her personal values when conducting a policy analysis? If so, describe ways in which this can be done.

4. What components should be added to the proposed policy framework presented in this chapter? Which of the components provided in this framework are the most important, and why?

5. Are most social policies analyzed rationally? If not, why not? Describe the factors that stand in the way of a systematic and rational analysis of

social policy in the U.S. context. How much value do decision makers place on social policy research? Why?

6. Because any analysis of social policy is by nature incomplete, should decision makers minimize policy studies? What alternatives, if any, can be used in lieu of a thorough and systematic policy analysis?

7. Because of its long reach and low costs, the Internet is the perfect breeding ground for the growth of hate groups. Should legislative controls be placed on the Internet to limit its use by hate groups?

8. What are some of the strengths and weaknesses of Internet research?

Notes

1. Thanks to Brene Brown for her ideas on environmental scanning. Dr. Brown has repeatedly pointed out that environmental scanning is a concept that successful agencies must adopt.

2. The Pew Center on the States, "One in 100: Behind Bars in America 2008," February 28, 2008. Retrieved 2008, from www.pewcenteronthestates.org/report _detail.aspx?id=35904

3. Gail Russell Chaddock, "US Notches World's Highest Incarceration Rate," *The Christian Science Monitor*, August 18, 2003, p. 16.

4. Lionheart Foundation, "Corrections in the U.S.—The Picture Today . . ." Retrieved 2004, from www .lionheart.org/prison_proj/corrections.html

5. Many social policy writers have developed excellent policy frameworks, among them Elizabeth Huttman, *Introduction to Social Policy* (New York: McGraw-Hill, 1981); Neil Gilbert and Harry Specht, *Dimensions of Social Welfare Policy*, 2nd ed. (Englewood Cliffs, NJ: Prentice Hall, 1986); Gail Marker, "Guidelines for Analysis of a Social Welfare Program," in John E. Tropman et al. (eds.), *Strategic Perspectives on Social Policy* (New York: Pergamon Press, 1976); David Gil, *Unraveling Social Policy* (Boston: Shenkman, 1981);

and Charles Prigmore and Charles Atherton, *Social Welfare Policy* (New York: D.C. Heath, 1979).

6. Richard Lakeman, "Using the Internet for Data Collection in Nursing Research," *Computers in Nursing* 15, no. 5 (1997), pp. 269–275.

7. Ibid.

8. John Grohol, "Best Practices in E-Therapy: Confidentiality & Privacy." Retrieved 1999, from www.ismho.org/issues/99901.htm

9. Elizabeth Weise, "Net Use Doubling Every 100 Days," *USA Today* (April 16, 1998), p. 6.

10. Joanne Yaffe, *Quick Guide to the Internet for Social Work* (Boston: Allyn & Bacon, 1998).

11. Lance Rose, *Netlaw: Your Rights in the Online World* (Berkeley, CA: McGraw-Hill, 1995).

12. Alan Parkin and David Stretch, "Facilities on the Internet May Be Abused," *British Medical Journal* 313, no. 4 (November 11, 1997), pp. 67–69.

13. Enrico Coiera, "The Internet's Challenge to Health Care Provision," *British Medical Journal* 312, no. 3–4 (January 6, 1996), pp. 8–16.

14. John Grohol, *The Insider's Guide to Mental Health Resources Online* (New York: Guilford Press, 1997).

15. Ibid.

CHAPTER 3

Religion and Social Welfare Policy

Howard Jacob Karger and Peter A. Kindle

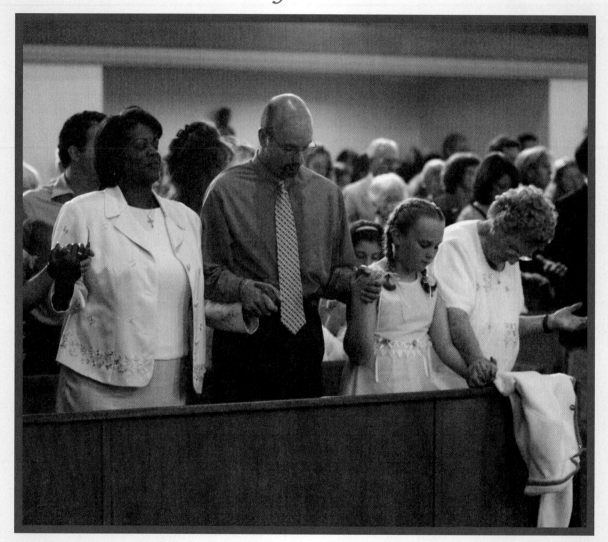

*E*very week more than 300,000 congregations, mosques, temples, and ashrams meet to conduct religious services across the United States.[1] Over 80 percent of the American population report a religious affiliation, over 90 percent report a personal belief in the existence of a supreme being, and more than $295 billion was donated to churches and charities in 2006.[2] Not only are the American people the most religious Western democracy in the world, the variety of religious expression in this country is unequaled.

There are more Jews practicing their faith in the United States than there are in Israel. By some estimates, there are more Muslim adherents in the United States than there are in Kuwait, Oman, Qatar, Lebanon, or the United Arab Emirates.[3] There were almost 1,200 congregations practicing the Bahai faith in 2000, over 1,600 Buddhist worship centers, and over 600 Hindu temples.[4] To one accustomed to the variety of religious expressions and practices that are part of contemporary America, it may be difficult to recognize that this diversity has not always been the case.

While we understand and appreciate the important contributions made by the world's religions to U.S. social policy, the vast majority of this chapter will focus on Christianity. This is not because we are Christocentric—on the contrary. However, U.S. social welfare history has been more strongly influenced by Christianity than by any other world religion. In order to understand how religion has influenced the development of social welfare policy, it is necessary to understand the major historical trends that have shaped religion in the United States. As such, this chapter examines the religious roots for the development of the welfare state, and how changes in religious thought and expression have been reflected in social welfare policies.

Religious Antecedents of Welfare Statism

The roots of social welfare go deep into the soil of Judeo-Christian tradition. It was the disfavored son Cain who repudiated his responsibility to his brother with the defensive, "Am I my brother's keeper?"[5] Societal structures in ancient Judaism encoded protections for the most powerless (e.g., the poor, the orphan, and the widow). The poor were allowed to glean the remains and corners of the fields at harvest time, and brothers-in-law were commanded to marry their brother's widow and to raise her children as his own.[6]

Christian traditions build on Jewish foundations. Jesus himself is said to value the "cup of cold water" given in faith, and early gatherings of Christians were reputedly communitarian in that they appear to have shared material provision for daily living in an egalitarian fashion.[7] "No one claimed that any of his possessions was his own, but they shared everything they had."[8] In fact, there are interpreters of religious history that attribute the survival of Jewish and Christian sects during the first and second centuries to this communitarian impulse.

There are other traditions of compassion that could be related to the development of welfare statism, but the dominance of Judeo-Christian compassion and community is without peer as the source in Western societies. The eventual dominance of the Christian tradition in Europe, and the near-identification of church with state government during the medieval period, led to the gradual assumption of government responsibility for social welfare.

The English Poor Laws

Early social welfare relief in England was considered a private and church matter. For example, individual benefactors took responsibility for building almshouses, hospitals, and even bridges and roads. Despite private philanthropy, the main burden for the poor rested on the shoulders of the church; however, it would be a mistake to interpret this to mean that the English government assumed little or no responsibility for the care of the poor. The Church of England has been an integral part of the English government since the sixteenth century, and there has been a sense in which government responsibility for social welfare has continually been, at least partially, discharged through this established church.

In 1601, the English government established the Elizabethan Poor Laws that were largely administered through church parishes. In essence, these laws, which remained active for almost 250 years, established the responsibility of the English government to provide relief to the needy. Furthermore, the laws decreed that the needy had a legal right to receive governmental assistance. In order to define the boundaries of government help, the law distinguished among three classes of dependents and proposed remedial measures: Needy children were given apprenticeships, the able-bodied were given work, and the worthy poor were provided either indoor (institutional) or outdoor (home) relief. Finally, the law ordered local governments to assume responsibility for the needy.[9] The English Poor Laws formed the basis for statutes that were enacted in both colonial and postcolonial America.[10]

Church, State, and Social Welfare in Colonial America

Most settlers in colonial America were poor; however, unlike their European ancestors, they were not destitute.[11] The undeveloped resources of the frontier provided opportunities for colonists that were not available in the social milieu of Europe, and, therefore, pauperism was not widespread. According to Robert Morris, less than 1 percent of American colonists received help from outside sources.[12] The new frontier provided ample opportunity for work, and the ready availability of work allowed for the reinterpretation of European religious perspectives.

European Protestants valued work. Martin Luther viewed work as a responsibility to God. Furthermore, work conferred dignity and was a "calling" by God. In Luther's view, a person served God by doing the work of his vocation. Therefore, those who are able-bodied and yet unemployed are sinners. John Calvin took Luther's argument one step further by claiming that work carried out the will of God and, as such, would ultimately help to create God's kingdom on earth. According to both Luther and Calvin, God-fearing people must work regardless of their wage or type of employment.[13] God commanded work, America provided opportunity, and economic success became a sign of divine favor. This Protestant ethic (Roman Catholics were less than 2 percent of the population in 1776) fueled the creation of a work-oriented society and provided a religious foundation for the condemnation of the poor.[14] If prosperity was a sign of God's favor, then poverty was a sign of God's judgment. When assistance was required, it was provided on a case-by-case basis in town meetings. When the number of cases increased as a result of indentured servants and abandoned children, the English system of overseers was introduced. It was not uncommon for the town council to auction off the poor to neighboring farmers, apprentice out children, place the poor in private homes at public expense, or send them to privately operated almshouses. Settlers believed that children should be part of a family unit, and thus the practice of indenture became widespread; however, by the end of the colonial period, the locus of responsibility for the poor began to shift from the town to the province.[15] It was inconceivable until the mid-1800s that there could be any federal responsibility for social welfare.

The Second Great Awakening

The nineteenth century opened (1800–1830) with a period of unusually intense religious fervor termed the *Second Great Awakening*. At least in part a reaction to the disestablishment of religion codified in the Bill of Rights (eight of the original 13 colonies had an established church on the European pattern) and in part millennial enthusiasm, the religion sparked by the Second Great Awakening contributed to the general spirit of reform.[16] The Puritans' vision of America as "a city set on a hill" was renewed across the nation. America's destiny was to be a pure and holy nation.

Church attendance doubled in comparison to the revolutionary era,[17] but the organizational structure of most denominations was still quite rudimentary. Those denominations with the most adherents in 1776 were in serious decline, and the more evangelistic denominations were on the rise. In 1776 Congregationalists, Episcopalians, and Presbyterians made up 55.1 percent of religious adherents; by 1850 these denominations represented only 19.1 percent. The Baptists and Methodists, who made up 19 percent of adherents in 1776, had grown to 55 percent by 1850. Catholics, who encompassed less than 2 percent of the population in 1776, in spite of western expansion into Texas and French Catholic lands to the Mississippi River, remained a modest minority of 14 percent in 1850.[18] Voluntary associations were formed to promote causes the existing denominational structures could not support. For example, the American Board for Foreign Missions (1810), the American Tract Society (1814), the American Bible Society (1816), and the American Sunday School Union (1824) were organized.[19] However, this optimistic religious fervor was not contained solely within the churches and religious endeavors, but was also channeled into moral and social reform.

From his pulpit at Hanover Street Congregational Church in Boston, Lyman Beecher (1775–1863) railed against moral license. Largely due to his efforts, the Connecticut Society for the Reformation of Morals (1823) and later the American Temperance Union (1836) were formed.[20] The casual and heavy drinking of alcohol that had been the American custom since the first colonists came under attack. Abstinence from all strong drink became the new moral standard, if not the actual practice, of the average American citizen. It would be more than a century before the temperance movement would culminate in the 18th Amendment prohibiting the manufacturing, transportation, or sale of alcoholic beverages.[21] The tone was set for future clashes between church and state by the New England Sabbatarian campaign (1828–1832). Although ultimately unsuccessful, the clergy-led campaign to end mail delivery on Sunday did "recruit moral reformers and give them their political baptism."[22] "They raised funds, held rallies, published tracts, signed petitions, and failed. . . ."[23] This experience was to prove invaluable for abolitionists that followed, and according to James A. Morone, established a new institutional symbiosis between private organizations and the public bureaucracy that was instrumental in melding local and national interests in this geographically dispersed nation.[24] Perhaps no reform movement shows more clearly the intricate interweaving of religion and politics more than the abolition movement. While the former editor of a small Baptist temperance journal, William Lloyd Garrison (1805–1879), thundered against the evils of slavery in his *Public Liberator and Journal of the Times* (in press from 1831 to 1843), Charles G. Finney (1792–1875) led religious revivals throughout the northern states that led converts to support the abolition movement. Many, if not the majority, of these converts were women who stepped forward with Garrison's support to take an active role in the leadership of the movement.[25] Even though there was little sympathy for the abolitionists in the southern states, the religious fervor of the Second Great Awakening had its influence. The Cane Ridge camp meeting in Kentucky (1801) is often cited as the beginning of the awakening, and its influence was felt in both Tennessee and Ohio.[26] The Baptists and Methodists were quick to adopt the revival patterns that fueled their rapid growth. For the first time, conversion efforts were directed toward the slave population of the south with considerable success. Sydney Ahlstrom notes that "the

evangelization of the slaves was prosecuted with increased vigor" as though it was a direct response to northern abolitionists.[27] Three products of the Second Great Awakening had a lasting influence on what was to become social welfare policy. First, the religious impulse for reform was channeled into private organizations attempting to affect public change. Second, a cadre of female leaders were mobilized and trained. Third, an African American clergy began to form to lead the African American converts. Even though the egalitarianism associated with the religious revival had produced tumult, social welfare reform proceeded at a slower pace.

The Civil War Era

Those denominations with national constituencies split over the slavery issue prior to the beginning of the Civil War. In 1845 the Methodists and Baptists divided into autonomous northern and southern denominations. The Presbyterians followed in 1857. Those denominations without national membership (e.g., Congregationalists, Unitarians, and Universalists), those whose congregational polity had yet to produce denominational structures (e.g., Jews and Disciples of Christ), and those who were withdrawn or isolated from public life (e.g., Latter Day Saints and Mennonites) did not separate into distinct denominations. Lutherans, Episcopalians, and Catholics did not take a denominational stand on slavery prior to the outbreak of war in 1860. They did not split into distinct national churches until there were two separate nations—the United States and the Confederate States of America.[28]

During the course of the Civil War (1860–1864), the evangelistic fervor of the Second Great Awakening was rekindled. Soldiers on both sides of the conflict required assistance, and the existing churches and private organizations were generous in meeting these needs. In the North the Christian Commission raised more than $3 million in cash and millions more in supplies and services, and recruited over 5,000 volunteers to assist Northern soldiers. The work of the Southern churches is less well documented, but the religious support was no less fervent. Linus P. Brockett wrote in his 1864 book, *The Philanthropic Results of the War in America*, "neither in ancient nor modern times has there been so vast an outpouring of a nation's wealth for the care, the comfort, and the physical and moral welfare of those who have fought the nation's battles or been the sufferers from its condition of war."[29]

This philanthropic impulse was to continue to influence America's early social welfare for some time.

For example, Dorothea Dix, a Sunday School teacher, led a campaign to reform the care of the mentally ill. She was successful in lobbying for state actions but became convinced that federal assistance was needed due to the large expenditures required. In 1854 both houses of Congress passed a bill to assist the mentally ill. It was vetoed by President Franklin Pierce with these words, "If Congress has the power to make provisions for the indigent insane . . . it has the same power for the indigent who are not insane. . . . I cannot find any authority in the Constitution for making the Federal Government the great almoner of public charity throughout the United States."[30] Federal responsibility for social welfare was to develop slowly and gradually.

However, the Civil War ushered in a new period for relief activities. Families who had lost a breadwinner or who had a breadwinner return from the war permanently disabled could not be blamed for their misfortunes. As a response to this hardship, localities passed laws that raised funds for the sick and needy and, in some instances, for the founding of homes for disabled soldiers. Another concern was the increasing numbers of freed slaves, and freedman relief societies with religious ties were organized in most northern cities during the first year of the war.[31] Other welfare issues during the Civil War included the disease and filth rampant in army camps and hospitals and the shortage of trained medical personnel. In an effort to remedy this situation, Unitarian minister Henry W. Bellows and a group of citizens (mainly women) organized the U.S. Sanitary Commission in 1861, the first important national public health group. Functioning as a quasi-governmental body, the commission was financed and directed by the private voluntary sector. Working initially in the area of preventive health education, the commission eventually became involved in serving the needs of soldiers.[32] Another social welfare institution that emerged from the Civil War was the Freedmen's Bureau. By the close of the war, political leaders realized that the emancipation of millions of slaves would create serious social problems. Former slaves having no occupational training, land, or jobs would require assistance. In 1865, following the earlier example of local freedman's relief societies, Congress established the Bureau of Refugees, Freedmen, and Abandoned Lands. The Freedmen's Bureau, as it was commonly called, was responsible for directing a program of temporary relief for the duration of the war and one year afterward. After a bitter struggle, Congress extended the Freedmen's Bureau for an additional six years.

Under General Oliver Howard, the bureau performed a variety of services designed to help African Americans make the transition from slavery to freedom. For example, the bureau served as an emergency relief center that distributed 22 million rations to needy Southerners. The bureau also functioned as an African American employment agency, a settlement agency, a health center that employed doctors and operated hospitals, an educational agency that encouraged the funding of African American colleges and provided financial aid, and finally, as a legal agency that maintained courts in which civil and criminal cases involving African Americans were heard. The Freedmen's Bureau set an important precedent for federal involvement in a variety of human services. In 1872 the bureau was dissolved by Congress.[33] Northern denominations continued the work, sponsoring thousands of educational missionaries to teach in African American schools, and founding Lincoln University in Pennsylvania, Morehouse College and Atlanta University in Georgia, Talladega College in Alabama, Tougaloo University in Mississippi, Hampton Institute in Virginia, and Fisk University in Tennessee.[34] Following the war and the end of Reconstruction in 1877, only the Catholic and Episcopal churches immediately reunited. Methodists reunited in 1939, Presbyterians in 1983, and the division between northern and southern Baptists continues to this day.[35] Further divisions occurred as each denomination tended to segregate African Americans. The Colored Primitive Baptists (1866), the Colored Cumberland Presbyterian Church (1869), and the National Baptist Convention (1895) joined the older African Methodist Episcopal Church, Bethel (1816), and the African Methodist Episcopal Church, Zion (1821), as institutional organizations for African Americans. By 1900, 2.7 million out of 8.3 million African Americans would identify with one of these denominations.[36]

The Late Nineteenth and Early Twentieth Centuries

Although Catholic immigration increased the size of this denomination until it was the largest in America by 1890, the Protestant hegemony over America was unchallenged. Protestant discrimination contributed to Catholic and Jewish sectarianism. Parochial schools, Catholic versions of professional organizations and semiprofessional guilds, even a Catholic alternative to fraternal lodges, "created a parallel society within which [Catholics] were protected from Protestant insults as well as from Protestant influences."[37] Jewish sectarianism, rooted as it was in European anti-Semitism, may have led to fewer institutions, but it was no less isolated from the Protestant mainstream. As late as 1866, white, American Protestant denominations were capable of forming into a single ecumenical association called the Evangelical Alliance to assert "the claim that Protestantism was the only true religion of the republic."[38] This alliance was short-lived but provided the development of a Protestant confidence in large-scale organizations and affirmed an "optimism about realizing God's kingdom in this world."[39] Other circumstances—social, philosophical, and theological—in the late nineteenth century would cause this optimism to crumble.

Immigration and industrialization made significant impacts on Protestant optimism. Prior to industrialization, most people lived in small, rural communities with an array of institutions that afforded a high degree of self-sufficiency. Chief among these institutions were the local churches. Survival necessitated a degree of solidarity, or interdependence, and the local churches were an apt institution to fill this need. From 1890 to 1920, 22 million immigrants came to the United States. At the same time, the American people became more urban. Seventy-five percent of foreign immigrants lived in the cities and, during the decade following 1920, 6 million people moved from farms to cities.[40] Community solidarity was no longer the norm. Millions of the new immigrants were Catholic and tens of thousands were Jewish. Numerical increases alone threatened Protestant hegemony. Even an urban/rural dichotomy became more apparent within the Protestant denominations.

Philosophically, many people looked to the developing social sciences for guidance in redefining social policy. There, prominent scholars drew lessons from the natural sciences that could be used for purposes of social engineering. Borrowing from biology, some American proponents of the new science of sociology applied the idea of natural selection to social affairs.

Social Darwinism was a bastard outgrowth of Charles Darwin's theory of evolution as described in his 1859 classic, *The Origin of Species*.[41] Social theorists such as Herbert Spencer and America's William Graham Sumner reasoned that if Darwin's laws of evolution determined the origin and development of species, then they might also be applied to understanding the laws of society.[42] Applying Darwin's rules to society and then adapting laissez-faire principles of economics to sociology led to a problematic set of assumptions. First, if the "survival of the fittest" (a term coined by Spencer) was a law governing the lower species, then it must also govern the higher species. Because subsidizing the poor allowed them to survive, this circumvented the law of nature, and because the poor reproduced more rapidly than the middle classes, society was thus subsidizing its own demise. Social Darwinists believed essentially that the poor would eventually overrun society and bring down the general level of civilization. The fact that many of the new urban poor were recent immigrants with Catholic or Jewish backgrounds did little to mitigate the harsh implications of Social Darwinism.

Social Darwinists believed that, although unfortunate, the poor must pay the price demanded by nature and be allowed to die out. According to the Social Darwinists, social welfare thwarts nature's plan of evolutionary progress toward higher forms of social life. Speaking for many intellectuals, the British theorist Herbert Spencer drew this conclusion:

> It seems hard that widows and orphans should be left to struggle for life or death. Nevertheless, when regarded not separately but in connexion with the interests of universal humanity, these harsh fatalities are seen to be full of beneficence the same beneficence which brings to early graves the children of diseased parents, and singles out the intemperate and the debilitated as the victims of an epidemic.[43]

Social Darwinism led to indifference toward the urban poor in the north, and white indifference to the freedman's condition in the south, and set a secular tone for the nation that denied the most basic assumption of Protestant optimism—that America was to be a holy nation, a "city set upon a hill." The Protestant establishment was not unanimous in its response to these threats and began to separate into what would become mainline and evangelical traditions. Lack of unanimity led to lack of a coordinated Protestant response to human need. Catholic charities developed to serve the immigrant poor in the north. Jewish social services expanded nationwide to provide assistance to the eastern European and Russian immigrants of that faith.[44] In the south, no comparable institutional relief was afforded the freedman who would remain marginalized until the latter half of the twentieth century.

This cleavage among Protestants was to be accelerated by theological conflicts. German higher criticism challenged the infallibility of scripture. Evolution provided a natural alternative to supernatural explanations as did Freudian psychology and Marxian socialism. The success of the scientific method elevated confidence in human reason. Protestants responded in two ways. First, conservative, evangelical theologians reverted to traditional interpretations. Biblical infallibility, miracles, and the existence of the supernatural were reasserted. Conversion and personal piety were emphasized as essential elements of Christian faith. Within this religious framework, poverty was related to improvidence: People were poor because they engaged in drinking, slothfulness, licentious behavior, and gambling.

This evangelical Protestant response to theological challenges was not without opposition. A movement known as the Social Gospel emerged. Composed of theologians concerned with the abuses created by industrialization and the excesses of capitalism, Social Gospelists such as Josiah Strong, Graham Taylor, and others, believed that the church should recapture the militant spirit of Christ by taking on the issues of social justice and poverty. The critique posed by the Social Gospelists called for fair play and simple justice for the worker.[45] Proponents of the Social Gospel movement maintained that churches wrongfully stressed spirituality rather than morality.[46] The condemnation of classical economics, business ethics, and the lawlessness of the plutocracy was centered on a moral rather than a spiritual plane. For the Social Gospelists, social reformation could not occur without a regeneration of character.[47] Although the movement contained degrees of radicalism, all Social Gospelists were moved by a sense of social crisis, and all believed in the necessity of a Christian solution.[48] At the turn of the twentieth century, an outside observer may have had great difficulty in identifying the distinction between these two Protestant factions. Both were heavily committed to the tradition of religious social relief. Postmillennialism, the belief that Christian preaching will result in a gradually and steadily improving society so that when Christ returns a second time, God's kingdom will be established without additional radical change, was the dominant eschatological

view.[49] The cleavage began to be apparent in 1908 when the more conservative and evangelical denominations declined to join the Federal Council of Churches.[50] Walter Rauschenbusch's 1907 book, *Christianity and the Social Crisis,* provided a ready statement of the Social Gospel that was later countered by publication of twelve volumes called *The Fundamentals* (1910–1915) that were distributed without charge to Protestant ministers.[51] Postmillennial optimism did not survive World War I among evangelical Protestants who began to embrace dispensational premillennialism. This new eschatological view, originating with the Englishman John Nelson Darby (1800–1882) and popularized by the Scofield Reference Bible, expected human society to become steadily more ungodly and evil until, in a secret rapture of the true Christians, a seven-year period of tribulation would signal the second return of Christ.[52] By 1920 evangelical Protestants had discontinued most social relief work, at least in part, as a means of distinguishing themselves from the more public and liberal theology of the mainline Protestants.[53]

The Rise of Social Work as a Profession

Religion and social welfare in nineteenth-century America were inextricably linked. Almost all forms of relief emanated from church groups, and all major denominations had some mechanism for providing social welfare, at least until the early twentieth century.[54] For example, as early as 1880 there were 500 private, church-related social welfare organizations in New York City alone, with the largest network for social services provided by Protestant churches. Christian charity suffused the Charity Organization Societies (COSs) and Settlement Houses that assumed a major share of the responsibility for urban social welfare during the late nineteenth century.

It was thought that in order to reclaim providence, the poor must be taught to live a moral and self-disciplined life. Although early religious social workers clung tenaciously to their desire to teach the moral life, they also understood the need to provide material assistance.[55] The major emphasis of the early social worker, however, was more often on spiritual guidance than on material aid.

The relief assistance provided by these religious social workers was often linked to harsh criteria. For example, it was not uncommon for social workers to appraise the worth of the family's possessions and then instruct them to sell off everything in order to qualify for relief. Nor was it uncommon for social workers to deny relief because they felt that the poor family was intemperate and not sufficiently contrite. Although social workers dispensed relief, they were basically opposed to the concept of it. In effect, they believed that distributing relief was imprudent because a reliance on charity would weaken the moral fabric of the poor and provide a disincentive for work.

Urban Needs during Industrialization

Life in late-nineteenth-century America was hard. The dream of milk and honey that motivated many immigrants to leave their homelands became, for many, a nightmare. The streets of American cities were not paved with gold; instead, they were overcrowded, rampant with disease and crime, and economically destitute. Many tenement houses in the larger cities contained neither windows nor indoor plumbing. Tuberculosis was widespread, and among some groups, infant mortality ran as high as 50 percent. Scant medical care existed for the poor; there was no public education; and insanity and prostitution rates among immigrants were high.[56] Industrial and economic prospects were equally bleak. Factory conditions were deplorable: Workers were expected to labor six or seven days a week (often on Sunday), and 18-hour days were not unusual, especially in summer.[57] Factories were poorly lit and unsanitary, easily turned into fire traps, and offered almost no job security. Moreover, homework (taking piecework home, usually for assembly by whole families in one- or two-room tenements) was common. Women were forced to work night shifts and then take care of their homes and children by day.[58] No special protective legislation for women existed until the early 1900s, and child labor was legal.

Charity Organization Societies

First evident in the 1870s, Charity Organization Societies (COSs) had offices in most American cities by 1900.[59] With the exception of meager state-sponsored indoor and outdoor relief, the COS movement was the major provider of care to the destitute. COSs varied in their structures and methods. In general, they coordinated relief giving by operating community-wide registration bureaus, providing direct relief, and "educating" both the upper and lower classes as to their mutual obligations.

The work of the COSs was carried out by a committee of volunteers and agency representatives who examined "cases" of needy applicants and decided on a course of action. The agent of the COS was the "friendly visitor," whose task was to conduct an investigation of the circumstances surrounding the cases and to instruct the poor in ways of better managing their lives. Friendly visitors, drawn from the upper classes, often held a morally superior attitude toward their clientele, and their intervention in the lives of the poor was interpreted by some observers as a form of social control as well as a means of providing assistance.[60] In any case, the charity provided by these organizations was often less than generous. Leaders of the movement drew an important lesson from Social Darwinism and the Protestant work ethic in believing that beneficent charity was counterproductive because it contributed to sloth and dependency. Josephine Shaw Lowell, president of the New York Charity Organization Society, believed that charity should be dispensed "only when starvation was imminent."[61] To be sure, it was difficult for friendly visitors to maintain a sense of Christian duty in the midst of immoral behavior. In such instances, when some wretched soul seemed beyond instruction and charity, more radical measures were in order.

Settlement Houses

Begun in the 1880s, the settlement house movement had emerged in most of the big cities over the next two decades. Settlement houses were primarily set up in immigrant neighborhoods by wealthy people, college students, unattached women, teachers, doctors, and lawyers, who themselves moved into the slums as residents. Rather than simply engaging in friendly visiting, the upper- and middle-class settlement leaders tried to bridge class differences and to develop a less patronizing form of charity. Rather than coordinating the existing charities like the COS movement, they sought to help the people in the neighborhoods to organize themselves. Because they actually lived in the same neighborhoods as the impoverished immigrants, settlement workers could provide fresh and reliable knowledge about the social and economic conditions of American cities.

One of the best-known settlement houses, Hull House was established by Jane Addams in 1889.

Jane Addams established Hull House in 1889. She approached the project and the Chicago ethnic community in which it was based with a sense of Christian Socialism that was derived from a "rather strenuous moral purgation"[62] rather than a sense of *noblesse oblige*. By 1915, this altruism was shared by enough settlement workers so that more than 300 settlements had been established, and most large American cities boasted at least one or more settlement houses.[63] Even though the larger settlements provided individual services to the poor, they were essentially reform oriented. These reforms were achieved not only by organizing the poor to press for change but also by using interest groups formed by elite citizens, as well as by the formation of national alliances. Settlement-pioneered reforms included tuberculosis prevention, the establishment of well-baby clinics, the implementation of housing codes, the construction of outdoor playgrounds, the enactment of child labor and industrial safety legislation, and the promotion of some of the first studies of the

urban black in America, such as W. E. B. Du Bois's *The Philadelphia Negro*.

The Social Casework Agency

Charity Organization Societies and settlement houses served as models for the delivery of social welfare services in the voluntary sector organizations that emerged during the Progressive Era. Similar in many respects, these organizations evolved to form the social casework agency. Both were of modest size in terms of staff, both were located in the communities of the clientele they served, both served a predominantly poor population, and both relied on contributions from a variety of sources for private donations, the Community Chest, and foundations.[64] Typically, workers in these agencies were female volunteers. COS techniques for investigation were refined, with their aim being the identification of a "social diagnosis" as the basis for case intervention.[65] Subsequently, these activities, along with the community-oriented work of the settlement reformers, gave birth to the profession of social work.

As predominant service delivery forms, COSs and settlement houses were shaped by two influences: the need for scientifically based techniques, and the socialization of charity. Together, these contributed to the emergence of the social casework agency. COSs and settlement houses had provided meaningful activity for upper- and middle-class women who found it necessary to ground their work in techniques derived from science. This necessity had been driven home in 1915 during the National Conference of Charities and Correction, when Abraham Flexner, a renowned authority on professional graduate education, was asked to address the question of whether social work was a profession. Much to the disappointment of the audience, Flexner judged that social work lacked all the requirements of a profession, particularly a scientifically derived knowledge base that was transmittable.[66]

The Progressive Movement

A reaction to the heartlessness that characterized a large segment of American society came in the form of the Progressive movement, a social movement

Spotlight 3.1

Jane Addams and Hull House

In 1889, Jane Addams established Hull House to serve residents of the Chicago community in which she lived. To learn more about Jane Addams and Hull House, go to **www.uic.edu/jaddams/hull/urbanexp.** Using historical photos and narrative, this website presents a comprehensive overview of Hull House and its surrounding neighborhoods.

that was popular from the early 1900s to World War I. Progressive Era philosophy intended to inject a measure of public credibility and Christian morality into social, political, and economic affairs. As a result, it reflected a unique blend of social reform encompassing anti–big business attitudes, a belief that government should regulate the public good, a strong emphasis on ethics in business and personal life, a commitment to social justice, a concern for the "common man," and a strong sense of paternalism. Progressives believed that the state had a responsibility to protect the interests of the public, especially those who were vulnerable. Supported by the nation's most respected social workers, including Jane Addams, Lillian Wald, and Paul U. Kellogg, the Progressive Party presented a presidential ticket in 1912. The advent of World War I diminished the liberal fervor that had characterized the Progressive Era of the late 1800s and early 1900s. In the wake of the disillusionment that followed the war, the mood of the country became conservative. Progressive ideas were treated skeptically by the 1920s, and activists were often accused of being Bolsheviks.

Religion and the Welfare State

On January 16, 1920, the 18th Amendment went into effect and Prohibition became the law throughout the country. This single event, the culmination of religious and moral reforms that had begun more than a century before, signaled the high point of Protestant dominance in the United States, but this was to be short-lived.

The Fundamentalist Controversy and Its Aftermath

The Protestantism of the 1920s held little resemblance to its nineteenth-century predecessor. Those mainline denominations that associated with the Federal Council of Churches were characterized by large denominational bureaucracies, significant interdenominational cooperation, and a new form of religious intellectualism.[67] Theologically, the mainline tended to embrace the findings of the natural sciences and the new social sciences in preference to biblical and historical traditions. Postwar patriotism was bolstered by economic prosperity, leading to the uncritical conclusion that capitalism and the Protestant work ethic had divine favor. Paradoxically, one-third of Americans continued to live in poverty.[68] Although the Social Gospel had waned, it maintained a presence in the larger urban congregations that were most proximate to those living in urban poverty and in the voices of social conscience best personified by Reinhold Niebuhr of Union Theological Seminary in New York.[69]

The cleavage in American Protestantism became the focus of national attention during the Scopes monkey trial. "In the course of a few days in July 1923 two million words of newspaper reportage were telegraphed from Dayton, Tennessee."[70] John Scopes, a recent college graduate and novice high school teacher, was on trial for teaching the theory of evolution in violation of Tennessee law. Conservative and evangelical Protestants were subjected to national scorn and ridicule as Fundamentalists, exacerbating sectarian tendencies. For the most part, conservative and evangelical Protestant organizations withdrew from public life. The prosperous twenties abruptly ended in late 1929 as stock market values crashed. Within four years over a quarter of Americans were unemployed, Prohibition had been repealed, and Franklin D. Roosevelt was president.

The Great Depression and New Deal

It is difficult to appreciate the significance of the Great Depression from the position of the relatively prosperous twenty-first century; however, it can be safely concluded that religion had a more significant impact on the private lives of Americans than it did on public policy. The economic crisis called for emergency measures, and Roosevelt's New Deal programs were the response. Social and policy changes took place with blinding speed as the federal government became "the great almoner of public charity."[71] Billions of dollars were spent on relief efforts to provide food, clothing, and shelter. Public works projects were to employ as many as 3.2 million a month by 1938. A minimum wage, a maximum work week, collective bargaining, and the abolishment of child labor were established in 1937. The apogee of the New Deal was the Social Security Act of 1935 that included a national old-age retirement system; federal grants to states for maternal, child, and disabled welfare services; and a federal-state unemployment system.[72]

Protestant churchmen could not keep pace, and even the liberal mainline tended to withdraw into a quiescent spirituality. At best the mainline waged an ineffective post hoc critique of the New Deal while the conservative and evangelical groups tended to become more isolated and sectarian. In contrast with the Protestant denominations, the Roman Catholic Church strongly supported many aspects of the New Deal. Roman Catholic social teaching was largely unaffected by Social Darwinism. Pius XI's encyclical *On the Reconstruction of the Social Order* (1931) advanced Leo XIII's ideas expressed in *On Capital and Labor* (1891) which promoted labor over capital, supported labor unions and minimum wage legislation, and positioned the Catholic Church in America as a champion of the poor.[73] Unfortunately, Catholicism in the United States was unable to escape sectarian marginalization during the 1930s, and the denominational support for labor and the poor was not replicated within the Protestant establishment.

Social workers and others with tenancy experience in a settlement house stepped to the forefront to provide the moral leadership previously provided by religion. Edith Abbott, president of the National Conference of Social Welfare and Dean of the University of Chicago School of Social Service Administration, participated in the drafting of the Social Security Act. Frances Perkins became the first Secretary of Labor. Harry Hopkins is credited as the primary architect of the New Deal. Both the National Association for the Advancement of Colored People (NAACP) and the National Urban League included key social workers in their early formation.[74]

Patterns of Religious Change

The abdication of public moral leadership did not mean that religious change did not occur. In a pattern that has held true since the Congregationalists yielded numerical dominance to the Methodists between 1776 and 1850, mainline denominations tended to decline in membership and sectarian groups tended to grow.[75] Dean M. Kelley, an executive with the National Council of Churches (which replaced the Federal Council in 1950), was the first to publicize this historical trend in his book *Why Conservative Churches Are Growing*. Although many aspects of Kelley's analysis were flawed, for example, his claim that the decline in mainline membership was a sudden change due to cultural shifts in the 1960s, his explanation for the trend has survived all challenges: Strong congregations are strict.[76] Finke and Stark explain:

> High cost [of association with sectarian groups] serve to screen out potential members whose commitment and participation would otherwise be low. The costs act as nonrefundable registration fees which, as in secular markets, measure seriousness of interest in the product. As a result the demanding sects speak of "conversions," "being born again," and "submitting their lives to the Lord." The less demanding churches refer to affiliations that are seldom life-altering events. Sectarian members are either in or out; they must follow the demands of the group or withdraw.[77]

Of course, it is not impossible for a sect to require too much of potential members, but in general, "the higher the costs of membership, the greater the material and social, as well as religious, benefits of membership."[78] Many, if not all, of the conservative and evangelical denominations benefited from their withdrawal from public life.

A comparison of the Methodist and Baptist traditions is one of the clearest examples of the declining trend associated with the mainline, and the corresponding growth associated with a more sectarian identity. Both groups grew during the first half of the nineteenth century, but the stricter Methodists clearly outshined the Baptists. Between 1776 and 1850, Baptist adherents grew by a respectable 21 percent and Methodists by more than 1,268 percent.[79] As the largest religious Protestant denomination in the late nineteenth century, Methodism began to change. Circuit-riding lay preachers gave way to seminary-trained ministers, the emotion-packed worship style of the camp meeting yielded to a more sedate middle-class conformity, and strict behavioral codes were relaxed.[80] By 1926, Baptists outnumbered Methodists.[81] This trend continued unabated in virtually every religious group in the United States throughout the twentieth century. For example, the market share for major mainline denominations (United Methodists; Presbyterian, USA; Episcopal; Christian [Disciples]; and United Church of Christ) declined by more than 50 percent from 1940 to 1985. During the same time period, the more sectarian conservative and evangelical groups (Southern Baptists, Assemblies of God, Church of the Nazarene, and Church of God [Cleveland, Tennessee]) grew by more than 47 percent. Catholics, despite massive Latin American immigration, grew by only 12 percent.[82] In the decades prior to World War II (1941–1945), there were specific individuals who made significant contributions that helped change the face of American religious life after the war. On the left, Reinhold Niebuhr, a theologian at Union Seminary in New York, articulated a neoorthodox theology aimed at reforming liberal thought. His work produced a renewed mainline appreciation for the reality of human evil and the need for social change.[83] Both Martin Luther King Jr. and President Jimmy Carter were to list Neibuhr as a major influence on their faith and political activism.[84] On the right, J. Gresham Machen authored *Christianity and Liberalism* (1923), which remains one of the crown jewels of the conservative evangelical defense of biblical inerrancy.[85] A controversial figure within his own Presbyterian tradition, he was defrocked in 1936, yet his impassioned defense of traditional Christian orthodoxy influenced many conservative and evangelical leaders.[86] Carl F. H. Henry honored Machen in 1956 by naming his new evangelical magazine, *Christianity Today*, after a failed publication founded by Machen.[87] Other theologians of public note included the Protestant Paul Tillich, the Catholic Jacques Maritain, and the Jewish Will Herberg. One historian concluded that "the 1950's were the last decade in which theologians played a major role in

American public life."[88] The careful words and fine distinctions characteristic of theological reflection could not prevail in the new religious arena dominated by radio and television.

Religion and the New Media

Regular radio broadcasting began in 1920, and from the start the Federal Communications Commission required specific time to be set aside for public service broadcasting. As the sole interdenominational organization available, the mainline churches of the Federal Council of Churches soon developed a near monopoly on this free, religion-based programming. By 1931, only one radio network was willing to sell commercial time to conservative and evangelical Protestants.[89] Despite such restrictions, Charles Fuller's *Old Time Gospel Hour* aired in 1937 and had captured a weekly audience of over 20 million by 1943.[90] When the mainline churches were successful in lobbying all broadcast companies to stop selling commercial time to conservative evangelicals in 1944, the conservative evangelicals went directly to local stations to buy airtime, thereby creating radio syndication.[91]

Ironically, the mainline monopoly on radio broadcasting served to strengthen conservative and evangelical commitment to the use of new media. Without the largesse of free public service airtime, the conservative evangelicals developed successful self-funded programs. When the Federal Communications Commission rules changed in 1960, the conservative evangelicals were best able to compete for available time slots on both television and radio.[92] Conservative evangelicals claimed their own television network that same year as Pat Robertson founded the Christian Broadcasting Network (CBN) with the purchase of a small UHF television station.[93] Today CBN broadcasts internationally in 77 different languages. Another network, Trinity Broadcasting (founded in 1973), currently boasts 5,000 local affiliates, 33 satellite links, and thousands of cable systems carrying their message worldwide.[94] By 1990, conservative and evangelical ministers controlled 90 percent of all religious broadcasting in the country.[95] Conservative evangelicals were not the only ones to take advantage of new media. As early as 1926, Father Charles Coughlin of Michigan, a Catholic priest, gained national attention for airing his "America First" isolationist, anticommunist, and ultimately anti-Semitic and anti-Roosevelt message.[96] The almost rabid anticommunist stance of the Roman Catholics may have been the primary means by which this once highly sectarian group merged more fully into the American mainstream.[97] In the 1950s, Bishop Fulton Sheen's popular television series, *Life Is Worth Living*, provided additional impetus.[98] By 1960, not only could a Catholic run for high office, but John F. Kennedy in fact became the first American Catholic president.

Television and radio were to make a significant impact on American religious life. For example, in 1955 only one out of 25 Americans had left their childhood faith for a new religious home. By 1985 one in three had done so.[99] Denominational growth was no longer merely a consequence of family size or immigration as Americans changed denominational affiliation as religious consumers. Religious use of the new media accelerated the commercialization of religious life and subordinated the relationship of pastor–pew to that of media–audience.

Secularization

The 1st Amendment to the U.S. Constitution states that "Congress shall make no law respecting an establishment of religion, or prohibiting the free exercise thereof."[100] Despite this sentence, often referred to as the establishment clause, Protestants had enjoyed considerable influence in virtually every public arena, and restrictions were few. Beginning in 1940 with the extension of the establishment clause to state governments in *Cantwell v. Connecticut*, but rapidly accelerating after the end of World War II in 1945, the Supreme Court began to dismantle Protestant privilege. Conservative and evangelical churchmen tended to view this loss of privilege as an attack on traditional Christian values. For example, public schools and public school teachers were prohibited from promoting religion in 1948, prayer in public schools was declared unconstitutional in 1962, and Bible reading was prohibited in 1963.[101] State laws preventing the teaching of evolution were overturned in 1968, and tax support of parochial schools was prohibited in 1971.[102] These cases specifically impacted long-standing, local privileges, but the social changes mandated by an activist court received even greater opposition. The 1954 *Brown v. Board of Education* decision undermining the legal foundation for segregation and the 1973 decision in *Roe v. Wade* banning state limits on abortion were particularly onerous to the conservative groups.[103] The first threatened white, Protestant dominance;

the second threatened the Christian ideal of the sanctity of human life.

The mainline response to this secularizing trend may be best exemplified by Harvey Cox's *The Secular City* (1965). As Patrick Allitt describes Cox's views:

> Christianity had itself been a powerful force for secularization. Ancient religions had had a great pantheon of gods. . . . Judaism and Christianity, however, had swept away the whole lot and left just one remote, omnipotent God presiding over the world. People were then free to manipulate and organize the world without fear that they were stepping on the gods' toes. And having learned that the world was not crammed with divinities, they had learned to take the logical next step of pushing back further and further their need for any god at all. Secularization and urbanization are the not the enemies of Christianity . . . but its logical end product.[104]

This radical theology culminated in the ultimate liberal claim: "God is dead." To conservative and evangelical ears, there could be no greater challenge.

The Reawakening of a Religious Social Conscience and the Great Society

The liberal, moral leadership provided during the New Deal yielded the framework for the modern social welfare state. Income disparities were mitigated and federal responsibility for social welfare was well established. Despite this progress, irreligious liberal thinkers recognized the disadvantages reason held in comparison with the conservatives' appeal to traditional faith. None attempted to face this disadvantage with more honesty than John Dewey in *A Common Faith* (1934) and *Liberalism and Social Action* (1935). His attempt to dislodge the "impulses of generosity and self-sacrifice, of humility and communal solidarity" from religious roots proved unsuccessful.[105] Liberal social action grinded to a halt following World War II until it was re-energized by a prophetic religious voice.

On December 1, 1955, Rosa Parks refused to give up her seat to a white man on a Montgomery, Alabama, city bus. Female coworkers at the local NAACP office and some local students distributed bus boycott leaflets to Montgomery's African American clergy that very day. Martin Luther King Jr. was elected president of the hastily organized Montgomery Improvement Association.[106] A prophet had been found.

Rejecting liberal, white leadership and, in most cases, counsel, King led a nonviolent activist movement confronting discrimination and segregation that was opposed by white southerners and his own African American denomination. Northern, white liberal churchmen offered weak support.[107] Recent scholarship has challenged the typical classification of this movement as mere civil protest:

> Participants often recalled the movement years as a heady, life-transforming era touched with divine significance. . . . Such testimony suggests that it may be misleading to view the civil rights movement as a social and political event that had religious overtones. . . . To take the testimony of intense religious transformation seriously is to consider the civil rights movement as part of the historical tradition of religious revivals.[108]

Lyndon B. Johnson, who became president following John F. Kennedy's assassination in 1963, tapped into the religious and moral ideals sparked by King and the sacrifices made in the name of desegregation. He declared a "War on Poverty" in his State of the Union address on January 8, 1964.[109] Over 1,000 pieces of legislation were passed as part of Johnson's Great Society including the Civil Rights Act in 1964 and the Voting Rights Act in 1965.[110] White churchmen continued to lag behind the waves of social change, and social workers were among those who stepped forward to lead. For example, the Secretary of Health, Education, and Welfare, Wilbur Cohen, played a major role in the passage of the Medicare and Medicaid Acts of 1965, only two of his 65 innovations in social welfare policy.[111] Even though the Vietnam War was to prove a fatal distraction, Johnson's War on Poverty and Great Society had some success. By 1969 the number of Americans living below the poverty line had fallen by more than half.[112]

The Continuing Decline of Mainline Influence

White religious leadership, in comparison to the courage and conviction of the African American churches, proved to be distracted by internal issues or radical irrelevancy. Roman Catholics were preoccupied with Vatican II (1962–1965). This reform movement, led by Pope John XXIII, ended the last vestiges of isolation and parochialism for American Catholics. Liturgical reforms included enhanced lay participation, the elimination of Latin during mass,

and the loosening of behavioral codes. Faithful Catholics were no longer required to avoid meat on Fridays, except during Lent. As American Catholicism lost its sectarian identity, church attendance and seminary enrollments dropped.[113]

Twenty-nine Protestant and Orthodox denominations had reorganized the mainline into the National Council of Churches in 1950, largely because the *cause celebre* of the Federal Council, the religious delivery of social services, had become the purview of government after the New Deal. The new focus was on ecumenism. The Consultation on Church Union (COCU) was initiated in 1960. Although COCU was largely ineffective at producing broad denominational merger, some progress was made within major historical traditions. Unitarians and Universalists merged in 1961. The Methodist Church and Evangelical United Brethren became the United Methodists in 1968. The Civil War breach between Presbyterian groups ended with the Presbyterian Church in the United States of America in 1984, and several Lutheran bodies created the Evangelical Lutheran Church in America in 1988.[114] Despite claims to the contrary, the National Council of Churches never represented a majority of religious adherents in the country, and the embrace of liberation theologies did little to maintain public influence or lay support. Developed in the class struggles and economic disparities of Latin America, "liberation theology employs a Marxist-style class analysis, which divides the culture between oppressors and oppressed. . . . But unlike Marxism, liberation theology turns to the Christian faith for bringing about liberation."[115] The goal is the radical transformation of society. James Cone applied the insights of liberation theology to the African American struggle for civil rights in his *Black Theology of Liberation* (1970), and Mary Daly did the same for women in her *Beyond God the Father* (1973).

The influence of liberation theology on mainline thought was evident as early as 1964 when the National Council of Churches criticized Great Society reforms as inadequate.[116] President Richard M. Nixon took office in 1968 and became an unlikely champion of the mainline goal—a guaranteed annual income as a fundamental right of citizenship. National Council of Churches' support quickly turned to opposition when Nixon refused to triple the proposed benefit level.[117] Nixon's Family Assistance Plan was ultimately to fail in the Senate. President Jimmy Carter (1976–1980) was to court mainline support for his own watered-down version that also failed.[118] Mainline influence has yet to recover. Martin Marty, a leading church historian, has written that "everybody knows that when the mainline churches take a position, it is only six people in a room on Riverside Drive."[119] Riverside Drive is the local address of the National Council offices in New York, and, hyperbole aside, political events since the presidential election in 1980 indicate that there is some truth in Marty's observation.

The New Christian Right

In 1965, the late Jerry Falwell, senior minister at Thomas Road Baptist Church in Lynchburg, Virginia, preached that "believing the Bible as I do, I would find it impossible to stop preaching the pure saving gospel of Jesus Christ and begin doing anything else—including fighting Communism, or participating in Civil Rights reforms."[120] By 1979 he had changed his mind and founded the Moral Majority, a political action group committed to overturning the secular trends Falwell interpreted as moral deterioration. The Moral Majority was for prayer and the

Jerry Falwell founded the Moral Majority, a political action group that supports prayer and the teaching of creationism in public schools and opposes abortion, the Equal Rights Amendment, and gay and lesbian rights.

teaching of creationism in public schools but was opposed to abortion, feminist issues such as the Equal Rights Amendment, homosexual rights, and even peace talks with the Soviet Union.[121]

Falwell had picked an opportune time to organize the Moral Majority. The two largest conservative evangelical denominations, Southern Baptists and Missouri-Synod Lutherans, had largely remained aloof from the fundamentalist controversy in the 1920s, but each had recently begun internal struggles over the challenges of theological liberalism. Each rejected liberalism in favor of a traditional conservative theology. The Missouri-Synod Lutherans purged its leading seminary of liberal influence in 1976,[122] and Paige Patterson and Paul Pressler led a well-coordinated and successful plan to gain control of the Southern Baptist Convention and its seminaries and agencies that began in 1979.[123] Lay support for theological conservatism was easily converted into sympathy for Falwell's political agenda.

The conservative dominance of religious media also furthered Falwell's agenda, as did the growth of megachurches across the country. With care, he nurtured relationships with the leading religious personalities of the day. Pat Robertson of *The 700 Club*, Jim and Tammy Fae Bakker of *The PTL Club*, and Jimmy Swaggert became colleagues in Falwell's campaign for moral and political reform, and even Catholics and Jews were included in Falwell's embrace.[124] While there have always been a few very large churches, the increase in megachurches is a peculiarly late twentieth-century phenomenon. Utilizing the best business management practices, the allure of charismatic preachers, a smorgasbord of family-oriented recreational services, contemporary professional music, and a traditional but undemanding theology, these large churches that number their members in the thousands have sprung up across the nation since the 1970s. In a country where the average non-Catholic church attendance is 84 persons a week (Catholics average 375 in mass), approximately 50 percent of all church attendance is in the top 10 percent of congregations in size.[125] In part, the lower levels of denominational loyalty noted earlier have been fueled by the existence of these megachurches. Those who prefer this style of worship are less concerned with denominational *brand* and more concerned with the megachurch *style*. The leaders of these new congregations also proved ready allies in Falwell's cause.

Was Falwell's Moral Majority a success? If success is measured by the number of column inches and the minutes of television and radio time devoted to the discussion of the Christian Right, the Moral Majority was an unqualified success. As previously stated, the conservative and evangelical perspective dominated religious broadcasting, and in like fashion, the colorful characters leading this movement were quick to provide useful sound bites and controversial opinions. Falwell, who passed away in 2007 at the age of 74 of a heart attack in his office at the Thomas Road Baptist Church, was the primary focus of at least 16 books since 1979.[126] Ralph Reed's Christian Coalition, the successor organization to Falwell's Moral Majority, coupled the Christian Right to Karl Rove's Republican apparatus.[127]

Has the public relations victory of the Christian Right been equally overwhelming at the polls? Beginning with Ronald Reagan's elections in 1980 and 1984, and through the election of George H. W. Bush in 1988, and again in George W. Bush's elections in 2000 and 2004, the Christian Right has been quick to claim credit for each victory. In fact, advocates of this viewpoint have interpreted Bill Clinton's election in 1992 as the consequence of the financial scandals and sexual improprieties of Jim and Tammy Bakker, Jimmy Swaggert, and Oral Roberts in 1987.[128] In part a reaction to these scandals and in part evangelical disillusionment that Pat Robertson did not claim the Republican nomination in 1987, Falwell disbanded the Moral Majority in 1989, and consequently, Clinton's 1992 victory was due to the absence of organized opposition by the Christian Right. Unsurprisingly, others offer alternative interpretations.

Even though a consensus has yet to develop among religious scholars, preliminary studies seem to indicate that the influence of the Christian Right on social policy and politics is not so simply determined. Analyses of the National Election Studies indicate that with the exception of conservative and evangelical support in 1976 for the Southern Baptist candidate, Jimmy Carter, there has been no significant change in the voting patterns of white, conservative Protestants. This group comprised 20 percent of the Democratic voters in 1972 and 18 percent in 1996, and it comprised 27 percent and 30 percent of Republican voters in 1972 and 1996, respectively. In comparison, the largest change was noted among white, mainline Protestants who were 45 percent of the Republican voters in 1972 but fell significantly to only 33 percent of the Republicans in 1996.[129] Other studies also seem to support a more limited political orientation, especially during congregational activities, for white, conservative Protestants.[130] If the Christian Right has influenced national elections since 1980, it has not been by changing the pattern of voting among white conservative evangelicals.

Since the 2006 midterm elections, commentators on religion and politics have often heralded the decline of the Christian Right.[131] In general, it is clear that America's tolerance for extreme religious voices is strained. John McCain, the Republican candidate for the 2008 presidential election, rejected the endorsement of televangelists John Hagee and Rod Parsley,[132] and Barack Obama, the Democratic candidate, resigned his two-decade-long church membership over comments made by his former pastor, Jeremiah Wright.[133] Despite this trend, 3 of 10 Republican candidates for president raised their hands to indicate disbelief in evolution at the May 3, 2007, debate in Simi Valley, California.[134] One of these, Mike Huckabee, formerly governor of Arkansas and an ordained Baptist minister, garnered the second-highest delegate count for the Republican presidential nomination.

Perhaps a greater threat to the political influence of the Christian Right is developing from within. Within the ranks of conservative evangelical leaders, especially the younger generation of megachurch leaders, many have begun to question their close association with the Republican Party and the reduction of religious values to issues of personal morality such as opposition to abortion and gay marriage.[135] This growing concern among conservative evangelicals ranks with poverty, war, environmentalism, and the harsh economic consequences often associated with globalization reflect a Catholic-like interpretation of biblical themes that extend beyond the personal to issues of economic, environmental, and social justice. The extents to which issues of justice may trump issues of personal morality have yet to be determined in national elections, yet it is clear that change is in the wind.

Conclusion

Progressives initially rejoiced at Clinton's election, the first time in 16 years that a Democrat had captured the presidency. By the end of Clinton's first term, many of those same liberals were left more cautious or, in some cases, despondent because even the important policy successes of the Clinton admin-istration were tinged with conservatism. For exam-ple, he signed into law the Personal Responsibility and Work Opportunity Reconciliation Act of 1996 (PRWORA), a bill that capped public assistance ben-efits, ended Aid to Families with Dependent Children (AFDC), and eliminated recipients' entitlement to public assistance. Equally important, Section 104 of the PRWORA contained what has been called the Charitable Choice provision:

> The purpose of this section is to allow States to con-tract with religious organizations, or to allow reli-gious organizations to accept certificates, vouchers, or other forms of disbursement . . . on the same basis as any other non-governmental provider without impairing the religious character of such organiza-tions, and with diminishing the religious freedom of beneficiaries of assistance funded under such pro-gram. [Section 104(b)]

George W. Bush has been a strong advocate of Charitable Choice. As governor of Texas, he aggres-sively pursued welfare reform through a faith-based initiative as early as 1996. In his second week in office as president, he established the White House Office of Faith-Based and Community Initiatives with units in the Departments of Labor, Justice, Housing and Urban Development, Education, and Health and Human Services.[136] Executive orders expanded faith-based involvement to the Department of Agriculture and the U.S. Agency for International Development in 2002.[137] Federal fund-ing is available for faith-based organizations (FBOs) through state channels, but the states have been almost unanimous in their tepid response. "For the most part, it appears that state officials have not felt that there is a need to make substantive changes—FBOs are already active players in delivering servic-es . . . and their involvement is not a subject of con-troversy. . . ."[138] Despite a lack of significant change in state policies and procedures, nearly two-thirds of states have pursued outreach efforts to FBOs and more than half have a faith representative on welfare advisory committees. On the other hand, less than one-third of the states provide technical assistance to FBOs, fewer than one-quarter have modified pro-posal notification processes, and only two states have provided capacity building or start-up grants.[139] Federal guidelines make funding poten-tially available through Temporary Assistance for Needy Families, Welfare-to-Work, the Emergency Food and Shelter Program, the Emergency Shelter

Grant program, and the Community Development Block Grant program. Educational funding is more problematic due to a long history of Supreme Court limitations on tax support for private schools.[140] Michigan, Ohio, and Texas have been most aggres-sive in facilitating funding for FBOs, but the research to date seems to indicate that most of this funding is directed to older, established nonprofit agencies with religious roots (e.g., Catholic Charities, Catholic Social Services, Jewish Family Services, Lutheran Social Services, Salvation Army, and Young Women's Christian Association).[141] Congregations of all denominational varieties have been reluctant to pursue Charitable Choice funding. Even though more than half of all congregations provide some type of social service, primarily emer-gency food and shelter, only 3 percent receive public funds.[142] In the mainline it seems reasonable to assume that the sense of congregational participa-tion in social services has been delegated to these volunteer associations for decades; among conserva-tive evangelicals the reluctance may be due to con-cerns about government intervention.[143] Marvin Olasky was among the first to advocate for faith-based provision of social services.[144] His rationale was clear: "holistic service delivery that focuses on personal transformation and provides long-term, lasting solutions to poor people's problems" are best provided in a faith context.[145] Besides, churches were awash in well-intentioned volunteers. The problem is that neither of these assumptions are actually correct. The National Congregations Study indicates that congregation-based social services are advanced by the smallest handful of volunteers, and that these services are overwhelmingly dispensed at arm's length. "If congregations' social services are imagined to be more effective than secular social services because they are more holistic, neither quantitative nor qualitative evidence supports the idea."[146] In fact, quantitative studies are beginning to appear that suggest that FBOs underperform in comparison with public agencies.[147] Is the availabil-ity of funding likely to change the attitudes of reli-gious organizations to social services? Frankly, it is too soon to tell. The decentralized channels through which the federal monies flow has hindered the col-lection of reliable information on the recipients; out-come studies have been rare, methodologically flawed, and frequently ambiguous; and there has been a tendency for Charitable Choice to simply expand the degree of competition for access to an ever-decreasing amount of social service funding.[148]

One conclusion does seem obvious. Provision of social services through FBOs will always be limited to some extent; if not by the fluctuating availability of resources, then by the vision of church leaders and the limitations of theological perspectives. Some have already reported reluctance by those with needs to obtain help through FBOs, and others have reported apparent abuses and financial irregularities by FBOs.[149] Charitable Choice may remain a permanent part of the federal provision of social services, but it is unlikely that FBOs have the capacity and commitment to sustain comprehensive and long-term services on a level comparable to federal and state bureaucracies.

Discussion Questions

1. Since the establishment of the English Poor Laws, there has been a tendency for social welfare programs to distinguish between the "worthy needy" and those less worthy of assistance. What, if any, are the religious foundations for such a distinction? Is this distinction still evident in U.S. social welfare policies?
2. How has the Protestant work ethic affected U.S. social welfare policy? Is there any recent evidence that suggests that this theological perspective has a continuing influence today? Is it compatible with macro- and micro-level social work practice? Give specific examples to support your answer.
3. What are the causes of the division of American Protestantism into mainline and evangelical camps? Describe the form of social welfare each camp is most likely to promote.
4. The authors present religion as having an important role in the development of professional social work. Does religion continue to have a significant influence on social work policies, values, and practice? If you agree, give specific examples. If you disagree, explain how social work now differs from its religious roots with specific policy and practice examples.
5. How would social welfare policy change if the theological movements of the Protestant mainline (the Social Gospel and liberation theology) were the dominant influences?
6. Interpret the Personal Responsibility and Work Opportunity Reconciliation Act from a religious perspective. What theological orientations seem to be most evident? Which religious groups are most likely to be pleased with its provisions?
7. The authors are pessimistic that Charitable Choice and faith-based initiatives are likely to solve U.S. social welfare problems. Why would they reach this conclusion?

Notes

1. American Religion Data Archive. Retrieved November 2004, from www.thearda.com
2. "U.S. Charitable Giving Reaches $285.02 Billion in 2006." Retrieved from the Planned Giving Design Center website at www.pgdc.com/pgdc/news-story/2007/06/26/u-s-charitable-giving-reaches-295-02-billion-2006
3. Authors' conclusion based on comparison of Allied Media Corp. demographic information (at www.allied-media. com) with population statistics reported in the CIA World Factbook (at https://www.cia.gov/library/publications/the-world-factbook/index.html).
4. American Religion Data Archive. Retrieved November 2004, from www.thearda.com
5. Genesis 4:7 (New International Version).
6. Gary V. Smith, "Poor, Orphan, Widow," in *Holman Bible Dictionary* (Nashville, TN: Holman Bible Publishers, 1991), pp. 1124–1125.
7. Matthew 10:41 (New International Version).
8. Acts of the Apostles 4:32 (New International Version).
9. Howard Karger and David Stoesz, *American Social Welfare Policy: A Structural Approach*, 3rd ed. (New York: Longman, 1998), p. 34.
10. Ibid., p. 35.
11. David Rothman and Sheila Rothman (eds.), *On Their Own: The Poor in Modern America* (Reading, MA: Addison-Wesley, 1972).
12. Robert Morris, *Rethinking Social Welfare* (New York: Ketev Press, 1972), p. 143.

13. David Macarov, *The Design of Social Welfare* (New York: Holt, Rinehart and Winston, 1978).

14. Roger Finke and Rodney Stark, *The Churching of America. 1776–1990: Winners and Losers in Our Religious Economy* (New Brunswick, NJ: Rutgers University Press, 1992).

15. Nathan Edward Cohen, *Social Work in the American Tradition* (New York: Holt, Rinehart and Winston, 1958), pp. 23–24.

16. Peter W. Williams, *American's Religions: From Their Origins to the Twenty-First Century* (Urbana, IL: University of Illinois Press, 2002), pp. 181–190.

17. Finke and Stark, *The Churching of America*, p. 16.

18. Ibid., p. 55.

19. Sydney E. Ahlstrom, *A Religious History of the American People* (New Haven, CT: Yale University Press, 1972), pp. 423–425.

20. Ibid., p. 426.

21. James Morone, *Hellfire Nation* (New York: Knopf, 2001), pp. 311–317.

22. Ibid., p. 189.

23. Ibid., p. 25.

24. Ibid., pp. 186–189.

25. Ibid., pp. 159–168.

26. Ahlstrom, *A Religious History*, pp. 432–435.

27. Ibid., p. 659.

28. Ibid., pp. 659–668.

29. Quoted in Ahlstrom, *A Religious History*, p. 681.

30. Quoted in Walter Trattner, *From Poor Law to Welfare State* (New York: Free Press, 1974), p. 62.

31. Ahlstrom, *A Religious History*, p. 680.

32. Trattner, *From Poor Law to Welfare State*, p. 63.

33. Ibid., p. 87.

34. Ahlstrom, *A Religious History*, pp. 694–695.

35. Peter J. Thuesen, "The Logic of Mainline Churches: Historical Background since the Reformation," in Robert Wuthnow and John H. Evans (eds.), *The Quiet Hand of God: Faith-Based Activism and the Public Role of Mainline Protestantism* (Berkeley, CA: University of California Press), p. 37.

36. Ahlstrom, *A Religious History*, pp. 707–709.

37. Finke and Stark, *The Churching of America*, p. 139.

38. Thuesen, "The Logic of Mainline Churches," p. 35.

39. Ibid., p. 35.

40. June Axinn and Herman Levin, *Social Welfare* (New York: Dodd, Mead, 1975), p. 129.

41. Charles Darwin, *On the Origin of Species by Means of Natural Selection* (London: John Murray, 1859).

42. See Herbert Spencer, *An Autobiography*, 2 vols. (New York: D. Appleton, 1904); William Graham Sumner, *Social Darwinism* (Englewood Cliffs, NJ: Prentice Hall, 1963); and Richard Hofstadter, *Social Darwinism in American Thought* (Boston: Beacon Press, 1959).

43. Spencer, *An Autobiography*, p. 186.

44. Robert Morris and Michael Freund (eds.), *Trends and Issues in Jewish Social Welfare in the United States,* *1899–1952* (Philadelphia: The Jewish Publication Society of America, 1966), p. 15.

45. Charles Howard Hopkins, *The Rise of the Social Gospel in American Protestantism, 1865–1915* (New Haven, CT: Yale University Press, 1940).

46. Ibid.

47. Henry F. May, *Protestant Churches in Industrial America* (New York: Octagon Books, 1963).

48. Howard Jacob Karger, *The Sentinels of Order: A Study of Social Control and the Minneapolis Settlement House Movement, 1915–1950* (Lanham, MD: University Press of America, 1987).

49. R. G. Clouse, "Views of the Millennium," *Evangelical Dictionary of Theology* (Grand Rapids, MI: Baker Book House, 1984), p. 714.

50. Ahlstrom, *A Religious History*, pp. 802–804.

51. C. T. McIntire, "The Fundamentals," *Evangelical Dictionary of Theology* (Grand Rapids, MI: Baker Book House, 1984), p. 436.

52. Clouse, "Views of the Millennium," p. 717.

53. George M. Marsden, *Fundamentalism and American Culture: The Shaping of Twentieth Century Evangelicalism, 1870–1925* (New York: Oxford University Press, 1980).

54. Macarov, *The Design of Social Welfare*.

55. Roy Lubove, *The Professional Altruist: The Emergence of Social Work as a Career, 1880–1930* (New York: Atheneum Books, 1975).

56. Robert Bremner, *From the Depths: The Discovery of Poverty in the United States* (New York: New York University Press, 1956).

57. David Montgomery, *Workers' Control in America* (Cambridge, UK: Cambridge University Press, 1979).

58. Ibid.

59. Lubove, *The Professional Altruist*, pp. 1–21.

60. Ibid., p. 14.

61. Axinn and Levin, *Social Welfare*, p. 100.

62. Hofstadter, *The Age of Reform*, p. 211.

63. Ibid., p. 92.

64. H. L. Weissman, "Settlements and Community Centers," *Encyclopedia of Social Work*, 18th ed. (Silver Spring, MD: NASW Press, 1987), p. 21.

65. Mary Richmond, *Social Diagnosis* (New York: Russell Sage Foundation, 1917).

66. Maryann Syers, "Abraham Flexner," *Encyclopedia of Social Work*, 18th ed. (Silver Spring, MD: NASW Press, 1987), p. 923.

67. Ahlstrom, *A Religious History*, pp. 895–917.

68. Clark Chambers, *Seedtime of Reform* (Ann Arbor, MI: University of Michigan Press, 1967), p. 211.

69. Ahlstrom, *A Religious History*, pp. 939–943.

70. Ibid., p. 909.

71. President Franklin Pierce quoted in Trattner, *From Poor Law to Welfare State*, p. 62.

72. Cohen, *Social Work in the American Tradition*, p. 169.

73. Chester Gillis, *Roman Catholicism in America* (New York: Columbia University Press, 1999), p. 72.
74. Biographical information from *Encyclopedia of Social Work,* 18th ed.
75. Finke and Stark, *The Churching of America,* pp. 66–71.
76. Dean M. Kelley, *Why Conservative Churches Are Growing* (New York: Harper and Row, 1972), pp. 95–96.
77. Finke and Stark, *The Churching of America,* p. 254.
78. Ibid., p. 255.
79. Ibid., p. 55.
80. Ibid., p. 161.
81. Ibid., p. 146.
82. Ibid., p. 248.
83. Ahlstrom, *A Religious History,* p. 942.
84. Patrick Allitt, *Religion in America since 1945: A History* (New York: Columbia University Press, 2003), pp. 48, 149.
85. Ahlstrom, *A Religious History,* p. 912.
86. D. R. Kelly, "John Gresham Machen," *Evangelical Dictionary of Theology* (Grand Rapids, MI: Baker Book House, 1984), pp. 673–674.
87. Ahlstrom, *A Religious History,* p. 958.
88. Allitt, *Religion in America since 1945,* p. 26.
89. Finke and Starke, *The Churching of America,* pp. 218–219.
90. Allitt, *Religion in America since 1945,* p. 13.
91. Ibid., p. 223.
92. Ibid.
93. Christian Broadcasting Network. Retrieved October 2004, from www.cbn.com
94. Trinity Broadcasting Network. Retrieved October 2004, from www.tbn.org/index.php/3/18.html
95. Ahlstrom, *A Religious History,* pp. 928–930.
96. Ibid., p. 151.
97. Allitt, *Religion in America since 1945,* p. 23.
98. Williams, *America's Religions,* p. 416.
99. Robert Wuthnow, *The Restructuring of American Religion: Society and Faith since World War II* (Princeton, NJ: Princeton University Press, 1988), p. 88.
100. Williams, *America's Religions,* p. 181.
101. The New York Public Library, *American History Desk Reference* (New York: MacMillan, 1997), p. 415.
102. See Allitt, *Religion in America since 1945,* p. 181; and New York Public Library, *American History Desk Reference,* p. 410.
103. Allitt, *Religion in America since 1945,* pp. 321–322, 356.
104. Allitt, *Religion in America since 1945,* p. 75.
105. David L. Chappell, *A Stone of Hope: Prophetic Religion and the Death of Jim Crow* (Chapel Hill, NC: University of North Carolina Press, 2004), pp. 12–18.
106. Allitt, *Religion in America since 1945,* pp. 47–48.
107. Chappell, *A Stone of Hope,* pp. 26–43.
108. Ibid., p. 87.
109. Michael B. Katz, *The Undeserving Poor: From the War on Poverty to the War on Welfare* (New York: Pantheon Books, 1989), p. 80.
110. New York Public Library, *American History Desk Reference,* pp. 112–113.
111. Charles Schottland, "Wilbur Joseph Cohen: Some Recollections," *Social Work* 32, no. 5 (September/October 1987), pp. 371–372.
112. Katz, *The Undeserving Poor,* pp. 113–114.
113. Finke and Stark, *The Churching of America,* pp. 255–261.
114. Williams, *America's Religions,* pp. 352–356.
115. See Gustavo Gutierrez, *A Theology of Liberatio* (Maryknoll, NY: Orbis, 1973). Quoted in D. D. Webster, "Liberation Theology," *Evangelical Dictionary of Theology* (Grand Rapids, MI: Baker Book House, 1984), p. 636.
116. Brian Steensland, "The Hydra and the Swords," in Robert Wuthnow and John H. Evans (eds.), *The Quiet Hand of God: Faith-Based Activism and the Public Role of Mainline Protestantism* (Berkeley, CA: University of California Press), p. 214.
117. Ibid., pp. 215–217.
118. Ibid., pp. 217–218.
119. Quoted in Finke and Stark, *The Churching of America,* p. 224.
120. Quoted in Allitt, *Religion in America since 1945,* p. 151.
121. "Moral Majority," *The Columbia Encyclopedia.* Retrieved November 2004, from www.bartleby.com/65/e-/E-MoralMajo.html
122. Williams, *America's Religions,* pp. 359–360.
123. Finke and Stark, *The Churching of America,* pp. 187–198.
124. Allitt, *Religion in America since 1945,* p. 153.
125. U.S. Congregational Life Survey, 2001. Retrieved November 2004, from www.uscongregations.org/myths.htm
126. Authors count of title available in subject search on Amazon.com on December 7, 2004.
127. E. J. Dionne, Jr., *Souled Out: Reclaiming Faith and Politics After the Religious Right* (Princeton, NJ: Princeton University Press, 2008), p. 91.
128. Allitt, *Religion in America since 1945,* pp. 194–195.
129. Jeff Manza and Clem Brooks, "The Changing Political Fortunes of Mainline Protestants," in Robert Wuthnow and John H. Evans (eds.), *The Quiet Hand of God: Faith-Based Activism and the Public Role of Mainline Protestantism* (Berkeley, CA: University of California Press), pp. 163–167.
130. Mark Chaves, *Congregations in America* (Cambridge, MA: Harvard University Press, 2004), pp. 94–126.
131. For examples, see Dionne, *Souled Out;* Amy Sulivan, *The Party Faithful: How and Why Democrats Are Closing the God Gap* (New York: Scribner, 2008); Jim Wallis, *The Great Awakening: Reviving Faith and*

Politics in a Post-Religious Right America (New York: HarperCollins, 2008); and Christine Wicker, *The Fall of the Evangelical Nation: The Surprising Crisis Inside the Church* (New York: HarperCollins, 2008).

132. Neela Banerjee and Michael Luo, "McCain Cuts Ties to Pastors Whose Talks Drew Fire," *New York Times* (May 23, 2008).

133. Michael Powell, "Following Months of Criticism, Obama Quits His Church," *New York Times* (June 1, 2008).

134. Katherine Q. Seelye, "At G.O.P. Debate, Candidates Play to Conservatives," *New York Times* (May 5, 2007).

135. David D. Kirkpatrick, "The Evangelical Crackup," *New York Times* (October 7, 2007).

136. Ram A. Cnaan and Stephanie C. Boddie, "Charitable Choice and Faith-Based Welfare: A Call for Social Work," *Social Work* 47, no. 3 (July 2002), p. 225.

137. Lisa M. Montiel, "The Use of Public Funds for Delivery of Faith-Based Human Services." The Roundtable on Religion and Social Welfare Policy, 2003, p. 18. Retrieved December 2004, from www.religionandsocialpolicy.org

138. Mark Ragan, Lisa M. Montiel, and David J. Wright, "Scanning the Policy Environment for Faith-Based Social Services in the United States." The Roundtable on Religion and Social Welfare Policy, 2003, p. 18. Retrieved December 2004, from www.religionandsocialpolicy.org

139. Ibid., p. 11.

140. Montiel, "The Use of Public Funds," pp. 4–11.

141. Ibid., p. 13.

142. Chaves, *Congregations in America*, p. 66.

143. Dave Donaldson and Stanley Carlson-Thies, *A Revolution of Compassion: Faith-Based Groups as Full Partners in Fighting America's Social Problems* (Grand Rapids, MI: Baker Books, 2003).

144. Marvin Olasky, *The Tragedy of American Compassion* (Washington, DC: Regnery Gateway, 1992).

145. Chaves, *Congregations in America*, p. 58.

146. Ibid., p. 65.

147. S. S. Kennedy and W. Bielefeld, *Charitable Choice at Work: Evaluating Faith-Based Job Programs in the States* (Washington, DC: Georgetown University Press, 2006).

148. See Montiel, "The Use of Public Funds," p. 22; Jason D. Scott, "The Scope and Scale of Faith-Based Social Services," The Roundtable on Religion and Social Welfare Policy, 2003, retrieved December 2004, from www.socialpolicyandreligion.org/docs/bibliographies/9-4-2002_scope_and_scale.pdf; and Byron R. Johnson, "Objective Hope: Assessing the Effectiveness of Faith-Based Organizations: A Review of the Literature," Center for Research on Religion and Urban Civil Society, 2002, retrieved December 2004, from www.manhattan-institute.org/pdf/crrucs_objective_hope.pdf

149. See Robert Wuthnow, Conrad Hackett, and Becky Yang Hsu, "The Effectiveness and Trustworthiness of Faith-Based and Other Service Organizations: A Study of Recipients' Perceptions," *Journal for the Scientific Study of Religion* 43, no. 1, 1–17; and Texas Freedom Network, "The Texas Faith-Based Initiative at Five Years: Warning Signs as President Bush Expands Texas-Style Program to National Level," 2002, retrieved December 2004, from www.tfn.org/site/PageServer?pagename=faithbased

CHAPTER 4

Discrimination in American Society

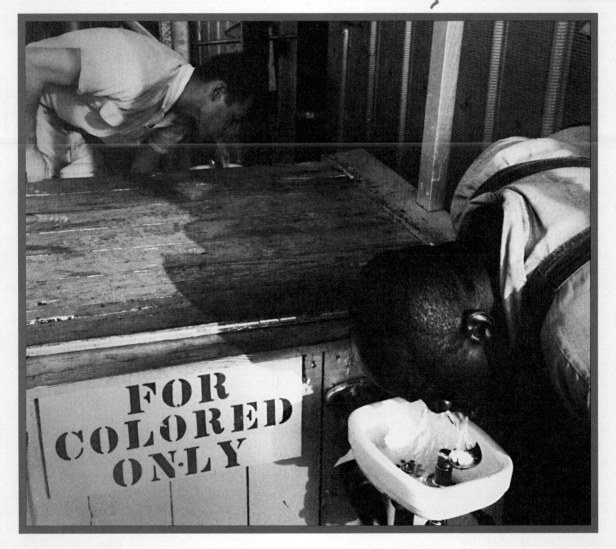

*D*iscrimination and poverty are inextricably linked to the fabric of U.S. social welfare. Economic, social, and political discrimination often leads to poverty, which, in turn, results in the need for income maintenance and other social programs. Realizing that discrimination leads to poverty, some policymakers have tried to address this cycle by attacking discrimination. These policymakers hope that if discriminatory practices and attitudes are curtailed, the result will be equal opportunities for achievement and success. This chapter probes discrimination based on race, gender, sexual orientation, disability, and age.

Discrimination

The causes of discrimination in U.S. society are complex. A range of literature explores the motives for discrimination. Broken down, the main theories fall into three broad categories: psychological, normative-cultural, and economic.

Psychological interpretations attempt to explain discrimination in terms of intrapsychic variables.[1] A theory called the frustration-aggression hypothesis, formulated by J. Dollard, maintains that discrimination is a form of aggression activated when individual needs become frustrated.[2] Dollard argues that when people cannot direct their aggression at the real sources of their rage, they seek a substitute target. Thus, relatively weak minority groups become an easy and safe target for the aggression and frustration of slightly stronger discontented groups. For example, poor Southern whites have been viewed as an outwardly racist group. Exploited by the rigid economic and social class system of the old South, they often focused their rage on African Americans, a group even weaker than themselves. African Americans therefore served a twin purpose for poor whites: On the one hand, they formed a lower socioeconomic group, making poor whites feel better about their own standing; on the other, they were scapegoats for the frustrations of poor whites. Women, racial minorities, homosexuals, and other disenfranchised groups often serve the same purpose for those on a slightly higher social rung.

Another psychological approach, the "authoritarian personality" theory developed by Theodore Adorno and other psychoanalysts, posited that discriminatory behavior is determined by personality traits that involve a reaction to authority.[3] Persons who exhibit the traits of irrationality, rigidity, conformity, xenophobia, and so forth are more likely to discriminate against minorities than are people lacking those traits. Other authors, such as Wilhelm Reich, argued that discriminatory attitudes arise from a sense of insecurity, self-hatred, deep-seated fears, and unresolved childhood needs and frustrations.[4]

The normative-cultural explanation suggests that individuals hold prejudicial attitudes because of their socialization. That is, through both overt and covert messages, a society teaches discrimination and rewards those who conform to prevailing attitudes and behaviors. Because of strong societal pressures to conform to established norms, resistance to discriminatory practices becomes difficult.[5] For example, special opprobrium in the old South was reserved for liberal whites who broke the norms governing interactions with African Americans. Often, societies are more tolerant of outsiders who break the norms than they are of insiders who "betray" the group. This theory suggests that as social and institutional norms that support discriminatory practices change, individual attitudes will follow suit.

One economic theory contends that dominant groups discriminate to maintain their economic and political advantages. For example, male workers may discriminate against female workers because they perceive them as encroaching on their employment prospects. These males may fear they will be replaced by a female worker at lower wages. Employers may promote discriminatory attitudes because as long as women workers are stigmatized, they will command a lower salary and are thereby a cheap labor pool. In that sense, contemporary racial tensions in U.S. society can be understood partly as reflecting the employment advancements made by minority groups. A Marxian analysis views discrimination as economically useful to the capitalist class. Specifically, capitalism requires an unskilled labor pool willing to take the jobs rejected by economically better-off groups.

By pitting stigmatized groups against each other, employers can suppress wage demands and force wage concessions by threatening to replace relatively well-paid employees with lower-paid workers from a disenfranchised group. Paradoxically, the lower economic status of disenfranchised groups increases their value to the economic order. Simply put, discrimination partly determines who will flip the burgers and supersize the drinks.

To maintain an air of legitimacy, discrimination must have moral, social, and theological underpinnings. To that end, some have used the Bible to explain the inferiority of women, the "sin" of homosexuality, and the necessity of separating the races. To augment or replace biblical interpretations, spurious scientific explanations have been developed, such as Social Darwinism and pseudoanthropological treatises around the attributes of stigmatized groups. For example, some people maintain that menstrual cycles cause severe mood swings that make women incapable of holding positions of power. Others believe that African Americans are descended from Ham and have therefore committed biblical sins that justify discrimination. Some members of the Ku Klux Klan claim that African Americans are racially inferior based on theories grounded in shaky anthropological research supported by dubious intelligence testing. Some white supremacist groups believe that Jews are descendants of Satan and that the "true Israelites" (i.e., the lost tribes of Israel) are Aryans. These stereotypes have little to do with reality. Moreover, it is unimaginable that skinheads or those living in white supremacist enclaves represent the hope of the white race or are the "true Israelites." Without the legitimation offered by moral, religious, social, and "scientific" sources, discrimination devoid of social validity becomes naked exploitation.

Social stigma and discrimination can lead to the transformation of disenfranchised groups into a lower socioeconomic class. Alternatively, as in the case of gays, lesbians, and the aged, social stigma and discrimination can result in social marginalization without triggering statistically observable economic discrimination. For example, although the individual incomes of gays and lesbians (and the assets of the elderly) are higher than the national averages, people in these groups often experience economic discrimination in the form of restricted career choices, including forced occupational clustering, limited access to upper managerial positions, discrimination in hiring practices, forced retirement, and so forth. The following sections will examine some core components of discrimination and social stigma, including racism, sexism, homophobia, ageism, and discrimination against people with disabilities.

Racism

Federal and state governments often accumulate data based on dividing U.S. society along the lines of whites and people of color. Today, however, clumping white Americans into a single category is as misleading as not understanding the important cultural differences among people of color. For example, in 1850 it was relatively easy to describe white Americans; in all probability they were Protestant and of Anglo-Saxon or Teutonic backgrounds. But after the Civil War, vast numbers of immigrants began to arrive from southern and central Europe. They were not Protestant, they were not Anglo-Saxon, and they had different languages and cultures from those who preceded them. About 200 million Americans can trace at least some of their ancestry back to the following groups (in descending size order): English, German, Irish, French, Italian, Scottish, Polish, Dutch, Swedish, Norwegian, Russian, Czech, Slovakian, Hungarian, Welsh, Danish, and Portuguese.[6] In addition, while some white Americans have an Hispanic surname, they have no Hispanic cultural memory. This is complicated by a large migration of those from Arabic-speaking countries, who even though they may experience discrimination, are classified as white. Although most white groups have generally assimilated into American culture, many still maintain some of the characteristics of their predecessors. Not surprisingly, the field of white studies has been studied at schools like the University of California at Berkeley, Northwestern University, Harvard University, and the University of Massachusetts.[7]

Throughout U.S. history, whites have been in the majority. But according to Census Bureau projections, this is rapidly changing. Although whites represented about 67 percent of the population in 2005, their growth is slowing because of low birth rates and high rates of immigration. By 2050 whites will make up only 50 percent of the population with minority groups expected to account for the other half of the population. The Census Bureau projects that between 2004 and 2050, Asians and Hispanics will see the most dramatic increases, as the U.S. population grows by almost 50 percent to reach 420 million.[8] A good deal of social history in the next several decades will demonstrate how the United

States addresses this changing demography and whether it will result in greater equality. Regardless, major social institutions will be transformed because of this demographic shift.

Racism refers to discrimination against and prejudicial treatment of a racially different minority group. This prejudicial treatment may take the form of differential hiring and firing practices and promotions, differential resource allocations in health care and education, a two-tier transportation system, segregated housing policies, discriminatory behavior of judicial and law enforcement agencies, or stereotypical and prejudicial media images. A pattern of racial discrimination that is strongly entrenched in a society is called *institutional racism*.

The Minority Middle Class

The Census Bureau has no official definition of the middle class. Although the idea of "middle class" is central to American life, there is no official definition of what constitutes the middle class and no reliable income figure that connotes a middle-class lifestyle. Consequently, the middle class has come to represent a large portion of the U.S. population with incomes between 200 percent of the federal poverty threshold and those in the nation's top 5 percent of income earners. Some analysts classify households with total annual incomes between $40,000 and $140,000 as middle class.[9] Other analysts categorize middle-class families as having annual incomes between $25,000 and $75,000. Still others use annual incomes of $50,000 as a marker. Middle-class incomes are also not adjusted geographically or by an urban/rural designation. In short, the designation of "middle class" has become virtually meaningless given the enormous income spread and the failure to adjust income levels to high- and low-cost regions.

Despite these definitional problems, the minority middle class is nearly invisible to the general public partly because of the intense (and generally negative) attention paid to poor urban populations. Debates about public assistance, child welfare, crime, school dropout rates, teenage pregnancy, and drug use are almost always directed toward the poor. Almost 25 percent of Hispanics and African Americans live below the poverty line, so this attention is not wholly unwarranted. However, social researchers rarely focus on the other three-fourths who are solidly middle or upper class. As a result, social researchers have relatively little information on who makes up the minority middle class and what their lives are really like.

spotlight 4.1

The Minority Middle Class

Minority groups have made concrete gains in entering the middle class. African Americans, for example, have not only improved their socioeconomic position in recent years, but they have done so at a relatively faster rate than whites. One of the most noticeable gains has been in the area of professional employment. There is a variety of media outlets that offer business and financial information to the African American community. One of these outlets is *Black Enterprise* magazine, which has been in existence since 1970. The magazine provides information on financial management, entrepreneurship, and careers to professionals, corporative executives, entrepreneurs, and decision makers. To learn more about *Black Enterprise*, visit its website at **www.blackenterprise.com**.

The Hispanic population has also experienced important economic successes. Hispanics have achieved impressive gains in household income, educational attainment, and homeownership. *Hispanic Business* magazine, a publication of Hispanic Business Incorporated, provides current business-related news, covers the growth of the U.S. Hispanic market, economic trends within the Americas, best business practices, and career development opportunities. To learn more about *Hispanic Business*, visit its website at **www.hispanicbusiness.com**.

Minority groups have made concrete gains in joining the middle class. Many African Americans have not only improved their socioeconomic position in recent years, but they have done so at a relatively faster rate than whites, a trend especially pronounced in the 1990s. The most noticeable gains have occurred in the areas of professional employment, incomes (including two-earner family incomes), higher education, and home ownership. For example, the number of black professionals increased from 3.3 million in 2001 to over 4 million in 2004, with the percentage of black full-time workers earning over $75,000 a year increasing from 4.4 percent to 5.7 percent.[10] The black median family income in 2002 was $29,177; nearly one-third of all African American families reported total income in 2001 of $50,000 or more (for African American married couples it was nearly 52 percent). On the other hand, per capita income for African Americans decreased 1 percent between 2002 and 2003 to $15,775.[11]

The number of black-owned businesses in 2002 increased by more than 370,000, or 45 percent, since 1997 (the nation's total number of firms increased by 10 percent between 1997 and 2002 to 23 million).[12] Partly resulting from increased

incomes, blacks recorded a 47 percent increase in home ownership during the 1970s compared to 30 percent for whites.[13] In 2007, 47.2 percent of black households owned their own homes.[14]

In 2004, over 80 percent of blacks aged 25 and over were high school graduates, and close to 18 percent had a bachelor's degree or higher.[15] By 2006, over 4 million African Americans had an advanced degree.[16] There is now no statistical difference in high school graduation rates between whites and blacks. A slightly higher percentage of black women than men aged 25 and over have at least a bachelor's degree (19 versus 18 percent).[17] By 2002–2004, there had been dramatic gains in the percentage of black high school graduate students attending college, increasing to 41 percent.[18]

The Hispanic population has also experienced important economic successes. The percentage of Hispanics living in poverty decreased from 29 percent in 1996 to 20 percent by 2006, while just over one-quarter of all Hispanic families earned between $50,000 and $100,000 in 2006. Hispanic high-income-earning families have done especially well. In 1986, only 5.9 percent of all Hispanic households had incomes of over $100,000 (2006 adjusted dollars), however by 2006 this had nearly

African Americans have made significant gains in professional employment.

doubled to 10.5 percent.[19] In 2006, 53 percent of *all* Hispanic households were owned.[20] Much of this economic growth was fueled by Hispanic business formation, which increased 39 percent from 1992 to 1997.

Much of the recent growth of the minority middle class has resulted from the prosperity of the middle 1990s, but this may be changing. The 2006 Census Bureau reported the real median income in the United States climbed between 2005 and 2006, reaching $48,200. Asian households had the highest median income ($64,200), followed by non-Hispanic whites ($52,400), Hispanic ($37,800), and black households ($32,000).[21] While, as previously mentioned, Hispanic households at the higher end of the earnings scale have been doing increasingly well over recent years, the percentage of those at the lower end of the scale, below $25,000, has remained the same since 2000, at around 30 percent.[22]

African Americans

The Demography of African Americans

The nation's African American population was estimated in 2008 to be 40.2 million (13.4 percent of the total U.S. population), an increase of half a million residents from just one year earlier.[23] According to projections, the African American population may increase to 61 million by 2050, a 50 percent rise. The black population is largely young, with almost 33 percent under age 18. This compares with 23 percent of the white population. In 2002, the median African American age was 30, five years younger than the U.S. population as a whole. Eight percent of African Americans were 65 years old and over versus 14 percent of whites.[24]

African Americans are concentrated in the South (55 percent) and are also more likely to live in metro areas (87.5 percent) than are whites (78 percent). More than 52 percent of African Americans live in central or inner cities. The 10 states with the largest African American populations in 2007 were New York (3.5 million), Florida (3.0 million), Texas (2.9 million), Georgia (2.6 million), California (2.7 million), Illinois and North Carolina (2.0 million each), Maryland (1.7 million), Virginia (1.6 million), Michigan (1.5 million), and Ohio (1.5 million).[25]

African Americans in Poverty

After dropping in the mid-1990s, the number of poor African Americans rose from 8.1 million in 2001 to 8.9 million in 2002, and their poverty rate increased from 22.7 to 23.9 percent. African American families with a female householder (no husband present) experienced a drop in both the number and percentage of families who were poor: 1.4 million and 35 percent in 2001, down from 1.5 million and 39.3 percent in 2000. Although the 2001 poverty rate for African Americans was 22.7 percent (or 8.1 million people), it represented the lowest rate since the Census Bureau began collecting poverty data in 1959.[26] By 2007, the African American poverty rate had increased to 24.3 percent.

The "Diswelfare" of African Americans

History was made on November 4, 2008 when Barack Obama was elected as the first African American president in U.S. history. Indeed, Barack Obama was the first black person elected to head any Western democracy. It was a watershed not only for the United States but for the world. Despite this important victory, intense problems continue to exist in the African American community.

Millions of African Americans have not seen positive changes in their living conditions; instead, they have experienced significant erosion in living standards. The effects of discrimination are illustrated by key socioeconomic indicators in the areas of poverty, family structure, African American businesses, labor force participation and income, crime, housing, health, education, and welfare dependency.

Poverty Despite a drop in the mid-1990s (and a rise in the early 2000s), black poverty rates continue to be much higher than those for non-Hispanic whites. Some 8 percent of whites were poor in 2002, a rate less than one-third that of blacks. Similarly, median household income in 2003 was more than 38 percent higher for non-Hispanic whites than for blacks.

Family Structure In 2002, 48 percent of African American families were married couples, 43 percent of families were single female–headed households, and 9 percent were maintained by men only. African American families are larger than non-Hispanic white families: 20 percent had five or more members in contrast to 12 percent of white families. (Larger family sizes result in lower per capita income.) Thirty-six percent of African American children resided with both parents in 1998. In 2002, 30 percent (1.1 million) of all children living in a grandparent's home were African American.[27]

African American Businesses Black-owned businesses grew 46 percent between 1987 and 1992, receipts in these businesses constituted only 1 percent of total U.S. business receipts in 1992. Receipts for black-owned firms averaged $52,000 per firm, compared with $193,000 for all U.S. firms. Overall, the annual combined revenue of the 25 largest U.S. black-owned businesses in 2002 was only $7.8 billion.[28]

Labor Force Participation and Income Discrimination continues in the areas of employment and wages. Although laws and regulations addressing employment racial discrimination have had some success, they have not adequately prevented widespread discrimination against African Americans. The Urban Institute compared the experiences of comparable African American and white male job seekers. Using hiring audits, the study found that black applicants were subject to unfavorable treatment during the application process 20 percent of the time, compared with 7 percent for white applicants. Unfavorable treatment included (1) not advancing to the next level of the hiring process, (2) encountering more questions or resistance before receiving an application form, (3) being steered toward less desirable positions than white

counterparts, (4) being forced to wait longer for interviews, (5) receiving only cursory interviews, (6) hearing discouraging or derogatory remarks, and (7) being turned down for a position when it was offered to a white applicant.[29]

Despite the narrowing of some important economic indicators, the unemployment rate for blacks is still almost twice that of whites. The national employment rate stood at about 5.4 percent in mid-2004, but the black adult unemployment rate was 10.4 percent, and among black teenagers it was 37 percent.[30]

Discrimination influences income, and not surprisingly, the narrowest income gap is found between blacks and whites without a high school diploma. The more education, the greater is the income gap. In 2005, white males with a master's degree earned $80,145 a year; African American males, $61,084. This $19,061 translates into a salary differential of almost 24 percent. In varying degrees, the same salary gap is evident between minority and white women. (See Table 4.1.)

Jared Bernstein offers several explanations for the African American wage gap, including discrimination in employment (aided by the lax enforcement of antidiscrimination laws); more frequent employment in vulnerable sectors of the labor economy; a combination of regional, industrial, and occupational choices; lower rates of overall unionization; and the general erosion of worker rights.[31]

Table 4.1

2005 Median Salary and Educational Attainment for Workers Age 18 and Over

	Asian		White		African American		Hispanic	
	Men	Women	Men	Women	Men	Women	Men	Women
No H.S. Diploma	26,090	21,833	25,011	18,563	23,431	19,036	21,897	16,894
H.S. Grad	30,295	24,485	36,518	26,899	27,833	23,933	26,866	22,413
Some College	36,052	30,608	42,276	31,619	36,021	30,061	35,131	28,602
Assoc. Arts Degree	36,877	38,383	48,042	35,039	43,129	31,736	40,143	31,699
BA Degree	56,578	43,280	61,859	43,138	46,083	45,314	49,992	37,796
Master's Degree	80,641	65,086	80,145	53,493	61,084	53,663	62,557	53,030
PhD	100,000+	NA*	92,188	71,113	NA	NA	NA	NA
Prof. Degree	100,000+	NA	100,000+	85,928	NA	NA	70,166	NA

*NA = The sample size was too small for accurate calculation.

Source: Adapted from American Council on Education (ACE), Center for Policy Analysis, *ACE Fact Sheet on Higher Education* (Washington, DC: American Council on Education, February 2007).

Another explanation suggests that as middle-class African Americans advance, greater unemployment occurs among those with less education and skills. But this explanation does not address the large African American/white unemployment differential among college-educated men, a disparity greater in central cities of the East and North. According to Franklin Wilson, the cause of this discrepancy can be found in two factors: (1) the decline during the 1980s in the number of jobs traditionally filled by college-educated African American men (e.g., public sector jobs dealing with affirmative action, social welfare, and criminal justice); and (2) the inability of educated African Americans to penetrate the professional/technical occupations that entail managerial or supervisory responsibilities. Also, any cutbacks in federal and state governments are likely to exacerbate the income differential of African Americans, because one of the major middle-class employment opportunities is in the governmental sector. Regardless of the causes, African Americans continue to earn less than whites, irrespective of household composition, education, region, or religion.

Crime In 2007, 2.3 million people were held in federal or state prisons or in local jails in the United States. The annual growth rate of people incarcerated in the United States between 2000 and 2006 was 2.6 percent. There were 773 white male sentenced prisoners per 100,000 white males, and there were 4,618 black male sentenced prisoners per 100,000 black males.[32] The lifetime likelihood of going to state or federal prison for blacks is about twice that of Hispanics and five times more than for whites. Based on rates of first incarceration, about 32 percent of black males will enter state or federal prison during their lifetime, compared to 17 percent of Hispanic males and 5.9 percent of white males.[33] In 2004, an estimated 12 percent of black males in prison were in their late twenties compared to 3.6 percent of Hispanics and 1.7 percent of whites. Black males in their twenties and thirties are found to have higher rates of incarceration with an estimated 576,600 black males aged between 20 and 39 incarcerated.[34] Moreover, the racial composition of the 3,517 people on death row in 2003 was 46 percent white, 42 percent African American, and 10 percent Latino. Given that African Americans make up only 13 percent of the U.S. population, they are overrepresented on death row by more than three times their number in the population.[35]

Blacks were six times more likely than whites to be murdered in 2002.[36] Although the homicide rate for black males in the United States has fallen in recent years, the rate remains unacceptably high. Black males 18 to 24 years old have the highest homicide rates. Compared to the next highest rates, their rates are more than three times the rates of black males 14 to 17 years old, and four times the rates of black males age 25 and older. In Washington, DC, 1 in 12 black 15-year-old males (about 8 percent) will be murdered before age 45. By comparison, the death rate for U.S. soldiers serving in the military during World War II was 2.5 percent; during World War I, it was 2.4 percent; and during the Vietnam War, 1.2 percent.[37]

Housing Housing patterns reflect the economic gulf between African Americans and whites. Minority (African American, Hispanic, and Native American) households are both poorer and more likely to be renters than white households. The home ownership rate in 2007 for whites was 68 percent, for Hispanic or Latino households this was 50 percent, and for African American households this was 47 percent.[38] About one in five non-Hispanic white married couples who rent can qualify to buy a modestly priced home compared with only 1 in 20 black married couples. Similarly, about 82 percent of non-Hispanic white married-couple homeowners could afford to relocate to a modestly priced home in the area in which they lived, but only 66 percent of black married-couple owners could. Hispanic married-couple homeowners could only afford to purchase a different modestly priced home 58 percent of the time, compared with 81 percent for non-Hispanic married-couple homeowners.[39]

Health The effects of racism are also evident in health issues. In 2002, the black infant mortality rate in the United States was 13.6 per 1,000 live births, more than twice that of whites (5.7 deaths). Taken by itself, the U.S. black infant mortality rate ranks high internationally (see Table 4.2). The rate of sudden infant death syndrome (SIDS) among African Americans was 113.5 deaths per 100,000 live infant births in 2001 compared to 45.6 for whites. In 2005, black men were nearly seven times higher than white men to be diagnosed with HIV, and black women more than 20 times that of white women.[40] Not surprisingly, life expectancy is lower for African Americans. In 2006, black males had a life expectancy of 70 years compared to 76 years for

Table 4.2

**Infant Mortality Rates and Ranks: Selected Countries, 2007
(Deaths per 1,000 Live Births)**

Rank	Country	Rank	Rank	Country	Rank
1	Singapore	2.3	19	South Korea	6.1
2	Sweden	2.8	20	Israel	6.8
3	Japan	3.2	*	United States (overall)	6.8
4	Finland	3.5	21	Cyprus	6.9
5	Germany	4.1	22	Poland	7.1
6	France	4.2	23	Slovakia	7.1
7	Spain	4.3	24	Hungary	8.2
8	Switzerland	4.3	25	Chile	8.4
9	Austria	4.5	*	United States (American Indian)	8.5
10	Denmark	4.5			
11	Australia	4.6	26	Costa Rica	9.5
12	Canada	4.6	27	Russia	11.1
*	United States (Asian and Pacific Islander)	4.7	*	United States (black)	13.3
			28	Panama	16.0
13	Portugal	4.9	29	Sri Lanka	19.5
14	United Kingdom	5.0	30	Mexico	19.6
15	Ireland	5.2	31	Albania	20.0
16	Greece	5.3	32	Venezuela	20.9
17	Italy	5.7	33	China	22.1
18	New Zealand	5.7	34	Ecuador	22.1
*	United States (white only)	5.7	35	Brazil	27.6

Sources: Adapted from Central Intelligence Agency, *The World Factbook, Rank Order—Infant Mortality Rate* (April 15, 2008). Retrieved April 2008, from www.cia.gov/library/publications/the-world-factbook/rankorder/2091rank.html; U.S. Census Bureau, International Database, "Life Expectancy and Infant Mortality in Selected Countries, 2007." Retrieved April 2008, from www.infoplease.com/ipa/A0004393.html; and Center for Disease Control and Prevention, "Infant Mortality Statistics from the 2004 Period Linked Birth/Infant Death Data Set," *National Vital Statistics Reports* 55, no. 14 (June 13, 2007). Retrieved April 2008, from www.cdc.gov/nchs/data/nvsr/nvsr55/nvsr55_14.pdf

whites. For African American women, the life expectancy was 76.9 years compared to 81 years for white women.[41]

A major factor affecting infant mortality is low birth weight. Although the cause is unknown, low birth weight (less than 5.5 pounds) increases the chances of infant death during the first month by 40 percent. In 2002, 7.8 percent of babies were born at low birth weight; for African American babies it was 13.4 percent.[42]

Education Continuing an upward trend in black educational attainment that began in 1940, there

was no statistical difference in high school completion rates between African American and white students (around 86 percent) in 2004. Although the high school dropout rate is now relatively low, it is still significant because the failure to complete high school is strongly correlated with poverty. Although roughly the same proportions of black and white students graduate from high school, college completion rates significantly differ. In 2006, 41 percent of all whites aged 18 to 24 were enrolled in higher education compared with 32.6 percent of all blacks. The percentage of whites aged 25 to 29 holding a bachelor's degree in 2007 was 35.5 percent compared with

19.5 percent for blacks.[43] As a high school diploma becomes less valuable in the marketplace, only educational upgrading can protect workers' incomes. On average, college graduates in 2004 earned almost $43,000 a year compared to $21,000 for high school graduates.[44] The strong correlation between higher education and higher salaries implies that the disparity between African American and white college completion rates will have a long-term impact on the economic well-being of minorities. In addition, fewer minority college graduates go on to obtain advanced degrees.[45] For example, only 1,604 African Americans earned a doctoral degree in 2001.[46]

Welfare Dependency Welfare dependency is another indicator of racism. Although welfare dependency is decreasing for African Americans, 7.7 percent received more than 50 percent of their total annual family income from means-tested public assistance programs compared to 1.9 percent of the non-Hispanic white population.[47]

Hispanic Americans

Although the history of race relations in the United States is older than the nation itself, the issue is rising in importance with the coming of a "minority majority"—the name given by some to the changing demographics expected in U.S. society over the next 50 years. There are "two Americas." One is the aging, white society still found in smaller metropolitan areas, smaller towns, and rural areas; the second is a younger, more multicultural society.

The Demography of Hispanic Americans

Hispanics became the nation's largest minority community in 2002. It is projected that from 2002 to 2050, Hispanics will increase their ranks by 188 percent to 102.6 million, or roughly one-quarter of the U.S. population. The Hispanic population in the United States is young, with more than one-third under age 18. Between 2000 and 2002, the nation's Hispanic population grew much faster than the population as a whole, increasing from 35.3 million to 38.8 million. According to Census Bureau estimates, Hispanics accounted for 3.5 million, or fully

one-half, of the population increase of 6.9 million from 2000 to 2002.[48]

The use of the term *Hispanic* masks a rich diversity within this group. U.S. Hispanics have roots in 22 different countries; their family histories are from Mexico, Puerto Rico, Cuba and other Caribbean islands, and Central and South America, as well as the United States.

The diversity of the various Hispanic groups is partly reflected in the percentages of those 25 and older who graduated from high school by 2002. These high school graduates ranged from 74 percent of "other Hispanic origin" to 71 percent for Cubans and 51 percent for Mexican Americans. Although Latinos pump $300 billion into the U.S. economy, 21 percent of Hispanics lived below the poverty line in 2001. Hispanic children represented 18 percent of all children in the United States but accounted for 28 percent of all children in poverty.[49] Of those living below the poverty line in 2001, nearly 21 percent were Mexican American, 26 percent were Puerto Ricans living in the U.S. mainland, 16.5 percent were Cuban Americans, and 15 percent were from Central and South America.[50] This compares to just 8 percent of whites and 24.4 percent of African Americans who lived below the poverty line.[51]

Because of the large number of undocumented workers coming from Central America and Mexico, the Hispanic population of the United States is difficult to measure accurately. Some estimate the number of undocumented workers in the United States (most of them from Spanish-speaking countries) to be 12 million. Nevertheless, it is known that the total Hispanic population is growing rapidly.[52] The Hispanic population is also geographically concentrated, with 65 percent living in just three states: California, Texas, and New York. Eighty-eight percent of all Latinos live in nine states, and 88 percent live in urban areas.

Hispanic Poverty and Income

The poverty status of Hispanics worsened from the 1980s onward in relation to other groups, including African Americans. Although their position has improved in recent years, they still are relatively poor compared to whites and experience much greater poverty. In 2006, the median income for all households in the United States was $48,451, with white median household income being $52,375. For Hispanic households, however, it was $38,747. About 13.3 percent of the United States as a whole was classed as living below the poverty threshold in 2006. Compared with non-Hispanic whites at 9.3 percent, Hispanics had a poverty rate more than double at 21.5 percent.[53]

In 2001, Hispanic children represented almost 18 percent of all U.S. children but made up 30 percent of all children living in poverty. By comparison, only 9.5 percent of white children were poor. All told, 28.6 percent of Hispanic children lived below the poverty line in 2007.[54]

Diversity in the Hispanic Population

Although for statistical purposes the Hispanic population is often considered as a single group, the various Latino subgroups have distinct social and historical backgrounds. For example, Cubans living in Florida may have little in common historically or politically with Mexican Americans living in California, and Puerto Ricans living in New York may have little understanding of the culture of either Cuban Americans or Mexican Americans. These differences are also reflected in income. Among Latino full-time, year-round workers in 2002, Mexicans had the lowest proportion of workers earning $35,000 a year or more.[55]

Mexican Americans constitute about 67 percent (17.1 million) of all Hispanics in the United States and are the fastest-growing Spanish-speaking subgroup. According to the Census Bureau, there were about 20.6 million Mexican Americans in the United States in 2000, a substantial increase over the 13 million in 1989.[56] In part, the poverty of Mexican Americans is correlated to deficits in educational attainment. More than two in five Hispanics 25 and older have not graduated from high school, and more than one-quarter had less than a ninth-grade education compared with only 4 percent of non-Hispanic whites. The proportion of Hispanics with a bachelor's degree or more was much lower (11 percent) than for non-Hispanic whites (29 percent). Educational attainment varies among Hispanics and among Latinos 25 and older. Cubans, Puerto Ricans, and Central and South Americans were more likely to have at least graduated from high school (74 percent, 67 percent, 71 percent, and 65 percent, respectively) than were Mexicans (51 percent). Similarly, the proportion that had attained at least a bachelor's degree ranged from 19 percent for Cubans, 17 percent for Central and South Americans, to 7.6 percent for Mexicans.[57]

In 2002 Puerto Ricans constituted 8.6 percent of the Hispanic population and less than 1 percent of the total U.S. population. They also had the highest unemployment rate (9.6 percent) among Hispanic groups, and their poverty rate was 26 percent, again the highest of any Hispanic group.[58]

The economic data on Hispanics suggest two subgroups with different characteristics. For example, although average household worth fell, the Latino community's total wealth rose. The number of Hispanic businesses increased 31 percent (from around 1.2 million to 1.57 million) from 1997 to 2002.[59] Overall, the economic data clearly suggest a worsening picture for most Hispanic communities in the United States, especially Mexican Americans and Puerto Ricans.

American Indians

American Indians, in some ways the poorest group in the United States, experience oppression similar to that of other disenfranchised populations. From 1970 to 2000, the reported American Indian population grew from 574,000 to more than 2 million. This population rise was due to a lower infant mortality rate, a high birthrate, and the fact that more individuals of mixed American Indian descent were reporting their race as American Indian. This last factor may be partly correlated with the resurgence of American Indian pride that began in the 1970s. In 2000, American Indian and Alaska Natives numbered about 2.5 million or 0.9 percent of the U.S. population. According to Bureau of Indian Affairs (BIA) estimates, about 1.5 million American Indians live on or near reservations with about another 356,000 living in urban areas.[60]

Despite the 562 federally recognized tribes (including 223 Alaskan Native groups) and 275 American Indian reservations, there is no single definition of an American Indian.[61] The BIA classifies someone as American Indian if they are a member of a recognized American Indian tribe and have one-fourth or more Indian blood. The Bureau of the Census uses self-identification.

The history of American Indians is marked by hardship, deprivation, and gross injustice. Before the arrival of Christopher Columbus, American Indians in the territorial United States numbered somewhere between 900,000 and 12 million.[62] This indigenous population was decimated as a result of disease, the

Table 4.3

Selected Indicators of American Indian Social and Economic Well-Being, 2003

	Native American Indian	All Races
Percent of single-parent households with children	45.4	31.8
H.S. dropout rate	15.5	9.0
Percent of those aged 16–19 not in school or working	14.8	8.0
Percent of children in poverty	32.8	17.0
Percent of married couples with children in poverty	46.6	24.0
Median income	$36,549	$43,318

Source: Adapted from A. Willeto, "Native American Kids: American Indian Children's Well-Being Indicators for the Nation and Two States," *Social Indicators Research* 83 (2007), pp. 149–176.

westward expansion of whites, and the resulting wars and genocidal policies. By 1880 the census reported only 250,000 American Indians.[63] Moreover, American Indians were not granted citizenship until 1924; New Mexico refused them the vote until 1940.

The social and economic problems faced by American Indians are similar to those of other at-risk minority populations (see Table 4.3). After generations as the nation's poorest and most overlooked minority, American Indians continue to suffer from what a 2003 U.S. Commission on Civil Rights report called a "quiet crisis" of discrimination, poverty, and unmet promises. Unemployment, substance abuse, and school dropout rates are among the highest in the nation, and American Indians face staggering health problems.[64] In 2004, American Indians were 770 percent more likely to die from alcoholism, 650 percent more likely to die from tuberculosis, 420 percent more likely to die from diabetes, 280 percent more likely to die from accidents, and 52 percent more likely to die from pneumonia or influenza than the rest of the United States, including other minority populations. As a result of high mortality rates, the life expectancy for American Indians is 71, nearly five years less than the rest of the U.S. population.[65]

American Indian tribes are sovereign nations under federal law and states may not enforce their civil codes on reservations. After the federal government gave tribes more control over their economic development, some began operating gaming places that conflicted with state and local laws. A number of states challenged these operations, but a series of Supreme Court cases were decided in the tribes' favor. To clarify the law, the Indian Gaming Regulatory Act was passed in 1988. Tribes could operate full-scale casino gambling on reservations

in any state that allowed such gambling anywhere within its borders, provided the details of the operation were set forth under a tribal–state compact.

By the late 1990s, there were over 310 gaming operations run by more than 200 of the nations' 562 federally recognized tribes. Of these operations, about 220 were "Las Vegas"–style casinos with slot machines and table games. Examining the effects of casinos after at least four years of operation, economists William Evans and Julie Topoleski found that positive changes included young adults moving back to reservations (a 12 percent population increase); adult employment increased by 26 percent; the number of working poor declined by 14 percent; and mortality rates fell by 2 percent. Evans and Topoleski concluded that tribal gaming operations had both positive and negative spillovers in the surrounding communities. Given the size of tribes relative to their counties, most of the employment growth was due to non–American Indian employment (most of those employed by casinos are not American Indians). The researchers found that four years after a casino opens, community changes include a 10 percent increase in auto thefts, larceny, and violent crime, and an increase in bankruptcies within 50 miles of a new casino. Because casino profits are nontaxable, their presence in many states diverts funds from taxable activities.[66]

Caught in the paternalistic web of the Bureau of Indian Affairs, American Indians continue to struggle to retain their identity. Having been robbed of their land, murdered indiscriminately by encroaching white settlers (as well as by the U.S. Cavalry), and treated alternately as children and pests by the federal government, for many years American Indians were further oppressed by having their children taken away by welfare officials. This widespread abuse by welfare workers, who evaluated American Indian child-rearing practices as neglectful in the context of white middle-class family values, was partially remedied by the **Indian Child Welfare Act of 1978**, which restored child-placement decisions to the individual tribes. As a result of this act, priority in placement choices for American Indian children was given to tribal members rather than white families.[67] In an attempt to remedy historical injustices, the Indian Self-Determination Act of 1975 emphasized tribal self-government, self-sufficiency, and the establishment of independent health, education, and welfare services.[68] Despite these limited gains, the plight of American Indians serves as a reminder of the mistakes made by the United States in both past and present policies toward disenfranchised minority groups.

Asian Americans

The 2000 census reported more than 25 Asian-Pacific subgroups in the United States, including Chinese, Filipino, Japanese, Asian-Indian, Korean, Vietnamese, Laotian, Thai, Cambodian, Polynesian (Hawaiian, Samoan, and Tongan), Micronesian, and Melanesian. The six largest Asian population groups in the United States are Chinese (2.7 million), Filipino (2.4 million), Japanese (1.1 million), Asian-Indian (1.9 million), Korean (1.2 million), and Vietnamese (1.2 million).[69] In 1970 there were 1.5 million Asians living in the United States; by 1980 that number rose to 3.7 million; and by 1990, 7.3 million. This growth represented an astounding 475 percent increase over 20 years and made Asians the fastest-growing minority group in the United States. It is projected that because of above-average birthrates and accelerating legal and illegal immigration, the Asian population will more than triple to 33 million by 2050.[70] In 2004 the Asian population was 12.3 million, an increase of 16 percent from four years earlier in 2000.[71]

Even though the social and economic data on Asians are mixed, perhaps the most striking feature is the high median family income (see Figure 4.1 on page 74). Economic and social data point to a population that has made great strides, especially in the educational area. In 2003, 88 percent of Asians were high school graduates, compared with 89 percent of whites, 80 percent of African Americans, and 57 percent of Hispanics.[72] Asians made up only 3 percent of the population in 1990, but they represented 12 percent of the students at Harvard University; 20 percent at Stanford; and in 2003, 45 percent at the University of California.[73] In 2003, 29 percent of all males had completed college. Of that number, 28 percent were white, 17 percent African American, 11 percent Hispanic, and 50 percent Asian.[74]

Impressive as these economic statistics are, they conceal several things. First, most Asians live in expensive urban areas where salaries are higher than the U.S. average. Second, economic statistics for Asian Americans obscure the problems of many low-wage recent immigrants who work in sweatshops in urban Chinatowns. A 2002 study by the Asian American Federation of New York found that garment workers in New York's Chinatown earned $112 a week. Restaurant workers, many of whom were illegal, earned only $124 a week.[75] Third, although many Chinese and Japanese Americans have achieved economic success, Southeast Asians are at higher risk of poverty than whites. Fourth, Asians are underrepresented in the higher-salaried public and private career positions, and their salaries tend to be lower than those of whites.[76] Fifth, although a large number of Asian immigrants have become successful entrepreneurs and own and operate their own small businesses, for some this role was forced on them as a result of discrimination.

Asian Americans have been stigmatized in U.S. society in many ways. Most dramatic was the internment of Japanese Americans in detention camps during World War II. Asians in the United States have also experienced more subtle forms of discrimination. For example, because of their economic and educational achievements, Asians are often thought of as a "model minority." Because of this status, many Asians experience pressure from within around achievement and sometimes external hostility. An example of this tension is evident in the hostility between Korean shopkeepers and inner-city African American residents. Last, some Asian Americans complain that they are discriminated against in colleges and universities because of their strong academic performance.[77] Facing this backlash, some Asians have redoubled their efforts to become mainstream U.S. citizens—to be in the center of the society rather than on the margins as "hyphenated Americans."

Many Asians point to contributions resulting from Oriental cultural values that include an emphasis on frugality, greater consideration for the feelings of others, and a balance between group and individual welfare. According to sociologist Tu

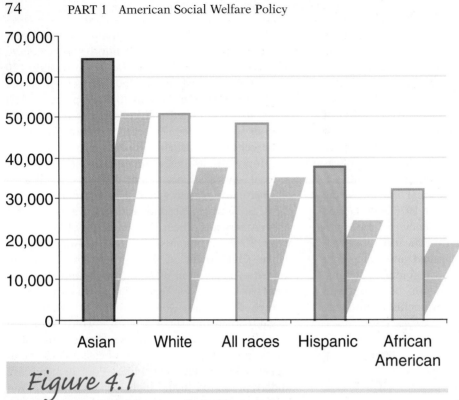

Figure 4.1

Median Household Annual Income, 2006

Source: U.S. Census Bureau, Current Population Survey (CPS), "Median Income of Households by Selected Characteristics and Income Definition." Retrieved June 2008, from http://pubdb3.census.gov/macro/032007/altinc/newinc03_000.htm

Weiming, the less individualistic culture of Asians, their lower sense of self-interest, their less adversarial nature, and their less legalistic approach have important lessons for the United States.[78]

Voter Registration and Discrimination

On July 27, 2006, President Bush signed into law The Voting Rights Act Reauthorization and Amendments Act of 2006 that extended federal oversight for specific state and local jurisdictions with historical patterns of discrimination against minority voters and continued to require the provisions of bilingual voting materials. These special provisions of the Voting Rights Act of 1965 were extended for an additional 25 years.[79] That right to vote is based upon permanent provisions of the 1965 Act that permit citizen-initiated suits in federal court to challenge discriminatory voting practices under the 15th Amendment to the Constitution.[80]

Unfortunately, there appears to be a continuing nationwide pattern of questionable voting practices that needs to be challenged. Georgia, Wisconsin, Missouri, and Arizona passed legislation requiring specific identification prior to voting which has been shown to discriminate disproportionately against minority citizens who are less likely to have the required identification documents. Electronic voting machines have been found to malfunction in Texas, Pennsylvania, Iowa, and North Carolina. By erasing votes and providing an inadequate backup paper system, voting machines have disenfranchised voters. Too few polling locations in poor neighborhoods is an old problem, but one that has recently been reported in Columbus, Ohio, New Orleans, and St. Louis. Inadequate polling locations inhibit voting by requiring long waits and effectively prohibiting some votes by closing before the line of waiting voters has completed their selections. Failure to provide adequate compensation and training for poll-workers can result in incompetence; dirty tricks can dissuade some from voting; gerrymandering can have the effect of disempowering minority voters by consolidating their votes into single districts or by diffusing their votes to minimize impact. Even the 2006 midterm elections suggest that civil rights, especially the right to vote, need to be constantly monitored in order to be adequately protected.

Immigrants and Immigration

The U.S. Census Bureau projects that immigration will cause the population of the United States to increase from 300 million to more than 400 million in less than 50 years. Between January 2000 and March 2002, about 3.3 million illegal immigrants arrived in the United States. Mexicans made up over half of undocumented immigrants (57 percent), with another 23 percent coming from other Latin American countries, 10 percent from Asia, 5 percent from Europe and Canada, and 5 percent from the rest of the world. Almost two-thirds (65 percent) of the undocumented population live in just six states: California (27 percent), Texas (13 percent), New York (8 percent), Florida (7 percent), Illinois (6 percent), and New Jersey (4 percent). However, the most rapid growth in the undocumented population since the mid-1990s has been outside these states.[81] In 2002, the foreign-born population of the United States was 33.1 million, equal to 11.5 percent of the U.S. population. The U.S. Office of Immigration Statistics (OIS) estimates that in 2002 the legal permanent resident (LPR) population and those eligible to naturalize numbered 11.4 million and 7.8 million, respectively.[82]

Although poverty rates are higher for immigrants, they are lower than those of naturalized citizens (10 percent) and native-born Americans (11.8 percent).[83] Moreover, a significant portion of Hispanic poverty is attributable to the large numbers of illegal immigrants entering the United States and to the low-paying jobs they occupy. Asian Americans have also felt the backlash from mainstream Americans worried about the consequences of admitting non-Europeans into U.S. society.

The pace of economic growth in the 1990s would have been impossible without the influx of immigration. Immigrants contributed to job growth in three ways: (1) by filling an increasing share of jobs, (2) by taking jobs in labor-scarce regions, and (3) by filling the types of jobs shunned by native workers. The labor force grew by 16.7 million workers in the 1990s, with 6.4 million of them being foreign-born. The majority of foreign-born workers (4.2 million) came during the boom of 1996–2000.

In fact, immigrants filled four of every 10 job openings at a time when the unemployment rate hit record lows in the mid-1990s.[84]

Not only is the number of jobs filled by immigrants important, but the location and kind of jobs is also important. In earlier years, most new immigrants from Latin America and Asia clustered in a few large cities, such as Los Angeles, New York, and Chicago. However, the 1990s witnessed a spread to the western Midwest, New England, and the Mid- and South Atlantic regions. In some parts of the country, almost all labor force growth between 1996 and 2000 was due to immigration.

Because a large number of new immigrants have less than a high school education, new immigrants commonly fill low-skill, blue-collar jobs. About 33 percent of immigrants have not finished high school compared with 13 percent of natives. Many immigrants are not only lower-skilled than native workers, but their skills do not translate into the U.S. workplace. Although immigrants overwhelmingly fill blue-collar jobs, they also account for as much as half the growth in categories such as administrative support and services.[85]

Legal immigration to the United States has undergone several important changes since the mid-1980s. The number of immigrants entering the United States remained relatively constant from 1985 to 1988 but then rose sharply from 1988 to 1991. The sharp rise was due to the impact of the Immigration Reform and Control Act of 1986 (IRCA), granting legal status to undocumented immigrants who had been in the United States continuously since 1982 or had worked in agriculture. But by 1995 the total number of immigrants admitted to the United States was 720,461, or less than half of the 1,827,167 admitted in 1991.[86]

Major changes have occurred in U.S. immigration since the 1950s. The most notable shift is the decrease in immigration from Europe to immigration from Asia. In 2007, Asians represented more than one-third of all persons obtaining permanent legal resident status in the United States, while it was just 11.5 percent for people from Europe. After Asians, the next highest was from North America (32.2 percent), followed by South America (10.1 percent), Africa (9 percent), and Oceania (0.6 percent). (See Figure 4.2 on page 76.) Most immigrants (65.3 percent) to the United States choose to settle in just six states: California (26.6 percent), New York (10.7 percent), Florida (9.8 percent), Texas (8.1 percent), New Jersey (5.6 percent), and Illinois (4.5 percent).[87]

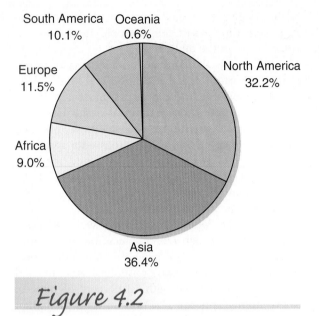

South America 10.1%
Oceania 0.6%
Europe 11.5%
North America 32.2%
Africa 9.0%
Asia 36.4%

Figure 4.2

Immigrants by Place of Origin, 2007

Sources: U.S. Department of Homeland Security, *Yearbook of Immigration Statistics: 2007*, "Persons Obtaining Legal Permanent Resident Status by Region and Country of Birth: Fiscal Years 1998 to 2007." Retrieved June 2008, from www.dhs.gov/xlibrary/assets/statistics/yearbook/2007/table03d.xls

In 1996, Congress passed the **Personal Responsibility and Work Opportunity Reconciliation Act (PRWORA).** This act was the most comprehensive welfare reform legislation passed since the New Deal of 1935. The 900-page bill contained profound implications for both legal and illegal immigrants (PRWORA will be discussed more fully in Chapter 11).[88] Specifically, the PRWORA disentitled most legal immigrants (including many who had been living in the United States for years but had not elected to become citizens) from food stamps, Aid to Families with Dependent Children (AFDC), and Supplemental Security Income (SSI). (Illegal immigrants were never entitled to these benefits.) Based on the PRWORA, the only immigrants still entitled to benefits were (1) those who had become citizens or who had worked in the United States and paid Social Security taxes for at least 10 years; and (2) veterans of the U.S. Army who were noncitizens. In addition, the bill allows states the option to deny Medicaid benefits to immigrants.[89] Even though some of the harsher provisions were later rescinded, anti-immigration sentiment remained.

In 1996, Congress revisited immigration, this time voting to double the size of the Border Patrol, stiffen penalties for document fraud and immigrant smuggling, bar illegal immigrants from qualifying for Social Security benefits or public housing, give states the right to deny illegal immigrants drivers' licenses, and slightly increase the earnings requirements for U.S. residents wishing to sponsor foreign family members.[90]

Immigration policy changed dramatically since the World Trade Center attacks of September 11, 2001. After 9/11 three important acts were passed: (1) the USA Patriot Act, (2) the Enhanced Border Security Act, and (3) the Homeland Security Act of 2002. These acts do not directly shape immigration policy per se, but they impact it by more carefully screening and monitoring foreigners who temporarily visit (and sometimes wish to settle in) the United States. The most important changes have been stricter background checks for visa applicants and requirements for tamper-proof, machine-readable travel documents. In addition, American consulates have raised fees, and wait times for visa approvals have gone from less than a month to several months. Those applying for visas are now paying more and are more likely to be denied entry.

Two other groups have also been impacted by stricter visa procedures: foreign students and refugees. Background checks on foreign students and stricter requirements on the universities and schools that admit them have impacted the number of student visas issued. For instance, applicants for student visas are advised to apply at the U.S. Embassy or Consulate with jurisdiction over their place of permanent residence rather than applying at just any U.S. consular office abroad, as it may be more difficult to qualify outside their own country.[91] These policies have also affected U.S. universities who rely on foreign students to fill graduate programs and for the tuition they generate.[92]

Refugee resettlement has also slowed. This decline is partly explained by stricter security procedures for natives of countries linked to terrorism, such as Sudan and Somalia.[93] A report released by the Migration Policy Institute analyzing post–9/11 policy changes found an emerging pattern of violations of due process and harsh law enforcement measures directed against males from Arab and Muslim countries. The report also investigated the impact of current policy on U.S. Arab and Muslim communities and found that governmental actions have frightened and alienated this community. Programs such as special registration became a vehicle to arrest those with even minor immigration

■ *Foreign students have been especially affected by stricter immigration procedures.*

violations, and the threat of deportation was always looming in the background.[94] According to report coauthor Muzaffar Chishti, "The experience of Muslim and Arab communities post–Sept. 11 is, in many ways, an impressive story of a community that first felt intimidated but has since started to assert its place in the American body politic."[95]

Guest Workers

Both the history and the current practice of guest worker programs question the assumption that socially just aims can be accomplished by such a program. From 1942 until 1964, Mexican nationals were recruited to enter the United States, primarily for agricultural work, under a treaty between Mexico and the United States. This "Bracero" program employed almost 450,000 workers at its peak in 1956,[96] with more than 4.5 million participating during the period of the program. The treaty provisions[97] provided significant protections for the guest worker, from standards for housing, compensation, and even the savings of a portion of earnings to be remitted once the worker returned to Mexico, but these provisions were known more for their violation than for their enforcement.[98] Housing was clearly substandard for the migrant workers. Wage

guarantees were almost never implemented, and the withheld savings were distributed to only a small proportion of the workers.

The abuse of guest workers continues today. Current immigration law permits the recruitment of temporary foreign workers under H2-A and H2-B programs that employed over 120,000 in 2005. Even small programs like these have been labeled "exploitative" by the Southern Poverty Law Center. Home country recruiters often require substantial payment for services; low skill employment in forestry, fishery, and agriculture are geographically dispersed and therefore frequently escape federal oversight; and lack of education and English proficiency severely limit the guest worker's ability to assert his or her legal rights. When visa and identity papers are held by the employer, a common practice, the employment approaches a form of slavery.[99]

Despite good intentions, legislative protections for guest workers have consistently failed in the case of H2-A and H2-B visas. To solicit the economic contribution of foreign nationals through employment without extending the same legal protections and services available to citizen employees is discriminatory. How the country chooses to rectify the structural inequities of a guest worker program may be the most important issue facing immigration reform.

Women and Society

Former Senator Hillary Clinton cracked, if not shattered, an important glass ceiling for women. Although in 1984 former Congresswoman Geraldine Ferraro ran for vice president with Walter Mondale on the Democratic party ticket, her candidacy was short-lived as they lost to Ronald Reagan in a landslide election. It took 23 years for another woman to achieve the political visibility to run as a serious candidate for the U.S. presidency. Hillary Clinton had that honor and in a tightly contested primary race she lost to Barack Obama, the first Afrian American president. For the first time in American history, a woman became a viable choice for U.S. president. Sexism is a term that denotes the discriminatory and prejudicial treatment of women based on their gender, and it is a problem U.S. society has wrestled with since the beginning of the nation. Sexism can manifest itself in a myriad of ways. For example, purposefully, women are kept out of military academies, private clubs, and certain sports. Occupational boundaries keep women from operating heavy construction machinery, being involved in skilled trades such as bricklaying, or flying commercial or military jets, or, women reach a glass ceiling from where they cannot rise any higher. It can take political forms, like appointing or electing token women to offices or cabinet positions or creating "special appointments" to placate feminist groups.

Violence and Sexism

Sexism can also manifest itself in crime and family violence (violence against women is primarily partner violence).[100] According to a study by Patricia Tjaden and Nancy Thoennes:

- Nearly 25 percent of surveyed women said they were raped or physically assaulted by a current or former spouse, cohabiting partner, or date at some time in their lifetime.
- Approximately five percent (1.5 million) of women are raped or physically assaulted by an intimate partner annually in the United States. Almost 5 million (victims are often victimized more than once) intimate partner rapes and physical assaults are perpetrated against U.S. women annually.

- Almost 5 percent of women reported being stalked by a current or former spouse, cohabiting partner, or date at some time in their lifetime.
- The researchers found that women who were physically assaulted by an intimate partner averaged almost seven physical assaults by the same partner. The survey also found that 41.5 percent of the women who were physically assaulted by an intimate partner were injured during their most recent assault.
- The U.S. medical community treats millions of intimate partner rapes and physical assaults annually. Of the estimated 4.9 million intimate partner rapes and physical assaults perpetrated against women annually, about 2 million will result in an injury to the victim, and one and a half million will result in some type of medical treatment.
- Most intimate partner victimizations are not reported to the police. Only one-fifth of all rapes, one-quarter of all physical assaults, and one-half of all stalkings against women by intimates are reported to the police.[101]

Congress passed the Violence against Women Act (VAWA), signed into law by President Bill Clinton in 1994. VAWA represents a comprehensive approach to domestic violence and sexual assault, combining a broad array of legal and other reforms. Specifically, it was designed to improve the response of police, prosecutors, and judges to these crimes; force sex offenders to pay restitution to their victims; and increase funding for battered women's shelters. VAWA mandates a nationwide enforcement of protection orders entered in any court and provides penalties for crossing state lines to abuse a spouse or violate a protection order. It also prohibits anyone facing a restraining order for domestic abuse from possessing a firearm.[102] The act provides grants for training police, prosecutors, and judges in domestic abuse; provides grants for battered women's shelters; assists victims of sexual assault, including providing educational seminars, hotlines, and programs to increase awareness (as well as targeted efforts to underserved racial and ethnic minority communities); provides grants for safety-related improvements to public transportation, national park systems, and public parks; funds efforts to prevent youth violence; assists funding for rape crisis centers; and allocates funds for the treatment and counseling of youth subjected to or at risk of sexual abuse (e.g., runaways, homeless youth, and street people).[103] In 2004, overall funding for VAWA was $567 million.[104]

The Feminization of Poverty

Sexism also has an economic face. Women's wages are generally lower than those of men, and women more often have to resort to public welfare programs. The term **feminization of poverty** was coined by Diana Pearce in a 1978 article in *Urban and Social Change Review* in which she argued that poverty was rapidly becoming a female phenomenon as women accounted for an increasingly larger proportion of the economically disadvantaged.[105]

The effects of female poverty are staggering. For example, in the United States in 2000, two out of three poor adults were women, and in 2003 nearly 4 out of 10 families headed by women lived in poverty.[106] There were almost 13 million female-headed families (about 7.5 million with children) in 2003—a figure more than double that of 1970.[107]

The causes of the feminization of poverty are complex. When women are deserted or divorced, many must find jobs immediately or go on public assistance. According to Ann Withorn, women generally enter the welfare system only after exhausting other possibilities for income support.[108] Those who choose welfare are held in poverty by the low benefits; those who opt to work are kept in poverty by the low wages that characterize service jobs. Low-paying service employment, such as jobs in fast-food outlets and retail stores, make welfare benefits seem attractive because at least staying at home involves no child care costs, transportation, clothing, and lunch costs.

Women and Low-Income Work

Women frequently enter the workforce through the service and retail trades, doing clerical jobs, cleaning, food preparation or service, personal service work, or auxiliary health service work. These occupations are marked by low pay, a low level of unionization, little status, meager workplace benefits, and limited prospects for job advancement. Thus, much of the increase of women in the workforce is in the "secondary labor market" (see Chapter 5), a marginal area of employment. When economists cite the creation of millions of jobs, much of what they refer to is the secondary labor market. For example, of the 18.8 million jobs created between 1979 and 1989, 14.4 million were in retail trade and in services, the two lowest-paid economic sectors.[109]

The economics of low-wage service work are gloomy. For instance, if a single mother[110,111] with one child in day care chooses to avoid the stigma of welfare and finds work at near the minimum wage, her prospects for economic survival are bleak. The mock budget in Table 4.4 illustrates the dilemma of

Table 4.4

Monthly Budget for a Working Mother with One Child in School and One Infant in Day Care (Gross Monthly Income for a Full-Time Worker at $6.00 an hour: $960)

Expenses	Monthly Total
Day care for 1 child	$ 540.83[a]
Rent	$ 337.53[b]
Health care	$ 93.75[c]
Utilities	$ 60.00[c]
Food	$ 259.00[d]
Clothing	$ 62.00[a]
Transportation	$ 200.00[c]
Entertainment	$ 50.00[c]
Sundry items (e.g., soap, cleaners, repairs, sheets, blankets, etc.)	$ 100.00[c]
Total approximate cost	$1,703.11[c]
Monthly deficit between income and budget	–$ 743.11[c]

a. Child care costs are calculated based on the average of the most and least expensive cities for child care according to the Runzheimer International survey of childcare costs. Retrieved September 2004, from www.runzheimer.com/corpc/news/scripts/012004.asp

b. Rent was calculated on the basis of the average of U.S. Department of Housing and Urban Development (HUD)-determined fair market rents in the lowest-cost metropolitan areas in a state. The average rent of all these states totaled $450. See HUD, "Fair Market Rents for the Housing Choice Voucher Program and Moderate Rehabilitation Single Room Occupancy Program Fiscal Year 2004," *Federal Register 68*, no. 190. Retrieved August 2004, from www.huduser.org/datasets/fmr.html

c. This amount was based on figures provided in John E. Schwartz and Thomas J. Volgy, "A Cruel Hoax Upon the Poor," *The San Diego Union Tribune* November 9, 1992, p. 5.

d. The amount for food is based on the maximum Food Stamp allocation that this mother would receive in 2004 if she had no countable income.

a single mother who finds full-time employment at $6.00 an hour.

Work at or slightly above the minimum wage is problematic, limiting the economic choices for the unskilled female household head. Moreover, the National Commission on Children estimates that the typical family spends about $6,000 annually on expenses associated with raising a child. This would mean that, excluding a mother's personal expenses, having two children requires a minimum income of $12,000 per year. According to the National Commission on Children, "If a single mother with two children moved from welfare to a full-time, minimum wage job in 1991, her net income would have increased by only about $50 per week."[112] The low minimum wage combined with inflation makes a single mother's plight even more dire. Neither welfare nor low-income work provides single female-headed households with viable economic choices.

Single-mother families in the United States fare worse than their counterparts in many European industrial nations. In a study of the relative economic well-being of single-mother families in eight nations, Yin-Ling Wong, Irwin Garfinkel, and Sara McLanahan found that compared with two-parent families, single mothers in the United States are considerably worse off financially than single mothers in the eight countries surveyed. The United States ranked last, surpassed by Canada, Australia, France, Germany, Norway, Sweden, and the United Kingdom.[113]

Inequities in **public transfer programs** also aggravate the economic problems of low-income women. For example, Social Security and public assistance are often the only viable options for women. Although median transfers to women are lower than to men, they constitute a higher share of the recipients' total income: about one-third for female-headed households compared to one-tenth for male-headed households. Moreover, Social Security is often the only source of income for elderly women. Like other public transfer programs, Social Security is riddled with pitfalls. In large part, many problems with Social Security are based on the assumptions that all families are nuclear and that families with young children need more per capita income than aged couples or single individuals. Some of the inequities in Social Security include the following:

- Because women's wages are lower than men's, their retirement benefits are also lower.

- Married female workers fare better on Social Security than single women. Married individuals who never worked can benefit from Social Security payments made by a spouse.
- Couples in which one worker earned most of the wages may fare better than couples in which the husband and wife earned equal wages.
- Homemakers are not covered on their own unless they held a job in the past. Widows do not qualify for benefits unless they are 60 years old or have a minor in the house.
- Regardless of the length of the marriage, divorced women are entitled to only one-half of their ex-husband's benefits. If this partial payment is the divorced woman's only income, it is usually inadequate. Furthermore, divorced women must have been married to the beneficiary of Social Security for at least 10 years to qualify for his benefits.
- Because of child care responsibilities, women typically spend less time in the workforce than men and their benefits are therefore usually lower.[114]

As a result of the Social Security amendments of 1983, several sex-based qualifications were eliminated: Divorced persons can qualify for benefits at age 62 (even if the ex-spouse has not yet claimed benefits), and divorced husbands can claim benefits based on the earnings records of their ex-wives.[115] Although these changes are important, they have led to only minor improvements in the system. Other reforms under discussion include an earnings-sharing option that would equally divide a couple's income between husband and wife (thereby eliminating the category of a primary wage earner and a dependent spouse) and a double-decker option in which everyone would be eligible for basic benefits regardless of whether they contributed to the system (individuals who contributed to the paid labor force would receive a higher benefit).

Women and Work

Myths abound in attempting to explain why women consistently earn less than men:[116]

Myth 1. A working mother's wages are not necessary to her family's survival; her job is a secondary activity that usually ceases with marriage or childbirth.

Fact. Most families require two paychecks to maintain the same standard of living as their parents.

Supreme Court Justice Clarence Thomas. Sexual harassment is defined as unwelcome sexual behaviors, including jokes, teasing, remarks, questions, and deliberate touching; letters, telephone calls, or materials of a sexual nature; pressure for sexual favors; and sexual assault. Although sexual harassment is illegal (Title VII of the 1964 Civil Rights Act has been interpreted as prohibiting sexual harassment) it remains all too common in the workplace.[137]

Finally, a major obstacle faced by many working women is the inflexibility of work. Because women frequently take on the major responsibility for child care, elder care, and home management, they often forgo educational or training opportunities. To help working women balance family and work responsibilities, options such as flexible hours, job sharing, and part-time work with benefits need to be expanded.

Fighting Back: The Equal Rights Amendment and Comparable Worth

The Nineteenth Amendment to the U.S. Constitution gave women the right to vote in 1920. That, however, did not end their economic and social plight, and shortly after winning the vote the Women's Party proposed the first **Equal Rights Amendment (ERA)** to the Constitution. In 1972, Congress passed a newly drafted ERA and set a 1979 date for state ratification. When the ERA had not been ratified by 1978, Congress extended the deadline to June 30, 1982. Despite the endorsement of 450 organizations representing 50 million members, opponents of the ERA were able to defeat the amendment in 1982, just three states short of the 38 required for ratification.

The ERA read as follows: "Equality of rights under the law shall not be denied or abridged by the United States or any other State on account of sex. . . . The Congress shall have the power to enforce, by appropriate legislation, the provisions of this article. . . . This amendment shall take effect two years after the date of ratification."[138]

The battle for women's rights has also been fought around **comparable worth**—the idea that workers should be paid equally for different types of work, if those jobs require the same levels of skill, education, knowledge, training, responsibility, and effort. The desire to equalize incomes through comparable worth is based on the belief that the **dual labor market** has created a situation whereby "women's work" (e.g., secretarial work, teaching,

social work, nursing, child care) is valued less than traditional male occupations.

An illustration of the debate around comparable worth is provided in Table 4.9 that lists average wages for jobs typically occupied by women and men. Although the policy is controversial, 20 states have passed laws making comparable worth a requirement or goal of state employment. Although a good idea in theory, comparable worth brings up a difficult question: What criteria should determine the comparability of different jobs? Moreover, some critics have rejected the idea of rigorously enforcing comparable worth on the grounds that the economic costs would be catastrophic.

In 1963 Congress passed the Equal Pay Act, requiring employers to compensate male and female workers equally for performing the same job under the same conditions (not all jobs were covered by the bill). Another protective measure was Title VII of the Civil Rights Act of 1964 that prohibited sex discrimination in employment practices and provided the right of redress in the courts. In 1972, Presidential Executive Order 11375 mandated that

Table 4.9

Comparable Worth and Average Annual Income, 2006

	2006 Mean Annual Income
Child care workers	$18,820
Teacher assistants	21,860
Nursing aides	22,960
Hairdressers and cosmetologists	24,550
Preschool teachers	25,900
Home health aides	20,100
Social and human services assistants	27,200
Fitness trainers	31,710
Auto mechanics	36,070
Truck drivers	36,320
Maintenance and repair workers	39,060
Machinists	35,810
Auto body mechanics	38,230

Source: U.S. Department of Labor, Bureau of Labor Statistics, "National Occupational Employment and Wage Estimates, All Occupations," May 2006. Retrieved April 2008, from www.bls.gov/oes/home.htm

employers practicing sex discrimination be prohibited from receiving federal contracts. Title IX of the Educational Amendments of 1972 prohibited discrimination in educational institutions receiving federal funds. Finally, the Equal Credit Act of 1975 prohibited discrimination by lending institutions on the basis of sex or marital status.

Abortion and Women's Rights

Feminists often point to the abortion debate as another area in which women's rights are threatened. Specifically, pro-choice advocates argue that where abortion is concerned, some male legislators and judges have promulgated laws and regulations to control the behavior of women by denying them full reproductive freedom. They argue that the choice of an abortion is a personal matter involving a woman and her conscience. Antiabortion forces claim that life begins at conception and that abortion is murder. Moreover, they point to the 1.2 million legal abortions performed in the United States in 2005, while at the same time pointing to the scarcity of adoptable infants.[139]

In 1973, Sarah Weddington, a young attorney from Austin, Texas, argued *Roe v. Wade* before the U.S. Supreme Court. Though her client had long since relinquished her child for adoption, Weddington argued that a state could not unduly burden a woman's right to choose an abortion by making regulations that prohibited her from carrying out that decision. The Court ruled in favor of Weddington, and abortion was legalized in the United States, thereby nullifying all state laws that made abortion illegal during the first trimester of pregnancy. (Before 1970, four states—New York, Alaska, Hawaii, and Washington—had already made abortion legal contingent upon the agreement of a physician.) Within a decade after *Roe v. Wade*, almost 500 bills were introduced in Congress, most of which sought to restrict abortions through a constitutional amendment outlawing abortion, by transferring the power to regulate abortion decisions to the states, or by limiting or terminating federal funding of abortions.[140]

The abortion question has been marked by several key issues: (1) clinic access, (2) fetus viability testing, (3) parental consent for minors, (4) waiting periods, (5) insurance regulations, (6) public funding, and (7) partial birth abortions (abortions beyond the first trimester). The abortion debate has also been marked by Byzantine maneuvers and complex twists. In 1977 the Hyde Amendment prohibited the federal government from funding abortions except to save the life of a mother. Also in 1977 the federal government lifted its ban on funding abortions for promptly reported cases of rape and incest and in cases where severe and long-lasting harm would be caused to a woman by childbirth. The 1980 Supreme Court decision in *Harris v. McRae* upheld the constitutionality of the Hyde Amendment. In 1981 the government again reversed its position, this time cutting federal funding of abortions except to save the life of the mother. By 1990 federal funds paid for only 165 abortions, a dramatic drop from the almost 300,000 federally funded abortions in 1977.[141] In 1994, the Freedom of Access to Clinic Entrances Act was signed into law. This bill expanded the civil liberty of persons to have unobstructed access to any abortion or reproductive health services clinic. Any person or group that interferes with the right of such persons is subject to legal penalties, which range from a high fine to imprisonment.

The strategy of the antiabortion movement has been to whittle away at *Roe v. Wade* by attempting to restrict abortions on the state level. For example, in Akron, Ohio, rules were promulgated that required a minor to receive parental consent for an abortion and imposed a one-day moratorium between a woman's signing the consent form and the actual performance of the abortion. In a 1989 landmark decision, the Supreme Court upheld a Missouri law that prohibited public hospitals and public employees from performing an abortion (except to save the life of the mother), required physicians to determine whether a woman who is at least 20 weeks pregnant is carrying a fetus able to survive outside the womb, and declared that life starts at conception. In 1991 the Court ruled in *Rust v. Sullivan* that the United States can prohibit federally financed family planning programs from giving out abortion information (i.e., the gag rule). On former President Clinton's second day in office, he signed a bill overturning this "gag rule;" on the same day, in another blow to antiabortion advocates, he overturned the federal ban on using fetal tissue matter gained from abortions in scientific experiments.

The U.S. abortion rate decreased from 1.31 million in 2000 to 1.21 million in 2005. A substantial proportion of this decline was due to the use of emergency contraception. Medication abortion accounted for 13 percent (161,000) of all abortions performed in 2005 and 22 percent of all eligible abortions.[142]

Sixty-one percent of women who have abortions are already mothers and more than half have two or more children. Many women who already have children want to be responsible and take care of their existing children and many become concerned that having another child would compromise the care given to existing children—financially, emotionally, and physically. Two-thirds of women who feel this way are at or below the poverty line and received little help from their partners.[143]

Since 1973, abortion has proved to be one of the most divisive issues in American public life. The public is ambivalent. According to a 2000 Gallup poll, 51 percent of American adults believe that abortions should be legal under some circumstances; 28 percent believe that they should be legal under all circumstances; and 19 percent believe they should be illegal, even to save the life of the mother. The same poll revealed that 50 percent of adults identified themselves as pro-choice and 40 percent as pro-life. Other polls directly contradict the 2000 Gallup poll.[144]

Gays and Lesbians: Two Populations at Risk

In today's culture wars, one of the most intense controversies surrounds the issue of whether homosexuality is an acceptable lifestyle and, if so, whether those who are openly gay and lesbian should enjoy protected minority status under civil rights laws. Forty years ago few people in public or religious life even dared to raise the possibility that it might be acceptable to be openly gay. For example, all 50 states in 1960 maintained laws criminalizing sodomy by consenting adults. In 1970, 84 percent of respondents to a national Gallup poll agreed that homosexuality was "social corruption that can cause the downfall of a civilization." Two-thirds of those polled thought homosexuals should not be allowed to work as schoolteachers, church pastors, or even government employees.

In recent decades there has been a slow but dramatic shift in public attitudes toward homosexuality. After years of concerted pressure by gay activists, the American Psychiatric Association in 1993 removed homosexuality from its *Diagnostic and Statistical Manual of Mental Disorders, 3rd edition (DSM-III)* list of "objective disorders" and declared it "a normal, if divergent lifestyle." Laws forbidding sodomy were repealed in state after state throughout the 1970s and 1980s. Although the United States has no federal law protecting against discrimination in employment by private sector employers based on sexual orientation, 14 states, the District of Columbia, and over 140 cities and counties have enacted laws banning discrimination. As of July 2003, the states banning sexual orientation discrimination in private sector employment included California, Connecticut, Hawaii, Maryland, Massachusetts, Minnesota, Nevada, New Hampshire, New Jersey, New Mexico, New York, Rhode Island, Vermont, and Wisconsin. Many of these laws also ban discrimination in other contexts, such as housing or public accommodation.[145] By 2004, 35 states had rescinded laws that criminalized consensual sodomy. In a crucial decision the U.S. Supreme Court invalidated the Texas sodomy law in 2003, holding private consensual sexual conduct to be constitutionally protected. In 2008, the California Supreme Court struck down two state laws that had limited marriage to be only between a man and a woman, making California the second state after Massachusetts to allow same-sex marriages.[146] These policies and polls reflect a significant shift in public opinion about homosexuality.

Despite these limited successes, many homosexuals continue to be forced to "live in the closet," concealing their sexual orientation in order to survive in a hostile world. Often the objects of ridicule, homosexuals have been denied housing and employment, harassed on the job, assaulted, and even killed because of their sexual orientation. In many states, homosexuality is still considered a criminal or felony offense, and in some of these states the police systematically raid homosexual bars and randomly arrest patrons. Discrimination and violence are still all too commonplace:

- Students describing themselves as lesbian, gay, bisexual, or transgendered are five times more likely to miss school because of feeling unsafe—28 percent are forced to drop out.
- The vast majority of victims of antilesbian/antigay violence—possibly more than 80 percent—never report the incident because they fear being "outed."
- Eighty-five percent of teachers oppose integrating lesbian, gay, and bisexual themes in their curricula.
- Due to discrimination, lesbians earn up to 14 percent less than their heterosexual female peers with similar jobs, education, age, and residence.

- Forty-two percent of homeless youth identify as lesbian, gay, or bisexual.
- Seventy-five percent of people committing hate crimes are under age 30—one in three are under 18—and some of the most pervasive anti-gay violence occurs in schools.
- Lesbian and gay youth are at a four times higher risk for suicide than their straight peers.
- A survey of employers found that 18 percent would fire, 27 percent would not hire, and 26 percent would refuse to promote a person thought to be lesbian, gay, or bisexual. [147]

In his 1999 State of the Union address, former President Clinton referred to the murder of Matthew Shepard: "We saw a young man murdered in Wyoming just because he was gay."[148] According to the National Coalition of Anti-Violence Programs, there were 1,393 anti-LGBT incidents in 2006.[149] Represented in all occupations and socioeconomic strata, gays and lesbians make up anywhere from 1 to 10 percent of the population. (Recent research suggests that the percentage of males and females that report themselves as being either homosexual or bisexual is about 4.1 percent.[150])

Gay Rights

When gays and lesbians have demanded equal rights under the law, the result has been mixed—and generally negative. During the 1970s, Miami gays tried to pass a civil rights amendment that would have prevented discrimination based on sexual orientation. This referendum failed, and similar efforts were defeated in St. Paul and other cities. Houston voters defeated two gay rights proposals in 1986, one calling for an end to discrimination in city employment practices based on sexual orientation, and the other calling for an end to the maintenance of sexual orientation data in city employment records. In Tampa, Florida, and in Portland, Maine, voters in the 1990s overturned city ordinances protecting gays and lesbians.[151] Conversely, in the late 1990s, 13 states had antidiscrimination laws. Municipalities across the country have also adopted civil rights ordinances to cover lesbians and gay men in areas such as employment, public accommodations, housing, and credit.[152]

For almost 20 years the Supreme Court refused to hear cases concerning gay rights, but in 1985 it heard *Oklahoma City Board of Education v. The National Gay Task Force*. The Supreme Court ruled that public schoolteachers cannot be forbidden to advocate homosexuality (e.g., by way of public demonstrations), but they can be prohibited from engaging in homosexual acts in public. In 1988 the Supreme Court ruled that the Central Intelligence Agency could not dismiss a homosexual without justifying the dismissal. In 1992 Colorado voters passed a referendum (Amendment 2) that prevented any law banning discrimination against gays. This amendment nullified gay rights laws that already existed in Aspen, Denver, and Boulder. On May 20, 1996, the U.S. Supreme Court ruled that Colorado's Amendment 2 was unconstitutional.

Gays and Lesbians in the Military

The U.S. armed forces have generally not tolerated homosexuality in their ranks. Draft board physicians in 1940 were ordered to screen out homosexuals on the basis of such characteristics as a man's lisp or a woman's deep voice. Because World War II created a desperate need for soldiers, these instructions were often overlooked. After the war, however, gay and lesbian military personnel were discharged, and exclusionary policies were again enforced. A similar situation occurred during the Vietnam War; once the conflict ended, gays and lesbians were again persecuted and their careers terminated.[153] The policy of the U.S. armed forces that excludes gays and lesbians from military service reads as follows: "Homosexuality is incompatible with military service. The presence in the military environment of persons who engage in homosexual conduct or who, by their statements, demonstrate a propensity to engage in homosexual conduct, seriously impairs the accomplishment of the military mission."[154] Those who admit to homosexuality at the time of enlistment are rejected; if homosexuality comes to light later on, the individual is separated. Although more liberal policies were put into effect during the 1970s and 1980s, they were directed at the type of separation, not the legitimacy of the separation.[155]

One of the principal justifications for excluding gays and lesbians from military service has been their supposed vulnerability to blackmail by enemy agents threatening to expose their secret. The Defense Department conducted at least three separate studies to justify this belief, but no findings supported the exclusionary policy.[156] In fact, the Personnel Security Research and Education Center of the Defense Department conducted an examination of the homosexual exclusion policy and found no evidence that gays and lesbians disrupt any branch of the military; instead, its report praised their dedication and superior performance.[157] Support for homosexuals in the military came from other sources, including conservative former senator Barry Goldwater, who argued that "you don't need to be straight to fight and die for your country, you just need to shoot straight."[158] By the 1990s the argument against gays and lesbians serving in the armed forces changed to the "unit cohesion" argument that predicted a breakdown of the social bonds necessary for accomplishing a military mission if combat groups include a homosexual. The underlying belief is that straight soldiers will place the good of their unit first, except when it comes to working with gay people because they cannot or are unwilling to set aside their personal prejudices.[159]

The U.S. military's policy of excluding homosexuals has far-reaching consequences. First, it adversely affects the career prospects of uniformed gays and lesbians. Second, people discharged from military service without an honorable discharge may have difficulty finding employment and may be ineligible to obtain benefits associated with military service. Even an honorable discharge given on the grounds of homosexual conduct carries grave consequences for the future of ex-service-people.

One campaign promise of former President Bill Clinton was to end discrimination against homosexuals in the military. As one of his first official acts, Clinton signed an order that prohibited military recruiters from inquiring about the sexual orientation of potential recruits. Shortly afterward, he proposed wide-ranging reforms aimed at ensuring equal rights for gays and lesbians serving in the military. Proponents of the plans argued that discrimination against homosexuals in the military was no different from the discrimination practiced against African American soldiers in World War I and World War II. For these activists, discrimination in the military was a civil rights issue. Critics argued that homosexuality was a lifestyle choice rather than a factor of birth such as skin color. Facing criticism from the Joint Chiefs of Staff and many influential members of Congress, Clinton retreated from his earlier position and instead supported a "don't ask, don't tell, don't pursue, and don't harass" policy that prohibited the military from asking questions as long as a homosexuals behaved discreetly. However, under this rule, servicepeople can be discharged if they state they are gay, lesbian, or bisexual or make a statement that indicates a propensity to engage in a homosexual act.

By the end of 2003, 9,682 service members were discharged from the military under the "don't ask, don't tell" policy. A 1999 report by the Servicemembers Legal Defense Network (SLDN), a gay rights group, noted that in the first five years of the "don't ask, don't tell" policy, there was a 92 percent increase in gay-related discharges. According to the military, these were the result of servicepersons' voluntarily "outing" themselves. The SLDN notes, however, that these "voluntary statements" include statements made in confidential settings such as counseling sessions, court testimony, and personal diaries. The SLDN report claims that many discharges are the result of coercion that circumvents the "don't ask, don't tell" policy.[160] An additional concern is violence directed toward gays in the military. In 1999 Pfc. Barry Winchell was murdered by soldiers on a Kentucky army base. The accused soldiers admitted that their motivation involved Winchell's sexual orientation. That murder spurred on the military to more proactively protect lesbian and gay service members. The two most significant outcomes of the Winchell murder were the addition of the "don't harass" prong and the Pentagon's adoption of an antiharassment action plan.[161]

The ban on gays and lesbians serving in the military puts the United States among interesting company. Countries that allow gays and lesbians to serve in the military include Australia, Austria, Bahamas, Belgium, Britain, Canada, the Czech Republic, Denmark, Estonia, Finland, France, Ireland, Israel, Italy, Lithuania, Luxembourg, the Netherlands, New Zealand, Norway, Slovenia, South Africa, Spain, Sweden, and Switzerland. In addition to the United States, countries that ban gay military service include Argentina, Belarus, Brazil, Croatia, Greece, Poland, Peru, Portugal, Russia, Turkey, and Venezuela. The list does not include countries in which homosexuality is banned outright, such as several Middle East nations.[162]

Gay and Lesbian Family Life

A long-standing issue for gays and lesbians has been the recognition of gay unions. In 2001, the Netherlands became the first country to recognize same-sex marriages (SSMs). Belgium followed suit, and by late 2004 six Canadian provinces and Massachusetts allowed SSMs. Denmark, Norway, Sweden, Finland, Greenland, Iceland, Germany, France, and Vermont allow same-sex couples to enter into legal partnerships, and although they have many of the benefits and protections of civil marriage, they are not legally married. Even though same-sex couples were able to obtain marriage licenses in San Francisco and in various towns in New Mexico and New York for short intervals during 2004, only Massachusetts allows SSMs. Conversely, 38 states had enacted legislation banning SSMs by late 2004.

• Twenty-six states have constitutional amendments explicitly barring the recognition of same-sex marriages.
• Forty-three states have statutes restricting marriage to persons of the opposite sex.
• Connecticut, New Jersey, Vermont, Maine, Hawaii, Oregon, Washington, and New Hampshire allow civil unions.
• Internationally, same-sex marriages are allowed in the Netherlands, Belgium, Spain, Canada, and South Africa. Same-sex marriages conducted abroad are recognized in Israel, Aruba, France, and the Netherlands Antilles.[163]

The question of gay marriages had become an issue in 1996, because it appeared that Hawaii might soon recognize such marriages. Other states were concerned that a same-sex couple could relocate to a state allowing such unions, fulfill whatever residency standards are required for marriage, and then move to another state that did not recognize the union. States were quick to react, and by late 1996 one-third of all states had passed legislation prohibiting the recognition of SSMs from another state. The federal government entered the fray by passing the Defense of Marriage Act (DOMA) that effectively established that the only legitimate marriage was with a member of the opposite sex. Ironically, in the same month that Congress passed DOMA, both IBM and the city of Denver extended domestic partnership benefits (e.g., health insurance) to their gay and lesbian employees.

A 1999 decision by the Vermont Supreme Court found no compelling reason to not recognize a civil union for same-sex couples and ruled that they should be granted the same rights and responsibilities as married Vermonters. The Vermont governor signed into law a "civil union" bill in 2002 granting Vermont gay and lesbian couples most of the rights and benefits available to married couples under the law.[164] These protections included insurance benefits, inheritance, medical decision-making rights, and state tax benefits and obligations. The one exception was the right to have a same-sex union

legally called a marriage; instead it was a civil union. The concept of civil union has been criticized because it creates a separate and thereby unequal set of rights.[165]

Seven Massachusetts gay and lesbian couples filed a lawsuit (*Goodridge et al. v. Department of Public Health*) in 2001 attempting to obtain the right to marry. In November 2003, the Massachusetts Supreme Judicial Court ruled that the state constitution allowed SSMs and that the state had to issue marriage licenses starting in May 2004. These marriages are recognized on the state level, but they are not recognized by the federal government.

In the 2004 elections, 11 states approved state constitutional amendments banning same-sex marriage. The antigay measures passed in Arkansas, Georgia, Kentucky, Michigan, Mississippi, Montana, North Dakota, Ohio, Oregon, Oklahoma, and Utah. Even though most of the states that passed the antigay marriage constitutional amendments already had laws on the books prohibiting same-sex marriage, antigay groups felt that amending the state constitutions would prevent court rulings like the one in Massachusetts. In a major blow to gay rights, California voters approved the California Marriage Protection Act, or Proposition, 8 on November 4,

■ *A long-standing issue for gays and lesbians has been the recognition of gay unions.*

2008. This proposition amended California's constitution to eliminate the right of same sex couples to marry by stating that only marriage between a man and a woman is valid or recognized in California. The proposition did not affect domestic partnerships in California. The Proposition 8 campaign raised more than $73 million (almost evenly split between supporters and nonsupporters), becoming the highest—funded campaign on any state ballot-spending on Proposition 8 was exceeded only by the presidential contest.[166]

Significant controversy arose around how different groups voted on the proposition. For instance, exit polls showed that most African Americans and Hispanics voted in favor of the measure. Religious attendance and affiliation were also strongly correlated with support of the measure. Regular church-goers supported the measure by a 4 to 1 ratio. A little less than 66 percent of both Protestants and Catholics voted yes, while 90 percent of those claiming no religion voted no. Republicans supported the proposition by a 4 to 1 margin.[167]

The question of parental rights is linked to the recognition of same-sex unions. Specifically, sexual orientation is often a factor in issues of family law, including custody, visitation, and foster/adoptive parent eligibility. Because homosexuality does not enjoy a constitutionally protected status, it can be considered in legal actions surrounding the rights of parents and would-be parents. In some jurisdictions it effectively blocks adoption and foster care placement. Although most states have no statute explicitly prohibiting gay and lesbian adoption or foster care placement, several states unofficially do not permit it.[168]

AIDS and the Gay Community

The AIDS crisis has been used to justify homophobic attitudes. In the early days of the epidemic (i.e., the 1980s), there were recommendations for quarantining AIDS victims, renewed attempts at punishing homosexual behavior, increased job discrimination, and a generally hostile climate for both gays and lesbians. At the federal level, former senator Jesse Helms successfully introduced a bill that prevented the Centers for Disease Control from using AIDS education funds in ways that could foster homosexuality. Although in the United States, AIDS still predominantly affects gay and bisexual men, intravenous drug users, and African American women, the movement of AIDS into the heterosexual community has fueled a certain sympathy toward the gay population. But positive change has come only after the documentation of more than a million AIDS cases in the United States, resulting in about 500,000 deaths through mid-2002.[169] Robert Walker writes of the early days of the AIDS epidemic:

> This was the time, the early 1980s, when the AIDS epidemic and its costs might have been contained, but effectively raising the alarm entailed serious political risks in all the affected communities—the political, the religious, and the homosexual. Political leaders took their cue from President Reagan's deafening silence, and most national, state, and local public and private institutions dithered through the critical years.[170]

Homophobia—the irrational fear of homosexuality—is a social phenomenon that has led to numerous attempts to limit the civil rights and legal protections of gays and lesbians. Justifications for this attitude have been found in traditional religious dogma that treats homosexuality as a sin against God, and in psychological explanations that view homosexuality as a disease or symptom of arrested development or a fear of intimacy. Nevertheless, the self-perception of gays and lesbians has undergone a dramatic shift since the 1960s. Gays and lesbians have begun to identify themselves as members of an oppressed minority, similar to other oppressed minority groups. As gays and lesbians have become more visible, they have organized support groups; religious groups such as Dignity (Roman Catholics), Integrity (Episcopalians), Mishpachat Am (Jews), and Lutherans Concerned; social service organizations; subchapters of professional associations; and political action groups. The political power of gays and lesbians had grown to the point that by 1984 activists were successful in inserting a gay civil rights plank in the Democratic Party platform. These changing attitudes have encouraged some political leaders to openly court the gay vote by supporting gay issues. The Clinton administration was the first to endorse gay rights openly (albeit erratically). For example, Clinton's administration backed the Employment Non-Discrimination Act (a gay civil rights bill); appointed more than 100 openly gay and lesbian persons to administrative jobs; nominated the first-ever open lesbian to the U.S. District Court; helped defeat antigay initiatives in Oregon, Maine, and Idaho; mandated that all federal agencies add sexual orientation to their affirmative action policies; stopped the practice of denying security clearance based on sexual orientation; granted political asylum to people at risk of persecution in their home countries based on their sexual orientation; and increased public health spending on AIDS.[171]

Gays and lesbians face discrimination in social and economic areas that is manifested in the absence of civil rights in employment and employment benefits, housing, immigration and naturalization, insurance, and custody and adoption.[172] Moreover, some social service agencies refuse to allow foster care in gay or lesbian homes; insurance companies deny workers the right to cover same-sex partners under their health insurance; and gays and lesbians are often refused the right to name their partner as next of kin in medical emergencies.

Gay and Lesbian Rights in an International Context

The tolerance and acceptance of gay, lesbian, bisexual, and transgendered (GLBT) peoples differ widely throughout the world. Along a continuum, many European nations have either legalized same-sex marriages or employ a system of registered partnerships. On the other end, homosexuality in countries like Saudi Arabia is theoretically punishable by death. In countries such as Egypt it can lead to prison sentences, and in some countries, very long sentences. Homosexuality is also forbidden in many sub-Saharan African nations like Nigeria and Uganda.

In other cases, homosexuality is simply denied. When Iranian president Ahmadinejad spoke in front of a Columbia University audience on September 24, 2007, he stated that: "In Iran, we don't have homosexuals like in your country. In Iran we don't have this phenomenon. I don't know who told you we had it."[173] In large measure, the United States seems to fall somewhere in the middle of the continuum between the most repressive and the most liberal countries regarding GLBT rights.

Legal recognition of same-sex relationships can be categorized in four main groups:

- *Marriage:* Same-sex couples have the same rights, responsibilities, and legal recognition given to married different-sex couples.
- *Registered Partnership:* Same-sex couples can enter into a formal registration agreement providing them with virtually (but not exactly) the equivalent status, rights, responsibilities, and legal recognition given to married couples. Typically this form of registration is open only

to same-sex partners, but some countries have also made it available to different-sex partners.
- *Registered Cohabitation:* A series of rights, responsibilities, and legal recognitions are given to couples who register their cohabitation. Often available to both same-sex and different-sex couples, this registration requires couples to prove they have lived together for a given period of time before they can register.
- *Unregistered Cohabitation:* Limited rights and responsibilities are automatically accrued after a specified period of cohabitation. These rights are almost always available to unmarried different-sex couples as well.[174]

In large measure, a nation's attitude toward gay and lesbian rights is reflective of their overall progressiveness. By 2008, five countries legalized same-sex marriages: Spain, Canada, South Africa, Belgium, and the Netherlands. Civil unions and registered partnerships are legal in Andorra, Czech Republic, Denmark, Finland, France, Germany, Hungary, Iceland, Luxembourg, New Zealand, Norway, Slovenia, Sweden, Switzerland, United Kingdom, and Uruguay. These kinds of unions are recognized in some regions or states of Argentina, Australia, Brazil, Mexico, and the United States. Unregistered cohabitation is recognized in Australia, Austria, Brazil, Colombia, Croatia, Israel, and Portugal.[175]

Ageism

Ageism is a problem in a consumer-oriented society that idolizes youth. Like other minority groups, the aged face significant social and economic barriers. For example, workers over 50 often find it difficult to find equivalent employment if they lose their jobs. The aged in the United States are seldom respected for their wisdom and experience and they do not occupy elevated social positions protected by tradition. Instead, once they have lost their earning potential, the aged are often perceived as a financial albatross around the neck of an economically productive society. Socially isolated in retirement communities, low-income housing, or other old-age ghettos, the aged often become invisible.

America is getting older—nearly 21 percent of the U.S. population will be 65 or older by 2050 compared with 12 percent in 2006. For the first 99 percent of human history, the average life expectancy was approximately 18 years. Life expectancy rose from age 47 in 1900 to 77.2 in 2002.[176]

Between 2000 and 2005, the population aged 55 and over increased by 13 percent to 67 million, more than four times the rate of people under 55. Due largely to the aging of the Baby Boom generation (those born between 1946 and 1964), the growth rate was especially rapid among those aged 55 to 65. While those aged 65 and older also increased (5 percent) in this five-year period, those aged 85 and older increased by 20 percent to 5.1 million. Among this older population over 55, there are 81 males for every 100 females; however, the number of males per 100 females for those aged 85 and older is less than half at 46.[177]

This aging trend will have important consequences for health care costs, because disabilities increase with age. Whereas only about 20 percent of people aged 65 to 74 need help with daily activities such as eating, bathing, and dressing, 52.5 percent of those over age 85 need assistance with daily activities.[178] Similarly, although only a small percentage (4.2 percent) of all elderly people live in nursing homes, these numbers vary dramatically with age.[179]

Elderly Poverty and Social Programs

The proportion of older people living in poverty and in low income has been declining in recent decades. In 1959, 35 percent of people aged 65 and over lived below the poverty threshold. In 2006, 9 percent lived in poverty, 26 percent were in the low-income group, 36 percent in the middle-income group, and 29 percent in the high-income group. Median household income has also increased, from $19,086 in 1974 to $27,798 in 2006.[180]

Poverty rates differ by age and sex in the older population. Older women (12 percent) were more likely than older men (7 percent) to live in poverty in 2006. Also, those aged 65 to 74 had a poverty rate of 9 percent, compared with 10 percent of those aged 75 and over. Race and ethnicity are also related to poverty in the older population. Older non-Hispanic whites (7 percent) were less likely than older African Americans (23 percent) and older Hispanics (19 percent) to be living in poverty. Older non-Hispanic white and African American women had higher poverty rates than their male counterparts.[181] As such, policymakers must calculate the impact of increasing numbers of minority elderly in determin-ing the future funding needs of health and income-based social programs.

In 2006, total income for those aged over 65 came largely from four sources: Social Security (37 percent); earnings (28 percent); pensions (18 percent); and asset income (15 percent). Most older people rely to some degree on Social Security. Nine out of 10 people age 65 and over live in families with income from Social Security, 60 percent are in families with income from assets, and almost one-half (45 percent) are in families with income from pensions. About one-third (36 percent) are in families with earnings, and 1 in 20 are in families receiving public assistance.[182] Other than the very poor, seniors are the only group with universal health coverage and the only group to receive non-means–tested government assistance. In contrast, younger workers today are less likely to have health insurance or pension benefits than are retired seniors.[183]

Health Care and the Elderly

As Judy Ochoa and Barbara Navarro point out, "In reality, both the stereotype from a few years ago of forgotten elders subsisting on dog food and the present day stereotype of 'country club' seniors have some basis in fact, but are only parts of a varied group with varying needs."[184] As the numbers of the very old and the minority elderly increase, we can expect a dramatic increase of seniors who are in financial need.

These trends have important implications for social welfare policy. For one, as the numbers of elderly increase, their demands on society for housing, health, and recreational services become greater. The stresses put on the health care system by an increasingly aging population are already evident in the near insolvency of Medicare. For example, the hospitalization rate increased from 306 hospital stays per 1,000 Medicare enrollees in 1992 to 350 in 2005, although the average length of a hospital stay decreased from 8.4 days to 5.7 days. Also, the number of Medicare-funded physician visits and consultations increased from 11,359 per 1,000 Medicare enrollees in 1992 to 13,914 in 2005.[185] As more of the population ages in the coming decades, and as the group aged 85 and over grows rapidly, the burden of health care expenses will become even more problematic.

Elderly women live longer than men, yet they have only 58 percent of their income. Hence, more of elderly women's health care costs will have to be paid by the government or by their families, putting increasing burdens on both. In addition, as people live longer and require more care—especially in-home care—more pressure will be put on family members to provide or pay for that care. Because families are already stressed by increasing work-loads, other family pressures, and the often large geographic distances between children and parents, the state may be pressed to provide even more care for greater numbers of the elderly.

The elderly vote in large numbers, and over the years their voices have been heard more clearly by politicians than those of minorities. In the 1960s policymakers responded to the needs of the elderly by passing the Older Americans Act (OAA) of 1965. The objectives of the OAA included (1) an adequate retirement income that corresponds to the general standard of living; (2) the promotion of good physi-cal and mental health, regardless of economic sta-tus; (3) the provision of centrally located, adequate, and affordable housing; (4) the availability of mean-ingful employment, with the elimination of age-specific and discriminatory employment practices; (5) the provision of civic, cultural, and recreational opportunities; and (6) adequate community servic-es, including low-cost transportation and supported living arrangements.[186]

Despite federal policies and vigorous advocacy by the American Association of Retired Persons (AARP) and other groups, ageism persists. Negative stereotypes of elderly persons continue to be perpetuated by the media and the film industry. Moreover, the elderly continue to be victimized by crime, domestic violence by family members, and job discrimination. Perhaps the clearest expression of continuing ageism is seen in employment poli-cies. The 1967 Age Discrimination in Employment Act (ADEA) protected most workers age 40 to 69 from discrimination in hiring, job retention, and promotion. However, for most workers the protec-tion of the ADEA stops when they reach age 70. Legislation to remove the "70 cap" has consistent-ly failed in Congress, as employer lobbies have argued that they require a free hand in personnel policies.

People with Disabilities

People with disabilities also experience the effects of discrimination. About 20 percent of the U.S. pop-ulation has disabilities that limit their ability to work.[187] (See Table 4.10 and Table 4.11.)

Table 4.10

Disabled Persons, Age 21–64

Disability	Percent Employed*
Difficulty hearing	68.1
Difficulty seeing	55.3
Mental disability	47.2
Difficulty walking	40.8

*Persons may have more than one type of disability.

Source: U.S. Census Bureau, *Americans with Disabilities: 2002* (Washington, DC: U.S. Department of Commerce, Economics, and Statistics Administration, May 2006). Retrieved April 2008, from www.census.gov/prod/2006pubs/p70-107.pdf

Disability is a difficult term to define. One med-ical definition is based on the assumption that a disability is a chronic disease requiring various forms of treatment. Another definition derived from the medical model—a definition used as a basis for determining eligibility in the Social Security Disability Insurance program—characterizes people with disabilities as those unable to work (or unable to work as frequently) in the same range of jobs as nondisabled people.[188] People with disabilities are viewed as inherently less productive than other members of society. A third model defines disability based on what those with disabilities cannot do, seeing the disabled in terms of their inability to per-form certain functions expected of the able-bodied population. As William Roth maintains, "The func-tional limitation, economic, and medical models all define disability by what a person is not—the med-ical model as not healthy, the economic model as not productive, the functional limitation model as not capable."[189]

A newer definition—the psychosocial model—views disability as a socially defined category. In other words, people with disabilities constitute a minority group, and if a person with disabilities is poor, it is because of discrimination rather than per-sonal inadequacy. This definition locates the prob-lem in the interaction between disabled people and the social environment. Therefore, the adjustment to disability is not a personal problem but a social challenge requiring the adjustment of society. This definition requires that society reevaluate its atti-tudes and remove the physical and transportation barriers placed in the way of people with disabili-ties. It also requires the elimination of stereotypes. In part, this newer definition of disability was expressed in Section 504 of the Rehabilitation Act of 1973 (PL 93–112).

Although the potential range of disabilities is vast, people with disabilities share a central experience rooted in stigmatization, discrimination, and oppression. Like other stigmatized groups, those with disabilities experience poverty in numbers disproportionately larger than the general population. Perhaps not surprisingly, rates of disability are greatest among the aged, African Americans, the poor, and blue-collar workers.[190] Compared to the able-bodied, people with disabilities tend to be more frequently unemployed and underemployed and, as a consequence, often fall below the poverty line. Because disability is often correlated with poor education, age, and poverty, it is not surprising that African Americans are twice as likely as whites to have some level of disability (their representation is even greater in the fully disabled population), and that more women are disabled than men. The problems of low wages and unemployment are exacerbated because people with disabilities often need more medical and hospital care than others, are less likely to have health insurance, and spend three times more of their own money on medical care than do the able-bodied.[191]

Although discrimination continues, major strides have been made to integrate people with disabilities into the social mainstream. These advances have often resulted from organized political activity on the part of the disabled and their families. For example, an outgrowth of this political activity is Title V of the Rehabilitation Act of 1973 mandating the following rules for all programs and facilities that receive federal funds:

- Federal agencies must have affirmative action programs designed to hire and promote people with disabilities.
- The Architectural and Transportation Barriers Compliance Board must enforce a 1968 rule mandating that all buildings constructed with federal funds, including buildings owned or leased by federal agencies, be accessible to people with disabilities.

Table 4.11

Characteristics of the Civilian Noninstitutionalized Population by Age, Disability Status, and Type of Disability, 2002

	Number (in thousands)	Percent
Total All Ages	**282,831**	**100.00**
With any disability	51,235	18.1
Total Population 6 years and older	**259,387**	**100.00**
With any disability	10,746	4.1
Total Population 15 years and older	**222,226**	**100.00**
With any disability	46,124	20.8
sensory	14,828	6.7
physical	43,555	19.6
mental	14,329	6.4
self-care	3,611	1.6
Total Population 25 to 64 years	**149,031**	**100.00**
With any disability	24,350	16.3
sensory	7,162	4.8
physical	20,853	14.0
mental	8,229	5.5
self-care	1,831	1.2
going outside the home	3,685	2.5
employment disability (age 16 to 64 years)	36,766	19.7
Population 65 years and over	**33,742**	**100.00**
With any disability	17,646	52.3
sensory	6,920	20.5
physical	21,733	64.4
mental	3,921	11.6
self-care	1,738	5.2
going outside the home	4,921	14.6

Source: U.S. Census Bureau, *Americans with Disabilities: 2002* (Washington, DC: U.S. Department of Commerce, Economics, and Statistics Administration, May 2006). Retrieved April 2008, from www.census.gov/prod/2006pubs/p70-107.pdf

- All businesses, universities, and other institutions having contracts with the federal government must implement affirmative action programs targeted for people with disabilities.
- Discrimination against people with disabilities is prohibited in all public and private institutions receiving federal assistance.

The greatest stride was made on July 26, 1990, when former President George H. W. Bush signed the Americans with Disabilities Act (ADA) (PL 101-336) into law (see Figure 4.4). This act is the most comprehensive legislation for people with disabilities ever passed in the United States. The ADA lays a foundation of equality for people with disabilities, and it extends to disabled people civil rights similar to those made available on the basis of race, sex, color, national origin, and religion through the Civil Rights Act of 1964. For example, the ADA prohibits discrimination on the basis of disability in private sector employment; in state and local government activities; and in public accommodations and services, including transportation provided by both public and private entities. Some policies of the ADA went into effect immediately, whereas others were to be phased in over several years.[192]

In spite of some serious loopholes, the ADA is an important step forward for disabled people. Nevertheless, some argue that even though the ADA is a good law in principle, abuses are stirring

I. Employment

   A. Employers may not discriminate against an individual with a disability in hiring or promotion if the person is otherwise qualified for the job.

   B. Employers can ask about one's ability to perform a job but cannot inquire if someone has a disability; nor can employers subject a person to tests that tend to screen out people with disabilities.

   C. Employers must provide "reasonable accommodation" to employees with disabilities. This includes job restructuring and modification of equipment. Employers are not required to provide accommodations that impose an "undue hardship" on business operations.

   D. All employers with 15 or more employees must comply with the ADA.

II. Transportation

   A. New public transit buses and rail cars must be accessible to individuals with disabilities.

   B. Transit authorities must provide comparable para-transit or other special transportation services to individuals with disabilities who cannot use fixed bus services, unless an undue burden would result.

   C. Existing rail systems must have one accessible car per train.

   D. New bus and train stations must be accessible. Key stations in rapid, light, and commuter rail systems must be made accessible. All existing Amtrak stations must be accessible by July 26, 2010.

III. Public Accommodations

   A. Private entities such as restaurants, hotels, and retail stores may not discriminate against individuals with disabilities.

   B. Auxiliary aids and services must be provided to individuals with vision or hearing impairments, unless an undue burden would result.

   C. If removal is readily achievable, physical barriers in existing facilities must be removed. All new construction and alterations of facilities must be accessible.

IV. State and Local Government

   A. State and local governments may not discriminate against individuals with disabilities.

   B. All government facilities, services, and communications must be accessible, consistent with the requirements of Section 504 of the Rehabilitation Act of 1973.

V. Telecommunications

   A. Companies offering telephone service to the general public must offer telephone relay services to individuals who use telecommunications services for the deaf (TDDs) or similar devices.

Figure 4.4

A Summary of the Americans with Disabilities Act

up widespread resistance. Specifically, disability is often defined so broadly that virtually anyone with a problem, regardless of its extent, can claim protection under the ADA. Moreover, some people seek to use this protection to excuse incompetence or inappropriateness on the job or in school. On the other hand, any social policy that addresses the widespread needs of a large constituent is inherently vulnerable to abuse.

Despite the ADA and other federal laws, discrimination is still widespread against people with disabilities. For instance, most buildings still do not meet the needs of the physically handicapped in terms of access, exits, restrooms, parking lots, warning systems, and so forth. Many apartment complexes and stores continue to be built without allowing for the needs of people with disabilities. The struggle for full social, political, and economic integration of the disabled remains an ongoing battle.

Legal Attempts to Remedy Discrimination

Attempts to eliminate discrimination are a relatively recent development. Although the 14th Amendment of the Constitution guaranteed all citizens equal protection under the law, it was also used to perpetuate discrimination on the basis of "separate but equal" treatment. Overt segregation existed in the South until the middle of the twentieth century, and separate but (supposedly) equal public facilities characterized much of the social and economic activity of the Southern United States. The extensive system of Southern segregation included public transportation, schools, private economic activities, and even public drinking fountains. It was only in the mid-1950s that the U.S. Supreme Court overturned the *Plessy v. Ferguson* (1896) decision that had formed the basis for the separate but equal doctrine.

Desegregation and the Civil Rights Movement

In a landmark decision on *Brown v. Board of Education of Topeka, Kansas,* the U.S. Supreme Court ruled in 1954 that separate but equal facilities in education were inherently unequal. The Court ruled that separating the races was a way of denoting the inferiority of African Americans. In addition,

the court ruled that segregation hindered the educational and mental development of African American children. Although the Supreme Court ruled against officially sanctioned segregation in public schools, **de facto segregation** was not addressed until the *Swann v. Charlotte-Mecklenburg Board of Education* ruling of 1971. This ruling approved court-ordered busing to achieve racial integration of school districts with a history of discrimination.

The gains made by African Americans were won through bitter struggle. Until the middle 1960s, Southern blacks enjoyed few rights, with total segregation enforced in almost all spheres of social, economic, political, and public life. Segregation in the North occurred through de facto, or unofficial, rather than de jure, or legal, means. The net effect was almost the same.

In 1955 Rosa Parks, too tired to stand in the "colored" section in the back of a bus in Montgomery, Alabama, sparked a nonviolent bus boycott led by Reverend Doctor Martin Luther King Jr. Still another protest was begun when African American students in North Carolina were refused service at an all-white lunch counter. The Civil Rights movement grew rapidly and resulted in widespread demonstrations (in Selma, Alabama, one march drew more than 100,000 people), picket lines, sit-ins, and other forms of political protest. Gaining international publicity, the protests of the late 1950s and early 1960s attracted Northern religious leaders, students, and white liberals—some of whom would lose their lives. By the time the Reverend Doctor Martin Luther King Jr. was assassinated in 1968, many demands of the Civil Rights movement had been incorporated in the Civil Rights Act of 1964. Ironically, Congress exempted itself from complying with the act until 1988. The 1964 Civil Rights Act had not lived up to its promise. Power had not shifted and African American and other minority groups continued to be disenfranchised economically, politically, and socially. It soon became apparent that other remedies were required. One of those was affirmative action, a set of policies designed to provide equal opportunities for minorities and women.

Affirmative Action

Two basic strategies have been employed to address racial, economic, and other injustices. The first is nondiscrimination, in which no preferential treatment is given to selected groups. The second is **affirmative action,** whose overall goal is to ensure that women and minorities are admitted, hired, and promoted in direct proportion to their numbers in the population. Affirmative action policies and legislation represent an aggressive step beyond the largely reactive stance taken by simple nondiscrimination policies. As such, affirmative action policies give preferential treatment to minority and female applicants. The ostensible goal is to right past wrongs done to groups of people throughout the country's history.

As a response to the Civil Rights movement, Presidents Kennedy, Johnson, and Nixon initiated affirmative plans to move the country toward nondiscrimination. Designed initially to address discrimination against African Americans, affirmative action policies were expanded to address discrimination based on gender, age, and disability.

There are three types of affirmative action programs: (1) employers and schools can adopt voluntary programs to increase the hiring of minorities and women; (2) the courts can order an employer or school to create an affirmative action plan; and (3) federal, state, and local governments can require contractors to adopt affirmative action plans to remain eligible for government contracts.[193]

As illustrated in Table 4.12, affirmative action and civil rights legislation affect a much wider group of Americans than minorities. Moreover, as demonstrated by the table, rulings on affirmative action and civil rights cases have been inconsistent, characterized by two steps forward and one or two steps backward. This has occurred partly because civil rights and affirmative action policies have emerged from often contradictory legislation or court decisions.

Opponents of affirmative action argue that it leads to racial quota systems, preferential treatment, and reverse discrimination. They argue that it violates the equal protection under the laws guaranteed in the Fourteenth Amendment. Still others argue that affirmative action benefits minority group members who do not need the help while placing whites who are innocent of any wrongdoing at a disadvantage. These critics maintain that rights inhere in individuals, not in groups. Other conservatives, such as Supreme Court Justice Antonin Scalia, argue that there never was a justification for affirmative action because the Constitution is "colorblind."[194] Moderates such as former President Bill Clinton note that "Affirmative action has been good for America. Affirmative action has not always been perfect, and affirmative action should not go on forever. . . . We

should reaffirm the principle of affirmative action and fix the practices. We should have a simple slogan: Mend it, but don't end it."[195] Yet attacks on affirmative action have also come from liberal quarters. Columnist Roger Hernandez argues:

> Admittedly, affirmative action offers protection from discrimination. But the price it exacts is too high. Affirmative action reinforces the degrading notion that certain cultures are so inferior they render all individuals brought up in it [sic]—regardless of their socioeconomic status—into incompetent fools who cannot get along without special attention. . . . The sense of ethnic inferiority such a philosophy encourages does more harm than the outright discrimination affirmative action is supposed to prevent. . . . Ending affirmative action attacks the idea that every member of certain ethnic groups is a muddle of social pathologies.[196]

William Julius Wilson, an African American sociologist, criticizes the ability of affirmative action strategies to help the most disadvantaged members of society:

> Programs based solely on [race-specific solutions] are inadequate . . . to deal with the complex problems of race in America. . . . This is because the most disadvantaged members of racial minority groups, who suffer the cumulative effects of both race and class subjugation . . . are disproportionately represented amongst the segment of the general population that has been denied the resources to compete effectively in a free and open market. . . . On the other hand, the competitive resources developed by the advantaged minority members . . . result in their benefitting disproportionately from policies that promote the rights of minority individuals by removing artificial barriers to valued positions. . . . [If] policies of preferential . . . treatment are developed in terms of racial group membership rather than real disadvantages suffered by individuals, then these policies will further improve the opportunities of the advantaged without necessarily addressing the problems of the truly disadvantaged such as the ghetto underclass.[197]

Affirmative action is one of the most controversial facets of U.S. social policy. Moreover, it is open to a wide array of moral conundrums. For example, how much discrimination does a group have to encounter before preferential treatment is justified? Although Asian Americans continue to encounter significant discrimination, their income levels and educational attainment arguably mitigate against the need for preferential treatment. Moreover, if historical social discrimination were a basis for

Table 4.12

Milestones in Civil Rights and Affirmative Action Rulings

Legislation or Court Ruling	Summary
Plessy v. Ferguson (1896)	The U.S. Supreme Court established the "separate but equal" doctrine.
Fair Employment Practices Committee (1935)	Employers are directed to not discriminate in hiring based on race.
Brown v. Board of Education of Topeka, Kansas (1954)	The Supreme Court ruled that "separate but equal" facilities in education were inherently unequal.
Equal Pay Act of 1963	Men and women have a right to equal pay for doing the same work
Civil Rights Act of 1964, including amendments added in 1972, 1978, and 1991	1. Voter registration is a legal right that cannot be tampered with. 2. It is unlawful to discriminate or segregate based on race, color, religion, or national origin in any public accommodation, including hotels, motels, theaters, and other public places. 3. The attorney general will undertake civil action on the part of any person who is denied access to a public accommodation. If the owner continues to discriminate, a court fine and imprisonment will result. 4. The attorney general must represent anyone who undertakes the desegregation of a public school. 5. Each federal department must take action to end discrimination in all programs or activities receiving federal assistance. 6. Public or private employers, employment agencies, or labor unions with more than 15 employees cannot discriminate against an individual because of their race, color, religion, national origin, or sex. An Equal Opportunity Commission will be established to enforce this provision. A 1968 amendment to this act prohibited discrimination in housing.
Age Discrimination Act of 1967	Persons over 40 may not be discriminated against in any terms or conditions of their employment.
Griggs v. Duke Power Co. (1971)	The Court prohibited discriminatory employment practices. It put the burden of proof on the employer to show that hiring criteria have a direct relationship to the job. Griggs was overturned by *Wards Cove Packing Co. Inc. v. Atonio* (1989), in which the Court imposed tougher standards for proving discrimination and shifted the burden of proof onto the employee.
Swann v. Charlotte-Mecklenburg Board of Education (1971)	The Court ruled in favor of court-ordered busing to achieve racial integration of school districts with a history of discrimination.
Title IX of Education Amendments of 1972	Institutions receiving federal financial assistance may not discriminate based on sex.
Rehabilitation Act of 1973	Discrimination on the basis of mental or physical disability is prohibited.
Vietnam Era Veterans Readjustment Act of 1974	Employers with federal contracts must take steps to employ and advance qualified disabled veterans.
Milliken v. Brady (1974)	The Court ruled that mandatory school busing across city-suburban boundaries to achieve racial integration was not required unless segregation had resulted from an official action.
Marco DeFunis v. University of Washington Law School (1974)	DeFunis claimed that he was denied admission to law school even though his grades and test scores were higher than those of minorities who were admitted. The Supreme Court ruled in his favor.

(Continued)

Table 4.12

(Continued)

Legislation or Court Ruling	Summary
Age Discrimination Act of 1975	Employers who receive federal financial assistance cannot discriminate based on age.
Regents of the University of California v. Bakke (1978)	The Supreme Court ruled that Alan Bakke was unfairly denied admission to the University of California–Davis Medical School. Like DeFunis, Bakke argued that his qualifications were stronger than those of many of the minority candidates who were admitted.
United Steelworkers v. Weber (1979)	The Court upheld an affirmative action plan to erase entrenched racial biases in employment.
Fullilove v. Klutznick (1980)	The court ruled that federal public works contracts may require 10 percent of the work to go to minority firms.
Firefighters Local Union No. 1784 v. Stotts (1984)	The Court ruled that an employer may use seniority rules in laying off employees, even when those rules adversely affect minority employees. This ruling was a blow to affirmative action, because it perpetuated the dilemma that minorities are the last to be hired and the first to be fired. The Department of Justice used this decision to force Indianapolis and 49 other jurisdictions to abandon their use of hiring quotas.
Wyatt v. Jackson Board of Education (1986)	An affirmative action plan must have a strong basis in evidence for remedial action.
United States v. Paradise (1987)	The Court found that a judge may order racial quotas in promoting and hiring to address "egregious" past discrimination.
Johnson v. Transportation Agency (1987)	The Court permitted the use of gender as a factor in hiring and promotion.
City of Richmond v. J. A. Croson (1989)	The Court imposed standards of "strict scrutiny." Racial or ethnic classifications must serve a compelling interest and be narrowly tailored.
Martin v. Wilks (1989)	The Court imposed tougher standards for Asian Americans to be included in affirmative action plans and made it easier to challenge settlements of those plans.
Metro Broadcasting, Inc. v. FCC (1990)	The Court allowed minority preferences to promote diverse viewpoints across the airwaves.
Adarand Constructors, Inc. v. Pena (1995)	The Court ruled that federal affirmative measures using racial and ethnic criteria in decision making must meet the same standards of strict scrutiny imposed in *Croson*.
Hopwood v. State of Texas (1996 5th Cir.)	The appeals court ruled that the University of Texas's goal of achieving a diverse student body did not justify its affirmative action program, suggesting that achieving diversity does not represent a compelling state interest.
California Proposition 209 (California Civil Rights Initiative) (1996). Now Article I, Section 31 of the California Constitution	Racial or gender preferences in public education, employment, and state contracting are prohibited. In 1997 a three-judge panel of the Ninth Circuit Court of Appeals upheld the referendum passed by California voters. The U.S. Supreme Court refused to consider the appeal.* The passage of the CCRI effectively put an end to affirmative action in California.
Washington State I-200 (1998)	"Preferences" in state and municipal hiring and recruitment to the state university system are prohibited. This 1998 ballot measure effectively repealed affirmative action in Washington state.

Table 4.12

(Continued)

Legislation or Court Ruling	Summary
One Florida Plan (1999)	Racial preferences in university admissions and state contracting are prohibited. In November 1999 Florida Gov. Jeb Bush ordered an end to racial preference programs in agencies under his control. The One Florida plan replaces race and ethnicity with criteria such as a student's socioeconomic background, geographical diversity, status as a first-generation college student, or preparation in a low-performing D or F school.
Grutter v. Bollinger and *Gratz v. Bollinger* (2003)	The U.S. Supreme Court ruled that race can be a factor in university admission decisions but limited the extent of it. In two separate but related decisions, the Court ruled that the University of Michigan's law school affirmative action policy (*Grutter v. Bollinger*) that favors minorities is legal. In the second decision (*Gratz v. Bollinger*) it ruled that the University of Michigan's undergraduate admissions, which awards 20 points on a 100 point scale to African Americans, Hispanics, and Native Americans, violated equal protection provisions of the Constitution.

*D. D. Gehring (ed.), *Responding to the New Affirmative Actions Climate: New Directions for Student Services* (San Francisco: Jossey-Bass, 1998).

Sources: Adapted from ACLU, "Affirmative Action," ACLU Briefing Paper No. 17 (New York: ACLU, n.d.); American Council on Education, "Major Civil Rights and Equal Opportunity Legislation Since 1963." Retrieved October 21, 2008, from www.acenet.edu/bookstore/descriptions/making_the_case/legal/legislation.cfm; Winnie Chen, Vilma Hernandez, Erin Townsend, and Carol Wyatt, "Affirmative Action," unpublished class paper, Graduate School of Social Work, University of Houston, 1996; Marjorie Blythe and Anna Conaty, "Affirmative Action and the State of America's Minorities," unpublished paper, Graduate School of Social Work, University of Houston, 2000; and National Public Radio, "Split Ruling on Affirmative Action High Court Rules on Race as Factor in University Admissions," June 23, 2003. Retrieved October 2004, from www.npr.org/news/specials/michigan

affirmative action, then Jews, Catholics, Irish, Eastern Europeans, and other groups who have historically been squeezed out of the U.S. social mainstream should also be eligible. Moreover, poor whites are discriminated against in U.S. society because of their class background. Should they be covered under affirmative action? Women who grow up in upper-class families and attend Ivy League universities are covered under affirmative action by virtue of their gender. Do they experience more discrimination than a poor white Appalachian male? These are some issues that plague the development of clear and fair affirmative action guidelines.

Conclusion

Discrimination takes many forms in the United States. It can be targeted against African Americans, Hispanics, Native Americans, Asians, women, gays and lesbians, the elderly, people with disabilities, and poor whites. Because discrimination often leads to poverty, it often results in the creation of income maintenance and poverty programs designed to curb its effects. Those who become beneficiaries of these programs soon find themselves with a second handicap—the stigma of being on public assistance, or just plain needing help.

Some policymakers have tried to reduce the need for long-term and expensive social welfare programs by attempting to arrest the cycle of discrimination and stigma. They often undertake this effort by advocating for policies and legislation designed to attack discrimination at its roots. Antidiscrimination programs, policies, and legislation often include affirmative action policies, women's rights legislation, city and state gay and lesbian ordinances, and legislation protecting the rights of the physically and mentally challenged. Policymakers hope that by curtailing discrimination, U.S. society can offer at-risk populations equal opportunities for achievement and success. At best, the scorecard on these well-intentioned policies has been mixed. Despite a strong start, affirmative action programs have not led to widespread economic success for women and minorities. Gays and lesbians continue to be discriminated against, even in places that have passed civil rights ordinances. Although women have made significant gains over the past few decades, they still earn less than males in comparable jobs. Poverty rates for minority groups are three times higher than for whites and their median family incomes are lower.

When added together, the vast majority of the U.S. population experiences discrimination: 51 percent of the population are women; almost 13 percent are over age 65; almost 20 percent are disabled; and roughly one in three Americans are Hispanic, African American, or Asian. Hence, discrimination in U.S. society is not about numbers, per se, but reflects the relative lack of political, social, and economic power of marginalized groups.

Discussion Questions

1. The effects of racism can take many forms, including overt discrimination, poverty, housing problems, high rates of underemployment and unemployment, wage differentials, family disruption, inferior educational opportunities, high crime rates, and welfare dependency. The relationship between racism and poverty is clear. Less clear, however, are the causes of racism. Describe what you believe to be the primary causes of both individual and institutional racism. How are these factors nourished or condemned by society?

2. In recent years there has been a marked increase in the number of racially based incidents, especially against African Americans, Asian Americans, gays and lesbians, Jews and Muslims, and those of Arabic descent. What factors explain the rise of such incidents?

3. Over the past four decades, numerous legal and judicial decisions have attempted to eradicate racism, including the 1964 Civil Rights Act and various Supreme Court rulings. Were these attempts successful? If not, why not? What, if anything, can be done to eliminate racism?

4. It is generally acknowledged that sexism is a powerful and pervasive force permeating much of U.S. society. How is sexism manifested? What strategies, if any, can be employed to lessen the impact of sexism in society?

5. Most women in U.S. society work to either provide a necessary second income or as the family's primary wage earner. Describe some of the major obstacles faced by working women. What can be done to eliminate some of these obstacles?

6. Gays and lesbians face severe economic and social problems apart from AIDS. What are some of the most important social, political, and economic hurdles standing in the way of full equality for gays and lesbians? What can be done to ameliorate these obstacles?

7. Being elderly in U.S. society is in many ways a social handicap. Describe some key social, economic, and political indicators that illustrate this belief.

8. It is generally agreed that people with disabilities face significant discrimination. What is the evidence, if any, to support this belief?

Notes

1. Billy J. Tidwell, "Racial Discrimination and Inequality," *Encyclopedia of Social Work*, 18th ed. (Silver Spring, MD: NASW, 1987), p. 450.

2. J. Dollard et al., *Frustration and Aggression* (New Haven, CT: Yale University Press, 1939).

3. Theodore W. Adorno et al., *The Authoritarian Personality* (New York: Harper & Row, 1950).

4. Wilhelm Reich, *Listen Little Man* (Boston: Beacon Press, 1971).

5. Tidwell, "Racial Discrimination and Inequality."

6. Stephanie Bernardo, *The Ethnic Almanac* (Garden City, NY: Doubleday, 1981).

7. V. Dion Haynes, "Movement Aims to Explain and Deflate White Power," *Daily Titan*, 1999. Retrieved 2000, from http://titanyearbook.com/archives/1998/1998-03-04.pdf

8. U.S. Census Bureau, "Population Profile of the United States: Dynamic Version by Race and Hispanic Origin in 2005." Retrieved April 2008, from www.census.gov/population/pop-profile/dynamic/RACEHO.pdf

9. See Andrew Cassel, "Black Middle Class Continues to Grow, but Gaps Remain," *Philadelphia Inquirer* (July 12, 2004), p. B6.

10. U.S. Census Bureau, "The Black Population in the United States: Population CPS Reports 2001–2004." Retrieved May 2008, www.census.gov/population/www/socdemo/race/black.html

11. See U.S. Census Bureau, "Census Bureau Facts for Features, African American History Month," Washington, DC; February 14, 2000; and U.S. Census Bureau, "Census Bureau Facts for Features, African American History Month 2004," January 7, 2004. Retrieved July 2004, from www.census.gov/Press-Release/www/releases/archives/facts_for_features_special_editions/002270.html

12. U.S. Census Press Release, "Minority Groups Increasing Business Ownership at Higher Rate than National Average, Census Bureau Reports," U.S. Census Bureau News, Public Information Office, Washington, DC, July 28, 2005.

13. William Julius Wilson, *The Truly Disadvantaged: The Inner City, the Underclass, and Public Policy* (Chicago: University of Chicago Press, 1987), p. 109.

14. U.S Census Bureau, "Housing Vacancies and Homeownership (CPS/HVS)—Homeownership Rates by Race and Ethnicity of Householder: 1994 to 2007." Retrieved May 2008 from www .census .gov/hhes/www/housing/hvs/annual07/ann07t20 .html

15. U.S. Census Bureau News, "College Degree Nearly Doubles Annual Earnings, Census Bureau Reports," Washington, DC, March 28, 2005. Retrieved April 2008, from www.census.gov/Press-Release/www/releases/archives/education/ 004214.html

16. U.S. Census Bureau, "Current Population Survey: 2006," Washington, DC, revised August 2007. Retrieved April 2008, from http://pubdb3.census.gov/macro/032007/perinc/new03_005.htm

17. U.S. Census Bureau, "Current Population Survey: 2006," Washington, DC, revised August 2007. Retrieved April 2008, from http://pubdb3.census.gov/macro/032007/perinc/new03_000.htm

18. American Council on Education, "Students of Color Make Dramatic Gains in College Enrollment but Still Trail Whites in the Rate at Which They Attend College" October 30, July 2006. Retrieved June 2008, from www.acenet.edu/AM/Template.cfm?Section=Search&template=/CM/HTMLDisplay.cfm&ContentID=21571

19. Carmen DeNavas-Walt, Bernadette D. Proctor, and Jessica Smith, "Income, Poverty, and Health Insurance Coverage in the United States: 2006." Economics and Statistics Administration, U.S. Census Bureau, issued August 2007. Retrieved June 2008, from www.census.gov/prod/2007pubs/p60-233.pdf

20. U.S. Census Bureau, "Current Population Survey: 2006," Washington, DC, revised August 2007. Retrieved April 2008, from http://pubdb3.census.gov/macro/032007/perinc/new03_009.htm

21. U.S. Census Bureau News, "Household Income Rises, Poverty Rate Declines, Number of Uninsured Up," Washington, DC, August 28, 2007. Retrieved April 2008, from www.census.gov/Press-Release/www/releases/archives/income_wealth/010583.html

22. DeNavas-Walt, Proctor, and Smith, "Income, Poverty, and Health Insurance Coverage in the United States: 2006."

23. U.S. Census Bureau, "Census Bureau Facts for Features, African-American History Month: February 2008," Washington, DC, December 03, 2007. Retrieved April 2008, from www.census.gov/Press-Release/www/releases/archives/facts_for_features_special_editions/010969.html

24. U.S. Census Bureau, "Projected Population of the United States, by Race and Hispanic Origin: 2000 to 2050," March 18, 2004. Retrieved July 2004, from www.census.gov/population/www/projections/usinterimproj

25. U.S. Census Bureau, "Minority Population Tops 100 Million," Washington, DC, December 03, 2007. Retrieved April 2008, from www.census.gov/Press-Release/www/releases/archives/population/010048.html

26. See "Family Income Finally Rises," *New York Times* (September 27, 1996), p. 18; and U.S. Census Bureau, "The Black Population in the United States, March 2002." Retrieved July 2004, from www.census.gov/prod/2003pubs/p20-541.pdf

27. U.S. Census Bureau, "Census Bureau Facts for Features, African American History Month, 2004."

28. "Vital Statistics," *The Journal of Blacks in Higher Education*, 40 (Summer 2003), p. 9.

29. Jared Bernstein, *Where's the Payoff?* (Washington, DC: Economic Policy Institute, 1995).

30. Bureau of Labor Statistics, Employment Situation Summary, 2003. Retrieved September 2004, from www.bls.gov/news.release/empsit.nr0.htm

31. Bernstein, *Where's the Payoff?*

32. Bureau of Justice Statistics, "Prison Statistics," June 2007. Retrieved June 2008, from www.ojp.usdoj.gov/bjs/prisons.htm

33. Bureau of Justice Statistics, "Criminal Offender Statistics." Retrieved June 2008, from www.ojp.usdoj.gov/bjs/crimoff.htm#inmates

34. U.S. Department of Justice, Bureau of Justice Statistics Bulletin, "Prison and Jail Inmates at Midyear 2004," April 2005. Retrieved April 2008, from www.ojp.usdoj.gov/bjs/pub/ascii/pjim04.txt

35. See American Bar Association, "A Statistical Look at Criminal Justice and Injustice," *Human Rights Magazine* (Winter 2004), p. 19; and Matthew Klein, "Death Row in Black and White," *American Demographics* 20, no. 5, pp. 39–40.

36. U.S. Department of Justice, Bureau of Justice Statistics, "Homicide Trends in the U.S.—Trends by Race, 2004." Retrieved September 2004, from www.ojp.usdoj.gov/bjs/homicide/race.htm

37. Gareth G. Davis and David B. Mulhausen, "Young African-American Males: Continuing Victims of High Homicide Rates in Urban Communities," The Heritage Foundation, Washington, DC.

38. U.S. Census Bureau, "Housing Vacancies and Home Ownership: Annual Statistics 2007." Retrieved June 2008, from www.census.gov/hhes/www/housing/hvs/annual07/ann07t20.html

39. Howard A. Savage, "Who Could Afford to Buy a Home in 2002?" July 2007. Retrieved June 2008, from www.census.gov/prod/2007pubs/h121-07-1.pdf

40. Centers for Disease Control and Prevention, CDC Features, "CDC Addresses the HIV/AIDS Epidemic among African Americans," February 2008. Retrieved April 2008, from www.cdc.gov/Features/BlackHIVAIDSAwareness

41. National Vital Statistics Reports, "Deaths: Preliminary Data for 2006," June 2008. Retrieved June 2008, from www.cdc.gov/nchs/data/nvsr/nvsr56/nvsr56_16.pdf

42. Center for Disease Control and Prevention, "Births: Final Data for 2002," *National Vital Statistics Reports* 52, no. 10 (2003). Retrieved September 2004, from www.cdc.gov/nchs/data/nvsr/nvsr52/nvsr52_10.pdf

43. "Vital Statistics," *The Journal of Blacks in Higher Education*, no. 59 (Spring 2008).

44. U.S. Census Bureau, "Earnings by Occupation and Education, 2004." Retrieved October 2004, from www.census.gov/prod/2004pubs/censr-15.pdf

45. Mishel and Frankel, *The State of Working America*, p. 253.

46. "Vital Statistics," *The Journal of Blacks in Higher Education*. 40 (Summer 2003), p. 9.

47. See U.S. Department of Health and Human Services, Indicators of Welfare Dependence: Annual Report to Congress, 2003, HHS, Washington, DC.

48. Department of Commerce, "Young, Diverse, Urban: Hispanic Population Reaches All-Time High of 38.8 Million."

49. Ibid.

50. U.S. Census Bureau, "The Hispanic Population in the United States: March 2002," June 2003. Retrieved August 2004, from www.census.gov/prod/2003pubs/p20-545.pdf

51. U.S. Census Bureau, "Income, Poverty and Health Insurance Coverage in the United States: 2003," August 2004. Retrieved September 2004, from www.census.gov/prod/2004pubs/p60-226.pdf

52. Hispanic News Link, "Hispanics Who Defy Averages," *The Numbers News* (September 1995), p. 1.

53. Bruce H. Webster Jr. and Alemayehu Bishaw, "Income, Earnings, and Poverty Data from the 2006 American Community Survey," August 2007.

54. Roberto R. Ramirez and G. Patricia de la Cruz, "The Hispanic Population in the United States: March 2002," *Current Population Reports*, U.S. Census Bureau, Washington, DC, June 2003.

55. U.S. Census Bureau, "Poverty, Income See Slight Changes; Child Poverty Rate Unchanged."

56. See Ramirez and de la Cruz, "The Hispanic Population in the United States: March 2002"; and Guadalupe Gibson, "Mexican Americans," *Encyclopedia of Social Work*, 18th ed. (Silver Spring, MD: NASW, 1987), p. 139.

57. Ramirez and de la Cruz, "The Hispanic Population in the United States: March 2002."

58. Ibid.

59. U.S. Census Bureau, "Summary Statistics for Changes in the Number of Hispanic-Owned Businesses and Their Receipts: 1997 to 2002." Retrieved June 2008, from www.census.gov/csd/sbo/summarychangehispanic.pdf

60. See Evelyn Lance Blanchard, "American Indians and Alaska Natives," *Encyclopedia of Social Work*, 18th ed. (Silver Spring, MD: NASW, 1987), p. 61; U.S. Bureau of the Census, *Census of Population and Housing Summary* (Washington, DC: U.S. Government Printing Office, 1990), p. 93; and U.S. Department of the Interior, Bureau of Indian Affairs, "Statistical Abstract on the Web."

61. Compiled from Bureau of Indian Affairs, Answers to Frequently Asked Questions, 2001. Retrieved August 2004, from http://usa.usembassy.de/etexts/soc/bia.pdf. See also U.S. Department of the Interior. Retrieved October 21, 2008, from www.doi.gov/bia

62. H. F. Dobyns, *Native American Historical Demography: A Critical Bibliography* (Bloomington, IN: Indiana University Press, 1976), p. 32.

63. H. E. Fey and D. McNickle, *Indians and Other Americans: Two Ways of Life Meet* (New York: Harper & Row, 1970), pp. 9–12.

64. Thomas Hayden, "A Modern Life: After Decades of Discrimination, Poverty, and Despair, American Indians Can Finally Look Toward a Better Future," *U.S. News and World Report* (October 4, 2004), p. 20.

65. U.S. Commission on Civil Rights, Office of the General Counsel, "Broken Promises: Evaluating the Native American Health Care System," Draft Report for Commissioners' Review, Washington, DC, July 2, 2004.

66. William N. Evans and Julie H. Topoleski, "The Social and Economic Impact of Native American Casinos," *NBER Working Paper No. w9198*, National Bureau of Economic Research, September 2002. Retrieved October 2004, from www.bsos.umd.edu/econ/evans/wpapers/evans_topoleski_casinos.pdf

67. B. J. Jones, "The Indian Child Welfare Act: The Need for a Separate Law," American Bar Association, 1995. Retrieved October 2004, from www.abanet.org/genpractice/compleat/f95child.html

68. U.S. Department of Justice, "Coverage Issues under the Indian Self-Determination Act," Memorandum for the Assistant Attorney General Civil Division, April 22, 1998. Retrieved October 2004, from www .usdoj.gov/olc/isdafin.htm

69. U.S. Census Bureau, "The Asian Population, 2000," February 2002. Retrieved September 2004, from www.census.gov/prod/2002pubs/c2kbr01-16.pdf

70. Felicity Barringer, "U.S. Asian Population Up 70% in 80's," *New York Times* (March 2, 1990), p. 1.

71. U.S. Census Bureau, "Population by Race and Hispanic Origin: 2000 and 2004." Retrieved June 2008, from www.census.gov/population/pop-profile/dynamic/RACEHO.pdf

72. U.S. Census Bureau, "Educational Attainment in the United States: 2003," June 2004. Retrieved August 2004, from www.census.gov/prod/2002pubs/c2kbr01-16.pdf

73. Daniel Goleman, "Probing School Success of Asian-Americans," *New York Times*, September 11, 1990, p. A8.

74. U.S. Bureau of the Census, "Educational Attainment in the United States: 2003."

75. U.S. Department of State, Bureau of International Information Programs, "September 11 Hurt New York's Chinatown, but Human Smuggling Continues to Flourish," June 17, 2004. Washington, D.C.

76. Bruce Brown, "Evidence of a Glass-Ceiling for Asian-Americans," Cal State Polytechnic University, WEAI Conference, Denver, CO, July 12, 2003. Retrieved October 2004, from www.csupomona.edu/~bbrown

77. Sussumu Awanchara, "Hit by a Backlash," *Far Eastern Economic Review* 155, no. 2 (March 26, 1992), p. 30.

78. Ibid.

79. "What Expires in 2007?" Retrieved March 20, 2007, from www.renewthevra.org/resources/reauthorization.html

80. "Myth: Voting Rights for African Americans Expire in 2007." Retrieved March 20, 2007, from www .renewthevra. org/resources/notexpire.html

81. Jeffrey S. Passel, Randy Capps, and Michael Fix, "Undocumented Immigrants: Facts and Figures," Urban Institute Immigration Studies Program, Washington, DC, January 12, 2004.

82. Nancy F. Rytina, "Estimates of the Legal Permanent Resident Population and Population Eligible to Naturalize in 2002," U.S. Department of Homeland Security, Office of Immigration Statistics, Washington, DC, May 2004.

83. U.S. Census Bureau, "Income, Poverty and Health Insurance Coverage in the United States, 2003," August 2004. Retrieved September 2004, from www.census.gov/prod/2004pubs/p60-226.pdf

84. Pia M. Orrenius, Federal Reserve Bank of Dallas, "U.S. Immigration and Economic Growth: Putting Policy on Hold," *Southwest Economy* (6), (November/December 2003), p. 3.

85. Ibid.

86. U.S. Department of Justice, Immigration and Naturalization Service, "Immigration to the United States in Fiscal Year 1995" (Washington, DC: USDOJ, August 5, 1996).

87. Office of Immigration Statistics, "2003 Yearbook of Immigrations Statistics," September 2004. Retrieved August 2004, from http://uscis.gov/graphics/shared/aboutus/statistics/2003Yearbook.pdf

88. HR 3734: Personal Responsibility and Work Opportunity Reconciliation Act (Immigration Provisions)—Conference Committee Version: Title IV, Restricting Welfare and Public Benefits for Aliens (Washington, DC: U.S. House of Representatives, Conference Committee, August 5, 1996), p. 16.

89. Patty Reinert, "Federal Welfare Plan Hits Legal Immigrants," *Houston Chronicle* (August 2, 1996), pp. 1A and 16A.

90. Greg McDonald, "House Passes $600 Billion Spending Bill," *Houston Chronicle* (September 29, 1996), pp. 1A and 32A.

91. "United States Immigration and Naturalization Law: Foreign Students." Retrieved June 2008, from www .studyoverseas.com/america/usaed/visa.htm

92. Orrenius, "U.S. Immigration and Economic Growth."

93. Ibid.

94. Muzaffar A. Chishti, Doris Meissner, Demetrios G. Papademetriou, Jay Peterzell, Michael J. Wishnie, and Stephen W. Yale-Loehr, *America's Challenge: Domestic Security, Civil Liberties, and National Unity After September 11* (Washington, DC: Migration Policy Institute, 2003).

95. Ibid., p. 18.

96. "Mexican Migration to the United States." Retrieved March 20, 2007, from www.farmworkers.org/migrdata.html

97. "The Official Bracero Agreement." Retrieved March 20, 2007, from www.farmworkers.org/bpaccord.html

98. Dick Meister, "Give Braceros Their Money," 2001. Retrieved March 20, 2007, from www.labornet.org/viewpoints/meister/braceros.htm

99. Matthew Bigg, "U.S. 'Guest' Worker Program Exploitative: Report," *Reuters*, March 12, 2007. Retrieved March 20, 2007, from www.reuters.com/article/topNews/idUSN1237714820070312?pageNumber=1

100. U.S. Department of Justice, "National Crime Victimization Survey," August 1995. Quoted in U.S. Department of Justice, "The Violence against Women Act," September 23, 1996. Retrieved 2000, from www.ovw.usdoj.gov/index.html

101. Patricia Tjaden and Nancy Thoennes, "Extent, Nature, and Consequences of Intimate Partner Violence: Findings from the National Violence against Women

Survey," National Institute of Justice, NCJ 181867, July 2000. Retrieved October 2004, from http://ncjrs.org/txtfiles1/nij/181867.txt

102. U.S. Department of Justice, National Crime Victimization Survey.

103. Update on VAWA, *National NOW Times* (January 1995). Retrieved 1999, from www.now.org

104. Jan Erickson, "Legislative Update: End of Year Funding Bills Leave Lives in the Balance," *National NOW Times* (Winter 2003/2004), p. 24.

105. Diana Pearce, quoted in S. Bianchi, "Feminization and Juvenilization of Poverty: Trends, Relative Risks, Causes and Consequences," *Annual Review of Sociology* 25 (1999), pp. 307–333.

106. Ruth Sidel, *Women and Children Last* (New York: Harper, 1984).

107. See Women's Bureau, "Women Who Maintain Families," U.S. Department of Labor, Washington, DC, June 1993; Appalachian Regional Commission, Households and Families in Appalachia, 2003. Retrieved October 2004, from www.arc.gov/index.do?nodeId=2166; and National Women's Law Center, "Many Women Still Not Benefitting from Overall Declines in U.S. Poverty," Washington, DC, September 30, 1999.

108. Ann Withorn, quoted in M. A. Jimenez, "A Feminist Analysis of Welfare Reform: The Personal Responsibility Act of 1996," *Affilia* 14 (Fall 1999), pp. 278–293.

109. Mishel and Frankel, *The State of Working America,* p. 105.

110. Although we have stressed single female-headed families here, it is important to acknowledge that single male-headed families are growing even more rapidly. From 1959 to 1989, single male-headed families grew from 350,000 to 1.4 million, compared with 7.4 million mother-only and 25.5 million two-parent households. From 1960 to 1990, the percentage of father-only households increased 300 percent. See Daniel R. Mayer and Steven Garasky, "Custodial Fathers: Myths, Realities, and Child Support Policy," Institute for Research on Poverty, Madison, WI, August 1992, Discussion Paper no. 982-992, pp. 8–9.

111. National Commission on Children, *Poverty, Welfare and America's Families,* p. 3.

112. National Commission on Children, *Beyond Rhetoric: A New Economic Agenda for Children and Families* (Washington, DC: National Commission on Children, 1991), p. 90.

113. Yin-Ling Irene Wong, Irwin Garfinkel, and Sara McLanahan, "Single-Mother Families in Eight Countries: Economic Status and Social Policy," Institute for Research on Social Policy, Madison, WI, 1992, Discussion Paper no. 970–992.

114. Martha N. Ozawa, "Gender and Ethnicity in Social Security," *Conference Proceedings*, Nelson A. Rockefeller Institute of Government, State University of New York at Albany, November 1985, pp. 2–6.

115. Ibid.

116. Much of the following section is based on information found in *Wider Opportunities for Women, Making Both Ends Meet* (Washington, DC: Wider Opportunities for Women, 1991), pp. 4–9.

117. AFL-CIO, "Ask a Working Woman Survey Report," Washington, DC, 2004.

118. Thomas A. Kochan, "Bringing Family Values to the Workplace," *The Boston Globe,* (August 29, 2004), p. 18.

119. U.S. Bureau of Labor Statistics, "Labor Force Participation of Mothers with Infants in 2003," April 22, 2004. Retrieved October 2004, from www.bls.gov/opub/ted/2004/apr/wk3/art04.htm

120. Family assistance was one of the major thrusts of the former Clinton administration. It is also an issue that crosses racial and social class lines.

121. AFL-CIO, "Ask a Working Woman Survey Report."

122. Ibid.

123. Department of Labor, Bureau of Labor Statistics, *Women in the Labor Force—A Databook,* 2007. Retrieved June 2008, from www.bls.gov/cps/wlf-databook-2007.pdf

124. Ibid.

125. Lynn C. Burbridge, United States Glass Ceiling Commission, "The Glass Ceiling in Different Sectors of the Economy: Differences Between Government, Non-profit, and For-profit Organizations," Washington, DC, June 1994.

126. U.S. Department of Labor, Women's Bureau, *Median Annual Earnings for Year-Round Full-Time Workers by Sex in Current and Real Dollars, 1951–98, 1999.* Retrieved 2000, from www.bls.gov/cps/wlf-table 16-2007.pdf

127. Associated Press, "Glass Ceiling Shows Some Cracks." *New York Times* (April 23, 2000). Retrieved 2000 from www.nyt.com

128. Feminist Majority Foundation, "Women in Business."

129. See P. Anderson and B. Levine, *Working Paper Series: Child Care and Mothers' Employment Decisions* (Massachusetts: National Bureau of Economic Research, 1999); and The White House, *America's Workforce: Ready for the 21st Century,* August 5, 2004. Retrieved October 2004, from www.whitehouse.gov/news/releases/2004/08/ 20040805–6.html

130. U.S. House of Representatives, "Child Care," *Green Book, 2004* (Washington, DC: U.S. Government Printing Office, 2004).

131. S. Hofferth, "Childcare, Maternal Employment and Public Policy," *Annals of the American Academy of Political and Social Sciences* 563 (May 1999), pp. 20–38.

132. The National Association of Child Care Resource & Referral Agencies "2007 Child Care Capacity."

Retrieved June 2008, from www.naccrra.org/randd/program.php?Page=1

133. The National Association of Child Care Resource & Referral Agencies, "2007 Price of Child Care." Retrieved June 2008, from www.naccrra.org/randd/docs/2007_Price_of_Child_Care.pdf

134. Children's Defense Fund, "The State of America's Children," p. 37.

135. Sidel, *Women and Children Last*, p. 123.

136. National Commission on Working Women of Wider Opportunities for Women, "Women, Work and Health Insurance" (Washington, DC: Wider Opportunities for Women, n.d.).

137. National Commission on Working Women, "Women and Nontraditional Work."

138. Jim Harris, *The Complete Text of the Equal Rights Amendment* (New York: Ganis & Harris, 1980), p. 7.

139. Guttmacher Institute, "An Overview of Abortion in the United States." Retrieved June 2008, from www.guttmacher.org/media/presskits/2005/06/28/abortionoverview.html

140. Nanneska Magee, "Should the Federal Government Fund Abortions? No," in Howard Jacob Karger and James Midgley (eds.), *Controversial Issues in Social Policy* (Boston: Allyn & Bacon, 1993).

141. Tanya Albert, "Abortion, Legal since 1973, Still Shapes, Divides Doctors," *AMNews*, January 27, 2003, p. 30.

142. Guttmacher Institute, "U.S. Abortion Rate Continues Long-Term Decline, Falling to Lowest Level Since 1974; More Effort Still Needed to reduce Unintended Pregnancy." Retrieved June 2008, from www.guttmacher.org/media/nr/2008/01/17/index.html

143. Guttmacher Institute, "Concern for Current and Future Children a Key Reason Women Have Abortions." Retrieved June 2008, from www.guttmacher.org/media/nr/2008/01/07/index.html

144. Religious Tolerance, "Abortion: Public Opinion Polls: Year 2000, 2004." Retrieved October 2004, from www.religioustolerance.org/abo_poll2.htm

145. Margaret S. Stockdale, "Patchwork Protections: Progress and Problems in Battling Sexual Orientation Discrimination in Employment," Southern Illinois University Carbondale, Society for Industrial Psychology. Retrieved October 2008, from, www.siop.org/tip/Jan08/02stockdale.aspx

146. "California Court Affirms Right to Gay Marriage," *New York Times*, May 16, 2008.

147. Cited in National Organization of Women, "Come out Against Homophobia! Did You Know?" Retrieved October 2004, from www.now.org/issues/lgbi/stats.html

148. "State of the Union Address 2000," *Washington Post.* Retrieved November 2001, from www.washingtonpost.com/wp-srv/politics/special/states/docs/sou00.htm

149. National Coalition of Anti-Violence Programs, "Annual Report on Anti-LGBT Hate Violence Released," May 07, 2007. Retrieved April 2008, from www.ncavp.org/media/MediaReleaseDetail.aspx?p=2285&d=2409

150. William D. Mosher, Anjani Chandra, Jo Jones, "Sexual Behavior and Selected Health Measures: Men and Women 15–44 Years of Age, United States, 2002." Retrieved June 2008, from www.cdc.gov/nchs/data/ad/ad362.pdf

151. Kent Kilpatrick, "Oregon Voters Reject Stigmatizing Homosexuals," *The Advocate* (November 5, 1992), p. 2C.

152. Human Rights and Equal Opportunity Commission, "Federal and State Anti-Discrimination Law." Retrieved October 2008, from www.hreoc.gov.au/info_for_employers/law/index.html

153. Much of the section on gays and lesbians in the military was derived from Rivette Vullo, "Homosexuals in the Military," unpublished paper, Louisiana State University School of Social Work, Baton Rouge, LA, December 4, 1991. See also K. Dyer (ed.), *Gays in Uniform: The Pentagon's Secret Reports* (Boston: Alyson, 1990).

154. Dyer, *Gays in Uniform*, p. xiv.

155. Joseph Harry, "Homosexual Men and Women Who Served Their Country," *Journal of Homosexuality* 10 (1984), pp. 117–125.

156. Dyer, *Gays in Uniform*, p. xv.

157. Conrad K. Harper and Jane E. Booth, "End Military Intolerance," *National Law Journal* 13 (1991), pp. 17–18.

158. Barry M. Goldwater, "Ban on Gays Is Senseless Attempt to Stall the Inevitable," *Los Angeles Times* (September 23, 1993), p. C7.

159. Gregory M. Herek, "A Shift from 'Don't Ask' to Heterosexual Exception," *San Francisco Chronicle* (March 6, 2000), p. A8.

160. Servicemembers Legal Defense Network, "Gay Discharge Figures at Highest Level Since 1987," 1999. Retrieved 2000, from www.sldn.org/scripts/sldn.ixe?page=alert_01_23_99

161. Travis D. Bone, "Serving in Silence: Don't Ask, Don't Tell Deconstructed," *San Diego Gay & Lesbian Times* (September 16, 2004), p. 2.

162. Center for the Study of Sexual Minorities in the Military, "Russia Joins U.S. & Turkey in Barring Gays from Military Service, New Data Analysis Finds American Policy Out of Step with Other Democratic Nations," University of California, Santa Barbara, 2003.

163. B. A. Robinson, "Same-Sex Marriages (SSM) & Civil Unions," Ontario Consultants on Religious Tolerance, August 30, 2004. Retrieved September 2004, from www.religioustolerance.org/hom_marr.htm

164. R. Sneyd, "Same-Sex Bill Not about Marriage, Legislators Say," *Patriot Ledger* (March 18, 2000), p. 18.

165. Ibid.

166. Dan Morain and Jessica Garrison, "Backers Focused Prop 8. Battle Beyond Marriage," *Los Angeles Times*, November 6, 2008.

167. CNN News, Election Center 2008, Exit Polls. Retrieved December 4, 2008, from http://edition.cnn.com/ELECTION/2008/results/polls/#val=CAI01p1.

168. See J. J. Sampson et al., *Texas Family Code Annotated* (Eagan, MN: West Group, August 1999); and N. D. Hunter et al., *The Rights of Lesbians and Gay Men: The Basic ACLU Guide to a Gay Person's Rights*, 3rd ed. (Carbondale & Edwardsville, IL: Southern Illinois University Press, 1992).

169. National Institute of Allergy and Infectious Diseases, "HIV/AIDS Statistics," National Institutes of Health, July 2004. Retrieved October 2004, from www.niaid.nih.gov/factsheets/aidsstat.htm

170. Robert Searles Walker, *AIDS: Today, Tomorrow* (Atlantic Highlands, NJ: Humanities Press International, 1992), p. 119.

171. Joann Szabo, Phyllis Tonkin, Veronique Vaillancourt, Philip Winston, and Deidre Wright, "The Clinton Scorecard," unpublished paper, University of Houston Graduate School of Social Work, Houston, TX, April 25, 1996.

172. Norman Wyers, "Is Gay Rights Necessary for the Well-Being of Gays and Lesbians?" in Howard Jacob Karger and James Midgley (eds.), *Controversial Issues in Social Welfare Policy* (Boston: Allyn & Bacon, 1994).

173. Australian Broadcasting Company (ABC) (September 25, 2007). "No Gays in Iran: Ahmadinejad." Retrieved May 12, 2008, from www.abc.net.au/news/stories/2007/09/25/2042189.htm

174. International Lesbian and Gay Association-Europe (ILGA), "Marriage and Partnership Rights for Same-Sex Partners: Country-by-Country." Retrieved May 13, 2008, from www.ilga-europe.org/europe/issues/marriage_and_partnership/marriage_and_partnership_rights_for_same_sex_partners_country_by_country

175. Ibid.

176. See K. Dychtwald, *Age Power* (New York: Putnam 1999); and National Center for Health Statistics, "U.S. Life Expectancy at All-Time High, But Infant Mortality Increases," Center for Disease Control and Prevention, February 11, 2004. Retrieved October 2004, from www.cdc.gov/nchs/pressroom/04news/ infantmort.htm

177. U.S. Census Bureau "Older Adults in 2005." Retrieved June 2008, from www.census.gov/population/pop-profile/ dynamic/OLDER.pdf

178. Ibid.

179. C. Cozic (ed.), *An Aging Population: Opposing Viewpoints* (San Diego, CA: Greenhaven Press, 1996).

180. Agingstats.gov, "Older Americans 2008: Key Indicators of Well-Being." Retrieved June 2008, from http://agingstats.gov/Agingstatsdotnet/Main_Site/Data/2008_Documents/Economics.aspx

181. Ibid.

182. Ibid.

183. Cozic, *An Aging Population.*

184. Ibid., p. 7.

185. Agingstats.gov, "Use of Healthcare Services." Retrieved June 2008, from http://agingstats.gov/agingstatsdotnet/Main_Site/Data/2008_Documents/Health_Care.pdf

186. L. D. Haber, "Trends and Demographic Studies on Programs for Disabled Persons," in L. G. Perlman and G. Austin (eds.), *A Report of the Ninth Annual Mary E. Switzer Memorial Seminar* (Alexandria, VA, 1985), pp. 27–29.

187. Bureau of the Census, "Disabilities Affect One-Fifth of All Americans Proportion Could Increase in Coming Decades," U.S. Department of Commerce, Economics and Statistics Administration, Washington, DC, December 1997.

188. William Roth, "Disabilities: Physical," *Encyclopedia of Social Work*, 18th ed. (Silver Spring, MD: NASW, 1987), p. 86.

189. Ibid.

190. Haber, "Trends and Demographic Studies," p. 32.

191. Winifred Bell, *Contemporary Social Welfare*, New York: MacMillan, 1983, p. 174.

192. Administration on Developmental Disabilities, *Fact Sheet* (Washington, DC: Administration on Developmental Disabilities, n.d.).

193. Kathy Brown, "Mend It, Don't End It," *Outlook* 90, no. 3 (Fall 1996), p. 9.

194. Ibid., p. 11.

195. Bill Clinton, "Mend, Don't End, Affirmative Action," *Congressional Quarterly Weekly Report* 53 (July 22, 1995), pp. 2208–2209.

196. Roger Hernandez, "End Affirmative Action, but for the Right Reason," syndicated column, King Features, 1995.

197. Wilson, *The Truly Disadvantaged*, pp. 146–147.

Poverty in America

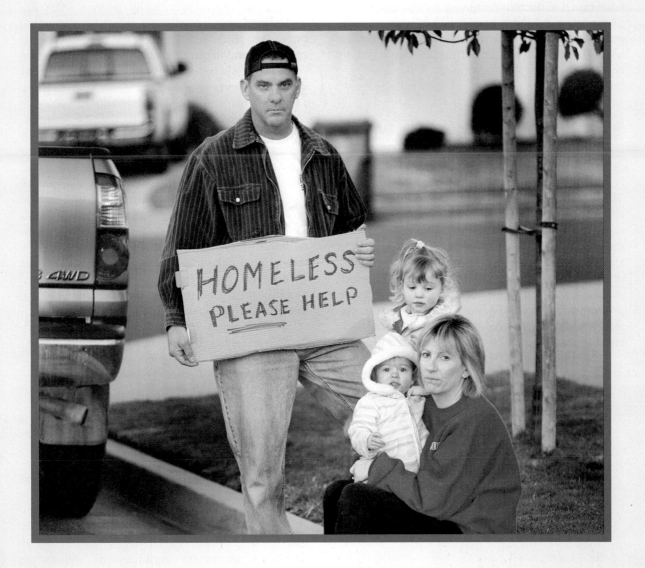

This chapter examines the characteristics of poverty in the United States, focusing particular attention on the wide range of theories that attempt to explain why some people become poor and why many remain poor. Also examined are demographic aspects and ways of measuring poverty; family constitution and poverty; child poverty and elderly poverty; the urban and rural poor; and the connections between poverty and work-related issues such as the minimum wage, structural unemployment, dual labor markets, job training programs, and the alternative financial sector or the fringe economy. Last, key strategies developed to combat poverty will be surveyed.

Some Theoretical Formulations about Poverty

The word "poverty" can be defined as deprivation—either absolute or relative. Absolute poverty refers to an unequivocal standard necessary for survival (e.g., the calories necessary for physical survival, adequate shelter for protection against the elements, and proper clothing). Those who fall below that absolute standard of poverty are considered poor. Relative poverty refers to deprivation that is relative to the standard of living enjoyed by other members of society. Although basic needs are met, members of a seg-

ment of the population may be considered poor if they possess fewer resources, opportunities, or goods than other citizens. Relative poverty (or deprivation) can be understood as inequality in the distribution of income, goods, or opportunities.

The Culture of Poverty

Culture of poverty (COP) theorists maintain that poverty and, more specifically, poverty traits are transmitted intergenerationally in a self-perpetuating cycle. According to this theory, the COP transcends regional, rural/urban, and national differences and everywhere shows striking similarities in family structure, interpersonal relations, time orientation, value systems, and patterns of spending.[1]

Oscar Lewis maintained that the COP flourishes in certain types of societies where there is a cash economy based on wage labor and production for profit; there is a high rate of underemployment and unemployment for unskilled workers; low wages are common; there is a failure to provide low-income groups with social, political, and economic organization, either on a voluntary basis or by governmental imposition; and there is a set of values held by the dominant class that stress the accumulation of wealth and property, the possibility of upward mobility, thrift, and the idea that low economic status results from personal inadequacy.

According to Lewis, the culture of poverty is characterized by hopelessness, indifference,

Spotlight 5.1

Poverty

People living in poverty fall into three general categories:

1. Those making only minimum wage (the working poor)
2. The unemployed
3. Those who have poor health or an occupational disability (e.g., a deficit in human capital such as poor education or a low quality and quantity of training and skills)

RESULTS is a nonprofit grassroots advocacy organization committed to creating the political will to end hunger and the worst aspects of poverty. RESULTS members lobby elected officials for effective solutions and key policies that affect hunger and poverty. To learn more about RESULTS, go to the organization's website at **www.results.org**.

alienation, apathy, and a lack of effective participation in or integration into the social and economic fabric of society. Key COP elements are a present-tense time orientation; cynicism toward and mistrust of those in authority; strong feelings of marginality, helplessness, dependence, and inferiority; a high incidence of maternal deprivation and a weak ego structure; lack of impulse control and the inability to defer gratification; a sense of resignation and fatalism; a widespread belief in male superiority; a high tolerance for psychological pathology of all kinds; the absence of childhood as a specially protected and prolonged state; early initiation into sexual unions or nonlegal marriages; a high incidence of abandonment of wives and children; a matriarchal family structure with an emphasis on family solidarity; a proclivity toward authoritarianism; and a minimal level of community organization combined with a strong sense of territoriality.

Opponents argue that COP theories divert attention away from the real factors causing poverty and that supposed characteristics of the COP are also evident in the middle and upper classes. For example, the inability to defer gratification underlies many credit card purchases. Sexual unions and informal marriages are a common occurrence among the middle classes and celebrities. The lack of community is an earmark of the modern suburb; the inability to achieve family solidarity is widespread in the United States; and feelings of indifference, helplessness, alienation, and dependence also afflict much of the middle class.

Eugenics and Poverty

Theories based on eugenics and genetic inferiority have periodically surfaced as explanations for poverty, crime, and disease. In 1877, Richard Dugdale reported on a study of the New York penal system that found crime, pauperism, and disease were transmitted intergenerationally.[2] Henry Goddard's *The Kallikak Family* was an account of a Revolutionary War soldier who had an affair with a feebleminded servant girl before marrying a "respectable" woman.[3] Goddard meticulously listed the disreputable descendants of the servant girl and compared them with the respectable achievers of the wife's descendants. Generations of students were taught the dogma of eugenics.

The eugenics movement lost favor when the racial and genetic theories that were used by Hitler to justify genocidal policies. However, the movement

reemerged with the publication of Arthur Jensen's 1969 article "How Much Can We Boost IQ and Scholastic Achievement?"[4] Jensen concluded that compensatory education was doomed to failure because 80 percent of intelligence (measured by IQ tests) was inherited; hence, money spent on compensatory education was badly spent.[5]

William Shockley, a Nobel laureate in physics who became interested in genetics, advocated paying the "unfit poor" (those who paid no income taxes) $1,000 for each point they fell below an IQ of 100, if they agreed to be sterilized.[6] Richard Herrnstein, a Harvard psychologist and a colleague of Shockley and Jensen, claimed that income and wealth are distributed among Americans based on their abilities which, in turn, are related to their IQ score. Herrnstein argued that the United States should become a "hereditary meritocracy," where the most capable citizens receive the greatest rewards as an incentive for assuming leadership.[7]

The eugenics argument was rekindled by Richard Herrnstein and Charles Murray's *The Bell Curve*, published in 1994, in which the authors argued that socioeconomic inequality in the United States was due to the lack of genetic intelligence.[8] Armed with statistics, tables, and charts, Herrnstein and Murray tried to demonstrate that those in the lower socioeconomic classes have lower IQ scores, which explains why white males (who test higher) control so many of society's institutions.[9] They argue that affirmative action programs overlook intellectual meritocracy. Moreover, spending money to educate the poor is wasteful given their innate deficiencies.

The scholarship in *The Bell Curve* has been attacked by a wide range of critics in the scientific and educational communities.[10] Critics argue that Herrnstein and Murray exaggerate IQ as a predictor of job performance, attribute inaccurate validities to IQ scores, and substitute hypotheticals for reality.[11] Assertions about genetic inferiority fail to hold up under scrutiny, and the theories of Shockley, Jensen, Herrnstein, and Murray have been repudiated by scores of educators, psychologists, sociologists, and anthropologists.[12]

The Radical School and Poverty

Radicals define poverty as resulting from exploitation by the ruling capitalist or dominant class. According to socialists (see Chapter 1), poverty provides capitalists with an army of surplus laborers who will depress the wages of similar workers. For example, employers can use an oversupply of workers to drive down wages knowing that there will be an abundance of job seekers. In an oversupply of labor, employers can more easily threaten recalcitrant workers with dismissal given the intense competition for jobs. Surplus labor is linked to poverty by using the *threat* of poverty (through unemployment) to discipline the labor force and demand concessions.

According to David Gil, poverty can be understood in terms of status, resource allocation, and the division of labor.[13] Most developed societies manipulate these factors. For instance, societies must develop resources—symbolic, material, life-sustaining, and life-enhancing goods and services. They must also develop a division of labor and must assign individuals or groups to specific tasks related to developing, producing, or distributing the resources of the society. This division of labor is used as the basis for assigning status to individuals and groups; that is, the more highly a society prizes the function an individual or group performs, the higher is the status reward. By manipulating the division of labor, a society is able to assign individuals to specific statuses within the total array of statuses and functions available.

The assignment of status roles is complemented by the distribution of rights. Higher-status roles implicitly demand greater compensation than lower-status roles, and such rewards come by way of the distribution of rights. Higher-status groups are rewarded by a substantial and liberal distribution of general entitlements and rights to material and symbolic resources, goods, and services. Conversely, lower-status groups are denied these resources through formal and informal constraints. Societies rationalize this form of status and goods allocation by an expressed belief in the omniscience of the marketplace. In other words, rewards are based on the value of contribution. This ideology is well masked and rarely questioned. Socialists argue that poverty will be omnipresent so long as society reproduces itself on the basis of the private ownership of the means of production. They believe that poverty cannot be altered without fundamentally rearranging the economic fabric of U.S. society.

Who Makes Up the Poor?

Poverty is a fluid rather than static process for most Americans. The University of Michigan's Panel Study of Income Dynamics (PSID) followed 5,000

U.S. families for almost 10 years (1969–1978) and found that only 2 percent of families were persistently poor throughout the entire period.[14] In fact, about one-third of the individuals poor in any given year escaped from poverty the following year, and only about one-third of the poor families in any given year had been poor for at least eight of the preceding years. The data showed that as people gained (or lost) jobs, as marriages were created (or dissolved), or as offspring were born (or left home), people were either pushed into poverty or escaped from it.[15] Changes in family composition, especially divorce or separation, were the leading causes of poverty. Conversely, **spells of poverty** were most often ended by family reconstitution (e.g., remarriage).

"Mobility in the United States is substantial, according to the evidence," concluded researchers from the Urban Institute. "Large portions of the population move into a new income quintile with estimates ranging from about 25 to 40 percent in a single year. The mobility rate is even higher over longer periods—about 45 percent over a 5-year period and about 60 percent over both 9-year and 17-year periods."[16] Bradley Schiller found that upward mobility is also experienced by the poor. According to Schiller, one-third of minimum wage workers had received a raise within a year, and 60 percent were beyond the minimum wage within two years. "The longitudinal experiences of minimum-wage youth . . . refute the notion of a 'minimum-wage trap,'" he concluded. "Youth who started at the minimum wage in 1980 recorded impressive wage gains over the subsequent seven years both in absolute and relative terms."[17] W. Michael Cox and Richard Alm confirmed significant upward movement of the poor:

> Only 5 percent of those in the bottom fifth in 1975 were still there in 1991. Where did they end up? A majority made it to the top three fifths of the income distribution—middle class or better. Most amazing of all, almost 3 out of 10 of the low-income earners from 1975 had risen to the uppermost 20 percent by 1991. More than three-quarters found their way into the two highest tiers of income earners for at least one year by 1991.[18]

Delving deeper into the labor market, David Howell and Elizabeth Howell constructed a matrix of "job contours" consisting essentially of self-employed, white-collar, blue-collar, and low-wage jobs, then analyzed the mobility of workers according to race, gender, and immigrant status. During a period of enormous compression in job opportunities due to an influx of immigrants, the researchers found that among workers who had worked at least 20 weeks in the previous year, "male and female African American and female new immigrant workers show[ed] substantial improvements in their employment distribution, shifting from the two 'worst' (secondary) job contours toward the two 'best' (independent primary) contours."[19] Income data show that poverty is not a permanent status for many, if not the majority, of the poor.

The following statistics from 2006 suggest some important trends in poverty in the United States:

- The poverty rate was 12.3 percent (36.4 million people), up from 11.8 percent in 1999.
- The poverty rate for children under 18 was 17.4 percent, up from 16.7 percent in 2002. The poverty rate for people over 65 was 9.4 percent.
- Beginning in 2001, the poverty rates also grew for nearly every racial and ethnic group. The poverty rate for blacks was 24.2 percent in 2006, more than twice the poverty rate for whites (10.3 percent). For Hispanics the poverty rate was 20.6 percent, but for children under age five it was 29.9 percent. The poverty rate for Asians and Pacific Islanders was 10.3 percent. These numbers represent an important shift because poverty rates had edged downward throughout the 1990s; by 2001 the cycle was reversing and poverty rates began to climb.
- Poverty rates were 11.5 percent in the Northeast, 11.2 percent in the Midwest, 13.8 percent in the South, and 11.6 percent in the West.
- Poverty rates were the lowest outside principal cities; they were high in inner cities (16.1 percent) and rural areas (15.2 percent).[20]

Table 5.1 on page 114 describes the characteristics and numbers of poor over a 50-year period.

Measuring Poverty

There are two versions of the federal poverty measure: (1) the poverty threshold and (2) the poverty guideline. The poverty threshold, also called the **poverty line,** is the official federal poverty measure and is used primarily for statistical purposes, such as estimating the number of Americans in poverty each

year. All official population figures are calculated using the poverty threshold. The poverty guideline uses a slightly lower poverty level than the weighted poverty threshold; for example, for a family of four in 2007 the poverty guideline was $20,650 versus $21,386. The poverty guideline is used for determining eligibility requirements for federal programs such as Head Start, food stamps, the National School Lunch Program, and Low-Income Home Energy Assistance Program. Other federal programs, including Temporary Assistance for Needy Families (TANF) and Supplemental Security Income, use the poverty threshold. As noted earlier, in 2007 the federal poverty index for a family of four was $21,386, up from $8,414 in 1980. (See Table 5.2 on page 115) These increases do not reflect more liberal standards but are due solely to the effects of inflation.

Set by the Social Security Administration (SSA), absolute poverty is defined by a poverty line drawn at a given income. The poverty threshold used by the federal government was developed by taking the cost of the least expensive food plan (the Thrifty Food Plan developed by the Department of Agriculture) and multiplying that number by 3. This formula was based on 1955 survey data showing that the average family spent about one-third of its budget on food. Formally adopted by the SSA in 1969, the official poverty measure provides a set of income cutoffs adjusted for household size, the number of children under age 18, and the age of the household head. To ensure constant purchasing power, the SSA adjusts the poverty line yearly, using the consumer price index (CPI).

The poverty index is plagued by a variety of structural problems. A 1995 National Academy of Sciences (NAS) report noted the following problems in calculating the current poverty threshold[21]:

- It excludes in-kind benefits when counting family income.
- It ignores the cost of earning income when calculating the net income of working families. For example, $5,000 in wage income does not include work-related costs such as clothing, transportation, and so on.
- It disregards regional variation in the cost of living, especially the cost of housing and food.
- It ignores the impact of tax payments, such as income, sales, payroll, and property taxes in states where those taxes are high.
- It ignores the effects of Earned Income Tax Credits (EITC).

Table 5.1

Persons Below the Poverty Line, Selected Years and Characteristics, 1959–2006 (number and percentage below poverty, in thousands)

Year	Overall	Aged	Children[a]	Individuals in Female Headed Families[b]	African Americans	Hispanic Origin[c]	White
2006*	36,460	3,394	12,827	13,199	9,048	9,243	24,416
	12.3%	9.4	17.4	30.5	24.3	20.6	10.3
2002	34,570	3,578	12,133	11,667	8,884	8,556	24,074
	12.1%	10.4	16.7	26.5	24.1	21.8	10.3
1999	32,258	3,167	12,109	12,687	9,091	7,439	21,922
	11.8%	9.7	18.9	27.8	22.7	22.8	9.8
1995	36,425	3,318	13,999	12,315	9,872	8,574	24,423
	13.8%	10.5	20.2	32.4	29.3	30.3	11.2
1990	33,585	3,658	14,431	12,578	9,837	6,006	22,326
	13.5%	12.2	20.6	37.2	31.9	28.1	10.7
1986	32,370	3,477	12,876	11,944	8,983	5,117	22,183
	13.6%	12.4	20.5	38.3	31.3	27.3	11.0
1980	29,272	3,871	11,543	10,120	8,579	3,491	19,699
	13.0%	15.7	18.3	36.7	32.5	25.7	10.2
1978	24,497	3,233	9,931	9,269	7,626	2,607	16,259
	11.4%	14.0	15.9	35.6	30.6	21.6	8.7
1969	21,147	4,787	9,961	6,879	7,095	NA	16,659
	12.1%	25.3	14.0	38.2	32.2	NA	9.5
1959	39,490	5,481	17,552	7,014	9,927	NA	28,484
	22.4%	35.2	27.3	49.4	55.1	NA	18.1

*These numbers may appear inconsistent because the U.S. Census Bureau changed the classification of races in the 2000 census to include the designation of more than one race. In addition, the statistics were calculated slightly differently in different years.

[a]All children, including unrelated children.

[b]Does not include females living alone.

[c]People of Hispanic origin may be of any race; it is an overlapping category.

Sources: Compiled from Committee on Ways and Means, U.S. House of Representatives, "Overview of Entitlement Programs",: *1992 Green Book* (Washington, DC: U.S. Government Printing Office, 1992), Tables 5.2 and 5.3, pp. 1274–1275; Joseph Dalaker and Bernadette D. Proctor, U.S. Census Bureau, "Poverty in the United States: 1999," Current Population Reports, Ser. P60-210 (Washington, DC: U.S. Government Printing Office, 2000); and Bernadette D. Proctor and Joseph Dalaker, U.S. Census Bureau, "Poverty in the United States: 2002, Demographic Programs," Current Population Reports: Consumer Income, U.S. Department of Commerce, Economics and Statistics Administration (Washington, DC: U.S. Government Printing Office, September 2003). Carmen DeNavas-Walt, Bernadette D. Proctor, and Jessica Smith, "Income, Poverty, and Health Insurance Coverage in the United States: 2006." Economics and Statistics Administration, U.S. Census Bureau, issued August 2007. Retrieved June 2008, from www.census.gov/prod/2007pubs/p60-233.pdf

Table 5.2

Changes in the Poverty Line Based on Income and Family Size, 1975–2007

Family Size	Income, Selected Years						
	1975	1980	1985	1990	1995	2003	2007
1	$2,724	$ 4,190	$ 5,250	$ 6,652	$ 7,763	$ 9,393	$10,787
2	3,506	5,363	7,050	8,509	9,933	12,015	13,884
3	4,293	6,565	8,850	10,419	12,158	14,680	16,218
4	5,500	8,414	10,650	13,359	15,569	18,810	21,386
5	6,499	9,966	12,450	15,572	18,408	22,245	25,791
6	7,316	11,269	14,250	17,839	20,804	25,122	29,664
7	9,022	13,955	16,050	20,241	23,552	28,544	34,132

Sources: Compiled from U.S. Census Bureau, *Technical Paper 56*, ser. P-60, nos. 134 and 149 (Washington, DC: U.S. Government Printing Office, 1992); Carmen DeNavas-Walt, Bernadette D. Proctor, and Robert J. Mills, U.S. Census Bureau, "Income, Poverty and Health Insurance Coverage in the United States: 2003," *Current Population Reports*, ser. p. 60–226. Retrieved October 2004, from www.census.gov/prod/2004pubs/p60-226.pdf; U.S. Census Bureau, "Poverty Thresholds 2007." Retrieved June 2008, from www.census.gov/hhes/www/poverty/threshld/thresh07.html

- It ignores the value of health coverage in determining family income, and ignores medical care costs both in terms of health insurance costs and out-of-pocket medical costs for those without health insurance.
- The index was never updated to account for changing consumption patterns and expenses. For example, although food accounted for one-third of all family expenditures in the 1950s, it now accounts for about one-seventh.[22]

The NAS panel made three important recommendations:

1. Change the measure of income by adding non-cash benefits and by subtracting taxes and work-related expenses, child support payments, and out-of-pocket medical expenses.
2. Create a new poverty threshold that is based on clothing, food, shelter, and "a little bit more." The panel also suggested new ways of estimating the poverty threshold for families of different sizes and composition, allowing for geographic variation. They further suggested that annual updates of the threshold be based not simply on inflation but on the growth of median expenditures on basic goods (food, clothing, and shelter).
3. Replace the current use of the *March Current Population Survey* with data from the *Survey of Income and Program Participation,* a measure that would change the percentage and distribution of the poor.

Legitimizing the NAS panel recommendations, former Democratic senator Daniel Patrick Moynihan introduced the *Poverty Data Correction Act of 1999* that would have required that any data relating to poverty be adjusted for geographic differences in the cost of living. Moynihan argued that because the current poverty calculations do not allow for geographical differences, they distort the true incidence of poverty.[23] Indeed, one would be hard-pressed to argue that the cost of living in Houma, Louisiana, is equivalent to that in Los Angeles or New York.

Families and Poverty

Family composition is strongly correlated to poverty, and families at greatest risk of poverty in the United States are those headed by single females. In 2007 the poverty rate for male-present families was 5.7 percent; for female-headed households it was 30.5 percent. These figures become even starker when disaggregated: Families headed by non-Hispanic white women had a poverty rate of 26.5 percent; families headed by African American and Hispanic women had poverty rates of 39.0 and 36.9 percent, respectively.[24]

More than 1 million American children see their parents divorce or separate each year, and more than half will spend some time in a single-parent family. Using six nationally representative data sets tracking more than 25,000 children, Sara McLanahan and Gary Sandefur found that children raised with only one biological parent are disadvantaged in myriad ways. Compared to children who grow up in two-parent families, they are (1) twice as likely to drop out of school; (2) 2.5 times as likely to become teen mothers; (3) 1.4 times as likely to be idle—out of work and out of school; and are (4) likely to have lower grade point averages, lower college aspirations, poorer academic attendance records, and higher rates of divorce in adulthood. These patterns persist even after adjustments for differences in race, the education of parents, the number of siblings, and the child's geographic location.[25]

■ *The families at greatest risk of poverty in the United States are those headed by single females. This poverty is compounded when child support payments are withheld.*

Child Support Enforcement

A 1995 Census Bureau study reported that slightly more than half of families with an absent parent have child support orders in place. Of those with orders, half received full payment and half received partial or no payment.[26] In 1975 Congress enacted Title IV-D, which was later amended by the Child Support Enforcement Amendments of 1984, the Family Support Act of 1988, and the Personal Responsibility and Work Opportunity Reconciliation Act of 1996. Title IV-D of the federal Social Security Act funds state programs designed to recover child support payments. A case is considered IV-D if the family has received public assistance benefits, or if an application for services was filed with a public welfare agency. The attention focused on "deadbeat dads" has important political overtones. Some argue that focusing on deadbeat dads has allowed policymakers to blame a variety of social ills, from poverty to high welfare costs to social pathology, squarely on fathers.[27]

Nevertheless, child support is important for families with only one custodial parent. According to the Census Bureau, 77 percent (5.26 million)

custodial parents received some child support in 2005. The proportion of custodial parents receiving every payment they were due increased from 37 percent in 1993 to 47 percent in 2005.[28] Of the 13.6 million custodial parents in 2006, 7.8 million (57.3 percent) had some type of agreement or court award allowing them to receive financial support from the noncustodial parent for their children. Most of these (7.2 million) were formal legal agreements (established by a court or other government entity). When custodial parents without any agreements and those with informal agreements were asked why a formal legal agreement was not established, the reasons most often cited were that they did not feel the need to go to court or get legal agreements (33.7 percent), the other parent provided what he or she could for support (27.9 percent), and they felt the other parent could not afford to pay child support (24.1 percent).[29] Arguably, child support is very important for low-income families:

- Child support constitutes 26 to 29 percent of the income of divorced families and reduces their poverty rate by 7 to 11 percent.

- Child support is an important income source for poverty-level families. About 66 percent of custodial parents with incomes below the poverty line that were due child support receive at least some payment. The average amount was $3,000 and constituted 40 percent of their total family income.
- Child support lifts about 500,000 children out of poverty and reduces the poverty rate by 8 percent.
- Child support is an important income source for families leaving welfare. About 42 percent of families leaving welfare receive child support, which makes up 30 percent ($2,562) of their income.
- Child support is important for families affected by welfare time limits. The percentage of these families receiving child support and the amounts they receive increase after public assistance is terminated.
- Child support is important for families leaving the TANF program for work. Between 25 and 33 percent of those leaving welfare for work receive between $250 and $400 a month in child support.
- One study of families leaving welfare with regular child support payments found that they had a slower rate of welfare reentry, a faster rate of finding work, and a slower rate of job loss compared to families without steady child support income.[30]

In 1996, President Clinton signed the Personal Responsibility and Work Opportunity Reconciliation Act (PRWORA) into law. The PRWORA was intended to broadly reform the public assistance system, but it also addressed child support enforcement. Specifically, failure to meet child support obligations could result in revocation of driver's and professional licenses; expanded wage garnishment; liens; and denial, revocation, or limitation of passports. Delinquent support obligations could also be collected through unemployment and disability insurance benefits.

Children in Poverty

There were 12.3 million poor children under the age of 18 in the United States in 2007. The poverty rate for children is higher than for any other age group: 17 percent in 2007 compared to an overall poverty rate of 12.5 percent. For children under age five, the poverty rate was even higher, at 20.4 percent (4 million children). While high, this rate is eclipsed by the almost 53.7 percent poverty rate for children five and under living in female-headed households. More than 7 percent of U.S. children live in extreme poverty (family incomes below 50 percent of the poverty line), and 38.5 percent of children live in or near poverty (family incomes below 200 percent of the poverty line).[31] Compared to poverty in later childhood, research indicates that extreme poverty during a child's first five years has especially deleterious effects on their future life chances.[32]

The probability of children growing up poor is strongly correlated with family composition. In 1987, for example, the Census Bureau estimated that 61 percent of the children born in that year would spend some part of their childhood in single-parent families, which are five times more likely to be poor than two-parent families.[33] This prediction turned out to be correct.

Poverty and the Elderly

On the surface, the poverty picture for the elderly (once the poorest group in the country) seems to be growing less bleak. In 1959 the poverty rate for those over 65 was 35.2 percent; the poverty rate and the number of people 65 and older in poverty decreased to 9.4 percent in 2006 from 10.1 percent in 2005. Despite the downward trend, more than 3.4 million elderly citizens live in poverty.[34]

Senior poverty is disproportionately experienced by minority groups. Almost 23 percent of African Americans over age 65 were poor in 2007. For African American women, those numbers were 26.7 percent. About 19.5 percent of elderly Hispanics were poor.[35] The federal government's estimate of the elderly poor is questionable. Specifically, the poverty line is calculated using two classifications: (1) families headed by persons under age 65, and (2) families headed by persons 65 or older, for whom the poverty line is set lower. For example, the poverty line in 2007 for an unrelated individual 65 or older was $9,944 compared to $10,782 for those under 65—a difference of $843 or 8 percent. This differential is based on the assumption that the elderly spend less on food because they require less food to absorb the same amount of nutrients. It does not take into account the higher drug bills for the aged.

The Urban and Rural Poor

About 7.2 million rural Americans live in poverty. This segment of the population is generally overlooked because of the national attention traditionally directed toward urban poverty. Although rural poverty lacks significant media attention, many rural areas have poverty rates equal to those of central cities. In 2007, the rural poverty rate of 15.2 percent almost paralleled the urban poverty rate of 16.1 percent.[36]

In 2007 more than half of the rural poor lived in the South (almost 4 out of 7.1 million), 24 percent in the Midwest, 13 percent in the West, and 8 percent in the Northeast. The farming population accounts for only 10 percent of the rural population, so, therefore, the rural poor are mostly nonfarmers.[37] The number of poor rural communities has dropped since 1960, when 2,083 counties had a poverty rate of 20 percent or more. By 2004 the number of persistently poor counties designated by the United States Department of Agriculture (USDA) as having poverty rates of 20 percent or more had dropped to 386. Traditionally poor rural areas include the Colonias of the Southwest, the Mississippi Delta, Appalachia, and Indian reservations.[38]

Rural minority members experience considerable poverty with figures as follows:

- More than 25 percent of nonmetro Hispanics, African Americans, and American Indians are poor.
- The nonmetro poverty rate in 2003 for African Americans was 30.5 percent. The rate for Hispanics was 25.4 percent.
- Sixty-eight percent of poor nonmetro Hispanics have less than a high school education, compared with 40 percent of nonmetro poor whites. Fifty-two percent of poor nonmetro American Indians have incomes less than half of the poverty line.
- Poverty rates for African Americans and American Indians are more than 10 percentage points higher in nonmetro areas than in metro areas, the largest gap among minority population groups.[39]

The rural poor are more likely than the urban poor to live in chronic long-term poverty. Despite higher unemployment in rural areas, the rural poor rely less on public assistance than the urban poor. Lack of information and access to services, fear of stigma, and reliance on informal employment may help explain some of this difference.[40] Family structure also has a significant bearing on poverty:

- The highest poverty rate by type of family is for female-headed, nonmetro families. More than one out of every three persons living in nonmetro families that are headed by a female is poor. This rate is much higher than the poverty rates for nonmetro families headed by a husband and wife, where only one out of every 14 persons is poor.
- Those persons living in families with a husband and wife present have the lowest rates of poverty with 7.1 percent poor in nonmetro areas and 6 percent poor in metro areas.
- The poverty rate for nonmetro female-headed families is more than 7 percent higher than for metro families.
- In 2003, the child poverty rate in nonmetro areas was 20.1 percent.[41]

Several factors contribute to chronic rural poverty, including high levels of illiteracy, low levels of education, a dearth of highly trained workers, high numbers of low-skill and low-paying jobs, high levels of underemployment and unemployment, and a deficient physical infrastructure. Rural county and city managers also find it difficult to attract major industries. Not surprisingly, the absence of economic opportunity has resulted in the net outmigration of many rural families, especially when the primary wage earner possesses higher-level skills and education.[42]

Work and Poverty

Almost one in four U.S. workers live in or around the edges of poverty. Thirty-five million Americans work full time but fail to make an adequate living. They are the nursing home aides, poultry processors, pharmacy assistants, child care workers, data entry keyers, janitors, and other employees of the secondary and tertiary labor markets.

A Profile of the Working Poor

As a group, the working poor represent a growing sector of the poverty population. The working poor are defined as individuals who spend at least 27 weeks in the labor force (working or looking for work) but whose family or personal incomes fall below the poverty line. About 7.7 million persons were classified as the working poor in 2005, nearly 400,000 more than in 2002. The following represents some of the demographics of the working poor in 2005[43]:

- 11.6 percent of the 23 million part-time workers were classified working poor.
- As workers achieve higher levels of education, their likelihood of being classified as working poor decreases. In 2005, the number of college graduates who were in the labor force for at least 27 weeks counted among the working poor was 1.7 percent, compared with 14.1 percent of those with less than a high school diploma.
- Among families with at least one member in the labor force for 27 weeks or more, those families including children under 18 years old were about four times more likely than those without children to live in poverty or to be among the working poor.
- The proportion of persons in the labor force for at least 27 weeks who lived below the poverty level was higher for women (6.1 percent) than for men (4.8 percent).
- Whites accounted for about 7 in 10 of the working poor in 2005. African Americans and Hispanics had the highest working-poor rates, 10.5 percent each. The rates for whites and Asians, at 4.7 percent each, were less than half as high. [44]

Why Are There Working Poor?

The large numbers of working poor are related to other factors, including the replacement of high-paying industrial jobs with low-paying service jobs. Millions of Americans who were working full time, year-round earned less than the official poverty level. In 2005, 118.7 million full-time workers (3.9 percent) were classified as working poor.[45]

This employment trend reflects a clear movement away from higher-paying manufacturing jobs to low-wage service employment. By the 1980s corporations had eliminated 300,000 manufacturing jobs. Continuing this trend, a million more manufacturing jobs were eliminated during the 1990s. In the 1950s, 33 percent of all workers were employed in primary manufacturing industries (e.g., cars,

radios, refrigerators, and clothing). By 1992 only 17 percent were employed in those industries. While manufacturing jobs have declined, service jobs have increased. According to the Bureau of Labor Statistics, service-providing industries are expected to account for approximately 20.8 million of the 21.6 million new wage and salary jobs generated from 2002 to 2012.[46]

Underemployment and Unemployment

The failure of the labor market to meet the economic needs of the population has been the source of important distinctions in employment policy. For example, those over 16 who are looking for work are counted by the Department of Labor as unemployed. But the **unemployment** rate does not assess the adequacy of employment. For example, part-time workers who wish to work full time are counted as employed; and workers holding jobs below their skill levels are not identified, even though such workers are **underemployed.** Finally, **discouraged workers** who simply give up and stop looking for work, relying on other methods to support themselves, do not appear in the unemployment statistics because they are not actively seeking work.

A second set of distinctions relates to economic performance. In a robust economy, businesses start up and close down in significant numbers, leaving workers temporarily out of work until they find other jobs. Such **frictional unemployment** is considered to be unavoidable, the cost of a constantly changing economy. **Structural unemployment,** in contrast, refers to "deeper and longer-lasting maladjustments in the labor market," such as changes in the technical skills required for new forms of production.[47] Because of swings in economic performance, some unemployment may be cyclical, as when recessions pitch the rate upward; but because certain groups of workers in certain regions have persistent difficulty finding work owing to an absence of jobs, some unemployment may be chronic. Michael Sherraden has examined how these components vary in the composition of the unemployment rate and concluded that structural and frictional factors account for about one-third, **cyclical unemployment** for about one-fourth, and **chronic unemployment** for about one-half.[48]

These distinctions are important because social welfare is directly connected to the employment experience of Americans. When people are out of work, they frequently rely on welfare benefits to tide them over. Thus, welfare programs are often designed to complement the labor market. This has led some observers to refer to welfare as a **social wage;** in other words, the amount the government pays to workers through welfare programs when they are not able to participate in the labor market. Logically, much of welfare could be eliminated if well-paying jobs were plentiful, but such has not been the case in the United States. Policymakers have tacitly accepted an unemployment rate of between 4 and 5 percent as normative, which means that at any given time, 5 to 8 million workers are unemployed.[49] Yet in 1978 Congress enacted the Humphrey–Hawkins Full Employment Act, which set an unemployment rate of 3 percent—equivalent to frictional unemployment—as a national goal. Since then, many government programs to aid unemployed, underemployed, and discouraged workers have been reduced or eliminated, leaving many Americans dependent on welfare programs for support.

The outsourcing of U.S. jobs to low-wage countries, such as India and China, may also exacerbate unemployment. A report by the U.S. Department of Labor on mass layoffs found that in the first quarter of 2004, 4,633 workers were laid off because their jobs were moved overseas. However, other economists argue that the report undercounted the total number of jobs lost offshore, with the real number being between 250,000 and 350,000 jobs a year. (This is still a relatively small number in a labor force of more than 130 million people.) The report also did not account for jobs created by U.S. companies overseas that did not involve direct layoffs in the United States. Nonetheless, the trend of outsourcing work overseas raises concerns about the potential loss of the high-wage white-collar jobs (especially in information technology) that were once considered safe from global competition. It also raises the specter that competition from less-expensive overseas workers will slow the wage growth of U.S. workers.[50]

The absence of employment opportunities contributes to other social problems. Research by M. Harvey Brenner shows that a seemingly small increase in the unemployment rate is associated with an increase in several social problems. During the 1973–1974 recession, for example, the unemployment rate increased by 14.3 percent, a change associated with the pathologies shown in Table 5.3. Brenner calculated that the combination of the 1973–1974 increase in the unemployment rate, the decrease in real per capita income, and the increase in the business failure rate was related to "an overall

Table 5.3

Consequences of Increases in Unemployment

Pathological Indicator	Percentage Increase due to Rise in Unemployment Increase	Rise in Incidence of Pathology
Total mortality	2.3	45,936
Cardiovascular mortality	2.8	28,510
Cirrhosis mortality	1.4	430
Suicide	1.0	270
Population in mental hospitals	6.0	8,416
Total arrests	6.0	577,477
Arrests for fraud and embezzlement	4.0	11,552
Assaults reported to police	1.1	7,035
Homicide	1.7	403

Source: Reprinted from M. Harvey Brenner, *Estimating the Effects of Economic Change on National Health and Social Well-Being* (Washington, DC: U.S. Government Printing Office, 1984), p. 2.

increase of more than 165,000 deaths [from cardio-vascular disease] over a ten-year period (the greatest proportion of which occurs within three years)."[51] Overall, the total economic, social, and health care costs of this seemingly slight increase in unemployment cost $24 billion.[52]

As noted earlier, underemployment and unemployment constitute a major factor in determining poverty. In 2006, employers laid off about 936,000 workers in 4,885 private (nonfarm) extended mass layoff events, similar to the previous year. The reasons for these included employers moving to other U.S. locations or to locations outside of the United States and permanent worksite closures. Extended mass layoffs refer to layoffs of at least 31 days duration that involve the filing of initial claims for unemployment insurance by 50 or more individuals from a single establishment during a consecutive five-week period. In 2006, there were 950,157 claimants for unemployment insurance associated with this type of layoff. Of these, 40 percent were women; 16 percent were African American; 14 percent were Hispanic; and 19 percent were 55 years of age or older. Benefit exhaustion rates were highest for claimants involved in worksite closures (24 percent), and claimants associated with layoffs from employers that did not expect a recall (18 percent) experienced a higher benefit exhaustion rate than workers in events from which a recall was expected (9 percent).[53] These types of events can result in former workers experiencing significant economic losses for a lengthy time after their jobs are lost.

Dual Labor Markets

According to Piore, the labor market can be divided into two segments, or "dual labor markets"—a **primary labor market** and a **secondary labor market:**

> The primary market offers jobs which possess several of the following traits: high wages, good working conditions, employment stability and job security, equity and due process in the administration of work rules, and chances for advancement. The other, secondary sector, has jobs which, relative to those in the primary sector, are decidedly less attractive. They tend to involve low wages, poor working conditions, considerable variability in employment, harsh and often arbitrary discipline, and little opportunity to advance. The poor are confined to the secondary labor market.[54]

Researchers calculated that in 1970, 36.2 percent of workers fell into the secondary labor market, a modest increase over 1950's 35 percent.[55] By the 2000s, however, two factors increased the proportion of workers in the secondary labor market. First, membership in labor unions—the best security for nonprofessional workers—fell from 30.8 percent of nonagricultural workers in 1970 to 12.1 percent in 2007, leaving millions of workers vulnerable to the vicissitudes of the secondary labor market. Second, a higher proportion of the new jobs created were in the service sector, which consists largely of secondary labor market jobs.[56]

Wages and Poverty

The Minimum Wage   The low minimum wage is another factor that explains the growth of the working poor. Before the 2006 midterm elections, Democrats promised they would raise the minimum wage within 24 hours if given control of the House.[57] They did not meet that deadline, but Congress did pass the Fair Minimum Wage Act of 2007 that, on July 24, 2007, raised the minimum wage to $5.85 an hour. The bill called for two more phased-in raises, going up to $6.55 an hour on July 24, 2008, and then again to $7.24 an hour on July 24, 2009.

Even with the recent increases, it is difficult for minimum wage employment to provide an adequate household income. Under the 2008 minimum wage of $6.55 an hour, a single parent working full time with two children would earn $12,576 a year and be at 71 percent of the poverty line. A four-person, two-parent family where both adults are working full time and earning the minimum wage would gross $25,152 a year, or only $3,952 above the poverty line. The Economic Policy Institute claims that 13 million workers are likely to be affected by an increase in the minimum wage to $7.24. This includes more than 1.2 million single parents. This legislation will positively impact African American and Hispanic workers. Almost 80 percent of the beneficiaries of the increased minimum wage are adults.[58]

Traditional labor economics assumes that minimum wage increases result in inflation and significant job losses among low-wage workers.[59] Empirical analysis is beginning to challenge this conclusion. The Economic Policy Institute did not find an increase in unemployment fol- lowing the last federal minimum wage increase in 1996–1997.[60] The Fiscal Policy Institute concluded that states that have enacted minimum wage increases higher than the federal stan- dard have experienced stronger small business and retail sector growth as a result.[61] Of course, these conclusions are not without challenge,[62] but the mere presence of an empirical argument against the standard economist's rejec- tion of higher minimum wages is wel- come news to progressives. Moreover, although a higher minimum wage will not eliminate the challenges faced by the working poor, it is a step in the correct direction. The following employment sectors have the highest proportion of minimum wage jobs:

Food service workers (26.6 percent)
Sales occupations (18.7 percent)
Office and administration support work-
    ers (13.1 percent)
Transportation and material moving workers (8.2
    percent)
Cleaning and building service workers (8.2 percent)
Personal care workers (7.5 percent)[63]

■ *The minimum wage has been criticized by both conservatives and liberals.*

The minimum wage is not adjusted annually to the cost of living. Congress must pass a bill and the president must sign it into law for the minimum wage to rise. Minimum wage increases have been signed into law by Presidents Truman, Eisenhower, Kennedy, Johnson, Nixon, Carter, George H. W. Bush, and Clinton. The minimum wage has risen only slightly during the past 18 years, increasing to $4.25 an hour by 1991 and then remaining at that level for more than five years. By 1996 approxi- mately 10 million American workers were earning between $4.25 and $5.14 per hour. In 1997 the fed- eral minimum wage was again raised, this time to $5.15 an hour. The minimum wage was frozen from 1997 to 2007.

In 1950 the minimum wage brought a worker to 56 percent of the median wage. Throughout the 1950s and 1960s (see Table 5.4.), the minimum wage hovered between 44 and 56 percent of the average wage. By 1980, however, the minimum wage had fallen to 46.5 percent of the average wage, and in 1988 it dropped even farther to 35.7 percent. Overall, from 1979 to 1996 the minimum wage

dropped 29 percent. Even the increase to $5.15 an hour in 1997 raised the minimum wage to only 42 percent of the average wage, bringing a family of three to 83 percent of the poverty line[64] (consider- ably lower than the 120 percent of the poverty level reached by the minimum wage in 1968).[65] Moreover, the minimum wage increase in 1997 needed to be $6.07 (almost $1.00 higher) to have the same purchasing power as in the 1970s.[66] Even the higher minimum wage of $7.24 projected for 2009 would bring a family of three to only 79 percent of the 2008 poverty line.

Companies in metropolitan areas experiencing labor shortages use a "real" minimum wage that is often $1 to $2 above the federal level. Jared Bernstein maintains that a rise in the minimum wage would affect workers making just above the minimum wage through a "spillover effect." Workers in this group are more likely to be older (87 percent are adults) and to work more hours (69 percent work full time) than minimum wage workers.

The Living Wage Movement An alliance between labor and religious leaders in Baltimore in 1994 led to a campaign for a local law requiring city service contractors to pay a living wage. These

Table 5.4

Value of the Minimum Wage, Selected Years

Year	Percent of Poverty Line for a Family of Three	Percent of Average Wage	Value of the Minimum Wage, 1995 Dollars	Minimum Wage, Nominal Dollars
1955	73	44	$3.94	$0.75
1960	88	48	4.75	1.00
1965	103	51	5.59	1.25
1968	120	56	6.49	1.60
1970	107	50	5.92	1.60
1975	101	46	5.71	2.10
1980	98	47	5.76	3.10
1985	81	39	4.76	3.35
1988	73	36	4.33	3.35
1989	71	35	4.13	3.35
1990	79	38	4.44	3.80
1993	75	39	4.50	4.25
1995	72	37	4.25	4.25
1997	83	42	4.89	5.15
2007	73	30	4.30	5.85

Sources: Based on data from Isaac Shapiro, *The Minimum Wage and Job Loss* (Washington, DC: Center on Budget and Policy Priorities, 1988), p. 3; U.S. Census Bureau, "Income 1995" (Washington, DC: U.S. Government Printing Office, September 26, 1996); Bureau of Labor Statistics, "May 2007 National Occupation Employment and Wage Estimates." Retrieved July 2008, from www.bls.gov/oes/current/oes_nat.htm#b00-0000; Carmen DeNavas-Walt, Bernadette D. Proctor, and Robert J. Mills, "Income, Poverty, and Health Insurance Coverage in the United States: 2003," August 2004. Retrieved October 2008, from www.census.gov/prod/2004pubs/p60-226.pdf

kinds of campaigns seek to pass local ordinances requiring private businesses that benefit from public money to pay their workers a living wage. Commonly, these ordinances cover employers who hold large city or county service contracts or receive substantial financial assistance from the city in the form of grants, loans, bond financing, tax abatements, or other economic development subsidies. Since the Baltimore campaign in 1994, community, labor, and religious coalitions have fought for and won similar ordinances in St. Louis, Boston, Los Angeles, Tucson, San Jose, Portland, Milwaukee, Detroit, Minneapolis, and Oakland. By 2000, there were more than 75 living wage campaigns under way in cities, counties, and states.

The justification for these campaigns is that when subsidized employers pay workers less than a living wage, taxpayers pay a double bill: the initial subsidy plus increased taxes to pay for food stamps and other social services that low-wage workers require to support themselves and their families. Many citywide campaigns have defined the living wage as equivalent to the poverty line for a family of four, although ordinances that have passed stipulate wages ranging from $6.25 to $11.42 an hour, with some campaigns pushing for even higher wages. Increasingly, living wage coalitions are proposing other community standards in addition to a wage requirement, such as health benefits, vacation days, community hiring goals, public disclosure, community advisory boards, environmental standards, and language that supports union organizing.[67]

In addition to the federal minimum wage, states can institute their own higher minimum wage. (See Table 5.5 on page 124.) By 2008, 29 states and the District of Columbia had a higher minimum wage, with Washington, Oregon, Arizona, Connecticut, Missouri, Montana, and Vermont linking it automatically to the cost of living.[68]

Table 5.5

States with Minimum Wages Above the Federal Rate, 2008

State	Minimum Wage	State	Minimum Wage	State	Minimum Wage
Alaska	$7.15	Hawaii	7.25	New Mexico	7.50 (2009)
Arizona	6.90	Illinois	7.75	New York	7.15
Arkansas	6.25	Iowa	7.25	North Carolina	6.15
California	8.00	Maine	7.00	Ohio	7.00
Colorado	7.02	Massachusetts	8.00	Oregon	7.95
Connecticut	7.65	Michigan	7.15	Pennsylvania	7.15
Delaware	7.15	Minnesota	6.15	Rhode Island	7.40
District of Columbia	7.55	Missouri	6.65	Vermont	7.68
		New Hampshire	7.25	Washington	8.07
Florida	6.79	New Jersey	7.15	Wisconsin	6.50

Source: U.S. Department of Labor, Employment Standards Administration Wage and Hour Division, Minimum Wage Laws in the States—January 1, 2008. Retrieved May 12, 2008, from www.dol.gov/esa/minwage/america.htm

Strategies Developed to Combat Poverty

Former Senator Bob Kerrey stated that "In a global economy, your economic health and security is measured by what you own in addition to what you earn."[69] Michael Sherraden concurs: "Despite the prominence of asset ownership in American values and American history, social policy in the modern welfare state—and especially means-tested policy for the poor—has been focused almost exclusively on the distribution of income for consumption. Indeed, means-tested policy usually prohibits savings and the accumulation of assets. . . . After more than 50 years of income maintenance policy, we have confirmed that it is correctly named—it provides only maintenance, not development."[70] Sherraden goes on to suggest that "We should consider a different approach. Social policy, including welfare policy, should promote asset accumulation. In addition to the income and consumption policy of the current welfare state, asset-based policy would focus on savings and investment."[71] For the vast majority of households, the road to ending poverty involves savings, accumulation and assets. These are important prerequisites for purchasing a home, sending a child to college, starting a small business, and for reaching other economic goals. Moreover, when people begin to accumulate assets, their thinking and behavior changes, leading to important psychological and social effects that are not achieved when simply receiving and spending regular income.[72]

Until recently, the importance of asset accumulation for the poor has been virtually ignored in welfare state policies. Nevertheless, the tax system supports asset accumulation for the nonpoor in two primary areas: tax benefits for home equity and for retirement pension accounts. In these two areas alone, the federal government spends well over $100 billion each year and the total is rising rapidly.[73] Unfortunately, poor people fail to benefit from asset accumulation tax policies because they have marginal tax rates that are either zero or too low to receive significant tax benefits. Even worse, means-tested welfare programs count assets and savings as income in calculating eligibility. As such, the poor who have accumulated assets or savings must spend these down in order to qualify for assistance.

IDAs

The concept of individual development accounts (IDAs) was introduced in 1991 by Michael Sherraden in *Assets and the Poor.*[74] IDAs are part of an asset-building policy strategy designed to reduce wealth inequality by enabling asset-poor individuals to accumulate assets. Low-income individuals establish savings accounts matched by public and private resources, which are then used for home purchases, business capitalization, and postsecondary education.[75]

In Sherraden's framework, IDA accounts would be established for all low-income individuals and would be tax benefitted to foster asset accumulation. Depending on the financial circumstances of the depositor, individual savings would be matched by federal, state, or private contributions at varying rates. For instance, a very low–income family might have a match as high as 90 percent while a working family with a relatively good income would receive no match but might receive tax benefits. The matching system would be flexible and permit the government to supplement savings as the economic circumstances of individuals change. IDA accounts would be managed by individuals so that they become familiar with investment options. Despite the flexibility, IDA withdrawals would be restricted to approved purposes such as home purchases, education, retirement, or the creation of a business. IDA assets could be transferred to children at death or prior to death.[76]

Three Approaches to Combat Poverty

Policy analysts identified three basic strategies for combating poverty. The first strategy, used by Lyndon Johnson in the War on Poverty and Great Society programs, was to apply a curative strategy to the problems of the poor. The **curative approach to poverty** aims to end chronic and persistent poverty by helping the poor to become self-supporting through changes in their personal lives and in their environment. By breaking the self-perpetuating cycle of poverty, the curative approach strives to initiate the poor into employment and, later, the middle class. The goal of the curative approach is rehabilitation, and its target is the causes of poverty.

The second strategy is the **alleviative approach to poverty,** which is exemplified by public assistance programs that attempt to ease the suffering of the poor rather than ameliorate the causes of poverty. The third strategy is the **preventive approach to poverty,** exemplified by social insurance programs such as Social Security. In this approach, people are required to utilize social insurance to insure against

the costs of accidents, sickness, death, old age, unemployment, and disability. The preventive strategy sees the state as a large insurance company whose umbrella shelters its members against the vicissitudes of life.

John Kenneth Galbraith's *The Affluent Society* identified two kinds of poverty: **case poverty** and **area poverty.** According to Galbraith, case poverty was the outgrowth of personal deficiencies (i.e., deficits in human capital). Area poverty was related to economic problems endemic to a region. "Pockets of poverty" or "depressed areas" resulted from a lack of industrialization in a region or the inability of an area to adjust to technological change. This kind of poverty was a function of the changing nature of the marketplace.[77]

One example of a case poverty approach is the federal government's attempt to promote education as a means to increase human capital. Poverty is highly correlated with educational deficits, and adolescent parenthood is strongly associated with low levels of basic skills and high school dropout rates.[78] To help address these educational deficits, the federal government initiated the Head Start program, targeted at poor children age three to five and their families.[79]

Area poverty is illustrated by reviewing poverty rates on a state-by-state basis (see Table 5.6 on page 126). The overall national poverty rate in 2006 was 12.3 percent, but some states that were poverty pockets had much higher poverty rates, including New Mexico (16.9 percent), Mississippi (20.6 percent), Alabama (14.3 percent), Louisiana (17 percent), Kentucky (16.8 percent), District of Columbia (18.3 percent), Arkansas (17.7 percent), West Virginia (15.3 percent), and Texas (16.4 percent). By contrast, other states like New Hampshire (5.4 percent), Alaska (8.9 percent), Connecticut (8 percent), New Jersey (8.8 percent), Delaware (9.3 percent), Maryland (8.4 percent), Minnesota (8.2 percent), Vermont (7.8 percent), and Washington (8 percent) had poverty rates below the national average.[80]

The various approaches to poverty are not merely hypothetical formulations; they formed the basis for social welfare policy throughout much of the 1960s and beyond. Between 1965 and 1980, social welfare policies were grounded in the view that public expenditures should be used to stimulate opportunities for the poor. As a result, major social welfare legislation was enacted and billions of dollars were earmarked for the remediation of poverty. However, beginning with the Reagan

Table 5.6

Strategies Developed to Combat Poverty: Percent of Persons in Poverty by State, 2006

State	Average Percentage in Poverty 2006	State	Average Percentage in Poverty 2006
United States	12.3	Missouri	11.4
Alabama	14.3	Montana	13.5
Alaska	8.9	Nebraska	10.2
Arizona	14.4	Nevada	9.5
Arkansas	17.7	New Hampshire	5.4
California	12.2	New Jersey	8.8
Colorado	9.7	New Mexico	16.9
Connecticut	8.0	New York	14.0
Delaware	9.3	North Carolina	13.8
District of Columbia	18.3	North Dakota	11.4
Florida	11.5	Ohio	12.1
Georgia	12.6	Oklahoma	15.2
Hawaii	9.2	Oregon	11.8
Idaho	9.5	Pennsylvania	11.3
Illinois	10.6	Rhode Island	10.5
Indiana	10.6	South Carolina	11.2
Iowa	10.3	South Dakota	10.7
Kansas	12.8	Tennessee	14.9
Kentucky	16.8	Texas	16.4
Louisiana	17.0	Utah	9.3
Maine	10.2	Vermont	7.8
Maryland	8.4	Virginia	8.6
Massachusetts	12.0	Washington	8.0
Michigan	13.3	West Virginia	15.3
Minnesota	8.2	Wisconsin	10.1
Mississippi	20.6	Wyoming	10.0

Source: U.S. Census Bureau, "POV46: Poverty Status by State: 2006." U.S. Census Bureau, Current Population Survey, 2007 Annual Social and Economic Supplement. Retrieved July 2008, from http://pubdb3.census.gov/macro/032007/pov/new46_100125_01.htm

administration in 1980, there was a move away from reliance on social welfare expenditures and toward an emphasis on ending poverty through overall economic growth.

Consequently, public expenditures for poverty programs decreased and tax cuts—intended to give people incentives to work and save money—increased. The Reagan approach belied the belief that the poor should wait for gains through increased economic activity rather than rely on welfare programs. This perspective assumed that the trickle-down effect of economic growth would benefit the poor more than direct economic subsidies. According to analyst Kevin Phillips, "Low-income families, especially the working poor, lost appreciably more by cuts in government services than they gained in tax reductions."[81] Despite the nation's long-standing belief in eradicating poverty through market incomes, the major factors influencing the general decrease in poverty from the 1960s to the late 1970s were governmental cash and in-kind transfers.[82]

Employment opportunities are increasingly being based on the proficiency of technological skills, something directly impacted by the relationship between poverty and the digital divide.

The Digital Divide

The Internet and related information technologies represent a major technological breakthrough. However, there are also important policy concerns arising from the use of new technologies, including the balance between social well-being and the free flow of information in a democracy. For those with access, the Internet has become a marketplace of ideas and a marketplace for a wide range of goods and services. But this technology is also leaving some people behind, especially some of the poor.

The term *digital divide* refers to the information "haves" and "have-nots"—the differential access to technology that exists along income, class, and racial lines. The digital divide in the United States is an important social equity issue. For example, those with telecommunications services, such as a home telephone and a computer with Internet access, can effectively engage the global economy, participate in political debates, and interact within the "global village." People bereft of this access risk being left behind, disconnected from the global community, the political system, and the information-driven market economy.

People use the Internet and related technologies for many different purposes: e-mail, information searches, and job searches. Pursuing online courses and school research is also popular. Despite the Internet's utility, certain groups still cannot access it and are unable to benefit from its growing list of uses.[83]

The digital divide cuts across income levels, race and ethnicity, and location. For example, in 2007, of all households with income over $150,000 only 2 percent did not use the Internet at all, while for those households earning between $5,000 and $10,000 per year it was 64 percent. Similarly, there are also significant differences in Internet access across racial and ethnic lines. Of those reporting they had access to the Internet *anywhere*, Asians had 82 percent access followed by whites (75 percent), African Americans (59 percent), and Hispanics (55 percent). Of those who had access *in the home*, the differences were similar with Asians (76 percent)

and whites (67 percent) having the highest access and African Americans (45 percent) and Hispanics (43 percent) having much less access. Internet use in rural homes is less than in urban homes. For example, urban households with incomes of $20,000 to $25,000 had 42 percent access while for rural households this was 37 percent.[84] America's digital divide is fast becoming a racial and class divide.

Digital access has occupied policy discussions in national legislative bodies, state capitals, industry boardrooms, and grassroots community organizations since 1998. These discussions, and the media attention surrounding them, are causing society to become increasingly aware of the detrimental effects of the lack of Internet access for e-commerce, civic engagement, political organization, and the like. Several organizations such as Jesse Jackson's Rainbow/PUSH, the Benton Foundation, and notably the National Telecommunications and Information Administration (NTIA) of the U.S. Department of Commerce have identified the digital divide as a major social problem.

To narrow the digital gap, the former Clinton administration initiated the E-Rate program, which was designed to provide schools and libraries with lower-cost Internet access and other telecommunication services. By 1999 E-Rate had funded more than 45,000 schools with more than $2.5 billion in telecommunications subsidies.[85] Despite these efforts, the digital divide between low-poverty schools and high-poverty schools still exists. Welfare retrenchment, deep federal and state budget cuts, the growth of the working poor, under- and unemployment, dual labor markets, and a frozen minimum wage have all conspired to create an alternative financial services sector, or a fringe economy.

America's Fringe Economy[86]

According to the U.S. Department of Commerce's Bureau of Economic Analysis, the personal savings rate of Americans went negative in the first quarter of 2005 and has continued to be negative ever since.[87] The Federal Reserve Bank of San Francisco reports that a negative savings rate means that Americans are spending more than they earn. The declining savings rate that began in the 1980s is partly explained by formerly rising home prices and a robust stock market.[88] In other words, why save when gains can be realized by disposing of an asset?

The problem is more than a failure to save. Since 1960, the ratio of household debt to personal disposable income has more than doubled as Americans have gone on the longest sustained spending spree in history.[89] For example, from 2001 to 2004, home equity loans funneled $425 billion a year into consumption. Inflation-adjusted aggregate household debt during this period increased by more than 26 percent, and measures of the ability of households to repay their debt suggest that it is getting harder for many to repay. Over 83 percent of all consumer debt is now secured by residential property that has been declining in value.[90]

What does all this mean? Basically, the average U.S. middle-class household has become accustomed to a lifestyle that cannot be sustained by their income alone. Instead of saving part of their income to accumulate wealth, the average U.S. family is borrowing to acquire a house and relying on its appreciation to substitute for savings. This means that the financial future for most Americans will depend on the vicissitudes of the housing market which has been on a downward spiral since 2007. Unlike investments in stocks and bonds that can be diversified to protect the investor against downturns, reliance on home appreciation cannot be protected. Converting the house to spendable cash is not a feasible solution if the value of the home has depreciated and is worth less than the mortgage. Relief from impossible debt in the form of personal bankruptcy has become more difficult due to the Bankruptcy Abuse Prevention and Consumer Act of 2005.[91]

Headlines have recently exploded with the phrase "housing bust." Indeed, new home starts have fallen[92] while repossessions have escalated to unparalleled heights.[93] The decline in the housing markets, the strongest non-military–related sector in the U.S. economy for the past few years, is threatening an economic recession.[94] When rent-to-own stores, pawn shops, cash exchanges, and payday lenders are advertising on television for middle-class customers, it is a clear sign that something is afoot and the anachronistic poverty line that focuses exclusively on household income fails to tell the full poverty story.

While much of the economic life of the middle class is rooted in credit,[95] many poor people encounter obstacles to basic credit and are vulnerable to exploitation by fringe businesses. The often shoddy storefronts of fringe economy hide the true scope of this economic sector. Ninety percent of payday lending revenues are based on fees from trapped borrowers. The typical payday borrower pays back $793 for a $325 loan. Predatory payday lending now costs U.S. families $4.2 billion per year in excessive fees.[96]

The past decade has been a good one for check cashers, payday lenders, pawnshops, rent-to-own stores, and the like. Their loans are now legal in 38 states. The number of payday loan outlets increased significantly from just 2,000 in 1995 to 24,000 in 2007. Funded largely by mainstream financial institutions, the total loan volume in 2005 was $40 billion, over 10 times that in 1998. Ten large companies, including listed companies, own or operate about 40 percent of payday loan stores in the United States. Among the industry leaders is QC Holdings Inc., which operates more than 600 Quick Cash and other payday loan stores in 25 states, backed by U.S. Bancorp, the nation's sixth largest commercial bank that provides QC with a $45 million line of credit.[97] The fringe economy is also robust in the housing sector. Subprime (loans to marginal borrowers that carry a higher interest rate) mortgages rose significantly throughout the 1990s, by 880 percent from 1993 to 1998.[98] For subprime mortgages originated from 1998 through to 2006, it has been projected that 2.2 million U.S. households will lose their homes to foreclosure, costing these households as much as $164 billion, and that one out of every five (19.4 percent) subprime loans made will fail.[99] By 2007 the number of subprime loans, many of them shaky at best, had threatened to bring down the international banking sector.

In short, the U.S. fringe economy is not a mom-and-pop operation composed of small storefronts that generate moderate family incomes; instead, it is a multibillion parallel economy that provides low-income consumers with a full range of cash, commodities, and credit lines. Pawnshops, check cashers, and payday lenders are a major part of the fringe economy, but they are only the tip of the iceberg. This subeconomy also includes mainstream banks issuing high-interest credit cards and expensive check overdraft protection, high-interest subprime home financing and refinancing loans, and deferred interest retail payments. Fringe economic services exist in every sector where people borrow or spend money.

The insularity of this sector means that the prices of commodities and financial services in the fringe economy are virtually removed from the real value of these goods and services in the mainstream marketplace. As such, prices in the fringe economy are based on the supposedly higher risk of serving a poor or credit-challenged population. In this economic bubble, used cars can cost twice their book value, housing prices are determined by the financial desperation of home buyers rather than the home's value, a 14-day $200 payday loan can cost $40 in interest/fees, and credit cards come with yearly and monthly service fees plus annual percentage rates (APR) of 30 percent or more. In the fringe economy, economic distress and low credit scores translate into high corporate profits.

The Unbanked and the Functionally Poor

Important clients in the fringe economy are the unbanked (e.g., individuals and families without accounts at deposit institutions). About 12 million U.S. households (one-fourth of all low-income families) have no relationship with a mainstream financial service provider, such as a bank, savings institution, or credit union.[100] The unbanked report they do not have checking accounts because (1) they do not write enough checks to warrant one, (2) they have almost no month-to-month financial savings to deposit, (3) they cannot afford high bank fees, (4) they cannot meet minimum bank balance requirements, (5) they want to keep their financial records private, and (6) they experience discomfort dealing with banks. Almost 85 percent of the unbanked have yearly incomes below $25,000.[101]

One industry-funded study found that the average payday-loan customer was female with children living at home, was between 24 and 44 years old, earned less than $40,000 a year, was a high school graduate, was a renter, was transient (most had lived in the same home for less than five years), and had little job tenure.[102] This group represents the lower- and moderate-income working class rather than the poorest of the poor.

The misconception that only the poor use the fringe economy overlooks the convergence of the traditional poor with growing segments of the middle class that can be categorized as the functionally poor. For instance, the functionally poor can include homeowners who use their houses like ATM machines, regularly drawing out equity to finance credit card debts or other purchases. It also includes the middle class with tarnished credit who carry high-interest-rate credit cards or finance their purchases through tricky time-deferred payments. In

that sense, a burgeoning sector of the middle class is economically closer to the traditional poor than to the traditional middle class.

Total U.S. household debt (including vehicles and mortgages) was $13.3 trillion in 2007 (the equivalent of $44,000 per person), a 500 plus percent increase since 1957. Personal savings rates and home equity were the lowest in recent history. In the 1980s, consumers saved roughly 10 percent of their disposable income; by 2003 it was only 2.5 percent, and by 2007 it was negative or close to it. In 2002, home owners initiated $97 billion in home equity loans, nearly five times the amount in 1993.[103] Consumers spent almost all of it, and about 500,000 home owners are in the foreclosure process.[104] Credit card debt is another factor in the new poverty. Consumers who did not pay off monthly balances in 2002 owed a median average of $2,200 in credit card debt and those who carried over balances owed close to $9,000. Overall, credit card holders carried more than $915 billion in debt in 2007.[105]

Credit and the Poor

Credit is a bridge between real household earnings and consumption decisions, offering relief during periods of economic distress and uncertainty.[106] Payment options are flexible for those with good credit, and collateral is not required. Hence, the middle class can purchase goods and services or borrow cash without losing their possessions. On the other hand, neither trust nor the presumption of goodwill exists in the fringe economy. A borrower with compromised credit typically must provide collateral such as a secured bank account, a post-dated check, household goods, or a car title. Those who manage to find unsecured credit are often charged high interest rates combined with onerous loan terms.

Credit card use has become almost mandatory in the United States. Renting a car or reserving a hotel room or flight is almost impossible without a credit card. The average U.S. credit card holder has ten cards—four retail cards, three bank cards, one phone card, one gasoline card, and one travel and entertainment card. Not surprisingly, bank write-offs for uncollectible credit card debt were 5.25 percent in 2007 ($1.2 billion could potentially be written off).[107]

There are two basic types of credit cards: unsecured and secured. The cornerstones of unsecured credit are the cardholder's creditworthiness, past use of credit, and ability to repay debt. Conversely, secured credit cards require cardholders to guarantee their credit line by providing cash collateral which makes it difficult for the borrower to default.

Unsecured Credit Cards   Widespread credit card use by consumers with poor credit is a relatively recent phenomenon. Until the 1990s, banks limited their exposure on credit cards by refusing poor credit risks. However, as the credit card market became saturated and more competitive, banks were forced to examine ways to make money from riskier customers. Because bankruptcy laws prevent refiling for six years, banks began to promote "special offers" to newly bankrupted consumers with an income source.[108] Although the default rate for these individuals is high, the cards carry such low credit lines—coupled with high interest rates and fees—that banks can still make money. Terms are strict, and only one late payment results in a cardholder being moved into the default rate category, which carries a 23 to 35 percent or higher APR.

Some credit cards require no security deposit but credit limits are low (in the $100 to $500 range) and cardholders must earn at least $12,000 a year. Fees on these unsecured cards can cost hundreds of dollars, and interest rates are close to 30 percent. For example, Centennial MasterCard/Visa advertised a low 9.9 percent APR. However, two late payments in six months results in the rate jumping to almost 24 percent. Fees for this credit card were $178, including a $48 annual fee and a $6 monthly participation fee. The maximum credit limit was only $250. The Plains Commerce Bank Visa charged $281 for a credit card with a limit of $300, leaving only $19 when the card arrived.[109] This is predatory lending, especially when compared to mainstream credit cards that charge no setup or monthly fees, charge nothing to increase credit limits, and have free electronic access for account management.

Secured Credit Cards   Responding to consumers with problematic credit, the industry created a class of credit cards securitized by a cardholder's collateral. Like their unsecured cousins, secured cards are emblazoned with Visa and MasterCard logos. Although these cards require a credit check, they are really quasi-credit cards, because no line of credit is actually extended. The major advantage of secured cards for credit card issuers (CCIs) is that they can easily liquidate a cardholder's collateral and apply it to the outstanding balance.

To receive a secured credit card, the customer must open an interest-bearing savings account for the amount of the credit line, usually a minimum of $200 to $5,000. (Some banks only allow customers a credit line equal to 50 percent of their collateral.) Funds in the savings account are jointly owned by the bank and cannot be accessed by the cardholder. In turn, cardholders are given a Visa or MasterCard with a credit line equal to the collateral. Credit card balances are not subtracted from the savings account; instead, cardholders pay those charges as they would any other credit card. Despite the collateral, fees and interest rates are high: Cross Country Bank charged a $50 origination fee, a 24 percent APR, and a hefty late fee. There was also a 50 cent minimum finance charge and a $10 monthly fee. Because this credit card had no grace period, interest began with each purchase. Wells Fargo's secured credit card had an $18 annual fee, a $300 security deposit, a late and over-the-limit fee of $30, and a 17 percent APR for purchases and 21.8 percent for cash advances.[110]

Preloaded or Stored Value Debit Cards   A variation of the secured credit card is the preloaded debit card, sometimes called a stored value card (SVC). Using a Visa or MasterCard logo, SVCs are similar to prepaid phone cards in that they are preloaded with funds. When the funds are exhausted, the card must be reloaded or it becomes inactive. Unlike secured credit cards, prepaid cards are not dependent on credit or banking history because they are not linked to a bank account. (Customers can use the entire amount loaded onto the card.) There is also no debt to repay. Like any fringe economy transaction, there is a downside. For example, WiredPlastic charged an initial $50 fee, a one-time activation fee of $30, a monthly maintenance fee of $7, and $2 for each cash withdrawal (plus any other fees charged by ATM owner/operators). Money could be loaded directly through payroll transfers and government checks, such as Social Security.[111]

Secured and preloaded debit cards reflect the inherent inequities in the fringe economy. For instance, if banks demanded that the middle class securitize their $10,000 Visa or MasterCard credit lines, most would return to cash or checks. Secured credit cards are exploitive in other ways. For instance, customers are compelled to deposit money in a low-interest-bearing savings account. Simultaneously, they are charged a 24 percent APR for purchases, plus other fees to essentially borrow against their own money. Because the credit line is guaranteed by collateral, banks cannot argue that high costs reflect an exceptional risk. The most viable explanation for the high costs is simple avarice. Moreover, secured credit cards are often marketed as a way to build or rebuild credit histories. However, if the CCI does not report the transaction to a credit bureau—which many do not—a cardholder cannot build or rebuild their credit history. In effect, stored value debit cards are often just like expensive gift cards.

Telecommunications and the Alternative Services Market The effects of poor credit are evident in the telecommunication services industry. Consumer telecommunications are divided into two groups: post- and pre-paid services. For post-paid (i.e., paying *after* a charge is accrued) telephone services, customers are required to undergo credit checks, and those without an acceptable credit score are denied local and long-distance service. Denied mainstream telecommunications services, consumers are forced into the more expensive prepaid sector.

Consumers can opt for alternative prepaid local phone service from Competitive Local Exchange Carriers (CLECs), which are small companies that compete with regional carriers such as the Bell companies and GTE. DPI, a CLEC, charged $39 a month for basic local phone service with no option for long distance or directory assistance. Others, such as Direct Telephone, charged $50 a month for local service bundled with some options.[112] In comparison, Southwest Bell charged about $19 a month for full-service local phone service.

Postpaid cell phone service is also dependent on good credit scores, and clients with problematic credit are a lucrative part of the wireless industry. For example, wireless consumers with good credit could get Sprint's $35 postpaid cell phone service, which included 300 daytime minutes and unlimited night and evening minutes. AT&T's $30 plan included 200 daytime and unlimited nighttime minutes.[113] On the other hand, Verizon charged prepaid customers 10 cents a minute and 25 cents for each call (35 cents for the first minute). Cingular (owned by AT&T) charged prepaid customers 35 cents a minute and 10 cents a minute on weekends or 10 cents a minute and $1 a day. AT&T bases its prepaid pricing on the amount of refills a customer bought. For example, customers who could only afford a $10 refill paid from 50 to 85 cents a minute while the costs for those who could afford a $100 refill ranged from 12 to 22 cents a minute.[114]

Because prepaying customers cannot default, the high costs of these services are based on the customer's economic vulnerability. Prepayment schemes are also unfair because they allow corporations to use a customer's money without paying interest. A single $100 prepayment to AT&T will not generate much interest, but multiplied by tens of thousands of prepaid cell phone customers, the float (i.e., the lag time between when money is received or requested and when the financial institution actually releases it) is sizable. Prepaid customers are therefore penalized twice—once by paying higher prices and then again when the company uses their money without paying interest. Consumers trying to build or rebuild their credit history derive little benefit from prepaying because no credit is extended and therefore there is nothing to report to a credit agency. Lacking cash and mainstream credit, many low-income and credit-impaired consumers also turn to the furniture and appliance rental industry.

The Furniture and Appliance Rental Industry The rent-to-own (RTO) sector targets low- and moderate-income consumers. RTOs advertise no credit checks, weekly or monthly payments, and a choice of appliances, furniture, and jewelry that would otherwise be unaffordable if low-income consumers bought them outright.[115] The $6.8 billion a year RTO industry served over 3 million customers in 2007 and is a major player in the fringe economy.[116] Rent-A-Center (the largest RTO) began with eight stores in 1986; by 2008 Rent-A-Center was the largest rent-to-own operator in the United States with over 3,000 stores nationwide, annual revenues of $2.9 billion, and approximately 37 percent market share.[117] Aaron Rents started in 1955 by renting folding chairs to auction houses for 10 cents a day. By 2008, it had 1,563 owned and franchised stores. Revenue for the first quarter of 2008 alone increased 13 percent to $437.3 million compared to $387.9 million for the first quarter of 2007.[118]

The RTO industry employs two approaches to transactions: (1) customers rent goods and pay weekly or monthly fees, or (2) they rent-to-own with payments extending from 12 to 24 months. In either case, customers can usually cancel the agreement without further cost or obligation. Customers take ownership of the property if the contract is renewed a prescribed number of times (usually 12 to 24 months) or if they complete the lease agreement. No credit bureau reports are obtained or filed because RTO customers make advanced payments.[119]

Renting or leasing is an expensive option. Rainbow Rentals, leased/rented a Frigidaire washer and dryer for $19 a week or $69 a month for 21 months. The total cost was between $1,450 and $1,600 for a washer and dryer that could be purchased for $700 to $800 at a local discount store. A Compaq Presario notebook rented for $38 a week or $144 a month for 24 months, raising the total cost to about $3,500. The same computer could have been bought for one-third of the price—about $1,200 to $1,300—at major discount stores. A 32-inch Toshiba flat screen television cost $1,800 to rent for 24 months while Best Buy sold the same set for $650. The list goes on and on. RTO customers generally pay at least two to three times more than the retail price for furniture or appliances.[120] The RTO industry argues that high prices reflect two variables: The cost of free repairs and the risk of doing business with customers who have poor credit histories and unstable incomes.

RTOs make money in other ways. For one, RTOs retailers offer merchandise at a "cash price and carry" price. According to a 1997 PIRG study, the typical RTO cash price on an item was $389 compared with the average department store price of $217.[121] For example, one Aaron Rents store in Houston, Texas, was selling a used GE refrigerator for $1,134—about the same price as a new one in a discount appliance store. RTOs also make money by repossessions and re-rents. For instance, a 32-inch Toshiba television may cost the RTO store $500. If the set is rented for $69 a month, they will make up the $500 in only seven months and realize a gross profit of $1,173 at the end of the two-year lease term. If the set is repossessed after seven months, the retailer can re-rent it for another two years at a slightly lower rental price. In this way, merchandise can be frequently recycled. One Rent-A-Center store had a $119 VCR that brought in more than $5,000 over a five-year period.[122] Typical RTO stores have revenues of almost $500,000 a year.[123]

The RTO industry is hounded by a controversy over whether transactions are credit sales or purchase option leases. As a credit sale, RTO transactions would carry a 100 to 200 percent APR and would therefore clash with many state anti-usury laws. In addition, federal truth-in-lending laws would apply in a credit sale, triggering interest rate disclosures and other consumer information. Forty-six states currently have laws regulating RTO transactions as leases, mandating a variety of disclosures and other requirements. Consumer groups argue that RTO transactions should be treated as credit sales.[124]

Many fringe businesses long ago realized the importance of treating low-income customers well. Good customer service is important to low-income consumers, especially those who have been subjected to humiliation by mainstream merchants after bad credit checks. Some consumers are so sensitive to poor treatment that they will pay more, sometimes much more, to feel they are being respected. As one former Rent-A-Center manager stated, "If you treat the customer like royalty, you can bleed them through the nose."[125]

Cash Loans   Cash loans serve the same purpose for the poor as credit card cash advances for the middle class in that they provide crisis cash for a medical or familial emergency, or when income is insufficient to make ends meet on a short-term basis. Cash loans can be divided into two categories: collateral-based loans and nonsecured or promissory loans. In the former, the borrower provides collateral (either property or guaranteed anticipated income) to the lender that is worth as much or more than the loan. Even though many in the middle class receive unsecured loans, this type of loan is often denied to the poor or those with bad credit. As such, loans available to the poor are generally collateral-based loans such as pawnshop transactions.

Pawnshops   Pawnshops are high-growth industries and at least five chains are publicly traded (i.e., EZ Pawn, Cash America Pawn, Express Cash, Famous Pawn, and First Cash Pawn). According to the National Pawnbrokers Association, the number of pawnshops in the United States has nearly doubled in the past ten years from 6,900 in 1988 to 13,000 in 2008, a reflection of the present tough economic times.[126]

A pawnshop loan is a relatively simple transaction. A pawnbroker makes a fixed-term loan that is guaranteed by collateral. The customer is given a pawn ticket that includes his or her name and address, a description of the pledged good, the amount lent, the maturity date, and the amount that must be repaid to reclaim the property. The property is returned when the customer presents the ticket and pays the loan and the fees within the agreed-on time. If the loan is not repaid, the collateral becomes the property of the pawnbroker and the customer's debt is extinguished. Customers can repay a loan at any time during the loan term and redeem the collateral. Pawnshops are typically regulated by state and sometimes local governments, and interest rates can range from 1.5 percent to 25 percent a month, depending on the regulations of the state. The average pawn shop loan is about $75 but can go as low as $15.[127]

In Houston, Texas, a pawnshop transaction works in the following way. A customer brings in an item that is then appraised by the broker. This appraisal is typically very low, with jewelry appraised at wholesale prices, guns appraised at less than 60 percent of their Blue Book value, and appliances at a fraction of their original cost. Many pawnshops have a maximum loan limit on items (usually $500 to $1,000) regardless of the value of the property. Hence, even if an item is worth $2,000, the pawnshop may only lend up to a maximum of $500 or $1,000 (although on higher priced items some pawnshops exercise flexibility).

Pawnshops allow customers to borrow all or part of the appraised value of an item for 30 days, at which time the loan is renewable for up to 90 days. However, many pawnshops have an open-ended policy whereby the customer can extend the pawn indefinitely by paying only the interest on the loan. In most Houston pawnshops, the interest on a $500 loan is $75 for the first month and $75 a month for the fixed term of the three-month loan. At the end of the first 30 days it would cost $575 to redeem the item; after 60 days the price would rise to $650; and at the end of 90 days it would cost $725, or 45 percent of the value of the collateral. One pawnshop manager stated that some people renew their loans for a year or more, which translates into $1,800 in interest charges on a $1,000 loan. Although some state laws cap interest rates, loopholes often allow "lease back" agreements to add fees, sometimes effectively doubling interest rates.[128]

Car Title Pawns Car title pawns (vehicle title lenders) operate similarly to pawnshops. A customer needs a short-term loan, but instead of using his or her television or stereo as collateral, they use their vehicle title. In most cases, this will substantially increase the amount that can be borrowed because vehicles generally have more value than televisions, stereos, or microwaves. Unlike pawnshop transactions, the borrower does not forego the use of his or her property during the course of the loan, even though the vehicle is technically owned by the lender until the loan is repaid.

Car title pawns operate in the following way. A borrower provides the lender with a free and paid-up vehicle title and an extra set of keys. In return for the loan, the borrower allows the title lender to keep the title or to put a lien on the vehicle.

The vehicle is appraised based on the lowest possible value, which is the wholesale price in poor condition. For example, a 1993 Oldsmobile Cutlass Ciera would have a retail value of $2,217 if bought from a dealer in June 2002. The resale value of the car to a private party would have been $1,530, and the dealer trade-in would have been $1,118.[129] Because car title pawn companies generally lend up to 50 percent of the value of a vehicle, the maximum loan would have been $559. A loan default would therefore provide the lender with a car worth $2,217 for $559 plus the interest payments already made by the borrower. Moreover, if a vehicle is repossessed, the borrower does not receive any proceeds from the sale, even if the resale amount exceeds the loan amount.

Vehicle title loans are usually for one month and often involve an APR of 300 percent or more. Although loan terms vary slightly between companies, one large title loan company operates in the following way. A vehicle is appraised at $2,000 (the wholesale price in poor condition) and a 30-day loan is given for 50 percent of the car's value or $1,000. After 30 days the loan payoff is $1,246.57 (almost 25 percent in interest and fees). If the loan is not repaid, the car is repossessed on the 31st day. The borrower may ask for a 30-day extension after paying the interest and fees. After only 60 days the interest and fees will total almost 50 percent of the original $1,000 loan. The borrower may then ask for a third extension after paying the interest charges of $493 for the first two loan periods. This extension is for a maximum of one year. At that point, the monthly payment rises to $346.57 because the borrower is now expected to pay down $100 a month toward the loan principal as well as pay the interest. By the fourth month, the principal will be only $900 and so on until the loan is paid off or the car is repossessed.[130] If the borrower keeps the loan for 12 months, he or she will have paid almost $3,000 in interest charges/fees for a $1,000 loan. Borrowers will have also paid more than the value of the vehicle.

Payday Loans Although pawnshops are profitable, the payday loan market (sometimes called deferred deposit services) is even more robust. For example, while the average pawnshop loan is $75, the average payday loan ranges from $100 to $500 or more.[131] As stated earlier, the number of payday loan outlets increased significantly from just 2,000 in 1995 to 24,000 in 2007 with a total loan volume of $40 billion, over ten times of what it was in 1998.

To qualify for a payday loan, the customer must have a valid checking account from which a check is issued (or electronically debited) to cover the interest and principal for the loan. On a $300 payday loan, the lender may ask for a $300 check and then deduct the interest from the amount received by the borrower. Borrowers must also provide recent pay stubs and valid identification. Many payday lenders consider benefits as income and will give loans to those on public assistance, recipients of child support or alimony, and Social Security beneficiaries.[132]

Payday loans are typically issued for a maximum of $300 ($500 to $1,000 for established customers) and are usually given for 14 or 18 days. The average fees are almost $20 per $100 borrowed (fees can be as high as $37 per hundred), or 20 percent for the two-week loan period. Since the borrower repays $360 on a $300 loan, this translates into a 500 percent APR. (Nationally, the average APR for payday loans is 474 percent.[133]) Because the lender may extend the loan (called a rollover) for additional 14- or 18-day periods (after the interest is paid), a $300 payday loan extended to 42 days or three loan periods will accrue $180 in interest charges alone, elevating the full loan repayment to $480 in less than two months. Unlike pawnshop transactions where a customer loses his or her collateral if he or she defaults, payday loans can inflict potentially greater damage on borrowers. For instance, defaulting on a payday loan will mar the creditworthiness of the borrower, if not destroy it. It may also result in criminal prosecution for writing a hot check.[134]

Collection tactics for payday loans can be aggressive. If a borrower cannot repay the loan, it may be turned over to a collection agency and result in the loss of a house, car, or the garnishing of wages. In some cases, the collection agency can add additional interest to the original debt.[135] The payday lender may prosecute the customer for writing a "hot check," even though they knew the customer did not have sufficient funds in his or her checking account when he or she wrote it. Some payday loan companies require borrowers to agree beforehand to pay all fees related to the collection of their account, including attorney fees, collection fees,

and court costs.[136] A default on a payday loan involves a worthless check, and some state credit laws allow for triple damages when a bad check is used in a retail transaction. Lenders may also require that customers sign statements authorizing them to go directly to the borrower's employer and ask for the amount owed to be deducted from their paychecks.

Tax Refund Anticipation Loans   Refund anticipation loans (RALs) are short-term loans secured by an expected tax refund. RALs are expensive and similar to other forms of fringe credit with an APR ranging from 67 to 774 percent.[137] Every year tax preparation services earn about $1 billion dollars in fees from these loans.[138]

RALs are common in low-income neighborhoods where there are a large number of tax refunds associated with the federal earned income tax credit (EITC) program (see Chapter 9). Under EITC, the working poor receive refunds that exceed what they paid in taxes. In addition to EITC, low- and moderate-income families with children are also eligible for the federal child tax credit (CTC), worth up to $1,000 a child. The EITC and CTC tax refunds created a powerful incentive for mainstream tax preparers to enter the poverty services market.

Sixty-eight percent of EITC- and CTC-eligible families use tax preparers and electronic return originators (EROs) that are authorized by the IRS to electronically transmit federal income tax returns. Low-income tax filers use EROs for several reasons: (1) the EITC and the CTC filing process is complicated;[139] (2) low-income working families can receive large tax refunds and many are eager to claim them quickly, sometimes the day they file; (3) tax preparers are ubiquitous in lower-income neighborhoods (there are 50 percent more EROs in zip codes with high numbers of EITC recipients than zip codes with fewer recipients);[140] (4) free tax assistance is scarce; and (5) the poor cannot afford to pay upfront the $100 plus in tax-preparation fees.

Commercial tax preparers earn high profits by providing financial services to some of the poorest of the poor. According to one study, RAL customers tend to have annual incomes between $10,000 and $15,000, are unemployed or employed in service occupations, and possess less than a high school education.[141] About 40 percent of taxpayers who use RALs are EITC recipients.[142] Moreover, many of the poor are unaware that RALs are actually loans because they are often advertised as "Quick Cash,"

"Super Fast Refunds," or "Instant Money." In April 2001, H&R Block received 2,230 citations from the New York City Department of Consumer Affairs for misrepresenting RALs and luring customers into accepting loans they did not fully understand. The company settled for $4 million and paid $2.4 million in restitution to 61,700 customers. Block also settled a RAL-related class-action suit in Texas for $41.7 million.[143]

RALs are expensive. For example, a tax filer eligible for a $1,900 EITC refund who takes out a RAL will pay $248 (see Table 5.7), thereby reducing the original $1,900 to $1,652.[144] Most of these costs are incurred simply to get an EITC refund a few days earlier compared to filing electronically and having the IRS directly deposit the refund into a checking account. RALs are also risky for low-income tax filers. Because a RAL is a loan from a bank in partnership with a tax preparer, it must be repaid even if the IRS denies or delays the refund, or if the refund is smaller than expected. Moreover, when tax filers apply for RALs, they give the lender the right to use the tax refund to pay for old tax-preparation debts that may be owed.

If low-income consumers are fleeced when they enter a tax-preparation office, they are ripped off again on their way out. About 45 percent of RAL customers use commercial check cashing outlets (CCOs) to cash their refund checks, paying fees that range from 3 to 10 percent of the face value of the check. Responding to this captive market, ACE Cash Express installed check-cashing machines in some

H&R Block lobbies and charged roughly 3 percent to cash a secure check, thereby further lowering the $1,900 refund to $1,602.[145] All told, EITC-eligible families using EROs and check cashers can lose more than 16 percent of the value of their tax refund.

Tax-preparation fees can take other forms. For example, a consumer is charged a tax-preparation fee of $100 to $118, which they are expected to pay out-of-pocket.[146] Because some families cannot pay the fee or do not have a checking account, tax preparers offer a "refund transfer." Although not a loan, per se, the filer pays about $28 to establish a dummy bank account into which the IRS directly deposits a tax refund check. After the deposit, the tax preparer subtracts their fees, issues a paper check, and closes the account. The $28 fee is high for a 10-day bank account designed for a single lump sum, especially because for a few dollars more the consumer can maintain a checking account for a full year. The advantage to low-income consumers is that tax-preparation fees can be deducted directly from the dummy account, thereby relieving them from paying those fees upfront. In effect, dummy accounts are actually disguised loans because they defer tax-preparation fees. Another variation is an assisted refund transfer or, as Jackson Hewitt calls it, "IRS Direct." With this product, a consumer pays the tax preparer to be an intermediary in processing a tax refund into the tax filer's *own* bank account.[147]

High tax-preparation and RAL fees hurt poor working families and substantially diminish the economic impact of the EITC and CTC. In 2001, tax

Table 5.7

Draining EITC: 2002 Tax Preparation, RAL Fees, and Check Cashing

Type of Fee	Cost to Tax Filer	Drain on EITC Program (in millions)
RAL loan fee	$75	$363
Electronic filing fee	40	194
Document preparation/ application/handling fee	33	160
Tax preparation fee	100	484
Check cashing fee	57	110*
Total	305	1,311

*This was based on 40 percent of low-income tax filers using a check cashing service.

Source: Based on Chi Chi Wu and Jean Ann Fox, "The High Cost of Quick Tax Money: Tax Preparation, 'Instant Refund' Loans, and Check Cashing Fees Target the Working Poor." (Washington, DC: National Consumer Law Center, Consumer Federation of America, January 2003). Reprinted with permission of the National Consumer Law Center, www.consumerlaw.org, 617-542-9595.

filers paid almost $1.8 billion in RAL and other fees,[148] which took a substantial chunk out of the $31 billion EITC program that Congress had targeted for the poor.[149] Table 5.7 illustrates the impact of tax-preparation fees and RALs on tax filers and the EITC program.

Check Cashing Outlets (CCOs)   In large urban areas, from 20 to 40 percent of the unbanked pay fees to cash their paychecks through CCOs.[150] Many larger CCOs are one-stop financial service centers in that they offer a wide range of services in one location: (1) check cashing; (2) utility and other bill pay services; (3) money transfers; (4) payday loans; (5) money orders; (6) telecommunications products (e.g., prepaid long-distance calling cards, prepaid local phone service, cell phones and beepers); and (7) other services such as fax transmissions, copy services, stamps and envelopes, notary services, mailboxes, and lottery tickets.[151]

CCOs with names like ACE Cash Express, Check 'N Go, Mr. Payroll, Dollar, and Money Mart are common sights in inner-city neighborhoods. Behind these 11,000 plus storefronts lies an industry that cashes upwards of 180 million checks a year with a face value of more than $55 billion. The CCO industry generates nearly $1.5 billion a year in revenues.[152]

CCOs are an expensive way to cash checks. Most check-cashing fees range from 1 to 10 percent (plus a service fee in some states) of the face value of a check.[153] Check-cashing charges are often based on a sliding scale, and Dollar—the second largest CCO—charges 3.5 percent, or $35, to cash a $1,000 payroll check.[154] Fees for cashing personal checks can run as high as 10 to 12 percent of the value of the check. If a customer cashes twenty $800 paychecks a year through Dollar, they will pay $560—far more than the costs of even a deluxe checking account. The price list at one ACE Cash Express in Houston, Texas, is typical of the industry:

Cashier's check	5.0%
Government check	2.7%
Handwritten payroll check	2.7%
Insurance drafts/checks	5.0%
Money orders	5.0%
Tax refund checks	3.9%
No I.D. checks	5.0%
Special risk	5.0%
Bank-processing fee	$0.49
Minimum charge per item	$1.99
Returned check charge	$25.00

High check-cashing fees do not correspond to high risk since about 70 to 90 percent of all checks cashed at CCOs are relatively secure payroll checks with an average value of $500 to $600.[155] Losses are also extremely low. For example, ACE uses a system for verifying and assessing the risk of each check-cashing transaction and reports losses of less than one quarter of 1 percent.[156] The profitability of the check cashing business is stunning. In 2002, 797 ACE company-owned stores posted average revenues of $237,000, or a store profit of almost 43 percent.[157] This profitability is leading even non-finance-related industries into the fray. For example, the Eastern Division of the Safeway supermarket chain was once the largest CCO in Maryland. Supermarket chains such as H.E.B. and Kroger's have also established check-cashing operations, although often charging slightly less than commercial CCOs.

Transportation in the Fringe Economy

For the poor who can afford a used vehicle, the path to car ownership is mined with high down payments, dead-end financing, extortionate interest rates, and overpriced insurance. Understanding the used-car industry is necessary to appreciate the obstacles faced by the poor. About 40 million used vehicles are sold annually in the United States—11 million by franchised new-car dealers and the remaining 29 million by independent used-car lots.[158] Used-car lots fall into two categories: independent lots and franchised dealerships. Independent or non-franchised dealers frequently sell older and less expensive vehicles. Franchised used-car lots are part of new-car dealerships and their cars tend to be newer, cleaner, and more expensive. Because of this market segmentation, most poor buyers end up in independent car lots, many of which are "here today and gone tomorrow."

A major obstacle faced by the poor is based on how mainstream financial institutions make loans in the $370 billion used-car industry. Most mainstream lenders like Bank of America, Wells Fargo Bank, and Chase refuse to lend money on vehicles four to six years or older, and those with more than 100,000 miles on them. Some lenders only finance vehicles purchased through dealerships, and some further restrict that to dealerships that also sell new cars. These restrictions limit the choices for the poor, because used cars sold by a dealer are more expensive than private-party sales. According to the Kelly Blue Book, a 1996 Chevrolet Lumina with 76,000 miles bought from an auto dealer in New York City in 2005 would have cost 30 percent more than one purchased privately.

Three tiers of financing exist for used-car buyers. The first is prime lending, which is offered to borrowers with a higher income and a good credit history. Interest rates are low because they are tied to the prime rate. The second tier is subprime lending, which is geared toward buyers with credit problems but who still have sufficient creditworthiness to secure a loan. Subprime loans carry higher interest rates, involve a substantial down payment, and often require that a vehicle be purchased from a franchised dealership. The third tier is nonprime lending or dealer financing, whereby vehicles are financed in-house. This type of financing often carries the highest interest rates and often requires weekly payments.

Buy-Here, Pay-Here used-car lots provide in-house financing, and they do not require buyers to undergo a credit check because the payment history is not reported to a credit bureau. Dealer-financed cars require a hefty down payment (typically $1,000 on a $5,000 vehicle) and late payments can result in immediate repossession.

Buy-Here, Pay-Here used-car lots are more profitable than franchised car dealerships. In 2002, the average retail price of used cars sold by franchised car lots was $11,793 with a gross profit of $1,741. In that same year, the average retail price of a used car in a Buy-Here, Pay-Here lot was $7,810, with a gross profit of $3,772—more than double that of franchised dealers. Lest one believe these dealerships are just small mom-and-pop operations, the National Association of Buy-Here, Pay-Here dealers held an annual convention in 2001 with over 800 attendees and 60 sponsors, including Bank of America, Bank One, SeaWest, and Wells Fargo. The Buy-Here, Pay-Here sector will likely grow as more subprime lenders—some of whom have lost money in recent years—further tighten their credit standards.

Auto insurance is another area where the poor are hard hit. For example, many people with older cars insure them only for state-mandated liability rather than for collision (damage to their vehicle) coverage. It makes little sense to pay $600 a year for collision coverage on a car worth $1,000, especially with a $500 deductible. Unfortunately, consumers who finance through Buy-Here, Pay-Here dealerships or subprime lenders must insure their vehicles

for liability *and* collision, regardless of whether it is cost effective.

The poor are hard hit by high auto-insurance rates. According to one study, 92 percent of large insurance companies run credit checks on potential customers, which translate into insurance scores.[159] These insurance scores determine whether the carrier will insure an applicant and for how much. Those with poor or no credit will be denied coverage, while those with limited credit will pay high premiums. Although there is no evidence that residents in low-income or high minority zip codes are involved in more accidents, they pay more for basic auto insurance, even if they have been accident-free and ticket-free for years.[160] Mounting consumer complaints have aroused the suspicion of some state insurance regulators that this may be a new form of redlining—a practice outlawed by the Fair Housing Act of 1968—because it discriminates against low-income, single-parent, young, and minority consumers whose credit histories may be less than perfect.[161]

While mainstream auto insurers calculate premiums based on a six-month or one-year period, fringe auto insurers usually provide only monthly quotations. Many also require a sizable down payment and a service fee. The premiums charged by fringe insurers are exorbitant compared with mainstream auto insurers. For example, in 2005 GEICO charged $700 a year for full coverage on a 1991 Chrysler minivan for a Houston driver with an excellent driving record. In comparison, minimally regulated, high-rate local insurance agencies like Houston's Alamo Insurance charged $2,100 a year for the same vehicle, or three times the $700 quoted by GEICO.

Fringe auto insurers get away with charging high premiums for several reasons. For one, they have captive consumers who are rejected by large insurance carriers. Second, the insurance demands of Buy-Here, Pay-Here dealers and subprime lenders create a steady stream of car buyers desperate for insurance. Third, many fringe auto insurers are minimally regulated and state insurance agencies are lax in rooting out predatory insurers, especially those serving the poor. Not coincidentally, fringe auto insurers take the pressure off mainstream carriers to provide coverage for the poor. Last, many state vehicle inspections require a proof-of-insurance card before a vehicle can pass inspection. Some car owners will pay the high monthly premium only to get the card and pass inspection, after which they drop the coverage. This may explain why fringe auto insurance rates are quoted monthly rather than biannually.

The low-income population pays more than the middle class for financial services in both absolute dollars and relative to their income.[162] These costs are exacerbated by the bifurcation of financial services that results in one system for the poor and another for the middle and upper classes. This bifurcated system leads to even greater inequality: Banks for the middle class and check cashers for the poor; access to savings tools for the middle class and barriers to savings for the poor; low-cost financial services for the middle class and high fee–based services for the poor. The fringe economy represents the financial exploitation of the poor by a predatory market designed to deplete rather than enhance the resources of poor families and communities. To better understand the poor, policy analysts must be aware of the myriad ways in which they are economically exploited. The regulation of the fringe economy is an economic justice issue that should be a central focus of any progressive social welfare agenda.

Conclusion

Poverty is one of the most intractable problems in U.S. society. Because poverty is both a political and a social issue, the policies surrounding it are often less than objective. For example, one can halve the poverty rate simply by redefining the poverty index. One can also cut poverty rates by placing a high dollar value on in-kind benefits such as food stamps and Medicaid. Conversely, one can swell the ranks of the poor by moving the poverty line upward; that is, by increasing the income level at which people are defined as poor. Like all social policies, poverty-related policies exist in a context marked by political exigencies, public opinion, the economic health of a society, and the complex mask of ideology.

Although various kinds of poverty-related data are available, policymakers remain uncertain as to the precise causes of poverty. What is known is that they are complex and involve, among other things, the effects of discrimination; the composition of family life, including the rise in single, female-headed families and teenage pregnancies; geographical location; and age. In large measure, the determination of whether a child is poor depends on chance; that is, on the family the child is born into. Policymakers also know that the skewed distribution of income in society and governmental tax and investment policies have major impacts on the numbers of people in poverty and on the extent of their poverty.

Most policymakers agree that employment is the best antipoverty program. Thus, work-related factors such as the value of the minimum wage (especially its relationship to mean incomes), the level of under- and unemployment, the rise or decrease in family incomes, and the general state of the economy all have a major impact on the level and extent of poverty. The availability of job training programs and the regulation of the dual labor market help determine the salaries workers will make. Taken together, these factors have caused poverty rates to remain higher in the United States than in many other industrialized nations. They have also helped make poverty seem like an intractable problem with few viable solutions.

Discussion Questions

Questions of poverty have long plagued social scientists. Specifically, these questions revolve around why some groups are able to rise out of poverty but others appear only to fall deeper into the poverty trap. Although several theorists have offered explanations for poverty, none hold up to empirical testing. This is because there is no simple or single answer to poverty. The causes of poverty involve a wide range of social, economic, political, and cultural factors. Poverty is one of the most elusive—if not the most elusive—problems facing U.S. social policy. Theories and strategies that address single explanations or single causes of poverty are doomed to failure, only aggravating a public that is already suspect of most antipoverty measures.

1. The measurement of poverty is both complex and controversial. Nevertheless, the way that poverty is measured has important consequences for the development of social policy in the United States. Describe some of the potential pitfalls in measuring poverty rates and discuss how the calculation of poverty rates affects the creation of social policy.

2. Working families make up an important and growing segment of the poor. What is causing the increase in the numbers of working poor? What specific policies should be implemented to reduce the number of working poor families?

3. Several theories have been advanced to explain why some individuals and groups of people are persistently poor while others are not. Theorists who have tried to tackle this problem include Daniel Patrick Moynihan, Oscar Lewis, and Edward Banfield. Although all theories of poverty have intrinsic flaws, which theory or combination of theories described in this book (or elsewhere) do you think best explains the dynamics of poverty?

4. Many strategies have been developed to fight poverty, including the curative approach, the alleviative approach, and the preventive approach. Of these strategies, which is the most effective in fighting poverty and why? What alternative strategies, if any, could be developed that would be more effective in combating poverty?

5. Policy analysts have traditionally argued that jobs are preferable to welfare and that the lack of employment opportunities results in increasing needs for social welfare. Is this relationship apparent in your community? What is the evidence?

6. A commonly held belief is that government make-work jobs are inferior to private sector employment. Yet many New Deal jobs programs have made important contributions to the infrastructure of the nation's cities. What New Deal projects are evident in your community? If a new governmental jobs program were initiated, what community needs might it address?

7. The fringe economy is a high-growth sector that is adversely affecting the economic lives of the poor. What policies or programs would you propose that could regulate, constrain, or abolish the fringe economic sector? What legislative or policy reforms are needed?

Notes

1. See Edward C. Banfield, *The Unheavenly City* (Boston: Little, Brown, 1966) and Oscar Lewis, La Vida (New York: Harper & Row, 1965).

2. Richard Dugdale, *The Jukes* (New York: G. P. Putnam's Sons, 1910).

3. Henry Goddard, *The Kallikak Family* (New York: Arno Publishers, 1911).

4. Arthur R. Jensen, "How Much Can We Boost IQ and Scholastic Achievement?" *Harvard Educational Review* 39 (Winter 1969), pp. 1–23.

5. Winifred Bell, *Contemporary Social Welfare* (New York: Macmillan, 1983), p. 261.

6. William Shockley, "Sterilization: A Thinking Exercise," in Carl Bahema (ed.), *Eugenics: Then and Now* (Stroudsburg, PA: Doidon, Hutchinson & Ross, 1976); see also Bell, *Contemporary Social Welfare*, p. 263.

7. Richard Herrnstein, *IQ and the Meritocracy* (Boston: Little, Brown, 1973).

8. Richard Herrnstein and Charles Murray, *The Bell Curve* (New York: Free Press, 1994).

9. Winnie Chen, Vilma Hernandez, Erin Townsend, and Carol Wyatt, "Affirmative Action," unpublished paper, University of Houston Graduate School of Social Work, Houston, TX, May 1, 1996.

10. T. Beardsley, "For Whom the Bell Curve Really Tolls," *Scientific American* 272, no. 1 (1995), pp. 14–17; Stephen Gould, "Ghosts of Bell Curves Past," *Natural History* 104, no. 2 (1995), pp. 12–19; and C. Lane, "The Tainted Sources of the Bell Curve," *The New York Review of Books* 41, no. 20 (1994), pp. 14–19.

11. Gould, "Ghosts of Bell Curves Past," p. 14.

12. Bell, *Contemporary Social Welfare*, p. 264.

13. David Gil, *Unraveling Social Policy* (Boston: Shenkman, 1981).

14. Blanche Bernstein, "Welfare Dependency," in Lee D. Bawden (ed.), *The Social Contract Revisited* (Washington, DC: Urban Institute Press, 1984), p. 129.

15. Greg J. Duncan et al., *Years of Poverty, Years of Plenty* (Ann Arbor, MI: Institute for Social Research, 1984).

16. Daniel McMurer and Isabel Sawhill, *Getting Ahead* (Washington, DC: Urban Institute, 1998), p. 33.

17. Bradley Schiller, "Relative Earnings Redux." Review of Income and Wealth 40, no. 4 (1994), p. 629.

18. W. Michael Cox and Richard Alm, *Myths of Rich & Poor* (New York: Basic Books, 1999), p. 73.

19. David Howell and Elizabeth Howell, *The Effects of Immigrants on African American Earnings* (New York: New School for Social Research, 1997), p. 23.

20. Carmen DeNavas-Walt, Bernadette D. Proctor, and Jessica Smith, "Income, Poverty, and Health Insurance Coverage in the United States: 2006," Economics and Statistics Administration U.S. Census Bureau, issued August 2007. Retrieved May 2008, from www .census.gov/prod/2007pubs/p60-233.pdf

21. Institute for Research on Poverty, "Improving the Measurement of American Poverty," Focus 19, no. 2 (Spring 1998), p. 2.

22. Ibid.

23. U.S. Senate, "Introduction of the Poverty Data Correction Act of 1999," p. 1. Retrieved 2008, from www.govtrack.us/congress/bill.xpd?bill=s106-204

24. DeNavas-Walt, Proctor, and Smith, "Income, Poverty, and Health Insurance Coverage in the United States: 2006."

25. Sara McLanahan and Gary Sandefur, *Growing Up with a Single Parent* (Cambridge, MA: Harvard University Press, 1997).

26. U.S. Department of Health and Human Services, Support Collections Up 40 Percent Since 1992: $24 Billion More Can Still Be Collected, Shalala Says," December 5, 1995. Retrieved 2008, from www.hhs.gov/news/press/1995pres/951205a.html

27. Ron Dean, "Myths, Legends and the American Way: Deadbeat Dads," August 15, 1995. Retrieved 2008, from www.vix.com/pub/men/child-support/commentar

28. Timothy S. Grall, "Custodial Mothers and Fathers and Their Child Support: 2005," U.S. Census Bureau, August 2007. Retrieved June 2008, from www.census.gov/prod/2007pubs/p60-234.pdf

29. Ibid.

30. Center for Law and Social Policy, "Child Support Substantially Increases Economic Well-Being of Low- and Moderate-Income Families," Washington, DC, 2004.

31. DeNavas-Walt, Proctor, and Smith, "Income, Poverty, and Health Insurance Coverage in the United States: 2006."

32. Neil G. Bennett Jiali Li, Younghwan Song, and Keming Yang, "Young Children in Poverty: A Statistical Update," New York: National Center for Children in Poverty, Columbia University, Mailman School of Health, June 17, 1999.

33. See Congressional Record, Senate, vol. 133, no. 120 (Washington, DC: U.S. Government Printing Office, July 21, 1987), pp. S10400–S10404; and Sheldon Danziger and Marcia Carlson, "Cohabitation and the Measurement of Child Poverty," Poverty Measurement Working Papers, U.S. Bureau of the Census, February 1998. Retrieved 2008, from www.census.gov/hhes/www/ povmeas/papers/cohabit.html

34. DeNavas-Walt, Proctor, and Smith, "Income, Poverty, and Health Insurance Coverage in the United States: 2006."

35. Ibid.

36. Ibid.

37. Ibid.

38. See Ibid. Economic Research Center, "Measuring Rurality: 2004 County Typology Codes," U.S. Department of Agriculture, 2004; Kathryn Porter, *Poverty in Rural America* (Washington, DC: Center on Budget and Policy Priorities, 1989), pp. 7–11; and Scott Barancik, *The Rural Disadvantage: Growing Income Disparities between Rural and Urban Areas* (Washington, DC: Center on Budget and Policy Priorities, April 1990), pp. ix–x.

39. Economic Research Center, "Rural Poverty at a Glance." U.S. Department of Agriculture, 2003. Retrieved October 2004, from www.ers.usda.gov/publications/rdrr100/rdrr100.pdf

40. Porter, *Poverty. in Rural America.*

41. United States Department of Agriculture, "Rural Income, Poverty and Welfare: Rural Poverty." Retrieved July 2008, from www.ers.usda.gov/ Briefing/incomepovertywelfare/RuralPoverty/

42. See Economic Research Service, "Rural America at a Glance," USDA, Rural Development Briefing Room. Retrieved 2008, from www.ers.usda.gov/publications/rdrr97-1/highres_rdrr97-1.pdf

43. U.S. Bureau of Labor Statistics, "A Profile of the Working Poor, 2005," September 2007. Retrieved July 2008, from www.bls.gov/cps/cpswp2005.pdf

44. Ibid.

45. Ibid.

46. Bureau of Labor Statistics, "Tomorrow's Jobs," U.S. Department of Labor, June 2, 2004. Retrieved October 2004, from http://stats.bls.gov/oco/oco2003.htm

47. Michael Sherraden, "Chronic Unemployment: A Social Work Perspective," *Social Work* (September–October 1985), p. 403.

48. Ibid., pp. 404–406.

49. As Sherraden notes, the common understanding that an unemployment rate of 5 percent is "normal" is not supported by economists, who calculate that structural and frictional unemployment can be reduced to 3 percent through astute social policies.

50. "Not Many Jobs Are Sent Abroad, U.S. Report Says," *New York Times* (June 11, 2004).

51. M. Harvey Brenner, *Estimating the Effects of Economic Change on National Health and Social Well-Being* (Washington, DC: U.S. Government Printing Office, 1984), pp. 2–4.

52. Ibid.

53. U.S. Bureau of Labor Statistics, "Extended Mass Layoffs in 2006," April 2008. Retrieved July 2008, from www.bls.gov/mls/mlsreport1004.pdf

54. Michael Piore, "The Dual Labor Market," in David Gordon (ed.), *Problems in Political Economy* (Lexington, MA: D.C. Heath, 1977), p. 94.

55. David Gordon, Richard Edwards, and Michael Reich, *Segmented Work, Divided Workers* (New York: Cambridge University Press, 1982), p. 211.

56. Michael Harrington, Robert Greenstein, and Eleanor Holmes Norton, Who Are the Poor?: A Profile of the Changing Faces of Poverty in the United States in 1987 (Washington, DC: Justice for All, 1987), p. 10.

57. James Parks, "Kennedy, Pelosi Promise Quick Action on Minimum Wage if Democrats Win Congress," October 24, 2006. Retrieved March 20, 2007, from http://blog.aflcio.org/2006/10/24/kennedy-pelosi-promise-quick-action-on-minimum-wage-if-democrats-win-congress/

58. "Minimum Wage: Facts at a Glance," Economic Policy Institute, March 2007. Retrieved March 20, 2007, from www.epi.org/content.cfm/ issueguides_minwage_minwagefacts

59. George. J. Borjas, *Labor Economics* (Boston: McGraw-Hill, 2005).

60. "Minimum Wage: Facts at a Glance."

61. "Sates with Minimum Wages above the Federal Level Have Had Faster Small Business and Retail Job Growth," Fiscal Policy Institute, March 30, 2006. Retrieved March 20, 2007, from http://fiscalpolicy.org/FPISmallBusinessMinWage.pdf

62. David Neumark and William Wascher, "Minimum Wages and Employment: A Review of the Evidence from the New Minimum Wage Research," National Bureau of Economic Research, Working Paper no. 12663, 2006.

63. The Bureau of Labor Statistics, "Characteristics of Minimum Wage Workers: 2007," Tables 4. Retrieved July 2008, from www.bls.gov/cps/minwage2007tbls.htm#5

64. Jared Bernstein and Isaac Shapiro, "Nine Years of Neglect: Federal Minimum Wage Remains Unchanged for Ninth Straight Year, Falls to Lowest Level in More than Half a Century," Center on Budget and Policy Priorities, August 31, 2006. Retrieved 2008, from www.cbpp.org/8-31-06mw.htm

65. Isaac Shapiro, *The Minimum Wage and Job Loss* (Washington, DC: Center on Budget and Policy Priorities, 1988).

66. Center on Budget and Policy Priorities, "Assessing the $5.15 an Hour Minimum Wage."

67. Acorn, National Living Wage Resource Center, "Introduction to ACORN's Living Wage Web Site." Retrieved 2000, from www.livingwagecampaign.org

68. U.S. Department of Labor, Employment Standards Administration Wage and Hour Division, Minimum Wage Laws in the States—January 1, 2008. Retrieved May 12, 2008, from www.dol.gov/esa/minwage/america.htm

69. Cited in Michal Grinstein-Weiss and Jami Curley, "Individual Development Accounts in Rural Communities: Implications for Research." Working Paper no. 03-21, Washington University, Center for Social Development, George Warren Brown School of Social Work, Washington University, St. Louis, MO, 2003.

70. Michael Sherraden, "Can Asset-Based Welfare Policy Really Help the Poor?" in Howard Jacob Karger, James Midgley, and Brene Brown, *Controversial Issues in Social Policy*, 2nd ed. (Boston: Allyn & Bacon, 2003), p. 50.

71. Ibid., p. 51.

72. Ibid.

73. Ibid.

74. Michael Sherraden, *Assets and the Poor: A New American Welfare Policy* (Armonk, NY: M.E. Sharpe, 1991).

75. Ibid.

76. Ibid.

77. John Kenneth Galbraith, *The Affluent Society* (Boston: Houghton Mifflin, 1958).

78. Harrington, Greenstein, and Norton, *Who Are the Poor?* p. 17.

79. Ibid., p. 22.

80. U.S. Census Bureau, "Poverty Status by State: 2006." U.S. Census Bureau, Current Population Survey, 2007 Annual Social and Economic Supplement. Retrieved July 2008, from http://pubdb3.census.gov/macro/032007/pov/new46_100125_01.htm

81. Kevin Phillips, *The Politics of Rich and Poor* (New York: Random House, 1990), p. 87.

82. Sheldon Danziger, "Poverty," *Encyclopedia of Social Work*, 18th ed. (Silver Spring, MD: NASW Press, 1987), pp. 301–302.

83. National Telecommunications and Information Agency, *A Nation Online: How Americans Are Expanding Their Use of the Internet*, U.S. Department of Commerce, February 2002. Retrieved August 2004, from www.ntia.doc.gov/ntiahome/dn/index.html

84. National Telecommunications and Information Agency, "Households Using the Internet In and Outside the Home, by Selected Characteristics: Total, Urban, Rural, Principal City, 2007." Retrieved July 2008, from www.ntia.doc.gov/reports/2008/Table_HouseholdInternet2007.pdf

85. Ekaterina Walsh, Shelley Morrisette, and Nicky Maraganore, "The Digital Melting Pot," *The Forrester Report*. Forrester Research Inc., Jupiter Communications, June 15, 2000.

86. For a fuller examination of the fringe economy see Howard Karger, *Shortchanged: Life and Debt in the Fringe Economy* (San Francisco: Berrett-Koehler, 2005).

87. "Personal Savings Rate," Bureau of Economic Analysis, U.S. Department of Commerce. Retrieved March 22, 2007, from www.bea.gov/briefrm/saving.htm

88. Kenneth J. Lansing, "Spendthrift Nation," *FRBSF Economic Letter*, November 10, 2005. Retrieved March 22, 2007, from www.frbsf.org/publications/economics/letter/2005/el2005-30.html

89. Ibid.

90. Brian K. Bucks, Arthur B. Kennickell, Kevin B. Moore, Gerhard Fries, and A. Michael Neal, "Recent Changes in U.S. Farmly Finances: Evidence from the 2001 and 2004 Survey of Consumer Finances," *Federal Reserve Bulletin*, 2006. Retrieved March 22, 2007, from www.federalreserve.gov/pubs/oss/oss2/2004/bull0206.pdf

91. "President Signs Bankruptcy Abuse Prevention, Consumer Protection Act," April 20, 2005. Retrieved March 22, 2007, from www.whitehouse.gov/news/releases/2005/04/20050420-5.html

92. Brian Louis, "KB Homes First Quarter Net Income Plunges in Slump (Update 3)," *Bloomberg,* March 22, 2007. Retrieved March 22, 2007, from www.bloomberg.com/apps/news?pid=20601087&sid=a13dV_1LQ1cI&refer=home

93. Bob Ivry, "Foreclosures May Hit 1.5 Million in U.S. Housing Bust," *Bloomberg*, March 12, 2007. Retrieved March 22, 2007, from www.bloomberg.com/apps/news?pid=20601109&sid=aoxvdkPVfUNo&refer=home

94. Gerard Jackson, "U.S. Economy: Will a Housing Bust Cause a Recession?" *Free Market News Network*, March 20, 2007. Retrieved March 22, 2007, from www.freemarketnews.com/Analysis/50/7152/gerard.asp?wid=50&nid=7152

95. Robert D. Manning, *Credit Card Nation* (New York: Basic Books, 2000).

96. Center for Responsible Lending, "Financial Quicksand: Payday Lending Sinks Borrowers in Debt with $4.2 Billion in Predatory Fees Every Year," November 30, 2006. Retrieved July 2008, from www.responsiblelending.org/pdfs/rr012-Financial_Quicksand-1106.pdf

97. National Consumer Law Center, "Utilities and Payday Lenders: Convenient Payments, Killer Loans." Retrieved July 2008, from www.consumerlaw.org/reports/content/payday_utility.pdf

98. Ibid.

99. Center for Responsible Lending, "Losing Ground: Foreclosures in the Sub-prime Market and Their Cost to Homeowners," December 2006. Retrieved July 2008, from www.responsiblelending.org/pdfs/foreclosure-paper-report-2-17.pdf

100. Fannie Mae Foundation, 2001.

101. Federal Reserve Board, 2002; IO Data Corporation, Payday Advance Customer Research: Cumulative State Research Report, September 2002. IO Data Corporation, Salt Lake City, UT.

102. IO Data Corporation, 2002.

103. Joint Center for Housing Studies of Harvard University, The State of the Nation's Housing (Cambridge, MA: Harvard University, 2003); Theresa Murray, "Experts Warn Against Milking Home Equity to Extend Debt," *Minneapolis St. Paul Star Tribune* (November 4, 2000), p. B-5.

104. See Noel Paul, "Culture of Consumption," *Christian Science Monitor* (June 12, 2003), 18; and Joint Center for Housing Studies of Harvard University, 2003.

105. Peter Gumbel, "The $915 Billion Bomb in Consumers' Wallets." Retrieved July 2008, from http://money.cnn.com/2007/10/29/magazines/fortune/consumer_debt.fortune/index.htm?postversion=2007103007

106. Manning, *Credit Card Nation*.

107. Murray Coleman, "Mortgage Meltdown Seen Spreading to Credit Cards," *MarketWatch*, November 19, 2007.

108. Joanna Stavins, "Credit Card Borrowing, Delinquency and Personal Bankruptcy," *Questia* (2000). Retrieved 2003, from www.questia.com

109. Ibid.

110. Cardweb.com. Retrieved 2003, from www.cardweb.com

111. Wired Plastic. Retrieved 2003, from www.wiredplastic.com

112. Direct Telephone Company, Inc., Houston, TX.

113. See Sprint PCS. Retrieved 2004, from www.sprintpcs.com; and AT&T Wireless. Retrieved 2004, from www.attwireless.com

114. Ibid.

115. See APRO, "RTO Industry Stats, 2003." Retrieved 2004, from www.aprovision.org/industrystats.html and James M. Lacko, Signe-Mary McKernan, and Manoj Hastak, *Survey of Rent-to-Own Customers, Federal Trade Commission* (Bureau of Economics, Washington, DC, 1999).

116. APRO, "About Rent-to-Own: Rent-to-Own Industry Overview." Retrieved July 2008, from www.rtohq.org/apro-rto-industry-overview.html

117. Rent-a-Center "Investor Relations." Retrieved July 2008, from http://investor.rentacenter.com/phoenix.zhtml?c=90764&p=irol-irhome

118. Aaron Rents, Inc., "2008 First Quarter Report." Retrieved July 2008, from http://media.corporate-ir.net/media_files/irol/10/104698/Chairman_letter_1Q08.pdf

119. Rent-A-Center. Retrieved January 2, 2004, from www.rentacenter.com; ColorTyme. Retrieved January 2, 2004, from www.colortyme.com; Aaron Rents. Retrieved 2004, from www.aaronrents.com; RentWay. Retrieved 2004, from www.rentway.com; Rent Rite. Retrieved 2003, from www.rentrite.com

120. Public Interest Research Group (PIRG), "Don't Rent to Own: The 1997 PIRG Rent-to-Own Survey," U.S. Public Interest Research Group, Washington, DC, June 11, 1997.

121. Ibid.

122. Alix M. Freedman, "Peddling Dreams: A Market Giant Uses Its Sales Prowess to Profit on Poverty," *Wall Street Journal* (September 22, 1993), p. D15.

123. APRO, 2003.

124. John Seward, "Tales of the Tape: Rent-to-Owns Seek Definition in Law," *Wall Street Journal* (October 22, 2003), p. D15.

125. Quoted in Freedman, 1993, p. D16.

126. UPI.com, "Tough Times Send Many to Pawnshops," June 16, 2008. Retrieved July 2008, from www.upi .com/Business_News/2008/06/16/Tough_times_send _many_to_pawn_shops/UPI-47261213629989/

127. American Financial Services Association, "Pawnshops Struggle, 2002." Retrieved 2002, from www.spot-lightonfinance.org/issues/August/Stories/story13.htm/

128. John Caskey, Fringe Banking (New York: Russell Sage Foundation, 1994).

129. *Edmund's Used Cars & Trucks Prices: 1992–2001, American & Import,* Spring/Summer, 2002 (Chicago, IL: Edmunds, 2002).

130. Personal communication with Car Title Loans of America, Inc., Missouri office, Columbia, MO, June 5, 2002.

131. American Financial Services Association, 2002.

132. Ibid.

133. Consumer Federation of America, "Predatory Lending, 2002," Retrieved 2002, from www .consumerfed.org/backpage/predatory.html.

134. AARP, "Payday Loans Don't Pay." Retrieved 2008, from www.aarp.org/money/wise_consumer/smartshopping/ a2002-10-02-FraudsPaydayLoans.html

135. See Howard Karger, *Shortchanged: Life and Debt in the Fringe Economy* (San Francisco: Berrett-Koehler, 2005), p. 156.

136. Quik Payday, "APR Disclosure, 2002." Retrieved 2002, from www.quikpayday.com/apr-disclosure .html

137. Consumer Federation of America, 2002.

138. Daniel P. McKernan, *The Monitor,* "The Real Cost of Tax Refund Anticipation Loans," December 20, 2007. Retrieved July 2008, from www.fbmonitor.com/ 2007/12december/122007/pdf/122007part5.pdf

139. Consumer Federation of America, 2002.

140. Ibid.

141. Alan Berube, Anne Kim, Benjamin Forman, and Megan Burns, *The Price of Paying Taxes: How Tax Preparation and Refund Loan Fees Erode the Benefits of the EITC.* Center on Urban & Metropolitan Policy, The Brookings Institution and The Progressive Policy Institute, Washington, DC: The Brookings Institution, May 2002.

142. Consumer Federation of America, 2002.

143. See Karger, *Shortchanged,* p. 93.

144. See Karger, *Shortchanged,* p. 98.

145. Ibid.

146. This is based on national averages.

147. Chichi Wu and Jean Ann Fox, "The High Cost of Quick Tax Money: Tax Preparation, 'Instant Refund' Loans, and Check Cashing Fees Target the Working Poor," National Consumer Law Center, Consumer Federation of America, January 2003. Washington, DC.

148. Ibid.

149. Ibid.

150. John Caskey, "Bringing Unbanked Households into the Banking System," *Capitol Xchange,* The Brookings Institution, January 2002. Retrieved 2002, from www .brookings.edu/articles/2002/01metropolitanpolicy _caskey.aspx

151. ACE Cash Express, "ACE Store Services, 2002." Retrieved 2002, from www.acecashexpress.com/ general/services.html

152. See Anne Kim, "The Unbanked and the Alternative Financial Sector. Discussion Comments to the Changing Financial Markets and Community Development Conference." Federal Reserve Bank of Chicago, transcript, April 5, 2001. Retrieved 2002, from www.ppionline.org/ppi_ci.cfm?cp=3&knlgAreaID =114&subsecid=236&contentid=3843; and Financial Service Centers of America, 2003.

153. Sougata MuKherjee, "Consumer Group Pushes for Regulation of Check Cashing Industry," *Houston Business Journal* (August 29, 1997), p. 25.

154. Kim, 2001, op cit.

155. Financial Service Centers of America (FiSCA), 2003.

156. See ACE Cash Express Inc., *Annual Report on Form 10-K for the Fiscal Year Ended June 30, 2000.* Filed with the Securities and Exchange Commission; and Dollar Financial Group, Inc., *Annual Report on Form 10-K for the Fiscal Year Ended June 30, 2000,* filed with the Securities and Exchange Commission.

157. ACE Cash Express, "ACE Cash Express Extends Money Order Relationship with Travelers Express, ACE to Receive $3.4 Million in Signing and Annual Bonuses," October 20, 2003. Retrieved 2008 from http://goliath.ecnext.com/coms2/gi_0199-4021692/ ACE- Cash-Express-Extends-Money. html

158. See Karger, *Shortchanged,* p. 145.

159. "Conning & Co. Study Says Auto Insurers Are Paying Closer Attention to Credit Scores," *Insurance Journal* (August 2, 2001).

160. Consumers Union, "Reducing the Number of Uninsured Motorists," *Consumers Union SWRO Issue Pages for the 77th Texas Legislature* (January 2001).

161. A.M. Best Company, Inc., "Insurers Expect Battle on Use of Credit Scores in About Half the United States," *BestWire* (January 30, 2002).

162. John Caskey, Lower Income Americans, Higher Cost Financial Services (Madison, WI: Filene Research Institute, 1997).

The Voluntary Sector Today

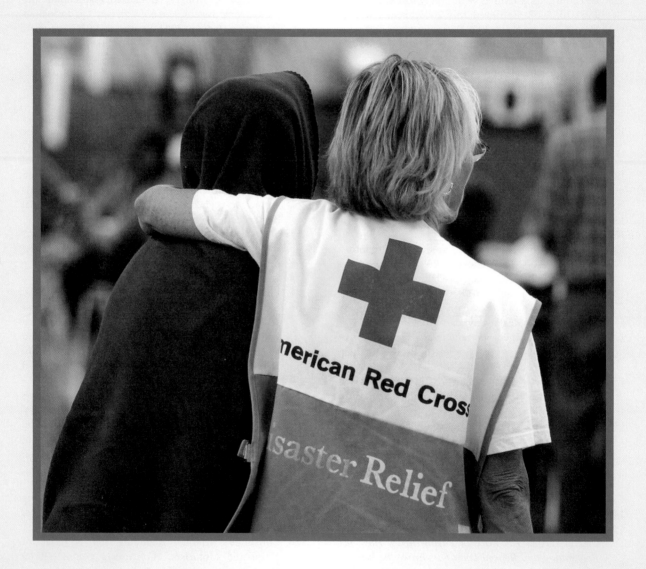

*T*his chapter locates the voluntary sector with respect to the other institutions involved in social welfare in the United States. The heart of the **voluntary sector** is made up of the private, non-profit organizations that are ubiquitous at the local level. Supporting the voluntary sector are philanthropic contributions that have been a mainstay for social service initiatives. In this chapter, the work of prominent human service agencies is described and the role of voluntary agencies in advocating social justice is examined. The fiscal crisis of the voluntary sector is discussed, as are the recession of the early 1980s and the scandal that shook the United Way during the 1990s, thus further compounding the funding problems of nonprofit service agencies. Finally, the responses to September 11, 2001, and Hurricane Katrina, as well as emerging trends in the voluntary sector are considered.

As the twenty-first century begins, welfare professionals are reassessing the capacity of the voluntary sector to meet the nation's social welfare needs. As governmental expenditures for social welfare fail to increase in the face of rising demand for human services, the voluntary sector has been called on to shoulder more of the welfare burden. This shift in responsibilities was stated explicitly by President Reagan, who appealed to the charitable impulses of Americans as a way for the nation to address human needs while reducing federal appropriations to social programs; the idea was restated by George H. W. Bush in his reference to "a thousand points of light" during his 1988 presidential campaign. Although President Clinton made no comparable gesture to the non-profit sector, his statement that "the era of big government is over" had enormous implications for nonprofit agencies. Finally, the emergence of "compassionate conservatism" and its corollary, "faith-based social services," by George W. Bush restates the conservative case for a reinvigorated voluntary sector.

Although many liberals of the 1980s were skeptical about the sincerity of conservatives in championing the virtues of the voluntary sector, suspecting that it was a ruse to gut governmental social programs, other events conspired to focus attention on this sector. A wave of conservatism since the 1980s and 1990s may have stalled the introduction of liberally inspired social legislation, but the conservative imprint on social welfare could be traced as far back as the late 1970s.

During the Carter presidency, conservatives began to challenge liberal welfare programs on the grounds that they divided the family, eroded the work ethic, and subverted communal norms. A widely distributed monograph by analysts from the American Enterprise Institute criticized social "megastructures" for contributing to alienation among Americans, and called for stronger "mediating structures"—voluntary entities—to empower people.[1] During the 1990s, Democrats responded to these conservative trends by jettisoning from their party platform traditional welfare planks that called for major new federal social programs in favor of more pluralistic strategies that included the voluntary sector.

Despite the altruism implicit in the voluntary sector, it has not been without controversy. The aftermath of scandals rocked established nonprofits. In 2005 the Atlanta Area Council of the Boy Scouts was found to have inflated enrollment by a factor of two in order to obtain greater funding.[2] The same year after accusations of sexual harassment, Habitat for Humanity founder Millard Fuller was replaced by Jonathan Reckford; having denied the accusations, Fuller and his wife decamped to establish a competing nonprofit.[3] In 2007, following financial improprieties of 2001, the United Way of the National Capital Area, which includes Washington, DC, slashed funding to member nonprofits after contributions plummeted more than 50 percent; five years later donations to the United Way remained flat.[4] After lobbyist Jack Abramoff was indicted for tax fraud, the nonprofit he had established, the U.S. Family Network, was found to have misappropriated over $3 million, including purchase of a townhouse which then-Congressman Tom DeLay used for fundraising, travel to resorts, purchase of artwork, and attack ads calling for the resignation of then-President Clinton.[5] When campaign finance reform included contributions to political parties, donors to candidates in the 2004 elections constructed nonprofit organizations, "527s"—named after the Internal Revenue Service (IRS) code authorizing their status—to do their bidding, contributing $685 million in 2004.[6] After the 2004 election, 60 tax-exempt organizations became the subject of investigations by the IRS.[7] Regardless, nonprofits were an ideal cover for issue-based political ads. The impact of 527s on the 2008 presidential campaign will not be determined until 2009.

Structural Interests within Social Welfare

Organized responses to the needs of Americans have undergone fundamental change since European settlement. In a sense, the voluntary sector is the first modern welfare institution, with a long legacy in American social welfare. Over the centuries the voluntary sector has witnessed the emergence of competing institutions: the state and federal governmental programs of the public sector, the private practices of professional entrepreneurs, and a corporate sector accountable to chief executive officers and stockholders. Reflecting this transformation, David Stoesz posited that four groups can be identified within U.S. social welfare: traditional providers, welfare bureaucrats, clinical entrepreneurs, and human service executives.[8] Because these groups have become integrated into the nation's political economy, they are termed *structural interests*.

Traditional Providers

The heart of the voluntary sector consists of professionals and laypersons who seek to maintain and enhance traditional relations, values, and structures in their communities through private, nonprofit agencies. **Traditional providers** hold an organic conception of social welfare, seeing it as tightly interwoven with other community institutions. According to traditional providers, voluntary nonprofit agencies offer the advantages of neighborliness, a reaffirmation of community values, a concern for community as opposed to personal gain, and freedom to alter programming so as to conform to changes in local priorities.

Much of the heritage of social welfare can be traced to early proponents of this structural interest—people such as Mary Richmond of the **Charity Organization Society (COS)** movement and Jane Addams of the settlement house movement. Charity Organization Societies and **settlement houses** were transformed by two influences: the need for scientifically based treatment techniques and the socialization of charity. Together, these factors functioned as an anchor for the social casework agencies in an industrializing society. The agency provided the grist for scientific casework that was instrumental in the emergence of the social work profession. The new schools of social work, in turn, relied on casework agencies for internship training, a substantial portion of a professional's education. Once graduated, many professionals elected to work in the voluntary sector, ensuring agencies of a steady supply of personnel.

Voluntary agencies routinized philanthropic contributions by socializing charity. Beginning with Denver's Associated Charities in 1887, the concept of a community appeal spread so rapidly that by the 1920s more than 200 cities had "community chests." The needs of social workers for effective treatment techniques and the economic imperatives for organizational survival functioned together to standardize the social agency. Perhaps the best description of the casework agency is found in the 1923 Milford Conference Report, *Social Casework: Generic and Specific*, which comprehensively outlined the organization through which professional caseworkers delivered services.[9] By the 1940s the social casework agency had become a predominant form of service delivery. Today, much social service provision exists in the form of United Way–subsidized sectarian and nonsectarian agencies, whose member groups collected $4.07 billion in 2006–2007.[10]

Welfare Bureaucrats

Welfare bureaucrats are public functionaries who maintain the welfare state in much the same form in which it was conceived during the New Deal. "Their ideology stresses a rational, efficient, cost-conscious, coordinated . . . delivery system."[11] Welfare bureaucrats view federal government intervention vis-à-vis social problems as legitimate and necessary, considering the apparent lack of concern by the private sector and local governments. Moreover, they contend that federal intervention is more effective than other forms, because authority is centralized, guidelines are standardized, and benefits are allocated according to principles of equity and equality.

The influence of welfare bureaucrats grew as a result of the Social Security Act of 1935. To a limited extent, the larger community chests "exerted a pressure toward rationalization of the professional welfare machinery,"[12] but this did not diminish the effect of the governmental welfare bureaucracy, which soon eclipsed the authority of traditional providers. Actually, a unilinear evolution between these interests could have occurred had Harry Hopkins, head of the Federal Emergency Relief Administration in the 1930s, not prohibited states from turning federal welfare funds over to private agencies.[13] Denied the resources to address significantly the massive social problems caused by the Great Depression, private agencies lapsed into a secondary role while federal and state agencies ascended in importance. An array of welfare legislation followed the Social Security Act, including the Housing Act of 1937, the G. I. Bill of 1944, the Community Mental Health Centers Act of 1963, the Civil Rights Act of 1964, the Food Stamp Act of 1964, the Economic Opportunity Act of 1964, the Elementary and Secondary Education Act of 1965, the Medicare and Medicaid Acts of 1965, Supplemental Security Income in 1974, Title XX of the Social Security Act of 1975, the Full Employment Act of 1978, the Americans with Disabilities Act of 1980, the No Child Left Behind Act of 2001, and the Medicare Modernization Act of 2003.

The flourishing of bureaucratic rationality concomitant with this legislative activity represented the institutionalization of liberal thought, which initially sought to control the caprice of the market, ensure a measure of equality among widely divergent economic classes, and establish an administrative apparatus to ensure the continuity of these principles. Confronted with a rapidly industrializing society lacking basic programs for ameliorating social and economic catastrophes, progressives perceived the state as a vehicle for social reform. Their solutions focused on "coordinating fragmented services, instituting planning, and extending public funding."[14] Implicit in the methods advocated by welfare bureaucrats is an expectation, if not an assumption, that the social welfare administration should be centralized, that eligibility for benefits should be universalized, and that social welfare should be firmly anchored in the institutional fabric of society.

The influence of welfare bureaucrats had been curtailed somewhat since the mid-1980s. The Reagan administration all but capped the growth of public social welfare expenditures as a percent of GDP. The presidency of George W. Bush transmitted a mixed message to welfare bureaucrats: while a series of tax cuts reduced federal revenues for social programs, the addition of a prescription benefit to Medicare and the augmentation of payments for managed care strengthened their relations to the pharmaceutical industry and health insurance companies. Smarting from election losses in the 1980s and 2000, liberal Democrats had begun to reconsider their objections to private sector solutions to social problems. Still, the volume of resources and the number of people dependent on public welfare and social insurance assure welfare bureaucrats of a dominant and continuing role in the foreseeable future.

Clinical Entrepreneurs

Clinical entrepreneurs are professional service providers, chiefly social workers, psychologists, and physicians, who work for themselves instead of being salaried employees. Important to clinical entrepreneurs in each specialty is the establishment of a **professional monopoly,** the evolution of which represents a concern on the part of practitioners that their occupational activity not be subject to political interference from the state or the ignorance of the lay public. In the United States, the professions found that a market economy was conducive to occupational success. In the most fundamental sense, private practice reconciles professionals' desire for autonomy with the imperatives of a market economy. The transition from entrepreneur to professional monopolist is a matter of obtaining legislation restricting practice to those duly licensed by the state. "Professionalism provides a way of preserving monopolistic control over services without the risks of competition."[15] As an extension of the entrepreneurial model of service delivery, professional monopoly offers privacy in practice, freedom to establish one's worth by setting fees, and the security ensured by membership in the professional monopoly.

The social worker as clinical entrepreneur is a relatively recent phenomenon, and the **National Association of Social Workers (NASW)** did not officially sanction this form of service delivery until 1964. Before that, privately practicing social workers identified themselves as psychotherapists and lay analysts. Typically, they relied on referrals from physicians and psychiatrists, and after World War II they began to establish "flourishing and lucrative"[16] practices. By the 1970s, **private practice** in social work was developing as an important form of service delivery, although analysts disagreed about the number of social workers engaged in independent practice. In 1975 NASW estimated that 10,000 to 20,000 social workers were engaged in private practice. By 1983 Robert Barker, author of *Social Work in Private Practice* and a columnist on private practice in *NASW News*, speculated that about 30,000 social workers, or 32 percent of all social workers, engaged in private practice on a full- or part-time basis.[17] By 1985 a large portion of psychotherapy was being done by social workers, and the *New York Times* noted that "growing numbers of social workers are treating more affluent private clients, thus moving into the traditional preserve of the elite psychiatrists and clinical psychologists."[18] Yet in the early 1990s, NASW reported that only about 15,000 of its members—11.1 percent—were in solo or partnership practice as private practitioners, compared to about one-third of NASW members employed in for-profit firms.[19]

Clinical entrepreneurs are an emerging interest in social welfare. While this group grew rapidly during the 1970s and 1980s due to the licensing of social workers in all 50 states and graduate students' interest, by the end of the twentieth century, their options were increasingly proscribed by managed care. Clinical entrepreneurs would be well positioned to become a more influential interest in social welfare in the United States were it not for the incursion of managed care: the attempt of human service corporations to diminish the influence of clinical entrepreneurs. Independently practicing social workers could emulate physicians who countered managed care by creating **independent practice associations,** but social workers have not done so.

Human Service Executives

Human service executives share an important characteristic with clinical entrepreneurs: Both groups represent ways of organizing service delivery in the context of the market. However, in some important ways they differ. Unlike clinical entrepreneurs, **human service executives** are salaried employees of proprietary firms and, as such, have less autonomy. As administrators or chief executive officers of large corporations, human service executives advance market strategies for promoting social welfare. Whereas welfare bureaucrats emphasize the planning and regulatory functions of the state, human service executives favor the rationality of the marketplace in allocating resources and evaluating programs. In the present circumstances, human service executives are advocating market reform of the welfare state—the domain of welfare bureaucrats—and thus are in a position to challenge the bureaucratic interest.

For-profit firms became prominent in social welfare in the United States during the 1960s, when Medicaid and Medicare funds were paid to proprietary nursing homes and hospitals.[20] Since then, human service executives have been rapidly creating independent, for-profit human service corporations that provide an extensive range of nationwide services. Human service corporations have established prominent, if not dominant, positions in several human service markets, including nursing home care, hospital management, health maintenance, child care, home care, and even corrections and welfare. Most recently, human service corporations have aggressively exploited the managed care market. In 1981 there were 34 human service corporations, reporting annual revenues above $10 million; by 1985 the number of firms had increased to 66; and by 2000 the number had soared to 268. Of these, 16 corporations reported revenues higher than the total annual contributions to all of the United Ways of America; by 2007 the number had exceeded 23.

As the proprietary sector expands to dominate different human service markets, oligopolies emerge and a fundamental change occurs. No longer passively dependent on government appropriations, proprietary firms are in a strong position to shape the very markets they serve, influencing not only consumer demand but also governmental policy through establishing and maintaining a **human services industrial complex.** This capacity to determine or control a market qualitatively distinguishes corporate welfare from the earlier form of business involvement in social welfare—that is, from philanthropic contributions to nonprofit agencies of the voluntary sector. For these reasons, human service executives are now well positioned to challenge the power of welfare bureaucrats.

The structural interests just described can be located in relation to two variables: span of influence and type of economy. As Figure 6.1 indicates, power shifts as a result of significant social influences: privatization and bureaucratization. The consequences of these forces will be evident throughout this book.

Marginal Interests

Social welfare in the United States is also populated by numerous groups that have not become as symbiotically attached to the social structure as have the structural interests just described. These marginal interest groups usually represent special populations that have been ignored, excluded, or oppressed by mainstream society. Their number reflects the capacity of U.S. culture to maintain its equilibrium while excluding many groups from full social participation. A partial list of marginal interest groups includes African Americans, poor women, Native Americans, homosexuals, residents of isolated rural areas, and Hispanic Americans. These groups are of concern to welfare professionals because typically they have not had the same

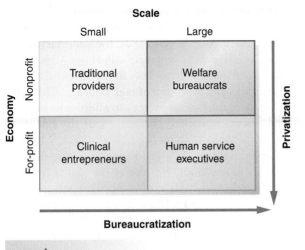

Scale

Figure 6.1

Dynamics of Structural Interests

Source: David Stoesz, "A Theory of Social Welfare," *Social Work* 34, no. 2 (March 1989), p. 106.

opportunities as mainstream populations; in other words, they have been denied social justice. Within the context of democratic capitalism, elevating marginal interests remains extraordinarily difficult.

The marginal status of many groups relates to the nature of the social welfare industry. In U.S. culture, groups excluded from the mainstream are expected to gather their resources and identify leaders who will mount programs to serve their particular group. Although this expectation is congruent with traditional values such as self-sufficiency and community cohesion, the solidarity approach does not necessarily ensure success. Significant variations are evident within regions of the United States with respect to generosity. For example, the Generosity Index reveals that residents of some states are more willing to contribute a portion of their income to social causes than others. For 2004 the most generous states were Mississippi, Arkansas, Oklahoma, Louisiana, and Alabama, and the stingiest were New Hampshire, Massachusetts, Rhode Island, New Jersey, and Wisconsin. The Generosity Index suggests that a state's charity is inversely related to its wealth.[21]

Metropolitan areas also vary significantly in their generosity toward those in need, as seen in Table 6.1. In light of such variations, the voluntary sector may be able to accommodate only a limited number of marginal interests because of financial restraints, or it may be unresponsive to groups that violate traditional community norms. Programs to aid victims of domestic violence and the homeless, for example, have often struggled to mount and sustain minimal services, because the United Way often has funding priorities consonant with the needs of clientele more highly regarded in the community.

In a democratic polity, marginal groups can also make claims on the social order by seeking benefits through governmental programs; but to do so presents other problems. Government programs are likely to be managed by welfare bureaucrats, who have their own understanding of what is best for the marginal interest. For a marginal group to get benefits through government programs, its claim must be mandated through legislation, which requires the approval of a majority of legislators. Once enacted, benefits for marginal groups must be programmed and monitored by agents of the welfare state, who often have a welfare ideology that differs from that of disadvantaged groups. The result is likely to be a program that is more consonant with the ideology of

Table 6.1

Donations by Metropolitan Area

Area	Percent (%) of Discretionary Income Given to Charity
Salt Lake City/Ogden	14.9
Grand Rapids, Michigan	10.0
Minneapolis/St. Paul	8.5
Greensboro/Winston-Salem	8.5
Memphis	8.4
Dallas/Fort Worth	8.4
Nashville	8.3
San Antonio	8.1
Houston/Galveston	8.1
Oklahoma City	8.0
Norfolk/Virginia Beach/ Newport News	8.0
Charlotte/Rock Hill	7.9
Seattle/Tacoma	7.7
Washington, DC/Baltimore	7.6

Source: Adapted from Jacqueline Salmon and Hamil Harris, "Pr. George's a Leader in Giving," *Washington Post* (April 29, 2003), p. A7.

the welfare bureaucrats than with that of the marginal group. During the 1980s, the effort to combat AIDS was plagued by volatile disagreements between gay advocacy organizations and the public health bureaucrats who run the Center for Disease Control and Prevention.

Despite such obstacles, members of marginal groups have powerful incentives to work within existing structures if their needs are to be met. Usually, their success in this regard is mixed. As a result of affirmative action, African Americans have been able to secure positions within the welfare bureaucracy in relatively significant numbers and are now well established among welfare bureaucrats. White women have found independent practice a desirable framework within which to provide services and are well represented among clinical entrepreneurs. In contrast, many marginal groups continue to struggle against a welfare industry that is controlled by structural interests indifferent to minority concerns. The structural interest of human service executives, for example, remains a bastion of white patriarchy. Activists from the African American community struggle to contain gang violence, reduce the number of teen pregnancies, and halt the scourge of illegal drugs, often with inadequate resources. Indeed, one of the most glaring contradictions of U.S. social welfare are state-of-the-art medical centers controlled by human-service executives located right next to inner-city ghettos inhabited by the poorest and most neglected Americans. How has the U.S. welfare state come to assure wealth for health and human service executives while generating, at the same time, an underclass?

The Forgotten Sector

As a result of the dynamic expansion of other structural interests over the course of the twentieth century, the voluntary sector lapsed in importance.[22] Following the triumph of the New Deal, leading welfare philosophers expected government to dominate in the creation and administration of the welfare state. In fact, so complete was the expectation that the government-driven welfare state would dominate social welfare in the United States that references to private voluntary agencies became scant in the professional literature. There was little room within welfare state ideology for a dynamic voluntary sector, and references to private, nonprofit agencies virtually disappeared from discussions of social welfare. When discussed, voluntary agencies were viewed as vestiges from an earlier time. Rediscovered during the 1980s, the voluntary sector quickly attracted converts. Perhaps the most notable of the new adherents to the promise of nonprofits was business guru Peter Drucker. Citing the capacity of the "social sector" to address local problems, Drucker recited the virtues of the nonprofit sector in books such as *The New Realities*;[23] in 1990 he even went so far as to establish the Peter F. Drucker Foundation for Nonprofit Management.[24] The Republican Party embraced the voluntary sector as a means to address social problems while containing federal social programs, subsequently serving as the institutional basis for "compassionate conservatism."

To the extent that the voluntary sector has been related to the governmental welfare state, it has been as a subcontractor of social services. This role was made possible through an amendment to the Social Security Act, Title XX, which allowed for the "purchase of service" from private providers. Under purchase-of-service contracts, the government could avoid the costs and responsibilities of administering programs directly. Because of an open-ended funding formula, however, federal costs for Title XX services escalated sharply. Congress later capped Title XX expenditures at $2.5 billion in order to contain program costs, and still later the Reagan administration was successful in having the program devolved to the states as the Social Services Block Grant, with further funding restrictions.[25] Consequently, in response to Title XX, many voluntary social service agencies secured purchase-of-service contracts, the funding for which allowed nonprofit agencies to expand programs in the late 1960s and early 1970s. Then, when funding was reduced, voluntary sector agencies were heavily penalized. Federal expenditures for Title XX fell from $2.8 billion in 1980 to $2.7 billion in 1992, a significant reduction in that it occurred at a time when demand for service was rising sharply.[26] By 2003, Title XX had eroded still further to only $1.7 billion.[27]

When policymakers turned to the voluntary sector in the 1980s to compensate for reductions in the governmental welfare effort, little was known about nonprofit social service agencies. Lester Salamon and Alan Abramson, authorities on the voluntary sector, observed that "despite their importance, these organizations have tended to be ignored in both public policy debates and scholarly research."[28] As government assumed a dominant role in U.S. social welfare, the voluntary sector receded in importance. If the Reagan and Bush presidencies rekindled interest in the voluntary sector, the 1994 Republican takeover of Congress created a small firestorm. As part of their Contract with America, congressional Republicans promised to reform welfare as part of an extensive overhaul of the whole welfare state. Government, they argued, had induced the dependency of millions of families on public assistance; welfare programs largely benefited the welfare professionals who worked in them; and all of this diminished the influence of community institutions. Congressional conservatives had a strategy in mind when they critiqued federal social programs: Replace governmental welfare programs with private, voluntary sector initiatives. "The crisis of the modern welfare state is not just a crisis of government," contended conservative scholar Marvin Olasky. "The more effective provision of social services will ultimately depend on their return to private and especially religious institutions."[29] Suddenly, after half a century of neglect, the "forgotten sector" was being called on to assume unprecedented responsibilities in caring for the needy.

Beginning in the 1970s, researchers had begun to investigate the scope of the voluntary sector. Their task has not been easy. The voluntary sector is composed of tens of thousands of organizations, many of which are not associated with any national umbrella association. The picture emerging from preliminary investigations reveals a sector that, if small by economic standards, is extraordinarily rich socially. Perhaps the most convenient measure of the scale of the voluntary sector is to count the voluntary and philanthropic associations that received tax-exempt status as social service agencies from the IRS—263 thousand in 2003, of which 35 thousand are engaged in human services.[30] Despite their proliferation, the voluntary sector accounts for only half of national economic activity attributed to government and one-tenth that of business.[31]

Generally, the expansion of the voluntary sector has paralleled economic growth (see Table 6.2). Philanthropic contributions account for a small portion of GDP ranging from 1.7

percent in the 1990s to 2.0 percent in 2005.[32] Three-fourths of contributions are made by individuals, with foundations accounting for about 10 percent and corporations about 5 percent. Religious institutions receive the most contributions although their portion has decreased from about half of all philanthropy to a little over one-third. Human service organizations received 8.6 percent of donations in 1990, but their receipts actually fell five years later, perhaps due to the Aramony scandal noted below. Subsequently, human services increased to account for 10.4 percent of all philanthropic gifts.

Like other subsectors of the economy, the nonprofit sector fluctuates with profound events. The economic reverberations of September 11, 2001, dampened philanthropic activity; between 2001 and 2002, charitable contributions actually fell by 1.2 percent.[33] Despite the infusion of $2.6 billion of charitable contributions to victims of the 9/11 attacks,[34] subsequent mismanagement of nonprofit organizations reduced public philanthropy. Eventually, the September 11 Victims Compensation Fund dispensed $7 billion to more than 5,000 families.[35] Yet, the upsurge in generosity was not without problems. A fundamental question arose with respect to compensation for victims: Should payments be made equally or on the basis of previous earnings? In order to reduce the likelihood of litigation, a flat award was rejected; as a result,

Table 6.2

Philanthropy by Source and Allocations

Funds (billions)	1990	1995	2000	2005
Total	101.4	124.0	227.7	260.3
Individuals	81.0	95.4	174.5	199.1
Foundations	7.2	10.6	24.6	30.0
Corporations	5.5	7.4	10.7	13.8
Allocations				
Religion	49.8	58.1	77.0	93.2
Health	9.9	12.6	18.8	22.5
Education	12.4	17.6	31.7	38.6
Human Svs	11.8	11.7	18.0	25.4
Arts	7.9	10.0	11.5	13.5
Public Benefit	4.9	7.1	11.6	14.0
Environment	2.5	3.8	6.2	8.9
International	1.3	2.9	3.7	6.4

Source: Adapted from *Statistical Abstract of the United States* (Washington, DC: US GPO, 2008), Table 562.

compensation varied widely from more than $4 million to less than $25,000.[36] A dispute about the use of contributions to aid victims of 9/11 led to the resignation of the director of the American Red Cross. Questionable practices in response to 9/11 were compounded by the Gulf Coast disaster of Hurricane Katrina. (Ultimately, the Red Cross would go through seven executives in as many years and have to cut up to one-third of its headquarter staff to address a $200 million deficit.[37]) Victims of the Oklahoma City bombing questioned why they were not able to get assistance for their losses, also attributable to terrorism.[38] Ultimately, such problems dampened Americans' support of the voluntary sector. After 9/11, a poll of Americans' attitudes toward charity revealed that the number of respondents who had no confidence toward organized charities had increased from 8 percent to 16 percent, compared to a drop in those who had a lot of confidence from 25 percent to 19 percent,[39] a response that seemed to reflect the ambivalence toward the voluntary sector registered during the 1990s. Despite financial fluctuations, the voluntary sector persevered, attracting the allegiance of millions of volunteers. In 2006 the nonprofit sector engaged more than 61 million volunteers, or 26.7 percent of the population. Of this volunteer effort, 35 percent was accounted for by religious organizations, followed by 26.4 percent for youth/education, and 12.7 percent for social/community service.[40]

The relationship between the nonprofit and governmental sectors has been the source of much debate in recent decades. Notably during the Reagan presidency, charitable revenues dropped because of a severe recession, reductions in government assistance, and adverse changes in tax law; yet, conservatives suggested that there was untapped capacity in the philanthropic sector for social welfare. This position was argued most aggressively by George W. Bush who undertook a "faith-based initiative" that would allow religious groups access to federal funding. Ultimately, most scholars of the voluntary sector concluded that rather than try to replace governmental social welfare activities, nonprofit agencies should adopt practices "in support of an expansion of the welfare state."[41]

During the last decades of the twentieth century, even though profound questions were raised about the plausibility that the voluntary sector could replace government social programs, there was little doubt that philanthropy would expand significantly during the twenty-first century. Aside

from normal economic growth, the massive tax cuts engineered by the administration of George W. Bush which favored the wealthy, presage a new era of philanthropy. The value of the four tax cuts enacted by the Bush administration is projected to total $1.9 trillion over ten years, much of it benefiting corporations and the wealthy.[42] Paul Schervish has outlined the philanthropic consequences of this massive expansion of wealth in America:

> We estimate that an unprecedented $45 to $150 trillion in wealth transfer is in the offing over the next five decades, that this will produce at least $21 trillion to $55 trillion of charitable giving, and that between 52 percent and 65 percent of this amount will be contributed by households with $1 million in net worth.[43]

The extent to which such unprecedented wealth will be used to amplify *moral citizenship*—fulfilling the inclinations and obligations of caring—will be one of the challenges of the twenty-first century.[44] Just as compelling is a recent question: Will traditional levels of philanthropic giving continue after the economic crisis of 2008?

Advancing Social Justice

In addition to providing social services, the voluntary sector has been important in U.S. social welfare because it has been the source of efforts to advance the rights of disenfranchised populations. In this respect, the voluntary sector is essential to the nation's culture, in that it is a correcting influence to the indifference often shown to marginal populations by governmental and corporate bureaucracies. This case was argued vigorously by John W. Gardner, former Secretary of Health, Education, and Welfare and chairman of the board of Independent Sector. According to Gardner, the voluntary sector fosters much of the pluralism in the life of this country, taking on those concerns that do not attract the broad spectrum of public support necessary for the legislation that mandates governmental programs, and concerns that do not represent the commercial prospects necessary to attract the interests of the business community. In other words, the voluntary sector serves as the best—and, in some cases, the only—vehicle for addressing certain social needs. Indeed, much of what Americans would identify as central to their culture can be attributed to organizations of the voluntary sector: hospitals, schools, religious institutions, welfare agencies, fraternal associations, symphonies, and museums, to name of few. According to Gardner,

> Institutions of the nonprofit sector are in a position to serve as the guardians of intellectual and artistic freedom. Both the commercial and political marketplaces are subject to leveling forces that may threaten standards of excellence. In the non-profit sector, the fiercest champions of excellence may have their say. So may the champions of liberty and justice.[45]

Gardner's last reference here is not merely rhetorical but has its basis in history. As Alexis deTocqueville observed in the 1830s, Americans have long depended on voluntary organizations to solve communal problems. And in addressing these problems, the voluntary sector has compiled an impressive list of positive additions to American life. Those seeking solutions to current problems often find inspiration in voluntary sector initiatives of the past. Gardner noted that "At a time in our history when we are ever in need of new solutions to new problems, the private sector is remarkably free to innovate, create, and engage in controversial experiments." He observed, "In fact, virtually every far-reaching social change in our history has come up in the private sector: the abolition of slavery, the reforms of populism, child labor laws, the vote for women, civil rights, and so on."[46]

Important social welfare initiatives have also originated in the voluntary sector. The inspiration for the Great Society initiative, during which new social programs such as Medicaid, Food Stamps, and the Job Corps were launched, can be traced to Mobilization for Youth, a voluntary sector poverty program in New York City funded by the Ford Foundation. Two champions of community organization, Saul Alinsky and César Chávez of the United Farm Workers Union, were also influenced by the privately run Industrial Areas Foundation of Chicago. More recently, services to battered women, patients with AIDS, and the homeless have been pioneered by voluntary sector organizations. Given public apathy toward these groups, for many years the voluntary sector was the only source of service for these groups.

That social change begins in the voluntary sector has a particular lesson for human service professionals: The openness of democratic American culture means that anyone is free to organize for purposes of rectifying past injustices. Well within the reach of social welfare professionals are the building blocks of every voluntary sector initiative—recruiting participants, forming a board of directors, filing for tax-exempt status under IRS Code section 501(c)(3) or (4), soliciting contributions, and applying for grants and contracts. Wendy Kopp's Teach for America (TFA) is a good illustration. In 1988, armed with a vision of a Peace Corps–like program for inner cities and rural areas, the then 23-year-old Kopp began to hustle corporate contributions to match idealistic professionals to disadvantaged communities. In 1996 TFA boasted a $5.5 million budget and was graduating 500 volunteers annually[47]; by 2004 3,500 volunteers were teaching 297,500 students through a TFA budget of $34 million.[48] What Wendy Kopp accomplished illustrates the promise of the voluntary sector in every U.S. community.

Contemporary Nonprofit Human Service Organizations

The voluntary human service sector consists of a large constellation of organizations that are instantly recognizable by most Americans (see Table 6.3 on page 154).

The United Way

Perhaps the best recognized of voluntary sector organizations is the United Way. Local United Ways, as well as the United Way of America, are nonprofit organizations. The purpose of local United Ways is to

■ *One of the most well-known nonprofit human service organizations is the United Way.*

Table 6.3

Nonprofit Human Service Organizations, 2008

Name	Revenues	Affiliates	Notes
Alliance for Children and Families	$5.1 million ($3.6 billion for all member organizations)	More than 350 members	Alliance members serve over 8,000 communities in over 2,700 locations.
Alzheimer's Association	$97.7 million	National organization has offices in Chicago and Washington, DC and 78 chapters around the country	Provide information, education, advocacy, and support including a 24/7 Helpline. Their mission is to eliminate Alzheimer's disease through the advancement of research; to provide and enhance care and support for all affected; and to reduce the risk of dementia through the promotion of brain health. Strategic goals include increasing concern and awareness of the disease; advancing advocacy; enhancing care and support; and accelerating research.
American Foundation for the Blind	$20.5 million	New York City headquarters; Public Policy Center in Washington DC; and four other offices	The primary focus of the American Foundation for the Blind's Public Policy Center is federal and state programs affecting education and rehabilitation of blind persons, as well as laws that relate to economic status and civil rights. AFB's priorities include broadening access to technology; elevating the quality of information and tools for the professionals who serve people with vision loss; and promoting independent and healthy living for people with vision loss by providing them and their families with relevant and timely resources.
American Red Cross	$6.009 billion (2006)	Over 700 locally supported chapters	Maintain quality of blood supply; disaster relief efforts, such as the tsunami, 9/11, and wildfires.
Arthritis Foundation	$74.8 million (national office)	National office and 47 chapters	Research, public policy, education.
The Arc of the United States	$3.8 million (national office)	More than 850 state and local chapters	Promoting and improving supports and services for people with mental retardation and their families.

Table 6.3

Name	Revenues	Affiliates	Notes
Boy Scouts of America	$182 million	More than 300 local councils	Character-building programs emphasizing leadership, citizenship, personal development, and physical fitness.
Camp Fire USA	$3.5 million	145 councils and community partners	Youth leadership, self-reliance, after-school groups, camping, environmental education, and child care for more than 750,000 youth. Serves nearly 750,000 children and youth annually.
Catholic Charities USA	$101 million	More than 1,700 Catholic Charities agencies and organizations	Launching "Campaign to Reduce Poverty in America." Advocacy on hunger, housing, family economic security, and health care have been established as major priorities. Also focused on fair and focused federal budget, protecting special populations, and disaster response.
Child Welfare League of America	$17.5 million (national office)	Six regional offices, 800 member agencies	Program and policy advocacy on a full range of child-related problems.
Girl Scouts of the United States of America	$113 million	More than 300 local councils	Values-based activities to enhance development of girls.
Goodwill Industries	$2.9 billion (2006)	184 member or affiliate organizations	Rehabilitation, training, placement, and employment services for those with disabilities and other barriers to employment. Last year, local Goodwills collectively provided employment and training services to more than 930,775 individuals.
National Council on Alcoholism and Drug Dependence	$0.9 million (national office)	Nearly 100 councils	Fights the stigma and the disease of alcoholism and other drug addictions.
Easter Seals	$86.2 million	More than 550 service centers	Medical rehabilitation, job training and employment, child care, camping and recreation, and adult day services.
Mental Health America (formerly known as the National Mental Health Association)	$8.2 million	More than 320 affiliates	Advocacy, education, research, and service to improve mental health.

(Continued)

Table 6.3

(continued)

Name	Revenues	Affiliates	Notes
National Urban League	$40.8 million	102 affiliates	Programs in education, job training and placement, housing, business development, and crime prevention.
Planned Parenthood Federation of America	$926.4 million (affiliates); $104.1 million (national office)	103 affiliates operate 860 health centers	Sexual and reproductive health care, education, and information.
The Salvation Army	$3.324 billion (2006)	In over 115 countries	Full range of Christian programming for those in need.
United Jewish Communities	$350.2 million	155 Jewish federations and 400 independent Jewish communities	Mission is to improve the quality of Jewish life worldwide, nurture Jewish learning, care for those in need, rescue Jews in danger.
United Service Organizations (USO)	$136.5 million	More than 130 centers worldwide	Services to military personnel and their families.
Young Men's Christian Association (YMCA)	$95 million (2006)	2,663 YMCAs serve more than 20.2 million people each year	Health, fitness, and recreation programs; child care and community development programs.
Young Women's Christian Association (YWCA)	$7.9 million	300 YWCA associations nationwide at over 1,300 sites; serving almost 2 million members and participants	Health, youth development, and women's leadership (nationwide initiatives). Sports and fitness programs for women and girls; shelter, support, and child care services for women and their families; advocacy for women and families.

raise funds that are then disbursed to nonprofit agencies in the community, most of which are United Way members. Local United Ways also contribute a small percentage of funds to the national headquarters, the United Way of America, which is located in suburban Washington, DC. Because the United Way is a confederation of organizations, power resides within the local United Ways. The United Way of America provides support services nationwide but has no direct authority over local United Ways.

In 2006–2007, the United Ways in the United States raised $4.04 billion. United Way contributions have oscillated over time, often failing to keep pace with inflation. Two events accounted for plunging contributions. First, the recession of the early 1980s, the worst since the Great Depression, accounted for a significant loss in contributions.

Second, revelations of managerial improprieties on the part of United Way CEO William Aramony in the early 1990s precipitated another reduction in donations (adjusted for inflation) to United Ways. Muckraking journalists reported that Aramony had supplemented his $390,000 annual salary by authorizing excessive perks, including a New York penthouse, limousine service, and European trips on the Concorde. Using United Way funds for seed money, Aramony had also authorized the creation of three independent corporations, which later employed his son.[49] The final chapter in the Aramony scandal was not written until 1995, when a jury found Aramony and two associates guilty of multiple counts of conspiracy, fraud, and filing false tax returns. Aramony was found to have misappropriated $1.2 million in United Way funds, was sentenced to seven years in federal prison, and was fined $522,000.[50] Ultimately, the regional United Ways would bear the brunt of Aramony's indiscretions. Between 1991 and 1997, United Way gifts in Los Angeles fell 41.3 percent, San Diego 35.6 percent, Cleveland 29.4 percent, Boston 25.3 percent, Chicago 24.3 percent, Detroit 23.1 percent, and New York 17.5 percent.[51]

In late 1995, leaders of major foundations met in New York to survey the damage. Noting that the philanthropic community "seems to have lost a large part of its claim on the sympathies of the American public," Lester Salamon, director of the Johns Hopkins Institute for Policy Studies, suggested the establishment of a special commission that would "rethink the role, function and operation of the nonprofit sector for the next century." Citing "a growing mismatch between the actual operation of the voluntary sector and popular conceptions of what this sector is supposed to be like," Salamon argued that the major philanthropies were vulnerable to "cheap shots and exposés" when a management scam hit the headlines.[52]

Yet administrative problems within the United Way continued. In 2003, Oral Suer, head of the United Way of the National Capital Area (Washington, DC), was found to have misappropriated $1.5 million through various financial arrangements. In the process, Suer had made himself a "paragon of personal virtue" by pledging $9,000 annually to the United Way, then paid off his pledge through unauthorized payments from the United Way.[53] Suer was subsequently sentenced to 27 months in prison; but the credibility of the United Way serving the nation's capital had been severely damaged. In 2001, the United Way of the National Capital Area had raised $90 million; after the Suer scandal, contributions fell

to $19 million, causing the organization to lay off half of its staff, close several satellite offices, and forfeit its lucrative fundraising contract with federal employees.[54] In a sector where credibility is a virtue, such damage requires years to repair.

At the same time, traditional United Way agencies were faced with diminishing revenues as a result of competition from nontraditional organizations that were also seeking charitable contributions. For example, until recently the United Way claimed about 90 percent of all contributions to the Combined Federal Campaign (a campaign directed at federal employees) that were not specifically designated for other purposes. As a result of challenges brought by agencies as diverse as environmental groups and the National Rifle Association, however, nondesignated contributions are now apportioned among a larger number of organizations. Consequently, the United Way receives less than it did in the past from the Combined Federal Campaign.[55] In response to increased competition for charitable dollars, most United Ways offer donor-option through which they will relay contributions to nonmember organizations.

Revenues of the United Way are derived from multiple sources. As is generally true of charitable contributions, about half of the funds contributed to the United Way are from employees and small businesses. Corporations account for somewhat less than a fourth of United Way revenues. Financial support that the United Way provides to local agencies is also varied. Health, family services, and youth services account for the largest categories of expenditures. Smaller percentages go to agencies providing food, clothing, and housing; day care; public safety; community development; income and jobs support; education; and other kinds of assistance.

spotlight 6.1

Nonprofit Human Service Organizations

Well-known nonprofit human service organizations include United Way, the American Red Cross, the Child Welfare League of America, Goodwill Industries, United Jewish Communities, and Catholic Charities. To learn more about each of these organizations, visit their websites using the links below:

The United Way: http://national.unitedway.org
The American Red Cross: www.redcross.org
The Child Welfare League of America:
www.cwla.org
Goodwill Industries: www.goodwill.org
United Jewish Communities: www.ujc.org
Catholic Charities:
www.catholiccharitiesusa.org

Of course, the amounts actually allocated in communities vary considerably according to the different priorities of each local United Way.

Elite Philanthropy

The United Ways that dot the nation's landscape, which pursue relatively modest goals, can be classified as "bourgeois" philanthropy. "Elite" philanthropy, on the other hand, has much grander expectations. During the late 1990s, Ted Turner announced an unprecedented $1 billion contribution to the United Nations; this gift was matched by Bill Gates, whose foundation pledged $1 billion for various disease prevention initiatives in the Third World, notably work on HIV/AIDS in sub-Saharan Africa.[56] By 2004 the Gates Foundation was investing $600 million annually for prevention of diseases that ravaged developing nations, significantly outspending other charities.[57] In 2006 Warren Buffett, reluctant to establish his own foundation, donated over $6 billion to the Gates Foundation, raising its assets to $44 billion.[58] Despite its magnitude, Gates' wealth paled in comparison to that of the captains of industrial America; John D. Rockefeller's fortune in inflation-adjusted dollars, for example, was more than twice as large.[59] The major philanthropic foundations are identified by the names of the titans of U.S. capitalism (see Table 6.4).

Even though the conspicuous generosity of large foundations generates high-visibility grants,[60] analysis of tax records reveals that the most generous Americans earn between $50,000 and $100,000 annually. Charitable contributions of the middle class exceed those earning more than $10 million by

Table 6.4

Largest Philanthropic Foundations

Rank	Name/(State)	Assets	As of Fiscal Year End Date
1.	Bill & Melinda Gates Foundation (WA)	$33,120,381,000	12/31/06
2.	The Ford Foundation (NY)	11,615,906,693	09/30/05
3.	J. Paul Getty Trust (CA)	9,618,627,974	06/30/05
4.	The Robert Wood Johnson Foundation (NJ)	9,367,614,774	12/31/05
5.	The William and Flora Hewlett Foundation (CA)	8,520,765,000	12/31/06
6.	Lilly Endowment, Inc. (IN)	8,360,760,584	12/31/05
7.	W. K. Kellogg Foundation (MI)	7,799,270,734	08/31/06
8.	The David and Lucile Packard Foundation (CA)	6,351,000,000	12/31/06
9.	The Andrew W. Mellon Foundation (NY)	5,586,112,102	12/31/05
10.	John D. and Catherine T. MacArthur Foundation (IL)	5,492,269,240	12/31/05
11.	Gordon and Betty Moore Foundation (CA)	5,308,627,945	12/31/05
12.	The California Endowment (CA)	4,405,938,934	02/28/06
13.	The Rockefeller Foundation (NY)	3,417,557,613	12/31/05
14.	The Starr Foundation (NY)	3,344,801,753	12/31/05
15.	The Annie E. Casey Foundation (MD)	3,265,655,271	12/31/06
16.	The Kresge Foundation (MI)	3,032,422,497	12/31/05
17.	The Duke Endowment (NC)	2,708,834,085	12/31/05
18.	The Annenberg Foundation (PA)	2,539,268,854	06/30/06
19.	Carnegie Corporation of New York (NY)	2,530,191,576	09/30/06
20.	Charles Stewart Mott Foundation (MI)	2,480,562,766	12/31/05

Source: "Top 20 U.S. Foundations by Asset Size," The World Bank Group. Retrieved December 12, 2008, from http://go.worldbank.org/5M7C7NGCMO

a factor of two to six.[61] Indeed, most foundations are modest ventures. Seventy-three percent of foundations have assets of less than $1 million, yet they represent only 13.1 percent of grants. About 70 percent of grants are made by foundations with assets exceeding $10 million.[62] In order to optimize their influence, many smaller foundations have merged.[63]

Despite the substantial philanthropic activity of foundations—gifts of $43 billion in 2007[64]—critics questioned their generosity. Accusations of impropriety, fraudulent activity, and stinginess plagued the foundation world. Subsequently, the Charitable Giving Act of 2003 was introduced which would require foundations to spend 5 percent of their endowments annually on charity. Under current law, foundations are allowed to include administrative expenses, such as rent, travel, and salaries, in that 5 percent requirement, so disallowing administrative expenses were projected to increase gifts to nonprofits by $4.3 billion.[65] In response, 18 major foundations secured the services of former congressman Bill Paxon who worked for a major lobbying firm.[66] The strategy succeeded; subsequently, the bill died in the House Ways and Means Committee.

In addition to criticisms of fund misuse, many people question the motives of large philanthropies and the individuals who support these organizations. "Elite American philanthropy serves the interests of the rich to a greater extent than it does the interests of the poor, disadvantaged, or disabled," argues Teresa Odendahl; it is "a system of 'generosity' by which the wealthy exercise social control and help themselves more than they do others."[67] Odendahl calculated that about one-half of all gifts itemized on income tax returns were made by the wealthy.[68] For what purposes do the rich demonstrate such beneficence? They give to institutions that "sustain their culture, their education, their policy formulation, their status-in short, their interests."[69] In other words, wealthy Americans usually use the tax code to maintain institutions of elite culture, such as private schools, museums, symphony orchestras, and opera companies. These institutions often announce generosity of sufficient magnitude to the public by naming an important structure or endowment after the benefactor, a tradition maintained by cultural elites in major U.S. cities. The use of funds that have been withdrawn from public use by the tax code in order to reproduce the social institutions of the rich is unacceptable to Odendahl, who proposes reforms that would require philanthropy to be put to public benefit in different ways.

The Future of the Voluntary Sector

Despite the visibility of elite philanthropy, most Americans voiced preference for voluntary efforts to address social problems. Of respondents to a 2001 poll of the public's perception of problem solving, 56 percent ranked sectarian agencies as important for "solving social problems in their communities," compared to 53 percent for local nonprofits, 39 percent for the United Way, 33 percent for state government, and 28 percent for the federal government.[70] The ability of the nonprofit sector to meet these public expectations is problematic, however. Although charitable contributions and elite philanthropy continue to increase, a leadership vacuum has emerged in the voluntary sector. A study of nonprofit executives conducted by Meyer Foundation revealed that one-third of executives are dissatisfied with their salaries and three-fourths plan to leave within five years (see Table 6.5).[71] In addition, several forces have transformed the nonprofit sector, including the intrusion of commercial firms, the rise of faith-based social services, and the emergence of social entrepreneurship.

Table 6.5

Compensation for Executives of Selected Foundations

Foundation	Executive	1997 Salary
Lilly Endowment	Thomas Lofton	$450,000
Ford Foundation	Susan Berresford	440,500
Packard Foundation	Colburn Wilbur	272,549
Kellogg Foundation	William Richardson	400,000
RW Johnson Foundation	Steven Schroeder	367,000
Pew Charitable Trusts	Rebecca Rimel	339,734
Rob't Woodruff Foundation	Charles McTier	270,000

Source: Adapted from Judith Havemann, "Top Foundations Gave Chiefs a Bountiful Raise," *Washington Post* (July 5, 1998), p. A1.

Commercialization

In the mixed welfare economy, the voluntary sector coexists with government but also competes with commercial providers. This places nonprofit organizations in an odd position: having secured a tax-exempt status from government in order to provide charity care, many voluntary sector agencies find themselves competing with for-profit corporations in the same market. The commercialization of health care, described in Chapter 7, is a case in point. Confronted with a segment of the population not served by for-profit hospitals that insist on payment for care, nonprofit hospitals in several metropolitan areas, such as Martin Luther King-Harbor Hospital in Los Angeles and Grady Memorial Hospital in Atlanta, have run serious deficits adhering to their commitment to provide charity care to the indigent.[72] Yet, other nonprofit hospitals have not been so generous. North Mississippi Medical Center in Tupelo, for example, harassed uninsured patients for outstanding debts, ultimately becoming the subject of suits brought on behalf of poor patients. In a tentative settlement, North Mississippi Medical Center agreed to provide free care to low-income patients and provide refunds to those who had paid for care.[73] In another instance, Seventh Day Adventist hospitals were sued for insisting that low-income patients pay prior to receipt of health care, often at inflated prices. By the end of 2005, attorneys in 22 states had sued nonprofit hospitals for violating provisions of their tax-exempt status.[74]

The **commercialization** issue is particularly important for nonprofit agencies desiring to enhance their incomes. Faced with static, if not declining, revenues, some voluntary sector agencies have experimented with commercial activities in order to supplement income derived from traditional sources (contracts, contributions, grants, and fees). That nonprofit organizations should be allowed to engage in commercial endeavors without restriction is "unfair competition," according to business operators, who note that nonprofits do not ordinarily pay taxes on their income. Business operators fear that, exempt from taxation, nonprofits could lower their prices, increasing pressure on tax-paying businesses operating in the same market, eventually driving them out of business.

Limits on the freedom of nonprofit organizations to engage in commercial activities were highlighted in a celebrated case involving New York University Law School and the Mueller Macaroni Company. Seeking a way to enhance revenues to the law school and

thereby lighten the burden of contributing to their alma mater, enterprising alumni acquired Mueller and reorganized it as a nonprofit organization registered in Delaware. Income from the macaroni company was thus redefined as nontaxable income and diverted to the law school as a charitable contribution. This clever arrangement, however, did not go unnoticed by Mueller's competitors, who saw the possibility that Mueller might be able to use its newly acquired tax-exempt status to cut prices and drive other macaroni companies from the market. Further, they argued, what was to prevent any well-endowed nonprofit institution from acquiring profitable businesses as a way of supplementing its income while dodging any tax obligation? The situation soon proved so embarrassing to the law school that it sent no representatives to the congressional hearings convened to deliberate on the ethics of the arrangement. Eventually the tax code was altered, making income from commercial activities that are not related to the service function of a nonprofit organization taxable.[75] Since 1950, revenue obtained by nonprofit organizations from commercial activity has been taxable under the unrelated business income tax (UBIT).

Conflicts between nonprofit and for-profit organizations were aired during hearings held by the House Ways and Means Committee in 1987.[76] At the hearings, representatives of the business community complained that nonprofits were engaging in "unfair competition" with for-profit businesses in two ways. First, they argued, the UBIT is inconsistent in distinguishing between related and unrelated business activities. For example, a nonprofit hospital's pharmacy is considered related to the hospital's mission and is therefore exempt from paying taxes on profit, but a for-profit hospital's pharmacy is part of the business and its profit is therefore taxable. Second, nonprofit organizations benefit from the "halo effect"—that is, the public's perception that their services are superior because they do not operate from the profit motive. Thus, health spas complain that YMCAs benefit from a philanthropic "halo," and the revenues of the Ys are tax exempt.

Although complaints of unfair competition on the part of nonprofit organizations appear to be academic, the accusations open the possibility of further restrictions on the revenue base of voluntary sector agencies. For example, some Ys have stopped advertising their programs for fear that local authorities may interpret those programs as commercial and thereby attempt to tax their income. Thus, the unfair competition issue presents some very disturbing questions for administrators of nonprofit organizations. "We can't ask nonprofits to be more like for-profits in the ways that we like—efficient, responsive, aggressive—without expecting that they will also become more like for-profits in the ways that we don't: rapacious, hardheaded and, yes, sometimes selfish," noted Jacob Hacker.[77]

Some of the practices of voluntary sector agencies resemble those of commercial enterprises and beg important questions. If a nonprofit family service agency bills a client's insurance company for a "usual, customary, and reasonable" fee, a fee comparable to what is charged by a private practice group that must pay taxes on such income, should this income remain tax exempt? Should tax-exempt income be limited to charitable contributions only? Do program outreach and public education activities constitute marketing and advertising? Questions like these strike at the heart of the function of the voluntary sector. How these questions are resolved will be of great concern to nonprofit community service agencies, particularly to organizations faced with dwindling revenues.

Faith-Based Social Services

The idea of government's contracting with voluntary sector agencies is not a novel concept; through purchase-of-service agreements dating to the late 1960s, government has negotiated arrangements for delivery of a range of social services, often with sectarian agencies. This liberal mechanism for decentralization, however, has given conservatives an entrée to pose more fundamental questions about the proper role of government in social welfare. Since the 1980s, conservative think tanks have, with increasing urgency, sought an alternative to federal social programs. Central to the conservative critique of conventional welfare has been William Schambra who makes a fundamental differentiation between scientific philanthropy and faith-based charity. A manifestation of Progressivism, scientific philanthropy provided the justification for elite foundations, the advocates of which believed that public problems could be analyzed scientifically and addressed effectively through social programs. By contrast, faith-based charity makes no such pretense, satisfied that donations to do good works come from a well-spring of faith and warrant no further justification.[78] Compared to charity's simple, direct approach to need, Schambra characterized elite philanthropy as obscured by "smug, opaque, apolitical jargon—the endless, sterile, process-based chatter about collaborations, partnerings, learnings, leveragings, outcomes, and best practices."[79]

A primary proponent of sectarian nonprofit agencies has been Marvin Olasky, a journalist who has argued that voluntary religious agencies provided efficient and effective services to the needy well before the New Deal and the deployment of the welfare state.[80] Another source of support has come from evangelical Christians, who have objected to the absence of moral standards that they see as characterizing traditional social service agencies managed by liberal welfare professionals. By the 2000 presidential election, centrist conservatives within the Republican Party identified the voluntary sector, and in particular sectarian agencies, as a way to appeal to independent voters. Since its resurgence with the 1980 election of Ronald Reagan, conservatism had been in opposition to liberal social policy; however, it lacked a positive stance with respect to a large segment of the electorate—the middle class, the elderly, and the ill, among others. Invoking the virtues of the voluntary sector provided a way to address this ideological deficit, an approach that George W. Bush enthusiastically proclaimed during his 2000 presidential campaign as "compassionate conservatism."

As governor of Texas, Bush had extensive experience in mobilizing the private sector to address social welfare needs. After passage of the 1996 welfare reform legislation, he proposed contracting out all of the state's public welfare programming, a deal valued at $500 million annually; but this was vetoed by the Clinton administration. Despite this reversal, Bush countered by advancing "faith-based social services" as an alternative to traditional social programs.[81] Eventually, Bush proposed a five-year, $5 billion federal program for faith-based organizations; however, Democrats objected because of the possibility of discrimination in hiring, and the proposal failed. Undaunted, Bush instituted part of the plan through executive order. By 2004 over $1 billion had been awarded through Bush's faith-based initiative (see Table 6.6 on page 162). A year later, the amount diverted to faith-based organizations had increased by $150 million to $2.1 billion.[82] Bush administration designs for faith-based services received a boost when a federal judge determined that sectarian agencies could dismiss employees who refused to adhere to religious precepts of their sectarian employers.[83] Ultimately, even conservatives expressed reservations about the "faith-based" policy initiative. David Kuo, deputy director of the White House Office of Faith-Based and Community Initiatives, expressed his reservations about the sincerity of the Bush administration in *Tempting Faith: An Inside Story of Political Seduction*, a book that noted the manipulation of

Table 6.6

Federal Grants to Faith-Based Organizations

Agency	Money for Grant Programs (in millions)	Money for FBOs (in millions)	Percent (%) for FBOs
HHS	$10,874.3	$567.9	5
HUD	2,197.7	532.1	24
Justice	791.7	51.6	7
Labor	512.4	11.3	2
Education	134.7	6.8	5

Source: Adapted from Alan Cooperman, "Grants to Religious Groups Top $1.1 Billion," *Washington Post* (March 10, 2004), p. A27.

initiative in order to curry the support of religious conservatives.[84]

Enthusiasm for faith-based initiatives notwithstanding, the approach had yet to demonstrate its superiority through research. Indiana researchers evaluated 2,830 people who enrolled in 27 employment programs and found no difference between sectarian and secular organizations with respect to placement rates and beginning wages; graduates of faith-based organizations tended to work fewer hours and were less likely to receive health insurance.[85]

Regardless, proponents of faith-based social services, including many traditional sectarian agencies with a long history of helping the needy such as the Salvation Army, insisted that government programs were too bureaucratic and impersonal, and that secular nonprofit agencies were populated by welfare professionals who failed to infuse services with adequate moral content to be effective. In office, Bush extended "compassionate conservatism" beyond the parameters of local social services to propose education reform through the No Child Left Behind Act, adding a prescription drug benefit to Medicare, and increasing assistance to fight AIDS in Africa. Although Bush's "faith-based" policy initiative may not have generated the revenue promised, it clearly demonstrates how appeals to the voluntary sector resonate with conservative Republicans.

Social Entrepreneurship

Many theologically inclined liberals endorsed the idea of faith-based social services, but others pursued innovations through capital and technology. A new generation of social entrepreneurs has emerged as experiments with markets reveal untapped

opportunities for program innovation, both locally and nationally. For example, the Ben & Jerry's ice cream company and Working Assets Long Distance (WALD) [now CREDO] represent an ethic in which business praxis is inextricably suffused with social consciousness.[86] In 2007 CREDO contributed $3.5 million to progressive organizations advocating in several areas: social justice, the environment, civil rights, and international justice.[87] Realizing that there was a minimal return on time invested in securing foundation grants, Peter Samuelson, founder of Starlight Starbright, an organization serving critically ill children, approached the marketing department of Colgate-Palmolive and convinced them to incorporate cause-related marketing in their products. "The results were astonishing," Samuelson reported. "Instead of receiving $25,000 from the corporation's foundation, we were suddenly receiving $250,000 from a cause-related marketing campaign."[88]

Concerned about the decline of civic institutions, particularly in urban areas, sociologists proposed

■ *Former President George W. Bush advanced faith-based social services as an alternative to traditional social programs.*

"social capital" as a vehicle for revitalization. For Robert Putnam, the term *social capital* referred to "features of social organization, such as networks, norms, and trust, which facilitate coordination and cooperation for mutual benefit. Social capital enhances the benefits of investment in physical and human capital."[89] At the nexus of social capital, community-based nonprofit organizations can facilitate the development of poor neighborhoods providing they exploit new markets and technologies. An illustration of the social capital approach to community development is the work of former congressman Floyd Flake, pastor of the Allen African Methodist Episcopal Cathedral in Jamaica, New York.[90] Flake has used his position as church pastor to construct a $34 million network of community development ventures. Seeing the future as a social entrepreneur, Flake recognizes the ideological implications of recent changes in social policy: "Those of us who have made a commitment to stay in an urban community have decided that *this* is our paradise," he observed. "We are going to rebuild that paradise—and we understand that it means some paradigm shifts, even politically, because the majority of statehouses today are in the hands of Republican governors and the majority of the assemblies are in the hands of Republicans. So we can either continue in a protest mode or we find ways to have entrée to deal with who is in power now."[91]

Flake served 11 years in Congress during which he authored the 1993 Community Development Financial Institutions Act that designated a revolving loan fund for economic development in low-income communities. A decade later 527 CDFIs had been established, but the number fell far short of what might have been possible. In his analysis of the fringe economy, Howard Karger has calculated that $125 billion is siphoned from poor communities by check-cashers, pawnshops, rent-to-own stores, and the like each year.[92] The National Community Capital Association reported in 2001 that a developing CDFI held capital of $7 million.[93] In other words, a fringe economy of that scale would have supported a network of over 17,500 CDFIs in 2001 alone. Unfortunately, the failure of welfare advocates to seize the promise of social entrepreneurship combined with unwillingness of the Bush administration to fully fund the CDFI program has left poor communities without financial services that could address their poverty. Exploited by the fringe economy, essential capital continues to hemorrhage from poor communities, a circumstance that is as tragic as it is unnecessary.

Although the social entrepreneur movement has been slow to evolve in relation to social welfare, it has captured the imagination of international development advocates. David Bornstein championed their cause in his best-selling book, *How to Change the World: Social Entrepreneurs and the Power of New Ideas*.[94] The Grameen Bank, described in Chapter 18, has become an iconic institution melding a business ethic with social responsibility and leveraging the upward mobility of peasant families in the Third World. The latent capacity of the commercial sector to provide micro-credit loans to low-income families has spawned financial institutions worldwide.[95] As social entrepreneur gospel spread, its proponents characterized it as qualitatively different from traditional nonprofit or commercial organizations. The director of the New Hampshire Community Loan Fund made the case for applying capital to resolve social problems: "I think what people are increasingly looking for, whether in the for-profit or nonprofit sector, is how you harness the vitality and promise of capitalism in a way that's more fair to everyone."[96] In contrast to the skepticism of traditional welfare advocates toward capitalism, social entrepreneurs embrace its advantages. "The new breed of philanthropic and social entrepreneurs want to see measurable results, and soon; they embrace business and businesslike methods; they want projects to be sustainable and scalable, capable of living and growing on their own."[97] In 2008, Oprah took the social entrepreneur concept one step further by introducing venture social capital to the nonprofit sector, developing a TV reality show in which $1 million would be awarded to the contestant with the most innovative charitable idea.[98]

Conclusion

As commercialization, faith-based social services, and social entrepreneurship indicate, the nonprofit sector has struggled to rebound from the lethargy that characterized it during the latter decades of the twentieth century. How the voluntary sector preserves its mission of caring for the disenfranchised without succumbing to the bottom-line ethos of the corporate sector, responds to the range of diverse populations without proselytizing to unbelievers, and adapts the latest innovations in technology while putting forth a human face are challenges that remain.

Discussion Questions

1. What are the most prominent nonprofit human service agencies in your community? Are they members of the United Way? What do agencies perceive to be the advantages of United Way membership? Do they perceive disadvantages to United Way membership?

2. Has the United Way in your community failed to achieve its goals in contributions in recent years? If so, what are the causes? The proposed solutions?

3. What are the newer nonprofit agencies in your community? What populations do they serve? Are these agencies members of the United Way? If not, how do they attract the necessary resources? What is their perception of the United Way?

4. If there are unmet needs in your community, how would you create a nonprofit agency to meet them? Whom would you recruit for your board of directors? Where would you solicit resources, both cash and in-kind? Whom would you recruit for staff? What would you name your agency? Would your agency focus on providing services or on advancing social change?

5. In response to diminishing resources, many nonprofit social agencies have resorted to entrepreneurial strategies to raise money. What innovative projects have agencies deployed in your community? What entrepreneurial strategies can you think of that might be successful for nonprofit agencies in your community?

6. What are the most prominent foundations in your community? What has been the source of revenues for their activities? How would you rank them with respect to the volume of their gifts versus assets? Which foundations have been most active with respect to social welfare? Have their gifts increased or decreased in recent years?

7. Thinking as a social entrepreneur, how would you apply a business ethic to address a social problem in your community? Are there local nonprofits that have undertaken commercial ventures to increase their revenues? How successful have they been?

Notes

1. Peter Berger and Richard Neuhaus, *To Empower People: The Role of Mediating Structures in Public Policy* (Washington, DC: American Enterprise Institute, 1977).

2. Daniel Yee, "Atlanta Scouts Inflated Numbers," *Washington Post* (June 1, 2005), p. A5.

3. Stephanie Strom, "Habitat for Humanity Picks New Leader Among Turmoil," *New York Times* (August 5, 2005), p. A11.

4. Philip Rucker, "United Way Fundraising rises After Scandal-Induced Plunge," *Washington Post* (Novermber 3, 2007), p. B3.

5. R. Jeffrey Smith, "Former DeLay Aide Enriched by Nonprofit," *Washington Post* (March 26, 2006), p. A1.

6. John Solomon and Matthew Mosk, "Nonprofits Become a Force in Primaries," *Washington Post* (December 5, 2007), p. A1.

7. Genaro Armas, "60 Tax-exempt Groups under Investigation," *Washington Post* (October 30, 2004), p. A4.

8. David Stoesz, "A Structural Interest Theory of Social Welfare," *Social Development Issues* 10 (Winter 1985), pp. 73–85.

9. National Association of Social Workers, *Social Casework: Generic and Specific* (Silver Spring, MD: NASW, 1974).

10. Retrieved April 21, 2008, from www.unitedway.org/about/index.cfm

11. Robert Alford, *Health Care Politics* (Chicago: University of Chicago Press, 1975), p. 204.

12. Roy Lubove, *The Professional Altruist* (New York: Atheneum, 1969), p. 197.

13. Walter Trattner, *From Poor Law to Welfare State* (New York: Macmillan, 1974), p. 237; and "The First Days of Social Security," *Public Welfare* 43 (Fall 1985), pp. 112–119.

14. Alford, *Health Care Politics*, p. 2.

15. Ibid., p. 199.

16. Trattner, *From Poor Law to Welfare State*, p. 250.

17. Robert Barker, "Private Practice Primer for Social Work," *NASW News* (October 1983), p. 13.

18. A. Goleman, "Social Workers Vault into a Leading Role in Psychotherapy," *New York Times* (April 3, 1985), p. C-1.

19. Per conversation with NASW staff, November 16, 1992.

20. Donald Light, "Corporate Medicine for Profit," *Scientific American* 255 (December 1986), pp. 81–89.

21. "Generosity Index, 2004." Retrieved November 18, 2004, from www.catalogueforphilanthropy.org/ofp/olb.generosity

22. Ralph Kramer, "The Future of Voluntary Organizations in Social Welfare," in *Philanthropy, Voluntary Action, and the Public Good* (Washington, DC: Independent Sector/United Way, 1986).

23. Peter Drucker, *The New Realities* (New York: HarperCollins, 1989).

24. Peter Drucker, "It Profits Us to Strengthen Nonprofits," *Wall Street Journal* (December 19, 1991), p. 18.

25. Neil Gilbert, *Capitalism and the Welfare State* (New Haven, CT: Yale University Press, 1983), pp. 6–7; Neil Gilbert and Harry Specht, *Dimensions of Social Welfare Policy*, 2nd ed. (Englewood Cliffs, NJ: Prentice Hall, 1989), pp. 46–47.

26. Committee on Ways and Means, U.S. House of Representatives, Overview of Entitlement Programs, *1992 Green Book* (Washington, DC: U.S. Government Printing Office, 1992), p. 830.

27. Committee on Ways and Means. U.S. House of Representatives, Overview of Entitlement Programs, *2004 Green Book* (Washington, DC: U.S. Government Printing Office, 2004), p. 10-2.

28. Alan Abramson and Lester Salamon, *The Nonprofit Sector and the New Federal Budget* (Washington, DC: Urban Institute, 1986), p. xi. See also Waldemar Nielsen, *The Third Sector: Keystone of a Caring Society* (Washington, DC: Independent Sector, 1980).

29. Marvin Olasky, "Beyond the Stingy Welfare State," *Policy Review* (Fall 1990), p. 14.

30. U.S. Census Bureau, *Statistical Abstract of the United States* (Washington, DC: US GPO, 2008), Table 566.

31. Virginia Hodgkinson and Murray Weitzman, *Nonprofit Almanac* (Washington, DC: Independent Sector, 1996), p. 40.

32. Ibid., Table 645.

33. Greg Winter, "Charitable Giving Falls for First Time in Years," *New York Times* (October 27, 2003), p. A11.

34. AAFRC, *Giving USA, 2003* (Indianapolis: University of Indiana, 2003), p. 55.

35. David Chen, "After Weighing Value of Lives, 9/11 Fund Completes Task," *New York Times* (July 16, 2004), p. A1.

36. Christopher Lee, "Report on Sept. 11 Fund Is Released," *Washington Post* (November 8, 2004), p. A3.

37. Stephanie Strom, "Short on Fund-Raising, Red Cross Will Cut Jobs," *New York Times* (January 16, 2008), p. A13; Philip Rucker, "Corporate Leader Named Red Cross CEO," *Washington Post* (April 9, 2008), p. A3.

38. Lisa Belkin, "The Grief Payout," *New York Times Magazine* (December 8, 2002).

39. Jacqueline Salmon, "Nonprofits Show Losses in the Public's Trust," *Washington Post* (November 9, 2002), p. A2.

40. U.S. Census Bureau, *Statistical Abstract of the United States* (Washington, DC: US GPO, 2008), Table 568.

41. Steven Smith and Michael Lipsky, *Nonprofits for Hire* (Cambridge, MA: Harvard University Press, 1993), p. 184.

42. Jonathan Weisman, "Congress Votes to Extend Tax Cuts," *Washington Post* (September 24, 2004), p. A7.

43. Paul Schervish, "The Cultural Horizons of Charitable Giving in an Age of Affluence" (Cambridge, MA: Boston College Social Welfare Research Institute, September 23, 2003), p. 1.

44. Paul Schervish, "The Sense and Sensibility of Philanthropy as a Moral Citizenship of Care" (Cambridge, MA: Boston College and Indiana University Center on Philanthropy, January 2004).

45. Gardner quoted in O'Connell, *Origins, Dimensions and Impact of America's Voluntary Spirit*, p. 6.

46. John W. Gardner, *Keynote Address* (Washington, DC: Independent Sector; 1978), p. 13.

47. Irene Lacher, "Teaching America a Lesson," *Los Angeles Times* (November 11, 1990), E1; personal communication, Teach for America, October 7, 1996.

48. Teach for America. Retrieved October 3, 2004, from http://teachforamerica.org

49. David Lauter, "United Way's Chief Quits in Funds Dispute," *Los Angeles Times* (February 28, 1992), p. A1.

50. "Key Dates in the Adjudication of Former Management" (Fairfax, VA: United Way of America, 1996).

51. David Johnston, "United Way, Faced with Fewer Donors, Is Giving Away Less," *New York Times* (November 9, 1997), p. 28.

52. Karen Arenson, "Woeful '95 Leads U.S. Charities to Introspection," *New York Times* (December 10, 1995), p. 38.

53. Jacqueline Salmon and Peter Whoriskey, "Audit Excoriates United Way Leadership," *Washington Post* (August 12, 2003), p. A1.

54. Jerry Markon, "Ex-Chief of Local United Way Sentenced," *Washington Post* (May 15, 2004), p. A1.

55. Judith Havemann, "Federal Charity Drive Opened to More Groups," *Washington Post* (January 2, 1988), p. A1.

56. Jean Strouse, "How to Give Away $21.8 Billion," *New York Times Magazine* (April 16, 2000).

57. Sebastian Mallaby, "Opening the Gates," *Washington Post* (April 5, 2004), p. A17.

58. Yuki Nogouchi, "Gates Foundation to Get Bulk of Buffett's Fortune," *Washington Post* (June 26, 2006), p. A1.

59. Louis Uchitelle, "The Richest of the Rich, Proud of a New Gilded Age," *New York Times* (July 15, 2007), p. A18.

60. Phillip Rucker, "How Groups of the Rich Diverge in Philanthropy," *Washington Post* (December 6, 2007), p. A12.

61. David Johnston, "Study Shows the Superrich Are Not the Most Generous," *New York Times* (December 19, 2005), p. A25.

62. U.S. Census Bureau, *Statistical Abstract of the United States* (Washington, DC: US GPO, 2008), Table 564.

63. Stephanie Strom, "Charities Trying Mergers to Improve Bottom Line," *New York Times* (November 11, 2007), p. A18.

64. Stephanie Strom, "Foundations Set Record for Giving in '07," *New York Times* (May 2, 2008), p. A13.

65. Jacqueline Salmon, "Foundations Anxious over Bill on Giving," *Washington Post* (July 8, 2003), p. A3.

66. Stephanie Strom, "Foundations Hire Ex-Lawmaker to Lobby against a Bill," *New York Times* (May 29, 2003), p. A17.

67. Teresa Odendahl, *Charity Begins at Home* (New York: Basic Books, 1990), pp. 3, 245.

68. Ibid., p. 49.

69. Ibid., p. 232.

70. Richard Morin, "Nonprofit, Faith-Based Groups Near Top of Poll on Solving Social Woes," *Washington Post* (February 1, 2001), p. A19.

71. Jeanne Bell, Richard Moyers, and Timothy Wolfred, *Daring to Lead 2006* (Washington, DC: Meyer Foundation, 2007), p. 3.

72. Shaila Dewan and Kevin Sack, "A Safety-Net Hospital Falls into Financial Crisis," *New York Times* (January 8, 2008), p. A1.

73. Ceci Connolly, "Tax-Exempt Hospitals, Practices Challenged," *Washington Post* (January 29, 2005), p. A1.

74. Ceci Connolly, "Forcing a Look at Hospitals' Mission," *Washington Post* (August 22, 2005), p. A3.

75. W. Harrison Wellford and Janne Gallagher, *Charity and the Competition Challenge* (Washington, DC: National Assembly of National Voluntary Health and Social Welfare Organizations, 1987), pp. 13–15.

76. Anne Swardson, "Hill Taking New Look at Nonprofits," *Washington Post* (June 21, 1987), p. F-9.

77. Jonathan Cohn, "Uncharitable?" *New York Times Magazine* (December 19, 2004), p. 55.

78. William Schambra, "What Philanthropists Expect from Nonprofits," comments during a panel discussion at Gallaudet University, Washington, DC, December 2, 2004.

79. William Schambra, "The New Politics of Philanthropy," *American Outlook Today* (December 4, 2003), p. 22.

80. Marvin Olasky, *The Tragedy of American Compassion* (Washington, DC: Regenery Gateway, 1992); *Renewing American Compassion* (New York: Free Press, 1996).

81. Hanna Rosin, "Putting Faith in a Social Service Role," *Washington Post* (May 5, 2000), p. A1.

82. Alan Cooperman, "Bush Touts Grants to Religious Charities," *Washington Post* (March 10, 2006), p. A5.

83. Alan Cooperman, "Bush's Faith Plan Faces Judgment," *Washington Post* (October 20, 2005), p. A25.

84. David Kuo and John DiIulio, "The Faith to Outlast Politics," *New York Times* (January 29, 2008), p. A27.

85. Alan Cooperman, "Faith-Based Charities May Not Be Better, Study Indicates," *Washington Post* (May 25, 2003), p. A7.

86. Bill Shore, *The Cathedral Within* (New York: Random House, 1999).

87. "Our Donations at Work," (San Francisco, CREDO, March 20, 2008).

88. Peter Samuelson, "The Robin Hood Effect," *Privilege* (November 2004), p. 1.

89. Robert Putnam, "The Prosperous Community," *The American Prospect* no. 13 (Spring 1993), p. 1.

90. Terry Neal, "Ex-Lawmaker Refuses to Be Boxed In," *Washington Post* (January 10, 1998), p. A8.

91. R. Baker, "The Ecumenist," *The American Prospect* (January 17, 2000), p. 28.

92. Howard Karger, *Shortchanged: Life and Debt in the Fringe Economy* (San Francisco: Berrett-Koehler, 2006).

93. "CDFIs Side-by-Side," (Philadelphia: National Community Capital Association, 2001), p. 48.

94. David Bornstein, *How to Change the World* (New York: Oxford University Press, 2004).

95. Elizabeth Malkin, "Microloans, Big Profits," *New York Times* (April 5, 2008), p. B1.

96. Stephanie Strom, "Make Money, Save the World," *New York Times* (May 6, 2007), p. BU1.

97. Jonathan Rauch, "'This is Not Charity'," *The Atlantic* (October 2007), p. 76.

98. Philip Rucker, "After Tasting Success Early He's Looking to Give Back," *Washington Post* (April 20, 2008), p. C1.

CHAPTER 7

Privatization and
Human Service Corporations

*T*his chapter reviews the privatization of social welfare, a dynamic that has accelerated in recent decades. Historically, much social welfare has been provided by the private not-for-profit sector, and many nonprofits contract with government to provide social services. Since the 1980s, however, conservatives have called for downsizing government, in the process shifting service responsibility to the private sector, providing opportunities to the for-profit sector. Increasing demand for services has further propelled the commercial social welfare sector. A prospective on eldercare, for example, notes that "current economic conditions, combined with the growing need for personal care, has fostered rapid expansion in senior housing, assisted living facilities, continuing care retirement communities and other housing arrangements where a number of social supports and services are available as part of their monthly payment."[1] Most eldercare providers are for-profit, and their fortunes will increase with the retirement of 77 million baby-boomers.

Historically, progressive business leaders have made important contributions to the health and welfare of their employees by envisaging utopian work environments and pioneering the provision of benefits to employees. Business leaders were also instrumental in fashioning early governmental welfare policies, including the Social Security Act. More recently, emphasis on the "social responsibility" of corporations has encouraged business leaders to assess the broader implications of corporate activities. Corporations also shape social welfare policy by influencing the political process and subsidizing policy institutes. Proprietary firms have become well established in several **human services** markets: nursing care, hospital management, managed medical care, child care, life/continuing care, and corrections. Finally, in this chapter we consider collective bargaining as a response to privatization. Health and human service professionals have been reluctant to join unions, primarily because they fear doing so would taint their professional status. Yet continuing privatization means that unions may be the only aggregate defense for professionals who have become employees of profit-making health and human service corporations.

As a function of public dissatisfaction with governmental social programs, increasing reliance on the private sector to finance and deliver social services has emerged as an important theme in American social welfare. **Privatization,** as this idea has been termed, addresses the problem of the proper relationship between the public and private spheres of the national culture. In this case, the concept of privatization has come to involve "the idea that private is invariably more efficient than public, that government ought to stay out of as many realms as possible, and that government should contract out tasks to private firms or give people vouchers rather than provide them services directly."[2] That government should not hold a monopoly on social welfare is not a novel idea. Even liberal policy analysts entertained ways in which the private sector could complement governmental welfare initiatives.[3] Liberal proponents of social programs are often willing to concede a viable role to the private sector—even an innovative role—but insist that government must be the primary instrument to advance social justice. Conservatives see the proper balance as one in which the private sector is the primary source of protection against social and economic calamity, and they believe that government activity should be held in reserve. According to conservative doctrine, government can deploy the "safety net" of social programs, but these should provide benefits only as a last resort.

A clear articulation of the conservative vision of reinforcing the role of the private sector in social affairs appeared in the 1988 report of the President's Commission on Privatization. "In the United States . . . the growth of government has been based on the political and economic design that emerged from the Progressive movement around the turn of this century," noted the report. "The American privatization movement has represented in significant part a reaction against the themes and results of Progressive thought."[4] Specifically, the report targeted government social programs and the professional administrators who manage them as the undesirable consequences of the Progressive movement—consequences that could be corrected by privatization. The implications of this analysis are broad: Not only should benefits be removed from government and provided by the private sector, but the administration of social programs should also be removed from the public sector and placed under private auspices. Accordingly, the President's Commission on Privatization identified three "techniques for the privatization of service delivery": (1) selling government assets; (2) contracting with private firms to provide goods and services previously offered by government; and (3) using vouchers, whereby the government would distribute coupons authorizing

spotlight 7.1

Techniques for the Privatization of Service Delivery

The President's Commission on Privatization identifies three techniques for the privatization of service delivery:

1. Selling government assets

2. Contracting with private firms to provide goods and services previously offered by the government

3. Using vouchers, whereby the government would distribute coupons authorizing private providers to receive reimbursement from the government for the goods and services they have provided

---

private providers to receive reimbursement from the government for the goods and services they had provided.[5] Although all these methods had previously been used, the report characterized social welfare as a "zero-sum game" in which an advantage to one party is at the expense of another.

In *Reinventing Government,* David Osborne proposed a more integrated and dynamic relationship between the public and private sectors: government should establish the objectives of public policy, assigning the execution to the private sector.[6] Osborne tapped into a theme that had been integral to U.S. social programs: reliance on the private sector to deliver the goods. Nowhere had this been more evident than in health care. When the social engineers of the War on Poverty crafted Medicare and Medicaid, they elected to reimburse private providers rather than deploy a government-owned health care system, such as the Veterans Administration. The result, as we shall see momentarily, was the emergence of a for-profit industry in health care that was uniquely American. Indeed, when the Clinton administration presented its Health Security Act, it not only conceded the existence of commercial health providers but structured the plan to amplify their position in the market.

Thus, views of privatization vary. On the one hand privatization can be viewed as load-shedding, on the other as a contractual relationship between the public and private sectors. In either event, there is no question that this relationship is being reassessed. "Governments in the United States spend roughly half a trillion dollars per year paying public workers to deliver goods and services directly," observed John Donahue. "If only one-quarter of this total turned out to be suitable for privatization, at an average savings of, say, 25 percent—and neither figure is recklessly optimistic—the public would save over $30 billion."[7] Such savings could be used to lower taxes or to extend existing programs. As state and local jurisdictions struggle to justify increasing service demand with static resources, privatization is an option that many local officials pursue.

Privatization Issues

Many health and human service professionals have trepidations about privatization. Liberal social activists have objected to privatization citing research that identifies risks in relying on the private sector for certain activities. The irony in such a critical stance toward privatization is that many professionals opt for private practice as a method of service delivery, an arrangement through which government subsidizes entrepreneurs. Thus, private practice is condoned, but privatization of governmental activities is met with skepticism. This issue raises a profound concern for the social work profession: To the extent that social workers engage in private practice, there are fewer human service professionals in the public sector to work with people presenting more serious disorders. As a result, what limited influence social work has is invested in promoting its self-interest at the expense of the poor—a point underscored by the late-Harry Specht and Mark Courtney in *Unfaithful Angels:*

...there has been an increasing tendency of the [social work] profession to use its political power to support licensing of clinical social workers and third-party payments for social workers who are so licensed, to the relative neglect of efforts to improve the lot of social workers employed in the public social services and their clients.[8]

For many human service professionals, then, private practice represents a retreat from a service ethic that transcends self-interest: the public's welfare.

The tension between private gain and public interest surfaced in provisions of the 1996 welfare reform act that allowed states to contract with for-profit firms to not only provide social services but also determine eligibility and benefits. Although privatization was evident in child support enforcement and in some sectors of child welfare, it had not been employed in public assistance. Not surprisingly, some corporations stood to make considerable profits from the privatization of public assistance. At the time Nina Bernstein observed, "The new [1996] welfare bill is still a matter of confusion in statehouses and city streets. But to some companies it looks like the business opportunity of a lifetime."[9] In the decade to follow, consulting firms such as MAXIMUS flourished. Similarly, several corporations emerged to provide managed care for recipients of Medicare, Medicaid, and State Children's Health Insurance Program (SCHIP). The introduction of the prescription drug benefit to Medicare became a gold mine for pharmaceutical companies.

Opponents to welfare privatization voice several criticisms. First, if a corporation's profits are linked to reducing the welfare rolls, the incentive to deny aid will be significant. According to Henry Freedman of the Center for Social Welfare Policy and Law, "No company can be expected to protect the interests of the needy at the expense of its bottom line, least of all a publicly traded corporation with a fiduciary duty to maximize shareholder profits."[10] Clearly, corporations will have strong incentives to use the letter of the law to ration services to improve their profits and performance.[11] Much of this fiscal incentive will be based on the fixed-price nature of government contracts, which will include penalties for a failure to perform. Second, corporations are apt to reduce personnel costs. They may cut staff and replace full-time professionals and managers with contingent, lower-wage workers. As a way to control salaries, corporations may try to dislodge public sector unions where they exist, and to prohibit them where they do not. Third, privatization could encourage corporations to use technology to save money, such as replacing welfare offices and state workers in rural areas with automated kiosks similar to automated banking. This would have enormous implications for people who are not technologically sophisticated or who would benefit from face-to-face services. Fourth, government would find itself in a quandary if commercial providers bailed out of contracts. At worst, corporations could declare bankruptcy, effectively voiding their contractual obligations, or commercial providers could reduce the availability of services as a way to leverage more resources. Finally, corporations with a major presence in a given market are in a strong position to shape social policy, defining such factors as eligibility for program benefits and allocations. Oligopolies in several markets have already emerged raising the prospect of a human services-industrial complex that shapes social policy toward its own benefit. All of these corporate strategies would have a major impact on the quality of services delivered.

A new question in the debate on the balance between private and public responsibility for welfare was introduced with the recent emergence of health and human service corporations: If government is to contract out its social welfare obligations, can the business sector pick up the slack? Logically, proponents of privatization have two options: the nonprofit, voluntary sector (Chapter 6) and the for-profit, **corporate sector.** Both sectors are well established in U.S. social welfare. Since President Lyndon Johnson's Great Society programs, government has been contracting out services through both nonprofit and for-profit providers. The for-profit corporate sector capitalized on the contracting-out provisions of the Medicare and Medicaid programs. At the same time, through the purchase-of-service concept introduced in Title XX, nonprofit agencies became contractors providing a range of social services on behalf of public welfare departments.

Unfortunately, studies comparing the performance of these sectors have been few and their findings debatable.[12] In the absence of definitive results showing the advantages of one sector over another, the privatization debate has become heated. Advocates of *voluntarization*, or reliance on the voluntary sector to assume more of the responsibility for welfare, point to its historical contribution to the national culture, the rootedness of its agencies in the community, and the altruistic motives behind its programs. Advocates of voluntarization received a boost when the second Bush presidency advocated "faith-based" initiatives in social welfare. Proponents of *corporatization*, or dependence on the corporate sector to provide welfare, argue that corporations offer more cost-effective administration, are more responsive to consumer demand, and pay taxes. Corporatists scored a major victory in the 2003 Medicare reforms that introduced the prescription drug benefit. Whether voluntarists or corporatists prevail in the privatization debate rests largely on the ability of each party to manipulate the social policy process in its favor. Whatever the outcome, this process is certain to be lengthy and complex, as one might expect with the remaking of an institutional structure that has become as essential as social welfare is in the United States. And whether voluntarization or corporatization defines the future of social welfare, privatization has already highlighted several important issues.

Commercialization

For welfare professionals, the idea of subjecting human need to the economic marketplace is often problematic. In one of the earliest treatments of the matter, Richard Titmuss's *The Gift Relationship* explored the differences in the ways nations manage their blood banks. Unlike the United Kingdom, blood in the United States is "treated in laws as an article of commerce;" that is, rules of the market affect the supply and quality of blood. Titmuss observed the growth of blood and plasma businesses with alarm, because these businesses bought blood from a population that was often characterized by poverty and poor health. Quite apart from the health hazard posed by a blood supply derived from such a population—a hazard highlighted by AIDS—Titmuss was concerned that the profit motive would disrupt the voluntary impulses of community life. "There is growing disquiet in the United States," he observed, that "expanding blood programs . . . are driving out the voluntary system."[13] Indeed, a majority of blood banks in the United States are commercial.[14]

With the passage of Medicare and Medicaid in 1965, the federal government was placed in the position of reimbursing and regulating a private industry that evolved rapidly. In both programs, scandals were exposed through which billions of dollars have been billed fraudulently and patients neglected, sometimes with fatal consequences.[15] Once for-profit providers gain a significant share of a market, even nonprofit providers are likely to adopt commercial practices. In 2006 Congress convened hearings about some nonprofit hospitals which, instead of providing charity care congruent with their tax exempt status, hired collection agencies to harass former patients into paying for their care. Also under scrutiny were executive salaries. In 2004 the salary and benefits of the president of New York-Presbyterian Hospital equaled $5.2 million, while that of the president of Montefiore Medical Center in the Bronx equaled $1.8 million.[16]

A poignant problem with commercialization relates to those tax-exempt providers who transition from nonprofit to for-profit status. Before the commercialization of health care, the largest health insurer was Blue Cross–Blue Shield; however, many state Blue Cross–Blue Shield plans have converted to commercial status. The transition from non-profit to for-profit status requires the approval of state regulators, often elected officials who are concerned that low-income citizens might be left uninsured. Consequently, states often require such companies to establish health care foundations as a condition for becoming corporate. When Wellpoint and Anthem merged in California, for example, the companies offered $265 million, much of it to assure the continuation of health care to underserved communities.[17] Subsequently, such foundations become an important resource for those who wish to diminish inequities in health care.

Commercialization has not been confined to health care. Since Milwaukee pioneered school choice as an option for public school students, privatization has become a volatile issue in education.[18] Consistently opposed by teachers' unions, school choice has been supported by significant majorities of minority parents. Recognizing the problems inherent in inner-city, public education, liberals proposed their own alternatives, initially magnet schools within the purview of public education, but subsequently, independent charter schools.[19] Not only are private charter schools a regular feature of the urban educational landscape, but several city school systems have contracted out the management of poorly performing schools to for-profit companies. Thus, as objectionable as market-related practices may be, commercialization is a reality that liberals cannot simply dismiss out of a sense of moral indignation.

Preferential Selection

The application of market principles to client service introduces strong incentives for providers to differentiate clients according to their effect on organizational performance. Such selection can be at variance with professional standards, which emphasize the client's need for service over organizational considerations. But the marketplace tends to penalize providers that are imprudent about client selection, at the same time rewarding providers that are more discriminating. The practice of choosing clients according to criteria of organizational performance—as opposed to client need—is known as **preferential selection.** Under marketplace conditions, providers that do not practice preferential selection are bound to serve a disproportionate number of clients with serious problems and with less ability to pay the cost of care, thereby running deficits. By contrast, providers that select clients who have less serious problems and who can cover the cost of care often claim surpluses. For example, an analysis of psychiatric patients admitted to a public and a private hospital found that the latter selected patients of higher social status. The researchers concluded that "patients in the marginal/uncredentialed social class were comparatively more likely to be admitted to state mental hospitals than to private hospitals."[20]

Critics of privatization complain that creaming the client population through preferential selection is unethical and should be prohibited. Simply ruling out the practice is, however, easier said than done. Accusations of preferential selection are not new; private nonprofit agencies were accused of denying services to welfare recipients long before proprietary firms became established.[21] In Denver, where public hospitals have sustained heavy deficits by caring for a disproportionate burden of the medically indigent, the problem has become critical. Jane Collins, director of clinical social work for the Denver Department of Health and Hospitals, described public hospitals in the city as having become "social dumps."[22] Reports of dumping when life-threatening injuries are evident have drawn the ire of many human service professionals. In some cases, private hospitals have transferred indigent patients with traumatic injuries to public facilities without providing proper medical care, thus contributing to the deaths of several patients. When the federal government prohibited such transfers, many hospitals responded by closing their emergency rooms rather than incur the cost of uncompensated care.

Preferential selection on the part of a large number of providers is likely to be adopted by others who wish to remain competitive. In analyzing the practice in health care, a team of researchers from Harvard University and the American Medical Association noted that "in the same way that competition from for-profit providers leads to reduction in access, the more competitive the market for hospital services generally, the more likely are all hospitals in that market to discourage admissions of Medicaid and uninsured patients."[23] In other words, even nonprofit providers—who are exempt from taxes because they contribute to the community's welfare—are compelled to adopt the discriminatory practices of for-profit providers in a competitive market, unless the nonprofits are willing to underwrite the losses that more costly clients represent to for-profit providers. "When competitive pressures are great," researchers from Yale and Harvard universities have noted, "the behavior of for-profit and nonprofit institutions often converge."[24]

Cost-Effectiveness

Proponents of privatization frequently cite the discipline imposed on organizational performance by a competitive environment as a rationale for market reforms in social welfare. A competitive environment provides strong incentives for organizations to adopt cost-effective practices that reduce waste. This claim has led to a handful of studies of for-profit versus nonprofit service providers. In a comprehensive review of the issue, the Institute of Medicine of the National Academy of Sciences concluded in the mid-1980s that there was "no evidence to support the common belief that investor-owned organizations are less costly or more efficient than are not-for-profit organizations."[25] Later, Robert Kuttner summarized analyses conducted by an association of nonprofit hospitals and found that "investor-owned hospitals in 1994 were 13.7 percent more expensive on a charge basis than nonprofit and public hospitals." Again, not only were for-profit hospitals more expensive, but they also provided less care to the poor, admitting only half as many Medicaid patients as nonprofit hospitals. Another analysis of proprietary hospitals by the nonprofit hospital association found that investor-owned hospitals were 30 percent more expensive than not-for-profit hospitals.[26] A study of 14,423 nursing homes found that even though public facilities had a significantly higher proportion of Medicaid patients, they, along with nonprofit providers, performed better than their for-profit counterparts.[27]

Moreover, the promise of cost containment through privatization has not been borne out, and this presents an enormous problem for the governmental

A competitive environment provides strong incentive for organizations to adopt cost-effective practices that reduce waste.

sector. Under a privatized system, government is in a weak position to control the prices charged by contracting agencies unless it is prepared to deploy its own set of public institutions, thereby avoiding the private sector altogether. A good example is provided by the Medicare program. Through Medicare the government subsidizes health care for elderly people, most of which is provided by the private sector. In response to runaway Medicare costs, in 1983 Congress enacted the **Diagnostic Related Groups (DRGs)** prospective payment plan, whereby hospitals are reimbursed fixed amounts for medical procedures. Three years after the DRG system was in place, the Congressional Budget Office reported that hospitals had increased their surplus attributed to Medicare by 15.7 percent during 1985. This surplus occurred despite a reduction in the number of Medicare patients admitted to hospitals.[28] In this instance, strengthened government regulation failed to contain the escalating costs of Medicare, but the possibility of the federal government nationalizing health care was inconceivable.

Standardization

Commercial provision of human services allows the wealthy to purchase concierge care while the poor are consigned to substandard services because government reimbursements are at such low levels that they encourage standardization. In this way, privatization can induce human service organizations to adopt an industrial mode of provision in which the accepted measure of success is not necessarily high quality of service rendered but the maximum number of people processed at the lowest cost. Thus, corporations can generate surpluses, essential for investor-owned facilities, by reducing the quality of care and lowering labor costs. Because the logic of the market dictates that the goal of production is to process the largest number of people at the lowest possible cost, the **standardization** of services is an important method for lowering organizational expenses. Such uniformity of care has become an issue in the nursing home industry. Because Medicaid regulations stipulate standards of care, nursing homes deriving a large portion of their revenues from Medicaid are induced to standardize care for all patients. A business professor noted the implications of standardized care:

> The nursing home industry's identical treatment of everyone creates a one-class social system for all patients. This constitutes a denial of the affluent person's rights to purchase the quality of life that had been his or hers until stricken with illness or infirmity. This phenomenon represents creeping socialism of a major order, and creates an atmosphere ripe for either legal or market reprisal.[29]

That standardization of care within an industry dominated by for-profit firms would be equated with socialism is perhaps the best measure of the acuity of the problem.

Under these circumstances, life care—the service offered by the continuing-care retirement community—has emerged as an attractive alternative to the nursing home. Under life care plans, residents can purchase cottages or apartments in self-contained communities, at prices comparable to that of a new home, which provide a range of human services. In many respects the life care community provides more affluent residents an opportunity to purchase a higher level of long-term care. Many continuing-care facilities boast such amenities as wall-to-wall carpeting, maid service, and designer landscaping. "Already, the facility has shown its first in-house movie . . . and soon residents will be soaking up steam in the saunas, relaxing in the Jacuzzi, exercising on the mechanical bicycles, or browsing in the library," noted a visitor to one facility.[30] Found in the more posh life care communities are cocktail lounges, billiards rooms, sports facilities, and elegantly furnished restaurants serving continental cuisine. Amenities such as these "provide a lifestyle of grace and activity for seniors with the ability to pay for it," observed an industry reporter.[31] "We sell a style of life," explained one corporate executive.[32]

The prospect of extensive proprietary involvement in life care troubles some analysts. Lloyd Lewis, director of a nonprofit life care community, feared that "well-funded proprietary interests" would "drain off the more financially able segment of our older population, widening the gap between the 'haves' and the 'have nots'."[33] To a significant extent this has already occurred. Robert Ball, former Commissioner of the Social Security Administration, noted that even life care communities operating under not-for-profit auspices are often beyond the means of "the poor, the near poor, or even the low-income elderly."[34] As human service corporations divert capital to care for those who represent profit margins, economic and political support for the care of those less fortunate diminishes. "Those who cannot gain admission to [a private] institution will be forced into boarding homes . . . or bootleg boarding homes," suggested one critic. "These boarding homes will be filled with what are literally social rejects. We're reverting back to the way the industry was in the fifties and sixties."[35] Left unchecked, this pattern is likely to divide long-term care into two clearly demarcated systems, with the affluent enjoying the generous care of completely—some would say excessively—provisioned life care communities and the elderly poor dependent on the squalid institutions willing to accept government payment for their care.

Oligopolization

The privatization of human services invites **oligopolization:** the control of a market by few providers as organizations seek to reduce competition by buying their competitors. Within the corporate sector three waves of acquisition can be identified: acquisitions affecting long-term care, hospital management, and health maintenance organizations (HMOs). As firms gain control of major shares of markets, they are in a strong position to leverage influence through trade associations to shape social policy. Notably, the Health Insurance Association of America spent millions of dollars to defeat the Clinton administration's 1993 Health Security Act—even though 40 million Americans were then without health insurance.[36] A decade later, debate about prescription drug benefits and universal health care funneled tens of millions of dollars into lobbying; five of the top twenty lobbying organizations in 2007 focused on health care: Pharmaceutical Research and Manufacturers of America, $22.7 million; American Medical Association, $22.1 million; American Hospital Association, $19.7 million; Amgen, $16.3 million; and Pfizer, $13.8 million.[37] Oligopolization of human services presents a daunting specter in that a small number of wealthy and powerful trade associations are in a strong position to shape social policy to conform to their interests. Within health care, this development has led Arnold Relman, former editor of *The New England Journal of Medicine,* to voice alarm at the growing influence of the "new medical-industrial complex" in defining health policy in the United States.[38]

The medical-industrial complex was instrumental in crafting the 2003 Medicare reforms in a manner that served its interests. Central to the passage of Medicare reform was Thomas A. Scully, the Director of the Centers for Medicare and Medicaid Services (CMS). Before taking the helm of CMS, Scully was president of the Federation of American Hospitals (FAH), a trade association of for-profit hospitals, for which he was paid $675,000 per year. At CMS, his salary was only $134,000 per year, so it is not surprising that Scully announced a swift exit after two-and-one-half years of federal service during which he helped pass the 2003 Medicare reforms,[39] battening the act with subsidies to health care corporations. Immediately after passage of the legislation, he left government service to work for Alston & Bird, an Atlanta law firm specializing in health care, for an undisclosed salary, though one that probably exceeds what he made at FAH.[40] Within a year, Scully was back on Capitol Hill lobbying on behalf of the Renal Leadership Council, a kidney dialysis trade association. Joining him were other Alston & Bird acquisitions: Colin Roskey, former adviser to the Senate Finance Committee, and Marc Scheineson, former associate commissioner of the Food and Drug Administration. Alston & Bird's head of DC operations and former Clinton White House official, Marilyn Yeager, stated, "It's a very nice team here. They have a lot of expertise."[41]

The 2003 Medicare reforms would have been chalked up as another Republican maneuver to co-opt a Democratic issue, had not the program's chief actuary, Richard Foster, revealed that his attempts to inform Congress of the program's true costs—$551.5 billion over 10 years—had been suppressed by Scully. Foster's expos, was newsworthy because the Medicare reforms had passed by a close margin, and many members of Congress voted in favor only after being assured that the health reforms were within the $400 billion parameter stated by the White House. Federal law prohibits the obstruction of communication between federal employees and Congress,[42] but that did not stop Scully from blocking access to Foster's memo explicating the more realistic costs of Medicare reform. "If Rick Foster gives that to you," a House Democratic aide who had requested the memo was told by Scully, "I'll fire him so fast his head will spin."[43] Foster, a career civil servant, stuck to his story, accusing the White House of having full knowledge of his projections, but favoring lower estimates generated by other agencies.[44] A subsequent House inquiry failed to clarify the matter, in large part because the Republican leadership was unwilling to grant subpoena power to the committee, making testimony voluntary. When the House committee asked Scully to testify about the suppression of Foster's projection, he said he was "unable to appear" because he was traveling.[45] Lacking a majority in the House at the time, Democrats were unable to get a full hearing on the scandal. By the time Democrats regained control of Congress, the prescription drug benefit had been introduced, millions of Medicare recipients were receiving medication, and the pharmaceutical trade associations were prepared to oppose any reforms to Part D. Its tawdry passage notwithstanding, the Medicare prescription drug benefit was a done deal.

The Challenge of Privatization

For many health and human service professionals, privatization is contrary to social welfare. Advocates of government's responsibility for ensuring social and economic equality contend that privatization is nothing less than a retreat from a century of hard-won gains in social programs. This case is argued cogently by Pulitzer Prize–winning sociologist Paul Starr:

> A large-scale shift of public services to private providers would contribute to further isolating the least advantaged, since private firms have strong incentives to skim off the best clients and most profitable services. The result would often be a residual, poorer public sector providing services of last resort. Such institutions would be even less attractive as places to work than they are today. And their worsening difficulties would no doubt be cited as confirmation of the irremediable incompetence of public managers and inferiority of public services. Public institutions already suffer from this vicious circle; most forms of privatization would intensify it.[46]

For defenders of government social programs, the problems inherent in privatization—commercialization, client creaming, inflated costs, standardization, and oligopolization—make it a poor vehicle for advancing social welfare. Most profoundly, privatization reinforces a tendency in market economies to evolve dual structures of benefits, services, and opportunities: adequate and varied services for the affluent, substandard and uniform services for the poor. As Robert Kuttner has pointed out, "in a purely for-profit enterprise or system, there is no place for uncompensated care, unprofitable admissions, research, education, or public health activities—all chronic money losers from a strictly business viewpoint."[47] For many human service advocates, the purpose of social welfare is to correct for the inherent tendency of markets to direct resources toward the affluent and away from the poor. From this left-leaning perspective, the idea of privatization of social welfare violates the essential meaning of social welfare because it is a government function.

Yet increased reliance on the private sector at a time when public social programs are under assault is a reality that must be faced by those concerned about social welfare. In the absence of a politically effective left and the diminishing influence of a progressive labor movement, there appears little chance of launching new government social programs that conform to traditional liberal priorities. Insofar as corporations have assumed ever larger responsibilities for social program activities, such as Medicaid, SCHIP, child welfare, and mental health, welfare professionals have little choice but to concede privatization as a basis for welfare provision. In some instances, private sector analogues to public services have demonstrated surprising success. In New York and Connecticut an innovative program called America Works has evolved through the private sector:

> Each year the company finds jobs for more than 700 of the state's hard-core unemployed, 68 percent of whom are (as a result) permanently weaned from the welfare rolls. The company gets paid only after the former welfare recipient has been working for four months and its $5,000 fee is less than half of what it costs New York State to support an average welfare family of three. All told, America Works is saving taxpayers approximately $4.5 million annually and providing many of the state's hard-core unemployed with meaningful work.[48]

Upon closer inspection, there are strong arguments in favor of privatization as a strategy for promoting social welfare. Through commercial loans and issuance of stock, for-profit organizations have faster access to capital than does the governmental sector (which requires a lengthy public expenditure authorization process) or the voluntary sector (which relies on arduous fund-raising campaigns) for purposes of program expansion. The private sector has also been the source of important innovations in programs and organizational administration that have often become models for effective administration.[49] Hence, welfare-conscious administrators have missed opportunities for promoting social welfare by ignoring opportunities for professional practice associated with privatization.

Privatization will continue to challenge the moral and rational impulses of human service professionals. "The impact of the privatization movement, broadly understood, is only beginning to be felt," noted the President's Commission on Privatization in 1992, "Privatization in this broad sense may well be seen by future historians as one of the most important developments in the American political and economic life of the late 20th century."[50] This has been a conspicuous development in U.S. health care. As noted in Table 7.1, private sector health organizations have become too large to ignore.

How health and human service professionals choose to respond to the challenge of privatization—whether reactively or innovatively—will be critical for the future of U.S. social welfare. Privatization may come to be a rallying cry for defenders of established programs that have been discredited as being wasteful and inflexible and currying the favors of special interests; or privatization may ultimately mean discovering new ways to exploit the social carrying capacity of the private sector. As David Donnison suggested, welfare professionals would be wiser to reconsider their aversion to the private sector and to try to find the "progressive potential in privatization."[51]

Unions and the Private Sector

Unions of health and welfare professionals are one response to privatization. Since the Great Depression, social welfare professionals have organized collectively in order to obtain better wages and benefits, to enhance working conditions, and to improve services

Table 7.1

Private Sector Health Providers, 2006

Entity/Auspice	Annual Revenues	Number of Employees
UnitedHealth/Corporate	$75.4 billion	67,000
Wellpoint/Corporate	61.1 billion	41,700
Kaiser/Secular Nonprofit	34.4 billion	156,000
HCA/Corporate	25.5 billion	186,000
Humana/Corporate	25.3 billion	25,000
Ascension/Catholic	12.3 billion	106,000
Catholic Healthcare West	6.7 billion	50,000
Trinity Health/Catholic	6.1 billion	45,800

Source: Hoover's Inc., http://hoovers.com/free/.

to clients. Two pioneers of U.S. social welfare, Bertha Capen Reynolds and Mary van Kleek, vigorously urged social welfare workers to view unions as a vehicle for social justice. Today, members of the Bertha Capen Reynolds Society advocate collective bargaining in order to empower human service professionals. Social workers in the public sector often hold memberships in unions—most often in the American Federation of State, County, and Municipal Employees (AFSCME), with 1.4 million members in 2008, or in the Service Employees International Union (SEIU) with 1.9 million members in 2008. Altogether about one in four social workers belong to a collective bargaining unit.[52] Because of the dispersion of social work activities, however, social workers have been less successful than nurses or teachers in using unions to achieve their ends.

Collective bargaining is the foundation of the union process. Collective bargaining is face-to-face negotiation between unionized employees and management for the purpose of arriving at a union contract. Such bargaining is supposed to be done in good faith, and the legal rights of workers are protected by the National Labor Relations Act. If these rights are attenuated, workers can petition the National Labor Relations Board to address grievances. The ultimate power of unions is to exercise the right to strike when the bargaining process breaks down. Theoretically, both parties have an interest in a successful collective bargaining process, because strikes hurt both union members and their employers. Collective bargaining can also address professional issues such as caseload size, educational benefits like tuition reimbursement, conference release time and reimbursements, payment for professional dues and subscriptions, and flexible work hours. One union leader noted, "To the professional—the teacher or caseworker—things like class size and caseload size become as important as the number of hours in a shift is to the blue collar worker."[53] In one union organizing campaign, for example, caseload size, career ladders and training, pay equity, and classification downgrading were the primary issues. In a nonprofit mental health clinic, safe working conditions, benefits for part-time workers, workloads, and participation in agency decision making were the focus of organizing efforts.[54]

A significant question before human service professionals has been the extent to which union objectives are consistent with professional values. Despite the constructive influence that unions could potentially exert in response to workplace problems in social welfare, social workers have approached unions with great apprehension. Opponents to collective bargaining contend that (1) unions cost employees money; (2) strike losses are never retrieved; (3) even when they are not purposely kept uninformed by union leadership, members have little voice in union affairs; (4) bureaucratic union hierarchies control the economic destiny of members; (5) union corruption is rampant; (6) union opposition to management attempts to increase productivity arrests organizational growth; (7) union featherbedding results in unneeded employees and unnecessary payroll expenses; (8) union activities foster conflict rather than collaboration; and (9) unions fail to extrapolate the effects of wage increases on future employment, inflation, and taxes.

A fundamental concern among social welfare professionals revolves around the ultimate tactic that unions can bring to employer–employee relations—job actions, particularly strikes. For social workers who have pledged to make client welfare a priority, the prospect of denying services as a result of job actions makes union membership and professional commitment contradictory. In covering a strike by Local 1199 of the Retail Drug Employees Union which included the social work staffs of more than 50 hospitals and nursing homes, Dena Fisher wrote:

> Standards for professional practice conflict with the [NASW] Code of Ethics with regard to behavior during a labor strike when the prescribed behavior includes withholding service, failing to terminate clients properly, and picketing activity directed toward consumers. . . . The problem is that participation in a strike is a nonprofessional activity. . . . Standards of professional behavior conflict with union membership requirements.[55]

Yet proponents of union membership cite ways in which collective bargaining can complement professional objectives. In an attempt to encourage a better relationship with professional social workers, Jerry Wurf, former AFSCME president, stated that:

> AFSCME's involvement [with social issues] is part of a larger commitment to improving public services and programs. But more importantly, these vital efforts prove the true mission of a labor organization to be closely linked to that of social work. AFSCME's growth in the last decade was due in large part to its role as a social missionary. This precious pursuit has undoubtedly been enhanced by the growing number of social workers in our ranks.[56]

As they have lost membership, unions have become more receptive to nonconfrontational methods to advance their objectives. Andy Stern, a caseworker who rose to the Presidency of SEIU, found job actions against employers inferior to alternative methods to advance his union's agenda. After losing a strike with the Beverly nursing home corporation, Stern convinced the company to sign a contract improving staff working conditions if SEIU convinced government to increase reimbursement to patients cared for by Beverly. In New Jersey, SEIU negotiated novel contracts with employers which were not binding until a majority of employers had also agreed, spreading the contract costs across a wide spectrum of companies.[57] SEIU's tactics have not been condoned by the AFL-CIO from which it had split. At a Michigan conference, SEIU members stormed a meeting of the California Nurses Association (CNA), an AFL-CIO affiliate, over organizing nurses in Ohio. In light of SEIU's failure to organize Ohio nurses after three years, the CNA dispatched organizers to Ohio, a move resented by the SEIU. The ensuing altercation sent one union member to the hospital.[58]

The few studies that examined the issue found little incongruity between the loyalties of social workers who belong to unions. Leslie Alexander and his colleagues studied 84 union members with MSW degrees and found that "they view their work as solidly professional and, for the most part, do not see unionism and professionalism as incompatible."[59] Ernie Lightman reported similar findings when studying 121 randomly chosen professional social workers in Toronto, Canada. According to Lightman, "the vast majority saw no incompatibility; indeed, many felt unionization may facilitate service goals, offsetting workplace bureaucracy."[60] Reporting on child welfare agencies in Pennsylvania and Illinois, Gary Shaffer found that "workers did not find unionism incompatible with their educational or professional goals."[61]

Such complementarity notwithstanding, the concept of social work "exceptionalism" pervades the debate about professionalism and unions. The exceptionalism premise implies that tasks performed by social workers are more important than those performed by many other workers, especially nonprofessionals, and that normal labor relations principles are therefore not applicable. Proponents of social work exceptionalism must address two matters: First, how is it that other semiprofessionals, such as teachers and nurses, have reconciled their professional priorities with union activities and become more powerful in the contexts of their work as a result? Are social service activities to be considered more essential than education or health care? Second, does the idea of social work exceptionalism contribute to the powerlessness of social workers? If social work places such value on the empowerment of clients, why should social workers not also be so empowered? The idea of social work's exceptionalism was put in bold relief in 1991 when members of Canada's Public Service Alliance—many of whom are social workers—participated in one of the largest strikes in the nation's history, inspired by the government's plan to reduce wage increases.[62] If Canadian human service professionals can reconcile professional and union differences, why is this a problem for U.S. social workers?

While social workers in the United States procrastinate about an alliance with unions, events such as privatization and government cuts in funding make the issue ever more urgent. Social workers and unions should be able to collaborate in problem solving, fostering a public debate on social issues and promoting class-aware groupings in an adverse social climate. Facilitating social change is a goal of several organizations, including Jobs with Justice. As Charles Heckscher points out, new approaches to unionization "are still in their infancy . . . [and] the rich variety of innovations being tried today has the potential to restore an essential pillar of labor's strength: the sense among the wider public that employee organization contributes to the general good."[63]

Corporate Welfare

The business community in the United States influences social welfare in several important ways. Benefit packages for employees, which are usually available to dependents, provide important health and welfare benefits to a large segment of the working population. Historically, this form of "welfare capitalism" has been an important complement to public social programs. "For much of the 20th century, indeed, the development of U.S. social policy has followed an identifiable second track of intervention, one to which scholars of the welfare state, orthodox or revisionist, have paid only limited attention," noted Jacob Hacker. "The legislative milestones along this track have not been large and highly prominent social programs, but public policies of diverse form—tax breaks, regulations, credit subsidies, and government insurance—designed to encourage and shape private responses to public social problems."[64] The implications of this are momentous. Once private sector activities are calculated as part of the national welfare effort, the United States is similar in scale to European nations. Politically, any welfare state with competing public and private sectors can evolve separate solutions to citizens' needs, evident in liberal defense of Social Security contemporaneous with conservative preference for private alternatives, such as 401(k) plans.[65]

Corporate philanthropy has sponsored important—and, in some cases, controversial—social welfare initiatives. Policy institutes reflecting the priorities of the business community have made substantial changes in U.S. "public philosophy." More recently, the corporate sector has begun to exploit the growing human service markets in hospital management, long-term care, health maintenance, child care, public welfare, and corrections. These instances reflect the significant role that the corporate sector has played in U.S. social welfare, a role that has been expanding rapidly.

Among welfare theorists, however, corporate activities have tended to be underappreciated. As discussed in Chapter 1, many progressive scholars attributed the cause of much social and economic dislocation to industrial capitalism, and thereby implicated capitalism's institutional representative, the corporation. Thus, the corporation was seen not as a source of relief but rather as the perpetrator of social and economic hardship. As a result, liberal theorists concluded that the government was the only institution capable of regulating capitalism and compensating the victims of its caprices. Welfare state ideology, as it evolved, left little room for the corporation, viewing it as the source of much suffering and as generally unwilling to pay its share of the tax burden to remediate the problems it had spawned. For example, advocacy groups such as the public interest research groups (PIRGs) associated with Ralph Nader and Citizens for Tax Justice regularly criticize the corporate sector for pursuing economic and political self-interest, sacrificing the general welfare in the process. Notorious examples of the sacrifice of civic values in pursuit of profits have been chronicled by liberal advocacy groups. These include the disruption, then abandonment, of Love Canal because of improper disposal of toxic waste; the exploitation of Mexican agricultural workers in the Southwest; the extortion of huge sums from New York City housing officials by landlords who provide single-room occupancy lodgings for the homeless; and the deceit of tobacco companies about the harmful effects of smoking. To corporate critics, chief executive officers (CEOs) flaunt their positions by commanding salaries way out of proportion to their productivity. When super-rich CEOs downsize production, lay off thousands of workers, and thereby decimate a local economy,[66] they become cultural pariahs. At the same time, few would doubt that wealth and status are enormously influential when wealthy executives leave private life and run for public office. "It's no accident that the Senate is a citadel of multi-millionaires," observed one longtime Washington journalist.[67]

Power and wealth notwithstanding, the corporate sector has made contributions to the **commonweal,** or public good. During the industrial era, major foundations were established that instituted important benchmarks in the development of the U.S. welfare state, and by the end of the twentieth century, minority Americans were making their mark in corporate philanthropy. Native American tribes contributed $35 million for the new Museum of the American Indian that opened in Washington, DC, in 2004. Jeong Kim used the sale proceeds from Yurie Systems for millions of dollars in aid to higher education. In 2003, African American publishing tycoon John Johnson contributed $4 million to Howard University's School of Communication.[68]

At this point, many welfare theorists began to reexamine the role of the corporate sector in U.S. social welfare. The concept of the "mixed welfare economy" combines the corporate proprietary sector with the governmental and voluntary sectors as primary actors in social welfare.[69] And the issue of privatization provoked a vigorous argument about the proper balance between the public and private (including corporate) welfare sectors.[70] Although Neil Gilbert's *Capitalism and the Welfare State* provided a timely review of the issues posed by "welfare capitalism,"[71] empirical investigations of for-profit human service corporations are in their infancy.[72]

History of the Corporate Sector

For most of the history of the United States, private institutions have been the basis of welfare provision. During the colonial era, the town overseer contracted out the poor to the resident who was willing to provide food and shelter at the lowest bid. Similarly, communities subsidized medical care for the poor through purchase of physicians' services. Through the eighteenth and nineteenth centuries, this practice contributed to the emergence of private institutions—hospitals and orphanages, among others—that served the needy.[73] Although many of these early welfare institutions were communal efforts and were not developed as private businesses, others were precisely that. Many early hospitals in the United States were owned and operated by physicians, who became wealthy by providing health care to the community. By 1900 approximately 60 percent of hospitals were privately owned by physicians.[74]

With industrialization, however, the business community took a new interest in the health and welfare of employees. To be sure, certain captains of industry saw employee welfare as a concession to be made as a last resort, sometimes only after violent confrontation with organized workers. Such was not always the case, however. Early in the Industrial Revolution, before government assumed a prominent role in societal affairs, altruistically minded businessmen saw little recourse but to use their business firms as an instrument for their social designs. In some cases, their experiments in worker welfare were nothing less than revolutionary. During the early 1820s the utopian businessman Robert Owen transformed a bankrupt Scotch mill town, New Lanark, from a wretched backwater populated by paupers into a "marvelously profitable" experiment in social engineering. Owen abolished child labor, provided habitable housing for his workers, and implemented a system to recognize the efforts of individual employees. Soon New Lanark attracted thousands of visitors, who were as awed by the contrast between the squalor of other mill towns and the brilliance of New Lanark as they were by the substantial profits Owen realized from the venture. A humanist and an irrepressible idealist, Owen believed that the solution to the problem of poverty lay not in the stringent and punitive English Poor Laws but in "making the poor productive." Owen later transported his utopian vision to the United States, where he attempted to establish a rural planned community in New Harmony, Indiana.[75]

Although Owen's U.S. experiment in local socialism did not survive, business leaders in the United States began to acknowledge that industrial production on a grand scale required a healthy and educated work force. Locating such workers was not easy amid the poverty and ignorance that characterized much of the population of the period. To improve the dependability of labor, several large corporations built planned communities for workers. During the early 1880s, for example, the Pullman Company, manufacturer of railroad sleeping cars, constructed "one of the most ambitiously planned communities in the United States—a company town complete with a hotel, markets, landscaped parks, factories, and residences for over 8,000 people."[76] Although some industries later built communities and facilities as a means of controlling and, in some cases, oppressing workers—as in the "company stores" operated by mining companies to keep miners forever in debt—many expressions of corporate interest in employee well-being clearly enhanced the welfare of the community.

In other instances, businesspeople experimented with alternative forms of business ownership. Current "workplace democracy" and "employee ownership" programs have a predecessor in the Association for the Promotion of Profit Sharing, established in 1892. In 1890, Nelson Olsen Nelson, a founder of this association, set aside a 250-acre tract in Illinois for workers in his company. Naming the village Leclair after a French pioneer of profit sharing, Nelson included in the town plan gardens, walkways, and a school, and he encouraged employees to build residences in the community. Consistent with his philosophy, Nelson offered employees cash dividends as well as stock in the company; and by 1893, 400 of the 500 employees held stock, thus earning 8 to 10 percent in dividends in addition to their wages. Not content with an isolated experiment in industrial socialism, Nelson advanced his ideas in a quarterly journal that promoted profit sharing. Eventually Nelson went so far as to convert his company into a wholly employee-owned cooperative, but overexpansion and irregular earnings led to his ouster in 1918.[77]

It is important to recognize that such experiments in the social function of the business firm were not solely the work of utopian crackpots, nor were they always the product of peculiar circumstances. **Welfare capitalism,** "industry's attending to the social needs of workers through an assortment of medical and funeral benefits, as well as provisions for recreational, educational, housing, and social services," was a popular idea among some business leaders before World War I.[78] Concern about the optimal purpose and value of business in the national culture was a frequent subject of discussion among the elite of U.S. commerce. Even a staunch capitalist such as John D. Rockefeller took a relatively progressive stance on the corporate role when, in 1918, he asked on behalf of the Chamber of Commerce of the United States:

> Shall we cling to the conception of industry as an institution, primarily of private interest, which enables certain individuals to accumulate wealth, too often irrespective of the well-being, the health and happiness of those engaged in its production? Or shall we adopt the modern viewpoint and *regard industry as being a form of social service*, quite as much as a revenue-producing process? . . . The soundest industrial policy is that which has constantly in mind the welfare of employees as well as the making of profits, and which, when human considerations demand it, *subordinates profits to welfare* [emphasis added].[79]

As fortunes, often ill-gotten, accumulated in the hands of the few, some wealthy individuals felt compelled to return a portion of their wealth to the commonwealth. In the late nineteenth century, "men who had great fortunes from the massive industrial growth of the post–Civil War period developed a humanistic concern which was manifested in lavish contributions toward social betterment."[80] Andrew Carnegie, who in 1886 had hired "an army of 300 Pinkerton detectives" to put an end to the violent Haymarket strike,[81] wrote seven years later that massive wealth was a public trust to be put toward the public interest. Carnegie eventually donated some $350 million through foundations for this purpose, most visibly for community libraries (often bearing his name) that began to dot towns across the country. For his part, John D. Rockefeller contributed about $530 million.[82]

Although largely based on the guilt associated with the great fortunes won by a handful of individuals in the midst of cruel circumstances for many, philanthropic foundations also fostered enduring contributions to social welfare. During the 1920s, the Commonwealth Fund proved instrumental in the execution of a series of child guidance experiments, and these served as prototypes for today's juvenile service departments.[83] The Russell Sage Foundation funded the publication of important works on the development of social welfare, including the classic *Industrial Society and Social Welfare* as well as a series of volumes that were precursors of the *Encyclopedia of Social Work*.[84]

The Rockefeller Foundation took a leading role in providing health care to a Southern black population that was neglected by state officials.[85] The active role of the Rockefeller Foundation in the eradication of hookworm warrants particular mention. Shortly after the turn of the century, Charles Wardell Stiles was appointed zoologist of the U.S. Department of Agriculture. Hypothesizing that a disease widespread in the South was caused by a parasite, Stiles convinced his superiors to fund a research trip. He succeeded in confirming his theory, but Congress refused to finance an eradication program. So Stiles turned to the Rockefeller Foundation. In 1909 the foundation established the Rockefeller Sanitary Commission for the Eradication of Hookworm Disease, naming Stiles as an officer. By World War I, having diagnosed and treated millions of the rural poor, mostly African Americans, the commission was well on its way to eradicating the disease that had caused such extensive malaise and listlessness among the poor—in the process contributing to one of the most vicious stereotypes about blacks in U.S. culture.[86]

The business community was also involved in early insurance programs designed to assist injured workers. Although court decisions initially absolved employers of liability for injuries incurred by employees, a swell in jury-awarded settlements to disabled workers convinced corporations of the utility of establishing insurance funds to pool their risk against employee suits. Eventually companies realized that they would pay lower premiums through state-operated workers' compensation programs than they had been paying through commercial insurance. Consequently, between 1911 and 1920, all 45 of the then-existing states enacted workers' compensation laws.[87] Later, when the Great Depression overtaxed voluntary social welfare agencies and when labor volatility resulting from high unemployment threatened political stability, politicians, businessmen, and labor leaders drew on their workers' compensation experience in designing the New Deal. Instrumental in creating federal social programs in the Roosevelt era was Gerald Swope, an executive with the General Electric Company. Having envisaged a "corporate welfare state," including "a national system of unemployment, retirement, life insurance, and disability programs and standards," Swope helped fashion the Social Security program from his position as chairman of Roosevelt's Business Advisory Council.[88] The Social Security program clearly bore the imprint of the business community. As the plan was conceived, only workers who had contributed to a "trust fund" would be able to draw benefits; this would ensure that no public funds would be required to operate the program.[89] What became known as the "social security concept" illustrated a public pension program that was in fact modeled on programs of the private sector. As such, it "represented the acceptance of approaches to social welfare that private businessmen, not government bureaucrats had created."[90] The Social Security Act, the crown jewel of the New Deal, meant that the social and economic security of millions of Americans would be underwritten by the federal government.

Although benefits from programs mandated by the Social Security Act became a staple of the U.S. welfare state, the business community continued to make independent decisions regarding the welfare of workers. Major corporations, such as General Electric, General Motors, and IBM, began to offer "fringe" benefits as supplements to salaries, which were frozen by wage controls during World War II, and these became important incentives in attracting desirable employees. By the standards of the mid-twentieth century, the benefits offered by large corporations were quite generous, including annual vacations, health care, recreation, life insurance, and housing. Business historians Edward Berkowitz and Kim McQuaid described the conscientiousness with which some corporations cared for their employees and suggested that it was "almost as if these firms were consciously demonstrating that the true American welfare state lay within the large and progressive American corporation."[91] Private sector activity in health, income maintenance, and education has grown in relation to the public sector. In 1980, social welfare expenditures represented 27.0 percent of GDP, of which the private sector represented 34.8 percent; in 1994, social welfare accounted for 34.5 percent of GDP, of which the private sector accounted for 39.1 percent.[92] Continued growth of the private sector is virtually assured insofar as the service sector of the U.S. postindustrial economy expands.

Corporate Social Responsibility

The corporation has also influenced U.S. social welfare as a result of accusations that it has been insensitive to the needs of minorities, the poor, women, and consumers. During the 1960s, criticism of the corporation focused on business's neglect of minorities and on urban blight. A decade later, issues relating to affirmative action, environmental pollution, and consumer rip-offs were added to the list. These problems contributed to a public relations crisis, as a leading business administration text noted:

> The corporation is being attacked and criticized on various fronts by a great number of political and citizens' organizations. Many young people accuse the corporation of failing to seek solutions to our varied social problems. Minority groups, and women, contend that many corporations have been guilty of discrimination in hiring and in pay scales.[93]

Melvin Anshen, a professor of public policy and business responsibility at Columbia University's Graduate School of Business, bemoaned the fact that "profit-oriented private decisions are now often seen as antisocial."[94]

In order to improve their public image, many businesses established policies on **corporate social responsibility.** Corporations that were reluctant to take seriously the social implications of their operations ran the risk of inviting the surveillance of public interest groups. As an example, the Council on Economic Priorities (CEP), founded in 1969, developed a reputation for investigating the social responsibility of U.S. corporations. CEP released *Rating America's Corporate Conscience*, which evaluated 125 large corporations based on their standing with respect to seven issues: charitable contributions, representation of women on boards of directors and among top corporate officers, representation of minorities on boards of directors and among top corporate officers, disclosure of social information, involvement in South Africa, conventional weapons-related contracting, and nuclear weapons-related contracting.[95] Subsequently, CEP served as the platform to launch Social Accountability International, which established workplace standards and monitored factories in developing nations.

Although public relations facades frequently gloss over businesses' substantive abuses, specific corporate social responsibility policies have advanced social welfare. During the late 1960s, General Electric and IBM instituted strong policies on equal opportunity for and affirmative action toward minorities and women. Under the title Public Interest Director, Leon Sullivan assumed a position on the General Motors board of directors, from which he presented principles governing ethical practices for U.S. corporations doing business in South Africa.[96] Ultimately, U.S. firms' adherence to the "Sullivan principles" contributed to the fall of apartheid in South Africa. More recently, financial consultants pioneered the concept of socially responsible investing. The practice of excluding certain industries from mutual fund portfolios because their activities are contrary to those of investors gained considerable ground during the 1980s. An illustration of socially responsible investing is the Domini Social Index (DSI), an investment strategy that screens out businesses in five areas: military contracting, alcohol and tobacco, gambling, nuclear power, and South Africa. After its inception in 1988, the DSI initially performed comparably to the Standard & Poor's 500 Index, but by the early 1990s it was generating a return on investment superior to Standard & Poor's.[97] In another instance, Control Data Corporation actually sought out "major unmet social needs, designed means for serving them within the framework of a profit-oriented business enterprise, and brought the needs and the means for serving them together to create markets where none had existed before."[98] These and other initiatives demonstrate that the corporate sector has been willing to undertake significant programs to support troubled communities.[99]

Corporate practices have also been applied directly to social problems, as evident in initiatives undertaken by the Enterprise Foundation, the Ford Foundation, and South Shore Bank. In 1981, in a venture reminiscent of Robert Owen, developer James Rouse established the Enterprise Foundation. Although this is technically a foundation that supports charitable projects, what makes it different is that within the foundation is the Enterprise Development Company, a wholly owned taxpaying subsidiary. Profits from the Development Company are transferred to the foundation to fund projects. Two decades later, this fiscally self-sufficient "charity corporation" had developed innovative projects for low-income housing in dozens of cities.[100] Recognizing the tendency of community institutions in poor areas to become dependent on government or philanthropy for continuing operations, the Ford Foundation sought contributions from corporations for a program to apply business principles to social problems. By 1983 the Local Initiatives Support Corporation (LISC) had developed investment funds in 24 regions supporting 197 community development projects.[101] Fifteen years after its inception, LISC had helped 1,400 community-based organizations leverage $2.9 billion. LISC contributions were credited with the construction of more

than 64,000 homes.[102] Chicago's South Shore Bank, for example, brought $270 million in new investments to deteriorating neighborhoods and rehabilitated 350 large apartment buildings. By the end of 1990, the bank had increased its assets fivefold and contributed to two important policy initiatives of the Clinton administration: the Empowerment Zone initiative and the Community Development Financial Institution Loan Fund. By the early 1990s, South Shore Bank also was consulting with community development activists in Poland, through collaboration in the Polish-American Enterprise Fund, and in Bangladesh, in partnership with the Grameen Bank, which has pioneered peer lending among poor women and in the process has become one of the largest development banks in the world. The concept of providing loans to low-income women in order to encourage self-employment also has been operationalized in the San Francisco metropolitan area through WISE, the Women's Initiative for Self-Employment. Since its inception in 1988, WISE has taught 3,500 poor women about running a business, in the process helping start or expand more than 500 businesses.[103] As South Shore Bank, the Polish-American Enterprise Fund, the Grameen Bank, and WISE indicate, the application of capital to promote social development has spawned a nascent network of international organizations.

In the light of such ventures, some business leaders have become enthusiastic about the activist responses to social problems on the part of the corporation. David Linowes, a corporate leader, foresaw a new role for business in public affairs:

> Mounting evidence proves that the private sector is uniquely well qualified to fulfill many of the social goals facing us more economically and expeditiously than government working alone. . . . I can visualize a wholesale expansion of existing incentives along with a spate of new reward strategies introduced to America's socio-economic system. Increasingly, I believe, this will help to change the attitude of businessmen regarding social involvement. I look forward to the day, in fact, when competition to engage in government-business programs will be every bit as spirited as competition for the consumer dollar is today.[104]

As chairman of the President's Commission on Privatization during the Reagan administration, Linowes worked to define ways in which the private sector could complement the responsibilities of government.[105]

Corporate Influence on Social Welfare Policy

Corporate social responsibility notwithstanding, it would be naive to think that the corporate sector is above self-interest in its orientation toward social welfare. The conservative political economist Irving Kristol stated as much when he wrote that "corporate philanthropy is not obligatory. It is desirable if and only if it serves a corporate purpose. It is expressly and candidly a self-serving activity, and is only legitimate to the degree that it is ancillary to a larger corporate purpose. To put it bluntly: There is nothing noble or even moral about corporate philanthropy."[106] And corporate influence in social welfare is not exerted simply through myriad corporations acting independently. Special interest organizations, such as the National Association of Manufacturers and the United States Chamber of Commerce, have routinely pressed for public policies that clearly reflect the priorities of the business community. The influence that the business community brings to public policy is discussed in greater detail in Chapter 8. Since the 1970s, certain foundations have made sizable contributions to conservative policy institutes, constructing the ideological infrastructure that would challenge liberalism in social policy (see Table 7.2).

At the turn of the century, conservative foundations continued to support think tanks associated with the Right. By the end of the twentieth century, such contributions placed conservative policy institutes at the center of the social policy debate. Not only were conservative think tanks well endowed with resources, but they were dispersed throughout the United States. As a result of these investments in the "marketplace of ideas," the conservative imprint on social policy has become indelible, and many of the most prominent conservative think tanks—AEI, Heritage, and Cato—have become household names (see Table 7.3).

Prominent policy institutes favored by the business community have been the American Enterprise

Table 7.2

Prominent Human Service Corporations

Company	Revenues 2004*	Revenues 2007	Market	Employees 2007
UnitedHealth	$25.9 billion	$75.4 billion	HMO	67,000
Wellpoint	18.4 billion	61.1 billion	Health care	41,700
Aetna	16.1 billion	27.6 billion	Health care	35,200
HCA	21.6 billion	25.5 billion	Hospital management	186,000
Humana	12.1 billion	25.3 billion	HMO	25,000
CIGNA	16.9 billion	17.6 billion	HMO	26,600
Health Net	10.0 billion	14.1 billion	Health care	10,068
Coventry	4.4 billion	9.9 billion	HMO	10,250
Tenet Healthcare	9.9 billion	8.9 billion	Hospital management	63,264
Magellan	1.4 billion	2.2 billion	Mental health	3,900
CCA	0.9 billion	1.5 billion	Corrections	16,000
Psych. Solutions	290.0 million	1.5 billion	Mental health	18,700
APS Healthcare	198.0 million	464.8 million	Mental health	1,200
Leisure Care	99.0 million	64.5 million	Assisted living	1,900
Sunrise	1.1 billion	1.6 billion	Assisted living	40,488
MAXIMUS	553.0 million	738.7 million	Consulting	6,120
Sierra Health	1.3 billion	1.7 billion	HMO	2,900
Matria Health	293.3 million	352.2 million	Women's health	2,602

*Revenues adjusted for inflation
Source: Hoover's Inc., http://hoovers.com/free/.

Institute for Public Policy Research (AEI) and the Heritage Foundation. Established as nonpartisan institutions for the purpose of enhancing the public's understanding of social policy, these policy institutes distanced themselves from the special interest connotations of earlier business advocacy groups. At the same time, conservative think tanks served as vehicles through which the business community could take a less reactive stance regarding social policy. Conservative policy institutes, then, addressed the complaint voiced by Lawrence Fouraker and Graham Allison of Harvard's Graduate School of Business Administration: "Public policy suffers not simply from a lack of business confidence on issues of major national import, but from a lack of sophisticated and balanced contribution by both business and government in the process of policy development."[107]

Table 7.3

Top Five Conservative Foundations, 1999–2001

Foundation	Assets	Contributions
Sarah Scaife Foundation	$323,029,669	$44,800,500
Bradley Foundation	584,752,379	38,858,118
Olin Foundation	71,196,916	17,403,240
Davis Foundation	78,314,656	13,013,125
DeVos Foundation	97,048,407	12,159,101

Source: Adapted from Jeff Krehely, Meaghan House, and Emily Kernan, *Axis of Ideology* (Washington, DC: National Committee for Responsive Philanthropy, 2004).

The American Enterprise Institute

Once noted for its slavish adherence to probusiness positions on social issues, the American Enterprise Institute (AEI), by the early 1980s, had developed an appreciation for U.S. "intellectual politics."[108] With a budget and staff comparable to that of a prestigious college, AEI was able to recruit an impressive number of notable scholars and individuals and to maintain projects in several domestic policy areas: economics, education, energy, government regulation, finance, taxation, health, jurisprudence, and public opinion. The significance of these activities for social welfare was stated by AEI's then-president, William J. Baroody Jr.:

> The public philosophy that has guided American policy for decades is undergoing change. For more than four decades, the philosophy of Franklin Delano Roosevelt's New Deal prevailed, in essence calling upon government to do whatever individual men and women could not do for themselves.
>
> Today we see growing signs of a new public philosophy, one that still seeks to meet fundamental human needs, but to meet them through a better balance between the public and private sectors of society.
>
> The American Enterprise Institute has been at the forefront of this change. Many of today's policy initiatives are building on intellectual foundations partly laid down by the Institute.[109]

For this ambitious mission, AEI impaneled a staff of influential and talented personnel. At the height of its influence, from the late 1970s through the mid-1980s, AEI had more than 30 scholars and fellows *in residence*, who prepared analyses on the various policy areas.[110] The institute's senior fellows included the previously mentioned Irving Kristol; Herbert Stein, an economist and chairman of the President's Council of Economic Advisors in the Nixon administration; and Ben Wattenberg, a veteran public opinion analyst. The AEI "distinguished fellow" was Gerald R. Ford, who had served as thirty-eighth president of the United States. Michael Novak, director of AEI's project on democratic capitalism, prepared analyses that focused on social welfare policy. Under the direction of Novak, the project on democratic capitalism intended to reform public philosophy by defining the corporation as a promoter of cultural enlightenment rather than as a perpetrator of inequality. "The social instrument invented by democratic capitalism to achieve social goals is the private corporation," he proselytized. "The corporation . . . is not merely an economic institution. It is also a moral and a political institution. It depends on and generates new political forms. . . . Beyond its economic effects, the corporation changes the ethos and the cultural forms of society."[111] At the same time, Novak took careful aim at the public sector, explaining, "I advise intelligent, ambitious, and morally serious young Christians and Jews to awaken to the growing danger of statism. They will better serve their souls and serve the Kingdom of God all around by restoring the liberty and power of the private sector than by working for the state."[112]

Through the late 1970s and early 1980s, AEI laid the groundwork for the conservative revolution in U.S. domestic policy. Much of the conceptual work was done by conservative scholars, but the execution depended on the building of a network between the business community and government. By the election of Ronald Reagan in 1980, that network was in place. This ensured that no social policy proposal would receive serious consideration without first passing the review and comment of AEI.

The Heritage Foundation

In 1986 AEI faltered, and organizational problems led to the resignation of Baroody. When AEI moved to the center, the Heritage Foundation assumed leadership in defining the probusiness and antigovernmental outlook favored by the Right. Established in 1973 by a $250,000 grant from the Coors family,[113] the Heritage Foundation had a 1983 budget of $10.6 million, already close to those of the liberal Brookings Institution and the conservative American Enterprise Institute.[114] Heritage espoused a militantly conservative ideology; it influenced social policy by proposing private alternatives to establishing governmental programs and by slanting its work to the religious right. By breaking new ground while building mass support for policy initiatives, Heritage complemented the less partisan analyses of AEI.

Heritage social policy initiatives emphasize privatization, which in this case means the transfer of activities from government to business. Implicit in this approach is an unqualified antagonism toward government intrusion in social affairs. Government programs are faulted for breaking down the mutual obligations between groups; for failing to attend to efficiencies and incentives in the way programs are operated and benefits awarded; for inducing dependency in the beneficiaries of programs; and for allowing the growth of the welfare industry and its special interest groups, particularly professional associations.[115]

This critique served as a basis for the aggressive stance taken by the Heritage Foundation in urban development, income security, and social welfare policies. With regard to urban development, Heritage proposed the Urban Enterprise Zone (UEZ) concept, which would ultimately find a home in the Clinton administration as Empowerment Zones. In the area of income security, the Heritage Foundation prepared an oblique assault on the

Social Security program, promoting a parallel system of individual retirement accounts (IRAs). The result would be a surefire formula for an attempt to privatize Social Security, a venture that would come to fruition early in the second term of George W. Bush's presidency. Regarding welfare policy, Heritage was instrumental in scouting Charles Murray, whose *Losing Ground* provided much of the rationale for the conservative assault on federal welfare programs. Murray's critique of family welfare would provide the impetus for Lawrence Mead, whose recommendation that welfare recipients be mandated to work was featured in the 1988 Family Support Act, as well as Newt Gingrich's Contract with America, the outline of which foretold the end of the family welfare entitlement through the 1996 federal welfare reform.

The conservative triumph in domestic policy was not coincidental. Not long after the Reagan inauguration, Heritage vice president Burton Pines had likened the conservative cause to a crusade. Pines noted the pivotal role of think tanks in the effort to transform public philosophy and acknowledged a debt to AEI, an organization he described as focusing "primarily on long (sometimes very long) range and fundamental transformation of the climate of opinion." Bringing the conservative Hoover Institution of Stanford into the fold, Pines characterized their work in military terms. "Together," he concluded, "Hoover, AEI and Heritage can today deploy formidable armies on the battlefield of ideas"[116]—forces that were to prove enormously influential in shifting domestic policy to the right.

The Future of Corporate Involvement in Social Welfare

Corporations will continue to influence social welfare policy, reflecting the preference of business leaders that businesses assume a primary role in activities of both the voluntary and governmental sectors. It follows that human service advocates, rather than outright rejecting corporate involvement in social policy and programming, should engage the business community proactively. A creative illustration of this kind of engagement appears in the "Decency Principles" proposed in 1988 by Nancy Amidei, a social worker and syndicated columnist. Noting that the Sullivan principles addressed the responsibilities of firms doing business in South Africa, Amidei wondered about the responsibilities of firms doing business in the United States. Her standards for responsible business practices included the following:

1. *Equitable wages.* Wages should be high enough to allow workers to escape poverty; there should be comparability across lines of race, age, sex, and handicapping conditions.
2. *Employee rights.* Employees should be provided equal opportunity, the right to organize for collective bargaining, affordable child care, safe working conditions, and health coverage.
3. *Housing.* Businesses should work for more affordable housing and help relocated or migrant workers obtain affordable housing.
4. *Environmental responsibility.* Business practices should include responsible use of resources, sound handling of dangerous substances, and conformance with environmental protection laws.

Amidei suggested that a corporation's adherence to the "Decency Principles" be a basis for government decisions on such matters as providing tax abatements to corporations to attract new industry or awarding government contracts.[117]

An advocate of fusing social needs and economic requirements was Clinton administration Secretary of Labor Robert Reich. According to Reich, much of the industrial malaise of the United States was attributable to underinvestment in human capital. However, human capital investments can be wasteful, leading to nonproductive dependency, when not coupled with the needs of industry. "Underlying many of the inadequacies of American social programs, in short, is the fact that they have not been directed in any explicit or coherent way toward the large task of adapting America's labor force."[118] The attachment of social needs to industrial productivity would fundamentally alter social welfare. "Government bureaucracies that now administer these programs to individuals will be supplanted, to a large extent, by companies that administer them to their employees," suggested Reich. "Companies, rather than state and local governments, will be the agents through which such assistance is provided."[119]

Significantly, industrial policy attracted conservative adherents as well. Influential analyst Kevin Phillips proposed a "business–government partnership" through which labor and business would

agree to work cooperatively with government so that the United States could regain its dominant role in the international economy. For Phillips, however, industrial policy conflicted with the traditional liberal orientation to social welfare:

> Political liberals must accept that there is little support for bringing back federal agencies based on New Deal models to run the U.S. economy, and that much of the new business-government cooperation will back economic development and nationalist (export, trade competition) agendas rather than abstractions like social justice or social welfare.[120]

The primacy of business interests in public policy has not been accepted by many social welfare advocates. Their argument has been that even though "corporatism" may seem plausible to corporate executives, government officials, and labor unions, it offers little to the unemployed or to the welfare or working poor.[121] This conventional wisdom, however, has been relegated to the historical dustbin by the proliferation of corporations that have provided a range of health and welfare services, often under contract by government. To the extent that corporations are contracted by government to serve the public, much as nonprofits have done so under purchase of service contracts, the traditional, liberal critique has less validity.

Human Service Corporations

Continued demand for human services in the postindustrial period has drawn the corporate sector directly into social welfare in the United States. Corporate exploration of the growing human services market has proceeded apace. In contrast, shackled by debt and denied revenue because of tax cuts, government social programs struggle to keep up with demand for services. Dependent on government support and on contributions of middle-income Americans who have experienced a continual erosion of their economic position, the voluntary sector is unlikely to meet future service demands. Relatively unfettered by government regulation and with easy access to capital from commercial sources, the corporate sector has made dramatic inroads into service areas previously reserved for governmental and voluntary sector organizations.

Significantly, the incentives for corporate entry into human services were initially provided through government social programs, especially with passage of Medicare and Medicaid in 1965. Between 1950 and 1991, government expenditures for social welfare increased from $23.5 billion to $1.16 *trillion,* a factor of 50. As a percentage of gross domestic product, public welfare expenditures more than doubled, from 8.8 percent in 1970 to 20.5 percent in 1991. Health care allocations figured prominently in the expansion of public welfare expenditures over this period. In 1970, government spent $24.9 billion on health care; by 1991 that figure had grown to $317.0 billion.[122] The potential profits for corporations entering the rapidly expanding health and human services market were unmistakable.

Concomitantly, public policy decisions encouraged proprietary firms to provide health and human services. By using a market approach to ensure the availability of health care for the medically indigent and the elderly, Medicaid and Medicare avoided the costs of constructing a system of public sector facilities and, in so doing, contributed to the restructuring of health care in the United States. What was essentially a haphazard collection of mom-and-pop nursing homes and small private hospitals was transformed, in a short period, into a system of corporate franchises, complete with stocks traded on Wall Street. And almost a decade later, incentives offered through Medicaid and Medicare to encourage the corporate sector to become involved in hospital care were replicated in the health maintenance industry. The Health Maintenance Organization Act of 1973 stimulated a sluggish health maintenance industry that has since grown at an explosive rate. As Pulitzer Prize–winning journalists Donald Barlett and James Steele noted, "Wall Street reasoned that a portion of America's hospitals could be assembled into national chains, much like department stores and auto-parts distributors, and investors could make a fortune."[123]

Initially dependent on government welfare programs, the corporate sector developed a life of its own. Exploitation of the nursing home, hospital management, and health maintenance markets has led to corporate interest in other markets. By the 1980s, human service corporations had established prominence in child care, ambulatory health care, substance abuse, psychiatric care, and home health care, as well as in life care and continuing care. By the 1990s, managed care firms were restructuring health and mental health services so as to batten corporate profits; by the end of the twentieth century, they had established beachheads in welfare

and corrections, as well. Increasingly, proprietary firms were able to obtain funds for facilities through commercial loans or sales of stock, and to meet ongoing costs by charging fees to individuals, companies, and nongovernmental third parties. Insofar as resources for human service corporations are not financed by the state, firms are free to function relatively independent of government intervention.

How big is the corporate sector in U.S. social welfare? Early in the twenty-first century, more than 20 of the largest firms reported annual revenues that were far greater than *all* contributions to the United Ways of America.[124] These corporations employed thousands of workers, some more than the number of state and local workers for public welfare programs in any state in the union.[125] Some salient statistics on the larger human service corporations are listed in Table 7.4.

Human service corporations in the United States are notable in several respects. First, virtually all were incorporated after World War II, the benchmark of the postindustrial era, with the great majority established after 1960. Second, the for-profit sector of health and human services has matured as a major industrial sector. By the early 1980s, 34 firms reported annual revenues exceeding $10 million apiece; by the beginning of the twenty-first century, the number had risen to 241, as shown in Figure 7.1. That the number of firms in 2008 was somewhat fewer than the 286 firms identified in 2000 or 2004 suggests that the sector was consolidating through mergers and acquisitions. Although most of the companies focus on health-related services, many diversify into other service areas; and in some instances, other types of corporations acquire human service firms in order to balance their operations.

Consolidation and Growth in New Human Service Markets

Human service corporations have become prominent, if not dominant, in several areas of social welfare: nursing homes, hospital management, health maintenance organizations (HMOs), child care, and home care. More recently, proprietary firms established beachheads in other markets, notably life and continuing care, corrections, and welfare. The

Table 7.4

Major Grant Recipients of Conservative Philanthropy, 1999–2001

Organization	State	Conservative Grants Received	Total Revenue, 2001
Heritage Foundation	DC	$28,569,700	$27,890,147
American Enterprise Institute	DC	7,613,741	24,095,354
Judicial Watch	DC	6,129,150	17,500,662
Manhattan Institute	NY	5,339,184	8,924,816
Cato Institute	DC	4,824,432	17,631,255
Hudson Institute	IN	4,681,592	7,818,439
Nat'l Ctr. for Policy Analysis	TX	3,818,700	4,770,562
Pacific Res. Inst. for Pub. Pol.	CA	3,272,389	4,424,316
Focus on the Family	CO	3,075,400	121,333,537

Source: Adapted from Jeff Krehely, Meaghan House, and Emily Kernan, *Axis of Ideology* (Washington, DC: National Committee for Responsive Philanthropy, 2004).

descriptions of the following subsectors are somewhat arbitrary because many companies diversify their operations, functioning across several subsectors. In health care, for example, a hospital management firm will also operate nursing homes as well as an HMO. Over time, these holdings can change significantly, reflecting the dynamic nature of the evolving health and human services market. For example, HealthSouth divested several assets after it was found to have defrauded Medicare in 2003, which proved a boon to Select Medical Corporation which acquired several assets, reporting $1.9 billion in revenues in 2007. Accompanying globalization, human service markets are also global; in 2007, Allied Healthcare International reported $277.8 million in revenues from 100 facilities in the United Kingdom; Sunrise Assisted Living generated $1.7 billion for elder care services in Britain, Germany, and the United States; the GEO Group earned $1 billion providing correctional services in Australia, Canada, South Africa, and the United Kingdom as well as the United States. The larger health and human service corporations are listed in Table 7.1.

Nursing Homes

Among corporate initiatives in social welfare, expansion into the nursing home industry is unparalleled. Between 1965 and 1978, expenditures for nursing home care increased 16.9 percent *annually*.[126] By the early 1980s, nursing homes had become a $25-billion-a-year industry, and the number of nursing

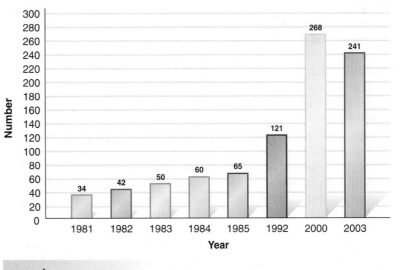

Figure 7.1

Human Service Corporations Reporting Annual Revenues above $10 Million

Sources: Standard and Poor's, 2000; Moody's, 2004; and Hoover's, 2008.

home beds exceeded those in acute care facilities for the first time.[127] At that time 70 percent of nursing homes were under proprietary management. Market conditions such as these led a writer in *Forbes* magazine to observe, "This is a guaranteed opportunity for someone. How the nursing home industry can exploit it is the real question."[128] Under favorable market conditions, nursing home corporations proliferated. David Vaughan, president of a real estate firm specializing in facilities for the elderly, noted:

> The overall affluence of the over fifty-five population makes investments in special care facilities an extremely attractive venture. The need of capital in meeting the housing needs of this segment of the U.S. population has been so great that we have been able to invest in these facilities with only limited competition.[129]

Guaranteed growth of the nursing home market led to the consolidation of proprietary firms and the emergence of an oligopoly. As early as 1981, each of the following three corporations held more than 10,000 nursing home beds: Beverly Enterprises, with 38,488 beds; ARA Services, 31,325; and National Medical Enterprises (NME), 14,534.[130] Beverly Enterprises attained first ranking by its 1979 purchase of Progressive Medical Group, which was the eleventh largest chain of nursing homes. NME attained the third ranking in 1979 by purchasing Hillhaven, then the third largest operation. ARA Services grew 26 percent in 1979, thereby attaining the second ranking, by consolidating smaller operations in Indiana, Colorado, and California.[131] Undeterred by the filing of the first antitrust action in the nursing home industry, nursing home firms continued such acquisitions and mergers.[132] In 1984, using its Hillhaven subsidiary, NME acquired Flagg Industries, which held 12 facilities in Idaho, bringing its total holdings to 339 health care facilities with 42,000 beds. Not to be outdone, Beverly Enterprises acquired Beacon Hill America for $60 million, thereby retaining its top ranking. By the mid-1980s Beverly Enterprises controlled 781 nursing homes with a total of 88,198 beds in 44 states and the District of Columbia.[133]

Given this trend, one industry analyst believed that the industry would eventually fall into the hands of "five or six corporations."[134] A decade later, Beverly continued as the largest corporation focusing on long-term care, managing 703 nursing homes, 30 assisted living centers, 6 hospices, 11 transitional hospitals, and 4 home health centers.

Yet Beverly's share of the nursing home market did not go unchallenged. On March 1, 1995, Beverly's primary competitor, NME, merged with American Medical International to form Tenet Healthcare Corporation, a $5.5 billion company.[135] Yet, Tenet would founder. In response to an FBI investigation into unnecessary heart surgeries performed at a California hospital, Tenet agreed to a $54 million penalty. Under new management, Tenet opted to sell one-third of its hospitals.[136]

The nursing care industry would be shaped largely by Manor Care, the largest long-term care provider with revenues of $3.6 billion and 59,500 employees, and the somewhat smaller Beverly which had been acquired by GGNSC Holdings ($2.5 billion). By 2007, Tenet had rebounded from its legal difficulties, posting a net income of $69 million from $8.9 billion in revenues.

2003 Medicare Reforms

The Medicare Modernization Act of 2003 included two provisions that were favored by corporate health providers: a prescription drug benefit and an 11 percent augmentation for Medicare beneficiaries who enrolled in managed care plans, Medicare Advantage. Immediately, pharmaceutical companies floated plans to attract subscribers; in many states as many as 50 plans vied to sign-up seniors.[137] Among the most aggressive were UnitedHealth and Humana. The fortunes of managed care companies have varied considerably, as shown in Table 7.5.

By gaining such a large share of recipients who need prescription drugs and desire managed care just a few years after passage of Medicare reform, UnitedHealth and Humana are well positioned to exploit the 77 million baby-boomers who began retiring in 2008. That managed care companies have so quickly addressed the needs of seniors makes alteration of the Medicare provisions from which they have profited less likely.

Hospital Management

The growth of the nursing home industry has been matched by corporate involvement in hospital management. Between 1976 and 1982, the number of investor-owned or investor-managed hospitals increased from 533 to 1,040, accruing gross revenues of approximately $40 billion.[138] Richard Siegrist Jr., a Wall Street analyst, concluded that the

Table 7.5

Managed Care and Medicare Reforms

Medicare Provision	UnitedHealth	Humana	Wellpoint	Aetna
Prescription Drugs				
Enrollment	4.7 million	3.5 million	1.6 million	0.3 million
Revenue	$5.4 billion	$3.6 billion	$1.2 billion	$0.3 billion
Earnings	$336 million	$87 million	$53 million	$28 million
Medicare Advantage				
Enrollment	1.3 million	1.1 million	0.4 million	0.2 million
Revenue	$12.3 billion	$11.0 billion	$2.8 billion	$2.3 billion
Earnings	$840 million	$786 million	$111 million	$107 million

Source: Adapted from Milt Freudenheim, "Two Insurers Increase Bet on Medicare," *New York Times* (December 5, 2007), p. C10.

future for the industry looked bright, noting that revenues and bed ownership for the five largest companies had roughly tripled between 1976 and 1981. Humana had doubled its size through an unfriendly takeover of American Medicorp (worth $450 million), gaining 39 hospitals and 7,838 beds. Meanwhile, Hospital Corporation of America (HCA) purchased Hospital Affiliates (worth $650 million), gaining 55 hospitals, 8,207 beds, and 102 hospital management contracts; General Care Corporation (worth $78 million) gained 8 hospitals with 1,294 beds; and General Health Services (worth $96 million) gained 6 hospitals with 1,115 beds. At the same time, American Medical International (AMI) acquired Hyatt Medical Enterprises (worth $69 million), with 8 hospitals, 907 beds, and 26 hospital management contracts, as well as Brookwood Health Services (worth $156 million), with 9 hospitals, 1,271 beds, and 5 hospital contracts.[139]

AMI's strategy of purchasing financially troubled community hospitals proved financially successful. Moreover, in 1984, AMI acquired Lifemark's 25 hospitals and three alcoholism treatment centers through a $1 billion stock transfer.[140] Despite such large-scale growth, AMI continued to rank second behind HCA, which owned 393 hospitals having 56,000 beds.[141] But Humana was to hold the trump card in hospital management. Boldly gambling on its offer to implant artificial hearts in 100 heart patients at no cost, Humana captured the public's attention in 1984. Even though the artificial hearts failed to perform as planned, the project reflected a management strategy that pushed Humana to the head of the pack. By 1993, Humana had forged ahead of its competitors to become the largest health and human service corporation in the world.

The mid-1990s witnessed the largest mergers among health care corporations that had occurred up to that point. As noted above, NME and AMI merged to form Tenet Healthcare Corporation, effectively approximating the market share controlled by Humana. This transaction paled, however, in comparison to the acquisition of HCA by Columbia. The Columbia/HCA merger created a $20 billion behemoth that dwarfed Tenet and Humana. By the mid-1990s the holdings of Columbia/HCA included 292 general hospitals, 28 psychiatric hospitals, and 125 outpatient and auxiliary facilities.[142] Being the largest health and human service corporation was not without its problems, however. An intensely competitive health market invited irregularities, the scale of which matched the size of the perpetrator:

> In June 2003, HCA agreed to pay $631 million in civil penalties and damages growing out of false claims to the government health care programs. That came on top of $840 million in criminal fines, civil restitution, and penalties the company paid in 2000. That same year, the company agreed to pay $250 million to settle other Medicare overbilling claims. In all, HCA has paid $1.7 billion as a result of its fraudulent practices.[143]

Despite such setbacks, HCA was well positioned with respect to federal programs that accounted for one-third of its revenue. The son of the company's founder, Thomas Frist Jr., was none other than Bill Frist, Senate Majority Leader.

After flirting with a presidential campaign, Bill Frist joined his father and brother in buying HCA for $33 billion, executing the largest purchase of a publicly held company in the nation's history.[144] By 2007, HCA was challenged by Humana, a company whose revenue had doubled from $12.2 billion in 2004 to $25.3 in 2007. Meanwhile, Tenet's fortunes had fallen, its revenues declining from $13.2 billion in 2004 to $8.9 billion in 2007.

Health Maintenance Organizations

Pioneered by the nonprofit Kaiser Permanente in California, the concept of **health maintenance organizations (HMOs)** was slow to attract the interest of the corporate sector. However, from 1973 to 1981, the Health Maintenance Organization Act of 1973 authorized funds for the establishment of these membership health plans in a large number of favorable marketing areas. This funding, coupled with the growth in the nursing home and hospital management industries, reversed investor apathy. By 1983, 60 HMOs were operating on a proprietary basis.[145] By the end of the century, the HMO industry was a commercial enterprise, save Kaiser-Permanente which had to adopt for-profit strategies in order to remain competitive.

An early leader in the HMO industry was HealthAmerica, a for-profit HMO begun in 1980.

Within a few years HealthAmerica enrolled almost 400,000 members in 17 locations across the nation, becoming the largest proprietary HMO (second in size only to nonprofit Kaiser Permanente). Seeking capital for further expansion, HealthAmerica offered stock publicly in July 1983 and raised $20 million for 1.5 million shares. One month later, Phillip Bredesen, chairman and president of HealthAmerica, reported that he anticipated "dramatic growth in the HMO segment of the health care business," and that "HealthAmerica [was] well-positioned with the people and systems that this growth [would] represent."[146] HealthAmerica's growth did not go unnoticed by Fred Wasserman, founder of Maxicare, another proprietary HMO. Wasserman suspected that Bredesen had stretched his company too thin in an ambitious expansion into new market areas. In November 1986, Maxicare purchased HealthAmerica for $372 million. Coupled with the earlier acquisition of HealthCare USA for $66 million, the purchase of HealthAmerica enabled Maxicare to claim more than 2 million members nationwide and annual revenues approaching $2 billion. After the HealthAmerica takeover, Wasserman spoke optimistically about overtaking Kaiser-Permanente in pursuit of a health maintenance market[147] expected to consist of 30 million members and $25 billion in revenues by 1990.[148]

■ *Health maintenance organizations such as Kaiser Permanente offer prepaid medical services. Members pay a monthly or yearly fee for all health care, including hospitalization. Because costs to patients are fixed in advance, preventive medicine is stressed to avoid costly hospitalization. One criticism of HMOs is that patients can use only doctors and specialists who are associated with the organization.*

Wasserman's optimism was misplaced, however. The firm proved unable to manage the debt incurred by its appetite for mergers. Maxicare sought protection against creditors, filing for bankruptcy under Chapter 11 in the late 1980s. The collapse of Wasserman's HMO empire was evident in his firm's revenues. Peaking in 1987, Maxicare reported earnings of $1.8 billion; three years later, the firm earned $387 million, less than a fourth of its earlier income.

In the late 1980s managed care became the method of choice for containing health care costs, and the HMO market surged. As business and labor groups attempted to limit the fiscal drain caused by escalating costs of health care, proprietary firms stepped forward to manage care more efficiently. By the mid-1990s more than a dozen managed care companies were reporting hefty revenues. Humana, for example, controlled 17 HMOs as well as the health care provided by some 40,800 physicians, in addition to its 630 hospitals. A rapidly growing competitor, PacifiCare, had established HMOs in six states and enrolled 1.2 million members. The largest firm focusing on health management was United HealthCare Corporation, with facilities in 24 states and Puerto Rico, and enrolling 13.5 million members. FHP International was in second place, reporting annual revenues of $3.9 billion. At the beginning of the twenty-first century, the insurance giant CIGNA dominated the industry, controlling 46 HMOs in which 3 million people were subscribers.[149]

CIGNA's reign was not to last. In November 2004, WellPoint and Anthem received permission from California regulators to consummate their merger announced a year earlier. Together, the new firm will serve 28 million consumers in 10 states and Puerto Rico. As a condition to the merger, the health providers agreed to pay $265 million to upgrade health care in California. Combined, WellPoint and Anthem eclipse CIGNA as the nation's largest health care insurer.[150] By 2007, Wellpoint and UnitedHealth Group International vied for dominance in corporate health care. Although Wellpoint reported $61.1 billion in revenues compared to UnitedHealth's $75.4 billion, it remained the nation's largest health insurer with 35 million members. But UnitedHealth was closing in as a result of its acquisition of PacifiCare for $8.1 billion, representing 3.3 million enrollees.[151]

The largest managed care company providing behavioral health services, Magellan, emerged from bankruptcy in 2004, having consolidated its position. Relying on 70 thousand mental health professionals, Magellan served 100 million members, reporting revenues of $2.2 billion in 2007. A primary competitor is Psychiatric Solutions, which manages 90 psychiatric hospitals in 30 states, reporting $1.5 billion in revenues in 2007, while a newcomer to the industry, Mental Health Network, claimed $53.5 million.

Child Care

As a human services market, child care has been exploited effectively by proprietary firms. In an important study of child welfare services delivery, Catherine Born showed the influence of for-profit providers relative to that of providers in the voluntary and public sectors. She noted the following:

> In the case of residential treatment, among all services purchased, 51 percent was obtained from for-profit firms, 26 percent from voluntary organizations, and 22 percent from other public agencies having contractual agreements with the welfare department. For contracted institutional services, 48 percent was provided by proprietary concerns, 14 percent by voluntary vendors, and 38 percent by other public agencies. The pattern was similar in the case of group home services where 58 percent was proprietarily contracted, 17 percent was obtained from the private, nonprofit sector, and 25 percent was purchased from other public agencies.[152]

The day care market, like its largest provider, KinderCare, expanded rapidly. Begun in 1969, KinderCare demonstrated prodigious growth, claiming approximately 825 "learning centers" representing $128 million in revenue in 1983. The net earnings for KinderCare in fiscal year 1983 represented a 68 percent increase over fiscal year 1982. The company executed a five-for-four stock split in November 1982 and a four-for-three stock split in May 1983. Also, during fiscal year 1983, the company entered the market of freestanding immediate medical care by purchasing First Medical Corporation and its 10 facilities for an undisclosed sum.[153] By the second quarter of 1984, KinderCare reported that more than 100 new learning centers and 20 new clinics were under construction.[154]

During the 1990s, KinderCare dominated the child care industry with more than 1,100 centers, but new competitors were emerging to serve a seemingly infinite need for organized child care. In 1991, Children's Discovery Centers of America claimed 93 centers and $57.2 million in revenues; Rocking Horse Child Care Center of America owned 87 preschool and elementary learning centers and reported earnings of $34.7 million; Sunrise Preschools—the new kid on the block—earned $10.4 million through its 15 preschool programs. The smaller Discovery Centers more than doubled the number of its facilities, claiming 193 centers serving 17,500 children. Sunrise Preschools actually lost market share, reporting 1995 revenues of $9.7 million from 29 facilities that cared for 2,700 children.[155]

Within a few years, KinderCare's command of the child care industry would be challenged by several upstarts that showed explosive growth. Bright Horizons Family Solutions managed more than 500 workplace centers in 37 states, reported revenue of $423 million, and had 16,000 employees; La Petite Academy boasted 650 centers, $383 million in revenue, and 12,000 employees; Learning Care Group reported $206 million in revenue and 7,500 workers. The increasing participation of mothers in the labor market has increased the demand for child care. Between 1979 and 2000, the number of hours worked by wives increased 50.7 percent,[156] a figure that would likely increase as a function of stagnating family income and the work mandate affixed to welfare reform. By 2007, KinderCare had been acquired by Knowledge Learning Corporation which boasted annual revenues of $1.6 billion, almost double what KinderCare had reported in 2004. Many of the smaller child care businesses were acquired by Learning Care Group which reported annual revenues of $522 million in 2007.

Home Health Care

Several companies in the **home health care** market replicated the success of corporations in the nursing home industry. Home Health Care of America, later renamed Caremark, began in 1979. A leader in the field, the company grew particularly quickly. Caremark generated net revenues of $1 million in 1980, $35.8 million in 1983, and $133.2 million in 1986. In 1983 Caremark increased the number of its regional service centers from 10 to 31; despite the costs incurred by this expansion, net income for the year increased 129 percent. By the mid-1990s Caremark was reporting annual revenues of $2.4 billion and claimed health care facilities in Canada, France, Germany, the United Kingdom, the Netherlands, and Japan.[157]

Growth of this magnitude led Elsie Griffith, chief executive officer of the Visiting Nurse Service of New York and chair of the board of the National Association for Home Care, to observe that home health care "is expanding at a phenomenal rate."[158] Expansion continued during the early 1990s, when home health companies adjusted their services to meet earlier hospital discharges resulting from implementation of Medicare's prospective payment system. That is, as patients went home sooner, the need for a range of specialized in-home health services grew. Quickly, home health companies began to offer a variety of these services to patients. In markets where conventional home health companies failed to offer such specialized care, new firms entered the market and expanded rapidly.

The diversification of elder care began to accelerate in anticipation of the retirement of the baby-boomers. Apria Healthcare Group, with revenue of $1.3 billion and more than 10,000 employees, included infusion and respiratory therapy in addition to medical equipment as a complement to home health. American HomePatient hired more than 3,400 caregivers to generate $336 million in 2003.

Although Caremark had been acquired by the CVS drugstore company, which claimed revenues of $76.3 billion in 2007, the home health industry was comprised of smaller providers. In 2007, the industry consisted of Tender Loving Care Health Care Services reporting $112.6 million in revenues, Assisted Living Concepts, $229.4 million, Altria Senior Living Group $183.6 million, and National Home Health Care Corporation, $110.8 million. Odyssey, a commercial hospice, reported revenues of $404.9 million in 2007.

Assisted Living

Increased longevity and improved health of the elderly spawned a special market for those who can afford it: life care. The graying of the population has led some corporations to construct special residential communities—assisted living—that include health care as a service. And despite well-publicized bankruptcies of several retirement communities, the potentially enormous market for life care facilities has attracted the interest of several corporations. The investment community has been enthusiastic about life care. Harold Margolin, a vice president of Merrill Lynch, stated that "the financial climate could impact on the growth of the continuing care segment of the health care industry, but only on the timing. It's going to be a very large industry."[159] By

2007 two companies had established prominence in this niche of the elder care industry: Brookdale, $1.8 billion, and Sunrise Senior Living, $1.6 billion.

Corrections

Among the more ambitious of human service corporations is the Correction Corporation of America (CCA), founded in 1983 by Tom Beasely with the financial backing of Jack Massey, founder of the Hospital Corporation of America. CCA officials noted that many states were unable to contend with overcrowding of prison facilities and proposed contracting with state and local jurisdictions for the provision of correctional services. As CCA acknowledged in its 1986 annual report, court orders to upgrade facilities, coupled with governmental reluctance to finance such improvements, provided strong incentives for jurisdictions to consider contracting out correctional services:

> Government response to [overcrowding] has been hampered by the administrative and budgetary problems traditionally plaguing public sector facilities. Most systems have suffered a lack of long-term leadership due to their ties to the political process, and many jurisdictions have placed a low priority on corrections funding. The outcome has been a proliferation of out-dated facilities with a lack of sufficient capacity to meet constitutional standards.[160]

By 1986 CCA operated nine correctional facilities with a total of 1,646 beds, and the company was negotiating with the Texas Department of Corrections "to build and manage two minimum security prisons which will provide an additional 1,000 beds."[161]

Most analysts expect that proprietary correctional facilities would continue to grow in popularity as governmental agencies recognize the cost savings of contracting out correctional services. For example, CCA's per diem charge in 1986 was $29.77, about 25 percent less than the cost in public facilities.[162] Texas, Oklahoma, and Arkansas soon put 3,000 correctional "beds" out to bid, an indication of the willingness of states to use proprietary firms on a large scale.[163] The most dramatic example of the possibilities of for-profit corrections dates from 1985, when CCA startled Tennessee state officials by offering to take over the state's entire prison system. As in 30 other states and the District of Columbia, Tennessee's system housed too many prisoners in cramped, archaic facilities and was operating under court supervision. When CCA offered the state a price of $250 million on a 99-year contract, state officials were hard pressed not to give the bid careful consideration. Ultimately, state officials balked at the idea, primarily because of a conflict of interest between CCA and leaders of state government.[164]

Undaunted, CCA moved steadily ahead, capitalizing on the dire need of local and state governments for greater prison capacity. By 1991, CCA managed 17 facilities and reported annual revenues of $67.9 million. Although these earnings were small compared with those of other human service firms, they were astonishing in light of the $7.6 million CCA had earned just six years earlier. By the mid-1990s CCA reported revenues of $207 million from holdings that had expanded to 49 correctional facilities, totaling 33,153 beds, with plans to develop or expand 16 more. Despite CCA's expansion, the largest for-profit provider of correctional services was Wackenhut, a firm with prisons and detention facilities in the United States, Great Britain, and Australia. For 1995 Wackenhut reported income of $796 million from 24 owned or managed facilities, representing 16,000 beds.[165]

By 2007 CCA's revenues of $1.5 billion had eclipsed that of Wackenhut (now GEO Group), $1.1 billion, as the largest incarceration provider. Undaunted, other firms were entering the market: Avalon Correctional Services saw its revenue increase from $25 million in 2004 to $27.3 million in 2007. Providing health care to inmates, Correctional Medical Services, claimed $150 million in revenue in 2002 which jumped to $240 million in 2007, and MHM Services, Inc., reported revenues of $24.4 million for the provision of mental health services at more than 250 institutions.

Public Welfare

Several companies have become profitable through contracts with state and local government. The largest consulting group, MAXIMUS, increased its revenues from $558.3 million in 2004 to $738.7 million in 2007. Several companies provide managed health care for populations eligible for Medicaid, Medicare, and SCHIP. For 2007, AMERIGROUP coordinated the services of 80,000 physicians in a dozen states, serving 1.7 million people, and claimed revenues of $3.9 billion. Cantene Corporation generated $2.9 billion, and Molina Healthcare reported $2.5 billion serving low-income people receiving Medicaid and SCHIP.

Implications for Health and Human Service Professionals

Most human service professionals have been skeptical about the provision of social welfare by human service corporations. According to the critics of proprietary human service delivery, the corporate sector is the organizational manifestation of a capitalist economy that is at the root of much social injustice and human need. For traditional welfare advocates, professional practice within a corporate context is antithetical to the very idea of "social" welfare. In fact, studies of the organizational practices of human service corporations raise important questions about their suitability for promoting the commonweal. Human service corporations have been found to be less cost-effective than nonprofit and governmental agencies; they engage in discriminatory selection of clients, which penalizes the poor; and they attract clients away from voluntary social service agencies.

The critique of corporate incursion in social welfare is perhaps best illustrated by examining health care policy. Currently, the United States spends 16 percent of GDP on health care, yet 47 million Americans lack health insurance. Liberals who have advocated universal health care as public policy have pointed their fingers at the commercialization of health care as a primary factor for this paradox. As a result of the fragmentation of U.S. health care, simply managing the complexity of such an incoherent arrangement imposes administrative costs of $1,059 per capita in the United States, compared to $307 in Canada.[166] David Himmelstein, a Harvard physician and universal health advocate, estimated that the administrative savings if the United States were to adopt a single-payer system, similar to Canada's, would realize annual savings of $375 billion, sufficient to provide health insurance to every American.[167]

Despite the critique of corporate involvement in health and human services, commercial providers are likely to play an active role in defining social welfare. The economy of the United States is, after all, capitalist, and entrepreneurs are free to establish businesses in whatever markets they consider profitable. Unless government strictly regulates—or prohibits—the for-profit provision of human services, human service corporations will influence U.S.

social welfare to an even greater extent in the future. Skeptics of the commercialization of social welfare may take comfort in holding the moral high ground, but practically speaking, they are losing territory with accelerating speed to for-profit entrepreneurs. If the expansion of health and human service corporations during the latter decades of the twentieth century is not sufficient evidence, then consider the Medicare reforms of 2003 that subsidized the pharmaceutical industry.

Despite the proliferation of human service corporations, health and human service professionals have been slow to adopt the corporate sector as a setting for practice. Considering that organizations under traditional auspices—the voluntary and governmental sectors—are increasingly limited in their capacity to provide services, it is unfortunate that health and human service professionals have been loathe to consider corporations as a suitable vehicle for delivering services and benefits. Actually, for-profit firms can be advantageous for several reasons. Proprietary firms may provide access to the capital needed for expanding social services, a primary explanation for their rapid growth. And human service corporations can reduce the cost of commercially derived capital by depreciating assets and writing off interest payments against income during the first years of operation. These present obvious advantages for human service administrators who are faced with diminishing revenues derived from charitable or governmental sources. Perhaps the best example of this advantage is the meteoric rise of long-term care corporations, which were almost nonexistent as recently as 1970. By convincing commercial lenders and investors that long-term care was viable, for-profit firms eventually gained control over the industry.[168]

In some instances, too, the corporate sector offers more opportunities for program innovation than are possible under other auspices. Governmental programs must be mandated by a public authority, and this requires a consensus on how to deal with particular concerns. Voluntary sector agencies are ultimately managed by boards of directors that reflect the interests of the community in organizational policy. When human service issues are controversial, welfare professionals can encounter stiff opposition to needed programs. Some of this difficulty can be obviated by a corporate structure that is not so directly wedded to the status quo. An example of how a human service corporation offers opportunities not possible through traditional human service organizations is: for-profit correctional companies are able to expand the scope of correctional facilities at a time when government is reluctant to finance new construction and the voluntary sector is unable to raise the necessary capital.

The corporate sector offers greater organizational flexibility than that usually found in governmental agencies and a level of sophistication in managerial innovation not often found in the voluntary sector. To be sure, economic advantages enjoyed by the corporate sector help make this possible; but the track record in organizational experimentation by the corporate sector is undeniable. In fact, ideas that could be of value to traditional welfare organizations are frequently derived from the corporate sector, as such popular books as *In Search of Excellence* and *The Changemasters* attest.[169] That comparable books do not emerge from the voluntary or governmental sectors reflects how noncompetitive they are with respect to entrepreneurs of the for-profit sector.

Private Practice

Despite their antipathy toward privatization, many social workers engage in private practice, a commercial activity. Indeed, mental health care has been an area in which social workers have emulated the success of psychiatrists and psychologists. As a form of independent practice, private practice is influenced by the policies of the states regulating it, by professional associations, by the insurance companies that pay clinicians for their services, and by managed care companies that have become established as providers of mental health services. Private social work practice in mental health has been controversial within the social work profession, as reflected in this depiction:

> In increasing numbers, social workers are flocking to psychotherapeutic pastures, hanging out their shingles to advertise themselves as psychotherapists just as quickly as licensing laws will permit. For the most part, professional associations of social workers and schools of social work are active participants in the great transformation of social work from a professional corps concerned with helping people deal with their social problems to a major platoon in the psychotherapeutic armies.[170]

Despite its detractors, private practice continues to be an attractive vehicle for delivering clinical social services. In 2001, 23 percent of social workers reported that their primary activity was in solo or group private practice; another 37 percent indicated they were "involved" in private practice. Of all National Association of Social Workers (NASW) members, the number working in for-profit settings increased from 19.8 percent in 1988 to 27.9 percent in 1995.[171] A subsample of NASW members indicated that in 2000, 35 percent were employed in the private, for-profit sector.[172]

For some time, many mental health services have been delivered by psychiatrists and psychologists who work predominantly out of private offices. The upsurge of social workers' interest in private practice is such that today a large portion of students entering graduate programs in social work—as many as 80 percent[173]—do so with the expressed intent of establishing a private practice. Professional schools of social work are specifically equipped to prepare graduate students for private practice. "M.S.W. programs appear to offer more to the practitioner bound for private practice than to the social worker who would prefer to work in an agency setting," concluded researchers in a study of private and agency-based social workers.[174]

The current enthusiasm for private practice can be attributed to several factors. First, private practitioners often enjoy a prestige and income that set them apart from salaried professionals.[175] In addition, private practitioners work significantly fewer hours per week compared to colleagues in public and nonprofit settings.[176] In 2002, 41 percent of social workers in private practice worked between 10 and 29 hours per week, a greater number than those working 30 hours or more, 32 percent.[177] It is not surprising that social workers, who are mostly female and usually underpaid—social work salaries are significantly less than those of nurses or teachers[178]—would see private practice as a way to increase their earnings and status. In fact, women are more likely to engage in private practice than to work in traditional social service agencies; two-thirds of private practitioners are women.[179]

Private practitioners also have a degree of autonomy that is not available to professionals who are bound by the personnel policies of traditional agencies. Srinika Jayaratne and associates found that "whereas 55 percent of the private practitioners report a high level of congruence between their expectations and their activities, only 18.3 percent of the agency practitioners do so."[180] This autonomy is important for experienced professionals who find continued supervision unnecessary or intrusive and who desire some flexibility in their work schedules to make room for other priorities. Finally, private practice allows professionals to specialize in activities at which they are best instead of having to conform to organizational requirements of the private agency or governmental bureaucracy. Again, 66.5 percent of private practitioners reported that they were able to do the things at which they excelled, whereas only 22.9 percent of agency practitioners said they could do so.[181]

The image of private practice that has emerged is one of freedom and opportunity, sans rules and regulations. This is somewhat misleading. Although private practice may involve comparatively fewer compliance requirements compared to salaried employment, it is anything but unfettered. In actuality, private practice involves many policies with which practitioners must be familiar if they are to be successful. The policies that affect private practice originate primarily from three sources: the professional community (a private entity); a government regulatory authority (a public entity); and, because of the role of managed care, corporate firms (commercial entities). This situation is complicated by the provision of service through the marketplace of a capitalist economy that traditionally discriminates against groups that do not participate fully in the labor market—minorities, women, elderly people, and people with disabilities. These groups frequently lack the resources to purchase the services provided by private practitioners. For this reason, private practice is not easily reconciled with the traditional values of social work, which emphasize service to the community and to the disadvantaged. So it is paradoxical that private practice has become a popular method of social work practice, and this development remains controversial.

The private practice of social work is a relatively recent phenomenon. The National Association of Social Workers did not officially sanction this form of service delivery for its members until 1964.[182] Before that, privately practicing social workers identified themselves as psychotherapists and lay analysts. Typically, they relied on referrals from physicians and psychiatrists,[183] and after World War II they began to establish "flourishing and lucrative" practices.[184] By 1987 all 50 states regulated social workers, with the majority of states requiring a master's degree in social work (M.S.W.). However, a social work license is not automatically awarded to those holding the M.S.W. degree. Many

states require candidates for licensure to have two years of post-M.S.W. experience under the supervision of a **licensed certified social worker** (LCSW) and to pass an examination. Beyond these common requirements, states vary greatly in their regulatory practices. Maryland, for example, has a three-tier system: the LCSW for M.S.W.s who have two years of post-M.S.W. experience and who have passed an examination; the Licensed Graduate Social Worker (LGSW) for newly graduated M.S.W.s; and the Social Work Associate (SWA) for those with baccalaureate degrees in social work.

To further complicate matters, new licensing legislation often allows candidates who have practiced professionally to become licensed without first meeting the requirements of the licensing legislation. This practice, called "grandfathering," is characteristic of new licensing legislation, and, in that social work licensing is a relatively recent development in many states, there are many LCSWs in practice who would not otherwise meet the technical requirements for a license. Moreover, because some states exempt state employees from licensing requirements, many "social workers" in public welfare do not meet the licensing requirements necessary for the title of social worker. As a result, many social workers are licensed but have not met the requirements with which their colleagues must comply. Consequently, states often establish additional requirements for professionals to be eligible for vendorship. Special registries for clinical social workers may be used to identify LCSWs who are eligible for third-party payments.

Professional associations also designate practitioners who have expertise in particular areas. In social work the most common distinction is membership in the Academy of Certified Social Workers (ACSW). Requirements for the ACSW are two years of post-M.S.W. experience under the supervision of an ACSW and passage of an examination. These are similar to the requirements for the LCSW, but the two designations should not be confused. Because states have the legal authority to license professions, special distinctions established by professional associations are neither equivalent to nor a substitute for state licensure. Thus, it is common for experienced clinicians to list both LCSW and ACSW after their names as indications of professional competence. Recently the NASW (which administers the ACSW) developed a "diplomate" designation, which identifies practitioners with skills above those required for the ACSW. Credentials such as the ACSW serve the function of distinguishing expertise among members of the professional community. But again, such credentials are determined by policies of the professional community and not by a public authority, as in the case of state licensure.[185]

Clinicians who successfully cultivate private practices stand to do quite well economically. Financial gain does not appear to be the sole motivation for social workers who enter private practice, however. In research on the motives of private social work practitioners versus social workers employed in agencies, stress reduction played an important part in the decision to go private. "Those in private practice reported fewer psychological and health strains, reported higher levels of performance, and, in general, felt better about their life circumstances," concluded researchers on private practice. "On every measure, those in private practice scored significantly better than those in agency practice."[186]

Despite the popularity of private practice, it has provoked a great deal of controversy within the professional community. There are several aspects to this controversy, not the least of which is that many practitioners who have committed themselves to helping the disadvantaged by working in voluntary and governmental sectors view the popularity of private practice as antithetical to everything that is "social" about social work. Donald Feldstein, head of the Federation of Jewish Philanthropies of New York, suggested that private social work practice is similar to private medical practice in that it presents "new opportunities for rip-offs by the privileged." Private practice, he maintained, was replacing social decision making with market decision making. According to Feldstein, "Social decision making is preferable to marketing human services like soap. . . . The private practice of social work is still against everything that is social about the term social work."[187] Another critic impugned the motives of social workers in private practice. "Over 15 years ago, when I first had exposure to private practitioners, they were objects of envy, never of nonacceptance. Obviously this envy has continued. For we see more social workers developing private practices. But why all the sham? Let's be honest enough to say it's usually done for the money."[188]

Defenders of private practice emphasize the benefits of the method for practitioners and clients. Why should social workers not enjoy the same professional freedom and responsibility as other professions that use private practice extensively, for instance, law, medicine, and psychiatry? Moreover,

"some clients prefer the opportunity to choose their own practitioner and a service they consider more personal and confidential."[189] Concern for the client's perceptions means that practitioners must be concerned about their image. This is evident in one privately practicing social worker's description of her office:

> It is decorated with comfortable chairs, built-in book cases, soft lighting, etc., and is arranged in such a way as to offer several different possibilities for seating. It is commensurate with most of the socio-cultural levels of my client group and provides him or her the opportunity for free expression without being overheard. . . . Dealing with only one socio-cultural client group allows me to provide physical surroundings which facilitate the client's identification with the worker.[190]

On the surface, then, private practice often provokes strong responses from welfare professionals, who perceive private practitioners as avoiding efforts by the voluntary and governmental sectors to advance social justice. On the other hand, some private practitioners believe that their work offers them an opportunity not only to enhance their status but also to provide mental health services to a middle class that the profession has neglected.

Beneath this surface issue, there are more substantive problems raised by private practice. Perhaps the most important of these is preferential selection. In an era of specialization, professionals will refer to other providers those clients with problems that are inappropriate for their practice. An important finding of Jayaratne's research was that private practitioners do not perceive their clients in the same way that agency-based social workers do. The latter "were significantly more likely to agree with the statement that 'my personal values and those of my clients differ greatly' than those in private practice."[191] Preferential selection becomes an issue when private practitioners elect to serve less troubled clients (who are able to pay the full cost of care) while referring multiproblem clients (who are unable to pay the practitioner's fee for service directly or through insurance) to agencies of the voluntary sector. Such "creaming" of the client population places an enormous burden on public agencies, which are left to carry a disproportionate share of chronically disturbed and indigent clients. In effect, then, the public sector absorbs the losses that private practitioners would suffer if they served this population. Preferential selection has become so pronounced that researchers have facetiously identified it as a syndrome. According to Franklin Chu and Sharland Trotter, the commercialization of private practice contributes to the **YAVIS syndrome**—the tendency of clients of private practitioners to be young, attractive, verbal, intelligent, and successful. One might add W to the syndrome, because the clients also tend to be disproportionately white.[192] Consequently, clients of private practitioners are less likely to be poor, unemployed, old, and uneducated.

The Business of Private Practice

Aside from preferential selection, another set of issues relates directly to the business nature of private practice. Because private practice is a business, economic considerations figure prominently in a professional's activities. Robert Barker, an authority on private social work practice, explains how economic factors shaped a new practice he established with a colleague: "We hired a good secretary, employed interior decorators to redo our offices and waiting room. We hired an investment counselor and established retirement accounts and insurance programs. Most of all we became more serious about getting our clients to meet their financial obligations."[193] The market nature of private practice, coupled with economic entrepreneurship, presents the possibility of questionable accounting practices, such as the creation of "uncollectible accounts," the use of "deliberate misdiagnosis," and the practice of "signing off." These practices involve income derived from third-party sources, usually health insurance. As private practitioners become dependent on insurance reimbursement, these questionable accounting practices become important for the professional community at large.

Health insurance frequently covers outpatient psychiatric care at a **usual, customary, and reasonable (UCR)** rate determined by the insurance companies. The UCR is what the therapist charges, not necessarily what he or she expects to collect from cash-paying clients. The practice of charging a fee higher than what is expected to be collected is termed holding an "uncollectable account," and it is frequently used with third-party fee payment arrangements. This practice is encouraged because insurance coverage rarely covers all of the practitioner's fee but leaves a certain percent to be paid by the client. For example, a social worker may have a UCR of $80 per session. The client may have insurance paying only 50 percent of the UCR, which leaves the client responsible for the remaining $40.

If the client is unable to pay $40 per session but can afford $10, a clinician will bill the insurance company directly, using an assignment of benefits procedure, for $80. Meanwhile, the client pays $10 per session, as opposed to the implied obligatory contractual amount of $40. Although the therapist may collect a total of $50 per session and not the UCR of $80, it may be economical to prefer that amount over an extended period of treatment or possibly until the client can afford the full amount of the copayment. At question here is a professional practice that is contrary to the implied contractual relationship among the client, the clinician, and the third-party payer. Yet it is in the interest of the clinician to establish this as a regular accounting procedure; the clinician depends on income from fees and may fear that the insurance company will lower the UCR if a significant number of billings (usually 50 percent) are below the customary rate.

A second questionable practice is **deliberate misdiagnosis,** an intentional error in client assessment on the part of clinicians. In a survey of clinical social workers, 70 percent of whom had engaged in private practice, Stuart Kirk and Herb Kutchins found that 87 percent of practitioners frequently or occasionally used a less stigmatizing, or "mercy," diagnosis to avoid labeling their patients. On the other hand, clinicians also frequently misdiagnose in order to collect insurance payments:

> Seventy-two percent of the respondents are aware of cases where more serious diagnoses are used to qualify for reimbursement. At least 25 percent of the respondents . . . indicated that the practices occurred frequently. Since reimbursement is rarely available for family problems, it is not surprising that 86 percent are aware of instances when diagnoses for individuals are used even though the primary problem is in the family. The majority of respondents said that this occurred frequently.[194]

Of course, such "overdiagnosis" is unethical because it places the economic benefit of the clinician before the service needs of the client. Still, overdiagnosis continues to be a prevalent practice. Kirk and Kutchins suggest that "reimbursement systems, which have become increasingly important for psychiatric treatment for the last decade, are undoubtedly a major factor in encouraging over-diagnosis."[195] The undesirable consequences of a reimbursement-driven diagnosis system are multiple. First, of course, is the possibility that clients will be done harm, particularly if confidentiality is breached and the diagnosis becomes known to others outside the therapeutic relationship. Second, if the prevalence of severe mental disorders is overreported, public officials may make errors in program planning as a result, concluding that mental disorders are worse than is actually the case. Third, and perhaps most important, overdiagnosis violates the "professionals' obligation to their profession to use their knowledge and skill in an ethical manner."[196] To be sure, individual digressions can be reported to professional and governmental bodies for investigation, but a greater problem exists for practitioners as a whole. Widespread misdiagnosis violates the social contract between the professional community and the state, and thus threatens to "corrupt the helping professions."[197] For these reasons, ethical problems associated with the relationship between diagnosis and reimbursement are of great concern to the professional community.[198]

Finally, there is the practice of signing off. Signing off has become important because some insurance covers only services provided by psychiatrists or psychologists. In other instances, insurance will reimburse at a higher rate when the services are provided by a psychiatrist or psychologist than when they are rendered by a social worker. The sign-off practice is one in which, in order to maximize reimbursement, the psychiatrist or psychologist signs the insurance claim even though the services were provided by a social worker. In some instances psychiatrists and psychologists may recruit social workers, paying them half the fees charged to insurance companies and pocketing the difference. Signing off is a type of fee splitting, and it is "unethical because it allows practitioners to refer clients not to the professional most suitable for the client's needs, but to the person who pays the highest fee."[199]

In a community in which many private practitioners compete for a limited number of paying clients, aggressive business practices, such as those above, are likely to raise questions about the ultimate concern of practitioners—whether it is the client's welfare or the clinician's income. Although the question is not ordinarily couched in such crude terms, the behavior of private practitioners may not be lost on the client population. Because clients usually seek services voluntarily, their impressions of practitioners are important; negative perceptions will eventually hurt practitioners as their clients seek services elsewhere. When unfavorable impressions emerge as a result of the practices described, practitioners will be prudent to take corrective action. Although the ethical code of the professional community can be a source for such action, much remains at the discretion of the individual practitioner.

Private practice is literally *private*, and practitioners enjoy "substantial discretion in conducting their activities."[200] Economic and other considerations may encourage private practitioners to engage in unethical or questionable practices. In such instances, other practitioners are obliged to report allegations of violations to the state licensing board or the professional association. Ultimately, it is in the interest of the professional community to address questionable practices of practitioners, and this includes the unethical business practices of private practitioners. When the media report that "routine falsification of insurance billings and other peculiarities of the mental health professions have caused acute anxiety among insurance companies . . . [who] now think they have little control over what they are paying for," more government regulation is probably not far behind.[201] In other instances, the consequences are acutely embarrassing for the professional community, as when a leading proponent of third-party reimbursement for social workers in Kentucky was found guilty of insurance fraud and ordered to return $37,000 to Blue Cross–Blue Shield.[202]

The Future of Private Practice

In response to the limitations imposed by traditional practice settings, many human service professionals have turned to private practice as a way of securing their economic and professional objectives. Private practice gives program administrators a chance to maintain their direct service skills, educators the opportunity to continue contact with clients, and clinicians with families the freedom to combine professional practice and attention to family life. More important, private practice may prove an adjunct to agency activities. "By fostering part-time practice," researchers have noted, "the profession can keep its main focus on agency services where there is a commitment to serve persons without regard to their ability to pay and where there can be a basis for social action and reform."[203]

As the growth of managed care illustrates, much of private practice is a result of larger social forces. Ellen Dunbar, former executive director of the California chapter of NASW, observed, "The major overriding trend that engulfs all others is that social work along with other service professions is becoming more commercial . . . [and] more an integral part of the free enterprise system."[204] In fact, the commercialization of social work attracted wide attention as the profession became more immersed in private practice. "There is concern," reported *Newsweek,* "that too many social workers are turning their backs on their traditional casework among the poor to practice therapy." *Newsweek* wondered at the consequences of "an apparent middle-class therapy explosion at the expense of public welfare and grassroots service."[205] How social work will reconcile its commitment to social justice with the new opportunities presented by private practice remains a central question before the professional community.

The interest in alternative methods of service delivery represents an implicit criticism of traditional ways in which social agencies provide services. Conventional contexts of direct practice evidence several faults. First, traditional agencies place constraints on employee discretion and professional autonomy. Second, rigid agency policies make few allowances for the demands of an employee's family life and community involvements. Third, the demands of increasing caseloads compounded by diminishing resources make traditional agencies a less desirable setting in which to practice. Although nonprofit agencies have been superior to governmental programs in the quality of services provided, these traditional auspices of service delivery are beginning to merge. Consequently, social work in smaller, voluntary agencies is not very different from the "proletarianized" work in larger, public agencies.[206] To the extent that traditional agencies become less desirable as contexts in which to practice, innovative models of service delivery surface.

As researchers on private practice have noted, rather than criticizing professionals who have opted for the private sector, the social work community should make it a priority to reform the means of service provision through traditional agencies. "The goal should be to make agency practice good for the health and well-being of the practitioner, because the ultimate beneficiary would be the client."[207] Stan Taubman, who has held direct practice and administrative positions and who couples county employment with private practice, states the matter succinctly: "Private practice isn't keeping social workers out of public services. Public services are."[208]

One service delivery innovation has been employee assistance plans (EAPs). Since the 1970s, social workers have been involved in EAPs that provide a range of services to workers, a population often neglected by traditional welfare programs.[209] By the late 1980s, occupational social welfare had become a popular specialization within social work, with graduate schools offering special curricula on the subject, a national conference inaugurated for specialists in the field, and a special issue of *Social Work* dedicated to it.[210] Although studies of EAPs are scarce,[211] there is evidence that occupational social work is likely to expand, particularly when located within the corporation. In a modest study of 23 "private-sector, management-sponsored" EAPs, Shulamith Straussner found that in-house programs demonstrated notable advantages over those contracted out. For example, EAPs located within the corporation cost one-third as much as contracted-out services. In-house EAPs proved adaptable to management priorities, developing "short-term programs to deal with company reorganization or retrenchment, special health concerns . . . [and] other organizational needs." Significantly, union representatives approved in-house EAPs twice as frequently as they did contracted-out programs.[212] These findings suggest that EAPs that are managed by employers are perceived by management and unions as superior to services provided by an external agency. If corporate executives and labor leaders develop personnel policies consistent with these findings, welfare professionals will find the business community a hospitable setting in which to practice. In that event, occupational social work within the corporation may become as prevalent an auspice of practice as are the voluntary and governmental sectors. Another service delivery innovation is employee ownership. Curiously, human service professionals occasionally advocate employee ownership as a method for empowering clients, they fail to see comparable benefits for themselves. For example, Cooperative Home Care Associates (CHCA) of New York City has been co-owned by employees since its inception in 1985. CHCA offers above-average wages as well as health and vacation benefits and has, as a result, served as a vehicle out of poverty for many workers who had been on public assistance.[213] By 2007, CHCA provided jobs for 1,600 home care workers and generated $60 million in annual revenue.[214]

An as yet unexplored innovation for human service professionals is the employee stock option plan (ESOP). Through ESOPs, workers gain ownership of a firm by gradually acquiring stock, the acquisition of which is granted certain tax advantages. Workers had used ESOPs to purchase wholly or in part several large corporations, such as J.C.

Penney, Kroger's, Avis, and United Airlines.[215] Inexplicably, human service professionals had not used ESOPs to gain control over the organizations that employ them. In part this can be explained by the fact that the traditional auspices of practice have been the nonprofit and governmental sectors. It may seem implausible for Department of Social Service employees to seek ownership of the local welfare department or for professionals hired by the local Family Service Agency to acquire that organization. Nevertheless, recent trends in privatization make employee ownership plausible.

In the absence of employee ownership alternatives, some private practitioners have undertaken competitive strategies vis-à-vis managed care corporations. The most obvious alternative is the creation of **Independent Practice Associations (IPA)** as alternatives to HMOs. If social workers provide such a large volume of mental health services and at reasonable cost, they could organize themselves into an IPA in order to counter competitive practices of HMOs. As managed care made in-roads into private medical practice, physicians organized IPAs, which now have larger enrollments than HMOs. Without a similar strategy, social workers are apt to remain vulnerable to behavioral managed care corporations. In the absence of alternatives, private practitioners have reacted defensively. The Virginia, California, New Jersey, and District of Columbia chapters of the American Psychological Association, for example, have sued HMOs for restricting the number of therapeutic sessions, limiting out-of-network referrals, and purging provider lists.[216]

If an issue within social work is the defection of private practitioners from their broader social responsibilities, licensing requirements could be altered to encourage involvement in community activities. Professionals are often required to demonstrate they are current with practice developments by acquiring Continuing Education Units (CEUs) for licensing. Following this logic, CEU requirements could be augmented to require professionals to demonstrate a minimal number of community service hours in order to obtain and keep a license. If mental health professionals—psychiatrists, psychologists, and social workers—were required to volunteer 20 hours annually with a nonprofit organization as a condition of licensing, a significant volume of mental health care would be available to the mentally ill. At this level of voluntary activity, 100 professionals are equivalent to one full-time staff person.

Continued growth of the for-profit sector is inevitable given expansion of the service sector, government reimbursement of private providers, and the willingness of corporations to explore new markets. Although social workers have been eager to engage in commercial activities through private practice, they have been reluctant to seize opportunities within the corporate sector. In this respect, social work has imposed its own glass ceiling on the prospects of its professional members. If social workers can make significant contributions through private forms of service delivery, such as the voluntary sector and private practice, there is no logical reason for them to write off the corporate sector.

Discussion Questions

1. Privatization is a hotly debated issue in social welfare. To what extent are some of the major concerns about privatization (e.g., unfair competition between nonprofit agencies and commercial firms, preferential selection and dumping of clients, superior performance of private providers, the emergence of an oligopoly of private providers) evident in your community? Should human service professionals practice in for-profit firms?

2. If you were inclined to establish a business providing a human service, what population would you focus on? How would you get capital to start the business? Would you own the business, or would you share ownership with stockholders? How would you market your service? What would you do with the profits— provide stockholders with dividends, enlarge the business, or make contributions to nonprofit agencies? What would be the name of your business?

3. Think tanks exist in Washington, DC, and in most state capitals. Obtain a copy of the annual report of a think tank. Who funds the think tank? Is there a relationship between the funding source and the ideological character of reports that the think tank publishes? What is the think tank's track record in social welfare issues?

4. In order to attain job security, many human service professionals join unions. What is the largest union to which social workers belong in your community? Do issues relating to service delivery figure in the union's negotiations with management? Under what conditions would human service professionals in your community engage in a strike?

5. The debate between private practice and agency-based practice continues as a heated issue within social work. What are the advantages and disadvantages of each? Is there a common base of social work practice? Can you foresee some ways to resolve the issue and bring private practitioners and agency-based practitioners together?

6. Private practice continues to be a focus of students in schools of social work. How many of your classmates are planning to become private practitioners? What are their motives? Do faculty members in your social work program who also have private practices serve as role models to students? Is there an opportunity in your studies to discuss the implications of private practice for social work?

7. How does your state regulate the practice of social work? What governmental unit is responsible for regulating social work? How is it constituted? Does your state have reciprocity arrangements with other states, honoring licenses granted in other jurisdictions? Has your state's social work licensing unit expelled professionals for unethical practices?

8. What is the position of your state chapter of the National Association of Social Workers on regulating professional practice? Are licensing and vendorship still high on the state chapter's priority list? If so, which social workers in your state remain concerned about the regulation of professional practice? Why?

9. What are the main concerns within your professional community about private practice—fees, misdiagnosis, licensing, image, competition with other professionals, vendorship? How are disagreements arbitrated, formally or informally?

10. Employee ownership is a way for human service professionals to attain control over their practices. Of the prominent social service agencies in your community, which ones might be candidates for employee ownership? If such a transition were accomplished, how would you ensure accountability to consumers? To the community?

Notes

1. Marilyn Hennessy, "Wanted: A Few Good Agencies" (Alexandria, VA: Odyssey Forum, 1998), p. 5.

2. Paul Starr, "The Meaning of Privatization," quoted in American Federation of State, County, and Municipal Employees, *Private Profit, Public Risk: The Contracting Out of Professional Services* (Washington, DC: AFSCME, 1986), pp. 4–5.

3. Charles Schultz, *The Public Use of Private Interest* (Washington, DC: Brookings Institution, 1977); Donald Fisk, Herbert Kiesling, and Thomas Muller, *Private Provision of Public Service* (Washington, DC: Urban Institute, 1978); Harry Hatry, *A Review of Private Approaches for the Delivery of Public Services* (Washington, DC: Urban Institute, 1983).

4. *Privatization: Toward More Effective Government* (Washington, DC: Report of the President's Commission on Privatization, March 1988), p. 230.

5. Ibid., pp. 1–2.

6. David Obsborne and Ted Gaebler, *Reinventing Government* (New York: Addison Wesley, 1992).

7. John Donahue, *The Privatization Decision* (New York: Basic Books, 1989), p. 216.

8. Harry Specht and Mark Courtney, *Unfaithful Angels* (New York: Free Press, 1994), p. 107.

9. Nina Bernstein, "Giant Companies Entering Race to Run State Welfare Programs," *New York Times* (September 15, 1996), p. 1.

10. Quoted in Bernstein, "Giant Companies Entering Race to Run State Welfare Programs," p. 1.
11. Ibid.
12. See Lawrence S. Lewin, Robert A. Derzon, and Rhea Margulies, "Investor-Owned and Nonprofits Differ in Economic Performance," *Hospitals* (July 1, 1981), pp. 65–69; Robert V. Pattison and Hallie Katz, "Investor-Owned Hospitals and Not-for-Profit Hospitals," *New England Journal of Medicine* (August 11, 1983), pp. 54–65; Robin Eskoz and K. Michael Peddecord, "The Relationship of Hospital Ownership and Service Composition to Hospital Charges," *Health Care Financing Review* (Spring 1985), pp. 125–132; J. Michael Watt et al., "The Comparative Economic Performance of Investor-Owned Chain and Not-for-Profit Hospitals," *New England Journal of Medicine* (January 9, 1986), pp. 356–360; Bradford Gray and Walter McNerney, "For-Profit Enterprise in Health Care: The Institute of Medicine Study," *New England Journal of Medicine* (June 5, 1986), pp. 560–563; Regina Herzlinger and William Kradker, "Who Profits from Nonprofits?" *Harvard Business Review* (January–February 1987), pp. 554–562.
13. Richard Titmuss, *The Gift Relationship* (New York: Pantheon, 1971), p. 223.
14. Theodore Marmor, Mark Schlesinger, and Richard Smithey, "A New Look at Nonprofits: Health Care Policy in a Competitive Age," *Yale Journal of Regulation* 3 (Spring 1986), p. 320.
15. Clifford Levy and Michael Luo, "New York Medicaid Fraud May Reach Into Billions," *New York Times* (July 18, 2005), p. A1; Clifford Gaul, "Bad Practices Net Hospitals More Money," *Washington Post* (July 24, 2005), p. A1; Charles Duhigg, "At Many Homes, More Profit and Less Nursing," *New York Times* (September 23, 2007), p. A1.
16. Robert Pear, "Nonprofit Hospitals Face Scrutiny Over Practices," *New York Times* (March 19, 2006), p. A14.
17. Milt Freudenheim, "California Backs Merger of 2 Giant Blue Cross Plans," *New York Times* (November 10, 2004), p. C1.
18. John Tierney, "City Schools That Work," *New York Times* (March 19, 2006), p. A25; George Will, "A Tide for School Choice," *Washington Post* (February 1, 2007), p. A15.
19. Sam Dillon, "Charter Schools Alter Map of Public Education in Dayton," *New York Times* (March 27, 2005), p. A15.
20. Charles Muntaner et al., "Psychotic Inpatients' Social Class and Their First Admission to State or Private Psychiatric Baltimore Hospitals," *American Journal of Public Health*, 84, no. 2 (February 1994), p. 287.
21. Richard Cloward and Irwin Epstein, "Private Social Welfare's Disengagement from the Poor," in Meyer Zald (ed.), *Social Welfare Institutions* (New York: John Wiley, 1965), pp. 628–629.
22. Emily Friedman, "The 'Dumping' Dilemma," *Hospitals* (September 1, 1982), p. 54.
23. Mark Schlesinger, "The Privatization of Health Care and Physicians' Perceptions of Access to Hospital Services," *The Milbank Quarterly* 65 (1987), p. 40.
24. Marmor, Schlesinger, and Smithey, "A New Look at Nonprofits," p. 344.
25. Gray and McNerney, "For-Profit Enterprise in Health Care," p. 1525.
26. Robert Kuttner, "Columbia/HCA and the Resurgence of the For-Profit Hospital Business," *New England Journal of Medicine* 335, no. 5 (August 1, 1996), pp. 365–366.
27. Anna Amirkhanyan, Hyun Kim, and Kristina Lambright, "Does the Public Sector Outperform the Nonprofit and For-Profit Sectors?" *Journal of Policy Analysis and Management*, 27, 2 (Spring 2008), pp. 326–353.
28. "Hospitals' Medicare Profits Up," *San Diego Union* (March 29, 1987), p. A5.
29. Richard Buchanan, "Long-Term Care's Pricing Dilemma," *Contemporary Administrator* (February 1981), p. 20.
30. Ann LoLordo, "Life-Care Centers Offer Seniors Worry-Free Living," *Baltimore Sun* (June 4, 1984), p. D4.
31. Carol Olten, "Communities Offering Seniors a Graceful Life," *San Diego Union* (March 13, 1988), p. D5.
32. Anthony Perry, "North County Housing Boom: A Lucrative Shade of Gray," *Los Angeles Times* (March 6, 1988), p. E5.
33. U.S. Senate Special Committee on Aging, *Discrimination against the Poor and Disabled in Nursing Homes*, (Washington, DC: U.S. GPO, 1984), p. 25.
34. Ibid., p. 10.
35. Quoted in William Spicer, "The Boom in Building," *Contemporary Administrator* (February 1982), p. 16.
36. Douglas Frantz, "Lobbyists, Interest Groups Begin Costly Health Care Battle," *Los Angeles Times* (May 24, 1993).
37. "Big Lobbying Spenders in 2007," *Washington Post* (April 15, 2008), p. A13.
38. Arnold Relman, "The New Medical-Industrial Complex," *New England Journal of Medicine* 303, no. 17 (1980), p. 80.
39. Robert Pear, "Health Industry Bidding to Hire Medicare Chief," *New York Times* (December 3, 2003), p. A1.
40. Robert Pear, "Medicare Chief Joins Firm with Health Clients," *New York Times* (December 19, 2003), p. A20.
41. Judy Sarasohn, "Special Interests," *Washington Post* (June 24, 2004), p. A23.
42. Robert Pear, "Agency Sees Withholding of Medicare Data from Congress as Illegal," *New York Times* (May 4, 2004), p. A17.

43. Sheryl Stolberg and Robert Pear, "Mysterious Fax Adds to Intrigue over Drug Bill," *New York Times* (March 18, 2004), p. A1.

44. Amy Goldstein, "Foster: White House Had Role in Withholding Medicare Data," *Washington Post* (March 19, 2004), p. A2.

45. Cheryl Stolberg, "2 Decline to Testify on Drug Cost," *New York Times* (April 2, 2004), p. A15.

46. Paul Starr, "The Limits of Privatization," in Steve Hanke, *Prospects for Privatization* (New York: Proceedings of the Academy of Political Science, 1987), pp. 82–107.

47. Kuttner, "Columbia/HCA," p. 363.

48. Reason Foundation, *Privatization 1992* (Los Angeles: Reason Foundation, 1992), p. 17.

49. David Stoesz, "Human-Service Corporations: New Opportunities in Social Work Administration," *Social Work Administration* 12 (1989), pp. 35–43.

50. Reason Foundation, *Privatization 1992*, p. 251.

51. David Donnison, "The Progressive Potential of Privatisation," in Julian LeGrand and Ray Robinson (eds.), *Privatisation and the Welfare State* (London: George Allen & Unwin, 1984), pp. 211–231.

52. Milton Tambor, "Unions," *Encyclopedia of Social Work*, 19th ed. (Washington, DC: National Association of Social Workers, 1995), pp. 2418–2419.

53. J. Weitzman, *The Scope of Bargaining in Public Employment* (New York: Praeger, 1975), p. 17.

54. Milton Tambor, "The Social Service Union in the Workplace," in Howard Karger (ed.), *Social Work and Labor Unions* (New York: Greenwood, 1988).

55. Dena Fisher, "Problems for Social Work in a Strike Situation," *Social Work* 32 (May–June 1987), pp. 253–254.

56. Jerry Wurf, "Labor Movement, Social Work Fighting Similar Battles," *NASW News* 25, no. 12 (December 1980), p. 7.

57. Bradford Plumer, "Labor's Love Lost," *The New Republic*, 238, 4,834 (April 23, 2008), p. 27.

58. Steven Greenhouse, "Conflict Between 2 Unions Intensifies," *New York Times* (April 16, 2008), p. A19.

59. Leslie Alexander et al., "Social Workers in Unions," *Social Work* 25 (May 1980), p. 222.

60. Ernie Lightman, "Professionalization, Bureaucratization, and Unionization in Social Work," *Social Service Review* 56, no. 1 (March 1982), p. 130.

61. Gary Shaffer, "Labor Relations and the Unionization of Professional Social Workers," *Journal of Education for Social Work* 15 (Winter 1979), p. 82.

62. "Public Service Workers' Strikes Disrupts Life in Canada," *Los Angeles Times* (September 10, 1991), p. A8.

63. Charles Heckscher, "Beyond Contract Bargaining: Partnership, Persuasion, and Power," *Social Policy* 25, no. 2 (1994), p. 29.

64. Jacob Hacker, *The Divided Welfare State* (New York: Cambridge University Press, 2002), p. 22.

65. Ibid., pp. 51, 339.

66. Jinlay Lewis, "CEOs' Presence in Bush Party Draws Attention to Their Pay," *San Diego Union* (January 13, 1992), p. E3.

67. Fred Barnes, "The Zillionaires' Club," *The New Republic* (January 29, 1990), p. 23.

68. Jacqueline Salmon, "Minorities Grab Fundraisers' Notice," *Washington Post* (November 7, 2004), p. F8.

69. Sheila Kamerman, "The New Mixed Economy of Welfare," *Social Work* 28 (January–February 1983), p. 76.

70. Paul Starr, "The Meaning of Privatization," and MDRC Bendick, "Privatizing the Delivery of Social Welfare Service" in *Working Paper 6* (Washington, DC: National Conference on Social Welfare, 1985); David Stoesz, "Privatization: Reforming the Welfare State," *Journal of Sociology and Social Welfare* 16 (Summer 1987), p. 139; Mimi Abramovitz, "The Privatization of the Welfare State," *Social Work* 31, no.4 (July–August 1986), pp. 257–264.

71. Neil Gilbert, *Capitalism and the Welfare State* (New Haven, CT: Yale University Press, 1983).

72. David Stoesz, "Corporate Welfare," *Social Work* 31, no. 4 (July–August 1986), p. 86; "Corporate Health Care and Social Welfare," *Health and Social Work* (Summer 1986), p. 158; "The Gray Market," *Journal of Gerontological Social Work* 16 (1989), p. 31.

73. Abramovitz, "The Privatization of the Welfare State," p. 257.

74. Marmor, Schlesinger, and Smithey, "A New Look at Nonprofits: Health Care Policy in a Competitive Age," p. 322.

75. Robert Heilbroner, *The Worldly Philosophers* (New York: Simon and Schuster, 1967), pp. 98–106.

76. Edward Berkowitz and Kim McQuaid, *Creating the Welfare State* (New York: Praeger, 1980), p. 4.

77. Ibid., pp. 5–10.

78. Gilbert, *Capitalism and the Welfare State*, p. 3.

79. Quoted in Norman Furniss and Timothy Tilton, *The Case for the Welfare State* (Bloomington: Indiana University Press, 1977), p. 156.

80. Murray Levine and Adeline Levine, *A Social History of Helping Services* (New York: Appleton-Century-Crofts, 1970), pp. 236–243.

81. Harold L. Wilensky and Charles N. Lebeaux, *Industrial Society and Social Welfare* (New York: Free Press, 1965), p. 88.

82. James Leiby, *A History of Social Welfare and Social Work in the United States* (New York: Columbia University Press, 1978), p. 170.

83. Levine and Levine, *A Social History of Helping Services*, pp. 236–243.

84. Wilensky and Lebeaux, *Industrial Society and Social Welfare*, p. 9; National Association of Social Workers,

Encyclopedia of Social Work, 18th ed. (Silver Spring, MD: NASW, 1987), p. 781.

85. James Jones, *Bad Blood* (New York: Free Press, 1981), p. 34.

86. Thomas DiBacco, "Hookworm's Strange History," *Washington Post* (June 30, 1992), p. 14.

87. Berkowitz and McQuaid, *Creating the Welfare State*, pp. 33–36.

88. Ibid., p. 83.

89. Michael Boskin, "Social Security and the Economy," in Peter Duignan and Alvin Rabushka (eds.), *The United States in the 1980s* (Stanford, CA: Hoover Institution, 1980), p. 182.

90. Berkowitz and McQuaid, *Creating the Welfare State*, p. 103.

91. Ibid, p. 136.

92. *Annual Statistical Supplement, Social Security Bulletin* (Washington, DC: US GPO, 1995), p. 151, (2002), p. 132.

93. Michael Misshauk, *Management: Theory and Practice* (Boston: Little, Brown, 1979), p. 6.

94. Melvin Anshen, *Managing the Socially Responsible Corporation* (New York: Macmillan, 1974), p. 5.

95. Steven Lydenberg, *Rating America's Corporate Conscience* (Reading, MA: Addison-Wesley, 1986).

96. Theodore Purcell, "Management and the 'Ethical' Investors," in S. Prakash Sethi and Carl Swanson (eds.), *Private Enterprise and Public Purpose* (New York: John Wiley, 1981), pp. 296–297.

97. Lloyd Kurtz, Steven Lydenberg, and Peter Kinder, "The Domini Social Index," in Peter Kinder, Steven Lydenberg, and Amy Domini (eds.), *The Social Investment Almanac* (New York: Henry Holt, 1992).

98. James Worthy, "Managing the 'Social Markets' Business," in Lance Liebner and Corrine Schelling (eds.), *Public–Private Partnership: New Opportunities for Meeting Social Needs* (Cambridge, MA: Ballinger, 1978), p. 226.

99. Melanie Lawrence, "Social Responsibility: How Companies Become Involved in Their Communities," *Personnel Journal* 61, no. 7 (July 1982), p. 381; James Chrisman and Archie Carroll, "SMR Forum: Corporate Responsibility-Reconciling Economic and Social Goals," *Sloan Management Review* 25, no. 2 (Winter 1984), p. 173.

100. Enterprise Foundation, *Annual Report 1983* (Columbia, MD: Author, 1983), p. 1.

101. Brian O'Connell, *Philanthropy in Action* (New York: The Foundation Center, 1987), p. 218.

102. Local Initiatives Support Corporation, *Making Change Happen: Annual Report* (New York: Author, 1995).

103. "Would You Like to Be Your Own Boss?" (San Francisco: Women's Initiative for Self Employment, n.d.).

104. David Linowes, *The Corporate Conscience* (New York: Hawthorn Books, 1974), p. 209.

105. *Privatization: Toward More Effective Government* (Washington, DC: U.S. Government Printing Office, 1988), pp. 2–3.

106. Irving Kristol, "Charity and Business Shouldn't Mix," *The New York Times* (October 17, 1982), p. 18.

107. Lawrence Fouraker and Graham Allison, "Foreword," in John Dunlop (ed.), *Business and Public Policy* (Cambridge, MA: Harvard University Press, 1980), p. ix.

108. Peter Steinfels, "Michael Novak and His Ultrasuper Democraticapitalism," *Commonweal* (February 15, 1983), p. 11.

109. William J. Baroody Jr., "The President's Review," *AEI Annual Report 1981–82* (Washington, DC: American Enterprise Institute, 1982), p. 2.

110. Peter Stone, "Businesses Widen Role in Conservatives' 'War on Ideas'," *Washington Post* (May 12, 1985), p. C5.

111. Ibid., p. 50.

112. Ibid., p. 28.

113. Richard Reeves, "How New Ideas Shape Presidential Politics," *New York Times Magazine* (July 15, 1984), p. 18.

114. Heritage Foundation, *The Heritage Foundation Annual Report* (Washington, DC: Heritage Foundation, 1983).

115. Interview with Stuart Butler at the Heritage Foundation, Washington, DC, October 4, 1984.

116. Burton Pines, *Back to Basics* (New York: Morrow, 1982), p. 254.

117. Nancy Amidei, "How to End Poverty: Next Steps," *Food Monitor* (Winter 1988), p. 52.

118. Robert Reich, *The Next American Frontier* (New York: Times Books, 1983), p. 223.

119. Ibid., pp. 247–248.

120. Kevin Phillips, *Staying on Top: The Business Case for a National Industrial Policy* (New York: Random House, 1984), pp. 5–6.

121. Yeheskel Hasenfeld, "The Changing Context of Human-Services Administration," *Social Work* 29, no. 4 (November–December 1984), p. 524.

122. Social Security Administration, *Social Security Bulletin, Annual Statistical Supplement* (Washington, DC: U.S. Government Printing Office, 1994), p. 140.

123. Donald Barlett and James Steele, *Critical Condition* (New York: Doubleday, 2004), p. 94.

124. David Stoesz, "Human-Service Corporations and the Welfare State," *Transaction/Society* 16 (1989), pp. 80–91.

125. Bureau of the Census, *Statistical Abstract of the United States, 1986* (Washington, DC: U.S. Government Printing Office, 1986).

126. U.S. Department of Commerce, *1982 U.S. Industrial Outlook for 200 Industries with Projections for 1986* (Washington, DC: U.S. Government Printing Office, 1982), p. 406.

127. Jerry Avorn, "Nursing Home Infections-The Context," *New England Journal of Medicine* (September 24, 1981), p. 759.

128. J. Blyskal, "Gray Gold," *Forbes* (November 23, 1981), p. 84.

129. D. Vaughan, "Health Care Syndications: Investment Tools of the '80s," *Financial Planner* (December 1981), p. 49.

130. Blyskal, "Gray Gold," p. 80.

131. V. DiPaolo, "Tight Money, Higher Interest Rates Slow Nursing Home Systems Growth," *Modern Health Care* (June 1980), p. 84.

132. National Senior Citizens' Law Center, "Federal Antitrust Activity" (Los Angeles: National Senior Citizens' Law Center, 1982), p. 2.

133. "NME Makes More Health Care Acquisitions," *Homecare News* (February 17, 1984), p. 4.

134. Quoted in W. Spicer, "The Boom in Building," *Contemporary Administrator* (February 1982), pp. 13–14.

135. "Beverly Enterprises" and "Tenet Healthcare Corp," Standard & Poor's Stock Report (October 1995), p. 89.

136. Donald Barlett and James Steele, *Critical Condition* (New York: Doubleday, 2004), pp. 106–108.

137. Richard Thaler and Cass Sunstein, *Nudge* (New Haven, CT: Yale University Press, 2008).

138. B. Gray, "An Introduction to the New Health Care for Profit," in B. Gray (ed.), *The New Health Care for Profit* (Washington, DC: National Academy Press, 1983), p. 2.

139. R. Siegrist, Jr., "Wall Street and the For-Profit Hospital Management Companies," in B. Gray (ed.), *The New Health Care for Profit*, p. 36.

140. American Medical International, *1983 Annual Report* (Beverly Hills, CA: AMI, 1983).

141. "GAO Says Proprietary Hospital Chain Mergers Raise Medicare/Medicaid Costs," *Home-Care News* (February 17, 1984), p. 6.

142. "Columbia/HCA" *Standard & Poor's Stock Reports* (October 1996), p. 80.

143. Barlett and Steele, *Critical Condition,* pp. 70–71.

144. Brooke Masters, "Hospital Chain Goes Private for $33 Billion," *Washington Post* (July 25, 2006), p. D1.

145. National Industry Council for HMO Development, *Ten Year Report* 1971–1983 (Washington, DC: Author, 1983).

146. HealthAmerica, *Company Profile* (Nashville, TN: HealthAmerica, 1983).

147. M. Abramowitz, "Maxicare HMO Soars with Farsighted Founder," *Washington Post* (November 30, 1986), p. 12.

148. National Industry Council, *Ten Year Report,* p. 22.

149. "PacifiCare," "United HealthCare Corp.," and "CIGNA," *Standard & Poor's Stock Reports* (October 1996), p. 102.

150. Milt Freudenheim, "California Backs Merger of 2 Giant Blue Cross Plans," *The New York Times* (November 10, 2004), p. C1.

151. Milt Freudenheim, "UnitedHealth to Buy PacifiCare in Push into Medicare," *The New York Times* (July 2, 2005), p. C1.

152. Catherine Born, "Proprietary Firms and Child Welfare Services: Patterns and Implications," *Child Welfare 62* (March–April 1983), p. 112.

153. Kinder-Care, *Annual Report 1983* (Montgomery, AL: Kinder-Care, 1983).

154. Kinder-Care, *Second Quarter Report* (Montgomery, AL: Kinder-Care, March 16, 1984).

155. "Kinder-Care," "Children's Discovery Centers," and "Sunrise Preschools," *Standard & Poor's Stock Reports* (October 1996).

156. Karen Kornbluh, "Americans Must Work Harder to Achieve the American Dream," (Washington, DC: New America Foundation, July 15, 2004), p. 2.

157. "Home Health Care of America," *Standard & Poor's Stock Reports* (March 1984, October 1995).

158. "Interview with Elsie Griffith," *American Journal of Nursing 18* (March 1984), p. 341.

159. "Merrill Lynch: Bullish on Health Care," *Contemporary Administrator* (February 1982), p. 16.

160. "Digest of Earnings Reports," *The Wall Street Journal* (August 13, 1987), p. 41.

161. Stephen Boland, "Prisons for Profit," unpublished manuscript, San Diego State University, School of Social Work, 1987, pp. 5–6.

162. Ibid., p. 8.

163. Eric Press, "A Person, Not a Number," *Newsweek* (June 29, 1987), p. 63.

164. D. Vise, "Private Company Asks for Control of Tennessee Prisons," *Washington Post* (September 22, 1985), p. D2.

165. "Correction Corporation of America" and "Wackenhut," *Standard & Poor's Stock Reports* (October 1996).

166. Barlett and Steele, *Critical Condition,* p. 170.

167. Steve Lohr, "The Disparate Consensus on Health Care for All," *New York Times* (December 6, 2004), p. C16.

168. Stoesz, "The Gray Market," p. 45.

169. Thomas J. Peters and Robert W. Waterman Jr., *In Search of Excellence* (New York: Harper & Row, 1982); and Rosabeth M. Kanter, *The Changemasters* (New York, Simon & Schuster, 1983).

170. Specht and Courtney, *Unfaithful Angels.*

171. Margaret Gibelman, *Who We Are: A Second Look,* 2nd ed. (Washington, DC: NASW Press, 1996), p. 69.

172. National Association of Social Workers, "Data on Practice Auspice" (Washington, DC: NASW, August 2000).

173. Philip Brown and Robert Barker, "Confronting the Threat of Private Practice," *Journal of Social Work Education 31,* no. 1 (Winter 1995), p. 106.

174. Srinika Jayaratne, Kristine Siefert, and Wayne Chess, "Private and Agency Practitioners: Some Data and Observations," *Social Service Review 62* (June 1988), p. 331.

175. Margaret Gibelman and Philip Schervish, *What We Earn: 1993 NASW Salary Survey* (Washington, DC: NASW, 1993), pp. 25, 27.

176. Diane Vinokur-Kaplan, Srinika Jayaratne, and Wayne Chess, "Job Satisfaction and Retention of Social Workers in Public Agencies, Non-Profit Agencies and Private Practice," *Administration in Social Work* 18, no. 3 (1994), p. 103.

177. Practice Research Network, Private Practice (Washington, DC: National Association of Social Workers, 2003).

178. Gibelman and Schervish, *What We Earn,* p. 32.

179. Vinokur-Kaplan, Jayaratne, and Chess, "Job Satisfaction," p. 103.

180. Ibid., p. 329.

181. Ibid.

182. Although Mark Courtney notes that a de facto private practice can be identified much earlier: "Psychiatric Social Workers and the Early Days of Private Practice," *Social Service Review* (June 1992), pp. 95–105.

183. M. A. Golton, "Private Practice in Social Work," *Encyclopedia of Social Work* (Silver Spring, MD: NASW, 1973), p. 949.

184. Walter Trattner, *From Poor Law to Welfare State* (New York: Free Press, 1974), p. 250.

185. For details on state licensure and professional certification, see Robert Barker, *The Business of Psycho-therapy* (New York: Columbia University Press, 1982).

186. Srinika Jayaratne, Mary Lou Davis Sacks, and Wayne Chess, "Private Practice May Be Good for Your Health and Well-Being," *Social Work* 36 (May 1991), pp. 226–227.

187. Donald Feldstein, "Debate on Private Practice," *Social Work* 22, no. 3 (1977), p. 3.

188. Ibid., p. 4.

189. Patricia Kelley and Paul Alexander, "Part-Time Private Practice: Practical and Ethical Considerations," *Social Work* 30, no. 3 (May–June 1985), p. 255.

190. N. T. Edwards, "The Survival of Structure and Function in Private Practice," *Journal of the Otto Rank Association* 13 (1979), pp. 12, 15.

191. Jayaratne, Sacks, and Chess, "Private Practice May Be Good for Your Health and Well-Being," *Social Work* 36 (May 1991), pp. 228–229.

192. Franklin Chu and Sharland Trotter, *The Madness Establishment* (New York: Grossman, 1974), p. 61.

193. Robert Barker, *The Business of Psychotherapy* (New York: Columbia University Press, 1982), p. xi.

194. Stuart Kirk and Herb Kutchins, "Deliberate Misdiagnosis in Mental Health Practice," p. 230.

195. Ibid., p. 234.

196. Ibid., pp. 232, 234–235.

197. Ibid., p. 235.

198. Kimberly Strom, "Reimbursement Demands and Treatment Decisions: A Growing Dilemma for Social Workers," *Social Work* 37 (September 1992), p. 18.

199. Robert Barker, *Social Work in Private Practice* (Silver Spring, MD: NASW, 1984), p. 113.

200. Kirk and Kutchins, "Deliberate Misdiagnosis in Mental Health Practice," p. 232.

201. Kathy Sawyer, "Insuring the Bureaucracy's Mental Health," *Washington Post* (April 10, 1979), p. A8.

202. "Signing Off Fraud Charge Warns Kentucky Clinicians," *NASW News* 32, no. 6 (June 1987), p. 1.

203. Kelley and Alexander, "Part-Time Private Practice," p. 254.

204. Ellen Dunbar, "Future of Social Work," *NASW California News* 13, no. 18 (May 1987), p. 3.

205. David Gelman, "Growing Pains for the Shrinks," *Newsweek* (December 14, 1987), p. 71.

206. Michael Fabricant and Steven Burghardt, *The Welfare State Crisis and the Transformation of Social Service Work* (Armonk, NY: M.E. Sharpe, 1992).

207. Jayaratne, Sacks, and Chess, "Private Practice May Be Good for Your Health and Well-Being," p. 229.

208. Stan Taubman, "Private Practice! Oh No!" *NASW California News* (March 1991), p. 8.

209. See Sheila Akabas, Paul Kurzman, and Norman Kolben (eds.), *Labor and Industrial Settings: Sites for Social Work Practice* (New York: Council on Social Work Education, 1979); Martha Ozawa, "Development of Social Services in Industry: Why and How?" *Social Work* 25 (November 1980), pp. 86–93; and Dale Masi, *Human Services in Industry* (Lexington, MA: D. C. Heath, 1982).

210. "Social Work in Industrial Settings," *Social Work* 33 (January–February 1988), p. 65.

211. But see J. Decker, R. Starrett, and J. Redhorse, "Evaluating the Cost-Effectiveness of Employee Assistance Programs," *Social Work* 31 (September–October 1986), p. 83.

212. Shulamith Straussner, "Comparison of In-House and Contracted-Out Employee Assistance Programs," *Social Work* 33 (January–February 1988), p. 53.

213. Francis Lappe and P. M. Dubois, *The Quickening of America: Rebuilding Our Nation, Remaking Our Lives* (San Francisco: Jossey Bass, 1994).

214. "About Us," retrieved April 18, 2008, from www.chcany.org/index-1.html

215. Ibid.

216. Lucette Lagnado and Nancy Jeffrey, "Psychologists Sue over Managed Care," *Wall Street Journal* (December 11, 1998).

CHAPTER 8

The Making of Governmental Policy

*T*his chapter describes the process by which governmental policy is made, exploring the phases of the policy process, examining the influence of various social groups on the policy process, and accounting for the role of key organizations. The public policy process is important because many social welfare policies are established by government, and decisions by federal and state agencies have a direct bearing on the administration and funding of social welfare programs that assist millions of Americans and employ thousands of human service professionals.

In an open, democratic society, **public policy** should reflect the interests of all citizens to the greatest extent possible. For a variety of reasons, however, this ideal is not realized. Although many Americans have the right to participate in the establishment of public policy, they often fail to do so. Policy made and implemented by the governmental sector may be perceived as being too far removed from the daily activities of citizens, or too complicated to warrant the type of coordinated and persistent efforts necessary to alter it. Moreover, many Americans with a direct interest in governmental policy are not in a position to shape it, as in the case of children and those with emotional impairments, who must rely on others to speak on their behalf. Consequently, governmental policy does not necessarily reflect the interests—indeed, the welfare—of the public, even though it is intended to do so. The discrepancy between what is constitutionally prescribed in making public policy and the way decisions are actually made leads to two quite different understandings of the policy process. For welfare professionals concerned with instituting change in social welfare, a technical understanding of how policy is made is essential. It is equally important for them to recognize that the policy process is skewed to favor powerful officials and interests rather than the interests of those who lack influence. Because social workers and their clients tend to be comparatively powerless, a critical analysis of the policy process is all the more important.

Technical Aspects of the Policy Process

Public policy in the United States is made through a deliberative process that involves the two bodies of elected officials that make up a legislature. This applies both to the federal government and to the states—with the singular exception of Nebraska, which has only one deliberative body, a unicameral legislature.

Aspects of the federal policy process can be found on the policyAmerica website (http://capwiz.com/policyamerica/index.html). Initially, a policy concern of a legislator is developed into a legislative proposal and usually printed in the *Congressional Record*. Because every legislator has a party affiliation and a constituency, legislators' proposals tend to reflect the priorities of those stakeholders. Often, several legislators will prepare proposals that are important to similar constituencies. Increasingly, policy institutes are instrumental in developing and vetting legislative options. Through a subtle interaction of ideas, the media, and legislative leadership, one proposal—usually a synthesis of several—is presented as a policy alternative. Other legislators are asked to sign on as cosponsors, and the measure is officially introduced. After the proposed bill is assigned to the appropriate committee, public hearings are held, and the committee convenes to "mark up" the legislation so that it incorporates the concerns of committee members who have heard the public testimony. Under propitious circumstances, the committee then forwards the legislation to the full body of the chamber that must approve it. While it is being approved by the full body of one chamber, a similar bill is often introduced in the other chamber, where it begins a parallel process. Differences between the measures approved by the two chambers are ironed out in a conference committee. The proposed legislation becomes law after it is signed by the chief executive—or, if the executive vetoes the bill, passed by a two-thirds vote of each legislative chamber. This process is always tortuous and usually unsuccessful. The eventual enactment of legislation under these conditions is a true testament to legislative leadership. A third branch of government, the judiciary, assesses legal challenges to existing legislation. In the upper levels of the judiciary, members can hold their posts for life. The primary features of the policy process of the federal government are illustrated in Figure 8.1 on page 212.

There are several critical junctures in a proposal's passage into legislation—or oblivion. First, most of the details in any proposal are worked out at the committee or subcommittee level. Different versions are negotiated and reconciled at the mark-up session, during which committee members and staff write their changes into the draft. This stage offers

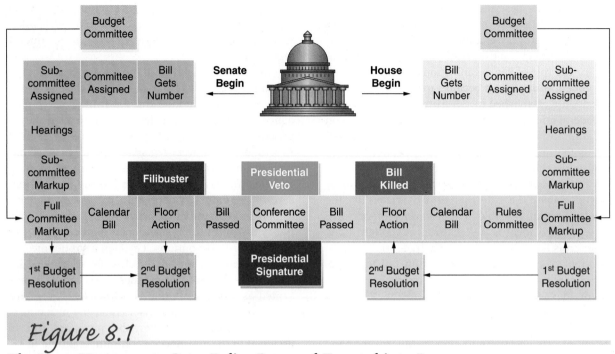

Figure 8.1

The Steps Necessary to Get a Policy Proposal Enacted into Law

an important opportunity to inject minor, and sometimes major, changes into the substance of the bill or to alter the intent of the bill's originator(s). Second, the viability of a proposal depends to a large extent on the numbers and weight of the witnesses who testify as to its merits at subcommittee and committee hearings. Obviously, public testimony will work to the advantage of well-financed interests; such interests can afford to pay lobbyists to do this professionally, whereas advocates for the disadvantaged often rely on volunteers. Nevertheless, the public testimony stage is an important opportunity to clarify for the record the position that human service professionals may take on a given proposal. Third, budget considerations figure heavily in the likelihood of a bill's passage. Other federal spending priorities, coupled with the unwillingness of elected officials to raise taxes, increase the likelihood that legislation will be underfunded or even passed with no additional funding whatsoever. Innovative revenue "enhancers," such as earmarked taxes or user fees, can make a proposal more acceptable during periods of fiscal belt-tightening. The policy process, then, is not necessarily intended to facilitate the passage of a proposal into law. Of the tens of thousands of bills presented in Congress, only 10 percent

were reported out of committee and only 5 percent became law.[1]

Beyond this general outline of the public policy process, multiple variations exist depending on historical and jurisdictional circumstances. In the federal government, all proposals related to taxation must originate in the House of Representatives, a provision the founders of the nation included in the Constitution in order to place revenue retrieval in the legislative body most representative of the people. The federal budget process begins each February when the President presents his/her proposed budget and culminates months later when he/she signs or vetoes the Congressional budget reconciliation bill that authorizes the budgets for 13 separate agencies. Typically, the ideal federal budget process is compromised in two ways: (1) a budget is not agreed upon, in which case a continuing budget resolution is passed extending funding at current levels until a complete budget is enacted; and (2) the amount of funds appropriated is less than that authorized, leaving programs with revenue shortfalls. This means that many welfare programs that receive discretionary funds are often beset with budgets that are not timely or adequately funded. The exceptions are social entitlements, such as Social Security, Medicare, and Medicaid, which are not subject to the budget cycle.[2]

Appointments of people for key executive posts, such as cabinet secretaries, ambassadors, and judges, must be ratified through the advice and consent of the Senate, a body less responsive to popular sentiment. States exhibit countless variations within the general outline of the tripartite balance of powers format. California, for example, has experienced chronic budget problems because the state government has been unable to raise sufficient revenue to keep up with mandated expenditures. Since the imposition of Proposition 13 in 1978, a two-thirds majority of the California legislature is required not only to raise property taxes but also to establish the state budget; this is a proportion far beyond the simple majority required in other states. Under these conditions, a small number of recalcitrant representatives can easily block the budget process. As these examples suggest, understanding the intricacies of the policy process is an essential step toward mastering public policy.

A few final points regarding the technical aspects of the policy process warrant mention. The decision-making process is defined by *Robert's Rules of Order,*[3] a text that lays out in detail the rules for democratic deliberation. Although *Robert's Rules* can appear obtuse, its value should not be underappreciated. Those who have mastered "the means of deliberation" are one step ahead of the rest of the crowd in seeing their ideas become public policy. Social activists who are optimistic that their proposal is working its way steadily through the legislative minefield may find their hopes exploded by an adroit procedural move on the part of an opponent who sidetracks a bill until the next legislative session. The elaborate rules of decision making, compounded by the traditions of deliberative bodies, may tend to deter citizens from participating in the democratic process. Yet there are means public policy novices can employ to become better acquainted with the ways in which elected officials go about the public's business. Citizen advocate organizations, particularly the League of Women Voters and Common Cause, can be helpful in making social policy more responsive to the public.

Congress and the legislatures of the larger states employ staff members as technical experts to aid them in decision making. Legislative staff members are frequently the experts most versed in an area of legislative activity, simply because they work through policy proposals on a regular basis. Staff reports researched as part of committee delibera-

tions can be valuable in that they often provide the most up-to-date data on particular programs or issues. A good example of this type of resource is the *Green Book* used by the U.S. House Ways and Means Committee in its consideration of social programs. Begun in the early 1980s to help committee members comprehend the vast number of social programs under their jurisdiction—Social Security, Medicare, child welfare, Temporary Assistance for Needy Families (TANF), Supplemental Security Income (SSI), and Unemployment Compensation, among others—the volume, *Background Material and Data on Programs within the Jurisdiction of the Committee on Ways and Means,* became essential reading for social program analysts. Because of its convoluted title, the volume became known by its standard-issue green paper cover, hence the Green Book. Fortunately, its popularity led to a (merciful) shortening of its title to *Overview of Entitlement Programs.*[4] In recent years the *Green Book* has been available online, making it more accessible.

A Critical Analysis of the Policy Process

Experience and sophistication notwithstanding, the public policy process often proves frustrating for social activists. Despite the most urgent of needs, the best of intentions, and the most strategic of proposals, the social welfare program output deriving from the legislative process often appears far short of what is required. Yet to conclude from this that public policy simply does not work would be an overstatement. A critical approach to public policy helps explain some of the limitations of the technical approach and suggests ways to make the legislative process a more effective strategy for those concerned with furthering social justice.

From a critical perspective, the policy process consists of a series of discrete decisions, each heavily conditioned by money and connections—in other words, by power. The extent to which governmental policy reflects the concerns of one group of citizens while neglecting those of others is ultimately a question of power and influence. Power is derived from several sources, and these have attracted the attention of philosophers over the centuries. Plato questioned the organization and execution of the civil authority of the state. Machiavelli focused on the limits of discretionary authority exercised by leaders of the state. The social contract philosophers of the Enlightenment—Hobbes, Locke, and Rousseau—considered the moral obligations of the state toward its citizens. Later, as the Industrial Revolution proceeded unchecked, Karl Marx attributed power inequities to control over the means of production, or capital. Subsequently, as governmental authority expanded to ameliorate the economic and social dislocation brought on by industrial capitalism, Max Weber identified bureaucratic administrators as a pivotal group. As the postindustrial era unfolded, such social critics as Marshall McLuhan and Alvin Toffler emphasized how the processing and uses of information can be a source of power and influence.

From these general speculations about social organization, other writers have turned to more specific aspects of social policy as subjects of inquiry. Several schools of thought have emerged. According to the *elitist* orientation, individuals representing a "power structure" control social policy in order to maintain a status quo that advantages them and, in the process, excludes marginal groups. In contrast, a *pluralist* orientation assumes that social policy in a heterogeneous democratic polity is the sum total of trade-offs among different interest groups, all of which have an equal opportunity to participate. At the program level, *incrementalists* have suggested that the more important questions about social policy are the product of bit-by-bit additions to the public social infrastructure. As counterpoint, other scholars have focused on "paradigm shifts" through which major changes, such as the inception of Social Security in 1935 and the devolution of welfare to the states through the Personal Responsibility and Work Opportunity Reconciliation Act of 1996, have altered the very foundation of social policy. With regard to program evaluation, *rationalists* have used the methods of social science to determine by objective standards to what extent policy changes bring about intended outcomes. By contrast, *social activists* use the political process as the measure of program performance, assuming that the optimum in program assessment is continued recertification and refunding by public decision makers. As might be expected in the investigation of any phenomenon as complex as social policy, a comprehensive explanation is likely to incorporate elements of more than one school of thought.

Underlying these varied approaches to interpreting social policy are assumptions about its very nature. In this regard, two orientations have become prominent. The first orientation might be labeled the *liberal evolutionary perspective*. According to this orientation, social policy reflects steady progress toward a desirable condition of human welfare for all. Most liberal analysts who have promoted the welfare state as an ideal have adopted an evolutionary perspective. Believers in the evolutionary perspective expect that the national government will progressively expand social programs until, eventually, the basic needs of the entire population are guaranteed as rights of citizenship. References to welfare state philosophy appear in many chapters of this book. The liberal evolutionary perspective dominated thinking about the U.S. welfare state from the New Deal until the rise of conservative ideology in the 1980s. The demise of Catastrophic Health Insurance in 1989 and the devolution of AFDC/TANF to the states in 1996 raise fundamental questions about the validity of this perspective. The liberal evolutionary perspective has been complemented by social systems theory, which assumes that welfare consists of basic institutions and processes that are related and are changed to suit environmental conditions. Reference to "social service delivery systems" was frequent during the 1960s and 1970s, when social programs were expanding, but this approach commanded less credibility when many public programs were thrown into chaos as a result of budget cuts during the Reagan and two Bush administrations. What had once been coordinated service delivery systems suddenly became disordered and fragmented clusters of agencies struggling for survival.

A competing orientation is the *conflict perspective* that emphasizes the differences between organized groups that compete for resources. The conflict perspective views social policy and resultant programs as the product of intense rivalry among various classes and groups. Applied to a capitalist economy and a democratic polity, the conflict approach goes a long way toward explaining the disparate distribution of goods, services, and opportunities within U.S. society. Accordingly, conflict theory is useful in two ways: It accounts for the quite substantial disadvantages experienced by some Americans—the poor, minorities of color, people with disabilities, and women—and it shows how such groups can be empowered to achieve a measure of social justice. Obviously, a conflict perspective accounts for the behavior of for-profit providers of health and human services, which compete intensively for market share, acquire other firms, and lobby public officials to shape policy favorably. The downside of the conflict perspective is that it fails to offer a unifying vision of future social policy.

Questions of governmental decision making often focus on three central aspects: (1) the degree of change in policy represented by a decision, (2) the rationality of the decision, and (3) the extent to which the disadvantaged benefit. First, governmental policies vary in the extent to which they depart from the status quo. It can be argued that, in the final analysis, there are no new ideas, but there *are* new governmental policies that have enormous implications for certain groups. Few could dispute that the Social Security Act and the Civil Rights Act were radical departures from the status quo and substantially changed the circumstances of older people and African Americans, respectively. On the other hand, such radical departures occur only under fairly unusual circumstances, and therefore rarely. As Charles Lindblom observed, the great bulk of decision making is "incremental," representing only marginal improvements in social policy already in place.[5] Amitai Etzioni proposed the term "mixed scanning" to refer to the way decision makers take a quick overview of a situation, weigh a range of alternatives—some incremental, some radical—and ultimately select the one that satisfies the most important factors impinging at the moment.[6] Thus, major shifts in public policy are the exception rather than the rule. Most social policy changes consist of relatively minor technical adjustments in program administration and budgeting.

Second, social policy does order human affairs, and to that extent the rationality or logic underlying the policy is of great significance. Historically, two basic forms of rationality have served to justify social policy: bureaucratic rationality and market rationality.[7]

Bureaucratic rationality refers to the ordering of social affairs by governmental agencies. Since Max Weber's work on the modern bureaucracy, this form of rationality has been central to governmental policy and hence to the maintenance of the welfare state. According to bureaucratic rationality, civil servants can objectively define social problems, develop strategies to address them, and deploy programs in an equitable and nonpartisan manner. Bureaucratic rationality takes its authority from power vested in the state, and bureaucracies have become predominant in social welfare at the federal (through the Department of Health and Human

Services) and state levels. A characteristic of bureaucratic rationality is a reliance on social planning. Several social planning methods have been developed to anticipate future problems and deal with existing ones. Generally, these can be classified under two headings: technomethodological and sociopolitical.

Technomethodological planning methods emphasize databases from which projections about future program needs can be derived. Such methods place a premium on relatively sophisticated social research methods and work best with programs that can be quantified and routinized, as in the case of cash payments through the Social Security program.

Sociopolitical planning approaches are more interactive, involving groups likely to be affected by a program. Community development activities, for example, frequently feature planners bringing together neighborhood residents, businesspeople, and local officials to create a plan that is relevant to the needs of a particular area.[8] Regardless of planning method, it is important to recognize the power and influence that governmental agencies have assumed in social welfare policy, much of it by exercise of bureaucratic rationality.

Market rationality refers to a reliance on the rule of "supply and demand" as a means for distributing goods and services. While on the surface this may appear to be antithetical to the meaning of rationality, a high degree of social ordering in fact occurs within capitalism. Such organization is implicit in the very idea of a market, entailing a large number of prospective consumers that businesses seek to serve. In a modern market economy, the success of a business depends on the ability of managers to survey the market, merchandise goods and services, shape consumer preferences through advertising, and reduce competition by buying or outmaneuvering competitors. Of course, market rationality is not a panacea for providing social welfare because the marketplace is not particularly responsive to those who may not fully participate in it, such as minorities, women, children, the elderly, or people with disabilities. Yet market rationality cannot be dismissed as a rationale for delivering social welfare benefits. Approximately half of Americans get their health and welfare needs met through employer-provided benefits that are ultimately derived from the market.[9] Since the late 1980s, commercial firms have conducted an ambitious campaign to ration health care benefits through "managed care," an idea that has become anathema to health and human service professionals. Another example of the impact of the market on social welfare benefits is the practice by governmental jurisdictions of contracting out certain human services to private sector businesses, usually with the rationale of reducing costs by taking advantage of efficiencies associated with the market.[10]

The third aspect of governmental decision making addresses disadvantaged populations. It is entirely possible, of course, for social policy to introduce radical change that is based on data but generates mixed effects with respect to the well-being of important groups. The 1996 welfare reform legislation, for example, ended the 60-year entitlement to income for poor families on the basis of evaluations of state welfare demonstrations allegedly showing that states could provide public assistance better if the federal government were not involved. Fearing the consequences of such welfare reform for poor minority children, advocacy groups such as the Children's Defense Fund lobbied ardently against the proposal, but to no avail. Of primary concern among children's advocates was the consequence of **time limits** on the receipt of welfare for poor children. Analysts from public and private research agencies projected that 1 million to 4 million children would be terminated from public assistance if a five-year time limit on receipt of aid were imposed. The 1996 welfare reform legislation included provisions for families that were chronically dependent on welfare—exempting 20 percent of the AFDC/TANF caseload from time limits—but children's advocates claimed these were inadequate. The 1996 welfare reform legislation was not welfare "reform," claimed children's advocates; it was welfare termination. Several years later, the consequences of welfare reform were less clear. Those beneficiaries who had entered the labor market earned low wages, but the earned income tax credit boosted most above the poverty line. More disturbing was the subgroup that had been diverted from public assistance. Caseloads dropped more than half during the 1990s; however, most of those who left were not employed full time, leaving their fate uncertain. Unfortunately, the scanty research on "leavers" failed to clarify the matter.[11]

The degree of change represented by any change in public policy, the extent to which it is rational with respect to bureaucratic or market criteria, and the consequences for disadvantaged populations make the social policy process a dynamic and sometimes volatile area of activity. Even though this process may be intimidating for the uninitiated,

it is essential for achieving social justice for the simple reason that it is the only means available within the governmental arena.

The Policy Process

A critical analysis of the policy process highlights the social stratification of the society, the phases through which policy is formulated, and the organizational entities that have become instrumental in the decision-making process. This section will describe and chart these factors in order to demonstrate how social policy is created in the United States.

Social Stratification

A variety of **social stratification** models differentiate groups with influence from those lacking it. The most simple of these schemes consists of a dual stratification: for instance, capitalists and the proletariat, such as Marx used. A stratification familiar to Americans defines three parts: an upper class, a middle class, and a lower class. Placement of individuals in the appropriate class is usually made on the basis of income, education, and occupational status. This three-part stratification is limited in its capacity to explain very much about U.S. social welfare, however. If asked, most Americans identify themselves as middle class, even if by objective criteria they belong to another stratum. Further, the designation *lower class* is not particularly informative about the social conditions of a large portion of the population with which human service professionals are concerned.[12]

A more informative stratification consists of six social groups, which he differentiated according to wealth, internal solidarity, and control over the environment, as elaborated in Table 8.1.[13]

As this stratification model indicates, some groups—the wealthy and executives—are able to influence the environment, but other groups—the working/welfare poor and the underclass—have virtually no influence. This distinction has important implications for social welfare, because those who are of lower status tend to be the recipients of welfare benefits that are the product of a social policy process in which they do not participate. The way in which these various groups influence the social policy process will be discussed in greater detail in the following section.

Table 8.1

Social Stratification of the Population

Name of Group	Examples	Characteristics
The wealthy	Upper elites, the independently wealthy, large stockholders	Ownership of resources is the main source of power; control over goals is very high, but control over means is through executives
Executives	Top administrators in business, government, the military	Organizational solidarity facilitates effective policy implementation; some control over goals and a high degree of control over means
Professionals	Middle-level managers, technical experts, private practitioners, community leaders	Environment encourages limited solidarity; control over means is high, and goal setting can be influenced if collective action is undertaken
Organized workers	Semiskilled workers, civic and political clubs, social action organizations	Environment encourages solidarity, groups have some control over the means by which goals are realized
Working/welfare poor	Temporary and part-time workers earning minimum wage and who use welfare as a wage supplement	A subjugated position with no control over the environment; frustration is shared and irrational, explosive behavior results
Underclass	Unemployables and illiterates; disabled substance abusers; itinerants, drifters, migrant workers	A subjugated position with no control over the environment; a sense of failure coupled with limited mobility reduces social interaction and leads to retreatism

Source: Dexter C. Dunphy, *The Primary Group: A Handbook for Analysis and Field Research* (Englewood Cliffs, NJ: Prentice Hall, 1972), pp. 42–44. Copyright © 1972. Reprinted by permission of Prentice Hall, Inc.

With these clarifications in mind, the policy process can be divided into four stages: formulation, legislation, implementation, and evaluation. Although these terms are somewhat self-explanatory, during the decision-making process certain organizational entities exert their influence at different times, making the process an uneven one characterized by fits and starts. Organizations correspond to the stratification groups that figure prominently in their organizational activities and thereby in the policy process.

Formulation

Before the nineteenth century it would have been accurate to state that policy formulation in this country began with the legislative phase. Clearly, this was the situation envisioned by the drafters of the Constitution; but theirs was a largely agrarian society with comparatively little institutional specialization.

With industrialization many complexities were injected into the society, and in time special institutions emerged to assist the legislature in evaluating social conditions and preparing policy options. Eventually, even constitutionally established bodies such as Congress lapsed into a reactive role, largely responsive to other entities that formulated policy.[14] Initially institutions of higher education provided technical intelligence to assist the legislative branch, and some still do. For example, the University of Wisconsin Institute for Research on Poverty provides analyses on important welfare policies.[15]

That legislators at the federal level, as well as those in the larger states, would rely on experts to assess social conditions and develop policy options is not surprising, given the fact that each legislator must attend to multiple committee and subcommittee assignments requiring expertise in particular matters, while at the same time contending with the general concerns of a large constituency. A typical day in the life of a legislator has been reconstructed by Charles Peters, a longtime Washington observer:

> The most striking feature of a congressman's life is its hectic jumble of votes, meetings, appointments, and visits from folks from back home who just drop by. From an 8 A.M. breakfast conference with a group of union leaders, a typical morning will take him to his office around 9, where the waiting room will be filled with people who want to see him. From 9 until 10:30 or so, he will try to give the impression that he is devoting his entire attention to a businessman from his state with a tax problem; to a delegation protesting their town's loss of air or rail service; to a constituent and his three children, who are in town for the day and want to say hello; and to a couple of staff members whose morale will collapse if they don't have five minutes alone to go over essential business with him. As he strives to project one-on-one sincerity to all these people, he is fielding phone calls at the rate of one every five minutes and checking a press release that has to get out in time to make the afternoon papers in his district.
>
> He leaves this madhouse to go to a committee meeting, accompanied by his legislative aide, who tries to brief him on the business before the committee meeting begins. The meeting started at 10, so he struggles to catch the thread of questioning, while a committee staff member whispers in his ear. And so the day continues.
>
> The typical day . . . usually ends around 11:30 P.M., as the congressman leaves an embassy party, at which he has been hustling as if it were a key precinct on election eve. He is too tired to talk about any but the most trivial matters, too tired usually to do anything but fall into bed and go to sleep.[16]

As a result of competing demands, legislators pay somewhat less attention to the policy process than their public image would have you believe, leaving much of the work to their staffs. Even then, public policy tends to get short shrift. Because reelection is a primary concern for legislators, their staffs are frequently assigned to solve the relatively minor problems presented by constituents. In fact, placating unhappy constituents has become so prominent a concern that one legislative observer notes that constituency services—called "casework" by elected officials—have become "more important than issues" for representatives.[17]

Gradually, institutions have begun to specialize in providing the social intelligence necessary for policy formulation. These policy institutes, sometimes called think tanks, now wield substantial influence in the social policy process. Not unlike prestigious colleges, think tanks maintain multidisciplinary staffs of scholars who prepare position papers on a range of social issues. With multimillion-dollar budgets and connections with national and state capitals, think tanks are well positioned to shape social policy. Generally, financial support for these institutes comes from wealthy individuals and corporations with particular ideological inclinations that are evidenced by the types of think tanks they support. Several prominent policy institutes are located on the ideological continuum in Figure 8.2.

Within policy institutes, prominent scholars, usually identified as senior fellows, hold endowed chairs, having often served in cabinet-level positions within the executive branch. For example, when a Republican administration comes into power, large numbers of senior fellows from conservative policy institutes assume cabinet appointments; their Democratic counterparts return to liberal institutes, where senior chairs await them. For junior staffers, an appointment in a think tank can provide invaluable experience in how the governmental policy process actually works. Despite their influence in public policy, however, it is important to recognize that think tanks are private, nongovernmental institutions.

Through much of the twentieth century, a first generation of largely liberal policy institutes, such

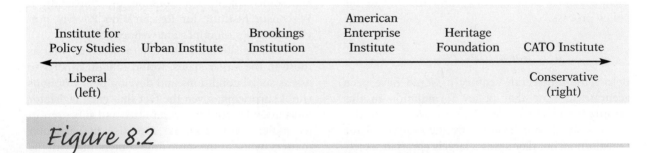

Figure 8.2

Place on the Ideological Continuum of Six Policy Institutes

as the Brookings Institution, contributed to the formulation of governmental welfare policy. Their role was essentially reactive, in that they provided technical expertise to legislators and governmental agencies upon request. By the mid-1970s, however, a second generation of conservative policy institutes, such as the American Enterprise Institute and the Heritage Foundation, moved aggressively forward to shape a public philosophy that was more consistent with their own values. The elections of Ronald Reagan and George H. W. Bush did much to further the influence of these organizations, and the work of scholars from these policy institutes became important to the implementation and continuation of the "Reagan revolution."[18] A third generation of policy institutes emerged later to promote programs for the poor. The Children's Defense Fund and the Center on Budget and Policy Priorities endeavor to reassert the needs of the disadvantaged in social welfare policy.[19] The election of Bill Clinton to the presidency in 1992 brought to the forefront the Progressive Policy Institute, a think tank responsible for much of the policy research Clinton used during the campaign, and later influential in establishing domestic policy. When George W. Bush used conservative policy institutes to move public policy further to the right, progressive groups responded by establishing the Center for American Progress, an avowedly liberal organization. Unlike the more ideologically oriented think tanks, the New America Foundation has established itself as a policy institute with a more bipartisan agenda. In 2002, policyAmerica was established as an Internet-based think tank committed to disseminating innovations in social policy.

Legislation

Much public policy work is conducted by legislators who are appointed to committees and subcommittees on the basis of their particular interests. An important and often unappreciated component of the legislative phase is the role played by the staffs of committees and subcommittees. Former legislative staffers are definitive experts in the subject area of a committee and are prized as lobbyists for special interest groups.[20] As a result of the increasing complexity of the policy process, the number of legislative staff has multiplied. In the late 1980s, 24,000 staff members served Congress, more than double the number in the late 1970s.[21] Committees are the loci of testimony on issues, and legislative hearings provide an opportunity for the official and sometimes the only input from the public on some matters. Accordingly, representatives of advocacy groups make it a point to testify before certain committees in order to ensure that their views are heard. At the federal level, the primary committees dealing with social welfare are as follows[22]:

Senate

Finance Committee. Subcommittees: Medicaid and Health Care for Low-Income Families; Medicare, Long-Term Care, and Health Insurance; Social Security and Family Policy

Agriculture. Subcommittee: Research, Nutrition, and General Legislation

Appropriations. Subcommittee: Labor, Health and Human Services, Education

Labor and Human Resources. Subcommittees: Aging, Children and Families, Disability Policy

Special Aging

Spotlight 8.1

The Policy Process

Public policy in the United States is made through a deliberative process that involves the U.S. Senate and House of Representatives. You can learn more about each of these bodies of elected officials at their respective websites: **www.senate.gov** and **www.house.gov**. For a detailed explanation of the legislative process and how laws are made, go to

http://thomas.loc.gov/home/lawsmade.toc.html. Political action committees (PACs) play an influential part in decisions on public policy. In the United States, PACs represent almost every group or interest imaginable. To review the various PACs, go to the Google search engine (**www.google.com**) and type in the words *political action committee*.

House of Representatives

Ways and Means. Subcommittees: Health; Human Resources; Social Security

Economic and Educational Opportunities. Subcommittees: Early Childhood, Youth, and Families; Employer/Employee Relations; Postsecondary Education, Training, and Lifelong Learning; Workforce Protections

Appropriations. Subcommittee: Labor, Health and Human Services, and Education

Throughout the process, representatives of special interests attempt to shape any given proposal so that it is more congruent with priorities of their members. Special interests can be classified according to the nature of their activities: During legislative sessions, interests can exert pressure strategically through **lobbying;** during elections, interest groups exert influence through **Political Action Committees (PACs).** As special interests learned to skirt federal campaign regulations, increasing amounts of "soft money" (nonregulated donations) influenced election activity.[23]

As indicated in Table 8.2, during the past two decades substantial funds have been expended in order to influence elections for the purpose of shaping public policy. Contributions are made to political parties and candidates who take positions that are congruent with a donor's interests. As a result, larger contributors tend to prefer one political party over another by channeling contributions through political action committees (PACs), as evident in Table 8.3. For all the money thrown into political campaigns, the consequences are remarkably static, reinforcing the status quo. In 2002, 98 percent of incumbents of the House and 86 percent of the Senate were reelected.[24]

In addition to contributions that are monitored by the Federal Election Commission, an increasing volume of "soft money," contributions that were not regulated, flooded into campaigns during the 1990s. For example, "soft money" contributions to the major political parties more than quadrupled from $79.1 million in 1991–1992 to $220.7 million in 1997–1998[25] to $450 million in 2000.[26] According to Common Cause, for 1999 "soft money" contributions by business eclipsed those of labor by a factor of 10.[27] For the 2000 election year the Democratic Party received $206.6 million in "soft money," an amount eclipsed by the Republicans who received $242.5 million.[28] Other patterns in the origins of "soft money" were discernable. Although contributions on the part of individuals were evenly split between the political parties, corporations and trade associations heavily favored Republicans over Democrats almost two-to-one. Two features of soft money donations contributed to the practice becoming controversial. First, donations were often of unknown origin, raising questions about the true origins of campaign contributions. Second, soft money was clearly partisan, often aiding one particular party of campaign exclusively. In 2004 campaign finance reform was enacted through the Bipartisan Campaign Reform Act of 2002 that prohibited "soft money" contributions to national political parties. Subsequently, political groups exploited section 527 of the Internal Revenue Service code that allowed nonprofits and corporations to advocate specific causes. By the next national election cycle "soft money" had been diverted to "527 groups" to influence elections, the largest of which are shown in Table 8.4 on page 222.

Although the "soft money" and "527 group" controversies commanded the headlines during the elections from 2000 through 2006, the real money was in lobbying. Unlike campaign contributions which are regulated, lobbyists can shift major amounts of cash depending on their particular

Table 8.2

Top 10 Donors, 1989–2007

American Federation of State, County & Municipal Employees	$39,106,885
AT&T Inc.	$38,473,085
National Association of Realtors	$31,242,406
American Association for Justice	$28,005,639
National Education Association	$27,327,970
Goldman Sachs	$27,172,482
International Brotherhood of Electrical Workers	$27,028,736
Laborers Union	$26,069,839
Service Employees International Union	$25,225,643
Carpenters & Joiners Union	$25,176,682

Based on data released by the Federal Election Commission (FEC) on Monday, October 29, 2007.

Source: Center for Responsive Politics. Retrieved January 2008 from www.opensecrets.org. Used by permission.

Table 8.3

Top 20 Political Action Committee (PAC) Contributors to Federal Candidates, 2007–2008

PAC Name	Total Amount	Democrat %	Republican %
Operating Engineers Union	$1,417,675	86	14
International Brotherhood of Electrical Workers	1,097,950	98	2
American Bankers Association	1,039,370	40	60
Machinists/Aerospace Workers Union	1,017,000	97	3
AT&T Inc.	1,010,550	39	61
National Beer Wholesalers Association	1,003,500	52	48
Laborers Union	974,000	91	9
American Federation of State, County & Municipal Employees	896,636	99	1
Credit Union National Association	874,849	59	41
American Association for Justice	833,000	96	4
National Air Traffic Controllers Association	823,900	77	23
Air Line Pilots Association	821,000	86	14
General Electric	793,500	49	51
United Parcel Service	787,787	42	58
National Association of Realtors	780,000	53	47
National Association of Home Builders	763,000	44	56
Plumbers/Pipefitters Union	706,800	93	7
American Hospital Association	706,080	62	38
International Association of Fire Fighters	704,800	75	25
American Crystal Sugar	689,000	66	34

Totals include subsidiaries and affiliated PACs, if any.

Source: Center for Responsive Politics. Retrieved January 2008 from www.opensecrets.org. Used by permission.

needs. As Table 8.5 on page 222 attests, vested interests expended vast sums to influence germane issues; during the past two Congresses, lobbyists sought to influence a range of issues: the future of Medicare, telecommunications deregulation, tort reform, and fuel mileage requirements for passenger cars. Lobbying allows industries to advocate for or defend against specific bills. Thus, anticipating the Medicare reforms of 2003, the health care and pharmaceutical industries pumped almost $300 million into lobbying activities. Lobbyists enjoy influence in several ways. Although the largest lobbying firms command millions of dollars in revenues, as shown in Table 8.6 on page 223, they account for but a small fraction of the scale of the industry. For

2004, lobbyists spent $2.1 *billion* ($176.7 million each month), employing 32,890 personnel, which is double the number in 1999.[29] Complementing the funding and staffing of lobbying firms has been their acquisition of former members of Congress. Between 1998 and 2005, 43.4 percent of former members became lobbyists.[30] A joke making the rounds of Capitol Hill was that being elected to Congress provided the apprenticeship necessary for a position in a lobbying firm, where the real money was.

In national politics, the key to influence is choreographing the resources of PACs, soft money, and lobbyists to attain party objectives. By way of illustration, having won control of Congress as a result of the 1994 midterm elections, Republicans

Table 8.4

Top Contributors to 527 Committees, 2006 Election Cycle

Contributor	Total
Service Employees International Union	$32,929,734
Perry Homes	9,150,000
Operating Engineers Union	4,331,720
Laborers Union	3,515,313
Soros Fund Management	3,515,000
United Food & Commercial Workers Union	3,164,955
America Votes 2006	2,345,000
Sheet Metal Workers Union	2,075,000
Chartwell Partners	2,000,200
Sustainable World Corp./Linda Pritzker	1,941,000
Peter B. Lewis/Progressive Corp.	1,624,375
John R. Hunting/Philanthropist	1,531,000
International Brotherhood of Electrical Workers	1,375,545
National Education Association	1,194,806
Gill Foundation	1,181,355
Jon Stryker/Jon Stryker Architecture	1,171,313
John Templeton Foundation	1,117,415
Media Fund	1,035,000
Conserving for the Future	1,011,400
Las Vegas Sands	1,000,000
Eagle Realty of SW Florida	1,000,000

This chart lists the top donors to these committees during the 2006 election cycle. Contributions may come from the organizations themselves or its individual members or employees or owners, and those individuals' immediate families. Organization totals include subsidiaries and affiliates. The data are based on records released by the Internal Revenue Service on Tuesday, December 11, 2007.

Source: Center for Responsive Politics. Retrieved January 2008 from www.opensecrets.org. Used by permission.

Table 8.5

Top Spenders, 1998–2007

Client	Total
U.S. Chamber of Commerce	$338,324,680
American Medical Association	157,247,500
General Electric	149,990,000
American Hospital Association	138,084,144
Pharmaceutical Research & Manufacturers of America	115,008,600
AARP	112,732,064
Edison Electric Institute	107,132,628
National Association of Realtors	103,890,000
Business Roundtable	101,660,000
Northrop Grumman	101,350,474
Blue Cross/Blue Shield	90,163,317
Lockheed Martin	87,797,702
Freddie Mac	86,164,048
Verizon Communications	83,407,022
Boeing Co.	82,038,310
General Motors	77,620,483
Philip Morris	75,500,000
Roche Group	74,888,942
Fannie Mae	73,857,000
Ford Motor Co.	71,312,808

Source: Center for Responsive Politics. Retrieved January 2008 from www.opensecrets.org. Used by permission.

moved swiftly to divert the flow of PAC money from the Democratic Party. Leading the effort was Representative Dick Armey, house majority leader, who, in April 1995, sent a letter to Fortune 500 CEOs complaining that their contributions to such "liberal" charities as the American Cancer Society were contrary to Republican intentions in social reform. In order to clarify his intentions, Armey's staff let PAC contributors know that contributions to Republican ventures were expected and that those to Democrats would also be tallied. Special interests seeking access to the new Republican leadership should be zeroing in on their contributions to Democrats. In the annals of special interest politics, Armey's brazen tactics broke new ground: "By imposing an ideological test on givers they have introduced a new level of coercion," observed journalist Ken Auletta.[31] Yet Armey's strategy violated no laws, and the money rolled in. In the first eight months of 1995 the Republican Party received $60 million in contributions, up from just $36 million in 1993.[32]

During the presidency of George W. Bush, Armey teamed up with Grover Norquist, president of Americans for Tax Reform, to launch the "K

Table 8.6

Top 10 Lobbying Firms

Rank of Firm	Revenues in Millions
1. Patton Boggs	$35.3
2. Van Scoyoc Associates	26.2
3. Akin Gump Strauss Hauer & Field	26.0
4. Cassidy & Associates	24.5
5. Barbour Griffith & Rogers	22.2
6. Dutko Worldwide	21.6
7. Hogan & Hartson	17.8
8. Quinn Gillespie & Assoc.	17.0
9. DLA Piper	16.6
10. PMA Group	16.3

Source: Jeffrey Birnbaum, "In the Loop," *Washington Post* (March 13, 2007), p. A15.

Street Project." Frustrated that lobbyists were frequently wedded to liberal social programs and the interests that sustained them, Norquist proposed routinizing Armey's vetting strategy: If the lobbying industry expected access to Capitol Hill, it needed to hire Republicans. In short order, K Street complied: Virtually all new hires by lobbying firms were card-carrying Republicans. In effect, the K Street Project cemented the relationship between conservative interests and Congress.

> Now the Republican Party is using its sway over both K Street and the wider business community to build a private sector equivalent to Roosevelt's machine. It hands out government contracts to businesses that fill its coffers: look at the way the pharmaceutical industry should gain from the new prescription-drug benefit in Medicare. It provides its most loyal foot soldiers, from congressional aides to congressmen, with a pot of gold on K Street when they retire.[33]

Having secured control of the three branches of the federal government, Republicans viewed consolidation of their power as the next goal. Strategists from the Right speculated that this could be achieved by bankrolling campaigns, coordinating lobbying, and investing in conservative think tanks. Ultimately, the objective was an era of political dominance that would rival—and reverse—the leg-islative triumphs of the New Deal coalition that engineered the American welfare state.[34] With the election of George W. Bush, the prospect of permanent conservative dominance in social policy appeared a distinct possibility. "The right has out-organized, out-fought and out-thought liberal America over the past 40 years. And the left still shows no real sign of knowing how to fight back," noted two British journalists.

> In theory, liberals have more than enough brain and brawn to match conservatives. The great liberal universities and foundations have infinitely more resources than the American Enterprise Institute and its allies. But the conservatives have always been more dogged. The Ford Foundation is as liberal as Heritage is conservative, but there is no doubt which is the more ruthless in its cause.[35]

Scrambling for purchase in domestic policy, a group of philanthropists established the Phoenix Group to encourage innovative thinking among Progressives. Tycoons George Soros and Peter Lewis "had come to view progressive politics as a market in need of entrepreneurship, served poorly by a giant monopoly—the Democratic Party—that is still doing business in an old, Rust Belt kind of way."[36] For Democrats, the 2004 election had come to symbolize more than a presidential campaign, but the very relevance of the party. The 2006 midterm election returned control of Congress to Democrats where they began to dismantle the Republican's "K Street Project." In order to curry favor with the new Democratic leadership, lobbyists hired Democrats, reversing Republican designs on attaining permanent governance.[37]

An open, democratic polity provides ample opportunities for groups to mobilize members to advance their cause. Emily's List, founded by Ellen Malcolm in the mid-1980s is illustrative. Established to increase the number of pro-abortion members of Congress, Malcolm started from scratch, raising funds to encourage Democratic women to enter politics. Coining an acronym for "early money is like yeast," Emily's List focused on primaries, figuring that "If we could raise enough early money to get women started then they could convince the traditional fundraisers that they were viable, and they could then raise the money they needed to win," Malcolm recalled. Forging strong relationships between female candidates and female donors augmented the focus on primaries and vaulted Emily's List to the forefront of Progressive politics. Two decades after its inception, Emily's List boasted a staff of 70, had leveraged $30 million for pro-abortion candidates, and increased the number of Democratic women in Congress fourfold.[38]

Compared to business, labor, and lobbyists, most social advocacy groups bring few assets to bear on the political process. Limited by meager resources, social advocacy groups usually rely on volunteer lobbyists. In addition to NASW, there are several advocacy groups within social welfare that have been instrumental in advancing legislation to assist vulnerable populations—among them the American Public Human Service Association, the Child Welfare League of America, the National Association for the Advancement of Colored People, the National Urban League, the National Assembly of Voluntary Health and Welfare Associations, and the National Organization for Women. Of these advocacy groups only one, AARP, ranks among the top 100 lobbyists on Capitol Hill. Despite the number of welfare advocacy organizations and their successful record in evolving more comprehensive social legislation, changes in the policy process hamper their work. Increases in the number of governmental agencies as well as in their staffs make it difficult to track policy developments and changes in administrative procedures. Worse, the escalating cost of influencing social policy, evident in the number of paid lobbyists and in the contributions lavished by PACs, is simply beyond the means of most welfare advocacy organizations. As one Democratic candidate for the Senate lamented, "only the well-heeled have PACs—not the poor, the unemployed, the minorities or even most consumers."[39]

Compared to more affluent interests, human service professionals have little clout. In social work, the PAC that provides assistance to candidates is Political Action for Candidate Election, or PACE, "the political arm of the National Association of Social Workers." PACE uses a variety of tactics to "expand social workers' activity in politics," including voter registration, support for political campaigns, and analysis of incumbents' voting records.[40] For the 1999–2000 election cycle, PACE budgeted total contributions of $225,000 to $240,000 to candidates running for national office,[41] an amount that, though not insignificant to candidates who received assistance, pales in comparison to the amounts wielded by more influential PACs.

This is not to say that proponents of social justice have been ineffectual. Among liberal advocacy organizations, the Children's Defense Fund (CDF) hoped to benefit significantly from the election of Bill Clinton; First Lady Hillary Rodham Clinton had been a former chair of its board of directors, and Clinton's Health and Human Services (HHS) secretary, Donna Shalala, had succeeded Rodham Clinton at CDF. CDF did claim a substantial victory with incorporation of the Children's Initiative in the Clinton 1993 economic package, but in 1996 children's advocates were distraught when Clinton signed the welfare reform law, PRWORA, which they thought was injurious to poor children. CDF fared little better under the administration of George W. Bush. In search of a label on which to hang its school reform initiative, the Bush White House apprehended CDF's comprehensive Leave No Child Behind initiative, and reworked it to become No Child Left Behind. Ultimately, CDF joined a coalition of liberal advocates and savored the defeat of George W. Bush's attempt to privatize Social Security.

Implementation

The fact that a policy has been enacted does not necessarily mean it will be implemented. Often governmental policies fail to provide for adequate authority, personnel, or funding to accomplish their stated purposes. This has been a chronic problem for social welfare programs. It is also possible that a governmental policy initiative will not be enforced even after it has been established. Many local jurisdictions have correctional and child welfare institutions now operating under court supervision because judges have agreed with social advocates that these institutions are not in compliance with state or federal law.

Implementation, difficult enough in the normal course of events, is that much more difficult when the public is disaffected with governmental institutions. The episodic nature of public endorsement of governmental institutions has been studied extensively by Albert O. Hirschman. In *Shifting Involvements*, Hirschman investigated the relationship between "private interest and public action." According to Hirschman, public endorsement of governmental institutions is a fundamental problem for industrialized capitalist societies, which emphasize individual competitiveness while generating social and economic dislocations that require collective action. "Western societies," Hirschman observes, "appear to be condemned to long periods of privatization during which they live through an impoverished 'atrophy of public meanings,' followed by spasmodic outbursts of 'publicness' that are hardly likely to be constructive."[42] Disenchantment with governmental solutions to social problems makes public welfare programs vulnerable to their critics, leading to reductions in staff and fiscal support, often followed by an escalation in the social problem for which the social program was initially designed. Thus, the episodic nature of public support for programs designed to alleviate social problems further impedes effective implementation.

Evaluation

The expansion of governmental welfare policies has spawned a veritable industry in program evaluation. Stung by the abuses of the executive branch during Watergate and the Vietnam War, Congress established additional oversight agencies to review federal programs.[43] As a result, multiple units within the executive and legislative branches of government have the evaluation of programs as their primary mission. At the federal level, the most important of these include the Government Accountability Office (GAO), the Office of Management and Budget (OMB), the Congressional Budget Office (CBO), and the Congressional Research Service (CRS). For example, OMB developed the Program Assessment Rating Tool (PART) to evaluate federal programs, concluding that one-third are inadequate. Among those evaluated by PART as inferior were several social programs, including the substance abuse prevention and treatment block grants, the community development block grant, juvenile accountability block grants, and Earned-Income Tax Credit compliance.[44] State governments have similar units. In addition, departments have evaluation units that monitor program activities for which they are responsible. Finally, federal and state levels of government commonly contract with nongovernmental organizations for evaluations of specific programs. As a result, many universities provide important research services to government. The University of Wisconsin's Institute for Research on Poverty is distinguished for its research in social welfare, and Chapin Hall at the University of Chicago evaluates child welfare programming. In the past three decades, private consulting firms, such as the Manpower Demonstration Research Corporation (MDRC), Abt Associates, MAXIMUS, and Mathematica, have entered the field, often hiring former government officials and capitalizing on their connections in order to secure lucrative research contracts. Of course, any politicization of the research process is frowned upon, because it raises questions about the impartiality of the evaluation. Is a former government official willing to assess rigorously and impartially a program run by an agency in which he or she was employed in the past or would like to be employed in the future? Questions about the closeness between governmental agencies and research firms and the validity of evaluation studies have become so common that the consulting firms located near the expressway surrounding Washington, DC, are often referred to as "the beltway bandits."

Whether conducted in-house or contracted out to universities or commercial firms, evaluation research has become a major industry, replete with its own vocabulary. Alice O'Connor recounted in her history of poverty studies that research had become a subsector of the welfare state:

> The technical jargon of recent decades has taken poverty knowledge to a level of abstraction and exclusivity that it had not known before. It is a language laced with acronyms that themselves speak of particular data sets, policies and analytic techniques (PSID, NLSY, TRIM, FAP, PBJI, EITC, and, albeit without a detectable sense of irony, Five Year Plans and a model known as the KGB). It also speaks of a self-contained system of reasoning that is largely devoid of political or historical context.[45]

The influence of evaluation research in social policy was sustained by the interaction of elite university social science departments that prepared researchers and liberal policy institutes which provided the setting for the application of their analyses. Annual conferences held by professional organizations such as the Association for Public Policy Analysis and Management, featured young researchers displaying their virtuosity in command of mathematics and logic.

Investigations by program evaluation organizations can be characterized as applied (as opposed to "pure") research, the objective being to optimize program operations. As a result of this emphasis on the function of programs, evaluation studies frequently focus on waste, cost-effectiveness, and goal attainment. Owing to the contradictory objectives of many welfare policies, the constant readjustments in programs, and the limitations in the art of evaluation research, evaluations frequently conclude that any given program has mixed results. Rarely does a program evaluation provide a clear indication for future action. Often the results of a single program evaluation are used by both critics and defenders in their efforts to dismantle or to advance the program.

The very inconclusiveness of program evaluation contributes to the partisan use to which evaluation research can be put. It is not uncommon for decision makers to engage in statistical arguments that have a great influence on social welfare policy. Of recent "stat wars," several relate directly to social welfare. One example is the question of whether underemployed and discouraged workers should be included in the unemployment rate. Currently, the Department of Labor defines as unemployed only those who are out of work and actively looking for jobs; and it considers part-time workers as employed. As a result, many African Americans, Hispanic Americans, young adults, and women are not considered unemployed, even though advocates for these groups contend that they are not fully employed. Liberals argue that including underemployed and discouraged workers in the unemployment rate would produce a more accurate measure of the employment experience of disadvantaged groups. Conservatives argue that the employment rate is not a good indicator of employment opportunity anyway, citing the millions of undocumented workers who come to the United States illegally every year to take menial jobs. Further, including underemployed and discouraged workers would increase the unemployment rate by as much as 50 percent and would prove unacceptably expensive, because extensions in the number of quarters for which workers are eligible for unemployment compensation are tied to the unemployment rate. Predictably, evaluations of employment programs vary considerably. Consultants have generated considerable data about the results of state and local welfare-to-work initiatives. Their studies evince a general theme: Although welfare caseloads have dropped more than 50 percent, heads of households who have found work (1) tend to remain stuck in sub-poverty-level wages, and (2) remain eligible for benefits such as food stamps and Medicaid. Such research serves ideological purposes, of course. Conservatives trumpet the reduction in welfare dependency, and liberals worry about the fate of families who continue to be poor despite full-time work.

Marginalization If the governmental decision-making process is somewhat irregular and irrational, it is also unrepresentative. As illustrated in Figure 8.3, groups in the upper levels of the social stratification populate the institutions through which policy is made. In the case of welfare policy, welfare beneficiaries must adjust to rules established by other social groups. The primary players in the social policy game are executives and professionals. The wealthy are able to opt out, leaving its social obligations in the hands of executives. Groups lower on the social stratification scale have less and less influence on governmental policy. The interests of these groups are left largely in the hands of professionals who work through advocacy organizations. Thus, the lower socioeconomic groups' lack of influence in the social policy process is virtually built into governmental decision making. The term *non-decision making* has been coined to describe this phenomenon—the system's capacity to keep the interests of some groups off the decision-making agenda.[46] Marginalization has a long history in the United States; generations of African Americans and women were legally excluded from decision making prior to emancipation and suffrage.

Policymakers' attempts to increase the influence of disadvantaged groups in decision making have not been well received. A classic illustration of this occurred during the Great Society initiative, when poor people were to be assured of "maximum feasible participation" in the Community Action Program (CAP). This stipulation was interpreted to mean that one-third of the members of CAP boards of directors must be poor people—a seemingly reasonable idea—but the militancy of poor people in some cities at the time led to utter chaos in many CAPs. As a result of pressure from mayors and other officials, lawmakers rescinded this requirement in order to make CAPs more compliant.[47] Since then, the representation of lower socioeconomic groups in decision making has been limited, for all practical purposes, to an advisory capacity at best.

The governmental policy process also poses problems for administrators and practitioners. Policies frequently reflect assumptions about the human condition that may seem reasonable to the upper socioeconomic groups that make them but bear little resemblance to the reality of the lower socioeconomic groups that are supposed to be beneficiaries. For example, child support enforcement policy assumes that fathers of children on TANF have the kind of regular, well-paying jobs that would allow them to meet the amounts of their court orders, whereas often their jobs are intermittent

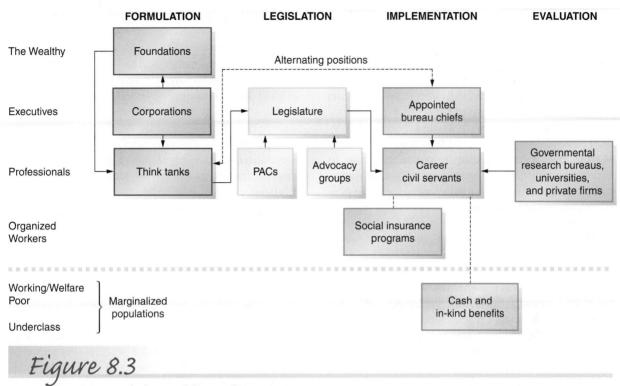

Figure 8.3

Stratification and the Public Policy Process

and offer low wages. Consequently, support payments to children who are dependent on welfare have been relatively disappointing. In 2002, $20.1 billion in child support was collected through the Child Support Enforcement (CSE) program, but most of this was for non-TANF families; only 14 percent of TANF benefits were recovered through child support enforcement.[48] For nonwelfare households, CSE's revenues exceeded administrative costs, but for welfare families, those for whom the program was initially justified, CSE lost money. An evaluation of Parents' Fair Share, a program designed to increase the child support paid by men whose dependents were on welfare, resulted in reduced child support payments despite the multiple interventions incorporated in the program.[49] To cite another example, welfare-to-work programs assume that young women want to complete their education and gain meaningful employment—but their socialization often instructs them that school and work are irrelevant and that having a child may be the most meaningful thing they can do. For many years, AFDC/TANF has provided financial support to poor teenage mothers, a benefit that many conservatives claim has actually induced girls to

become pregnant. But an evaluation of New Chance, a teen pregnancy prevention program, resulted in outcomes that were contrary to the intent of the program: Young mothers enrolled in New Chance were more likely to become pregnant again and less likely to participate in the labor market than those in the control group.[50] In sum, the preliminary studies on child support and teen pregnancy suggest that the poor do not necessarily comply with the bourgeois assumptions that are implicit or explicit in social policy.

It is not surprising, then, that welfare programs are not well received by many of the people who depend on them. Instead of being grateful, beneficiaries are frequently resentful. In turn, upper-income taxpayers find this ingratitude offensive and are inclined to make programs more punitive. Ironically, beneficiaries of welfare programs tend to respond to punitive policies with indifference and defiance because, for many of them, welfare programs have never been particularly helpful. The perception that welfare programs are only minimally helpful is occasionally validated when, under exceptional circumstances, someone from an upper socioeconomic group falls into the social safety net and suddenly appreciates the importance of welfare programs for daily survival.

Not all social programs are perceived in such a negative light. Generally, programs that benefit persons who are solidly in the working class fare better. The social insurance programs, such as Social Security, Unemployment Compensation, and Medicare, are usually regarded more highly by beneficiaries. Of course, the insurance programs require people to first pay into the program in order to claim benefits later, so they are designed to be different from the means-tested, welfare programs intended for the poor.

A particular consequence of governmental policy making falls on the shoulders of welfare professionals. "Workers on the front lines of the welfare state find themselves in a corrupted world of service," wrote Michael Lipsky in his award-winning *Street-Level Bureaucracy*. According to Lipsky, "Workers find that the best way to keep demand within manageable proportions is to deliver a consistently inaccessible or inferior product."[51] In response to the irrelevance often characteristic of governmental welfare policies, personnel in public welfare offices consequently deny benefits to people who are eligible for them, a process labeled **bureaucratic disentitlement**.[52] It should come as no surprise, then, that public welfare programs mandated by governmental policy have acquired an undesirable reputation within the professional community. The executive director of the California chapter of NASW candidly stated that "Public social services are being abandoned by M.S.W. social workers. It seems to be employment of last resort."[53] Another veteran observer was even more graphic: "To work in a public agency today is to work in a bureaucratic hell."[54] Within the context of public welfare, it is not surprising to find that burnout has become pervasive among welfare professionals. The inadequacy of public welfare policies for both beneficiaries and professionals is an unfortunate consequence of the governmental policy process as it is currently structured.

Making the public policy process more representative is a primary concern of welfare advocates. Since the Civil Rights movement, African Americans and the poor have recognized the power of the ballot, and voter registration has become an important strategy for advancing the influence of these groups. The registration of Hispanic Americans in the Southwest has been the mission of the Southwest Voter Research Institute, founded by the late Willie Velasquez. Under the visionary leadership of Velasquez, Latino voter registration grew steadily and was reflected in an increase in the number of Hispanic elected officials. Fifteen years of voter registration campaigning by the institute contributed to a doubling of the number of Hispanic elected officials in the Southwest by the late 1980s.[55] As the attempts to increase the registration of minority voters suggest, reengaging Americans in the political process is a difficult undertaking. In national elections, only about half of eligible U.S. voters exercise the franchise, the lowest turnout among industrialized nations. Explanations of voter apathy are multiple. The Republican and Democratic parties have lost the allegiance of increasing numbers of voters who identify themselves as independents. Between 1987 and 2004 the number of Democratic voters declined from 52 percent to 44 percent, while Republican voters held constant at about 33 percent; yet, the unaffiliated voters increased from 17 percent to 24 percent. Although both Democratic and Republican parties boasted modest growth during the period—4.8 percent and 8 percent—respectively, they were eclipsed by independent voters who grew 11 percent.[56]

Political parties and campaign managers who contend with the growing ranks of independent voters have come to appreciate segmentation of the voting public. The Pew Research Center for the People and the Press has divided the electorate into nine groups, shown in Table 8.7. The Pew study has enormous implications for the future of U.S. social welfare. The bad news is that despite the extensive benefits of social programs, just two groups clearly support them, comprising only one-fourth of the electorate. The good news is that conservatives who are struggling economically and discouraged independents might support social programs if they viewed them in their self-interest. Clearly, advocates of social and economic justice cannot afford to rest on their laurels if they wish to be competitive in the marketplace of political ideas.

Within the voting population, more affluent voters are more than twice as likely to exercise their franchise as are those who are poor: In 1996, 65.7 percent of voters with incomes above $50,000 voted in the presidential election, versus only 28.6 percent of those with incomes less than $10,000.[57] To a troubling degree, younger voters are disengaged from the political process, a circumstance that will be exacerbated by the aging of the baby boomers. In 2002, voters over age 65 outnumbered voters under age 30 by a factor of two; in 2022, that is expected

Table 8.7

Who's Who in the Electorate

Group Label	Defined as	Percent of Electorate
Enterprisers	Staunch conservatives	11
Social conservatives	Religious, critical of business	13
Progovernment conservatives	Struggling social conservatives	10
Liberals	Secular, antiwar	19
Disadvantaged Democrats	Social welfare loyalists	10
Conservative Democrats	Latter-day New Dealers	15
Upbeats	Positive outlook, moderate	13
Disaffecteds	Working class, discouraged	10
Bystanders	10 percent of populace	Did not vote

Source: Dan Balz, "Disparate Coalitions Now Make Up Two Parties, Study Finds," *Washington Post* (March 16, 2005), p. A15.

to increase to a factor of four.[58] A survey conducted by the Pew Research Center for the People and the Press revealed that substantial majorities of respondents agreed with such statements as "government is inefficient and wasteful," "politicians lose touch pretty quickly," and "government controls too much of daily life."[59] Such perceptions bode ill for the democratic process, of course. Some 30 million prospective voters are inactive, a group made up disproportionately of minorities and the poor.[60] Increasing the involvement of apathetic voters not only would make inroads against marginalization, but also would make public social programs more responsive to their circumstances.

Social Workers and Social Reform

As a result of marginalization and voter apathy, advocates of social justice view themselves as instrumental in correcting for a skewed political process. Throughout the history of U.S. social welfare, advocates of care for vulnerable populations have been shaping social policies. If we look beneath the surface of policy statements, we find a rich and often exciting account of the skirmishes fought by advocates for social justice. In some respects, social policy innovations can be looked upon as individual and collective biographies written in official language. In an age of mass populations that are often manipulated by private and public megastructures, it is easy to forget how powerful some individuals have been in shaping social welfare policy in the United States. Many of these leaders are known because they achieved national prominence; yet some of the more heroic acts to advance social justice were performed by individuals whose names are not widely recognized. As just one example not to be forgotten in this regard is Michael Schwerner, a social worker who was murdered while working in a voter registration drive in the South during the Civil Rights movement.[61]

Early social welfare leaders emerged during the **Progressive era,** a period when educated and socially conscious men and women sought to create structures that would advance social justice in the United States. The settlement house gained a reputation as the locus for reform activity, leading one historian to conclude that "settlement workers during the Progressive Era were probably more committed to political action than any other group of welfare workers before or since."[62] From this group Jane Addams quickly surfaced as a leader of national prominence. Through her settlement, Hull House, she fought not only for improvements in care for slum dwellers in inner-city Chicago, but also for international peace. For Jane Addams, social work was social reform. Instead of focusing solely on restoration and rehabilitation, Addams claimed that there was a superior role for the profession: "It must decide whether it is to remain behind in the area of caring for the victimized," she argued, "or whether to press ahead into the dangerous area of conflict where the struggle must be pressed to bring to pass an order of society with few victims."[63] In that struggle Addams served nobly, receiving an honorary degree from Yale University and serving as president of the Women's International League for Peace and Freedom. In 1931, Jane Addams was awarded the Nobel Peace Prize, a suitable distinction for a social worker who once had herself appointed a garbage collector in order to improve sanitation in the slums around Hull House.

Hull House proved a remarkable institution, and among its residents were women who made lasting and important contributions to the New Deal:

- Edith Abbott, president of the National Conference of Social Welfare, dean of the University of Chicago School of Social Service Administration, and participant in the drafting of the Social Security Act of 1935
- Grace Abbott, organizer of the first White House Conference on Children, director of the U.S. Children's Bureau, and participant in the construction of the Social Security Act
- Julia Lathrop, developer of the first juvenile court and of the first child mental health clinic in the United States, and the first director of the U.S. Children's Bureau
- Florence Kelley, director of the National Consumer League, cofounder of the U.S. Children's Bureau, and a member of the National Child Labor Committee
- Frances Perkins, director of the New York Council of Organizations for War Services, director of the Council on Immigrant Education, and the first Secretary of Labor[64]

The activity around Hull House was never limited to those with a narrow view of reform. A regular participant in the settlement was John Dewey, in his time "America's most influential philosopher, educator, as well as one of the most outspoken champions of social reform."[65] As a result, pragmatism, America's most distinctive contribution to philosophy, was infused with the promise of social reform.

Settlement experiences crystallized the motivations of other reformers as well. Harry Hopkins, primary architect of the New Deal and of the social programs that made up the Social Security Act, had resided in New York's Christadora House Settlement. Ida Bell Wells-Barnett led the Negro Fellowship League to establish a settlement house for African Americans in Chicago. Lillian Wald, with Florence Kelley, had earlier established New York's Henry Street Settlement, an institution that

was to achieve distinction within the African American community. Under the guidance of Mary White Ovington, a social worker, the first meetings of the National Association for the Advancement of Colored People were held at the Henry Street Settlement.[66]

Early social welfare leaders not only championed causes that improved the conditions of children and immigrants, but they also advocated racial equality. When it became apparent that Booker T. Washington's program of "industrial education" was unable to contend effectively with ubiquitous racial discrimination, social reformers Jane Addams, Ida B. Wells-Barnett, and John Dewey joined W.E.B. DuBois in the Niagara Movement. The early organizations spawned by the Niagara Movement were later consolidated into the National Urban League, with George Edmund Haynes, a social worker, as one of its codirectors. In 1910 Haynes had been the first African American to graduate from the New York School of Philanthropy, so it is not surprising that an important Urban League program was the provision of fellowships for African Americans to the school.[67] Later, during the height of the Civil Rights movement, the National Urban League, under the direction of social worker Whitney Young Jr., collaborated in organizing the August 28, 1963, march on Washington, memorialized by the ringing words of Martin Luther King Jr., "I have a dream!"[68]

If the New Deal bore the imprint of social workers, the Great Society was similarly marked some 30 years later. Significantly, one leader of the War on Poverty was Wilbur Cohen, a social worker who had been the first employee of the Social Security Board created in 1935. Eventually Cohen was to be credited with some 65 innovations in social welfare policy, but his crowning achievement was the passage of Medicare and Medicaid in 1965. The secretary of Health, Education, and Welfare during the Johnson administration, Cohen was arguably the nation's most decorated social worker, receiving 18 honorary degrees from American universities.[69]

Social Work and Advocacy Organizations

The formulation of social welfare policy in the United States, as this chapter has shown, is a complicated and often arduous process. Much of this can be attributed to the nature of U.S. culture: to the competing interests inherent in a pluralistic society; to the multiple systems of government that make social policy at the same time; to public and private bureaucracies that serve large numbers of consumers; to economic and technological developments that lead to specialization. Under these circumstances, changing social welfare policy to improve the circumstances of disadvantaged groups can be a daunting task. Regrettably, few human service professionals consider social policy advocacy an enterprise worthy of undertaking. Most social workers prefer direct service activity, in which they have little opportunity for direct involvement in social policy. Some social workers attain important positions in federal and state human service bureaucracies and are close to the policy process. Unfortunately, however, these managers are often administering welfare policies that have been made by legislatures and that do not necessarily represent either clients or human service professionals. Perhaps most troubling, the involvement of social workers in the formulation of social policy has been diminishing in recent years. In a provocative statement, June Hopps, former-dean of the Boston College School of Social Work and former Editor-in-Chief of *Social Work*, acknowledged that "Since the late 1960s and early 1970s, the [social work] profession has experienced a dramatic loss of influence in the arenas where policy is shaped and administered."[70] That this should occur is not only a reversal of the profession's Progressive era legacy, but also an abnegation of a rapidly expanding service sector. Paradoxically, opportunities to enter the upper levels of the federal civil service have become available through the Presidential Management Internship and Department of Health and Human Services Emerging Leaders programs, but social work has not found a way to systematically exploit these.

If one indicator of good social policy is the correspondence between the policy and the social reality of its intended beneficiaries, then social welfare policy would be enhanced by the input of social workers. However, social workers have left much of the decision making about social welfare to professionals from other disciplines. "There are increasing numbers of non-social workers, including psychologists and urban planners," observed Eleanor Brilliant, "taking what might have been social work jobs in service delivery and policy analysis."[71] The consequences of welfare professionals' opting to leave social policy in the hands of others are impor-

tant. For direct service workers, these consequences can mean having to apply eligibility standards or procedures that, although logical in some respects, make little sense in the social context of many clients. For the public, they may mean a gradual disenchantment with social programs that do not seem to work. The causes of the retrenchment affecting social programs since the late 1970s are complex, of course; but it is worth noting that public dissatisfaction with social programs has escalated as social welfare professionals have retreated from active involvement in public policy.

The rebuilding of a role for social workers in social policy will take concerted effort. Individual leadership is a necessary, but no longer sufficient, precondition for this objective. Essential to the undertaking will be social workers' ability to understand and manipulate complex organizations and programs. In fact, this skill may be the most critical for welfare professionals to acquire if they are to advance social justice, for it addresses a question central to the postindustrial era. During the Industrial Revolution, Karl Marx suggested that the central question was "Who controls the means of production?" A mature industrial order and the expansion of civil bureaucracy led Max Weber to ask, "Who controls the means of administration?" The evolution of a postindustrial order, in which primary economic activity occurs in a service sector dependent on processed information, raises a new question: "Who controls the means of analysis?" If social workers are to shape social policy as effectively as they had in the past, they will have to learn to control the means of analysis. This means conducting research on social problems, surveying public opinion about welfare programs, analyzing existing social policy for opportunities to enhance welfare provision, and winning elected office in order to make decisions about proposed social welfare policies.

Advocacy Organizations and the New Policy Institutes

Policy analysis organizations have been instrumental in shaping social policy since the New Deal. Subsequently, policy institutes have had liberal or conservative labels ascribed to them, with the liberal organizations achieving dominance up until the late 1970s—when, as we have seen, conservative

2

PART 3 The Government Sector

institutes ascended. The failure of government social programs to expand during the Carter presidency, followed by the profoundly negative impact of the Reagan years and the two Bush presidencies, led social reformers to look to traditional policy institutes such as the Brookings Institution and the Urban Institute for leadership. But the inability of these organizations to shape the debate on U.S. social welfare policy compelled increasingly impatient reformers to establish a new group of policy analysis organizations.

Children's Defense Fund   Begun by Marian Wright Edelman in 1974, the Children's Defense Fund (CDF) sought to address the health, income, and educational needs of the nation's children.[72] By the mid-1980s CDF had become a major voice in children's policy and had successfully advocated programs at the federal and state levels. In 1984 CDF helped pass the Child Health Assurance Program, which expanded Medicaid eligibility to poor women and children. It also advocated for the 1998 State Children's Health Insurance Program (SCHIP). CDF is noted for its educational publications, particularly for eye-catching posters depicting injustices inflicted on poor, minority children. Its annual report, the State of America's Children, is an authoritative compendium of issues and programs concerning children.

The Center on Budget and Policy Priorities   Established in 1981 by Robert Greenstein, former administrator of the Food and Nutrition Service in the Agriculture Department, CBPP has fought to defend social programs for low-income people against budget cuts. With a modest staff, CBPP distributes its analyses to congressional staffs, the media, and grassroots organizations. Despite its small size, CBPP provided much of the program analysis to refute arguments presented by conservative officials in their efforts to cut means-tested social programs. Significantly, CBPP and CDF have developed a close working relationship. CBPP regularly provides data to CDF on the health and income status of children.[73]

Economic Policy Institute   In 1986 Jeff Faux convinced labor-oriented liberals to establish a policy institute to represent "the perspective of working families and the poor."[74] During the subsequent decade EPI expanded rapidly and published reports depicting a widening chasm between the economic circumstances of working families and the affluent. Notable among EPI publications is its annual volume *The State of Working America,* which contains current data on income, taxes, wages, wealth, and poverty.

Institute for Women's Policy Research   Created in 1987 by Heidi Hartmann, a social program researcher and director of the Women's Studies Program at Rutgers University, IWPR quickly attained a respected position in Washington, DC. The IWPR research and advocacy agenda relating to women is extensive, including retirement, family leave, health insurance, welfare reform, and pay equity. In 1994 Hartmann received a MacArthur "genius" fellowship award for her advocacy of gender equity.

New America Foundation   In 1999, Ted Halstead launched the New America Foundation in order to develop policy options congruent with the information age. With Michael Lind, Halstead wrote *The Radical Center,* a book that outlined the need for an ideological orientation that was postliberal as well as postconservative.[75]

policyAmerica   In 2002, policyAmerica was established by David Stoesz, Howard Karger, and Jack Hansan as an Internet-based think tank designed to disseminate innovations in social policy. In addition to posting developments on its website, policyAmerica organized conferences on Bootstrap Capitalism, Rebuilding Communities, and Reinventing Children's Services.

Center for American Progress   Smarting from reversals attributed to conservative think tanks, John Podesta convinced other liberals to establish the Center for American Progress in 2003. Drawing on an annual budget of $10 million and many policy experts who had served in the Clinton administration, the Center for American Progress is well positioned to compete with policy institutes from the Right.[76]

Political Practice

The capacity of social workers to reassert their role in social welfare policy depends on the willingness of individuals to consider public office as a setting for social work practice. Although many welfare pioneers began their careers advocating for social welfare policy and then assumed administrative positions managing social programs, others used elected office to advance social reform. The first woman elected to the House of Representatives was Jeannette Rankin, who won a seat in 1916 running as a Republican in Montana. As a social worker who had studied under Frances Perkins, Rankin voted for early social welfare legislation and against military expansion. More recently, social workers in **political practice** have included Maryann Mahaffey, a member of the Detroit City Council, and Ruth Messinger, a former member of the New York City Council.

By 2008, six social workers had attained national office:

■ *Debbie Stabenow*

- Edolphus "Ed" Towns received his Master of Social Work degree in 1973. Elected as a Democratic state committeeman and then as the first African American deputy borough president in Brooklyn's history, Towns was elected in 1982, with 90 percent of the vote, to serve in Congress as the representative of the eleventh Congressional District of New York. Towns' work on congressional committees overseeing government operations, public works, and narcotics directly addresses the primary concerns of his inner-city constituents.[77]

■ *Edolphus Towns*

- Barbara Mikulski received her M.S.W. degree in 1965 and then served on the Baltimore City Council and in the U.S. House of Representatives. In 1986 Mikulski became the first Democratic woman to be elected to the U.S. Senate in her own right. Through appointments to the powerful Appropriations and Labor and Human Resources Committees, Mikulski is well positioned to advocate programs in health and social services.[78]

■ *Barbara Mikulski*

- Debbie Stabenow was awarded her M.S.W. from Michigan State University, after which she was elected to the Ingham County Commission, the Michigan House, and the Michigan Senate. In 1996 Stabenow ran to represent the Eighth Congressional District of Michigan on a platform opposing the extremes of the Republican Congress elected in 1994. Having won election to the House of Representatives, in 1999 Stabenow challenged an incumbent to become the second social worker to be elected to the U.S. Senate in her own right.

- Barbara Lee was elected in 1998 to fill the House seat of Ron Dellums, a social worker on whose staff she had served. Lee received her M.S.W. from the University of California, Berkeley, and established a community mental health center while completing her graduate studies. Subsequently she was elected to the California State Senate. Congresswoman Lee now serves on the House Committee on Banking and Financial Services and on the House Committee on International Relations, the Congressional Progressive Caucus, the Congressional Black Caucus, and the Congressional Women's Caucus.

■ *Barbara Lee*

- In 2000, Susan Davis defeated an incumbent to represent California's 49th Congressional District. Davis received her graduate degree in social services from the University of North Carolina in 1968; she subsequently moved to San Diego, where she chaired the school board. As a new member of Congress, Davis attained a coveted seat on the Armed Services Committee. Among her primary concerns are education and campaign finance reform.

■ *Susan Davis*

• Ciro Rodriquez, M.S.W. 1978 from Our Lady of the Lake University, was first elected to Congress in 1997, but lost his seat after a controversial redistricting of Congressional districts. In 2006, he won re-election, and has since represented the 23rd Congressional district of Texas. Representative Rodriguez serves on the Appropriations and Veterans' Affairs Committees.

■ *Ciro Rodriguez*

Conclusion

Perhaps the best indicator of social work's potential future influence on social policy appears at the local level. For example, social workers have lobbied successfully on behalf of nonprofit agencies facing threats to their tax-exempt status,[79] encouraged students to engage in election campaigns and to become more knowledgeable about politics,[80] and managed a campaign for the election of a state senator.[81] In each of these instances, social workers were gaining the kind of experience that is essential to political involvement at higher levels. By 2000 such activity was paying off: More than 200 social workers had been elected to state, county, municipal, and judicial offices. In response to increasing political activity at the state level, social work professor emeritus Bob Schneider established Influencing State Policy in order to empower human service professionals.[82]

Social workers disinclined to engage in high-visibility activities such as campaigning for public office could make their imprint on politics through legislators' "constituent services." Pulitzer Prize–winning journalist Hedrick Smith observed that members of Congress are increasingly relying on constituent services in place of pork barrel projects as domestic expenditures dry up. Using a term familiar to most social workers, politicians call constituent services "casework"—that is, "having your staff track down missing Social Security checks, inquire about sons and husbands in the armed services, help veterans get medical care, pursue applications for small-business loans."[83] The importance of political "casework" has been noted by political scientists, who attribute up to 5 percent of the vote to such activities, a significant amount in close elections. David Himes of the National Republican Congressional Committee claimed that "our surveys have shown that constituency service, especially in the House, is more important than issues."[84]

The cultivation of practice skills in the political arena at the local level offers perhaps the most promising way for social workers to regain influence in social welfare policy. Such activity can be undertaken by virtually any professional interested in the opportunity. On a volunteer basis, social workers would find few politicians who would turn down their professional assistance in the provision of constituent services. With experience, enterprising social workers might find that political practice could be remunerative, providing that they possessed skills needed by elected officials—such as conducting surveys, maintaining data banks of contributors, organizing public meetings, and keeping current on legislation important to constituents. From another perspective, however, the prospect of political practice should be taken seriously. If social workers are sincere about making essential resources available to their clients—a responsibility stated in the NASW Code of Ethics—then some form of political practice is a professional obligation. "To do less," noted Maryann Mahaffey, "to avoid the political action necessary to provide these resources, is to fail to live up to the profession's code of ethical practice."[85]

Discussion Questions

1. Clicking on "For Students" on the policyAmerica website, select a social welfare policy and identify its primary components. Which elected members of Congress were cosponsors of the legislation? What committees were instrumental in its passage? Which special interests benefited from its passage?

2. Clicking on "Advocacy" on the policyAmerica website, identify your Representative and Senators. E-mail them about an issue that is important to you. Do any of your members of Congress have any important health and human service committee assignments? Do your representatives have committee assignments that

could make them influential on issues important to you? Do your representatives have position statements available to constituents about specific social programs?

3. Politicians elected to your state legislature have responsibilities similar to members of Congress. Identify your state representatives. Do they have assignments on health and human service committees? Do they have position statements they could send to you on health and human service issues?

4. Select a health and human service bill of interest to you and follow it in your state legislature. Which committees and interest groups supported or fought the proposed legislation? How was the bill changed to make it more acceptable to special interests? Have local interests, such as a major newspaper, endorsed or objected to the proposed legislation? Why?

5. Does your state chapter of the National Association of Social Workers make legislation a high priority for the professional community? What are the legislative goals of the state NASW chapter? How are those goals reflected in the resources allocated? How would you prioritize health and human services in your community?

6. If marginalization leaves many clients of social programs impotent in the public policy process, how could these people be made more influential? How could the local professional community assist in empowering beneficiaries of social programs? What could you do?

7. Identify social workers who serve in local elected offices. What led them to pursue elective office? What are their future political plans? Could you provide constituent services for these persons or help with their reelection?

Notes

1. U.S. Congress, *U.S. Congress Handbook 1992* (McLean, VA: Barbara Pullen, 1992), p. 184.
2. "The Long Path to a Federal Budget," *Washington Post* (April 5, 2005), p. A21.
3. *Robert's Rules of Order* is available from several publishers.
4. The latest annual edition of *Overview of Entitlement Programs* can be obtained through the Government Printing Office in Washington, DC.
5. Charles Lindblom and David Braybrooke, *Strategy of Decision* (New York: Free Press, 1970).
6. Amitai Etzioni, *The Active Society* (New York: Free Press, 1968), pp. 282–288.
7. For a description of these forms of rationality, see Robert Alford, "Health Care Politics," *Politics and Society* 2 (Winter 1972), pp. 127–164.
8. Neil Gilbert and Harry Specht, *Dimensions of Social Welfare Policy* (Englewood Cliffs, NJ: Prentice Hall, 1986), pp. 206–210.
9. "Nuking Employee Benefits," *Wall Street Journal* (August 29, 1988), p. 16.
10. For example, see Harry Hatry, *A Review of Private Approaches for Delivery of Public Services* (Washington, DC: Urban Institute, 1983).
11. David Stoesz, *A Poverty of Imagination* (Madison, WI: University of Wisconsin Press, 2000).
12. Even Marx, who used a two-part classification, conceded the existence of a "lumpen-proletariat," although he did little to develop the concept.
13. Dexter Dunphy, *The Primary Group* (New York: Appleton-Century-Crofts, 1972), pp. 42–44.
14. Charles Peters, *How Washington Really Works*, rev. ed. (Reading, MA: Addison-Wesley, 1983), p. 112.
15. See, for example, Sheldon Danziger and Daniel Weinberg, *Fighting Poverty* (Cambridge, MA: Harvard University Press, 1986).
16. Peters, *How Washington Really Works*, pp. 101–102, 116.
17. Hedrick Smith, *The Power Game: How Washington Works* (New York: Random House, 1988), p. 152.
18. David Stoesz, "Policy Gambit: Conservative Think Tanks Take on the Welfare State," *Journal of Sociology and Social Welfare* 16 (1989), pp. 8–16.
19. David Stoesz, "The New Welfare Policy Institutes." Unpublished manuscript, School of Social Work, San Diego State University, 1988.
20. Peters, *How Washington Really Works*, p. 114.
21. Smith, *The Power Game*, p. 24.
22. *Congress at Your Fingertips* (McLean, VA: Capitol Advantage, 1996).
23. First established in 1944, PACs are political organizations that are regulated by federal law: Individual candidate contributions are limited to $5,000 per election, contributions to other PACs are restricted to $5,000 annually, and funding of national party committees cannot exceed $15,000 annually. Because of these restrictions, "soft money"—contributions outside the prohibitions of the Federal

Election Campaign Act—have become more prominent in federal elections.

24. Charles Noble, *The Collapse of Liberalism* (Lanham, MD: Rowman & Littlefield, 2004), p. 36.

25. "Overall Campaign Finance Statistics" (Washington, DC: Common Cause, June, 11, 1999).

26. "The Power of 'Soft Money,' " *Washington Post* (February 13, 2002), p. A25.

27. Ruth Marcus and Mike Allen, "Democrats' Donations from Labor Up Sharply," *Washington Post* (July 17, 2000), p. A1.

28. "The Power of Soft Money," p. A25.

29. Todd Purdum, "Go Ahead, Try to Stop K Street," *New York Times* (January 8, 2006), Section 4, p. 1.

30. Jeffrey Birnbaum, "Hill a Steppingstone to K Street for Some," *Washington Post* (July 27, 2005), p. A19.

31. Ken Auletta, "Pay Per Views," *New Yorker* (June 5, 1995), p. 56.

32. Nancy Gibbs, "Where Power Goes . . ." *Time* (July 17, 1995), p. 21.

33. John Micklethwait and Adrian Wooldridge, *The Right Nation* (New York: Penguin, 2004), p. 258.

34. Adam Clymer, "Buoyed by Resurgence, G.O.P. Strives for an Era of Dominance," *New York Times* (May 25, 2003).

35. John Micklethwait and Adrian Wooldridge, "For Conservatives, Mission Accomplished," *New York Times* (May 18, 2004), p. A25.

36. Matt Bai, "Wiring the Vast Left Wing Conspiracy," *New York Times Magazine* (July 25, 2004), p. 34.

37. Jeffrey Birnbaum, "Democrats' Stock is Rising on K Street," *Washington Post* (August 17, 2006), p. A6.

38. Chris Cillizza, "Emily's List Celebrates Clout as It Turns 20," *Washington Post* (October 18, 2005), p. A13.

39. Smith, *The Power Game*, p. 254.

40. Interview with Toby Weismiller, NASW, Washington, DC, January 11, 1988.

41. Personal communication with Dave Dempsey, NASW, Washington, DC, July 21, 2000.

42. Albert O. Hirschman, *Shifting Involvements* (Princeton, NJ: Princeton University Press, 1982), p. 132.

43. Peters, *How Washington Really Works*, p. 111.

44. Sam Coates, "Another White House, Another Yardstick Against Government," *Washington Post* (July 28, 2005), p. A23.

45. Alice O'Connor, *Poverty Knowledge* (Princeton, NJ: Princeton University Press, 2001), p. 15.

46. Peter Bachrach and Morton S. Baratz, *Power and Poverty* (New York: Oxford University Press, 1979), p. 7.

47. For a review of the CAP experience, see Daniel Patrick Moynihan, *Maximum Feasible Misunderstanding* (New York: Random House, 1973).

48. House Ways and Means Committee, *Overview of Entitlement Programs* (Washington, DC: U.S. GPO, 2004), p. 8-6.

49. Dan Bloom and Kay Sherwood, *Matching Opportunities to Obligations: Lessons for Child Support Reform from the Parents' Fair Share Pilot Phase* (New York: Manpower Demonstration Research Corporation, 1994).

50. Janet Quint, Denise Polit, Hans Bos, and George Cave, *New Chance: Interim Findings on a Comprehensive Program for Disadvantaged Young Mothers and Their Children* (New York: Manpower Demonstration Research Corporation, 1994).

51. Michael Lipsky, "Bureaucratic Disentitlement in Social Welfare Programs," *Social Service Review* 33, no. 4 (March 1984), pp. 81–88.

52. Quoted in Robert Kuttner, *The Economic Illusion* (Boston: Houghton Mifflin, 1984), p. 86.

53. Ellen Dunbar, "Future of Social Work," *NASW California News* 13, no. 18 (May 1987), p. 3.

54. Harris Chaiklin, "The New Homeless and Service Planning on a Professional Campus" (University of Maryland, Chancellor's Colloquium, Baltimore, December 4, 1985), p. 7.

55. "Willie's Vision for Chicano Empowerment," *Southwest Voter Research Notes* 2, no. 3 (June 1988), p. 1.

56. Rhodes Cook, "Moving On," *Washington Post* (June 27, 2004), p. B1.

57. Dale Russakoff, "Cut Out of Prosperity, Cutting Out at the Polls," *Washington Post* (October 24, 2000), p. A12.

58. Amy Goldstein and Richard Morin, "Young Voters' Disengagement Skews Politics," *Washington Post* (October 20, 2002), p. A1.

59. "Deconstructing Distrust," The Pew Research Center. Retrieved from www.people-press.org/trustrpt.htm

60. David Broder, "The 30 Million Missing Voters," *Washington Post* (July 16, 2000), p. B7.

61. Maryann Mahaffey, "Political Action in Social Work," *Encyclopedia of Social Work*, 18th ed. (Silver Spring, MD: NASW, 1987), p. 290.

62. Allen Davis, "Settlement Workers in Politics, 1890–1914," in Maryann Mahaffey and John Hanks (eds.), *Practical Politics: Social Work and Political Responsibility* (Silver Spring, MD: National Association of Social Workers, 1982), p. 32.

63. Allen F. Davis, *American Heroine: The Life and Legend of Jane Addams* (New York: Oxford University Press, 1973), p. 292.

64. Biographical information from *Encyclopedia of Social Work*, 18th ed. (Silver Spring, MD: NASW, 1987).

65. Richard Bernstein, "John Dewey," in Paul Edwards (ed.), *Encyclopedia of Philosophy, Vol. II* (New York: Macmillan and The Free Press, 1967), p. 380.

66. Mahaffey, "Political Action in Social Work," p. 286.

67. John Hope Franklin, *From Slavery to Freedom* (New York: Knopf, 1979), pp. 319–321.

68. Ibid., pp. 471–472.

69. Charles Schottland, "Wilbur Joseph Cohen: Some Recollections," *Social Work* 32, no. 5 (September/October 1987), pp. 371–372.

70. June Hopps, "Reclaiming Leadership," *Social Work* 31 (September/October 1986), p. 323.

71. Eleanor Brilliant, "Social Work Leadership: A Missing Ingredient?" *Social Work* 31 (September/October 1986), p. 328.

72. For details on CDF, see Joanna Biggar, "The Protector," *Washington Post Magazine* (May 18, 1986), p. C-4; and *The Children's Defense Fund Annual Report 1984–85* (Washington, DC: Children's Defense Fund, 1985).

73. Information on CBPP was obtained from an interview with David Kahan at CBPP on March 12, 1984.

74. *1998 Annual Report* (Washington, DC: Economic Policy Institute, 1998).

75. Ted Halstead and Michael Lind, *The Radical Center* (New York: Doubleday, 2001).

76. David Von Drehle, "Liberals Get a Think Tank of Their Own," *Washington Post* (October 23, 2003), p. A29.

77. Biographical sketch, courtesy of Congressman Ed Towns' office, n.d.

78. Biographical sketch, courtesy of Senator Mikulski's Office, n.d.

79. Elliot Pagliaccio and Burton Gummer, "Casework and Congress: A Lobbying Strategy," *Social Casework* 69 (March 1988), pp. 321–330.

80. Grafton Hull, "Joining Together: A Faculty-Student Experience in Political Campaigning," *Journal of Social Work Education* 23 (Fall 1987), pp. 116–123.

81. William Whittaker and Jan Flory-Baker, "Ragtag Social Workers Take On the Good Old Boys and Elect a State Senator," in Maryann Mahaffey and John Hanks (eds.), *Practical Politics: Social Work and Political Responsibility* (Silver Spring, MD: National Association of Social Workers, 1982).

82. For details, see the ISP website at www.statepolicy.org.

83. Smith, *The Power Game*, p. 124.

84. Ibid., p. 152.

85. Mahaffey and Hanks, *Practical Politics*, p. 284. (See Chapter 10, "Political Action in Social Work.")

CHAPTER 9

Tax Policy and Income Distribution

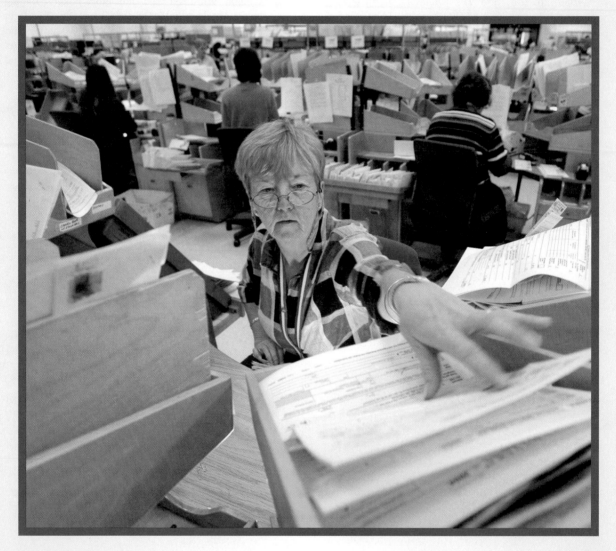

*T*ax policy, the use of legislation to define how revenues are generated in order to achieve social objectives, is fundamental to the structure of social welfare in the United States. Although this function may seem prosaic, in fact tax policy has been the flash point of major historical events, as evident in the Boston "tea party" when colonists objected to taxation without representation. Recently, the massive tax cuts of the George W. Bush administration have provoked dire warnings by liberals and conservatives alike about the fiscal health of the republic. Although tax policy is an instrument of government, its influence is not limited solely to generating revenues for federal and state social programs: Through "tax expenditures," areas exempted from taxation, tax policy provides significant incentives not only for specific industries, as in "corporate welfare," but also for individual behavior, as in the mortgage interest deduction. For this reason tax policy is of increasing interest to advocates of social justice. As support for direct benefits through traditional social programs has waned, social advocates have turned to "targeted tax expenditures"—preferably, refundable tax credits—as a means to advance economic justice. As a vehicle for funding social programs, tax policy is also an important barometer for social equity; and indeed, policy analysts have long used income distribution—and more recently wealth distribution—as an indicator of how fair the economy has been for various groups. Changes in income and wealth over time influence the economic mobility of Americans, some of whom fare better than others.

History of U.S. Tax Policy

All governments levy taxes to meet their legislated obligations. Because taxation appropriates income from private parties—individuals and corporations—and puts it to public use, it has been controversial and, at times, volatile. Ever since the establishment of the republic, various groups have objected to government taxation, challenging the authority to appropriate private property. Such challenges have usually been sorted out through the courts, but on occasion they have led to violent armed confrontations, as in the Whiskey Rebellion that divided the nation shortly after its creation. Although tax policy has traditionally been of professional interest primarily to the "green-eyeshade" accountants at the Internal Revenue Service, the radical Right also have

a keen interest in it because it recognizes that tax money is the lifeblood that allows government to function. A precept of American conservatism has been minimal taxation. Speaking about the American colonies, Edmund Burke observed that taxes, by their very nature, tended to be imprudent: "To tax and to please, no more than to love and to be wise, is not given to men."

Progressives and liberals understood the relationship between taxes and social programs differently, citing Oliver Wendell Holmes: "Taxes are what we pay for civilized society." Ever since the creation of the welfare state with the passage of the Social Security Act of 1935, social program expenditures have grown; and all these programs have been paid for by increasing taxes. The optimal welfare state, as liberals conceived it, would provide essential benefits as a right of citizenship. These benefits would be funded by progressive taxes—taxes that derived their revenues disproportionately from the wealthy. Implicit in this vision was the political calculus that was captured by Harry Hopkins, whose synopsis has become part of welfare folklore: "Tax, tax; spend, spend; elect, elect!" For half a century, this strategy produced solid electoral support for liberal social programs: The wealthy were taxed at higher rates, the revenues were diverted to social benefits for the middle and working classes through social programs, and social program beneficiaries expressed their gratitude by voting Democratic. Ultimately, however, liberal Democratic hegemony in social policy foundered on the shoals of its own success. As working families rose into the middle class, they tended to individualize their achievements, discounting the role of social programs and, in the process, becoming more receptive to conservative proposals to reduce social programs and their tax burden. By the 1980s this scenario led to the election of Ronald Reagan, who had a visceral dislike for federal social programs. The Reagan presidency was revolutionary in several respects, one being profound changes in tax policy, increasing economic inequality.

While the Clinton interregnum restored a measure of fairness in tax policy, the presidency of George W. Bush has viewed tax cuts as the centerpiece of its domestic agenda, achieving one for each year of its first term. The intent of the Bush White House has been summarized by Grover Norquist, who as president of Americans for Tax Reform has proposed that the Bush White House implement annual tax cuts: "I don't want to abolish government. I simply want to reduce it to the size where I can drag it into the bathroom and drown it in the bathtub."[1] Accordingly, conservatives have viewed tax cuts as essential to rolling back social programs, "starving the beast." As Paul Krugman observed, "Starving-the-beasters believe that budget deficits will lead to spending cuts that will eventually achieve their true aim: shrinking the government's role back to what it was under Calvin Coolidge."[2] For intellectuals of the Right, tax reform is ultimately the vehicle for dismantling the U.S. welfare state. "Instead of sending taxes to Washington, straining them through bureaucracies and converting what remains into a muddle of services, subsidies, in-kind support, and cash hedged with restrictions and exceptions," argued Charles Murray, "just collect the taxes, divide them up, and send the money back in cash grants to all American adults." According to Murray, a $10,000 grant to each nonincarcerated U.S. citizen, of which $3,000 would be for health care, would cost $355 billion more than current expenditures. By 2011, however, Murray's thought experiment would be revenue neutral; by 2020 it would save a half trillion dollars.[3] How this dispute between social entitlements and tax revenues will be worked out has implications far beyond beneficiaries of social welfare programs. Issues, such as the federal deficit, global economic competition, and the fate of discretionary programs, make the resolution extraordinarily complex.

As a creation of the legislative process, tax policy is most visible in the passage of major bills. Over time these become the basis of the state and federal tax codes, those notoriously confounding labyrinths of accounting rules. Periodically, attempts to reform tax policy emerge, such as the 1986 federal tax reform, which simplified the tax code and eliminated—at least temporarily—provisions for special interests. Indeed, the lobbying around deletion of special tax provisions was so intense that the 1986 tax reform became known as the "showdown at Gucci gulch," after the impeccable dress of the professionals populating the lobbying firms on Washington's K Street.

As this overview suggests, tax policy is dense and at the same time dynamic. Historically, three tax policies have been central to U.S. social policy: the income tax, the withholding tax, and the earned income tax credit.

- The federal income tax was instituted after approval of the 16th Amendment to the Constitution in 1914. A *progressive tax*, in that the wealthy were taxed at a higher rate, the income tax was initially levied on less than 1 percent of the population and had a top rate of only 7 percent. On average, the income tax is 8.2 percent, but it is higher for upper-income families, 11.7 percent. Because a threshold on taxable income has been set, low-income families are exempt from paying the federal income tax.[4]

- The Social Security withholding tax, the payroll tax, was established in 1935. For employed workers, the withholding tax was initially set at 2 percent of the first $3,000 in wages, paid equally between employers and workers. Since then Social Security withholding has increased to 12.4 percent of the first $97,500 in wages in 2007, increasing to $102,000 in 2008. The wage cap was established at the outset, under the presumption that Social Security was a public pension plan for workers who would not have recourse to retirement provisions available to the wealthy.[5] The withholding tax is a regressive tax, in that lower-income workers pay the same rate as higher-wage employees. Most taxpayers now pay more in Social Security withholding than they do in income taxes.

- The **earned income tax credit (EITC)** was enacted in 1975 after the failure of a "negative income tax" plan advanced by the Nixon administration. A *refundable tax credit*, the EITC instructs the IRS to send a check to low-wage workers, especially those with children, who have earned income below a certain level. In 2003, for example, a worker with two children could receive a maximum refund of $4,204.[6] Since the creation of the EITC, other tax credits have been introduced: A child care tax credit allows low-wage workers to deduct the costs of day care, and 22 states and the District of Columbia have introduced tax credits for low-income workers, some of which are refundable.

The interaction of these basic tax policies is complex, as evident in Table 9.1. Although the top quintile claims over 60 percent of income, it also bears the weight of paying most of the income, payroll, corporate, and estate taxes. On the other hand, the effective tax rate of the top quintile—almost 26 percent—is considerably less than its share of income. The negative income tax entries for the lowest quintiles can be attributed to rebates paid them through the earned income tax credit, a negative income tax for low-wage families with children.

Tax provisions fund social programs that exist within an economy that is also shaped by economic

Table 9.1

Distribution of Federal Taxes by Quintiles, 2007

	Economic Income	Individual Income Tax	Payroll Tax	Corporate Income Tax	Estate Tax	All Federal Tax
			Share of Total			
Top quintile	61.1	96.7	51.2	84.9	94.2	73.0
Fourth quintile	19.5	13.1	25.5	7.8	0.8	17.0
Middle quintile	11.2	3.1	14.4	3.4	1.2	7.4
Second quintile	6.2	−1.7	6.7	2.2	0.1	2.1
Lowest quintile	2.4	−1.2	2.1	0.9	0.2	0.4
			Average Effective Tax Rate			
Top quintile		14.5	6.9	4.2	0.3	25.9
Fourth quintile		6.8	10.8	1.2	0.0	18.8
Middle quintile		2.8	10.7	0.9	0.0	14.4
Second quintile		−2.8	8.9	1.1	0.0	7.3
Lowest quintile		−5.0	7.3	1.2	0.0	3.4
All		10.2	9.3	3.0	0.2	21.7

Source: Adapted from "Current-Law Distribution of Federal Taxes by Economic Income Percentiles, 2007: Table T04-0093," Urban-Brookings Tax Policy Center, Microsimulation Model (Version 0304-2). Retrieved September 28, 2004, from www.taxpolicycenter.org. Used by permission.

policy; thus, economic policy, through tax policy, influences social programs. A classic example was the conservative enthusiasm about "supply-side economics" during the 1980s. As advocated by Arthur Laffer, optimal economic policy would consist of minimal taxation, so as not to impede capital formation and expansion. Given the relatively higher tax rates that preceded his presidency, Ronald Reagan endorsed tax reform that incorporated a one-third cut in the income tax, assuming that the cut would reinvigorate a sluggish economy.[7] But although the tax cut of 1981 jolted the economy out of recession, it also cut off tax revenues to the Treasury, which then had to sell bonds to service the federal debt. Soon the federal government plunged further into debt, the depth of which was unprecedented for peacetime. By 1983 the annual deficit was $207 billion, 6.3 percent of **gross national product,** and growing. Debt service on government bonds grew commensurately, so that by the end of the 1980s, annual interest payments on the debt were $150 billion, the second largest item in the federal budget.[8]

Annual debt service overshadowed domestic policy discussions during the early 1990s. The congressional response was to impose a cap on domestic spending, an effort to stem the hemorrhaging of cash leaving the Treasury during a period when inflowing revenues had been stemmed by tax cuts. Liberal Democrats insisted that entitlement spending for social programs be exempt from the spending cap, with the result that federal budget decisions subsequently penalized discretionary programs—those with fixed budgets that are subject to the appropriation process annually—disproportionately. Because discretionary programs include research and development, student loans, public transportation, and the entire defense budget, the spending cap created intense pressure between social entitlements and discretionary programs. Thus, several years after a sharp cut in federal taxes, the effects took the form of pressure to cut an array of discretionary programs.

Looming federal deficits cast a pall over the incoming Clinton administration. After campaigning on a platform that emphasized investments in human capital, President Clinton was confronted with the massive deficits left over from the Reagan and Bush administrations. Clinton's nascent liberal tendencies, evident in his support for public works and national health insurance, were redirected by Alan Greenspan, chair of the Federal Reserve. Greenspan argued that the economy in general, and financial markets in particular, would respond negatively to new social programs that carried high price tags, because such programs would either (1) worsen the federal debt or (2) require significant tax increases. Although Clinton balked at Greenspan's position, economic reality was making short work of the new president's campaign rhetoric. Cornered between forces that advocated social investments and groups demanding deficit reduction, Clinton blew up during a staff meeting, as Bob Woodward recounted in *The Agenda:*

> "Where are all the Democrats?" Clinton bellowed. "I hope you're all aware we're all Eisenhower Republicans," he said, his voice dripping with sarcasm. "We're Eisenhower Republicans here, and we are fighting the Reagan Republicans. We stand for lower deficits and free trade and the bond market. Isn't that great?"
>
> The room was silent once more.
>
> He erupted again, his voice severe and loud, "I don't have a goddamn Democratic budget until 1996. None of the investments, none of the things I campaigned on."[9]

Capitulating to Greenspan's insistence on deficit reduction, Clinton put his social investment plans on hold, a decision that contributed to an unprecedented economic expansion that promised to make possible the eventual elimination of the federal debt by generating a surplus projected at $2 trillion over 10 years.

After a hotly disputed 2000 presidential election, many anticipated that George W. Bush would govern in a bipartisan manner, yet this was not the case. With Republican control of Congress, the White House was positioned to move aggressively on domestic policy; among its primary concerns was tax policy. During its first term, four tax cuts were passed reducing federal revenues $1.9 trillion over 10 years. Because the federal government had to honor its obligation to social entitlements while increasing spending for national security and mounting a war on terrorism, the federal government not only spent the surplus inherited from the Clinton presidency but also slid rapidly back into debt. As a result, the federal debt skyrocketed. With passage of the 2004 tax cut, the federal debt was projected to increase from $4.3 trillion to $8 trillion by 2014.[10] Conservatives minimized the fiscal consequences of the federal deficit, noting that as a

percentage of gross domestic product the Bush deficit was only 1.8 percent in 2007 while the Reagan deficits were much higher, 6 percent.[11] Adherents to supply-side economics in the Bush White House bet that economic growth would shrink the deficit—in the words of Vice President Cheney: "Reagan proved that deficits don't matter." Liberals were less sanguine. "Bush's policies may, in fact, best be explained by another, more radical agenda. Extensive tax cuts will require Congress to limit the growth of social programs and public investment and undermine other programs altogether," argued Jeff Madrick, "Rising deficits will inevitably force Congress to starve those 'wasteful' social programs. The prospective high deficits may even make it imperative to privatize Social Security and Medicare eventually."[12] In 2008 the first of 77 million baby boomers began collecting Social Security, incurring future obligations that current social insurance programs will not be able to meet. The prospects would be to either trim social insurance benefits severely or convert them to public assistance programs, neither of which are desirable outcomes for liberals who have sought to extend social program coverage. The continuation of the Bush tax cuts past 2010, when they are scheduled to expire, looms as a critical fiscal issue; assuming continuation of tax cuts and contemporary expenditures, there will be insufficient revenues for Medicaid and Medicare by 2030; by 2040 Social Security will be underfunded and net interest on federal debt will approximate 15 percent of GDP.[13]

Tax Policy and Special Interests

Tax policy has always contained provisions that benefit specific interests. Bending the tax code in response to lobbying is a long-standing practice in the United States, though today it is most often associated with corporate influence. Actually, the exclusion of pension plans from taxation began in 1921, and these provisions have been updated to include provisions such as individual retirement accounts. Tax expenditures that benefit individuals have now grown to the point that they exceed allocations for many prominent social welfare programs. In 2003, for example, tax expenditures for pension contributions were projected to be $279.1 billion, for health insurance $561.9 billion, and for mortgage interest deductions $362.9 billion. By comparison, in 2002

Spotlight 9.1

Tax Policy

The Tax Policy Center is a joint venture of the Urban Institute and the Brookings Institution. The center is comprised of nationally recognized experts in tax, budget, and social policy who have served at the highest levels of government. The center provides analysis and facts about tax policy to policymakers, journalists, citizens, and researchers. To learn more about this group, go to its website at **www .taxpolicycenter.org.**

---

allocations for Supplemental Security Income were $38.5 billion, Medicaid $258.2, and federal housing programs $25.7 billion. Even the largest tax credits available for low-income taxpayers for 2003 are dwarfed by middle-class tax expenditures: The EITC costs $34.4 billion, child care $44.1 billion, and housing $4.1 billion.[14]

Realizing that the tax code can be manipulated to serve the interests of the affluent, many social justice advocates have targeted "corporate welfare," or the special provisions directed at specific industries, for reform. The libertarian CATO Institute reported that the federal government spends $92 billion, directly and indirectly, to subsidize private sector activities.

This list might rankle many taxpayers, but efforts to downsize corporate welfare have been frustrating. As long as there is pork in politics, there is the opportunity to customize tax policy to serve the concerns of individual legislators—who, after all, are often influenced by constituent requests. Thus, tax policy is crafted both to meet the Appalachian Regional Commission's need for roads and to respond to Sonoma Valley vintners' desire to export their products to France.

Tax law also has a significant influence, directly and indirectly, on the revenues of nonprofit organizations. By allowing taxpayers to deduct charitable contributions from taxable income, tax law directly encourages support of philanthropy. Lower tax rates work indirectly, at least in theory, by leaving taxpayers with more discretionary income and assets that they may then donate to nonprofit causes. Comparatively, policy analysts are more confident

Corporate Welfare by Federal Agency

Department	2001 Outlays Millions	2006 Outlays Millions	% Change
Dept. of Agriculture	$44,103	$43,732	−.1
Dept. of Commerce	2,024	1,726	−14
Dept. of Defense	7,691	11,814	54
Dept. of Energy	1,930	1,875	−3
Dept. of Housing and Urban Development	5,988	5,116	−15
Dept. of State	4,310	4,610	7
Dept. of Transportation	2,849	5,749	102
Others	14,201	17,326	22
Total	83,096	91,967	11

Source: Stephen Slivinski, "The Corporate Welfare State," (Washington, DC: CATO Institution, 2007), Table 2.

about the effectiveness of direct support through tax deductions than about indirect support via lower taxation. In 1981, for example, taxpayers who did not itemize their tax deductions were allowed to deduct contributions to nonprofit organizations; at the same time significant reductions in income and estate taxes were instituted. In 1986 legislation removed the deduction for charitable contributions on the part of nonitemizers; concurrently, income and corporate tax rates were reduced sharply, although many tax shelters were also eliminated. The effects on charitable giving proved ambiguous. Despite his celebration of "compassionate conservatism," George W. Bush failed to change the tax code to allow nonitemizers to claim deductions for charitable contributions. As a result, fewer low-income families contribute less than do upper-income families. In 2004, 56.3 percent of families earning less than $50,000 contributed to charities while 93.3 percent of those with incomes above $100,000 did so. For lower-income families, the average annual contributions totaled $1,186, compared to $3,886 for wealthier families.[15] Yet the charitable impulse of Americans has continued despite changes in tax policy. "Giving as a percent of income has remained remarkably constant in the face of increases in the cost of giving," concluded tax policy analysts.[16]

As noted in Chapter 6, the story on charitable giving as a function of tax reduction is less unilinear than conservatives might wish. The idea is that as taxes on individual and corporate income are lowered, private wealth increases, creating a larger pool of resources against which nonprofits can lay claim. This, of course, is a mantra that conservatives have chanted since the 1980s—indeed, to the point that some ideologues have proposed that private charity actually replace government activity in social welfare. Deep tax cuts introduced during the 1980s significantly reduced federal social welfare funding; and indeed, until the early 1990s, these were made up for by increases in charitable giving. During the 1990s, however, although both private giving and federal support of nonprofits increased significantly, these sources never compensated for the total revenue losses attributed to direct federal funding cuts. After the election of George W. Bush, conservatives proposed repeal of the estate tax, the consequence of which the Congressional Budget Office predicts would be between $13 billion and $25 billion in reduced charitable contributions because the wealthy would no longer count gifts against their tax obligations.[17]

Federal Tax Policy

Despite the mammoth size of the federal budget of the United States, it is predicated on a tax base that is minimal compared to those of other industrialized nations. As shown in Table 9.2 on page 246, the 2002 tax burden of the United States was lower than that in most industrialized nations. Another way to assess the fairness of tax policy is to compare nations with respect to their income equality by use of the Gini index. This index calibrates the extent to which a nation's income distribution varies from a perfectly equal distribution; the closer the Gini index is to zero the greater the equality—higher values indicate greater inequality. Table 9.3 on page 246 ranks the nations of the Organization for Economic Cooperation and Development (OECD), the most developed of national economies.

The relatively low tax rate of the United States largely accounts for the nation's skewed **income distribution.** A tenet of the welfare state has been the progressive taxation of income and its redistribution to the poor through social programs. By definition, a welfare state with a low tax rate is unable to generate revenues sufficient to level the differences between rich and poor; thus, the question of income distribution has become integral to the discussion of tax policy. Income distribution changes over time; most recently, wealthier families have benefited significantly.

Economic growth during the latter decades of the twentieth century exacerbated income inequality; while the lowest two quintiles treaded water with respect to family income, the top quintile fared significantly better. The fortunes of the wealthiest 20 percent of families were battened by the tax cuts during the presidency of George W. Bush, which favored the rich. By 2006 the top 10 percent of American families claimed almost half of family income, second only to that figure in 1929! By one calculation, the top 1 percent claimed 53 percent of the growth in income in 2004.[18] Significantly, the new rich are less likely to have inherited their wealth and more likely to be executives.

The evidence suggests that top income earners are not "rentiers" deriving their incomes from past wealth but rather are "working rich," highly paid employees or new entrepreneurs who have not yet accumulated fortunes comparable to those accumulated during the Gilded Age. Such a pattern might not last for very long. The possible repeal of

Changes in Family Income

Quintile	1973	1979	1989	2000	Percent Change 1973–79	1979–89	1989–2000
Highest	$92,160	$94,752	$107,925	$132,487	2.8	13.9	22.8
Fourth	52,696	53,715	56,068	59,657	1.9	4.4	6.4
Middle	35,980	35,563	35,861	36,576	−1.2	0.8	2.0
Second	21,408	21,256	20,979	21,567	−0.7	−1.3	2.8
Lowest	8,417	8,324	8,146	8,216	−1.1	−2.1	0.9

Source: Committee on Ways and Means, Overview of Entitlement Programs (Washington, DC: US GPO, 2004), p. H-19.

the federal tax on large estates in coming years would certainly accelerate the path toward the reconstitution of the great wealth concentration that existed in the U.S. economy before the Great Depression.[19]

Thus, the demise of the estate tax, cleverly called the "death tax" by its opponents, may reintroduce a degree of income inequality not seen in eight decades. Income is skewed according to gender, race, and ethnicity, although in ways that are sometimes unexpected. The following table shows changes in wages from 1989 to 2005.

White men earned more than any income group until they were eclipsed by Asian men at the beginning of the twenty-first century. Among male workers, Hispanics consistently earned least. The earnings of Asian women have not only exceeded other groups of female workers since at least 1989, but

Median Hourly Wages by Gender, Race/Ethnicity, 1989-2005 (2005 Dollars)

	1989	1995	2000	2005
Men				
White	$16.51	$15.88	$17.28	$17.42
Black	11.94	11.61	12.64	12.48
Hispanic	11.10	10.12	11.09	11.14
Asian	15.42	15.29	17.18	18.49
Women				
White	11.56	11.84	12.96	13.78
Black	10.30	10.18	11.33	11.22
Hispanic	9.19	9.00	9.58	9.99
Asian	11.96	12.18	13.81	14.49

Black and Hispanic men as well. Among all groups, Hispanic women had the lowest wages. At different points in time, the earnings of every one of these groups actually fell, except for White and Asian women whose incomes steadily increased. This would help explain how, between 1973 and 2005, the ratio of women's wages to those of men has increased from 63.1 to 82 percent.[20]

Yet, income is only one component of economic justice; another measure of affluence is assets. Although considered in discussions of social policy less often than income, assets are important insofar as they are an indication of real wealth. Consisting of savings, real estate, stocks and bonds, and related property, assets not only can be liquidated during periods of adversity, thus offering the owner a buffer against poverty, but also appreciate in value, thus generating additional wealth. The distribution of assets is even more skewed than income distribution, with the highest quintile owning more than 80 percent. By contrast, the wealth of the lowest quintile is negative, indicative of debt. As has been the case with income, the distribution of assets has become more skewed during recent decades, the wealthiest quintile controlling more wealth with the lowest remaining in debt. And as with income, the distribution of assets is relatively constant; moderate changes occur, but the distribution pattern remains essentially the same over time. Consider the period following the Great Society efforts of the mid-1960s: Despite a major expansion of social programs for the poor, the lowest quintile still showed negative wealth, remaining mired in debt. For these reasons, a critical examination of wealth is essential for assessing economic justice.[21] If income distribution is skewed in favor of the affluent, assets are even more so. Notably, the bottom quintile is chronically in debt, its obligations

Table 9.2

Tax Revenue of OECD* Countries as a Percent of GDP, 2002

Rank	Country	Total Tax Rate
1	Sweden	50.2
2	Denmark	48.9
3	Belgium	46.4
4	Finland	45.9
5	Austria	44.0
5	France	44.0
7	Norway	43.5
8	Italy	42.8
9	Luxembourg	41.8
10	Czech Republic	39.3
11	Netherlands	39.2
12	Hungary	38.3
13	Iceland	38.1
14	Germany	36.0
15	Greece	35.9
16	Spain	35.8
17	United Kingdom	35.6
18	New Zealand	34.9
19	Canada	33.9
19	Portugal	33.9
21	Slovak Republic	33.1
22	Poland	32.8
23	Australia	31.5
24	Turkey	31.1
25	Switzerland	30.3
26	Ireland	28.4
27	United States	26.4
28	Japan	25.8
29	Korea	24.4
30	Mexico	18.1
	European Union	40.6
	OECD	36.3

*Organization for Economic Cooperation and Development

Table 9.3

Gini Index of OECD Member Nations

Rank	Nation	Gini Index
1	Denmark	24.7
2	Japan	24.9
3.5	Belgium	25.0
3.5	Sweden	25.0
5	Finland	25.6
6	Norway	25.8
7	Austria	30.5
8	Canada	31.5
9	Spain	32.5
10	Netherlands	32.6
11	France	32.7
12	Switzerland	33.1
13	Australia	35.2
14	Ireland	35.9
15.5	Italy	36.0
15.5	United Kingdom	36.0
17	New Zealand	36.2
18	Germany	38.2
19	Portugal	38.5
20	United States	40.8

Source: Adapted from United Nations Development Program, *Human Development Report, 2003* (New York: Oxford, 2003), p. 282.

(compared to an increase of 17.4 percent for non-Hispanic whites).[22]

The fact that assets are consistently negative for the lowest quintile reflects the difficulty of poorer families to buffer themselves from economic shocks. Thus, asset poverty, the wealth needed to survive for three months at the poverty level, exceeds income-based poverty. In 1999 the official poverty level was 11.8 percent, and the asset poverty rate was 27.9 percent; however, the asset poverty rate for minorities was much higher, for blacks 57.6 percent and Hispanics 52.3 percent.[23] In 2000 the asset poverty rate was 25.5 percent, twice the conventional poverty level, 12.7 percent.[24] The consequences of the tax cuts engineered during the second Bush presidency would be expected to widen the chasm between rich and poor.

exceeding its assets. Wealth is also skewed in relation to race and ethnicity. Between 1996 and 2002, the wealth of African Americans fell 16.1 percent, while that of Hispanics increased 14 percent

Changes in the Distribution of Wealth (Household Assets Minus Debts), 1962–2004

Quintile	1962	1983	1989	2001	2004	Percent Change			
						1962–83	1983–89	1989–2001	2001–2004
Highest	81.0%	81.3%	83.5%	84.4%	84.7%	0.4	2.2	0.9	0.2
Fourth	13.4	12.6	12.3	11.3	11.3	−0.8	−0.3	−1.0	0.0
Middle	5.4	5.2	4.8	3.9	3.8	−0.2	−0.4	−0.9	−0.1
Second	1.0	1.2	0.8	0.7	0.7	0.2	−0.3	−0.1	0.0
Lowest	−0.7	−0.3	−1.5	−0.4	−0.5	0.4	−1.2	1.1	−0.1

Change in Average Wealth (Thousands of 2004 dollars)					Annualized Growth			
Top	$680.8	$1,001.9	$1,178.7	$1,711.6	$1,822.6	1.8	2.7	3.2	2.1
Fourth	112.7	154.8	173.9	229.6	243.6	1.5	1.9	2.3	2.0
Middle	45.7	64.3	68.2	80.0	81.9	1.6	1.0	1.3	0.8
Second	8.0	14.5	11.9	14.9	14.4	2.9	−3.3	1.9	−1.0
Lowest	−6.1	−3.7	−21.3	−8.7	−11.4	2.4	−33.9	7.2	−9.2

Source: Lawrence Mishel, Jared Bernstein, and Sylvia Allegretto, The State of Working America 2006–2007 (Washington, DC: Economic Policy Institute, 2007), pp. 254–55.

State Tax Policy and the Poor

Federal taxes are important in social welfare policy because they subsidize the major social entitlements, but states also levy taxes in order to meet their legislative obligations. Historically, states have held major responsibility in social programs, areas such as mental health, child welfare, and corrections; and to a great degree the adequacy of a state's social programs depends on its tax collections. Unlike federal taxation, which is uniform across the nation, state tax policy varies significantly. By way of illustration, consider the income tax. Whereas the federal income tax is uniform nationwide, 43 states have income taxes, but 7 do not (Florida, Nevada, South Dakota, Tennessee, Texas, Washington, and Wyoming). State income taxes provide general revenues that can be used for a range of social programs, but this is not the only reason that state tax policy is important. State tax policy can establish an income floor for taxation or exempt low-income families from any tax liability altogether, thus allowing them to keep more of their income. Disparities among states are striking; in 2006, the state income threshold in Alabama was only $4,600, for example,

while that of California was $44,700. Of states that levy an income tax, the more progressive jurisdictions actually provide a rebate, similar to the federal Earned Income Tax Credit. As Table 9.4 on page 248 indicates, some states have been much more generous with respect to low-income families, while others have been downright punitive.

The Efficiency of Tax Policy in Reducing Poverty

In the larger context of social policy, tax policy is one of several strategies that apportion societal resources. Within social welfare, more traditional benefits have consisted of social insurance such as Social Security, cash public assistance (means-tested cash benefits) such as Temporary Assistance for Needy Families (TANF), in-kind public assistance (means-tested noncash benefits) such as Food Stamps, and the Earned Income Tax Credit (tax rebates). These different strategies vary in terms of their efficiency in poverty reduction over time. For elders, social insurance—compulsory contributions to social programs like Social Security and

Table 9.4

State Income Tax at Poverty Line of $20,615 for Two-Parent Families of Four, 2002

Rank	State	Tax	Rank	State	Tax
1	Alabama	$573	20	Colorado	$0
2	Hawaii	546	20	Connecticut	0
3	Arkansas	427	20	Delaware	0
4	West Virginia	406	20	Idaho	0
5	Oregon	319	20	Maine	0
6	Michigan	242	20	North Dakota	0
7	Indiana	239	20	Pennsylvania	0
8	Iowa	236	20	South Carolina	0
9	New Jersey	219	20	Utah	0
10	Montana	211	20	Virginia	0
11	Illinois	192	32	New Mexico	(40)
12	Louisiana	169	33	Rhode Island	(140)
13	Georgia	160	34	Nebraska	(299)
14	Ohio	159	35	Kansas	(363)
15	Oklahoma	139	36	Wisconsin	(373)
16	Missouri	83	37	Maryland	(423)
17	Kentucky	82	38	Massachusetts	(447)
18	North Carolina	78	39	District of Columbia	(708)
19	Mississippi	30	40	Vermont	(1,195)
20	Arizona	0	41	New York	(1,436)
20	California	0	42	Minnesota	(1,587)

Source: Adapted from Jason Levitis, *The Impact of State Income Taxes on Low-Income Families in 2006* (Washington, DC: Center on Budget and Policy Priorities, 2007), p. 17.

Medicare—makes the biggest dent in poverty, and means-tested in-kind benefits and tax policies are more important for children and families. Regardless, more than twice the number of elders are removed from poverty than are children and families by these different strategies (see Table 9.5).

Tax Expenditures as Poverty Policy

The use of federal tax policy to alleviate poverty and the increase in states' use of tax policy to augment the income of poor families are relatively new features of U.S. social policy. In the past quarter centu-ry, a significant shift in social welfare policy has been witnessed: gradually, direct welfare transfers are being augmented with indirect expenditures through tax credits. While the family welfare alloca-tion was restricted to $16.5 billion when AFDC was replaced by TANF, the EITC expanded to over $34 billion. This created a major disconnect in poverty policy insofar as many of the families transitioning from welfare to work do not claim EITC benefits even though they would be eligible for them. In 1999, 61.6 percent of TANF/AFDC families had heard of the EITC, but only 33.3 percent had received an EITC refund.[25] If welfare departments were truly concerned about poverty, as opposed to simply distributing public assistance benefits, they would make certain that all families with earned income claimed the EITC, but few welfare workers

Table 9.5

Impact of Safety Net on Poverty Reduction, 2002

Category	Individuals, over 65 (in thousands)	Percent over 65	Children under 18 (in thousands)	Percent under 18	Persons in Unmarried Households (in thousands)	Percent in Unmarried Households
Number of poor	17,082		14,314		14,425	
Number removed due to:						
Social Insurance	13,133	76.9	1,676	11.7	535	3.7
Means-tested cash benefits	373	2.2	505	3.5	1,103	7.6
Means-tested in-kind	508	3.0	1,392	9.7	546	3.8
Federal taxes and refunds	−10	−0.1	1,565	10.9	1,544	10.7
Total removed	14,004	82	5,138	35.9	1,573	36.8

Source: House Ways and Means Committee, Overview of Entitlement Programs (Washington, DC: U.S. GPO, 2004), adapted from Tables H-19, H-20, and H-21.

are familiar with the program. As a result, it is underutilized by the welfare poor.

Tax expenditures in the form of deductions for families' housing and health insurance costs have been enjoyed by the middle class for more than a half century, but it has not been until relatively recently that tax expenditures have been targeted for low-income families. The list of tax credits available to the poor has grown to include credits for earned income, child care, the welfare-to-work transition, care for the elderly and disabled, and adoption expenses. As the number of tax credits targeted to the poor has increased, tax credits have emerged as a contender to replace, at least partially, direct income transfers to aid the poor.

Although promises of federal tax credits for low-income families were conspicuous during the 2000 presidential campaign, many advocates of social justice had already enjoyed success lobbying state legislatures. Because many state legislatures were controlled by conservatives, a tax credit strategy proved more effective than a traditional appeal for increases in welfare transfers. By 2000 almost a dozen states had complemented the federal EITC with comparable state programs, and several had introduced other tax credits. Notably, Minnesota enacted a state EITC, a refundable child care credit, a property tax credit for renters, and a subsidized health insurance program. Paul Wilson and Robert

Cline note that 27 percent of Minnesotans take advantage of at least one of these programs; the Minnesota array of tax credits thus extends important income and health assistance to families ranging from the welfare poor to the working poor.[26]

As might be expected by a transition of such magnitude, the replacement of welfare transfers with tax credits raises several policy issues:

- Tax and revenue agencies replace welfare departments as the source of benefits, a role that many departments of social services are either unprepared for or may resist outright.
- Beneficiaries of tax credits must participate in the tax system in order to claim benefits, a status that is unfamiliar for many.
- Because much tax preparation is done by commercial firms, low-income workers may fall prey to unscrupulous preparers, particularly those advancing a refund as a loan.
- Tax credit refunds are almost always paid after the fact, requiring the recipient's willingness to wait, unlike traditional welfare that arrives monthly.
- As tax expenditures, tax credits are no less consequential for the federal and state treasuries than are traditional welfare transfers.

An important advantage of tax credits is that their allocations are not fixed; like open-ended entitlements, the amount awarded is determined by the volume of valid claims.

Tax credits offer new opportunities in areas historically understood as "welfare." In order to accelerate the upward mobility of the poor, for example, tax credits could be connected directly to asset-accrual strategies, such as individual development accounts, by encouraging low-income taxpayers to split their refund, directing a portion to a savings instrument. The tax preparation necessary for people to access tax credits could be one of several basic services—checking, savings, financial planning—offered by community financial services that could replace current welfare departments and serve as alternatives to marginal financial outfits that exploit the poor. Integrated with other capital formation strategies such as electronic benefit transfer, deposits by commercial banks to meet their Community Reinvestment Act obligations, and deposits by government and nonprofit agencies, tax credits could be part of a broad community development initiative that would finance projects in poor neighborhoods, thereby providing jobs to residents. In this respect, tax credits may not only begin to replace traditional welfare transfers, but in so doing may well introduce a new era of basic supports for poor families.[27]

Other tax credits have been proposed to augment poverty policy. Martha Ozawa and Baeg-Eui Hong suggested using the EITC to establish a $1,000 income floor for poor children and adjusting the benefit according to family size. "The modified EITC and children's allowances combined would improve the income status of all EITC-recipient children by 23.6 percent, with black and Hispanic children benefiting more than white children," Ozawa and Hong concluded.[28] Robert Cherry and Max Sawicky proposed a universal unified child credit that would augment the EITC and child care tax credit with an additional child credit.[29] Thus, the integration of refundable tax credits and calibrating them according to family size could reduce poverty significantly.

The Anti-tax Movement

Proponents of publicly funded social programs assume that tax-generated revenues are prudent investments toward the public good. Within the larger policy context, there are differing views on this assumption, however. It is worth acknowledging that some of the most egregious violations of personal decency, to say nothing of civil rights, have occurred under the auspices of public programs—such as the sterilization of "feeble-minded" people during the eugenics movement, the Tuskegee

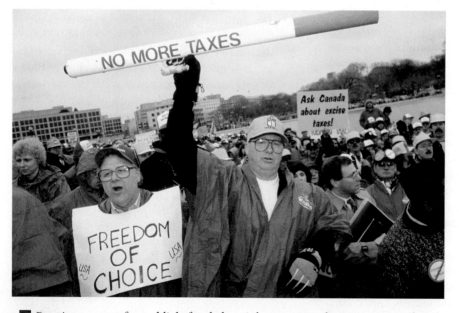

■ *Despite support for publicly funded social programs, there are some who believe that Americans should not pay any taxes.*

"experiment" on syphilitic African American men, and the warehousing of chronically mentally ill patients as well as of prison inmates.

For conservatives, particularly libertarians, government activities are likely to attenuate individual liberties, a likelihood encouraged by the fragmentation of modern society. The oppressive capacity of the state has long been a concern of political philosophers; in a recent statement of the issue, Jared Diamond noted that all societies try to balance the provision of essential services with measures aimed at thwarting the kleptocratic inclinations of those in power:

> These noble and selfish functions are inextricably linked, although some governments emphasize much more of one function than of the other. The difference between a kleptocrat and a wise statesman, between a robber baron and a public benefactor is merely one of degree: a matter of just how large a percentage of the tribute extracted from producers is retained by the elite, and how much the commoners like the public uses to which the redistributed tribute is put.[30]

To the extent that government enriches the powerful and mistreats citizens, a logical reform strategy is to de-fund the state by cutting off its tax revenues. By way of illustration, Michael Tanner of the Cato Institute calculates that $3.5 trillion has been spent on poverty programs since the Great Society period, yet with little success. "We are not going to solve our welfare problems by throwing more money at them," he concludes. "It is time to recognize that welfare cannot be reformed. It should be ended."[31]

An equally compelling critique of government taxation can be found in classic liberalism, a philosophic doctrine that emphasizes the freedom of individuals to act in their own best interests. Isaiah Berlin's distinction between "positive liberty" and "negative liberty" was framed within the context of twentieth-century state socialism, in an era when public programs were ascendant. Advocates of public programs justified them on the basis that they protected the vulnerable from poverty, idleness, and sickness, but Berlin noted that such "positive liberty" invariably strengthened the state. Berlin preferred "negative liberty," because it emphasized the ability of free citizens to act in their own interests.[32] Although dichotomies such as Berlin's may seem to be of limited application in social work practice or, worse, to be a rationale for gutting essential social programs, it is worth noting that a primary ethical value in social work is client self-determination.

The obvious question raised by conservatives is, why tax at all? Beyond central functions of the state, conservatives contend that citizens should be allowed to retain earned income and use it as they see fit. The liberal rebuttal to this suggestion has been that unregulated capitalism inevitably skews the distribution of resources and opportunities, leaving subgroups vulnerable to insecurity with respect to income, employment, and health. The result, liberals have contended, is that specific populations suffer disproportionate and protracted poverty, thus providing the rationale for social programs. For more than a half century, they note, social insurance and public assistance programs have buffered low-income families from poverty.

Conservative ambitions in domestic policy are to reverse liberal dominance of government in the lives of citizens and allow them to do more for themselves. At best, the Right contends, government consumes tax revenues that could be otherwise used for personal purposes; at worst, social programs inflict not only acute damage on individuals but long-term harm on society as well. The inverse relationship between citizen autonomy and government social programs is at the heart of the conservative social policy strategy. By favoring autonomy, tax cuts provide individuals with discretionary income with which they can choose the services they desire. This is shrewd politics, as Jonathan Rauch noted, "by repudiating the Washington-knows-best legacy of the New Deal, Republicans will empower the people, and the people will empower Republicans." And the consequences for welfare liberalism are equally profound:

> If the Democrats dig in their heels and fall back on stale rants against greed, inequality, and privatization, so much the better. The voters will know whom to thank for empowering choices that Republicans intend to give them. As for which is the "party of nostalgia," the voters will also remember who defended, until the last dog died, single-payer Medicare, one-size-fits-all Social Security, schools without accountability, bureaucratic government monopolies, static economics, and Mutually Assured Destruction.[33]

The success of the antitax movement seems evident with the relatively wide support that the Bush tax cuts have received, even if they benefit the wealthy disproportionately. In this respect, voter support of tax cuts can be interpreted as a referendum on the welfare state; given the choice, rather than divert income to public programs through taxes, many voters prefer to keep their income for themselves.

Having seized on the strategy, the Right has been ruthless in its application. Movement conservatives, such as Grover Norquist, hoped to pass a new tax cut every year of George W. Bush's presidency.[34] Ultimately, conservatives intend to amplify the strategy through control of state and federal legislatures, eventually securing "an era of Republican dominance."[35] In all this, the second Bush administration had not only veered farther to the Right but had shown more organizational discipline in pursuing its objectives than even the avatar of contemporary conservatism, Ronald Reagan.[36]

Upward Mobility

If people kept more of their income instead of having it taxed to support social programs, would this be prudent public policy? Obviously, there are events that afflict individuals, communities, and societies that, being unexpected, warrant a governmental safety net; but, beyond such circumstances, can people be expected to act in their own best interests economically?

Recently, economists have approached these questions through examining the concept of "social mobility." Their research has raised profound questions about the embeddedness of poverty as well as the permanence of being poor. The policy issue is simple: To the extent that poor people of working age are upwardly mobile, the case for social programs is weakened. Brad Schiller, the author of a standard text on poverty and discrimination, examined the upward mobility of the poorest Americans and, in its absence, the intractability of the underclass. Using a national data set, Schiller examined the experience of young workers earning the minimum wage and their subsequent earnings, finding that one-third of minimum wage workers had received a raise within a year and that 60 percent were beyond the minimum wage within two years. Of those who entered the labor market in 1980, a recession year, only 15 percent continued earning the minimum wage after three years.[37] Furthermore,

> . . . the available perceptions of minimum-wage youth seem to dispel the notion that minimum-wage jobs offer low wages and nothing more. Over 85 percent of the minimum-wage entrants stated that they liked their jobs, and over 60 percent felt that they were earning skills that would be valuable in attaining

better jobs. Only one out of eight minimum-wage youth perceived a total lack of on-the-job training—a condition compatible with the notion of "dead-end" jobs. Over half (56 percent) of the minimum-wage workers perceived opportunities for promotion with the same employer.[38]

Seven years after beginning a minimum wage job, the average worker had seen an increase in his or her wages of 154 percent, about 15 percent per year. Although non-minimum-wage job entrants were earning more, the minimum wage entrants had closed the gap significantly. Notably, Schiller concluded that race did not appear to retard the wage increases of youth. "The longitudinal experiences of minimum-wage youth . . . refute the notion of a 'minimum-wage trap,'" concluded Schiller. "Youth who started at the minimum wage in 1980 recorded impressive wage gains over the subsequent seven years both in absolute and relative terms."[39]

The upward mobility of low-wage workers thus parallels that of the general population. Daniel McMurer and Isabel Sawhill noted that upward mobility is more pronounced than data on a stagnating income distribution would suggest. Mobility in the United States is substantial, according to the evidence. Large portions of the population move into a new income quintile, with estimates ranging from about 25 to 40 percent in a single year. As one would expect, the mobility rate is even higher over longer periods—it averages about 45 percent over a 5-year period and about 60 percent over both 9-year and 17-year periods.[40]

Mobility is also pronounced among the poor. Reporting on data from the mid-1990s, the U.S. Census Bureau found that although 30.3 percent of Americans lived below the poverty line for at least two months during a three-year span, only 5.3 percent were poor continuously for two years. On average, families were below the poverty line for four and a half months.[41] Using data from the Panel Survey on Income Dynamics, W. Michael Cox and Richard Alm conclude that upward mobility, even of the poorest Americans, is striking:

> Only 5 percent of those in the bottom fifth in 1975 were still there in 1991. Where did they end up? A majority made it to the top three-fifths of the income distribution—middle class or better. But most amazing of all, almost 3 out of 10 of the low-income earners from 1975 had risen to the uppermost 20 percent by 1991. More than three-quarters found their way into the two highest tiers of income earners for at least one year by 1991.[42]

Family Income Mobility Over Three Decades

Quintile in 1969	Quintile in 1979				
	Top	Fourth	Middle	Second	Lowest
Top	49.1	23.7	13.2	9.0	5.0
Fourth	23.7	27.4	24.1	15.0	9.9
Middle	18.7	23.0	24.8	23.4	10.2
Second	7.7	16.2	25.2	27.8	23.2
Lowest	3.3	9.1	13.8	24.5	49.4

Quintile in 1979	Quintile in 1989				
	Top	Fourth	Middle	Second	Lowest
Top	50.9	26.1	13.4	5.4	4.2
Fourth	25.3	27.6	24.3	16.1	6.8
Middle	15.0	24.6	25.0	23.3	12.1
Second	7.6	15.8	23.8	31.5	21.3
Lowest	3.2	7.4	15.0	24.1	50.4

Quintile in 1989	Quintile in 1998				
	Top	Fourth	Middle	Second	Lowest
Top	53.2	23.2	14.9	5.7	3.0
Fourth	25.8	31.1	23.7	12.9	6.5
Middle	12.6	27.5	28.3	20.7	10.9
Second	4.3	11.0	22.6	36.3	25.7
Lowest	4.3	6.4	12.4	23.6	53.3

Source: Adapted from Lawrence Mishel, Jared Bernstein, and Sylvia Allegretto, *The State of Working America 2006–2007* (Washington, DC: Economic Policy Institute, 2007), p. 106.

On average, children tend to have higher income than their families of origin with those at the bottom of the income distribution doing better. Of all children, 67 percent have higher incomes than their parents' families; but that was true for only 43 percent of children in the top quintile, compared to 82 percent in the bottom quintile.[43] Despite increased income across generations, economic mobility slowed during the last quarter of the twentieth century.

During the last decades of the twentieth century a larger number of individuals in the top quintile remained in place as did those in the bottom quintile. Had the nation experienced more upward mobility economically, the opposite would have occurred: The percent of people in the top quintile would have dropped and those in the lowest quintile would have risen. Yet, the table also reveals an anomaly: Of those in the lowest quintile in 1969, 3.3 percent rose to the top quintile by the end of the decade, a figure that lagged a bit 10 years later and then increased to 4.3 percent in 1998.

An artifact of segregation, race adversely affects economic mobility. If economic mobility has stagnated for all families, the mobility of African American families has actually worsened (see Table 9.6 on page 254). While middle income status protects white families from downward, this does not occur with African American families. "Startlingly, almost half (45 percent) of black children whose parents were solidly middle class end up falling to the bottom of the income distribution compared to only 16 percent of white children." Over half of all African American children born to families in the bottom quintile (54 percent) stay there.[44]

The research on economic mobility suggests that if the American dream is to be valid for all, strategies are necessary to accelerate the upward mobility of low-income families. These not only include methods for augmenting earned income, such as the minimum wage, but also strategies for accruing assets, such as Individual Development Accounts. The 1995 Assets for Independence Act allocated $125 million over five years to encourage poor families to save for specific activities, yet the amount budgeted was miniscule compared to tax expenditures that favor wealthier families. Still, initiatives such as the SEED (Saving for Education, Entrepreneurship, and Downpayment) Initiative, which encourages low-income families to build assets, illustrate how the tax code can be an instrument of economic justice.[45]

Conclusion

Tax policy, often undervalued in discussions of social welfare, serves a vital function because it provides the revenues through which public programs operate. Increasing fluency in tax policy has significant benefits for advocates of social justice. At the national level, for example, introducing progressive features to the Social Security withholding tax, adjusting the tax rate for income, and lifting the cap on taxable income, would generate significant new

Table 9.6

Parents' Income of Children by Race

Percent of Children Living in Each Income Quintile

Quintile	White	African American
Parents in top quintile, $81,200	23	*
Parents in fourth quintile, $65,100–$81,200	23	7**
Parents in middle quintile, $48,800–$65,100	22	8
Parents in second quintile, $33,800–48,800	19	23
Parents in lowest quintile, $0–$33,800	13	62

*Too few observations to report entry.
**Treat data with caution due to small sample size.

Source: Julia Isaacs, *Economic Mobility of Black and White Families* (Washington, DC: Brookings Institution, 2007), p. 4.

revenues that could make minimal Social Security benefits more adequate. This could serve a strategic purpose, as well, by providing a counterpoint to conservative contentions that Social Security should be privatized.

Leveraging tax policy to advance social justice requires sophistication in social policy, however. Historically, two streams of poverty policy have evolved in the United States. The first—public welfare—was legislated through the Social Security Act of 1935 and consists of TANF, SSI, Medicaid, Food Stamps, and the like. Much of public welfare is managed by HHS and parallel agencies at the state level. The second—Bootstrap Capitalism[46]—was enacted through the 1975 Earned Income Tax Credit and consists of an array of tax credits for individuals as well as businesses. Bootstrap Capitalism is operated by the Treasury Department and the Federal Reserve System. By understanding poverty policy exclusively through the public welfare paradigm, human service professionals omit from the realm of possibility a set of policy options that have enormous promise. Thus, if social welfare professionals are to enhance their role in the domestic policy debate, they will have to master the financial, procedural, and accounting nuances of tax policy. These are daunting fields, to be sure, but the potential payoff makes the effort worthwhile.

Discussion Questions

1. Click on the "Student Section" link of the policyAmerica website (http://capwiz.com/policyamerica/index.html) and explore tax cuts that have passed during the Bush administration. Who have they benefited? Who has been disadvantaged? What changes in tax policy could advance economic justice?

2. Why has Harry Hopkins's political calculus, "Tax, tax, spend, spend, elect, elect!" lost its political currency in more recent times?

3. Should the federal government expand its spending on social programs despite the large and ongoing federal debt? What are the effects of increased spending, and what are the effects of stable or even decreasing spending, on social programs?

4. What are the positive and negative effects of increasing corporate taxation? How would it affect the poor in both the short term and the long term?

5. Should nonprofit human service corporations be required to pay taxes just as for-profit firms do? What would be the possible consequences of restructuring the tax code to mandate that nonprofits lose their nonprofit tax status?

6. Should the altruism of Americans be rewarded by tax codes that permit charitable contributions, cash as well as in-kind, to be deducted from

taxes? Do the long-term effects of this tax deduction encourage or discourage real altruism?

7. Some welfare advocates concerned with income inequality argue that the function of the welfare state is to equalize incomes and assets through social welfare programs. Others believe it is unrealistic to expect that welfare state programs can do more than alleviate human suffering by providing resources to those in need.

Should the goal of social welfare programs be to reduce income and asset inequality, or should that function be relegated to tax and labor policy?

8. Has the social work profession been successful in lobbying efforts and in promoting a more just society? If not, why? What strategies should social workers employ to move society toward more equitable income and asset redistribution?

Notes

1. Paul Krugman, "Duped and Betrayed," *New York Times* (July 6, 2003), p. A31.
2. Paul Krugman, "The Tax-Cut Zombies," *New York Times* (December 23, 2005), p. A27.
3. Charles Murray, "A Plan to Replace the Welfare State," *Focus* 24, 2 (Spring–Summer 2006), p. 2.
4. Thomas Dye, *Understanding Public Policy*, 9th ed. (Upper Saddle River, NJ: Prentice Hall, 1998), pp. 242–243.
5. That part of the withholding tax dedicated to Medicare Health Insurance is levied on all income, though that for Social Security has a cap on taxable income. Committee on Ways and Means, *Overview of Entitlement Programs* (Washington, DC: U.S. GPO, 1998), p. 58.
6. Committee on Ways and Means, *Overview of Entitlement Programs* (Washington, DC: U.S. GPO, 2004), pp. 13–36.
7. Reynolds Farley, *The New American Reality* (New York: Russell Sage Foundation, 1996), p. 85.
8. *The Economic and Budget Outlook: Fiscal Years, 1991–1995* (Washington, DC: CBO, 1990), pp. 112, 122.
9. Bob Woodward, *The Agenda* (New York: Simon & Schuster, 1994), p. 165.
10. Jonathan Weisman, "Congress Votes to Extend Tax Cuts," *Washington Post* (September 24, 2004), p. A7.
11. Lori Montgomery and Nell Henderson, "Burden Set to Shift on Balanced Budget," *Washington Post* (January 16, 2007), p. A1.
12. Jeff Madrick, "The Iraqi Time Bomb," *New York Times Magazine* (April 6, 2003), p. 50.
13. "The Bottom Line: Today's Fiscal Policy Remains Unsustainable" (Washington, DC: Government Accountability Office, September 2006).
14. Committee on Ways and Means, *Overview of Entitlement Programs* (Washington, DC: U.S. GPO, 2004), pp. 13-4–13-5.
15. "Key Findings Center on Philanthropy Study" (Indianapolis, IN: Center on Philanthropy, 2005), pp. 6–7.
16. Alan Abramson, Lester Salamon, and C. Eugene Steuerle, "The Nonprofit Sector and the Federal Budget," in Elizabeth Boris and C. Eugene Steuerle (eds.), *Nonprofits and Government* (Washington, DC: Urban Institute, 1999), p. 122.
17. David Kamin, "New CBO Study Finds That Estate Tax Repeal Would Substantially Reduce Charitable Giving," (Washington, DC: Center on Budget and Policy Priorities, 2004), p. 1.
18. Aviva Aron-Dine and Isaac Shapiro, "New Data Show Extraordinary Jump in Income Concentration in 2004" (Washington, DC: Center on Budget and Policy Priorities, 2007), p. 3.
19. Emmanuel Saez, "Striking It Richer," *Pathways* (Winter 2008), p. 7.
20. Lawrence Mishel, Jared Bernstein, and Sylvia Allegretto, *The State of Working America, 2006–2007* (Washington, DC: Economic Policy Insitute, 2007), pp. 163–164.
21. Thomas Shapiro and Edward Wolff (eds.), *Assets for the Poor* (New York: Russell Sage Foundation, 2001).
22. Rakesh Kochhar, "The Wealth of Hispanic Households: 1996–2002" (Washington, DC: Pew Hispanic Center, 2004), p. 5.
23. Asena Caner and Edward Wolff, "Asset Poverty in the United States," *Public Policy Brief* 76A (Annandale-on-Hudson, New York: Jerome Levy Economics Institute, 2004), p. 4.
24. Ray Boshara (ed.), *Building Assets* (Washington, DC: Corporation for Enterprise Development, 2001), p. 2008.
25. Katherin Phillips, "Who Knows about the Earned Income Tax Credit?" (Washington, DC: Urban Institute, January 2001).
26. Paul Wilson and Robert Cline, "State Welfare Reform: Integrating Tax Credits and Income Transfers." Paper presented at the 1994 National Tax Symposium, Washington, DC, May 24, 1994.
27. David Stoesz and David Saunders, "Welfare Capitalism," *Social Service Review* (September 1999).
28. Martha Ozawa and Baeg-Eui Hong, "The Effects of EITC and Children';s Allowances on the Economic

Well-Being of Children," *Social Work* 27, no. 3 (September 2003), p. 171.

29. Robert Cherry and Max Sawicky, "Giving Tax Credit Where Credit Is Due," (Washington, DC: Economic Policy Institute, n.d.).

30. Jared Diamond, *Guns, Germs, and Steel* (New York: Norton, 1997), p. 276.

31. Michael Tanner, "Ending Welfare as We Know It" (Washington, DC: Cato Institute, 1994), p. 24.

32. Michael Ignatieff, *Isaiah Berlin* (New York: Henry Holt, 1998), pp. 202–203.

33. Jonathan Rauch, "The Accidental Radical," *The National Journal* 35, no. 30 (July 26, 2003).

34. Dana Milbank and Dan Balz, "GOP Eyes Tax Cuts as Annual Events," *Washington Post* (May 11, 2003), A1.

35. Adam Clymer, "Buoyed by Resurgence, G.O.P. Strives for an Era of Dominance," *New York Times* (May 25, 2003), p. A1.

36. Bill Keller, "Reagan's Son," *New York Times Magazine* (January 26, 2003).

37. Bradley Schiller, "Moving Up: The Training and Wage Gains of Minimum-Wage Entrants," *Social*

Science Quarterly 75, no. 3 (September 1994), p. 629.

38. Ibid., p. 627.

39. Ibid., p. 634.

40. Daniel McMurer and Isabel Sawhill, *Getting Ahead* (Washington, DC: Urban Institute, 1998), p. 33.

41. "Poverty Short-Lived for Most, Study Finds," *Richmond Times Dispatch* (August 10, 1998), p. A3.

42. W. Michael Cox and Richard Alm, *Myths of Rich and Poor* (New York: Basic Books, 1999), p. 73.

43. "Economic Mobility of Families across Generations," (Washington, DC: Brookings Institution, 2007), p. 3.

44. Julia Isaacs, "Economic Mobility of Black and White Families" (Washington, DC: Brookings Institution, 2007), p. 2.

45. "Banking on SEED: Lessons from Financial Institutions in the SEED Initiative" (Washington, DC: Corporation for Enterprise Development, 2007).

46. David Stoesz, "Bootstrap Capitalism," *Families in Society*, 88, 3 (July–September 2007), pp. 375–379.

CHAPTER 10

Social Insurance Programs

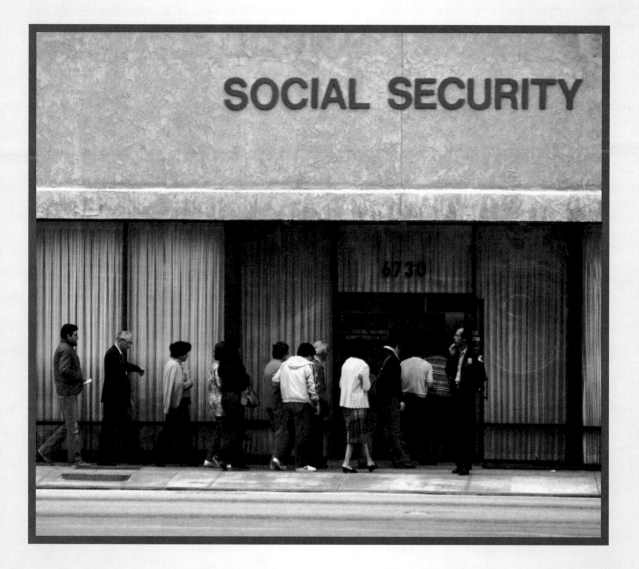

This chapter explores the major forms of social insurance in the United States: Old Age, Survivors, and Disability Insurance (OASDI), Unemployment Insurance (UI), and Workers' Compensation. In addition, this chapter explores some of the major issues and problems surrounding social insurance programs.

Definition of Social Insurance

Social insurance is the cornerstone of U.S. social welfare policy. Specifically, it is a system whereby people are compelled—through payroll or other taxes—to insure themselves against the possibility of their own indigence, such as might result from the economic vicissitudes of retirement, the loss of a job, the death of the family breadwinner, or physical disability. Based in part on the same principles used in private insurance, social insurance sets aside a sum of money that is held in trust by the government and earmarked for use in the event of workers' retirement, death, disability, or unemployment. The major goal of social insurance is to help maintain income by replacing a portion of lost earnings. It is a pay-as-you-go system whereby the workers and employers of today pay for those who have retired, are ill, or who have lost their jobs. Although originally designed to replicate a private insurance fund, the original Social Security program has been broadened to include a variety of programs that provide a minimal level of replacement income. Because the benefits paid to some retired workers exceed their contributions to the system, Social Security has

taken on some of the characteristics of an income redistribution or public assistance program.

Unlike Social Security, public assistance programs are subject to **means tests** and are based entirely on need. The rationale for public assistance is grounded in the concept of *safety nets* designed to ensure that citizens receive basic services and do not fall below a given poverty level. Social insurance, on the other hand, requires beneficiaries to make contributions to the system *before* they can claim benefits. Because social insurance affects a larger number of people and benefits are generally higher, expenditures for social insurance are far greater than for public assistance (see Figure 10.1 on page 260). Social insurance is also universal; that is, people receive benefits as legal entitlements regardless of their personal wealth. Table 10.1 shows federal spending for major social insurance programs. Because the social insurance benefit structure is linked to occupationally-defined productive work, most programs tend not to be stigmatized, but in contrast, public assistance recipients are usually highly stigmatized. Perhaps this stigma occurs because public assistance programs are financed from general tax revenues; they are not occupationally linked or based on a previous work record; and eligibility is determined by means tests.

Although some people complain about the costs of public assistance programs, social insurance programs consume many times more resources as public welfare. For example, in 2007, OASDI cost $580.8 billion compared to just $126.3 billion for public assistance and related programs (Earned Income Tax Credit [EITC], low-income home energy assistance, among others).[1] The average OASDI beneficiary benefit in 2007 was about $962 a month

Table 10.1

Past, Current, and Projected Federal Spending for Major Social Insurance Programs, Selected Years (expenditures in billions)

Programs	2002	2004	2006	2008	2010
OASDI	$452	$494	$539	$598	$670
Medicare	254	287	319	366	421
Unemployment Insurance	51	46	43	45	49
Total	757	827	901	1,009	1,140

Source: Committee on Ways and Means, U.S. House of Representatives, *2004 Green Book* (Washington, DC: U.S. Government Office, 2004), pp. I-2, I-8.

compared to the national average Temporary Assistance for Needy Families (TANF) payment of about $400 to $450. Looking at it another way, in 2001 total means-tested programs accounted for 2.5 percent of U.S. gross domestic product (GDP) compared to 8.3 percent of all non-means-tested programs. Broken down, Social Security accounted for 4.2 percent of the GDP; Medicare, 2.3 percent; Unemployment Compensation, 0.3 percent; and other retirement and disability, 0.9 percent.[2]

The Background of Social Insurance

The first old-age insurance program was introduced in Germany in 1889 by Chancellor Otto von Bismarck. The program was originally designed to curb the growing socialist trend in Germany, and by the onset of World War I nearly all European nations had old-age assistance programs of one sort or another. In 1920 the U.S. government began its own Federal Employees Retirement program. By 1931, 17 states had enacted old-age assistance programs, although these often had stringent eligibility requirements. For example, benefits were denied in some cases in which relatives were capable of supporting an elderly person. These state-administered retirement programs were often restrictive and punitive, and elderly people applying for assistance had to agree to sign over their assets to the state when they died.[3] Nevertheless, the concept of governmental responsibility for welfare grew during the early part of the twentieth century; by 1935 all states except Georgia and South Carolina had programs providing financial assistance to widows and children.[4]

Spurred on by the Great Depression of the 1930s and prompted by the growing rebellion inspired by California physician Francis Townsend (who advocated a flat $200 per month for each retired worker), President Franklin Roosevelt championed a government assistance program that would cover both unemployed and retired workers.[5] The result of Roosevelt's efforts was the Social Security Act of 1935, through which the federal government established the basic framework for the modern social welfare state.

The original 1935 Social Security Act was relatively modest compared to its present scope. It established categorical assistance to the elderly

poor, dependent children, the blind, and some disabled children. Title IV earmarked money for vocational rehabilitation, rural public health, and training for public experts. Two titles covered eligibility and financing for old-age retirement; two others established UI under joint state and federal government auspices. Title VII established a Social Security Board, whose job it was to monitor the fund. Title XI gave the legislature the right to alter any part of the act.[6]

The current Social Security Act provides for (1) OASDI; (2) UI programs under joint federal and state partnership; (3) federal assistance to aged, blind, and disabled persons under the Supplemental Security Income (SSI) program; (4) public assistance to families with dependent children under the Aid to Families with Dependent Children (AFDC) program (now TANF); (5) federal health insurance for the aged (Medicare); and (6) federal and state health assistance for the poor (Medicaid). Although all these programs fit under the rubric of the Social Security Act of 1935, not all are true social insurance programs (e.g., Medicaid, TANF, and SSI).

The insurance feature of Social Security emerged as the result of an intense debate between progressives who wanted Social Security funded out of general revenue taxes and conservatives who wanted it funded solely out of employee contributions. The compromise reached in 1935 was that old-age insurance would be financed by employer and employee contributions of 1 percent on a base wage of $3,000, with a maximum cap for worker contributions set at $30 a year. At age 65, single workers would receive $22 a month and married workers $36. No benefits were paid out until 1940 to allow the program to accumulate reserves.

The Social Security Act of 1935 has been repeatedly modified, almost always in the direction of increasing its coverage. The original Social Security Act of 1935 provided retirement and survivor benefits to only about 40 percent of the labor force. Farm and domestic workers, mariners, bank employees, the self-employed, and state and local government employees were excluded. In 1950 farmers and self-employed persons were added, thereby bringing the coverage to more than 90 percent of the labor force. Congress made survivors and dependents of insured workers eligible for benefits in 1939, and in 1956 disability insurance was added to include totally and permanently disabled workers. In 1965 Health Insurance for the Aged (Medicare)—a prepaid health insurance plan—was incorporated into the law. In later years the act was amended to allow workers to retire as early as age 62, provided they agreed to accept only 80 percent of their benefits. In 1977 an automatic cost-of-living index was attached to benefit payments.

With the amendments of 1939 (extending coverage to widows, elderly wives, surviving children, etc.), Social Security technically became bankrupt because it was no longer self-financed. As such, the federal government assumed responsibility for any financial shortfalls and thus implicitly assumed responsibility for promoting the general welfare. By 1996, more than 43 million Americans and more than one-quarter of all U.S. households depended on a monthly Social Security check.[7] As illustrated in Figure 10.1, only 69 percent of Social Security beneficiaries were retired workers in March 2008.[8]

The Financial Organization of Social Insurance

The organization of social insurance is relatively straightforward. Covered workers pay taxes into Social Security while they work, and when they retire or become disabled, they (or their family members) collect monthly benefits. Social Security taxes are used to pay for retirement, disability, or Medicare benefits. General revenue taxes are used to finance SSI, which, despite its name, is actually a means-tested public assistance program rather than social insurance.

Social Security and Medicare taxes are divided among several trust funds. Two funds include (1) the Old-Age and Survivors Insurance (OASI) trust fund (pays for retirement and survivor benefits), and (2) the federal Disability Insurance (DI) fund (pays benefits to people with disabilities and their families). There are also two Medicare trust funds: (1) The federal Hospital Insurance (HI) trust fund pays for services covered under the hospital insurance (Part A) provisions of Medicare, and (2) the federal Supplementary Medical Insurance (SMI) trust fund pays for services covered under the medical insurance (Part B) provisions of Medicare.

The trust funds are governed by a board of trustees made up of the Secretary of the Treasury, the Secretary of Labor, the Secretary of Health and Human Services, the Commissioner of Social Security, and two public trustees who serve four-year terms. The board of trustees reports annually to Congress on the condition of the funds and on estimated future operations.

Before 1983 the system operated on a pay-as-you-go system, with taxes flowing into one end of the pipeline and flowing out the other end. However, since 1983 Social Security has operated under a partial reserve system in which inflows exceed outflows, thereby building up a reserve to help pay benefits to an increasing number of retired workers.

Social Security revenues are deposited daily into trust funds and benefits are paid out. Surplus income (i.e., income not needed to pay benefits) is invested in U.S. government bonds that earn the prevailing rate of interest and whose principal and interest are guaranteed by the federal government. Almost all securities held by the trust funds are "special issue" bonds available only to the funds. The DI trust fund also holds a relatively small number of public issue stocks (marketable securities

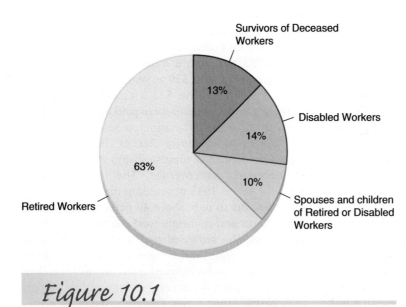

Figure 10.1

Number of Social Security Beneficiaries by Type, September 2008 (total 49.8 million)

Source: Social Security Administration, Office of Research, Evaluation, and Statistics, "Fast Facts & Figures About Social Security, 2008," SSA Publication No. 13-11785, Washington, DC, August 2008.

available to the general public). The OASI trust fund holds no public issue stocks. Unlike marketable securities, special issues can be redeemed at any time at face value. Consequently, investments in special issues provide the trust funds with the same flexibility as having cash. The amount of earned interest can be substantial. In 2007 the Social Security trust funds earned $110.2 billion, nearly $30 billion more than in 2002.[9]

Key Social Insurance Programs

OASDI

OASDI is a combination of Old Age and Survivors Insurance (OASI) and Disability Insurance (DI). Commonly referred to as Social Security, it is the largest social program in the nation and covers approximately 9 out of 10 workers. OASDI is a federal program administered by the Social Security Administration, which in 1994 became an independent agency headed by a commissioner and a board appointed by the U.S. president for a six-year term.

Social Security is a stellar example of a program that has worked. In 2006:

- Social Security served more than 54 million people and paid out about $585 billion in benefits.
- Social Security provided at least half of the income for 65 percent of the aged.
- 84 percent of women were fully insured, up from just 63 percent in 1970.
- Women accounted for 56 percent of adult Social Security beneficiaries.[10]

As recently as 1969, before the Social Security **cost-of-living adjustments (COLAs)** took effect, the poverty rate for the elderly was double that of the general population, 25 versus 12 percent.[11] According to the Social Security Administration, the poverty rate for the elderly would have been 52 percent without Social Security.[12] In that sense, Social Security has a strong redistributive effect, transferring resources from those with high lifetime earnings to those with low lifetime earnings.[13]

Unlike prefunded private annuity plans, where a worker draws off money already invested, Social Security benefits are paid by today's workers rather than by the retirees. Benefits under OASDI are entitlement based; that is, they are based on the beneficiaries' earnings rather than the amount of the revenue in the trust fund. If benefits in a given period exceed revenues, the difference is made up from the reserves in the trust funds. OASDI operates in the following manner:

- On an employee's first $102,000 in earnings in 2008, the employee and his or her employer each paid an OASDI tax equal to 6.2 percent and a Medicare hospital insurance (HI) tax equal to 1.45 percent of earnings. Employees therefore paid a total of 7.65 percent. Self-employed persons paid 15.3 percent. In general, increases in the wage base are automatic and are based on the increase in average wages in the economy each year. For example, the highest Social Security tax a worker could pay in 2008 was $6,324 (not including the HI tax). Self-employed persons had their taxes computed on a lower base (net earnings from self-employment less 7.65 percent), and half of that tax was deductible for income tax purposes already eliminated.
- Based on their age at retirement and the amount earned during their working years, workers receive a monthly benefit payment. Retired workers aged 62 receive a reduction of 5/9 of 1 percent for each month of entitlement

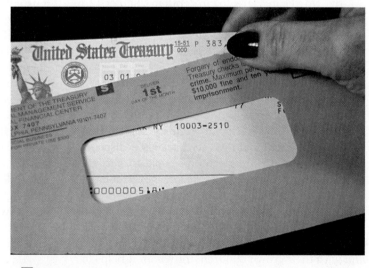

■ *Social Security is the key social insurance program in the United States.*

before age 65, with a maximum reduction of 20 percent. Benefits are modest; the average retired worker received $1,083 a month in 2008. The maximum benefit in 2008 for a retired worker at age 65 was $2,185 a month.

- Under the OASI program, a monthly payment is made to an unmarried child or eligible dependent grandchild of a retired worker or a deceased worker who was fully insured at the time of death, if the child or grandchild is (1) under age 18; (2) a full-time elementary or secondary school student under age 19; or (3) a dependent or disabled person aged 18 or over whose disability began before age 22. A grandchild is eligible only if the child was adopted by the insured grandparent.
- A lump-sum benefit of $255 is payable to a spouse who was living with an insured worker at the time of his or her death.
- Under the Disability Insurance (DI) program, monthly cash benefits are paid to disabled workers under age 65 and to their dependents. The purpose of the DI program is to replace lost income when a wage earner is no longer able to work. Monthly cash benefits are paid and computed generally on the same basis as they are in the OASI program; that is, they are calculated on the basis of past earnings. Medicare benefits are provided to disabled workers, widows or widowers, or adult children after they have been entitled to disability benefits for 24 months.
- Almost all people, whether they paid into Social Security or not, are eligible for Medicare benefits. (Medicare is treated in depth in Chapter 12.)
- Social Security beneficiaries are required to have completed at least 40 quarters of work (10 years) before they are eligible to draw benefits.[14]

Social Security, especially OASDI, has been a heated topic for much of its relatively short history. Political conservatives and laissez-faire economists are troubled because Social Security socializes a portion of the national income. Because it discourages savings and causes retired people to become dependent on a supposedly fragile governmental system, other critics claim that Social Security will lead to moral and economic ruin, The Social Security system, on the other hand, is popular with the elderly who rely on it for much of their income, and with their grown children, for whom it helps to provide peace of mind.

Unemployment Insurance

The first line of defense for workers fired or laid off from their jobs is unemployment insurance (UI). Part of the Social Security Act of 1935, UI is a federal/state program whose objectives are (1) to provide temporary and partial wage replacement to involuntarily and recently unemployed workers, and (2) to help stabilize the economy during recessions. Although the U.S. Department of Labor oversees the general program, each state administers its own UI program.[15] The current guidelines of the UI program require employers to contribute to a trust fund that is activated if an employee loses his or her job. The average weekly number of workers claiming UI in 2006 was 2.48 million at a total cost of $5.55 billion for the year. In 2006 the average duration of unemployed workers in the UI program was 15.2 weeks.[16]

The Unemployment Insurance System and Benefits The UI system consists of two basic parts: (1) regular state-funded benefits, generally provided for a maximum of 26 weeks; and (2) a federal/state extended benefits program. The second part provides an additional 13 weeks of benefits to unemployed workers who have used up their regular benefits and are still searching for a job. Extended benefits in the UI system are activated when the level of unemployment insurance claims in a state rises above a specified threshold. The extended benefits program is based on the assumption that when a state's unemployment rate is high, it usually takes longer to find a new job.[17] States pay 50 percent of the benefits provided by the UI extended benefits program.

To be eligible for UI benefits, a worker must be unemployed, be ready and willing to work, be registered for work with the state employment service, and have been working in covered employment during a base eligibility period. Conversely, a worker who is fired for misconduct, quits a job without a legally acceptable reason, fails to register with the state employment service, refuses a job equal to or better than the one previously held, or goes on strike is ineligible for unemployment benefits. States cannot, however, deny benefits to workers who refuse to be strikebreakers or who refuse to work for less than the prevailing wage rate.[18]

Basic decisions concerning the amount of benefits, eligibility, and length of benefit time are made by the states. In January 2008 the average weekly benefit check was $298. State unemployment benefits varied widely, ranging from a weekly average of $186 in Alabama to $343 in Minnesota.[19]

Problems in Unemployment Insurance Congress created the UI system in 1935, and since then the program has remained essentially the same despite changes in the economy and in the nature of unemployment. There are several problems endemic to the UI program:

1. *Part-time workers.* Part-time workers are 59 percent less likely than full-time workers to collect UI benefits. In 23 states, people looking for part-time work are not considered to be looking for "suitable work" and are therefore ineligible for benefits. This occurs even though their employers pay UI payroll taxes for them, and they often meet minimum earnings requirements. Additionally, 32 states do not consider workers eligible for UI if they are only available for part-time work.[20]

2. *Temporary workers.* Temporary workers are 28 percent less likely than all other workers to receive UI benefits. The number of temporary workers has been increasing, and by 2003 the number of temporary workers totaled 2.2 million. Those who work at temporary agencies face several difficulties when applying for UI benefits. First, they may not have worked enough hours or earned enough to qualify for benefits. Second, because they were employed at temporary agencies they have difficulty proving they did not voluntarily quit the job. Last, to remain eligible for benefits, a worker cannot refuse "suitable work," or work of the same nature at or above the same pay rate that the worker was earning before. Some temporary workers have been denied benefits because they refused a different type of temporary assignment than they had previously been doing.

3. *Low-wage workers.* Only 18 percent of low-wage workers (those earning $8 an hour or less) receive UI benefits compared to 40 percent of high-wage workers. These workers are often ineligible because they fail to meet minimum earnings requirements. Another reason low-wage workers are often ineligible is that not all of their earnings are considered when determining eligibility. In most states, up to six months of a worker's earnings do not count toward the earnings requirements because the state ignores the last completed quarter and the current quarter of earnings. By 2003, 19 states had adopted low-wage worker eligibility reforms based on an "alternative base period," which expands eligibility for workers who need their most recent earnings to qualify for UI.[21]

4. *Limited coverage.* In 1975, 75 percent of jobless workers received benefits. By 1986, 33 percent of jobless workers received benefits and the situation remained much the same in 2007 with 37 percent of unemployed workers (2.5 million people) receiving benefits.[22]

5. *Benefit decline.* In 1986 total UI benefits were 59 percent lower than in 1976 (after adjusting for inflation). In 2006 only about 35 percent of the average worker's lost wages were replaced by UI benefits.[23] As such, many families cannot afford to live on these benefits. In 2004 the average weekly UI benefits were too low to lift a one-parent, one-child family above the poverty line in 22 states. In another 11 states, the benefit level was less than $1,000 above the poverty line for a two-person family. A 2004 study by the Congressional Budget Office found that almost 25 percent of UI recipients out of work for four months or more fell into poverty despite UI benefits.[24]

6. *Longer spells of unemployment.* UI was based on the assumption that layoffs are temporary and that employers will typically recall workers. Now, however, many people are losing their jobs because of long-term structural changes in the economy. UI is based on the belief that workers will find suitable reemployment that matches their skills and experience. However, those who receive assistance longer than the norm question this assumption. In July 2007, 1.3 million people had been unemployed for 27 weeks or more and therefore were beyond the standard eligibility period for regular unemployment insurance benefits. That compares with just 696,000 long-term unemployed workers in March 2001. In addition, the median duration of unemployment in July 2007 was 8.9 weeks. This compares with a median duration of unemployment of 6.6 weeks in March 2001.[25]

In a forced response to the continuing economic downturn in the United States, President Bush in June 2008 signed a bill that included an extension of jobless benefits for long-term unemployed workers, called Emergency Unemployment Compensation (EUC). Under the bill, workers still unable to find jobs after having exhausted their regular state benefits are eligible for up to 13 weeks of extended federal benefits (or half their state benefits, whichever is less), reaching back to cover still-unemployed workers who first filed for their state unemployment benefits on May 7, 2006, or later. The program will remain in effect for workers exhausting their state benefits through March 2009.[26]

7. *Women and unemployment.* Sixty-seven percent of part-time workers are women, and one-third of all women work part time. Women are also more likely to be employed by temporary agencies than are men, and their lower wages make them less likely to meet minimum UI earnings requirements. Finally, many women leave their jobs for voluntary reasons that are not considered "good cause" in many states. In other states, a woman is ineligible for UI benefits if she quits to escape a violent domestic partner, because of a schedule change that makes child care arrangements impossible, to take care of a sick child, or to follow a spouse to another location. Because of these factors, only 33 percent of unemployed women receive UI benefits compared to 37 percent of men.[27] By 2003, 24 states had adopted family-friendly UI policies covering domestic violence as "good cause" for leaving work and collecting unemployment benefits, and 14 states adopted a "dependent allowance," permitting workers to increase their unemployment benefits based on the number of children being cared for.

8. *Meeting its financial obligations.* The UI system has difficulty in meeting its financial obligations during economic downturns without federal aid or deficit spending. Employers pay into a general fund that is supposed to have adequate financial reserves. Yet, many states borrow billions from the federal government to cover benefits in times of high unemployment. According to the Department of Labor, states have less money in their trust funds than they did in the 1940s and 1950s, thereby creating the potential for serious liability problems.[28]

9. *Tightened eligibility requirements.* In recent years, many states have tightened UI eligibility requirements. In addition, the UI program often fails to help the states with the most severe unemployment problems. For example, the calculation of unemployment rates is based on a study conducted by the Department of Labor in which 60,000 households (individuals 16 years or older are included in the survey) are interviewed each month. Part-time workers are counted as being employed, and discouraged workers who dropped out of the labor force are not counted. Although the UI program includes mechanisms that allow states to receive more federal reimbursement when unemployment rates are unusually high, the official state rate is lowered because many of the unemployed are not counted. The consequence is that this artificially low rate of unemployment may not set off the extended benefits mechanism.[29] Furthermore, states with "pockets of poverty" receive no additional help when the overall state unemployment rate is not high enough to set off the triggers.

One conservative approach to UI reform transfers the primary responsibility for unemployment insurance to individual workers through the creation of individual unemployment accounts (IUAs). The IUA would be a portable individual trust that belongs to the employee and would work much like an individual retirement account (IRA). IUA holders would be personally responsible for investing and managing their IUA funds. The funds would be created by voluntary tax-free contributions from each worker or the employer or both. In turn, the worker would have access to the funds any time he or she was without a job.[30]

Workers' Compensation

The U.S. Bureau of Labor Statistics reported that in 2006, 5,840 workers were killed on the job—about 16 workers a day.[31] There are currently 6.8 million work-related injuries and about 50,000 workers a year die from workplace-related illnesses.[32]

Workers' Compensation (WC) programs began in 1911 in Wisconsin and New Jersey. By 1948 every state operated some form of WC program. WC programs provide cash, medical assistance, rehabilitation services, and disability and death benefits to persons (or their dependents) who are victims of industrial accidents or occupational illnesses. By the 2000s, WC laws protected more than 97 million workers, or 87 percent of the labor force.[33] Although laws vary from state to state, the basic principle is that employers should assume the costs of occupational disabilities without regard to fault.[34] Although most workers are covered in the majority of states, business owners and independent contractors are often excluded, as are volunteer, farm, railroad, maritime, and domestic workers. Federal employees are covered under a special program.

Not only do the specific laws governing WC vary from state to state; there is little consistency either in benefit levels or in the administration of the programs. For example, some states require employers to carry insurance, other states provide a state-sponsored insurance fund, others allow employers to act as self-insurers, and still others do not require compulsory WC coverage. Some state programs do not cover employees of nonprofit, charitable, or religious institutions. Because of the potential for large claims, most employers transfer their responsibility by purchasing insurance from private companies that specialize in WC.

WC programs are problematic in several ways. First, benefit levels are established on the basis of state formulas and are usually calculated as a percentage of weekly earnings (generally about 66.66 percent). As such, each state sets its own annually adjusted benefit level, and these levels vary widely across states. For example, in 2005, total benefits were $1.59 per $100 of covered wages in California, compared to $1.06 for the nation as a whole, and wage-replacement benefits were $0.85 compared to $0.56.[35] Second, the cost to employers for providing WC insurance has been rising rapidly. Employers paid $88.8 billion to insure their workers in 2005, up from $60.1 billion in 2000. Medical benefits were a primary factor behind the rising cost of workers' compensation increasing by about 25 percent from $20.9 billion in 2000 to $26.2 billion in 2005.[36] Third, there is great variability among states in the way claims are handled. Workers are often encouraged to settle out of court for attractive lump sums, even though the amounts may not equal their lost wages. Often, benefits are uneven. For example, the price attached to the loss of a body part has been interpreted differently from state to state. Charles Prigmore and Charles Atherton note that in 1978 in

Hawaii the loss of a finger was valued at $5,175, more than the courts in the state of Wyoming allowed for the loss of an eye.[37] In addition, there are often long delays between the time an injury occurs and the period in which benefits start. Finally, in some states, employers are exempt from the WC tax if they can demonstrate that they are covered by private insurance. Unfortunately, private insurance coverage may prove inadequate after a disability benefit is determined. Even though injured workers or their survivors received $55.3 billion in benefits and medical payments in 2005,[38] WC may not provide adequate protection for many disabled workers.

The Social Security Dilemma

Because of its widespread public support, Social Security was long perceived by policy analysts and legislators as the third rail of politics—touch it and you die. Besides, the immediate focus of conservative Republicans and Democrats was on the more vulnerable public assistance programs that enjoyed less public support. Nevertheless, emboldened by the successful passage of the Personal Responsibility and Work Opportunity Reconciliation Act of 1996, conservatives turned their attention to social insurance, the real welfare giant.

Criticisms leveled at the Social Security system were particularly pointed during the 1990s. Opponents argued that Social Security was depressing private savings (and thereby providing less capital

spotlight 10.1

Major Social Insurance Programs

In the United States, there are three *major* social insurance programs:

- OASDI (also known as Social Security) covers the elderly, survivors, and those people unable to work due to a disability.

- Unemployment Insurance covers workers who have been fired or laid off from their jobs.
- Workers' Compensation provides case, medical assistance, rehabilitation services, and disability and death benefits to persons (or their dependents) who are victims of industrial accidents or occupational illnesses.

for investment) by giving people a retirement check financed by the working population rather than interest on accumulated savings. The average retired Social Security recipient in 2008 would have needed a savings account of about $260,000 (at 5 percent interest) to collect interest equal to the average benefit ($12,996) in that year.

Arguments against the Current Social Security System

Social Security in the United States is a pay-as-you-go system, and as such it is an intergenerational wealth transfer plan based on demographic factors. Specifically, birthrate and longevity determine the solvency of pay-as-you-go retirement systems.

The U.S. birthrate at the time of the creation of Social Security was 2.3, but it rose to 3.0 by 1950 and continued to climb throughout that decade. Today it has dropped back to 2.1. The average life expectancy in 1935 was 63; today it is about 78. As a result of these demographic factors, the number of workers paying Social Security payroll taxes has gone from 16 for every retiree in 1950 to just 3.3 for every Social Security beneficiary in 1997. That ratio is expected to decline to just 2 to 1 by 2025.

Social Security is also exacerbating intergenerational tensions. Younger workers are skeptical about the ability of Social Security to support them upon retirement. They are nervous that Social Security will buckle when the baby boomers start retiring around 2010. Some are also anxious because they are saving less than their parents. In short, some younger workers fear that they will be denied Social Security benefits despite having made enormous contributions. Ted Dimig sums up the dilemma: "So, where does this leave my generation? First of all, it leaves us with a huge resentment over the idea that our elders might saddle us with the debt for their retirement . . . while shortchanging us on our own retirement."[39]

Although OASDI is an important part of economic security for the nation's retired, serious problems threaten its future viability. The original strategy of the Social Security Act of 1935 was to create a self-perpetuating insurance fund, with benefits to the elderly being in proportion to their contributions. That scenario did not materialize. For example, in 1992 a single man retiring at age 65 would have received a maximum Social Security benefit of $13,056 per year, plus an additional $1,756 yearly in Medicare benefits. If the worker had started contributing to the Social Security fund in 1950 and contributed regularly at the maximum level until he retired in 1992, the total contribution would have been about $52,000. Yet in three and a half years this worker would have received his entire contribution back in benefits. If the worker survived to age 72, his benefits would exceed his contributions by $51,000. That amount does not include any cost-of-living increases. Put another way, a man who retired in 1980 could expect to receive Social Security benefits 3.7 times greater than his contributions would have generated if invested in low-risk government securities. For a similar woman, this ratio was even higher—4.4 times—given her longer life expectancy.[40] On the other hand, this windfall is not true for current workers, because both the tax and the wage base upon which the tax is determined have increased dramatically since the 1970s. Whether current workers will recover their entire investment will depend on how long they live, whether they are married, and whether they earned a high or low wage.

Arguments for the Current Social Security System

The Social Security program serves four main functions: (1) It supports more than 7 million survivors of deceased workers and 4 million disabled Americans. (2) Social Security is the nation's most successful antipoverty program. Largely because of Social Security, the poverty rate among the nation's elderly has fallen over the last 50 years from more than 40 percent to 10.4 percent. Today, only 40 percent of elderly Americans have access to public or private pension plans or annuities.[41] Without Social Security about half of elderly Americans would have incomes below the poverty level. For two-thirds of the elderly, Social Security is their major source of income. For a third of the elderly it is virtually their only income. (3) Social Security is important to working as well as retired Americans. Financially solvent seniors are viable consumers which is good for businesses. Few children would trade the burden of payroll taxes for the onus of supporting destitute retired parents. (4) Social Security is a special kind of "investment" unavailable in the private sector: a lifetime retirement annuity with benefits that rise with inflation. Almost all corporate pensions (many which run out after 20 years) are not indexed to compensate for the erosion of purchasing power caused by inflation. The belief that the basic protection provided by Social Security is analogous to private savings and would be unnecessary if people just saved more is spurious. And as a disability insurance policy, Social Security provides coverage equivalent to a $203,000 policy in the private sector; a similar dependent and survivor policy for a 27-year-old average-wage worker with two children would be equivalent to a $295,000 private sector policy.[42] About one in three Social Security beneficiaries is not a retiree.

Social Security has also been accused of overpaying the elderly, slighting younger workers (who could get a better return if they invested privately), and leading the nation to financial collapse. Merton and Joan Bernstein challenge the criticisms leveled at Social Security. They claim that rather than discouraging private savings, Social Security actually stimulates financial planning for retirement and thus encourages savings.[43] Others counter the overpayment argument by noting that in 2002, 52 percent of families over age 65 had total annual incomes under $35,000, while only 30 percent had annual incomes exceeding $50,000. Almost 32 percent of elderly nonfamily households (persons living alone or with relatives) had annual incomes below $10,000.[44] These numbers hardly suggest an elderly population becoming wealthy by exploiting an overly generous Social Security system.

Social Security in Trouble

Social Security began to show signs of fiscal trouble in the mid-1970s. Between 1975 and 1981, the Old-Age and Survivors Insurance fund suffered a net decrease in funds and a deficit in the reserve of between $790 million and $4.9 billion a year. This imbalance between incoming and outgoing funds threatened to deplete the reserve by 1983. Moreover, the prospects for Social Security seemed bleak in other ways. Whereas the ratio of workers to supported beneficiaries (the dependency ratio) was then three to one, estimates at the time indicated that by the end of the century (with the retirement of the baby boom generation) that ratio would be only two to one. In short, the long-term costs of the program would exceed its projected revenues. The crisis in Social Security was fueled by demographic changes (a dropping birthrate plus an increase in life expectancy), more liberal benefits paid to retiring workers, high inflation, high

unemployment, and the COLAs passed by Congress in the mid-1970s.

Facing these short- and long-term problems, Congress moved quickly to pass PL 98–21, the Social Security Amendments of 1983. Among the newly legislated changes were a delay in the cost-of-living adjustments and a stabilizer placed on future COLAs. Specifically, if trust funds fell below a certain level, future benefits would be keyed to the consumer price index (CPI) or the average wage increase, whichever is lower. A second change was that Social Security benefits became taxable if taxable income plus Social Security benefits exceeded $25,000 for an individual or $32,000 for a couple. A third change increased the 2027 retirement age to 67 to collect full benefits. Although workers could retire at age 62, they would receive only 70 percent of their benefits instead of 80 percent. Finally, coverage was extended: New federal employees were covered for the first time, as well as members of Congress, the president and vice president, federal judges, and employees of nonprofit corporations.

In the mid-1990s the Social Security rules were again changed, this time easing the historic Social Security penalty for about one million beneficiaries aged 65 to 67 who are still working. Previously, annual earnings that exceeded $11,250 would result in $1.00 of benefits lost for every $2.00 earned.[45] The new rules meant that by 2008, for those who had reached their full retirement age, the limit was $36,120 with a loss of $1.00 of benefits for every $3.00 earned.[46]

The Long-Term Prospects for Social Security

Despite these reforms, the fiscal viability of the OASDI system remains in question. Some analysts suggest that Social Security is on sound footing. They point to the fact that the income and assets reserve in the combined OASDI trust funds reached $2.24 trillion in 2007. At the end of 2007, the OASDI trust fund income was $785 billion while outgoing expenses were $594 billion. By 2017 the OASDI assets are expected to peak at $4.3 trillion.[47]

Under the intermediate assumptions of the Social Security Administration (SSA), OASDI costs will increase faster than tax income due to the retirement of the large baby boomer generation. After 2030, increases in life expectancy and low fertility rates of the baby boomers will continue to

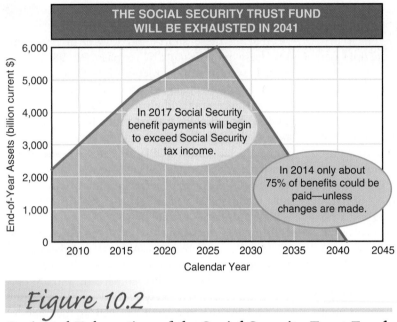

Figure 10.2

Projected Exhaustion of the Social Security Trust Fund

Sources: Social Security Administration, "The Future of Social Security," SSA Publication No. 05-10055, Washington, DC, May 2008.

increase Social Security system costs relative to tax income, albeit more slowly. Annual costs of OASDI will exceed tax income starting in 2015, at which time the gap will be covered by redeeming the Treasury bills that make up the trust fund assets. By 2042 those assets will be exhausted (see Figure 10.2). More specifically, the DI fund is projected to be exhausted in 2029 followed by the OASI fund in 2044 (see Table 10.2 and Table 10.3). However

Table 10.2

Key Dates for the Trust Funds

	OASI	DI	OASDI	HI
First year outgo exceeds income excluding interest	2018	2008	2018	2004
First year outgo exceeds income including interest	2029	2017	2028	2010
Year trust funds are exhausted	2044	2029	2042	2019

Source: Social Security Administration. Retrieved September 2004, from www.ssa.gov/OACT/TRSUM/trsummary.html

bleak, these figures reflect the SSA's improving long-range view of OASDI as a result of changes in immigration methods and assumptions.[48]

Annual cost will exceed tax income in 2015 for the OASDI Trust Funds, which are projected to become exhausted and unable to pay benefits in 2042. For the trust funds to remain solvent for the 75-year projection period, the combined payroll tax rate must be permanently raised 1.7 points, benefits would have to be permanently reduced by 11.5 percent, and general revenue transfers equivalent to $4.3 trillion would have to be made. Alternatively, a combination of approaches could be adopted.[49]

Medicare's financial status is even worse than OASDI's because its financial difficulties will come sooner and be more severe. In 2008 Medicare's Hospital Insurance (HI) Trust Fund is expected to pay out more in benefits than it receives. The difference will be made up from general revenues. Growing annual deficits are projected to exhaust HI reserves in 2019. In addition, the Medicare Supplementary Medical Insurance (SMI) Trust Fund that pays for physician services and the prescription drug benefit will continue to require general revenue financing and charges on beneficiaries that grow substantially faster than the economy and beneficiary incomes. Medicare's annual costs were 3.2 percent of GDP in 2007 (almost 75 percent of Social Security's) but are projected to exceed Social Security expenditures in 2028 and reach a whopping 10.8 percent of GDP in 2082.[50]

According to the trustees, the Medicare program could be made solvent over the next 75 years by an immediate 122 percent increase in the payroll tax (from 2.9 percent to 6.44 percent), or an immediate 51 percent reduction in program outlays or some combination of them. Part B of the Supplementary Medical Insurance (SMI) Trust Fund, which pays doctors' bills and other outpatient expenses, and Part D, which pays for access to prescription drug coverage, are both expected to be adequately financed because current law automatically provides financing each year to meet next year's expected costs.[51]

Table 10.3

Year of Trust Fund Exhaustion Using Social Security Administration Estimates

Set of Assumptions	OASI	DI	OASDI	HI
Alternative I (low cost)	Never	Never	Never	Never
Alternative II (best estimate)	2044	2028	2042	2025
Alternative III (high cost)	2033	2015	2031	2012

Source: Committee on Ways and Means, U.S. House of Representatives, *2004 Green Book* (Washington, DC: U.S. Government Office, 2004), pp. 1–60.

Some critics complain that the federal government is borrowing from the current Social Security surplus to fund other programs and is thereby hiding the real extent of the federal deficit. Money in the Social Security trust funds was intended to be invested and to be set aside for future years, not to be used to finance other government spending. But in 1990, for example, $65 billion in Social Security surpluses went for non–Social Security spending. As a result, part of almost every federal program is paid for by the Social Security payroll tax. In that sense, the real budget deficit—and the absence of a *real* Social Security surplus to pay for future benefits—has been hidden from the public.[52]

Although some Social Security reforms have provided a short-term solution, structural problems continue to plague the system. As already discussed, one problem is the "graying of America." Since 1900 the percentage of Americans 65 years and older has more than tripled (from 4.1 percent in 1900 to 12.3 percent in 2006), and the absolute number has increased 11.5 times (from 3.1 million to 35.6 million).[53] Demographic projections suggest that by 2030 the number of persons over age 65 will increase to 70.5 million. In other words, by 2030 the percentage of elderly is expected to climb from the current rate of 12.34 percent to 19.4 percent. Furthermore, the elderly are living longer. Between 1900 and 1990 the 75- to 84-year-old group increased 16 times, and the 85-and-over group was 38 times larger.[54] These demographic trends suggest that the **dependency ratio** will significantly increase, as will the pressures on the Social Security system. For example, in 1960 the worker-to-beneficiary ratio was

5 to 1; by 2007 it had dropped to 3.4 to 1. By 2025 the dependency ratio is expected to be 2 to 1.[55] A question arises whether two workers in 2040 will be able to support one retired person, and whether the Social Security system—as it is presently structured—can support 20 percent of the U.S. population.

Projections about the future of Social Security are predicated on the belief that certain economic and demographic factors will be in play for the next 50 years. However, economics and demographics could easily shift, invalidating the most earnest predictions. For example, a recession (such as the one in 2008), changing demographic trends, an oil crisis, or major changes in immigration patterns would all have profound consequences for the future of Social Security. However, there is nothing inviolate about the way Social Security is currently funded. An act of Congress could easily eliminate the insurance feature of Social Security and replace it with general revenue taxes. Given the widespread dependence on Social Security, it seems highly unlikely that policymakers and the public will allow the system to go bankrupt.

Another issue in Social Security involves the competition between public (compulsory) and private (voluntary) pension plans. Some critics argue that private pension plans are preferable to public plans because they are not dependent on the government and have greater potential for yielding higher returns. Private pensions originated as a means of encouraging employee loyalty and as a way of easing out aging workers. However, only about one-third of all workers and one-fourth of current employees are covered under private pension plans. Moreover, only a small fraction of these plans are indexed for inflation.

Critics of private pension plans argue that they are basically unreliable. Employees can switch jobs and thus lose their pension rights; companies can go bankrupt; corporations can raid pension funds, many of which are based on the vicissitudes of company stock (e.g., Enron) and workers risk losing their entire retirement savings if the corporate stock drops; and corrupt or incompetent pension managers can wreak havoc on pension plans. The 20 largest U.S. pension funds hold 10 percent of the equity capital of the largest U.S. companies; in total, they own assets worth well over $2.5 trillion.[56]

Despite federal tax subsidies to private pension plans totaling more than $64 billion in 1988, coverage under these plans has actually decreased since 1980. Supporters of Social Security argue that unlike the riskier private pension plans, OASDI benefits are portable and indexed for inflation; also, workers are immediately vested in Social Security, and benefits are not contingent on the financial condition of the employer.[57]

Although originally intended to supplement private pension funds and to operate as a pay-as-you-go insurance plan, OASDI has taken on many characteristics of a public welfare program. Specifically, most current retirees are realizing benefits far in excess of their contributions. (Those who retired in 1993 were the first group of workers to receive less in benefits, Social Security payroll, than they paid in taxes.)

The question remains: Should social insurance be modified to reflect social assistance and income redistribution goals? If the answer is yes, then benefits must be structured to reflect the current needs of retired workers rather than their past contributions. Furthermore, if Social Security is viewed as a public welfare program, then its regressive tax structure must be modified along more progressive lines. For example, Social Security is the single largest tax paid by a low-income worker, yet that same worker receives the lowest benefits when they retire. In short, the workers hurt most by the tax receive the fewest benefits. Using that same line of reasoning, if Social Security is designed for social assistance, then should everyone, regardless of income, be eligible? More particularly, should the very wealthy be allowed to be beneficiaries? Unfortunately, there are no simple answers to these questions.

Should We Privatize Social Security?

Proposals to fully or partially privatize Social Security with individually managed accounts have emerged from several quarters, including the former Clinton administration. Supporters argue that privatization would provide the individual with control of the Social Security portion of their retirement plan, and that successful investors who never touched their accumulations could achieve higher rates of return and higher benefits than Social Security provides.

The question of privatizing Social Security played an important role in the 2000 and 2004 presidential campaigns. By early 2005 the largely theoretical debate about privatizing Social Security came to a head when the former Bush administration released its Social Security reform plan. In one

■ *Critics argue that privatization would replace the guaranteed economic security of Social Security with risky stock market accounts.*

of the greatest challenges to Social Security since its inception in 1935, the Bush plan would divert some payroll taxes into private accounts that could be invested in the stock market. Specifically, the plan would let younger workers divert up to two-thirds of their Social Security taxes into private accounts, which they could invest in stocks and bonds. At the same time, the guaranteed Social Security benefit would be cut by up to 40 percent. The following is a brief summary of the Bush plan.

The Bush Plan   The plan would have restructured Social Security to allow workers under age 55 to divert a portion of their Social Security payroll taxes into private investment accounts in exchange for lower guaranteed future benefits. Workers would invest this money in stocks and bonds in hopes of earning higher returns. There would be no change in the current system or benefit levels for those born before 1950.

The Bush administration asserted that Social Security payroll taxes belong to the people and they should decide what to do with them. Over the long haul, individuals can expect to earn higher returns by investing in stocks, or a mix of stocks and bonds, than from what is generated now by the low-yielding Treasury bonds held by the Social Security trust fund. The accounts are individually owned, so they could be passed along to heirs—with certain exceptions. Personal accounts would be administered publicly. Accounts would be modeled on the Thrift Savings Plan, a retirement system for federal workers in which there are five investment options, all mutual funds. A person could hold a mix of the funds. Workers would continue to get traditional benefits from the Social Security system because the private accounts would represent only a percentage of benefits. Future benefit levels from the traditional system would be cut. Nothing could be withdrawn from the personal accounts before retirement, and the money could not be borrowed from them. People entering retirement would have to buy an investment annuity that would assure that their income would at least reach the poverty level when the accounts and the traditional benefits are combined. The clincher was that the government would borrow money to pay benefits during the phase-in to personal accounts; estimates ranged as high as $2 trillion over 10 years.

The Bush plan was virtually dead on arrival as even stalwart Republicans distanced themselves from such a radical departure in social policy. These Republicans knew full well that messing with Social Security was the third rail of politics. Older people vote and they do not like their income support fiddled with. This was especially important in an upcoming election year where Republicans knew they would be fighting an uphill battle. Also, the presumed vast gains in Social Security through a privatized system are predicated on a vibrant and predictable stock market. Having been burned in the stock market crash of 2001, many people were wary about trusting their future retirement to the market.

Critics contend that limited privatization would open the door to full privatization, which in the end would create a purely voluntary system that would destroy Social Security. In that scenario, worker benefits would be entirely dependent on the performance of the stock market. Critics also claim that privatization is a draconian solution to the problems of Social Security. The system needs changes, but not ones that are so major. They also argue that the problems in the system are overblown to make the case for privatization. Last, they argue that for privatization to work, the economic system must be robust so that stock dividends are high. In that case, the current Social Security system would also be doing well—incomes would be rising, which would then translate into higher revenues flowing into the system.[58]

The Pension Protection Act of 2006   August 17, 2006, may well be remembered as the day privately defined benefit pensions died. The Pension Protection Act of 2006 signed into law by former President Bush required sweeping changes in how employers account for and fund defined benefit pensions.[59] This reform legislation was a reaction to $11 billion in claims to the Pension Benefit Guaranty Corporation (PBGC) from 2002 to 2004.[60] The PBGC is a federal corporation funded through employer premiums that provides pension benefit protection for over 44 million Americans in defined benefit pension plans.[61] The failure of several large pension programs including WorldCom and Enron resulted in potential insolvency for the PBGC. Most of the pension programs that failed did so due to underfunding.[62] The most important change enacted in the Pension Protection Act of 2006 is the requirement that employers significantly increase the funding for defined benefit plans.

Funding of defined benefit pension plans can be quite confusing to someone unaccustomed to thinking like an accountant. Basically, there are two different ways to think of funding retirement. An employer can fund on a cash or as-needed basis, putting just enough money into the pension fund to meet the distribution requirement to those retirees currently receiving benefits. The other extreme requires the employer to estimate the future liability for all existing employers and to put enough money into the pension fund so that there will be money sitting in the bank waiting on each employee when he or she retires. Historically, most defined benefit pension plans were a little closer to the cash or as-needed basis than they should have been, meaning that they were underfunded. The Pension Protection Act of 2006 requires the employers to estimate future liabilities using reasonable interest rates and actuarial tables which will have the effect of requiring substantially higher funding for defined benefit plans for many. For example, the defined benefit plans for the Standard and Poor's 500 were estimated to be underfunded by more than $140 billion in 2005.[63]

Corporations are beginning to escape defined benefit obligations by reorganizing under Chapter 11 bankruptcy.[64] Corporations in two industries have been quick to pursue bankruptcy protection: auto parts suppliers (Collins & Aikens Corporation[65] and Delphi Corporation[66]) and airlines (Delta and Northwest).[67] It may not be long before other major corporations "reorganize" to escape their legal obligations to fund retirees' pensions and health care.

The alternative for the employer is simple—convert the defined benefit plan into a defined contribution plan. In the latter, the employer commits to current year funding of an employee-owned account like a 401K retirement account and, by doing so, has no future liability toward the employee.

The Pension Protection Act of 2006 was not intended to end defined benefit pension plans, but the large funding requirements mandated by this new law provide ample incentive to major corporations to eliminate traditional pensions, thereby eroding the corporate sector's role in the provision of social insurance.

Conclusion

Social insurance programs are replete with contradictions and difficulties. Nevertheless, social insurance programs, especially OASDI, have become a mainstay of the U.S. social welfare state. Despite the original intent of its architects, Social Security has become a primary source of financial support for elderly Americans. Moreover, OASDI has demonstrated the ability not only to curb the poverty rate for its constituents, but to actually reduce it. A majority of Americans have come to view Social Security as a right and to count on its benefits.

Social insurance programs represent a major source of security for both elderly Americans and present-day workers. Over the past 50 years, Americans have come to believe that regardless of the ebb and flow of economic life, Social Security and Unemployment Insurance embody a firm governmental commitment to care for workers and the elderly. Economic gains made by elderly people since the mid-1960s have validated this belief. Because Social Security is clearly linked to past contributions, beneficiaries experience little stigma. This is not true for the highly stigmatized beneficiaries of public assistance programs, and it is to this population that we will turn in Chapter 11.

Discussion Questions

1. Social insurance programs, especially Social Security, are among the most popular social programs in the nation. Part of the reason for this popularity is that unlike income maintenance programs, social insurance is not stigmatized. What are other reasons for the popularity of social insurance programs?

2. Serious questions exist about the future of Social Security. Some critics argue that Social Security is doomed, because the trust funds are expected to be depleted by the middle of the next century. Other observers argue that Social Security is sound, because the federal government is backing it. Is Social Security on solid ground, and can we expect it to be healthy in the future? If so, why? If not, why not? What can be done to make the system more stable?

3. The Social Security system is currently plagued by several different problems. What are the three most important problems facing the system?

Notes

1. U.S. Government, "Historical Tables: Budget of the United States Government Fiscal Year 2009." Retrieved July 2008, from www.whitehouse.gov/omb/budget/fy2009/pdf/hist.pdf

2. Congressional Budget Office (CBO), "The Budget and Economic Outlook: Fiscal Years 2003–2012," January 2002. Retrieved October 2004, from www.cbo.gov/showdoc.cfm?index=3277&sequence=14#tableF-10

3. Frances Fox Piven and Richard A. Cloward, *Regulating the Poor: The Functions of Public Welfare* (New York: Vintage Books, 1971).

4. David P. Beverly and Edward A. McSweeney, *Social Welfare and Social Justice* (Englewood Cliffs, NJ: Prentice Hall, 1987).

5. Ibid., p. 100.

6. W. Andrew Achenbaum, "Social Security: Yesterday, Today and Tomorrow," The Leon and Josephine Winkelman Lecture, School of Social Work, University of Michigan, March 12, 1996.

7. Ibid.

8. U.S. Social Security Administration, "Number of Social Security Beneficiaries." Retrieved July 2008, from www.segurosocial.gov/OACT/ProgData/icpGraph.html

9. U.S. Social Security Administration, "Status of the Social Security and Medicare Programs." Retrieved July 2008, from www.ssa.gov/OACT/TRSUM/index.html

10. See Social Security Administration, "Fast Facts and Figures about Social Security, 2007." Retrieved July 2008, from www.socialsecurity.gov/policy/docs/chartbooks/fast_facts/2007/fast_facts07.pdf

11. Department of the Census, *Current Population Reports, 1981*, Series P-60, No. 125 (Washington, DC: U.S. Government Printing Office, 1981).

12. Social Security Administration, "Fast Facts: SSI." Retrieved November 2001, from www.ssa.gov:80/statistics/fastfacts/pageii.html

13. Ibid.

14. Social Security Administration, "Monthly Statistical Snapshot, May 2008." Retrieved July 2008, from www.socialsecurity.gov/policy/docs/quickfacts/stat_snapshot/

15. U.S. House of Representatives, Committee on Ways and Means; *Overview of Entitlement Programs, 1992 Green Book* (Washington, DC: U.S. Government Printing Office, 1992), p. 485.

16. Social Security Administration, "9.A Unemployment Insurance." Retrieved July 2008, from www.socialsecurity.gov/policy/docs/statcomps/supplement/2007/9a.pdf

17. Isaac Shapiro and Marion Nichols, *Far From Fixed: An Analysis of the Unemployment Insurance System* (Washington, DC: Center on Budget and Policy Priorities, March 1992), p. viii.

18. Diana M. DiNitto, *Social Welfare: Politics and Public Policy* (Englewood Cliffs, NJ: Prentice Hall, 1991), p. 87.

19. U.S. Department of Labor, "Summary Data for State Programs, By State, Report Period for 01/2008." Retrieved July 2008 from, http://workforcesecurity.doleta.gov/unemploy/5159report.asp

20. U.S. GAO, "Unemployment Insurance—Low Wage and Part-time Workers Continue to Experience Low Rates of Receipt," September 2007. Retrieved July 2008, from www.gao.gov/new.items/d071147.pdf

21. Economic Policy Institute, "EPI Issue Guide, Unemployment Insurance."

22. Center on Budget and Policy Priorities, "Addressing Longstanding Gaps in Unemployment Insurance Coverage," August 7, 2007. Retrieved July 2008, from www.cbpp.org/7-20-07ui.pdf

23. National Center for Children in Poverty, "Unemployment Insurance." Retrieved July 2008, from www.nccp.org/profiles/index_37.html

24. Committee on Ways and Means, *2004 Green Book*, pp. 4–7.

25. Center on Budget and Policy Priorities, "Addressing Longstanding Gaps in Unemployment Insurance Coverage," August 7, 2007. Retrieved July 2008, from www.cbpp.org/7-20-07ui.pdf

26. National Employment Law Project, "Extended Unemployment Benefit Checks Reaching Jobless Workers Soon," posted July 1, 2008. Retrieved July 2008, from www.nelp.org/ui/federal/benefits/euc.cfm

27. Institute for Women's Policy Research, "Women and Unemployment Insurance: Outdated Rules Deny Benefits That Workers Need and Have Earned," January 2008. Retrieved July 2008, from www.iwpr.org/pdf/A132_WomenandUI.pdf

28. U.S. Department of Labor, "UI Data Summary," 2000.

29. Ibid.

30. Stephen M. Colarelli and Lawrence Brunner, "Solving Problems in Unemployment Insurance," Mackinac Center for Public Policy, 1994. Retrieved October 2001, from www.mackinac.org/13

31. Bureau of Labor Statistics, "Census of Fatal Occupational Injuries, 2006." Retrieved July 2008, from www.bls.gov/iif/oshcfoi1.htm

32. See Bureau of Labor Statistics, "Census of Fatal Occupational Injuries." Retrieved October 2004, from www.bls.gov/iif/oshwc/cfoi/cfch0002.pdf; and

Joseph Dear, "Partner, Not Problem," *TechNews* 1, no. 1 (January/February 1995), p. 1.

33. DiNitto, *Social Welfare.*

34. Ways and Means Committee, *1992 Green Book,* pp. 1707–1709.

35. National Academy of Social Insurance, "Workers' Compensation in California and in the Nation: Benefit and Employer Cost Trends, 1989–2005," April 2008. Retrieved July 2008, from www.nasi.org/usr_doc/California_Brief_April_2008.pdf

36. Ibid.

37. Charles Prigmore and Charles Atherton, *Social Welfare Policy* (Lexington, MA: D.C. Heath, 1979) pp. 66–67.

38. National Academy of Social Insurance, "Workers' Compensation in California and in the Nation."

39. Ted Dimig, "Social Security on the Brink," *Houston Chronicle* (August 4, 1996), pp. 1F and 4F.

40. Joseph F. Quinn and Olivia S. Mitchell, "Social Security on the Table," *The American Prospect* 26 (May–June 1996), pp. 76–81.

41. AARP, *A Profile of Older Persons: 2003,* 2004. Retrieved September 2004, from http://assets.aarp.org/rgcenter/general/profile_2003.pdf

42. C. Eugene Steuerle, "Why Are Social Security Benefits Adjusted Every Year?" AARP Webplace, 2000. Retrieved October 2001, from www.aarp.org

43. C. Merton and Joan Broadshaug Bernstein, *Social Security: The System That Works* (New York: Basic Books, 1987).

44. AARP, *AARP Profile of Older Persons: 2003.*

45. Michael Doerflein, Angela Garner, Niki Gober, and Stacy Lochala, "Social Insurance." Unpublished paper, Graduate School of Social Work, University of Houston, Houston, TX, May 1996.

46. Social Security Administration, "How Much Can I Earn and Still Receive Social Security Benefits?" Retrieved July 2008, from http://ssa-custhelp.ssa.gov

47. Social Security Administration, "2008 OASDI Trustees Report," March 25, 2008. Retrieved May 24, 2008, from www.ssaonline.us/OACT/TR/TR08/II_highlights.html#76460

48. Ibid.

49. Ibid.

50. Social Security Administration, "Status of the Social Security and Medicare Programs: A Summary of the 2008 Annual Reports, Social Security and Medicare Boards of Trustees," April 3, 2008. Retrieved May 24, 2008, from www.ssa.gov/OACT/TRSUM/trsummary.html

51. Ibid.

52. Robert J. Shapiro, "The Right Idea for 1990: Cut Social Security Taxes," *Economic Outlook,* 4 (January 29, 1990).

53. See AARP, *AARP Profile of Older Persons: 2003*; and Committee on Ways and Means, *2004 Green Book,* p. A-2.

54. See AARP, *AARP Profile of Older Persons: 2003.*

55. Committee on Ways and Means, *2004 Green Book.*

56. Peter F. Drucker, "Reckoning with the Pension Fund Revolution," *Harvard Business Review* (March 1, 1991), pp. 1–9.

57. Bernstein and Bernstein, *Social Security.*

58. Laura Meckler, "Republicans Voice Doubt about Bush Plan. And in the Senate, Not a Single Democrat Has Signed On," Associated Press (February 4, 2005); Terence Hunt, "Bush Pushes Social Security Overhaul," *Chicago Sun-Times* (February 3, 2005), p. 6; and Richard W. Stevenson, "Vast Borrowing Seen in Altering Social Security," *New York Times* (November 28, 2004), p. 2.

59. "Fact Sheet: The Pension Protection Act of 2006: Ensuring Greater Retirement Security for American Workers," The White House, August 17, 2006. Retrieved March 31, 2007, from www.whitehouse.gov/news/releases/2006/08/20060817.html

60. "Securing Retirement: An Overview of the Pension Protection Act of 2006," Deloitte Tax LLP, Washington, DC, August 3, 2006. Retrieved March 31, 2007, from www.deloitte.com/dtt/cda/doc/content/us_gre_securingretirement_310806.pdf

61. "Mission Statement," Pension Benefit Guarantee Corporation. Retrived March 31, 2007, from www.pbgc.gov/about/about.html

62. "Securing Retirement."

63. Robert Brokamp, "The End of Retirement," *Motley Fool,* March 31, 2007. Retrieved March 31, 2007, from www.fool.com/personal-finance/retirement/2007/03/31/the-end-of-retirement.aspx

64. Ibid.

65. "U. S. Agency Taking Over Pension Plan," Bloomberg News, *Chicago Tribune,* March 31, 2007. Retrieved March 31, 2007, from www.chicagotribune.com/business/chi-0703300359mar31,0,2486636.story?coll=chi-business-hed

66. Katie Merx, "Are Delphi Pensions Secure?" *The Buffalo News,* March 31, 2007. Retrieved March 31, 2007, from www.buffalonews.com/145/story/43811.html

67. Charles Leocha, "Airlines in Bankruptcy Land," MSNBC, March 30, 2007. Retrieved March 31, 2007, from www.msnbc.msn.com/id/17858408/

CHAPTER 11

Public Assistance Programs

*T*his chapter examines key public assistance programs, including the former Aid to Families with Dependent Children (AFDC); AFDC's replacement, Temporary Assistance to Needy Families (TANF); Supplemental Security Income (SSI); and general assistance (GA). The chapter also investigates and analyzes the problems and issues inherent in public assistance programs.

The U.S. social welfare state is a complex mix of programs, policies, and services. Perhaps few people, including many policymakers, fully appreciate the complexity of the welfare system. One reason is that unlike many European countries that operate under a comprehensive and integrated welfare plan, the United States relies on a patchwork quilt of social welfare programs and policies. Because of the nation's historical ambivalence toward providing public relief, most welfare legislation has emerged from compromises and adroit political maneuvering rather than from a systematic and coordinated plan. In short, public assistance in the United States is not a comprehensive, integrated, and nonredundant system of social welfare services; instead, it is a disorganized mix of programs and policies.

Public assistance programs are one of the most misunderstood elements of the U.S. welfare state. Although expenditures for public assistance programs are far less costly than social insurance programs, they tend to be more controversial. Unlike social insurance, public assistance programs are based entirely on need and are therefore means

Most of Budget Goes Toward Defense, Social Security, and Major Health Programs

Figure 11.1

Where Federal Dollars Go, 2007

Source: Matt Fiedler, "Where Do Our Tax Dollars Go?", Center on Budget and Policy Priorities, Revised May 15, 2007. *Original Source:* Office of Management and Budget Data.

tested. Figure 11.1 illustrates the major federal governmental spending areas and the relative expenditures on each.

Public assistance programs that offer cash, medical, and other forms of assistance are based on the concept of safety nets—that is, plans designed to ensure that citizens receive basic services so they

spotlight 11.1

Key Public Assistance Programs in the United States

In the United States there are three major public assistance programs:

1. Temporary Assistance to Needy Families (TANF): a block grant based on workfare, time-limited benefits (a maximum of five years), and strict work participation rates

2. Supplemental Security Income (SSI): provides cash assistance to the elderly and to disabled poor people, including children

3. General Assistance (GA): state or locally run programs designed to provide basic benefits to low-income people who are ineligible for federally funded public assistance programs

remain above a certain poverty level. There are 51 separate safety nets—one in each state and in the District of Columbia. Although federal guidelines help determine the level of aid for the poor, individual states have extensive freedom to fashion their own safety nets. States differ as to benefit levels, and the vast majority lack an adequate safety net to help the poor and the jobless.[1] Nevertheless, a major component of the safety net includes programs designed to ensure that families and individuals receive the resources necessary to meet subsistence needs.

Assumptions and Myths about Public Assistance

American attitudes toward public assistance can be characterized as a mixture of compassion and hostility. This ambivalence plays out in a series of harsh and often conflicting assumptions about public assistance recipients. The struggle around public assistance programs is symbolic, reflecting the tensions in Americans' ideas about wealth, opportunity, and privilege.

On the hostility side, the argument goes like this: If privilege is earned by hard work, then people are poor because they are lazy and lack ambition. Those driven by the powerful American spirit of competitiveness see the inability of the poor to compete as a serious character flaw. On the other hand, only a few paychecks separate the welfare recipient from the average citizen—thus the compassion.

Although democratic capitalism is rooted in the belief that hard work guarantees success, real life often tells a different story. The following assumptions, among others, underlie much of the discussion around public assistance: (1) Because generous benefits create a disincentive to work; recipients must always receive less cash benefits than the minimum wage. (2) Welfare recipients need prodding to work because they lack internal motivation. (3) Work is the best antipoverty program. (4) Public assistance programs must be highly stigmatized lest people will too readily embrace them. (5) Women receiving public assistance should work and their children should not have the luxury of being raised by a full-time homemaker. These assumptions about public assistance—many of which are remarkably

similar to those found in the Elizabethan Poor Laws—are rife with serious misconceptions.

The many myths surrounding public assistance make it imperative to discriminate between fact and fiction. (Note that in the items that follow, AFDC and TANF are used interchangeably because they served and serve the same clientele.)

Myth 1. Many families on the public assistance rolls include an able-bodied father who refuses to work.

Fact. In 2007, only 58,082 of the monthly average 1.7 million TANF families were two-parent families. This was a significant drop from the 342,000 two-parent TANF families in 1995. The vast majority of TANF families are headed by one parent—mostly mothers who are unmarried, divorced, widowed, or separated. Ninety percent of TANF children live with their mothers and 10 percent with their fathers. In the 2007 fiscal year, the average monthly recipients of TANF included 908,357 adults and 3,044,586 children, a total of nearly 4 million.[2]

Myth 2. Most poor people are on public assistance, and the number is growing.

Fact. In 2007 only 1.7 million families were receiving TANF assistance on average in any given month, representing less than one-quarter of the 7.6 million families living below the poverty line and millions more living just above it. Clearly, many low-income families do not turn to TANF for support. Also, states are responsible for meeting targets in relation to how much they distribute in TANF payments and focus their efforts on decreasing caseloads, as well as encouraging families to become self-sufficient.

Many states developed policies that attempt to divert assistance from those applicants needing the least amount of state help to become self-sufficient. As of July 2006, about three-fifths of states had created formal diversion programs where families could choose to receive lump-sum cash payments to deal with immediate needs instead of receiving monthly TANF benefits. Families that accept diversion payments are typically barred from applying for monthly TANF benefits for some period.[3]

Myth 3. Recipient mothers have more children in order to collect greater benefits; therefore, families on public assistance are large and steadily growing in size.

Fact. According to the Current Population Survey (CPS) the average size of TANF families in 2005 was 2.2 persons, a decrease of 0.1 from 2.3 in 2000. One-third of families had only one child. The average age of children was 5.4 years. The average size of families receiving TANF payments in 2005 was 3.8 persons.[4] Many states have **family cap** legislation that prohibits TANF families from receiving additional assistance for any child born after the mother has enrolled in the program. In 2006, 21 states had family cap limitations.[5]

Myth 4. Once on welfare, always on welfare.

Fact. This is now a moot point since the 1996 TANF regulations instituted a five-year lifetime benefit cap for recipients. Even before TANF, more than half of all AFDC recipients left the rolls within one year of going on welfare; by the end of two years, the percentage increased to 70 percent. Within the first year after leaving welfare, 45 percent returned; almost 66 percent returned by the end of three years. Over the course of seven years, more than 75 percent of those who left welfare returned at some point.[6]

Myth 5. Welfare programs create dependency, which is transmitted intergenerationally.

Fact. Given the lifetime cap on cash assistance, the dependency issue has become less relevant. Nevertheless, even before TANF the vast majority of AFDC recipients stayed on public assistance less than four years, those who stayed eight years or more accounted for half the number of people on the rolls at any given point in time.[7]

Research on **welfare dependency** is inconclusive. Robert Moffitt found that the length of welfare spells varied with demographic characteristics, the generosity of the state's public assistance program, and local labor market conditions.[8] P. J. Leahy, T. F. Buss, and J. M. Quane found that previous work experience, age at entry to welfare, and number of children were the best predictors of long-term welfare use.[9] Mary Jo Bane and David Ellwood found that race, education, marital status, work experience, and disability influenced first-spell durations. These same variables influenced recidivism. Bane and Ellwood also point out that many of the long-term users cycled in and out of welfare, apparently trying to leave but unable to do so permanently.[10]

The phenomenon of intergenerational dependency is not yet fully understood. According to Duncan and Hoffman, only 19 percent of African American and 26 percent of white women coming from households that were heavily dependent on welfare were heavily dependent on welfare themselves. The 19 percent of second-generation dependent African American women was the same percentage as that of African American women heavily dependent on welfare who did not grow up in households that were heavily dependent on welfare.[11]

On the other hand, Peter Gottschalk found a positive intergenerational relationship between welfare use by mothers and daughters.[12] M. Ann Hill and June O'Neill also found persistence in welfare dependency across generations. Looking at data from the National Longitudinal Survey of Youth (NLSY), these researchers found that young white women from welfare families had a 24 percent chance of being on welfare, compared with a 2 percent chance for non-Hispanic white women coming from families that were not on welfare. Comparable figures for African Americans were 42 and 15 percent; for Hispanics, 34 and 8 percent.[13] In their study of men's earnings, Mary Corcoran, Roger Gordon, Deborah Laren, and Gary Solon found

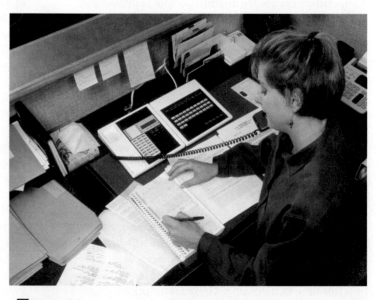

■ *One of the most commonly held myths about public assistance is that recipients don't want to work.*

that "One of our strongest results is the large negative association between a son's outcomes and welfare receipt in his family of origin."[14] A correlation may exist between welfare receipt and family of origin, but what remains unanswered is whether parental welfare receipt was the cause of the children's behavior.

Myth 6. Most welfare recipients are African Americans and Hispanic Americans.

Fact. In 2005 non-Hispanic whites constituted 43.3 percent of recipients, 30.3 percent were African American, and 26.4 percent were Hispanic. The remaining recipients were Asian, American Indian, or of another ethnicity.[15] Although the percentages of African Americans and Hispanics on the welfare rolls were larger than these groups' representation in the population, this is not surprising, because people of color are statistically poorer than whites.

Myth 7. Public assistance benefits provide a disincentive to work; people on welfare either do not want to work or are too lazy to work.

Fact. In 2005, one-quarter of recipients were employed and 6 of every 10 were in school, leaving only 15 percent who were not employed but looking for work. Of those who worked, 60 percent worked over 35 hours per week. Only 10 percent of TANF recipients worked less than 10 hours per week.[16]

Myth 8. Public assistance recipients are doing better than ever.

Fact. The reverse is true. From 1972 to 1992, AFDC benefit levels failed to keep pace with inflation, falling 43 percent in the typical state. This decline reflected a benefit loss of $279 a month, or more than $3,300 a year.[17] TANF benefits are exceedingly small; the maximum monthly benefit for a family of three with no income in most states in 2006 was between $300 and $500 a month. This can vary significantly between states. For example, the maximum monthly benefit may be $691 in New York, $625 in New Hampshire, and $640 in Vermont, but it is just $215 in Alabama, $204 in Arizona, and $170 in Mississippi.[18]

Myth 9. Never-married teen mothers constitute the bulk of welfare recipients.

Fact. In 2005 most adult TANF recipients were women (men represented only 6 percent of adult recipients) with an average age of 34.3, up from 33.1 in 2000. Of these, only one-quarter (24.9 percent) were under the age of 25, down

from 27.2 percent in 2000. Over 40 percent were 35 years or older.[19] According to Duncan and Hoffman, the most important causes for beginning AFDC spells were (1) divorce or separation (45 percent), (2) an unmarried woman becoming a pregnant household head (30 percent), and (3) a drop in earnings of the female head of the household (12 percent). Conversely, the predominant reasons for terminating public assistance spells were (1) remarriage (35 percent), (2) an increase in the earnings of a female householder (21 percent), and (3) children leaving the parental home (11 percent).[20]

Myth 10. It is easy to get on public assistance and too many undeserving people are receiving benefits.

Fact. According to the Center for Local Self-Reliance, before someone can apply for TANF in Georgia they must first get a form signed by six employers stating that they applied in good faith for a minimum wage job and were turned down. Once enrolled, if they are penalized twice for failure to meet administrative/work requirements, they are barred for life from seeking aid. David Morris stated: "In the early 1990s about 75 percent of those who walked into the welfare office to apply wound up on welfare rolls. Today it is closer to 25 percent. A growing number of states (13 at last count) now drop entire families from the welfare rolls after the first instance of non-compliance by the adult recipient."[21]

According to the Census Bureau in 2008, in addition to having to provide extensive documentation and meet verification requirements, applicants for food stamps can qualify for this program only if the household has less than $2,000 in disposable assets ($3,000 if one member is aged 60 or older), gross income below 130 percent of the official poverty guidelines for the household size, and net income below 100 percent of the poverty guidelines. Households with a person aged 60 or older or a disabled person receiving SSI, social security, state general assistance, or veterans' disability benefits may have gross income exceeding 130 percent of the poverty guidelines. All households in which all members receive TANF or SSI are categorically eligible for food stamps without meeting these income or resource criteria. Households are certified for varying lengths of time, depending on their income sources and individual circumstances.[22]

Myth 11. Public assistance recipients migrate to states where benefits are high.

Fact. A study by economist James Walker found no compelling evidence in support of the welfare magnet theory.[23] Other studies indicate that poor people migrate for a variety of reasons, including proximity to family and friends, the desire for a better life, and the hope of finding work. Although research by the Wisconsin's Institute for Research on Poverty concluded that some poor people migrate across state lines to receive higher benefits,[24] it failed to demonstrate that high benefits per se cause migration. According to Henry Freedman of the Center for Social Policy, "Census data on migration show that poor people move in the same direction as those who are not poor, usually toward states with jobs and booming economies rather than those offering higher welfare benefits."[25] Nevertheless, the question of whether poor people migrate for higher welfare benefits remains unanswered.

Myth 12. Welfare spending consumes a large portion of state budgets.

Fact. During the mid-1990s most states experienced large welfare-related budget surpluses. In 1999 this surplus reached $400 million in Texas alone. Specifically, federal TANF funding levels were set at 1994 to 1995 levels, while states were experiencing a 47 percent drop in TANF caseloads. Even before the TANF surplus, states spent roughly 3.4 percent of their total budgets on AFDC in 1991. Because about 1.5 percent of state budgets came from the federal government, they only spent about 2 percent on AFDC.[26]

State governments now, however, have to do more with less. For example, in Georgia the poverty rate has increased from 12.7 percent in 2002 to 14.4 percent in 2005, giving Georgia the 14thhighest poverty rate in the United States. Georgia's total federal and state TANF grant per poor child was $1,383 in 2002 and decreased by 16 percent to $1,160 by 2005. Georgia has more individuals living in poverty and using food stamps and low-income Medicaid, but a substantially smaller amount of individuals accessing the program that should assist in bridging poverty and employment—TANF. This means that Georgia is faced with having more families in need and less supports available to assist them, as funding is continually shifted away from work assistance and devalued by inflation.[27]

Myth 13. TANF benefits influence decisions relating to family composition (i.e., childbearing, marriage, divorce, and living arrangements) by encouraging women to head their own households.

Fact. Under the TANF guidelines, teenage mothers under age 18 are not entitled to benefits unless they are living at home or in a supervised facility. Although some empirical studies found a small correlation between public assistance benefits and the number of women who choose to head households or remarry, most researchers believe that the evidence does not support the view that generous benefits are responsible for high illegitimacy rates or the growth of single-female-headed households. For example, although total welfare benefits have declined since 1975, the number of single-female-headed households has remained relatively constant.[28]

Aid to Families with Dependent Children

AFDC was arguably the most controversial program in the U.S. welfare system. Its purpose was to maintain and strengthen family life by providing financial assistance and care to needy dependent children in their own homes or in the homes of responsible caregivers. Despite these modest goals, AFDC served as a symbol in the ideological battle between liberals and conservatives and caused recipients to be victimized in two ways: (1) by their own poverty, and (2) by ideologically motivated assaults against their character and motives.

The requirement for receiving AFDC was that a child be deprived of the parental support of one parent because of death, desertion, separation, or divorce. (In the case of the AFDC Unemployed Parent program, the criterion was deprivation of parental economic support because of unemployment or illness.) In 1992 AFDC served 4.8 million families (about 13.6 million individuals); of those 13.5 million recipients, about 67 percent were children.

The Evolution of the AFDC Program

Welfare reform has been a heated topic, and most presidents since John F. Kennedy have either offered welfare reform proposals or at least given lip service to the need for reform. To understand the issues surrounding welfare reform, it is important to examine the history of the AFDC program.

Originally called Aid to Dependent Children (ADC), the AFDC program was part of the Social Security Act of 1935 and was designed to provide support for children by dispensing aid to their mothers. In 1950 the adult caregiver (usually the mother) was made eligible for ADC benefits.[29] Also in the 1950s, medical services paid for in part by the federal government were made available for ADC recipients. Beginning in the late 1950s, some critics argued that ADC rules led to desertion by fathers, because only families without an able-bodied father were eligible. In 1961 a new component was added that allowed families to receive assistance in the event of a father's incapacity or unemployment. The new program, Aid to Families with Dependent Children-Unemployed Parent (AFDC-UP), was not made mandatory for the states, and until the welfare reform act of 1988, only 25 states and the District of Columbia had adopted it. In 1962 ADC was changed to AFDC to emphasize the family unit.

By 1962 the focus of the AFDC program had shifted to rehabilitation, and new policies mandated casework and treatment services. Although historically AFDC services were delivered by one worker, beginning in 1972 federal policy dictated that the AFDC program be divided into social services and **income maintenance programs.** This policy required that one worker be assigned the AFDC paperwork while the other assumed responsibility for social services.

The number of AFDC recipients tripled from 1960 to 1970. From 1971 to 1981 that number rose another 50 percent, and in 1992 it reached an all-time high of 13.6 million recipients. In 1950 AFDC recipients constituted 1.5 percent of the population; by 1992 that number reached 5 percent.

One notorious chapter in AFDC history involved the man-in-the-house rule. This policy mandated that any woman with an able-bodied man in the house would be terminated from AFDC because, regardless of whether the man was the father, it was supposedly his responsibility to support the family. This policy was manifested in "midnight raids" whereby social workers made late-night calls to determine if a man was present. Even a piece of male clothing found on the premises could justify cutting off aid. In some states the man-in-the-house rule was extended to include rules on dating. In 1968 the U.S. Supreme Court struck down the rule in Alabama, and the Court later reinforced its decision in a California case.[30]

The Family Support Act (FSA) of 1988 was an important piece of welfare legislation.[31] The FSA (budgeted at only $3.3 billion over a five-year period) attempted to change AFDC from an income support to a mandatory work and training program. To accomplish this, the bill established the **Job Opportunities and Basic Skills (JOBS)** program that required recipient women with children under age three (or, at state option, age one) to participate in a work or training program. By 1990 each state was to enroll at least 7 percent of its recipients (increasing to 20 percent by 1993) in a basic state education program, job training, a work experience program, or a job search program.[32]

Adoption of the AFDC-UP program became mandatory for all states, although they could choose to limit enrollment for two-parent families to 6 out of 12 calendar months in a year. Moreover, one family member of an AFDC-UP household was required to participate at least 16 hours a week in a community or make-work job in return for benefits. In addition, the FSA called for mandatory child support payments to be automatically deducted from an absent parent's paycheck. Finally, the FSA allowed states to require a teenage recipient to live with a parent or in a supervised environment to be eligible for assistance.[33]

The FSA's promise soon faded. Instead of declining, AFDC caseloads actually rose by 2.1 million from 1990 to 1992. By the end of 1991 the states had spent less than half of the available federal JOBS funds. Underappreciated at the time was the FSA component that permitted states to request waivers to existing AFDC rules, an option that opened the door for the radical welfare reforms that emerged in 1996.[34]

In his 1992 presidential campaign, Bill Clinton promised to "end welfare as we know it" by implementing a two-year cap on AFDC benefits. In 1993 Clinton appointed a working group on welfare reform, headed by White House advisor Bruce Reed and well-known poverty researchers David Ellwood and Mary Jo Bane. Completed in 1994, the Work and Responsibility Act called for expanding the JOBS program to help recipients move from welfare to work. Based on a personal plan, each AFDC recipient would enter into an agreement with a public assistance agency in return for subsidized child care, health care benefits, and other supportive services. This plan included a two-year limit on cash assistance, after which recipients would be expected to become employed (preferably in the private sector). Those unable to find employment after two years would enter an employment program based on subsidies to public or private employers to hire recipients in "worklike" positions. In turn, employers would provide a paycheck equaling the recipient's former welfare check as compensation for a given number of weekly work hours at the minimum wage. Participants would be required to change jobs every 12 months and undergo reassessment every two years. In addition, participants would be eligible for AFDC benefits if their wages were low enough, and they would continue to receive Medicaid and subsidized child care. Although time limits and work requirements would be national, states would have had considerable flexibility for innovation.[35] The election of the ultraconservative 104th Congress in 1994 ruled out the possibility of passing any welfare reform bill that included liberal components such as subsidized employment.[36]

The Personal Responsibility and Work Opportunity Reconciliation Act of 1996

In 1996, former President Bill Clinton signed the Personal Responsibility and Work Opportunity Reconciliation Act (PRWORA) (H.R. 3734), a complex 900-page document that confused even seasoned welfare administrators.[37] In effect, the PRWORA replaced AFDC, JOBS, and the **Emergency Assistance Program** with the Temporary Aid for Needy Families (TANF) program.

One of the most radical features of the PRWORA was among the least understood. Under the PRWORA, federal **entitlement** to public assistance was ended. In contrast, the former AFDC program operated under the principle of entitlement. This meant that states must provide assistance to anyone eligible under the law. This did not mean that states were required to provide something for nothing. In fact, states could have required recipients to participate in work, education, training, or job search programs as a condition for receiving aid. Under TANF, no family or child is *entitled* to assistance.[38] In effect, the TANF **disentitlement** rescinded the 60-year-old federal entitlement for support to poor children and families. TANF operates in the following manner:

- In order to receive a TANF grant, each state must submit a plan to the Department of Health and Human Services (HHS). In turn, HHS determines whether the plan conforms to the law. Plan requirements are generally limited, and much operational detail is omitted.

- TANF provides lump-sum federal **block grants** for states to operate their own welfare and work programs. Each state receives a block grant based on federal spending for a **fiscal year (FY)** for the state's former AFDC program, the JOBS program, and the Emergency Assistance Program. A minority of states receive annual adjustments in the form of supplemental grants; but for most states the amount of the TANF block grant is frozen, except for adjustments due to bonuses or penalties. Under limited circumstances, a state experiencing an economic downturn may qualify for additional federal funding.

- Maintenance of effort provisions require that to receive a full block assistance grant, the state must spend nonfederal funds at no less than 80 percent of a historic spending level based on 1994 spending. This requirement is reduced to 75 percent for a state that meets the act's **work participation rate** (percentage of TANF recipients in the workforce) requirements. A state that does not maintain the required spending level risks a dollar-for-dollar reduction in its block grant funding.

- States are prohibited from using TANF funds to assist certain categories of families and individuals. The most important prohibition involves the use of TANF funds to assist families in which an adult has received assistance for 60 months or more. (States can choose to pay beneficiaries with their own monies.) States can provide exceptions for up to 20 percent of their caseloads. Although the PRWORA mandates a maximum five-year lifetime limit on cash assistance, it allows states to set a shorter time limit. Other restrictions include a prohibition on assisting minor parents unless they are attending school and living at home or in an adult-supervised living arrangement (subject to limited exceptions), and a requirement to reduce or eliminate assistance if an individual does not cooperate with child support–related requirements, such as identifying the father.

- The TANF block grant has four specific work requirements. First, a state must require nonexempt unemployed parents or caregivers to participate in community service after receiving assistance for two months. Second, states must outline how they will require a parent or caregiver receiving benefits to engage in work not later than 24 months after they receive assistance. Third, a state must meet a work participation rate for all families of 50 percent. Fourth, states must meet a 90 percent work participation rate for two-parent families. Failure to comply with the last two work requirements results in a 5 percent penalty the first year and 2 percent thereafter (capped at 21 percent).

- States can spend their block grants on cash assistance, noncash assistance, services, and administrative costs in connection with assistance to needy families with children. States can also choose to spend up to 30 percent of their TANF funds to operate programs under the Child Care and Development Block Grant and the Title XX Social Services Block Grant. No more than one-third of that amount can be used for programs under Title XX, and the funds must be spent on programs for children or families whose incomes fall below 200 percent of the poverty line.

• When parents participate in required work activities, the state may (but is not required to) provide child care assistance. However, a state may not reduce or terminate a family's assistance if a single parent of a child under age six refuses to comply with work requirements because of a demonstrated inability of the state to provide needed child care.

• Recipients are not automatically eligible for Medicaid. However, states are required to provide Medicaid coverage for single-parent families and qualifying two-parent families with children if they meet the income and resource eligibility guidelines that were in effect in the state's AFDC Program on July 16, 1996. (States may modify these guidelines to a limited extent.)

• The TANF program attempted to address the dramatic increase in nonmarital births (especially teen births). First, state TANF plans must demonstrate how they will establish goals and take action to prevent and reduce out-of-wedlock pregnancies. Second, the act provides financial incentives to states to reduce their out-of-wedlock birth rates. The act authorizes HHS to give $20 million apiece to the five states that show the greatest success in reducing their nonmarital birth rates, while at the same time lowering their abortion rates below the states' 1995 levels.[39]

• The PRWORA allows states to impose a family cap that denies assistance to children born into families already receiving public assistance.

• States must permanently deny all Title IV-A cash assistance and Food Stamp Program benefits to recipients convicted of felony drug possession, use, or distribution. Other members of the family can continue to receive benefits. States may opt out of this provision or limit the period of denial by passing legislation.

In addition to TANF, the PRWORA included other reforms:

• Amended in 1997, the law makes immigrants who arrived in the United States before August 22, 1996, eligible for Medicaid and SSI benefits.

However, immigrants who arrived after that date are barred from all means-tested, federally funded public benefits for the first five years they are in the country. After five years states can, at their discretion, offer Medicaid to immigrants. Accordingly, aged, blind, and disabled immigrants are not categorically eligible for Medicaid. There are exceptions made for persons who have worked for 40 quarters in covered employment or served in the military. States cannot deny coverage of emergency medical services to either illegal or legal aliens.

• Illegal immigrants are barred from the following federal public benefits: (1) grants, contracts, loans, and licenses; and (2) retirement, welfare, health, disability, public or assisted housing, post-secondary education, food assistance, and unemployment benefits.

• SSI eligibility was tightened for children. The new standard eliminated the comparable severity standard, the individual functional assessment, and references to maladaptive behavior. Children can qualify for SSI only if they have "a medically determinable physical or mental impairment which results in marked and severe functional limitations."

• The Food Stamp Program retained its structure as an uncapped individual entitlement. However, Food Stamp Program benefits were limited to three months every three years for unemployed able-bodied single adults aged 18 to 50. An additional three months of eligibility was granted to adults who were laid off from their jobs.

• Child support collection efforts were strengthened through a number of provisions. First, one condition for receiving assistance is that families must assign child support collection rights to the state.[40] Second, states must operate automated centralized collection and disbursement units. Third, noncustodial parents who are $5,000 or more in arrears are subject to passport revocation. Fourth, states must accord full faith and credit to out-of-state child support orders and liens. Federal income withholding, liens, and subpoena forms must be used for interstate cases. Fifth, states must have laws in effect that establish authority to withhold, suspend, or restrict drivers, professional, occupational, and recreational licenses of individuals who owe overdue support. Other provisions include automated state directories of new hires, expansion of income withholding requirements, access to locator information networks such as that of law enforcement, use of Social Security numbers on licenses and other government-issued documents, and expedited **establishment of paternity**.[41]

The conservative 104th Congress effectively pushed through the passage of the PRWORA. The rapidly approaching presidential election also may have played a role, especially since former President Clinton had already vetoed a similar welfare reform bill in January 1996. The rhetorical slogans of the 1992 Clinton presidential campaign, calling for "an end to welfare as we know it" and "two years and off to work," were viewed by the public as endorsements of the distaste for AFDC. Frances Fox Piven argues that Clinton's rhetoric created a maelstrom of which he eventually lost control. Moreover, by the time Clinton signed the PRWORA, he had already approved draconian state waivers that were in some cases even more punitive than TANF.[42]

State Welfare Reform Waivers

Radical welfare reform was well under way even before the PRWORA became law. In fact, Clinton had granted 43 state waivers during his first term, more than all previous administrations combined. By mid-1996, 43 of the 50 states had approved or pending AFDC waivers that incorporated many of the TANF reforms. Pointing to the flood of AFDC waivers signed by the Clinton administration, the Enterprise Institute's Douglas Besharov observed, "Based on what happened in the last year, President Clinton can justifiably claim that he has ended welfare as we know it." Besharov, describing the waiver requests as "welfare reform on the cheap without an increase in spending for child care or a penny for job training," concluded that "the revolutionary result is an end to personal entitlement."[43] Along with a robust economy, state waivers that included time limits, benefit cuts, and widespread sanctions for disapproved behaviors had already resulted in a 10 percent drop in the AFDC rolls in 1996.

Has the PRWORA Worked?

Both Democrats and Republicans have pronounced the PRWORA a raging success. They point to the dramatic decline in welfare caseloads—60 percent for individuals and 53 percent for families—since the passage of the PRWORA in 1996. The number of white families on welfare showed the steepest decline, falling by 63 percent; the number of African American families fell by 52 percent; and the number of Hispanic families by 44 percent.[44] Despite this drop, important questions remain. First, caseloads had already begun to drop—from a high of 5 million

in 1994 to 4.5 million in 1996. These declines occurred before the PRWORA was fully in effect. Second, other factors such as the strong labor market in the 1990s and changes in welfare policy help explain the drop in caseloads. In the late 1990s the nation was in the midst of the longest peacetime expansion in its history, with low unemployment and rising wages. Because of this, gains in employment and wages were experienced by groups with typically high rates of welfare use. Third, it is difficult to ascertain the success of the PRWORA because it has been largely in effect during a strong economic period. For example, beginning in mid-2001 caseloads rose in 28 states, most likely because of the weakening economy. In 2003 caseloads began dropping again (3 percent for individuals and 1.8 percent for families).[45] However, this drop occurred during a period of rising poverty rates and higher unemployment, suggesting that a large number of people were either discouraged from receiving public assistance, or their time limit had ran out. Perhaps more importantly, this trend broke the traditional link between increased need and increased welfare spending.

There are three primary avenues for leaving TANF: (1) voluntary termination because of employment, marriage, and so forth; (2) reaching the end of the federal or state time limit; and (3) being terminated for failure to comply with work or administrative rules. Research on TANF has found the following:

- Most recipients leaving public assistance (50 to 60 percent) take jobs that pay just over minimum wage. Because of this, many low-income families continue to receive some form of public assistance, such as food stamps. Between 2001 and 2006 the percentage of households receiving food stamps increased from 47.4 percent to 55.6 percent.[46]

- Families that left welfare in 2001 or earlier were more likely than those leaving after this period to find employment. Employment of recent leavers increased between 20 and 30 percent between 1996 and 2001. However, an Urban Institute report found that even though 54.5 percent of former TANF recipients were employed in 2000, by 2005 this had decreased to 39.3 percent.[47]

- Families that remained on TANF welfare also experienced a decline in employment status after the first five years of reform. In 2000, 31 percent of families were employed but by 2005 this had fallen to 24.5 percent. Only some of this decline can be attributed to increased (4 percent) school attendance.[48]

- Former TANF recipient families have not done well when it comes to average family income, with such income having decreased significantly over time. The average income in 2005 was $22,733, a decrease of $2,795 per annum from the average $25,528 in 2000.[49]

- An Urban Institute report also shows that there has been an increase in the health barriers to work of former welfare recipients. In 2000, 13.1 percent of former recipients had a health condition that limited their work; however, by 2005 this had increased 2.8 percent to 15.9 percent. There has also been a decrease in the number of former recipients who have own-employer health insurance. In 2000, this was 26.3 percent; however, by 2005 only 21.8 percent had insurance, a decrease of 4.5 percent.[50]

Arguably, too much emphasis is placed on caseload reduction and insufficient attention is paid to income and poverty outcomes. Between 2000 and 2003, the number and percentage of single mothers living in poverty increased while the percentage of single mothers with jobs fell. At the same time, poverty among children rose, and the number of children living below half of the poverty line increased by nearly one million. In response to this increase in poverty and need, the number of families receiving food stamps and Medicaid rose. The number of poor families receiving TANF cash assistance, however, continued to fall, and it provided assistance to 845,000 fewer people in 2003 than in 2000. The former Bush administration portrays TANF's lower caseloads as a positive development and suggested that unemployment insurance was replacing TANF. Even if this was true, fewer than 2 out of every 100 poor, single-mother families were lifted out of poverty by the unemployment insurance program in 2003.[51]

The Deficit Reduction Act of 2005

On February 8, 2006, former President Bush signed The Deficit Reduction Act (DRA) of 2005 that, among other things, reauthorized the TANF program. The DRA strengthened work requirements, shifted the base year for measuring work-related progress from 1996 to 2005, and authorized the use of $150 million of the TANF block grants to be used to sustain and support Healthy Marriage

programs. Up to $50 million of that money was eligible to support Responsible Fatherhood programs.[52]

The final rules were promulgated by the Department of Health and Human Services on June 29, 2006, and significantly modified work-eligible definitions. The all-families work participation requirement for each state remained at 50 percent and the two-parent requirement remained at 90 percent; however, shifting the base year from 1996 to 2005 meant that there would be far fewer allowances permitted for states to remain in compliance with work eligibility rules. Furthermore, even sanctioned or otherwise ineligible adults living with TANF-eligible children would be required to be included in the work eligibility determination. Documentation of work eligible hours has been restricted as well. For example, job search, vocational training, community service, and unpaid work experience not only must meet strict documentation standards, but they also must be "supervised daily."[53] Failure to meet work eligibility requirements potentially subjects states to a retroactive financial penalty that can become as large as 21 percent of the State Family Assistance Grant through which states receive the federal funding for TANF.[54]

With the TANF reauthorization included in the DRA, it could be said that the conversion of welfare to workfare was nearing completion. Prior to DRA, less than half of the families with children who qualified were receiving TANF benefits,[55] and the number would surely drop under the new administrative rules. Unfortunately, few of the families that left TANF have also left poverty. States have little choice but to direct the majority of TANF funds toward work programs even at the expense of providing supportive income and services to recipients facing serious barriers to employment due to mental or physical disability, substance abuse, and unstable housing.[56]

Supplemental Security Income (SSI)

SSI is designed to provide cash assistance to the elderly and to disabled poor individuals, including children. Although a public assistance program, SSI is administered by the Social Security Administration.

The SSI program at the end of 2007 was serving 7.36 million people at a cost of over $3.7 billion in monthly benefits.[57] Unlike OASDI, SSI is a means-tested, federally administered public assistance program funded through general revenue taxes. Unlike TANF, the basic SSI payment level is adjusted annually for inflation. A portion of elderly people receive SSI in conjunction with Social Security. Age is not an eligibility criterion for SSI, and children may receive benefits under the disabled or blind portion of the act. Among others, the following people are eligible for SSI: (1) mentally retarded individuals, (2) people at least 65 years old who have little or no income, (3) the legally blind, (4) disabled adults with a physical or mental impairment expected to last for at least 12 months, (5) the visually impaired who do not meet the criteria for blindness, (6) drug addicts and alcoholics entering treatment, and (7) children under age 18 who have a severe impairment comparable to that of an eligible adult. Of the persons receiving federally administered SSI payments in 2006, over 1.2 million were aged, nearly 6 million disabled, and over 73,000 with blindness. However, nearly 790,000 of those receiving benefits on the basis of disability or blindness were also over the age of 65.[58]

To qualify for SSI, an applicant must have limited resources. In 2008, SSI applicants were allowed to own resources valued at less than $2,000 for an individual and $3,000 for a couple (excluding, e.g., a house; a car, depending on use and value; burial plots; and certain forms of insurance). These resource limits are set by statute, are not adjusted to allow for inflation, and have not changed since 1989. SSI benefits are not generous, although they can be higher than TANF benefits. In December 2006, the average monthly federal benefit was $423. The maximum payment for an individual in 2008 was $637 a month; for a couple, it was $936 a month.[59]

The SSI program began during the Nixon administration. When Richard Nixon took office in 1972, he attempted to streamline the welfare system by proposing a Family Assistance Plan (FAP) that included a guaranteed annual income replacing AFDC, Old Age Assistance (OAA), Aid to the Blind (AB), and Aid to the Permanently and Totally Disabled (APTD). Although Congress rejected the overall plan, the OAA, AB, and APTD programs were federalized in 1972 under a new program— Supplemental Security Income—with the federal government taking over the operation of those programs from state governments. No longer would state governments set eligibility levels, establish minimum payment levels, or administer the programs.

In 1974 there were 3.25 million SSI recipients; by 2007 that number had more than doubled to 7.4 million. Concomitantly, SSI expenditures increased from $5 billion in 1974 to more than $44 billion in 2007. In large part these increases resulted from the rapid growth in the numbers of disabled persons receiving SSI, a population that rose from 2.4 million in 1984 to over 6 million in 2006.[60]

Two groups of SSI recipients that have shown dramatic growth in their numbers are children with disabilities and adults with disabilities relating to drug addiction and alcoholism. One reason for this growth was the Supreme Court's decision in the *Sullivan v. Zebley* case that made children eligible for SSI if they had a disability that was comparable to that of an eligible adult. Children are now the fastest-growing population on SSI, and by 2006, 858,917 children were recipients. Of those children, 17.9 percent were mentally retarded and 8.6 percent had diseases of the nervous system or organs.[61]

The other group of SSI recipients that have drawn attention are individuals whose drug or alcohol addiction (DAA) is the primary contributing factor in their disability. Between 1980 and 1994, the number of DAA recipients on SSI rose from 23,000 to 86,000, bringing the number to more than 250,000. By 1994, this group cost the federal government $1.4 billion.[62]

As a response to SSI's rapid growth, Congress passed the Social Security Independence and Program Improvements Act in 1994, which, among other things, restricted SSI and Disability Insurance benefits to individuals disabled by drug and alcohol addiction. The new restrictions required SSI beneficiaries with a DAA diagnosis to participate in a substance abuse program. In addition, beneficiaries (except those for whom treatment was not available) would receive benefits for only 36 months. Beneficiaries removed from the SSI rolls would continue to receive Medicare or Medicaid unless they failed to comply with their treatment program for 12 successive months.[63] In addition, the law established a Commission on Childhood Disabilities to reevaluate the SSI definition for childhood disability and to look into possible alternative definitions.[64]

Major concerns regarding SSI involve the low level of income and the stringent requirements for eligibility. SSI payments are so low that, as of 2008, all but seven states and jurisdictions provide some form of optional state supplementation. States that provide no supplement are Arkansas, Kansas, Mississippi, North Dakota, Commonwealth of the Northern Mariana Islands, Tennessee, and West Virginia.[65] States may choose to set their own requirements for supplementary SSI payments, thereby including only certain beneficiaries or limiting disabilities. Stringent eligibility requirements and red tape have kept many people off the SSI rolls. For example, SSI cases are reviewed every three years (a process that usually involves a medical review), and "continuing disability reviews" may be required. Some critics believe that the federal government has purposely made entrance and continued maintenance in SSI difficult to discourage participation. Moreover, only couples receiving a combination of SSI, Social Security, and food stamps are raised to or above the poverty line. In 2008 an individual who received SSI was raised to only 73.5 percent of the poverty threshold, and couples were raised to 81.9 percent (see Table 11.1).

Table 11.1

TANF Work Participation Rates

Fiscal Year	Percentages
Work Participation for All Families	
1997	25
1998	30
1999	35
2000	40
2001	45
2002 and beyond	50
Work Participation for Two-Parent Families	
1997	75
1998	75
1999 and beyond	90

Source: Mark Greenberg and Sharon Parrott, "Summary of TANF Work Participation Provisions in the Budget Reconciliation Bill," Center on Budget and Policy Priorities and Center for Law and Social Policy, January 9, 2006.

General Assistance

General assistance (GA) programs, also known as General Relief programs in some states, are cash and in-kind assistance programs financed and administered entirely by the state, county, or locality in which they are located. They are designed to meet the short-term or ongoing needs of low-income persons ineligible for (or awaiting approval for) federally funded assistance such as Temporary Assistance for Needy Families (TANF) or Supplemental Security Income (SSI). Most states limit GA eligibility to the severely poor, without children. Although income eligibility varies across states, a majority of state GA programs limit assistance to only those with incomes less than half the poverty level. Most states set resource limits between $1,000 and $2,000, regardless of family size. However, states generally disregard some earned income and certain resources (e.g., a home and a car) in determining eligibility.[66]

The GA program in Minnesota in 2008, for example, acts as the primary safety net for single adults and childless couples. It provides monthly cash grants for vulnerable persons whose net income is less than $203 per month for singles and $260 for couples and whose resources are less than $1,000. GA participants are also eligible for help with medical costs through the General Assistance Medical Care (GAMC) or the Medical Assistance (MA) programs and Food Support. Program participants in Minnesota must fit at least one of the 15 categories of eligibility specified in state statutes which are primarily defined in terms of disability and unemployability. Most applicants and recipients are required to apply for benefits from federally funded disability programs for which they may qualify, such as Retirement, Survivors, and Disability Insurance or SSI. The maximum benefit for a single adult in Minnesota is $203 per month and for a married couple is $260 per month. Special funding is available for emergency situations when a person or family lacks basic need items, such as a lack of shelter or food, and threatens the person's or family's health or safety. In fiscal year 2003, an average of 11,600 people per month at a total cost of $28.4 million for the year were assisted in Minnesota under GA.[67]

Although states are generally responsible for GA, some devolve responsibility and administration to their counties. California is a good example of a state that does this. It describes its GA program as being designed to provide relief and support to indigent adults who are not supported by their own means, other public funds, or assistance programs. GA in each one of California's counties is established and 100 percent funded by its own board of supervisors. As the state is not involved in this program, benefits, payment levels, and eligibility requirements vary among each of the 58 counties.[68]

In Los Angeles county, GA is called General Relief Opportunities for Work (GROW). It is not simply a matter of signing a form and receiving financial assistance but seen as a pathway to employment. An Employment Needs Evaluation is conducted to identify job readiness and barriers to employment. The interview is conducted at application by an employment specialist, a designated eligibility worker. The evaluation is later reviewed by a GROW case manager during an orientation and job skills assessment. People who do not attend the evaluation have their application denied. Applicants also attend a half-day motivational component that provides them with an overview of the program and its services.[69]

Some states administer GA programs at the state or county level, and others delegate this responsibility to individual municipalities or towns. This is the case in Maine. Each town has a GA program to help people in emergencies where people contact their town office. Skyrocketing oil prices in 2008 led to a huge increase in people seeking GA. In 2001 Mainers paid just $1.33 for a gallon of home heating oil. In 2008 they paid an average $3.37. In some towns in Knox County, the budget could be as low as $500 per year due to the minimal two or three requests per year. In recent years, however, demand for GA has increased by 300 to 500 percent.[70] In 2007 $6.45 million was disbursed by the state for GA, an increase of almost $1 million from the previous year.[71]

Trends and Issues in Public Assistance

The basic principle underlying the PRWORA was transferring the responsibility for managing social programs from Washington to the states. Promoted early by the Reagan administration, this ideological perspective has been labeled the "devolution revolution" or the "new federalism."[72] Energized by the omnipresent cry of "states' rights," the new federalism trades off long-term and stable federal funding for increased state control through block grants.

The responsibility of states to care for their poor is not new. In part, it was the failure of states to meet that responsibility that originally led to the creation of the 1935 Social Security Act, legislation that federalized most state public assistance and social insurance programs. Devolving welfare responsibility to the states is neither new nor novel. Nevertheless, the question remains: If states were unable to mount compassionate social welfare programs before 1935, why should they do so today, especially in difficult economic times?

Transforming Public Assistance Policy into Labor Policy

It can be argued that income maintenance programs should be housed under the Secretary of Labor rather than the Secretary of Health and Human Services. Beginning almost 30 years ago, the transformation of public assistance policy into labor policy reached fruition with the passage of the PRWORA, essentially a labor policy clothed in welfare terminology.

AFDC had been a sore spot for conservatives since its inception. This antagonism persisted even though in 1995 combined AFDC and food stamps costs accounted for only 3 percent of the federal budget compared to 22 percent for Social Security, 18 percent for defense, and 10 percent for Medicare.[73] The real concern about public assistance was not about excessive spending; instead, it was a reaction to AFDC as a symbol of governmental responsibility to provide a cash proxy for labor market earnings. The very existence of AFDC was a thorn in the side of economic conservatives because it implied that the marketplace was somehow incapable of meeting the needs of all Americans.

Early federal attempts to transition recipients into the labor force were stillborn for several reasons. For one, between 1979 and 1994 the average wages of the lowest 30 percent of U.S. wage earners decreased by 12 percent.[74] The infusion of 3 or more million unskilled former welfare recipients into the labor force would have resulted in greater job competition and an even steeper drop in wages. Moreover, high unemployment rates in the late 1970s and early 1980s led to an oversupply of labor resulting in little incentive to drive more workers into the labor market. On the contrary, sound public policy dictated that more people be kept out of the workforce to not further aggravate unemployment. Hence, the conservative preference for labor market employment over public assistance was held in abeyance by the economic realities of the period.

A unique confluence of events came together in 1996 to complete the transformation of public assistance into labor policy. Frustrated by repeated failures of federal welfare-to-work efforts and the ignominious death of the FSA, the newly elected conservative 104th Congress was determined not to repeat past mistakes. First and foremost was to disentitle public assistance. Second, the PRWORA removed the fiscal responsibility of government to provide income support to public assistance recipients beyond a five-year lifetime cap. The Clinton welfare reform panel's proposed safety net (i.e., government as employer of the last resort) was eliminated. Under the PRWORA, the only option for those who exhaust their benefits is labor market participation or penury.

The PRWORA was passed in a period of robust economic growth. In 1996, the unemployment rate was 4.5 percent and the economy was growing steadily at over 2.5 percent a year.[75] The low unemployment rate combined with a strong economy meant that the 138-million-member U.S. labor force could easily absorb the 4.2 million AFDC recipients without driving down wages or increasing unemployment. The economic giddiness of the mid-1990s reinforced the conservative belief that a job existed for anyone who wanted it.

Removing the federal responsibility for providing long-term cash assistance to the poor shifted the problem of poor support away from social welfare and into labor policy. The PRWORA represented the culmination of the long-standing conservative goal of deracinating public assistance: When the poor exhaust time-limited public assistance benefits, they become a labor market rather than a welfare problem. With that change, U.S. public assistance policy became a short-term, transitional step in the march toward the full labor market participation of the poor.

The conservative push toward labor policy is not entirely without merit. First, one would be hard-pressed to argue that a well-paying job with full benefits is not the best antipoverty program. Moreover, Sweden—historically considered a progressive welfare state—has frequently used labor policy as a proxy for aggressive public assistance programs.[76] Second, the push toward workforce participation is congruent with current labor market trends for women. For instance, in 1955 only 18 percent of all U.S. mothers with children under age six were in the labor force. By 1985 that number rose to 54 percent, and by 2002, it was 64.1 percent.[77] Given these trends, welfare advocates are hard-pressed to justify non-employment-based public assistance programs when more than three-fifths of all mothers with children under age six are in the labor force. Despite these conservative arguments, the absence of sound federal labor policy, a lack of guaranteed health care insurance, and few workplace protections have resulted in most former recipients going from the frying pan into the fire. Many former recipients now occupying secondary labor market jobs face an even shakier economic future than under tainted AFDC policies.

Despite some positive gains, the substitution of labor policy for public assistance policy has led to serious problems. For one, the absence of sound labor policy rewards low-wage employers while punishing low-income workers forced into poorly paid dead-end jobs that provide little, if any, benefits. Specifically, low-wage employers are rewarded by not being required to provide employees with a minimum number of hours, benefits, or employment perks. These employers are subsidized by not having to pay the requisite salary to support a worker and his or her family. In effect, low-wage employers are subsidized by the earned income tax credit (EITC), child tax credit, food stamps, Medicaid, and the Child Health Insurance Program (CHIPs), which partially make up the shortfall between low salaries and the real cost of living. For example, combined EITC and food stamp benefits alone can provide a maximum yearly supplement of $9,600 for a family of four, or almost the $10,000 minimum wage earned by a single worker.

Data from employer surveys administered in several large metropolitan areas suggest that in a severe recession, job vacancy rates decline by two-thirds or more, and by somewhat less in a milder recession.[78] Accordingly, the new hire and employment rate of former welfare recipients is expected to decline by large amounts as well. At the same time, many unemployed low-income workers will be ineligible for TANF once they have exhausted their lifetime limits. In addition, neither TANF nor unemployment insurance benefits will be available to many noncustodial fathers whose contributions to family income are crucial. This is especially problematic because the labor market experiences of low-income noncustodial fathers generally improved much less than those of single mothers in recent years.[79]

Compelling former recipients to become engaged in the workforce by way of a lifetime benefit cap will not ensure permanent labor force attachment, especially if the economy exhibits weakness. According to the U.S. Census Bureau, the poverty rate rose from 11.3 percent in 2000 to 12.3 percent in 2006, after dropping for four consecutive years. The number of poor families also increased from 6.4 million in 2000 (or 8.7 percent of all families, a record low rate) to 7.7 million (9.8 percent) in 2006.[80]

The transition from public assistance to labor policy does not bode well for the "hard to employ," a group of recipients that have significant barriers to employment and difficulty in finding and sustaining work. Some of these barriers include substance abuse, physical disabilities, domestic violence, learning disabilities, mental health issues, language barriers, chronic health problems, and multiple barriers.[81] Many of these recipients who have been exempted from work participation under the former AFDC program are now subject to work requirements under PRWORA.

No single policy will ensure that former recipients maintain a viable attachment to the workforce. And, no single measure will compensate for the lack of a comprehensive labor policy for low-income workers. David Stoesz sums up the dilemma: "Welfare reform that offers the welfare-poor an opportunity to become the working-poor is no *real* reform at all. The challenge that remains is to devise policies that will accelerate the upward mobility of welfare families so that they can partake in the American dream."[82] Family composition affects welfare receipt, which, in turn, is strongly influenced by teenage pregnancy.

Teenage Pregnancy

Teenage birthrates in this country have declined steadily since 1991. Although this is good news, teen birthrates in the United States nevertheless remain high, exceeding those in most developed countries. For example, U.S. rates are nearly twice as high as those in England and Wales or Canada, and nine times as high as those in the Netherlands or Japan:

- More than 10 percent of all U.S. births in 2004 were to mothers under age 20. Most teenage births (about 67 percent) are to girls aged 18 and 19.

- More than 750,000 teenagers become pregnant each year, and about 420,000 give birth. About 3 in 10 teenage girls become pregnant at least once before age 20.

- The teenage birthrate is declining. Between 1991 and 2004, the rate fell by one-third (from 61.8 per 1,000 women to 41.1). Still, in 2004, about 4 teenage girls in 100 had a baby.

- Between 22 and 30 percent of teen mothers under age 18 have a second baby within two years after the birth of their first baby.

- Teen mothers are more likely than mothers over age 20 to give birth prematurely (before 37 completed weeks of pregnancy). Between 2002 and 2004, preterm birthrates averaged 14.3 percent for women under age 20 compared to 11.7 percent for women ages 20 to 29. Babies born too soon face an increased risk of newborn health problems, long-term disabilities, and even death.

- Teen mothers are more likely to drop out of high school than girls who delay childbearing. Only 40 percent of teenagers who have children before age 18 go on to graduate from high

Although teenage birthrates in the United States have declined, they still remain high, exceeding those in most developed countries.

school, compared to 75 percent of teens from similar social and economic backgrounds who do not give birth until age 20 or 21.

- Teen mothers are more likely to live in poverty than women who delay childbearing, and more than 75 percent of all unmarried teen mothers go on welfare within five years of the birth of their first child.[83]

Out-of-wedlock births have grave economic consequences. This is especially true because teenage mothers, regardless of their income, are now more likely to keep their children.[84] The high out-of- wedlock birthrate translates into important economic realities. For one, teenage mothers are twice as likely to be poor as are nonteen mothers, and a teenage mother earns only half the lifetime wage of a woman who waits until she is 20 to have her first child.[85] Second, as mentioned above, a strong correlation exists between young single motherhood and high welfare dependency. Mothers with children age three and under are at the greatest risk of long-term welfare dependency. According to the Brookings Institute, teenage childbearing cost U.S. taxpayers $7 billion a year.[86] Moreover, teen mothers who grew up on public assistance were more than twice as likely to be dependent on welfare themselves.[87]

Although numerous programs have been developed to reduce teenage pregnancy, evaluations of these attempts have shown mixed results. One early teen pregnancy prevention program was Project Redirection. From 1980 to 1982, 805 AFDC-eligible mothers aged 17 or younger received intensive services to optimize educational, employment, and life management skills. Evaluation of Project Redirection mothers one, two, and five years after their participation in the program was mixed. Project Redirection teens fared no better than the control group in obtaining a high school diploma or GED certificate. Although participants were more likely to be employed one year after exiting the program, their weekly earnings five years later were only $23 more than those in the control group. Five years later, the household income of the control group exceeded that of the Project Redirection group by $19. Two years after participation, 7 percent of Project Redirection teens were on welfare; five years later, 10 percent fewer of the control group were on welfare. Regarding childbearing, Project Redirection teens reported fewer pregnancies in the first and second years after the program; yet five years after

the program, they exceeded the control group in their number of pregnancies as well as their number of live births. Researchers concluded that "the program impacts were largely transitory."[88]

From 1989 to 1992 researchers randomly assigned 2,322 poor young mothers, ages 16 to 22, either to New Chance—a program through which the women received health, education, and welfare assistance coordinated by a case manager—or to a control group that received no special services. At the 18-month follow-up, the experimental group fared worse than the control group in two important respects. First, New Chance mothers were less likely to be using contraception, were more likely to become pregnant, and were more likely to abort their pregnancies than the control group. Second, participants were less likely to be working after entering the program; were earning less; and, during the fourth to the sixth months, were more likely to be on public assistance.[89] To compound matters, New Chance cost $5,073 per participant, excluding child care. (If child care were included, an average of $7,646 was spent.)[90]

Not surprisingly, the antiteen pregnancy movement is highly politicized. On one side are those who support comprehensive sex education that promotes abstinence as an alternative but includes information about contraception and condoms. On the other side are those who favor abstinence-only-until-marriage programs that promote abstinence from sexual activity outside marriage as the expected standard of behavior. Proponents of abstinence-only programs believe that providing information about the benefits of condoms or contraception contradicts the message of abstinence and undermines its impact. As such, abstinence-only programs provide no information about contraception beyond failure rates. Included in the 1996 PRWORA was a provision (later set out in Title V of the Social Security Act) that appropriated $250 million over five years for state initiatives that promote sexual abstinence outside of marriage as the only acceptable standard of behavior for young people. From 1998 to 2003, almost a half a billion dollars in state and federal funds were used to support the Title V initiative. The findings of 11 states with evaluations that were available in 2003 showed few short-term benefits and no lasting, positive impact. Specifically, abstinence-only programs showed little evidence of sustained (long-term) impact on attitudes and intentions. Worse, they showed some negative impacts on the willingness of participants to use contraception, including condoms, to prevent untoward sexual health outcomes. Only in one state did any program demonstrate any short-term success in delaying the initiation of sex and none of the programs demonstrated evidence of long-term success in delaying sexual activity among adolescents.[91] The apparent failure of these prevention programs illustrates how little policymakers understand the motivation and the behaviors associated with teenage pregnancy. It also illustrates how little is known about the interpersonal, social, and cultural components that lead to teenage pregnancy.

Welfare Behaviorism

Behavioral Poverty   The TANF program is predicated on a form of **welfare behaviorism:** an attempt to reprogram the behaviors of the poor. Current welfare reform efforts, however, are unlikely to deliver on the promises of this approach. Despite data demonstrating the marginal economic benefits of making welfare conditional, conservatives effectively leveraged a moral argument that public policy should change the behavior of the welfare poor. By the mid-1980s, conservative theorists had arrived at a new consensus on poverty; namely, that although the liberally inspired public assistance programs might once have been appropriate for the "cash poor," they were counterproductive for the "behaviorally poor."[92] As poverty programs expanded, conservatives contended, the social dysfunctions of the behaviorally poor metastasized: Beginning as teen mothers, women dominated family life, ultimately becoming generationally dependent on welfare; young men dropped out of school, failed to pursue legitimate employment, and resorted to sexual escapades and repetitive crime to demonstrate prowess; children, lacking adult role models of effective parents at home and capable workers on the job, promised to further populate the underclass.

Conservatives differed in how to respond to behavioral poverty. In *Losing Ground,* Charles Murray suggested "scrapping the entire federal welfare and income support structure for working-aged persons."[93] Not long after, Lawrence Mead offered a less draconian measure in *Beyond Entitlement:* Make receipt of public aid contingent on conventional behaviors, particularly work.[94] Eventually, both prescriptions were to be incorporated in

welfare policy. Following Mead's admonition, TANF required recipients to participate in work-related activities. As states secured federal waivers for "experiments," welfare mothers often had to meet a number of other requirements or risk losing aid: Through "Learnfare" children on public assistance had to demonstrate regular school attendance; through the family cap additional assistance for children born after a mother became eligible for assistance would be denied, inducing family planning; the establishment of paternity was required before a child could receive benefits, so as to enable the state to pursue child support; as a method for protecting public health, recipient children were required to have immunizations in order to attend school; to dissuade teenagers from becoming pregnant, states required teen mothers to live with their parents in order to receive welfare.[95]

The ending of the 60-year federal entitlement to an income floor for poor families has had extensive political fallout. Die-hard conservatives justified the termination of welfare with George Gilder's contention that what the poor needed most was "the spur of their own poverty,"[96] and "compassionate conservatives" found a rationale in "tough love." Either way, conservative welfare reformers conceded that terminating benefits would probably worsen deprivation but argued that was necessary.

Personal and Parental Responsibility   The welfare behaviorism inherent in TANF reflects a belief in the importance of personal and parental responsibility. This philosophy harks back to supposedly traditional "Main Street" values of self-reliance, independence, and individual responsibility. It is based on the idea that the United States offers a level playing field replete with abundant economic and social opportunities. It also includes a de facto belief in the limited role of government.

The view of parental responsibility reflected in the PRWORA focuses on several themes: (1) fathers who beget children have a responsibility to financially support them; (2) mothers requesting public aid have a responsibility to establish paternity for the purpose of collecting child support; (3) mothers who have physical custody of children have a responsibility to provide for them financially through work efforts; (4) custodial parents have a responsibility to ensure that their children receive and appropriately respond to educational opportunities; and (5) custodial parents have a responsibility to provide basic public health protection for their children, including immunizations. These tenets of parenthood are neither extreme nor especially controversial. In fact, they are in part the glue that holds society together. Controversy arises, then, not on the correctness of these values but in their operationalization. More specifically, significant controversy surrounds the question of whether attempts at engineering appropriate social behaviors are successful or whether they simply function as punishment.

Examples of social engineering as social punishment abound. Learnfare, introduced in Wisconsin in the fall of 1988, targeted teenagers who had more than two unexcused absences from school. Under Learnfare sanctions, such absences would cause the family's AFDC benefits for a dependent teen to be reduced by $77 a month; for an independent teen with a child, the penalty was $190 a month. Wisconsin officials contended that such sanctions would result in the return of 80 percent of teens on AFDC who had dropped out of school. Rhetoric notwithstanding, an independent agency's subsequent evaluation of the Milwaukee demonstration "did not show improvement in student attendance that could be attributed to the Learnfare requirement." Undeterred, state officials wrote to the evaluators and demanded that they suppress the parts of the study detailing the failure of Learnfare to enhance teen school attendance. When the researchers refused, Wisconsin officials canceled the contract, in the process impugning the professionalism of the evaluators.[97]

In Ohio another demonstration program promised teens a $62-a-month carrot for good school attendance, coupled with a $62-a-month penalty (stick) for truancy. Three years after the program's inception, LEAP (Learning, Earning, and Parenting) was heralded as a major victory in the battle against teen truancy. A closer examination of the LEAP evaluation was not encouraging. The glowing results were reported only for teens currently enrolled in school and excluded those who had dropped out, even though both groups were part of the study's population. Including dropouts, LEAP's outcomes plummeted: The number completing high school was not 20 but 6.5 percent; the number employed was not 40 but 20 percent. Because of the benefit reduction sanction levied against truant teens, a significant number of all mothers in the study reported "diminished spending on essentials for their families, especially clothing and food."[98] In their concluding observations, evaluators conceded that

changing adolescent behavior is difficult and admitted that LEAP produced some "perverse effects."[99]

Another issue underlying the new welfare reforms involves (re)marriage. According to several studies, no more than a fifth of mothers voluntarily leave public assistance as a result of earnings increases; most exits result from a change in marital status.[100] Yet public assistance programs punish marriage in two ways: (1) by how they treat a married couple with children, and (2) by how they treat families with stepparents. First, a needy two-parent family with children is less likely to be eligible for aid than a one-parent family. Although the nonincapacitated two-parent family can apply for TANF, many states' restrictions involving work expectation and time limits make the program inaccessible to many poor families. Second, a stepparent has no legal obligation to support the children of his or her spouse in most states. Nevertheless, TANF cuts or limits benefits when a woman remarries by counting much of the stepparent's income when calculating the family's countable income, thus jeopardizing the mother's eligibility status.[101] In effect, there is a strong economic disincentive for a low-income woman to marry a man with low earnings. According to the Heritage Foundation's Robert Rector:

> The current welfare system has made marriage economically irrational for most low-income parents. Welfare has converted the low-income working husband from a necessary breadwinner into a net financial handicap. It has transformed marriage from a legal institution designed to protect and nurture children into an institution which financially penalizes nearly all low-income parents who enter into it. Across the nation, the current welfare system has all but destroyed family structure in the inner city. Welfare establishes strong financial disincentives, effectively blocking the formation of intact, two-parent families.[102]

Welfare to Work

TANF is predicated on the long-standing belief that recipients should be moved off public assistance and into private employment as quickly as possible. Whereas conservatives argue that paid work is the best antipoverty program, some liberals have asserted that child rearing is also a productive form of work. These pro-welfare liberals have contended that although it is socially acceptable for middle-class mothers to stay at home with young children, poor mothers are considered lazy and unmotivated if they do the same.

Workfare programs have been a constant feature of the welfare landscape since 1967, when new AFDC amendments were added to pressure recipient mothers into working. As part of those new rules, work requirements became mandatory for unemployed fathers, mothers, and certain teenagers. AFDC recipients who were deemed employable and yet refused to work could be terminated.[103] A work incentive program (WIN) was developed to provide training and employment for all welfare mothers considered employable (recipients with preschool-age children were exempt). Day care was made available to facilitate the WIN program. Partly because of a lackluster federal commitment (in 1985 the total federal contribution to WIN was only $258 million), the performance of work programs was generally disappointing. In addition, many states were reluctant to enact mandatory job requirements, because they believed that enforcing them would prove more costly than simply maintaining families on AFDC.

Workfare again resurfaced in 1988 when it formed the backbone of the Family Support Act. By the early 1990s, however, the Manpower Demonstration Research Corporation (MDRC) had amassed considerable evidence about the performance of state welfare-to-work programs, and the results fell far short of what supporters had promised. Out of 13 welfare-to-work programs evaluated in 1991, most boosted participants' earnings little more than $700 per year. Although most programs also experienced reductions in AFDC payments, these were modest and typically less than $400 a year. Significantly, in only two programs were AFDC payment reductions greater than the programs' cost per welfare-to-work participant.[104]

For welfare reform researchers, the welfare-to-work bandwagon was less of a star-spangled apparatus than its proponents had made it out to be. Before his assignment to the Clinton working panel on welfare reform, Harvard's David Ellwood admitted as much, writing that the typical welfare-to-work program increased earnings between $250 and $750 per year. "Most work-welfare programs look like decent investments," he concluded, "but no carefully evaluated work-welfare programs have done more than put a tiny dent in the welfare caseloads, even though they have been received with enthusiasm."[105] A similar sentiment was expressed by workfare expert Judith Gueron:

> [Although] welfare-to-work programs have paid off by increasing the employment and earnings of single mothers and reducing their receipt of public

assistance . . . MDRC's research also reveals the limits of past interventions. Whether the targeted group were welfare mothers, low-income youth who dropped out of high school, teenage parents with limited prospects, or unemployed adult men, the programs had little success in boosting people out of poverty. . . . Often, welfare recipients who get jobs join the ranks of the working poor.[106]

If the reality of welfare-to-work diverges from the rhetoric of welfare reform, it is because of the assumption that TANF mothers are so welfare dependent that they have no experience with the labor market. In fact, many mothers have worked and have, as a result, come to see welfare benefits as a form of unemployment or underemployment assistance. To explain the relationship between work and welfare, labor economist Michael Piore split workers into primary and secondary labor markets. As explained earlier, workers in the primary labor market hold down salaried jobs that include health and vacation benefits, are full time, and incorporate a career track. Workers in the secondary labor market work for hourly wages—often at the minimum wage—without benefits in jobs that are part time or seasonal and are not part of a career track.

Other research has captured the erratic relationship between work and welfare for many mothers on TANF. Findings of the Institute for Women's Policy Research reveal that 43 percent of former AFDC mothers were either peripherally attached to the labor market, augmenting welfare with wages, or drifting on and off of welfare depending on the availability of work. Once AFDC mothers who were seeking work were coupled to those above, 66 percent of welfare mothers were either participating in the labor market or were trying to.[107]

But conditions of the secondary labor market make this problematic.[108] Given the reality of the secondary labor market, the trick of welfare reform is to catapult TANF mothers beyond the secondary labor market and into the primary labor market. If this could be done, earnings would increase enough to assure economic self-sufficiency. The sticking point is that substantial investments are necessary to achieve such program performance. But to do so creates two problems: First, a "moral hazard" emerges as welfare beneficiaries become recipients of benefits that are not available to the working poor not on welfare. While working people often grumble about the welfare dependent obtaining benefits not available to them, they also suspect that ample benefits induce those who should be working to apply for public assistance. Second, a "political hazard" is created for any elected official who states a willingness to support welfare recipients over the working poor. In such circumstances, the prudent politician favors the least costly and most expedient option—push welfare recipients into the labor market and celebrate doing so with paeans to the work ethic. These moral and political hazards thus prescribe the boundaries of plausibility: perforce, welfare reform is limited to elevating the welfare poor up to the level of the working poor.

Finally, TANF work-to-welfare programs are flawed in another way. Specifically, they fail to take into account barriers to employment. A study of welfare recipients by Sandra Danziger and her colleagues found high levels of barriers to work, such as physical and mental problems, domestic violence, and lack of transportation, but relatively low levels of other barriers, such as drug or alcohol dependence or a lack of understanding of work norms. Their study also found that recipients commonly have multiple barriers and that the number of barriers is strongly and negatively associated with employment status. Almost two-thirds of the study respondents had two or more potential barriers to work, and more than one-quarter had four or more. Finally, Danziger and her colleagues found that the barrier hypothesis is a better predictor of employment than traditional models that rely on education, work experience, and welfare history. For example, they found that the number of years of prior welfare receipt is not associated with current employment, once health and mental health factors, transportation, work skills, and perceived discrimination experiences are taken into account.[109]

Conclusion: The Evolution of Public Assistance

For a half century, AFDC did little more than dispense checks; not until relatively recently has recipient behavior been a target for systematic intervention. Because of its lack of direction, AFDC became the source for derogatory colloquialisms such as "welfare mess" and "welfare queen." Instilling some order in welfare was bound to produce some desirable outcomes. It is the extent of positive outcomes that is questionable.

Welfare analysts suspect that most of the improvement in welfare program performance is attributable to those recipients who are relatively well educated, have employment experience, and are upwardly mobile. Such welfare beneficiaries are good candidates for the secondary labor market, and some will even find secure employment in the primary labor market. Of the remaining welfare families, most may be socially mainstreamed with adequate inducements and supports. The welfare behaviorism articulated through initiatives such as welfare-to-work has been testing the malleability of this population. Some of this group will respond positively to incentives and sanctions; some will not. In all likelihood, many—perhaps 20 percent—will fail to negotiate the procedural thicket imposed by the welfare reforms of the mid-1990s. Although the PRWORA allows states to exempt 20 percent of families from time limits, there is no requirement that those on the lowest social stratum be allowed to stay on aid indefinitely. And indeed, there is no assurance that states will exempt the most troubled families from time limits. It is just as plausible that savvy state welfare administrators will exempt mothers who are in lengthy educational/training programs, on the basis that they represent a better long-term investment of public resources. Even some conservatives are opposed to arbitrary time limits. At a 1996 conference on welfare reform, Lawrence Mead stated his opposition to time limits, primarily on the basis that virtually no research had been done to determine the consequences of terminating poor families from public assistance.[110]

Despite its age and relative maturity, a core question involves the extent to which states can be expected to comply with the federal work requirements, especially given a severe economic downturn. This problem is exacerbated as work participation rates increase under TANF reauthorization. Fractures in TANF could be seen in 2004 as most states had either exhausted their TANF funds or were approaching the need to augment federal funds with state funds. In the event of a continuing economic downswing, this will produce an enormous compression effect on the states. Squeezed between static resources and increasing demands for job placement, the initial response will be to remove families from welfare or to discourage new families from enrolling.

Whenever possible, states will attempt to transfer the most troubled families to SSI, a program that is fully federally funded. This, however, will require certification of disability, and the federal government will resist SSI's becoming a dumping ground for the states' welfare reform failures. Indeed, PRWORA tightens the eligibility requirements for SSI in a manner that makes transfers from welfare more difficult. Without the SSI transfer option, states will be induced to reduce the number of cases not in compliance with work requirements. Given difficulties in operationalizing the federal five-year lifetime limit, states will be induced to consider ever shorter limits. Terminating families as soon as possible on the basis of noncompliance will ultimately screen out those families least likely to become employed. Eventually such families will cease seeking aid; and to the extent that large numbers of the more disorganized families disappear from state welfare rolls, states will avoid federal penalties for failing to meet employment requirements.

The future of families dumped from state welfare programs is bleak. Many have ended up in the tertiary job market, or worse, in shelters or on the streets. Like the deinstitutionalized, some former TANF families have been swallowed up in the urban landscape and have become virtually invisible, leading lives of quiet desperation. Conservative scholars, such as Marvin Olasky, have promised that private, especially religious, agencies will pick up the slack,[111] but this has not happened. Contributions to nonprofit agencies such as the United Way have stagnated in recent years. Ineligible for state aid and unable to get necessary assistance from the nonprofit sector, former welfare families have turned to metropolitan government as the last resort. Big-city mayors are already dreading the impact that such families will have on their already overburdened city budgets.[112]

Despite the problems, certain incremental benefits of welfare reform must be acknowledged. For example, the PRWORA allows states to establish individual development accounts (IDAs), a strategy to increase the assets of poor families and help vault them out of poverty. Unfortunately, the welfare reform plan makes no specific allocations for IDAs, leaving funding the option of state and local governments or philanthropy.

At this point, the negatives outweigh the positives. For instance, PRWORA benefits are denied for life to parents convicted of felony drug offenses unless they are participating in a drug treatment program, even though family-oriented drug treatment for addicts who are also mothers is rare. Several of the provisions of PRWORA target teenagers on welfare: Teen mothers are required to live with their parents and stay in school to receive benefits; HHS is required to mount a teen pregnancy prevention initiative; and the Justice Department is required to identify older men (some of whom may be only a few years older than the mother) who impregnate female teenagers and prosecute them for statutory rape. Several provisions address child support, including the requirement that states establish registries for child support and streamline the process for establishing paternity. States are encouraged to be more aggressive in withholding income from noncustodial parents in arrears for child support. Furthermore, more vigorous penalties are directed at noncustodial parents to encourage them to pay up, such as revocation of professional, driver's, occupational, and recreational licenses.[113]

Given the track record of demonstration programs designed to prevent teen pregnancy and increase child support, the stiff penalties directed at adolescents and deadbeat dads would seem to be more of rhetorical value to elected officials than of practical use to save the public revenues now allocated to welfare programs. Regarding a larger issue, no one seems to have taken the trouble to calculate the ultimate cost of deploying a state-administered welfare apparatus with tracking, surveillance, and sanction capacities designed to reprogram the behavior of the 2.7 million families on public assistance.

Finally, PRWORA includes funding for further research on welfare reform, most of it for the benefit of children. For example, if the child poverty rate increases by 5 percent or more for a given year, HHS must prepare a plan for corrective action. Significantly, there are no specific requirements for states to study the consequences of deleting families from welfare as a result of time limits, particularly as this action affects children. Moreover, while HHS has studied welfare leavers, the results of these investigations have not been translated into policy reform. On the contrary, the 2005 TANF reauthorization plan directly contradicted research findings.

Recipients of public assistance programs fare less well than those covered under the social insurances. Public assistance programs include a large dose of stigma, and the character of recipients is often maligned because of their need. Moreover, the relative success of Social Security in arresting poverty among the elderly has not been replicated in public assistance programs. In fact, the reverse is true; the poorest of the poor have endured greater levels of poverty from 1980 onward. Indeed, the legacy of welfare reform signed by former President Clinton bodes badly for the future prospects of America's poor.

The U.S. welfare system has undergone a dramatic transformation over the past 20 years marked by several important themes: (1) the conversion of public assistance policy into labor policy, (2) the conversion of public assistance policy into tax policy, and (3) the increased privatization of social welfare services. By converting AFDC into workfare through TANF, the PRWORA eliminated the boundary between public assistance and labor policy and became a feeder system to supply the secondary labor market with manpower. The result is fewer protected islands left for those who cannot compete in the labor market.

The conversion of public assistance policy into labor policy is shored up by tax policy through the expansion of EITC benefits, the only public assistance program that has been purposely enlarged in the past 20 years. In fact, EITC is not the largest public assistance program in the nation. By expanding EITC benefits through the tax code while at the same time eliminating AFDC, the legislature has shifted the focus from the nonworking poor to the working poor, a group more marginally acceptable

to conservatives and the larger society. Public assistance payments to the poor will likely be increasingly routed through tax policy for low-income workers rather than direct cash or in-kind subsidies for the nonworking poor.

Privatized social services have encroached upon most welfare domains, including health care, public education, mental health and chemical dependency services, nursing home care, corrections, and child care. Many of these markets are already glutted by the influx of corporations seeking to increase their profits and their corporate reach.

This is clearly a difficult time for the U.S. welfare state. Even after huge expenditures on social welfare services, basic human needs remain unmet. Given the present economic trend—in which vast numbers of service jobs are produced, many of which are part time, have few if any benefits, and pay the minimum wage—long-term welfare benefit packages will likely be required for an increasing number of citizens. How much help these income benefit packages will contain, and at what cost, will be a matter for future discourse in public policy.

Discussion Questions

1. Public assistance programs are arguably the most controversial programs in the U.S. welfare state. Critics frequently lambaste them for encouraging everything from welfare dependency to teenage pregnancy. Supporters argue that public assistance programs are poorly funded and barely allow recipients to survive. Why is public assistance so controversial? What, if anything, can be done to make the TANF program less controversial?

2. Numerous myths have arisen around the TANF program. In your opinion, what myths have been the most harmful to the programs and to recipients? Why?

3. Since the 1970s, most strategies for reforming public assistance have revolved around implementing mandatory work requirements. This strategy was evident in the programs of Presidents Carter and Reagan and was the centerpiece of the 1988 Family Support Act. More recently, the TANF program mandated that benefits should last for a maximum of five years, after which a recipient would be required to work. Is establishing a mandatory work requirement a viable strategy for reforming

public assistance? If so, why? If not, why not? What would be a better strategy for reforming public assistance?

4. TANF benefit levels vary widely from state to state because the federal government has refused to establish a national minimum benefit level. Moreover, there is little federal pressure on states to increase benefit levels and thereby curtail the erosion of public assistance benefits that has taken place since the 1970s. Should the federal government establish a minimum national benefit level for TANF and compel states to meet that level? If not, why not? If you agree, what should that level be?

5. Public assistance programs are increasingly being designed to change the behavior of poor recipients. Can and should the behavior of poor people be changed through social policy legislation? Will this legislation work? If not, why?

6. Although administered by the Social Security Administration, the SSI program carries a stigma similar to public assistance programs like food stamps or the TANF. Why does this stigma exist? What can be done to diminish it?

Notes

1. Isaac Shapiro and Robert Greenstein, *Holes in the Safety Nets* (Washington, DC: Center on Budget and Policy Priorities, 1988).
2. U.S. Administration for Children & Families, "Case Load Data 2007." Retrieved July 2008, from www.acf.hhs.gov/programs/ofa/data-reportscaseload/caseload_current.htm
3. The Urban Institute, "Welfare Rules Databook: State TANF Policies as of July 2006," September 2006. Retrieved July 2008, from www.urban.org/UploadedPDF/411686_welfare_databook06.pdf
4. The Urban Institute, "TANF Caseload Composition and Leavers Synthesis Report," March 28 2007. Retrieved July 2008, from www.urban.org/UploadedPDF/411553_tanf_caseload.pdf
5. The Urban Institute, "Welfare Rules Databook: State TANF Policies as of July 2006."
6. "Welfare Reform Issue Paper," Working Group on Welfare Reform, Family Support and Independence, U.S. Department of Health and Human Services, February 26, 1994; and Peter Gottschalk, "Achieving Self-Sufficiency for Welfare Recipients—The Good and Bad News," in *Select Committee on Hunger, Beyond Public Assistance: Where Do We Go From Here?* Serial No. 102-123 (Washington, DC: U.S. Government Printing Office, 1992), p. 56.
7. Mary Jo Bane and David T. Ellwood, *Welfare Realities: From Rhetoric to Reform* (Cambridge, MA: Harvard University Press, 1994).
8. Robert Moffitt, quoted in Hillary Hoynes and T. McCurdy, "Has the Decline in Benefits Shortened Welfare Spells," *AEA Papers and Proceedings* 84, no. 2 (May 1994), pp. 43–48.
9. P. J. Leahy, T. F. Buss, and J. M. Quane, "Time on Welfare: Why Do People Enter and Leave the System," *American Journal of Economics and Sociology* 54 (January 1995), pp. 33–46.
10. Bane and Ellwood, *Welfare Realities;* see also Greg J. Duncan and Saul D. Hoffman, "Welfare Dynamics and Welfare Policy," unpublished paper, Institute for Social Research, Ann Arbor, MI, 1985.
11. Ibid.
12. Peter Gottschalk, "Is Intergenerational Correlation in Welfare Participation across Generations Spurious?" Boston College, November 1990, Conference Papers, 1990 ASPE-JCPES Conference on the Underclass (Washington, DC: U.S. Department of Health and Human Services).
13. M. Ann Hill and June O'Neill, "Underclass Behaviors in the United States: Measurement and Analysis of Determinants," City College of New York, March 1990, Conference Papers, 1990 ASPE-JCPES Conference on the Underclass (Washington, DC: U.S. Department of Health and Human Services).
14. Mary Corcoran, Roger Gordon, Deborah Laren, and Gary Solon, "Problems of the Underclass: Underclass Neighborhoods and Intergenerational Poverty and Dependency," University of Michigan, 1991, Conference Papers, 1990 ASPE-JCPES Conference on the Underclass (Washington, DC: U.S. Department of Health and Human Services).
15. The Urban Institute, "TANF Caseload Composition and Leavers Synthesis Report."
16. Ibid.
17. Iris Lav and Steven Gold, *The States and the Poor* (Washington, DC: Center on Budget and Policy Priorities, 1993), p. 11.
18. The Urban Institute, "Welfare Rules Databook: State TANF Policies as of July 2006."
19. The Urban Institute, "TANF Caseload Composition and Leavers Synthesis Report."
20. Duncan and Hoffman, "Welfare Dynamics."
21. David Morris, "Ask Dr. Dave," Institute for Local Self-Reliance, 2003. Retrieved October 2004, from www.americanvoice2004.org/askdave/26askdave.html
22. U.S. Census Bureau, 2008 "Section 11—Social Insurance and Human Services." Retrieved July 2008, from www.census.gov/prod/2007pubs/08statab/socins.pdf
23. James R. Walker, *Migration Among Low-Income Households: Helping the Witch Doctors Reach Consensus,* Institute for Research on Poverty, Discussion Paper no. 1031-94, University of Wisconsin–Madison, April 1994.
24. Thomas Corbett, "The Wisconsin Welfare Magnet: What Is an Ordinary Member of the Tribe to Do When the Witch Doctors Disagree?" *Focus* 13, no. 3 (Fall/Winter 1991), pp. 2–4.
25. Quoted in Diane Rose, Terri Sachnik, Josie Salazar, Eunice Sealey, and Virginia Wall, "Welfare Reform II," unpublished paper, University of Houston Graduate School of Social Work, Houston, TX, 1996.
26. U.S. House of Representatives, "Myths and Realities," p. 58.
27. Georgia Budget and Policy Institute, "TANF Budget 2002–2007: The Shifting Priorities," June 2007. Retrieved July 2008, from www.gbpi.org/pubs/gabudget/20070612.pdf
28. Robert Moffitt, "Incentive Effects of the U.S. Welfare System: A Review," *Journal of Economic Literature* 30 (March 1992), pp. 1–61; see also Barbara Vobejda, "Decline in Birth Rates for Teens May Reflect Major Social Changes," *Houston Chronicle* (October 29, 1996), p. 13A.

29. W. Joseph Heffernan, *Introduction to Social Welfare Policy* (Itasca, IL: F.E. Peacock, 1979).
30. Elizabeth D. Huttman, *Introduction to Social Policy* (New York: McGraw-Hill, 1981), p. 168.
31. William Eaton, "Major Welfare Reform Compromise Reached," *Los Angeles Times* (September 27, 1988), p. 15.
32. American Public Welfare Association, *Conference Agreement on Welfare Reform* (Washington, DC: American Public Welfare Association, September 28, 1988), pp. 1–3.
33. See David Stoesz and Howard Karger, "Welfare Reform: From Illusion to Reality," *Social Work* 35, no. 2 (March 1990), pp. 141–147; and Spencer Rich, "Panel Clears Welfare Bill," *Washington Post* (September 28, 1988), p. A6.
34. See David T. Ellwood, "Welfare Reform as I Knew It: When Bad Things Happen to Good Policies," *The American Prospect 26* (May–June 1996), p. 240.
35. Ellwood, "Welfare Reform as I Knew It."
36. Ibid.
37. "Legal Immigrants to Carry Burden of Welfare Reform," *El Paso Times* (August 3, 1996), p. B1.
38. Mark H. Greenberg, "No Duty, No Floor: The Real Meaning of 'Ending Entitlements,'" Washington, DC: Center for Law and Social Policy, 1996. Retrieved 1997, from http://epn.org/clasp/clduty-2.html
39. Paula Roberts, "Relationship between TANF and Child Support Requirements," Washington, DC: Center for Law and Social Policy, September 1996. Retrieved 1997, from http://epn.org/clasp/cltcsr.html
40. "Welfare Reform," *NASW News* (September 1996), pp. 1, 12.
41. NACo Legislative Priority Fact Sheet, New Welfare Reform Law, "The Personal Responsibility and Work Opportunity Reconciliation Act of 1996," Washington, DC: NACo, 1996.
42. Frances Fox Piven, "Was Welfare Reform Worthwhile?" *The American Prospect* 27 (July–August 1996), pp. 14–15.
43. Quoted in Ibid., p. 14.
44. Douglas J. Besharov, "The Past and Future of Welfare Reform," *Public Interest* (Winter 2003), pp. 18–25.
45. U.S. Department of Health and Human Services, "Secretary Thompson Announces TANF Caseloads Declined in 2003," August 23, 2004. Retrieved October 2004, from www.hhs.gov/news/press/2004pres/20040823.html
46. U.S. Social Security Administration, "The Food Stamp Program and Supplemental Security Income," 67(4), 2007. Retrieved July 2008, from www.socialsecurity.gov/policy/docs/ssb/v67n4/67n4p71.html
47. The Urban Institute, "TANF Caseload Composition and Leavers Synthesis Report."
48. Ibid.
49. Ibid.
50. Ibid.
51. Shawn Fremstad, Sharon Parrott, and Arloc Sherman, "Unemployment Insurance Does Not Explain Why TANF Caseloads Are Falling as Poverty and Need Are Rising," Center on Budget and Policy Priorities, Washington, DC, October 12, 2004.
52. "Welfare Reform Reauthorized," Office of Public Affairs, Administration for Children and Families. Retrieved March 31, 2007, from www.acf.hhs.gov/opa/spotlight/welfarereauthorized.htm
53. Sharon Parrott, Liz Schott, Eileen Sweeney, Allegra Baider, Evelyn Ganzglass, Mark Greenberg, Elizabeth Lower-Basch, Elisa Minoff, and Vicki Turetsky, "Implementing the TANF Changes in the Deficit Reduction Act: 'Win-Win' Solutions for Families and States, Second Edition," Center on Budget and Policy Priorities and Center for Law and Social Policy, February 2007. Retrieved March 31, 2007, from www.cbpp.org/2-9-07tanf.pdf
54. Ibid., p. 19.
55. Ibid., p. 1.
56. Ibid., p. 2.
57. Committee on Ways and Means, *2008 Green Book*, p. 3–2. Available at http://waysandmeans.house.gov/Documents.asp?section=2168.
58. Committee on Ways and Means, *2008 Green Book*, p. 3–21.
59. Committee on Ways and Means, *2008 Green Book*, p. 178.
60. Ibid.
61. Committee on Ways and Means, *2008 Green Book*, p. 3–25.
62. See Social Security Administration, "Fast Facts and Figures about Social Security; and Committee on Ways and Means," *2004 Green Book*, pp. 3–38
63. Jeffrey Katz, "Social Security, Conference OKs Bill Creating Independent Agency," *Social Policy* (July 23, 1994), pp. 6–9.
64. Ibid.
65. Committee on Ways and Means, *2008 Green Book*, p. 3–15.
66. L. Jerome Gallagher, Cori E. Uccello, Alicia B. Pierce, and Erin B. Reidy, "State General Assistance Programs 1998," Washington, DC: The Urban Institute, April 1999. Retrieved from http://newfederalism.urban.org/html/ga_programs/ga_full.html#exesum
67. Minnesota Department of Human Services, "General Assistance Program." Retrieved July 2008, from www.dhs.state.mn.us/main/idcplg?IdcService=GET_DYNAMIC_CONVERSION&RevisionSelectionMethod=LatestReleased&dDocName=id_002558
68. California Department of Social Services, "General Assistance or General Relief." Retrieved July 2008, from www.cdss.ca.gov/cdssweb/PG132.htm
69. Los Angeles County, "GAINS." Retrieved July 2008, from www.ladpss.org/dpss/grow/gr_home.cfm

70. Maine Emergency Management Agency, "Knox County EMA Taking on a Different Kind of Emergency," March 7, 2008. Retrieved July 2008, from www.maine.gov/mema/mema_news_display.shtml?id=52174

71. Maine State Legislature, "Summary of Major State Funding Disbursed to Municipalities and Counties," October 2007. Retrieved July 2008, from http://mainegov-images.informe.org/legis/ofpr/Municipal07/2007_full_report.pdf

72. Thomas Corbett, "The New Federalism: Monitoring Consequences," *Focus* 18, no. 1 (1996), pp. 3–6.

73. *Economic Report of the President*, (Washington, DC: U.S. Government Printing Office, 1995).

74. T. Hilton and P. Huffaker, "Welfare Reform, Low-Wage Jobs and the U.S. Economy," *The Advocate's Forum* 3 (1996), p. 1. Retrieved 2004, from www.ssa.uchicago.edu/publications/advforum/v3n1/advocates3.1.2.html

75. Public Broadcasting System, "Transcript of Economic Growth 101" (October 1996), Washington, DC. Retrieved 2004 from www.pbs.org/newshour/bb/economy/october96/growth_10-30.html

76. Richard Friedmann, Neil Gilbert, and Moshe Sherer (eds.), *Modern Welfare States* (New York: New York University Press, 1987).

77. Infoplease.com. "Mothers Participating in the Labor Force, 1955–2002." Retrieved November 2002, from www.infoplease.com/ipa/A0104670.html

78. Harry Holzer and Michael Stoll, "Employer Demand for Welfare Recipients by Race," Discussion Paper 1213-00, Institute for Research on Poverty, Madison, WI, 2000.

79. R. Lerman, S. Riegg, and L. Aron, *Youth in 2020: Trends and Policy Implications* (Washington, DC: The Urban Institute, 2000).

80. Carmen DeNavas-Walt, Bernadette D. Proctor, and Jessica Smith "Income, Poverty, and Health Insurance Coverage in the United States: 2006," Economics and Statistics Administration U.S. Census Bureau, issued August 2007. Retrieved July 2008, from www.census.gov/prod/2007pubs/p60-233.pdf

81. Office of Inspector General, "State Strategies for Working with Hard-to-Employ TANF Recipients," July 2002. Department of Health and Human Services, OEI-02-00-00630, Washington, DC.

82. David Stoesz, *A Poverty of Imagination: Bootstrap Capitalism, Sequel to Welfare Reform* (New York: Oxford University Press, 2004), p. 106.

83. March of Dimes, "Teenage Pregnancy." Retrieved July 2008, from www.marchofdimes.com/professionals/14332_1159.asp

84. "Teenaged Childbearing and Welfare Policy," *Focus* 10, no. 1 (Spring 1987), p. 16.

85. Michael Harrington, with the assistance of Robert Greenstein and Eleanor Holmes Norton, *Who Are the Poor?* (Washington, DC; Justice for All, 1987), p. 12.

86. See Ibid., p. 1100; and Children's Aid Society, "Adolescent Pregnancy Prevention Program, 2004." Retrieved October 2004, from www.stopteenpregnancy.com/news/news_wsj.html

87. U.S. House of Representatives, *Overview of Entitlement Programs, 1994* (Washington, DC: U.S. Government Printing Office, 1994), p. 448.

88. Denise Polit, Janet Quint, and James Riccio, "The Challenge of Serving Teenage Mothers," New York: Manpower Demonstration Research Corporation, 1988, Tables 2 and 3, p. 17.

89. Janet Quint, Denise Polit, Hans Bos, and George Cave, *New Chance* (New York: Manpower Demonstration Research Corporation, 1994), Tables 5 and 6.

90. Ibid., p. xxxi.

91. Debra Hauser, "Five Years of Abstinence-Only-Until-Marriage Education: Assessing the Impact, Advocates for Youth," October 26, 2004. Retrieved October 2004, from www.advocatesforyouth.org/publications/state evaluations/index.htm

92. Michael Novak, *The New Consensus on Family and Welfare* (Washington, DC: American Enterprise Institute, 1987).

93. Charles Murray, *Losing Ground* (New York: Basic Books, 1984), pp. 227–228.

94. Lawrence Mead, *Beyond Entitlement* (New York: Free Press, 1986).

95. Center on Budget and Policy Priorities, "The New Welfare Law," Washington, DC: Center on Budget and Policy Priorities, 1996.

96. George Gilder, *Wealth and Poverty* (New York: Basic Books, 1981), p. 118.

97. Lois Quinn and Robert Magill, "Politics versus Research in Social Policy," *Social Service Review* (December 1994), pp. 83–90.

98. David Long, Judith Gueron, Robert Wood, Rebecca Fisher, and Veronica Fellerath, "LEAP," New York: Manpower Demonstration Research Corporation, 1996, p. ES6.

99. Ibid., p. ES13.

100. Robert Moffitt, "Incentive Effects of the U.S. Welfare System: A Review," *Journal of Economic Literature* (March 1992) p. 30.

101. Mark Greenberg, testimony before the Domestic Task Force, Select Committee on Hunger, U.S. House of Representatives, April 9, 1992, in *Federal Policy Perspectives on Welfare Reform: Rhetoric, Reality and Opportunities*, Serial No. 102-25 (Washington, DC: U.S. Government Printing Office, 1992), pp. 52–53.

102. Robert Rector, "Strategies for Welfare Reform," Testimony before the Domestic Task Force, Select Committee on Hunger, U.S. House of Representatives, April 9, 1992, in *Federal Policy Perspectives on Welfare Reform: Rhetoric, Reality and Opportunities*, Serial No. 102-25, Washington, DC: U.S. Government Printing Office, 1992, pp. 67–68.

103. Huttman, *Introduction to Social Policy*.

104. Judith Gueron and Edward Pauly, From Welfare to Work (New York: Russell Sage Foundation, 1991).

105. David Ellwood, *Poor Support* (New York: Basic Books, 1988), p. 153.

106. Judith M. Gueron, "Statement by the President," *Manpower Demonstration Research Corporation, 1991 Annual Report* (New York: MDRC, 1991), p. 2.

107. Roberta Spalter-Roth, Beverly Burr, Heidi Hartmann, and Lois Shaw, *Welfare That Works: The Working Lives of AFDC Recipients* (Washington, DC: Institute for Women's Policy Research, 1995), p. 18.

108. LaDonna Pavetti, *Questions and Answers on Welfare Dynamics* (Washington, DC: Urban Institute, 1995).

109. Sandra Danziger, Mary Corcoran, Sheldon Danziger, Colleen Heflin, Ariel Kalil, Judith Levine, Daniel Rosne, Kristin Seefeldt, Kristine Siefert, and Richard Tolman, "Barriers to the Employment of Welfare Recipients," Poverty Research and Training Center, University of Michigan, January 1999.

110. Personal discussion at a conference on welfare reform, the Jerome Levy Economics Institute, Bard College, Annandale-on-Hudson, NY, July 12, 1996.

111. Marvin Olasky, "Beyond the Stingy Welfare State," *Policy Review* (Fall 1990), p. 14.

112. Robert Pear, "Giuliani Battles Congress on Welfare Bill," *New York Times* (July 27, 1996), p. A7.

113. *Personal Responsibility and Work Opportunity Reconciliation Act of 1996* (Washington, DC: National Association of Social Workers, 1996).

CHAPTER 12

The American Health Care System

*F*ifty-five percent of Americans surveyed in February 2007 said that the most important domestic policy for the President and Congress to focus on is making health insurance available for everyone. In the same survey, 90 percent said that the present health care system requires fundamental changes or needs to be completely rebuilt.[1] This chapter examines the U.S. health care system—specifically, the organization of medical services; key governmental health programs such as Medicare and Medicaid; the crisis in health care, including attempts to curb health care costs; the large numbers of uninsured people; the impact of the American Medical Association on health care; the growing role of managed care; and the ramifications of the AIDS epidemic in the health care system. The chapter also surveys various proposals designed to ameliorate the problems in U.S. health care and considers how medical services are organized in Great Britain and Canada.

The Uninsured

Health care in the United States is marked by several contradictions. According to Census Bureau data, the number of people *with* health insurance rose to 249.8 million in 2006, up from 240.1 million in 2000. The number *without* such coverage rose from 38.4 million to 47 million in the same period. The percentage of the nation's population without health care coverage was 15.8 percent in 2006, and the percentage of people covered by government health insurance programs (Medicaid and Medicare) was 27 percent. The proportion of uninsured children in 2006 was 11.7 percent of all children, or 8.7 million.[2] Although the vast majority of Americans have easy access to a wide range of health care services through employment-based or public insurance programs, more than 47 million people remain without coverage. The medically uninsured have the following characteristics:

- Children under age 18 in poverty were more likely to be uninsured—19.3 percent in 2006 compared to 11.7 percent of all children. Adults between the ages of 18 and 44 made up three-quarters (76 percent) of the uninsured.
- Young adults (18 to 24 years old) were the least likely of any age group to have health insurance in 2006. Nearly 30 percent of uninsured persons were in this six-year age bracket.
- The poor are three times more likely to be uninsured as those who are not poor. One-quarter of people in households with annual incomes under $25,000 had no health insurance in 2006 compared with only 8.5 percent for those with incomes over $75,000.

spotlight 12.1

The National Center for Health Statistics

The National Center for Health Statistics (NCHS) is a key resource of information about the health of Americans. As the principal health statistics agency in the United States, the organization compiles statistical information to guide action and policies to improve the health of people living within the United States. The information provided by NCHS helps to do the following:

- Document the health status of the population and of important subgroups
- Identify disparities in health status and use of health care by race/ethnicity, socioeconomic status, region, and other population characteristics
- Describe various experiences with the health care system
- Monitor trends in health status and health care delivery
- Identify health problems
- Support biomedical and health services research
- Provide information for making changes in public policies and programs
- Evaluate the impact of health policies and programs

To learn more about NCHS, go to its website at **www.cdc.gov/nchs.**

- The uninsured rate for African Americans in 2006 was 20.5 percent; for Asians, 15.5 percent; for whites, 10.8 percent; for Hispanics 34.1 percent; and for American Indians or Alaska Natives it was 31.4 percent.
- The proportion of the foreign-born population without health insurance (33.8 percent) was about two-and-a-half times that of the native population (13.2 percent) in 2006.
- The South (19 percent) and West (17.9 percent) have a higher uninsured rate than either the Northeast (12.3 percent) or the Midwest (11.4 percent).
- The number of people who received health insurance coverage through their employers fell slightly from 60.2 percent in 2005 to 59.7 percent in 2006, while the number of people covered by government health insurance programs (e.g., Medicare and Medicaid) was 80.3 million or 27 percent.[3]

The relatively high number of uninsured Americans is not surprising, given that family health insurance premiums cost on average $9,320 annually in 2004—a high cost for a family trying to make ends meet.[4] In 35 states average premium costs for workers rose three times faster than average earnings from 2000 to 2004. Purchasing affordable, accessible insurance is a particular challenge for many older people, for workers in transition between jobs, and for small businesses and their employees. For example, premiums for COBRA (transitional health insurance allowed a worker when they terminate employment) average almost $700 a month for family coverage and $250 for individual coverage, a huge expenditure given the average $1,100 monthly unemployment check.[5]

The uninsured are three times more likely than the privately insured not to receive needed medical care, 50 to 70 percent more likely to need hospitalization for avoidable acute conditions like pneumonia or uncontrolled diabetes, and four times more likely to rely on an emergency room or to have no regular source of care.[6] At least one million Americans seeking medical care are turned away each year because they cannot pay, and millions more forgo preventive services.[7] This exists even though every major city has at least one major medical center.[8] The uninsured face other problems:

- Uninsured children have a higher incidence of developmental delays than those with health coverage.
- They are more likely to put off seeking care; to not receive care when needed; and to not fill a prescription or get a recommended treatment because of the expense.
- They are more likely to have problems paying their medical bills, and to be contacted by a collection agency.
- Uninsured adults hospitalized for heart attacks are 25 percent more likely to die while in the hospital than privately insured adults.
- Even after controlling for the severity of the injury, uninsured adults hospitalized for a traumatic injury are more than twice as likely to die in the hospital as insured adults.
- The diagnosis of a serious new health condition, including cancer, diabetes, heart attack, chronic lung disease, or stroke, reduced the wealth of uninsured households by 20 percent. Insured households with a similar diagnosis suffered a 2 percent decline in overall wealth.
- Insured households paid about $26,957 in total medical spending after the diagnosis of a serious new health condition; uninsured households paid $42,166.
- Americans who lack health insurance cost the economy between $65 and $130 billion a year in lost productivity.[9]
- The cost of medical care for the uninsured totaled around $125 billion in 2004.[10]

The Organization of Medical Services

Most health care costs in the United States are paid for by private insurers, public plans, and the direct public provision of health care. Only about 25 percent of health care costs are paid for directly by consumers. The dominant form of health care coverage in the United States is private insurance, which covers about 70 percent of the population (of whom three-quarters are covered by employer-based plans). Many elderly people use private health insurance plans to supplement the coverage offered by Medicare. Medical services in the United States consist of six major components:

1. Physicians in solo practice. These are typically the traditional physicians who may employ a nurse and receptionist. This form of medical

organization is becoming increasingly rare in an age of group practices and managed care.

2. Group outpatient settings, including groups of physicians sharing facilities. This setting is becoming common as physicians are forced to pool resources—capital, equipment, office staff, and so forth—in order to compete in an increasingly difficult health care marketplace. Group outpatient settings may also include health maintenance organizations (HMOs), physicians in industrial Employee Assistance Plan (EAP) settings, or doctors operating under university auspices. During the past few decades, physicians have increasingly worked in group practices or other organized settings.[11]

3. Physicians employed in corporate-owned for-profit clinics or in nonprofit clinics.

4. Hospitals—private, nonprofit, or public.

5. Public health services delivered on the state, local, regional, national, or international level. These services include health counseling; family planning; prenatal and postnatal care; school health services; disease prevention and control; immunization; referral agencies; STD (sexually transmitted diseases) services; environmental sanitation; health education; and maintenance of indexes on births, deaths, and communicable diseases. Government-sponsored health services include the Veterans Administration Hospitals (the largest network of hospitals in the United States); Community and Migrant Health Centers; services provided under the Title V Maternal and Child Health Block Grant; and the Title X Family Planning Program.

6. Sundry and corollary health services. This category includes home health services, physical rehabilitation, group homes, nursing homes, and so forth.

Major Public Health Programs: Medicare, Medicaid, and SCHIP

Health care spending is the second fastest-growing component of the federal budget, overshadowed only by the growth in the public debt. Overall, health care spending accounts for about one-fifth of total governmental expenditures at the state and federal levels. In 2006, 40.3 million people were covered by Medicare (13.6 percent) and 38.3 million (12.9 percent) were covered by Medicaid.[12]

Medicare

After Social Security, Medicare is the largest social insurance program in the United States with expenditures of $408.3 billion in 2006. It is also the largest public payer of health care, financing close to 20 percent of all health care spending. When Medicare began in July 1966, approximately 19 million people were enrolled; by 2007 more than 44 million people were enrolled in one or both of Parts A and B, and 8 million chose to participate in the Medicare+Choice (renamed Medicare Advantage) plan. In 2006, HI benefits totaled $189 billion.[13]

Medicare was added to the Social Security Act in 1965 and was designed to provide elderly people with prepaid hospital and optional medical insurance. The modern Medicare system is composed of four parts: compulsory Hospital Insurance (HI), known as Part A; Supplemental Medical Insurance (SMI), known as Part B; the Medicare Advantage program, known as Part C; and the Medicare Prescription Drug, Improvement, and Modernization Act of 2003, known as MMA or Part D. Although traditionally consisting of two parts (HI and SMI), Part C (established by the Balanced Budget Act of 1997) expanded beneficiaries' options for participation in private sector health care plans. The MMA or Part D was added in 2003.

Surrounded by controversy, the MMA was signed into law in 2003. As a 700-page document, this complex bill proved difficult for Medicare beneficiaries to understand. Apart from prescription drug coverage, Part D also includes changes for beneficiaries such as increases in the Part B deductible, increased income standards relating to the Part B premium, and new preventive health benefits. Like SMI, participation in the MMA is voluntary.

From mid-2004, beneficiaries had access to Medicare-endorsed drug discount cards estimated to save consumers 10 to 15 percent. For beneficiaries with incomes below 135 percent of poverty, the federal government provided $600 a year toward drug expenses plus the annual enrollment fee. This temporary plan was phased out in 2006. Part D now provides subsidized access to prescription drug insurance coverage on a voluntary basis, upon payment of a premium, to individuals entitled to Part A or enrolled in Part B. Premium and cost-sharing subsidies are available for low-income enrollees. People may enroll in either a stand-alone prescription drug plan (PDP) or an integrated Medicare Advantage plan that offers Part D coverage.[14]

The standard benefits for the MMA include the following:

• Beneficiaries pay about $25 a month in premiums for basic drug coverage (these are likely to vary across plans) in addition to the Part B premium. They also pay a $180 to $265 annual deductible and 25 percent (or approximate flat copayment) of full drug costs up to $2,400. After the initial coverage limit of $2,400 is met, a "doughnut hole" begins where the beneficiary may be responsible for up to the full amount of his or her drug costs. The "doughnut hole" ends once the beneficiary has met an out-of-pocket expense of $3,850. In the final post–"doughnut hole phase," enrollees pay only 5 percent of their total drug costs.

• Beneficiaries are required to find a private prescription drug plan that has contracted with the Medicare program. Managed care plans, like those currently in Medicare Advantage, may also provide the drug benefit. In areas where only one (or no) private plan exists, the government will provide a "fall-back" plan that provides the standard benefit.

• Medicare beneficiaries receive preventive benefits, including an initial routine physical examination, cardiovascular blood screening tests, and diabetes screening tests and services.

• The deductible, the size of the "doughnut hole," and catastrophic thresholds grow each year based on increased MMA spending. Thus, if Medicare drug costs skyrocket, the deductible and the "doughnut hole" will increase. For example, the benefit gap is projected to be $5,066 in 2013 and the annual premium is expected to jump to $696 by 2013. Because drug costs rise faster than inflation— and are projected to continue to do so—most Medicare beneficiaries will see their drug costs rise faster than their income. In the end, it is estimated that the MMA will only pay for about 25 percent of seniors' drug costs.

• Medicare will provide additional assistance to beneficiaries who qualify based on low incomes and limited assets. There are multiple levels of low-income assistance. For example, beneficiaries with incomes below 135 percent of the poverty line and assets under $6,000 for an individual or $9,000 for a couple (not including the value of a home or car), will be eligible to get drugs at $1 to $2 per generic prescription and $3 to $5 per brand-name prescription. Many of these six million people (called dual

eligibles) will have to pay higher copayments for prescription drugs. This is compounded by the fact that, unlike Medicare, there are no due process clauses for lodging complaints.

• MMA plan providers are permitted to offer an alternative benefit design provided it is actuarially equivalent and does not raise the Part D deductible or out-of-pocket limit. Plan providers are also required to provide drugs in each therapeutic category but have flexibility to establish preferred drug lists. In addition, companies offering drug plans can change formularies at any time, while a beneficiary can only change cards once a year. Plans may utilize a preferred network of pharmacies to reduce beneficiary cost-sharing. They may also offer supplemental benefits for an additional premium. Medicare has guidelines for the type of drugs plans must cover, but they do not require that all plans offer the same drugs. Beneficiaries will be required to ascertain whether the plan they enroll in covers the drugs they need.

Critics charge that the MMA does not curb skyrocketing drug costs. In fact, the MMA may actually increase costs by prohibiting Medicare from using its purchasing power to negotiate lower drug prices for beneficiaries. Private plan providers seek discounts for enrollees, but they lack Medicare's purchasing power. This stands in contrast to the Veterans Administration which has successfully negotiated lower prices with drug companies. In effect, the "no negotiation" clause increases program costs, which in turn adds to the deficit. The one-sided bill also prohibits consumers from buying cheaper drugs from Canada or Mexico. Under the Medicare legislation, drugs can only be reimported from Canada, and then only if the Secretary of Health and Human Services certifies that the reimportation is safe and would significantly reduce costs.

Drug companies and the managed care industry stand to reap huge profits from this legislation. Not only are there no mechanisms to effectively control rising drug costs, but the new drug benefit means much larger sales volume. Private insurance companies that participate in the Medicare program also realize windfall profits as they attempt to enroll the healthiest and youngest seniors, thereby lowering their costs. The MMA also includes an opportunity for private providers to gain more ground by allowing demonstration programs that lay the groundwork for privatizing Medicare. For instance, in 2010 Medicare will begin a demonstration project in six metropolitan areas in which traditional fee-for-service Medicare will bid competitively against private plans. Because traditional Medicare serves an older, sicker, and more expensive population, its costs will undoubtedly be higher.[15]

The Medicare bill was passed under a cloud of impropriety. In July 2004, Medicare administrator Thomas Scully admitted to ordering Richard Foster, a Medicare actuary, to withhold information from Congress. Foster had projected that the bill would cost at least $139 billion dollars more than the White House was claiming.[16] Even that estimate would climb as the costs of the MMA are expected to rise 11.5 percent a year until 2015.[17]

Perhaps the most important part of the MMA has nothing to do with Medicare. It is a little-noticed component called health savings accounts (HSAs) that could cost the federal government $6.4 billion over the next decade. Basically, the HSAs offer a tax-free shelter for those with high-deductible insurance. When a person puts money into the account it is not taxed. Nor is it taxed when the money is removed to pay for medical costs. Critics argue that this adds to the federal budget deficit. Moreover, this plan removes the owners of these accounts from the shared risk that is at the core of the health insurance system. Conservatives claim health savings accounts will encourage people to more closely monitor their health care spending and bring down medical costs. Critics call the accounts a tax shelter that benefits the wealthy and draws young, healthy workers out of health care plans, potentially doubling the cost of insurance for everyone else. For conservatives, a key selling point of health savings accounts is its potential effect on the future of health care. Specifically, polls show that two-thirds of Americans support government-run, universal health care. By giving a large segment of the population the option to withdraw from the health insurance system, health savings accounts can serve to prevent another Clinton-style health care reform proposal. Simply put, it would be hard to reform the health care system if a large number of people opted out and were self-insured.[18]

Medicare Coverage HI or Part A is provided free to persons aged 65 or over who are eligible for Social Security or Railroad Retirement benefits. It is a compulsory **inpatient care** (hospital) insurance plan (it also includes some nursing and home health care) with premiums coming out of a payroll tax that is part of the Social Security deductions. Most Americans 65 or older are automatically entitled to

Part A, and workers and their spouses with a sufficient period of Medicare-only coverage in federal, state, or local government employment are also eligible beginning at age 65. In addition, HI coverage is provided to insured workers (and spouses and children) with end-stage renal disease (ESRD), and to some otherwise ineligible aged and disabled beneficiaries who voluntarily pay a monthly premium. In 2006 the HI program covered about 43 million people (36 million aged and 7 million disabled enrollees).[19] The following health care services are covered under Medicare's HI program:

- Inpatient hospital care includes the costs of a semi-private room, meals, regular nursing services, operating and recovery rooms, intensive care, inpatient prescription drugs, laboratory tests, X-rays, inpatient rehabilitation, long-term care hospitalization, and all other medically necessary services and supplies.
- Skilled nursing facility (SNF) care is covered only if it follows within 30 days of a hospitalization of three days or more and is certified as medically necessary. Covered services are similar to those for hospitalized patients but also include rehabilitation services and medical appliances.
- Home health agency (HHA) care may be provided for a home-bound beneficiary if deemed medically necessary. Certain medical supplies and durable medical equipment may also be provided but require a copayment. Full-time nursing care, food, blood, and drugs are not provided as HHA services. Home health agency (HHA) care is covered by both HI and SMI and requires no copayment or deductible.
- Hospice care is available to terminally ill persons with life expectancies of six months or less who forego the standard Medicare benefits. Such care includes pain relief, supportive medical and social services, physical therapy, nursing services, and symptom management. If a hospice patient requires treatment for a condition not related to the terminal illness, Medicare will pay for all covered services necessary for that condition. Beneficiaries pay no deductible for the hospice program but do pay a small coinsurance for drugs and inpatient respite care.[20]

By paying a monthly premium, U.S. citizens (and certain legal aliens) over age 65 and all disabled persons entitled to HI are eligible to enroll in the SMI program. Almost all persons entitled to HI enroll in SMI. In 2006 the SMI program covered about 40 million (34 million aged and 6 million disabled) people with benefits totaling $165.9 billion.[21] The SMI program covers the following:

- Physicians' and surgeons' services, including some covered services furnished by chiropractors, podiatrists, dentists, and optometrists; also covered are services provided by nonphysician Medicare-approved practitioners, such as nurse practitioners in collaboration with a physician, clinical psychologists, clinical social workers (other than in a hospital or skilled nursing facility), and physician assistants.
- Services in an emergency room or outpatient clinic, including same-day surgery, and ambulance services
- Home health care not covered under HI
- Laboratory tests, X-rays, and other diagnostic radiology services, as well as certain preventive care screening tests
- Ambulatory surgical center services in a Medicare-approved facility
- Most physical and occupational therapy and speech pathology services
- Comprehensive outpatient rehabilitation facility services, and mental health treatment in a partial hospitalization psychiatric program
- Radiation therapy, renal dialysis, and certain (e.g., heart, lung, liver, pancreas, bone marrow, kidney, and intestinal) transplants
- Approved durable medical equipment for home use, such as oxygen equipment, wheelchairs, prosthetic devices, and surgical dressings, splints, and casts
- Drugs that cannot be self-administered[22]

Funding   Medicare finances are handled by two trust funds in the U.S. Treasury, one for the HI program and the other for SMI. The HI program is financed primarily through a mandatory payroll tax. Almost all employees and self-employed persons pay taxes to support benefits for aged and disabled beneficiaries. In 2008 the HI tax rate was 1.45 percent of earnings (paid by each employee with a matching amount paid by the employer) and 2.90 percent for self-employed persons. Unlike Social Security, there is no earnings cap on taxable wages.

The SMI program is financed by beneficiary payments ($96.40 a month in 2008) and contributions from general tax revenues. Beneficiary premiums are generally set at a level that covers 25 percent of the average expenditures for aged beneficiaries. As such, the contribution from general tax revenues is the largest source income for the SMI program. Beneficiary premiums and general fund payments are determined annually to match estimated program costs for the following year. Capitation payments to Medicare Advantage plans are financed from the HI and SMI trust funds.

Gaps in Medicare Coverage   Fee-for-service beneficiaries pay for charges not covered by Medicare and for various cost-sharing aspects of both HI and SMI. These liabilities may be paid by beneficiaries out-of-pocket, by a third party (an employer-sponsored retiree health plan or private "Medigap" insurance), or by Medicaid (if the person is eligible). "Medigap" insurance refers to private insurance plans that pay most of the charges not covered by Medicare. For beneficiaries enrolled in Medicare Advantage plans, the beneficiary's payment share is based on the cost-sharing structure of the specific plan selected by the beneficiary. Most plans have lower deductibles and coinsurance than that required for fee-for-service beneficiaries. Beneficiaries pay the monthly Part B premium and may pay an additional plan premium.

For HI hospital care, a fee-for-service beneficiary's payment share includes a one-time deductible at the beginning of each benefit period ($1,024 in 2008). This deductible covers the beneficiary's part of the first 60 days of each instance of inpatient hospital care. If continued inpatient care is needed beyond the 60 days, additional coinsurance payments ($256 a day in 2008) are required through the 90th day of a benefit period. Each HI beneficiary also has a lifetime reserve of 60 additional hospital days that may be used when the covered days within a benefit period have been exhausted. Lifetime reserve days may be used only once, and coinsurance payments are required.

Medicare covers the first 20 days of skilled nursing care (SNF) in a benefit period. But a copayment is required ($128 a day in 2008) for days 21 through 100. Medicare's obligation ends after 100 days of SNF care per benefit period. Home health care has no deductible or coinsurance payment.

For SMI, the beneficiary's payment share includes one annual deductible ($135 in 2008), the monthly premiums, the coinsurance payments for

SMI services (usually 20 percent of the medically allowed charges), a deductible for blood, certain charges above the Medicare-allowed charge, and payment for any services not covered by Medicare. The beneficiary is liable for 50 percent of the approved charges for outpatient mental health treatment services.

Reimbursements to Providers Medicare payments for most inpatient hospital services are made under a reimbursement mechanism known as the prospective payment system (PPS). Under PPS, a predetermined amount is paid for each inpatient hospital stay based on a diagnosis-related group classification. In some cases the payment to the hospital is less than the actual costs, while in other cases it is more. The hospital absorbs the loss or makes a profit. Adjustments are made for unusual or costly hospital stays. Payments for skilled nursing care, home health care, inpatient rehabilitation, and long-term hospital care are made under separate PPSs.[23]

If a doctor or medical supplier agrees to accept the Medicare-approved rate as payment in full, they may not request any additional payments from the beneficiary. If the provider does not take assignment, the beneficiary is charged for the excess (sometimes paid by Medigap insurance). Limits exist on the excess that doctors or suppliers can charge. Medicare reimbursements to health care providers are subject to maximum payments by level of service, which are often less than some physicians will accept. In these cases, patients pay the difference between the physician's charge and the Medicare reimbursement. Because of paperwork and limited reimbursement, many physicians choose not to participate in Medicare.

Medicare payments to Medicare Advantage plans are based on a blend of local and national capitated rates. Actual payments to plans vary depending on the demographic characteristics of the enrolled population. Although Medicare provides important services, the gaps in coverage are extensive, which is why many beneficiaries opt for HMOs or supplement Medicare with private **Medigap** insurance.

Since 1980 Medicare costs have risen about 10 percent a year. Total Medicare expenditures more than doubled from 1989 to 1998, and they are rising faster than the wages on which the payroll tax is based. Medicare's annual costs in 2007 equaled

3.2 percent of the gross domestic product (GDP) but are expected to reach almost 10.8 percent by 2082. In turn, the projected date of the HI trust fund exhaustion is 2019. Part B of the SMI trust fund and the MMA are both expected to remain adequately funded into the future because current law automatically sets financing to meet the next year's expected costs (something not true for the HI program). The Medicare program is expected to experience even greater hardships when the baby boom generation begins retiring around 2010 (see Figure 12.1).[24]

Medicaid

Before 1965, medical care for those unable to afford it was primarily a responsibility of charitable institutions and state and local governments. In 1950 the federal government authorized states to use federal/state funds under the Social Security Act of 1935 to provide medical care for the indigent. In 1957 the Kerr-Mills Act provided for a federal/state matching program to provide health care for the elderly and the poor. However, Kerr-Mills was not

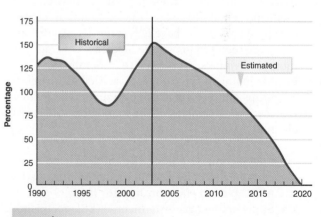

Figure 12.1
Hospital Insurance Trust Funds Assets (assets at beginning of year as percentage of annual expenditures)
Source: House Committee on Ways and Means, Statement of Rick Foster, Chief Actuary, Centers for Medicare and Medicaid Services, Testimony before the House Committee on Ways and Means, March 24, 2004.

mandatory, and many states chose not to participate. As a compromise to ward off more far-reaching health policies, President Lyndon Johnson signed the Medicaid and Medicare programs into law in 1965.[25] Replacing all previous governmental health programs, Medicaid became the largest public assistance program in the nation. In 2006 Medicaid served about one in every six people at a combined federal and state cost of $319.6 billion.[26]

Medicaid is a means-tested public assistance program. Eligible persons receive services from physicians who accept Medicaid patients (in many places a minority of physicians) and other health care providers. These providers are reimbursed by the federal government on a per-patient basis. Alternatively, several states require Medicaid recipients to enroll in state-contracted HMOs.

Medicaid is a federal/state program. States determine eligibility within broad federal guidelines. For instance, each state establishes its own eligibility standards; determines the type, amount, duration, and scope of services; sets the rate of payment for services; and administers its own program. Medicaid policies can be complex and vary widely among states. For instance, a person eligible for Medicaid in one state may be ineligible in another, and the services provided by one state may differ in the amount, duration, or scope of services compared to other states. State legislatures may change Medicaid eligibility, services, or reimbursement during the year. To be eligible for federal funds, states are required to provide Medicaid coverage for most individuals who receive federally assisted income maintenance payments, as well as for related groups not receiving cash payments. The following are some examples of the mandatory Medicaid eligibility groups:

- Low-income families with children who meet certain eligibility requirements in the state's AFDC plan in effect on July 16, 1996
- Supplemental Security Income (SSI) recipients
- Infants born to Medicaid-eligible pregnant women. Medicaid eligibility continues throughout the first year of life, as long as the infant remains in the mother's household and she remains eligible, or would be eligible if she were still pregnant.
- Children under age 6 and pregnant women whose family income is at or below 133 percent of the federal poverty level. The maximum mandatory income level for pregnant women

and infants in certain states may be higher than 133 percent if the state has established a higher percentage for covering those groups. All poor children under age 19 are covered.
- Recipients of adoption assistance and foster care under Title IV-E of the Social Security Act
- Certain Medicare beneficiaries and special protected groups; for example, those who lose SSI payments due to earnings from work or increased Social Security benefits
- Other "categorically needy" groups as decided by the state. These optional groups share characteristics of the mandatory groups, but the eligibility criteria are somewhat more liberally defined. Examples of these optional groups are (1) infants up to age 1 and pregnant women not covered under the mandatory rules whose family income is below 185 percent of the federal poverty level; (2) certain targeted low-income children; (3) certain elderly, blind, or disabled adults who have incomes above those requiring mandatory coverage but below the federal poverty level; (4) children under age 21 who meet income and resources requirements for Temporary Assistance for Needy Families (TANF) but who otherwise are not eligible for TANF; (5) institutionalized individuals with income and resources below specified limits; (6) persons who would be eligible if institutionalized but are receiving care under home- and community-based services waivers; (7) recipients of state supplementary payments; and (8) tuberculosis (TB)-infected persons who would be financially eligible for Medicaid at the SSI level.[27] (Table 12.1 shows the numbers and eligibility categories of the Medicaid population.)

The medically needy (MN) option allows states to extend Medicaid eligibility to additional persons. These persons would be eligible for Medicaid under one of the mandatory or optional groups, except that their income or resources are above the eligibility level set by their state. Persons may qualify immediately or may "spend down" by incurring medical expenses that reduce their income to or below their state's medically needy level. By 2008, 24 states had elected to have a medically needy program. All remaining states utilize the "special income level" option to extend Medicaid to the "near poor" in medical institutional settings.

Table 12.1

Medicaid Recipients by Category, 1985–2005, Selected Years (in thousands)

Year	Total	Age 65 or Older	Blind/Disabled	Children	Adults	Other
1985	21,814	3,061	3,017	9,757	5,518	1,214
1988	22,907	3,159	3,487	10,037	5,503	1,343
1990	25,255	3,202	3,718	11,220	6,010	1,105
1993	33,432	3,863	5,016	16,285	7,505	763
1997	34,872	3,955	6,129	15,791	6,803	2,195
2000	42,886	4,289	7,479	21,086	10,543	862
2005	57,643	4,396	8,210	26,337	12,529	6,171

Source: Social Security Administration, "Unduplicated Number of Recipients, Total Vendor Payments, and Average Payment by Type of Eligibility Category, Fiscal Years 1985–2005"*Annual Statistical Supplement, 2007.* Retrieved July 2008, from www.socialsecurity.gov/policy/docs/statcomps/supplement/2007/8e.pdf

Medicaid is funded by federal/state matching funds. In every state the federal government pays at least half, and in some states far more, of state Medicaid spending. Title XIX of the Social Security Act allows considerable flexibility within the states' Medicaid plans. However, some federal services are mandatory if matching funds are to be received:

- Inpatient hospital services
- Outpatient hospital services
- Prenatal care
- Vaccines for children
- Physician services
- Nursing facility services for persons aged 21 or older
- Family planning services and supplies
- Rural health clinic services
- Home health care for persons eligible for skilled-nursing services
- Laboratory and X-ray services
- Pediatric and family nurse practitioner services
- Nurse midwife services
- Federally qualified health center (FQHC) services, and ambulatory services of an FQHC that would be available in other settings
- Early and periodic screening, diagnostic, and treatment (EPSDT) services for children under 21 years[28]

States may also receive federal matching funds to provide certain optional services:

- Diagnostic services
- Clinic services
- Intermediate care facilities for the mentally retarded (ICFs/MR)
- Prescribed drugs and prosthetic devices
- Optometrist services and eyeglasses
- Nursing facility services for children under age 21
- Transportation services
- Rehabilitation and physical therapy services
- Home- and community-based care to certain persons with chronic impairments[29]

Medicaid was designed as a federal/state program to pay for health care for low-income and disabled citizens. On average Medicaid pays for about one-third of all births in the United States and, in some states, pays as much as 55 percent. Almost half of Medicaid recipients are children. Despite this number, the greatest single outlay of Medicaid funds goes to the elderly. For example, in 2004, Medicaid payments for services for 4.7 million aged, who constituted 8 percent of all Medicaid beneficiaries, was about $13,295 per person compared to the average 4,640 per person.[30] Payment for long-term nursing home care alone accounted for 37 percent of the Medicaid budget. Of the almost 1.8 million nursing home beds in the United States in 2004, 1.33 million were certified as Medicare/Medicaid beds, and 286,000 were certified as Medicaid only.[31] Although Medicaid pays only 48 percent of the cost of nursing home care nationally, the program covers 70 percent of nursing home residents and it pays something toward the cost of nearly 80 percent of all patient days.[32] Not surprisingly, the growth of the nursing home industry parallels the creation of Medicaid. From 1965 (the year Medicaid was created) to 1970, the number of nursing home residents rose by 18 percent. From 1970 to 1975 that number rose another 17 percent; from 1975 to 1980 it rose 14 percent; and from 1980 to 1985 it rose about 12 percent. Because 75 percent of nursing homes are for-profit facilities, Medicaid functions as a de facto subsidy for the nursing home industry. Medicaid also functions as a subsidy for the middle class. Namely, when elderly parents of today's middle class spend down their assets they become eligible for Medicaid. Without Medicaid the children of elderly parents would be responsible for paying the average national rate of $150 a day for nursing home care. A nursing home resident lives on average 2.4 years, so the total cost to a middle-class family would be more than $128,000. If their elderly parents lived in Alaska, Connecticut, District of Columbia, Hawaii, Massachusetts, New Jersey, or New York, they would pay from $189,000 to $381,000 for the nursing home care of their parents.[33]

Despite federal guidelines, four important gaps exist in Medicaid coverage: (1) the low eligibility limits set for Medicaid; (2) the refusal of many states to adopt most or all of the Medicaid options; (3) the gaps in coverage for the elderly and disabled; (4) the general ineligibility of poor single persons and childless couples for Medicaid unless they are elderly or disabled; and (5) state cutbacks in Medicaid coverage because of lower state revenues. Even though Medicaid covered about one in every six people in 2006, it does not provide health care services even for some very poor persons unless they are in a designated group.[34]

For all its shortcomings, the Medicaid program has led to important gains in the nation's health. In 1963, 54 percent of poor people did not see a physician and only 63 percent of poor pregnant women received prenatal care (by 1976 that number had increased to 76 percent). Between 1964 and 1975 the use of physicians' services by poor children increased 74 percent. The increased health care utilization helped bring about a 49 percent drop in infant mortality between 1965 and 1988. For African American infants the drop in mortality was even sharper: Infant mortality dropped by only 5 percent in the 15 years before Medicaid, but it dropped by 49 percent in the 15 years after the program began. Ongoing preventive care also cut program costs for Medicaid-eligible children by 10 percent.[35] Medicaid is one of the most important governmental health programs in the United States.

The State Children's Health Insurance Program (SCHIP)

As part of the Balanced Budget Act of 1997, Congress created the State Children's Health Insurance Program (SCHIP), a federal–state partnership that allocated $48 billion over 10 years to expand health care coverage to uninsured children under age 19 who are ineligible for Medicaid or are not covered by private insurance. In 2007, $6.04 billion was spent on SCHIPs and 4.4 million children were enrolled (as at June 2007).[36] The SCHIP program gives states three options for covering uninsured children: designing a new children's health insurance program, expanding current Medicaid programs, or a combination of both strategies. By 2007, 19 states had chosen to implement a separate SCHIP program, 18 states had a combined SCHIP and Medicaid program, and the remainder expanded their Medicaid program. SCHIP is a block grant program financed by federal/state matching funds. Each state with an approved plan receives enhanced federal matching payments for its SCHIP expenditures up to a fixed state allotment. However, the largest share of SCHIP funds come from the federal government, and in 2007, the federal share accounted for 65 percent of the program's funding.[37] SCHIP allows states to charge premiums and copayments and covers a more limited set of benefits than Medicaid.

Before SCHIP, Medicaid eligibility was largely linked to welfare receipt. In large measure, Medicaid-eligible children had to be in an SSI or a TANF family. Perhaps the most important policy change in SCHIP is that it delinked state-subsidized child health care from welfare receipt. Before SCHIP only four states covered children whose family incomes were at least 200 percent of the federal poverty line. Now, SCHIP enables states to insure children from working families with incomes too high to qualify for Medicaid but too low to afford private health insurance. In 2008, 44 states including the District of Columbia covered children in families with incomes up to 200 percent of the federal poverty line ($42,400 per year for a family of four in 2008) or higher. Of the 38 states with separate SCHIP programs, nearly two-thirds (25 states) apply at least one type of disregard when determining eligibility.[38]

The Tobacco Settlement

Public policy is occasionally made by the court system rather than the legislature. This was the case in the 1998 tobacco industry settlement. For 40 years tobacco companies had won every lawsuit brought against them. The long march toward a national tobacco settlement began in April 1994, when representatives from seven of the leading American tobacco companies stood before Congress and swore that nicotine was not an addictive substance. The presentation was astounding even in the eyes of many people who were neutral toward cigarette companies. In 1998 the tobacco companies were forced to accept a 600-page Master Settlement Agreement (MSA) requiring them to pay $206 billion to 46 states over a 25-year period. (That amount did not include $40 billion in separate settlements reached by four other states.) From 2000 to 2004, states realized $37.5 billion in tobacco company payments. The MSA was the largest civil settlement in U.S. history. Payments are based on states' shares of the cost of smoking-related illnesses paid for through the Medicaid program. In exchange for the fine levied by the MSA, 39 states with pending individual lawsuits agreed to drop their cases. Following are some highlights of the MSA:

• Public health initiatives prohibit youth targeting in advertising and promotion; ban the use of cartoon characters in advertising, promotion, packaging, and labeling; restrict sponsorship by brand names; ban outdoor advertising; ban sales of merchandise with tobacco brand names; ban free samples to youth; and set minimum pack size at 20 cigarettes.
• Tobacco companies must develop corporate principles committed to compliance with the MSA, such as reducing youth smoking, designating an executive manager to identify ways to reduce youth access, and encouraging employees to identify alternative methods to reduce youth access.
• The MSA disbands tobacco trade associations, including the Council for Tobacco Research, the Tobacco Institute, and the Council for Indoor Air Research. It creates regulations and oversight for any new trade organizations.
• The settlement limits industry lobbying by prohibiting tobacco companies from opposing legislation aimed at restricting youth access and reducing consumption, specifically at the state and local levels.
• It includes the creation of a $1.45 billion public education fund to carry out a sustained nationwide advertising and education program to counter youth tobacco use and educate consumers about tobacco-related disease.[39]

States accrued significant revenues from the tobacco settlement: $6.4 billion in 2000, $6.9 billion in 2001, $8.3 billion in 2002, and $8.4 billion in 2003. Contrary to the hopes of many public health advocates, there are no restrictions on the use of MSA funds by the states. Some criticism of the tobacco settlement has centered on the following issues:

• The tobacco settlement did not require the money be spent on antismoking or health care programs. In 2003, 31 states used their tobacco settlement funds to fill budget gaps for 2004. Only a handful of states spent all of their tobacco money for health purposes in 2003. Only six states earned "A" grades from the American Lung Association in its 2004 report card for their antismoking programs. By 2008 states spent $717 million in tobacco prevention and cessation. Even though this is the highest figure in six years, it is less than half of what the Centers for Disease Control and Prevention (CDC) recommend.
• California, Connecticut, New Jersey, New York, Oregon, Rhode Island, Washington, and Wisconsin have cashed in a big chunk of their share of the settlement, selling future tobacco payments to investors for an upfront lump sum, known as securitization.
• Fewer people are smoking and hence states receive less because their yearly allotment from the settlement fund is based on the number of cigarettes sold in the state. Nationwide, the number of smokers has dropped to 13 percent of adults, down from about 50 percent 40 years ago. State allotments also will go down as smokers turn to cigarettes from off-brand manufacturers and online retailers that do not pay into the settlement fund. Given the fiscal crunch experienced by states, many are turning to raising cigarette taxes because studies have shown that this often causes people to stop smoking. Instead of curbing advertising, the tobacco industry actually raised its marketing budget to a record $14 billion from 1998 to 2004.[40]

(For some facts on the U.S. tobacco industry, see Figure 12.2 on page 314.)

Cigarettes account for over 90 percent of spending on tobacco products in the United States; in 1998 Americans smoked 24 billion packs. In 1995 U.S. spending for all tobacco products totaled about $49 billion.

Five American companies–Philip Morris, R.J. Reynolds, Brown and Williamson, Lorillard, and Liggett–produce almost all of the cigarettes sold in the United States. Two companies, Philip Morris and R.J. Reynolds, account for more than 70 percent of industry sales. About 36 billion packs of cigarettes were produced by U.S. firms in 1997; about 12 billion packs were exported to other countries and about 280 million shipped to U.S. territories and to U.S. armed forces stationed overseas. The rest were consumed by domestic smokers. Smokeless tobacco products are also produced by only five domestic manufacturers: U.S. Tobacco, Conwood, Pinkerton, National, and Swisher. Over 120 million pounds of chewing tobacco and snuff were produced in the United States in 1996; in 1995, smokeless tobacco companies posted revenues of $1.7 billion. About 2.5 billion large cigars and cigarillos and 14.2 million pounds of pipe and roll-your-own tobacco were produced by U.S. companies in 1995.

The United States is the second largest tobacco producer in the world, well below China. In 1996 tobacco was grown on over 124,000 U.S. farms, with a crop value of $2.9 billion. The tobacco industry supports more than 600,000 jobs.

Figure 12.2

Tobacco at a Glance

Source: CNN, "A Brief History of Tobacco." Retrieved 2001, from www.cnn.com/US/9705/tobacco/history/index.html

The Health Care Crisis

Health care in the United States is plagued with problems such as eroding coverage, rising costs, cost shifting, and an increasing number of anxious citizens. This and the following sections will explore some parameters of the health care crisis, including health care spending and cost efficiency, the effectiveness of the U.S. health care system, attempts at cost cutting, the growing role of managed care, and the impact of AIDS on the health care budget.

Overview of U.S. Health Care Expenditures

U.S. health care cost $2.26 trillion in 2007, up from $73 billion in 1970. This translates into about 16 percent of the total gross domestic product (GDP). (Health expenditures as a percentage of the GDP measure the proportion of all resources devoted to health care.) It is projected that by 2013 health care spending will rise to $3.4 trillion and make up 18.4 percent of the GDP. In comparison, health care spending in 1970 was only 7.1 percent of the GDP. From 1970 to 2007, per capita health care costs rose from $341 to $7,439, an increase of more than 2,000 percent (see Figure 12.3).

Health care spending accounted for about 14 percent of the GDP in 2001 compared to education which was only 4.8 percent. Moreover, the costs of providing health care have risen faster than the rate of inflation. From 1980 to 1992, annual increases in per capita expenditures on health care were approximately five points above the yearly inflation rate. The growth rate in health care expenditures decelerated somewhat in 1992 (registering less than three points above the rate of inflation)[41]—but it accelerated again in the late 1990s. In 2002 health care expenditures rose by 9.5 percent or more than four times the rate of inflation.

When health care expenditures are broken down, the largest share (31 percent) goes to hospitals.[42] (See Figure 12.4.) An increase in the cost of hospital care has been a key factor in driving up health care costs, and in 2004 that rose 6.5 percent which outpaced overall inflation. By comparison, in 1965 the average daily hospital room charge was

Figure 12.3

National Health Care Expenditures Selected Years, 1970–2006 (dollar amount in billions)

Source: HHS, Centers for Medicare & Medicaid Services, "National Health Expenditures Aggregate, Per Capita Amounts, Percent Distribution, and Average Annual Percent Growth, by Source of Funds: Selected Calendar Years 1960–2006". Retrieved July 2008, from www.cms.hhs.gov/NationalHealth ExpendData/downloads/tables.pdf

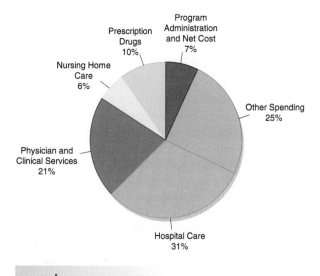

Figure 12.4

The Nation's Health Dollar, Calendar Year 2006: Where It Went

Note: "Other Spending" includes dental services, other professional services, home health, durable medical products, over-the-counter medicines and sundries, public health, other personal health care, research and structures, and equipment.

Source: HHS, Centers for Medicare & Medicaid Services. Retrieved July 2008, from www.cms.hhs.gov/National HealthExpendData/downloads/PieChartSourcesExpendit ures2006.pdf

$41; by 1994 it was $1,127. In 1965 the average cost per hospital stay was $315. By 2003 it rose to $11,700 for an average stay of less than five days.[43]

Of the total amount spent on health in 2006, 34 percent came from private insurance, 19 percent from Medicare, 15 percent from Medicaid and SCHIP, and 12 percent from out-of-pocket expenses. The remaining 19 percent came from other public (workers' compensation, Department of Defense, etc.) and other private (including philanthropy) sources.[44] Premiums increased only 2 percent yearly from 1994 to 1998, but then jumped to 8.2 percent in 1998. In 2002 premiums shot up by 11.4 percent and then dropped to about 7.1 percent in 2004.[45]

U.S. Health Care in International Perspective

Health care costs are higher in the United States than in any other industrialized nation.[46] The United States spends more than other countries on health care, both in absolute dollars and in the share of total economic activity. Health spending per capita in the United States was almost $7,500 in 2007, more than twice the average for the other industrial nations in the Organization for Economic Cooperation and Development (OECD). Specifically, health spending in the United States in 2006 was 15.3 percent of the gross domestic product, nearly twice the percentage of Australia and the United Kingdom and by far the highest of 30 OECD countries.[47] (See Table 12.2 on page 316.) Although high expenditures are often equated with excellent medical treatment, the health of the average American—as measured by life expectancy and infant mortality—is below that of other major industrialized nations. More specifically, despite the high costs of U.S. medical care, life expectancy ranks only in the middle of the 30 OECD nations. This is due to a variety of factors, including diet, low levels of physical activity, births to teenage mothers, and the high number of violent deaths.[48]

The data clearly suggest that the U.S. health care system does not perform as well as health care systems in other industrialized countries. For one,

Table 12.2

Total Health Care Expenditures as a Percentage of GDP

Country	1975	2006	Percentage Point Change
United States	7.9	15.3	7.4
France	6.4	11.1	4.7
New Zealand	6.7	9.3	2.6
Germany	8.4	10.6	2.2
Canada	7.0	10.0	3.0
Australia	6.5	8.8 (2005)	2.3
United Kingdom	5.5	8.4	2.9

Source: OECD Health Data 2008, www.oecd.org

the United States is the only major industrialized country that fails to provide health coverage for all its citizens, yet spending on health is extremely high compared to other nations. The United States emphasizes private markets as a strategy for cost containment, yet health care costs are growing rapidly. Private spending as a share of total health care expenditures is far higher in the United States than in other industrialized nations. Moreover, out-of-pocket per capita health care spending in the United States was $707 in 2000, more than twice ($328) that of other industrialized nations.[49]

A common perception is that other industrialized countries control costs by rationing patient care. In fact, Americans receive fewer days of hospital care than residents of other industrialized nations and have about the same amount of physician visits. Americans are, however, more likely to undergo specialized medical procedures.[50]

According to the Commonwealth Fund, the United States falls short in access to needed services. The Fund ranked the United States last among five English-speaking countries on measures of equity and first for access problems due to costs. Americans are much more likely than their counterparts in other countries to say they did not visit a physician, fill a prescription, or get a recommended test, treatment, or follow-up care because of costs. Disparities between people in above-average and below-average income groups were greatest in the United States and the uninsured were much more likely to report problems in obtaining needed care.[51]

Infant mortality rates also illustrate troubling trends. In 2002 the United States had one of the highest infant mortality rates among OECD countries (6.69 per 1,000 live births). This compared unfavorably to Greece (6.25), New Zealand (6.18), Portugal (5.84), Italy (5.76), Czech Republic (5.46), United Kingdom (5.45), Ireland (5.43), Canada (4.95), and other nations. Another health indicator is premature deaths, or deaths that would have been preventable had appropriate medical knowledge been applied or had risky behavior been less prevalent. The United States had the most preventable deaths per 100,000 people, with Japan having the least.[52] In short, Americans are neither healthier nor live longer than people in similar industrial nations where health care spending is 50 percent lower.[53]

Explaining the High Cost of U.S. Health Care

Although accounting for the enormous costs of the U.S. health care system is complicated, some policy analysts attribute at least some of these costs to the following factors:

• High costs of medical malpractice.

• The former Bush administration argued that medical malpractice suits drove up health care costs from $60 to $80 billion a year. The Bush Administration maintains that this waste could be eliminated by passing legislation that limited (i.e., up to $250,000) what injured patients could collect in lawsuits. In contrast, both the General Accounting Office and the Congressional Budget Office criticized the 1996 study the Bush administration used as their main support, instead maintaining that any savings would be relatively small.[54]

• The United States leads the world in the development and use of medical technology, but these advances have come at a high price. For example, between 1980 and 1991, the number of coronary bypass operations for men increased from 108,000 to 206,000. By 2006, the number of bypass operations had reached 365,000 and the number of "stent" operations (an alternative to bypasses) had soared to nearly one million.[55] The treatment is now available for some diseases that were formerly untreatable, albeit at a high price. For example, some technologies are introduced before being sufficiently tested to determine their cost effectiveness and superiority to existing technologies.

• The administrative costs involved in processing millions of insurance claims also add to rising health care expenditures. Harvard Medical School researchers reported in 2004 that the United States spent $399 billion a year on its health care bureaucracy, essentially the administrative costs of insurers, hospitals, doctors, nursing homes, and other institutions. In California, $45 billion of the $163 billion spent on health care (28 percent) went to administration.[56]

Hospital Costs

As noted earlier, 31.7 percent of all health care expenditures go toward hospital costs. The total costs of hospital care reached $648 billion in 2006, up from $28 billion in 1970. Since 2000, spending

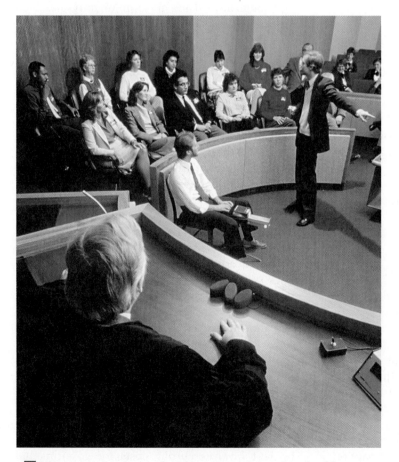

■ *The increasing costs of malpractice suits against health care providers are felt most directly by consumers, who must pay higher medical costs to offset these suits.*

on hospital services has grown by over 7 percent each year.[57] According to the American Hospital Association, nearly 60 percent of hospital costs go to wages and benefits of caregivers and others. Labor costs account for the largest share of spending growth for hospital services from 2001 to 2003. In addition, the costs of technology, construction, and regulatory compliance account for a growing share of hospital costs. Predictions from the Centers for Medicare and Medicaid Services suggest that hospitals' share of national health expenditures will decline to less than 28 percent in 2012. However, much of this decline may be attributable to cuts in federal and state health programs.[58]

Physicians' Salaries

The second largest health care expenditure is for physicians' services. From 1970 to 1999, the cost of physicians' services rose by almost 1,800 percent. From 1980 to 1990 alone, the cost of physicians' services rose by 300 percent.[59] By 2008 the average salary for a number of specialist physicians was approaching $400,000 (see Table 12.3 on page 318).

Physician organizations argue that high salaries are necessary to repay the high debts incurred by medical students. In 2003, medical students graduated with 4.5 times more debt than in 1984. Moreover, in that same year the median debt was $100,000 and $135,000 for public school and private medical school graduates, respectively.[60] Despite this debt, the American Medical Association claims that "Even though the cost of medical school has risen faster than physician salaries, physicians still earn a decent return on their investment, roughly 6% for the $1.2 million a physician bears for the assorted costs of a public education and the wages lost while in school. Also, becoming a doctor is typically a higher paying investment when comparing average educational costs and salaries of business and law school graduates."[61]

The problem of high physician salaries is aggravated by the growth in the number of expensive medical specialists. Beginning in 1997 fewer medical students chose **primary care** tracks.

Table 12.3

Average Salaries of Selected U.S. Practicing Physicians, 2008

Specialty	Salary
Orthopedic surgery	$439,000
Anesthesiology	336,000
Urology	387,000
Gastroenterology	379,000
Otolaryngology	362,000
General surgery	321,000
CRNA	185,000

Source: ASC Review, "Average Salaries for Top Recruited Specialties," June 27, 2008. Retrieved July 2008, from www.beckersasc.com/healthcare-business/healthcare-business-issues/average-salaries-for-top-recruited-specialties.html

By 2002, 20 percent fewer medical students were in a primary care track compared to 1997. For example, from 2000 to 2001 the number of medical students pursuing a family practice track dropped by 9.1 percent and the number of those pursuing internal medicine dropped by 2 percent. On the other hand, students pursuing neurological surgery increased by 36 percent, pathology by almost 27 percent, anesthesiology by almost 14 percent, and diagnostic radiology by 10 percent.[62] By 2005, approximately 60 percent of physicians were specialists and 40 percent primary care (12.3 percent in family medicine and general practice)—a reversal of the ratio that existed 30 years ago.[63]

The Pharmaceutical Industry

The high cost of prescription drugs is also driving up health care costs. Over the past decade, the share of health expenditures spent on pharmaceuticals in the United States increased from 8.9 percent of total health spending in 1995 to 12.6 percent in 2006. Consumers pay more for medicine in the United States than in any other country. The United States was the top spender on pharmaceuticals in 2006, with spending of $843 per person, followed by Canada, Belgium, and France.[64] Two-thirds of doctor visits result in a drug being prescribed, and overreliance on drugs is a major factor contributing to medical care being the third leading cause of death in the United States. Many of these people are exposed to financial

catastrophe as a result of highly inflated drug prices. In contrast, manufacturers of the top 20 drugs have increased their profits at rates much higher than the average rate of Fortune 500 companies.[65]

Harvard physician Marcia Angell disputes the drug industry's reputation as an "engine of innovation," arguing that the top U.S. drug makers spend 2.5 times as much on marketing and administration as they do on research. According to Angell, at least a third of the drugs marketed by the industry were discovered by universities or small biotech companies but are sold to the public at inflated prices. Angell cites Taxol, the cancer drug discovered by the National Institutes of Health but sold by Bristol Myers Squibb for $20,000 a year, reportedly 20 times the manufacturing cost. Angell attacks the pharmaceutical industry—whose top ten companies make more in profits than the rest of the Fortune 500 combined—for using free market rhetoric while opposing competition.[66]

Though advertising prescription drugs has been legal for years, Food and Drug Administration (FDA) guidelines released in 1997 clarified the rules for advertising directly to consumers. Since the mid-1990s, pharmaceutical companies have tripled the amount of money spent on advertising prescription drugs directly to consumers. From 1996 to 2000, spending on these ads more than tripled, rising from $791 million to nearly $2.5 billion.[67]

In 1999 the drug industry spent $8.3 billion promoting its products—nearly half as much as the $17 billion it spent on research and development. Direct consumer advertising accounted for $1.3 billion of the total, with the rest being aimed at medical professionals. The advertising paid off. Posting huge increases in sales between 1993 and 1998 were heavily advertised drugs that included antihistamines (sales increases of $1.9 billion), antidepressants ($5 billion), cholesterol reducers ($3.4 billion), and anti-ulcer drugs ($2.7 billion).[68] Health care costs almost doubled in a decade, and prescription drug prices increased by 152 percent.[69]

Cutting Health Care Costs

There are two aspects to cutting health care costs. The first involves cutting costs for governmental health care programs; the second involves lowering overall medical costs.[70] The rising costs of Medicare have led the federal government to seek alternative ways to lower hospital costs, including the Diagnostic Related Group system (DRG). In 1983 Congress enacted the DRG form of medical payment. Although earlier Medicare rules had restricted the fees hospitals could charge, the government generally reimbursed them for the entire bill. This style of reimbursement was called retrospective (after-the-fact) payment. By contrast, DRGs are a form of **prospective payment system**, or payment before the fact, whereby the federal government specifies in advance what it will pay for the treatment of 468 classified illnesses or diagnosis-related groups.[71]

Developed by health researchers at the Yale-New Haven Hospital, the DRG system was designed to enforce economy by defining expected lengths of hospital stays. This system provides a treatment and diagnostic classification scheme, using the patient's medical diagnosis, prescribed treatment, and age as a means for categorizing and defining hospital services. In other words, the DRG system determines the length of a typical patient's hospital stay and reimburses hospitals only for that period of time. (Exceptions to the DRG classification system are made for long hospital stays, certain kinds of hospital facilities, hospitals that are the only facility in a community, and hospitals that serve large numbers of poor people.) Additional costs beyond the DRG allotment must be borne by the hospital. Conversely, if a patient requires less hospitalization than the maximum DRG allocation, the hospital keeps the difference. Hence, patients not yet ready for discharge (e.g., patients who do not have appropriate aftercare services available) may be discharged—a situation that can result in patient dumping.

Managed Care

Managed care became a household word in the 1990s. By 2008 more than 70 million Americans were enrolled in HMOs, up from 33.3 million in 1990. An estimated 90 million more are enrolled in PPOs, which cost more but allow patients more flexibility. Managed care and HMOs have been touted by the nation's large employers as a way to control health care costs. However, while managed care cut costs for most of the 1990s, by the end of the decade costs started climbing again, increasing by more than 7 percent in 2000.[72] From 2002 to 2004 managed care costs rose from 7 to 10 percent.

Paul Schmolling Jr., Merrill Youkeles, and William Burger define **managed care** as "an umbrella for health care insurance systems that contract with a network of hospitals, clinics, and doctors who agree to accept fees for each service or flat payments per patient. The advantage to providers is that they are given a ready source of referrals."[73] Figure 12.5 on page 320 lists various types of managed care systems.

Proponents of managed care argue that the system has effectively lowered health care costs without reducing the quality of health care services. They maintain that the system encourages more efficient and less expensive medical care and that it can stress prevention over treatment. Because doctors reimbursed by managed care organizations have little incentive to overtreat patients or recommend unnecessary medical care, the health care system is expected to be more efficient. This suggests that in some degree the proponents are correct. For example:

- The per capita growth in health care expenditures was 2.7 percent in 1994, dropping from 5 percent in the 1980s and early 1990s (before managed care had gained a strong foothold). Per capita national expenditures on health care were $3,510 in 1994, only $100 more than in 1993 and half the increase of 1992 to 1993.
- Physicians' salaries dropped 3.6 percent from 1993 to 1994—the first recorded drop in the history of the American Medical Association.[74]

Managed care is clearly shaping U.S. medicine. According to the AMA, the percentage of doctors who had contracts with managed-care plans increased from 61 percent in 1990 to 92 percent by 1997. Among doctors with such contracts, the proportion of their income resulting from those plans rose from 35 percent to 40 percent between 1996 and 1997.[75] Broadly defined, private managed plans now cover two-thirds of all privately insured Americans. Jumping on the bandwagon, the federal and many state governments have encouraged (and, in some states, required) Medicare and Medicaid beneficiaries to join managed care plans. By 2003, there were 179 Medicare plans with 5 million members, 1 million less than five years previously because of HMOs dropping elderly consumers.[76] Insurers have charged that the federal government's Medicare reimbursement rate is too low to keep pace with medical inflation and thus ensure the financial solvency of Medicare HMOs.[77]

Critics of managed care (including HMOs) maintain that they are plagued with serious problems.[78] Indeed, managed care has not won the hearts and minds of the public. In a 1999 survey, only 46 percent of Americans said they were very confident their treatment would be based on their

- **Health Maintenance Organizations (HMO)**—a prepaid or capitated insurance plan in which individuals or their employers pay a fixed monthly fee for services rather than a separate charge for each visit or service.

- **Preferred Provider Organizations (PPO)**—a type of HMO whereby an employer or insurance company contracts with a selected group of health care delivery providers for services at preestablished reimbursement rates. Consumers have the choice of who to contact to provide the service. If a doctor is not on the provider list, higher out of pocket expenses will result.

- **Exclusive Provider Organization (EPO)**—a type of HMO where members must get care only from the EPO doctors who may only treat members of the plan.

- **The Independent Practice Association (IPA)**—a type of HMO which has large numbers of independent doctors in private practice. Physicians are paid a fixed fee for treating IPA members but also can treat patients who are not members of the plan.

- **The Network Model**—multispecialty groups of doctors who have contracts with more than one HMO. Doctors work out of their own offices.

- **Point of Service (POS)**—an option that can be offered by any type of HMO. If patients use doctors in their HMO network, and if referrals are made only by the primary care physician, only nominal fees are charged. If patients use doctors outside their HMO network the cost is higher.

- **Physician–Hospital Organization (PHO)**—organized groups of doctors affiliated with a particular hospital who provide services to patients enrolled in their plan as they would in an HMO.

Figure 12.5

Types of Managed Care Plans

Source: Naomi Brill and Joanne Levine, *Working With People*, 7th ed. (Boston: Allyn & Bacon, 2001).

health care needs rather than on the cost of their care. Another national poll found that 61 percent of Americans agreed with the statement "I'm frustrated and angry about the state of the health care system in this country." In addition, only a third of people who had been ill in the previous year said they were completely happy or very happy about the care they received through their HMO.[79]

Many physicians believe the quality of care has gotten worse under managed care. Some physicians have joined unions, and others have formed networks to negotiate contracts with managed care. Still others have stopped taking HMO patients. Hospitals say they are squeezed by slow and low payments from HMOs and cuts to Medicare. Many have had to cut staff. Nurses say that hospitals often are so short staffed that patient care is seriously compromised. One study found that nearly 70 percent of nurses worry about inadequate staffing levels.[80]

Managed care plans generally gate-keep the access to specialists for consumers. These plans do this by pressuring primary physicians to not refer or by limiting specialist care to one or two visits. Some managed care plans are reluctant to cover costly procedures or experimental treatments, especially those relating to cancer. Still other plans refuse to pay for medical care clients receive while out of state, even if it was required in an emergency. Some enrollees complain that managed care forces them to use only primary care physicians, hospitals, and specialists that are on an approved list, which restricts their freedom of choice. And some managed care operations do not provide the same level of benefits as Medicare, especially when it comes to home health care, physical therapy, and nursing home care.[81] Critics also note that the size of managed care operations has led to greater bureaucratization and impersonality.[82]

During the late 1990s many HMOs were in financial trouble and the industry posted $1.25 billion in net losses in 1998. To compensate, HMOs raised premiums, cut services, or many left the business. Several large managed care companies across the country went bankrupt, leaving state officials and consumers scrambling to find replacement coverage. From the mid-1990s onward the health insurance market consolidated at a rapid pace. Between 1995 and 2001 there were over 350 mergers involving health insurers and managed care organizations. The result is that more than half of all commercially insured Americans are now covered by the 10 largest health insurers. In many parts of the country health insurance markets are dominated by a few companies that have significant power over the marketplace. According to one AMA study, there is at least one insurer with a market share in excess of 30 percent in 89 percent of highly concentrated metropolitan areas. In 40 percent of these markets a single insurer has a market share in excess of 50 percent; and in 15 percent they have a market share of more than 70 percent.[83] This trend has resulted in the profit margins of health insurers rising, albeit in fits and starts.[84]

Managed care companies are boxed in to a degree. Specifically, HMOs cannot reprise their 1990s role as gatekeepers that restrict care to boost the bottom line. Regulations on the state and federal level have dampened that idea, and after bad publicity in the 1990s, managed care companies became somewhat more lenient and paid for more care. Instead of gate-keeping, these companies simply passed along premium hikes plus a few percent for profits. In short, instead of cutting costs, managed care companies simply pass on rate hikes. On the other hand, managed care companies cannot survive by simply passing along high rate hikes each year. Their role of belt-tightening has been lost, and with it, their justification for providing affordable health care.

The Underinsured

The U.S. medical system provides high-quality care for most people in the upper and upper-middle classes, who are protected by adequate health insurance. Although most Americans are covered by private insurance plans,[85] gaps in private health insurance may include high deductibles and copayments, limits on the length of hospital stays, dollar limits on payments to hospitals and physicians, exclusion of certain laboratory tests, refusal of coverage for office visits and routine health care, noncoverage for mental health services, refusal of coverage to persons who are found to be in poor health when applying for insurance, and a lack of coverage for dental and eye care. Because privately purchased health insurance has become almost unaffordable, the availability of health insurance may be a major factor in an individual's job search or decision to continue in a job.[86] Moreover, employers may be reluctant to hire people with high-risk conditions, because of the negative effect on their insurance premiums. Finally, one of the most dramatic gaps is the frequent failure of some private health insurance plans to cover catastrophic medical costs—those costs that could reduce a middle-class family to "medically indigent" status within only a few months.

AIDS and Health Care

The U.S. health care crisis is aggravated by the AIDS epidemic that first surfaced during the presidency of Ronald Reagan. The Reagan administration initially saw the AIDS problem as being of little consequence. Indeed, expressing public concern for the suffering of homosexuals was a political liability—especially given that the Republican Party was actively courting the religious right, some of whose leaders saw AIDS as a divine punishment for the sin of homosexuality.[87] Unlike the Reagan and Bush administrations, the Clinton administration was unafraid to address the AIDS crisis head-on. President Clinton pushed for full funding for the Ryan White Care Act, created the National Task Force on AIDS Drug Development, strengthened the Office of AIDS Research at the National Institutes of Health, and placed HIV/AIDS victims under the protection of the Americans with Disabilities Act.

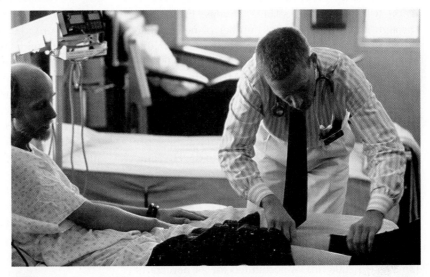

■ *According to a Rand study, not all people with HIV are treated equally. Among adults with HIV, women receive inferior care compared to men, as do African Americans and Hispanics compared to non-Hispanic whites.*

Table 12.4

Characteristics of Male and Female Adults/Adolescents Living with AIDS in the U.S., 2006

Exposure Category	White (not Hispanic) Male	White (not Hispanic) Female	African American (not Hispanic) Male	African American (not Hispanic) Female	Hispanic Male	Hispanic Female
Sex between men	101,299	NA	57,520	NA	36,087	NA
Injecting drug use	13,168	7,407	33,911	18,531	14,795	5,025
Sex between men and injecting drugs	12,393	NA	10,121	NA	4,352	NA
High risk heterosexual contact	6,081	11,350	24,205	41,741	7,816	11,092
Other	1,743	508	1,602	1,456	574	413
Total	134,684	19,265	127,359	61,728	63,624	16,530

Source: Centers for Disease Control and Prevention, "Estimated Numbers of Persons Living with AIDS at the End of 2006, by Race/Ethnicity, Sex, and Transmission category—50 States and the District of Columbia," Basic Statistics, HIV/AIDS Surveillance Report. Retrieved July 2008, from www.cdc.gov/hiv/topics/surveillance/resources/reports/2006report/pdf/2006SurveillanceReport.pdf

The epidemiological data on AIDS are striking. At the end of 2006, the prevalence rate of AIDS among adults and adolescents in the United States was estimated at 178.6 per 100,000. Among male adults and adolescents, male-to-male sexual contact is a key characteristic for people living with AIDS (nearly 200,000) and for African American females, heterosexual contact (over 40,000) (see Table 12.4).[88] Marked declines in AIDS deaths began in 1996 because of the widespread use of potent combination antiretroviral therapies. By 2002 AIDS prevalence was continuing to rise, with almost 400,000 persons living with AIDS in the United States. From 2002 through 2006 the estimated number of newly diagnosed AIDS cases remained stable with the estimated rate of AIDS cases in 2006 being 12.3 per 100,000.[89]

The prevalence of HIV/AIDS in African Americans and Hispanics is much higher than for other groups. In 2006, African Americans accounted for 49 percent of all HIV/AIDS cases diagnosed, and their rate of HIV/AIDS was the highest at 67.7 per 100,000, followed by 25.5 per 100,000 in the Hispanic population, 8.8 per 100,000 for American Indians/Alaska Natives, 8.2 per 100,000 for whites, and 6.7 per 100,000 for the Asian/Pacific Islander population. From 2003 through 2006, the estimated number of HIV/AIDS cases increased approximately 5 percent among males and decreased 6 percent for females. In 2006, males accounted for 74 percent of all HIV/AIDS cases among adults and adolescents. From 2002 through 2006, the estimated number of AIDS cases decreased 10 percent in the West, 6 percent in the Northeast, and remained stable in the South and the Midwest.[90]

According to a recent Rand study, not all people with HIV are treated equally. Among adults with HIV in the United States, women receive inferior care compared to men, as do African Americans and Hispanics compared to non-Hispanic whites. Uninsured and Medicaid-insured HIV victims receive inferior care compared to the privately insured. Patients infected through heterosexual, gay, or bisexual contacts receive superior care compared to patients infected through injection drug use. In sum, disparities in HIV care are frequently associated with insurance status, gender, race, ethnicity, exposure group, income, education, age, and even geographical region.[91]

HIV/AIDS has spread at an alarming rate over the past few decades, although it has slowed slightly in recent years (see Table 12.5). In 2007, about 2.5 million people were newly infected with HIV. In 2007, around 2.1 million people died from AIDS (over 30 million have died since the first cases of AIDS were identified in 1981). According to the World Health Organization, about 33 million people were living with HIV/AIDS worldwide in 2007.[92]

Nowhere has the impact of HIV/AIDS been more severe than in sub-Saharan Africa:

- HIV/AIDS has reduced life expectancy by more than 20 years in Botswana, Lesotho, Swaziland,

Table 12.5

Regional HIV/AIDS Statistics, 2007

Region	Adults and Children Living with HIV/AIDS	Adults and Children Newly Infected with HIV	Adult Prevalence Rate
Sub-Saharan Africa	20.9–24.3 million	1.4–2.4 million	4.6–5.5%
North Africa and the Middle East	270,000–500,000	16,000–65,000	0.2–0.4%
South and Southeast Asia	3.3–5.1 million	180,000–740,000	0.2–0.4%
East Asia	620,000–960,000	21,000–220,000	< 0.2%
Oceania	53,000–120,000	11,000–26,000	0.3–0.7%
Latin America	1.4–1.9 million	47,000–220,000	0.4–0.6%
Caribbean	210,000–270,000	15,000–23,000	0.9–1.2%
Eastern Europe and Central Asia	1.2– 2.1 million	70,000–290,000	0.7–1.2%
Western and Central Europe	600,000–1.1 million	19,000–86,000	0.2–0.4%
North America	480,000–1.9 million	38,000–68,000	0.5–0.9%
Total	33.2 million	2.5 million	0.8%
	(30.6–36.1 million)	(1.8–4.1 million)	(0.7–0.9%)

Source: UNAIDS/WHO, "AIDS Epidemic Update," December 2007. Retrieved July 2008, from http://data.unaids.org/pub/EPISlides/2007/2007_epiupdate_en.pdf

and Zimbabwe. By 2015 the disease will have reduced populations of the 38 most affected countries by 10 percent or some 91 million people.

- Young adults aged 15 to 24 account for half of all new HIV cases; the majority are women.
- Women are biologically two to four times more likely to contract HIV during unprotected sex than men, and teenagers are even more biologically vulnerable.
- AIDS has orphaned at least 14 million children. By 2010 a number expected to double.
- AIDS is directly or indirectly responsible for up to 60 percent of all child deaths in Africa.
- Fewer than 5 percent of all the people with HIV/AIDS in the developing world have access to lifesaving antiretroviral (ARV) therapy.[93]

Reforming U.S. Health Care

The Business Roundtable is a Washington, DC–based organization of the Chief Executive Officers of leading U.S. corporations. Together they represent more than 10 million employees and $4.6 trillion in annual revenues.[94] On January 16, 2007, Business Roundtable joined with AARP and the Service Employees International Union (SEIU) to create the Divided We Fail partnership.[95] Among other things, the Divided We Fail platform includes, "All Americans should have access to affordable health care, including prescription drugs, and these costs should not burden future generations."[96] The U.S. Chamber of Commerce, the world's largest association of businesses with more than 3 million corporate members, echoes this sentiment in their Policy Priorities for 2004 that include "passage of legislation to help business continue to provide affordable coverage for their employees."[97] Even the National Agenda of the smaller National Federation of Independent Businesses, traditionally an opponent of attempts to expand mandatory health insurance coverage, states that "finding and affording quality health insurance is a top concern of small-business owners."[98] In the past there has been a large gap between access/affordability and universal coverage; however, there are signs that this gap is narrowing.

In 2007 Andy Stern, President of SEIU, and Lee Scott, CEO of Wal-Mart, together announced the good of universal health care coverage by 2012.[99] Prior to that in December 2006, Steve

Burd, chairman and CEO of Safeway, stood with Senator Ron Wyden and Andy Stern to advocate for universal coverage. Burd even announced the creation of a new advocacy group composed of businesses to be called the Coalition to Advance Health Care Reform.[100] What Burd came to realize is that access to affordable health care cannot be achieved without universal participation. Universal health care is not simply a moral issue. It represents a major cost in operating a business and has a significant impact on international competitiveness. For potential employees it is a jobs issue, with escalating health costs impacting the ability of the business sector to create and sustain new jobs.

In January 2004, a coalition of associations representing medical providers, pharmaceutical companies, insurance companies, businesses, and leading nonprofits began working to see if they could come to a consensus on how to reform health care. On January 18, 2007, this new Health Coverage Coalition for the Uninsured (HCCU) (www .coalitionfortheuninsured.org) issued "Expanding Health Care Coverage in the United States: A Historic Agreement."[101] The policy recommendations advocated by HCCU have the goal "to expand health coverage to as many people as possible as soon as possible."[102] The specific proposals rely heavily on tax credits to fund the cost of health insurance. Signatories to this agreement include the American Medical Association, the American Hospital Association, America's Health Insurance Plans, Kaiser Permanente, Pfizer, and the U.S. Chamber of Commerce. The policy proposals by HCCU are more incremental than the universal coverage being advocated by Burd, yet the mere existence of a policy consensus by associations this diverse suggests that some form of health care reform cannot be too far away, and HCCU does have the same goal as Burd—coverage for everyone.

The U.S. health care system is driven by a combination of ideological and fiscal variables. Primary among these is whether **health care access** should be a right or a privilege. Conservatives generally believe that access to medical care is a privilege that must be earned through past or present labor force participation. Democrats, in turn, believe that health care should be a right that is somehow tied to labor force participation, except in instances in which people are not linked to the workforce. Progressive thinkers, grounded in a European tradition, argue that health care is a right that should be bestowed upon each individual at birth.

Another issue in the health care debate is the role of the private marketplace in the provision of medical care. Conservatives support the **commodification** of health care and believe that medical care should be lodged squarely in the private marketplace. Conservatives argue that medical institutions and drug companies should be free to establish the prices of health care and medical goods. They believe that in medical care, as with other commodities, increased competition lowers the price of goods and increases quality. Government regulation of the health care market is therefore seen as leading to more inefficiencies, lower quality or poorer service, and higher prices. Some liberals believe the private marketplace is the proper venue for the delivery of health care, but they also recognize that health care is a commodity that does not respond to market conditions in the same way as other commodities. For example, if a person is immobilized by cardiac arrest, it is unlikely that he or she will shop around for the cheapest cardiac care prices. Likewise, most patients facing serious surgery will not choose a surgeon based on price point. These conservatives believe that the health care marketplace must be somewhat regulated by government to ensure quality, price, and access.

More progressive thinkers argue that health care is too important to be left to the vicissitudes of the marketplace. For them, health care should be removed from the context of a market in which decisions are made solely on economic precepts. Health care must therefore be free or heavily subsidized at the point of access, universal in its coverage, and administered and controlled by government.

During the past 30 years, most proposals designed to reform or transform health care in the United States fall into three basic categories: (1) removing health care from the marketplace, (2) maintaining the private health care system while providing universal coverage through national health insurance, and (3) incremental reforms designed to soften the harder features of the U.S. health care system.

National Health Service

The most radical proposal for reforming the U.S. health care system involved the creation of a National Health Service (NHS). Proposed in the mid-1970s by left-wing health planners and members of Congress, the plan was promoted by Congressman Ronald Dellums (a social worker). The NHS would have established health care as a right of citizenship. Similar to the British model, it would have provided free (no fee at the point of access and no payments from third-party vendors) and comprehensive health care coverage, including diagnostic, therapeutic, preventive, rehabilitative, environmental, and occupational health services. To improve the maldistribution of medical services, the NHS would have provided free medical education in return for required periods of service in medically underserved areas.[103] The goal of the NHS was the elimination of private profit in the health care system.

Supporters argue that socialized health care would allow for the coordination of health services and reduce profiteering by professionals and corporations. Moreover, they contend that the experience of other countries illustrates that a system incorporating strict budgeting, nationalization, and the elimination of the profit motive arrests the growth of health care costs and, in the end, will prove less expensive than the current privatized system.

National Health Insurance

Single Payer System   Another proposal for restructuring U.S. health care as a **single-payer system** was the National Health Care Act of 1992. As in the Canadian model, states would have had responsibility for ensuring the delivery of health services, for paying all providers, and for planning in accordance with federal guidelines. Although this plan would have allowed the practice of private medicine, the act would have discontinued private health insurance coverage.[104] Supporters of this bill claimed that it would immediately reduce health care spending by 18 percent, and that a single payer approach would reduce the fraud endemic to a multiple-payer system.[105]

Another strategy to restructure the U.S. health care system is **national health insurance (NHI).** According to Paul Starr, the United States was on the brink of establishing national health insurance several times during the twentieth century, but each time factors unique to the country's political and social institutions prevented its adoption.[106] In the 1930s, for example, NHI plans began to proliferate as part of Roosevelt's New Deal; but the idea was abandoned because of the strident opposition of the AMA—originally a supporter of NHI—and the fear that NHI's inclusion would jeopardize passage of the 1935 Social Security Act. President Harry Truman took up the NHI banner in the days

following World War II, but by that time most middle-class and unionized workers were covered by private insurance plans. Moreover, the AMA again set its powerful lobbying machine into motion, this time equating national health insurance with socialized medicine and with Communism.[107]

The most recent incarnation of NHI occurred in the Health Security Act (HSA) proposed by former President Bill Clinton in 1993. Although the HSA was not a NHI per se, it contained important components of national insurance. Clinton's bill was based partly on the ideas of the Jackson Hole Group, who reiterated the need for cost consciousness in health care and the need for substantial investment in outcome and evaluation research.[108]

To formulate the health care bill, Hillary Clinton and Ira Magaziner led a 500-person task force charged with (1) extending medical insurance to the uninsured at a reasonable cost; (2) guaranteeing continued coverage when workers change jobs or get sick; (3) curbing and controlling steadily rising health care costs by developing health care networks; (4) addressing the problems of the insurance industry; (5) stopping drug companies from inflating drug prices; (6) developing a basic benefits package for every American; and (7) providing universal health care coverage. The result of this task force was the 1,342-page Health Security Act.

The HSA would have worked in the following manner: All citizens and legal immigrants would get a card guaranteeing them a comprehensive lifelong package of health care benefits, including inpatient and outpatient medical care, prescription drugs, dental and vision care, long-term care, mental health services, and substance abuse treatment. Coverage would be continuous regardless of employment status. All participants would buy into large purchasing pools called Health Care Alliances. Each alliance would offer separate plans for consumers: (1) a **fee-for-service** option allowing consumers to choose their doctors; (2) a plan based on joining a network of doctors and hospitals; and (3) the choice of an HMO. Charges for low-income self-insurers would be based on a sliding scale. Those on public assistance would have their fees paid by Medicaid. Employers would pay 80 percent of the premium of the standard benefit package and workers would pay the additional 20 percent.

Despite a promising start, the HSA bill faltered almost from the moment of its inception. Opposition came from several quarters. Smaller health insurers felt they were being maneuvered out of the industry and took to the airwaves. Almost immediately, the Health Insurance Association of America (HIAA) broadcast $2 million worth of "Harry and Louise" commercials attacking the HSA as rationing health care under socialized medicine.[109] Within days HIAA claimed that more than 40,000 callers had phoned their 800 number to register complaints about health care reform.[110] On the congressional side, small business lobbyists argued that the costs of the employer mandate would bankrupt thousands of small companies. Within weeks, dozens of lobbyists from such groups as pharmaceutical companies, tobacco companies, restaurants, and labor unions besieged Congress. Anticipating the 1994 elections, health industry interest groups contributed $26 million to congressional campaigns.[111] Observers put the price tag on defeating the HSA at $100 million.[112] The conservative 104th Congress of 1994 killed the possibility of comprehensive health care reform.

Critics of NHI plans charge that they would modify payment mechanisms rather than encourage major changes in the health care system. Although NHI schemes would equalize the ability of patients to pay, they would not improve the accessibility or the quality of services. Furthermore, most NHI proposals call for coinsurance (copayments) in amounts that many poor people could not afford.[113] Contrary to what some critics claim, NHI schemes are not socialized medicine: Hospitals would remain private, doctors would continue to be private practitioners, and most NHI plans reserve a major role for private insurance companies.

Incremental Reform

Incremental health care reform has proved more acceptable to the general public and policymakers than sweeping reforms. This approach has generally focused on remedying the more troubling aspects of the private health care system and on fine-tuning public health care programs.

A conservative approach to incremental health care reform is based on the concept of the individual medical savings account (MSA). The MSA is a form of self-insurance whereby individuals can purchase high-deductible health insurance while setting aside pretax dollars to pay for medical expenses. Opponents of MSAs fear, however, that these plans would benefit only the healthy and wealthy, leaving those with less money and more health problems behind in an increasingly costly insurance pool.

Congress also passed legislation in 1996 to require insurers to pay for a 48-hour hospital stay following a vaginal birth and a 96-hour stay after a cesarean section. In addition, Congress passed an amendment designed to create some level of parity between mental health and physical health benefits. The amendment requires insurers to set the same levels for annual and lifetime caps on mental health benefits as on physical health benefits. However, the bill stipulates that plans are not prohibited from requiring preadmission screening before authorization of services; nor are they prohibited from restricting mental health coverage to only those services that are medically necessary.[114]

Other reforms have been enacted on state levels. In Hawaii, employers are required to insure employees who work more than 20 hours a week.[115] A Health Rights program in Minnesota extends health care coverage to all noncovered low-income residents and charges them on a sliding-scale basis.[116]

Barack Obama's health care plan fits squarely under the category of incremental reform. Building on the existing system, Obama's plan is based on using current providers, doctors, and insurance plans. Under this plan, those who liked their health insurance would keep it with no changes except lower premiums. The 40 million plus Americans without health insurance would have a choice of health insurance options. Obama's plan would:

- Require insurance companies to cover preexisting conditions.
- Create a new Small Business Health Tax Credit to help small businesses provide health insurance to their employees.
- Lower business costs by covering a portion of the catastrophic health costs they pay in return for lower employee premiums.
- Prohibit insurers from overcharging doctors for malpractice insurance.
- Make employer contributions fairer by requiring large employers not offering health insurance to contribute a percentage of payroll costs toward employee health care.
- Establish a National Health Insurance Exchange allowing individuals and small businesses to buy affordable health coverage.
- Allow cheaper medicines from abroad, increase the use of generic drugs in public programs, and take on drug companies that block generic medicines from the market.

Obama proposed to pay for his $50 to $65 billion health care reform by ending the Bush tax cuts for those earning more than $250,000 per year and retaining the estate tax at its 2009 level.[117]

Comparative Analysis: Health Care in Canada and Britain

Americans often fail to look at what is happening in other parts of the world. This section briefly explores medical systems in Canada (a single-payer system), Great Britain (National Health Service), and Australia which has a hybrid public–private system.

The Canadian Health Care System

The current Canadian health care system began less than 50 years ago when a hospital insurance plan in Saskatchewan evolved into a network of plans developed by Canada's 10 provinces and 2 territories.[118] In 1966 Canada passed the Medical Care Act (Medicare), which instituted a nationwide federal/provincial health insurance system that is publicly funded, privately delivered, and free at the point of access.[119] Each province is responsible for administering its own health care plan.[120] Although each of the 10 provinces and 2 territories has its own unique plan, all plans are essentially universal and comprehensive, covering all residents for inpatient and outpatient hospital and physician services. To receive federal funds, every plan must meet basic national eligibility standards:

1. *Universal coverage.* Every provincial resident must be covered under uniform terms and conditions.
2. *Portability.* Plans must be portable, in that they must cover residents who are temporarily away from home or who have moved to another province.
3. *Comprehensiveness.* All approved hospital and physicians' services must be covered, including medical and hospital care, mental health services, and prescription drugs for those over 65 and for those with catastrophic illnesses.
4. *No cost to patient at point of access.* Services must be free at point of access and include no financial barriers to care.
5. *Nonprofit administration.* Plans must be nonprofit and publicly administered.
6. *Freedom of choice.* Each Canadian is free to choose his or her provider.[121]

Unlike the U.S. system, the Canadian system is grounded in universal entitlement rather than linked to employment. Accordingly, all of Canada's 33 million residents are eligible for provincial health insurance, regardless of their employment status, except for people covered by other federal programs such as the military.[122] Questions arose in the 1980s about direct charges made to patients beyond the level paid by the provincial health care plan. The 1984 Canada Health Act eliminated all extra billing and user charges. Today virtually every Canadian is covered by a comprehensive medical and hospital plan with no copayment.[123]

General practitioners (GPs) make up the majority of physicians in Canada and provide most of the nation's health care. Specialists can be used only if a referral is received from the GP. Although patients may choose their primary care physician, the choice is contingent upon whether the physician has openings for new patients. Patients also use the hospital in which the physician has admitting privileges. In addition to providing free physician and hospital care, most provinces cover the cost of travel and medical services if the treatment cannot be obtained in the area where the patient resides. Although covered health care is free at the point of access, some elements not covered include out-of-hospital drugs, dental care, eyeglasses, physical therapy, and chiropractic care not ordered by a medical doctor.[124]

Contrary to some misconceptions, the Canadian health care system is not a form of socialized medicine; instead, it is a social insurance model that mixes public funds with private health care delivery. Canada's single-payer model is based on the idea that provincial governments function as single-source payers of health care with a centralized locus of control. As such, Canada's provincial governments reimburse both hospitals and physicians on a prospective budgeting basis. Specifically, private physicians' fees are negotiated between the provincial governments and the medical associations. Reimbursements for physicians are on a fee-for-service basis. The salaries of physicians in Canada are generally lower than those of their U.S. counterparts. Because of budgetary problems, several provinces have limited payments to physicians who earn above a certain income by lowering the reimbursement rates.[125]

There are more than 1,250 hospitals in Canada, of which 57 percent are run by religious orders or nonprofit organizations. Hospital reimbursements are made on a global prospective basis. In other words, hospitals operate on a negotiated but fixed yearly budget. As such, they must stay within the budgetary allotment granted by the province regardless of the number of patients seen in a year.[126]

Canada's Medicare system is paid for with a mixture of federal and provincial funds. Federal funds go to the provinces in the form of block grants and transfer payments. The provinces obtain funds to operate the medical system from general revenue taxes and, in the case of Alberta and British Columbia, from insurance premiums paid for by employers. Provinces that charge such premiums provide exemptions or subsidies for the aged, the unemployed, and the indigent.[127]

Critics of Canadian health care point to numerous problems facing the system. One of the most important is the question of funding. Cutbacks in government spending (from 1981 to 1992 the Canadian government cut transfer payments to the provinces by almost $8 billion), increasing demands for services, and the high cost of technology have made controlling costs the number one issue facing the Canadian health care system.

Some critics have charged that Canada's prospective global budgeting system for hospitals has caused health care rationing. These critics argue that to cope with budgetary constraints, Canadian hospitals are closing down hospital wards during certain times of the year; filling up one-third of hospital beds with long-term elderly patients to keep high-volume (and expensive) traffic down; using cheaper medical materials; rushing medical procedures and thus jeopardizing accuracy; providing substandard hospital care; not investing in technology or capital improvements; and prioritizing illnesses into "urgent," "emergent," and "elective" categories, thereby causing artificial queues for treatment.[128] According to these critics, health care rationing is having a dramatic effect on Canada's medical system.[129]

Some health care analysts have suggested that the United States adopt a health care reform plan similar to the Canadian model.[130] They argue that a single-payer system allows for greater control of systemwide health care capacity—that is, supply, distribution, and costs—than does a fragmented insurance system in which no party has the overall authority for controlling the production and distribution of medical goods and services. Health care analysts also point to the uneven coverage provided to Americans under the current patchwork of private and public health insurance plans. In comparison to the universal, comprehensive, and publicly funded health care system that Canadians enjoy, most Americans are forced to purchase employer-based health insurance offering coverage that ranges from minimal to comprehensive, depending on the type of policy. Moreover, a significant number of Americans fall through the cracks in health insurance: They receive no employment-based health insurance, they cannot afford to insure themselves, and they are ineligible for Medicaid or Medicare. Critics claim that a Canadian-style universal health care policy would ensure all Americans adequate medical care without regard to their ability to pay or the generosity of their employers.

Perhaps the most formidable argument for the United States adopting a Canadian-style health care system is provided by an examination of leading health indicators and per capita health care spending. Before the Canadian Medicare system became operational in 1971, Canada lagged behind the United States in the important indicators of infant mortality and life expectancy. Impressive gains now place Canada ahead of the United States on both health indicators. Moreover, Canada has been able to achieve those gains while spending less of its GNP on health care than the United States. Although health care costs are rising in Canada, they are doing so at a slower rate than in the United States.[131]

Factors that influence lower health care costs in Canada include lower physician and administrative costs and less concern with malpractice litigation. According to the *Journal of the American Medical Association*, the higher per capita expenditure in the United States is explained entirely by higher fees, because the per capita number of physician visits is actually lower in the United States than in Canada. Fees for procedures in the United States are more than three times as high as in Canada.

In addition, fees for evaluation and management services are about 80 percent lower in Canada. Part of the difference in fee structures may be related to the lower rates of malpractice litigation in Canada. Also, because Canadian health care is based on a single-payer system, overhead costs are lower.[132] In part, this is due to the significant portion of the U.S. health care budget that is spent on advertising and billing.[133] The single-payer system also lessens the paperwork load on physicians, thereby freeing them up to see more patients. One indicator of the success of Canada's health care system is that the majority of Canadians are generally satisfied with it and show no inclination of giving it up.[134]

Britain's National Health Service

The National Health Service (NHS) is the most enduring aspect of the British Labour Party's postwar welfare state. The direct inspiration for the NHS was a 1944 white paper written for the wartime coalition government by Sir William Beveridge. The Beveridge Report maintained that a "comprehensive system of health care was essential to any scheme for improving living standards."[135]

After initial resistance from the British Medical Association, the National Health Service Act was passed in 1946 and took effect in 1948. In the words of the act, the aim was to promote "the establishment of a comprehensive health service designed to secure improvement in the physical and mental health of the people . . . and the prevention, diagnosis and treatment of illness."[136] The principle of freedom of choice was upheld in that people could either use the NHS or seek outside doctors. Doctors were guaranteed that there would be no interference in their clinical judgment, and they were free to take private patients while participating in the service. The main goal of the NHS was to provide free medical service to anyone in need. The NHS Act was based on a tripartite system: (1) hospital service with specialists; (2) general medical doctors, dentists, and eye doctors, maintained on a contractual basis; and (3) prevention and support systems, provided by local health departments.

Under the leadership of Minister of Health Anuerin Bevan, all Britain's hospitals were nationalized. Because most hospitals were owned by local governments or were heavily subsidized nonprofit institutions, nationalization was not difficult. General medical practitioners were brought into a new governmentally subsidized plan that provided universal basic medical care that was free at the point of access. This was not a major change, as physicians' services had been subsidized for industrial workers since before World War II. The NHS Act simply extended this coverage to the whole population. British physicians generally came to support the act because it guaranteed a steady income.

The NHS Act does not eliminate private medicine, and a small percentage of NHS hospital beds are reserved for private patients. As mentioned, general practitioners (GPs) and specialists are permitted to treat private patients while working in the NHS. Moreover, affluent patients are permitted to purchase private health insurance and private care. The major advantages of private care are more attractive hospital rooms and quicker service for elective surgery. About 15 percent of Britons currently have private health insurance, which businesses often provide as a fringe benefit for upper-level management.

The backbone of the NHS is the GP. Every patient in Britain is registered with a GP who provides family care. Patients may change their GPs unless they are diagnosed with a chronic illness such as AIDS. GPs are paid by the NHS on the basis of an annual **capitation** fee (per-person fee) for each registered patient. Roughly half of a GP's income comes from capitation payments, with the rest made up by allowances for services such as contraceptive advice and immunization. The role of the GP is to provide primary medical care; GPs are forbidden to restrict their practice to any special client group. Individuals can register with any GP provided he or she is willing to accept them. GPs see almost 75 percent of their registered patients at least once a year; and, because mobility is relatively low in Britain, many people retain the same GP for a considerable period of time.[137]

The GP has wide professional latitude and equips his or her own office, hires staff, and may choose to work singly, in pairs, in groups, or in a government health center. Close to 50 percent of all GPs practice in groups of three or more. Health centers, part of the original National Health Service Act, mushroomed in the late 1960s and 1970s, and by 1975 there were 600 nationally. Sweeping changes in 1967 gave GPs increased benefits, including a higher capitation rate if they had a patient load of 2,500 to 3,500. In addition, extra remuneration was provided for each person on a doctor's list who was over 65, for night calls, for transients, for maternity care, for family planning services, and for certain preventive measures. GPs also receive partial reimbursement for secretaries, receptionists, and nurses, as well as for the rental costs of their offices. Extra payments are also provided for seniority, postgraduate education, and vocational training; for working in groups of three or more; and for practicing in underdoctored areas.[138]

The second tier of the British health care system is the physician consultant (specialist). Most referrals to consultants—except for accidents or emergency care—are made through GPs. Although employed by the government and under contract to a public hospital, a physician specialist is allowed a small private practice. In effect, patients in the community are served by GPs, whereas in the hospital they are under the care of specialists. As in the U.S. health care system, physician specialists are accorded greater prestige and remuneration.[139]

The NHS is funded from general taxes, with the proceeds divided among regional health authorities that plan local health services. The regions, in turn, divide their money among districts that pay for hospitals through global prospective budgets.[140] Health services under the NHS are relatively comprehensive, with hospital and primary medical care being free. However, there are significant patient charges for adult dentistry and eyeglasses and a small charge for prescriptions. Drug prices are agreed upon between the health department and the pharmaceutical industry according to a specific pricing formula based on company profits. In addition, government subsidies for medical education mean that students' direct educational costs are low.[141]

Critics complain that NHS hospital funds are dispersed in a haphazard manner. One reform suggested a way to remedy this problem was to create "internal markets," whereby the distribution of NHS money would follow patients rather than the other way around. Another important problem was that hospitals received nothing extra for efficiently treating more patients at less cost; as a result hospitals had little incentive to improve efficiency.[142]

Another criticism of the NHS is that its funding is based not on the medical needs of consumers, but rather on how much the British treasury believes it can afford to spend on health care. The result is de facto health care rationing and long waiting lists for elective procedures—caused not by inefficiencies in the system but by limited resources. In addition, consumers complain of long waits in GP offices and of hospital buildings that are often in poor repair. There are also long waiting lists for elective surgeries such as hip replacements, routine treatment of varicose veins, and repairs of hernias. (There is believed to be little wait for urgent surgery.) Long waiting lists can be misleading to some extent because they sometimes include people who have died, have moved, have already had their operations, or who have been kept waiting by consultants who want to secure more resources or private patients.[143]

Other critics charge that despite government efforts, there are serious shortages of doctors in certain parts of Britain. In addition, expenditures and resources under the NHS seem to be slanted toward hospitalization rather than toward primary, first-level care. Critics also complain about the lack of accountability of doctors and about strong unions that have supported restrictive practices and fought attempts to privatize support services.[144] Finally, other critics charge that the inequality in the British health system has resulted in higher disease and mortality rates for lower socioeconomic groups.

Under the original NHS Act, Parliament allocated money and power to local health authorities that managed the hospitals and contracted with specialists for services.[145] Passed in 1990, the National Health and Community Care Act was designed to reduce the long queues for the treatment of nonacute illnesses and procedures by introducing market efficiencies. Loosening the knot between funders and providers, this bill permitted some hospitals (called *trust hospitals*) to operate independently of the local health authority in setting fees, managing budgets, developing personnel packages, and purchasing goods. The theory was that independently managed hospitals would be more efficient than centrally planned ones. To further encourage efficiency, these trust hospitals were allowed to sell their services to any local health authority, private patients, or to private insurance companies. In addition, GPs with large practices were permitted to become fundholders of NHS grants from which they could purchase hospital or specialized services for their clients. It was expected that GPs would refer their patients to those hospitals or specialists that were the most efficient. Inefficient hospitals would get fewer referrals and thus would be forced to increase their quality of care while reducing costs.[146] Unfortunately, the hoped-for results have not been achieved.

Much of the reporting on the NHS in the U.S. press has tended to emphasize its flaws. Although some GPs express dissatisfaction with the system, the British people continue to use it in large numbers. For example, although 15 percent of Britons have private insurance, most use it as a supplement rather than as a substitute for the NHS.[147] Despite the criticisms, the NHS appears to be serving the majority of the British population as well as, and in some ways better than, the U.S. health care system. For instance, in 2005 per capita health care expenditures were only 8.3 percent of Britain's GDP compared to 15.3 percent for the United States.[148] Much of this lower cost is attributable to the success of GPs in keeping down hospital admission rates and to the relatively low administrative costs of the NHS. Notwithstanding the lower cost of the British health care system, most health indicators, such as life expectancy and infant mortality rates, are equivalent to or better than those found in the costlier U.S. health care system. Enoch Powell, a former British health minister, summed up the contradictions of the NHS: "One of the most striking features of the NHS is the continual, deafening chorus of complaints which rises day and night from every part of it, a chorus only interrupted when someone suggests that a different system altogether might be preferable . . . it presents what must be a unique spectacle of an undertaking that is run down by everyone engaged in it."

The Australian Health Care System

The current Australian health care system is a hybrid public–private system. Introduced in 1984, Medicare provides Australia's residents with high-quality universal health care. The Medicare system was predicated on the idea that all Australians should contribute to the cost of health care according to their ability to pay. As such, it is financed by a progressive income tax and an income-related Medicare levy. As a supplement to Medicare, Australians are strongly encouraged to purchase private health insurance, which in 2008 cost up to $250 a month for a family to get top-level coverage.[149]

Medicare provides comprehensive benefits such as consultation fees for doctors, including specialists; medical tests like X-rays, MRIs, and pathology tests; eye tests performed by optometrists; most surgical and therapeutic procedures performed by doctors; and some surgical procedures performed by approved dentists. From 2006 mental health services paid for by Medicare have broadened to include services to families and schools. The Australian Government's Better Access to Psychiatrists, Psychologists and General Practitioners program through the Medicare Benefits Schedule initiative is slated to cost $538 million over five years.[150]

One can enter an Australian hospital either as a public or private pay (using health insurance) patient. Public hospital patients are not charged for care and treatment by attending physicians or specialists, or aftercare by the treating doctor. However, the treatment they receive is from doctors and specialists nominated by the hospital. Those admitted to a public or private hospital as a private patient (i.e., using private health insurance) have a choice of doctors to treat them. Medicare pays 75 percent of the Medicare Schedule fee for services and procedures provided by the treating doctor. With private health insurance, some or all of the outstanding balance is covered. Private patients are charged for hospital accommodation and items such as surgery and medicines, which are often covered by private health insurance.[151]

Medicare does not cover private patient hospital costs (e.g., surgery or accommodation); most dental examinations and treatment; ambulance services; home nursing; acupuncture (unless part of a doctor's consultation); glasses and contact lenses; hearing aids and other appliances; prostheses; medicines (except those subsidized by the Pharmaceutical Benefits Scheme which covers most classes of medicines); and cosmetic surgery.

Criticism leveled against Medicare is similar to that directed at the British NHS. Namely, long waits for elective surgery as a public patient (private patients have no wait); inefficiencies, staff shortages, and underfunding. The new Labor government under Kevin Rudd has promised to significantly increase funding for public hospitals and medical services. Other criticisms involve copayments and gaps in services, such as dental. All told, Australians seem to be relatively pleased with their system.[152]

It is difficult to compare the quality of the Canadian, British, and Australian health care systems with that of the United States. For affluent or middle-class Americans with good health insurance, the U.S. system of health care may well provide the best medical care in the world; and for complex medical procedures involving sophisticated equipment and technology, U.S. health care is unequaled. Moreover, unlike the long queues characteristic of the UK and Canadian systems, the waiting period for surgery, tests, and other procedures is relatively short in the United States. Finally, physicians in this country are among the best trained in the world. However, the emphasis on costly equipment and technology is not without a price. A medical approach that emphasizes specific diseases over primary care and preventive medicine usually results in good care, but for fewer people. Health care systems that emphasize personal and primary care, accessibility, and free or inexpensive services often reach more people. Given that, the health care systems of Canada, Britain, and Australia appear to distribute health resources more equitably than does the U.S. health care system.

Conclusion

The examination of health care in the United States raises important questions. What is this nation's responsibility for providing health care to all its citizens? How much high-tech medicine can our society realistically afford? How should U.S. medical resources be allocated? What, if any, limitations on personal freedom are permissible in the name of promoting health and preventing disease? These and other questions require urgent answers.

The U.S. health care system is facing an acute crisis. This crisis is grounded in the failure of the marketplace to curb health care expenditures, the system's overreliance on medical technology at the expense of providing primary health care services, the huge amount spent on growth, health care administrative costs, and the large numbers of working people and their families who cannot afford health care coverage. Moreover, compared to industrialized countries with less-costly health care systems, the higher-cost U.S. health care system is not producing greater longevity, lower rates of infant mortality, or other indicators of improved public health.

The United States is one of the few industrialized countries without a national health insurance system. Moreover, it is also one of the few industrialized nations where medical expenses can cause poverty. Terri Combs-Orme suggests that a progressive reconstruction of the U.S. health care system must be grounded in the following principles:

1. Accessible health care should be a universal right of all Americans, not a privilege to be purchased or earned.
2. The quantity, quality, and accessibility of health care should be equal for all, not dependent on income or categorical status. No health care system should result in differential quantity, quality, or accessibility of care based on income, gender, age, or any other criterion.
3. Health care should not be linked to employment. A majority of Americans purchase health care insurance through their place of employment, but the fear of job loss or other issues not under their control undermines the security of this arrangement and limits their job mobility.
4. The quality, quantity, and accessibility of health care should not vary on a state-by-state basis.
5. A progressive health care system must balance the needs and rights of children and the elderly in a fair and rational way.
6. A comprehensive health care system should include coverage for and accessibility to long-term care for the elderly.[153]

If commodification and high costs are left unchecked, health care in the United States may someday be out of reach for the majority of citizens. Although the likely outcome of the U.S. health care crisis is unknown, left solely to the caprice of the marketplace, the problems will undoubtedly worsen.

Discussion Questions

1. In 2008 U.S. health care expenditures were more than $2 trillion a year. This cost has risen dramatically over the past 25 years in terms of the amount spent, the percentage of the GDP used for health care, and the per capita costs of health care. What are the main factors that have driven up health care costs? How can these factors be controlled?
2. Medicare has experienced large increases in costs. What are the major factors contributing to the steep rise in Medicare costs? What can be done to slow these rises?
3. Some critics believe that the costs of Medicare and Medicaid cannot be brought under control without radically reforming the entire health care system. They argue that incremental reforms in the Medicare and Medicaid programs have only a minuscule impact on the rise in federal and state expenditures for health care. Are these critics correct?

4. Evidence of the effectiveness of cost-controlling mechanisms such as DRGs has been mixed. Critics charge that not only has the DRG system failed to substantially reduce health care costs, but it has also led to a reduced level of patient care. Is the DRG system successful? If so, should it be a model for future health care reforms?

5. Many critics argue that there is a serious health care crisis in the United States. Describe the main characteristics of that crisis (e.g., health care costs, accessibility issues, uninsured populations, U.S. health indicators compared with those of other nations).

6. The AIDS epidemic is one of the most important public health issues facing the global community. Some critics insist that more money should be spent on basic AIDS research, outreach, and treatment. Other critics argue that AIDS is only one of many health care problems facing the United States and other countries around the world. They argue that the money spent on AIDS research should be in proportion to the numbers of people affected by the disease, which, in the United States, are relatively small compared to the numbers of people suffering from cancer and heart disease. Is AIDS a significantly more important public health problem in the United States than cancer, heart disease, or the effects of drugs, alcohol, and tobacco? Should the federal government spend proportionally more on AIDS research than on other diseases?

7. Some health care analysts are calling for radical reform in the U.S. health care system. Many of them insist that the nation's free market health care system should be replaced by a more cost-effective and comprehensive system. Assuming that these health care analysts are correct, which of the health care systems described in this chapter would be the best model for the United States to emulate? Why?

8. Why has the United States not developed a health care system that is universal and publicly funded, like those of its industrial counterparts? What, if anything, can be done to reform or radically transform U.S. health care?

Notes

1. "New York Times/CBS News Poll," February 23–27, 2007.
2. U.S. Census Bureau, "Income, Poverty, and Health Insurance Coverage in the United States: 2006," Economics and Statistics Administration, issued August 2007. Retrieved July 2008, from www.census.gov/prod/2007pubs/p60-233.pdf
3. Ibid.
4. C. P. Pandya, "Study: Health Insurance Premiums Rising Much Faster Than Average Wages," *The New Standard* (September 28, 2004), p. 3.
5. National Coalition on Health Care, "Health Insurance Coverage."
6. Health Care Financing Administration, "President Clinton Announces Approximately 2.5 Million Children Have Enrolled in the State Children's Health Insurance Program, Praises the Decline in Uninsured, Urges Congress to Expand Coverage, Unveils New Funds for Outreach" (Washington, DC: Health Care Financing Administration, 2000).
7. Terri Combs-Orme, "Should the Federal Government Finance Health Care for All Americans?: Yes," in Howard Jacob Karger and James Midgley (eds.), *Controversial Issues in Social Policy* (Boston: Allyn & Bacon, 1993).
8. Irving J. Lewis and Cecil G. Sheps, *The Sick Citadel* (Boston: Oelgeschlager, Gunn, and Hain, 1983), p. 16.
9. National Coalition on Health Care, "Health Insurance Coverage."
10. J. Hadley and J. Holahan, "The Cost of Care for the Uninsured: What Do We Spend, Who Pays, and What Would Full Coverage Add to Medical Spending?", 2004. Retrieved July 2008, from www.kff.org/uninsured/upload/The-Cost-of-Care-for-the-Uninsured-What-Do-We-Spend-Who-Pays-and-What-Would-Full-Coverage-Add-to-Medical-Spending.pdf
11. Sumner A. Rosen, David Fanshel, and Mary E. Lutz (eds.), *Face of the Nation 1987* (Silver Spring, MD: NASW, 1987), p. 75.
12. U.S. Census Bureau, "Income, Poverty, and Health Insurance Coverage in the United States: 2006."
13. Centers for Medicare & Medicaid Services, "Brief Summaries of Medicare and Medicaid," November 1, 2007. Retrieved July 2008, from www.cms.hhs.gov/MedicareMedicaidStatSupp/downloads/07BriefSummaries.pdf
14. Ibid.
15. See Families USA, "Understanding the New Medicare Prescription Drug Benefit," The Medicare Road

Show, Washington, DC, Spring 2004; Kaiser Family Foundation, "The Medicare Prescription Drug Law," March 2004, retrieved November 2004, from www .kff.org/medicare/loader.cfm?url=/commonspot/ security/getfile.cfm&PageID=33325; and Egyptian Area Agency on Aging, "Medicare Prescription Drug Benefit," Cartersville, IL, May 20, 2004, retrieved November 2004, from www.egyptianaaa.org/ MedicareDrugBill.htm.

16. Ceci Connolly, "OMB Says Medicare Drug Law Could Cost Still More, White House Estimates Show a $42 Billion Increase over 10 Years," *Washington Post* (September 19, 2004), p. A04.

17. Ibid.

18. Michael Scherer, "Medicare's Hidden Bonanza," *Mother Jones* (March/April 2004), p. 11.

19. Centers for Medicare & Medicaid Services, "Brief Summaries of Medicare and Medicaid."

20. Centers for Medicare & Medicaid Services, "Medicaid: A Brief Summary," September 16, 2004. Retrieved October 2004, from www.cms.hhs .gov/-publications/overview-medicare-medicaid/ default4.asp

21. Centers for Medicare & Medicaid Services, "Brief Summaries of Medicare and Medicaid."

22. Centers for Medicare & Medicaid Services, "Medicaid: A Brief Summary."

23. Ibid.

24. David E. Rosenbaum, "Gloomy Forecast Touches off Feud on Medicare Fund," *New York Times* (June 6, 1996), pp. A1 and B14.

25. For a good historical analysis of the Medicare program, see Theodore R. Marmor, *The Politics of Medicare* (Chicago: Aldine, 1973).

26. Centers for Medicare & Medicaid Services, "Brief Summaries of Medicare and Medicaid."

27. Health Care Financing Administration, "Medicaid Eligibility." Retrieved 2001, from www.hcfa.gov/ medicaid/meligib.htm

28. Centers for Medicare & Medicaid Services, "Medicaid: A Brief Summary."

29. Ibid.

30. Social Security Administration, "Medicaid," *Annual Statistical Supplement, 2007.* Retrieved July 2008, from www.socialsecurity.gov/policy/docs/statcomps/ supplement/2007/medicaid.pdf

31. American Health Care Association, "Nursing Facility Beds by Certification Type," June 2004. Retrieved November 2004, from www.ahca.org/research/oscar/ rpt_certified_beds_200406.pdf

32. Stephen A. Moses, "Denial Is Not a River in Egypt," *Health Insurance Underwriter* 50, no. 11 (December 2002), pp. 36–40.

33. American Association of Retired Persons (AARP), "Average Daily Cost for Nursing Home Care by State, 2001," 2004. Retrieved November 2004, from www.aarp.org/bulletin/longterm/Articles/a2003-10-30-dailycost.html

34. Social Security Administration, "Medicaid."

35. See Children's Defense Fund, *A Children's Defense Budget,* p. 109; and Barbara Wolfe, "A Medicaid Primer," *Focus* 17, no. 3 (Spring 1996), pp. 1–6.

36. Kaiser Family Foundation, "State Health Facts." Retrieved July 2008, from www.statehealthfacts.org

37. Ibid.

38. Kaiser Family Foundation, "Determining Income Eligibility in Children's Health Coverage Programs: How States Use Disregards in Children's Medicaid and SCHIP," May 2008. Retrieved July 2008, from www.kff.org/medicaid/upload/7776.pdf

39. Kentucky Farm Bureau, "Summary of Master Tobacco Settlement," April 1, 1999. Retrieved 2001, from www.kyfb.org/FactTobSett040199.htm

40. See Andrew Garber, "Tobacco Settlement Gregoire Negotiated Not Popular with All," *Seattle Times* (October 4, 2004), p. A6; and Pamela M. Prah, "Smokers Help to Balance State Budgets," *Stateline,* March 3, 2004, retrieved November 2004, from www .stateline.org/stateline/?pa=story&sa=showStoryInfo &print=1&id=354303

41. U.S. House of Representatives, *Overview of Entitlement Programs: 1996 Green Book.*

42. U.S. House of Representatives, *1996 Green Book,* p. 995.

43. See Ibid.; and U.S. Bureau of the Census, *Statistical Abstract of the United States, 1991* (Washington, DC: U.S. Government Printing Office, 1991), p. 107.

44. HHS, Centers for Medicare & Medicaid, "The Nation's Health Dollar, Calendar Year 2006: Where It Came From." Retrieved July 2008, from www.cms .hhs.gov/NationalHealthExpendData/downloads/Pie ChartSourcesExpenditures2006.pdf

45. Julie Appleby, "What Happens after the Band-Aids Run Out?" *USA Today* (December 8–10, 2000), pp. 1–2.

46. See Health Care Financing Administration, "Actuarial Products, N.H.E. Projections, Table 1;" and G. J. Schieber and J. P. Poullier, "International Health Care Spending: Issues and Trends," *Health Affairs,* 10 (1991), p. 110.

47. OECD Health Data 2008, "How Does the United States Compare." Retrieved July 2008, from www .oecd.org/dataoecd/46/2/38980580.pdf "

48. Alliance for Health Reform, "Covering Health Issues: 2003, A Sourcebook for Journalists," January 2003. Retrieved November 2004, from www.allhealth .org/sourcebook2002/ch8_8.html

49. The Commonwealth 2003 Annual Report, "A Look in the Mirror," 2003. Retrieved November 2004, from www.cmwf.org/annreprt/2003/msg_pres02_lookin mirror.htm

50. Ibid.

51. Ibid.

52. Ibid.

53. Ibid.

54. Annenberg School of Communication, "President Uses Dubious Statistics on Costs of Malpractice Lawsuits, Two Congressional Agencies Dispute Findings That Caps on Damage Awards Produce Big Savings in Medical Costs," University of Pennsylvania, January 29, 2004. Retrieved November 2004, from www.factcheck.org/article133.html

55. Michael Clemens, "Rising Costs Reflect Many Instances," USA Today May 5, 1993, p. B2.; and Barnaby J. Feder, "Heart Specialists Reconsider the Bypass," February 25, 2007. Retrieved July 2008, from www.iht.com/articles/2007/02/25/news/surgery.php

56. Victoria Colliver, "In Critical Condition: Health Care in America," *San Francisco Chronicle* (October 11, 2004), p. A8.

57. HHS, Centers for Medicare & Medicaid Services, "National Health Expenditures Aggregate, Per Capita Amounts, Percent Distribution, and Average Annual Percent Growth, by Source of Funds: Selected Calendar Years 1960–2006." Retrieved July 2008, from www.cms.hhs.gov/NationalHealthExpendData/downloads/tables.pdf

58. American Hospital Association, "Rising Demand, Increasing Costs of Caring Fuel Hospital Spending," Press Release, February 19, 2003. Retrieved November 2004, from www.aha.org/aha/hospital connect/search/pressrelease.jsp?dcrpath=AHA/Press _Release/data/PR_030219_Costs&domain=AHA

59. Health Care Financing Administration, "Actuarial Products, N.H.E. Projections, Table 2." Retrieved 2001, from www.hcfa.gov/stats/NHE-Proj

60. Myrle Croasdale, "High Medical School Debt Steers Life Choices for Young Doctors," *AMA News* (May 17, 2004), pp. 2–5.

61. Ibid., p. 6.

62. Jay Greene, "Primary Care Matches Down Again; Fourth Year of Decline Worries Some," *AMA News* (April 9, 2001), p. 16.

63. Bureau of Labor Statistics, "Occupational Handbook Outlook 2008–9 Edition." Retrieved July 2008, from http://stats.bls.gov/OCO/OCOS074.HTM

64. OECD Health Data 2008, "How Does the United States Compare."

65. Katherine van Wormer, *Social Welfare: A World View* (Chicago: Nelson-Hall, 1997), p. 412.

66. Marcia Angell, *The Truth About the Drug Companies: How They Deceive Us and What to Do About It* (New York: Random House, 2004).

67. Meredith Rosenthal and John H. Foster, "Drug Ads Take Increasing—Though Still Small—Share of Pharmaceutical Promotion Budget," *The New England Journal of Medicine* (February 14, 2002), pp. 498–505.

68. Nancy McVicar, "Drug Costs Go Up but Coverage Comes Down," *Sun-Sentinel* (February 23, 2000). Retrieved 2001, from www.sun-sentinel.com/news/daily/detail/0,1136,27000000000116737,00.html

69. "Melinda Beck, "Doctors under the knife," *Newsweek* (April 5, 1993), p. 29.

70. John H. Goddeeris and Andrew J. Hogan, "Nature and Dimensions of the Problem." In John H. Goddeeris and Andrew J. Hogan (eds.), *Improving Access to Health Care: What Can the States Do?* (Kalamazoo, MI: W. E. Upjohn Institute for Employment Research, 1992), pp. 14–15.

71. Quoted in Marie A. Caputi and William A. Heiss, "The DRG Revolution," *Health and Social Work 3*, no. 6 (June 1984), p. 5.

72. McVicar, "Drug Costs Go Up but Coverage Comes Down."

73. Paul Schmolling, Merrill Youkeles, and William R. Burger, *Human Services in Contemporary America* (Pacific Grove, CA: Brooks/Cole Publishing Co., 1997), p. 54.

74. U.S. House of Representatives, *1996 Green Book*.

75. Amy Goldstein, "Cutting Health Costs Slices into Charity," *Washington Post* (April 5, 1999), p. A1.

76. Weiss Ratings Inc., "Consumers Continue to Choose Medicare HMOs Despite High Risk of Being Dropped," 2004. Retrieved November 2004, from www .weissratings.com/News/Ins_HMO/20021209 hmo.htm

77. Vicki Lankarge, "Seniors Dropped from Medicare HMOs Shouldn't Rejoin Others, Weiss Warns," *insure.com* (November 14, 2000). Retrieved 2001, from www.insure.com/health/medicare/fewoptions1100 .html

78. Howard Waitzkin, *The Second Sickness: Contradictions of Capitalist Health Care* (New York: Free Press, 1983), p. 220.

79. Nancy McVicar, "Medical Care Is There—If You Can Afford It," *Sun-Sentinel* (February 24, 2000). Retrieved 2001, from www.sun-sentinel.com/news/daily/detail/0,1136,27500000000104840,00.html

80. Ibid.

81. Ellyn E. Spragins, "Simon Says, Join Us," *Newsweek* (June 19, 1995), pp. 55–58.

82. Thomas H. Ainsworth, *Live or Die* (New York: Macmillan, 1983), p. 89.

83. American Medical Association, *Competition in Health Insurance: A Comprehensive Study of U.S. Markets*, 2nd ed. (Chicago: American Medical Association, January 2003).

84. Ibid.

85. John M. Herrick and Joseph Papsidero, "Uncompensated Care: What States Are Doing," in Goddeeris and Hogan (eds.), *Improving Access to Health Care: What Can the States Do?* (Kalamazoo, MI: W.E. Upjohn Institute for Employment Research, 1992), pp. 139–140.

86. W. Greenberg, "Elimination of Employer-Based Health Insurance," in R. B. Helms (ed.), *American Health Policy: Critical Issues for Reform* (Washington, DC: AEI Press, October 1992), pp. 1–4.

87. Robert Searles Walker, *AIDS: Today, Tomorrow* (New Jersey: Humanities Press International, 1992), p. 134.

88. Centers for Disease Control and Prevention, "Cases of HIV infection and AIDS in the United States and Dependent Areas, 2006." Retrieved July 2008, from www.cdc.gov/hiv/topics/surveillance/resources/reports/2006report/pdf/2006SurveillanceReport.pdf

89. Ibid.

90. Ibid.

91. Martin Shapiro and Samuel Bozzette, "Privileged Treatment Inequities in HIV Care Demand Remedies for U.S. Health Care," 1999. Retrieved 2001, from www.rand.org/publications/RRR/RRRfall99/privilege.html

92. UNAIDS/WHO, "AIDS Epidemic Update," December 2007. Retrieved July 2008, from http://data.unaids.org/pub/EPISlides/2007/2007_epiupdate_en.pdf

93. World Health Organization, *The World Health Report 2003*, Geneva, 2003.

94. "About Business Roundtable." Retrieved April 2, 2007, from www.businessroundtable.org/aboutUs/index.aspx

95. "AARP, Business Roundtable, and SEIU Partner to Spur Action on Health Care, Long-Term Financial Security," January 16, 2007. Retrieved April 2, 2007, from www.businessroundtable.org//taskForces/taskforce/document.aspx?qs=7025BF159FC4951448113 8A74EA1851159169FEB56A37B2AC

96. "The Divided We Fail Platform." Retrieved April 2, 2007, from www.businessroundtable.org//taskForces/taskforce/document.aspx?qs=7025BF159FC4951448 1138A74EA1851159169FEB56A37B2AC

97. "U.S. Chamber Policy Priorities for 2007," U.S. Chamber of Commerce, p. 3. Retrieved April 2, 2007, from www.uschamber.com/NR/rdonlyres/ehu6b2fp4 efxznrpxdt2jk3db22imtentbak7wuiyqhvfposezwt ma4a7gh64w7rg5nyi55zup6xilm4wrrplkmldhf/0701priorities.pdf

98. "Health Care: Introduction." Retrieved April 2, 2007, from www.nfib.com/page/healthcare.html

99. Jonathan Cohn, "What's the One Thing Big Business and the Left Have in Common?" *New York Times*, April 1, 2007. Retrieved April 2, 2007, from www .nytimes.com/2007/04/01/magazine/01Healthcare.t.html?ref=health

100. Ibid.

101. "Expanding Health Care Coverage in the United States: A Historic Agreement," Health Coverage Coalition for the Uninsured, January 18, 2007. Retrieved April 2, 2007, from www.coalitionfortheuninsured.org/pdfs/agreement.pdf

102. Ibid, p. 1.

103. Ronald V. Dellums et al., *Health Services Act* (H. R. 2969) (Washington, DC: U.S. Government Printing Office, 1979). For a good summary of the act, see Waitzkin, *The Second Sickness*, pp. 222–226.

104. "Summary of S. 2817, The National Health Care Act of 1992," *NASW-LA News* 16, no. 5 (September/October 1992), p. 2.

105. Thomas Daschle, Rima Cohen, and Charles Rice, "Health Care Reform: Single-Payer Models," *American Psychologist* 48, no. 3 (March 1993), pp. 265–267.

106. Paul Starr, *The Social Transformation of American Medicine* (New York: Basic Books, 1984).

107. Ibid.

108. Jeff Bingaman, Robert G. Frank, and Carrie L. Billy, "Combining a Global Health Budget with a Market-Driven Delivery System," *American Psychologist* 48, no. 3 (March 1993), pp. 271–272.

109. Robin Toner, "'Harry and Louise' Ad Campaign Biggest Gun in Health Care Battle," *San Diego Union-Tribune* (April 7, 1994), p. A7.

110. Sara Fritz, "Ads Are Designed to Counter Health Care Proposals," *Los Angeles Times* (May 15, 1993), p. A16.

111. Dana Priest, "The Slow Death of Health Reform," *Washington Post Weekly* (September 5–11, 1994), p. 11.

112. Douglas Frantz, "Lobbyists, Interest Groups Begin Costly Health Care Battle," *Los Angeles Times* (May 24, 1993).

113. Waitzkin, *The Second Sickness*, p. 218.

114. C. Sabatino, "Kassebaum-Kennedy Health Insurance Bill Clears Congress: Medical Savings Accounts Limited to Demonstration Program," Families USA (Washington, DC: Families USA).

115. Wolfe, "Changing the U.S. Health Care System," p. 17.

116. Diane M. DiNitto, *Social Welfare: Politics and Public Policy* (Boston: Allyn & Bacon, 1995), p. 270.

117. Obama–Biden, "Health Care." Retrieved December 6, 2008, from www.barackobama.com/issues/healthcare

118. W. Barnhill, "Canadian Health Care: Would It Work Here?" *Arthritis Today* 6, no. 6 (November–December 1992), p. 8.

119. Elaine Vayda and R. B. Deber, "The Canadian Health Care System: An Overview," *Social Science and Medicine* 18, no. 3 (1984), pp. 191–197.

120. Callaway, "Canadian Health Care: The Good, the Bad, and the Ugly," *Health Insurance Underwriter* (October 1991), pp. 18–35.

121. See Tracy Falwell, Suzy Carter, Jodie Daigle, Renee Mills, Lissa Cameron, and Leticia Gonzalez-Castro, "International Health Care Systems Analysis: Canada, Britain, Germany, Sweden, France, Mexico and South Africa," unpublished paper, Graduate School of Social Work, University of Houston, Houston, TX, April 30, 1996; and T. Mizrahi, R. Fasan, and S. Dooha, "National Health Line," *Health and Social Work* 18, no. 1 (1993), pp. 7–12.

122. Jonathan S. Rakich, "The Canadian and U.S. Health Care Systems: Profiles and Policies," *Hospital and Health Services Administration* 36, no. 1 (Spring 1991), pp. 26–27.

123. Falwell et al., "International Health Care Systems Analysis."

124. Barnhill, "Canadian Health Care," p. 19.

125. Ibid.

126. Ibid.

127. Rakich, "The Canadian and U.S. Health Care Systems," p. 32.

128. See Barnhill, "Canadian Health Care;" I. Munro, "How Not to Improve Health Care," *Reader's Digest* (September 1992), p. 21; and B. Gilray, "Standing Up for American Health Care," *Health Insurance Underwriter* (February 1992), p. 10.

129. Robert E. Moffitt, "Should the Federal Government Finance Health Care for All Americans?: No," in Howard Jacob Karger and James Midgley (eds.), *Controversial Issues in Social Policy* (Boston: Allyn & Bacon, 1993).

130. For example, David Himmelstein and Steffie Woolhandler, "A National Health Care Program for the United States: A Physicians' Proposal," *The New England Journal of Medicine* 320 (January 12, 1989), pp. 102–108; and Combs-Orme, "Should the Federal Government Finance Health Care for All Americans?: Yes."

131. Combs-Orme, "Should the Federal Government Finance Health Care for All Americans?: Yes."

132. van Wormer, *Social Welfare,* p. 419.

133. See Combs-Orme, "Should the Federal Government Finance Health Care for All Americans?: Yes;" and "How Does Canada Do It?: A Comparison of Expenditures for Physicians' Services in the United States and Canada," *Journal of the American Medical Association* 265, no. 19 (May 15, 1991), p. 2474.

134. See W. Caragata, "Medicare Wars," *Maclean's* 108, no. 14 (1995), p. 4; and Leger Marketing, "Canadian Perceptions of Their Health Care System," Executive Report, Ottawa, June 2001. Retrieved November 2004, from www.legermarketing.com/documents/spclm/010709eng.pdf

135. Ruth Levitt, *The Reorganised National Health Service* (London: Croom Helm, 1979), p. 15.

136. Quoted in Ibid. p. 17.

137. Victor W. Sidel and Ruth Sidel, *A Healthy State* (New York: Pantheon Books, 1983), p. 144.

138. Ibid., pp. 144, 157–159.

139. Ibid., p. 172.

140. Ibid.

141. Ibid.

142. "Nye Bevan's Legacy," *The Economist* (July 6, 1992), p. 12.

143. Ibid.

144. Ibid.

145. Levitt, *The Reorganized National Health Service,* p. 27.

146. "Nye Bevan's Legacy."

147. Ibid., p. 12.

148. OECD, Health Data 2007.

149. See www.iselect.com.au.

150. Australian Government, Medicare Australia, About Medicare, 2008. Retrieved June 10, 2008, from www.medicareaustralia.gov.au/public/register/index.jsp

151. Ibid.

152. Ibid.

153. Combs-Orme, "Should the Federal Government Finance Health Care for All Americans?: Yes."

CHAPTER 13

Mental Health and Substance Abuse Policy

*T*his chapter reviews the provision of mental health and substance abuse services to people with serious impairments. Before the emergence of the community mental health movement, states were solely responsible for the care of their mentally disturbed residents. When the movement to improve mental health services through federal assistance to the states stalled, many who suffered from serious mental illness were left without care. This lack of adequate care was made worse by a series of legal decisions that reinforced the civil rights of mental patients while requiring the states to provide adequate services. As a result of these developments, many former mental patients are now living on the streets or in squalid single-room-occupancy hotels. In 1996 mental health advocates were encouraged by passage of the Mental Health Parity Act, which mandated that employers offer employees mental health benefits that were comparable to physical health care benefits. Despite this incremental reform, problems associated with chronic mental illness as well as with alcohol and drug abuse have become more prevalent. The lack of adequate support for substance abuse prevention and treatment efforts, coupled with the economic collapse of inner-city neighborhoods, left many urban areas subject to unprecedented levels of street violence and social deterioration. And while social workers in the public sector struggled to care for their seriously impaired clients, private practitioners providing mental health services prospered—although the more recent advent of managed care has attenuated their prospects.

Throughout the history of U.S. social welfare, states have played a prominent role in mental health services. During the nineteenth century, social problems attributable to immigration, urbanization, and industrialization overwhelmed local poorhouses that had been established during the colonial era. Dorothea Dix championed the humane treatment of people with mental illness in the United States, and by the 1840s she was instrumental in convincing many states to construct special institutions to provide asylum to the emotionally deranged. In fact, Dix's leadership was so persuasive that Congress passed legislation authorizing federal aid to the states for mental institutions. However, because President Franklin Pierce thought that the federal government should not interfere with the responsibility of the states to ensure social welfare, he vetoed the legislation in 1854.[1] It would not be until more than a century later that the federal government, through the Community Mental Health Centers Act, would assume a central role in determining mental health policy.

As a result of federal abnegation, states assumed responsibility for care of the mentally ill. During the latter decades of the twentieth century, states built large asylums for the mentally impaired to replace local poorhouses. Originally, state mental hospitals were intended to be self-sufficient communities offering good air, clean water, nutritious food, and healthful activities consistent with the dictates of "moral treatment." Considering the quality of life experienced by many Americans at that time, such refuges were sorely needed. Conditions in rural settings were no less dire than conditions in urban centers in the nineteenth century. An adverse social climate, coupled with the absence of welfare programs to cushion people against poverty, joblessness, inadequate housing, and illness, served to swell the population of state hospitals. Often these institutions provided care for 2,000 or more residents; and, while Dorothea Dix would have appreciated the demise of the poorhouse, she would have condemned the quality of care provided to residents. "The large state asylums for the chronic insane certainly were cold, impersonal, and often brutal bins for warehousing the mentally ill," reflected Michael Katz.[2]

In this milieu, the eugenics movement provided some of the scientifically minded reformers of the Progressive Era a straightforward and surgically precise solution to the problem of state institutions being inundated by "mental defectives." Proponents of eugenics believed that the human race could be improved by selective breeding. With respect to the mentally impaired, they argued that patients often suffered from hereditary deficiencies and that generational transmission should be interrupted by sterilization. Because adherents of eugenics were less concerned about the civil rights of individual mental patients than they were about the future of civilization, the fact that some patients might object was merely an inconvenience. In such instances, eugenicists obtained court permission to sterilize patients without their consent. Many patients, of course, lacked the mental capacity to comprehend sterilization and had no idea that the surgical procedures to which they were subjected would terminate their reproductive lives. By the 1930s, 30 states had passed laws authorizing involuntary sterilization, and by 1935 20,000 patients had been sterilized, almost half of them in California. Involuntary sterilization of the feebleminded generated great controversy, eventually culminating in a Supreme Court decision, *Buck v. Bell* (1927), written by Oliver Wendell Holmes, which validated the practice.

The case upon which Holmes based his decision included an essential report prepared by a social worker, involving a young woman in Virginia who was sterilized, only to be judged psychologically normal years later.[3] A reconstruction of the case showed that in 1906 a Charlottesville, Virginia, woman named Emma Buck had a daughter, Carrie. A widow and social outcast, Emma was brought before a Commission on Feeblemindedness in 1920 where she was committed to the Colony for Epileptics and Feebleminded. Daughter Carrie was placed in the care of a family for whom she did housework; in school, Carrie received good grades until her foster family withdrew her so that she could do housework for other families. When she was 17, Carrie became pregnant, having been raped by her boyfriend, she alleged. Such untoward behavior was unacceptable to her foster family; ominously, Carrie was brought before the same commission that had committed her mother. That same year the Superintendent of the Colony intoned on such immoral behavior: "These women are never reformed in heart and mind because they are defectives from the standpoint of intellect and moral conception and should always have the supervision by officers of the law and properly appointed custodians."[4] On January 23, 1924, Carrie was committed to the Colony; on March 28 she delivered a daughter, Vivian. Frustrated by lower court appeals to involuntary sterilization, eugenicists had been seeking a case to appeal to the Supreme Court in order to legitimize the practice, and Carrie Buck appeared an ideal candidate. Two of the Buck family women had been judged feebleminded; if Vivian were determined to be impaired as well, the mental impairment would have affected three generations. Providing questionable representation for Carrie Buck was a eugenicist and founder of the Colony. Only seven months old, Vivian was evaluated by a social worker who, when asked if the infant was normal, replied, "There is a look about it that is not quite normal, but just what it is, I can't tell."[5] But it was sufficient evidence for the justices of the Supreme Court who ruled 8 to 1 in favor of involuntary sterilization of Carrie Buck. Writing for the majority, Justice Holmes wrote famously, "Three generations of imbeciles are enough."[6] As if to rebuke the justices, Vivian did well in school, earning a place on the honor roll before dying of an infectious disease at age 8.[7]

With medical advances in neurology, physicians assumed a prominent role in addressing mental disorders, sometimes in ways that would later be refuted. The frontal lobotomy, promoted by Walter J. Freeman as a method for dealing with mental disorders, was a case in point. Based on the preliminary work of a Nobel laureate physician, Freeman developed a 10-minute operation in which a lance was inserted behind the eye socket into the frontal lobe of the brain. Pioneering the procedure at George Washington University Hospital in 1936, Freeman eventually performed lobotomies on 2,900 patients, the youngest a four-year-old. However, permanent disability and death were often the outcomes of Freeman's work, and it fell into disrepute. His admitting privileges at a California hospital were suspended after the death of a past lobotomy patient of his in 1967.[8]

Mental Health Reform

More humane efforts to reform state institutions invariably involved the National Association for Mental Health (NAMH). Begun early in the twentieth century as an extension of the work of Clifford Beers, who had recovered after being hospitalized for mental illness, NAMH became critical of the custodial institutions operated by state governments. The issue of mental health attracted wide public attention during World War II, when approximately one in every four draftees was rejected for military service because of psychiatric or neurological problems.[9] In response to public outcry about mental health problems immediately after the war, Congress passed the Mental Health Act of 1946, which established the National Institute of Mental Health (NIMH). Accompanying the Mental Health Act was an appropriation for an exhaustive examination of the mental health needs of the nation. In 1961 NIMH released *Action for Mental Health*, a report that called for an ambitious national effort to modernize the U.S. system of psychiatric care.[10]

Action for Mental Health was a utopian vision of mental health care, the idealism of which coincided perfectly with a set of extraordinarily propitious circumstances. First, the postwar economy was booming, and, with cutbacks in military expenditures, a surplus existed that could be tapped for domestic programs. Second, a new generation of drugs—psychotropic medications—showed promise of being able to stabilize severely psychotic patients who before had been unmanageable. Third, a literature was emerging that was critical of the "total institution" concept of the state hospital and implied that noninstitutional—and presumably community—care was better. Finally, because of his experience with mental retardation as a family problem, a sister who was seriously impaired after a lobotomy, President John F. Kennedy was supportive of programs that promised to improve mental health care.[11]

These political and social circumstances did not go unnoticed by Dr. Robert H. Felix, a physician who had grown up with the Menninger family in Kansas and had developed a sharp critique of the state mental hospital as an institution for the care of emotionally disturbed patients. Felix was later to become director of NIMH. A primary architect of the community mental health movement, Felix was able to draw on his extensive experience in the Mental Hygiene Division of the U.S. Public Health Service as well as on the breadth of professional and political contacts that three decades of public service afforded.[12] Felix's objective was as simple as it was radical. He intended to pick up the banner last advanced by Dorothea Dix and reassert the role of the federal government in the nation's mental health policy. Through the community mental health movement, Felix would use federal legislation to reform the archaic state mental hospitals. The laws that enabled NIMH to reform mental health care were the Community Mental Health Centers Acts of 1963 and 1965.

The Community Mental Health Centers Acts

Under the propitious circumstances of the postwar era, the first Community Mental Health Centers (CMHC) Act was passed by Congress and signed by President Kennedy on October 31, 1963. The enactment of CMHC legislation was not, however, without obstacles. To allay the American Medical Association's fears that the act represented socialized medicine, the CMHC Act of 1963 appropriated funds only for construction purposes. It was not until 1965, when the AMA was reeling from governmental proposals to institute federal health care programs for the aged and the poor, that funds were authorized for staffing CMHCs. Advocates of the CMHC Acts of 1963 and 1965

maintained that a constant target of the legislation was "to eliminate, within the next generation, the state mental hospital, as it then existed." The strategy of the mental health leadership and their allies was to "demonopolize" the state role in the provision of mental health services and attempt to establish a triad of federal, state, and local support for mental health services. At this time, federal bureaucrats planned to blanket the whole country with comprehensive community mental health services. Their intention was not to federalize the total program through its financing, but to obtain a degree of control through the resulting federal regulations and standards.[13]

The philosophical basis for transferring mental health care from the state hospital to the community was borrowed from public health, which had developed the concept of prevention. In adopting this formulation, proponents of community mental health presumed that services provided in the community would be superior to the warehousing of patients in state institutions. Prevention, according to the public health model, was of three types: **Primary prevention** efforts were designed to eliminate the onslaught of mental health problems. Certain psychiatric disturbances, such as depression and anxiety disorders, seemed to be caused by stress, which could be reduced by eliminating the source of stress. **Secondary prevention** consisted of early detection and intervention to keep incipient problems from becoming more debilitating. For example, screening schoolchildren for attention deficit disorders and providing corrective treatment could enhance a child's educational career and thereby enhance development throughout adolescence. **Tertiary prevention** consisted of "limiting the disability associated with a particular disorder, after the disorder had run its course." Typically, tertiary prevention activities sought to stabilize, maintain, and—when possible—rehabilitate those with relatively severe impairments.[14] It was clear to the community mental health activists that the state hospital addressed only tertiary prevention (and then poorly), whereas community mental health offered the prospect of combining primary and secondary intervention with a more adequate effort at tertiary prevention. The structure through which prevention would be implemented was the community mental health center (CMHC).

According to the CMHC Acts, the United States was to be divided into catchment areas, each with a population of 75,000 to 200,000 persons.[15]

Eventually, NIMH planned a CMHC for each catchment area, some 2,000 in all.[16] Programmatically, each CMHC was to provide all essential psychiatric services to the catchment area: inpatient hospitalization, partial hospitalization, outpatient services, 24-hour emergency services, and consultation and education for other service providers in the community. Soon after initial passage of the CMHC Act, child mental health as well as drug abuse and alcoholism services were added to the array of services provided. To assure that patients were not lost between programs within the CMHC network, **case management** was included, whereby every case was assigned to one professional who monitored the patient's progress throughout treatment. Financially, NIMH provided funding to disadvantaged catchment areas through matching grants over an eight-year cycle. At the end of the cycle, the catchment area was supposed to assume financial responsibility for the CMHC.[17] With this framework, mental health reformers believed that the CMHC was an effective alternative to the state hospital.

Deinstitutionalization

Enthusiasm for community mental health reform ebbed when a series of circumstances that were beyond the control of the CMHC architects began to subvert the movement. Despite promising growth in the number of CMHCs during Johnson's presidency, the Nixon administration did not look favorably on CMHCs and impounded funds appropriated for mental health programs. Although funds were later released, the Nixon administration had clearly stated its disapproval of governmental mental health initiatives. Subsequent legislation to restore momentum to the flagging CMHC movement was crushed by a veto from President Ford. By the time a more sympathetic Carter administration assumed office, general economic problems were so serious that additional appropriations for mental health were not authorized.[18] Still, at the end of Carter's term, 691 CMHCs continued to receive federal assistance. With the Omnibus Budget and Reconciliation Act of 1981, however, the Reagan administration collapsed all mental health funding into a block grant available to states for any mental health services they deemed fundable. As a result, the designation of CMHCs for direct receipt of federal funds ceased in 1981.[19]

In the meantime, however, many states had planned to shift responsibility for the mentally ill to the CMHCs. In fact, the community mental health movement had proved a timely blessing for officials in states where the maintenance of archaic state hospitals was an increasing economic burden. As states discharged patients from state institutions, they realized immediate savings: "the continuing fall in the numbers of patients to be housed provided state governments with plausible reasons for abandoning expensive schemes of capital investment designed to extend and (or) renovate their existing state hospital systems."[20] In all, 14 state hospitals were closed between 1970 and 1973. The prospect of substantial cost savings through the **deinstitutionalization** of patients received wide support. As governor of California, Ronald Reagan proposed closing all state hospitals by 1980.[21] Unfortunately, the transfer of patients from state institutions to settings in the community was not well planned. Through the mid-1970s, the deinstitutionalization movement was characterized by "severe fragmentation of effort and distribution of activity broadly throughout government with little effective coordination at the state or national level."[22] For purely economic reasons, then, state officials were strongly encouraged to facilitate deinstitutionalization regardless of whether or not alternative forms of care were available for those discharged from state hospitals. Ominously, by the end of the 1990s, 93 percent of the state psychiatric beds that had existed in 1955 had been lost to deinstitutionalization.[23]

Deinstitutionalization was further confounded by a series of judicial decisions in the mid-1970s that enhanced the civil rights of mental patients while at the same time requiring states to provide them with treatment. In **Wyatt v. Stickney,** Alabama District Court Judge Frank Johnson ruled that the state of Alabama was obliged to provide treatment to patients in state hospitals and ordered Governor Wallace and the state to appropriate millions of dollars for that purpose—a judgment with which the state subsequently failed to comply. Shortly thereafter, in **Donaldson v. O'Connor,** the Supreme Court determined that "the state could not continue to confine a mentally ill person who was not dangerous to himself or others, who was not being treated, and who could survive outside the hospital." Finally, in **Halderman v. Pennhurst,** the Third District Court established that institutionalized patients deserved treatment in the "least restrictive alternative."

As a group, these rulings had a profound effect on institutional care for patients with mental impairments. Only persons dangerous to themselves or others could be hospitalized involuntarily. For those hospitalized, involuntarily or otherwise, states were obliged to provide adequate treatment in the manner that was least restrictive to the patient. These decisions promised to be enormously costly to state officials who were trying to curb mental health expenditures. To comply with the court decisions, states would have to pump millions of dollars into the renovation of institutions that had been slated for closure. The solution, in many instances, was to use a narrow interpretation of *Donaldson* to keep emotionally disturbed people out of state institutions. In other words, judicial decisions, coupled with the fiscal concerns of state officials, provided a convoluted logic that served to justify first emptying state hospitals of seriously disturbed patients and then requiring the manifestation of life-threatening behavior for their rehospitalization. If people were not hospitalized in the first place, the states bore no obligation to provide the adequate, but expensive, treatment demanded by *Wyatt*. The criteria for hospitalization specified the most serious self-destructive behaviors; once admitted, however, patients were stabilized as quickly as possible and then discharged. As a result, those in greatest need of mental health services—patients who were seriously mentally ill—were often denied the intensive care they needed. The consequences for the mentally ill were substantial. In his interpretation of the legal decisions influencing mental health services, Alan Stone, a psychiatrist and a professor at Harvard Law School, observed that the true symbol of the Supreme Court *Donaldson* decision was a bag lady.[24] Thus, legal decisions favoring the mentally ill often proved illusory; in the name of enhancing the human rights of people with mental illness—but with no corresponding improvement in services—they offered those people nothing more than the right to be insane.[25]

The Revolving Door

The shortfall of the community mental health movement, states' transfers of patients from mental hospitals, judicial decisions assuring patients of their civil rights, and the deinstitutionalization movement all combined to leave tens of thousands of former mental patients adrift. Although some former mental hospital patients were able to deal with community agencies in order to obtain mental health care, many of the seriously mentally ill were left to themselves.[26] By the late 1970s some 40,000 poor, chronically ill mental patients had been "dumped" in New York City. The 7,000 on the Upper West Side of Manhattan represented "the greatest concentration of deinstitutionalized mental patients in the United States."[27] Former patients presented such problems, that special units of nursing homes were designated for them. In 2002 the *New York Times* reported that "hundreds of patients released from state psychiatric hospitals in New York in recent years are being locked away on isolated floors of nursing homes, where they are barred from going outside on their own, have almost no contact with others and have little ability to contest their confinement."[28] Of the 5,000 residents of homes, 946 had died between 1995 and 2000: "some residents died roasting in their rooms during heat waves. Others threw themselves from rooftops, making up some of at least 14 suicides in that . . . period. Still more, lacking the most basic care, succumbed to routinely treatable ailments, from burst appendices to seizures."[29] By authorizing special homes for mental patients, state officials had effectively replaced large state institutions with a dispersed network of small private ones.

New York was not alone in routinizing the neglect of those who had resided in institutions. In 1999, Katherine Boo investigated the care of residents with mental retardation who lived in group homes in the District of Columbia. During the 1990s, 350 incidents of theft, abuse, neglect, and molestation of residents had been reported, yet not a single fine had been levied against the companies that operated the group homes. Worse, during the late 1990s, 53 residents had died in incidents related to substandard care; of these, three received only a cursory review by the District or the federal government.[30] Eventually, it was discovered that the deaths of 116 group home residents with mental retardation had never been investigated, resulting in a series of lawsuits by families of the residents.[31] For her muckraking series on the subject, Boo was awarded a Pulitzer Prize.

Deinstitutionalization marginalized many patients. Reporting in *Scientific American*, two mental health researchers described their experiences with deinstitutionalized patients:

> Time and time again we see patients who were released from state hospitals after months or years of custodial care; who then survive precariously on

■ *The high incidence of readmissions for psychiatric hospital patients is a chronic problem in mental health care.*

welfare payments for a few months on the fringe of the community, perhaps attending a clinic to receive medication or intermittent counseling; who voluntarily returned to a hospital or were recommitted . . . who were maintained in the hospital on an antipsychotic medication and seemed to improve; who were released again to an isolated "community" life and who, having again become unbearably despondent, disorganized, or violent, either present themselves at the emergency room or are brought to it by a police officer. Then the cycle begins anew.[32]

The high incidence of readmissions for psychiatric patients—the "revolving door"—had become an unavoidable problem in mental health.

Meanwhile, resources for state mental hospitals dwindled, leaving patient care uncertain. In an attempt to manage patients more cost-effectively, state mental institutions relied more heavily on psychoactive medication, sometimes with disastrous consequences. In California, for example, a federally funded group that oversees mental health care complained of unnecessary deaths of mental patients who had been left unsupervised after receiving medication. A typical fatality was a 28-year old man who died after being locked in his room for three and a half hours: "In addition to lithium and Valium, he was given Cogentin, which can cause vomiting, and Thorazine, which can suppress the body's natural coughing reflex. He suffocated on his own vomit and a piece of Christmas candy."[33] The first nationwide review of such deaths revealed that 142 psychiatric patients had died between 1988 and 1998 as a result of institutional abuses; 33 percent of the deaths were attributed to asphyxiation and 26 percent to cardiac problems. More than one-fourth of the patients who died were children.[34]

By the end of the 1980s, the United States lacked a coherent mental health plan. Psychiatrist E. Fuller Torrey and his associates observed that "services for individuals with serious mental illness in the United States are a disaster by any measure used. Not since the 1820s have so many mentally ill individuals lived untreated in public shelters, on the streets, and in jails."[35] State hospitals had been divested of much of their responsibility for patients with serious psychiatric problems, but a complete system of CMHCs was not in place to care for many of those who had been deinstitutionalized. As a result of this institutional transformation, the last half of the twentieth century witnessed a radical change in mental health care. In 1955 the vast majority of mental health care was inpatient, with less intensive care representing a minority of episodes; by 1997 this had been reversed.

As state hospitals converted from long-term custodial care to short-term patient stabilization, psychotropic medication came to be a routine form of treatment. But the psychopharmacological revolution, though congruent with the relatively orderly march toward deinstitutionalization in the late 1960s, actually exacerbated the psychiatric chaos of two decades later. Shown to stabilize psychotic patients until interpersonal treatment methods could be employed, the major tranquilizers—Prolixin, Thorazine, Haldol, and Stelazine, to name a few—seemed clinically indicated within the controlled environment of the hospital. In a community setting, however, psychotropic medication became problematic. Once stabilized on major tranquilizers, patients frequently found the side effects of the medication—dry mouth, nervousness, torpor, lactation in women, and impotence in men—unacceptable and stopped taking the medication.

Yet without medication such patients frequently decompensated, and without the regular supervision of psychiatric personnel, patients disappeared into inner-city ghettos or rural backwaters, adding to an already growing homeless population. Definitive data on the psychological condition of the homeless are difficult to generate, but a study of the homeless in Fresno, California, revealed that "34 percent were rated severely impaired and urgently in need of [psychiatric] treatment. An additional 33 percent were rated moderately impaired so that treatment would be of substantial benefit."[36] A Baltimore study found that 80 percent of the homeless were mentally ill, and most of these were also abusing illicit drugs and alcohol.[37] A Housing and Urban Development (HUD) census of the homeless revealed that 62 percent had problems with alcohol abuse, 58 percent with drugs, and 57 percent with mental health.[38]

In the absence of mental health care, increasingly desperate former mental hospital patients turned to petty crime to gain income, thus clogging local courts. Commenting on the surge in arrests of the mentally ill, one mental health worker became exasperated: "These people are forced to commit crimes to come to the attention of the police and get help."[39] By 2000 the Justice Department reported that 283,800, or 16 percent, of inmates in local and state correctional facilities suffered from mental disorders,[40] and another 550,000 were on parole.[41]

In 2003 Human Rights Watch reported that U.S. prisons contained three times more psychiatric patients than mental hospitals. This institutional mismatch had come to the point that the largest psychiatric facility in the nation was the Los Angeles County Jail which held 3,400 mentally ill inmates; second was New York's Rikers Island with 3,000.[42] At the end of 2006 the director of Florida's social services agency quit after being fined $80,000 for a contempt of court citation due to having failed to transfer mentally ill inmates to state hospitals. Bernard Harcourt quite aptly noted that "prisons have become the new asylums."[43]

By 2000, reformers were attempting to change judicial policy in regard to mentally ill convicts by creating special courts to deal with nonviolent offenders who had mental disorders. Paralleling special drug courts that had emerged in several metropolitan areas during the 1990s to contend with nonviolent drug abusers, the mental health court concept was advocated by the National Alliance for the Mentally Ill (NAMI) as well as the National Mental Health Association.[44] In 2000 Congress passed America's Law Enforcement and Mental Health Project Act. Drawing on mental health courts already established in Seattle, Washington, Anchorage, Alaska, Fort Lauderdale, Florida, and San Bernardino, California, the Act instructed the Attorney General to make grants for mental health courts in other locations. The Mental Health Courts Grant Program subsequently supported the creation of 23 mental health courts in 2002 and 14 more in 2003. By the end of 2004 a consortium of mental health advocacy organizations reported that 99 mental health courts were operating.[45] Federal funding lagged behind the initiative, however; in 2003, $2.98 million was appropriated for mental health courts, but the following year the amount was zero.[46]

CMHCs under Siege

The discharge of patients from state mental hospitals imposed an enormous burden on the CMHCs. Because the seriously mentally ill were often unable to get care from hospitals, the CMHCs provided the only service these people received. A Philadelphia CMHC reported that 44 percent of its patients were chronically disturbed and that these patients consumed 70 percent of the mental health services provided.[47] CMHCs had to restructure their activities so as to focus on immediate care for seriously disturbed patients, with the result that "indirect" services, such as prevention and evaluation, were cut back. A study of 94 CMHCs showed that increasing demand for direct services to the seriously mentally disturbed began to skew mental health service delivery.[48] Thus, rather than being a mental health agency that provided a comprehensive range of services to all persons in a catchment area, the CMHC rapidly became an outpost for individuals with serious mental disturbances—a population that CMHCs were not intended to serve, at least not exclusively.

As client demand escalated, CMHCs faced significant cuts in federal funding. The Reagan administration moved to consolidate mental health funding in the form of block grants that were devolved to the states, but in the process reduced federal funding 21 percent.[49] With funding from the federal government diminishing, CMHCs became more dependent on the states, which had historically defined mental health care in the United States. CMHCs were able to compensate for federal reductions to some extent by obtaining more funding from government assistance programs. Significantly, nongovernmental sources, such as client fees and private insurance, continued to account for a relatively minor portion of CMHC operating expenses. Precisely how this reduction in federal funds affected the CMHC effort varied, of course, with individual programs. CMHCs in wealthier states, for example, were better able to weather the fiscal turmoil than were those in poorer states. Generally, however, CMHCs reduced staffing and programming through such strategies as layoffs and hiring freezes, staff reassignments, and internal reorganization.[50]

By the mid-1980s, CMHCs seemed to have made the necessary organizational adjustments to funding changes; but these were at the expense of staffing and programming needs that had been increasing. CMHCs were able to hire some new staff to make up for earlier reductions, but programming was compromised. In San Diego, for example, county officials decided to target scarce resources for only the most seriously disturbed, which drew this editorial response from a CMHC staff member:

> In the future . . . the community mental health clinics will provide little or no talking therapy to their thousands of clients. Instead, most patients will find their treatment limited to a 15-minute visit with a psychiatrist and a prescription for expensive psychotropic medications—bought, incidentally, at taxpayer expense.[51]

A decade after the devolution of mental health block grants to the states, CMHCs had changed their priorities, targeting **chronic care** services and services for people who were insured, while reducing services to children, adolescents, and the elderly who were uninsured.[52]

By 1990, CMHCs maintained an important institutional role, yet no longer served as the focus of mental health reform. CMHCs not only had failed to replace the state hospital system, but accounted for less than 5 percent of inpatient episodes. CMHCs were more visible in the realm of outpatient care, yet provided only a third of care by private practitioners.[53] Within two decades, the momentum had gone out of the CMHC movement, leaving thousands of former patients with mental illness adrift. It was perhaps inevitable that more intrusive methods would evolve to manage them.

Preventive Commitment

By the early 1990s, governmental mental health policy was in disarray. Deinstitutionalization had contributed to the homelessness problem, with at least 50 percent of the homeless being people with severe mental illness by the late 1980s.[54] When winter threatened the safety of some homeless people in New York City, a team of mental health workers were authorized to pick up those who posed a danger to themselves and to commit them to Bellevue Hospital for a three-week observation period, a policy referred to as **preventive commitment.** The first person picked up was Joyce Brown, who "was dirty, malodorous and abusive to passersby, and defecated on herself."[55] To the chagrin of then-Mayor Ed Koch, when Brown had been stabilized in Bellevue, attorneys from the American Civil Liberties Union challenged her involuntary commitment. The prospect that pending litigation might cancel the program led one supporter to observe that "for the severely mentally ill, liberty is not just an empty word but a cruel hoax."[56]

Despite initial setbacks in preventive commitment, 41 states would eventually authorize the practice.[57] The high number of treatment dropouts from outpatient therapy and the revolving door of hospitalization served to encourage local authorities to find some method for ensuring that seriously mentally ill persons would not deteriorate because of lack of intervention by mental health professionals. Preventive commitment provides for commitment of individuals who do not meet the statutory standard for involuntary hospitalization but who are mentally ill, are unable to voluntarily seek or comply with treatment, and need treatment in order to prevent deterioration that would predictably result in dangerousness to self or others or grave disability.[58]

A tragic incident in early 1999 strengthened the cause of preventive commitment: In New York City a 32-year-old receptionist, Kendra Webdale, was pushed under a subway train and killed by a 29-year-old patient with mental illness, Andrew Goldstein. During the two years prior to the incident, Goldstein not only experienced persistent hallucinations but also acted violently, once assaulting a psychiatrist. Having been discharged from inpatient care, Goldstein had fared poorly in a basement apartment without a phone; he had sought residential services in a group facility to no avail, as there were no vacancies.[59] Within a year, the New York legislature enacted Kendra's Law, authorizing $30 million for preventive commitment.[60]

An increasingly popular mental health policy, preventive commitment nevertheless presents serious problems when there are inadequate resources to ensure that it is used properly. When a facility lacks staff, preventive commitment can become a form of social control—as opposed to therapy—in which treatment "consists of mandatory medication and little else."[61] One authority on preventive commitment speculated that mental health professionals would have little choice but to use "forced medication" as "the treatment of choice" for those in preventive commitment and that they would have to "actually track down noncompliant patients at their place of residence or elsewhere and administer medication as part of a mobile outreach team."[62]

For those concerned with the civil rights of those with mental impairment, such an eventuality is nothing less than ghoulish, an exercise in state tyranny in the name of social welfare.[63] Even under conditions of adequate staffing, preventive commitment remains problematic. The side effects of psychoactive medications are so pronounced for many patients that they simply refuse to take the drugs, even under duress. Among the contraindications of early psychoactive medications is **tardive dyskinesia,** permanent damage to the central nervous system resulting from long-term use of medications

such as Prolixin and Stelazine. Because tardive dyskinesia is irreversible and is manifested by obvious symptoms—"protrusion of tongue, puffing of cheeks, puckering of mouth, chewing movements"[64]—the disorder raises a haunting specter: In an attempt to control psychological disturbances, psychiatry has created a host of physiological aberrations. Fortunately, a new generation of psychoactive medication, such as Zyprexa, has shown less evidence of tardive dyskinesia; however, these drugs are more expensive, and this raises another problem. In 2003 Kentucky reduced the cost of its Medicaid program by excluding Zyprexa from its list of approved medications, leaving poor persons with mental illness dependent on cheaper medications that are more likely to have adverse side effects.[65]

Mental Health Service Delivery

The Substance Abuse and Mental Health Services Administration (SAMHSA) of the Department of Health and Human Services oversees the federal Alcohol, Drug Abuse, and Mental Health block grants. These grants consolidate several separate or "categorical" programs established earlier, such as the CMHC Acts. Since 1981 all mental health expenditures have been in block grants to states. By using a block grant strategy, the federal government removed the power from federal agencies and transferred it to the individual states. Since the creation of mental health block grants, funding for mental health services has increased only incrementally, particularly in comparison with substantially greater funding for substance abuse services. During the mid-1990s, the mental health block grant remained static; since 2003 the annual appropriation has been $436 million.[66]

Static federal funding for mental health services signaled declining leadership in mental health reform. By the 1990s, several states were exploring innovative methods for delivery of mental health services.[67] One approach involved the integration of services and payment through a capitation method, through which agencies are awarded a predetermined amount per client with which they must provide a range of services. Agencies are funded the capitation amount regardless of the actual cost of serving an individual client, thus encouraging them to optimize care. Capitation in mental health care would mimic health maintenance organizations

(HMOs), which have a successful track record in providing preventive and primary health care. "Mental health HMOs would centralize financing and delivery system responsibility, create financial incentives to reallocate resources from inpatient to outpatient settings, and reduce system fragmentation, as perceived by patients."[68] Such an arrangement has the advantage of being easy to administer, and it builds into the reimbursement scheme certain incentives that do not exist in other arrangements. Under a capitation reimbursement method, for example, agencies are encouraged to cut down on expensive services, such as hospitalization, because a surplus can be realized when the actual cost of care is below the capitation amount. "Money can be used to develop walk-in crisis centers, step-down units that provide intermediate care after an acute hospitalization, special case management programs for coordinating services, and rehabilitation or special housing services."[69] In addition, agencies are penalized for neglecting to serve clients, because every capitated client represents a resource base for the agency.

An example of how a capitation method of payment could be used in mental health service delivery was the integrated mental health (IMH) concept pioneered in New York State and Philadelphia. Capitated mental health care under IMH would have three major features: First, current **categorical grants**—Medicaid, Supplemental Security Income, Food Stamp Program, local funding—would be aggregated into a common fund from which capitation "premiums" would be paid. Second, a nonprofit planning and coordination agency would be established to oversee mental health care and in so doing negotiate contracts with providers, monitor performance, and evolve innovative programs. Third, particularly high-usage clients would be targeted for provision of less costly services in order to generate surpluses for less-intensive services.[70]

The magnitude of cost savings that can be realized through IMH is illustrated by the deployment of a capitated system in two New York counties during the 1990s. In order to induce CMHCs to participate in the capitation arrangement, the counties established payment rates for levels of service for three types of patients: for "continuous patients," who had been hospitalized for some time, $39,000 per year; for "intermittent patients," who generally required intermediate care, two rates, $18,000 and $13,000; and for "outpatients," who needed the least intensive care, $5,000. State officials calculated that such payments would represent savings, because state hospital care exceeded $100,000 per patient

annually. Eventually, the continuous patient rate was reduced to $28,000; the intermittent rate was combined and lowered to $15,600; and the outpatient rate was increased to $11,600. Initial assessment of the program indicated cost savings and improved patient functioning. Participating CMHCs planned to use their revenue surpluses to extend mental health services to children and the elderly.[71]

The idea of integrating services through an arrangement such as the IMH may become a source of innovation in future mental health policy. Such an eventuality has significant implications for human service professionals, who may miss an important opportunity to shape mental health programs unless they are willing to sharpen their administrative skills. The capitation of mental health services, as might be suspected, places a premium on fiscal analysis, cost accounting, and strategic planning. In a policy environment in which capitation is an increasingly prevalent method of ensuring access to service while containing program costs, mental health administrators who are not knowledgeable about fiscal management may well lose control of programs to professionals from business and public administration. For example, the Threshold Jail Program, which provides care for mentally ill inmates, calculates a per diem of $26, compared to $70 for incarceration and $400 for mental hospital hospitalization. Although the program has been extant for only a few years, it has helped all of its 45 members avoid re-arrest, an accomplishment that resulted in a grant of $495,000 from the state of Illinois.[72] Constructing incentives to reduce more expensive forms of care through methods such as capitation would place social workers at the forefront of mental health service innovation.

Mental health policy that emphasizes innovations such as capitation presents a paradox for social workers: while they have been integrally involved in direct practice through case management, they have been less visible in program development. Thus, while case management services for people with serious mental illness "have enjoyed a rapid increase in prominence within the mental health system,"[73] social workers have been reluctant to become managers in human service corporations.[74] As conventionally structured, managed care in mental health has been subject to the same problems as managed physical health care, often attenuating services by limiting the number of therapeutic sessions. At worst a mental health corporation can collapse, as has Charter Behavioral Systems, leaving hundreds of patients adrift.[75] Regardless, unless mental health professionals increase their understanding of human service markets, they may find themselves working under the direction of business executives and using methods that are not optimal with respect to patients' well-being. Such a development is unlikely to be in the best interests of patients who are seriously emotionally disturbed.

Parity for Mental Health Care

Although managed care defined much of the coverage for mental health care during the late 1980s and early 1990s, many who had received mental health services in the past found their options rationed, attenuated, or eliminated.[76] In response, a group of parents and relatives of people with mental illness organized NAMI and fought for extended mental health coverage,[77] placing mental health provision on par with physical health services. The demise of the proposal left mental health advocates searching for a vehicle for obtaining parity. Health insurers opposed parity in mental health care, because it would increase the cost of premiums; the Congressional Budget Office projected that parity would raise premiums by 4 percent, or about $12 billion.[78] Given its aversion to increased health costs, to say nothing of its objections to government meddling in health care, few expected the conservative 104th Congress to move toward parity.

Yet, smarting from negative ratings associated with an overzealous conservative agenda, Congress suddenly reversed field in the closing days of the legislative session and in 1996 delighted mental health advocates by agreeing on legislation establishing parity for mental health care. Effective January 1, 1998, employers with more than 50 employees who offer any mental health coverage must include mental health benefits that are comparable to health benefits.[79] The consequences of legislatively mandating parity in mental health coverage were immediately disputed. Opponents warned of significant increases in health insurance premiums and the likelihood that employers would eliminate mental health coverage in order to dodge the parity mandate.[80] Defenders, on the other hand, minimized the implications for premium increases, noting that mental illness was, for the first time, being interpreted as a physiological disorder.

An evaluation of the Mental Health Parity Act released by the General Accounting Office in May 2000 tempered the enthusiasm of mental health advocates. Although 86 percent of employers surveyed were in compliance with the legislation, most— 87 percent—had altered employee benefits so that mental health benefits were more restrictive. Significantly, only 3 percent reported that compliance had resulted in increased costs and none had dropped mental health coverage altogether in response to mandated mental health parity.[81] Achieving parity in mental health may have been an important development in social policy; but its provisions were quite modest. Parity was predicated on employment so it did nothing for those who were not in the labor market; moreover, because it applied only to employers with more than 50 workers, its provisions were evaded by small employers. Thus, parity did little for those with mental illness who were not working, and even less for those hired by small businesses.

Parity for mental health care may have marked the end of the downsizing of mental health care, yet much remained to be done. The devolution of mental health care to the states beginning in the early 1980s, and the rationing of resources for mental health under managed care through the remainder of the decade, had effectively checked the expansion of mental health care, and the incarceration of mentally impaired offenders recalled the horrors against which Dorothea Dix had fought during the nineteenth century and which Frederick Wiseman depicted in his documentary *Titicut Follies*. Providing essential mental health services for poor people who evidence severe psychological disorganization remains a primary challenge to mental health advocates, although resources remained inadequate for the task at hand. In 2003 President Bush's New Freedom Commission on Mental Health released its report on the status of mental health services in the United States. For all practical purposes the report was an admission of institutional inadequacy, admitted Mike Hogan the Commission Chair, "We have an unintended conspiracy to keep people disabled."

Issues in Mental Health Policy

According to a study commissioned by NIMH, just over half of all Americans will experience a mental disorder during their lifetime. Most prevalent was anxiety, followed by impulse control, mood disorders, and substance abuse (Table 13.1 on page 350). Mental disorders are ubiquitous, and treatment options have expanded commensurately.

Table 13.1

Mental Health Census

Disorder	Lifetime Prevalence (%)
Anxiety disorder	28.8
Impulse control disorder	24.8
Mood disorder	20.8
Substance disorder	14.6

Source: Benedict Carey, "Most Will Be Mentally Ill at Some Point, Study Says," *New York Times* (June 7, 2005), p. A17.

With advances in pharmaceuticals that have reduced annoying side effects, medication has become a popular intervention. The advent of managed care in mental health has contributed to the medicalization of psychiatry, particularly the use of psychoactive medications to control patient behavior.[82] Yet, psychoactive medication has become controversial. In 2004 a dispute erupted about the use of psychoactive medication with children. Prozac had been demonstrated to be effective in alleviating depression with adolescents,[83] but the efficacy research of other medications—Paxil, Zoloft, and Effexor—had not been made public. Regardless, mental health professionals had prescribed these medications with increasing frequency, often citing research conducted by pharmaceutical companies. When British researchers reported a link between suicidal ideation and the use of unapproved medications, concerns by American parents were transmitted to the Food and Drug Administration (FDA).[84]

In response to subsequent FDA queries, the pharmaceutical companies refused to release their research on clinical trials on the basis they were trade secrets.[85] As the dispute festered during the Spring of 2004, the FDA assigned an epidemiologist to evaluate 22 studies involving 4,250 children to determine the efficacy of psychotropic medication for children. When the scientist concluded that children taking antidepressants were more than twice as likely to be suicidal, the FDA refused to allow him to testify at congressional hearings on the matter.[86] In March an embarrassed FDA ordered drug companies to affix warnings of suicidal side effects on labels. Despite the publicity, the number of children on antidepressants increased 15 percent during the first three months of 2004.[87]

Four years of war in Iraq and Afghanistan resulted in serious mental health problems among returning veterans. Unlike the Vietnam conflict, the prevalence of PTSD was significantly higher,[88] although this was disputed by psychiatrist Sally Satel who contended that "a culture of trauma has blossomed," largely attributable to bonuses for veterans with PTSD.[89] More disturbing, the incidence of suicide among members of the uniformed services, particularly the Army, had increased.[90] Mental health analysts reached an alarming conclusion: not only were mental health disorders among returning soldiers delayed, but they were more prevalent among reservists (Table 13.2).

Increases in war trauma coincided with loss of mental health personnel within the uniformed services, about 10 percent between 2003 and 2006. In response, Congress authorized $600 million for enhanced mental health services for veterans.[91]

Table 13.2

Mental Health Disorders among Returning Soldiers

Type of Disorder	Return from Iraq (%)		3 to 6 months later (%)
Interpersonal conflict	Active duty	3.5	14
	Reserves	4.2	21.1
PTSD	Active duty	11.8	16.7
	Reserves	12.7	24.5
Depression	Active duty	4.7	10.3
	Reserves	3.8	13
Overall mental health	Active duty	17	27.1
	Reserves	17.5	35.5

Source: Ann Scott Tyson, "Troops' Mental Distress Tracked," *Washington Post* (November 17, 2007), p. A3.

That so many veterans were reservists scattered throughout the country underscored the need for an integrated system of mental health services. Speaking for many, Pete Earley, an award-winning author whose son was diagnosed with mental illness, advocated for better inpatient care: "What is missing in our system today are modern, long-term treatment facilities where the chronically mentally-ill can receive good medical attention and, if necessary, can live safely until they can be moved to less restrictive facilities."[92] Similarly, Andrew Solomon called for a network of university-based research centers that would study mental disorders, such as depression.[93] Building on the adoption of mental health parity, Art Levine advocated for "parity-plus," expanding mental health care through a five-part strategy: implement mental health parity, promote proven treatments for mental illness, fund patients not programs, provide early screening for children, and encourage mainstream activities such as work.[94] A half-century after the Community Mental Health movement, the question of mobilizing mental health advocates around a coherent, comprehensive of reform remained.

Substance Abuse

Mental health services are often associated with substance abuse. Human service professionals in direct services are familiar with clients who have chosen to anesthetize themselves from stress or misery with alcohol, tobacco, and other substances. Individuals' psychological problems are of course compounded by reliance on such substances, and these problems not only affect the families of substance abusers but also become more severe when addiction is manifested. Ordinarily, addiction is associated with alcohol and drugs, less often with tobacco. Substance abuse has become an important area of public policy not only because of the necessity for appropriations for treatment programs but also because of the enormous costs that substance abuse extracts from society. As these costs have escalated, substance abuse policy has attained a higher profile in domestic affairs.

The interaction of emotional difficulties, alcoholism, and substance abuse is reflected in social welfare policy and has been institutionalized in the Substance Abuse and Mental Health Services Administration. The consolidation of categorical grants into a federal block grant program under SAMHSA reflected the preference of many human service professionals for preventive programs that apply generically to all forms of substance abuse. This approach has been argued persuasively by Mathea Falco:

> An estimated 18 million Americans are alcoholics and 55 million are regular smokers, compared to 5.5 million serious drug abusers. Each year alcohol causes 200,000 deaths from disease and accidents, while more than 400,000 Americans die from smoking. By contrast, deaths from all illicit drugs range from 5,000 to 10,000. The costs of health care and lost productivity caused by tobacco-related illnesses are estimated at $60 billion a year, and those attributed to

Spotlight 13.1

The Substance Abuse and Mental Health Services Administration

Substance abuse is an important area of public policy not only because of the appropriations for treatment programs, but also because of the enormous costs that substance abuse extracts from society. To address substance abuse issues and their toll on society, the federal government established the Substance Abuse and Mental Health Services Administration (SAMHSA) in 1992. The goal of this agency is to focus attention, programs, and funding on improving the lives of people with, or at risk for, mental and substance abuse disorders.

To learn more about SAMHSA and its programs, go to its website at **www.samhsa.gov.**

alcoholism exceed $100 billion. For all illegal drugs, the National Institute of Drug Abuse sets the annual bill to society at $40 billion.[95]

What is the logic in having separate preventive programs for tobacco, alcohol, and illegal drugs when effective prevention programs can be developed for all of them? In the light of diminishing resources for social programs, Falco's book *The Making of a Drug-Free America: Programs That Work*—a call for integrating prevention efforts—is compelling.

History of Substance Abuse

Although most societies have incorporated addictive substances into their religions or social conventions, the use of these substances is ordinarily circumscribed. For historical and demographic reasons, U.S. culture has been accepting of certain substances, ambivalent about some, and phobic about others. Tobacco, a crop the colonists were encouraged to cultivate by their European sponsors, has been a legal commodity since Europeans first settled in North America. Alcoholic beverages appear in most agrarian societies, and these are a fixture in American folklore. Still, the consequences of excessive alcohol consumption on family life led some religiously inspired Prohibitionists to call for the banning of alcohol. From 1919 to 1933, the 18th Amendment to the Constitution prohibited the manufacture and sale of alcoholic beverages in the United States. Cocaine was a common ingredient in many early patent medicines and in popular beverages such as Coca-Cola. Concern about quality in production, however, led to the Pure Food and Drug Act of 1906, which required that ingredients be listed on product labels. When the public learned that there was cocaine in some products, local jurisdictions prohibited their sale. Opium, imported with the Chinese laborers who built the western rail system, was initially ignored in this country until reports surfaced that women from upright families were frequenting "opium dens." The Hague Opium Convention of 1912, of which the United States was a leader, subsequently controlled the production and sale of opium internationally. In the United States, restrictions on the manufacture and sale of cocaine, heroin, and marijuana were first established through the 1914 Harrison Narcotic Act. Marijuana was effectively made illegal through the Marijuana Tax Act of 1937.[96]

Despite this legacy, governmental control of mind-altering substances is anything but consistent.

Although the federal government wages a "drug war," some states, for all practical purposes, disregard marijuana possession; some jurisdictions have legalized marijuana for medical purposes. The sale and use of cocaine and heroin have become so essential to the economy of many poor inner-city communities that the police are ineffectual in controlling trade, able at best to harass users.[97] During the 1980s cocaine was commonly used by young urban professionals (yuppies) as the drug of choice and was glamorized by Hollywood. Meanwhile, a substantial market emerged in prescription drugs, such as Valium, which were available as widely as there were corrupt physicians willing to prescribe them. Most recently, misuse of drugs by athletes has resulted in calls for the prohibition of all performance-enhancing substances.

Public intolerance of drug abuse escalated because of several factors. Continued carnage on the nation's highways because of drunk drivers led to the founding of Mothers Against Drunk Driving (MADD), a voluntary group that fought aggressively for stiffer penalties for drivers under the influence of alcohol. The alcohol- and drug-related deaths of entertainers such as Janis Joplin, Jimi Hendrix, and Elvis Presley were sobering experiences for many young people. When sports stars Len Bias and Don Rogers died from cocaine overdoses, drug abuse took center stage in the United States. In the meantime, an ominous development served to underscore drug abuse as a public health problem, not simply as an individual moral problem. AIDS, initially associated with male homosexuals in this country, was increasingly prevalent among inner-city intravenous drug users (IDUs). Needle sharing among cocaine and heroin addicts was identified as a primary means of HIV transmission. Indiscriminate injections by IDUs quickly spread AIDS within the African American and Hispanic communities in major urban centers. When IDUs practiced unsafe sex, AIDS was passed to minority heterosexuals. As women who had contracted AIDS became pregnant, they bore infants who were HIV positive. By century's end, concerns about substance abuse drew together diverse groups of Americans. The anguish of the white suburban mothers of MADD was shared by African American inner-city mothers with AIDS.

Alcohol Abuse

Americans steadily increased their consumption of alcohol from the end of World War II until the 1980s, when drinking began to decrease. By 1987 average per capita consumption was a little more than 2.5 gallons of alcoholic beverages a year.[98] However, that amount was not evenly distributed throughout the population. One-third of the adult population abstains from alcohol consumption; one-third of people who do drink consider their consumption to be light; and the remaining third are considered moderate to heavy drinkers. The 2006 National Survey on Drug Use and Health revealed that 57 million Americans were binge drinkers on occasion and that 17 million were heavy drinkers.[99] These statistics are directly related to serious social problems. Forty-eight percent of all convicted criminals used alcohol just before committing a crime, and 64 percent of offenses against public order are alcohol related.[100] Yet substance abuse services often are not available for drinkers who are subsequently incarcerated. Substance abuse services were available at 93.8 percent of federal correctional facilities but at only 60.3 percent of state prisons, 33.5 percent of jails, and 36.6 percent of juvenile facilities.[101] Perhaps the most significant adverse consequence of alcohol consumption is highway accidents. The tragic death toll on U.S. highways not only provoked the establishment of MADD but also demands for stronger penalties for drunk drivers and public education campaigns to dissuade people from drinking while driving. This combination of motivators seemed to have a positive effect: Between 1982 and 1986 the number of inebriated drivers involved in fatal accidents dropped significantly. By 2006 the percent of people age 12 and over who drove under the influence dropped to 12.4 percent, down from 14.2 percent in 2002.[102]

Among the most pernicious effects of alcohol consumption is fetal alcohol syndrome (FAS), a physiological and mental deformation in infants caused by their mothers' ingestion of alcohol during pregnancy. FAS children exhibit behaviors that make them extraordinarily difficult to manage: limited attention span, slow response to stimuli, and an inability to incorporate a moral code. Because of these deficiencies, FAS children tend to have difficulty in the early socialization experiences of elementary school. Children with FAS frequently fail to understand complicated instructions; they tend to wander about; and they take the property of classmates without understanding the inappropriateness of such behavior. FAS is particularly difficult to diagnose in that its milder form, fetal alcohol effect (FAE), does not cause any physiological abnormality

in facial structure. The National Institutes of Health estimated in 1990 that the incidence of FAS among children of heavy-drinking women was as high as 25 per 1,000 births and that the annual cost of coping with the disorder was almost one-third of a billion dollars.[103]

Although FAS has been recognized by pediatric researchers since 1973,[104] the syndrome was not widely known to the public until Michael Dorris's account of his adopted son's FAS condition was published in *The Broken Cord*. The husband of award-winning author Louise Erdrich, Dorris wrote poignantly about his adoption of Adam, a Native American infant. Ignorant of Adam's condition, Dorris spent years consulting with teachers, having his son tested by psychologists, and transferring Adam to special schools. It was not until he visited an Indian reservation and a special education bus discharged a group of FAS children for school that Dorris learned about FAS from a friend. Suddenly, Dorris understood that Adam was suffering from a permanent disorder brought about by his birth mother's drinking.

In *The Broken Cord*, Dorris and Erdrich wrote movingly about the consequences of FAS. Being Native Americans, their observations were as acute as they were controversial. Noting that as many as 25 percent of the children born on the Sioux Pine Ridge Reservation suffered from FAS, Dorris contended that Indian women's alcohol consumption during pregnancy represented a kind of genocide. In order to contain FAS, Dorris suggested that pregnant women who have previously given birth to FAS children and who demonstrate an inability to control their drinking be incarcerated until they give birth. Erdrich concurred, her rationale being that the health of the fetus had primacy over the mother's freedom to consume alcohol:

> Knowing what I know now, I am sure that even when I drank hard, I would rather have been incarcerated for nine months and produce a normal child than bear a human being who would, for the rest of his or her life, be imprisoned by what I had done. And for those so sure, so secure, I say the same thing I say to those who would not allow a poor woman a safe abortion and yet have not themselves gone to adoption agencies and taken in the unplaceable children, the troubled, the unwanted: If you don't agree with me, then please, go and sit beside the alcohol-affected while they try to learn how to add.[105]

The idea of restraining women during pregnancy to prevent fetal damage triggered a debate in the popular media. This controversy was fueled by two related issues. First, a rapid increase in the number of infants who tested positive for cocaine at birth raised the specter of a "bio-underclass" consisting of a generation of minority children condemned to disability by maternal substance abuse.[106] Second, arrests of women for exposing their infants to substance abuse in utero enraged feminists who had watched the cutbacks in maternal health and social services during the 1980s. "It has become trendy," columnist Ellen Goodman observed acidly, "to arrest pregnant women for endangering their fetuses."[107] An unstable truce that had evolved between proponents of fetal health and women's rights was broken when a prosecutor in rural Alabama jailed mothers whose infants tested positive for illegal substances.[108] Clearly, both camps favored aggressive public education and early treatment for substance abuse before, during, and after pregnancy, but lack of funding made such initiatives unlikely.

As a result, the question of how to manage substance-abusing women during pregnancy has been passed down to program managers and clinical staff. As the number of infants testing positive for substance abuse increased, opposition to social control intervention on the basis that it violated women's rights became less tenable for human service professionals. Indeed, the possibility of compulsory treatment for pregnant drug abusers became an unavoidable issue when drug abuse was associated with the transmission of AIDS.[109] Compulsory treatment, of course, runs contrary to the individual liberties guaranteed by the Constitution, because it is possible only through some commitment procedure. Proponents of compulsory treatment and preventive commitment have argued that it is the only way to protect potential victims against the uncontrolled and hazardous behavior of addicts. Critics, on the other hand, insist that effective public education and treatment would make such draconian measures unnecessary.

This dilemma has serious implications for clients of substance abuse programs as well as practitioners. Compulsory treatment is likely to deter some people from seeking treatment that they might have sought voluntarily, though perhaps at a later date. Compulsory treatment also places the practitioner in the role of social control agent, a role not conducive to building a client's trust. Compulsory treatment is likely to drive the substance abuse problem underground, further exacerbating the very problem it is intended to remedy.

Without adequate investments in education and treatment, the future of substance abuse policy appears likely to be plagued by a series of such negatively reinforcing decisions.

Drug Abuse

By contrast with alcohol abuse, the prevalence of drug abuse is more difficult to ascertain because the use of controlled substances—the focus of drug abuse—is illegal. It appears that general drug abuse has begun to decline after peaking during the 1979–80 period. In 2006 almost 20.4 million Americans reported use of illicit drugs, a significant decrease from the 25 million abusers estimated in 1979 (see Table 13.3). Among younger Americans aged 12 to 17, drug abuse has been declining (from 11.6 percent in 2002 to 9.8 percent in 2006); drug abuse by young adults aged 18 to 25 remained static (from 20.2 percent in 2002 to 19.8 percent in 2006).

Table 13.3

Types of Illegal Substances

Type of Substance	Millions of Users in Past Month
Marijuana	14.8
Illicit drugs other than marijuana	9.6
Psychotherapeutics	7.0
Pain relievers	5.2
Cocaine	2.4
Tranquilizers	1.8
Stimulants	1.2
Hallucinogens	1.0
Inhalants	0.8
Methamphetamine	0.7
Crack	0.7
Ecstasy	0.5
Sedatives	0.4
Heroin	0.3
OxyContin	0.3
LSD	0.1
PCP	0.0

Source: "2006 National Survey on Drug Use and Health" (Washington, DC: SAMHSA, 2006), p. 18.

Types of illegal substances vary considerably. Next to marijuana, cocaine is the most prevalent illicit drug, accounting for 1.7 million users, followed by pain relievers, 1.6 million users; heroin is far less prevalent with 323,000 addicts.[110] Even if heroin is less prevalent, it remains a major problem if only because of the health problems associated with its use: As many as 25 percent of people who contract AIDS in this country are IDUs.[111] A haunting scenario takes shape: IDUs can no longer be thought of solely as tortured souls in the slow process of self-destruction; they have become transmitters of an epidemic that promises to be as costly as it is deadly.

The federal response to illicit drug use has been twofold, involving both interdicting the supply of illegal substances and reducing the demand through treatment and public education. Government strategies have oscillated wildly between the interdiction and prevention approaches. Before Ronald Reagan came to power, federal policy emphasized treatment and public education, assuming that these strategies would diminish demand. During the early 1970s, for example, two-thirds of federal appropriations for drug abuse were for treatment and education. A decade later, however, supply interdiction had superseded demand reduction as the prime strategy, consuming 80 percent of federal drug funds. Illegal drug use is considered in greater detail in Chapter 14.

For human service professionals, an emphasis on prevention over interdiction would be a positive development in drug abuse policy; $500 million for school drug abuse prevention programs became available through the Drug Free Schools Act in the early 1990s. Applying the prevention trinity used in public health to drug abuse, it is evident that most treatment funding has been directed toward rehabilitating addicts (tertiary prevention) or treatment of abusers (secondary prevention). Limited primary prevention efforts have been field tested, but these are only now being widely adopted. Mathea Falco notes that not all have been equally effective. Life Skills Training (LST), developed in New York City, and STAR (Students Taught Awareness and Resistance), deployed in Kansas City, have been superior to DARE (Drug Abuse Resistance Education). But the real test of school prevention programs comes in poor neighborhoods where drug abuse is part of the community fabric. Programs such as the Westchester Student Assistance Program in New York, Smart Moves of

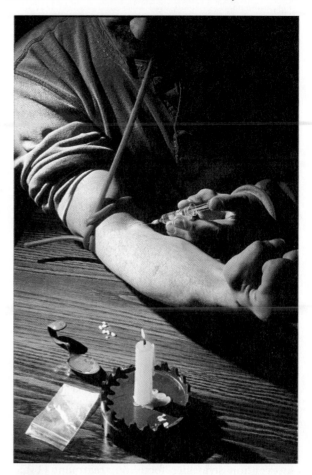

The federal response to illicit drug use has been twofold: cutting off the supply of illegal substances and reducing the demand through treatment and public education.

the Boys and Girls Clubs, and the Seattle Social Development Project show promise; yet, upon evaluation, program graduates tend to report resistance to "soft" drugs—tobacco, alcohol, marijuana. Avoidance of "hard" drugs has not been clearly demonstrated through these programs.[112] This inability of prevention programs to produce resistance to hard drugs in high-risk neighborhoods may be due to methodological problems. High-risk youth who are susceptible to hard drug use are probably unlikely to complete a prevention program, nor are they good candidates to report hard drug usage through an outcome instrument. Instead, they are likely to be casualties of the research process for the same reasons they are casualties of substance abuse. Therefore, some researchers have contended that substance abuse

Table 13.4

Location of Substance Abuse Treatment

Location	Numbers (in thousands)
Self-help group	2,183
Outpatient rehabilitation	1,621
Outpatient mental health center	1,104
Inpatient rehabilitation	934
Hospital inpatient	816
Private doctor's office	606
Prison or jail	420
Emergency room	397

Source: "2006 National Survey of Drug Use and Health" (Washington, DC: SAMHSA, 2006), p. 62.

prevention efforts will not be successful until a much more expansive definition of primary prevention, including social, economic, and institutional factors, is adopted.[113]

In the absence of major prevention initiatives, intervention strategies focus on treatment (Table 13.4). Generally, employees with generous health insurance have been able to gain ready admission to drug abuse treatment programs. The poor, by contrast, have found treatment available irregularly, often through self-help groups. Treatment eludes large numbers of substance abusers. In 2006 over one million youth age 12 to 17 would have received substance abuse treatment had it been available.[114]

Although treatment lags behind demand, research continues to demonstrate the wisdom of investing in rehabilitation. Columbia University's Center on Addiction and Substance Abuse has reported that 32.3 percent of Medicaid hospitalization days were due to neonatal complications attributed to substance abuse. Cardiovascular and respiratory disorders associated with substance abuse accounted for another 31.4 percent of Medicaid hospitalization days. Significantly, when substance abuse was noted as a secondary diagnosis, the length of hospitalization doubled.[115] A comprehensive investigation of substance abuse treatment programs in California claimed savings of $7 for every $1 dollar in program costs. "Treatment is a good investment!" affirmed the California director of alcohol and drug programs. In a 1997 review of drug use treatment, SAMHSA reported that 12 months after treatment, illicit drug use dropped significantly: 48.2 percent for users of a primary drug (e.g., marijuana), 50.8 percent for crack, 54.9 percent for cocaine, and 46.6 percent for heroin.[116] As is often the case with addiction services, the subsequent question of long-term abstinence has not been thoroughly evaluated.

A major expansion of substance abuse treatment through employer insurance plans, mandated through mental health parity, would inject substantial private resources into a service area that has been dominated by governmental programs and self-help groups. Yet because such insurance is connected to employment, it will not influence the treatment of abusers who are marginal to the labor market—those most impaired and most in need of intensive rehabilitation. Arguably, the greatest impact would be among inmates incarcerated due to drug-related offenses, yet the effectiveness of prison treatment programs has not been substantiated.

Conclusion

Mental health and substance abuse policies have been complex in part because they have addressed behaviors that are not well understood. Compounding this have been major policy disputes that have made it more difficult to reach a consensus about optimal programming. Mental health care has been compromised by a fundamental disconnect in American social welfare policy: Should responsibility for the aberrant rest with the federal government or the states? Since the 1980s, mental health care has been devolved to the states; yet, the states have been unwilling to pick up the costs for an adequate array of mental health services. Moreover, the aftermath of deinstitutionalization is still evident in the prevalence of homelessness and substance abuse. Substance abuse services have been compromised by a different disconnect: Should the focus be on treatment or interdiction? Since the advent of the war on drugs, the emphasis has been on law enforcement, resulting in underinvestment in treatment.

Discussion Questions

1. Click on the "For Students" link on the policyAmerica website (http://capwiz.com/policyamerica/index.html) and identify a mental health or substance abuse policy that is of interest to you. Are the provisions of the policy adequate? What could be done to make services more effective?

2. In the early 1980s funding for community mental health centers (CMHCs) was converted to mental health block grants. To what extent did your community develop CMHCs? What has happened to them since the 1980s? What priorities have been established through the mental health block grant system? How has this changed mental health services in your community?

3. The misuse of psychoactive medication has been implicated in several undesirable consequences. Has tardive dyskinesia become a significant problem among mental health patients in your community? If so, what is being done to prevent it? Are more or fewer mental patients going through the "revolving door"?

4. The effects of substance abuse on innocent people present difficult policy dilemmas for decision makers. What policies could be put in place to prevent the birth of infants with FAS or AIDS? How could the rights of mothers be protected? What should be the role of human service professionals in such cases?

5. Prevention and treatment of substance abuse vary from locality to locality. What has your community done to dissuade young people from substance abuse? Have these initiatives been successful? According to what indicators?

6. What resources has your community committed to dealing with substance abuse? Have these resources been adequate? Which organizations support or oppose increasing treatment for substance abuse?

Notes

1. Jean Quam, "Dorothea Dix," *Encyclopedia of Social Work*, 18th ed. (Silver Spring, MD: NASW, 1987), p. 921.
2. Michael Katz, *In the Shadow of the Poorhouse* (New York: Basic Books, 1986), p. 102.
3. Stephen Gould, "Carrie Buck's Daughter," *Natural History* (July 1984), pp. 85–92.
4. Quoted in Edwin Black, *War against the Weak* (New York: Four Walls Eight Windows, 2003), p. 110.
5. Black, *War against the Weak*, p. 115.
6. Ibid., p. 121.
7. Ibid., p. 122.
8. Sandra Boodman, "'Lobotomist' Serves as a Warning," *Washington Post* (January 15, 2008), p. F4.
9. Walter Trattner, *From Poor Law to Welfare State* (New York: Free Press, 1974), p. 175.
10. Joint Commission on Mental Illness and Health, *Action for Mental Health* (New York: Basic Books, 1961).
11. David Mechanic, *Mental Health and Social Policy* (Englewood Cliffs, NJ: Prentice Hall, 1969), pp. 59–60.
12. Henry Foley, *Community Mental Health Legislation* (Lexington, MA: D. C. Heath, 1975), pp. 13–14.
13. Ibid., pp. 39, 40.
14. Bernard Bloom, *Community Mental Health* (Monterey, CA: Brooks/Cole, 1977), pp. 74–75.
15. National Institute of Mental Health, *Community Mental Health Center Program Operating Handbook* (Washington, DC: U.S. Department of Health, Education, and Welfare, 1971), pp. 2–6.
16. Foley, *Community Mental Health Legislation*, p. 126.
17. The description of CMHCs is derived from the *Community Mental Health Centers Policy and Standards Manual*, 1988; see *Community Mental Health Centers Program Operating Handbook*, 1989.
18. Bloom, *Community Mental Health*, pp. 46–56.
19. U.S. Census Bureau, *Statistical Abstract of the United States*, 108th ed. (Washington, DC: U.S. Government Printing Office, 1987), p. 104.
20. Andrew Scull, *Decarceration* (Englewood Cliffs, NJ: Prentice Hall, 1977), p. 71.
21. Ibid., p. 69.
22. Donald Stedman, "Politics, Political Structures, and Advocacy Activities," in James Paul, Donald Stedman, and G. Ronald Neufeld (eds.), *Deinstitutionalization* (Syracuse, NY: Syracuse University Press, 1977), p. 57.

23. E. Fuller Torrey and Mary T. Zdanowicz, "Deinstitutionalization Hasn't Worked," *Washington Post* (July 9, 1999), p. A29.

24. Alan Stone, *Law, Psychiatry, and Morality* (Washington, DC: American Psychiatry Press, 1984), pp. 116, 117.

25. Jean Isaac Rael, "'Right' to Madness: A Cruel Hoax," *Los Angeles Times* (December 14, 1990), p. E5.

26. Uri Aviram, "Community Care of the Seriously Mentally Ill," *Community Mental Health Journal* 26, no. 1 (February 1990), pp. 23–31.

27. Peter Koenig, "The Problem That Can't Be Tranquilized," *New York Times Magazine*, (May 21, 1978), p. 15.

28. Clifford Levy, "Mentally Ill and Locked Up in New York Nursing Homes," *New York Times* (October 6, 2002), p. A1.

29. Clifford Levy, "For Mentally Ill, Death and Misery," *New York Times* (April 28, 2002), pp. 1, 34.

30. Katherine Boo, "Forest Haven Is Gone, But the Agony Remains," *Washington Post* (March 14, 1999); "Residents Languish; Profiteers Flourish," *Washington Post* (March 15, 1999).

31. Katherine Boo, "U.S. Probes DC Group Homes," *Washington Post* (May 4, 1999); Marcia Greene and Lena Sun, "Deaths Put DC Group Home Firm under Scrutiny," *Washington Post* (May 18, 2000).

32. Ellen Bassuk and Samuel Gerson, "Deinstitutionalization and Mental Health Services," *Scientific American* 238, no. 2 (February 1978), p. 18.

33. "State Blamed for 3 Deaths at Mental Hospitals," *Los Angeles Times* (October 2, 1991), p. A4.

34. Eric Weiss, "Mental Patients' Deaths Probed," *Washington Post* (October 11, 1998), p. A28

35. Cited in Glenn Yank, David Hargrove, and King Davis, "Toward the Financial Integration of Public Mental Health Services," *Community Mental Health Journal* 8, no. 2 (April 1992), p. 99.

36. Joseph Sacks, John Phillips, and Gordon Cappelletty, "Characteristics of the Homeless Mentally Disordered Population in Fresno County," *Community Mental Health Journal*, (Summer 1987), p. 114.

37. "Survey of Homeless Shows Mental Illness and Addiction," *New York Times* (September 10, 1989), p. 16

38. "Homeless in America: A Statistical Profile," *New York Times* (December 12, 1999), p. WK3.

39. Hector Tobar, "Mentally Ill Turn to Crime in a Painful Call for Help," *Los Angeles Times* (August 26, 1991), p. A1

40. Edward Walsh, "16% of State, Local Inmates Found Mentally Ill," *Washington Post* (July 12, 1999), p. A6

41. Kari Lydersen, "For Jailed Mentally Ill, a Way Out," *Washington Post* (June 28, 2000), p. A3.

42. Sally Satel, "Out of the Asylum, into the Cell," *New York Times* (November 1, 2003), p. A29.

43. Bernard Harcourt, "The Mentally Ill, Behind Bars," *New York Times* (January 15, 2007), p. A19.

44. "Mental Health Courts," National Mental Health Association. Retrieved October 7, 2004, from www.nmha.org

45. "Survey of Mental Health Courts," NAMI. Retrieved October 7, 2004, from http://nami.org

46. "Mental Health Courts," Bureau of Justice Assistance. Retrieved October 7, 2004, from www.ojp.usdoj.gov/BJA

47. A. Anthony Arce and Michael Vergare, "Homelessness, the Chronic Mentally Ill and Community Mental Health Centers," *Community Mental Health Journal* (Winter 1987), p. 9.

48. Judith Larsen, "Community Mental Health Services in Transition," *Community Mental Health Journal* (Winter 1987), pp. 19, 20.

49. Trevor Hadley and Dennis Chulhane, "The Status of Community Mental Health Centers Ten Years into Block Grant Financing," *Community Mental Health Journal* (April 1993), p. 96.

50. Larsen, "Community Mental Health Services in Transition," p. 22.

51. Donald Woolson, "Policy Makes Short Shrift of Mentally Ill," *Los Angeles Times* (November 2, 1986), p. C4.

52. Hadley and Chulhane, "The Status of Community Mental Health Centers," p. 97.

53. Ronald Manderscheid and Mary Sonnenschein (eds.), *Mental Health, United States, 1994* (Rockville, MD, Substance Abuse and Mental Health Administration, 1994), pp. 37, 38.

54. Community for Creative Non-Violence, *Homelessness in America* (Washington, DC: CCNV, 1987).

55. Josh Barbanel, "Homeless Woman to Be Released after Being Forcibly Hospitalized," *New York Times* (January 19, 1988), p. 8.

56. Charles Krauthammer, "How to Save the Homeless Mentally Ill," *The New Republic*, (February 8, 1988), p. 23.

57. Paul Stavis, "Treatment by Cooperation," *Washington Post* (August 19, 1999), p. A21.

58. "Developments in Mental Disability Law: 1986," *Clearinghouse Review* 20 (January 20, 1987), p. 1148. Quoted in Ruta Wilk, "Involuntary Outpatient Commitment of the Mentally Ill," *Social Work* (March–April 1988), p. 133.

59. Michael Winerip, "Bedlam in the Streets," *New York Times Magazine* (May 23, 1999).

60. Stavis, "Treatment by Cooperation," p. A21.

61. "Developments in Mental Disability Law: 1986"; and Wilk, "Involuntary Outpatient Commitment," p. 134.

62. Wilk, "Involuntary Outpatient Commitment," p. 136.

63. See, for example, Thomas Szasz, *The Myth of Mental Illness* (New York: Harper and Row, 1961); David

Ingleby (ed.), *Critical Psychiatry: The Politics of Mental Health* (New York: Pantheon, 1980).

64. *Physician's Desk Reference* (Oradell, NJ: Medical Economics Company, 1986), p. 2014.

65. Gardiner Harris, "Drug Makers Resist State Efforts to Cut Medicaid Expenses," *New York Times* (December 18, 2003), p. A1.

66. Retrieved March 18, 2008, from www.samhsa.gov/budget/B2005/spending/

67. Glenn Yank, David Hargrove, and King Davis, "Toward the Financial Integration of Public Mental Health Services," *Community Mental Health Journal* 28, no. 2 (April 1992), pp. 2–12.

68. Jon Christianson and Muriel Linehan, "Capitated Payments for Mental Health Care: The Rhode Island Programs," *Community Mental Health Journal* 25, no. 2 (Summer 1989), p. 122

69. A. P. Schinnar, A. B. Rothbard, and T. R. Hadley, "Opportunities and Risks in Philadelphia's Capitation Financing of Public Psychiatric Services," *Community Mental Health Journal* 25, no. 4 (Winter 1989), p. 256.

70. Ibid., pp. 257–258.

71. Phyllis Marshall, "The Mental Health HMO: Capitation Funding for the Chronically Mentally Ill. Why an HMO?" *Community Mental Health Journal* 28, no. 2 (April 1992), pp. 9–14.

72. Kari Lydersen, "For Jailed Mentally Ill, a Way Out," *Washington Post* (June 28, 2000), p. A3.

73. Charles Rapp and Ronna Chamberlain, "Case Management Services for the Chronically Mentally Ill," *Social Work* (September–October 1985), p. 417

74. David Stoesz, "Human Service Corporations: New Opportunities for Administration in Social Work," *Administration in Social Work* (Fall 1993), pp. 8–16.

75. Barry Meier, "A Price Too High?" *New York Times* (February 16, 2000), p. C1.

76. Charles Hall, "What Price Peace of Mind?" *Washington Post* (April 23, 1996), p. A7.

77. Agnes Hatfield, "The National Alliance for the Mentally Ill: A Decade Later," *Community Mental Health Journal* 27, no. 2 (April 1991), pp. 89–106.

78. Robert Samuelson, "Mental Health's Gray Areas," *Washington Post Weekly* (June 10–16, 1996), p. 5

79. Helen Dewar and Judith Havemann, "Conferees Expand Insurance for New Mothers, Mentally Ill," *Washington Post* (September 20, 1996), p. A1.

80. Stuart Auerbach, "The Cost of Increased Coverage," *Washington Post Weekly* (September 30–October 6, 1996), p. 19.

81. "Mental Health Parity," (Washington, DC: General Accounting Office, May 10, 2000).

82. T. M. Luhrman, *Of Two Minds: The Growing Disorder in American Psychiatry* (New York: Knopf, 2000).

83. Gardiner Harris, "Antidepressants Seen as Effective for Adolescents," *New York Times* (June 2, 2004), p. A1.

84. Shankar Vedantam, "FDA Links Antidepressants, Youth Suicide Risk," *Washington Post* (February 3, 2004), p. A1.

85. Shankar Vedantam, "Antidepressant Makers Withhold Data on Children," *Washington Post* (January 29, 2003), p. A1.

86. Gardiner Harris, "Expert Kept from Speaking at Antidepressant Hearing," *New York Times* (April 16, 2004), p. A16.

87. Milt Freudenheim, "Behavior Drugs Lead in Sales for Children," *New York Times* (May 17, 2004), p. C9.

88. Benedict Carey, "Review of Landmark Study Finds Fewer Vietnam Veterans with Post-Traumatic Stress," *New York Times* (August 18, 2006), p. A11; and Rick Weiss, "Few Vietnam Vets Are Found to Have Stress Disorder," *Washington Post* (August 18, 2006), p. A3.

89. Sally Satel, "For Some, the War Won't End," *New York Times* (March 1, 2006), p. A25.

90. Dana Priest, "Solder Suicides at Record Level," *Washington Post* (January 31, 2008), p. A1.

91. Ann Scott Tyson, "Pentagon Report Criticizes Troops' Mental-Health Care," *Washington Post* (July 16, 2007), p. A2.

92. Pete Earley, *Crazy* (New York: Berkley Books, 2006), p. 356.

93. Andrew Solomon, "Our Great Depression," *New York Times* (November 17, 2006), p. A31.

94. Art Levine, "Parity-Plus: A Third Way Approach to Fix America's Mental Health System" (Washington, DC: Progressive Policy Institute, 2005), p. 4.

95. Mathea Falco, *The Making of a Drug-Free America* (New York: Times Books, 1992), p. 24.

96. Mathea Falco, *Winning the Drug War* (New York: Priority Press, 1989), pp. 19–20.

97. David Simon and Edward Burns, *The Corner: A Year in the Life of an Inner-City Neighborhood* (New York: Broadway Books, 2000).

98. *Alcohol and Health: Seventh Special Report to the U.S. Congress* (Washington, DC: U.S. Government Printing Office, 1990), p. 14.

99. "2006 National Survey on Drug Use and Health" (Washington, DC: SAMHSA, 2006), p. 10.

100. *Alcohol and Health: Sixth Special Report to the U.S. Congress* (Washington DC: Department of Health and Human Service, 1987), p. 13.

101. "1997 Survey of Correctional Facilities" (Washington, DC: SAMHSA, 1997).

102. "2006 National Survey of Drug Use and Health," p. 10.

103. "1997 Survey of Correctional Facilities," pp. 140, 139.

104. Ibid., p. 139.

105. Louise Erdrich, "Foreword" to Michael Dorris, *The Broken Cord* (New York: Harper and Row, 1989), p. xviii.

106. Charles Krauthammer, "The Horror of Addicted Newborns," *San Diego Tribune* (July 31, 1992), p. B7.

107. Ellen Goodman, "Community Begs Off, But Prosecutes Mom," *Los Angeles Times* (February 9, 1992), p. B9.

108. Adam Nossiter, "Rural Alabama County Cracks Down on Pregnant Drug Users," *New York Times* (March 15, 2008), p. A9.

109. Department of Health and Human Services, *Compulsory Treatment of Drug Abuse* (Washington, DC: U.S. Government Printing Office, 1989).

110. Ibid., p. 58.

111. Carl Leukefeld and Frank Tims, "An Introduction to Compulsory Treatment for Drug Abuse: Clinical Practice and Research," in *Compulsory Treatment of Drug Abuse: Research and Clinical Practice* (Rockville, MD: Department of Health and Human Services, 1988), p. 2.

112. Falco, *The Making of a Drug-Free America*, Chapters 3 and 4.

113. Derek Mason, Mark Lusk, and Michael Gintzler, "Beyond Ideology in Drug Policy: The Primary Prevention Model," *Journal of Drug Issues* 22, no. 4 (Fall 1992), pp. 81–89

114. "2006 National Survey of Drug Use and Health, Detailed Tables," p. 35.

115. Center on Addiction and Substance Abuse, *The Cost of Substance Abuse to America's Health Care System* (New York: Center on Addiction and Substance Abuse, 1993), pp. 33, 42.

116. *National Treatment Improvement Evaluation Study* (Washington, DC: SAMHSA, 1997).

CHAPTER 14

Criminal Justice

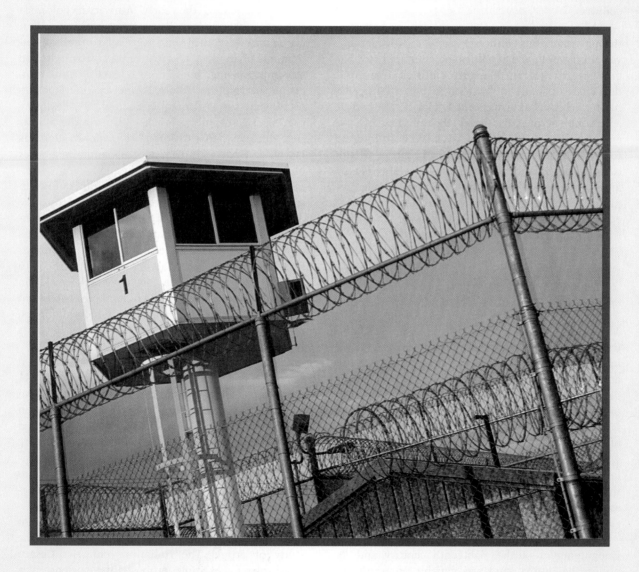

*T*his chapter provides an overview of crime and corrections in the United States, beginning with the history of U.S. criminal justice. Chapter sections explore the roles of various governmental jurisdictions in criminal justice; recent data on crime and justice expenditures; important developments and issues that include juvenile justice, the underclass and crime, the War on Drugs, the "new penology," and the future of criminal justice in this country.

All societies respond to norm-defying behavior through sanctions, although there is considerable variation among the penalties societies apply to specific behaviors. In Western cultures irrational deviance is usually understood as a mental health matter, whereas anormative behavior on the part of a rational actor falls under the purview of law enforcement. In either case, deviance is of interest to human service professionals because clients often engage in anormative activity. Deviance is also an issue of social justice, because poor people and minorities of color are disproportionately represented among those incarcerated in mental or correctional institutions.

History of U.S. Criminal Justice

Modern criminal justice in the United States can be traced to the faith in social science that originated in the West in the eighteenth century. Before the advent of classical criminology, justice was predicated on vengeance: Illegal acts brought the wrath of authority on the deviant. In premodern societies in which deviance was understood to be a product of evil influences, vicious and barbaric methods were justified as ways to exorcise Satan or to maintain archaic social structures. Thus, mutilation, torture, and capital punishment were often employed, sometimes in grotesque public displays, in order to rid society of malevolent influences.

Modern criminology dates from the Enlightenment of the eighteenth century and its notion that humankind was capable of producing the methods for its own perfectibility. The radical jurist and philosopher Jeremy Bentham (1748–1832) contended that scientific methods could be the vehicle for "the rational improvement of the condition of men." Accordingly, Bentham successfully advocated a series of reform laws in Great Britain, including several pertinent to penal institutions.[1] In the United States, Cesare Beccaria applied Bentham's utilitarian philosophy to corrections, arguing that crime could be measured in its severity, that prevention was more important than punishment, that the purpose of punishment was deterrence (not revenge), and that incarceration should segregate prisoners so as not to exacerbate lawlessness.[2] Liberal, humanistic values in criminal justice can thus be traced to the earliest thinkers in criminology.

Nevertheless, the early American colonists imported traditional European thinking about crime and its control. Jails were a fixture of all settlements of any size, and justice was often swift and uncompromising. In 1776, in response to the dungeons that typified colonial America, the Quakers established the Philadelphia Society for Alleviating the Miseries of Public Prisons.[3] During the following decades, institutional reformers such as Dorothea Dix sought to make jails and almshouses more humane. Unfortunately, the reformer's accomplishments were often subverted. An influx of immigrants, many of whom were unable to adjust to the American experience, became incarcerated in mental and correctional institutions. An American ethos of rugged individualism left little room for compassion, particularly when adults were concerned. In 1854, President Franklin Pierce vetoed legislation that would have involved the federal government in institutional care for people with mental illness, effectively leaving institutional control of deviants in the hands of the states.

Midway through the nineteenth century, an unlikely pioneer in U.S. corrections emerged. In 1841 a Boston shoemaker, John Augustus, negotiated an arrangement with the courts to use his own money in order to supervise petty criminals, post bail, and report to the courts on the offenders' rehabilitation. The services provided by Augustus were less expensive than prison, and many of his charges seemed to benefit from rehabilitation. Thus, a modest shoemaker began what was to become a nationwide system of probation.[4] Some early criminologists sought more direct applications of emerging sciences to the study of crime. The Italian psychiatrist Cesare Lombroso, for example, proposed the existence of a "criminal type," a construct of inferior intelligence, exaggerated physical features, and a taste for amoral activities, including tattooing. The idea that a criminal could be physiologically identifiable and criminal behavior genetically transmitted subsequently preoccupied some criminologists. For example, in 1913 Charles Goring studied English convicts, and during the 1920s Earnest Hooton evaluated American criminals; both concluded that prisoners were "organically inferior" to their law-abiding compatriots.

The notion of a genetic origin of deviant behavior was popularized by the eugenics movement before World War I. Proponents of natural selection, some of them esteemed scientists and jurists, convinced state legislators to pass legislation allowing for involuntary sterilization of "mental defectives." By the mid-1950s more than 58,000 mental patients and convicts had been forcibly sterilized.[5] The practice of involuntary sterilization abated during the Civil Rights movement when it became recognized that many of the victims were women and minorities of color. That most victims of the eugenics movement were disadvantaged populations was not coincidental. Race suffused the thinking of eugenicists, as Lombroso illustrated when he wrote in 1871, "Only we white people have reached the most perfect symmetry of bodily form."[6] The suggestion that crime was organically determined generated a firestorm of criticism during the 1960s when it was pointed out that an increasing number of criminals were minorities of color, the same populations that had been victimized by discriminative social policies. Despite this recognition, the contention that criminogenic behavior is hereditary continues to surface in the popular literature. A well-known popularization of genetically transmitted deviance was *The Bell Curve* (1994) by Richard Herrnstein and Charles Murray. The authors contended that, to a significant extent, poverty is hereditary; as a result, many social program expenditures are wasteful. Herrnstein and Murray argued that U.S. society is becoming stratified by intellectual ability, with a "cognitive elite" overseeing a degenerative underclass.[7] Another review of research on genetically transmitted crime revealed that heredity had a slightly positive influence on criminal behavior; however, the researcher suspected that future research would be more productive if it focused on the interaction between environment and genetic attributes.[8]

The Criminal Justice System

The U.S. criminal justice system is similar to education and mental health programs in that states and localities provide a significantly larger portion of services than the federal government. The Constitution, of course, reserves public functions to the states unless they are ceded to the federal government; in the case of criminal justice, this means that state and local government expenditures exceed those of the federal government by a factor of four.[9] During the 1980s expenditures for criminal justice more than doubled, a fact that warrants clarification. Much of the increase was attributable to corrections (as opposed to police protection and judicial and legal costs) which, on a per capita basis, increased from $30.34 in 1980 to $442.10 in 1999, increasing more than tenfold. Moreover, there was considerable variation in state expenditures. In 1999, for example, the per capita cost of criminal justice in the District of Columbia was $1,212.30; that of nearby West Virginia was $228.00.[10]

The last decades of the twentieth century witnessed a boom in prison construction, a development that drew the wrath of opponents of incarceration. Prison is an expensive way to manage deviants, costing $22,000 on average per inmate annually.[11] Since states pay most of the costs for incarceration, prisons vie with schools for funding, a competition that is decidedly skewed. "While the state government of Virginia spends upward of $70,000 per year to incarcerate each child in a juvenile prison," noted critics of imprisonment of juvenile offenders, "it contributes only about $3,400 to provide for the education of that child."[12] Such disparities have led liberals to argue for greater funding of education and youth services as a way to prevent incarceration, and some conservatives have come to appreciate the enormous expense of a criminal justice system in which prisons are dominant. Between 1995 and 2003, state correctional budgets increased by 50 percent, primarily because of prison construction and maintenance, leading several states to revise more punitive sentencing practices, such as mandatory minimums, three-strikes provisions, and abolishing parole.[13] Both rates of crime and types of offense have varied over time. During the 1990s all categories of crime decreased significantly as shown in Table 14.1 on page 364; during the early years of the twenty-first century, however, crime rates stabilized. It appeared that the falling crime rates of the 1990s were over. The reasons for the drop in crime during the 1990s were unclear. Demographers noted that younger, more crime-prone people were aging and less likely to be violent as a result; the Clinton administration cited its crime policies; conservatives claimed that increased incarceration rates removed criminals from the streets. In all likelihood, the proliferation of a drug economy in inner cities, the easy availability of firearms, and escalating gang violence contributed

Table 14.1

Crime and Crime Rates, by Type of Offense: 1980 to 2003, thousands

Year	Total	Murder	Rape	Robbery	Assault	Property
1980	1,345	23	83	566	673	12,064
1985	1,328	19	88	498	723	11,108
1990	1,820	23	103	639	1,055	12,655
1995	1,799	22	97	581	1,099	12,064
2000	1,425	16	90	408	912	10,183
2003	1,381	17	93	413	858	10,436

Source: U.S. Census Bureau, *Statistical Abstract of the United States*, 2006 (Washington, DC: U.S. GPO, 2007), p. 194.

to an increasing crime rate during the 1980s; as these were better controlled, the crime rate dropped.

But how accurate are crime figures? Traditionally, crime data have been aggregated by the Federal Bureau of Investigation (FBI) from the reports of state and local law enforcement agencies in the form of the Uniform Crime Report (UCR). Since 1973, however, an annual National Crime Survey (NCS) has been conducted as an alternative to the UCR. By 1990 it was evident that quite different portraits of crime were emerging from the two compilations. With regard to burglary and auto theft, shortly after its inception the NCS reported significantly higher rates than the UCR, but the path of both surveys merged by the late 1980s. With regard to larceny and assault, the NCS and UCR diverged significantly over time, failing to merge.

In the case of rape, the results were even more perplexing. In 1973 the UCR rape rate was 24 per 100,000 population; the NCS rate was more than 50 percent higher at 38. By 1990 the surveys had reversed: The UCR reported more than 105 rapes per 100,000 population, but the NCS had dropped to 24. According to the UCR, rape had increased fourfold in 17 years, but the NCS documented a reduction of 50 percent. The data indicated that law enforcement authorities were escalating their campaign against sexual assault; at the same time, households were reporting a significant decline in rape. In their attempt to sort out the differences in UCR and NCS rape rates, Gary Jensen and Maryaltani Karpos speculated that an escalating UCR documentation led law enforcement to take rape more seriously, the results eventually eclipsing the rape rate reported by the NCS.[14] If this explanation endures, it is rather

dramatic evidence of the possibility of the deterrence of crime when victims, in this case women, press upon law enforcement, primarily men, the import of specific types of crime.

The Jensen and Karpos interpretation of the sharp downturn in rape has policy implications as well. For example, in 1994 the Violence against Women Act (VAWA) was passed, and in the following year $26 million was allocated to the states, the first of $800 million over a five-year period.[15] During the period when the UCR documented reductions in rape, the incidences of child abuse—a different indicator of domestic violence—continued to climb. Thus, while domestic violence against women seemed to be diminishing, violence directed at children escalated. If law enforcement is effective at containing rape, then a case can be made for diverting funding to reduce domestic violence targeted at abused children.[16] The disposition of offenders varies, of course. Those who have not been convicted of violent offenses and who have no previous criminal record are likely to be granted probation. Those who have been convicted of offenses under local or state jurisdiction may be jailed or imprisoned in facilities that have often been determined to violate minimal humane standards of care. Federal convicts, on the other hand, may be incarcerated in prisons that are qualitatively better, some of which have a decidedly pleasant ambiance. Having served time for good behavior, many prisoners earn early release and go on parole, during which time they must report regularly to a supervising officer. These various statuses are depicted in Table 14.2. In less than two decades the numbers of incarcerated offenders more than tripled.

Table 14.2

Adults on Probation, in Jail or Prison, or on Parole

Year	Total	Probation	Jail	Prison	Parole
1980	1,840,400	1,118,097	182,288	319,598	220,438
1985	3,011,500	1,968,712	254,986	487,593	300,203
1990	4,348,000	2,670,234	403,019	743,382	531,407
1995	5,355,100	3,077,861	499,300	1,078,541	679,421
2000	6,448,300	3,839,532	613,534	1,309,661	725,527
2003*	6,900,000	4,073,987	684,432	1,394,319	774,588

*Projected.

Source: U.S. Census Bureau, Statistical Abstract of the United States, 2002 (Washington, DC: U.S. GPO, 2002), p. 214.

Prisons have been a signal concern in criminal justice, both because of the cost of incarceration and because of what imprisonment rates say about the preponderance of serious precipitating offenses. Among the nations of the world, the incarceration rate of the United States is second only to that of Russia. Russia imprisons 687 inmates per 100,000 population; the United States 682. The rates for other nations are strikingly lower: South Africa 321, Canada 115, France 90, and Japan 39.[17] Beyond these figures, the United States passed a benchmark coinciding with the new millennium in 2000, when 2 million people were behind bars.[18] In this population, gender and race emerge prominently: roughly 90 percent of inmates are men,[19] and two-thirds are minorities of color. Virtually half of all inmates are African American;[20] in 2002 about 12 percent of African American men between 20 and 34 were behind bars.[21] In light of the fact that two-thirds of inmates return to prison within a few years of release,[22] recidivism poses an enormous burden on the African American community.

The U.S. criminal justice system was shaken during the 1990s when increasing numbers of inmates were exonerated from crimes for which they had been convicted. In 1992 Barry Scheck and Peter Neufeld started the Innocence Project, reviewing convictions in light of recent developments in DNA technology. By 2007, the Innocence Project marked the release of 212 wrongfully convicted inmates. Of those released, 128 were African Americans, and their average length of incarceration was 12 years, yet fewer than half had been compensated for their wrongful convictions.[23] Because most wrongful convictions were based on

Because the majority of adult offenders were also known to the juvenile justice system, it stands to reason that diverting youngsters from juvenile crime may keep them out of the adult criminal justice system.

questionable confessions and evidence, police departments were in the process of videotaping confessions and taking precautions to retain evidence with DNA.[24]

Juvenile Justice

Juvenile justice is a significant feature of U.S. criminal justice for several reasons. Young deviants are good candidates for becoming adult deviants, in which case they become subject to the adult criminal justice system. Because the majority of adult offenders were also known to the juvenile justice system, it stands to reason that diverting youngsters from juvenile crime may well keep them out of the adult criminal justice system. From a crime prevention standpoint, reaching young people early, when their understanding of themselves in relation to social norms is still being formed, is a more plausible strategy than attempting to intervene with adult offenders, who have a less malleable sense of themselves vis-à-vis social institutions.

The first institution for juvenile delinquency was the New York City House of Refuge established in 1825. Massachusetts followed suit with a facility for boys established in 1847 and one for girls in 1854.[25] These institutions paralleled other institutions designed to care for neglected children, such as Charles Loring Brace's New York Children's Aid Society, established in 1853. Such institutions were not known for indulging children; furnishings were spartan, the discipline harsh, and escapes common. The orphanage asylum for children became the subject of scathing parody under the pen of Charles Dickens. During the Progressive Era, reformers contended that youth should be adjudicated separately from adults, and the first juvenile court was established in Chicago in 1899.[26] Institutional care for adolescent deviants remained virtually unchanged until the 1960s, when critics of warehousing children advocated for community alternatives. In 1972 Congress passed the Juvenile Justice and Delinquency Prevention Act, a measure that intended, in part, to remove children who were "status offenders" from the more serious deviants who had actually committed felonies or violent crimes. According to Jerome Miller, a youth service advocate, the act ultimately failed. However, it gave impetus to those who were proponents of noninstitutional care for delinquents.

In 1969 Miller assumed the directorship of the Massachusetts Division of Youth Services (DYS), a position that was to become symbolic of correctional reform in the United States. A social worker, Miller had been an officer in the U.S. Air Force, trained in the Menninger Clinic, and earned a doctorate at Catholic University. His initial plan, to seek incremental reforms in Massachusetts, faded as the structural flaws of state juvenile justice became more apparent. All of the personnel positions were filled through political patronage, and very few human service professionals could be found at DYS. Staff routinely resorted to cruel and inhumane treatment—such as breaking fingers of escapees, smearing feces on incorrigibles, and placing miscreants in solitary confinement—that would have been unconstitutional in an adult institution. As Miller learned during his first months on the job, rather than instituting changes, staff and administration subverted attempts to reform DYS. The institutional conspiracy of DYS was becoming as evident as it was implacable. At the same time, Miller was becoming aware of a compelling research finding: The longer children were institutionalized in DYS facilities, the *more* likely they were to become more serious adult offenders. As Miller saw it, not only were his reforms being disregarded, but also he was managing an institution that made youth worse. This seemed especially counterproductive when it became evident that the vast majority of adolescents in DYS institutions were not violent felons but teens who had a knack for getting into trouble.

Miller responded to the intransigence of DYS staff with the most radical of plausible solutions: If DYS was not amenable to reform and continued to damage adolescents, the most conscionable act would be simply to close it down. Thus, over a period of months, Miller and a hand-picked staff discharged the children to alternative community-based care programs. With the exception of a handful of violence-prone adolescents, all of the youth were removed from DYS by the end of Miller's tenure in the 1970s.

The consequences of such an abrupt transformation were predictable. Legislators objected to closing DYS facilities, particularly when an institution was in a legislator's district and thereby an employer of constituents. Law-and-order activists condemned Miller for turning loose on the Massachusetts public the next generation of felons. Researchers recorded a different experience. Using recidivism as an outcome measure, Lloyd Ohlin and Bob Coates of Harvard's Center for Criminal Justice found that in districts of the state in which strong community-based alternatives had been deployed, recidivism was markedly lower.[27] Eventually the Massachusetts experiment was to become a benchmark in juvenile justice in the United States, a case study used by several prominent professional schools. In writing a postscript on the experience, Miller targeted the indiscriminate labeling of youthful deviants by human service professionals who were oblivious to the fates their judgment brought on young offenders: "Our prisons and reform schools are filled with fabricated aliens made yet more alien by those who should know better, but who insufficiently understand the subjects of their research beyond narrow methodological parameters or highly controlled settings which demean and impoverish human experience."[28]

Incarceration as the intervention of choice for youthful offenders continues to be a source of disagreement within juvenile justice. Research on conventional as well as innovative programs yields mixed outcomes. An analysis of the closing of Maryland youth detention facilities revealed that youth who were not institutionalized had higher recidivism rates—although this held only for crimes against property, not for crimes against persons or involving drugs.[29] Early proponents of another initiative, boot camps, promised that discipline, exercise, and routine would deter adolescents from future offending. At boot camp "inmates would receive physical training, military discipline, and drug abuse treatment, all under the direction of military personnel and with the aim of preparing them for a life that would combine . . . the requirement of regular drug tests and the opportunity for gainful employment."[30] By 1993 boot camps had been established in 25 states, but just as rapidly enthusiasm faded. A study of Georgia facilities commissioned by the Justice Department concluded that boot camps failed to deter young offenders.[31] In 1994 Connecticut closed its National Guard boot camp, citing "rampant gang activity, assaults on weaker inmates, marijuana use, sexual activity, and gambling."[32] An analysis of boot camps in eight states concluded that alumni of boot camps were neither more nor less likely to commit future offenses.[33] Eventually, child fatalities provoked a federal inquiry. In 2007 the Government Accountability Office released a report of 10 children who had died in private juvenile detention facilities. The agency reported "thousands of allegations of abuse, some of which evolved death, at residential treatment programs across the country . . . During 2005 alone, 33 states reported 1,619 staff members involved in incidents of abuse in residential treatment programs."[34] Subsequently, Congressional hearings led to proposals to regulate such facilities, which were rejected by the National Association of Therapeutic Schools

and Programs, the trade association for residential correctional facilities.[35]

Despite the lack of success of boot camps, elected officials redoubled their efforts to contain what was perceived as an explosion in the number of juveniles who were engaged in violent crime. Many resorted to treating juvenile offenders as adults. Since 1992, 45 states have altered adjudication of juveniles in order to facilitate treating them as adults. "As a result, the number of youths under 18 held in adult prisons, and in many cases mixed in with adult criminals, has doubled in the last 10 years or so, from 3,400 in 1985 to 7,400 in 1997. Of the juveniles incarcerated on any given day, 1 in 10 are in adult jails or prisons."[36] Many youth advocates objected to increasing the severity of punishment for adolescents, citing evidence that some violent juvenile crime was abating. In 2007 the Task Force on Community Preventive Services reported that the juveniles incarcerated as adults were "33.7 percent more likely to be re-arrested for a violent or other crime" compared to juveniles residing in nonadult facilities. The Task Force concluded that "transferring juveniles to adult courts does harm to them, which diminishes their life chances, thereby increasing their likelihood of committing crimes in the future."[37] As Table 14.3 on page 368 shows, juvenile arrests have changed dramatically since 1980. Murder, rape, and robbery peaked during the mid-1990s but have since dropped back to levels proximate to those of 1980. On the other hand, arrests for sale and possession of illegal drugs show alarming increases; although arrests for selling drugs began to decline late in the 1990s, arrests for possession continue to climb.

Within a context of high juvenile crime and rampant drug use, in 1992 Boston juvenile authorities imposed an innovation that sparked the interest of criminologists across the country. Under Operation Night Light, an aggressive initiative targeting high-risk youth, Boston juvenile authorities precipitated a reduction in youth homicides, which numbered 70 from 1992 through 1995, to zero from 1996 through 1998. As one journalist described the effort, "Juvenile law enforcement in Boston has become a community-sized octopus that embraces teenagers who are temporarily troubled and ensnares (without necessarily jailing) those who are chronically violent."[38] Subsequently, several cities attempted to replicate the Boston model. A few years later, proponents of the Boston approach were less sanguine. By October 2004, 53 homicides had been committed in Boston, making it one of 10 cities experiencing escalating rates of youth violence.[39]

Table 14.3

Juvenile Arrests for Selected Offenses

Offense	1980	1990	1995	2000	2003
Violent crime	77,220	97,103	123,131	78,450	69,060
Murder	1,475	2,661	2,812	1,027	960
Rape	3,668	4,971	4,556	3,402	3,195
Robbery	38,529	34,944	47,240	24,206	18,960
Assault	33,548	54,527	68,523	49,815	45,955
Weapon violations	21,203	33,123	46,506	28,514	29,512
Drug abuse	86,685	66,300	149,236	146,594	134,746
Sale	13,004	24,575	34,077	26,432	21,987
Possession	73,681	41,725	115,159	120,432	112,759

Source: U.S. Census Bureau, *Statistical Abstract of the United States,* 2006 (Washington, DC: U.S. GPO, 2007), p. 205.

The War on Drugs

By the 1980s, events had propelled the control of drug abuse to a top priority in U.S. criminal justice. The deterioration of inner cities had been accompanied by an alarming degree of social dysfunction. Illegal drugs were not only prevalent in the poorest minority neighborhoods but had also become an essential, if not the predominant, part of the local economy. As gangs vied over turf and ever more profitable drug peddling, violence exploded. Drive-by shootings became commonplace in larger cities. Gang-bangers invaded previously neutral territory—hospitals, mortuaries, cemeteries—in pursuit of enemies. Innocent people became victims of a rash of holdups, carjackings, and seemingly random shootings. In response, President Reagan declared a war on drugs. Despite unrelenting efforts to contain drug abuse, during the 1990s the Department of Justice witnessed skyrocketing increases in drug seizures. Between 1990 and 2000, the number of drug seizures increased fourfold from 745,002 to 2.98 million.[40]

Two strategies dominated the War on Drugs: government interdiction of supplies, aimed at eliminating the substance, or treatment programs deployed to diminish the demand for illegal drugs. Appropriations for drug control increased substantially during the 1980s, but much of the funding was allocated for interdiction and comparatively less for treatment. For example, federal funds for law

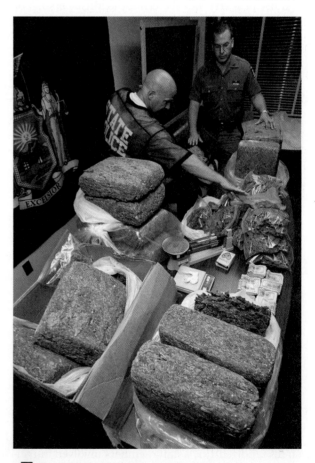

■ *Two strategies dominate the War on Drugs: government interdiction of supplies and treatment programs to diminish the demand for illegal drugs.*

enforcement increased from $800 million in 1981 to $1.9 billion in 1986; yet funding for prevention, education, and treatment decreased from $404 million in 1981 to $338 million in 1985, a 40 percent drop when adjusted for inflation.[41] Despite massive infusions of funds for the Drug Enforcement Administration (DEA) and the Coast Guard, by the late 1980s most analysts agreed that supply interdiction had failed. Experts contended that emphasizing law enforcement would not solve the nation's drug problem. "It would be naive to assume that this well-meant legislative effort will be an end to our drug dilemma," concluded the late Sidney Cohen, former director of the Division of Narcotic Addiction and Drug Abuse of the National Institute of Mental Health:

> We have not yet come to understand the resolute, determined, amoral nature of the major traffickers or their enormous power. Perhaps we do not even recognize that, for tens of hundreds of thousands of field workers, collecting coca leaves or opium gum is a matter of survival. At the other end of the pipeline is the swarm of sellers who could not possibly earn a fraction of their current income from legitimate pursuits. If they are arrested, they are out after a short detention. If not, many are waiting to take their place.[42]

If efforts to reduce the propagation of coca in South and Central America proved futile, attempts to reduce street trafficking were similarly unsuccessful. A kilogram of cocaine wholesaled in Miami for $60,000 in 1981; at the height of the crack epidemic of the late 1980s, the cost had plummeted to $10,000.[43] The price of cocaine was so low that crack houses were able to offer cocaine free to new customers, charging regulars as little as $2.[44]

To compound the problem, attempts at street-level interdiction led to arrests of users and petty distributors, swelling already overcrowded prisons. The arrest rate per 100,000 inhabitants increased from 435.3 in 1990 to 587.1 in 2000, an increase of 35 percent. In 2000, drug abuse violations accounted for one of eight arrests, more than any other offense. In every metropolitan area, a majority of arrestees tested positive for illegal drugs.[45] Thus, the focus on interdiction and enforcement proved perverse. To contain drug use through law enforcement, the country was imprisoning thousands of peddlers and addicts at enormous cost, yet funding for prevention and treatment lagged far behind allocations for incarceration. Most ironic, drug treatment for incarcerated addicts was virtually nonexistent.

The mismatch between the needs of drug addicts and the eligibility requirements of social programs was captured by journalist Barry Bearak, who followed a group of junkies in New York City. Scavenging what funds he had left, one junkie decided to get admitted to a detox program. After a full day's bouncing from one welfare agency to another seeking eligibility for "special" Medicaid, which would pay for the detox services, Georgie, a middle-aged Hispanic man, found himself in a line for public assistance only a few minutes before closing time. While Georgie waited, a friend who had come with him also to get into detox was shooting up in the restroom:

> The line moved slowly. Georgie's turn finally came a few minutes before 5 p.m. It was a short discussion. He had been in the wrong spot. He needed to be at the Application Desk, back over by Table Five where he had started.

spotlight 14.1

The Office of National Drug Control Policy

Established in 1988, the Office of National Drug Control Policy (ONDCP) sets policies, priorities, and objectives for the nation's drug control program. The goals of the program are to reduce illicit drug use, manufacturing, trafficking, drug-related crime and violence, and drug-related health consequences.

To learn more about this federal agency, go to its website at **www.ondcp.gov.**

He hurried across the big room. "Can I ask you a question?" he said to a clerk. "I'm sorry," she answered, her fingers busy in a file drawer. "I need to get this out of the way."

Georgie spoke up with more urgency: "I want to get into detox."

The woman turned to face him now. "You came too late," she said, shaking her head. "We're not giving out any more appointments."

"We've been getting the runaround all day."

She eyed him more carefully, looking over his sweaty face. She spoke slowly and distinctly for the junkie's benefit. "When you come back in, all they'll give you is an appointment," she said. "You won't get emergency Medicaid. Then, with an appointment, you have to come back in a week or so and see an interviewer. Then, after they have reviewed the case, the client is contacted by mail, and that takes three weeks or a month."

Georgie took this in and was stunned. "So the mumbo jumbo about getting on Medicaid the same day is bull—?" he said without anger, but with resignation.

"That's right. The only way to get on is with HIV [the AIDS virus]."

At last, good news. His face brightened. "Well, I'm HIV," he said.

The clerk took a step back from him. "You'd have to be able to prove it with a certified letter from your doctor," she said.

With that, Georgie was beaten. His shoulders sagged. And the clerk knew she could shift her attention back to the end-of-the-day filing.[46]

How Georgie came to drug addiction is speculative, of course; yet many social observers cite social and economic conditions in the poorest inner-city neighborhoods that conspire to make self-administered anesthesia desirable for many adolescents. By the early 1990s, for the first time, the number of young African American adults who were neither in school nor employed exceeded 50 percent in every section of the United States.[47] During the 1980s the combination of reductions in governmental assistance to cities through social programs and the prevalence of drug trafficking had a pronounced effect on inner-city neighborhoods. Gradually, once squalid but quiet urban neighborhoods began to echo with gunfire as rival gangs fought over turf; areas in many industrial cities virtually imploded.[48] Gang killings in Los Angeles soared 69 percent during the first eight months of 1990.[49] In 1992 Los Angeles reported more than 800 drug-related homicides.[50] Gang-related murders in the nation's capital, which reached a three-year high

in 1990, led a police department spokesperson to quip, "At the rate we're going the next generation is going to be extinct."[51]

Observers of urban poverty described a serious deterioration in inner-city communities of the 1980s as contrasted with those of the 1960s. When Claude Brown returned to Harlem 20 years after the publication of his *Manchild in the Promised Land,* he was shocked by the casual viciousness of gang members toward their victims.[52] "In many if not most of our major cities, we are facing something very like social regression," wrote the late-Senator Daniel Patrick Moynihan. "It is defined by extraordinary levels of self-destructive behavior, interpersonal violence, and social class separation intensive in some groups, extensive in others."[53] In the socioeconomic vacuum that had developed in the poorest urban neighborhoods, the sale and consumption of drugs became central to community life. The toll this conversion has taken on young African Americans was astonishing. As of 1988, 43 percent of those convicted of drug trafficking were African American. In New York, Hispanics and African Americans accounted for 92 percent of arrests for drug offenses in 1989. In 1990, the Sentencing Project, a criminal justice reform organization, reported that one-fourth of all African Americans between the ages of 20 and 29 were incarcerated, on parole, or on probation. Yet the Sentencing Project data scraped only the top of what was a very large statistical iceberg.

In *Search and Destroy: African-American Males in the Criminal Justice System,* Jerome Miller identified the frequency with which young African American males were likely to run afoul of the law, reporting that:

> on an average day in 1991, more than four in ten (42%) of all the 18-35-year-old African-American males who lived in the District of Columbia were in jail, in prison, on probation/parole, or being sought on arrest warrants; on an average day in Baltimore, 56% of all its young African-American males were in prison, jail, on probation/parole, on bail, or being sought on arrest [emphasis in original].[54]

According to Miller, incarceration was damaging enough, but arresting all these young men inflicted substantial harm simply because most employment applications inquire about an arrest record, and research demonstrates that employers avoid candidates who had been arrested.

For Miller the War on Drugs was just another **moral panic,** the sort of melodrama that an insecure middle class creates in order to retain its social standing. A moral panic is manifested by the emergence of policies and professionals that seek to reestablish social control over a phantom threat. In the case of the War on Drugs, conservative politicians and law enforcement officers convinced the public that the nation suffers from a new generation of violent minority youth that must be held in check. The evidence presented for the law-and-order agenda consisted largely of the arrest rates for violent and repeat offenders; yet Miller contended that most "violent" offenses represented the overcharging of miscreants by overzealous police, and most "repeat" offenders were rearrested for drug-related offenses. Not coincidentally, Miller contended, African Americans were the target of the War on Drugs. Many of the arrests were drug related,

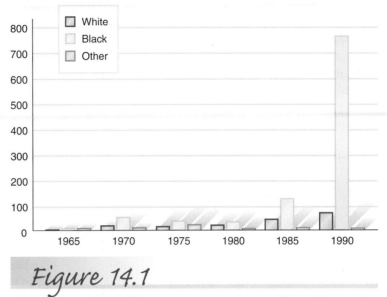

Figure 14.1

Tracking Racial Bias

Source: Adapted from Jerome Miller, Search and Destroy (New York: Cambridge University Press, 1996).

a category that was increasing dramatically among African American youth. Per 100,000 population, drug arrests for African American youth increased from 683 in 1985, to 1,200 in 1989, to 1,415 in 1991.[55] The racial disparity in juvenile drug arrests is shown in Figure 14.1. The social consequence of the arrest and incarceration of so many African American youths, Miller alleged, was the cultivation of an oppositional culture, replete with violence, in which engaging the criminal justice system was "something of a puberty rite, a transition to manhood."[56] Drawing an Orwellian conclusion, Miller predicted that jails would soon morph into "simple internment camps" for minority youth who were refugees from an alienating culture.

Other observers also documented the grim circumstances of poor minority families in urban centers. A common denominator of these portrayals was drug-related violence that seemed to metastasize throughout inner-city communities, extracting a horrifying toll on minority populations. The effect on African American family life was depicted poignantly by Alex Kotlowitz, who followed the daily activities of two youngsters, Lafayette and Pharaoh Rivers. The boys ventured out of their mother's apartment in one of Chicago's housing projects at the risk of being shot by drug dealers.[57] In New York City, a popular elementary school principal, Patrick Daly, was shot to death while walking

through a drug-infested neighborhood searching for a nine-year-old who had left school in tears after a fight.[58] During the summer of 1992, drug-related street violence in Baltimore reached the point where the state chapter of the National Association for the Advancement of Colored People formally requested that the governor of Maryland declare a state of civil emergency and call out the National Guard to restore order in the city.

By 2000, drug abuse had stabilized, yet the war on drugs continued amid escalating controversy. Since 1985 the United States had invested several hundred billion dollars in attempting to control the drug trade, but the results were hotly disputed.[59] Most of the arrests for drug abuse occurred at the local level, and the number of offenders quickly clogged the courts.[60] In the absence of corrective legislation, the U.S. Sentencing Commission voted unanimously to alter sentences for cocaine possession. Racial disparities in sentences for cocaine possession had become controversial since 85 percent of inmates imprisoned for crack cocaine were African American versus 27 percent for powder cocaine. As a result, 19,500 inmates were expected to be able to petition for reduced sentences.[61] Regardless, high demand for drugs fueled international drug cartels, with those in nearby Mexico and Colombia provoking diplomatic tensions around extradition and interdiction.[62] More fundamental issues emerged as traditional conservatives expressed concern about the involvement of the military in nondefense activities,[63] and libertarians and the Left proposed legalization of drugs as a more realistic alternative.[64] Thus, although the War on Drugs seemed to do little to reduce substance abuse, it not only increased the incarceration of minority youth, but it also generated diplomatic problems.

The Underclass and "Moral Poverty"

The contention that "crime" was largely a bourgeois contrivance to maintain control over hostile minority youth, as argued by liberals like Jerome Miller, was challenged by conservative crime theorists in the 1990s. Conservatives argued that the chronic poor suffered from problems qualitatively different from those of the temporarily poor. The latter lacked basic resources, and the provision of cash benefits was a prudent response to their circumstances. The chronic poor, however, evidenced a "behavioral" poverty that differentiated them from the transient poor. The behaviorally poor engaged in habits—teen pregnancy, drug abuse, petty theft, unmarried parenthood, and welfare dependency—that not only ensured continual destitution, but also subverted the intent of well-intended social programs.[65] Behavioral poverty sustained oppositional culture, and, in doing so, fostered the underclass.

Accordingly, William Bennett, John DiIulio Jr., and John Walters argued that the upsurge in crime could be attributed to "moral poverty":

> The poverty of being without loving, capable, responsible adults who teach right from wrong; the poverty of being without parents and other authorities who habituate you to feel joy at others' joy, pain at others' pain, satisfaction when you do right, remorse when you do wrong; the poverty of growing up in the virtual absence of people who teach morality by their own everyday example and who insist that you follow suit. In the extreme, moral poverty is the poverty of growing up severely abused and neglected at the hands of deviant, delinquent, or criminal adults.[66]

To substantiate their argument, Bennett, DiIulio, and Walters cited data on the behavior of state prisoners in 1991. For that year, 45 percent of prisoners were on probation or parole when they committed their latest offense. During community

supervision in the previous 17 months, the 162,000 probation violators committed some 6,400 murders, 7,400 rapes, 10,400 assaults, and 17,000 robberies. During community supervision of the previous 13 months, the 156,000 parole violators committed some 6,800 murders, 5,500 rapes, 8,800 assaults, and 22,500 robberies. "Together, probation and parole violators committed 90,639 violent crimes while 'under supervision' in the community."[67] These data revealed the evolution of a new breed of criminal, conservatives argued:

> At the core of the crime wave is a new category of "super-predators"—radically impulsive, brutally remorseless youngsters, including ever more pre-teenage boys, who murder, assault rape, rob, burglarize, deal deadly drugs, join gun-toting gangs, and create serious communal disorders. They do not fear the stigma of arrest, the pains of imprisonment, or the pangs of conscience. They perceive hardly any relationship between doing right (or wrong) now and being rewarded (or punished) for it later.[68]

Bennett, DiIulio, and Walters averred that much of the increase in crime could be attributed to a proliferation of drugs that had become so extensive as to represent de facto normalization of drug abuse. The severe damage associated with heroin and cocaine justified increasing drug interdiction efforts and getting tough with street criminals who peddle drugs. Regarding treatment, Bennett, DiIulio, and Walters noted that funding increases for treatment had not been accompanied by a significant decrease in the number of addicts seeking rehabilitation. Although existing treatment capacity was serving only half the nation's addicts, conservatives proposed few changes other than eliminating bureaucratic waste in order to extend treatment resources. Beyond that, little could be done, given the poor track record of treatment programs in getting addicts into recovery. For many addicts, treatment was a cyclical experience, not an end to their substance abuse, the authors concluded. They cited the California Civil Addict Program, which reported that more addicts eventually died after receiving treatment (27.7 percent) than became drug free (25 percent).[69]

The conservative prescription for moral poverty was as extensive as it was sometimes implausible. Bennett, DiIulio, and Walters advocated reinforcing work as opposed to unconditional welfare, removing young children from dysfunctional homes, and encouraging adoption as an alternative to foster care. Although public policy might prove instrumental in reducing "criminogenic" influences, it was less apropos, if not irrelevant, as a vehicle for other suggestions, such as limiting children's TV time or reasserting the importance of religious values in daily life.[70] Subsequently, DiIulio moderated his position about juvenile delinquents, recognizing the environmental deficits that contributed to their misconduct. In researching programs that served delinquents, DiIulio found that religious groups were often the most effective in treating delinquents,[71] and became an advocate of "charitable choice," the contracting out of social services through community-based religious organizations. By conceding that the compassion of religious intercession was more effective than punishment through incarceration, DiIulio reversed his earlier position with respect to juvenile delinquency.[72]

To the extent that social and economic factors—particularly the skewing of opportunities of minority youth who become adult offenders—are associated with crime, an argument can be made for environmental influences in criminal conduct, an argument congruent with a liberal orientation to criminal justice. This is the logic that John Hagan adopted in developing the concept of the "social embeddedness" of crime. In reviewing research on juvenile delinquency and adult offenders, Hagan noted the interaction of family and environment in the transmission of criminal behavior. Poor neighborhoods generated delinquents, often from families in which a parent had been an offender. Such intergenerational transmission of crime might be attributed to heredity; but, as noted earlier in this chapter, the relationship is too weak to be anywhere near conclusive. Consequently, Hagan took a more direct, and more useful, route in explaining how poor communities harbored crime-prone families that produced delinquents, many of whom became adult criminals. In poor communities, Hagan contends, two developmental paths evolve for children. Kids from working families with effective adult supervision are socialized in school and through early employment into a world in which there is the likelihood of success. By contrast, children from families in which an adult is an offender are more likely to encounter the juvenile justice system; and not only does that system label them as delinquent, but the punishment of juvenile offenders—incarceration or its surrogates—also interferes with kids' completing school or building a sound foundation for future employment. Essentially, young people from families with adult offenders are doubly burdened. As Hagan writes:

Involvements of parents in crime likely provide youths with more promising connections to illegal than legal labor markets. As well, contacts with criminal friends are more likely to integrate youths into the criminal underworld than into referral networks for legal employment. And youthful delinquent acts are likely to distance actors further from the job contacts that initiate and sustain legitimate occupational careers.[73]

So oriented, it is understandable how delinquency-prone youth could find gang involvement a natural progression in socialization. Drug-related gang activities, frequently targeted by law enforcement, bring arrests and sentences that label youngsters and disrupt education and employment. Before the end of high school, a delinquent has accumulated sufficient negative attributes to subvert any interest in conventional rewards. In place of education and employment, gang activity alternates with incarceration, producing a vicious circle. Measures of the intractability of the delinquent's circumstance can be found in the "oppositional culture" that flourishes among poor minority youth. The popularization of vulgar "gangsta" rap, a pattern of claiming the loyalty of young women by impregnating them, and "dissing" enemies (including authority figures)—even at the risk of bodily harm—are all part of the capitulation that young minority males make in the face of overwhelming odds militating against traditional means of success. Oppositional culture reproduces itself in children born to young minority women whose aspirations have been sabotaged. Such children experience little that is nurturing or dependable, least of all fathers—given that their fathers, knowing the tentativeness of life on the streets, expect to be dead or incarcerated well before their offspring reach adolescence. The scenario is as tragic as it is "embedded" in the social reality of its perpetrators and victims.

The evolution of liberal policies that divert youth from delinquency and subsequently prevent adult lawlessness has been advocated eloquently by William Julius Wilson. Mainstreaming the underclass, Wilson argues, requires enhanced educational opportunity; the realization of educational standards in inner-city schools; an increase in earned income tax credits for poor working families; and, in the end, a WPA-type public employment program. Eventually, improved educational and employment opportunities will overcome current inducements to engage in lawlessness.

As more people become employed, crime, including violent crime, and drug use will subside; families will be strengthened and welfare receipt will decline significantly; ghetto-related culture and behavior, no longer sustained and nourished by persistent joblessness, will gradually fade.[74]

Thus, Wilson reiterated a major finding from the research on opportunity and crime: Lawlessness declines as rates of employment and marriage rise.

Other African Americans were less sanguine about the role of public programs in reversing the damage attributed to oppositional minority youth. Coming to the defense of comedian Bill Cosby who initially criticized African American youth who defied mainstream conventions, Juan Williams veered away from traditional social programs, criticizing African American leaders in the process:

> The nation's leaving civil rights groups . . . are locked into arguing that "the system" is causing the continued high level of poverty in black America. Their goal seems to be to get government money for programs, grants, and scholarships for the black community. That money has done some good. But at this point a blind pursuit of government money to help the poor is a tired, failed strategy. It encourages patterns of dependency among black people.

Rather than expand discredited social programs, Williams called for new initiatives through which "the poor can be empowered to help themselves."[75]

Legalization of Drugs

During the 1980s, seemingly endless retreats in the War on Drugs led some analysts to propose legalizing controlled substances.[76] Drug legalization had been a standard demand among Libertarians, who argued that individuals should be free to engage in any activity so long as it does not harm others. Then, during the Reagan presidency, a small number of leaders representing law, economics, and politics complemented the Libertarian position with their own arguments. Noting the massive sums pumped into law enforcement and the meager results demonstrated by interdiction and treatment, proponents of legalization argued that U.S. policy on substance abuse was at best naive and at worst counterproductive. They contended that the current policy was little more than a replication of Prohibition's futile effort to ban alcohol from American culture. A more mature and pragmatic policy would be to admit that certain sub-

stances were part of contemporary lifestyles and simply to regulate them, they contended, much as tobacco and alcohol are regulated. According to its proponents, legalization would have several benefits. Legalizing drugs would enable substantial sums to be freed from law enforcement and put toward abuse prevention and treatment programs. Legalization would decriminalize drug use, thereby cutting the prison population significantly and, by destigmatizing users, making it more likely that users would enter treatment. Additional revenues could be raised by government because illegal substances would be available legitimately and taxed accordingly. Advocates of legalization questioned the claims of the defenders of the status quo who argued that prevention, treatment, and interdiction were effective strategies that would show positive results in the long run. Legalization of drugs, claimed its adherents, could produce substantial results immediately.

Momentum toward legalizing drugs reached its peak during the mid-1980s and then flagged. Public policy scholars raised questions for which there were no ready answers. Should all drugs be legalized? Or should legalization be limited to soft drugs, such as marijuana and minor tranquilizers, while restrictions on hard drugs were maintained? Should availability be unlimited, or should age restrictions apply, as they do now with tobacco and alcohol? If there were taxes on drugs and restrictions on their purchase, would not the government still have to fund law enforcement, regulate product safety, and maintain a taxing authority in order to contain an illicit market? If the government were to attempt to counter a black market by supplying drugs directly, it would be in the contradictory position of supplying drugs while also offering treatment for users of those same drugs.[77] Further confounding the issue of drug legalization was the firestorm of controversy over crack cocaine and, later, crystal meth. Proponents of legalization visualized drugs as substances analogous to tobacco and alcohol. People dependent on marijuana, heroin, and many psychedelics could use their drugs discreetly, they contended, without disrupting society. The proliferation of crack cocaine and crystal meth, however, presented a completely different picture. Not only were crack and meth implicated in violent incidents, but the craving for them was more intense than that for many other drugs. Methamphetamine in rural states was implicated in a significant increase in the number of children placed in foster care.[78] The prospect of legalizing a substance over which users seemed to have so little control and which, moreover, was connected to homicides, addicted infants, and family destruction seemed inconsistent with the vision implied by drug legalization.

By the 1990s, the legalization of drugs had drifted to the margin of the substance abuse debate, although it was still advocated by a small coterie of prominent people, such as New Mexico's then-Governor Gary Johnson and financier George Soros. Despite obvious contradictions represented by the status of tobacco and alcohol, few suggested that other substances should be legalized. In fact, pressure increased to contain the use of tobacco and alcohol. Municipalities expanded the areas they designated as smoke-free and stricter standards and fines were established for driving under the influence of alcohol. Increasingly, authorities came to believe that soft drugs served a "gateway" function, introducing young users to more addictive substances. Rather than loosening the regulation of such substances, continued restrictions were called for.[79] Finally, the most limited form of legalization—allowing physicians to prescribe certain substances for addicts—faltered when the country that had pioneered this strategy, Great Britain, halted the practice.[80] If a consensus had begun to emerge about not legalizing controlled substances, there was far less unanimity about how to reclaim neighborhoods in which drugs had become central to social and economic life. Aggressive action by law enforcement officers appeared to have reached an apex and then degenerated in the face of a lawless netherworld, as when DEA agents raided the wrong house and critically wounded a San Diego man in a drug bust gone wrong. The strategy of handing down severe sentences for even first-time offenders began to lose its luster when the cost of incarceration proved to exceed by far the value of taking small-time drug traffickers off the street. The seizure of property belonging to persons who had been implicated in drug transactions became a small scandal when newspapers reported that innocent people had lost belongings to overzealous law enforcement officers.[81] The promise of paramilitary boot camps for first-time offenders who had been convicted of drug-related crimes, although it looked like an appealing solution to a public frustrated by increasing numbers of crime-prone youth, failed to demonstrate any long-term changes in behavior.[82]

By the end of the twentieth century, many inner-city neighborhoods were more lethal for minority Americans than they had been at any time in the nation's history. Children learned that they could make hundreds of dollars a day carrying crack between dealers, easily eclipsing the income of conventionally employed adults in the community. This made a joke of the work ethic; no one with any self-respect would consider a dead-end job paying the minimum wage. Young men who had little hope of finding a good job traded their future for quick wealth and community notoriety in the drug trade. Drug-related violence made a mockery of already fragile community institutions. Gang members were shot to death in funeral homes, schools, even hospitals. Most tragically, infants born of crack-addicted mothers writhed and screamed at birth as they experienced withdrawal, only to be diagnosed later with HIV. Unwanted, many suffered in group homes and died at an early age.

While academics debated the finer points of drug legalization, the quality of life for the urban poor grew increasingly desperate. What had once been a grim struggle to reconcile meager income with daily living requirements had become a frantic scramble for safety. At best, the drug scourge forced inner-city residents to sharply curtail their expectations. At worst, it terminated expectations altogether. Eventually, the degradation of life attributed to the proliferation of drugs entered the popular media, clashing with cherished images of America. For too many of the urban poor, the American dream had not just faded from memory; it had been replaced by an antithetical image—the American nightmare.

The "New Penology"

While academics debated the merits of drug legalization, the public was growing increasingly intolerant of crime. Since the mid-1980s the nation witnessed a significant increase in prison construction, the passage of new laws requiring incarceration of repeat offenders, and the reinstitution of capital punishment in some states. Approaching the end of the twentieth century, the United States boasted an incarcerated population that exceeded 2 million. In 1970 the number of inmates in state and federal correctional facilities was 96.7 per 100,000 population; by 1993 the number had more than tripled, at 352.9[83]; by 1997 it had more than quadrupled, to 445.[84] In 1994 the Violent Crime Control and Law Enforcement Act introduced the "three strikes" penalties for repeat offenders and increased the number of federal crimes to which the death penalty applies.[85] The number of prisoners under the death sentence soared. In 1980, 688 inmates were on death row; by 2000 the number had increased fivefold to 3,593.[86] Of these, 43.7 percent were non-white;[87] the number of people of color with death sentences thus was more than double their proportion of the general population.

The rapid expansion in correctional facilities led criminologists Malcolm Feeley and Jonathan Simon to identify the advent of a "new penology." In contrast to the old penology that focused on individual rehabilitation (via probation or parole) or deterrence (via incarceration), the new penology eschewed these for the efficient management of large populations of high-risk offenders. The mission of criminal justice, contended Feeley and Simon, was "managerial, not transformative;"[88] the social function of criminal justice was "rabble management,"[89] or controlling "unruly groups."[90] As a managerial phenomenon, the new penology required a method for classification and incarceration, and the federal sentencing guidelines incorporated in the 1984 Comprehensive Crime Control Act (implemented on November 1, 1987) served just that purpose. The U.S. Sentencing Commission established an elaborate system of 258 categories for determining the punishment for an offense according to its severity and the offender's previous convictions.[91] The use of sentencing guidelines was consistent with the new penology, because the purpose of criminal justice was not to arbitrate punishment in relation to lawlessness, but to incapacitate large numbers of high-risk offenders selectively. Accordingly, prisons became warehouses for the offenders who were judged to represent the highest risk to society. Because a high-risk designation is positively associated with race and indigence, the new penology functioned to regulate the most troublesome—and allegedly dangerous—elements of the underclass, and drug involvement served to identify those among the underclass who presented the highest risk. Thus, within the contemporary urban milieu, the new penology became an instrument of racial and class oppression.

It could be argued that in the United States, prisons have historically served as institutions of last resort for incorrigible populations that have proved difficult to socialize. In that respect, the large numbers of African Americans who dominate the prisons today are little different from the Irish or Italian immigrant inmates who disproportionately populated correctional facilities decades ago. If there is a qualitatively different aspect to contemporary corrections, however, it lies in the merging of systems management with the rapid expansion of the correctional corporations. The fundamental difference between the old, government-maintained penology and the new, corporate-managed penology is that the latter has a financial stake in an expanding correctional market, whereas the incentives under the old penology were such that the state attempted to limit criminal justice expenditures. When George W. Bush announced tightened restrictions on illegal immigration, stock on the Correctional Corporation of America (CCA) rose 27 percent while that of competitor Geo Group (formerly Wackenhut) climbed 68 percent. Operating 8 of 16 detention facilities for immigrants, a spokesperson from CCA was confident that the company could grow to meet expanded need for incarceration: "We believe as [federal government's] demand increases, they will need to rely on providers who have bed space available," she said. "The company feels it is well positioned."[92]

Thus, an analysis of corrections produced by Steven Donziger for the National Criminal Justice Commission targeted the emerging "prison-industrial complex." According to Donziger, the prison-industrial complex consisted of an "iron triangle" of "government bureaucrats, private industry leaders, and politicians who work together to expand the criminal justice system."[93] In the United States in 1996 there were 21 companies with annual revenues exceeding $250 million, managing some 88 prisons in which 50,000 inmates were incarcerated—a 20-fold increase in the number of inmates managed by for-profit correctional firms since 1984.[94] The passage of the "three strikes" legislation targeting repeat offenders, the war on drugs, and the consequences of the sentencing guidelines provided the prison-industrial complex with a more-than-adequate supply of inmates. Because most inmates were nonviolent offenders, incarceration in the minimum- and medium-security facilities that were favored by for-profit firms proved ideal. Contrasted to the archaic prisons typical of the old penology, the facilities managed by for-profit firms were not only more adequate with regard to basic amenities, but they were also more likely to provide educational and other services as methods to maintain a compliant population.

The prison-industrial complex is not without its detractors, however. Prison guard unions have emerged as staunch critics of for-profit corrections, because a primary means by which for-profit firms reduce their costs is by hiring staff who are less expensive than state correctional officers who benefit from state civil service regulations and higher pay. Regardless, corrections has become big business, involving 2.2 million people in apprehending and incarcerating miscreants. "Major companies, such as Wackenhut Corrections Corporation [now the Geo Group] and Corrections Corporation of America employ sophisticated lobbyists to protect and expand their market share," observed Alan Elsner. "The law enforcement technology industry, which produces high-tech items such as the latest stab-proof vests, helmets, stun guns, shields, batons and chemical agents, does more than a billion dollars a year in business."[95] Although prisoners tend to benefit from correctional facilities managed by for-profit firms, especially when the alternative has been state-run facilities that are so retrograde that they have been found by the courts to violate the constitutional rights of inmates, the new penology brings with it a classic conflict between labor (prison guards) and management (CEOs).

The Future of Criminal Justice

With the expansion of correctional facilities in response to escalating crime, calls for reform of the criminal justice system have become increasingly shrill. Among the most prominent reforms are community policing, victim assistance, harsher sentences, and death sentence reviews. Competing views of criminal justice have driven these policy changes.

Community Policing Conceived in Houston, community policing reassigned law enforcement officers from patrol cars and specialty units, which had isolated them from the public, to beats on the streets of high-crime areas. As mayors[96] and the public noted the benefits of community policing,[97] the reform spread, eventually becoming a prominent feature of federal crime policy. President Clinton promised federal funding to deploy 100,000 more police officers to combat crime, and in 1995 the attorney general boasted that the Clinton administration had placed more than 25,000 police officers in the Community Oriented Policing Services (COPS) program.[98] In 2002 the Department of Justice awarded $720 million in grants through its COPS Office. Since its creation in 1994, COPS has awarded $12 billion in grants to communities for an array of crime prevention activities.

Victim Assistance Created through the 1984 Victims of Crime Act, the Justice Department's Office for Victims of Crime receives funds derived from settlements of federal civil cases, forfeited bail bonds, and special assessments, and makes grants for two purposes: victim compensation and victim assistance. Each year up to $20 million is reserved for child abuse and $50 million for victims of domestic terrorism; the remainder of funding—47.5 percent is set aside for state compensation programs and

47.5 percent for state assistance programs. Since its inception, funds available through the Office of Victims of Crime have increased from $68.3 million in 1985 to $520 million in 2004. A Congressional cap on fund allocations effectively limits benefits to victims, however. For 2004, for example, $1.3 billion were available, yet half that amount could be used as benefits for victims of crime.[99]

Sex Offender Registries As a result of crimes committed by sexual offenders, jurisdictions have stiffened sentencing. In response to the murders of Megan Kanka and Polly Klaas, the Violent Crime Control and Law Enforcement Act of 1994 included mandatory registration of sexual offenders with local law enforcement, information that is available to the public.[100] Subsequently, many states and localities have placed restrictions on residency of sexual offenders, often prohibiting them from living near schools, parks, and other public places where children congregate. Increasing restrictions on people convicted of sexual offenses have generated constitutional questions about possible violations of their civil rights.[101]

Death Sentence Review During the 1990s, an increasing number of death penalty convictions were reversed, some within days, if not hours, of scheduled executions. To dramatize the prospect of executing an innocent person, the Northwestern University Law School convened a conference on the issue in November 1998, featuring more than 30 former death-row inmates.[102] In a related development, the introduction of DNA evidence resulted in the release of 70 inmates, including eight from death row, who had been wrongfully convicted.[103] In 1999 the governor of Illinois announced a moratorium on executions, because so many of the state's death-row inmates had been found innocent.[104] Ultimately, an exhaustive study of capital punishment revealed that two-thirds of death sentences had been reversed on appeal, suggesting that the sentencing process was rife with irregularity.[105] Of the 3,600 inmates on death row, approximately 10 percent were mentally retarded, a status recognized by only 13 of the 38 states permitting capital punishment; since 1976, 34 mentally retarded inmates had been executed. As details about mentally impaired inmates became known, momentum grew to restrain capital punishment. For example, in 1995, Mario Marquez, who had an IQ of 60 and the aptitude of a seven-year-old, was executed in Texas for the murder of his niece. Hours before his execution he said, "I want to be God's gardener and take care of the animals." His attorney later said, "It was like talking to a five-year-old."[106] In 2002 the

Supreme Court ruled that executing retarded inmates was unconstitutional; two years later the Court agreed to hear the appeal of an inmate who had received a death sentence for a crime committed as a juvenile, ultimately determining that the execution of inmates for crimes committed as juveniles was also unconstitutional.[107] Opponents to the death penalty, such as the Death Penalty Information Center, fought for additional prohibitions against capital punishment. Late in 2007 the U.S. Supreme Court granted a stay of execution to an inmate scheduled to be put to death by lethal injection. The Court's decision effectively placed a moratorium on executions until the constitutionality of lethal injection could be determined.[108]

Reentry Services   Fundamental questions about the validity of the death penalty have contributed to the growth of mitigation investigations, in which social workers have played an important role.[109] If conservatives defined criminal justice policy through the 1980s and 1990s, two developments marked the possibility of an ideological shift. About 95 percent of current inmates locked up during the past two decades—585,000 by 2000—will require some type of reentry service if they are to avoid notoriously high recidivism rates: Of state prisoners, for example, 62 percent are rearrested within three years, and 41 percent are reincarcerated.[110] Yet, apart from experimental pilot demonstrations such as drug courts, comparatively little attention has been directed at services for ex-cons. Among the most successful services is the Delancey Street Foundation, a nonprofessional residential program, conceived in San Francisco in 1971. Delancey Street boasts that 90 percent of its graduates become productive citizens, although its capacity is limited to only 1,000 residents.[111]

Compstat   In the early 1990s, Dennis Smith, a policy professor at New York University, teamed up with New York Police Chief, William Bratton, to apply computer technology to create real-time depictions of crime in New York City. Having trained precinct commanders to promptly deploy officers in response to clusters of crime, Compstat proved remarkable successful, between 1994 and 1999 all categories of crime fell in all precincts. Serious crime, such as murder and manslaughter, motor vehicle theft, burglary, and robbery fell by more than 50 percent.[112] Soon Compstat was being exported to other cities, including Baltimore and Los Angeles.

Hate Crimes   The FBI collects data on hate crimes voluntarily submitted by local and state police departments. Data for 2007 reveal that most hate crimes are related to race, religion, sexual orientation, and ethnicity (Table 14.4). Federal hate crime

Table 14.4

Hate Crimes by Category, 2006

Bias Motivation	Incidents	Victims
Race	4,000	5,020
Anti-White	890	1,054
Anti-Black	2,640	3,332
Anti-American Indian	60	75
Anti-Asian/Pacific Islander	181	239
Anti-Multiple Races	229	320
Religion	1,462	1,750
Anti-Jewish	967	1,144
Anti-Catholic	76	86
Anti-Protestant	59	65
Anti-Islamic	156	208
Anti-Other Religion	124	147
Sexual orientation	1,195	1,472
Anti-Male Homosexual	747	913
Anti-Female Homosexual	163	202
Anti-Homosexual	238	307
Anti-Heterosexual	26	29
Anti-Bisexual	21	21
Ethnicity	984	1,305
Anti-Hispanic	576	619
Anti-Other	408	486
Disability	79	95
Anti-Physical	17	21
Anti-Mental	62	74
Total	7,722	9,652

Source: FBI, Hate Crime Statistics, www.fbi.gov/ucr/hc2006/table1.html.

data should not be assumed to provide a comprehensive portrait of social malevolence. Because data are provided voluntarily, some jurisdictions report higher incidents than others. For example, much of the South reports lower numbers than the Northeast. For 2006, Mississippi reported zero hate crimes![113]

Conclusion

Despite a burgeoning number of Americans becoming intimately acquainted with the criminal justice system, the prospect of radical reform appears dim. Other than driving down unemployment through its economic policies and encouraging community policing, the Clinton presidency was unwilling to propose any viable alternative to prison expansion. For its part, the administration of George W. Bush, intent on a "get tough" approach to crime, used the attacks of September 11, 2001, as a pretext for attenuating civil liberties through the U.S. Patriot Act. During the past two decades, the prison-industrial complex has expanded to process and capitalize on the legions of young African American men sentenced and placed in its care. Despite the enormous institutional and psychological costs associated with incarceration, momentum has yet to build in the direction of community-based services. Thus, criminal justice remains one of the greatest institutional challenges facing U.S. social policy.

Discussion Questions

1. Click on the "Student Section" link on the policyAmerica website (http://capwiz.com/policyamerica/index.html), identify legislation related to criminal justice, and trace its implications for social welfare. Has the policy been effective? What are its costs? How might it be made more adequate?

2. Crime varies considerably in terms of both the nature of offenses and the characteristics of offenders. How prevalent is crime in your community? What are the primary offenses? Who are the offenders?

3. State and local governments vary regarding the management of juvenile delinquency. Does your community have a juvenile court? Are its deliberations open to the public? What are the usual offenses that bring a youth to juvenile court?

4. Many communities are building new correctional facilities. Is your community upgrading corrections? To what extent do new facilities reflect the new penology? Are for-profit correctional firms active in your state? If not, should they be? Should they be allowed to contract to manage probation and parole?

5. Legalization of drugs has become a heated issue. What are the implications of drug legalization for substance abuse programs? How could drug legalization be structured in your state? How would substances be taxed? How would tax revenues from legalization be allocated?

6. In many poor urban communities, drug-related street violence has escalated to unprecedented heights. How has your community balanced resource allocations for supply interdiction versus resources for demand reduction? To what extent is substance abuse treatment available to inmates in local correctional facilities? Have specific neighborhoods in your community organized to contain and reduce drug trafficking? Which agencies have supported such initiatives?

7. As the war on drugs has failed to live up to its promise, more attention has been focused on prevention, particularly among children. What models have agencies in your community adopted to prevent substance abuse among kids? How much money has been allocated for prevention programs? What is the track record of the prevention programs adopted in your community?

8. How prevalent are hate crimes in your community? Is there any attempt to organize initiatives encouraging citizens to become more tolerant?

Are victims of hate crimes in your community encouraged to take advantage of victim assistance benefits?

9. To what extent are social workers involved in community reentry activities? Does the local chapter of the National Association of Social Workers have a position on reentry programs? If not, what should it consist of? How would you encourage NASW to take up a reentry initiative?

Notes

1. *Encyclopedia of Sociology* (Guilford, CT: Dushkin Publishing Group, 1974).

2. D. Stanley Eitzen and Doug Timmer, *Criminology* (New York: John Wiley, 1985), pp. 15–16.

3. Phyllis Day, *A New History of Social Welfare* (Englewood Cliffs, NJ: Prentice Hall, 1989), p. 181.

4. Ibid., p. 182.

5. Jerome Miller, *Search and Destroy: African-American Males in the Criminal Justice System* (New York: Cambridge University Press, 1996), p. 207.

6. Quoted in Ibid., p. 185.

7. Richard Herrnstein and Charles Murray, *The Bell Curve* (New York: Free Press, 1994).

8. Glenn Walters, "A Meta-Analysis of the Gene–Crime Relationship," *Criminology* 30, no. 4 (1992), pp. 8–16.

9. *Justice Expenditures and Employment Abstracts* (Washington, DC: U.S. Department of Justice, 1992).

10. U.S. Census Bureau, Statistical Abstract of the United States, 2002 (Washington, DC: U.S. GPO, 2002), p. 199.

11. "The Growing Inmate Population," *New York Times* (August 1, 2003), p. A22.

12. Andrew Block and Virginia Weisz, "Choosing Prisoners over Pupils," *Washington Post* (July 6, 2004), p. A19.

13. John Broder, "No Hard Time for Prison Budgets," *New York Times* (January 29, 2003), p. WK5.

14. Gary Jensen and Maryaltani Karpos, "Research on the Behavior of Rape Statistics," *Criminology* 31, no. 4 (1993), p. 382.

15. *Annual Report, Attorney General of the U.S.* (Washington, DC: Department of Justice, 1995), p. 4.

16. Lela Costin, Howard Karger, and David Stoesz, *The Politics of Child Abuse in America* (New York: Oxford University Press, 1996).

17. "Behind Bars," *Washington Post* (June 3, 2000), p. A9.

18. "Nation's Prison Population Climbs to over 2 Million," *Washington Post* (August 10, 2000), p. A4.

19. U.S. Census Bureau, *Statistical Abstract of the United States*, 1999 (Washington, DC: U.S. Government Printing Office, 1999), p. 231.

20. David Masci, "Prison-Building Boom," *Issues in Social Policy* (Washington, DC: Congressional Quarterly, 2000), p. 138.

21. Fox Butterfield, "Prison Rates among Blacks Reach a Peak, Report Finds," *New York Times* (April 7, 2003), p. A11.

22. "The Price of Prisons," *New York Times* (June 26, 2004), p. A26.

23. Retrieved February 5, 2008, from www.innocence project.org

24. Darryl Fears, "Exonerations Change How Justice System Builds a Prosecution," *Washington Post* (May 3, 2007), p. A3.

25. Day, *A New History of Social Welfare*, p. 180.

26. James Leiby, *A History of Social Welfare and Social Work in the United States* (New York: Columbia University Press, 1978), p. 147.

27. Jerome Miller, *Last One over the Wall* (Columbus, OH: Ohio State University, 1991), p. 222.

28. Ibid., p. 243.

29. Denise Gottfredson and William Barton, "Deinstitutionalization of Juvenile Offenders," *Criminology* 31, no. 4 (1993), pp. 98–117.

30. James Q. Wilson and John DiIulio, Jr., "Crackdown," *The New Republic* (July 10, 1989), p. 54.

31. Rhonda Cook, "Georgia's Prison Boot Camps Don't Work, Study Says," *San Diego Union Tribune* (May 8, 1994), p. A32.

32. "Connecticut Suspends Gang-Riddled Youth Boot Camp," *San Diego Union Tribune* (June 12, 1994), p. A6.

33. Doris Mackenzie et al., "Boot Camp Prisons and Recidivism in Eight States," *Criminology* 33, no. 3 (1995), p. 78.

34. "Residential Treatment Programs: Concerns Regarding Abuse and Death in Certain Programs for Troubled Youth" (Washington, DC: Government Accountability Office, 2007), p. i.

35. Diana Schemo, "Report Recounts Horrors of Youth Boot Camps," *New York Times* (October 11, 2007), p. A19.

36. Margaret Talbot, "The Maximum Security Adolescent," *New York Times Magazine* (September 10, 2000), p. 42.

37. Michael Tonry, "Treating Juveniles as Adult Criminals," *American Journal of Preventive Medicine*, 32, 48, p. S3.

38. Blaine Harden, "Boston's Approach to Juvenile Crime Encircles Youths, Reduces Slayings," *Washington Post* (October 23, 1997), p. A3.

39. Fox Butterfield, "Triple Murder in Boston Points to Unsettling Rise in Homicides," *New York Times* (October 12, 2004), p. A18.

40. U.S. Census Bureau, *Statistical Abstract of the United States,* 2002, p. 193.

41. Mathea Falco, *Winning the Drug War* (New York: Priority Press, 1989), pp. 26–27.

42. Sidney Cohen, "The Drug-Free America Act of 1986," *Drug Abuse and Alcoholism Newsletter* (San Diego, CA: Vista Hill Foundation, 1987), pp. 1–3.

43. Falco, *Winning the Drug War,* p. 29.

44. Barry Bearak, "A Room for Heroin and HIV," *Los Angeles Times* (September 27, 1992), p. A18.

45. U.S. Census Bureau, *Statistical Abstract of the United States,* 2002, pp. 191, 193.

46. Barry Bearak, "Road to Detox: Do Not Enter," *Los Angeles Times* (September 30, 1992), p. A18. Used by permission.

47. John Kasarda, "Industrial Restructuring and the Consequences of Changing Job Locations," in Reynolds Farley (ed.), *Changes and Challenges: America 1990* (New York: Russell Sage Foundation, 1995), Table 5.15.

48. Christopher Jencks, "Deadly Neighborhoods," *The New Republic* (June 13, 1988), p. 18; Juan Williams, "Hard Times, Harder Hearts," *Washington Post* (October 2, 1988), p. C4.

49. Louis Sahagun, "Gang Killings Increase 69%, Violent Crime up 20% in L. A. County Areas," *Los Angeles Times* (August 21, 1990), p. B8.

50. Jesse Katz, "County's Yearly Death Toll Reaches 800," *Los Angeles Times* (January 19, 1993), p. A23.

51. Gabriel Escobar, "Slayings in Washington Hit New High, 436, for 3rd Year," *Los Angeles Times* (November 24, 1990), p. A26.

52. Claude Brown, *Manchild in the Promised Land* (New York: Macmillan, 1965); and Claude Brown, "Manchild in Harlem," *New York Times* (September 16, 1984), p. 16.

53. Daniel Patrick Moynihan, *Came the Revolution* (San Diego, CA: Harcourt Brace Jovanovich, 1988), p. 291.

54. Miller, *Search and Destroy,* pp. 7–8.

55. Ibid., p. 85.

56. Ibid., p. 99.

57. Alex Kotlowitz, *There Are No Children Here* (New York: Doubleday, 1991).

58. Barry Bearak, "Brooklyn Neighborhood Grieves for Its Mr. Chips," *Los Angeles Times* (December 19, 1992), p. A6.

59. Glenn Frankel, "The Longest War," *Washington Post Weekly* (July 7, 1997), p. 6.

60. David Simon and Edward Burns, "Too Much Is Not Enough," *Washington Post* (September 7, 1997), p. C1.

61. David Stout, "Retroactively, Panel Reduces Drug Sentences," *Washington Post* (December 12, 2007), p. A1.

62. Pamela Frank, "Drugs across the Border: A War We're Losing," *Washington Post Weekly* (September 29, 1997), p. 27.

63. Jim McGee, "Military Seeks Balance in Delicate Mission: The Drug War," *Washington Post* (November 29, 1996).

64. George Soros, "The Drug War 'Cannot Be Won'," *Washington Post* (February 2, 1997).

65. Michael Novak, *The New Consensus on Poverty and the Family* (Washington, DC: American Enterprise Institute, 1987).

66. William Bennett, John DiIulio Jr., and John Walters, *Body Count* (New York: Simon and Schuster, 1996), p. 56.

67. Ibid., p. 105.

68. Ibid., p. 27.

69. Ibid., pp. 175–176.

70. Ibid., Chapter 5.

71. Jim Wallace, "With Unconditional Love," *Sojourners* (September–October 1997).

72. James Traub, "The Criminals of Tomorrow," *New Yorker* (November 4, 1996).

73. John Hagan, "The Social Embeddedness of Crime and Unemployment," *Criminology,* 31, no. 4 (1993), p. 469.

74. William Julius Wilson, *When Work Disappears* (New York: Knopf, 1996), p. 238.

75. Juan Williams, *Enough* (New York: Crown, 2006), pp. 220, 222.

76. Ethan Nadelmann, "The Case for Legalization," *Public Interest* 92 (1988), pp. 3–17.

77. James Jacobs, "Imagining Drug Legalization," The Public Interest 101 (Fall 1990), pp. 27–34.

78. Kate Zernike, "A Drug Scourge Creates Its Own Form of Orphan," *New York Times* (July 11, 2005), p. A1.

79. Mathea Falco, *The Making of a Drug-Free America* (New York: Priority Press, 1989), p. 100.

80. Jacobs, "Imagining Drug Legalization," p. 30.

81. Jim Newton, "Seizure of Assets Leaves Casualties in War on Drugs," *Los Angeles Times* (October 14, 1992), p. A1; and David Savage, "Drug-Case Forfeitures Will Be Reviewed," *Los Angeles Times* (January 16, 1993), p. A2.

82. David Lamb, "Last Shot to Salvage Their Lives," *Los Angeles Times* (January 17, 1993), p. A1.

83. U.S. Census Bureau, *Statistical Summary of the United States* (Washington, DC: U.S. Census Bureau, 1995), Table 349.

84. U.S. Census Bureau, *Statistical Abstract of the United States,* 1999, p. 231.

85. *Annual Report of the Attorney General of the U.S.,* 1995.

86. U.S. Census Bureau, *Statistical Abstract of the United States,* 2002, p. 204.

87. U.S. Census Bureau, *Statistical Abstract of the United States,* 1999, p. 233.

88. Malcolm Feeley and Jonathan Simon, "The New Penology," *Criminology* 30, no. 4 (1992), p. 452.

89. Miller, *Last One over the Wall,* p. 76.

90. Feeley and Simon, "The New Penology," p. 455.

91. Mary Flaherty and Joan Biskupic, "Justice by the Numbers," *Washington Post Weekly* (October 14–20, 1996), p. 88.

92. Meredith Kolodner, "Private Prisons Expect a Boom," *New York Times* (July 19, 2006), p. C1.

93. Steven Donziger, "The Prison-Industrial Complex," *Washington Post* (March 17, 1996), p. C3.

94. Ibid., p. C3.

95. Alan Elsner, "America's Prison Habit," *Washington Post* (January 24, 2004), p. A19.

96. Office of Community Oriented Policing Services, Department of Justice. Retrieved October 14, 2004, from www.usdoj.gov

97. Janet Vinzant and Lane Crothers, "Street-Level Leadership: The Role of Patrol Officers in Community Policing," *Criminal Justice Review,* 19, no. 2 (Autumn 1994), pp. 56–71.

98. *Annual Report of the Attorney General of the U.S.,* 1995.

99. "OVC Fact Sheet" (Washington, DC: Office for Victims of Crims, n.d.), pp. 1–2.

100. Hans Selvog, "Moral Panic and Sex Offenders," (Richmond, VA: Virginia Commonwealth University, School of Social Work, 2000).

101. Jennifer Medina, "Move to Commit Sex Offenders Raises Rights Issues in Albany," *New York Times* (February 6, 2006), p. A23.

102. Mary Cooper, "Death Penalty," in *Issues in Social Policy* (Washington, DC: Congressional Quarterly, 2000).

103. Brooke Masters, "DNA Testing in Old Cases Is Disputed," *Washington Post* (September 10, 2000), p. A1.

104. Bob Herbert, "Criminal Justice Breakdown," *New York Times* (February 14, 2000), p. A27.

105. Brooke Masters, "A Death Sentence, Then a Reversal," *Washington Post Weekly* (June 19, 2000), p. 34.

106. Raymond Bonner and Sara Rimer, "Executing the Mentally Retarded Even as Laws Begin to Shift," *New York Times* (August 7, 2000), p. 1.

107. Linda Greenhouse, "Justices Consider Executions of Young Killers," *New York Times* (October 14, 2004), p. A1.

108. Linda Greenhouse, "Supreme Court Stays Execution in a Sign of a Broader Halt," *Washington Post* (October 30, 2007), p. 30.

109. Julie Schroeder, "Forging a New Practice Area: Social Work's Role in Death Penalty Mitigation Investigations," *Families in Society* 84, no. 3 (2003).

110. Peter Slevin, "Life after Prison," *Washington Post* (April 24, 2000), p. A1.

111. Ray Rivera, "On Delancey Street," *The Santa Fe New Mexican* (October 19, 1997).

112. Dennis Smith and William Bratton, "Performance Management in New York City: Compstat and the Revolution in Police Management" (New York: New York University, n.d.), p. 455.

113. Darryl Fears, "Hate Crime Reporting Uneven," *Washington Post* (November 11, 2007), p. A3.

CHAPTER 15

Child Welfare Policy

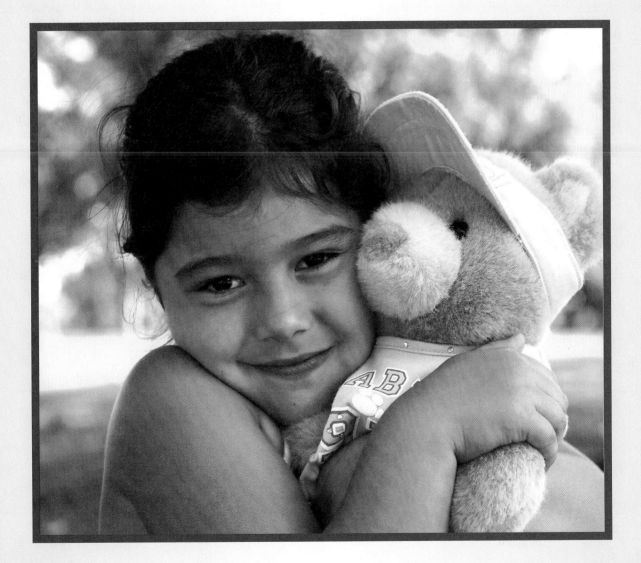

*T*his chapter examines the evolution of child welfare policy in the United States. Child protective services, foster care, adoption, and Head Start have been the focus of child welfare policy since the 1960s. The devolution of welfare to the states through the Personal Responsibility and Work Opportunity Reconciliation Act of 1996 has introduced questions about the prospects of poor children whose mothers are entering the labor market.

In U.S. social welfare, the condition of children is inextricably linked to the status of their families. Because the United States has failed to establish a family policy that ensures basic income, employment, and social service supports to parents, parents frequently have difficulty in caring for their children. As families are less able to care for their children, the demand for child welfare services escalates. The commitment that national governments make toward reducing poverty among children varies considerably. Among industrialized nations, the United States fares poorly. A UNICEF study of child well-being among the 21 most developed nations ranked the United States just above the United Kingdom along six dimensions: material well-being, health and safety, educational well-being, family and peer relationships, behaviors and risks, and subjective well-being.[1] The Luxembourg Study, which rated the number of children in poverty, found that the United States ranked highest, as indicated in Table 15.1.

In the United States in recent years, the proportion of children living in poverty, the proportion of children in single-parent households, the percentage of mothers in the workforce, and the birthrate of women in minority groups have all remained high. In 2002, 12.1 million children were living in poverty in this country, a significant increase from the 10.4 million poor children in 1970.[2] Although child poverty diminishes when family incomes increase during economic expansion, improvement slowed between the 1993–1995 period, when 1.2 million children per year were lifted out of poverty,

Table 15.1

Ranking Child Poverty in 17 Developed Countries

Rank	Country	Children in Poverty*	Elderly in Poverty*	Total Poverty*
1	United States	21.9%	24.7%	17.0%
2	Ireland	17.2	35.8	16.5
3	Italy	16.6	13.7	12.7
4	Spain	16.1	23.4	14.3
5	Australia	15.8	29.4	14.3
6	United Kingdom	15.3	20.5	12.4
7	Canada	14.9	5.9	11.4
8	Netherlands	9.8	2.4	7.3
9	Germany	9.0	10.1	8.3
10	Denmark	8.7	6.6	9.2
11	France	7.9	9.8	8.0
12	Austria	7.8	13.7	7.7
13	Belgium	6.7	16.4	8.0
14	Switzerland	6.7	18.4	7.6
15	Sweden	4.2	7.7	6.5
16	Norway	3.4	11.9	6.4
17	Finland	2.8	8.5	5.4

*For purposes of comparison, poverty equals 50 percent or less of median income.

Source: Lawrence Mishel, Jared Bernstein, and Sylvia Allegretto, *The State of Working America*, 2006–07 (Washington, DC: Economic Policy Institute, 2007), p. 350.

and the 1995–1998 period, when only 400,000 per year rose from the ranks of the poor.[3] More troubling, the Children's Defense Fund reported that the number of children in families with incomes less than half of the poverty line increased sharply during the late part of the 1990s.[4]

Poverty has adverse consequences for infants, contributing to insufficient prenatal care and high infant mortality. This fact explains, in part, the relatively high infant mortality rate of the United States for 2004, 6.6 deaths per 1,000 live births, compared to Japan's 3.3, Germany's 4.2, Canada's 5.2, and the United Kingdom's 5.3.[5] Despite the chronically poor showing of child welfare in the United States relative to other industrialized nations, the most recent federal accounting that included such variables as violent crime, poverty, mortality, teen pregnancy, and overall health, indicated that U.S. children were faring somewhat better than in the past.[6] The Child Well-Being Index, which tracks the welfare of children over time through 28 variables, has shown significant improvements since the mid-1990s.[7] Between 1996 and 2001, *Kids Count*, a project of the Annie E. Casey Foundation, reported improvement on eight of ten variables used to evaluate child welfare.[8]

Although an increase in a broad range of family and child welfare services might be expected in view of the chronic negligence that has typified the nation's care for its children, the societal response has been extremely varied. As Jeanne Giovannoni notes, "at best we have a hodgepodge of funding and regulatory mechanisms, and we rely predominantly on market mechanisms dictating both the amount and variety of care available."[9] Others have been less charitable. Alvin Schorr, a veteran welfare scholar, has observed, "From the 1960s on, child welfare suffered a series of blows that left [conventional] ideology and the program in shambles."[10]

A classification of child welfare services completed by the Child Welfare League of America identified nine diverse components: services in the home, day care, homemaker services, foster care, adoption, group home care, institutional care, protective services, and services to unmarried parents.[11] Of these, protective services, foster care, and adoption are most frequently identified as being related exclusively to child welfare and, therefore, are the focus here, though emerging issues are addressed as well.

Spotlight 15.1

Advocacy for Children

Of the many organizations advocating for children and families, three have become pivotal.

The Child Welfare League of America

Established in 1920, the Child Welfare League of America (CWLA) is an association of 1,000 public and private nonprofit agencies that assist abused and neglected children and their families each year with a wide range of services. To learn more about this agency, go to its website at **www.cwla.org.** CWLA also offers a timeline of events in the history of child welfare at **www.cwla.org/whowhat/history.htm.**

The Children's Defense Fund

Founded by Marian Wright Edelman, the Children's Defense Fund (CDF) develops and advocates in several program areas: health care, education, child welfare, and families. In addition, CDF convenes meetings of advocates in order to leverage federal legislation. More information can be found at **www. childrensdefense.org.**

Children's Rights

Founded in 1995 by Marcia Robinson Lowry to improve the plight of children through litigation, Children's Rights has been at the forefront of class action suits that resulted in numerous consent decrees whereby states have agreed to upgrade child welfare programs. Details about Children's Rights can be found at **www.childrensrights.org.**

Child welfare services are often controversial, because they sanction the intervention of human service professionals in family affairs that are ordinarily assumed to be private matters and the prerogative of parents. This dilemma places extraordinary demands on child welfare professionals, who are mandated to protect the best interests of the child while not intruding on the privacy of the family.[12] Recently, this conundrum has become more pronounced: advocates for child welfare services demand more programs, but traditionalist groups attempt to cut programs that they see as designed to subvert the family. Ironically, much of this argument could be defused if the United States adopted a family policy that helped parents care for children more adequately, thus reducing the need for the more intrusive child welfare interventions. For the moment, however, the adoption of any family policy is unlikely, leaving services to children fragmented. This historical reluctance to allow government to intrude into the privacy of the family has been compounded by scandals involving underfunded, overburdened, and mismanaged child welfare departments in several states as well as the District of Columbia.

■ *Child welfare policy in the United States began in the 1870s. An early program led by Charles Loring Brace, founder of New York's Children's Aid Society, moved thousands of children from deleterious urban conditions in New York City to farm families in the Midwest. Under intense criticism, this program would later be replaced with programs that were less divisive to family and community.*

History of U.S. Child Welfare Policy

Although many states established orphanages during the eighteenth century, current child welfare policy in the United States has its origins in the 1870s.[13] The large number of child paupers led Charles Loring Brace, founder of New York's Children's Aid Society, to move thousands of children from deleterious urban conditions in New York City to farm families in the Midwest. Eventually, criticism of Brace's methods, which were divisive of family and community, contributed to more preventive approaches to children's problems. By the beginning of the twentieth century, most large cities had children's aid societies that practiced the "boarding out" of children (the payment of a fee for child rearing) to sponsors in the community.[14] The boarding out of children until adoption (except in the case of children with disabilities, who were unlikely to be adopted) was the forerunner of today's foster care and adoption programs in the United States.

Protective services for children began with one of the more unusual incidents in U.S. social welfare. In 1874 a New York church worker, Etta Wheeler, discovered that an indentured nine-year-old child, Mary Ellen, was being tied to a bed, whipped, and stabbed with scissors. On investigating what could be done for Mary Ellen, Wheeler spoke with the director of the New York Society for the Prevention of Cruelty to Animals (NYSPCA) on behalf of the child. Although it was subsequently misreported that intervention on behalf of Mary Ellen was predicated on her status as an animal, rather than as a child, a careful review of the case indicated that Mary Ellen's case was adjudicated consistently with legal precedents involving abused children.[15] The following year, the New York Society for the Prevention of Cruelty to Children was established.[16] By 1922, 57 societies for the prevention of cruelty to children had been established to protect abused youngsters.[17]

Child welfare proved an effective rallying issue for Progressives, who advocated intervention on the part of the federal government. In 1909, James E. West, a friend of President Theodore Roosevelt and later head of the Boy Scouts of America, convinced Jane Addams and other welfare leaders to attend a two-day meeting on child welfare. This first White House Conference on Children focused attention on the plight of destitute families, agency problems with the boarding out of children, and the importance of home care. The conference proved so successful that it was subsequently repeated every 10 years—with the exception of 1981, when the conference was canceled by the Reagan administration. The White House Conference on Children served as a model for legitimating and attracting attention to social welfare needs. One significant product of the White House Conference on Children was the call to establish a federal agency to "collect and exchange ideas and information on child welfare." With an initial appropriation of $25,640, the U.S. Children's Bureau was established in 1912 under the auspices of the Department of Commerce and Labor.[18] Instrumental in the early years of the Children's Bureau were Lillian Wald, of New York's Henry Street Settlement House, and Florence Kelley, an alumna of both the Henry Street Settlement and Hull House. Julia Lathrop, a former resident of Hull House, was the bureau's first director.[19]

Because of the economic circumstances of poor families, child labor emerged as a primary concern of early child welfare advocates. The absence of public relief meant that families were compelled to work at whatever employment might be available, however wearing and demeaning. Children worked full shifts in coal mines and textile mills; women labored in sweatshops. Neither were protected from dangerous or unhygienic working conditions. Under the guidance of Florence Kelley, the National Consumer League fought for children and women using a dual strategy. First, the league lobbied for reform in the working conditions of women through regulation of sweatshops and factories, and for ending the exploitation of children by prohibiting child labor. Second, it advocated ameliorating the grinding poverty of many families by means of a family subsidy that would make such deplorable work less necessary. For Kelley, the family subsidy was a preventive measure with which she was quite familiar; in Illinois in 1911, she had successfully lobbied for passage of the Funds for Parents Act. This act was a precursor of the Aid to Dependent Children program, part of the original Social Security Act of 1935.[20]

Before the Great Depression, welfare advocates could boast of a series of unprecedented initiatives designed to improve the conditions of poor families in the United States. The Children's Bureau Act of 1912 established a national agency to collect information on children. The Child Labor Act of 1916 prohibited the interstate transportation of goods manufactured by children. The Maternity and Infancy Act of 1921 assisted states in establishing programs that dramatically reduced the nation's infant and maternal mortality rates. Yet these hard-won successes were constantly at risk of being subverted. The Supreme Court ruled the Child Labor Act unconstitutional in 1918, and the Maternity and Infancy Act was terminated in 1929, when Herbert Hoover and Congress refused further appropriations.[21] Child and family welfare initiatives remained unsuccessful until the Social Security Act of 1935 ushered in an array of welfare policies.

The Social Security Act addressed child welfare in two of its provisions. Title IV introduced the Aid to Dependent Children program, which provided public relief to needy children through cash grants to their families. Cash benefits were to be authorized and overseen by welfare caseworkers who were also to provide social services to welfare families. Title V reestablished Maternal and Child Welfare Services (which had expired in 1929) and expanded the mandate of the Children's Bureau, whose goal was now to oversee a new set of child welfare services "for the protection and care of homeless, dependent, and neglected children, and children in danger of becoming delinquent."[22] Significantly, both family relief and child welfare services were to be administered by the states through public welfare departments. As a result, as of 1935 the provision of child welfare services shifted largely from the private, voluntary sector to the public, governmental sector.

Within public welfare, the responsibility for child welfare has shifted between the federal and state governments. Since 1935 the state and federal governments have shared responsibility for social services provided to families, but the role of the federal government has changed with respect to income maintenance benefits to poor families. From 1935 until 1996, federal and state government shared the funding and administration of the AFDC program. With devolution of public assistance to the states through the 1996 Personal Responsibility and Work

Opportunity Reconciliation Act (PRWORA), however, the federal government limited its role to one of funding and limited oversight. PRWORA instituted a block grant program, Temporary Assistance for Needy Families (TANF), which is primarily under the control of state government. Consistent with the residual conception of welfare, primary responsibility for children rests with their parent(s) with state intervention as a backup. Ominously, in 2003 a significant number of states had reduced TANF appropriations for transition to work, assistance to the poorest families, transportation aid, and cash assistance. Thirty-two states had restricted eligibility, instituted waiting lists, and reduced payments for child care, and four states had reduced support of teen pregnancy prevention programs.[23] Thus, although PRWORA has contributed to a sharp drop in welfare rolls, reduced support for children and youth may imperil their futures. The long-term prospects of child welfare are also problematic. Open-ended entitlements for the elderly—Social Security, Medicare, and Medicaid—are likely to squeeze discretionary funding, resulting in lower appropriations for child welfare. Between 2007 and 2017, federal funding for children is expected to decline from 2.6 to 2.1 percent of gross domestic product (GDP), while benefits for the elderly increase from 7.6 to 9.5 percent. In 1960 federal funding for elders eclipsed that for children by 2 percent; by 2017 the gap is projected to increase to 31.5 percent.[24]

Protective Services for Children

Through the Social Security Act, states proceeded to develop services to children independently of one another and within the relatively loose specifications of the act. In the absence of a centralized authority that would ensure standardized care throughout the United States, child welfare services varied greatly from state to state and even within states. In the two decades following the passage of the Social Security Act, child welfare services had become established within American social welfare, but with a high degree of fragmentation.

In the 1960s the status quo in child welfare was upset by increasing reports of child abuse and neglect. A pediatrician, C. Henry Kempe, identified nonaccidental injuries to children as the "battered child syndrome." As more states began to address the problem, child welfare advocates built a compelling

case for a national standard for child protective services. This lobbying led to the passage of the Child Abuse Prevention and Treatment Act of 1974, which established the National Center for Child Abuse and Neglect within the Department of Health and Human Services and presented a model statute for state child protective programs. All 50 states eventually enacted the model statute that, among its provisions, specified the following:

- A standard definition of child abuse and neglect
- Methods for reporting and investigating abuse and neglect
- Immunity for those reporting suspected injuries inflicted on children
- Prevention and public education efforts to reduce incidents of abuse and neglect

As a result of these national standards, the National Center for Child Abuse and Neglect was able—for the first time—to report trends in child abuse and the need for protective services for children. Alarmingly, the data collected by the National Center revealed a dramatic increase in reports of child abuse; these more than doubled between 1976 and 1986, when reports of child abuse numbered 2 million.[25] In 1991 Chicago's National Committee for the Prevention of Child Abuse reported that 1,383 children died as a result of abuse, 50 percent more than the number reported in 1986.[26] Most troubling was that reports of child abuse continued to climb through the mid-1980s, while at the same time expenditures for child protective services were decreasing.[27]

Increases in child abuse reports and decreases in expenditures led to a crisis in child welfare services. The magnitude of this crisis was mapped in 1987 by Douglas Besharov, an authority on child welfare policy:

> Of the 1,000 children who die under circumstances suggestive of parental maltreatment each year, between 30 and 50 percent were previously reported to child protective agencies. Many thousands of other children suffer serious injuries after their plight becomes known to authorities. . . . Each year, about 50,000 children with observable injuries severe enough to require hospitalization are not reported [emphasis in original].[28]

A consequence of this disintegration of children's services was a volatile debate over the definition of child abuse and neglect. One solution to the widening disparity between dwindling resources for children's services and increasing reports of abuse and neglect, of course, would be to redefine the criteria in accordance with which emergency services for children were deployed. If conservatives could promulgate a more restrictive definition of abuse and neglect, they would benefit directly, in that such a change would effectively subvert demands for greater funding for children's services because the incidence of child maltreatment would drop, and parents would retain wider latitude for discipline in the home. Contending that confirmed reports of child abuse had consistently declined since implementation of the Child Abuse Prevention and Treatment Act, Besharov subsequently argued for a more restrictive definition.[29] Countering this claim, David Finkelhor of the University of New Hampshire's Family Research Laboratory noted that annual data from the American Humane Association indicated fairly steady rates of validated abuse and neglect, from 40 to 43 percent of all reports. Because more specific research on the nature of general abuse and sexual abuse suggested increasing incidence, Finkelhor argued for more resources for child protection.[30]

The rapid deterioration of child welfare services led children's advocates to call for more funding of social services. But proposals for increased support for child welfare services did not go unchallenged. Ambiguity in the definition of what constituted child abuse and neglect had contributed to incidents in which child welfare workers appeared to disregard parental rights in their eagerness to protect children. Perhaps the most notorious instance of such overzealousness occurred during the summer of 1984, when social workers from the Vermont Department of Social and Rehabilitation Services and the state police rounded up 112 children from "a radical Christian sect" and detained them for three days to search for indications of abuse. When the American Civil Liberties Union threatened to sue the state on behalf of the religious community, state officials reconsidered, and the children were returned to their parents.[31] Similar but less newsworthy incidents enraged parents who, feeling unjustly accused, formed VOCAL (Victims of Child Abuse Laws) in an attempt to restore traditional parental rights in the face of what they perceived to be the intrusiveness of the state.

Conservative scholars contributed to the grassroots indignation that fueled VOCAL. Sociologists Bridgitte and Peter Berger contended that social services, such as child welfare, were the vehicle through which middle-class professionals evangelized among lower-class clients. In disputes between professionals and parents over parents' versus children's rights, the Bergers' recommendation was to "trust parents over against experts."[32] With momentum building during the 1980s, the 3,000 members of VOCAL took their complaints into the public arena. In Arizona, for example, VOCAL held up a $5.4 million appropriation for child protective services.[33]

Further distracting public attention from child maltreatment, during the 1980s some family therapists suggested that therapy could "recover memories" of childhood abuse. By the end of the decade, showcase trials of child day care providers, teachers, clergy, and parents resulted in a series of convictions based on incidents that had been previously forgotten but were later retrieved during clinical treatment. Later, as appeals raised questions about the veracity of allegations, the "recovered memory" movement came under scrutiny. By the time a Wenatchee, Washington, minister and his wife were found innocent in 1996 of charges that they had run a satanic cult that abused children, judgments for virtually all of the perpetrators convicted in earlier trials had been reversed on appeal.[34]

While academics, policy wonks, and therapists debated definitional, ideological, and clinical aspects of child maltreatment, child protective services deteriorated. New York City's child welfare services became the focus of scrutiny in the cases of a series of children who died despite having been active child protection cases. In 1992 five-year-old Jeffrey Harden died from broken ribs and burns caused by scalding water. Although Jeffrey's family had been known to child welfare authorities for 18 months, intervention by four different caseworkers failed to identify the risk to the child. By the time of his death, all four workers had left the agency.[35] During Thanksgiving 1995, young Elisa Izquierdo was beaten to death by her demented mother. Despite repeated calls by neighbors and school officials, the city's child protection workers had failed to prevent her murder. Within a year, four-year-old Nadine Lockwood had starved to death. Again, child welfare workers had failed to confirm Nadine's deteriorating health even though neighbors had complained about her neglect. An investigation into the Child Welfare Administration showed the magnitude of agency failure: in a fifth of reported cases, workers failed to interview all of the children in the family; in two out of five cases, workers ignored previous reports of child abuse; almost one-fifth of cases were closed despite the risk of future abuse.

Following the exposé, Mayor Rudolph Giuliani announced plans to restructure child welfare in the city.[36] Despite the appointment of a new commissioner of children's services, Nicholas Scoppetta,[37] a subsequent report found that 40 percent of abused and neglected children were returned home and mistreated again.[38]

Virtually every major metropolitan area featured at least one scandal involving a child who died while under the care of protective services. The District of Columbia's Child and Family Service Agency (CFSA) had been so mismanaged that it was placed under a court-appointed receiver. After several years, the staff was upgraded until virtually all were M.S.W.'s, yet the agency continued to show serious performance problems,[39] chief among them high caseloads and high turnover.[40] By 2000 a deteriorating work environment had resulted in "foster care panic," in which CFSA workers removed children from parents, leading the *Washington Post* to accuse social workers of "flight from professional judgment and responsibility." "Social workers are abandoning their training as well as the children and families they've been hired to serve," the paper intoned.[41] Six months later the General Accounting Office reported that CFSA had failed to investigate 1,200 cases of suspected neglect and abuse within 30 days, among other structural problems.[42] Soon, the reporting of CFSA children placed with families outside the district was so poor that Maryland suspended accepting CFSA children for foster care. Meanwhile, another case was unnecessarily delayed, and a judge issued an order for the CFSA receiver, a social worker, to appear in court. The receiver ignored the order, which led to her arrest, handcuffing, and quick retreat to a restroom to dodge reporters.[43] More composed, the receiver announced that she would legally challenge the judge's authority to hold her accountable, a statement that was widely derided.[44] As the entire spectacle occurred in the nation's capital, congressional Republicans convened hearings to investigate misfeasance on the part of CFSA as well as the judgment of the receiver.[45] Eventually the receiver apologized to the court, paid fines that included reimbursement of parties inconvenienced by her absence at the hearing, and subsequently resigned. None of this reflected well on child welfare professionals, who appeared inept under the scrutiny of the federal lawmakers responsible for oversight of federal child welfare policy.

In 2001 the death of a 23-month-old African American infant due to child abuse led reporters from the *Washington Post* to investigate other child deaths. Within a year, reporters had identified the outline of a rather imposing iceberg; their research revealed that between 1993 and 2001, 229 children had died as a result of maltreatment in the District of Columbia, but the deaths had gone without proper investigation on the part of the Metropolitan Police Department and DCFS[46]—a story that would receive a Pulitzer Prize. Yet, reform of child protection in the District lagged. The State of Maryland threatened to return 1,500 District foster children because of inadequate documentation on the part of CFSA.[47] Punctuating CFSA lapses in accountability, the family of one of the children who had died of abuse—a 15-year-old whose deformed spine crushed her internal organs because corrective surgery had not been performed—initiated a $120 million suit against CFSA. In a perverse action on the behalf of the District, attorneys argued that CSFA was not liable because the agency had been placed under federal court supervision![48]

Not long thereafter, the nation witnessed another illustration of child welfare in disarray: A five-year-old Miami girl in foster care, Rilya Wilson, had been missing for 15 months, yet Florida child welfare workers were unable to locate her.[49] Although the head of the Florida family service agency admitted that the performance of child welfare workers was "appalling," she had no explanation for the whereabouts of the 374 other foster children whom the state was unable to locate.[50] Florida child welfare workers replicated the performance of those who had been encountered by reporters elsewhere: Rather than admit the extent of problems in children's services, workers used confidentiality as an excuse to avoid public accountability. Years after the exposé, Rilya Wilson had yet to be found.[51]

In January 2003 the decomposing body of seven-year-old Faheem Williams was found in a Newark basement; his two brothers had been locked in a nearby room, "emaciated and with burn scars on their bodies."[52] Although Williams had been an active protective services case with the New Jersey Division of Youth and Family Services (DYFS), multiple agency errors failed to save him. Subsequently, the *New York Times* obtained case records on 17 children which documented the deaths of four children and "the sometimes brutal, prolonged abuse of 13 more."[53] As the *Times* would learn, the culture at DYFS conspired to expose children to risk. Rather than redoubling efforts to protect maltreated children, child welfare workers were so intent on closing cases that they often took shortcuts, contravening agency policy and state law. In a grim parody of street slang, workers came to refer to the rush to eliminate cases as "drive-by closings." For years, DYFS used confidentiality to avoid public scrutiny: "one of the most serious offenses committed by [DYFS] over the years has been its ability to keep the full dimensions of its failings secret—from parents of children in its care, from lawyers acting on behalf of children who have been raped or killed and from legislators seeking to reform the agency's practices." When confidentiality and stonewalling failed to discourage court inquiries into its operations, DYFS simply defied court demands to turn over records.[54] Though the exposé of DYFS brought the agency's defensive practices to light, it did little to correct for its malfeasance. Within a year of the Williams tragedy, Matthew Calbi was beaten to death by his mother, despite four investigations of the family during the previous two years.[55]

In October 2003 a New Jersey couple was arrested for starving two boys they had adopted; the oldest was 19 years old, 4 feet tall, and weighed 45 pounds. Despite 38 visits by a DYFS caseworker during the previous two years, no evidence of malnourishment had been reported.[56] Although agency policies called for annual medical checkups, none of the six children that the couple had adopted had seen a doctor during the previous six years.[57] The case file documented that one emaciated child beseeched his caseworker for food and rooted through the glove box in the caseworker's car in search of something to eat. "When he ate away from home, he begged the caseworkers not to tell his adoptive parents," reported the *New York Times.* "The family was nevertheless allowed to adopt three more children; each came with a government subsidy."[58] In fact, the previous year the couple obtained more than $30,000 in welfare benefits for the children they had adopted and one foster child.[59] Reflecting on a suit her advocacy agency brought against DYFS for its neglect of foster children, Marcia Robinson Lowry, founder and director of Children's Rights, expressed her exasperation: "Either people were purposely flouting a federal court order or the depths of their incompetence was so profound that people didn't know what they were supposed to do."[60] Immediately, the governor of New Jersey announced a two-year plan to right the state's foundering child welfare agency.[61] A subsequent review of cases in which child abuse had been suspected revealed that 110 children had disappeared

from New Jersey's child protection system.[62] A year later, the four malnourished boys who had underscored New Jersey's tawdry child welfare services had doubled in weight and were recovering from years of maltreatment.[63]

In March 2004 Children's Rights filed a suit against the State of Mississippi for exposing maltreated children to further risk. The state had closed 34 child abuse prevention centers, and caseloads of child welfare workers were skyrocketing. Even though the Child Welfare League of America suggested that caseloads not exceed seventeen, in several Mississippi counties caseloads had risen to 100 per worker; in Forrest County the caseload exceeded 200. Ominously, services were provided to fewer than half of families in which neglect or abuse had been confirmed. Due to a shortage of caseworkers, the state could ensure that only half of reported cases of child maltreatment were even investigated; as a result in 2004 the percent of substantiated cases was less than half what it was in 1997.[64] Mississippi seemed poised to replicate the debacles that have befallen Florida, New Jersey, and Washington, DC.

Tragically, the deaths of children due to abuse and neglect were not a local problem but one that had become nationwide. By the mid-1990s the U.S. Advisory Commission on Child Abuse and Neglect concluded that some 2,000 children were dying of abuse and neglect annually,[65] far above the 1,400 deaths counted by the National Center on Child Abuse and Neglect in 2002.[66] In rating the child homicide rates for industrial nations, a British researcher concluded that the child fatality rate of the United States was double that of the second most lethal nation for children, Australia.[67] The rate of reported as well as confirmed cases of abuse and neglect in the United States were more than double those of the United Kingdom or Canada.[68]

Regardless of increases in injury and death to children due to abuse and neglect, child welfare professionals were embracing a new approach to serving at-risk families, "family preservation." Initially demonstrated in the late 1970s through the Homebuilders program, family preservation called for the provision of intensive services for a brief period, usually six weeks, by a worker assigned four to six cases. Services provided ranged from crisis intervention to home repair to child day care—all intended to stabilize the family and prevent out-of-home placement of a child. Family preservation was greeted enthusiastically by child welfare professionals because of the multiple benefits it offered.

Foremost, by keeping a family intact, this approach avoided out-of-home placement of a child who had been abused or neglected. Because of the high cost of out-of-home placement, family preservation thus offered financial benefits: the cost of mounting a family preservation program was quickly recovered through savings from the reduction in out-of-home placements. Finally, in valuing family unity over child removal, family preservation allied child welfare agencies with conservative traditionalists who placed family rights over those of children.

The relationship between family preservation and child protective services was oblique but nonetheless consequential. Child welfare professionals understood family preservation as a preventive strategy that could preclude the most dramatic disposition of child protective services, out-of-home placement. As family preservation captured the allegiance of child welfare professionals, the focus on child protection began to lapse. Even as fatalities due to child abuse mounted, children's advocates pressed for policy changes focusing on family preservation. Consequently, when the 1993 Clinton economic package was passed, it included $930 million for family support and preservation services over five years, but only a footnote reference to child protective services.[69] After a decade, family preservation had been incorporated into child welfare through the Promoting Safe and Stable Families program, budgeted at $505 million annually,[70] yet failure to intervene effectively on behalf of maltreated children contributed to CPS scandals that erupted across the United States.

Despite policies intended to ameliorate child abuse, the number of confirmed cases of maltreated children climbed steadily, more than quadrupling from 10 per 1,000 in 1976 to 47 in 1996.[71] In 2001, 2.7 million children were alleged to have been maltreated; two-thirds of those were investigated, and 903,000 were determined to have been victims of abuse or neglect. This computed to an incidence rate of 12.4 per 1,000 children. Children are much more likely to have been neglected than abused. For 2001 the rate of neglect was 7.1 per 1,000 children, and the abuse rate was 2.3. Thus, 59 percent of maltreated children had been victims of neglect, and 19 percent had been abused. Approximately 10 percent had been sexually abused, and 7 percent were psychologically abused.[72] Girls (52.3 percent of victims) were more likely to be maltreated than boys (46.7 percent). Although the majority of abused children, 56.4 percent, were white, African American

children were disproportionately overrepresented at 26.4 percent of victims. The vast majority of perpetrators were parents, 79.2 percent.[73]

Since 1996 the incidence of child maltreatment has decreased somewhat, although data on child abuse and neglect are notoriously inadequate. Prior to 1996, state reports on child maltreatment were voluntary; subsequently, states have been required to provide data to the "maximum extent possible." The refusal of the federal government to insist on regular reporting by the states, combined with the variation among states with respect to their data collection capacity, makes a hodgepodge of child maltreatment statistics. The result is evident in data provided by the states on alleged and founded incidents of maltreatment (see Table 15.2). The totals from state reports would suggest slight reductions in reports of maltreatment, –1 percent, as well as confirmed cases, – 4 percent. An examination of the experiences of individual states, however, suggests a situation bordering on chaos. Several states provided suspect data or no data. In 1998 North Dakota reported zero victims of maltreatment, an achievement as unprecedented as it was unlikely. For 2001 Kansas and Maryland failed to provide data on allegations of maltreatment. For those states reporting, allegations ranged from Kentucky's high of 159.5 per 1,000 children in 1998 to Pennsylvania's low of 7.9 in 1998. In 2001 founded cases ranged from Alaska's high of 82.6 per 1,000 children to Pennsylvania's low of 1.6. From these data one might conclude that in 1998 Kentuckians were 20 times more likely than Pennsylvanians to report allegations of abuse, and that in 2001 Alaskans were 50 times more likely than Pennsylvanians to victimize their children. To the contrary, it is more likely that statistics such as these reflect the failure of federal and state government to provide a minimally adequate portrait of the welfare of the nation's most at-risk population—maltreated children.

In 2005 the federal Administration on Children and Families (ACF) released an assessment of the performance of the states with respect to seven basic outcomes central to child welfare, the Child and Family Services Reviews (CFSRs). Not one state was able to assure that maltreated children had a permanent and stable living arrangement; not one state was in compliance with regard to families having improved their ability to care for their children; and only one state demonstrated that it adequately met a child's physical and mental health needs. As a result of their poor performance, states risked

Table 15.2

Incidents of Child Maltreatment Allegations and Victimization, by State, 1998–2001

State	Children Alleged to Be Victims per 1,000 Children		Percentage Change in Allegation Rate 1998–2001	Child Victims per 1,000 Children		Percentage Change in Victimization Rate 1998–2001
	1998	2001		1998	2001	
Alabama	33.1	26.6	–20	15.4	8.2	–47
Alaska	58.9	95.4	62	37.1	82.6	123
Arizona	48	38.4	–20	7.1	3.8	–46
Arkansas	45.2	37.6	–17	13.1	10.1	–23
California	46.4	51.7	11	17.7	13.6	–23
Colorado	37.6	27.5	–27	6.7	4.3	–36
Connecticut	51.7	56.2	9	21.4	14.4	–33
Delaware	54.1	42.8	–21	16.2	8.5	–48
DC	95.8	64.3	–33	47.7	25.5	–47
Florida	52.8	71.4	35	23.2	33.3	44
Georgia	36.7	51.7	41	12.1	16.6	37
Hawaii	12	24.2	102	7.3	13.2	81
Idaho	76	26.6	–65	22.6	9.5	–58
Illinois	34.7	44	27	11.2	8.5	–24
Indiana	67.3	33.9	–50	12.5	13.4	7
Iowa	38.9	51.6	33	10.1	17.5	73
Kansas	38.4	NA	NA	7.6	10.2	34
Kentucky	64.2	56.6	–12	23.1	16.6	–28
Louisiana	38	31.3	–18	11.6	9.2	–21
Maine	31	30.2	–3	12.3	14.4	17
Maryland	43.5	NA	NA	11.1	14.4	30
Massachusetts	36.3	40.9	13	18.9	22.1	17
Michigan	61.3	66.3	8	8.9	11.0	24
Minnesota	19.7	18.4	–7	8.4	7.6	–10
Mississippi	42.8	40	–7	8	5.9	–26
Missouri	53.4	56.4	6	8.9	6.5	–27
Montana	84.7	65.4	–23	14.7	8.4	–43
Nebraska	32.9	23.8	–28	9.5	7.4	–22
Nevada	49.7	41.9	–15	17.2	9.2	–47
New Hampshire	30.1	38.6	28	3.9	3.5	–10
New Jersey	38.2	33.8	–12	4.9	4.1	–16
New Mexico	26.6	45.6	71	8.4	13.6	62
New York	53.4	53.7	1	18.6	16.6	–11
North Carolina	65.6	61.5	–6	19.5	18.4	–6
North Dakota	43.7	43.8	0	0	8.5	NA

(continued)

Table 15.2

(continued)

State	Children Alleged to Be Victims per 1,000 Children		Percentage Change in Allegation Rate 1998–2001	Child Victims per 1,000 Children		Percentage Change in Victimization Rate 1998–2001
	1998	2001		1998	2001	
Ohio	47.7	39.5	−17	20.4	17.7	−13
Oklahoma	68.6	71.1	4	18.9	15.3	−19
Oregon	33.5	29.9	−11	12.3	10.5	−15
Pennsylvania	7.9	7.9	0	1.9	1.6	−16
Rhode Island	41.5	45.7	10	14.5	13.3	−8
South Carolina	39.9	36.2	−9	8.8	11.0	25
South Dakota	26.4	49.2	86	13.2	18.3	39
Tennessee	24.2	36.2	50	7.5	6.8	−9
Texas	30.7	32.9	7	7.1	7.4	4
Utah	38.8	39	1	11.4	14.0	23
Vermont	14	24	71	6.3	7.7	22
Washington	32.1	23.2	−28	8.8	3.9	−56
West Virginia	159.5	67.2	−58	19.3	19.8	3
Wisconsin	16.5	29.3	78	6	8.7	45
Wyoming	17.1	32.4	89	6.2	7.7	24
Total	42.5	41.9	−1	12.9	12.4	−4

Source: House Ways and Means Committee, *Overview of Entitlement Programs,* 2004 (Washington, DC: U.S. GPO, 2004), p. 11–76.

losing millions of dollars in federal funds; however, this appeared a symbolic threat because it is improbable that the federal government would step in and assume direct control of services for abused and neglected children. But there was little reason to expect dramatic improvement in state compliance with the seven standards: "Many states said they did not have enough caseworkers to investigate reports of abuse and neglect or to monitor children in foster care. They have difficulty recruiting and retaining workers because salaries are low," reported the *New York Times,* "But some states, grappling with what they describe as their worst fiscal problems in more than 50 years, have cut spending for some child welfare services."[74] Regardless, states were expected to mount Program Improvement Plans (PIPs) which would chart how they would address CFSR deficiencies. States were given two years to address CFSR deficits or suffer funding penalties in relation to the number of measures in noncompliance.[75]

Inadequate resources for child welfare affected the capacity of local agencies to address their mandated responsibilities. For decades the Annie E. Casey Foundation had invested tens of millions of dollars in children's services, identifying and supporting model programs across the nation. Unfortunately, the exemplary programs it subsidized remained just that, isolated from the mainstream and failing to catalyze system-wide reforms. In 2003 the Foundation identified a significant impediment to progress: the human services workforce:

Human services is reaching a state of crisis. Frontline jobs are becoming more and more complex while the responsibility placed on workers remains severely out of line with their preparation and baseline abilities. Many are leaving the field while a new generation of college graduates shows little interest in entering the human services sector. Millions of taxpayer dollars are being poured into a compromised system that not only achieves little in the way of real results, but its interventions often do more harm than good. It is *spotlight 15.2*

The National Foster Parent Association

The National Foster Parent Association (NFPA) is a national nonprofit organization that supports foster families through legislative advocacy, training and education, publications, networking among foster parents, state and local foster parent associations, and child welfare associations. To learn more about NFPA and read more about the history of foster care in the United States, go to its website at **www .nfpainc.org.**

clear that frontline human services jobs are not attracting the kinds of workers we need, and that regulations, unreasonable expectations, and poor management practices mire workers and their clients in a dangerous status quo.[76]

A companion report released by the Brookings Institution echoed the Casey Foundation's conclusions: "Unfortunately, there is a vast gulf between what these human services workers are asked to do and how they are equipped for that task," wrote Paul Light. "Workloads often exceed recommended limits, turnover rates among the most qualified workers are high, and human services employees describe their work as both frustrating and unappreciated."[77]

In 2003 Congress passed the Keeping Children and Families Safe (KCFS) Act, Public Law 108-36, as a reauthorization of CAPTA. Among its provisions, the Act doubled funding for child abuse prevention and treatment to $200 million for 2004. Funds were intended to enhance staff training and supervision as well as tracking systems. Significantly, KCFS authorized completion of the fourth National Incidence Study of Child Abuse and Neglect, updating the last such study of 1993. In order to subsume child maltreatment under the broader concept of family violence, the Act authorized $175 million to enhance public awareness about harm to families and children due to domestic violence. Finally, KCFS provided additional resources for adoption of special needs children and services to abandoned infants, particularly those with AIDS.[78] Whether the funding and compliance provisions of KCFS are sufficient to forge a more adequate network of services for maltreated children remains to be seen.

Foster Care for Children

When parents are unable to care for their children, foster care is often used to provide alternative care. As an extension of the practice of boarding out children, most foster care in the United States is at no cost to the parents, and children are placed in the homes of other families. There is an important relationship between child protective services and foster care: Foster care is primarily a service for victims of child abuse; more than half of children in foster care were placed there by child protective service workers. The second most prevalent reason for child foster care is the "condition or absence of the parent," accounting for about 20 percent of foster care placements.[79]

As in the case of protective services, foster care for children was not coordinated under the provisions of the Social Security Act. States adopted separate policies and, unfortunately, took few measures to monitor children in foster care. During the early 1960s a series of studies began to document a disturbing development: rather than being a temporary arrangement for child care, foster care had become a long-term experience for many youngsters, with 70 percent of children in foster care for more than one year.[80] Not only had states planned poorly for the reunification of children with their original families, but in many instances child welfare agencies lost track of foster care children altogether. During the summer of 1992, the District of Columbia's Department of Human Services was rocked by a foster care scandal when it was reported that the department had literally no idea of the location of one out of every four children it had placed in foster care.[81]

In response to the deterioration of children's services, several "family preservation" demonstration projects were begun. As discussed earlier, these efforts offered intensive services to families in order to prevent children from being placed in foster care or to effectively reunite children with their biological parents. The demonstrations seemed to be cost-effective. In Virginia, 14 pre-foster-care placement service projects concluded that family functioning improved in 69 percent of the families receiving intensive support services. Moreover, the cost of support services was $1,214 per child, substantially less than the cost of foster care ($11,173) or residential care ($22,025) over the average length of time (4.6 years) a child was in these out-of-home settings.[82] As a result of such field demonstrations, "permanency planning" became a central feature of the Adoption Assistance and Child Welfare Act (AACWA) of 1980.

Permanency planning is "the systematic process of carrying out, within a brief time-limited period, a set of goal-directed activities designed to help children live in families that offer continuity of relationships with nurturing parents or caretakers and the opportunity to establish lifetime relationships."[83] AACWA was an ambitious effort, and one expert heralded it as making it "possible to implement at state and local levels a comprehensive service delivery system for children."[84] As a result of permanency planning, the number of children in foster care plummeted. In 1971, 330,400 children were in foster care; by 1982 the number had dropped to 262,000, a reduction of 20.7 percent.[85] Welfare workers swiftly removed children from foster care and reunited them with their biological families under the rationale that community support services would assist parents. Early research on family preservation services indicated cost savings; but some families needed extensive service costing as much as $2,600. As costs associated with reunification increased, public agencies struggled to pay for necessary services. An analysis of a model family reunification program found that deficits in agency resources—gaps in service, large caseloads and high worker turnover, and inadequate family preparation, among others—presented problems in more than half of all cases. The researchers were "unaware of any reported successful permanency planning program that has high caseloads as a program component."[86]

Tragically, inadequate resources sometimes created a vicious circle: When biological parents received few support services, they were less able to care for their children, thereby contributing to the need for child protective services. In the absence of intensive support services, permanency planning for many children meant a revolving door—placement in foster care, reunification with the biological parent(s), and then a return to foster care. In 1982, 43 percent of children had been in multiple placements, but by 1983 53.1 percent had been in more than one placement; 20.1 percent had been placed twice, 24.2 percent three to five times, and 8.8 percent six or more times.[87] The National Association of Social Workers newsletter reported the instance of a four-year-old New York boy who was placed in 37 different homes in two months and described another child who had been placed in 17 homes in 25 days.[88] By 2001 the number of multiple placements had dropped; 39 percent of children had been in three or more placements.[89]

In large measure, the permanency planning movement faltered because of lack of support services to families. Not long after passage of AACWA, Ronald Rooney observed prophetically that "if the promise of permanency planning is to be realized, those who allocate funds must provide money for a continuum of services that are delivered from the point of entry into foster care and include programs designed to prevent the removal of children from their homes."[90] Yet in 1981 an important source of family support services, Title XX, was cut 21 percent. For 1992 the Title XX appropriation, $2.8 billion, was $100 million less than the amount funded in 1981, despite a 58 percent increase in reports of child abuse and neglect since that time.[91] And the decline in gross appropriations for Title XX reveals only a small part of the defunding of the program: Once inflation is factored in, it can be seen that between 1977 and 1992, Title XX actually lost $3.2 billion, or 55.4 percent of its funding.[92] (By 2003 Title XX had been whittled down to $1.7 billion, further hampering child welfare service delivery.[93]) A decade after the early permanency planning demonstration projects, Theodore Stein feared that the movement was being subverted by budget cuts and a reliance on crisis services in child welfare.[94]

Limited funding for child welfare under Title XX induced states to become more dependent on other federal sources of revenue. Because it was funded completely by the federal government and did not require any state matching funds, Title XX was the optimal funding source for child welfare program administrators, but it had one important limitation: Revenues were capped. Other available federal assistance included Title IV-B of the Social Security Act, which allocated a fixed amount of funds for children's services and required a 25 percent state matching contribution. Most of the programs under Title IV-E of the Social Security Act were not capped, but federal funds required a matching state contribution ranging from 25 to 50 percent; the exception was the Chaffee Foster Care Independence Program, which was capped and required a state match of 20 percent. Moreover, the two programs that child welfare program administrators looked to under Title IV-E, foster care and adoption assistance, were reserved for poor children who would have been eligible for welfare had they stayed at home. In other words, beyond Title XX, child welfare administrators could try to address increases in service demand through other federal programs, but Title IV-B funds were capped and required a state match, and open-ended Title IV-E funds were earmarked for welfare children in addition to requiring a state match.

Under these circumstances, Byzantine patterns of service funding evolved during the 1980s as child welfare officials exploited matching formulae that optimized federal reimbursement. Imaginative program managers from affluent states first matched federal requirements for welfare children in order to capture Title IV-E funds, and then funded the state match for IV-B funds, reserving Title XX funds to the extent possible for nonwelfare children. Program managers from states unwilling to meet the federal matching requirements had little choice but to use scarce Title XX funds, sometimes for welfare children. Table 15.3 shows trends in three

Table 15.3

Federal Funding for Child Welfare, Foster Care, and Adoption (in millions of dollars)

Year	IV-B Child Welfare	IV-B/2 Safe & Stable Families	IV-E Foster Care	IV-E Independent Living	IV-E Adoption
1986	198	—	605	—	55
1987	223	—	793	45	74
1988	239	—	891	45	97
1989	247	—	1,153	50	111
1990	253	—	1,473	60	136
1991	274	—	1,819	70	175
1992	274	—	2,233	70	220
1993	295	—	2,547	70	272
1994	295	60	2,607	70	325
1995	292	150	3,050	70	411
1996	277	225	3,114	70	485
1997	292	240	3,692	70	590
1998	291	255	3,704	70	697
1999	292	275	4,012	70	843
2000	292	295	4,256	140	1,012
2001	292	305	4,382	140	1,197
2002	292	375	4,519	140	1,342
2003	290	404	4,690	182	1,525
2004	292	505	4,917	200	1,692
2005*	292	505	5,044	200	1,871
2006*	292	505	5,276	200	2,064

*Estimated

Source: House Ways and Means Committee, *Overview of Entitlement Programs*, 2004 (Washington, DC: U.S. GPO, 2004), p. 11–5.

sources of federal revenues for children's services from 1986 to 2006. The rapid expansion of funds for foster care of welfare children under Title IV-E, an open-ended entitlement, contrasts with capped funding under Title IV-B and Title XX,[95] creating the risk that states may be induced to place poor, and disproportionately minority, children in foster care rather than help them stay at home by funding in-home support services.

To compound the problems faced by foster care workers, quality foster care placements became scarce. A declining standard of living forced many women into the job market, thus restricting the pool of families with a parent at home to supervise children[96]—a requisite for desirable foster care. Between 1979 and 2000 the number of hours worked by wives increased 50.7 percent; no-longer-at-home wives were working to shore-up eroding family finances.[97] Soon the shortage of foster homes became critical. In the mid-1980s the director of the Illinois Department of Children and Family Services pleaded for 1,000 new foster parents to prevent the collapse of the state's foster care program.[98] In an investigation into the death of one foster care child, a Virginia grand jury cited "the acute shortage of suitable shelter for the 6,000 neglected, abused, and disabled children" in the state as a factor contributing to the child's death.[99] Thus, by the late 1980s, with permanency planning beset with multiple problems, foster care was an unreliable way of serving many of the most endangered children in the United States.

With passage of the Family Support and Preservation Program in 1993, extended by the Promoting Safe and Stable Families Act, policymakers gave priority to supporting troubled families in order to prevent foster care placements. Two decades after the passage of AACWA, the parameters of permanency planning were fairly clear: almost half of children were returned to their immediate or extended families and slightly more than one-fifth were slated for adoption; however, more than 20 percent remained in long-term foster care or had yet to have a permanent plan established. Of plans executed, almost three-fourths remained in foster care; one in ten children remained in institutional care. (See Table 15.4.)

Several issues have emerged to dampen enthusiasm about foster care as a solution for children from very troubled families. Although many mothers negotiate return of their children who had been placed in foster care, some overcoming the considerable hurdles associated with drug abuse,[100] others

Table 15.4

Permanency Plans of Children (in percentages)

Disposition	1999	2000	2001
Permanency Plan			
Reunify	42	42	44
Live with relative(s)	4	4	5
Adoption	21	21	22
Long-term foster care	8	8	9
Emancipation	6	6	6
Guardianship	3	3	3
Not yet established	17	15	11
Placement Setting			
Pre-adoptive home	4	4	4
Foster home (relative)	27	25	24
Foster home (non-relative)	47	47	48
Group home	7	8	8
Institution	11	10	10
Supervised independent living	1	1	1
Runaway	1	1	2
Trial home visit	3	3	3

Source: House Ways and Means Committee, *Overview of Entitlement Programs,* 2004 (Washington, DC: U.S. GPO, 2004), pp. 11–105, 11–107.

experience protracted difficulties. In some instances, children who have been placed in foster care are returned to mothers who are poor candidates for resuming care. A celebrated case involved Cornelious Pixley, a two-year-old African American toddler who had been placed with a white policewoman after his mother was convicted of murdering his infant sister. Following a judge's order that Cornelious be returned to his mother, the foster mother challenged the decision with the assistance of child advocacy organizations. The challenge was based not only on the mother's homicide conviction, but also on her violation of probation as well as her difficulty stabilizing her household. Eventually, custody was remanded to the foster mother.[101]

Too often, foster care has emerged as the catalyst of family dramas that become the grist of journalistic accounts of a child welfare system that "is infected with mistrust, backbiting and second-guessing," hardly the ambience that builds public confidence. One reporter summarized his impression of child welfare:

> As soon as a complaint is received, a virtual industry of social workers, lawyers, judges and administrators goes to work, and no matter how pure the intentions are, the process often deteriorates into chaos. A central goal of child welfare is permanence and stability for the child, but cases routinely become so mired in complications, and legalities, and indecision, and nastiness, and the necessity of trying to understand a specific moment of horror in the larger context of societal issues, that the focus can shift from the search for permanence to the mere passage of time. Months pass. Years pass. Rather than resolution, there is drift, so much that nationally, on average a third of the children entering foster care will be there in excess of two years, creating, instead of stability, an ambiguity that can be damaging.[102]

Increasing demand for foster parents and homosexual rights collided in a controversy about the suitability of gays and lesbians as parents. A Texas child welfare supervisor ordered the removal of a foster child from a lesbian foster parent, arguing that the state's antisodomy statutes defined homosexual households as unacceptable.[103] An Arkansas judge ruled unconstitutional a state ban on placing foster children with families having a gay member.[104] Yet, the U.S. Supreme Court refused to sort out conflicting state policies, letting stand a Florida prohibition on adoption by same-sex parents.[105] The *Washington Post*'s Colbert King undoubtedly spoke for many when he observed, "I couldn't care less what those [foster] parents look like as long as they are strong in themselves and are giving that kid the sense of security, belonging, and love that every child on this earth needs."[106]

Although a desirable outcome for children in foster care would be reunification with biological parents better able to care for them, about 25,000 foster children simply aged out of care each year. Their prospects were often grim. A 1998 study of "graduates" of foster care revealed that 37 percent had not graduated from high school, 18 percent had been incarcerated, and 12 percent had been homeless.[107] A subsequent study of children who have aged out of foster care in the Northwest revealed that, within the 12 months prior to being interviewed, 20 percent had a major depressive episode, 12 percent suffered from alcohol and drug dependence, and

25 percent were diagnosed with posttraumatic stress disorder.[108] In 1999 the Foster Care Independent Living Act provided funding for education and employment services for children who were aging out of foster care; foster youth were entitled to vouchers worth up to $5,000 per year for higher education, for example.[109] Voluntary sector organizations contributed to the Independent Living Program by launching the Saving for Education, Entrepreneurship, and Downpayment (SEED) Initiative, which encouraged states to develop matching savings programs for foster youth in order to assist their economic independence.[110]

Adoption

From the standpoint of permanency planning, adoption has become an important child welfare service. In the early 1980s the Children's Bureau noted that 50,000 "hard-to-adopt" children were waiting for homes. Many of these children were of minority origin, had disabilities, or were older and had been in foster care for several years.[111] Because such children posed a financial burden for adoptive parents, the Adoption Assistance and Child Welfare Act of 1980 provided subsidies to adoptive parents. In 1983, 6,320 children were being subsidized each month at a cost of $12 million.[112] Between 1995 and 2002 the number of agency-involved adoptions virtually doubled from 25,693 to 50,950, respectively.[113] Providing incentives for parents to adopt hard-to-adopt children clearly supported the concept of permanency planning, as "90 percent of subsidized adoptions involve foster parents whom the subsidy has enabled to adopt children with whom they had formed a relationship . . . and most of these are minorities or have special needs."[114] Moreover, subsidized adoption proved cost-effective, costing 37 percent less than foster care.

Still, adoption is not without controversy. Because children come from a variety of racial and cultural groups, questions have been raised about transcultural adoption. Should agencies give consideration to maintaining the cultural identity of children placed for adoption by finding them homes in their birth culture? This question was at the heart of the Indian Child Welfare Act of 1978. Native Americans were disturbed that "25 to 35 percent of all American Indian children [were] separated from their families and placed in foster homes, adoptive homes, or institutions."[115] The fact that 85 percent of such placements were in non-Indian families and left the children "without access to their tribal homes and relationships" raised the specter of partial cultural genocide.[116] To reinforce the cultural identity of Native American children, the Indian Child Welfare Act provided for:

> minimal Federal standards for the removal of Indian children from their families and the placement of such children in foster or adoptive homes which will reflect the unique values of Indian culture, and for assistance to Indian tribes in the operation of child and family service programs.[117]

Equally important, the Indian Child Welfare Act established tribes, rather than state courts, as the governing bodies responsible for Indian foster children.

A similar argument for culturally appropriate placement of children was advanced during the 1980s by the National Association of Black Social Workers (NABSW). Noting a high percentage of African American children placed with white families, NABSW contended that cross-racial adoptions deprived individual children of their racial identity and would eventually result in a degree of cultural genocide for the African American community. Research on cross-racial adoption, however, consistently found that African American children did not suffer adverse consequences from growing up in white families. In 1996 President Clinton signed legislation forbidding interference in child placement for reasons based on race, except by Indian tribes.[118] Although provisions to reinforce the cultural identity of children have unquestionable merit in a pluralistic society, the circumstances of many racial and cultural minorities leave the implementation of such policies in doubt.[119] Without basic health, education, and employment supports, many minority families are likely to have difficulty adopting children. For example, the number of African American children available for adoption far outstrips the number of African American families able to adopt children, despite the fact that African American families "adopt at a rate 4.5 times greater than white or Hispanic families."[120] The number of minority children not only exceeds the portion of the population represented by minorities as a whole, but the percent of adopted children as well. (See Table 15.5.)

Changes in family composition further cloud the picture. The pool of adoptive families has diminished with the increase in the number of female-headed households. The combination of low wages

Table 15.5

Race/Ethnicity of Children Waiting to be Adopted and Adopted, 2001 (in percentages)

Race/Ethnicity	Waiting Children	Adopted Children
White	32	38
African American	42	35
Hispanic	11	16
Two or more races	2	3
Other	2	2
Unknown	4	5
Missing data	6	0

Source: House Ways and Means Committee, *Overview of Entitlement Programs,* 2004 (Washington, DC: U.S. GPO, 2004), p. 11–125.

for women and a shortage of marriageable men means that mothers are encouraged to maintain small families, not to expand them through adoption. In the mid-1980s Esther Wattenberg of the University of Minnesota Center for Urban and Regional Affairs observed prophetically that the future of child welfare:

> will be dominated by a sorting out of "the best interests of the child" in the extraordinarily complex family relationships that develop out of extending family boundaries to stepparents, several sets of grandparents, and an assortment of new siblings from remarried families that join and unjoin family compositions.[121]

Head Start

In response to concerns about the lack of educational preparation of poor children, Head Start was incorporated in the Economic Opportunity Act of 1964. The first Head Start programs were established in poor communities a year later. Intended to compensate for a range of deficits displayed by poor children, Head Start offered health and dental screening, nutrition, and socialization experiences in addition to preschool academic preparation. Of the Great Society programs, Head Start was one of a few that captured the imagination of the nation.

Table 15.6

Head Start: Participation and Federal Funding, Selected Years

Fiscal Year	Enrollment	Budget Authority (in millions)
1965 (summer only)	561,000	$96.4
1970	477,400	325.7
1975	349,000	403.9
1980	376,300	735.0
1985	452,080	1,075.0
1990	548,470	1,552.0
1995	750,077	3,534.1
2000	857,644	5,266.2
2002	912,345	6,536.6

Source: House Ways and Means Committee, *Overview of Entitlement Programs,* 2004 (Washington, DC: U.S. GPO, 2004), p. 15–124.

Despite wide public support, however, participation in Head Start was somewhat uneven, as shown in Table 15.6. Significantly, it was not until 1995 that the enrollment of Head Start eclipsed that of 1966; today, fewer than half of eligible children participate in the program.[122]

During the 1980s, when government assistance to the poor was reduced, many poor families dispatched both parents to the labor market to stabilize family income, and this increased the need for Head Start. Even the Deficit Reduction Act of 1990, which held spending for most social programs in check, provided for modest increases in Head Start.[123] In large measure, this funding reflected a growing appreciation that Head Start was a proven investment in human capital. Award-winning author Sylvia Ann Hewlett noted that "Head Start ($3,000 a year per child) is much less expensive than prison ($20,000 a year per inmate)."[124] The 1996 welfare reform act, which required recipients of family cash assistance to participate in the labor market, increased Head Start enrollments even further.

Early Head Start was introduced in 1995 to provide early education, health, and parental support to toddlers to age three. Supporters of expanding Head Start to younger children than those traditionally served pointed to a longitudinal, experimental study showing that serving younger children had long-term

benefits. Significantly, Early Head Start provided services through vouchers, allowing parents to use home-based, instead of center-based, services. By 2007 only 51 percent of funding for Early Head Start went to center-based care, while 41 percent went to care in the home. In addition, Early Head Start targeted pregnant mothers to encourage them to receive dental and mental health care as well as increasing the educational credentials of teachers. Despite the program enhancements of Early Head Start, the program enrolled only 62,023 children in 2006, only three percent of eligible children.[125]

Since its inception, Head Start has largely become a pre-kindergarten program for the minority poor. In 2002, 52 percent of children enrolled were age four, and 36 percent were age three; 33 percent were African American, 30 percent were Hispanic, 3 percent were American Indian, and 3 percent were Asian. Thirteen percent of Head Start children have disabilities.[126] Few dispute the value of Head Start programming for at-risk children, persistent questions about the long-term benefits of the program notwithstanding. Rather than subverting Head Start, research on such questions has become central to the growing conservative critique of public education. Accordingly, in 2003 the Bush administration proposed transferring Head Start from the U.S. Department of Health and Human Services (HHS) to the Department of Education, reducing health and family features in order to emphasize literacy.[127] Proponents of the transfer cited research indicating cognitive improvements among three-year-olds enrolled in Early Head Start.[128] Ultimately, the Bush gambit failed. In the absence of effective federal leadership, many states moved to universalize preschool education.

Emerging Issues in Child Welfare

Changes in the economic and social circumstances of families in the United States have broadened the scope of the issues that traditionally defined child welfare policy. Of these changes, three are likely to shape child welfare in the future: day care, maternal and child health, and teenage pregnancy.

Day Care

Day care for children has risen in importance as more and more parents with children work. In 1998

Day care for children has become more important as more and more parents with children work.

families in which both parents worked exceeded more than half of all married couples with children, up from 33 percent in 1976.[129] At the same time the number of working mothers with young children has skyrocketed; in 1947 only 12 percent of mothers with children under age six worked outside the home, but by 2002 64.1 percent did.[130] The need for child day care is felt both by middle-income families, in which both parents work in order to meet the income requirements of a middle-class lifestyle, and by low-income families, in which a parent is encouraged or required to participate in a welfare-to-work program. Yet the child care available is often unreliable, expensive, and of questionable quality. Thus, by 1994, almost twice as many children were cared for in a family home as in organized child care facilities.[131] Although poor families typically find family care of their children less expensive than organized child care, on average, child care costs consume 28.5 percent of their income.[132] Even then, available child care often does not conform to the work schedules of parents. A study of New York City families found that half had to patch together day care from multiple providers. Low wages fail to attract the more skilled providers to the day care field, leading the Children's Defense Fund to observe ruefully that "despite their higher levels of education, child care

providers are paid less than animal-caretakers, bartenders, or parking lot and amusement park attendants."[133] In 2000 the median wage for a center-based child care worker was $7.43 per hour. Low wages and poor benefits contribute to staff instability; in 1977 the turnover rate of child care staff was 31 percent.[134]

The crisis in child day care received nationwide attention in 1986 when two Miami children, unsupervised because their mother had to work and could not locate child care, climbed into a clothes dryer in which they "tumbled and burned to death."[135] This incident was cited in the introductory remarks to a proposed $375 million Child Care Services Improvement Act. An indicator of the severity of the day care crisis was that the legislation was sponsored by Orrin Hatch, a conservative senator noted for his prior opposition to social welfare legislation.[136] Regardless, by 1999 many children were caring for themselves: 3 percent of five- to eight-year-olds, 14.1 percent of nine- to 11-year-olds, and 39.4 percent of 12- to 14-year-olds.[137]

The primary programs assisting parents with child care are the federal dependent care tax credit, the child care tax credit, the Child Care and Development Block Grant, and Title XX. The dependent care tax credit allows families to deduct

$3,000 for one child or $6,000 for two children spent on child day care for a given year; the child care tax credit of $1,000 per child is refundable and phased out with increased income. As "tax expenditures"—de facto allocations the Internal Revenue Service creates by not taxing income spent for a specific purpose—the child care tax credit is budgeted at $44.1 billion for 2004, the largest form of federal assistance for child care.[138] Unfortunately, only a small portion of the child care tax credit is refundable, allowing poor families a cash refund for child care expenses. With passage of the 1996 welfare reform act, several child care programs were consolidated under the Child Care and Development Block Grant (CCDBG), funding for which was set at $3.7 billion for 2002.[139] By 2006 the number of children covered under CCDBG remained unchanged, yet the number of eligible children resulted in a waiting list in many states. In California 207,000 children would have had their child care reimbursed under more generous provisions.[140] Under Title XX states are able to purchase day care for poor families; but as of 2001, for example, only $129 million, or 7.6 percent, of the $1.7 billion in Title XX funds was expended for child care.[141]

Maternal and Child Health

Maternal and child health has emerged as an issue among child welfare advocates as younger, poor women give birth to low-birth-weight babies who have received inadequate prenatal care. Low birth weight is a concern because such infants have a higher incidence of developmental disabilities, some of which are permanent and eventually require institutional care. The relationship between low birth weight and developmental disabilities, long recognized by public health officials, resurfaced in Hunger in America, a 1985 report by the Physician Task Force on Hunger in America funded through the Harvard University School of Public Health. The task force noted that "low birth-weight is the eighth leading cause of death in the United States." Efforts to sustain premature and low-birth-weight infants are expensive and, even when successful, often cannot forestall "long-term growth and developmental problems." Infants born small and premature suffer 25 percent more major neurological problems and 117 percent more minor neurological problems than do normal infants.[142] Despite such documentation, the incidence of low birth weight among infants in the United States is relatively high, comparable to that of many poorer nations; that among African Americans parallels the rate of many African nations. Between 1996 and 2001, a period when many child welfare indicators were improving, the percent of low-birth-weight babies increased by 4 percent; for non-Hispanic African Americans, 13.1 percent of babies were low birth weight, compared to 7.7 for all births.[143] Low birth weight in minority infants is of particular concern, because it relates to lack of adequate prenatal care: since 1970 the rate of late or no prenatal care among African Americans has been more than twice the rate for whites.[144] Given the relatively high number of teen pregnancies in the nonwhite population, these figures translate to a disturbing reality: Substantial numbers of nonwhite infants in the United States are born with serious neurological deficits.

The primary federal program to enhance prenatal care for low-income families is WIC, the Special Supplemental Nutrition Program for Women, Infants, and Children. Under WIC, low-income pregnant and nursing women and their young children are eligible for food coupons through which they may obtain especially nutritious foods. Even though the WIC program would seem a logical method for addressing the low-birth-weight problem of infants born to poor women, participation in the WIC program is not at desirable levels. Nationwide, only about half of the people financially eligible to participate in WIC do so.[145] Participation and expenditures for WIC are listed in Table 15.7. Our failure to address inadequate nutrition of the most vulnerable of Americans, poor children, remains one of the most striking paradoxes of the nation's social welfare effort.

Medicaid and the State Child Health Insurance Program (SCHIP) also subsidize health care for low- and middle-income children. Like many welfare programs, these have not proved ideal. Medicaid reimburses health care providers who agree to the programs' procedures and payments; but, if providers refuse to accept Medicaid, the benefit is reduced to symbolic value. This was demonstrated graphically in 2007 when a 12-year-old Maryland boy died from a dental infection, his mother having been unable to locate a dentist despite having Medicaid.[146] Restrictive eligibility provisions introduced by the 2006 Deficit Reduction Act required beneficiaries to produce a birth certificate or passport in order to retain Medicaid. Because the parents of many children, especially immigrants, were unable to produce the necessary documentation,

Table 15.7

WIC Participation and Spending

Year	Participation (in thousands)				Spending in Constant Dollars (in millions)
	Women	Infants	Children	Total	
1980	411.0	507.0	995.0	1,913.0	$1,620.5
1985	665.0	874.0	1,600.0	3,138.0	2,497.7
1990	1,035.0	1,412.5	2,069.4	4,516.9	2,955.1
1995	1,576.8	1,817.3	3,500.1	6,894.2	4,078.0
2000	1,750.0	1,894.2	3,554.0	7,198.1	4,166.0
2002	1,812.2	1,928.2	3,748.2	7,488.6	4,372.3

Source: House Ways and Means Committee, *Overview of Entitlement Programs,* 2004 (Washington, DC: U.S. GPO, 2004), p. 15–115.

tens of thousands of children were deleted from Medicaid.[147] Thus, while 11.2 percent of all children are without health insurance, 21.9 percent of Hispanic children are uninsured.[148]

Teen Pregnancy

Problems relating to maternal and infant health are exacerbated by the sharp rise in the numbers of adolescent females having children. Out-of-wedlock births became an important family issue in the 1980s, when the incidence of unwed motherhood increased so rapidly that by 1983 half of all non-white births were outside of marriage.[149] In 2001, the number of births per 1,000 unmarried women was 43.8 for women of all races, 68.2 for African American women, 87.8 for Hispanic women, and 27.5 for non-Hispanic white women.[150] Even though the absolute number of births to teenagers declined between 1973 and 1991, the decline in the total number of adolescent females meant that the teen pregnancy rate was increasing substantially.[151] Most troubling was that the percentage of unmarried teenage mothers was rising so rapidly that by 1984 it was triple what it had been 25 years before.[152]

Conspicuously, the number of unwed births tripled during the last decades of the twentieth century, as seen in Table 15.8. Although the number of

Table 15.8

Births to Unmarried Women by Age, 1970 and 2001

Age	1970		2001	
	Number of Nonmarital Births	% of Nonmarital Births	Number of Nonmarital Births	% of Nonmarital Births
Under 15	9,500	2.4	7,494	0.6
15–19	190,400	47.8	352,026	26.1
20–24	126,700	31.8	514,959	38.2
25–29	40,600	10.2	257,702	19.1
30–34	19,100	4.8	135,040	10.0
35–39	9,400	2.8	65,257	4.8
Over 40	3,000	0.8	16,771	1.2
Total, all ages	398,700	100.0	1,349,249	100.0

Source: House Ways and Means Committee, *Overview of Entitlement Programs,* 2004 (Washington, DC: U.S. GPO, 2004), p. M–6.

teen births increased substantially, the percent of nonmarital births for teens actually declined. Moreover, the modal age increased; in 1970 most unwed births were among teens aged 15 through 19, but by 2001 most were aged 20 through 24.

Childbearing among very young unmarried women poses a serious problem for public policy for two basic reasons. First, teenage mothers are more likely to drop out of school and thus fail to gain skills that would make them self-sufficient. Adolescent mothers, particularly those who are African American or Hispanic, are apt to have less command of these basic skills. Poor skill development represents an especially critical problem when the skills in question involve parenting. Second, teenage mothers are more likely to have to depend on welfare, the benefits of which are at levels lower than the actual cost of raising children. This combination of inadequate skill development and dependence on public welfare presents the specter of poor teenagers bearing poor children in an endless cycle of hopelessness. The consequences are particularly tragic for the children, who have little prospect of escaping the poverty trap. Reductions in the numbers of working African American and Hispanic males who are marriageable means that many of these children have little hope that their mother will marry and thus pull them out of poverty, which had been the most prevalent way for mothers to become independent of public welfare.[153] The loss of buying power of the income support provided by Aid to Families with Dependent Children (now TANF) has meant that public assistance does not provide an adequate economic base for poor children.[154]

In response to the high teen pregnancy rate, the Clinton administration moved on several fronts. The 1996 welfare reform act required that unmarried teen parents live at home or in a supervised setting in order to receive cash assistance; in addition, states were encouraged to establish Second Chance homes for pregnant teens. One billion dollars in bonuses were to be made available to states that had achieved a decline in the unwed birth while also reducing the incidence of abortions; in addition $250 million over five years was allocated for abstinence education.[155] In 1999 HHS Secretary Donna Shalala announced a national campaign to prevent teen pregnancy, focusing on the role of local nonprofit organizations in pregnancy prevention. These initiatives, in conjunction with strengthened child support enforcement, were credited with helping sustain a steady decline in African American teen

pregnancy, which in 1999 fell for the eighth straight year.[156] Although doubts were raised about the validity of abstinence-only sex education,[157] the teen pregnancy rate plummeted 30 percent from 1991 to 2002. Had the rate not fallen, an additional 1.2 million children would have been born to teen mothers, 460,000 of whom would have lived in poverty.[158]

Conclusion: The Future of Child Welfare

After a half century of federal legislation, many child welfare advocates had become pessimistic about the care provided to youngsters in the United States. Hopes for using the family as the primary institution for child welfare had faded in the absence of economic and social supports to keep families intact. Lacking such supports, most families were reliant on the labor market to generate income to meet essential needs. Although some of the benefits of unprecedented prosperity and low unemployment began to trickle down to poor families by the end of the twentieth century, many welfare and working poor families continued to struggle. The 1996 imposition of welfare time limits cast a long shadow over poor families. In the absence of a coherent national family policy, poor families were less able to care for children; as a result, child welfare services—protective services, foster care, and adoption—have attempted to compensate for severe family deficits.

During the 1990s three strategies emerged in child welfare: the concept of child support assurance as a way to address income maintenance for poor families, and the idea of a children's authority as a way to restructure child welfare. As early as 1991 the National Commission on Children recommended the deployment of a demonstration program to test an enhanced child support enforcement and insurance scheme. Irwin Garfinkel, a social work professor at Columbia University, proposed a child support enforcement and assurance program (CSEAP) to replace family welfare. The CSEAP would reform child support in three ways: (1) The amount of child support would be calculated as a percentage of the absent parent's income; (2) support payments would be automatically withheld from paychecks; and (3) a minimum benefit to children would be provided by the federal government.[159] A federal CSEAP initiative with these components, Garfinkel reasoned, could replace most of the highly stigmatized family welfare program. The CSEAP concept is not without its critics, however. One critic opposed the idea because it placed the federal government in the same awkward position it has had with cash welfare, namely, subsidizing broken families.[160]

Meanwhile, states were experimenting with various methods for stretching their dollars to do more for children. Gradually, these efforts evolved into a potent critique of the traditional ways in which children's services had been delivered. "What's needed is a complete overhaul of children's services, bringing together public and private organizations to meet the comprehensive needs of children, adolescents, and parents," stated Stanford University's Michael Kirst.[161] Noting that many children from problem families were known to several separate health and human services agencies—none with sufficient resources to substantively help any one child—children's advocate Sid Gardner called for collaborative efforts among service providers: "In fact, we are ultimately failing our children not only because we haven't invested in them, but also because as communities we have failed to work together to hold ourselves accountable for the substantial resources we do invest—and for the outcomes of our most vulnerable residents."[162] Social worker Bonnie Bernard of the Far West Laboratory for Educational Research and Development observed that collaboration or restructuring, however defined, targets power relations. "True restructuring means the redistribution of policymaking power, not only from the central office administration to the local school, but to professionals and ultimately to consumers and their communities."[163] In New York City, Geoffrey Canada created the Harlem Children's Zone by coordinating 20 health, education and social service providers to better care for 3,400 inner-city children. "We've got to really do something radically different if we're going to save these kids," observed Canada.[164]

In 1996 Lela Costin, Howard Karger, and David Stoesz proposed that in every jurisdiction children's services be restructured and placed under a Children's Authority, a local body that would provide a comprehensive array of services under performance-based management.[165] Since the early 1980s, the Savannah/Chatham Youth Futures Authority has demonstrated the merits of such an approach. Not only has the Youth Futures Authority integrated a variety of child and family programs, but it has been able to provide data on program outcomes. According to the Youth Futures Authority, the teen pregnancy rate for ages 10 to 19 decreased from 47.7 in 2001 to 42.6 in 2002, and birth rates decreased from 2.3 in 2001 to 1.2 in 2002. Unfortunately, the percent of low-birth-weight infants increased from 2001 to 2002. Although the number of CPS investigations increased slightly during the period, the number of out of home placements fell from 450 to 360.[166] The Youth Futures Authority is not a panacea for enhancing services to vulnerable children and their families, of course, but it has shown that programming can demonstrate improvements with respect to vital indicators of child well-being. Thus, the Youth Futures Authority shows how localities can make important steps in improving child welfare services.

Absent radical restructuring of child welfare, children's advocates have promoted home visiting as an incremental reform. Pioneered by David Olds, periodic home visiting on the part of trained nurses endeavored to enhance the knowledge and skills of parents of vulnerable skills. Although field trials initially demonstrated multiple benefits of home visiting, a rigorous review of the research literature suggested that the strategy produced modest improvements at best.[167] Like family preservation, home visiting may prove to be a fad that produces marginal benefits, effectively distracting advocates from the need to radically reform child welfare.

To an alarming extent, child welfare innovations have been based more on the enthusiasm of children's advocates than on sound field research. New York City's field experiment with minority contracting of child welfare services serves as a case in point. Beginning in the 1980s, child welfare agencies managed by African Americans and Latinos received preferential treatment as well as contracts in the tens of millions of dollars to provide foster care to troubled youth. Under the pretext that traditional white agencies had been incapable of comprehending the cultural nuances related to family disorganization and child maltreatment, minority child welfare agencies avoided strict oversight as they expanded exponentially. Two decades later the de facto field experiment on minority foster children began to unravel. At St. Christopher's, "city investigators found that workers at the agency had doctored case files for children in its care—forging signatures and inserting made-up notations about whether foster homes had been inspected for safety, or whether children were receiving things as basic as clothing."[168] At Miracle Makers, journalists reported that "there has never been a full public accounting at what went wrong . . . or how it spent millions of dollars in government funds and private donations before child welfare officials lost patience with its performance and canceled its foster care contract in 2005."[169] By the end of 2007 the city's child welfare commissioner had notified six of the eight minority-run child welfare contractors that they would be subjected to rigorous program and fiscal audits, and possibly closed. The decision was met with resistance by minority child welfare advocates even though a formal evaluation "reflected problems across more than a dozen measures—from the levels of abuse in foster homes to adoption rates to how well the agencies kept track of whether children were being fed and clothed, attending school and receiving medical care."[170] Minority social workers clung to their belief in the virtues of minority contracting even as the welfare of minority children, victims of abuse and neglect, received substandard care from the very agencies designed to help them.

Poorly substantiated professional ideologies, such as family preservation and minority contracting, invite legal jeopardy for practitioners when children are harmed. The qualified immunity of child welfare workers established through *DeShaney v. Winnebago County Department of Social Services* (1989) was successfully challenged in *Currier v. Doran* (2001) in which child welfare workers were found liable when their actions "created the danger" that harmed a child. *Currier* has momentous implications for child welfare professionals. Foremost, "social workers who blatantly fail to heed warning signs of abuse or potential abuse will not be protected from liability."[171] But *Currier* has much broader implications. Workers cannot claim that high caseloads due to agency underfunding provide an excuse for negligence. Moreover, supervisors are legally liable if their "deliberate indifference" to clients' welfare is reflected in their failure to adequately train subordinates.[172] Thus, *Currier* underscores the need for child welfare professionals to demand adequate resources in order to meet their obligations to provide adequate care for at-risk children.

The import of *Currier* was underscored by the tragic deaths of four girls, aged five to 17, in Washington, DC in the winter of 2007–2008. Despite two calls to the DC Child and Family Services Agency (CFSA), social workers failed to assess adequately the risk to the children, failing to open a child protection case; the girls' mother was arraigned for their murder.[173] Among the agencies involved with the family, the *Washington Post* targeted the District's child welfare agency specifically: "Most culpable is [CFSA] the very organization charged with protecting abused and neglected children,"[174] The tragedy was all the more alarming since CFSA had been removed from oversight by a federal court just a few years earlier as a result of meeting the conditions of a court decree. Despite an overhaul in personnel and procedures, a failure in child welfare provision not only resulted in the deaths of four girls, but exposed CFSA's social workers to legal liability as well. As this tragic incident attests, child welfare professionals must be increasingly vigilant because they are increasingly being held accountable for their performance.

Discussion Questions

1. Using the "Student Section" link on the policyAmerica website (http://capwiz.com/policyamerica/index.html), identify a child welfare policy of interest to you. How has programming changed? Have budget appropriations been adequate to address the problem? What could be done to make the policy more effective?

2. Much of child welfare—protective services, foster care, and adoptions—is funded through a complex array of categorical programs. How does your welfare department optimize reimbursement through these funding sources? As a result of reimbursement systems, what are the priorities for children's services? How would you reconcile discrepancies between categorical funding priorities and community needs?

3. Maintaining the cultural identity of minority children who receive foster care and adoption services is a heated issue in child welfare. When there are too few minority families for the children needing foster care and adoption, what should the policy of the welfare department be in placing minority children? How consistent is your answer with current child welfare policy in your community?

4. Providing preschool programs for children is an increasingly important issue as more mothers enter the workforce. How adequate is day care provision in your community? Who is responsible for the oversight of day care? To what extent are the needs of low-income families considered in day care arrangements? What percentage of families eligible for Head Start actually participate in this program in your community?

5. Among health-related child welfare concerns are infant mortality and low birth weight. How do the statistics in your community compare with the state and national incidence of these two important indicators of child welfare? What are the incidences of infant mortality and low birth weight for children of teenage and minority mothers in your community? What plans does your community have for improving the health status of infants of minority and low-income families?

6. What is the plausibility of reforming child welfare by instituting a child support enforcement and assurance program, consolidating existing services under a Children's Authority, or mounting a home visiting program? If you favor one of these, how would you convince the public that it constitutes real child welfare reform?

7. *Currier* holds child welfare workers liable in the event a child is harmed. To what extent have child welfare workers in your community become aware of this judicial decision? How could it be used to empower child welfare workers?

Notes

1. UNICEF, *An Overview of Child Well-Being in Rich Countries* (Florence, Italy: UNICEF, 2007), p. 1.

2. U.S. House of Representatives, Ways and Means Committee, *Overview of Entitlement Programs* (Washington, DC: U.S. GPO, 2004), p. H-5.

3. Kathryn Porter and Wendell Primus, *Changes since 1995 in the Safety Net's Impact on Child Poverty* (Washington, DC: Center on Budget and Policy Priorities, 1999), p. v.

4. Arloc Sherman, *Extreme Child Poverty Rises Sharply in 1997* (Washington, DC: Children's Defense Fund, 1999), p. 2.

5. U.S. Census Bureau, *Statistical Abstract of the United States, 2006* (Washington, DC: U.S. GPO, 2006), p. 868.

6. Dale Russakoff, "Report Shows Children's Well-Being Is Improving," *Washington Post* (July 14, 2000), p. A1.

7. Kenneth Lamb, "The 2005 FCD Index of Child Well-Being" (New York: Foundation for Child Development, 2005).

8. *Kids Count* (Baltimore: Annie E. Casey Foundation, 2004), p. 33.

9. Jeanne Giovannoni, "Children," *Encyclopedia of Social Work*, 18th ed. (Silver Spring, MD: NASW, 1987), p. 247.

10. Alvin Schorr, "The Bleak Prospect for Public Child Welfare," *Social Service Review* 74, no. 1 (March 2000), p. 125.

11. Alfred Kadushin, "Child Welfare Services," *Encyclopedia of Social Work*, 18th ed. (Silver Spring, MD: NASW, 1987), p. 268.

12. Dale Rusakoff, "Assessing an Ambiguous Threat: Parents," *Washington Post* (January 19, 1998), p. A1.

13. Walter Trattner, *From Poor Law to Welfare State* (New York: Free Press, 1974), p. 100.

14. Ibid., pp. 106–107.

15. Sallie Watkins, "The Mary Ellen Myth," *Social Work* 35 (November 1990), p. 503.

16. Diana DiNitto and Thomas Dye, *Social Welfare* (Englewood Cliffs, NJ: Prentice Hall, 1987), p. 153.

17. Kathleen Faller, "Protective Services for Children," *Encyclopedia of Social Work*, 18th Ed. (Silver Spring, MD: NASW, 1987). p. 386.

18. Trattner, *From Poor Law to Welfare State*, pp. 181, 183.

19. James Leiby, *A History of Social Welfare and Social Work in the United States* (New York: Columbia University Press, 1978), pp. 148–149.

20. June Axinn and Herman Levin, *Social Welfare* (New York: Harper and Row, 1982), p. 159.

21. Trattner, *From Poor Law to Welfare State*, p. 186.

22. Axinn and Levin, *Social Welfare*, pp. 224–228.

23. Sharon Parrott and Nina Wu, "States Are Cutting TANF and Child Care Programs" (Washington, DC: Center on Budget and Policy Priorities, 2003), pp. 1–2.

24. Adam Carasso, C. Eugene Steuerle, and Gillian Reynolds, *Kids' Share 2007* (Washington, DC: Urban Institute, 2007), pp. 3, 8.

25. Barbara Kantrowitz et al., "How to Protect Abused Children," *Newsweek* (November 23, 1987), p. 68.

26. Sandra Evans, "Increase in Baby Killings Attributed to Family Stress," *Washington Post* (June 23, 1992), p. A1.

27. Faller, "Protective Services for Children," pp. 387, 389.

28. Douglas Besharov, "Contending with Overblown Expectations," *Public Welfare* (Winter 1987), pp. 7, 8.

29. Douglas Besharov, "Right versus Rights: The Dilemma of Child Protection," *Public Welfare* 43 (1985), pp. 19–46.

30. David Finkelhor, "Is Child Abuse Overprotected?" *Public Welfare* 48 (1990), pp. 22–29.

31. Fox Butterfield, "Sect Members Assert They Are Misunderstood," *New York Times*, (June 24, 1984), p. 16.

32. Bridgitte Berger and Peter Berger, *The War Over the Family* (Garden City, NY: Anchor, 1983), p. 213.

33. Besharov, "Contending with Overblown Expectations," p. 8.

34. William Claiborne, "Child Sex Ring or Witch Hunt: Charges Divide Town," *Washington Post* (November 14, 1995), p. A1; "A Northwest Town's Nightmare Continues," *Washington Post Weekly* (June 24–30, 1995), p. 31; and Lela Costin, Howard Karger, and David Stoesz, *The Politics of Child Abuse in America* (New York: Oxford University Press, 1996).

35. Douglas Besharov with Lisa Laumann, "Child Abuse Reporting," *Society* (May/June 1996), p. 43.

36. David Stoesz and Howard Karger, "Suffer the Children," *Washington Monthly* (June 1996), p. 20.

37. Dale Russakoff, "Protector of N.Y. City's Children Knows the System Well," *Washington Post* (December 19, 1996), p. A3.

38. Rachel Swarns, "Court Experts Denounce New York's Child Agency," *New York Times* (October 22, 1997), p. A19.

39. LaShawn A. V. Williams, "A Progress Report" (Washington, DC: Center for the Study of Social Policy, March 7, 2000).

40. Sari Horwitz and Scott Higham, "Foster Care Caseloads 'Horrible,'" *Washington Post* (March 27, 2000), p. A1.

41. "Foster Care Panic," *Washington Post* (March 1, 2000), p. A16.

42. Scott Higham and Sari Horwitz, "GAO Study Faults D.C. Child Care," *Washington Post* (September 20, 2000), p. A1.

43. Scott Higham and Sari Horwitz, "D.C. Child Welfare Official Arrested," *Washington Post* (August 15, 2000), p. A1.

44. Sari Horwitz and Scott Higham, "Child Welfare Chief Drops Lawsuit," *Washington Post* (August 24, 2000), p. B3.

45. Sari Horwitz and Scott Higham, "DeLay Lambastes Foster Care in D.C.," *Washington Post* (September 21, 2000), p. A1.

46. Sari Horwitz, Scott Higham, and Sarah Cohen, "'Protected' Children Died as Government Did Little," *Washington Post* (n.d.).

47. Sewell Chan, "Md. Threatens to Return D.C. Foster Children," *Washington Post* (April 18, 2002), p. B2.

48. Scott Higham, "District Says It's Not Liable in Girl's Death," *Washington Post* (March 28, 2002), p. B5.

49. Sue Pressley, "5-year-old Missing 15 Months, and No One Noticed," *Washington Post* (May 4, 2002).

50. Carol Miller, "Miami Welfare Workers Held Off Notifying Police of Missing Child," *Washington Post* (May 6, 2002).

51. Dana Canedy, "Two Years after Girl Disappeared, Little Has Changed in Florida Agency," *New York Times* (January 19, 2003), p. 18.

52. Matthew Purdy, Andrew Jacobs, and Richard Jones, "Life behind Basement Doors," *New York Times* (January 12, 2003), p. A1.

53. Richard Jones and Leslie Kaufman, "New Jersey Shows Failures of Child Welfare System," *New York Times*. Retrieved April 15, 2003, from www.nytimes.com

54. Richard Jones and Leslie Kaufman, "Foster Care Secrecy Magnifies Suffering in New Jersey Cases," *New York Times* (May 4, 2003), pp. 1, 32.

55. Richard Jones, "For Family of Beaten Boy, Tears, Not Finger-Pointing," *New York Times* (August 20, 2003), p. 1.

56. Lydia Polgreen and Robert Worth, "New Jersey Couple Held in Abuse," *New York Times* (October 27, 2003), p. A1.

57. Richard Jones, "Adopted Boys Were Starved, and Caseworkers Did Little, Report Finds," *New York Times* (February 13, 2004), p. A21.

58. "Watching as the Children Starved," *New York Times* (June 24, 2004), p. A26.

59. Leslie Kaufman, "Cash Incentives for Adoptions Seen as Risk to Some Children," *New York Times* (October 29, 2003), p. A1.

60. Jones, "Adopted Boys," p. A21.

61. Richard Jones, "New Jersey Plan on Child Welfare," *New York Times* (February 19, 2004), p. A1.

62. Michael Powell and Christine Haughney, "Kids in N.J.'s Care Missing," *Washington Post* (January 11, 2003), p. A8.

63. Geoff Mulvihill, "A Year Later, Four Boys Are Recovering Quickly From Neglect," *Washington Post* (October 11, 2004), p. A24.

64. Andrew Jacobs, "Lawsuit Challenges Mississippi's Short-of-Resources Child Protection System," *New York Times* (April 1, 2004), p. A14.

65. Costin, Karger, and Stoesz, *The Politics of Child Abuse in America*.

66. "The Deaths of Foster Children," *New York Times* (April 27, 2004), p. A24.

67. Costin, Karger, and Stoesz, *The Politics of Child Abuse in America*.

68. Jane Waldfogel, *The Future of Child Protection: How to Break the Cycle of Abuse and Neglect* (Cambridge, MA: Harvard University Press, 1998).

69. Costin, Karger, and Stoesz, *The Politics of Child Abuse in America*.

70. House Ways and Means Committee, *Overview of Entitlement Programs, 2004* (Washington, DC: U.S. GPO, 2004), p. 11–5.

71. Miringoff, *Social Health*, p. 75.

72. House Ways and Means Committee, *Overview of Entitlement Programs, 2004*, pp. 11-75–11-77.

73. National Center on Child Abuse and Neglect, *Child Maltreatment, 1994* (Washington, DC: U.S. Department of Health and Human Services, 1996), pp. 2–10.

74. Robert Pear, "U.S. Finds Fault in All 50 States' Child Welfare Programs, and Penalties May Follow," *New York Times* (April 26, 2004), p. A17.

75. *Improving the Performance and Outcomes of Child Welfare* (Washington, DC: Center for the Study of Social Policy, 2003).

76. Annie E. Casey Foundation, *The Unsolved Challenge of System Reform* (Baltimore: 2003), p. 2.

77. Paul Light, *The Health of the Human Services Workforce* (Washington, DC: Brookings Institution, 2003), p. 6.

78. *Keeping Children and Families Safe Act of 2003*. Retrieved October 22, 2004, from www.naswdc.org

79. Theodore Stein, "Foster Care for Children," *Encyclopedia of Social Work*, 18th ed. (Silver Spring, MD: NASW, 1987), pp. 641–642.

80. Ibid., p. 643.

81. Keith Harriston, "D.C. Foster Children Are Missing," *Washington Post* (August 6, 1992), p. C1.

82. *A Children's Defense Budget* (Washington, DC: Children's Defense Fund, 1988), p. 179.

83. Anthony Maluccio and Edith Fein, "Permanency Planning: A Redefinition," *Child Welfare* (May–June 1983), p. 197.

84. Duncan Lindsey, "Achievements for Children in Foster Care," *Social Work* (November 1982), p. 495.

85. House Ways and Means Committee, *Overview of Entitlement Programs*, 2004, pp. 11-86–11-87.

86. Peg Hess, Gail Folaron, and Ann Jefferson, "Effectiveness of Family Reunification Services," *Social Work* 37 (July 1992), pp. 306, 310.

87. Stein, "Foster Care for Children," p. 641.

88. "Foster Care Duty vs. Legal Vulnerability," *NASW News* (July 1988), p. 3.

89. House Ways and Means Committee, *Overview of Entitlement Programs, 2004*, p. 11–111.

90. Ronald Rooney, "Permanency Planning for All Children?" *Social Work* (March 1982), p. 157.

91. Children's Defense Fund, *A Children's Defense Budget*, p. 54.

92. U.S. House of Representatives, *1992 Green Book* (Washington, DC: U.S. Government Printing Office, 1992), p. 830.

93. House Ways and Means Committee, *Overview of Entitlement Programs*, 2004, p. 10-2.

94. Stein, "Foster Care for Children," p. 649.

95. Title XX amounts are not included in the table because the federal government does not collect data on how much is expended by states for child welfare.

96. Esther Wattenberg, "The Fate of Baby Boomers and Their Children," *Social Work* (January–February 1986), pp. 85–93.

97. "Americans Must Work Harder to Achieve the American Dream" (Washington, DC: New America Foundation, 2004), p. 2.

98. Kantrowitz et al., "How to Protect Abused Children," p. 71.

99. Mary Jordan, "Foster Parent Scarcity Causing Crisis in Care," *Washington Post* (July 20, 1986), p. A9.

100. Dale Russakoff, "One Child's Chaotic Bounce in Mother Government's Lap," *Washington Post* (January 18, 1998); and "Against the Odds, a Failed Mother Returns to Her Children," *Washington Post* (January 20, 1998), p. A1.

101. Steve Vogel, "Md. Custody Debate: Did Law Force Judge to Return Child to Killer?" *Washington Post* (January 1, 1998), p. B1; and Manuel Perez-Rias, "Pixley Denied Custody of Son," *Washington Post* (January 12, 2000), p. A1.

102. David Finkel, "'Now Say Goodbye to Diane,'" *Washington Post Magazine* (May 4, 1997), pp. 10–11.

103. Sam Verhovek, "Homosexual Foster Parent Sets Off a Debate in Texas," *New York Times* (November 30, 1997), p. 20.

104. David Hammer, "Arkansas Foster Child Law Stricken," *Washington Post* (December 30, 2004), p. A5.

105. Charles Lane, "Gay-Adoption Ban in Florida to Stand," *Washington Post* (January 11, 2005), p. A4.

106. Colbert King, "What Every Child Needs," *Washington Post* (March 11, 2000), p. A19.

107. House Ways and Means Committee, *Overview of Entitlement Programs*, 2004, pp. 11-50–11-51.

108. Peter Pecora, "Improving Family Foster Care: Findings from the Northwest Foster Care Alumni Study" (Seattle: Annie E. Casey Foundation, 2005).

109. House Ways and Means Committee, *Overview of Entitlement Programs*, 2004, p. 11–48.

110. Barbara Rosen, "SEED Accounts for Foster Youth" (Washington, DC: Corporation for Enterprise Development, 2007).

111. Elizabeth Cole, "Adoption," *Encyclopedia of Social Work*, 18th ed. (Silver Spring, MD: NASW, 1987), p. 70.

112. House Ways and Means Committee, *Overview of Entitlement Programs, 1985* (Washington, DC: U.S. Government Printing Office, 1985), p. 494.

113. House Ways and Means Committee, *Overview of Entitlement Programs*, 2004, p. 11–124.

114. Cole, "Adoption," p. 71.

115. Ronald Fischler, "Protecting American Indian Children," *Social Work* (September 1980), p. 341.

116. Evelyn Lance Blanchard and Russell Lawrence Barsh, "What Is Best for Tribal Children?" *Social Work* (September 1980), p. 350.

117. Fischler, "Protecting American Indian Children," p. 341.

118. Spencer Rich, "Wage Bill Includes Provisions Intended to Increase Adoptions," *Washington Post* (August 10, 1996), p. A4.

119. Patricia Hogan and Sau-Fong Siu, "Minority Children and the Child Welfare System," *Social Work* (November–December 1988), pp. 312–317.

120. Cole, "Adoption," p. 70.

121. Wattenberg, "The Fate of Baby Boomers and Their Children," p. 24.

122. Children's Defense Fund, *The State of America's Children,* 1991 (Washington, DC: Children's Defense Fund, 1991), p. 44.

123. Paul Leonard and Robert Greenstein, *One Step Forward: The Deficit Reduction Package of 1990* (Washington, DC: Center on Budget and Policy Priorities, 1990), p. 34.

124. Sylvia Ann Hewlett, *When the Bough Breaks* (New York: HarperCollins, 1992), p. 300.

125. Elizabeth Hoffmann and Danielle Ewen, "Supporting Families, Nurturing Young Children: Early Head Start Programs in 2006" (Washington, DC: Center on Law and Social Policy, 2007), pp. 2–3, 10.

126. House Ways and Means Committee, *Overview of Entitlement Programs,* 2004, p. 15–25.

127. Valerie Strauss and Amy Goldstein, "Head Start Changeover Proposed," *Washington Post* (February 1, 2003), p. A1.

128. Jay Matthews, "Early Head Start Offers an Edge," *Washington Post* (June 4, 2002), p. A9.

129. "Two-Income Families Now a Majority," *Richmond Times-Dispatch* (October 24, 2000), p. A3.

130. House Ways and Means Committee, *Overview of Entitlement Programs,* 2004, p. 9-2.

131. Ibid., pp. 9-8–9-9.

132. Ibid., p. 9–16.

133. Children's Defense Fund, *The State of America's Children,* 1988 (Washington, DC: Children's Defense Fund, 1988), p. 207.

134. House Ways and Means Committee, *Overview of Entitlement Programs,* 2004, pp. 9-18, 9-20.

135. Ibid., p. 214.

136. Ibid., p. 32; also National Association of Social Workers, *1986 Voting Record* (Silver Spring, MD: NASW, 1987).

137. House Ways and Means Committee, *Overview of Entitlement Programs,* 2004, p. 9–10.

138. Ibid., p. 13–5.

139. Ibid., p. 9–28.

140. Hannah Matthews, "Child Care and Development Block Grant Participation in 2006" (Washington, DC: Center for Law and Social Policy, 2007), p. 1.

141. House Ways and Means Committee, *Overview of Entitlement Programs, 2004*, p. 10-9.

142. Physician Task Force on Hunger in America, *Hunger in America* (Cambridge, MA: Harvard University Press, 1985), p. 65.

143. *Kids Count*, pp. 33, 34.

144. Miringoff and Miringoff, *The Social Health of the Nation*, p. 52.

145. Ibid., p. 84.

146. Mary Otto, "Hearing on Boy's Death Shows Little Dental Care for the Poor," *Washington Post* (May 3, 2007), p. B6.

147. Robert Pear, "Lacking Papers, Citizens Are Cut from Medicaid," *New York Times* (March 12, 2007), p. A1.

148. Christopher Lee, "Number of Uninsured Children Rises," *Washington Post* (September 5, 2006), p. A6.

149. Michael Novak (ed.), *The New Consensus on Family and Welfare* (Washington, DC: American Enterprise Institute, 1987), p. 135.

150. House Ways and Means Committee, *Overview of Entitlement Programs,* 2004, p. M-3.

151. U.S. House of Representatives, *1998 Green Book,* p. 1245.

152. Lisbeth Schorr, *Within Our Reach* (Garden City, NY: Doubleday, 1988), p. 13.

153. William Julius Wilson, "American Social Policy and the Ghetto Underclass," Dissent (Winter 1988), pp. 80–91.

154. David Ellwood, *Poor Support: Poverty and the American Family* (New York: Basic Books, 1988), p. 58.

155. House Ways and Means Committee, *Overview of Entitlement Programs,* 2004, p. M-10.

156. "Preventing Teenage Pregnancy" (Washington, DC: U.S. Department of Health and Human Services, August 8, 2000).

157. Laura Stepp, "Study Casts Doubt on Abstinence-Only Programs," *Washington Post* (April 14, 2007), p. A2.

158. Ceci Connolly, "As Teen Pregnancy Dropped, So Did Child Poverty," *Washington Post* (April 14, 2005), p. A10.

159. Irwin Garfinkel, "Bringing Fathers Back In: The Child Support Assurance Strategy," *The American Prospect* (Spring 1992), p. 75.

160. Mickey Kaus, *The End of Equality* (New York: Basic Books, 1992).

161. Michael Kirst, "Improving Children's Services," *Phi Delta Kappan* (April 1991), p. 616.

162. Sid Gardner, "Failure by Fragmentation," *California Tomorrow* (Fall 1989), p. 19.

163. Bonnie Benard, "School Restructuring Can Promote Prevention," *Western Center News* (December 1991), p. 8.

164. Paul Tough, "The Harlem Project," *New York Times Magazine* (June 20, 2004), p. 66.

165. Costin, Karger, and Stoesz, *The Politics of Child Abuse in America.*

166. Youth Futures Authority, "Children's Profile." Retrieved October 2004, from www.youthfuturesauthority.org

167. Deanna Gomby, "Home Visitation in 2005: Outcomes for Children and Parents" (Washington, DC: Committee for Economic Development, 2005).

168. Leslie Kaufman, "Foster Children at Risk, and an Opportunity Lost," *New York Times* (November 5, 2007), p. A20.

169. Benjamin Weiser, "City Is Slow to Limit Damage as a Hope for Children Fails," *New York Times* (November 6, 2007), p. A26.

170. Leslie Kaufman and Benjamin Weiser, "In Foster Care Reckoning, Vows and Help and Vigilance," *New York Times* (November 7, 2007), p. A22.

171. Daniel Pollack and James Marsh, "Social Work Misconduct May Lead to Liability," *Social Work* 9, 4 (October 2004), p. 611.

172. Ibid., p. 611.

173. Sue Montes, "Fenty Describes Missteps Before Girls Died," *Washington Post* (January 12, 2008), p. A1.

174. "A Deadly Failure," *Washington Post* (January 12, 2008), p. A16.

CHAPTER 16

Housing Policies

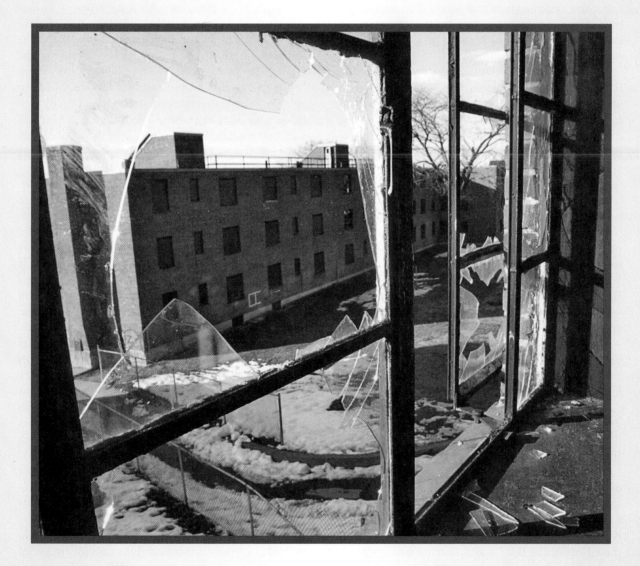

A house represents more than a mere address of domicile in America: It is the primary asset accumulated by most American families. Acquiring a house results in more stability—renters are 2.7 times more likely to relocate in a given year than are home owners.[1] The stability encouraged by home ownership may be a necessary prerequisite to the development of neighborhood identity, involvement in local social networks, and the investment in local institutions and organizations that strengthen social support. Among other things, this chapter discusses the large number of federal housing programs directed toward home ownership.

Most of the recent attention on housing has focused on the middle class. Yet, housing problems affect millions of Americans. Persistent problems include a lack of low-income affordable housing, dilapidated and dangerous housing, and high numbers of homeless people. Although housing discussions have frequently focused on homelessness, finding and maintaining adequate and affordable housing is also problematic for people on public assistance, for the working poor, and for a large section of the middle class. This chapter examines housing problems in the United States, with particular emphasis on low-income housing, affordability, homelessness, and proposals for housing reform. But before discussing these issues, it is important to examine perhaps the worst housing disaster in modern U.S. history, Hurricane Katrina.

New Orleans and Katrina

Hurricane Katrina made landfall in Louisiana on August 29, 2005. It was the costliest and one of the five deadliest hurricanes in the history of the United States,[2] the sixth-strongest Atlantic hurricane ever recorded, and the third-strongest hurricane on record that made landfall in the United States.[3] The extent of the devastation wrought by Katrina is mind-boggling. At least 1,836 people lost their lives in the floods, and Katrina was responsible for $81.2 billion in damage, making it the costliest natural disaster in U.S. history. In New Orleans, over 80 percent of the city had flooded and nearly 275,000 Gulf Coast residents were housed in group shelters.[4] Major or severe damage was reported for 123,000 homes and 82,000 rental units; 18,000 businesses had been destroyed.[5] One year after the storm, the Federal Emergency Management Agency (FEMA) reported distributing $6 billion for temporary housing (through the Individuals and Household Assistance Program) to more than 650,000 households.[6] By 2006, the population of the New Orleans Parish had fallen more than half to only 223,000.[7]

The Road Home Program developed by the Louisiana Recovery Authority and the state's Office of Community Development is an attempt to distribute $7.5 billion (up to $150,000 per eligible home owner) in funds provided by the U.S. Department of Housing and Urban Development (HUD) to compensate home owners for their losses.[8] Eligibility requirements are modest, but the substantial documentation needed is difficult for those who fled the storm without their records. Not surprisingly, the Road Home Program procedures have undergone criticism by HUD and the National Mortgage Bankers Association (NMBA). HUD determined that the Road Home is a rebuilding program, not a compensation program, and that distribution of funds should follow rebuilding efforts. Mortgage companies tend to agree. Because 80 percent of the damaged homes had an unpaid mortgage, NMBA suggests that property abandonment may escalate if rebuilding is not required.[9]

New Orleans Mayor Ray Nagin has been vocal in denouncing what he perceives to be racism in the New Orleans rebuilding effort. Pre-Katrina New Orleans was 67 percent African American but is now only 47 percent African American. Nagin claims that more than 12,000 people are eligible for compensation from the Road Home Program, but only 3,000 received checks. He attributes racism to the slow progress in reopening public housing and the closure of Charity Hospital, the primary health care provider for the poor in New Orleans.[10]

The story of the depopulation of the Gulf Coast is still being written. The impact on housing availability and price has ramifications as far away as Houston, Texas, and Atlanta, Georgia. Backed by FEMA vouchers, evacuees have increased rental occupancy rates and stretched the capacity of social service delivery systems. The reaction of some communities has been heroic; the reputations of others have not fared as well. It is too soon to tell if the final chapter in this story will point to a vibrant and stronger Gulf Coast, but if it does, it will be because of massive federal resources directed toward rebuilding homes.

Overview of Housing Legislation

Federal housing legislation began in 1937. As illustrated in Figure 16.1, this legislation developed into a tangle of laws that often evolved in conflicting directions.

In 1990 Congress passed the Cranston-Gonzales National Affordable Housing Act, which authorized housing-related block grants to state and local governments. The goals of the 1990 legislation included (1) decentralizing housing policy by allowing states to design and administer their own housing programs; (2) using nonprofit sponsors to help develop and implement housing services; (3) linking housing

The Housing Act of 1937	The United States had no national housing policy prior to the Housing Act of 1937. The objective of the act was to: "provide financial assistance to the states and political subdivisions thereof for the elimination of unsafe and unsanitary housing conditions, for the eradication of slums, for the provision of decent, safe, and sanitary dwellings for families of low income, and for the reduction of unemployment and the stimulation of business activity, to create a United States Housing Authority and for other purposes."
The Housing Act of 1949 (Amended 1937 Act)	This amendment called for federal money for slum clearance and urban redevelopment and for the creation of a public authority charged with building and administering low-income housing units. Specifically, this bill required each locality to develop a plan for urban redevelopment that contained provisions for "predominantly residential dwellings." The wording of this bill was interpreted by localities to mean that only one-half of new construction was to be devoted to low-income housing.
Housing Act of 1954 (Amended the 1949 Act)	"Urban development" was changed to urban renewal, and localities were required to submit a master plan for removing urban blight and for community development. The act removed the requirement that new federally subsidized urban construction be "predominantly residential," clearing the way for massive slum clearance projects. It also allowed localities to more easily lease or sell land and to avoid the construction of public housing. Through renewal projects, localities tried to revitalize inner cities by attracting middle- and upper-income families at the expense of displaced poor families. From 1949 to 1963, urban renewal projects removed about 243,000 housing units and replaced them with 68,000 units, of which only 20,000 were for low-income families.
The Demonstration Cities and Metropolitan Development Act (Model Cities)	Passed in 1966 as part of President Lyndon Johnson's War on Poverty, the Act focused on deteriorated housing and blighted neighborhoods. The Model Cities legislation promised to "concentrate public and private resources in a comprehensive five-year attack on social, economic, and physical problems of slums and blighted neighborhoods." The Model Cities Act and virtually all neighborhood development acts were superseded by the Housing and Community Development Act of 1974.

Figure 16.1

Historical Highlights of Pre-1990 Housing Legislation

Source: Quoted in Charles S. Prigmore and Charles R. Atherton, *Social Welfare Policy: Analysis and Formulation* (Lexington, MA: D. C. Heath, 1979), pp. 146–147; Robert Morris, *Social Policy of the American Welfare State,* 2nd edition. (New York: Longman, 1985), p. 131; Barbara Habenstreit, *The Making of America* (New York: Julian Messner, 1971), p. 46; Richard Geruson and Dennis McGrath, *Cities and Urbanization* (New York: Praeger, 1977), pp. 6–7; and National Training and Information Center, *Insurance Redlining: Profits v. Policyholders* (Chicago: NTIC, 1973), p. 1.

The Housing and Community Development Act of 1974	This wide-ranging bill included provisions for urban renewal, neighborhood development, model cities, water and sewer projects, neighborhood and facility grants, public facilities and rehabilitation loans, and urban beautification and historic preservation. Although spending priorities were determined at the national level, communities were required to submit a master plan, including specific reference to their low-income housing needs.
Home Mortgage Disclosure Act (HMDA)	This Act focused on mortgage redlining. Advocates argued that a major cause of community deterioration was a "lending strike," or redlining, by financial institutions. Redlining is defined as "an outright refusal of an insurance company, bank, or other financial institution to provide its services solely on the basis of the location of a property." The term is derived from the practice of marking in red the area on a map avoided by insurance or financial institutions. As a result, families seeking to purchase a home in a redlined neighborhood may be denied a mortgage, insurance, or other necessary services. In 1976, President Gerald Ford signed the Home Mortgage Disclosure Act, which required virtually every bank or savings and loan association to annually disclose where it made its loans.
Community Reinvestment Act (CRA) of 1977	Broader than the HMDA, the CRA established the principle that each bank and savings institution has an obligation to make loans in every neighborhood of its service area. Virtually all lending institutions are covered under the CRA, and the law requires the federal government to annually evaluate the performance of each lending institution. Primary enforcement involves control by federal regulatory agencies over new charters, bank growth and mergers, relocations, and acquisitions. Only a handful of the CRA challenges result in punitive action against lenders. The power of the Act rests with the ability of community groups to win concessions from lending institutions, usually in the form of negotiated settlements.

Figure 16.1

(continued)

assistance more closely with social services; (4) facilitating home ownership for low- and moderate-income people; (5) preserving existing federally subsidized housing units; and (6) initiating cost sharing among federal, state, and local governments and nonprofit organizations.[11] This Act also introduced the HOME investment partnerships block grant program, the Home ownership and Opportunity for People Everywhere (HOPE) program, and the national home ownership trust demonstration.

The centerpiece of the National Affordable Housing Act was the HOME program, designed to increase the supply of affordable housing for low-income families by providing federal grants to state and local governments. All states and more than 300 local jurisdictions receive HOME funds and 90 percent of HOME-assisted units in a jurisdiction must be affordable for families with incomes below 60 percent of the area median. The remaining units

must be affordable for families with incomes up to 80 percent of the median.[12]

The second component, the HOPE program, is designed to facilitate home ownership by low-income families through the sale of publicly owned or held homes to current residents or other low-income households. The HOPE program has four components: (1) HOPE I finances the sales of public housing apartments to residents; (2) HOPE II finances the sales to low-income persons of other apartment buildings held by the federal government; (3) HOPE III finances the sale of single-family homes owned by federal, state, or local governments; and (4) HOPE IV represents an effort to combine social services with housing assistance for households of the elderly and disabled who would otherwise be unable to live independently.[13]

The linkage between housing and social services was strengthened by the Family Sufficiency program that called for public housing authorities (PHAs) to help residents obtain coordinated social services to assist them in gaining employment. Participating families must complete these programs or risk losing their housing assistance. In return, as a participant's income increased, the money that would normally go toward a higher rent (calculated at 30 percent of income) was set aside in a special escrow account to be used for the purchase of a home. The legislation also included modest funds to create "Family Investment Centers" that provided social services in or near public housing projects.[14]

In 1998 former President Clinton signed the Quality Housing and Work Responsibility Act of 1998 (QHWRA), in some ways the housing equivalent of the 1996 PRWORA. In line with the PRWORA, the federal government devolved its responsibility as the primary agent for publicly assisted housing to 3,400 semiautonomous local PHAs. With input from public housing residents, these strengthened PHAs determine rents, admissions policies, and what (if any) social services are provided. The QHWRA also ties workforce participation into housing benefits. For example, (1) PHAs can consider prospective tenants' employment history in the admissions decision; (2) TANF recipients who fail to fulfill their work requirement can lose Section 8 or public housing benefits; and (3) PHAs are encouraged to recruit "good" working-class families to act as role models for welfare-dependent families (the legislation decreases the percentage of public housing units earmarked for very low-income families from 75 to 70 percent). The QHWRA also mandates that low-income tenants take personal responsibility for moving into better living conditions (e.g., a single-family home).[15]

The Federal Government and Low-Income Housing Programs

Housing is a fixed cost that is often paid before food, clothing, and health care bills.[16] For poor families, the precious little that remains after rent or mortgage payments is used to buy food and other necessities for the rest of the month. The important impact of housing costs on family finances has fueled the federal government's involvement with low- and non–low-income housing programs. By 2003 the HUD budget was $38 billion. Table 16.1 provides an overview of key HUD programs relating to the housing problems of low-income households.

Apart from HUD-administered programs, there is also the Low Income Housing Tax Credits (LIHTC). Created by the Tax Reform Act of 1986, the LIHTC was a way for the federal government to encourage the development of affordable housing without having to allocate direct federal expenditures. Apartments supported by the LIHTC cannot be rented to anyone whose income exceeds 60 percent of the area median income. Each year, the LIHTC leverages about $6 billion of private investment and produces more than 125,000 affordable apartments for working families, seniors, homeless people, and those with special needs. Overall, the LIHTC has assisted in the production of 1.6 million apartments with affordable rents for low-income families. This has been accomplished by providing investors in eligible affordable housing developments with a dollar-for-dollar reduction in their federal tax liability. The LIHTC now accounts for most new affordable apartment production and drives up to 40 percent of all multifamily apartment development.[17]

Despite its importance, governmental assistance for housing was never provided as an entitlement to all households that qualify for aid. Unlike income maintenance programs such as Supplemental Security Income (SSI) and the former Aid to Families with Dependent Children (AFDC), housing programs are not automatically provided to all eligible applicants. Congress appropriates funds yearly for various new commitments, most of which run from 5 to 50 years. Because funding levels are usually low, only a portion of eligible applicants actually receive assistance. According to NLIHC's *Losing Ground*, nationally there are only 43 units both affordable and available to every 100 renter households with incomes less than 30 percent of the area median income. According to HUD, more than 5 million very low income renter households pay more than 50 percent of their incomes toward rent or live in severely substandard housing. Recent NLIHC research shows that waiting lists for public housing and rental assistance vouchers far surpass anticipated availability of affordable units[18] (see Figure 16.2 on page 420).

Relatively low levels of funding have been earmarked for housing programs. The cumulative shortfall to PHAs in operating subsidies between 1993 and 2003 was more than $1.9 billion, and the cumulative shortfall in capital improvement funding was more than $20.3 billion.[19] This low funding level has also resulted in long waiting lists for public housing and Section 8 vouchers. The Council of Large Public Housing estimated that waiting lists for public housing nationwide in 2000 included 2.35

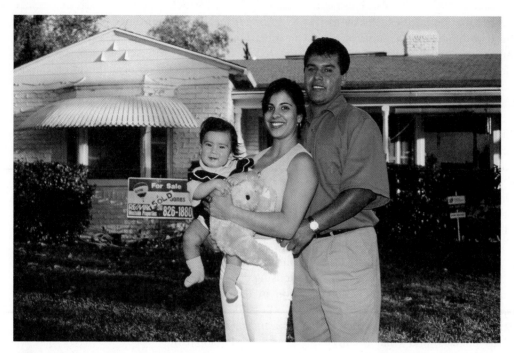

■ *For many families, the cost of housing represents the single largest expenditure in the household budget.*

Table 16.1

Overview of HUD's Major Grant, Subsidy, and Loan Programs

The Housing Choice Voucher Program (Section 8 Rental Assistance) is HUDs largest program. The Section 8 program is based on a voucher system that allows low-income tenants (50 percent or less of the area median income) to occupy existing and privately owned housing stock. The voucher covers the difference between a fixed percentage of a tenant's income (30 percent) and the fair market rent of a housing unit. The HUD subsidy goes to the local PHA, which then pays the landlord, provided that the unit meets quality standards. Contract terms for subsidies last for from five to fifteen years. About half of Section 8 is project-based, meaning that tenants have to live in specific apartments. The other half is tenant-based, allowing tenants to take their subsidies and move. Section 8 also provides funds for new construction and for substantial and moderate rehabilitation of existing units. Only a minority of eligible applicants are served and most are on a waiting list when they apply. In 2007 about 2 million low-income families received HUD vouchers. For fiscal year 2007, the Congress provided almost $16 billion for rent subsidies.

Community Development Block Grants (CDBG) were funded at about $4 billion in 2007. CDBGs are provided to units of local government and states for the funding of local community development programs that address housing and economic development needs, primarily for low- and -moderate-income persons.

Public and Indian Housing (PIH) Grants and Loans were funded at about $3.6 billion in 2006. Public Housing Operating Subsidies (totaling another $3.2 billion in 2006) are financial assistance provided for project operations to approximately 3,160 housing authorities managing approximately 1.2 million units. Public Housing was established by the U.S. Housing Act of 1937 and is restricted to households whose incomes are too low to find suitable private housing. The income of most families in public housing is less than 25 percent of the area median income and about one-half rely primarily on public assistance (TANF, SSI, and General Assistance) for their income; the other half rely on earned incomes, pensions, or Social Security. Residents pay 30 percent of their monthly adjusted income on rent. Public housing is concentrated in high poverty areas.

Affordable Housing Programs (HOME Investment Partnerships) were funded at $1.9 billion in 2007.

Table 16.1

(continued)

From 1992 to 2007, more than 600 communities have completed more than 834,000 affordable housing units, including 352,000 for new home-buyers. In addition, 186,000 tenants have received direct rental assistance. HOME Investment Partnership Grants provide assistance to renters, existing home owners, and first-time homebuyers, build state and local capacity to carry out afford-able housing programs, and expand the capacity of nonprofit community housing organizations to develop and manage housing. The Housing Opportunities for Persons with AIDS provides affordable housing and related assistance to persons with HIV/AIDS. The Homeless Programs consists primarily of grants to public and private entities to establish comprehensive systems for meeting the needs of homeless people.

Section 202/811 Capital Grants were funded at less than 1 billion in 2007. The program is designed to provide funds for the construction and long-term support of housing for the elderly and persons with disabilities. Advances are interest-free and do not have to be repaid providing the housing remains available for low-income persons for at least 40 years.

Native American Housing Block Grants and Home Loan Guarantees assist Native Americans in building or purchasing homes on Trust Land; obtaining affordable housing; implementing local housing strategies to promote home ownership; and developing communities.

Fair Housing Assistance Program (FHAP) provides grants to state and local agencies that administer fair housing laws that are equivalent to the Federal Fair Housing Act.

Fair Housing Initiatives Program (FHIP) provides funds competitively to private and public entities to carry out local, regional and national programs that assist in eliminating discriminatory housing practices and educate the public and housing providers on their fair housing rights and responsibilities.

Government National Mortgage Association (Ginnie Mae). Through its mortgage-backed securities program, Ginnie Mae facilitates the financing of residential mortgage loans by guaranteeing the timely payment of principal and interest to investors of privately issued securities backed by pools of mortgages insured or guaranteed by FHA, the Department of Veterans Affairs, and the Rural Housing Service.

The Ginnie Mae guarantee gives lenders access to the capital market to originate new loans.

Brownfields Redevelopment provides competitive economic development grants for qualified Brownfields (i.e., the cleanup and economic redevelopment of contaminated sites) projects.

Revitalization of Severely Distressed Public Housing (HOPE IV) makes awards to public housing authorities on a competitive basis to demolish obsolete or failed developments or to revitalize, where appropriate, sites upon which these developments exist.

Housing Opportunities for Persons With AIDS (HOPWA) is designed to provide states and localities with resources and incentives to devise long-term comprehensive strategies for meeting the housing needs of persons living with HIV/AIDS and their families.

The Office of Rural Housing and Economic Development (FmHA Section 502) was established to ensure that HUD has a comprehensive approach to rural housing and rural economic development issues. The office funds technical assistance and capacity-building in rural, underserved areas, and provides grants for Indian tribes, state housing finance agencies, and state economic development agencies to pursue strategies designed to meet rural housing and economic development needs. Section 502 makes low-interest loans available for home purchases in rural areas.

Homeless Assistance Grants provides funding to break the cycle of homelessness and to move homeless persons and families into permanent housing. This is done by providing rental assistance, emergency shelter, transitional and permanent housing, and supportive services to homeless persons and families.

Empowerment Zones/Enterprise Communities (EZ/EC) is designed to create self-sustaining, long-term development in distressed urban and rural areas. The program uses a combination of federal tax incentives and flexible grant funds to reinvigorate declining communities.

Office of Lead Hazard Control is authorized to make grants to states, localities, and Native American tribes to conduct lead-based paint hazard reduction and abatement activities in private low-income housing.

Source: Various documents downloaded from U.S. Department of Housing and Urban Development, www.hud.gov.

Section 8

• Section 8 Housing Choice Voucher Program served around 4.7 million seniors, people with disabilities, and low-income families with children.

• More than 324,000 seniors relied on Housing Choice Vouchers for affordable housing, representing 16 percent of all Section 8 households. Twenty-three percent of Section 8 seniors were 80 years or older. The median annual income for an elderly household in Section 8 was $8,550 and 90 percent relied on Social Security or Supplemental Security payments as their primary source of income.

• Section 8 recipients included almost 400,000 households in which one or more members had a disability, representing 22 percent of all voucher households. Almost 40,000 Section 8 households had a child with a disability.

• Sixty-one percent of all Section 8 households were families with children. More than 2.4 million children lived in Section 8, representing over 50 percent of all residents. Almost 50 percent of households with children obtained their primary income from wages, with the average income being $11,390.

Public Housing

• Public housing was home to almost 3 million seniors, people with disabilities, and low-income families with children. The average household size was 2.3 people.

• Thirty-one percent of public housing residents were seniors; more than 400,000 seniors relied on public housing and supportive services; 27 percent of public housing's seniors were 80 years of age or older. The median annual income for an elderly household in public housing was $8,250 and 72 percent of seniors relied on Social Security payments as their primary source of income.

• Thirty-two percent of all public housing residents (400,000 households) were disabled. Almost 18,000 public housing households had a child with a disability.

• About 1.2 million children lived in public housing, representing 43 percent of all public housing residents.

• The mean income for a public housing household was $9,531, which on average was about 24 percent of the median income for their area. Close to 43 percent of nonelderly households obtained their primary source of income from wages.

Figure 16.2

Characteristics of Section 8 Recipients and Residents in Public Housing, 2004

Source: Council of Large Public Housing Authorities, *Quick Facts on Public Housing* (Washington, DC: Author, 2004).

million households, many of whom waited two or more years before getting a unit.[20]

The United States spends less on housing assistance than any other Western industrial nation. Not only does the United States fail to adequately assist poor people with housing, but most housing subsidies benefit the nonpoor. For example, individuals can deduct interest on up to $1 million in mortgage indebtedness, plus interest on another $100,000 in home equity loans. In 2005 the deduction depleted an estimated $72.6 billion from the U.S. Treasury. The home mortgage deduction is the third-largest single "tax expenditure" behind the deductions companies take for contributions to pension plans and health care premiums.[21]

The home mortgage interest deduction accounts for a big chunk of cash in terms of federal housing policies. In 2005 the federal government provided $200 billion in subsidies for housing,

including $150 billion in tax breaks. At $70 billion the mortgage-interest deduction alone was one of the biggest government housing programs. The richer the home owner is, the better the deal. For every $1,000 in deductions, a family in the 35 percent tax bracket sees its taxes go down by $350, while a family in the 15-percent bracket sees its taxes go down by only $150. And families taking the standard deduction get no tax break. Hence, more than 80 percent of the major tax incentives for housing go to the top 20 percent of Americans while less than 5 percent go to the bottom 60 percent.[22] Nearly half of all families with mortgages receive no housing tax benefit. Last, because the mortgage cutoff of $1 million is much higher than the cost of a basic home, the bulk of the subsidies end up encouraging families who would have bought a home anyway to buy a larger house or to borrow more against it.[23]

Spotlight 16.1

The Department of Housing and Urban Development

Established in 1965, the Department of Housing and Urban Development (HUD) offers various programs to increase home ownership, support community development, and increase access to affordable housing free from discrimination. To learn more about HUD and its many programs, visit its website at **www.hud.gov.**

Issues in Housing Policy

The equity in home ownership is the cornerstone of wealth for most U.S. families. According to the Joint Center for Housing Studies of Harvard University, two-thirds of Americans list their home as their single biggest asset. In 2006 home equity hit a record high of $10.9 trillion while mortgage debt rose to $9.7 trillion.[24] Concurrently, the average home owners' equity—the mortgage balance as a proportion of the home's market value—fell to 48 percent at the end of 2007. The Federal Reserve reported for the first time since their record keeping began in 1945, home equity was below 50 percent for 2007. By early 2008 about 8.8 million home owners or 10 percent of homes will have mortgage balances that equal or exceed the value of their property.[25]

Trends in U.S. Housing

The following are some highlights of the often contradictory U.S. housing trends:

• Home ownership rates remained relatively stable since the early 1980s, inching upward to a high of 69.2 percent in 2005 and then dropping slightly to 67.7 in 2007.[26] Home sales and the value of residential construction reached new highs in 2003[27] but declined significantly beginning in 2006. By early 2008 homes had lost more than 11 percent of their value.

• When broken down, the differences in home ownership between races is stark. The home ownership gap between African American and white households was larger in 2006 than in 1990. In 2005 the white home ownership rate was 75.8 percent compared to less than 50 percent for African American and Hispanic households. Households with very low incomes had a home ownership rate that was 37 percentage points below the rate for high-income households. These gaps have changed little over the past 50 years.[28] Although persistent disparities between whites and minorities narrowed only slightly, minorities still accounted for nearly 40 percent of the net growth in owners between 1994 and 2003.[29] Unfortunately, much of that ownership occurred by way of subprime mortgages.

• From 2000 to 2006 the biggest population growth nationwide occurred in urban hubs (especially metropolitan suburbs) in the South and the West—now home to 7 of the 10 highest populated cities. With a population of 1.5 million, Phoenix officially edged out Philadelphia to become the nation's fifth most populous city, after New York, Los Angeles, Chicago, and Houston. Conversely, Detroit, Cleveland, Pittsburgh, Buffalo, Rochester, and other cities in the Rust Belt and upstate New York recorded population losses of more than 5 percent since 2000. Some of these older cities recorded smaller losses since 2005, suggesting that their population declines may have slowed. The gains in the West and the South demonstrate the nation's population shift. Only 3 of the 10 most populous cities in 1910—New York, Chicago, and Philadelphia—remain on the latest list of the top 10. Three of the 2007 top 10—Phoenix; San Jose, California; and San Diego, California—were not even among the 100 most populous in 1910.[30]

• In 2005 the number of such severely cost-burdened households jumped by 1.2 million to a total of 17 million. This brings the increase since 2001 to 3.2 million households. By 2007, one in seven U.S. households was severely housing cost burdened.

Federal assistance to very low-income households reaches only about one-quarter of eligible renters and virtually no home owners.[31]

• Houses are larger today than in the past. The size of newly constructed single-family homes rose from a median of 1,535 square feet in 1975 to 2,263 square feet in 2006, a 47 percent increase.[32]

• In 1940 almost half of all housing units lacked complete plumbing facilities. The percentage of households without complete plumbing dropped from 36 percent in 1950 to 17 percent in 1960. In 1940 three-fourths of households used either coal/coke or wood to heat their homes. By 1990 fewer than 1 percent of households heated their homes with coal/coke, and only about 4 percent with wood. More than three-fourths of households now rely on either utility-based gas or electricity to heat their homes.[33]

Problems in Home Ownership

Beginning in the 1970s, many people were forced to spend a higher percentage of their income on housing than they could reasonably afford. Some of these people became so financially overextended that they were vulnerable to mortgage default or eviction—or lacked the necessary cash to purchase other necessities.

Between 1967 and 2004, the median income for first-time home buyers rose from $28,011 to $54,500, and the median home price went from $56,466 to $168,500. In 1967 the average annual mortgage payment was $3,400; by 2004 it had risen to roughly $12,000.[34] The price increase of single-family homes is even sharper when not adjusted for inflation. In 1970 the average new single-family home was $26,600; in 2007 it cost $299,700 (see Table 16.2). The median price of housing also varies widely by city and region. For example, from 1985 to 2007 the median price for an existing single-family home in Los Angeles County went from $119,000 to $528,000, dropping down to $460,000 in early 2008.[35]

As a result of these and other factors, the home ownership rate for families in the bottom two-fifths of the income scale was only 42.4 percent in 2005, which was three percentage points less than it was 25 years earlier and 26 percentage points below the national average.[36] More than half of these households are headed by females or include at least one elderly member. In addition, nearly one-quarter are headed by minorities. Nearly 60 percent of very low-income home owners pay more than 30 percent of their incomes for housing; 10 percent pay more than 50 percent.[37]

Table 16.2

Average U.S. Housing Prices, Mortgage Rates, and Median Family Income in Non-Inflation Adjusted Dollars, Selected Years

Period	New SF Homes*	Existing SF Homes	Mortgage Rates	Median Income	Cost of Existing SF Home as proportion of income
1970	$26,600	$25,700	8.35%	$9,867	2.5
1975	42,600	39,000	9.21	13,719	2.9
1980	76,400	72,800	12.95	21,023	3.5
1985	100,800	86,000	11.74	27,735	3.1
1990	149,800	118,600	10.04	35,353	3.4
1995	158,700	139,000	7.85	39,558	3.5
2000	201,100	179,400	8.02	40,816	4.4
2004	263,100	186,500	5.83	43,318	4.3
2007	299,700	255,300	6.50	48,201	5.3

*SF = Single Family

Source: Based on data from U.S. Department of Housing and Urban Development, *U.S. Housing Market Conditions* (Washington, DC: HUD, Office of Policy Development and Research, 2nd Quarter 2004 and 2007); and *The State of the Nation's Housing: 2007*, retrieved November 2007, from www.jchs.harvard.edu/publications/markets/son2007.pdf.

Home Ownership and the Subprime Mortgage Crisis

Anyone who has given recent headlines a passing glance knows the mortgage industry is in deep trouble. Since 2006 more than 90 subprime lenders have quit or gone bankrupt. Many more are in serious trouble. Even mainstream financial institutions felt the impact as Countrywide, the nation's largest mortgage lender, was sold to Bank of America in 2007 for the "fire sale" price of $4 billion. Only a year earlier Countrywide had been worth $27 billion. The subprime crisis is also hitting Wall Street brokerages that invested in these loans, with reverberations being felt from Tokyo to London to Sydney. The losers and the amounts they lost in 2007 are stunning: Merrill Lynch faced $14 billion in mortgage-related write-offs; Citigroup wrote off $19 billion; UBS 13.5 billion; and Morgan Stanley $9.4 billion. Other banks that lost money include HBSC ($3.4 billion), Deutsche Bank ($3.2 billion), Bank of America ($3 billion), Barclays ($2.6 billion), JP Morgan Chase ($3.2 billion), and the list goes on and on.[38] In March 2008 the Federal Reserve was forced to bail out the investment banking house of Bear Stearns, the first time a bank was bailed out since the Great Depression. Shortly afterward, Bear Stearns was bought by JP Morgan for "fire sale" price.[39]

At least $2 trillion in adjustable rate mortgages came up for reset between 2006 and 2007. A recent study by First American Corporation projects that about one in eight households with adjustable-rate mortgages that originated in 2004 and 2005 will default on their loans. Other sources put that as high as one in five.[40]

It is important to examine the housing crisis not only from the perspective of banks and other financial institutions, but also from the families whose homes are on the line. Why did millions of families sign up for mortgage loans that were likely to end in failure and foreclosure?

Like most Americans, the authors grew up believing that home ownership is an important rite of passage in U.S. society. Most Americans view home ownership as the best choice for everyone, everywhere, and at all times. Common wisdom suggests that the more people who own their homes, the more robust the economy, the stronger the community, and the greater the collective and individual benefits. Home ownership is a ticket to the middle class.

For the most part, this is an accurate picture. Home owners gain a foothold in a housing market that—until recently—had the appearance of an almost infinite price ceiling. Others enjoy important tax benefits. Owning a home is often cheaper than renting. Most important, home ownership builds equity and assets for the next generation by promoting forced savings. According to the National Housing Institute's Winton Picoff and Sheila Crowley, the median wealth of low-income home owners is 12 times higher than that of renters with similar incomes.[41] Less tangibly, home ownership is a status symbol that supposedly distinguishes winners from losers.

Home ownership may also have positive effects on family life. Ohio University's Robert Dietz found that owning a home contributes to household stability, social involvement, environmental awareness, local political participation and activism, good health, and low crime. According to Dietz, home owners are better citizens, are healthier both physically and mentally, and have children who achieve more and are better behaved than those of renters.[42]

Johns Hopkins University researchers Joe Harkness and Sandra Newman looked at whether home ownership benefits kids even in distressed neighborhoods. Their study concluded that "Home ownership in almost any neighborhood is found to benefit children. . . . Children of most low-income renters would be better served by programs that help their families become homeowners in their current neighborhoods instead of helping them move to better neighborhoods while remaining renters."[43] The study was unable to determine whether owning a home leads to positive behaviors or whether owners are already predisposed to those behaviors.[44]

Faith in the benefits of home ownership—along with low interest rates and a plethora of governmental incentives—produced a surge in the number of low-income home owners. In 1994 former President Bill Clinton set, and eventually surpassed, a goal to raise the nation's overall home ownership rate to 67.5 percent by 2000. By the early 2000s there were 71 million U.S. home owners representing close to 68 percent of all households. By 2003, 48 percent of African American households owned their own homes, up from 34.5 percent in 1950. Much of this gain has been among low-income families.[45] In 2008 Americans owed about $13 trillion in mortgages, more than a 50 percent jump in just seven years.[46]

Government efforts to increase home ownership for low-income families include both demand-side (e.g., home owner tax credits, housing cost assistance programs) and supply-side (e.g., developer incentives) strategies. Federal housing programs insure more than a million loans a year to help low-income home buyers. Fannie Mae and Freddie Mac—the large, federally chartered but privately held corporations that buy mortgages from lenders, guarantee the notes, and then resell them to investors—increasingly turned their attention to low-income home buyers as the upper-income housing market became saturated. Banking industry regulations such as the Community Reinvestment Act and the Home Mortgage Disclosure Act encourage home ownership by reducing lending discrimination in underserved markets.

HUD modified some of its renter-based programs to focus on home ownership. For instance, cities and towns can now use the federal dollars they receive through HOME and Community Development Block Grants to provide housing grants, down payment loans, and closing cost assistance. Passed by Congress in 2003, the American Dream Downpayment Initiative authorized up to $200 million yearly for down payment assistance to low-income families. Private foundations followed suit. The Ford Foundation viewed owning a home as an important part of asset-building and the best option for low-income people, thereby focusing its housing grants on that rather than rental housing. While home ownership has undeniable benefits, many low-income families find the burdens can sometimes outweigh the positives.

The Downside of Home Ownership

Low-income families are vulnerable to wide-ranging risks when purchasing a home, including:

- Housing that is often affordable is rundown, with high maintenance costs.
- Neighborhoods that are affordable for low-income home buyers are frequently economically distressed with few jobs, a dearth of services, high crime rates, and poor schools. Houses appreciate slowly (if at all) compared to higher-income neighborhoods.
- Mortgage financing for low-income home buyers frequently includes high interest rates, high fees, and risky financial gimmicks.
- Low-income home buyers often work in unstable and recession-prone jobs. Even slight employment interruptions can mean the difference between keeping and losing a home.

Taken together, these factors make home buying a far riskier proposition for low-income families than for middle- and upper-income households.

Contrary to popular myth, home ownership is not an automatic hedge against rising housing costs. Too often, low-income families pay inflated prices for homes beset with major structural or mechanical problems masked by cosmetic repairs. Affordable homes are frequently old, in need of repair, and expensive to maintain. A study by NeighborWorks found that almost half of low-income home buyers experienced major unexpected costs due to the age and condition of their homes.[47] Unlike renters, homeowners cannot sue themselves because of a leaky roof, bad plumbing, or a dodgy furnace.

Apart from maintenance and repair costs, home ownership expenses also include property taxes and home owners insurance, both of which have skyrocketed in the last decade. Between 1997 and 2002 property tax rates rose nationally by more than 19 percent. Ten states (including giants Texas and California) saw their property tax rates rise by 30 percent or more during that period. In New York City suburbs, property tax rates grew two to three times faster than personal income from 2000 to 2004.[48]

The average home insurance premiums rose nationally by 62 percent from 1995 to 2005. Low-income home owners in distressed neighborhoods are especially hard hit by high insurance costs.[49] According to a Conning Company study, 92 percent of large insurance companies run credit checks on potential customers, which then translates into insurance scores used to determine whether the company will insure an applicant, and if so, what they will cover and how much they will charge. Those with poor or no credit are denied coverage, and those with limited credit pay high premiums.[50] Credit scoring also partly explains why, according to HUD, "Recent studies illustrate that compared to homeowners in predominantly white-occupied neighborhoods, homeowners in minority neighborhoods are less likely to have private home insurance, more likely to have policies that provide less coverage in case of a loss, and are likely to pay more for similar policies."[51]

With few cash reserves, low-income families are a heartbeat away from financial disaster if their wages fall because of unemployment, if their property taxes or insurance rates rise, or if expensive repairs are needed. With their savings in their homes, these families often have no cushion for emergencies. According to HUD data, between 1999 and 2001 the only group whose housing conditions worsened were low- and moderate-income home owners. The National Housing Conference reported that in 2005 about 50 percent of working families with critical housing needs were home owners.[52]

Most people who purchase a home believe they will live there for a long time and thus benefit from a secure and stable housing arrangement. This is not the case for many low-income families. According to a 2005 study by University of Washington researcher Carolina Katz Reid, from 1976 to 1993, 36 percent of low-income home owners gave up or lost their homes within two years and 53 percent exited within five years. Reid found that very few low-income families bought another house after returning to renting.[53] A 2004 HUD study by Donald Haurin and Stuart Rosenthal reached similar conclusions. Following a national sample of African Americans from youth (ages 14 to 21) in 1979 to middle age in 2000, the researchers found that 63 percent of the sample owned a home at some point, but only 34 percent still did in 2000.[54]

Low-income home owners employed in unstable jobs with stagnant incomes, few health care benefits, limited or no sick days, and little vacation time, may find it almost impossible to keep their homes if they experience a temporary job loss or a change in family circumstances, such as the temporary loss of a wage earner. Home ownership can also limit financial opportunities. A 1999 study by economists Richard Green and Patric Hendershott found that states with the highest home ownership rates also had the highest unemployment rates. Their report concluded that home ownership may constrain labor mobility because the high costs of selling a house make unemployed homeowners reluctant to relocate to find work.[55]

Special tax breaks are touted as a key selling point in deciding to become a home owner. But, if mortgage interest and other expenses come to less than the standard deduction ($10,700 for joint filers in 2007) there is no tax advantage to home ownership. This is one reason why only 34 percent of taxpayers itemize their mortgage interest, local property taxes, and other deductions. Even for families who itemize, the effective tax saving is usually only 10 to 35 cents for every dollar paid in mortgage interest. In short, the mortgage deduction primarily benefits those in high income brackets who need to shelter their income; it has little value to low-income homeowners.

Finally, home ownership promised growing wealth as housing prices in various parts of the United States soared from the late 1990s until 2007. However, homes bought by low-income families generally do not appreciate as rapidly as middle-income housing. For instance, Reid's longitudinal study survey of low-income minority home owners from 1976 to 1994 found that they realized a 30 percent increase in the value of their homes after 10 years; middle- and upper-income white home owners enjoyed a 60 percent jump.[56]

spotlight 16.2

The Brave New World of Home Loans

The new home loan products marketed widely in recent years to low- and moderate-income families are generally adjustable-rate mortgages (ARMs) with some kind of twist. Here are a few "creative" mortgage options:

- *Option ARMs* are loans whereby borrowers can choose which of three or four different fluctuating payments they will make (A) Full (principal + interest) payment based on a 30-year or 15-year repayment schedule. (B) Interest-only payment that does not reduce the loan principal or build home owner equity. Borrowers who pay only interest for a period of time soon face a big jump in the size of their monthly payments and some

are forced to refinance or lose their home. Refinancing only works if the home has appreciated in value or a substantial part of the mortgage has been paid off. If the home's value has remained stagnant or decreased (negative equity) it cannot be refinanced because little or no money can be drawn out.

Not all negative equity is bad. One of the newer variations of refinancing endorsed by HUD is a reverse mortgage for senior citizens, called a Home Equity Conversion Mortgage (HECM). This program unlocks the equity the elderly have built up in their property. Homeowners aged 62 or older can borrow against the value of their property. They receive payments from lenders monthly, in a lump sum, or as a line of credit. The size of the reverse mortgage is determined by the borrower's age, the interest rate, and the value of the home. The older the home owner, the larger the percentage of a home's value they can borrow. For example, a 65-year-old can borrow up to 26 percent of a home's value, a 75-year-old up to 39 percent, and an 85-year-old up to 56 percent. The amount owed increases over time, but no payment is due until the end of the loan term. When the loan term expires, the total loan amount plus interest is due in full. This lump sum payment is usually paid for by selling the property. No repayments are required while a borrower lives in the home and the monthly income is tax free.

(C) The minimum payment may be lower than one month's interest. If that occurs, the shortfall is added to the loan balance and results in "negative amortization," whereby over time the principal goes up, not down. Eventually the borrower may have an "upside down" mortgage where the debt is greater than the market value of the home.

According to the credit rating firm Fitch Ratings, up to 80 percent of all option arm borrowers choose the minimum monthly payment option, so it is not surprising that in 2005 20 percent of option arms were "upside down." When a negative amortization limit is reached, the minimum payment jumps up to fully amortize the loan for the remaining loan term. In other words, the borrower suddenly has to start paying the real bill.

Even borrowers who pay more than the monthly minimums can face payment shocks. Option arms often start with a temporary super-low teaser interest rate (and correspondingly low monthly payments) that allows borrowers to qualify for "more house." The catch? Because the low initial monthly payment (sometimes based on interest rates as low as 1.25 percent) is not enough to cover the real interest rate, the borrower will soon face a sudden sharp increase in monthly payments.

- *Balloon loans* are written for a five- to seven-year term during which time the borrower pays either interest and principal each month or, in a more predatory form, interest only. At the end of the short loan term, the borrower must either pay off the entire loan balance (i.e., a balloon payment),

refinance, or walk away from the home. Balloon mortgages are known as "bullet loans" because if the loan comes due during a period of high interest rates, it is like getting a bullet in the heart. About 10 percent of all subprime loans are balloon mortgages.

Balloon loans are sometimes structured with monthly payments that fail to cover the interest, much less pay down the principal. Although the borrower makes regular payments, the loan balance increases each month. Many borrowers are unaware that they have a negative amortization loan until they have to refinance.

- *Shared appreciation mortgages (SAMs)* are fixed-rate loans for up to 30 years that have easier credit qualifications and lower monthly payments than conventional mortgages. In exchange for a lower interest rate, the borrower relinquishes part of the future value of the home to the lender. Interest rate reductions are based on how much appreciation the borrower is willing to give up. SAMs discourage "sweat equity" because the home owner receives only a fraction of the appreciation resulting from any improvements. The nature of these loans has been likened to sharecropping.

- *Stated-income loans* are aimed at borrowers who do not draw regular wages but live on tips, casual cash jobs, commissions, or investments. Often called "liar loans" in the trade, these loans do not require W-2 forms or other standard wage documentation. The trade-off is higher interest rates.

- *No-ratio loan.* The debt–income ratio (the borrower's monthly payments including the planned mortgage, divided by monthly income) is a standard benchmark used by lenders to determine how large a mortgage they will write. In return for a higher interest rate, no-ratio loans abandon this benchmark. These loans are aimed at borrowers with complex financial lives or those who are experiencing divorce, the death of a spouse, or a career change.

Luckily, most of these dodgy loans ignominiously died when the subprime market crashed in 2007. However, when the credit market is stabilized, they could reappear again in various forms.

Tricky Mortgages

Buying a home is the largest purchase most families will make in their lifetimes and the biggest expenditure in a family budget. Real estate assets represent about one-third of the net worth of U.S. households.[57] Real estate transactions are also the most fraught with danger, especially for low-income families. The primary reason for this is the large gap between high home prices and the stagnant income of millions of working-class Americans. During the last decade, an unprecedented surge in home prices was seen, rising 35 percent nationally. The housing bubble was largely confined to specific metropolitan areas in the South, the Southwest, and the two coasts (home prices rose 50 percent in the Pacific states and 60 percent in New England); there are also bubbles in Midwestern cities like Chicago and Minneapolis. While the housing bubble were the most pronounced in high-end properties, the prices of low-end homes also spiked in many areas.[58]

Despite the current drop in housing prices, incomes still do not support persistently inflated home prices. Even the fall in mortgage interest rates in the 1990s and early 2000s was largely neutralized by higher property taxes, higher insurance premiums, and rising utility costs. At the end of the day, home buyers were spending almost as much monthly as when home prices were lower and interest rates higher. Housing costs operate like a shell game: Low interest rates and high housing prices lead to higher property taxes and home insurance costs. High interest rates and lower home prices lead to lower taxes and lower home insurance costs. At the end of the day, what matters most to home buyers is their total monthly housing expenses, which may or may not be different under these scenarios.

The growing disparity between relatively stagnant incomes and rapidly rising housing prices might have crushed the mortgage finance industry except for "creative financing." Over the past decade, the mortgage industry developed creative schemes designed to squeeze potential home buyers, albeit often temporarily, into houses they could not afford. It was a sleight of hand that required imaginative and risky financing for both buyers and financial institutions.

Most of the "creative" new mortgage products fell into the category of subprime mortgages—those offered to people whose problematic credit, lack of assets, or low income dropped them into a lower lending category. Subprime mortgages carried interest rates ranging from a few points to 10 points or more above the prime or market rate, plus onerous loan terms. Until the crash in 2007, the subprime mortgage industry was growing with lenders originating $173 billion in subprime loans in 2005, up from only $25 billion in 1993. Before the crash in 2007, the subprime market was valued at $600 billion, one-fifth of the U.S. mortgage market in 2006.[59]

Before the subprime collapse, the rate of return for subprime lenders was spectacular. *Forbes* claimed that subprime lenders could realize returns up to six times greater than the best-run banks.[60] In the past there were two main kinds of home mortgages: fixed-rate loans and adjustable rate mortgages (ARMs). In a fixed-rate mortgage, the interest rate stays the same throughout the 15- to 30-year term of the loan. In a typical ARM the interest rate varies over the course of the loan, although there is usually a cap. Both kinds of loans traditionally required borrowers to provide thorough documentation of their finances and a down payment of at least 10 percent (and often 20 percent) of the purchase price.

Adjustable-rate loans can be complicated, and a Federal Reserve study found that fully 25 percent of home owners with ARMs were confused about their loan terms. Nonetheless, ARMs are attractive because in the short run they promise a home with an artificially low interest rate and affordable payments.[61]

Despite the flexibility, traditional ARMs proved inadequate to the task of pushing more low-income families into the housing market and keeping home sales buoyant in the face of skyrocketing prices. To meet this challenge, the mortgage industry created a whole range of "affordability" products with names like "no-ratio loans," "option ARMS," and "balloon loans" that it doled out like candy to people never fully apprised of the intricacies of these complicated loans. New mortgage options opened the door for almost anyone to secure a mortgage, regardless of their capacity for repayment.

Beyond the higher interest rates that characterized the new "affordability" mortgages, low-income home buyers faced other costs as well. For instance, predatory and subprime lenders often required borrowers to carry credit life insurance, which pays off a mortgage in the event the home owner dies. This insurance is frequently sold either by the lender's subsidiary or by a company that pays the lender a commission. Despite low payouts, lenders frequently charge high premiums for this insurance.

As many as 80 percent of subprime loans included prepayment penalties if the borrower pays off or refinances the loan early, a scam that costs low-income borrowers about $2.3 billion a year and increases the risk of foreclosure by 20 percent. Prepayment penalties lock borrowers into a loan by making it difficult to sell the home or refinance with a different lender. And while some borrowers face penalties for paying off their loans early, others discover their mortgages have "call provisions" that permit the lender to accelerate the loan term even if payments are current. Newfangled mortgage products are often sold not by banks directly, but by a rapidly growing crew of mortgage brokers who act as finders or "bird dogs" for lenders. In 2006 there were approximately 53,000 mortgage brokerage companies in the United States employing almost half a million people. *BusinessWeek* notes that brokers now originate up to 80 percent of all new mortgages.[62]

Largely unregulated, mortgage brokers live off loan fees. Their transactions are primed for conflicts of interest or even downright corruption. For example, borrowers pay brokers a fee to help them secure a loan. Brokers can also receive kickbacks from lenders for referring a borrower, and many brokers steer clients to the lenders that pay the highest kickbacks rather than those offering the lowest interest rates. Closing documents use arcane language ("yield spread premiums," "service release fees") to hide these kickbacks. And some hungry brokers find less-than-kosher ways to make the sale, including fudging paperwork, arranging for inflated appraisals, or helping buyers find cosigners who have no intention of guaranteeing the loan.

Whether or not a broker is involved, lenders can inflate closing costs in a variety of ways: charging outrageous document preparation fees; billing for recording fees in excess of the law; and by "unbundling" (closing costs are padded by duplicating charges already included in other categories). Housing is highly susceptible to the predations of the fringe economy.

Subprime lending can be risky as borrowers and lenders soon realized. In the 37 years since the Mortgage Bankers Association (MBA) began conducting its annual national mortgage delinquency survey, the highest share of home loans entering foreclosure was seen in 2006. In early 2007, according to the MBA, 13.5 percent of subprime mortgages were delinquent (compared to 4.95 percent of prime-rate mortgages) and 4.5 percent were in foreclosure.[63] From July to September 2007, 446,726 homes nationwide were undergoing some kind of foreclosure activity, up 100 percent from the third quarter in 2006.[64] Some analysts are predicting that foreclosures will increase by at least 1.4 million homes in 2008.[65]

If the housing market continues to drop, by the end of 2008 up to 15 million U.S. households may owe more on their mortgages than their homes are worth. Thirty-nine percent of people who purchased a home two years ago already owe more than they can sell it for. Almost half of the borrowers who took out subprime mortgages in the last two years will not have any equity left if home prices drop an additional 10 percent.[66] If people owe more on their mortgage than their house is worth, a substantial number will simply send their keys back to the lender.

Refinancing or home equity loans have been a major vehicle for paying off credit card or other debt by periodically stripping equity in the home. About $2.2 trillion of home equity has been liquidated since 2001. U.S. property owners removed about $318 billion of equity from their homes in 2006 by refinancing home loans, with another $146.2 billion being lent in home equity lines of credit (HELOCs).[67]

Refinancing is not an option for home owners with negative equity and spiking mortgage rates. Strained borrowers who lack refinancing ability can only watch as their interest rates adjust upward. Because the home is often the last thing to go, financially strapped borrowers may engage in credit card and car loan delinquencies to try to stave off foreclosure. As more borrowers go into foreclosure, banks are likely to sell these foreclosed properties at discount prices, thereby further depressing housing prices.

Despite the hype, home ownership may not be a cure-all for low-income families who earn low wages and have poor prospects for future income growth. According to economist Dean Baker, given that mortgage delinquencies and foreclosures are at record levels among low-income households, millions of people would be better off today remaining renters.[68]

Instead of focusing almost exclusively on home ownership, a more progressive and balanced housing agenda would address the diverse needs of communities for both homes and rental units, and facilitate new forms of ownership such as community land trusts and cooperatives. A balanced housing policy would certainly aim to expand the stock of affordable rental units which has been decreasing partly to feed low-income home ownership programs. From 2004 to 2006, former President Bush and the Congress cut federal funding for public housing by 11 percent and cut 150,000 rental housing vouchers.

The reason the United States lacks a sound housing policy is evident when following the money. Overheated and rising home prices produce many winners. Real estate agents reap higher commissions, and mortgage brokers, appraisers, real estate attorneys, title companies, lenders, builders, home remodelers, and everyone else with their hand in the housing pie make money. Cities raise more money in property taxes, and insurance companies enroll more clients at higher premiums. Housing has buffered the economy, and moving more low-income families into homes regardless of the consequences has, in the short-term, helped keep the economy ticking.

Problems in Finding Affordable Rental Housing

If finding affordable housing is difficult for poor and moderate-income homeowners, it has reached crisis proportions for extremely low-income (ELI) renters. There are four major reasons for the affordability gap in rental housing: (1) Real incomes of ELI renter households have dropped; (2) the number of renter households has increased; (3) the number of low-cost unsubsidized rental units is dropping (federal housing assistance has not compensated for these losses); and (4) rents have increased or remained high for much of the 1990s and early 2000s.

The standard benchmark for "affordability" is that households should pay no more than 30 percent of their after-tax income for housing. Households paying between 30 and 50 percent for housing have moderate cost burdens; households paying more than 50 percent have severe cost burdens. Almost 30 million U.S. households pay more than 30 percent of their income for housing.[69] The robust economy of the late 1990s did little to relieve the housing problems of low-income renters. Renters in the bottom quarter of the income distribution saw their real incomes decline between 1996 and 1998, while rents increased by 2.3 percent.[70] Although the rental market cooled somewhat in the early 2000s, rents continued to remain high.

Rents follow similar trajectories as other market commodities. As more people entered the housing market through subprime loans and easy credit, the demand for rentals softened and rental prices dropped in some areas. As credit is tightened and subprime mortgages all but evaporate, fewer people can become home owners, which leads to rental shortages and higher prices.

Although most Americans are well housed, nearly a third of all households spend 30 percent or more of their incomes on housing and 13 percent spend 50 percent or more. In addition, crowding is on the increase, some 2.5 to 3.5 million people are homeless at some point in a given year, and nearly 2 million households still live in severely inadequate units. Housing challenges are most severe among those at the bottom of the income distribution. Fully half of lowest-income households spend at least 50 percent of their incomes on housing. Affordability pressures are likely to increase because wages in many low-wage jobs are insufficient to cover (at 30 percent of income) even a modest one-bedroom apartment in most parts of the country.[71]

Evidence of the crisis in affordable rents is illustrated by the relationship of the fair market rents (FMRs) to monthly minimum wage income and public assistance benefits. The FMR, a HUD designation, is defined as the dollar amount below which 40 percent of the standard quality rental housing units rent. In short, the FMR is what HUD determines it costs to rent modest, safe, and healthy housing in a specific county or metropolitan statistical area (MSA). The housing wage is based on the wage required by each county to rent a two-bedroom unit at the FMR. In 1999, the national two-bedroom housing wage was $11.08; by 2003, it rose to $15.21 in 2006, a 37 percent increase. This means that on average there must be almost three full-time minimum wage workers to enable a household to afford a two-bedroom unit at the FMR. The most serious housing problems are faced by the lowest income households. For ELI families—those with incomes less than 30 percent of the area median income (AMI)—the mean combined national hourly wage was $8.34 in 2003, only 45 percent of the national housing wage.[72] The loss of modest rental housing stock continues as market forces drive up the cost of housing and government fails to intervene to level the playing field.

In no state can an ELI household afford a two-bedroom home at the FMR. Looking below the state level reveals greater variation. In no MSA can a household with the ELI threshold afford the FMR for a two-bedroom home. In 43 MSAs, home to one-third of U.S. renters, a household earning the ELI threshold is able to afford only 50 percent or less of the MSA's FMR. At the county level, a household at the ELI threshold can afford a two-bedroom home at the FMR in only 27 largely rural counties that contain less than two-tenths of one percent of the renters in the nation.[73]

As mentioned earlier, when poor households live in adequate housing, they usually pay for it by spending an excessive proportion of their income on rent. Hence, many of these households have little left over for other necessities such as heat, food, clothing, and health care. Some of these families find themselves in a "heat or eat" situation. Little research has been done on the health effects of rent burdens, but Dr. Alan Meyers, a pediatrician at Boston Medical Center, studied 200 poor children and found that only 3 percent of children whose families received rent subsidies were underweight for their age. In contrast, 22 percent of children whose families were on the subsidized housing wait list were underweight for their age. After examining the records of 11,000 poor children, Meyers found that children were most likely to be underweight in the 90 days after the coldest month of the year; this finding bolstered his theory that families make the choice of whether to "heat or eat."[74]

Severe housing problems are related to the dwindling supply of affordable unsubsidized housing units available to very low-income households. Losses of units to either rising rents or demolition have intensified the housing problems of very low-income renters who receive no rent subsidies. Adding to the pressures on these households is the cost of supplying new affordable housing. Restrictive regulations and public resistance to high-density development make it difficult to replace or add lower-cost units. Between 1993 and 1995, for example, the number of unsubsidized units affordable by very low-income households dropped 8.6 percent—a decrease of nearly 900,000 units. At the same time, the number of units affordable by extremely low-income households—those with incomes less than 30 percent of the area median—fell by 16 percent.[75]

In 1999 there were 4.9 million affordable and available rental units for 7.7 ELI households. Three million low- to moderate-income working families spent more than half of their income on housing in 1997. By 2001 that number jumped to 4.8 million—a 67 percent increase. Overall, 14.4 million families have critical housing needs. It would take annual production of more than 250,000 units for more than 20 years to close the housing affordability gap. On the other hand, Congress has denied requests

and provided no funding since 1995 for new rental assistance to serve families with worst case needs.[76]

Several other factors have converged to deplete low-income housing stock, including the commercial renovation of central-city downtown areas. Developments consisting of new office buildings, large apartment complexes, shopping areas, and parking lots often replace low-income housing bordering on downtown areas. Traditionally affordable (and often run-down) apartment buildings, cheap single-room occupancy (SRO) hotels, rooming houses, and boardinghouses are razed as new office buildings and shopping complexes are erected. Displaced longtime residents are forced to find housing in more expensive neighborhoods; to double up with family or friends; or, in some cases, to become homeless.

The loss of SROs units has exacerbated the homeless problem. In the past SROs were home to many poor people (including those suffering from substance abuse and mental illnesses) who were not living in public or low-income subsidized housing. But between 1970 and the mid-1980s, an estimated 1 million SRO units were demolished. San Francisco lost 43 percent; Los Angeles lost more than 50 percent; New York lost 87 percent; and Chicago experienced the total elimination of its SRO housing units and hotels. These demolitions left many poor persons homeless, particularly those suffering from mental illness and substance abuse.[77]

Gentrification

According to George Sternlieb and Jones Hughes, "a new town may be evolving in-town."[78] This new town, or "gentrified" neighborhood, is a major component of the urban renaissance taking place in many U.S. cities. Attracted by old houses amenable to restoration; good transportation facilities; and close proximity to employment and artistic, cultural, and social opportunities, young professional and white-collar workers have begun to resettle the poor, aging, and usually heavily minority sections of central cities in the process called **gentrification.** As part of the process, upscale condos are built, houses are rehabbed, dusty lofts are modernized and sold for small fortunes, and trendy candle-lit restaurants and boutiques replace mini-marts and used furniture stores. Critics argue that a valuable piece of city real estate is being cleansed of its working class residents.

Although the renovation of central-city areas, such as New York's SoHo district, often makes a neighborhood more attractive (and potentially a tourist attraction), the effect on the indigenous—and frequently poor—population can be devastating. As homes become renovated, the price of surrounding housing increases. Even though low-income home owners can command a high price for their homes, they may find few suitable places to relocate. As neighborhoods become more affluent, property taxes rise, thus creating a burden on existing low-income homeowners. Previously affordable rental housing undergo large rent increases as neighborhoods become more desirable, thereby driving out older and poorer residents. Moreover, as the baby boomers age, the reason that many moved to the suburbs—good schools and safe neighborhoods for their children—may be eclipsed by the stress and exhaustion of long commutes and highway gridlock. Large numbers of these couples without children at home are opting to move closer to work and cultural amenities. Although gentrification has been selective, with the main demographic movement continuing to be suburban, it has had a striking impact on growing numbers of central-city neighborhoods.

The conversion of apartment buildings into condominiums represents another threat to low-income renters. As a consequence of tax breaks and income shelters, previously affordable rental housing is rapidly being converted into condominiums. Whether initiated by tenants or by developers, condominium conversion represents the serious depletion of good quality rental stock. Because units in these conversions may cost upwards of $100,000 or much more, low-income tenants can rarely afford the benefits of condominium living; and although long-term renters are sometimes offered a separation fee when a building undergoes conversion, this may barely cover the costs of moving, much less make up for the difference between renters' current rent and a higher alternative rent.

Overcrowded and Deficient Housing

Problems of overcrowding and structural inadequacy affect a significant number of U.S. households. HUD defines a housing unit as overcrowded if there is an average of more than one person per room. According to this definition, almost 3 million households live in overcrowded conditions, sometimes as a result of families' doubling up to avoid becoming homeless. In 1995 HUD classified 2 million housing units as seriously inadequate.

"Inadequate" housing is marked by severe physical deficiencies; for example, it may lack hot water, electricity, or a toilet or may have neither a bathtub nor shower. Years of neglect have led to a serious backlog of repairs among the 1.1 million assisted and 350,000 unassisted HUD-insured units. A study estimates that restoring systems in these buildings to adequate working condition would have cost $4.2 billion in 1995. In the suburbs both owners and renters make up substantial shares of households suffering from inadequate housing. That is, the number of suburban households living in these conditions equals that in central cities, but a larger share are home owners.[79]

Lead paint is one of the principal problems in units needing rehabilitation. The Centers for Disease Control and Prevention note that lead poisoning is one of the most common and devastating environmental diseases that affect young children, causing developmental and behavior problems. Children are exposed to lead poisoning by living in older homes with peeling, chipping, and flaking paint. According to the U.S. Environmental Protection Agency (EPA), there were nearly three to four million children with elevated blood lead levels in the United States in 1978; by the 1990s that number had dropped to 434,000 children. Because low-income families often occupy poorly maintained older homes, their children are four times more likely to have lead poisoning than children in high-income families.[80]

Other Factors Affecting Housing

Another problem affecting affordable housing is property taxes—the heart of local revenues. The escalating costs of providing governmental services have resulted in significant increases in property taxes, which landlords generally pass along to renters in the form of higher rents. In response, many states have tried to reduce property tax burdens for low-income households. The most common form of property tax relief occurs through **circuit breaker programs.** A typical circuit breaker is activated when taxes exceed a specified proportion of a home owner's income, and in some states, low-income households are sent a yearly benefit check that covers all or part of the property taxes they paid. Circuit breaker programs for low-income renters operate in a similar manner. Typically, a portion of the rent paid by a low-income household is considered to represent the property tax passed on by the landlord and is thus refunded by the state or local government. Although circuit breakers provide relief, they are often restricted to the elderly or disabled. For example, even though 31 states and the District of Columbia have circuit breaker programs, 21 states restrict eligibility to elderly and disabled households. Twenty-seven of these 31 states cover both renters and homeowners; six states restrict eligibility to home owners.[81]

Housing costs are also aggravated by high utility rates. Nationwide, the average family paid about $2,860 in utility bills in 2007.[82] However, in many parts of the country, especially the Northeast and the Midwest, an average family may pay considerably more, because of high heating costs. For example, the Energy Information Administration forecast that heating a home with natural gas in 2005 cost an average of $1,010; heating with oil, $1,114; and heating with propane, $1,335.[83] Low-income consumers spend anywhere from 13 to 44 percent of their total household income on utilities, whereas average-income Americans spend only 4 percent.[84] Increases in home energy bills disproportionately affect the poor, and in some cases, lead to utility shutoffs.[85] In 2007 about 1.2 million households had their utilities shut off. On average, each family owed $835 for a combined total of about $1 billion.[86]

To mitigate the effects of the federal deregulation of oil prices and the large oil price increases of the 1970s, Congress passed the Low-Income Home Energy Assistance Program (LIHEAP) in 1981. This legislation permits states to offer three types of assistance to low-income households: (1) funds to help eligible households pay their home heating or cooling bills; (2) allotments for low-income weatherization; and (3) assistance to households during energy-related emergencies. States are required to target LIHEAP benefits to households with the lowest incomes and the highest energy costs relative to income and family size. In 2003 LIHEAP was funded at almost $2 billion (this was cut to $1.88 billion in 2004) and served roughly 4.6 million households. This was less than the $2.1 billion spent in 1985 and represents more than an 11 percent cut in LIHEAP funds.[87]

Housing discrimination, another barrier facing the poor, takes two forms: racial discrimination and discrimination against families with children. Although illegal, racial discrimination in housing is still prevalent. In addition, many landlords and real estate agents refuse to rent to families with children. Even when these families find housing, they are often required to pay higher rents, provide exorbitant security deposits, or meet qualifications not required of renters without children.[88] Discrimination against families with children continues despite its ban by Congress in 1988.[89]

Homelessness

Simply put, homelessness is the lack of housing. As such, it represents both a simple and a complex problem. Specifically, homeless people are not a homogeneous group. Homelessness for some individuals is a lifestyle choice, the freedom to roam without being tied down to one place. For others, particularly people with mental illness and chronic alcoholism, homelessness reflects the deterioration of an overburdened public mental health system. The breakdown in the mental health system is aggravated by an influx of previously healthy people who, when reduced to economic deprivation and homelessness, develop symptoms of mental illness. For others, homelessness is rooted in cuts in federally subsidized housing programs and in the cost/income squeeze of the housing market. Finally, large numbers of people are homeless because public assistance benefits have failed to keep pace with the cost of living, especially in housing and utilities. Despite diverse causes, almost all forms of homelessness are tied to poverty.

The actual number of homeless people in the United States is difficult to ascertain. First, the definition of homelessness varies from study to study, and different methods for counting homeless people yield different results. Second, many of the homeless are "hidden" because they live in campgrounds, automobiles, boxcars, caves, tents, boxes, and other makeshift housing. Or the homeless may temporarily live with family members or friends. Such arrangements make it nearly impossible for agencies to count every person without stable housing. Studies of how many people are homeless on any given day or week (point-in-time studies) or of how many have experienced homelessness over a given time period (prevalence counts) are somewhat more valuable. These studies measure the magnitude of homelessness and therefore reflect the number of people who experience homelessness over a period of time, rather than an exact count. Most studies count people who are homeless in a given community by tracking people who use the services of soup kitchens and shelters.

Third, the homeless population is often undercounted in federal surveys for political reasons: If

spotlight 16.3

The National Coalition for the Homeless

The National Coalition for the Homeless (NCH) was established to end homelessness in America. To that end, this organization engages in public education, policy advocacy, and grassroots organizing. The work of NCH is focused in the following four areas: housing justice, economic justice, health care justice, and civil rights. To learn more about NCH, go to its website at **www.nationalhomeless.org.**

the true extent of homelessness were acknowledged, local, state, and federal authorities would have to target more services and funds for this population. For example, the U.S. Census Bureau estimated that in 2000 the homeless numbered only 280,527, based on those counted in homeless shelters, soup kitchens, on the streets, and at other venues.[90] A study by the Urban Institute put the number of homeless minimally at 2.3 million people, and as many as 3.5 million will experience homelessness at least once over the course of a year. The Joint Center for Housing Studies of Harvard University noted that on any given night some 750,000 Americans are homeless.[91]

Characteristics of the Homeless Population

Homelessness has been a long-standing problem in most urban areas, propelled onto center stage by media images of bag ladies, the mentally ill, chronic alcoholics, street people, and uprooted families. These images make for interesting copy, but popular

■ *Homelessness in America is both a simple and complex problem.*

stereotypes obscure both the extent and true nature of the problem. The homeless are generally the poorest of the poor. They include single-parent families and, occasionally, two-parent families. They are often people who work but who earn too little to afford housing. They are women and children escaping from domestic violence. They are runaway youngsters or "throw-away kids." They are unemployed people—some who are looking for work and some who have never worked. The homeless include retired people on small fixed incomes, many of whom have lost their cheap SRO hotel rooms to gentrification; school dropouts; drug addicts; disabled and mentally ill people lost in a maze of outpatient services; those who have worn out their welcome with family or friends; young mothers on welfare who are on long waiting lists for public housing; families who have lost their overcrowded quarters; and those who have "doubled up" and are temporarily sharing an apartment. In 2002 families comprised 41 percent of the urban homeless population, an increase of 5 percent over 2000. Nationally, children make up approximately 39 percent of the homeless population. In rural areas families, single mothers, and children make up the largest group of people who are homeless.[92]

The list below summarizes data from the National Survey of Homeless Assistance Providers and Clients conducted by the Census Bureau in 1996 for 12 federal agencies. Released in a 1999 HUD report, this survey interviewed representatives of almost 12,000 homeless programs and more than 4,000 clients. It is the most comprehensive study conducted on the homeless population to date and the picture it paints is bleak.

- *Families.* Sixty percent of homeless women had children ages 0 to 17; 65 percent of them lived with at least one of their minor children. Forty-one percent of homeless men had children ages 0 to 17; 7 percent of them lived with at least one of their minor children. Most of these homeless children were young; 20 percent were ages 0 to 2, 22 percent were ages 3 to 5, 20 percent were ages 6 to 8, 33 percent were ages 9 to 17, and age was not given for 5 percent. Parents reported that 45 percent of the 3- to 5-year-olds attended preschool and that 93 percent of school-age children (ages 6 to 17) attended school regularly. Fifty-one percent of children were in households receiving AFDC, 70 percent were in households receiving food stamps, 12 percent were in households receiving SSI, and 73 percent received Medicaid.

- *Gender and Marital Status.* Most homeless clients (85 percent) were single (that is, they did not have any of their children with them); 48 percent never married; 9 percent were married; 15 percent were separated; 24 percent were divorced; and 7 percent were widowed. Sixty-eight percent of the homeless were male and 32 percent were female.

- *Race.* Forty-one percent of the homeless were white, 40 percent African American, 11 percent Hispanic, 8 percent Native American, and 1 percent were other races.

- *Age.* Thirteen percent of the homeless were between the ages of 17 and 24; 80 percent were from 25 to 54; and 8 percent were 55 and older.

- *Education.* Thirty-eight percent of the homeless had less than a high school education; 34 percent had completed high school; and 28 percent had some education beyond high school.

- *Food Intake.* Twenty-eight percent of the homeless said they sometimes or often did not get enough to eat (compared with 12 percent of poor U.S. adults); 20 percent ate one meal a day or less. Thirty-nine percent of the homeless said that in the previous 30 days they had been hungry but unable to afford food (compared with 5 percent of poor Americans); 40 percent had gone without anything to eat for a day or longer in the previous 30 days because they could not afford food (compared to 3 percent of poor Americans).

- *Chemical Dependency and Mental Illness.* Thirty-eight percent of the homeless reported indicators of alcohol use problems; 26 percent reported indicators of drug use problems. Thirty-nine percent reported indicators of mental health problems; 75 percent reported indicators of one or more of these problems.

- *Physical Health.* Three percent of the homeless reported having HIV/AIDS; 3 percent reported tuberculosis; 26 percent reported acute infectious conditions such as a cough, cold, bronchitis, pneumonia, tuberculosis, or sexually transmitted disease other than AIDS. Eight percent reported acute noninfectious conditions such as skin ulcers, lice, or scabies; 45 percent reported having chronic health conditions such as arthritis, high blood pressure, diabetes, or cancer. Fifty-five percent had no medical insurance.

- *Crime.* Thirty-eight percent of the homeless claimed someone had stolen money or things from them; 22 percent had been physically assaulted; 7 percent had been sexually assaulted.

• *Income.* Single homeless clients reported a mean income of $348 in the previous 30 days, an amount only 51 percent of the 1996 federal poverty level of $680 a month for one person. Clients in family households reported a mean income of $475 during the previous 30 days, an amount only 46 percent of the 1996 federal poverty level of $1,023 a month for a family of three. Single homeless clients had only 12 percent of the median monthly income of all U.S. households in 1995 ($2,840), and homeless families only 17 percent.

• *Work.* Forty-four percent of the homeless had done paid work during the previous month. Twenty percent had worked in a job lasting at least three months; 25 percent worked at a temporary or day labor job; and 2 percent earned money by peddling or selling personal belongings. Three percent reported more than one source of earned income; 21 percent received income from family members or friends; 1 percent received child support. Eight percent reported income from panhandling in the previous 30 days.

• *Public Assistance.* Thirty-seven percent of the homeless received food stamps; 52 percent of households received AFDC; 11 percent received SSI; and 9 percent received General Assistance. Six percent of homeless veterans received veteran-related disability payments, and 2 percent received veteran-related pensions. Thirty percent received Medicaid, and another 7 percent received medical care from the Department of Veterans Affairs.

• *Locations.* Although there are homeless clients in every type of community, 71 percent were in central cities; 21 percent were in the suburbs and urban fringe areas; and 9 percent were in rural areas.

• *Shelter and Food.* Within the week previous to the interview, 31 percent of the homeless had slept on the streets or in other places not meant for habitation; 66 percent used an emergency shelter, transitional housing program, or program offering vouchers for emergency accommodation. Thirty-six percent used soup kitchens, and 10 percent used other homeless assistance programs (e.g., drop-in centers, food pantries, outreach programs, mobile food programs).

• *Episodes of Homelessness.* Forty-nine percent of clients were in their first episode of homelessness; 34 percent had been homeless three or more times. Single homeless clients and clients in families were equally likely to be in their first homeless episode, but single clients were more likely than clients in families to have been homeless three

times or more. For 28 percent of homeless clients, the current episode had lasted three months or less, but for 30 percent it had lasted more than two years. Clients in families were more than twice as likely as single clients to have been homeless for three months or less; single clients were almost three times as likely as clients in families to be in homeless spells that had lasted more than two years.

• *Veterans.* Thirty-three percent of male homeless clients were veterans. Forty-seven percent of veterans had served during the Vietnam era; and 17 percent had served since the Vietnam era. Many had served in more than one time period. Thirty-three percent of the male veterans were stationed in a war zone, and 28 percent were exposed to combat.

• *Childhood.* Twenty-seven percent of homeless clients had lived in foster care or in a group home or other institutional setting for part of their childhood; 25 percent reported childhood physical or sexual abuse; 21 percent reported childhood experiences of homelessness; 33 percent reported running away from home; and 22 percent reported being forced to leave home.

• *Homeless Services.* There are about 40,000 homeless assistance programs offered at about 21,000 locations in the United States. Food pantries, estimated at close to 9,000, are the most common type of program. Emergency shelters are next with an estimated 5,700 programs, followed closely by transitional housing programs (4,400), soup kitchens and other distributors of prepared meals (3,500), outreach programs (3,300), and voucher distribution programs (3,100). On an average day in February 1996, emergency shelters expected 240,000 program contacts, transitional housing programs expected 160,000, permanent housing programs expected 110,000, and voucher distribution programs expected 70,000. Expected contacts include those made by both homeless and other people who use services. Forty-nine percent of all homeless assistance programs are located in central cities, 32 percent in rural areas, and 19 percent in suburban areas. Because central-city programs serve more clients, a larger share of program contacts occur there.[93]

Trends in Homelessness

As noted earlier, homelessness and poverty are inextricably linked. Because poor families have limited resources that only cover a portion of their basic needs, they are forced to make difficult choices between housing, food, clothing, or health care. Housing costs absorb the greatest percentage of a poor family's income, which can leave them only a paycheck away from living on the streets if faced with a crisis. Families who have moved from welfare to work under the 1996 welfare reform law are not doing as well as projected (see Chapter 11) due to inadequate work supports and low wages. Moreover, the five-year TANF lifetime cap may lead to even greater numbers of homeless people in coming years, especially in the event of a recession.

Lack of affordable health care can cause many struggling families to spiral into homelessness when a serious illness or injury causes extended absence from work, job loss, or depletion of savings to pay for health care. Mental illness and drug and alcohol addiction also play a role. The increasing number of mentally ill homeless individuals is not entirely due to the deinstitutionalization of mentally ill patients from mental hospitals; rather, homelessness results because mentally ill people experience difficulty in accessing supportive housing along with treatment services. People who are both poor and addicted also face a high risk of homelessness.[94]

Domestic violence has been linked to homelessness. Specifically, many poor women are forced to choose whether to stay in an abusive relationship or become homeless. Several studies demonstrate the contribution of domestic violence to homelessness, particularly among families with children. A 1990 Ford Foundation study found that 50 percent of homeless women and children were fleeing abuse. Another study of 777 homeless parents (the majority of whom were mothers) in ten U.S. cities, found that 22 percent had left their last place of residence because of domestic violence. In addition, 46 percent of cities surveyed by the U.S. Conference of Mayors identified domestic violence as a primary cause of homelessness.

Another disturbing trend is the rise of homeless youth. Unaccompanied youth may account for as much as 3 percent (300,000) of the urban homeless population. Many homeless youth run away because of physical or sexual abuse, strained relationships, addiction of a family member, and parental neglect. In one study, more than half of the youth in shelters reported their parents either told them to leave or knew they were leaving but did not care. In another study, 46 percent of runaway and homeless youth had been physically abused and 17 percent had been forced into sexual activity by a household member. A history of foster care has also been correlated with becoming homeless at an earlier age and remaining so for a longer period of time. Some youth living in residential placements become homeless after discharge—they are too old for foster care and leave with no housing or income support. One national study found that more than 20 percent of youth who arrived at shelters came directly from foster care, and that more than 25 percent had been in foster care in the previous year. Many homeless adolescents find that survival on the streets requires exchanging sex for the necessities. In turn, they are at a greater risk for contracting AIDS/HIV. Studies suggest that the HIV prevalence rate for homeless youth may be 2 to 10 times higher than for other adolescents.[95]

Attempts to Address Homelessness

On July 22, 1987, President Ronald Reagan signed the McKinney-Vento Homeless Assistance Act into law. The McKinney Act created more than 20 separate programs to be administered by nine federal agencies. Some highlights of the current Act include the following:

• *Emergency Shelter Grants Program (ESGP).* This program provides formula (block grant) funding for emergency shelter and essential services.

• *Supportive Housing Demonstration Program (SHDP).* This competitive program funds a variety of grantees to provide transitional and permanent housing, particularly for homeless families and persons with special needs or handicaps. Initially funded as a demonstration, the program was renamed the Supportive Housing Program and made permanent in the Housing and Community Development Act of 1992. The program was also expanded to fund services only, Safe Havens, and Rural Homeless Housing.

• *Section 8 Moderate Rehabilitation for Single-Room Occupancy Dwellings.* This competitively awarded program provides funding to owners of SRO housing in the form of rental assistance payments on behalf of homeless individuals, in conjunction with the rehabilitation of the facility. The program provides permanent housing for previously homeless tenants.

• *Shelter Plus Care.* Congress added this program to HUD in 1990 and provided the first funding in 1992. Funds are competitively awarded for rental assistance. Grantees must match the value of rental assistance with an equal value of supportive services. The target population is homeless persons living on the streets or in emergency shelters with severe mental illness, chronic substance abuse problems, or AIDS.

• *Supplemental Assistance for Facilities to Assist the Homeless.*   This competitive program funds projects that meet the immediate and long-term needs of the homeless, as well as projects already receiving funds under ESGP and SHDP. The flexible range of assistance permits program expansion, capital improvement, and startup of new, needed supportive services. In 1992, this program was incorporated into the Supportive Housing Program.

• *Single Family Property Disposition Initiative.* Originally, this program was not a McKinney program. It was created in 1983 under the HUD Secretary's broad legislative authority to dispose of single-family properties. In 1985, it was broadened to allow HUD to sell or lease foreclosed single-family properties to nonprofit organizations, or to state or local governments to provide temporary shelter for homeless persons. In 1992, the Housing and Community Development Act recognized it as a McKinney initiative.[96]

In 1990 Congress amended the McKinney-Vento Act to remove requirements that kept homeless children from attending school, including proof of immunization, former school records, and proof of residency.[97]

Apart from the McKinney Act, several broader proposals emerged to alleviate the problem of homelessness. Chester Hartman has proposed a nine-point solution for ending homelessness: (1) massively increase the number of new and rehabilitated units offered to lower-income households; (2) lower the required rent/income ratio in government housing from 30 to 25 percent; (3) arrest the depletion of low-income housing through neglect, abandonment, conversion, and sale; (4) preserve the SRO hotels; (5) establish a national "right to shelter;" (6) require local governments to make available properties that can be used as shelters and second-stage housing; (7) create legislation that gives tenants reasonable protection from eviction; (8) provide governmental assistance to home owners facing foreclosure; and (9) provide suitable residential alternatives for mentally ill people.[98]

The 1991 "Federal Plan to Help End the Tragedy of Homelessness," prepared under the auspices of the Interagency Council for the Homeless, provides a set of objectives aimed at reducing homelessness: (1) Increase the participation of homeless families and individuals in mainstream programs that provide income support, social services, health care, education, employment, and housing; agencies should monitor these programs to gauge their impact on homelessness. (2) Improve the efficiency and effectiveness of homelessness-targeted programs in addressing the multiple needs of homeless persons. (3) Increase the availability of support services in combination with appropriate housing. (4) Improve access to quality, affordable, and permanent housing for homeless families and individuals. (5) Develop strategies for preventing homelessness by improving the methods for identifying families and individuals at risk of imminent homelessness; change current policies that may contribute to homelessness; and propose other initiatives to prevent people from becoming homeless.[99]

Housing First is an alternative approach to the current system of emergency shelter/transitional housing. It is premised on the belief that homeless families are more open to interventions and social service *after they are in their own housing*, rather than while living in a temporary or transitional facility. This model is grounded in the view that with permanent housing, distressed families can regain the control over their lives they lost when becoming homeless. In contrast to traditional emergency programs, Housing First: (1) helps homeless families move quickly and directly into affordable rental housing in residential neighborhoods; and (2) in order to help families transition into stability, each family receives six months to a year of individualized, home-based social services support after the move.

The process is divided into four stages:

- **Crisis Intervention and Short-Term Stabilization.** Helps families access emergency shelter services or short-term transitional housing while addressing crisis needs.
- **Screening, Intake, and Needs Assessment.** Creates an action plan for clients that encompasses short- and long-term goals and objectives.
- **Provision of Housing Resources.** Families are moved into permanent, affordable housing in a safe neighborhood after screening and assessment.
- **Provision of Case Management.** Before moving into permanent housing, case management

services identify clients' needs to ensure that they have a stable source of income by way of employment or public benefits.

Supporters argue that the combination of housing relocation services and home-based case management enables families to break the cycle of homelessness. This model facilitates long-term stability and provides formerly homeless families at risk of another episode of homelessness with the support necessary to remain in permanent housing.[100]

Homelessness cannot be eradicated without basic changes in federal housing, income support, social services, health care, education, and employment policies. Benefit levels for these programs must be made adequate; the erosion of welfare benefits must be stopped; residency and other requirements that exclude homeless persons must be changed; and programs (including outreach) must be made freely available to the homeless and the potentially homeless. Moreover, a real solution to the homeless problem must involve the provision of permanent housing for those who are currently or potentially homeless. Federal programs and legislation should be coordinated and expanded to provide decent, affordable housing, coupled with needed services, for all poor families. Finally, both the states and the federal government should intervene directly in the housing market by controlling rents, increasing the overall housing stock, limiting speculation, and providing income supports.

Housing Reform

The housing crisis faced by low-income people has led to numerous suggestions for housing reform. Some conservative critics argue that low-income housing assistance should be abolished, thereby allowing the law of supply and demand to regulate rents and, eventually, to drive down prices. Free market economic philosophy suggests that as rents increase, demand will slacken, and rents will drop eventually. Another argument is that government intervention in housing should occur only through the supply side. In other words, the government should stimulate production of rental housing by offering financial incentives such as tax breaks to builders, entrepreneurs, and investors. If rental housing is made more profitable, more units will be built, and the increase in the housing stock will lower prices.

Some liberal critics contend that because housing is a necessity and the demand is relatively inelastic, marketplace laws should not be allowed to dominate. For example, in 1995 the National Low-Income Housing Coalition called for:

- Guaranteeing housing assistance to people who need it
- Ending homelessness by linking housing with services to support recovery and self-sufficiency
- Providing a permanent and adequate supply of affordable housing
- Preserving and improving federally assisted affordable homes for people with low incomes
- Providing the opportunity for resident control of housing
- Preserving neighborhoods and ending displacement
- Ending economic and racial segregation through affirmative housing programs and the enforcement of fair housing laws
- Reforming federal tax laws to give priority to aiding people with the greatest housing needs
- Providing the financing needed to preserve, build, and rehabilitate housing[101]

Much of the housing innovation in recent years has come from the nonprofit sector. There are now more than 2,000 nonprofit housing groups that have built or renovated more than half a million housing units, most of them since 1990. These nonprofits operate with a combination of government subsidies and private contributions. They also get help from two important foundations—the Local Initiatives Support Corporation and the Enterprise Community Partners. According to Jason De Parle, the nonprofits' "impressive track records address the fear that more subsidized housing would mean more government-financed slums."[102]

Although nonprofit housing organizations are making an important impact on the country's housing problem, they have limitations. For example, many of the housing groups focus their attention on the "less needy"—those with incomes at 50 percent of the median. This occurs partly because no one group knows how to house large numbers of the poorest people, especially those on public assistance. If the poorest people are grouped together too tightly, neighborhoods may collapse. If they are spread out in the suburbs, the new neighbors complain. Perhaps more importantly, the scope and pace of building or renovating under nonprofits is inadequate to meet the need. Nonprofits are building or renovating about 50,000 units a year, and at that rate it would take a century to house the millions of families with rent burdens.[103]

Conclusion

The housing crisis is a structural problem based on the failure of incomes to keep pace with housing costs; an overdependence on credit to build and buy houses; a profit-making system that drives home ownership, development, and management; and the failure of states and the federal government to intervene actively in the housing market through more and higher subsidies or stricter regulation. Profit and speculation have driven up the price of rental and residential property faster than income growth. As a profit is made by each link in the housing chain (real estate agents and developers, lenders, builders, materials producers, investors, speculators, landlords, and home owners), renters and home buyers are forced to pay the costs. Put another way, the cost of every rental unit or home reflects the profits made by all parties who have come directly or indirectly into contact with that property.

The provision of adequate low- and moderate-income housing is an important challenge in modern society. The poor have difficulty finding decent affordable housing; blue-collar workers and the lower-middle class are caught in the cost/income squeeze and are having a hard time buying and holding onto their homes. In an economic downturn, this "affordability squeeze" results in increased mortgage foreclosures, higher rates of property tax and delinquency defaults, more evictions and homelessness, more overcrowding and doubling up of families, decreases in the consumption of other important necessities, deteriorating neighborhoods, increased business failures, higher rates of unemployment in the building trades, and the collapse of some financial institutions.

Past and current government programs have had minimal impact on the affordable housing crisis. Current housing programs are seriously underfunded, fragmentary, and without clear or focused goals. Because the federal government has often been viewed as an arbiter of last resort, some housing advocates contend that the government has the responsibility to ensure that adequate housing becomes a right rather than a privilege, and that healthy, sound, and safe neighborhoods become a reality.

An adequate housing policy for the United States must address cost burden, overcrowding, and housing quality. It must also provide opportunities for true housing choice and an end to the discriminatory practices that have led to de facto housing segregation. The nation will not have achieved the 1949 housing goal of "a decent home and suitable living environment for every American family" until all households live in adequate housing located in safe neighborhoods.

Discussion Questions

1. From 1937 until the present, the history of federal housing policy has been marked by evolving priorities and programmatic shifts. Describe the dominant trends in federal housing policy from 1937 onward and show how they led to the creation of current housing policies. What is the current direction of federal housing policy?
2. Describe the more serious shortcomings in federal low-income housing policy and discuss alternative policies to rectify those shortcomings.
3. Home ownership is important because it can lead to asset growth. For example, a renter has nothing to show for a long-term rental except rental receipts. In contrast, a poor family that owns a home will have a major asset after paying off their mortgage. What are some of the obstacles standing in the way of home ownership for the poor? What policies can help these families overcome the barriers?
4. Propose some federal or state policies that might help poor families find affordable rental housing.
5. HUD has created guidelines to evaluate whether a particular housing unit has "severe" physical deficiencies. Are these criteria adequate? If not,

what other criteria should be added to HUD's guidelines?

6. Homelessness has been described as just another housing problem and a manifestation of poverty. Others contend that its roots are psychological and it should be treated as a social service problem. Where do you stand on the issue?

7. Several proposals have been developed to eradicate homelessness. Which of these programs (or combination of programs) has the best chance for success?

8. Many experts believe the housing situation has reached crisis proportions for low-income renters and homeowners. Do you agree?

9. Should housing be considered a right and therefore be removed from the marketplace?

10. Housing is the largest expense for most American families. Whether one is looking at affluent suburbs or working-class rentals, more families are paying a larger portion of their income than financial advisors suggest is prudent. Look at the available housing in your community using your Internet search engine. Is affordable housing available? Could low-income single parents find housing in your community?

11. On March 31, 2006, HUD issued a new HUD Strategic Plan for 2006 to 2011. Using your Internet search engine, locate this document on HUD's website (www.hud.gov). Do you agree with the department's priorities? Why do you think home ownership is so important to HUD? What are the advantages of home ownership for people with low resources?

12. A disproportionately large portion of mortgages for low-income people have been subprime. In less than a decade the default rate on these subprime mortgages has escalated, more than quadrupling in some sections of the country. What degree of responsibility should creditors have for making loans to those without strong credit? What responsibility should low-income home buyers have for entering into such a mortgage?

Notes

1. "Historical Census of Housing Movers," U.S. Census Bureau, 2000. Retrieved April 9, 2007, from www.census.gov/hhes/www/housing/census/historic/movers.html

2. "Hurricane Katrina—One Year Later," Federal Emergency Management Agency, August 22, 2006. Retrieved April 9, 2007, from www.fema.gov/news/newsrelease.fema?id=29108

3. Richard Knabb, Jamie Rhome, and Daniel Brown, "Tropical Cyclone Report: Hurricane Katrina: 23-30 August 2005." National Hurricane Center.

4. "Effect of Hurricane Katrina on New Orleans," *Wikipedia.* Retrieved April 9, 2007, from http://en.wikipedia.org/wiki/Effect_of_Hurricane_Katrina_on_New_Orleans

5. "LA Hurricane Facts and Figures," The Road Home. Retrieved April 9, 2007, from www.road2la.org/la-hurricanes.htm

6. "Hurricane Katrina—One Year Later."

7. Stephan Ohlemacher, "La: Katrina Counties Slow to Repopulate," *Forbes* (Associated Press), March 22, 2007. Retrieved April 9, 2007, from www.forbes.com/feeds/ap/2007/03/22/ap3541676.html

8. "About the Road Home Program." Retrieved April 9, 2007, from www.road2la.org/about-us/default.htm

9. David Hammer, "Road Home Faces Detour: Lenders Want to Keep Installment Option," *The Times Picayune*, April 2, 2007. Retrieved April 9, 2007, from http://nola.live.advance.net/news/t-p/frontpage/index.ssf?/base/news-8/117549264173650.xml&coll=1&thispage=1

10. Hazel Trice Edney, "Nagin Tells Black Press, 'Tragedy is Still not Over,'" *The Louisiana Weekly*, March 26, 2007. Retrieved April 9, 2007, from www.louisianaweekly.com/weekly/news/articlegate .pl?20070326r

11. Edward B. Lazere, Paul A. Leonard, Cushing N. Dolbeare, and Barry Zigas, *A Place to Call Home: The Low-Income Housing Crisis Continues* (Washington, DC: Center on Budget and Policy Priorities and Low-Income Housing Information Service, December 1991), pp. 45–47.

12. Charles S. Prigmore and Charles R. Atherton, *Social Welfare Policy: Analysis and Formulation* (Lexington, MA: D.C. Heath, 1979), pp. 48–50.

13. National Training and Information Center, *Insurance Redlining, Profits v. Policyholders* (Chicago: NTIC, 1973), p. 1.

14. Ibid., pp. 52–53.

15. Center for Community Change, "Solutions," 1999. Retrieved December 29, 2000, from www.communitychange.org/pahcrisis2.html

16. Joint Center for Housing Studies of Harvard University, *The State of the Nation's Housing* (Cambridge, MA: Harvard University, 2003), p. 22.

17. National Low Income Housing Coalition (NLIHC), *2004 Advocates' Guide To Housing and Community Development Policy: Low Income Housing Tax Credit* (Washington, DC: NLIHC, 2004).

18. National Low Income Housing Coalition, *NLIHC's Comments to FDIC on Proposed Changes to the Community Reinvestment Act* (Washington, DC: NLHIC, September 20, 2004).

19. Council of Large Public Housing Authorities, *Quick Facts on Public Housing* (Washington, DC: Author, 2004).

20. National Coalition for the Homeless, "Why are People Homeless?" June 1999, retrieved December 29, 2000, from http:/nch.ari.net; see also Laura Waxman, *A Status Report on Hunger and Homelessness in America's Cities: 1995* (Washington, DC: U.S. Conference of Mayors, 1995); and Children's Defense Fund, *The State of America's Children,* 1991 (Washington, DC: Children's Defense Fund, 1991).

21. Jason Furman, "End the Mortgage-Interest Deduction! Why the Left Should Embrace the Bush Tax Commission's Most Radical Proposal," *Slate,* November 10, 2005. Retrieved March 20, 2008, from www.slate.com/id/2130017

22. Daniel Gross, "Location, Location—Deduction. The Mortgage-Interest Deduction Costs Taxpayers Billions, but It Won't Go Away Anytime Soon," *Slate,* April 14, 2005. Retrieved March 20, 2008, from www.slate.com/id/2116731

23. Jeff Schneppe, "10 Big Tax Breaks for the Rest of Us," *MSN Money,* 2004. Retrieved November 2004, from http://moneycentral.msn.com/content/Taxes/Taxshelters/P75680.asp

24. Joint Center for Housing Studies of Harvard University, *The State of the Nation's Housing, 2007* (Cambridge, MA: Harvard University, 2007), p. 35.

25. Sandra Block, "Home Equity Below 50% Level. Falling Prices Sap Owners' 'Wealth,'" *USA TODAY,* March 7, 2008, p. 1A.

26. Robert Callis and Linda Cavanaugh, "Census Bureau Reports on Residential Vacancies and Home ownership," U.S. Census Bureau News, U.S. Department of Commerce, January 29, 2008, Washington, DC.

27. Joint Center for Housing Studies of Harvard University, *The State of the Nation's Housing, 2003.* Retrieved November 2004 from www.jchs.harvard.edu/publications/markets/son2004.pdf

28. Donald Haurin, Christopher Herbert, and Stuart Rosenthal, "Home ownership Gaps among Low-Income and Minority Households," *Cityscape* 9, no. 2, 2007, pp. 26–35.

29. Ibid.

30. Sam Roberts, "Biggest Urban Growth Is in South and West," *New York Times,* June 28, 2007, B8.

31. *The State of the Nation's Housing,* 2007, p. 56.

32. Ibid, p. 58.

33. Ibid.; David Leonhardt, "In Most of the U.S., a House Is a Home But Not a Bonanza," *New York Times* (August 6, 2003), p. 19; Ohio Association of Realtors, "Better, Bigger Homes Available for Today's Buyers," retrieved December 29, 2000, from www.ohiorealtors.org/news/prez_col/0403.html; George Sternlieb and James W. Hughes, "Housing in the United States: An Overview," in George Sternlieb, James W. Hughes, Robert W. Burchell, Stephen C. Casey, Robert W. Lake, and David Listokin (eds.), *America's Housing* (New Brunswick, NJ: Rutgers University, Center for Urban Policy Research, 1980), pp. 5–7; Sumner M. Rosen, David Fanshel, and Mary E. Lutz (eds.), *Face of the Nation, 1987* (Silver Spring, MD: NASW, 1987), p. 68; and Joint Center for Housing Studies of Harvard University, *The State of the Nation's Housing,* (Boston, MA: Joint Center for Housing Studies of Harvard University, 1992), p. 12.

34. Joint Center for Housing Studies of Harvard University, *The State of the Nation's Housing,* pp. 28–31.

35. See U.S. Census Bureau, *Statistical Abstract of the United States,* 1991 (Washington DC: U.S. Government Printing Office, 1991), pp. 715–717; and MSNBC, "SoCal Median Home Price Falls to $408,000," KNBC-TV, March 13, 2008. Retrieved March 23, 2008, from www.msnbc.msn.com/id/23614434

36. Eduardo Porter and Vikas Bajaj, "Mortgage Trouble Clouds Home ownership Dream," *New York Times* (March 17, 2007), p. 16.

37. Joint Center for Housing Studies at Harvard University, *The State of the Nation's Housing: 2000.*

38. Harold Maass, "A Countrywide Sale, a Mess at Merrill." Yahoo Blogs, January 12, 2008. Retrieved March 10, 2008, from http://au.blogs.yahoo.com/business/722/a-countrywide-sale-a-mess-at-merrill

39. Kevin G. Hall, "Bankers Blame Feds for Forcing Bear Stearns Fire-Sale Price," McClatchy Newspapers, April 3, 2008. Retrieved April 10, 2008, from www.mcclatchydc.com/homepage/story/32562 .html

40. James R. Hagerty, "Millions Are Facing Squeeze on Monthly House Payments," *Wall Street Journal Online.* Retrieved March 10, 2008, from www.realestatejournal.com/buysell/mortgages/20060315-hagerty.html?mod=RSS_Real_Estate_Journal&rejrss=frontpage

41. Winton Picoff and Sheila Crowley, "Rental Housing for America's Poor Families: Farther Out of Reach Than Ever," National Low Income Housing Coalition (2002). Available at www.nlihc.org/oor2002

42. Robert Dietz, "Estimation of Neighborhood Effects in the Social Sciences: An Interdisciplinary Literature Review," URAI Working Paper No. 00–03, Urban and Regional Analysis Initiative, Ohio State University January 1, 2001.

43. Joseph Harkness and Sandra Newman, "Effects of Home ownership on Children: The Role of

Neighborhood Characteristics and Family Income," *Economic Policy Review* 9, no. 2 (June 2003), p. 51.

44. Ibid.

45. Howard Karger, "The Home ownership Myth," *Dollars & Sense*, 270, Spring (March/April and May/June 2007), pp. 2–11.

46. Bankrate.com, "Countrywide, the Mortgage Mess and You," August 17, 2007. Retrieved March 12, 2008, from MSNMoney, http://articles.moneycentral.msn.com/Banking/HomeFinancing/CountrywideTheMortgageMessAndYou.aspx?page=all

47. NeighborWorks, "Improving Incurability Through Rehab," Washington, DC, 2004.

48. Howard Karger, *Shortchanged: Life and Debt in the Fringe Economy* (San Francisco: Berrett-Koehler, 2005).

49. Ibid.

50. Ibid.

51. Ibid., p. 168.

52. National Housing Coalition, "The Housing Landscape for America's Working Families, 2007." NHC, Washington, DC, August 2007.

53. Carolina Katz Reid, "Studies in Demography and Ecology: Achieving the American Dream? A Longitudinal Analysis of the Home ownership Experiences of Low-Income Households," University of Washington, CSDE Working Paper No. 04-04, 2004.

54. Donald Haurin and Stuart Rosenthal, "The Sustainability of Home ownership: Factors Affecting the Duration of Home ownership and Rental Spells," Office of Policy Development & Research, U.S. Department of Housing and Urban Development, 2005; and Donald Haurin and Stuart Rosenthal, "The Influence of Household Formation on Home ownership Rates Across Time and Race," Office of Policy Development & Research, U.S. Department of Housing and Urban Development, 2005.

55. Richard Green and Patric Hendershott, "Home-ownership and Unemployment in the U.S.," *Urban Studies*, 38, no. 9, pp. 1509–1520, 2001.

56. Reid, "Studies in Demography and Ecology."

57. Kathleen Howley, "Americans Selling Homes See Prices Go Below Mortgage," February 13, 2008. Retrieved March 12, 2008, from www.bloomberg.com/apps/news?pid=20601109&refer=home&sid=aaKqieyMLwnc

58. Karger, *Shortchanged*.

59. Ibid.

60. Ibid.

61. Ibid.

62. Ibid.

63. Ibid.

64. "Foreclosure Rates Surge in Third Quarter," *Wall Street Journal*, November 1, 2007. Retrieved March 12, 2008, from http://blogs.wsj.com/developments/2007/11/01/foreclosure-rates-surge-in-third-quarter

65. Global Insight, "The Mortgage Crisis: Economic and Fiscal Implications for Metro Areas." Prepared for The United States Conference of Mayors and The Council for the New American City, Lexington, MA, November 26, 2007.

66. Howley, "Americans Selling Homes."

67. Ibid.

68. Dean Baker, "The Housing Bubble: A Time Bomb in Low-Income Communities?" Shelterforce Online, Issue #135, May/June 2004, www.nhi.org/online/issues/135/bubble.html

69. National Low-Income Housing Coalition, *NLIHC Background on Housing Issues* (Washington, DC: National Low-Income Housing Coalition, 2002).

70. Consumer Federation of America, "While Home ownership Rises, Home Equity Stagnates."

71. Joint Center for Housing Studies of Harvard University, 2004.

72. National Low-Income Housing Coalition (NLIHC), *Out of Reach 2003*, (Washington, DC: NLIHC, 2003).

73. Ibid.

74. Tracy L. Kaufman, *Out of Reach: Can Americans Pay Rent?* (Washington, DC: NLIHC, 1996), p. 57.

75. U.S. Department of Housing and Urban Development, *Finding 2: The Stock of Rental Housing Affordable to the Lowest Income Families Is Shrinking and Congress Has Eliminated Funding for New Rental Assistance since 1995*, HUD. Retrieved November 2004, from www.huduser.org/publications/affhsg/worstcase/finding2.html

76. The National Coalition for the Homeless, "Facts about Homelessness, People Need Affordable Housing." Retrieved November 2004, from www.nationalhomeless.org/facts/housing.html

77. National Coalition for the Homeless, "Why Are People Homeless?" NCH Fact Sheet #1, June 1999. Retrieved December 2000, from http://nch.ari.net

78. George Sternlieb and James W. Hughes, "Back to the Central City: Myths and Realities." In George Sternlieb et al. (eds.), *America's Housing* (New Brunswick, NJ: Rutgers University, Center for Urban Policy Research, 1980), p. 173.

79. Habitat for Humanity, "U.S. Affordable Housing Statistics" (Washington DC: Author, 2000); and Joint Center for Housing Studies at Harvard University, *The State of the Nation's Housing: 2000*.

80. See National Low-Income Housing Coalition, *NLIHC Background on Housing Issues;* and U.S. Environmental Protection Agency, "Shut the Door on Lead Poisoning," EPA November 2, 2004. Retrieved November 2004, from www.epa.gov/lead

81. Ibid., pp. 43–44.

82. Eugene Trisko, "The Rising Burden of Energy Costs on American Families, 1997–2007." Center for Energy and Economic Development, November 2006. Retrieved April 13, 2008, from www.ceednet

.org/docs/ABEC%20ENERGY%20COSTS%201997%202007%20FINAL.pdf

83. Ibid.

84. Carol Biedrzycki, "Residential and Low-Income Electric Customer Protection," *Texas Ratepayers' Organization to Save Energy, Inc.* Retrieved December 2000, from www.ncat.org/liheap/pubs/txreport.htm

85. Center on Budget and Policy Priorities, *Smaller Slices of the Pie* (Washington, DC: CBPP, November 1985), p. 33.

86. Mark Wolfe, "State Energy Directors Est. 1.2 million Households Disconnected from Utility Services: Call on Congress and the Administration to Provide Additional Funds for Energy Assistance," Press Release July 11, 2007. National Energy Assistance Directors' Association, Washington, DC.

87. See Committee on Ways and Means, U.S. House of Representatives, *2004 Green Book,* (Washington, DC: U.S. Government Office, 2004), pp. 15–128, 129; and Senator Paul Wellstone, "Senate Coalition Taking Offensive in Anticipated LIHEAP Funding Fight," March 25, 1999. Retrieved December 2000, from http://wellstone.senate.gov/liheap7.htm

88. Wellstone, "Senate Coalition."

89. Children's Defense Fund, *The State of America's Children, 1992* (Washington, DC: Children's Defense Fund, 1992), p. 38.

90. Quoted in Diana M. DiNitto, *Social Welfare: Politics and Public Policy* (Boston: Allyn & Bacon, 1995), p. 87.

91. See Joint Center for Housing Studies at Harvard University, *The State of the Nation's Housing: 2007*; and National Coalition for the Homeless (NCH), *The 2000 Census and Homelessness,* 2001. Retrieved November 2004, from www.nationalhomeless.org/census2001.html

92. The National Coalition for the Homeless, *Facts about Homelessness.*

93. U.S. Department of Housing and Urban Development, *Homelessness: Programs and the People They Serve,* retrieved November 2004, from www.huduser.org/publications/homeless/homelessness/figs_tbls.html; and National Coalition for Homeless Veterans

"Background Statistics," retrieved November 2004, from www.nchv.org/background.cfm

94. See National Coalition for the Homeless, "Domestic Violence and Homelessness," April 1999, retrieved November 2004, from www.nationalhomeless.org/domestic.html; and Institute for Children and Poverty, *Homes for the Homeless—Ten Cities 1997–1998,* Homes for the Homeless and Institute for Children and Poverty, New York, 1999.

95. See National Coalition for the Homeless, "Homeless Youth," April 1999, retrieved November 2004, from www.nationalhomeless.org/youth.html; Institute for Health Policy Studies, *Street Youth at Risk for AIDS: 1995* (San Francisco: University of California, 1999); and National Association of Social Workers, *Helping Vulnerable Youths: Runaway and Homeless Adolescents in the United States* (Washington, DC: NASW, 1992).

96. U.S. Department of Housing and Urban Development, "Stuart B. McKinney Homeless Programs: Introduction," July 11, 2002. Retrieved November 2004, from www.huduser.org/publications/homeless/mckin/intro.html

97. National Low-Income Housing Coalition, *1996 Advocate's Resource Book* (Washington, DC: NLIHC, 1996).

98. Chester Hartman, "The Housing Part of the Homelessness Problem." In Boston Foundation, *Homelessness: Critical Issues for Policy and Practice* (Boston: Boston Foundation, 1987), pp. 17–19.

99. National Low-Income Housing Coalition, *1996 Advocate's Resource Book.*

100. Tanya Tull, "The 'Housing First' Approach for Families Affected by Substance Abuse," *The Source* (National Abandoned Infants Assistance Resource Center), 13, no. 1 (Spring 2004).

101. See National Low-Income Housing Coalition, *NLIHC Background on Housing Issues*; and National Low-Income Housing Coalition, 1995 Advocate's Resource Book (Washington, DC: NLIHC, 1995).

102. Jason De Parle, *American Dream* (New York: Viking, 2004), p. 94.

103. Ibid.

The Politics of Food Policy and Rural Life

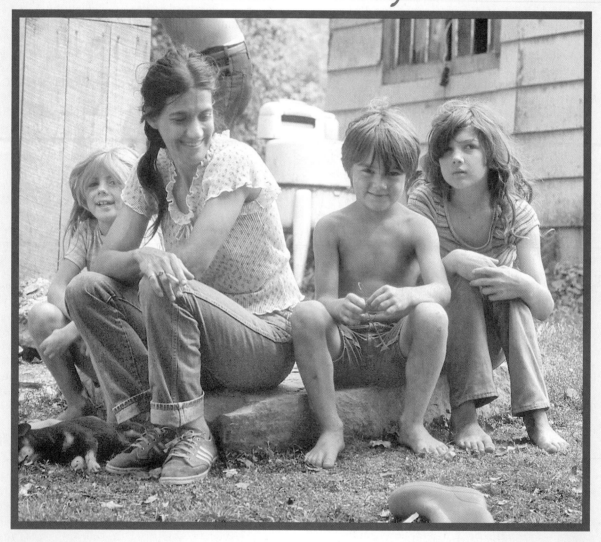

*H*ow can a nation as affluent as the United States allow food insecurity and even starvation to occur? Irregular diets impair the cognitive faculties, medication efficacy, and work readiness of far too many Americans. Improper nutrition also has an adverse impact on the emotional, mental, and social development of children and leads to increased rates of obesity and diabetes in adults. Despite medical cautions, most Americans are swimming in a sea of *trans* fats. Work schedules make it nearly impossible to escape the convenience of fast foods.

The policies related to the production and distribution of food form an important part of the U.S. welfare state. For example, over the course of a year an estimated one in five Americans participates in at least one of the 15 food assistance programs administered by the U.S. Department of Agriculture (USDA). Expenditures for these 15 food assistance programs totaled almost $60 billion in 2008.[1] This chapter examines the federal response to hunger and the government's attempts to distribute food-stuffs to the poor. Topics considered include the Food Stamp Program, WIC and other food programs, U.S. farm policy, the plight of farmworkers in the United States, and the overall problems of food production and distribution. Although the issues around food may initially seem disparate, they are tied together in a complex mosaic that is basic to the well-being of the nation.

Food policy in the United States is marked by important contradictions. In 2006, 35.5 million people lived in households that were unsure where their next meal was coming from (i.e., the food insecure). On the other hand, 24.4 percent of the U.S. population in 2006 was obese.[2] The Centers for Disease Control and Prevention (CDC) labels the obesity problem an epidemic. Almost 65 percent of Americans are either overweight or obese and the number is growing. The increase in overweight children is twice that seen in adults. In 2001, Americans spent $110 billion on fast food, more money than on higher education, personal computers, computer software, and new cars.[3] Directly and indirectly, obesity costs the United States $117 billion and results in 39 million lost work days a year. Three-fourths of the $1.4 trillion the United States spends on health care is to treat chronic illnesses, many of which are tied to obesity and being overweight.[4] Diets of burgers and fries are bringing the nation's steady rise in life expectancy to a grinding halt. The CDC predicts that 29 million Americans will be diagnosed with diabetes in 2050 compared with about 11 million in 2003. Twenty years ago the United States led the world's longevity league. Today, American women rank only 19th; males only 28th, alongside men from Brunei.[5]

The Contradictions of American Food Policy

With an annual budget in fiscal year 2008 of $124.4 billion,[6] the U.S. Department of Agriculture (USDA) is responsible for distributing more federal resources than the U.S. Department of Health and Human Services (DHHS) spends outside of Medicare and Medicaid.[7] Almost 46 percent of the USDA budget is comprised of means-tested food and nutrition programs; however, the balance is largely commodity price supports ($19.7 billion); soil conservation programs ($2 billion); crop insurance ($7.2 billion); export credit guarantees ($2.4 billion); rural development of utilities, housing, and businesses ($14.9 billion); and natural resource and environmental protection ($7.5 billion).[8]

Commodity price supports, conservation programs, crop insurance, and export credit guarantees are largely direct financial subsidies to the 2.1 million farms in America[9]; however, these subsidies are not supporting the small, family-owned and -operated farms so frequently mentioned in Congressional appeals for more funding. Nine percent of farms are large family-owned operations with annual revenues over $250,000 or corporate farms. Another 42 percent are identified as "residential/lifestyle" farms indicating that farming is not the primary focus. Another 28 percent of farms have annual revenues under $100,000 a year and are categorized as "limited resource" or "low sales." Another 6 percent are "medium sales" with $100,000 to $250,000 in annual revenue.[10] This means that only 734,000 farms may fit the popular image of a family farm, but even this number could be pared down by eliminating those operations that exist primarily to gain the tax advantages associated with farming.

To put this into perspective, the USDA manages $31.3 billion in subsidies that are justified in support of what may be less than half a million family farms. In comparison, Temporary Assistance for Needy Families (TANF) provides $17.1 billion[11] to provide income security to the almost 6 million families with children who have incomes below the poverty line.[12]

Questions about the expenditures of the USDA are a common occurrence in the *Washington Post*. Gilbert Gaul reported in October 2006 that the USDA not only subsidizes 60 percent of crop insurance premiums for American farms, insurance claims are regularly supplemented by disaster relief payments.[13] Since 2000 when the insurance subsidies began, an additional $24 billion has been designated by Congress in disasters. "A major share of the money goes to parched and flood-prone areas where farming is tenuous at best and 'disasters' seem to happen every year."[14] The question becomes, are American farmers raising food or are they raising crops of federal aid?

Hunger in the United States

One of the most striking aspects of poverty in the United States is hunger. The terms *hunger* and *malnutrition* conjure up images of emaciated Third World children with bloated bellies and protruding eyes. Americans often think of hunger as a problem that pertains mainly to developing countries. Hunger exists in the United States, but it typically occurs in subtle ways. For example, poor people may eat only once a day or skip meals for several days; they may be subject to chronic malnutrition; women may bear low-birth-weight babies, and babies may be at risk from high infant mortality rates. Crossing age, race, and gender lines, hunger in the United States affects children, the elderly, the unemployed and the underemployed, homeless people, people with disabilities, and both two-parent and single-parent families. The single common thread connecting these diverse groups to the problem of hunger is poverty.

Cheap and plentiful food is an American tradition, which may partly explain why most Americans older than age 25 are overweight.[15] Americans spend a smaller percentage of their income on food than any other nation, and we feed much of the world with our surplus (the value of U.S. agricultural imports was estimated at $52 billion in 2004).[16] Consumers, retailers, restaurants, and farmers throw away one-quarter of the U.S. food stock (almost 100 billion pounds of edible food) each year. Yet in 2006, 10.9 percent (about 12.6 million) of U.S.

households were food insecure. In other words, they had one or more persons who reported experiencing reduced food intake because of a lack of financial resources. Moreover, these households were unsure where their next meal would come from. Of that number, about one-third of food-insecure households (4.6 million) had very low food security, essentially unchanged from 2005 (3.9 percent).[17] Women and children make up about three-fourths of this population.[18] Food pantries, shelters, soup kitchens, and other emergency food providers serve at least 23 million people a year.[19]

Children who are denied an adequate diet are at a greater risk than other low-income children of not reaching their full potential as individuals. Undernourished youngsters have trouble concentrating and bonding with other children and are more likely to suffer illnesses that cause them to be absent from school. They consistently perform more poorly on standardized tests. Poor performance early in school is a major risk factor for dropping out of school. Studies have also shown that even mildly undernourished children may potentially suffer brain, cognitive, and psychological impairment that, if not corrected, can be irreversible. Research conducted by the Center on Hunger, Poverty and Nutritional Policy at Tufts University found compelling evidence that improved nutrition can modify and even reverse these effects. John Cook and Katie S. Martin found that millions of poor children have substandard intakes of important major nutrients. Analysis of government data revealed major differences between poor and nonpoor children's intakes of 10 out of 16 essential nutrients.

Cook and Martin also found that millions of poor children suffer from chronic undernutrition, the underconsumption of essential nutrients and food energy.[20] Intake of these nutrients is considered crucial to sound health and normal development. Inadequate food energy intake (caloric intake) can cause problems with attention, concentration, learning, and other important daily activities. For children who have not eaten breakfast, the educational value of a morning spent in the classroom may be lost. Repeated episodes of inadequate food energy intake can lead to cumulative deficits in learning, lower academic achievement, higher rates of school failure, and cognitive impairment.[21] Six- to 11-year-old children from food insufficient households have significantly lower arithmetic scores and are more likely to repeat a grade. Teenagers who are food insufficient are more likely to have seen a psychologist, have been suspended from school, and have difficulty getting along with other teenagers. Food insufficiency is also associated with increased risk of suicide in teenagers.[22]

The following data provide a snapshot of America's hungry in 2006:

- In 2006 on an average day in November, an estimated 600,000 to 877,000 households experienced very low food security, and children went hungry in 29,000 to 33,000 households.
- The median food-insecure household spent only 1 percent more than the cost of the Thrifty Food Plan, and the median food-secure household spent 32 percent more.
- Just over half of food-insecure households in 2006 had participated in the previous month in one or more of the three largest federal food and nutrition assistance programs—the National School Lunch Program, the Food Stamp Program, and the Special Supplemental Nutrition Program for Women, Infants, and Children (WIC).
- About 21 percent of food-insecure households obtained emergency food from a food pantry at some time during the year, and 2.2 percent ate one or more meals at an emergency kitchen in their community.
- Very low food security is more prevalent among African American and Hispanic households (8 and 5.7 percent, respectively).
- Low-income households with children (41.1 percent) were more likely to be food insecure than low-income households without children (27.1 percent). Low-income households with children headed by single women were especially vulnerable to food insecurity (46 percent).
- The prevalence of food insecurity varies geographically. Food insecurity for households located in principal cities of metropolitan areas (13.2 percent) and in nonmetropolitan areas (12 percent) by far exceeded the rate for households in suburbs and other metropolitan areas outside principal cities (9 percent). The prevalence of food insecurity was higher than the national average in the South (12.3 percent) and lower than the national average in the Northeast (9.2 percent), and the Midwest (10.7 percent) and West (10.5 percent) were near the national average.[23]

The extent of hunger and food insecurity is reflected in the number of people seeking food from emergency food providers, such as food pantries and soup kitchens. A 2007 study by the U.S. Conference of Mayors found that 16 (80 percent) of surveyed cities reported that requests for emergency food assistance increased during the last year. Among 15 cities that provided data, the median increase was 10 percent.[24]

Government Food Programs

The politics of food—or the way food is distributed in U.S. society—is complex. Like all resources in a free market society, food is a commodity that is bought and sold. In a pure market sense, those who cannot afford to purchase food are unable to consume it. Left to the caprice of the marketplace, many poor people would face malnutrition or even starvation. This problem is particularly acute in an urban environment, in which most people lack gardening skills and in any case have little or no access to land. Providing the poor with food is a redistributive function of the welfare state. As such, the governmental obligation to provide food to the poor is similar to its obligation to provide economic opportunity: When either or both are unavailable in adequate quantities, it is the responsibility of the welfare state to respond.

A Short History of Food Stamps and a Description of the Program

In 1933 Congress established the Federal Surplus Relief Corporation, an agency designed to distribute surplus commodity foods plus coal, mattresses, and blankets, and it established a food Stamp (FS) program that was terminated in 1943, when a commodity food distribution program was reestablished. A new pilot FS program began in John F. Kennedy's presidency, and in 1964 the current FS Act was passed.

Receiving FS increases the nutritional value of a low-income household's home food supply by 20 to 40 percent. Food stamp households that participate in the program on average spend more on food and acquire more food than low-income nonparticipating households. Figure 17.1 on page 448 describes the current eligibility rules for the FS program.

The federal government funds 100 percent of FS program benefits, with federal and state governments sharing 50 percent of administrative costs. Although administered by the USDA, state and local welfare agencies qualify applicants and provide

Assets and Income

Calculating Eligibility: Households may have no more than $2,000 in countable resources, such as a bank account ($3,000 if at least one person in the household is age 60 or older, or is disabled). Certain resources are not counted.

The *gross* monthly income of most households must be 130 percent or less of the federal poverty guidelines. For example, gross income includes all cash payments to the household, with a few exceptions.

The *net* monthly income must be 100 percent or less of federal poverty guidelines. Net income is figured by adding all of a household's gross income, and then taking a number of approved deductions for child care, some shelter costs and other expenses. Households with an elderly or disabled member are subject to the net income test, except where elderly disabled are a separate household and then are subject to the gross monthly income at 165 percent of the poverty level.

Countable assets include bank accounts, certificates of deposits, investments, and valuable art work, antiques, and other valuables.

Countable assets do not include:

• Homesteaded property that the claimant intends to return to if they are in a nursing home, or property occupied by a spouse, siblings, minor child, or disabled child of any age.

• Personal effects and household goods up to $2,000.

• One automobile of unlimited value if used for employment (long distance travel, not daily commute), medical purposes or as the family home. The FS program currently exempts any vehicle whose equity value is less than $1,500. For other vehicles, FS rules count either the fair market value over $4,650 or the equity value, whichever is greater. Some states use their TANF rules to determine vehicle eligibility, so these federal rules can vary from state to state.

Countable income does not include:

• Allowed deductions such as a 20 percent deduction from earned income; a standard deduction of $134 for all households (higher for some larger households); a dependent care deduction when needed for work, training, or education but not more than $200 for each child under age 2 and not more than $175 for each other dependent.

• Medical expenses for elderly or disabled members that are more than $35 for the month if they are not paid by insurance or someone else.

• Legally owed child support payments.

• Shelter costs for homeless households of $143 (some states only).

• Excess shelter costs that are more than half of the household's income after the other deductions. Allowable costs include the cost of fuel to heat and cook with, electricity, water, the basic fee for one telephone, rent or mortgage payments and taxes on the home. (Some states allow a set amount for utility costs instead of actual costs.) The amount of the shelter deduction cannot be more than $417 unless one person in the household is elderly or disabled.

Legal Immigrants and Rules of Work

A person must be a U.S. citizen, a member of a small group of certain non-citizens, or an eligible non-citizen to qualify for food stamps.

Citizenship/Alien Status

• The 2002 Farm Bill restores food stamp eligibility to most legal immigrants that: have lived in the country for 5 years; or are receiving disability related assistance or benefits, regardless of entry date; or starting 2003, are children regardless of entry date.

• Certain noncitizens such as those admitted for humanitarian reasons and those admitted for permanent residence are also eligible for the program. Eligible household members can get food stamps even if there are other members of the household who are not eligible.

• Noncitizens that are in the United States temporarily, such as students, are not eligible.

• A number of states have their own programs to provide benefits to immigrants who do not meet the regular Food Stamp program eligibility requirements.

Figure 17.1

Food Stamp Eligibility and Benefit Guidelines, 2007

Source: U.S. Department of Agriculture, "Food Stamp Program." Retrieved July 2008, from www.fns.usda.gov/pd/fspmain.htm

Work

With some exceptions, able-bodied adults between ages 16 and 60 must register for work, accept suitable employment, and take part in an employment and training program to which they are referred by the food stamp office. Failure to comply with these requirements can result in disqualification from the FS program. In addition, able-bodied adults between ages 18 and 50 who do not have any dependent children can get food stamps only for 3 months in a 36 month period if they do not work or participate in a workfare or employment and training program other than job search. This requirement is waived in some locations.

Benefits

An individual household's food stamp allotment is equal to the maximum allotment for that household's size, less 30 percent of the household's net income. Households with no countable income receive the maximum allotment. Allotment levels are higher for Alaska, Hawaii, Guam, and the Virgin Islands, reflecting higher food prices in those areas. The average monthly benefit was $96 per person and $215 per household in 2007.

Figure 17.1 (continued)

them with Electronic Benefit Transfer (EBT) cards. (Over 90 percent of FS recipients received EBT cards in 2007.) Recipients are given an allotment of stamps based on family size (see Table 17.1) and income, with eligibility requirements and benefits determined at the federal level. Food stamp eligibility is based on a means test (see Table 17.2 on page 450). Recipients originally had to pay a set price (depending on family size and income) for their stamps. For example, some families or individuals could purchase $75 worth of food stamps for $35; the difference between the cost and the face value of the stamps was called a "bonus." This system proved unwieldy because many poor people could not afford to purchase stamps. When purchase requirements were dropped in 1977 the participation rate rose by 30 percent.

Food Stamps: Who Is in the Program and What Does It Cost?

About 26.5 million people participated in the FS program in 2007 at a cost of $33.2 billion (see Table 17.3 on page 450). This represented a significant increase from previous years (17 million people received FS benefits in 2000) and was due to continuing high rates of joblessness; states improving access to low-income populations, including legal immigrants; and better outreach. Nevertheless, nearly half of all eligible people do not receive FS benefits.[25] The FS program is targeted toward those most in need:

• In 2006 the vast majority of food stamp households (87 percent) lived in poverty. Most FS

Table 17.1

U.S. Maximum Monthly Food Stamp Allotments, 2007–2008

Household Size	Maximum Allotment Level (48 states and DC)
1	$162
2	298
3	426
4	542
5	643
6	772
7	853
8	975
Each additional member	+122

Source: U.S. Department of Agriculture, "Food Stamp Program: How Much Could I Receive?" Retrieved July 2008, from www.fns.usda.gov/fsp/applicant_recipients/BEN.HTM

households (84 percent) contained a child under age 18, an elderly person (aged 60 and over), or a disabled nonelderly person.

• The average food stamp household in 2006 received a monthly FS benefit of $208, had a gross monthly income of $673, had a net monthly income of $328, had countable resources of $137, and was entitled to a total deduction of $411 per month.

• The average household size was 2.3 people in 2006.

Table 17.2

Gross and Net Income Eligibility Standards for the Continental United States, 2007–2008

Household Size	Gross Monthly Income (130 percent of poverty)	Net Monthly Income (100 percent of poverty)
1	$1107	$851
2	1484	1141
3	1861	1431
4	2238	1721
5	2615	2011
6	2992	2301
7	3369	2591
8	3746	2881
Each additional member	+377	+290

Note: Eligibility levels are higher for Alaska and Hawaii.

Source: USDA, "Food Stamp Program: Frequently Asked Questions." Retrieved July 2008, from www.workworld.org/wwwebhelp/food_stamp_benefit_levels.htm

• Children who received food stamps in 2006 tended to live in households that were headed by a single female adult. Nearly two-thirds (63 percent) of all food stamp households with children were headed by a single adult, representing 33 percent of all food stamp households.

• In 2006 the FS program served an average of 2 million households containing elderly people (aged 60 and over) each month, representing 18 percent of all households. These households received an average food stamp benefit of $91 per month and had an average household size of 1.3 people.[26]

Several of the provisions and rules of the FS program have remained unchanged for many years, but in June 2008 the FS program was reauthorized as part of The Food, Conservation and Energy Act of 2008 (FCEA). This legislation changes a number of provisions that will affect FS eligibility, benefits, and program administration, from October 1, 2008. For example, EBT cards will be the sole method of benefit delivery as of June 19, 2009, and food stamp coupons will not be accepted at stores from that time. The Food Stamp Program is also being renamed the Supplemental Nutrition Assistance Program (SNAP) and the Food Stamp Act of 1977 renamed the Food and Nutrition Act of 2008.[27]

Table 17.3

Food Stamp Statistics, Selected Years, 1975–2007 (participants and cost figures in millions)

Year	Total Cost of FS	Number of Participants	Percentage of Population Using FS	Average Monthly Benefits per Person
1975	$4,624	16.3	7.6	$21.40
1978	5,573	14.4	6.5	26.80
1981	11,812	20.6	9.0	39.50
1984	13,275	20.9	8.8	42.70
1987	13,535	19.1	7.8	45.80
1990	17,686	20.0	8.0	59.00
1991	21,012	22.6	9.0	63.90
1993	23,653	26.9	9.3	67.97
1995	20,500	26.7	8.9	71.50
2000	16,956	17.1	6.0	72.77
2003	23,880	21.2	7.5	83.93
2007	33,204	26.5	8.8	95.63

Sources: USDA, Food and Nutrition Service, "Food Stamp Participation and Costs," October 26, 2004. Retrieved November 2004, from www.fns.usda.gov/pd/fssummar.htm; and USDA, "Food Stamp Program Participation and Costs." Retrieved July 2008, from www.fns.usda.gov/pd/fssummar.htm

Special Supplemental Nutrition Program for Women, Infants, and Children (WIC)

The WIC program, enacted in 1972, was originally designed as a two-year pilot program to provide nutritional counseling and supplemental foods to pregnant and breastfeeding women, infants, and young children at nutritional risk. The goal of WIC is to address areas of child development that are most affected by poor health and inadequate nutrition, including impaired learning.[28] Specifically, the twin goals of WIC are (1) to enrich the food intake of participants by providing food or with coupons or food cards that are redeemable at local grocery stores, and (2) to educate mothers (individually and in groups) on how to prevent nutritional difficulties.

WIC is not an entitlement program. In other words, Congress does not set aside funds to allow every eligible individual to participate in the program. Instead, WIC is a federal grant program for which Congress authorizes a specific amount of funds each year. WIC is administered at the federal level by USDA's Food and Nutrition Service (FNS) and by state WIC agencies. WIC operates in all 50 states, 34 Indian Tribal Organizations, American Samoa, the District of Columbia, Guam, Puerto Rico, the Virgin Islands, and the Northern Mariana Islands. Each State agency is responsible for authorizing stores to accept WIC checks. At a minimum, the state agency will consider the prices of foods, the business integrity of the store's owner, and the variety and quantity of foods available in the store. In 2008, nearly 49,000 stores were authorized to accept WIC checks.[29] Income eligibility is less restrictive than for public assistance programs because federal guidelines target families whose pretax income is at or below 185 percent of the federal poverty line. Pregnant, breastfeeding, and postpartum women, infants, and children up to five years of age are eligible if they (1) are individually determined by a health professional to be at nutritional risk; (2) meet a state residency requirement; and (3) meet an income standard, or are determined automatically income eligible. A person who participates or has family members who participate in certain other benefit programs, such as the Food Stamp Program, Medicaid, or Temporary Assistance for Needy Families, automatically meets the income eligibility requirement (see Table 17.4).

Qualified beneficiaries receive supplemental foods each month in the form of actual food items or, more often, are given vouchers for the purchase of specific items in retail stores. Items that may be part of a food package include milk, cheese, eggs, infant formula, cereals, and fruits and vegetables. The USDA requires food packages that provide specific types and amounts of food appropriate for six categories of participants: (1) infants from birth to

Table 17.4

WIC Income Eligibility Guidelines, Effective from July 1, 2008 to June 30, 2009 (48 contiguous states, DC, Guam, and territories)

Household Size	Annually	Monthly	Twice-Monthly	Bi-Weekly	Weekly
1	$19,240	$1,604	$802	$740	$370
2	25,900	2,159	1,080	997	499
3	32,560	2,714	1,357	1,253	627
4	39,220	3,269	1,635	1,509	755
5	45,880	3,824	1,912	1,765	883
6	52,540	4,379	2,190	2,021	1,011
7	59,200	4,934	2,467	2,277	1,139
8	65,860	5,489	2,745	2,534	1,267
Each additional member	+6,660	+555	+278	+257	+129

Source: USDA, Food and Nutrition Service, "WIC Income Eligibility Guidelines, 2008–2009." Retrieved July 2008, from www.fns.usda .gov/wic/howtoapply/incomeguidelines.htm

■ *The National School Lunch Program is a federally assisted meal program that provides lunches to school-age children.*

three months; (2) infants from 4 to 12 months; (3) women and children with special dietary needs; (4) children from one to five years of age; (5) pregnant and nursing mothers; and (6) postpartum nursing mothers. In addition to receiving food benefits, WIC participants receive nutritional counseling.[30] In 2007 WIC served nearly 8.3 million women and children and cost $5.4 billion.[31]

Other Food Programs

Augmenting the FS program and WIC are a range of programs targeted at various constituencies. For instance, snacks are available to children and teenagers in after-school programs through the National School Lunch Program (NSLP) and the Child and Adult Care Food Program (CACFP). The

spotlight 17.1

Responding to Hunger in America

The federal government's response to hunger and malnutrition in the United States consists of several major programs—the food stamp program; the commodity distribution program; the national school lunch and breakfast programs; the Special Milk Program; the Special Supplemental Nutrition Program for Woman, Infants, and Children (WIC);

the Child and Adult Care Food Program; the Summer Food Service Program; Meals on Wheels; and the Congregate Meal Dining program.

To learn more about each of these programs and the specific services they provide, go the USDA's Food, Nutrition, and Consumer Services website at **www.fns.usda.gov/fns.**

Child Nutrition and WIC Reauthorization Act of 2004 (PL-108-265) enhances nutrition benefits for all children—with a special emphasis on older children—by authorizing reimbursement for snacks served to children through age 18 and to individuals, regardless of age, who are determined by the state agency to be mentally or physically disabled who participate in organized after-school programs.[32]

Although some low-income elderly receive food stamps, they can also be served by Meals on Wheels and the Congregate Meal Dining program. Begun in 1972, the Meals on Wheels program delivers meals for adults 60 years or older unable to take care of their own nutritional needs. Various community agencies arrange the daily delivery of meals to elderly persons living at home, and aged persons who receive food stamps can use them to purchase the meals. In some locations, meal services are also provided for nonsenior handicapped people. A donation of $2 is suggested for each meal, although there is no means test for the program. The Congregate Meal Dining program provides meals at such places senior like citizen centers. Figure 17.2 on page 454 examines other food programs.

Have the Food Programs Worked?

Because WIC is a discretionary rather than an entitlement program, it can serve only as many people as its budget allows. Consequently, it is estimated that only about half of those eligible receive WIC benefits.[33] Moreover, some counties have no WIC program; many others turn people away or have long waiting lists.[34] Although states may provide additional funds for WIC, only a minority do so.[35]

According to USDA studies, WIC saves lives and improves the health of nutritionally at-risk women, infants, and children. The results of studies conducted by FNS and other nongovernment entities demonstrate that WIC is one of the nation's most successful and cost-effective nutrition intervention programs. Some highlights of the findings are that WIC improves diet and diet-related outcomes; improves infant feeding practices; improves immunization rates and regular medical care; improves cognitive development; and improves preconceptional nutritional status. USDA research has also shown that the WIC program is playing an important role in improving birth outcomes and thus in containing health care costs. USDA reports found that Medicaid-eligible pregnant women in five states who participated in WIC during their pregnancies had longer pregnancies, fewer premature births, lower incidence of low-birth-weight infants, fewer infant deaths, and a greater likelihood of receiving prenatal care. Health care savings ranged from $1.77 to $3.13 for each dollar spent on WIC.[36]

The number of FS participants grew dramatically from 1989 (19 million) to 1994 (28 million) but then declined throughout the rest of the 1990s to 17.1 million in 2000. Food stamp caseloads decreased by 40 percent between 1994 and 2000. Studies showed that the caseload declined during this period of economic growth not only because many households' circumstances improved enough to make them ineligible for benefits, but also because a smaller percentage of the potentially eligible households were participating in the program. Since 2000, however, participation has increased dramatically to 26.5 million in 2007, almost to where it was in 1994, largely due to the economic downturn currently experienced in the United States.

Conservatives have also attacked the WIC program. In 2002 Douglas Besharov, director of the Project on Social and Individual Responsibility at the American Enterprise Institute, argued that the WIC program contributed to childhood obesity. He contended that real hunger is found mainly among people with behavioral or emotional problems such as drug addicts and the dysfunctional homeless. Besharov criticized liberal advocacy groups, unions, and farmers for standing in the way of "reform and modernization," code words used for dismantling a program while making it appear like an improvement.[37]

Food programs for the elderly have suffered a steep decline in federal appropriations after adjusting for inflation. In 2002 the government spent $716.5 million on home-delivered meals and on meals provided at senior centers. Ten years earlier it spent $767 million (in 2002 dollars), which explains why older Americans remain on waiting lists for months for a home-delivered hot meal. Trudy Lieberman maintains that New York City's budget for home-delivered meals illustrates the problem: "Twenty years ago Washington funded 80 percent of the program and the city funded the rest. Today the federal government provides less than 20 percent, and city and private sources provide the balance."[38]

Welfare reform and welfare-to-work programs are clearly not working if working people cannot afford to buy food. Hunger relief agencies report that since the early 1990s the greatest increase in

| National School Lunch Program (NSLP) | The NSLP provides lunches and the opportunity to practice skills learned in classroom nutrition education. NSLP is a federally assisted meal program operating in around 100,000 public and nonprofit private schools and residential child care institutions.

School districts and independent schools that take part in the lunch program receive cash subsidies and donated commodities from the USDA for each meal they serve. Free students are not charged and reduced price students are not charged more than 40 cents for lunch. In return, educational institutions must serve lunches that meet federal requirements. Children from families with incomes at or below 130 percent of the poverty level are eligible for free meals. Those between 130 percent and 185 percent of the poverty level are eligible for reduced-price meals. Children from families with incomes over 185 percent of poverty pay a full price, although their meals are still subsidized to some extent. Local school food authorities set their own prices for full-price meals, but most operate their meal services as nonprofit programs. In 2007 about 30.5 million children participated in the NSLP through more than 100,000 schools and residential child care institutions. Since the program began, more than 187 billion lunches have been served. The cost of the program in 2007 was $8.7 billion. |
| School Breakfast Program (SBP) | The SBP provides breakfasts to promote learning readiness and healthy eating behaviors. In 2007, 10.1 million children in more than 85,000 schools and institutions used the SBP, a federal program that provides states with cash assistance for nonprofit breakfast programs in schools and residential child care institutions. The program is administered at the federal level by the USDA through its FNS. State education agencies and local school food authorities administer the program at the local level.

Breakfasts served as part of the SBP provide one-fourth or more of the daily recommended levels for key nutrients that children need. They are required to provide no more than 30 percent of calories from fat and less than 10 percent of calories from saturated fat. Research shows that children who have school breakfast eat more fruits, drink more milk, and consume less saturated fat than those who don't eat breakfast or have breakfast at home.

Children whose families meet income criteria may receive free or reduced-price breakfasts. Those from families with incomes at or below 130 percent of the federal poverty level are eligible for free meals. Children whose family income is between 130 percent and 185 percent of the poverty level are eligible for reduced-price meals. Those from families over 185 percent of poverty pay a full price, although their meals are still subsidized to some extent. Schools may not charge more than 30 cents for a reduced-price breakfast. Schools set their own prices for breakfasts served to students who pay the full meal price though they must operate their meal services as nonprofit programs. The cost of the SBP program in 2007 was $2.2 billion. |
| Special Milk Program (SMP) | The SMP offers milk to children who lack access to other meal programs. The program provides milk to children in schools and child care institutions that do not participate in other federal child nutrition meal service programs. Schools or institutions may choose pasteurized fluid types of unflavored or flavored whole milk, low-fat milk, skim milk, and cultured buttermilk |

Figure 17.2

Other USDA Food Programs

Source: USDA, Food and Nutrition Service, "Program Fact Sheets." Retrieved July 2008, from www.fns.usda.gov/cga/FactSheets/ProgramFactSheets.htm

that meet state and local standards. All milk is to contain vitamins A and D at levels specified by the Food and Drug Administration.

When local school officials offer free milk under the program, any child from a family that meets income guidelines for free meals and milk is eligible. 4,914 schools and residential child care institutions participate in the SMP, along with 853 summer camps and 533 nonresidential child care institutions. Each child's family must apply annually for free milk eligibility. In 2007 over 90 million half pints of milk were served. The cost of the program in 2007 was $13.6 million.

Summer Food Service Program (SFSP)

The SFSP serves meals and snacks to low-income children during long school vacations. The FNS administers the SFSP at the federal level; state education agencies administer the program in most states, although in some areas the state health or social service department or an FNS regional office may be designated. Locally, SFSP is run by approved sponsors, including school districts, local government agencies, camps, or private nonprofit organizations. Sponsors provide free meals to a group of children at a central site, such as a school or a community center. States approve SFSP meal sites as open, enrolled, or camp sites. Open sites operate in low-income areas where at least half of the children come from families with incomes at or below 185 percent of the federal poverty level, making the children eligible for free and reduced-price school meals. Children 18 and younger may receive free meals and snacks through SFSP. Meals and snacks are also available to persons with disabilities who are over age 18 but who participate in school programs for mentally or physically disabled people. In 2007 about 118 million meals were served at over 31,000 sites. The cost of the program in 2007 was $285.9 million.

Child and Adult Care Food Program (CACFP)

CACFP is a key source of support for serving nutritious meals and snacks in child care centers, family child care homes, Head Start, after-school programs, shelters and adult day care centers. The program provides reimbursement for food and meal preparation costs, ongoing training in the nutritional needs of children, and onsite assistance in meeting the program's strong nutritional requirements.

Children aged 12 and younger are eligible to receive up to two meals and one snack each day at a day care home or center through CACFP. Children who reside in homeless shelters may receive up to three meals a day. Migrant children aged 12 and younger, and persons with disabilities regardless of their age, are also eligible for CACFP. Public Law 105-336 made CACFP snacks available to children and youth through age 18 in eligible afterschool care programs, while Public Law 108-265 raised the age limit for meals served to children residing in emergency shelters from 12 to age 18.

The Emergency Food Assistance Program (TEFAP)

TEFAP was first authorized to distribute surplus commodities in 1981. The 1988 Hunger Prevention Act required the USDA to purchase additional commodities for low-income households and local emergency feeding organizations.

TEFAP provides USDA commodities to states who distribute the food through local emergency food providers. Available foods vary depending on market conditions. Each state determines the criteria for household eligibility, and may adjust income criteria based on need in the state. Eligibility criteria may include participation in existing food or other assistance programs for which income is considered as a basis for eligibility. In FY 2008 Congress appropriated $189.65 million for TEFAP.

Figure 17.2 (continued)

hunger has been among the working poor. Among working people in emergency food recipient households, almost 56 percent work full time. According to the U.S. Conference of Mayors, 39 percent of people requesting emergency food assistance in U.S. cities are employed.[39]

A General Accounting Office (GAO) study on food stamps found that the need for food assistance has not diminished. Rather, needy individuals and families are increasingly relying on sources other than food stamps, such as food banks, soup kitchens, and emergency pantries. These findings were corroborated by other data. A Wisconsin study found that more than one-third of former welfare recipients had problems paying for food despite a high incidence of employment. Fewer than half of the former recipients reported having more money than when they were receiving public assistance, and 68 percent reported that they were "barely making it." A South Carolina Department of Social Services study reported that after leaving TANF, 17 percent of former welfare recipients had no way to buy food some of the time. This is twice the number of families who reported such problems while receiving assistance. An analysis of former welfare recipients in Massachusetts found that 18 percent of families leaving the rolls were back on welfare after three months, and 21 percent were back after a year; and the same study found that food insecurity increased for many families after they went off welfare. Forty percent of the families interviewed did not have enough food or enough of the right kinds of food after being off welfare for one year. More than 20 percent of families who remained off welfare after one year used food banks or had to borrow money to buy food. In short, as poor Americans transition from welfare to work and their benefits are cut or reduced, they are finding their wages insufficient to meet basic needs, including child care, transportation, and housing costs. As a result, working poor families may cut their food budget or turn to local charities for aid.[40]

Food stamp participation is also hampered by excessive red tape. In reviewing the application process for food stamps in 50 states, Second Harvest found that:

- More than half of all states and the District of Columbia have FS applications that run 10 to 36 pages long.
- Food stamp applications are difficult to read and complete, and they include excessive and invasive questions—often with little or no legal connection to the FS program.
- The average length of a state food stamp application is 12 pages. Ten states have applications between 19 and 28 pages long. Most food stamp applications are longer than the applications for a federal firearms permit, a federal home mortgage loan, or a school bus driver's license.
- Only 15 states have two-part applications in which the first part, generally shorter, may be used to initiate the process and begin the accrual of benefits once certified.
- FS applications in 49 of the 50 states and the District of Columbia contain certification statements that must be signed by the applicant (under penalty of perjury) that are written at the ninth- to twelfth-grade reading level. Some state FS applications require applicants to provide accurate information (under penalty of perjury) using terms that many are unlikely to understand.
- Some applications require information regarding children's income and bank accounts; income from babysitting; charity and gifts from churches and synagogues; income from panhandling, bingo, and plasma donation; and garage sale receipts.[41]

Farming in the United States

The 1980s were a tumultuous time for American farmers, and in many places the 1980s rivaled the Great Depression of the 1930s.[42] Some estimates were that 3.8 percent of all farmers had filed for bankruptcy in 1985 alone.[43] Other farm indicators were equally bleak. In 1981 the total asset value of U.S. agriculture was $1 trillion; by 1985 it decreased to $692 billion—a 30 percent drop and the steepest fall since the Great Depression. Although U.S. farms had declined in number by a modest 16,000 between 1978 and 1982, between 1982 and 1987 they declined by 151,000, or at a rate of about 30,000 a year.[44] U.S. farmers made a relative comeback in the late 1980s, due in part to the worldwide drought in 1987. By early 1990 farmland prices in the United States had risen, and net cash farm income went from $48.5 billion in 1987 to about the same level as in the mid-1970s. More importantly, the farm debt stabilized.[45]

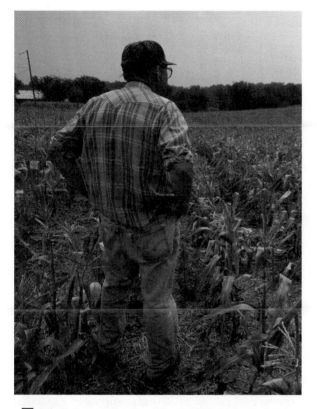

■ *Of all the occupations in the United States, farming today is facing the greatest decline.*

Farmers have historically demanded that agricultural commodity price supports be set at parity levels—in other words, an equal ratio between farm prices and input/output costs.[46] In 1942, Congress established the price support levels at 90 percent of parity. From 1942 to 1953, average prices paid to farmers were at 90 to 100 percent of parity, thereby raising market prices, ensuring a secure income for farmers, reducing the need for excessive debt, and encouraging stabilization in the price of grain.

By the end of World War II, powerful corporations, academics, and free traders had begun to wage war on the farm parity program. Soil conservation, supply management, and parity were characterized as socialist ideas that interfered with a free market economy. Grain companies called for lower prices to help foreign sales, arguing that expanded exports and food aid programs would compensate farmers for lower commodity prices. Industrialists argued that low food prices would translate into cheaper labor costs, and agribusiness believed that lowered commodity prices would result in more production, thereby increasing the use of their products.

The small farmer eventually lost to this powerful coalition, and farm parity was terminated in 1953. As a result, the purchasing power of net farm income decreased even as exports rose. Held constant in 1967 dollars, the purchasing power of net farm income dropped from an annual average of $25 billion from 1942 to 1952 (the years of farm parity) to an average of $13.3 billion from 1953 to 1972. In 1952 net farm income was greater than total farm debt; by 1983 net farm income was less than farm interest payments.[47]

Family farming embodies many of America's most cherished values—hard work, independence, strong family life, close-knit communities, and democratic institutions. For many rural families, farming is not a vocation but a way of life. Working the land, often a legacy from parents or grandparents, creates a commitment to both place and family heritage.[48] This psychological connection to farming means that many farmers see themselves as farmer-caretakers. Financial failure therefore leaves farmers not only with a sense of personal failure, but also with shame for having failed their families and their heritage. This loss can result in emotional problems ranging from stress and depression to self-destructive or aggressive behavior.[49] The Reverend Paul Tidemann, a Lutheran minister who studied the farm crisis of the 1980s, reported that "The loss of a farm . . . is not the same as a loss of a job. It signals the loss of a personal and family connection to the land. It prompts a sense of betrayal, in many cases, of generations of farmers, past, present, and future."[50]

Governmental Farm Policies

Former President Ronald Reagan signed the Food Security Act into law in 1985. This legislation was distinctive in three ways: (1) It was the most complicated farm bill ever passed; (2) it cost the federal government more than previous farm bills had (about $80 billion from 1986 to 1990); and (3) the price supports, at least in terms of parity, were lower than they had been in previous legislation.[51] In turn, farmers lost money on every bushel of corn harvested and were forced to borrow to cover their losses. Grain corporations and foreign buyers were allowed to purchase corn at prices below the cost of production. Federal policy was subsidizing the grain corporations at the expense of farmers, taxpayers, and the general public.

spotlight 17.2

The National Farmer's Union

The National Farmer's Union is a general farm organization that represents farmers and ranchers in the United States. The goal of this organization is to sustain and strengthen family farm and ranch agriculture. To learn more about this organization, go to its website at **www.nfu.org.**

The United Farm Workers Association

The United Farm Workers Association (UFW) represents the interests of farm workers throughout the United States. To learn more about this organization, go to its website at **www.ufw.org.**

In 1996, former President Bill Clinton signed the Federal Agricultural Improvement and Reform (FAIR) Act, replacing earlier farm bills. This legislation enjoyed wide support from Republicans, who wanted an agricultural free market, and from urban liberals, who wanted to end farm subsidies. The 1996 farm bill was based on a similar ideological premise as the Personal Responsibility and Work Opportunity Reconciliation Act (PRWORA). Namely, it was designed to wean farmers off governmental subsidies in the same way that TANF attempted to wean welfare recipients off public assistance. For free marketers, subsidy-dependent farmers were all too similar to subsidy-dependent welfare recipients.

The heart of the FAIR Act was the "Freedom to Farm" commodity program that replaced traditional farm subsidies (i.e., those that reimburse farmers when market prices drop) with a system of fixed annual payments that declined over seven years. The bill also severed the connection between subsidies and current farm prices. The government delivered these payments to all farmers who grew wheat, feed grains, cotton, rice, and soybeans/oilseed. The total payments of $36 billion declined over a seven-year period, thus ending the open-ended entitlement of previous legislation. The success was not long lived. In 1998 production grew, demand fell, and prices declined. The price of a bushel of wheat at the Chicago Board of Trade dropped from $7.16 in 1996 to less than $3.00 in 1998.[52] The 1996 farm bill was supposed to save taxpayers money, but instead it cost more than the legislation it replaced.[53] Congress retreated from the Agricultural

Market Transition Assistance (AMTA) spending caps and approved emergency relief payments.[54]

In 2002 former President George Bush signed the Farm Security and Rural Investment Act, which governed federal farm programs until 2008. The bill altered the farm payment program and introduced countercyclical farm income support; expanded conservation land retirement programs; emphasized on-farm environmental practices; relaxed rules to make more borrowers eligible for federal farm credit assistance; restored food stamp eligibility to legal immigrants; added various commodities to those requiring country-of-origin labeling; and introduced provisions on animal welfare. One of the more contentious issues in the bill was mandatory country-of-origin labeling for meat and other foods, something that was not implemented.[55]

Biofuels and Farming

Biofuel production (ethanol) has been a boon to the American farmer. Touted as a greener alternative to gasoline, ethanol can be made from corn, barley, wheat, sugarcane, or beet. Proponents argue that ethanol is a clean-burning renewable energy source that can help the United States switch from dwindling oil wells worldwide to boundless fields of crops. By 2008 about 25 percent of the nation's corn went into ethanol production.[56]

Critics argue that biofuel crops, such as corn, are grown with the help of fossil fuels in the form of fertilizers, pesticides, and the gasoline needed for farm equipment. One estimate is that corn needs 30 percent more energy than the finished fuel it produces. Another problem is the land required to produce it. Still others estimate that the grain needed to make enough ethanol to fill the gas tank of an SUV is sufficient to feed a person for a year. Critics argue that this biofuel production is helping to usher in worldwide food shortages. Other critics have questioned the role fertilizer is playing in climate change, claiming that using fertilizer on biofuel crops will emit enough nitrous oxide (more than 296 times more powerful heat trapping gas than Carbon dioxide) to eliminate all the carbon savings biofuels produce.[57]

Although biofuels are more carbon dioxide neutral than fossil fuels, the United Nations warns that land use, food supply, and water supply issues can be problematic in biofuel production. The dangers of biofuels involve the loss of biodiversity as forests are cleared to grow crops for ethanol, the exacerbation of water shortages, the distortion of food prices, and the competition with local food production. By 2008, increased biofuel production from corn had already dramatically raised the price of corn in many developing countries to the point of rioting. Despite these problems, when properly managed, biofuels can, in the short-term, help to foster an orderly transition from a fossil-based fuel economy to a sustainable energy system.

The Face of U.S. Farming

The following highlights important trends in U.S. agriculture:

• *Dwindling Farms.*   Of all the occupations in this country, farming today is facing the greatest decline. There are about 2 million farms remaining in the United States; between 1993 and 1997, the number of mid-sized family farms dropped by 74,440. In the 1930s, 25 percent of the population lived on farms; by 2004 that number dropped to 2 percent. Between 1978 and 2002, some 86,479 U.S. farms disappeared. In 1920 the United States had over 925,000 African American-operated farms; by 2002, there were less than 36,000. The rate of agricultural loss by African American farmers is over twice that of other farmers. Farms operated by hobby farmers account for 35 percent of all farms.

• *Farm Incomes.*   More than half of all U.S. farm operators work off-farm, with 80 percent of these working full-time jobs. Nearly half of all spouses are also employed off the farm. A source of income, farming has played an increasingly smaller role in determining the well-being of farm households. Those farmers who remain on their land often face the prospect of working off the farm just to stay on the land. In 2004, the USDA estimated that 98 percent of total farm operator income comes from off farm sources and only 7 percent of all farm families reported 100 percent "on-farm" income.

• *The Graying of U.S. Farms.*   Half of all current farmers are likely to retire in the next two or three decades. Nearly half of all farmers are between the ages of 45 and 65, with the average age being 54.3 years. Just 6 percent of farmers are under age 35. Farmers in the United States over age 55 control more than half the farmland; since 1987 the number of entry-level farmers replacing them has fallen by 30 percent and now makes up only 10 percent of all farmers. These trends suggest the absence of a new generation of beginning farmers.

• *Consolidation and Control.*   Nearly half of all U.S. land is farmland (more than 1 billion acres) and 4 percent of landowners hold 47 percent of it. In California, the nation's largest agricultural producer, 3 percent of California farms control 60 percent of the market. Nationwide the figures are similar— 7 percent of U.S. farms received 60 percent of the net cash farm income in 1992. The top 10 percent of farm-subsidy recipients collect two-thirds of the money, and the bottom 80 percent get just one-sixth.

• *Women and Farming.*   Ownership and control in U.S. agriculture contains distinct gender bias. Of those who control U.S. farmland, only 9 percent are women. Women tend to own smaller farms; the average size of properties held by men is one-third larger than farms held by women.

• *Crop Prices.*   The small farmer's share of each food dollar has dropped steadily over the past half century. Since 1985 farm prices in inflation-adjusted dollars have dropped steadily for commodities such as corn, wheat, and soybeans.

• *Rural Health and Food Quality.*   Many rural residents are exposed to excessive odors from factory farms and often suffer from nausea, vomiting, coughing, and headaches. In more extreme cases, people living near factory farms have developed neurological diseases and women have suffered from miscarriages as a result of water and air contamination. Employees working inside factory farms have died from exposure to manure lagoons. The factory farms' extreme confinement and increased levels of production of animals intensify the opportunity for contamination of meat and poultry with bacteria, such as *Escherichia coli* and salmonella, which can cause illness and death. Crowded livestock conditions lead to a reliance on antibiotics to maintain animal health, and more than 70 percent of all antibiotics consumed in the United States are fed to healthy farm animals. This indiscriminate use of drugs has contributed directly to the evolution of antibiotic-resistant bacteria that the American Medical Association considers an impending public health crisis.

• *Farm Subsidies.*   Large farms receive nearly twice as much in government subsidy payments as small farms. A USDA study found that one-fourth of farm subsidies go to the largest 1 percent of producers. The outbreaks of *E. coli* in spinach and tomatoes in the mid-2000s can be partly attributed to this large-scale production.

• *Efficiency.*   Because they often farm small acreages using greater crop diversity and careful management of natural resources, family farmers are more efficient than large, industrialized food producers. Moreover, the per unit cost for agricultural production is no better in larger commercial operations than in family farms. Factory farms add many real costs, such as increased use of fossil fuels, environmental damage, health threats, and threats to the safety of the food supply.[58]

Farmworkers

The efforts of millions of farmworkers are essential to the multibillion-dollar U.S. fruit and vegetable industry. Because agricultural production depends on the influx of seasonal labor, each year anywhere from 3 to 5 million families leave their homes to follow the crops. The wages and conditions they labor under are in many cases scandalous.

The $28 billion U.S. produce industry is largely cultivated by hand, mostly through the labor of America's farmworkers. Some Americans assume that farmworker poverty results in lower food prices, but Eric Schlosser notes that "Maintaining the current level of poverty among migrant farmworkers saves the average American household (just) $50 a year."[59]

Thousands of migrant farmworkers risk death and incarceration each year by crossing the U.S.–Mexico border. In the blistering Arizona heat of 2001, 14 immigrants died after smugglers abandoned them. In 2003, 17 immigrants, including a five-year-old boy, died of dehydration in the back of an abandoned truck in Texas. Despite the danger, illegal immigration rates have soared.

More than two million year-round and seasonal migrant farmworkers, including 100,000 children, work in the United States. About two thirds are immigrants, of whom 80 percent are from Mexico. Just 14 percent of all farmworkers have full-time work.[60] The following represents an overview of U.S. farmworkers in 2002:

• *Demographics.*   Sixty-one percent of farmworkers were U.S. born. The average age of farmworkers was 31, and half were under age 35. Almost 83 percent of farmworkers were men; 53.1 percent were married; and slightly less than half were parents.

• *Education and language.*   Eighty-four percent of farmworkers spoke Spanish and they typically completed six years of education. Thirty-one percent had less than nine years of schooling, and 52 percent had less than 12 years. Only 10 percent spoke or read English fluently.

• *Labor and conditions.*   Sixty percent of all farmworkers held just one U.S. farm job a year and spent roughly half their time doing farm work. Farmworkers earned $5.94 an hour on average. About 20 percent reported being covered by unemployment insurance, but only 3 percent had employer-provided health insurance. Seventy-seven percent of farmworkers were paid by the hour and 20 percent by the piece.

• *Wages and poverty.*   Three out of four U.S. farmworkers earn less than $10,000 annually, and 61 percent of families live below the federal poverty line. The median income of farmworkers was less than $7,500 a year. This is particularly striking because the largest 1.5 percent of U.S. farms employ more than half of the farm labor. Archer Daniels Midland, the world leader in the production of soy meal, corn, wheat, and cocoa, reaped $1.7 billion in profits in 2003; its chief executive officer (CEO), Allen G. Andreas, received over $2.9 million in compensation. Dole, the world's largest producer of fresh fruit, vegetables, and cut flowers generated $4.8 billion in revenues in 2003.

• *Use of social services.*   Despite their poverty, few farmworkers use social services. Just 20 percent of farmworkers report using unemployment insurance. Just 13 percent of farmworker families receive Medicaid, 10 percent get food stamps, and 10 percent participate in WIC.

- *Assets.* Few farmworkers have assets. Fewer than 44 percent of farmworkers own a vehicle. Because of this, many were forced to pay for rides to work. Home ownership also had declined. In the mid-1990s, one-third of all farmworkers owned or were buying a house; by the end of the decade that number was only 14 percent.
- *Women.* Women farmworkers have lower personal incomes than men. The median income for women farmworkers is typically only half to two-thirds that of males.[61]

On average, farmworkers spend more than 30 percent of their income on housing, often substandard. One study showed that 26 percent of farmworker homes were adjacent to pesticide-treated fields.[62] More than 35 percent of housing for farmworkers in eight major agricultural labor states (California, Florida, Texas, Washington, Colorado, Michigan, New York, and Ohio) lacked inside running water. Despite regulations, it is estimated that one-third of U.S. farm laborers work in fields without drinking water, hand-washing facilities, or toilets. And at the end of the workday, many farmworkers do not have a home to go to. The number of farmworkers needing housing often exceeds the available housing units. In addition, migrant farmworkers face barriers in obtaining private housing. For example, rural communities may not have enough rental units available, or they may be unwilling to rent to migrant farmworkers because they cannot provide deposits, qualify for credit checks, or make long-term rental commitments.[63]

Education is also problematic for migrant farmworkers. Constant mobility makes it hard for the children of farmworkers to complete their education. Children who move often are two and a half times more likely to repeat a grade than are children who are stationary. Changing schools is emotionally difficult for children, and youngsters are more likely to drop out of school if they change schools four or more times; educators who work with migrant children say that 55 percent of these children graduate nationwide. Migrant children also face intense economic pressure to drop out of school.[64]

The poverty experienced by migrant families requires all able family members to work. In fact, agriculture is the only industry that allows workers under age 16: The Fair Labor Standards Act sets age 12 as the legal limit for farm work, with exemptions available for children as young as 10 or 11. It has

been estimated that 43,000 children accompanied by family members, and an additional 55,000 unaccompanied minors, are involved in farm labor. When children work in the fields, occupational injury presents an even more significant risk than for adults because of their inexperience.[65]

The health problems experienced by farmworkers are staggering. One of the many health risks they face is the exposure to pesticides, herbicides, and fungicides. National estimates of the number of farmworkers, farmers, and their families potentially exposed to toxic chemicals range from 3.2 to 4 million people. In California the average death rate for farmworkers is five times higher than workers in other industries.[66] Approximately 300,000 farmworkers in the United States are poisoned by pesticides annually. The Environmental Protection Agency (EPA) estimated that 300,000 acute illnesses and injuries each year are attributable to the use of pesticides. Children work and play in the fields, and are thus exposed to the same occupational hazards as adults. Research has shown that because of lower weight and higher metabolism, children are more susceptible to the harmful effects of toxic chemicals than adults. One study found that 48 percent of children had worked in fields still wet with pesticides; 36 percent had been sprayed either directly or indirectly (by drift); and farm operators had sprayed 34 percent of the children's homes in the process of spraying nearby fields. A 2002 California study shows that 51 percent of pesticide poisoning cases were due to drift.[67] A 1988 study of 460 farmworkers in Washington State found that 89 percent did not know the name of a single chemical to which they had been exposed; 76 percent had never received any information on appropriate protection measures.[68]

As a result of the exposure to pesticides, farmworkers frequently suffer stomach ailments, headaches, rashes, burns, and other toxic chemical-related problems. Many die from environmentally caused cancer, and too often workers' babies are born with severe birth defects. Many families must sleep, bathe, and cook near the fields where they work and have no option but to use water that may be contaminated with toxic chemicals.[69] The following illustrates some of the health and safety problems faced by America's farmworkers:

- Agriculture is the most dangerous occupation in the United States; between 1979 and 1983 about 23,800 children and adolescents were injured. In 2002 an average of 103 children had died from agricultural injuries. Twenty-nine out of every 100,000 agricultural workers died of unintentional work-related injuries in 2001.[70]

• One study found that about 34 percent of migrant children were infected with intestinal parasites or suffered severe asthma, chronic diarrhea, vitamin A deficiency, chemical poisoning, or continuous bouts of otitis media leading to hearing loss. Other commonly reported health problems included lower height or weight, respiratory disease, skin infections, and undiagnosed congenital and developmental problems. Researchers found an 11 percent rate of chronic health conditions among migrant children, compared to the national rate of 3 percent. The majority of preschool-aged children of farmworkers are not appropriately vaccinated for their age level.

• Water-related parasitic infections afflict migrant farmworker adults and children an average of 59 times more often than the general population.

• More than any other workers, farmworkers suffer and die from heat stress and dehydration.

• Health centers rank alcohol and drug abuse as the fourth largest health problem among adult patients of migrant health centers.

• Death rates from influenza and pneumonia are as high as 20 percent and 200 percent higher, respectively, for farmworkers than the national average.

• In a study conducted by the CDC, 44 percent of farmworkers had positive tuberculosis (TB) tests. Regional studies show that 41 percent tested positive in North Carolina, 44 percent in Florida, and 48 percent in Virginia.

• It is estimated that as few as 42 percent of female farmworkers receive prenatal care during the first trimester of pregnancy, even though many migrant pregnancies are classified as high risk with multiple indicators. The infant mortality rate among migrant farmworkers is 125 percent higher than in the general population.[71]

In the 1960s the conditions faced by farmworkers led to the creation of the United Farm Workers union (UFW) in California, a movement led by the charismatic Cèsar Chávez. At its peak in the 1970s, the UFW had about 120,000 workers under contract, and between 1966 and 1980 it obtained two 40 percent wage increases in the grape industry, among other gains. But during the 1980s contracts began to expire and successive Republican administrations stacked the California Agricultural Labor Relations Board with pro-industry members, effectively gutting the law that had created the board. In the midst of a hostile political climate and internal differences, the UFW went into a decade-long slump. By the mid-1990s the UFW had only about 20,000 workers under contract in California, Texas, and Florida; and in 2003 fewer than 10 percent of all strawberry pickers were unionized.[72]

Farm labor contractors now hire 20 percent of farmworkers nationwide and 40 percent in California. In the 1980s a rise of independent labor contractors as key players in the farm industry was seen. Hired by growers, these middlemen round up laborers and deliver them to the fields. Contractors pay less than growers, offer few benefits, and provide little job security. They also have a reputation for mistreating farmworkers and cheating them in wages. Contractors shield large growers from labor actions and legal claims, distancing them from the actual hiring of workers.[73] If a judgment comes down against a labor contractor, the contractor often vanishes or puts the businesses into bankruptcy, only to emerge in a new place or under a new name. The labor subcontracting system is an important obstacle to improving the welfare of farmworkers. One issue being pressed by farmworker activists is the creation of legislation that would make growers legally responsible for their workers, regardless of whether they use contractors.

Issues in U.S. Farming

There are a number of important issues affecting U.S. farming, including the corporatization of agriculture, genetic engineering, global trade, mad cow disease, local selling, organic farming, sustainable agriculture, and global warming.

The Corporatization of American Farming

U.S. family farms are rapidly being replaced by corporate farms, a trend spanning all agricultural sectors. Corporate agriculture is a system wherein the farm owner, the farm manager, and the farmworker are different people. This system represents a dramatic shift from the historic structure of traditional agriculture, in which individual farmers make the decisions and reap the profits. Industrial agriculture encourages large-scale, highly specialized farms where uniformity is emphasized over quality, and where many costs are shifted from the farm operation to society. There are also attendant environmental risks in large-scale agriculture. In North Carolina, for example, a 25-million-gallon hog manure spill at a factory farm in 1995 killed thousands of fish, destroyed crops, and severely damaged a local river. A single Utah hog operation raises 2.5 million hogs a year, producing more waste than the entire city of Los Angeles.[74]

Corporatization leads to closed markets where prices are fixed not by open, competitive bidding but by negotiated contracts. Small volume producers are discriminated against in price or other terms of trade. Under these conditions, many smaller farmers who cannot participate in "vertical integration" are forced out of business because they have no place to sell their products. Moreover, in traditional food markets, 91 cents of every dollar spent on food goes to suppliers, processors, middlemen, and marketers, most of whom are not based in the community. As such, only nine cents of each dollar goes to the farmer.[75]

An integral part of corporate farming is vertical integration, whereby agricultural corporations control all aspects of production, including raising, owning, slaughtering, and marketing livestock or agricultural products. One example is ConAgra, the largest distributor of agricultural chemicals in North America and one of the largest fertilizer producers in the world. In 2007 ConAgra's gross revenues were just over $12 billion and it owned more than 100 grain elevators, 2,000 railroad cars, and 1,100 barges. It is the largest of the three corporations that mill 80 percent of North America's wheat. ConAgra is also the largest turkey producer and the fourth largest broiler producer, producing its own poultry feed as well as other livestock feed. The company hires growers to raise its birds and then processes them in their own facilities. This poultry can then be purchased as fryers, under the name of Butterball, or in further processed foods such as TV dinners and pot pies under the label of Banquet, Marie Callender's, or Healthy Choice. ConAgra also owns 73 well-known brand names such as Armour, Banquet, Blue Ribbon, Fleischmann's, Parkay, Hunt's, Chef Boyardee, Chung King, Wolfgang Puck, Egg Beaters, Healthy Choice, Hebrew National, Kid Cuisine, Knott's Berry Farm, La Choy, Libby's, Louis Kemp, Marie Callender's, Orville Redenbacher, Peter Pan, Wesson, Reddi-Whip, and Ranch Style.[76] The extent of corporate agriculture is illustrated in Figure 17.3.

- By 2003 the largest 9 percent of farms generated 73 percent of all U.S. farm output.

- In 2005 the top 10 commercial seed companies controlled more than 50 percent of the world's commercial seed sales. This was an increase of 17 percent in only two years.

- The top 10 biotech companies control 75 percent of world biotech crop sales. This is also an increase of 50 percent in two years.

- Among pesticide manufacturers, the top six companies account for 70 percent of the global market.

- The top 10 pesticide manufacturers control 84 percent of the pesticide market.

- Among agrochemical companies, the top 10 control 80 percent of global sales.

- In the vegetable seed market, one corporation dominates: Monsanto. It controls 31 percent of bean seed sales, 38 percent of cucumber seed sales, 34 percent of hot pepper sales, 29 percent of sweet pepper sales, 23 percent of tomato seed sales, and 25 percent of onion seeds.

- As of 2004 Monsanto accounted for 88 percent of the total land acreage producing genetically modified (GM) seeds: 91 percent of GM soybean lands; 97 percent of GM maize lands; 63.5 percent of GM cotton lands; and 59 percent of canola.

- Among grocery retailers, one company, Wal-Mart, is four times the size of its nearest competitor in terms of food sales, and bigger than the combined sales of the next four leading retailers.

Figure 17.3

Facts about Corporate Agriculture

Source: The International Forum on Globalization, "The Rise and Predictable Fall of Globalized Industrial Agriculture," 2007. Retrieved July 2008, from www.ifg.org/pdf/ag%20report.pdf

Genetic Engineering

Genetic engineering, which sparked a global controversy since its introduction in 1995, is the manipulation of specific genes that are moved from one species to another to create a trait that did not previously exist. For example, crops such as corn have been engineered to contain pesticides in every cell of the plant. As a result, these crops are not registered as food and are actually considered pesticides.[77] Even though the Food and Drug Administration claims genetically modified (GM) products are safe, there has been no thorough analysis of their long-term effects. Moreover, GM products are not labeled. Critics argue that GM crops are increasingly threatening the biodiversity in the seed supply and making crops more vulnerable to disease outbreaks and pest infestations. Two multinational companies, Monsanto and DuPont, dominate the U.S. seed industry.[78]

Farmers buy GM crops based on promise of lower costs and higher yields, but they often find additional costs in veterinary bills, medications, unstable markets, and extra pesticides. Specifically, farmers that buy GM seeds enter into a contract that dictates how and when the crop can be grown. This contract also forbids the farmer to save any seeds, which is contrary to traditional farming practices. Many farmers have been sued for allegedly saving seeds, while neighboring farmers whose crops have been contaminated by GM pollen drift have been sued by Monsanto for unknowingly possessing GM seeds.[79] In countries like New Zealand, GM food products are labeled as such.

Global Trade

The global trade in food has emerged as a serious threat facing family farmers in the United States and around the world. Agricultural free trade agreements, like the North American Free Trade Agreement (NAFTA)—which linked the economies of the United States, Mexico, and Canada—promote agricultural trade with little regard to its impact on local communities and family farmers. As a result, several countries, including the United States, have been flooded with cheap food imports (2004 marked the first year since 1986 that food imports exceeded food exports). These low-cost imports have caused small farmers to lose their local markets, and family farmers worldwide have been forced off their land. In turn, this weakened local food production.[80]

Since the passage of NAFTA in 1994, family farmers in all three countries have felt the negative impacts of a free trade agreement designed to benefit agribusiness. In the United States, 100,000 family farmers were forced out of farming between 1996 and 2001. During that same period, Canada lost 11 percent of its family farms.[81] NAFTA and other trade liberalization policies have dramatically increased rural poverty and hunger in Mexico. Between 1992 and 2002, the number of rural Mexicans living in extreme poverty grew from 36 to 52 percent. Almost 2 million subsistence farmers were pushed off their land and migrated to export factories, maquiladoras, or to fields and cities in the United States. NAFTA critics estimate that as many as 15 million more Mexican farmers—one in six—could be displaced.[82] On the other hand, Archer Daniels Midland's profits rose from $383 million in 2001 to $451 million in 2003, and Cargill's net earnings jumped from $333 million to $1.2 billion.

Mad Cow Disease

Mad cow disease (bovine spongiform encephalopathy, or BSE) is a neurological disease that affects cattle by attacking the brain and central nervous system. It is believed that cattle become infected with BSE by eating feed that contains remnants of other infected cattle. Humans can become infected with a BSE-like illness, called Creutzfeldt-Jakob disease (CJD) by eating meat from infected cows. There is no known cure for CJD and cooking at high temperatures or treating meat with radiation is not effective in preventing the disease. Because organic livestock producers adhere to strict feed requirements, which exclude animal by-products in the feed, it is believed that BSE is absent in this kind of meat.[83] Some consumers have become wary of purchasing and eating beef.

Local Selling

Because many small farmers cannot compete directly with agribusiness, they are realizing the importance of selling their products locally. Since 1995 the number of farmers' markets has increased by 79 percent, and in 2004, they numbered more than 3,000 nationwide. Community Supported Agriculture (CSA) programs—where local residents buy a seasonal share of produce directly from family farms—are also growing. Beginning with only one CSA in 1985, the program is now available through more than 1,000 family farms nationwide. By selling directly to consumers, farmers realize as much as 80 cents of each food dollar.[84]

Organic Farming

Started by family farmers, the organic movement is the fastest-growing sector of U.S. agriculture. Since 1992, the total amount of farmland dedicated to organic crops has quadrupled. This trend has created some confusion for consumers who are unsure of what the various labels mean (see Figure 17.4).

Sustainable Agriculture

The environmental challenges facing the United States are greater than at any time in the nation's history. Global environmental threats such as climate change; stratospheric ozone depletion; and the loss of biological diversity (through accelerating extinctions of species), forests, and fish stocks are affecting all countries regardless of their stage of economic development.

In June 1993 former President Bill Clinton appointed 25 leaders from business, government,

---

- *Organic.* Regulated by the USDA, the National Organic Standards assure that food products contain at least 95 percent organic ingredients and that no synthetic growth hormones, antibiotics, pesticides, biotechnology, synthetic ingredients, or irradiation were used in production or processing. Organic labels can be found on produce, dairy, meat, processed foods, condiments, and beverages.

- *Fair Trade.* Fair trade standards are enforced by the Fairtrade Labeling Organization International (FLO). Fair trade products are produced in accordance with several guidelines. For example, workers must receive decent wages, and housing, health, and safety standards must be adhered to. Workers must have the right to join trade unions and child or forced labor is prohibited. Crops must also be grown, produced, and processed in an environmentally friendly manner. Fair trade standards have been established for coffee, tea, cocoa, honey, bananas, orange juice, and sugar. Some producers have established alternative fair trade-type labels. Most are little more than marketing pitches.

- *Free Farmed.* This certification program was created by the American Humane Association in 2000 to ensure that animals raised for dairy, poultry, and beef products are treated in a humane manner. These guidelines ensure that livestock have access to clean and sufficient food and water as well as a safe, healthy living environment.

- *Feel Good Buying* (not certified). Some meat and dairy products are now being marketed as hormone free. In dairy products, this means that the farmer has chosen not to inject their cows with the artificial growth hormone called rBGH. On beef products this label indicates that the animal was raised without growth hormones or steroids.

- *Raised without Antibiotics.* This meat and dairy label indicates that the animal was raised entirely without the use of low-level and/or therapeutic doses of antibiotics.

- *GE Free, Non-GMO.* Food products that use GE Free or Non-GMO labels are regulated by individual companies, distributors or processors. Often, the companies require certification or affidavits from farmers that the materials were not genetically modified in any way.

- *All Natural.* There is no universal standard or definition for this claim.

- *Free Range.* This label claims that a meat or poultry product (including eggs) comes from an animal that was raised in the open air or was allowed to roam. However, the regulations do not specify how much of each day animals must have access to fresh air. In poultry the USDA considers five minutes adequate exposure to be considered free range. In beef the use of the label is completely unregulated or standardized.

Figure 17.4

What the Food Labels Mean

Source: Adapted from Farm Aid, Inc., "Issues in Farming," 2004. Retrieved November 2004, from www.farmaid.org/site/PageServer?pagename=info_facts_global. Used by permission.

environmental, civil rights, and Native American organizations to the Council on Sustainable Development. Their charge was to transform the idea of sustainable development into a concrete plan of action. As a benchmark, the council adopted the definition of sustainable development proposed by the UN Brundtland Commission in 1987. This stated that **sustainable development** must "meet the needs of the present without compromising the ability of future generations to meet their own needs." The final vision statement of the council noted that "Our vision is of a life-sustaining earth. We are committed to the achievement of a dignified, peaceful, and equitable existence. We believe a sustainable United States will have an economy that equitably provides opportunities for satisfying livelihoods and a safe, healthy, high quality of life for current and future generations. Our nation will protect its environment, its natural resource base, and the functions and viability of natural systems on which all life depends."[85]

Sustainable development theories also address the crisis of farmland mismanagement in the United States and abroad. Farming and related activities are the foundation of the U.S. food and fiber industry, which provides jobs for 17 percent of the workforce and contributes more than $1 trillion to the GNP. Moreover, the 1 billion acres of land in agricultural production is responsible for feeding, clothing, and housing 300 million people in the United States and millions more abroad. Yet, every minute, the United States loses two acres of productive farmland to urban sprawl—shopping malls, housing subdivisions, and the like. Since the first Earth Day in 1970, the United States has lost more than 40 million acres of farmland to development. Net cropland losses in the United States between 1992 and 1997 alone covered an area the size of Maryland.[86]

Urbanization is a leading cause of the loss of cropland. The spread of roads, buildings, and industrial parks consumes precious farmland. Cropland is also lost because of the depletion or diversion of irrigation water. In many water-scarce areas, water is supplied from nonrenewable aquifers. If farmers deplete the water stock or if it is siphoned off by large cities, agricultural land will either be abandoned or become less productive. Although irrigated land accounts for only 16 percent of all cropland worldwide, it supplies 40 percent of the world's grain.[87]

Each year the United States loses almost 3 billion tons of topsoil to wind and water erosion. As many as 1 billion tons wash into nearby waterways, carrying away natural nutrients and the fertilizers and pesticides contained in the soil.[88] This erosion damages water quality, fish and wildlife habitat, and recreational opportunities. Farmers spend an estimated $8 billion on fertilizers and $6 billion on fuel each year. Thus, the use of fertilizers, toxic chemicals, and fuel strains already tight farm budgets as well as threatens the environment. The overuse and misapplication of fertilizers and fuel threatens both the land and the farmers' profitability.[89]

The impressive success of the intensified agriculture that began in the 1960s has led to a complacent attitude toward cropland loss. Specifically, some people believed that farm yields were rising so quickly that they more than compensated for the loss of arable land. However, by 1984 the growth in crop yields had slowed. This trend was intensified in the 1990s as the amount of productive U.S. cropland per person fell to less than one-sixth the size of a soccer field.[90] Moreover, the shrinking supply of cropland and the slowing of yield increases come on the brink of the largest projected increase in food demand in history. In 25 years farmers will be required to feed 2.2 billion more people than they do today; yet most governments continue to allow land that could be used to grow food to be developed or washed away by erosion.[91]

Sustainable development is seen by many as an alternative to environmental degradation. According to social worker Richard Estes, the concept of *sustainable development* has succeeded in uniting differing theoretical and ideological perspectives into a single conceptual framework.[92] In an ecological context, sustainable development promotes a process whereby natural resources are replenished and future generations continue to have adequate resources to meet their needs.[93] Although sustainable development is an important concept, its wide use by different groups in the development process gives some pause for concern. For example, some groups use the term *sustainable development* to designate a radical restructuring of society with regard to environmental development and economic growth. Others simply use the idea of sustainable development to signal a change in attitudes and emphasis. Such different approaches are sometimes labeled "dark green strategies" versus "light green strategies." Although some policy analysts claim that sustainable development can be the basis for a new developmental and ecological paradigm, others caution that the concept is not yet fully developed.[94]

Climate Change

Despite the skepticism of the former George W. Bush administration, climate change has become an accepted fact among the vast majority of scientists and the general public. Environmental consciousness arose as early as the first Earth Day on April 22, 1970, and was bolstered by *An Inconvenient Truth*, the documentary partly based on Al Gore's presentations.

The effects of climate change are striking. For instance, Australia's worst drought in more than 100 years is threatening to make a desert of some of its verdant coastline. Climate change in America's northeast has seen summer temperatures climb into the upper 90s or above for months at a time. Climate change is causing rising sea levels, dramatic glacial retreat, arctic shrinkage exceeding even some of the most aggressive computer projections, significant slowing of the ocean circulation that transports warm water to the North Atlantic, and altered patterns of agriculture (prolonged droughts punctuated by extreme flooding). Other predicted effects include extreme weather events (hurricanes, cyclones, floods, intense droughts), an expansion of tropical diseases as subtropical areas heat up, and drastic economic changes including starvation as marginal croplands become deserts. Overall, the consequences of global warming result from one of three changes: rising sea levels, higher local temperatures, and changes in rainfall patterns.

Climate change is having a major impact on farming and food production. The greenhouse effect—a naturally occurring phenomenon—is the way the atmosphere traps part of the sun's heat and stops it from going back into space. It makes Earth warm enough for life, and without it, Earth would be about 86°F colder. Although global warming is a common term used to describe these changes, climate change is a better description because some areas may in fact cool. Global warming also describes other effects such as rising sea levels and wilder weather.[95]

Many scientists believe that increased emissions of greenhouse gases have contributed to the rise in global temperatures and sea level. These scientists maintain that we are adding dangerously to the natural greenhouse effect as the gases from industry and agriculture—chiefly carbon dioxide, methane, and nitrous oxide—trap more solar heat. Indeed, the average global surface temperature has risen by 1°F in the last 100 years, and scientists say

Earth is warming faster than it has in the last thousand years. The Arctic Climate Impact Assessment, produced by a council of nations with arctic territory that includes the United States, Canada, Russia, and several Nordic countries, reflects the work of more than 300 scientists. Leaked in late 2004, the report found that the arctic is warming much faster than other areas of the world and that much of this change is linked to human-generated greenhouse gas emissions. The report concluded that temperature increases in some parts of the arctic increased tenfold compared with the last century's worldwide average rise of 1°F.[96]

The Kyoto Protocol is a global treaty on tackling climate change. It commits industrialized nations to reduce their emissions of six greenhouse gases by an average of 5.2 percent below their 1990 levels within a decade. Scientists say it would take carbon cuts of 60 percent or more to prevent dangerous climatic instability, so Kyoto is only a modest start. The United States pollutes more, absolutely and per head, than any other country. Its greenhouse emissions have risen by more than 13.1 percent from 1990 to 2002, despite the Kyoto commitment to reduce them by 6 percent.[97]

In 2001 the Bush administration rejected the Kyoto Protocol claiming that the agreement was fatally flawed because it excluded developing nations, such as China and India. Bush maintained that forcing U.S. businesses to reduce their emissions while letting companies in those countries off the hook would drive up the cost of American products and cost jobs. In effect, the Bush administration was opposed to mandatory requirements for reducing emissions, instead favoring plans to push private industry to voluntarily reduce them. Of all the industrialized Western nations, only the United States and Australia refused to sign the Kyoto Protocol. In 2007 the new Australian Labor government signed the Kyoto Protocol almost immediately after taking office, under Prime Minister Kevin Rudd. Despite the U.S. rejection, the Kyoto accord took effect in 2005 as a result of Russia's ratification.

Conclusion

The production, distribution, and consumption of food have historically been rooted in political economy. Through various forms of legislation, the U.S. government has traditionally responded to the needs of diverse groups that have an interest in food—farmers, consumers, the poor or their advocates, food distributors, grain traders, and the Third World and wealthier countries that depend on U.S. food production.

The federal government has responded to these interests by creating a patchwork quilt of policies and programs. One of the most important is the FS program, an ingenious strategy that helps keep food affordable for low-income consumers, helps stabilize farm prices, slows agricultural surpluses by subsidizing consumption, and allows food retailers and distributors to increase their profits by ensuring a volume of subsidized consumers. The nation's food problems persist, however. These problems, which are serious for many poor people and farmers, have reached crisis proportions for others—including the very poor, farmworkers, and marginal farmers. Tragically, many farmers in the United States now profit from food stamps not because the program helps them control surplus farm goods but because it provides them with coupons redeemable in food. It is a sad commentary when the producers of food are unable to purchase what they grow.

Discussion Questions

1. WIC and the FS program are similar in many respects. What are the specific differences between them? Is it necessary for WIC to be a separate program?
2. Serious questions exist as to the effectiveness of U.S. food programs for the poor. What alternatives, if any, exist to the confusing matrix of food programs that make up the nutritional safety net?
3. U.S. farming has historically been economically volatile. For example, farming was reasonably good in the 1970s, after which it spun into a depression in the early and mid-1980s. What programs and policies might be implemented to stabilize U.S. farming?
4. Some advocates claim that sustainable development should be the basis for a new developmental and ecological paradigm. Is sustainable development a viable enough theory to serve as the basis for a set of development policies? Why?
5. The problem of how to deal fairly with farmworkers in the United States is both difficult and chronic. What are some possible solutions for promoting equity and fairness for farmworkers in this country?
6. Proponents of biofuels see it as a potential solution to America's energy dependency of imports. Supporters of biofuels argue that the production of ethanol might balance the foreign trade imbalance, eliminate agricultural surpluses, reduce agricultural subsidies, and reduce the emission of hydrocarbons that contribute to global warming. Are they right?
7. The FY 2007 U.S. Department of Agriculture budget for the Food Stamp program was almost $34.8 billion or more than double the $17.1 billion budgeted for Temporary Assistance for Needy Families in the U.S. Department of Health and Human Services budget. This makes the Food Stamp program one of the largest and most important means-tested social welfare programs in the country. What obstacles exist to clients receiving food stamps?

Notes

1. U.S. Department of Agriculture, "The Emergency Food Assistance Program," June 2008. Retrieved July 2008, from www.fns.usda.gov/fdd/programs/tefap/pfs-tefap.pdf
2. United Health Foundation, "America's Health Rankings," 2006. Retrieved July 2008, from www.unitedhealthfoundation.org/ahr2006/2006ahr.pdf
3. Eric Schlosser, *Fast Food Nation* (New York: Perennial, 2002), p. 3.
4. United Health Foundation, *America's Health: State Health Rankings, 2004 Edition*, 2004. Retrieved November 2004, from www.unitedhealthfoundation.org/shr2004/commentary/obesity.html
5. Robin McKie, "Lifespan Crisis Hits Supersize America," *Observer* (September 19, 2004), p. 2.

6. "FY 2008 Budget Summary and Annual Performance Plan," U.S. Department of Agriculture. Retrieved April 9, 2007, from www.obpa.usda.gov/budsum/fy08budsum.pdf

7. Calculated from "FY 2008 President's Budget for HHS," U.S. Department of Health and Human Services. Retrieved April 9, 2007, from www.hhs.gov/budget/docbudget.htm

8. "FY 2008 Budget Summary and Annual Performance Plan," pp. 4-5.

9. "Structure and Finances of U.S. Farms: 2005 Family Farm Report: U.S. Farms: Numbers, Size and Ownership," Economic Research Service, USDA, p. 11. Retrieved April 9, 2007, from www.ers.usda.gov/publications/EIB12/EIB12c.pdf

10. Ibid., p. 11.

11. "FY 2008 President's Budget for HHS," p. 73.

12. "S 1702: Poverty Status in the Past 12 Months of Families," U.S. Census Bureau, American FactFinder. Retrieved April 10, 2007, from http://factfinder.census.gov/servlet/STTable?_bm=y&-geo_id=01000US&-qr_name=ACS_2005_EST_G00_S1702&-ds_name=ACS_2005_EST_G00_

13. Gilbert M. Gaul, "Aid Is a Bumper Crop for Farmers," *Washington Post* (October 15, 2006), A01.

14. Ibid.

15. CNN, "Poll: Most Americans Older than 25 Are Overweight," March 5, 2002. Retrieved November 2004, from http://archives.cnn.com/2002/HEALTH/03/05/obesity.poll

16. Scott Kilman, "U.S. Tastes Could Bring Trouble, Americans' Desire for Imported Foods May Help Worsen Trade Imbalance," *Kansas City Star* (November 10, 2004), p. A8.

17. U.S. Department of Agriculture, "Household Food Security in the United States, 2006," November 2007. Retrieved July 2008, from www.ers.usda.gov/Publications/ERR49/ERR49_ReportSummary.pdf

18. Ibid.

19. Trudy Lieberman, "Hungry in America," *The Nation* (July 31, 2003), p. 2.

20. John T. Cook and Katie S. Martin, "Differences in Nutrient Adequacy among Poor and Non-Poor Children" (Summary of Findings), Tufts University, School of Nutrition-Center on Hunger, Poverty & Nutrition Policy, March 1995.

21. Ibid.

22. See Katherine Alaimo, Christine M. Olson, and Edward A. Frongillo, "Food Insufficiency and American School-Aged Children's Cognitive, Academic and Psychosocial Development," *Pediatrics* 108 (2001), pp. 44–53; and Katherine Alaimo, Christine M. Olson, and Edward A. Frongillo, "Family Food Insufficiency, but Not Low Family Income, Is Associated with Dysthymia and Suicide Symptoms in Adolescents," *Journal of Nutrition* 132 (2002), pp. 719-725.

23. U.S. Department of Agriculture, "Household Food Security in the United States, 2006."

24. City Mayors Society, "Hunger and Homelessness Persists in American Cities: A Report by the U.S. Conference of Mayors." Retrieved July 2008, from www.citymayors.com/features/uscity_poverty.html

25. Food Action Research Council, "Food Stamp Program," October 22, 2004. Retrieved November 2004, from www.frac.org/html/federal_food_programs/programs/fsp.html

26. U.S. Department of Agriculture, "Characteristics of Food Stamp Households: Fiscal Year 2006," September 2007. Retrieved July 2008, from www.fns.usda.gov/oane/MENU/Published/FSP/FILES/Participation/2006Characteristics

27. U.S. Department of Agriculture, "Food Stamp Provisions of the Farm Bill," July 3, 2008. Retrieved July 2008, from www.fns.usda.gov/fsp/rules/Memo/08/070308.pdf

28. Illa Tennison, "WIC Policy Analysis," unpublished paper, University of Missouri–Columbia, School of Social Work, 1987, p. 5.

29. U.S. Department of Agriculture, "WIC and Retail Grocery Stores." Retrieved July 2008, from www.fns.usda.gov/wic/WICRetailStoresfactsheet.pdf

30. U.S. House of Representatives, Committee on Ways and Means, *Overview of Entitlement Programs, 1992 Green Book* (Washington, DC: U.S. Government Printing Office, 1992), p. 1687.

31. U.S. Department of Agriculture, Food and Nutrition Service, "WIC Program Participation and Costs," June 26, 2008. Retrieved July 2008, from www.fns.usda.gov/pd/wisummary.htm

32. U.S. Department of Agriculture, Food and Nutrition Service, "Nutrition Assistance Programs," February 6, 2000. Retrieved January 2001, from www.fns.usda.gov/fns

33. See U.S. House of Representatives, *1992 Green Book*, p. 1688; and Kristin Cotter, "Texas WIC: Strategy for Outreach Policy," unpublished paper, University of Houston, Graduate School of Social Work, Houston, TX, Fall 1996.

34. Children's Defense Fund, *The State of America's Children, 1988* (Washington, DC: Children's Defense Fund, 1988), p. 186.

35. Isaac Shapiro and Robert Greenstein, *Holes in the Safety Nets* (Washington, DC: Center on Budget and Policy Priorities, 1988), pp. 33–34.

36. U.S. Department of Agriculture, Food and Nutrition Service, "How WIC Helps," May 15, 2000. Retrieved December 2001, from www.fns.usda.gov/wic/CONTENT/howwichelps.htm

37. Douglas J. Besharov, "We're Feeding the Poor as If They're Starving," American Enterprise Institute, Washington, DC, December 2002.

38. Lieberman, "Hungry in America," p. 2.

39. See Second Harvest, "Hunger in America, 2001," retrieved November 2004, from www.secondharvest.org/site_content.asp?s=81; and U.S. Conference of Mayors, "Hunger and Homelessness Survey," December 2003, retrieved October 2004, from www.usmayors.org/uscm/hungersurvey/2003/online report/Hunger AndHomelessnessReport2003.pdf

40. Second Harvest, "Who We Are," December 2000. Retrieved December 2001, from www.secondharvest.org/whoshungry/who_we_serve.html

41. Second Harvest, "State-by-State Review of Food Stamp Applications," November 2000. Retrieved November 2001, from www.secondharvest.org/policy/food_stamp_study.html

42. M. Drabenstott and M. Duncan, "Another Troubled Year for U.S. Agriculture," *Journal of the American Society of Farm Managers and Rural Appraisers* 49, no. 1 (1985), pp. 58–66.

43. Cited in Joanne Mermelstein, "Criteria of Rural Mental Health Directors in Adopting Farm Crisis Programming Innovation," unpublished Ph.D. dissertation, Public Policy Analysis and Administration, St. Louis University, Missouri, 1986, p. 3.

44. "U.S. Farm Sector, in Annual Checkup, Shows Strong Pulse," Farmline (December–January 1991), p. 2.

45. Ibid., pp. 4–5; see also Jim Ryan and Ken Erickson, "Balance Sheet Stable in 1992," *Agricultural Outlook* 46 (January-February 1992), pp. 29-30.

46. U.S. Department of Agriculture, "History of Agricultural Price Support and Adjustment Programs, 1933-84," *Bulletin No. 485* (Washington, DC: Economic Research Service, 1984), pp. 8–9.

47. Steve Little, "Parity: Survival of the Family Farm." Unpublished paper, University of Missouri-Columbia, School of Social Work, 1986, pp. 8–9.

48. Mermelstein, "Criteria of Rural Mental Health Directors," pp. 5–6.

49. Ibid., p. 7.

50. Quoted in John M. Herrick, "Farmers' Revolt! Contemporary Farmers' Protests in Historical Perspective: Implications for Social Work Practice," *Human Services in the Rural Environment* 10, no. 1 (April 1986), p. 9.

51. Ibid.

52. See Ford Runge and Stuart Kimberly, *Agricultural Policy Reform in the United States: An Unfinished Agenda* (Washington, DC: Center for International Food and Agricultural Policy, October 1996), pp. 1–30; and James Bovard, "Farmers Harvest Bumper Crop in Beltway," *Wall Street Journal* (October 21, 1998), pp. 1, 2.

53. American Farmland Trust, "1996 Farm Bill Review," 1996. Retrieved December 1999, from http://farm.fic.niu.edu/aft/fbreview.html

54. R.A. Wirtz, "Farm Crisis: Here We Go Again?" *Fedgazette*. Retrieved December 2001, from www.minneapolis fed.org/pbus/fedgaz/99-10/cover.html

55. Anuradha Mittal, "Giving Away the Farm: The 2002 Farm Bill," *Backgrounder* 8, no. 3 (Summer 2002), p. 1.

56. Gregory Lamb, "Biofuels Show Promise, But Also Present Problems," *The Christian Science Monitor* (May 10, 2007), p. 6; and Claudio Langone, Brazilian Ministry of the Environment, United Nations Commission on Sustainable Development, 14th Session, United Nations, New York, May 10 and 12, 2006.

57. Ibid.

58. See U.S. Department of Agriculture, "2002 Census of Agriculture," Retrieved December 2004, from www.nass.usda.gov/census/census02/volume1/us/index1.htm; U.S. Department of Agriculture, "Farms and Land in Farms," February 2004, retrieved June 2004, from http://usda.mannlib.cornell.edu/reports/nassr/other/zfl-bb/fmno0204.txt; U.S. Department of Agriculture, "2002 Census of Agriculture;" U.S. Department of Agriculture, "Income, Wealth, and the Economic Well-Being of Farm Households," ERS Agricultural Economic Report No. AER812, July 2002, retrieved May 2004, from www.ers.usda.gov/publications/AER812; U.S. Department of Agriculture, "Structural and Financial Characteristics of U.S. Farms: 2001," Family Farm Report, ERS Agriculture Information Bulletin No. 768, May 2001, retrieved April 2004, from www.ers.usda.gov/publications/aib768; Farm Aid, "Factory Farms: The Worst of Industrial Agriculture, 2004," retrieved November 2004, from www.farmaid.org/site/PageServer?pagename=info_facts_factory; Andrew Nelson, *From a Lifestyle to a Business, Small Farming in Transition: A Case Study Analysis of Small Farming in the Upper Midwest*, unpublished paper; Larry Keller, "Family Farming: An Endangered Career," CNN.com, October 30, 2000, retrieved October 2001, from http://fyi.cnn.com/2000/fyi/news/10/30/family.farms; Center for Rural Affairs, "Corporate Farming and Industrialization"; Farm Aid, "Family Farm Numbers," 2000, retrieved October 2001, from www.farmaid.org/org/farm/facts.asp; Farm Aid, "Factory Farming," 2000, retrieved December 2001, from www.farmaid.org/org/farm/factory.asp; and Farm Aid, "Questions and Answers," 2000, retrieved December 2001, from www.farmaid.org/org/farm/q_a.asp

59. Eric Schlosser, *Reefer Madness: Sex, Drugs, and Cheap Labor in the American Black Market*, (Houghton Mifflin, 2003), p. 56.

60. Christine Ahn, Melissa Moore, and Nick Parker, "Migrant Farmworkers: America's New Plantation Workers," *Backgrounder* 10, no. 2 (Spring 2004), pp. 2–11.

61. See Ahn, Moore, and Parker, "Migrant Farmworkers;" U.S. Department of Agriculture, "2002 Census of Agriculture;" U.S. Department of Labor, "Findings from the National Agricultural Workers Survey (NAWS) 1997-1998," Research Report No. 8, March 2000, retrieved November 2001, from www.dol.gov/dol/asp/public/programs/agworker/

report_8.pdf; and Richard Mines, Susan Gabbard, and Anne Steirman, "A Profile of U.S. Farm Workers, Demographics, Household Composition, Income and Use of Services (April 1997)," U.S. Department of Labor, Office of the Assistant Secretary for Policy, prepared for the Commission on Immigration Reform, retrieved December 2001, from www.dol.gov/dol/asp/public/programs/agworker/report/major.htm

62. Christopher Holden, "Migrant Health Series: Housing, 2001." Retrieved May 2004, from www.ncfh.org/docs/08%20-%20housing.pdf

63. See V.A. Wilk, *The Occupational Health of Migrant and Seasonal Farmworkers in the United States* (Washington, DC: Farmworkers Justice Fund, 1985); Juan Ramos and Celia Torres, "Migrant and Seasonal Farm Workers," Encyclopedia of Social Work, 18th ed. (Silver Spring, MD: NASW, 1987), p. 151; and National Center for Farmworker Health, *Facts about America's Farmworkers* (Washington, DC: National Center for Farmworker Health, 1996).

64. Wilk, *The Occupational Health.*

65. Ibid.; and Bureau of Primary Health Care, "The Children's Health Initiative, Migrant and Seasonal Farmworker Children: The Current Situation and the Available Opportunities," Health Resources and Services Administration, October 24, 1997, retrieved December 2001, from www.bphc.hrsa.gov/mhc/MIGRANT.HTML

66. Ahn, Moore, and Parker, "Migrant Farmworkers."

67. Margaret Reeves, Anne Katten, and Martha Guzman, "Fields of Poison, 2002: California Farmworkers and Pesticides," United Farmworkers, 2003. Retrieved August 2004, from www. ufw. org

68. Bureau of Primary Health Care, "The Children's Health Initiative, Migrant and Seasonal Farmworker Children: the Current Situation and the Available Opportunities."

69. Gary Huang, "Health Problems among Migrant Farmworkers' Children in the U.S." ERIC Digests, January 1, 1993. Retrieved December 1999, from www.ed.gov/databases/ERIC_Digests/ed357907.html

70. National Center for Farmworker Health, "Fact Sheets about Farmworkers, 2002." Retrieved June 2004, from www.ncfh.org/factsheets.php

71. Ibid.

72. Schlosser, *Reefer Madness.*

73. Ahn, Moore, and Parker, "Migrant Farmworkers."

74. Center for Rural Affairs, "Corporate Farming and Industrialization," 2000. Retrieved January 2001, from www.cfra.org/Issues.htm#Corporate

75. Stewart Smith, "Farming Activities and Family Farms: Getting the Concepts Right." Presented to the U.S. Congress Symposium, Agricultural Industrialization and Family Farms, Washington, DC, October 21, 1992.

76. ConAgra, "Our Foods," 2004. Retrieved November 2004, from www.conagrafoods.com/brands/index.jsp

77. Farm Aid, "Genetic Engineering," 2004. Retrieved November 2004, from www.farmaid.org/site/PageServer?pagename='info_facts_genetic

78. Ibid.

79. Ibid.

80. Farm Aid, "Issues in Farming," 2004. Retrieved November 2004, from www.farmaid.org/site/PageServer?pagename=info_facts_global

81. Ibid.

82. Ahn, Moore, and Parker, "Migrant Farmworkers."

83. Farm Aid, "Genetic Engineering," 2004.

84. Ibid.

85. The Council on Sustainable Development, "Sustainable America: A New Consensus," 1995. Retrieved December 1998, from www.whitehouse.gov/WH/ EOP/pcsd/info/highlite.html

86. American Farmland Trust, "Farming on the Edge: Sprawling Development Threatens America's Best Farmland," 2003. Retrieved June 2004, from www.farmland.org/farmingontheedge/downloads.htm#foodchart

87. Ibid.

88. Richard Magleby, "Agricultural Resources and Environmental Indicators: Soil Management and Conservation," No. AH722, February 2002. Retrieved August 2004 from www.ers.usda.gov/publications/arei/ah722/arei4_2/DBGen.htm

89. American Farmland Trust, "Why Save Farmland?" 1996. Retrieved January 6, 2001, from http://farm.fic.niu.edu/aft/aftwhysave.html

90. American Farmland Trust, "What's Happening to America's Agricultural Resources?" 1996. Retrieved January 6, 2001, from http://farm.fic.niu.edu/aft/aftwhathap.html

91. Ibid.

92. Richard Estes, "Toward Sustainable Development: From Theory to Praxis," *Social Development Issues* 15, no. 3 (1993), pp. 1-22.

93. Katherine van Wormer, Social Welfare: A World View (Chicago: Nelson-Hall, 1997).

94. James Midgley, *Social Development: The Development Perspective in Social Welfare* (London: Sage, 1995).

95. BBC News, "Global Climate Change, A Changing World," 2001. Retrieved July 2003, from http://news.bbc.co.uk/hi/english/static/in_depth/sci_tech/2000/climate_change/impact/default.stm

96. See Stevenson Swanson, "States May Lead Action against Global Warming, Manufacturers Reduce Emissions; Local Policies Try to Bypass Bush Stance," *Chicago Tribune* (November 14, 2004), p. 8A; and Juliet Eilperin, "Cool to Global Warming, Bush Administration Challenges Evidence, Tries to Keep Council from Endorsing Plans to Curb Climate Change," *Washington Post* (November 8, 2004), p. 10.

97. Swanson, "States May Lead Action against Global Warming, Manufacturers Reduce Emissions."

CHAPTER 18

The American Welfare State
in International Perspective

Various models have evolved to depict the comparative levels of development of nations. In recent times a three-part classification has enjoyed extensive use: a First World, consisting of the industrial nations of the capitalist West; a Second World, made up of the communist nations that constructed political economies as an alternative to the market-dominated First World; and a Third World, comprising nations that were former colonies of the First World and later achieved independence, often through revolutions of liberation. This tri-part formulation became prevalent after World War II as the Cold War intensified. Many developing nations adopted the slogans of revolution, if not outright insurrection, in order to shed the influences of First World colonial nations. The Second World viewed the Third World as a theater of independence, an arena in which the exploitation of capitalism would be summarily ended and the colonized nations would be brought into the communist sphere of influence. On the defensive, the First World deployed foreign aid, technical assistance, cultural exchange, and, on occasion, diplomatic subterfuge to neutralize Second World incursions into the Third World. In several regions—Central America, Southeast Asia, and sub-Saharan Africa—the First and Second Worlds recruited insurgents who acted as their surrogates, engaging the opposition in armed conflict at considerable cost in arms and human life.

With the fall of the Berlin Wall in 1989, the Three World formulation lost utility. Foremost, the collapse of the Soviet Union and its Warsaw Pact satellites halved the scale of the Second World. The remaining communist nations—the People's Republic of China, Vietnam, North Korea, and Cuba—posed little immediate threat to the First World and were unlikely to serve as models for Third World nations. At the same time, some nations of the Third World had been transformed substantially from their colonial era status. Several Arab nations, despite feudal forms of governance, had prospered through oil exports, achieving levels of income that mirrored those of industrial nations. And despite the absence of natural resources, a handful of nations in Southeast Asia—Hong Kong, South Korea, Taiwan, and Singapore—experienced such consistently high levels of growth that they became known as the "Four Tigers." Tragically, many Third World nations lost ground. By the end of the millennium, several of the nations of sub-Saharan Africa and Southeast Asia were significantly less developed than they had been a generation earlier, when they achieved independence from the First World. Nations such as Cambodia, Bangladesh, Afghanistan, Somalia, and Sierra Leone had lost so much capital, their infrastructure had deteriorated to such an extent, and their polity had become so unstable that development analysts began to speculate about the emergence of a Fourth World. Further confounding the prospects of Fourth World nations, the end of the cold war led the affluent industrial nations of the First World, particularly the United States, to expend relatively less on foreign aid than they had during the Soviet threat.

Typologies of Welfare States

The welfare states of the industrialized West vary structurally. With his colleague Charles Lebeaux, Harold Wilensky sought to summarize the differences between the European and American welfare states by constructing a typology of social welfare systems. The typology contrasts **residual welfare** with **institutional welfare.** The residualist approach is concerned with providing a minimal safety net for the poorest sections of the population rather than catering for the population as a whole. Residualists argue that people can enhance their well-being through their own efforts, through the help of neighbors or their families, by purchasing services on the market, or by obtaining help from voluntary organizations.[1] They point out that in the United States people make effective use of nongovernmental agencies, and that international comparisons should not be limited to government social programs. They also point out that although the United States may lag behind in public welfare provision, people enjoy exceptionally high standards of living and unequaled opportunities. This is why the country remains a magnet for immigrants from all over the world, people who come not to receive government handouts but to share in the American dream. Wilensky and Lebeaux believed that social policy in the United States is essentially residualist in nature. On the other hand, the institutional approach, which typifies European social welfare, seeks to provide a variety of social programs for the whole population and to combine economic and social objectives in an effort to enhance the well-being of all.[2]

These ideas were developed by the British social philosopher Richard Titmuss. Titmuss agreed that the residual approach typified social welfare in the United States and that an institutional approach was dominant in Europe. However, Titmuss noted that some countries did not fall into the residual and institutional dichotomy. For this reason he added a third category to the typology, which he called the industrial performance model. He believed that this approach characterized social policy in the former Soviet Union and communist Eastern European countries.[3]

Several subsequent attempts have been made to construct typologies of welfare states that go beyond Wilensky and Lebeaux's twofold category. One of the first was by Norman Furniss and Timothy Tilton, who provided a threefold classification that encompassed what they called the "positive state," the "social security state," and the "social welfare state." The United States exemplified the first, Britain the second, and Sweden the third.[4]

Canadian writer Ramesh Mishra, who has written extensively about international social welfare, retained the twofold approach developed by Wilensky and Lebeaux, but he stressed the efforts of some countries to forge strong alliances among government, labor, and business in order to reach a consensus on social welfare issues. This approach is known as *corporatism*. In corporatist societies, social welfare is integrated into the economy and other institutions of society. Countries such as Sweden, Austria, and Australia are typical of the corporatist approach. Mishra used the term *integrated welfare state* to connote the corporatist approach. On the other hand, Britain and the United States were noncorporatist in that they did not integrate social and economic policy or seek to forge a consensus around welfare issues. For this reason, Mishra called them *differentiated welfare states*. Mishra was one of the first writers to suggest that Britain was not, as Titmuss believed, like the rest of Europe but rather more like the United States in its approach to social welfare.[5]

Gosta Esping-Andersen's typology also recognized the corporatist type when classifying welfare states. However, Esping-Andersen grouped countries somewhat differently from Mishra. In addition to the corporatist category (Italy, Japan, France, and Switzerland), Esping-Andersen identified two other types—the liberal welfare state (Australia, Britain, and the United States) and the social democratic welfare state (Austria, the Netherlands, and the Scandinavian countries).[6] More recently, Norman Ginsburg constructed a fourfold typology comprising the social democratic welfare state (typified by Sweden), the social market welfare state (Germany), the corporate market welfare state (United States), and the liberal collectivist welfare state (Britain).[7] Of the various typologies of welfare states that have been developed by social policy investigators, Esping-Andersen's is perhaps the most widely accepted.[8]

Although the typologies differ, they use similar criteria when classifying countries. All emphasize government social programs and neglect the role of voluntary organizations and other nonstatutory activities in social welfare. The typologies also reveal the normative preferences of the authors. That is, although the typologies are intended to classify countries for analytical purposes, it is clear that they give expression to beliefs about the desirability of the role of government in social welfare. Analysts who favor extensive government involvement in social welfare have represented countries with extensive public programs more favorably in the typologies than countries that do not place as much emphasis on government involvement. For this reason, it is not surprising that most of the typologies depict the United States negatively in comparison to European welfare states.

American Exceptionalism

The apparent unwillingness of the United States to emphasize government social welfare programs has been described by Edwin Amenta and Theda Skocpol as "welfare exceptionalism."[9] These authors also summarized explanations of the country's reluctance to create an institutional European-style welfare state. One such explanation is that the racial, ethnic, and religious diversity of the United States has prevented the emergence of a comprehensive welfare state. In European nations people are more united and have a stronger sense of civic responsibility; in contrast, the pursuit of separate interests by a great number of different groups in the United States militates against the emergence of a single national system of provision that caters to all citizens.

Another explanation is based on the country's high degree of political decentralization that impedes the emergence of strong central political institutions. Combined with a high degree of diversity, the tradition of decentralization in which the states assume much responsibility for social welfare, creates cleavages in U.S. society that effectively prevents the emergence of a strong, centralized, and comprehensive welfare state. It has also been noted that the United States does not have a long tradition of bureaucratic government that can support centralized welfare programs. Some have claimed that this is because of the absence of a feudal tradition. Developing this idea, others have pointed to the unique role of the courts in policymaking in this country, the separation of the executive and legislative branches, and the role of powerful political interest groups—all of which impede the emergence of a strong, centralized welfare state. Another factor is the role of individualism in the United States, which is fundamentally antithetical to the collectivist assumption underlying the welfare state. It has also been argued that trade unions are weaker in the United States than in Europe and that the political left, which has played a major role in the emergence of the European welfare states, has not been strong in this country.

Although the notion of **welfare state exceptionalism** offers interesting insights into social policy in the United States, it can be criticized. For example, the idea that the United States is a welfare laggard is based largely on a comparison of social programs

such as health insurance and family allowances. The absence of these programs is usually emphasized by those claiming that the United States does not have a comprehensive welfare state. Although it is true that government health care and family income maintenance programs are poorly developed in the United States, the role of indirect support for families through tax relief and tax deductions for medical expenses is often ignored, as is the significance of Medicare and state and local health care programs. Jacob Hacker evaluated the extent to which private sector health and welfare benefits effectively augmented public social programs, concluding that their inclusion put the United States on a par with European welfare states. On public benefits alone, the United States expended 17.1 percent of gross domestic product, less than half that of Denmark's 37.6 percent. An analysis of after-tax public and private social welfare expenditures showed a different picture, however; the United States expended 24.5 percent of gross domestic product (GDP) compared to Denmark's 24.4 percent.[10] Thus, the United States is different from other advanced nations with respect to social welfare provision because of its reliance on the private sector.

During the nineteenth century, the United States led the world in the development of public education. Today it still compares favorably well with many other countries in terms of access to education, particularly at the college and university level.

In addition, the United States has excelled in other social fields. Historical research reveals that in the late nineteenth century, the United States was ahead of other Western countries in developing income maintenance programs for veterans and for women with children. At the turn of the century, no other industrializing country had introduced mother's pensions, and none came as close to creating a "maternal" rather than "paternal" welfare state.[11] During the nineteenth century it led the world in the development of public education; and it still compares favorably with many other countries in terms of access to education, particularly at the tertiary (college and university) level. Comparative studies have also shown that when particular social programs such as retirement pensions are compared, the United States fares quite well.[12]

Another problem is that comparisons between Europe and the United States are often characterized by strong personal biases. For example, a strong pro-British bias pervades Titmuss's writings. He has been criticized for presenting his arguments in a way that ensures the moral superiority of the institutional welfare state model.[13] It is also apparent that the European countries have widely varied welfare systems and that not all European welfare states are centralized, comprehensive, or highly activist. Studies of welfare policies in other parts of the world also have shown the U.S. welfare state in more favorable terms. For example, unlike the United States, Australia did not until recently have a universal Social Security system, and it relied extensively on means-tested social programs.[14] Nevertheless, it is difficult to reach the conclusion that the United States is one of the world's welfare leaders. Despite its extensive educational and Social Security provisions, the country does not compare favorably to the other industrial nations in the extent, comprehensiveness, or coverage of its welfare system. In fact, its position has deteriorated in recent years as social programs were retrenched since the Reagan administration.

The Welfare State in Transition

As a result of the globalization of capital, welfare states—however they are classified—have made structural adjustments to remain competitive. Welfare states grew steadily during the relatively stable economic period of the 1950s to the early 1970s; but by the mid-1970s most industrial economies began to experience high inflation, high rates of unemployment, sluggish economic growth, and unacceptably high levels of taxation. During this difficult period, Western governments were forced to reassess their overall economic strategies, including the resources allocated to welfare activities. Hence, beginning in the early 1970s, most Western governments either cut welfare programs or arrested their growth.[15]

All Western nations are experiencing a crisis rooted in the need to compete in a new global economy.[16] According to conservative policy analysts, national survival in the new economic order can be achieved only if government cuts costs and becomes more efficient. In addition, these analysts argue for the creation of government policies that encourage the accumulation of the capital necessary for investment, industrial modernization, and corporate growth. Conservatives maintain that this precondition for economic survival is possible only when government freezes or lowers personal and corporate tax rates. The subsequent loss of tax revenue, however, often results in heavy governmental debt, cuts in all services (including social services), a deterioration of the infrastructure, and myriad social problems. The general emphasis on efficiency and profitability also leads to industrial reorganization, which in turn leads to rapidly changing production technologies that displace workers and result in plant closures and downsizing. Thus, the effects of conservative policy changes are exacerbated as cuts in governmental services coincide with the increased demand for social services by victims of the global-based economic changes. In other words, Western industrial nations face a two-pronged assault on the welfare state: (1) the impact of the global economy on government spending, and (2) an increase in the use of social services by workers dislocated by global economic changes.

Western industrialized nations pursued liberal social policies after World War II.[17] In the United States most presidents following Franklin D. Roosevelt tolerated—and in some cases even promoted—a liberal social welfare agenda. Although the general belief in the United States was that people should adjust to the market rather than the other way around, the social consensus also dictated that the nation should strengthen human capital in order to make people more economically competitive.[18] Thus, social welfare programs were developed to increase human capital through education, employment, health, and housing. The belief was that as human capital increased, the dependent person (or at least his or her children) would eventually be able to compete in a free market. For those who could not compete because of serious deficits (such as disabilities or old age), a system of social insurance or public assistance was developed to ensure a minimum level of subsistence. Thus, the dual focus of the welfare state was (1) to create programs to increase human capital; and (2) to create programs to subsidize people unable to participate in the workforce. Even conservative presidents like Richard Nixon acquiesced to this welfare consensus.

But a more conservative welfare consensus emerged during the 1980s. This new consensus called for (1) making welfare benefits conditional on employment and other norms; (2) transforming open-ended entitlements to discretionary programs; (3) containing the growth of the governmental sector while retaining (in curtailed form) fundamental programs that affect the elderly and the working poor; (4) replacing government with other institutions, such as families and community-based organizations; and (5) contracting out services and benefits to the private sector. In effect, ideologues of the new right argued that the liberal welfare state was a failed social experiment.[19] During the 1990s, the conservative critique of the welfare state, introduced first by Margaret Thatcher in the United Kingdom and Ronald Reagan in the United States, prompted a reassessment of public welfare within liberal circles, with the result that Bill Clinton and Tony Blair (nominal liberals) essentially continued the conservative vector in social policy. Most recently, the implications of this trend have been explored by Anthony Giddens, who contends that this represents a "third way" in British social policy.[20] In the United States, Neil Gilbert observed the emergence of an "enabling state," which conditions social welfare benefits on participation in mainstream activities, particularly work.[21]

By the end of the twentieth century, it was evident that the welfare state was on the wane. "Across all of Europe and North America, the social democratic century has come to an end," observed Alan Wolfe:

> Solidarity, social citizenship, the gift relationship, and the difference principle—as all of them representing formulations of the idea that those who live in a society are obligated to insure the welfare of everyone else—are terms bandied about in academic circles, but they no longer make much of an appearance in real politics.[22]

The subsequent retrenchment of the welfare state is paradoxical. Reductions in welfare benefits have contributed to the formation of an "underclass" within the most prosperous of nations. Thus, in the major cities of the West, communities of squatters can be found, people whose poverty is not unlike that seen in the shantytowns that have been characteristic of the developing world. If the globalization of capital has resulted in the internationalization of prosperity, it has also produced an international class of paupers.

Ranking National Development

Various frameworks have been proposed to gauge the progress of nations. Among the first was the Gini coefficient, a figure denoting the extent to which the distribution of income diverges from perfect equality; a Gini ranking of developed nations appears in Chapter 9. Critics of the Gini coefficient cite the limitations of a portrait of development that is based solely on income. Other indicators, such as longevity, education, opportunity, and environment, should be included, they claim. Although this argument has obvious merit, defenders of the Gini coefficient cite its value when the disparity between the rich and poor has become such a chasm. By way of illustration, 1 billion people survive on less than $1 per day; yet, "the assets of the world's 358 billionaires exceed the combined annual incomes of countries with 45 percent of the world's people."[23]

The Human Development Index

Since 1990 the United Nations has published the Human Development Index (HDI) as a ranking of the development of nations. The HDI is a composite of three variables: life expectancy, educational attainment, and income. A nation's HDI score, an average of the sum of the three variables, has a maximum possible value of 1. In constructing the HDI, researchers arbitrarily designated the 70 nations with HDI scores above .800 as high in human development. (See Table 18.1 on page 478.) Nations classified as medium, between .799 and .500, numbered 85. The 22 countries below .499 were identified as low in human development.

Table 18.1

Human Development Index, 2005

Rank	Nation	Life Expectancy (years)	Adult Literacy	School Enrollment	GDP Per Capita	HDI Value
1	Iceland	81.5	99%	95.4%	$36,514	.968
2	Norway	78.7	99	99.2	41,420	.968
3	Australia	80.9	99	113.0	31,794	.962
4	Canada	80.3	99	99.2	33,375	.961
5	Ireland	78.4	99	99.9	38,505	.959
6	Sweden	80.5	99	95.3	32,525	.956
7	Switzerland	81.3	99	85.7	35,633	.955
8	Japan	82.3	99	85.9	31,267	.953
9	Netherlands	79.2	99	98.4	32,684	.953
10	France	80.2	99	96.5	30,386	.952
11	Finland	78.9	99	101.1	32,153	.952
12	U.S.	77.9	99	93.3	41,890	.951
13	Spain	80.5	99	98.0	27,169	.949
14	Denmark	77.9	99	102.7	33,973	.949
15	Austria	79.4	99	91.9	33,700	.948
16	U.K.	79.0	99	93.0	33,328	.946
17	Belgium	78.8	99	95.1	32,119	.946
18	Luxembourg	78.4	99	64.7	60,226	.944
19	New Zealand	79.8	99	108.4	24,996	.943
20	Italy	80.3	98.4	90.6	28,529	.941
21	Hong Kong	81.9	99	76.3	34,833	.937
22	Germany	79.1	99	88.0	29,461	.935
23	Israel	80.3	97.1	89.6	25,864	.932
24	Greece	78.9	96.0	99.0	23,381	.926
25	Singapore	79.4	92.5	87.3	29,663	.922
26	Korea	77.9	99	96.0	22,029	.921
27	Slovenia	77.4	99.7	94.3	22,273	.917
28	Cyprus	79.0	96.8	77.8	22,699	.903
29	Portugal	77.7	94.8	89.8	20,410	.897
30	Brunei	76.7	92.7	77.7	28,161	.894
31	Barbados	76.6	99.7	89	17,297	.892
32	Czech Rep.	75.9	99	82.9	20,538	.891
33	Kuwait	77.3	93.3	74.9	26,321	.891
34	Malta	79.1	87.9	80.9	19,189	.878
35	Qatar	75.0	89.0	77.7	27,664	.875
36	Hungary	72.9	99.3	89.3	17,887	.874
37	Poland	75.2	99.7	87.2	13,847	.870
38	Argentina	74.8	97.2	89.7	14,280	.869

Table 18.1

(continued)

Rank	Nation	Life Expectancy (years)	Adult Literacy	School Enrollment	GDP Per Capita	HDI Value
39	United Arab Emirates	78.3	88.7	59.9	25,514	.868
40	Chile	78.3	95.7	82.9	12,027	.867
41	Bahrain	75.2	86.5	86.1	21,482	.866
42	Slovakia	74.2	100	78.3	15,871	.863
43	Lithuania	72.5	99.6	91.4	14,494	.862
44	Estonia	71.2	99.8	92.4	15,478	.860
45	Latvia	72.0	99.7	90.2	13,646	.855
46	Uruguay	75.9	96.8	88.9	9,962	.852
47	Croatia	75.3	98.1	73.5	13,042	.850
48	Costa Rica	78.5	94.9	73.0	10,180	.846
49	Bahamas	72.3	95.5	70.8	18,380	.845
50	Seychelles	72.7	91.8	82.2	16,106	.843
51	Cuba	77.7	99.8	87.6	6,000	.838
52	Mexico	75.6	91.6	75.6	10,751	.829
53	Bulgaria	72.7	98.2	81.5	9,032	.824
54	St. Kitts	70.0	97.8	73.1	13,307	.821
55	Tonga	72.8	98.0	80.1	8,177	.819
56	Libya	73.4	84.2	8994.1	10,335	.818
57	Antigua	73.9	85.8	69	12,500	.815
58	Oman	75	81.4	67.1	15,602	.814
59	Trinidad	69.2	98.4	4.9	14,603	.814
60	Romania	71.9	97.3	76.8	9,060	.813
61	Saudi Arabia	72.2	82.9	76.0	15,711	.812
62	Panama	75.1	91.9	79.5	7,605	.812
63	Malaysia	73.7	88.7	74.3	10,882	.811
64	Belarus	68.7	99.6	88.7	7,918	.804
65	Mauritius	72.4	84.3	75.3	12,715	.804
66	Bosnia	74.5	96.7	69	7,032	.803
67	Russia	65	99.4	88.9	10,845	.802
68	Albania	76.2	98.7	6968.8	5,316	.801
69	Macedonia	73.8	96.1	70.1	7,200	.801
70	Brazil	71.7	88.6	87.5	8,402	.800
71	Dominica	75.6	88.0	81	6,393	..798
72	Saint Lucia	73.1	94.6	74.8	6,707	.795
73	Kazakhstan	65.9	99.5	93.8	7,857	.794
74	Venezuela	73.2	93	75.5	6,632	.792
75	Colombia	72.3	92.8	75.1	7,304	.791

Table 18.1

(continued)

Rank	Nation	Life Expectancy (years)	Adult Literacy	School Enrollment	GDP Per Capita	HDI Value
76	Ukraine	67.7	99.4	86.5	6,848	.788
77	Samoa	70.8	98.6	73.7	6,170	.785
78	Thailand	69.6	92.6	71.2	8,677	.781
79	Dominican Republic	71.5	87	74.1	8,217	.779
80	Belize	75.9	75.1	81.8	7,109	.778
81	China	72.5	90.9	69.1	6,757	.777
82	Grenada	68.2	96	73.1	7,843	.777
83	Armenia	71.7	99.4	70.8	4,945	.775
84	Turkey	71.4	87.4	68.4	8,407	.775
85	Suriname	69.6	89.6	77.1	7,722	.774
86	Jordan	71.9	91.1	78.1	5,530	.773
87	Peru	70.7	87.9	85.8	6,039	.773
88	Lebanon	71.5	86.5	84.6	5,584	.772
89	Ecuador	74.7	91	72	4,341	.772
90	Philippines	71.0	92.6	81.1	5,137	.771
91	Tunisia	73.5	74.3	76.3	8,371	.766
92	Fiji	68.3	93.2	74.8	6,049	.762
93	St. Vincent	71.1	88.1	68.9	6,658	.761
94	Iran	70.2	82.4	72.8	7,968	.759
95	Paraguay	71.3	93.5	69.1	4,642	.755
96	Georgia	70.7	100	76.3	3,365	.754
97	Guyana	65.2	98.6	85	4,508	.750
98	Azerbaijan	67.1	98.8	67.1	5,016	.746
99	Sri Lanka	71.6	90.7	62.7	4,595	.743
100	Maldives	67.0	96.3	65.8	5,261	.741
101	Jamaica	72.2	79.9	77.9	4,291	.736
102	Cape Verde	71.0	81.2	66.4	5,803	.736
103	El Salvador	71.3	80.6	70.4	5,255	.735
104	Algeria	71.7	69.9	73.7	7,062	.733
105	Vietnam	73.7	90.3	63.9	3,071	.733
106	Palestinian Territories	72.9	92.4	82.4	2,788	.731
107	Indonesia	69.7	90.4	68.2	3,843	.728
108	Syria	73.6	80.8	64.8	3,808	.724
109	Turkmenistan	62.6	98.8	81	3,838	.713
110	Nicaragua	71.9	76.7	70.6	3,674	.710
111	Moldova	68.4	99.1	69.7	2,100	.708
112	Egypt	70.7	71.4	76.9	4,337	.708

Table 18.1

(continued)

Rank	Nation	Life Expectancy (years)	Adult Literacy	School Enrollment	GDP Per Capita	HDI Value
113	Uzbekistan	66.8	99.2	73.8	2,063	.702
114	Mongolia	65.9	97.8	77.4	2,107	.700
115	Honduras	69.4	80	71.2	3,430	.700
116	Kyrgyzstan	65.6	98.7	77.7	1,927	.696
117	Bolivia	64.7	86.7	86	2,819	.695
118	Guatemala	69.7	69.1	67.3	4,568	.689
119	Gabon	56.2	84	72.4	6,954	.677
120	Vanuatu	69.3	74	63.4	3,225	.674
121	South Africa	50.8	82.4	77	11,110	.674
122	Tajikistan	66.3	99.5	70.8	1,365	.673
123	Sao Tome	64.9	84.9	65.2	2,176	.654
124	Botswana	48.1	81.2	69.5	12,387	.654
125	Namibia	51.6	85	64.7	7,568	.650
126	Morocco	70.4	52.3	58.5	4,555	.646
127	Equatorial Guinea	50.4	87	58.1	7,874	.642
128	India	63.7	61	63.8	3,452	.619
129	Solomon Islands	63.0	76.6	47.6	2,031	.602
130	Laos	63.2	68.7	61.5	2,039	.601
131	Cambodia	58.0	73.6	60	2,727	.598
132	Myanmar	60.8	89.9	49.5	1,027	.583
133	Bhutan	64.7	47.0	33	1,833	.579
134	Comoros	64.1	56.0	46.4	1,993	.561
135	Ghana	59.1	57.9	50.7	2,480	.553
136	Pakistan	64.6	49.9	40	2,370	.551
137	Mauritania	63.2	51.2	45.6	2,234	.550
138	Lesotho	42.6	82.2	66	3,335	.549
139	Congo	54.0	84.7	51.4	1,262	.548
140	Bangladesh	63.1	47.5	56	2,053	.547
141	Swaziland	40.9	79.6	59.6	4,824	.547
142	Nepal	62.6	48.6	58.1	1,550	.534
143	Madagascar	58.4	70.7	59.7	923	.533
144	Cameroon	49.8	67.9	62.3	2,299	.532
145	Papua New Guinea	56.9	57.3	40.7	2,563	.530
146	Haiti	59.1	50.8	52	1,663	.529
147	Sudan	57.4	60.9	37.4	2,083	.526
148	Kenya	52.1	73.6	60.6	1,240	.521
149	Djibouti	53.9	65.5	25.3	2,178	.516
150	Timor	59.7	50.1	72	—	.514

Table 18.1

(continued)

Rank	Nation	Life Expectancy (years)	Adult Literacy	School Enrollment	GDP Per Capita	HDI Value
151	Zimbabwe	40.9	89.4	52.4	2,038	.513
152	Togo	57.8	53.2	55	1,506	.512
153	Yemen	61.5	54.1	55.2	930	.508
154	Uganda	49.7	66.8	63	1,454	.505
155	Gambia	58.8	37.8	50.1	1,921	.502
156	Senegal	62.3	39.3	39.6	1,792	.499
157	Eritrea	56.6	56.7	35.3	1,109	.483
158	Nigeria	46.5	69.1	56.2	1,128	.470
159	Tanzania	51.0	69.4	50.4	744	.467
160	Guinea	54.8	29.1	45.1	2,316	.456
161	Rwanda	45.2	64.9	50.9	1,206	.452
162	Angola	41.7	67.4	25.4	2,334	.446
163	Benin	55.4	34.7	50.7	1,141	.437
164	Malawi	46.3	64.1	63.1	667	.437
165	Zambia	40.5	68	60.5	1,023	.434
166	Cote d'Ivoire	47.4	48.7	39.6	1,648	.432
167	Burundi	48.5	59.3	37.9	699	.413
168	Congo	45.8	67.2	33.7	714	.411
169	Ethiopia	51.8	35.9	42.1	1,055	.406
170	Chad	50.4	25.7	37.5	1,427	.388
171	Central African Rep.	43.7	48.6	29.8	1,224	.384
172	Mozambique	42.8	38.7	52.9	1,242	.384
173	Mali	53.1	24	36.7	1,033	.380
174	Niger	55.8	28.7	22.7	781	.374
175	Guinea-Bissau	45.8	39.6	36.7	827	.374
176	Burkina Faso	51.4	23.6	29.3	1,231	.370
177	Sierra Leone	41.8	34.8	44.6	806	.336

Source: "Table 1: Human Development Index," from *Human Development Report,* 2003. Copyright © 2003 by the United Nations Human Development Program. Used by permission of Oxford University Press, Inc.

The HDI demonstrates that nations with somewhat lower incomes are nonetheless able to sustain longevity and mount educational programs. Cuba's per capita GDP is 40 percent that of Saudi Arabia, yet Cubans enjoy greater longevity and more educational opportunity than Saudis. Still, the HDI is a less than optimal classification. An important qualification is that nations evidence significant variations internally that are not registered by the national HDI score. Ordinarily, national capitals, industrial cities, and ports elevate a nation's HDI score; rural and remote areas have a depressive effect. Although the "medium" developing nations rank higher than those ranked "low," the rural areas of the "medium" HDI-scoring nations tend to parallel those nations that rank lowest.

The Fourth World

To address important issues related to social progress, the United Nations developed other indices to assess national development. A Human Poverty Index incorporates nations' percentages of people not expected to reach age 40, their percentages of illiterate adults, the resources they have available in the form of health services and safe water, and their percentages of underweight children under age five. A general indicator of entrenched poverty is the percent of a nation's population living on less than $1 per day. Table 18.2 ranks those nations with at least 10 percent of the population living on less than $1 per day.

That so many remained in abject poverty despite global prosperity prompted a rigorous debate about development efforts in the Fourth World. Jeffrey Sachs proposed a global strategy for ending poverty by 2025, expanding on the UN's Millennium Development Goals. Sachs suggested a range of minimum standards:

- Primary education for all children
- Adequate nutrition for vulnerable populations
- Access to antimalarial bed nets

Table 18.2

Ranking of Nations with More than 10 Percent of Their Population Living on Less Than $1 per Day

Rank	Nation	% Living on Less than $1/day	Rank	Nation	% Living on Less than $1/day
1	Nigeria	70.8	23	Laos	27.0
2	Central African Republic	66.6	24	Mauritania	25.9
3	Cambodia	66.0	25	Nepal	24.1
4	Zambia	63.8	26	Bolivia	23.2
5	Madagascar	61.0	27	Ethiopia	23.0
6	Niger	60.8	28	Kenya	22.8
7	Rwanda	60.3	29	Malawi	20.8
8	Tanzania	57.8	30	El Salvador	19.0
9	Sierra Leone	57.0	31	Venezuela	18.5
10	Zimbabwe	56.1	32	Ecuador	17.7
11	Burundi	54.6	33	Cameroon	17.1
12	Haiti	53.9	34	Pakistan	17.0
13	Swaziland	47.7		Senegal	17.0
14	Nicaragua	45.1	36	Yemen	15.7
15	Ghana	44.8	37	Honduras	14.9
16	Bangladesh	41.3	38	Philippines	14.8
17	Mozambique	36.2		Cote d'Ivoire	14.8
18	Mali	36.1	40	Paraguay	13.6
19	Namibia	35.9	41	Guatemala	13.5
20	India	34.3	42	Mongolia	10.8
21	Benin	30.9	43	South Africa	10.7
22	Burkina Faso	27.2	44	Peru	10.5

Source: World Development Report (Washington, DC: World Bank, 2008), Table 2.

- Access to potable water and sanitation
- A half-kilometer of paved road per 1,000 population
- Access to cooking fuels and stoves that reduce indoor pollution

Adopting the UN's expectation that developed nations dedicate 0.7 percent of gross national product (GNP) for foreign aid, Sachs calculated that ending poverty by 2025 could cost $124 billion.[24] The agenda set forth by Sachs received notoriety once it was endorsed by Bono and other celebrities.

Within a year, another developmental economist, William Easterly, published a rebuttal to "the Plan," the attempt by elite planners from developed nations to dictate the route to prosperity for citizens in developing nations. "The Big Plans are attractive to politicians, celebrities, and activists who want to make a big splash, without the Western public realizing that those plans at the top are not connected to the reality at the bottom," Easterly wrote. Too often, Easterly argued, the best of intentions on the part of experts from the West are sabotaged by circumstances of "the Rest," citing antimalarial mosquito nets that are diverted to the black market where they are sold for wedding veils and fishing nets.[25] Instead of planners formulating, implementing, and evaluating development projects from afar, Easterly stated a preference for searchers, development experts whose ideas spring organically from the circumstances of indigent populations. "The aid agencies would be forced to act as social entrepreneurs, trying to offer innovative services that would prove attractive to the poor."[26]

Inevitably, the debate degenerated into an ideological polemic with liberals favoring Sachs and conservatives supporting Easterly, an unfortunate development because both had valid points to make with respect to traditional development strategies. A more strategic analysis by Paul Collier appeared in 2007. Collier contended that the bottom billion should be the focus of aid because of four traps: chronic civil conflict, the discovery of natural resources, being geographically landlocked, and having corrupt governance. Under these circumstances, neither strategies proposed by Sachs or Easterly are likely to address the needs of the most impoverished people on the planet. Massive aid from developed nations becomes a spoil for corrupt and inept governments of developing nations and local projects are insufficiently coordinated or funded to rise to the scale necessary to reverse protracted poverty. Instead, Collier calls for a series of international charters—a social contract on development—agreements between donor nations and developing nations which structure development:

- A charter for natural resources designed to optimize transparency in extraction contracts, even out economic fluctuations, and set aside revenues for future generations
- A charter for democracy that would not only assure fair elections but would also institute the civil institutions necessary for checks and balances in decision making
- A charter for budget transparency that would identify how funds are to be appropriated as well as track the outcomes of expenditures
- A charter for postconflict situations which establishes institutions and procedures for the reconciliation of disputes
- A charter for investment that precludes populist dictators from confiscating private holdings

In addition to development charters, Collier concedes that innovations are necessary to aid the most destitute, such as "independent service authorities," an alternative network of basic services for the poor.

> The authority would be a wholesale organization for purchasing basic services, buying some from local governments, some from nongovernmental organizations (NGOs), such as churches, and some from private firms. It would finance not just the building of schools and clinics but also their day-to-day operations. Once such an organization was put into place, managed jointly by government, donors, and civil society, both donors and government would channel money through it.[27]

So configured, such an authority would be similar to an airport or port authority in a developed nation.

Few would dispute the validity of Sach's contention that the developed world could contribute more for development, or Easterly's insistence on projects that have immediate relevance for the poor; Collier provides an essential third component of reform: infrastructure. The reassessment of development accounts, at least in part, for the Millennium Challenge Account initiative launched by the George W. Bush administration. Initially budgeted at $5 billion per year, those developing countries meeting minimal standards of good governance are eligible for special assistance. During a 2008 trip to Tanzania, Bush announced one of the largest grants, $698 million over five years, primarily for schools, roads, and utilities.[28] Unfortunately, Congressional reluctance to fund the initiative has left it between $1.2 billion and $1.8 billion—insufficient to realize its objectives.[29]

Capability Poverty

The idea that development is a multifaceted phenomenon has eclipsed a more circumscribed notion based on simple economic parameters. Using the HDI as a basis, development researchers began to evolve a more inclusive and dynamic understanding of authentic progress and to promulgate the idea of "capability poverty." The philosophical rationale for capability poverty was stated fully by Amartya Sen, who noted two profound historical truths: There are no records of famine within democratic societies, nor are there instances of war waged between them. Rather, these most severe events can be attributed to nondemocratic decision making that excludes large groups of people, who then bear the brunt of flawed policies. Sen's contention that freedom was a precondition of development, not a by-product to be enjoyed long after industrialization, earned him the Nobel Prize in economics in 1998.

The capability approach to development advocates "the expansion of the 'capabilities' of persons to lead the kind of lives they value—and have reason to value," Sen proposed, "Greater freedom enhances the ability of people to help themselves and also to influence the world, and these matters are central to the process of development."[30] Logically, however, deprivation of elemental requirements of survival subverts the possibility of full social participation, as do inadequate institutions that deny education, health, and recreation to subgroups. In constructing his argument for a "support-led process," Sen diverged with proponents of an economic model in which health, education, and labor benefits were viewed as being secondary. He contended that:

> [T]he success of the support-led process as a route [to development] does indicate that a country need not wait until it is much richer (through what may be a long period of economic growth) before embarking on rapid expansion of basic education and health care. The quality of life can be vastly raised, despite low incomes, through an adequate program of social services. The fact that education and health care are also productive in raising economic growth adds to the argument for putting major emphasis on these social arrangements in poor economies, without having to wait for "getting rich" first.[31]

■ *Among the 10 elements of a capability approach is play—enjoying activities that are entertaining and rejuvenating.*

Sen's pathbreaking work was soon elaborated by his colleague, Martha Nussbaum. In *Women and Human Development,* Nussbaum states the philosophical rationale for an absolute standard of social justice for the most chronically oppressed among the world's poor: women. "The core idea is that of the human being as a dignified free being who shapes his or her own life in cooperation and reciprocity with others, rather than being passively shaped or pushed around by the world in the manner of a 'flock' or 'herd' animal," contends Nussbaum. "A life that is really human is one that is shaped throughout by these human powers of practical reason and sociability."[32] Thus, optimal development is not only freedom from want but also the full enjoyment of a range of social and political opportunities. Nussbaum lists 10 elements of a capability approach to development:

1. Life: enjoying full longevity
2. Bodily health: having good health, including reproductive freedom
3. Bodily integrity: appreciating freedom of movement, security from assault, and pleasure in sexual relations
4. Senses, imagination, and thought: using the mind to explore rational and emotive bases for life as well as to advance their enhancement
5. Emotions: enjoying attachments to others that are not controlled nor censored by others
6. Practical reason: forming a conception of what is desirable and planning one's life
7. Affiliation: respecting and living with others without fear of discrimination
8. Other species: living in harmony with all features of the environment
9. Play: enjoying activities that are entertaining and rejuvenating
10. Control over one's environment: owning property and engaging politically in order to prosper[33]

So formulated, the capability approach to development provides a blueprint for achieving and maintaining progress. This approach is particularly compelling in an era of rapid international changes attributable to shifts in capital, production, and labor. "Especially in an era of rapid economic globalization, the capabilities approach is urgently needed to give moral substance and moral constraints to processes that are occurring all around us without sufficient moral reflection," Nussbaum concludes. "It may be hoped that the capabilities list

will steer the process of globalization, giving it a rich set of human goals and a vivid sense of human waste and tragedy, when choices are pondered that would otherwise be made with only narrow economic considerations in view."[34]

Among the most compelling issues in international social welfare has been the status of women. Notably in traditional, rural cultures women's opportunities have been circumscribed, but their options have also been attenuated in wealthy, industrialized nations. In this respect, the United Nations calculated the extent to which nations optimize opportunities for women, as evident in Table 18.3. Unlike most components of development, women's status does not necessarily parallel national prosperity. This has been particularly evident within the Arab world where women do not enjoy the same opportunities as their sisters in other nations. For example, the Gender Empowerment Measure of Saudi Arabia (.254), Egypt (.263), and Yemen (.129), is approximately half the HDI ranking of comparable nations.

Such low scores for women are indicative of their exploitation. During the later decades of the twentieth century, human trafficking became a critical international issue. Each year between 600,000 and 800,000 people are smuggled and kidnapped across national borders; most are women and children.[35] The U.S. State Department's Office to Monitor and Combat Trafficking in Persons is responsible for prevention, interdiction, and prosecution of human traffickers.[36] Through a separate program, the Department of Health and Human Services awarded $1.7 million in 2006 for local programs in Florida, California, Wisconsin, and Minnesota to provide services to victims of human trafficking.[37]

International Aid

Historically, intergovernmental transfers have accounted for most foreign aid although other intermediaries are being employed with increasing frequency. The recent performance of the industrialized nations demonstrates several trends in international aid. Foremost, nations with the largest economies, notably Japan and the United States, lag behind smaller industrialized nations with respect to the percent of GNP committed to international aid. The Scandinavian welfare states have consistently demonstrated international citizenship superior to that of

Table 18.3

Gender Empowerment Measure

Rank	Nation	GEM Value	HDI Ranking	Seats in Parliament, %	Legislators/ Senior Officials, %	Professional/ Technical Workers, %	Female to Male Earned Income
1	Norway	.910	2	37.9	30	56	.72
2	Sweden	.906	6	47.3	30	51	.81
3	Finland	.887	11	42.0	30	55	.71
4	Denmark	.875	14	36.9	25	53	.73
5	Iceland	.862	1	31.7	27	56	.72
6	Netherlands	.859	9	36.0	26	50	.64
7	Belgium	.850	17	35.7	32	49	.55
8	Australia	.847	3	28.3	37	56	.70
9	Germany	.831	22	30.6	37	50	.58
10	Canada	.820	4	24.3	36	56	.64
11	New Zealand	.811	19	32.2	36	53	.70
12	Spain	.794	13	30.5	32	48	.50
13	Austria	.788	15	31.0	27	49	.46
14	United Kingdom	.783	16	19.3	34	47	.66
15	United States	.762	12	16.3	42	56	.63
16	Singapore	.761	25	24.5	26	44	.51
17	Argentina	.614	37	19.1	33	61	.64
18	France	.718	10	13.9	37	47	.64
19	Ireland	.699	5	14.2	31	52	.53
20	Bahamas	.696	49	22.2	46	60	.70

Source: Human Development Report 2007/2008 (New York: United Nations, 2008), Table 29.

the more laissez-faire economies, as is evident in Table 18.4 on page 488. Compounding this pattern has been a downward trend in allocations for international aid. Since 1990 international aid from national governments has dropped in most of the nations for which longitudinal data are available. This retreat from aid has contributed to a reassessment of international assistance. As governments have donated less, reliance has increased on private **NGOs** (nongovernmental organizations) and on **quangos** (quasi-NGOs) such as the World Bank, the International Monetary Fund, and regional development banks. Although the United States is the largest donor, not only is its percent of GNP allotted to international aid the lowest among industrialized nations, but that ratio roughly halved since the mid-1980s.

Global Capital

The foundation for global markets was laid after World War II with an international agreement for currency stabilization and debt financing that was negotiated at Bretton Woods, New Hampshire. The Bretton Woods agreement established the International Monetary Fund (IMF), an international agency accountable to its member nations. With the expansion of capital to overseas markets during the 1960s, the IMF initiated a program of Special Drawing Rights (SDRs) or loans that encouraged expansionary policies in developing nations. This program, however, collided with the acute economic

Table 18.4

Net Official Development Assistance Disbursed, as a Percent of GNI, 1990 and 2005

Rank	Nation	Total (millions)	% of GNI 1990	% of GNI 2005	HDI Rank 2005
1	Norway	$2,786	1.17	.94	2
2	Sweden	3,362	.91	.94	6
3	Netherlands	5,115	.92	.82	9
4	Luxembourg	256	.21	.82	18
5	Denmark	2,109	.94	.81	14
6	Belgium	1,963	.46	.53	17
7	Austria	1,573	.11	.52	15
8	France	10,026	.60	.47	10
9	United Kingdom	10767	.27	.47	16
10	Finland	902	.65	.46	11
11	Switzerland	1,767	.32	.44	7
12	Ireland	719	.16	.42	5
13	Germany	10,082	.42	.36	22
14	Canada	3,756	.44	.34	4
15	Italy	5,091	.31	.29	20
16	Japan	13,147	.31	.28	8
17	New Zealand	274	.23	.27	19
18	Spain	3,018	.20	.27	13
19	Australia	1,680	.34	.25	3
20	United States	27,622	.21	.22	12
21	Portugal	377	.24	.21	29
22	Greece	384	—	.17	24

contraction of the 1970s due to the oil embargo, driving much of the developing world into severe debt. Subsequent IMF policies to restructure debt payments have stressed "conditionalities," or internal economic reforms, often requiring controversial reductions in domestic spending for health, education, and related social programs.

The World Bank, also accountable to its member nations, provides resources to enhance infrastructure, initially through the International Bank for Reconstruction and Development (IBRD). Following the dramatic success of the Marshall Plan that rebuilt postwar Europe, the World Bank instituted the International Development Association (IDA) in 1960 to redirect activities to developing nations. Focusing on the poorest nations, World Bank aid is often in the form of credits, long-term loans that are interest free.[38]

Both the IMF and World Bank presume that international markets will be a means for development, a strategy that, although markedly successful for industrialized nations, has been less so for developing nations. With the demise of state socialism, international markets have, nonetheless, become the primary means for economic growth of the Third World. Two entities have facilitated this growth: The General Agreement on Tariffs and Trade (GATT), established in 1947, enjoyed only modest success in reducing tariffs until 1967, but in that year impediments against international trade were cut drastically. And in 1995 the World Trade Organization (WTO) was created to accelerate the emergence of global markets, augmenting GATT. Since then, membership in GATT/WTO has increased dramatically. Between 1980 and 1999 the number of GATT member nations increased from 85 to 134.[39] Globalization has accelerated with the increasing flow of private capital into developing nations. Between 1980 and 1998, governmental aid was eclipsed by private capital.[40]

The Future

Although the unprecedented expansion of global markets has furthered economic growth internationally, the benefits have not been evenly distributed. During the last decades of the twentieth century, the per capita GDP of the most developed one-third of nations increased significantly; in contrast, that of the middle third dropped from 12.5 to 11.4 percent, and that of the lowest third fell 3.1 to 1.9 percent. "Such findings are of great concern," observed authors of the World Bank's development report, "because they show how difficult it is for poor countries to close the gap with their wealthier counterparts."[41] Between 1993 and 2002 the number of people living on less than $1 a day has almost halved in East Asia and the Pacific, while it has increased significantly in Africa and South Asia.[42]

Critics of global capitalism perceived such disparities as more than the inevitable consequences of international markets, however. Citing a crushing debt burden that required some Third World nations to repay international lenders sums that exceeded their nation's annual economic growth, as well as imposing program restructuring as a condition for future loans, opponents of international capital took to the streets in a series of demonstrations. In 1999 demonstrators seriously hampered WTO meetings in Seattle, Washington; several months later attempts to disrupt meetings of the World Bank in Washington, DC, were less successful. High on the demonstrators' lists of demands were debt relief for developing nations and a restructuring of international aid organizations in order to make assistance more just. In demanding a restructuring of global finance, many demonstrators pointed to the $1 trillion traded daily by currency speculators, on which a trivial tax of .1 percent would generate $1 billion each day that could be put to work in development projects.[43]

Given the infeasibility of deconstructing the organizations at the top of the global financial empire, development strategists have focused their energies on nongovernmental organizations. Jessica Mathews, a senior fellow at the U.S. Council on Foreign Relations, has contended that NGOs provide a bond among peoples whose relations have been abraded by the competitiveness of international markets and the retraction of aid from industrialized governments:

> At a time of accelerating change, NGOs are quicker than governments to respond to new demands and opportunities. Internationally, in both the poorest and richest countries, NGOs, when adequately funded, can outperform government in the delivery of many public services. Their growth, along with that of the other elements of civil society, can strengthen the fabric of many still-fragile democracies.[44]

During recent decades, hundreds of NGOs have emerged to facilitate development in the Third World. As is typical of voluntary ventures, these initiatives have both positive and negative features. On the positive side, their aggregate budgets and staffs eclipse the projects of many governmental projects; on the negative side, they tend to be fragmented, with any coordination being a product of volition. Three NGOs that either have become well established in development circles or show promise of breaking new ground are Habitat for Humanity, the Grameen Development Bank, and First Nations Development Institute:

• *Habitat for Humanity.* Established by Millard Fuller in 1976, Habitat for Humanity is a Christian organization that enlists volunteer labor and donated supplies to build housing for the world's homeless. In 2006 Habitat for Humanity celebrated the construction of 200,000 homes in areas from rural sub-Saharan Africa to colonias in Latin America to ghettos in the United States. International efforts have been central to the organization's agenda; in 2006 Habitat spent $357.2 million for housing.[45] Not operated as a welfare program, Habitat for Humanity requires that future home buyers provide sweat equity in constructing houses for others before they become eligible for one themselves. Home purchase is then arranged through zero-interest loans.

• *Grameen Development Bank.* In 1976, economics professor Muhammad Yunus made a small loan to a peasant woman in Bangladesh so that she could purchase materials for making bamboo

Spotlight 18.1

Nongovernmental Organizations Making a Difference

Three NGOs that have made a difference internationally for the disadvantaged are Habitat for Humanity, Grameen Development Bank, and First Nations Development Institute.

Established in 1976, Habitat for Humanity enlists volunteer labor and donated supplies to build housing for the world's homeless. To learn more about this organization, go to its website at **www.habitat.org.**

Grameen Development Bank created a banking system based on mutual trust, accountability, participation, and creativity. Grameen provides credit to the poorest of the poor in rural Bangladesh, without any collateral. To learn more about the Grameen Development Bank, go to its website at **www.grameen-info.org.**

Founded in 1980, First Nations Development Institute (FNDI) assists indigenous peoples in the control and development of their assets and, through that control, builds their capacity to direct their economic futures in ways that fit their culture. To learn more about FNDI, go to its website at **www.firstnations.org.**

stools. Pioneering a peer lending strategy whereby small groups of peasants receive a loan for which the entire group is responsible, the Grameen Bank not only enhanced the productivity of poor people but also reinforced solidarity. Soon, borrowers whom commercial banks had written off as too risky demonstrated a repayment rate above 95 percent. In 2005 the Grameen Bank boasted 1,735 branches, 5 million members, and cumulative disbursements exceeding $612 million.[46] Unique to the Grameen Bank is a social compact, "the 16 decisions," to which members must subscribe in order to become members. Addressing issues ranging from sanitation to birth control, education, and nutrition, the "16 decisions" provide a moral scaffolding for the bank's social architecture. Not a welfare program, Grameen Bank loans are interest bearing; the expectation is that, once repaid, they will make the borrower's loan group eligible for larger loans in the future. As a model of microfinance, the Grameen Bank not only inspired capital formation strategies in Africa and Latin America, but also prompted the United Nations to adopt it as a way to promote grass roots development in the poorest nations.[47] Yunus won the 2006 Nobel Peace Prize for his work in micro-credit.

• *First Nations Development Institute.* Established in 1979 by Rebecca Adamson, a Cherokee Indian who wanted to end forever the dependence of Native Americans on the federal government, First Nations Development Institute (FNDI) has become an advocate for indigenous peoples worldwide. In addition to organizing community development banks on reservations in the United States, FNDI has advocated the rights of Aborigines in Australia as well as nomads of the Kalahari Desert. The FNDI paradigm integrates four components—community, nature, subsistence, and culture—into a unity that is antithetical to the exploitive, individualistic model typical of the industrial West. In so doing, FNDI eschews welfare, associating it with the demise of traditional kinship patterns: "The government welfare systems, superimposed on a complex and existing system of giving, sharing and reciprocity has facilitated the breakdown of the kinship system," contends FNDI Vice President Sherry Salway Black, an Oglala Sioux.[48] In advocating for the world's indigenous populations, or first peoples, FNDI serves a population that is often neglected by traditional development projects. In 2006 FNDI made grants totaling $630,576 to native populations.[49]

NGOs cannot, of course, be expected to replace military forces or compensate for government inaction in the face of genocide. History will be a harsh

Table 18.5

Regions without Access to Potable Water or Adequate Sanitation

Region	% of Population	
	Without Safe Drinking Water	Lacking Adequate Sanitation
Africa	35–50	50–60
Asia	35–50	45–60
Latin America and Caribbean	20–30	25–40

Source: Adapted from Worldwatch Institute, *State of the World, 2007* (Washington, DC: Author, 2007), p. 27.

judge on the West for its diffidence at Srebrenica,[50] and it will be condemning of the West's utter disinterest in the ongoing slaughter in the Congo,[51] to say nothing of its complicity in the butchery in Sierra Leone.[52] An unanswered question is whether NGOs can address the infrastructure deficits that were once the province of industrialized governments or their international intermediaries. By way of illustration, consider these situations:

- Equatorial Guinea, an African backwater best known through Robert Klitgaard's scathing caricature of corruption, *Tropical Gangsters*,[53] has been blessed by the discovery of a large oil field, yet has virtually no civic infrastructure through which to ensure that oil revenues become translated into national development.[54]
- Parasitic disease is pandemic in regions without potable water and sanitation, impeding education and productivity, as evident in Table 18.5. Annually, waterborne parasites account for the deaths of two million children living in developing nations.[55]
- Remittances from workers sent to their home countries exceed $300 billion annually, more than formal foreign assistance from developed nations, yet such individual gifts are not integrated with development policy.[56]
- Deaths in Africa due to AIDS exceeded 2 million by 2001,[57] and the HIV infection rate for adults exceeds 20 percent in five nations in sub-Saharan Africa, constituting an epidemic that rivals the Black Death of fourteenth-century Europe; yet international efforts to contain the disease have been sporadic, resulting in the preventable infection of millions of adults and children.[58]
- Debt on development loans placed a crippling burden on several nations, prompting calls for relief. On October 1, 2004, the United States grudgingly agreed to a British plan to forgive $40 billion in loans owed to the World Bank and IMF primarily by nations in sub-Saharan Africa. The previous year African nations paid $15 billion in interest on those loans, impeding the fight against AIDS.[59]
- The widening digital divide—the disparity in access to computer technology between industrialized nations and the developing world—is furthering the gap between rich and poor nations. For example, the United States and Canada boast 1,396 web servers, compared to 142 for Europe, 22 for Latin America, and 11 for Asia.[60]

As these circumstances suggest, the emerging issues in international development demand innovative solutions, and they demand them urgently.

Conclusion

Nations vary developmentally both as individual entities and as clusters. Thus, the United States is more developed than Niger, just as the countries of the industrialized West are more affluent than those of sub-Saharan Africa. At the same time, countries and regions influence one another, contributing to the dynamism of international relations. A common tendency in the West has been to regard the welfare states of North America and western Europe as ideals to which the developing nations should aspire.

Yet a series of events challenged this assumption. First, since the 1980s the welfare states of the West have retrenched, reducing their fiscal commitments to social programs. Second, among developing nations, subgroups have emerged. The oil embargo of the 1970s highlighted a small group of nations, the oil-exporting countries, which have comparatively high per capita income despite relatively low industrialization. Another subgroup consists of Southeast Asian nations that have prospered by aggressively pursuing capitalist strategies of development. As for the nations of sub-Saharan Africa: Most of them are worse off today than when they achieved independence during the 1960s, a tragedy that has been exacerbated by the HIV/AIDS epidemic. Third, international development agencies, such as the United Nations and the International Monetary Fund, have begun to explore alternative scenarios to prosperity—scenarios, such as sustainable development[61]—that are often contrary to the alienating individualism and narcissistic consumption characteristic of the traditional welfare state.

A world in which inequality and strife contribute to social instability poses enormous challenges for human service professionals, as regards both direct services and development theory. Social workers who have served in the Peace Corps have an immediate appreciation for the intractability of problems in the Third and Fourth Worlds, of course. But immigrants seeking better opportunities in developing nations are presenting new problems to human service workers in industrialized nations. Social workers in the United States, for example, are confronted with human trafficking, undocumented workers, and refugee families in increasing numbers.[62] As James Midgley advised, addressing such problems requires strategies that focus on human capital, social development, and self-sufficiency, interventions that are not commonly taught in First World schools of social work.[63]

Discussion Questions

1. What are the limitations of the Human Development Index in measuring a nation's development?
2. Is examining a nation's material conditions the best way to evaluate social development? If not, what other indicators should be used?
3. What are the main reasons that Fourth World countries are less developed now than before they achieved independence?
4. Which welfare state typology provides the best explanation for the development of welfare states?
5. Compared to those of other nations, is the U.S. welfare state really "exceptional"? Why or why not?
6. In the light of international data, how important is foreign aid to development relative to private capital?
7. Select a developing nation and investigate the adequacy of its social infrastructure. What is the level of provision of welfare, health, and education services? How does it compare to the benefits and services of the United States?

Notes

1. See Martin Rein and Lee Rainwater (eds.), *Public/Private Interplay in Social Protection* (Armonk, NY: M.E. Sharpe, 1986); Sheila Kamerman, "The Mixed Economy of Welfare." *Social Work* 29 (1983), pp. 5–11; David Stoesz, "A Theory of Social Welfare," *Social Work* 34 (1989), pp. 101–107; Neil Gilbert and Barbara Gilbert, *The Enabling State: Modern Welfare Capitalism in America* (New York: Oxford University Press, 1989); and Richard Rose, "Common Goals but Different Roles: The State's Contribution to the Welfare Mix," in R. Rose and R. Shiratori (eds.), *The Welfare State East and West* (New York: Oxford University Press, 1986), pp. 13–39.
2. Harold Wilensky and Charles Lebeaux, *Industrial Society and Social Welfare* (New York: Russell Sage Foundation, 1965).
3. Richard M. Titmuss, *Social Policy: An Introduction* (London: Allen and Unwin, 1971).
4. Norman Furniss and Timothy Tilton, *The Case for the Welfare State* (Bloomington, IN: Indiana University Press, 1977).
5. Ramesh Mishra, *The Welfare State in Crisis* (Brighton, England: Wheatsheaf Books, 1984).
6. Gosta Esping-Andersen, *Three Worlds of Welfare Capitalism* (Cambridge, England: Polity Press, 1990).
7. Norman Ginsburg, *Divisions of Welfare: A Critical Introduction to Comparative Social Policy* (London: Sage, 1992).
8. These typologies seek to classify the social welfare systems of the industrial societies and do not refer to the developing countries of the Third World. Attempts to construct comprehensive typologies that

include the developing countries are still preliminary. See James Midgley, "Models of Welfare and Social Planning in Third World Countries," in Brij Mohan (ed.), *New Horizons in Social Welfare and Policy* (Cambridge, MA: Schenkman, 1985), pp. 89–108; and Stewart MacPherson and James Midgley, *Comparative Social Policy and the Third World* (New York: St. Martin's Press, 1987).

9. Edwin Amenta and Theda Skocpol, "Taking Exception: Explaining the Distinctiveness of American Public Policies during the Last Century," in Francis C. Castles (ed.), *The Comparative History of Public Policy* (New York: Oxford University Press, 1989), pp. 292–333.

10. Jacob Hacker, *The Divided Welfare State* (New York: Cambridge University Press, 2002), pp. 13–14.

11. Theda Skocpol, *Protecting Soldiers and Mothers: The Political Origins of Social Policy in the United States* (Cambridge, MA: Harvard University Press, 1992).

12. In 1975 Harold L. Wilensky noted that the United States "allocates a larger fraction of its total welfare spending to pensions that any of the twenty two richest nations [in the world]." However, more recent expenditure data from the Organization for Economic Cooperation and Development (OECD) show that while pension expenditures remain comparatively high, the United States is by no means a world leader. See Harold L. Wilensky, *Welfare State and Equality* (Berkeley, CA: University of California Press, 1975), p. 105; and OECD, Social Expenditure, 1960–1990, retrieved from www. oecd. org

13. Robert Pinker, *The Idea of Welfare* (London, Heinemann, 1979).

14. M. A. Jones, *The Australian Welfare State: Growth Crisis and Change* (Sydney, Australia: Allen and Unwin, 1980); and Terry Carney and Peter Hanks, *Social Security in Australia* (Melbourne: Oxford University Press, 1994).

15. Howard Glennester and James Midgley (eds.), *The Radical Right and the Welfare State* (London: Wheatsheaf Books, 1991).

16. See Barry Bluestone and Bennett Harrison, *The Deindustrialization of America* (New York: Basic Books, 1982); Samuel Bowles, David Gordon, and Thomas E. Weisskopf, *Beyond the Wasteland* (Garden City, NY: Anchor Press, 1983); Bennett Harrison and Barry Bluestone, *The Great U-Turn* (New York: Basic Books, 1988); Robert Reich, *Tales of a New America* (New York: Times Books, 1987); and Lester C. Thurow, *The Zero-Sum Solution* (New York: Simon and Schuster, 1985).

17. See Charles Atherton, "The Welfare State: Still on Solid Ground," *Social Service Review* 63 (Fall 1989), pp. 167–179; and Joel Blau, "Theories of the Welfare State," *Social Service Review* 63 (March 1989), pp. 226–237.

18. Atherton, "The Welfare State."

19. Martin Anderson, "Welfare Reform," in Peter Duignan and Alvin Rabushka (eds.), *The United States in the 1980s* (Stanford, CA: Hoover Institution, 1980), pp. 145–164; George Gilder, *Wealth and Poverty* (New York: Basic Books, 1981); Lawrence Mead, *Beyond Entitlement* (New York: Free Press, 1986); and Charles Murray, *Losing Ground* (New York: Basic Books, 1984).

20. Anthony Giddens, *The Third Way* (London: Polity Press, 2000).

21. Neil Gilbert, *Transformation of the Welfare State* (New York: Oxford University Press, 2002).

22. Alan Wolfe, "Paths of Dependence," *The New Republic* (October 14, 2002), p. 41.

23. *Human Development Report* (New York: Oxford University Press, 1996), p. 2.

24. Jeffrey Sachs, *The End to Poverty* (New York: Penguin, 2005), pp. 266–293.

25. William Easterly, *The White Man's Burden* (New York: Penguin, 2006), p. 17.

26. Ibid., p. 379.

27. Paul Collier, *The Bottom Billion* (New York: Oxford University Press, 2007), p. 119.

28. Peter Baker, "Pride in Obama Aside, Tanzanians Praise Bush," *Washington Post* (February 18, 2008), p. A10.

29. "The Millennium Challenge," *Washington Post* (July 16, 2007), p. A14.

30. Amartya Sen, *Development as Freedom* (New York: Knopf, 1999), p. 18.

31. Ibid., pp. 48–49.

32. Martha Nussbaum, *Women and Human Development* (New York: Cambridge University Press, 2000).

33. Ibid., pp. 78–80.

34. Ibid., p. 105.

35. "Facts about Human Trafficking," U.S. Department of State, Bureau of Public Affairs, May 24, 2004. Retrieved February 13, 2008, from www.state.gov/r/pa/ei/rls/33109. htm

36. "Modern Abolitionists at the U.S. State Department," January 17, 2008. Retrieved February 13, 2008, from www.america.gov/st/hr-english/2008

37. "Over $1.7 million Awarded to Fight Human Trafficking, Provide Assistance to Victims," U.S. Department of Health and Human Services, Administration for Children & Families. Press release, October 25, 2006. Retrieved from www.acf.hhs.gov/news/press/2006

38. Todaro, 1994, pp. 476–481.

39. World Bank, *Entering the 21st Century* (Washington, DC: World Bank, 2000), pp. 6–7.

40. World Bank, *Global Development Finance* (Washington, DC: World Bank, 1999).

41. World Bank, *Entering the 21st Century*, p. 18.

42. World Bank, *World Development Report, 2008* (Washington, DC: World Bank, 2008), p. 3.

43. David Stoesz, Charles Guzzetta, and Mark Lusk, *International Development* (Boston: Allyn & Bacon, 1999), pp. 260–261.

44. Jessica Mathews, "The Age of Nonstate Actors," *Foreign Affairs* 76, no. 1 (January/February 1997), p. 63.

45. Habitat for Humanity, "Annual Report, 2006." Retrieved February 20, 2008, from www.habitat .org/report/2006/AnnualReport

46. "Grameen Bank, Performance Indicators," Grameen Bank. Retrieved August 28, 2006, from www .grameen-info.org/bank/permanceindicators.html

47. Felicity Barringer, "U.N. Will Back Entrepreneurs in Bid to Lift Poor Nations," *New York Times* (July 27, 2003), p. 5.

48. Cited in Stoesz, Guzzetta, and Lusk, *International Development*, p. 191.

49. First Nations Development Institute, "FNDI Annual Report 2006." Retrieved February 20, 2008, from http://firstnations.org/publications/FNDIanrep.html

50. Chuck Sudetic, *Blood and Vengeance* (New York: Penguin, 1999).

51. Peter Gouveritch, *We Wish to Inform You That Tomorrow We Will Be Killed with Our Families* (New York: Farrar Straus and Giroux, 1998).

52. Ryan Lizza, "Where Angels Fear to Tread," *The New Republic* 223, no. 4 (July 24, 2000).

53. Robert Klitgaard, *Tropical Gangsters* (New York: Basic Books, 1990).

54. Norimitsu Onishi, "Oil Riches, and Risks, in Tiny African Nation," *New York Times* (July 23, 2000).

55. Jan Eliasson and Susan Blumenthal, "Dying for a Drink of Clean Water," *Washington Post* (September 20, 2005), p. A23.

56. Karin Brulliard, "Migrants Sent Home $300 Billion in 2006," *Washington Post* (October 18, 2007), p. A20.

57. Worldwatch Institute, *Vital Signs, 2003* (Washington, DC: Author, 2003), p. 69.

58. Barton Gellman, "The World Shunned Signs of Coming Plague," *Washington Post* (July 5, 2000).

59. Elizabeth Becker, "Debt Relief Deal for Poor Nations Seems to Be Near," *New York Times* (October 1, 2004), p. C1.

60. Anthony Faiola and Stephen Buckley, "Poor in Latin America Embrace Net's Promise," *Washington Post* (July 9, 2000), p. A25.

61. World Bank, *Sustainable Development in a Dynamic World* (Washington, DC: Author, 2003).

62. Lynne Healy, *International Social Work* (New York: Oxford University Press, 2001).

63. James Midgley, *Professional Imperialism* (London: Heinemann, 1981); and James Midgley, *Social Development* (London: Sage, 1995).

Glossary

absolute poverty A measurement and classification of poverty that is based on the minimal standard of living (including food, shelter, and clothing) necessary for survival

affirmative action Programs designed to redress past or present discrimination against minorities (including women) through criteria for employment, promotion, and educational opportunities that give these groups preferential access to such resources or opportunities

ageism Age-based discrimination against elderly persons

alleviative approach to poverty Strategies designed to ease the suffering of the poor rather than to eliminate the causes of poverty. Examples include AFDC, SSI, and the Food Stamps Program

annual percentage rate (APR) The annualized interest rate for a loan. Most credit card, mortgages and car loans are calculated at the APR.

area poverty Geographic regions that are economically depressed

block grants A method of funding social programs by which the federal government makes monies available to states for a wide range of services, including social services. Block grants usually allow states more freedom by diminishing or eliminating federal program regulations. Block grants are usually fixed in terms of the amount available

Brown v. Board of Education of Topeka, Kansas A 1954 landmark U.S. Supreme Court decision ruling that "separate but equal" facilities in education were inherently unequal

bureaucratic disentitlement The denial of benefits to eligible recipients by agents of public agencies

bureaucratic rationality The ordering of social affairs by governmental agencies

capitalism An economic system in which most of the production and distribution of goods and services occurs under private auspices

capitation The method of payment in which the provider is paid a fixed amount for each person served regardless of the actual number or nature of services delivered

case management The process by which all related matters of a case are managed by a single professional, often a social worker

case poverty Individual deficits in human capital such as illness, illiteracy, etc.

categorical grants A method of funding social services through which the federal government makes available to the states monies that must be spent for very narrowly specified service needs

charity organization society (COS) A voluntary organization active in the late nineteenth and early twentieth centuries that attempted to coordinate private charities and promote a scientific approach to philanthropy

chronic care Long-term care of individuals with long standing, persistent diseases or conditions

chronic unemployment The rate of unemployment attributable to persons who have persistent trouble finding work because of an absence of low-skilled jobs or because they have severe deficiencies in basic social and work skills

circuit breaker programs Tax rebate programs designed to relieve the low-income, elderly, or disabled home owner or renter from the burden of property or utility taxes

clinical entrepreneurs An interest group within American social welfare that is associated with private practice and the provision of social welfare in the private marketplace

commercialization The consequence of subjecting social welfare to the marketplace, including advertising for services, marketing services, and pricing services

commodification Term describing a governmental policy that takes social needs formerly met in the public sector (e.g., health care, counseling services) and places them within the private market sector

comparable worth The idea that workers should be paid equally when they do different types of work that require the same level of skill, education, knowledge, training, responsibility, and effort

corporate sector   That part of the mixed welfare economy consisting of large, for-profit human-service corporations

corporate social responsibility   The concept that corporations should be held accountable for practices and decisions that adversely affect those communities in which they do business. In addition, corporate social responsibility refers to the responsibility of corporations to promote the general well-being of society

cost-of-living adjustments (COLAs)   Adjustments designed to keep income maintenance and social insurance benefits in line with inflation. COLAs affect Food Stamps, Social Security, and SSI benefits

cost shifting   Charging one group of patients more in order to make up for underpayment by others

culture of poverty   Term used by a theoretical school that maintains that poverty is transmitted intergenerationally and that certain of its traits are found in diverse cultures and societies

curative approach to poverty   An approach designed to rehabilitate the poor through attacking the causes of poverty, for example, illiteracy, poor nutrition, or lack of employment

cyclical unemployment   A type of unemployment attributable to swings in economic performance, such as recessions

de facto segregation   Racial segregation that is not legally mandated by the state but that characterizes school systems and residential housing patterns

deinstitutionalization   Term used to describe the removal, in the late 1960s, of many mentally ill or mentally retarded patients from state institutions and their placement in community settings

deliberate misdiagnosis   The intentional distortion of a diagnosis in order to avoid labeling a client or for the purpose of collecting insurance payments

democratic capitalism   The type of political-economy characteristic of the United States, with a democratic polity and a capitalist economy

dependency ratio   The number of workers required to pay into the Social Security system to support one retired worker living on Social Security

diagnostic related groups (DRGs)   A prospective form of payment for Medicare-incurred charges. Specifically, DRGs are a classification scheme whereby hospitals are reimbursed only for the maximum number of days an illness or surgical procedure is designated to take

discouraged workers   Those who have stopped seeking work out of frustration with their poor employment prospects

disentitlement   The removal of an entitlement status for a group of people. Specifically, the PRWOA disentitled poor beneficiaries from receiving lifetime benefits

Donaldson v. O'Connor   The court decision ruling that mental patients could not be confined unless they were dangerous to themselves or others, and also that they should not be confined unless they are being treated and cannot survive without hospitalization

dual labor market   A labor market divided into two classes of workers. See Primary Labor Market and Secondary Labor Market

earned income tax credit   A federal program that functions somewhat like a negative income tax. Specifically, qualified working families or single people receive a tax rebate from the federal government that exceeds the taxes they paid

electronic benefit transfers (EBT)   The attempt by the federal government to use technology in the delivery of benefits. This can include automatically depositing public assistance benefits into the savings accounts of recipients, the use of debit cards in food stamp benefits, and so forth

emergency assistance program   A program that operated under AFDC and was intended to provide short-term cash assistance to families in crisis

entitlements   Governmental resources (cash or in-kind) to which certain groups are entitled, based on their ability to meet the established criteria. Entitlement programs have open-ended resources in that people cannot be denied benefits because of governmental resource constraints

Equal Rights Amendment (ERA)   An act that if passed would give women the same rights under the law as men

establishment of paternity   Policies that require unwed mothers to identify the fathers of their children in order to aid states in their efforts to collect child-support

family cap   Usually refers to the policy that recipient mothers will not receive any (or only partial) benefits for any children born while they are on public-assistance

fee-for-service   A method of reimbursement based on payment for services rendered. Payment may be made by an insurance company, the patient, or a government program such as Medicare or Medicaid

feminization of poverty   A social trend marked by the increasing frequency of poverty among women. It is thought to be related to the high incidence of women relying on governmental aid, the low wages that characterize traditional female employment, occupational segregation, and family decomposition (divorce, desertion, or death)

fiscal year (FY)   A term used by government and social service agencies in reference to a budgetary rather than a normal year. Fiscal years often begin on July 1 rather than January 1

frictional unemployment   The rate of unemployment, usually about 3 percent, considered inevitable for a viable economy

fringe economy   Predatory lenders and service providers (i.e., rental outlets, check cashers, etc.) who cater to a financially disadvantaged population

general assistance State or locally run programs designed to provide basic benefits to low-income people who are ineligible for federally funded public assistance programs

gentrification Resettlement of existing low-income neighborhoods by middle- and upper-class home owners or investors. This development can result in forcing poor and indigenous residents out of their neighborhoods

governmental sector That part of the mixed welfare economy consisting of social programs administered by government, particularly the federal government

Great Society Formerly called the War on Poverty, the Great Society comprehended a series of social welfare programs (including community development, training and employment, and health and legal services) enacted between 1963 and 1968 during the administration of President Lyndon Baines Johnson

Greens An environmental political party. Their orientation to social policy, *greening*, often incorporates an environmental awareness with a social justice perspective

gross domestic product (GDP) A measure of the total output of goods and services produced by a country's economy

gross national product (GNP) A measure of the total domestic and foreign output claimed by residents of a country. It is made up of the Gross Domestic Product (GDP) and of incomes accruing to foreign residents

Halderman v. Pennhurst The court decision ruling that institutionalized patients were entitled to treatment in the least restrictive environment

health care access The patient's ability to obtain medical care. Access is determined by the availability of medical services, the location of health care facilities, transportation, hours of operation cost of care, and so forth

health maintenance organizations (HMOs) Membership organizations that typically provide comprehensive health care. Members usually pay a regular fee and are thus entitled to free (or minimal-cost) hospital care and physicians' services

home health care Full range of medical and other health related services such as physical therapy, nursing, counseling, and social services that are delivered in the home of a patient by a provider

homophobia The fear of (and subsequent discrimination against) homosexuals on the basis of their sexual preference

housing starts Number of new houses begun in a given period

human capital Productive investments that are embodied in humans. These include education, training, skills, experience, knowledge, and health. Increases in human capital result from expenditures on education, job training, and medical care

human service executives An interest group within American social welfare that is associated with human service corporations and advocates the provision of social welfare through large-scale for-profit programs

human services A recent concept equivalent to social welfare

ideology A set of socially sanctioned assumptions, usually unexamined, explaining how the world works and encompassing a society's general methods for addressing social problems

income distribution The pattern of how income is distributed among the various socioeconomic classes in a society

income maintenance programs Social welfare programs designed to contribute to or supplement the income of an individual or family. These programs are usually means-tested and thus based on need

Indian Child Welfare Act of 1978 Legislation that restored child-placement decisions to the individual tribes

in-kind benefits Noncash goods or services provided by the government that function as a proxy for cash, for example, Food Stamps, Section 8 housing vouchers, and Medicare

inpatient care Care given in a hospital, nursing home, or other medical institution

institutional welfare A conception of welfare holding that governmental social programs that assure citizens of their basic needs (for food, housing, education, income, employment, and health) are essential to an advanced economy. Such programs are considered a right of citizenship

job lock Individuals' inability to change jobs because they would lose crucial health benefits

Job Opportunities and Basic Skills (JOBS) This program was created in the Family Support Act of 1988. The bill required a portion of a state's welfare caseload (usually AFDC mothers) to participate in a work or training program

Keynesian economics An economic school that proposes government intervention in the economy through such activities as social welfare programs to stimulate and regulate economic growth

libertarians A small but influential group that advocates more individual responsibility and a very limited role for government in social and economic affairs

licensed certified social worker A social worker holding the Master of Social Work degree who has practiced for two years under supervision and who has passed an examination. Twenty-nine states license social workers

managed care A loose umbrella term for the organization of networks of health care providers (e.g., doctors, clinics, and hospitals) into a system that is cost-effective. Institutions or individual health care providers who are in managed care systems agree to accept set fees for each service or flat payments per patient. HMOs are one example of managed care

market rationality   The ordering of human affairs by corporate institutions within the marketplace

means test   Income and asset tests designed to determine whether an individual or household meets the economic criteria necessary for receiving governmental cash transfers or in-kind services

Medigap   Private health insurance plans that supplement Medicare benefits by covering some costs not paid for by Medicare

mixed welfare economy   An economy in which governmental, private nonprofit, and private for-profit providers of social welfare coexist within the same society

National Association of Social Workers (NASW)   The major national organization of professional social workers

national health insurance   Various insurance-based proposals that incorporate comprehensive health coverage for the entire nation

neoconservatism   A recent American ideology, based on conservatism, that recognizes the necessity for social welfare but designs social programs so that they are compatible with the requirements of a market economy and traditional values

neoliberalism   A recent American ideology, based on liberalism, that assumes that universal social programs, such as those advanced by liberals, are implausible because of current social, political, and economic limitations. Neoliberals opt for more modest changes in social welfare programs

New Deal   The name given to the massive Depression-era social and economic programs initiated under the presidency of Franklin Delano Roosevelt

NGOs   Nongovernmental organizations (private or voluntary) that plan, deliver, or fund social services

occupational segregation   The domination of low-wage sectors of the labor market by a minority group. For example, women are thought to be occupationally segregated in "pink-collar" jobs, as secretaries, receptionists, typists, and so forth

Office of Economic Opportunity (OEO)   The federal agency that was charged with the responsibility for designing and implementing the Great Society programs

oligopolization   The process through which a small number of organizations effectively control a market

pay-go   A system for determining federal budgetary allocations that emerged out of the 1991 Omnibus Budget Reconciliation Act. In short, funding for any new program (or enhanced funding for an existing program) must come from reallocating existing money

permanency planning   A strategy for helping foster children to live in families that offer continuity of relationships and the opportunity to establish lifetime relationships

Personal Responsibility and Work Opportunity Reconciliation Act (PRWORA)   Passed in 1996, the PRWORA is a comprehensive act that created the TANF program, limited benefits to both legal and illegal immigrants, changed the qualifications for SSI, and established the precedent that government no longer had the responsibility for maintaining the poor indefinitely. In effect, it disentitled the poor from income support programs

Plessy v. Ferguson   The 1896 U.S. Supreme Court decision that formally established the "separate but equal" doctrine in race relations

policy framework   A systematic process for examining a specific policy or a set of policies

political action committees (PACs)   Organizations, usually associated with special interest groups, that divert campaign contributions to candidates running for public office in order to influence their later decisions on public policy

political economy   The blending of economic analysis with practical politics. In effect, political economy views economic activity within a political context

political practice   A method of social work practice by which social workers advance their priorities either by assisting those in political office or by running for office themselves

poverty line   A yearly cash income threshold (based on family size) set by the federal government to determine if an individual or household can be classified as poor. Sometimes called the poverty threshold or poverty index

preexisting condition   A physical condition of an insured person that existed prior to the issuance of his/her policy or his/her enrollment in a health plan

preferential selection   The selection of clients for treatment according to the organizational needs of the provider as opposed to the needs of the client; usually used to describe the practice of private providers who prefer insured clients with less severe problems

preventive approach to poverty   Social welfare strategies (e.g., social insurance programs) designed to prevent people from becoming poor

preventive commitment   The institutionalization of persons who do not meet the requirements for involuntary hospitalization but who are likely to deteriorate without inpatient care

primary care   Basic or general health care rendered by general practitioners, family practitioners, internists, obstetricians, and pediatricians

primary labor market   The full-time jobs that provide workers with an adequate salary, a career track, and benefits

primary prevention   Efforts designed to eliminate the causes of social problems

prime rate loans Loans or mortgages given to credit-worthy borrowers at low interest rates that reflect the prime rate set by the Federal Reserve.

private practice The provision of clinical services through the marketplace by individual practitioners or small groups of practitioners

privatization The ownership or management of social services by the private sector, either nonprofit agencies or proprietary corporations. Privatization of public assistance refers to attempts by individual states to have for-profit corporations manage the delivery of their public assistance benefits

professional monopoly The right to exclusive practice granted an occupational group in exchange for its promise to hold the welfare of the entire community as its ultimate concern

progressive movement A social movement popular in the United States from the late 1800s to World War I. Progressives stressed the need for morality, ethics, and honesty in all social, political, and economic affairs. This movement advocated numerous progressive reforms. It was also successful in establishing progressive legislation, including the progressive income tax

prospective payment system (PPS) A payment method that establishes rates, prices, or budgets before services are rendered and costs are incurred

public choice school A school of political economies that suggests that because interest group demands inevitably lead to budget deficits, government should therefore limit concessions to these groups as much as possible

public policy Policies designed by government that contain a goal, a purpose, and an objective. Public policy may also incorporate a standing plan of action toward a specific goal

public transfer programs Programs such as AFDC, SSI, and Social Security that transfer money from the governmental sector to families or individuals who are either entitled to it or who have earned it

quangos Quasi-governmental organizations that have some affiliation with government but that are predominately private

racism Discrimination against or prejudicial treatment of a racially different group

relative poverty A measurement and classification of poverty that is based on and related to the standard of living enjoyed by other members of a society

residual welfare A conception of welfare holding that the family and the market are the individual's primary sources of assistance, but that governmental "safety-net" programs may provide temporary help

secondary labor market Jobs that are characterized by irregular, seasonal, or part-time employment and that pay relatively low hourly wages, provide no benefits, and offer no career track

secondary prevention Early detection and intervention to keep incipient problems from becoming more debilitating

self-reliance school A relatively new school of political-economy advocating low-technology and local solutions to social problems

settlement houses Organizations that began in the late nineteenth century as an attempt to bridge the class differences marking American society. Based on the residence of middle-class volunteers in immigrant neighborhoods, settlement houses emphasized the provision of social services as well as reform activities

sexism Discrimination against women based solely on their gender. Sexism can also be directed at men

single-payer system A centralized system of health care payment in which the government assumes the costs (but not the delivery) for health services. People choose their doctor and hospital, and the government pays the bill according to a fixed-fee schedule. Coverage is often universal and is rights-based rather than employment-based. Canada is the best-known example of a single-payer system

social insurance A system that compels individuals to insure themselves against the possibility of indigence. Similar to private insurance, social insurance programs set aside a sum of money that is held in trust by the government to be used in the event of a worker's death, retirement, disability, or unemployment. Individuals are entitled to social insurance benefits on the basis of their previous contributions to the system

socialism A school of political-economy that attributes the need for social welfare to the social problems caused by capitalism. Socialists advocate restructuring the political economy—in the American case, capitalism—as the most direct way of promoting social welfare

social justice Connotes equity and fairness in all areas of social, political, and economic life, as well as the provision of basic necessities to all without regard to their participation in the market, an objective of liberals and progressives

social services Programs designed to increase human capital by ameliorating problems in psychosocial functioning, providing necessary goods and services outside normal market mechanisms, and providing cash supplements for the lack of market income

social stratification The vertical segmentation of the population according to income, occupation, and status

social wage A term used to refer to the additional "wage" a worker receives as part of the universal benefits paid out by a welfare state (e.g., health care coverage or housing loans)

social welfare policy The regulation of the provision of benefits to people who require assistance in meeting their basic life needs, such as for employment, income, food, health care, and relationships

sociopolitical planning   Methods for anticipating program needs that are interactive, involving groups likely to be affected by a program

spells of poverty   Periods of time (often limited) in which individuals or families fall below the poverty line

standardization   The reduction of services to a common denominator in order to lower provider costs

structural unemployment   The rate of unemployment attributable to long-lasting and deep maladjustments in the labor market

subprime loans   Loans or mortgages given to borrowers with problematic credit (previous bad loans, insufficient credit history, unstable employment, etc.). These loans tend to have higher interest rates and conditions not found on prime rate or conventional loans.

supply-side economics   A school of political-economy that proposes reductions in social programs so that tax dollars can be reinvested in the private sector to capitalize economic growth

sustainable development   A theory that stresses the need to develop an appropriate balance between material needs and future resource availability. It calls for a form of balanced economic development

Swann v. Charlotte-Mecklenburg Board of Education   A 1971 U.S. Supreme Court ruling that approved court-ordered busing to achieve racial integration in school districts with a history of discrimination

tardive dyskinesia   Permanent damage to the central nervous system, evidenced by involuntary movements, caused by psychotropic medication

technomethodological planning   Methods of anticipating program requirements using data bases from which projections of future program needs can be derived

Temporary Assistance for Needy Families (TANF)   TANF was included as part of the Personal Responsibility and Work Opportunity Reconciliation Act (PRWOA) and is a replacement for the AFDC program. It is a block grant program based on workfare, time-limited benefits (a maximum of five years), and strict work participation rates. The TANF program was instituted in 1996

tertiary prevention   Efforts to limit the effects of a disorder after it has become manifest

think tanks   Popular name for policy institutes

time limits   The length of time a recipient (or a recipient's family) is allowed to remain on welfare. The federal government has instituted a five-year lifetime cap on benefits; several states have set shorter caps

traditionalism   A social movement that gained increased strength during the 1970s. Traditionalists seek to make social policy conform with their conservative social and religious values

traditional providers   An interest group within American social welfare associated with voluntary nonprofit agencies that promotes local institutions as a preferred method of solving social problems

underemployed   Individuals who are working at jobs in which their skills are far above those required for the position. It may also refer to those who are employed part-time when their desire is to be employed full time

unemployment   The condition of individuals over 16 years of age who are looking for work

usual, customary, and reasonable (UCR)   That fee established by a majority of practitioners in a given community for a given procedure. The UCR is defined by insurance companies to determine the proper level of payment for covered procedures

voluntary sector   That part of the mixed welfare economy consisting of private, nonprofit agencies

welfare behaviorism   Refers to the attempts of public officials to modify the behavioral patterns (through instituting specific social policies) of low-income people, especially beneficiaries

welfare bureaucrats   Interest groups within American social welfare associated with governmental social programs that advocate the provision of social welfare through large-scale public social programs

welfare capitalism   An advanced system of social welfare existing in progressive capitalist countries

welfare dependency   The economic dependence of a family or individual on the provision of governmental welfare services, especially cash grants

welfare state   A welfare state is one in which the national government ensures essential goods, services, and opportunities to residents as a right of citizenship

welfare state exceptionalism   A term often used to characterize the U.S. welfare system and the differences between it and other welfare states, especially those of Western Europe

workfare   A system begun in the late 1960s whereby AFDC or AFDC-UP recipients were required either to work or to receive work training (sometimes in the form of higher education). The concept of workfare underlies the welfare reform bills passed in 1988 and in 1996

working poor   Those families or individuals who are in the work force (full- or part-time) but who are still at or below the poverty line

work participation rate   This refers to the percentage of individuals on public assistance that states are required to have in the workforce under TANF guidelines

Wyatt v. Stickney   The court decision requiring states to provide adequate levels of treatment to hospitalized mental patients

YAVIS syndrome   The tendency of clinicians to prefer clients who are young, attractive, verbal, intelligent, and successful

Index

Note: Page numbers followed by f denote figures; t, tables.

Photo Credits